W9-CDX-484

THIRD EDITION

Adult Development and Aging

John C. Cavanaugh

University of Delaware

Brooks/Cole Publishing Company

I(T)P® ***An International Thomson Publishing Company***

Pacific Grove • Albany • Belmont • Bonn • Boston • Cincinnati • Detroit
Johannesburg • London • Madrid • Melbourne • Mexico City • New York • Paris
Singapore • Tokyo • Toronto • Washington

Sponsoring Editor: *Jim Brace-Thompson*
Marketing Team: *Gax Meixel, Margaret Parks*
Marketing Representative: *Art Minsberg*
Editorial Assistant: *Terry Thomas*
Production Editor: *Marjorie Z. Sanders*
Manuscript Editor: *Kathy Pruno*
Permissions Editor: *Ben Greensfelder*
Design Coordinator: *E. Kelly Shoemaker*

Interior and Cover Design: *Katherine Minerva*
Interior Illustration: *Susan Breitbard, Lori Heckelman*
Cover Photo: *Shinichi Hiraki/Photonica*
Art Editor: *Lisa Torri*
Typesetting: *Graphic World, Inc.*
Cover Printing: *Color Dot Graphics, Inc.*
Printing and Binding: *R.R. Donnelly & Sons Company/Crawfordsville*

For more information, contact:

BROOKS/COLE PUBLISHING COMPANY
511 Forest Lodge Road
Pacific Grove, CA 93950
USA

International Thomson Publishing Europe
Berkshire House 168-173
High Holborn
London WC1V7AA
England

Thomas Nelson Australia
102 Dodds Street
South Melbourne, 3205
Victoria, Australia

Nelson Canada
1120 Birchmount Road
Scarborough, Ontario
Canada M1K 5G4

International Thomson Editores
Seneca 53
Col. Polanco
México, D.F., México
C.P. 11560

International Thomson Publishing GmbH
Königswinterer Strasse 418
53227 Bonn
Germany

International Thomson Publishing Asia
221 Henderson Road
#05-10 Henderson Building
Singapore 0315

International Thomson Publishing Japan
Hirakawacho Kyowa Building, 3F
2-2-1 Hirakawacho
Chiyoda-ku, Tokyo 102
Japan

Printed in the United States of America

10 9 8 7 6 5 4 3 2 1

Library of Congress Cataloging-in-Publication Data
Cavanaugh, John C.
Adult development and aging / John C. Cavanaugh.—3rd ed.
p.——cm.
Includes bibliographical references and index.
ISBN 0-534-34423-2
1. Adulthood—Psychological aspects. 2. Aging—Psychological aspects. 3. Adulthood—Physiological aspects. 4. Aging—Physiological aspects. 5. Aging—Social aspects. I. Title.
BF724.5.C38 1996
155.6—dc20 96-19648
CIP

To Patrice,
my soul mate,
my lover,
my best friend

ABOUT THE AUTHOR

John C. Cavanaugh is a Professor of Individual and Family Studies at the University of Delaware. He received his undergraduate degree from the University of Delaware, and his Ph.D. from the University of Notre Dame. Cavanaugh is a fellow of the American Psychological Association, the American Psychological Society, and the Gerontological Society of America. He has been an American Council of Education Fellow, and served as President of the Adult Development and Aging Division (Division 20) of the APA. Cavanaugh has also co-authored *Human Development* with Rob Kail of Purdue University. His research interests in gerontology concern family caregiving as well as the role of beliefs in older adults' cognitive performance. For enjoyment he backpacks, writes poetry, and, while eating chocolate, ponders the relative administrative abilities of James T. Kirk, Jean-Luc Picard, Kathryn Janeway, and Benjamin Sisko.

BRIEF CONTENTS

CONTENTS

CHAPTER 10

CHAPTER 11

CHAPTER 12

CHAPTER 13

CHAPTER 14

PREFACE

The mid-1990s demonstrated that having a solid grounding in research and theory about adult development and aging is essential even for understanding the evening news. Stories about changes in health care for older adults, genetic research on Alzheimer's disease, and the maintenance of cognitive abilities require familiarity with the research evidence in order to separate myth from fact. It is clear that such information will only increase in frequency as we head into the 21st century, as the average age of individuals in industrialized nations continues to increase. New paradigms will need to be created through the combined efforts of people in many occupations—academics, gerontologists, social workers, health care professionals, financial experts, marketing professionals, teachers, factory workers, technologists, government workers, human service providers, and nutritionists, to mention just a few. Every reader of this book, regardless of his or her area of expertise, will need to understand older adults in order to master the art of living.

This need to know about adult development and aging has resulted in an explosion of knowledge. Since the publication of the second edition of *Adult Development and Aging*, several new and important scientific journals have begun publication, hundreds of books have appeared, and the rate of discovery keeps increasing. These developments led to the creation of this third edition, which provides an up-to-date look at these interesting and sometimes controversial findings. As was the case in the first two editions, I have attempted to provide in-depth coverage of the major issues in the psychology of adult development and aging. The third edition of *Adult Development and Aging* adds numerous topics and provides expanded coverage of many existing ones.

MAJOR NEW FEATURES

While maintaining the basic chapter order from the second edition, the third edition includes many new features. Perhaps the most obvious at first glance is the comprehensive inclusion of pedagogical aids throughout the text. These include chapter outlines; learning objectives and concept checks in each major section; key terms in bold italics with the definitional sentence in boldface; chapter summaries organized with section heads; review questions organized by section heads; integrative questions at the end of each chapter that require students to pull together information from various sections within the chapter or from multiple chapters; key terms; and suggested readings. The effect is to build a study guide into the text, with the goal of making the text not only more student-friendly, but easier to learn from.

Throughout the text, the new organizing theme is the four basic forces on human development: biological, psychological, sociocultural, and life-cycle. A new box feature has also been added; "Discovering Development" provides ways for students to find examples in their everyday experience of the principles and concepts described in the text. Terminology has been updated, and recent research has been added (while classic studies have been retained).

Among the many new topics included in the third edition, the most important changes in each chapter are:

- Chapter 1 now includes a discussion of whether developmental changes are universal or reflect specific contextual differences; observational and case studies; and a discussion of research bias and ethics.
- Chapter 2 includes a discussion of age as a dimension of diversity; the material on ethnicity is now organized by ethnic group.
- Chapter 3 has a new chapter opener and a major section on biological theories of aging, as well as a thorough updating of research.
- Chapter 4 now includes a detailed discussion of gender differences in longevity; more information about the stress and coping paradigm; information on screening for prostate cancer; and a new major section on health, functioning, and prevention that includes a theoretical model and research on disability.
- Chapter 5 has a major updating on attention and automatic processing, as well as reorganized sections on home safety and accident prevention.
- Chapter 6 has several topics that have been reorganized; a new chapter opener; more details on autobiographical memory and text memory; a new subsection on memory self-efficacy; new findings from neuroscience on retention and encoding; and new research and theory on memory remediation.
- Chapter 7 has new subsections on reflective judgment and other approaches to postformal thought including gender differences; a new major section on problem solving; thoroughly rewritten sections on psychometric intelligence; and expanded discussions on expertise and wisdom.
- Chapter 8 has been reorganized around contemporary views of personality, with major expansions on life stories (based on work of McAdams and of Whitbourne); a new subsection on generativity; more detail on self-presentation; a new subsection on religiosity; and a new major section on social cognition.
- Chapter 9 has a new title to reflect a broader coverage of the issues; a new section using a multidimensional approach to psychopathology; a new section on ethnicity, aging, and mental health; inclusion of personality disorders; and more detail on the latest research on Alzheimer's disease.
- Chapter 10 now includes Carstensen's theory of socioemotional selectivity to explain developmental differences in the number of relationships; a new section on sibling relationships; a new and extensive section on violence in relationships; a thoroughly rewritten section on gay and lesbian relationships; a new subsection on caring for one's spouse; a new subsection on alternative styles of parenting; and a new subsection on male-female friendships.
- Chapter 11 now has a more focused discussion of the meaning of work, occupational choice, and occupational development; a new major section on gender, ethnicity, bias, and discrimination; a new section on retraining workers; and expanded coverage of long-term unemployment.
- Chapter 12 has additional discussion of the effect of the decline of rural towns; a new subsection on how a nursing home can become "home" for residents; and a major new section on communication with older adults in nursing homes.
- Chapter 13 includes a new subsection on a contextual approach to dying; a new subsection on comparing types of loss; a discussion on the use and effectiveness of advance directives for medical intervention; and more discussion on assisted suicide.
- Chapter 14 has been reorganized and includes updated discussions of health care and prevention; the need for research; and important psychological and social issues.

WRITING STYLE

Although *Adult Development and Aging* covers complex issues and difficult topics, I use clear, concise, and understandable language. I revised all of the chapters to achieve this goal, and many were completely rewritten. I examined all terms to make sure that their use was essential; otherwise they were eliminated.

The text is aimed at upper-division undergraduate students. Although it will be helpful if students have completed an introductory psychology or a course in human development across the life span, the text does not assume this background.

INSTRUCTIONAL AIDS

As noted earlier, many new instructional aids have been included in the third edition, which are described in more detail here.

Learning Helps in the Chapter Text

Each chapter begins with a chapter outline. At the start of each new major section, learning objectives are presented. These objectives are keyed to each primary subsection that follows, and they direct the student's attention to the main point(s) to be discussed. At the conclusion of each major section are concept checks, one for each primary subsection, which help students spot-check their learning. Key terms are defined in context; the term itself is printed in ***bold italic;*** with the sentence containing the term's definition in **boldface.** The study guide that accompanied the second edition has been replaced with in-text study aids.

End-of-Chapter Learning Helps

At the end of each chapter are summaries, organized by major sections and primary subsection heads. This approach helps the student match the chapter outline with the summary. Numerous review questions, also organized around major sections and primary subsections, are provided to assist students in identifying major points. Integrative questions are included as a way for students to link concepts across sections within and across chapters. Key terms with definitions are listed. Suggestions for additional readings from both the scientific and popular literatures are provided for students who would like to enrich their knowledge. Estimates of difficulty level are included based on undergraduates' evaluations.

Boxes

The third edition includes three types of boxes. Those entitled "How Do We Know?" draw attention to specific research studies that were discussed briefly in the main body of the text. These boxes supply additional information about the methodology and theory underlying the research to provide students with a more complete look at how empirical data are generated and with some alternative interpretations where appropriate.

"Something to Think About" boxes raise controversial and provocative issues, pose reflective questions, or draw attention to a social problem. These boxes get students to think about the implications of certain research findings or conclusions and may be used effectively as points of departure for class discussions.

"Discovering Development" boxes give students a way to see developmental principles and concepts in the "real world" as well as some suggestions as to how to find others. These boxes provide a starting point for applied projects in either individual or group settings.

INSTRUCTOR'S MANUAL

The third edition of *Adult Development and Aging* is accompanied by an instructor's manual. Each chapter begins with a lecture outline that highlights the main points of the chapter. In addition, supplemental information is included, as are suggested activities and discussion topics. A list of suggested videos is also provided. Included in the manual are numerous test items. The test items in the instructor's manual are also available in electronic format.

ACKNOWLEDGMENTS

As usual, it takes many people to produce a textbook; such is the case with the third edition. The editorial group at Brooks/Cole is simply the finest in the business. Jim Brace-Thompson (fossil-lover extraordinaire) is a real joy to work with, and he even provided many useful suggestions for the revision. Marjorie Sanders is a fun production editor; just enough drill sergeant to keep the schedule moving, but with enough good humor to keep it all in perspective. Kelly Shoemaker has the knack for knowing what colors and layouts look good together; it's fortunate they didn't ask me to handle this detail. Once upon a time in a galaxy far, far away, Cat Collins masterminded the permissions with help from Ben Greensfelder. Sue C. Howard did a great job locating the photographs.

I would also like to thank the reviewers of the second edition, as well as those who helped improve the manuscript for the third edition, all of whom provided insightful commentary and improved the work:

Bradley Caskey, University of Wisconsin–River Falls; Linda R. Conover, St. Joseph's College; Paul Foos, University of North Carolina–Charlotte; Andrew Futterman, College of the Holy Cross; A. R. Herzog, University of Michigan–Ann Arbor; William J. Hoyer, Syracuse University; Shirley Lupfer, Memphis State University; Kevin MacDonald, California State University–Long Beach; Jasmin Tahmuseh McConatha, West Chester University of Pennsylvania; Romy Nocera, Bowling Green State University; Rosellen Rosick, University of Alaska at Anchorage; Diedrick Snoek, Smith College; Irene Staik, University of Montevallo; and Debra Steckler, Mary Washington College.

This book would not have been possible without the support of Patrice, my wife. The long hours at night and on weekends took tremendous tolerance and patience. She is even getting used to my perpetual piles of papers, journals, and books. She was always there with words of encouragement (and more) just when I needed it. She is the most wonderful wife in the whole universe.

Finally, to a group too often overlooked—the sales representatives. Without you none of this would have any payoff. You are an extension of me and the whole Brooks/Cole editorial team. What a great group of hard-working folks you are!

Thanks to you all. Live long and prosper.

John C. Cavanaugh

THIRD EDITION

Adult Development and Aging

CHAPTER 1

Studying Adult Development and Aging

Cape Cod Evening; Edward Hopper; National Gallery of Art, Washington; John Hay Whitney Collection.

"To be 70 years young is sometimes far more cheerful and hopeful than to be 40 years old," wrote Oliver Wendell Holmes. In the late 19th century when he lived, being "70 years young" was unusual. Since then, countries around the world have experienced an unprecedented explosion in the number of older adults. As a result, we are squarely in the midst of a monumental revolution, especially in industrialized countries: the fundamental restructuring of the population from one that is dominated by youth to one that is increasingly "gray." You have probably heard a great deal about this shift in the media: The median age in the United States passed 30 in the late 1980s, whole industries sprang up that target middle-aged and older adult consumers, and services to older adults have increased in scope and cost.

The dramatic population change has placed unprecedented emphasis on the three-fourths of the average person's life spent in adulthood. The theories and research summarized in this text provide an overview of the kinds of changes that occur during this period of life. Unlike texts on child development and on adolescence, this book focuses on events that you have probably not yet experienced. In that sense, we will be looking into your future, and hope to provide opportunities for you to plan accordingly.

Adulthood and aging represent the longest part of our journey through life. We begin our journey with a description of some basic concepts and a discussion of how adulthood must be viewed as part of the life span as a whole. This life-span perspective provides the connections we need to earlier periods and reminds us that each of us comes into adulthood with a unique history.

PERSPECTIVES ON ADULT DEVELOPMENT AND AGING

Learning Objectives:

- What is gerontology? How does ageism relate to stereotypes of aging?
- What is the life-span perspective?

The dramatic shifts in the characteristics of the population have resulted in an equally rapid increase in studying about adult development and aging. Overall, there are three especially noteworthy reasons why it is important to learn as much as possible about what happens between the time one first becomes an adult and the time one dies:

1. *Older adults constitute a rapidly growing segment of the population.* At present, older adults represent the fastest growing age group in the United States as well as in many other countries. The consequence of this is not only that the number of older adults will increase dramatically, but also that older adults will wield increasingly political and economic power as we enter the 21st century. Their priorities and plans may differ from those of younger and middle-aged adults, which will require creative use of the limited resources available. The heated debates in the United States in the mid-1990s over the future of Medicaid and Social Security reflect these trends.
2. *We want to understand older adults.* What is it like to grow old? Why are older people the way they are? What changes as people age? Why are there so many differences among people of the same age? These and many other questions about the nature of older adults point to a need to understand the adult developmental process and how this process unfolds for each individual. This text will help you learn about older adults.
3. *More older people means new jobs.* The increasing number of older adults will create employment opportunities. Many social service agencies, businesses, consumer product manufacturers, advertisers, and companies in the health care industry are increasingly targeting older adults for new areas of growth. New jobs will be created as organizations begin to meet the needs of older adults. In the coming years, experts predict, this may well be the fastest growing segment of the economy.

This book deals with all of these issues by summarizing what scholars have learned about traversing adulthood and growing old. We have an advantage that most people in the current population of older adults did not have: We are able to study what growing old will be like. Never before have we had the chance to prepare as well for old age.

This opportunity is provided by scientists in many disciplines who are all interested in a common goal: understanding the aging process. The field of study that examines the aging process is gerontology. **More formally, *gerontology* is the study of aging from maturity (young adulthood) through old age, as well as the study of older adults as a special group.** Gerontology is a fairly new scientific discipline. For example, before the 1950s, researchers in the United States conducted only a handful of studies involving older adults (Freeman, 1979). One reason the study of older adults was so long in coming, as Freeman points out, is that authors and scientists throughout history conceptualized the aging process as one of inevitable, irreversible decline. Consequently, nothing was to be gained by studying aging, as it was already thought to be beyond our power to improve or change the process.

We now know that this picture of aging was distorted and oversimplified. As we will see repeatedly in this book, aging involves both growth and decline. Still, many myths concerning old people survive: Older adults are often thought to be incompetent, decrepit, and asexual. **These myths of aging lead to negative stereotypes of older people, which may result in *ageism*, a form of discrimination against older adults simply because of their age.** Ageism comes in many forms (Butler & Lewis, 1982). It may be as blatant as believing that all old people are senile and are incapable of making decisions about their

DISCOVERING DEVELOPMENT

Myths and Stereotypes About Aging

As we have noted, we are surrounded by misconceptions of older adults. We have all seen cartoons making jokes about older adults whose memories are supposedly poor or whose physical abilities have declined. Most damaging are the ideas portrayed in the media that older adults are incapable of leading productive lives and of making a difference. As a way to discover something about development, try to find several examples of myths or stereotypes about aging. Look at advertisements and articles in popular magazines, television, and music. Gather as many as you can, and then check them against the research on the topic discussed in this text. See how many myths and stereotypes you can show to be wrong by the end of the course.

---

lives. Or it may be as subtle as dismissing an older person's physical complaints with the statement, "What do you expect for someone your age?" As you will learn by doing the activities in the Discovering Development feature, such stereotypes surround us.

This book will rebut these erroneous ideas, but it will not replace myths with idealized views of adulthood and old age. Rather, it will strive to paint an accurate picture of what it means to grow old today, recognizing that development across adulthood brings with it growth and opportunities as well as loss and decline. To begin, we will consider the life-span perspective, which helps place adult development and aging into the context of the whole human experience. Afterward, we will consider the fundamental developmental forces, controversies, and models that form the foundation for studying adult development and aging. In particular, we will examine the biological, psychological, sociocultural, and life-cycle forces; the nature-nurture and continuity-discontinuity controversies; and the mechanistic, organismic, and contextual models. We will consider some basic definitions of age and will see that it can be viewed in many different ways. Finally, by examining various research methods, we will see how the information presented in this book was obtained.

The Life-Span Perspective

Adult development and aging does not happen in isolation from the rest of the human experience. Indeed, we cannot understand adults' experiences without appreciating what came before in childhood and adolescence. Placing adulthood in this broader context is what the life-span perspective is all about. **The *life-span perspective* divides human development into two phases: an early phase (childhood and adolescence) and a later phase (consisting of young adulthood, middle age, and old age).** The early phase is characterized by relatively rapid age-related increases in people's size and abilities. During the later phase, changes in size are slow, but abilities continue to develop as people continue adapting to the environment (Birren & Cunningham, 1985).

Viewed from the life-span perspective, adult development and aging are complex phenomena that cannot be understood within the scope of a single disciplinary approach. Understanding how adults change requires input from a wide variety of perspectives. Moreover, aging is a lifelong process, meaning that human development never stops.

Riley (1979) also points out the mutual influences of sociocultural, environmental, and historical change. These influences relate to three concepts of time described by Neugarten and Datan (1973). ***Life time* refers to the number of years a person has lived.** Both genetic (for instance, "long-life" genes) and environmental (such as pollution and lifestyle) factors influence life time. ***Sociocultural time* refers to the way that society determines the appropriate age for certain events to occur (such as the right time to get married) and sets the kinds of age-

related expectations on behavior (such as how older people are supposed to behave). Finally, *historical time* refers to the succession of social, political, economic, and environmental events through which people live (such as the Great Depression, the Vietnam War, and the AIDS epidemic). Our lives are anchored in the major events of particular historical periods. These events affect people differently depending on their age and position in society when they occur.

These different notions of time come together for each of us in our social clock (Hagestad & Neugarten, 1985; Neugarten & Hagestad, 1976). **A *social clock* is a personal timetable by which we mark our progress in terms of events in our lives.** A social clock is based on our incorporation of biological markers of time (such as menopause), sociocultural aspects of time (such as graduating from college), and historical time (such as a particular presidential election).

The mutual influence between people and society is seen best in the concept of socialization. ***Socialization* refers to the ways in which people learn to function in society.** Socialization demands that members of society conform their behavior, values, and feelings to society's expectations (Featherman, 1981). The roles we play as adults—such as parent, worker, grandparent, and retiree—reflect what we have incorporated from our observation of how society deals with people in these various positions. As people change their behaviors in particular roles, they in turn change society's expectations. For example, men have significantly changed how they feel about taking care of children. Whereas a few generations ago sociocultural expectations dictated that men not change diapers, today many fathers report doing just that.

Finally, *adaptation* refers to modifying behavior in response to changing physical and sociocultural environments. For example, changing the nursing home environment to allow residents to have a stronger sense of control may actually help them live longer. Adults of all ages respond to changes in their environment, and flexibility is a key aspect of healthy functioning.

Concept Checks

1. What are three reasons why it is important to study adult development and aging?
2. What are life time, sociocultural time, and historical time, and how do they relate to the social clock?
3. What is socialization?

FORCES, CONTROVERSIES, AND MODELS IN ADULT DEVELOPMENT AND AGING

Learning Objectives:

- What are the three main forces that shape development? What are normative age-graded influences, normative history-graded influences, and nonnormative influences?
- What are the nature-nurture, continuity-discontinuity, and universal versus context-specific development controversies?
- What are the mechanistic, organismic, and contextual models?

How do some people manage to remain thin while other people seemingly gain weight merely looking at food? Why do some people remain very active mentally well into later life? How does growing up in a Spanish-speaking culture affect one's views of family caregiving? Answering these questions requires us to consider the various forces that shape us as we mature. Developmentalists place special emphasis on four forces: biological, psychological, sociocultural, and life-cycle. These forces direct our development much as an artist's hands direct the course of a painting or sculpture.

Following from the forces that shape development are questions such as: What is the relative importance of genetics and environment on people's behavior? Do people change gradually or do they change more abruptly? Do all people change in the same way? These questions reflect three core controversies that underlie the study of human development (Lerner, 1986): the nature-nurture controversy, the continuity-discontinuity controversy, and the universal versus context-specific development controversy.

How developmentalists make sense of adult development and aging tends to fall into three views or models (Pepper, 1942): mechanistic, organismic, and contextual. **A *model* is a metaphorical representation of reality that allows very complex phenomena, such as human development, to become more understandable.** Models are not testable; that is, they cannot be subjected to an experimental examination and be falsified. But models are very important because they stimulate the creation of ideas, concepts, issues, and questions that result in testable *hypotheses;* in addition, models may suggest specific methods that can be used to address the issues.

Having a firm grasp on the forces, controversies, and models of development is important, as it provides a context for understanding why researchers and theorists believe certain things about aging or why some topics have been researched a great deal and others have been hardly studied at all. For example, one who believes that a decline in intellectual ability is an innate and inevitable part of aging is unlikely to search for intervention techniques to raise performance. Similarly, one who believes that personality characteristics change across adulthood would be likely to search for life transitions.

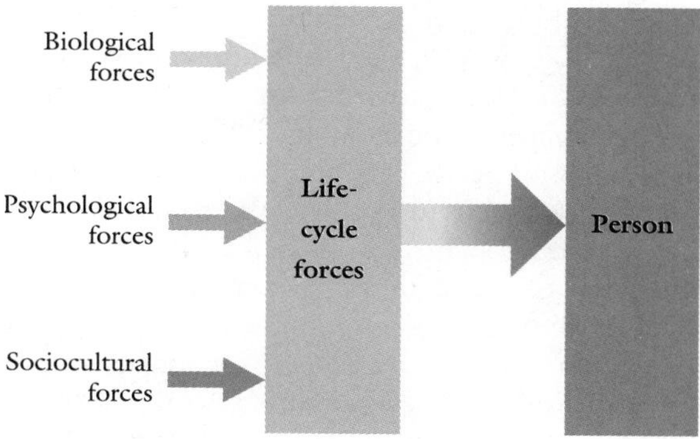

Figure 1.1 It is the interaction of biological, psychological, and sociocultural forces, through life-cycle forces, that shape a person's development.
Source: Kail and Cavanaugh, 1996

The Forces of Development

Why do some people develop gray hair in young adulthood? Why do some older adults continue to perform well on intelligence tests? Why are some older adults very active whereas others withdraw? Why might reactions to an unplanned pregnancy be different for a 26-year-old woman compared to a 46-year-old woman? These questions require us to understand the basic forces that shape us. Developmentalists typically consider four interactive forces:

- ***Biological forces* include all genetic and health-related factors that affect development.** Examples of biological forces include menopause, facial wrinkling, and changes in the major organ systems.
- ***Psychological forces* include all internal perceptual, cognitive, emotional, and personality factors that affect development.** Collectively, psychological forces provide the characteristics we notice about people that make them individuals.
- ***Sociocultural forces* include interpersonal, societal, cultural, and ethnic factors that affect development.** Sociocultural forces provide diversity and the network of people with whom we interact.
- ***Life-cycle forces* reflect differences in how the same event or combination of biological, psychological, and sociocultural forces affects people at different points in their lives.** Life-cycle forces provide the context for the developmental differences of interest in adult development and aging.

As depicted in Figure 1.1, each one of us is a product of a unique combination of these forces. Even identical twins growing up in the same family eventually have their own unique friends, partners, occupations, and so on. To see why all of these forces are important, imagine that we want to know how people feel about forgetting. We would need to consider several biological factors, such as whether the forgetting was due to an underlying disease. We would want to know about such psychological factors as what the person's memory ability has been throughout his or her life, as well as about his or her beliefs about what happens to memory with increasing age. We would need to know about sociocultural factors, such as the influence of social stereotypes about forgetting. Finally, we would need to know about the age of the person when forgetting experience occurs. Focusing on only one (or even two or three) of the forces would provide an incomplete view of how the person feels.

Interrelations Among the Forces: Developmental Influences

All of the forces we have discussed combine to create the developmental experiences people have. One way to consider these combinations is to consider the degree to which they are common or unique. Based on this approach, Baltes (1979) identifies three sets of influences that interact to produce developmental change over the life span: normative age-graded influences, normative history-graded influences, and nonnormative influences.

Normative age-graded influences **are those experiences caused by biological, psychological, and sociocultural forces that are highly correlated with chronological age.** Some of these—such as puberty, menarche, and menopause—are biological. These normative biological events usually indicate a major change in a person's life; for example, menopause is an indicator that a woman can no longer bear children without medical intervention. Normative psychological events would include focusing on certain concerns at different points in adulthood, such as a concern with socializing the younger generation when a person is middle-aged. Other normative age-graded influences involve sociocultural forces, such as the time when first marriage occurs and the age at which one retires. Normative age-graded influences typically correspond to major time-marker events, which are often ritualized. For example, many younger adults formally celebrate turning 21 as the official transition to adulthood; getting married is typically surrounded with much celebration; and retirement is often begun with a party celebrating the end of one's employment. These events provide the most convenient way to judge where we are on our social clock.

This middle-aged mother of a young child illustrates that chronological age alone does not provide very much information about a person.

Normative history-graded influences **are events that most people in a specific culture experience at the same point in time.** These events may be biological (such as epidemics), psychological (such as particular stereotypes), or sociocultural (such as changing attitudes toward sexuality). Normative history-graded influences often endow a generation with its unique identity, such as the baby-boom generation (people born roughly between 1946 and 1960) or generation X (people born after roughly 1965). These influences can have a profound effect. For example, the emergence of acquired immune deficiency syndrome (AIDS) during the 1980s fundamentally changed the attitudes toward dating and casual

SOMETHING TO THINK ABOUT

Developmental Forces in Action

One may assume from our discussion about the four basic forces of development that most research would incorporate all of them as a matter of course. This is not the case. Considering all four forces requires researchers to adopt a multidisciplinary view of adult development and aging, a view that is relatively new. Before this, most developmentalists regarded aging as an inevitable decline due to biological deterioration and did not see the need for other views.

Incorporating all four forces in multidisciplinary research is a departure from the past. Working within this approach also means accepting that aging is an extraordinarily complex process. For one thing, it means that biological aging, psychological aging, and sociocultural aging are not isolated phenomena; they must be viewed as part of a whole process.

What would an approach to adult development and aging look like from this multidisciplinary approach? As an example, let's consider what happens to intelligence as people grow older. Age differences in intelligence must be considered in the context of ongoing normative changes in the brain and in the context of developmental differences in other psychological abilities. Moreover, these intellectual differences must also be regarded in terms of the culture in which an individual lives and the important historical changes in education and technology that could affect the way people think. For example, the availability of the World Wide Web and multimedia educational software profoundly affect the way people learn, which in turn affects what they learn, dramatically influencing underlying intellectual abilities.

To make a multidisciplinary approach more personally relevant, take a minute to think about your own development. Think about the complex ways your life has been changed due to the interplay of biological, psychological, sociocultural, and life-cycle forces. See if you can identify why it makes more sense to think about all four of these forces being included in an explanation of your development than trying to account for yourself with only one of them. It's something to think about.

sexual relationships that had developed during the preceding decades.

***Nonnormative influences* are random or rare events that may be important for a specific individual but are not experienced by most people.** These may be favorable events, such as winning the lottery or an election, or unfavorable ones, such as an accident or layoff. The unpredictability of these events makes them unique. It is as if one's life is turned upside down overnight.

Life-cycle forces determine the relative importance of these three influences, as it depends on the specific behaviors examined and the particular point in the life span when they occur (Hultsch & Plemons, 1979). For example, history-graded influences may produce generational differences and conflict; parents' experiences years ago as young adults may have little to do with the complex issues faced by today's young adults. In turn, these interactions have important implications for understanding differences that are apparently age related. That is, differences may be explained in terms of differential life experiences (normative history-graded influences) rather than as an integral part of the aging process itself (normative age-graded influences). We will return to this issue when we discuss age, cohort, and time-of-measurement effects in research on adult development and aging.

The combined interactive effects of the four forces shape the course of human development across the life span. For an example of how this process works in intellectual development, take a minute to read the Something to Think About feature.

Controversies in Development

The forces of development provide the basis for building more general questions about how people develop. Many of these questions have to do with the basic plan of development, especially in terms of the relative importance of genetics and the environment, and whether development proceeds smoothly or occurs in a more segmented fashion. These more general questions form the three most important controversies in development: the nature-nurture controversy, the continuity-discontinuity controversy, and the universal versus context-specific development controversy.

The Nature-Nurture Controversy

The extent to which inborn, hereditary characteristics (nature) and experiential, or environmental, influences (nurture) determine who we are define the *nature-nurture controversy.* The two positions are captured well in the notions: "Your genes determine who you are, and that's that," and "You are a product of your environment."

Until the 1970s and 1980s, most theorists viewed adult development and aging from a nature position: Certain changes occur inevitably as people grow older, and one can do little to alter their course. This approach to aging can be seen in the works of such divergent writers as Shakespeare, who described old age in *As You Like It* as a second childhood, and David Wechsler, who believed that intellectual development in adulthood meant an inevitable loss of skills. More recently, the pendulum has shifted to the nurture side. Evidence is growing that the decline in performance on intelligence tests is not inevitable and is potentially remediable, at least for healthy older adults on some tasks.

How do nature and nurture interact? Anastasi (1958) points out that any specific hereditary factor can be reflected in any of several possible behaviors. Which behavior is observed depends on the environment present at any given time. For example, children born with Down syndrome have a specific genetic defect: an extra chromosome in the 21st pair. Although Down syndrome results in mental retardation, the degree of retardation depends in part on the child's environment. Children placed in an unstimulating environment are likely to be more severely retarded than children placed in a stimulating environment.

This same principle is being adapted in the study of some diseases associated with aging. For example, one theory of Alzheimer's disease holds that the illness has a genetic component (see Chapter 9). However, whether one actually gets Alzheimer's disease, and possibly even the course of the disease itself, may be influenced by the environment. Specifically, the genetic predisposition hypothesis states that an environmental trigger is needed for the disease to occur. Moreover, some evidence indicates that providing a supportive environment for persons with Alzheimer's disease improves their performance on cognitive tasks, at least for a while (Camp et al., 1993).

One difficulty in focusing on nature in studying adult development and aging is determining whether a particular behavior or disease has a genetic component. Having lived for many years already, older adults pose tough problems for geneticists. Documenting a genetic component in a behavior that may have been part of their repertoire for many years is very difficult. For this reason, most research on genetics and aging focuses on disorders, such as Alzheimer's disease, that show some evidence of a genetic component (such as an abnormal gene) that can be linked to certain behavioral patterns.

Anastasi (1958) also points out the range of effects of heredity on behavior. When the influences of heredity are strong and direct, effective intervention may not be possible. For example, there currently is no effective treatment for Huntington's disease, a genetic disorder that ultimately results in severe mental decline and death (see Chapter 9).

In contrast, in many situations the effects of heredity are indirect, such as susceptibility to a disease such as AIDS. In these cases, people's behavior and the environment in which they live are especially important in understanding how people get a disease, and effective means of prevention often lie outside the biological realm. For example, increased education about how to have safe sex can reduce the risk of getting AIDS.

Just as the effects of heredity must be understood by considering the environment, so the effects of environment must be understood by considering heredity (Lerner, 1986). The issue is the breadth of the influence of the environment (Anastasi, 1958). In some cases environmental effects are narrow, having a minimal, temporary impact on only a few specific aspects of behavior. In other cases environmental factors affect a wide range of behaviors, and their influence lasts a long time.

As is the case with hereditary influences, environmental influences vary in how directly they influence behavior. For instance, the outcome of a specific type of environmental effect, such as social class, depends on the individual's inherited characteristics. Given equally supportive and cognitively rich environments, we would not expect a person in the late stages of Huntington's disease to profit from intervention as much as a normal middle-aged adult. Thus, even when we consider environmental influences, our genetic inheritance is important (Lerner, 1986). For example, assuming that all older adults will profit equally from cognitive training without taking into account their inborn characteristics is a mistake, as is assuming that a person cannot do a particular task simply because he or she is 70 years old.

In general, to understand behavior we must *simultaneously* consider the individual's inborn, hereditary characteristics and the individual's environment. Each of us is genetically unique and has unique interactions with a given environment. Both factors have to be considered together to yield an adequate account of why we behave the way we do. To explain an individual's behavior and discover where to focus intervention, we must look at the unique interaction for that individual between nature and nurture.

The Continuity-Discontinuity Controversy

The second major issue in developmental psychology is a derivative of the nature-nurture controversy. Given that people change over time, and given that rules govern these changes, how do these rules hold up across the life span? Can the same rules that describe a person at one point be used to describe that person at another point, or do we need to use different rules? If we can use the same rules to account for behavior at two different points, we have *continuity.* But if we need to use different rules at different times, we have *discontinuity* (Lerner, 1986).

The *continuity-discontinuity controversy* is reflected in the competing views that adulthood is largely a matter of stability in behaviors and characteristics or that it is marked by significant and fundamental changes. The debate over the relative stability or change in behavior is especially heated in the areas of intellectual and personality development. The continuity-discontinuity issue lies at the heart of accounting for change within individuals. As we will see, two additional aspects of the controversy have major theoretical implications: description versus explanation and quantitative change versus qualitative change.

Think for a moment about the way you behaved when you were 5 years old. You can probably come up with a list of behaviors that have changed, as well as a list of behaviors that have stayed with you. The first things that may come to mind are specific behavioral differences, such as being less able to express yourself and being less able to open large doors. On the other hand, you may still cry sometimes when you are very happy or sad. Noting specific differences and similarities such as these *describes* the changes that have occurred. To *explain* the differences, you would have to offer some reason, such as brain development (for language) and height (for opening doors).

Most of the research we will consider in this book focuses on describing adults. Careful description is essential because we first need to know the areas in which adults change or stay the same before we can develop reasons why these patterns occur. Still, a few attempts at explanation have been made, most notably in cognitive development and personality development.

The second subissue concerns whether developmental change is quantitative or qualitative. This distinction can be understood more easily by consider the following situation: A person is presented with a hypothetical dilemma concerning whether to stay with an alcoholic spouse. The nonalcoholic partner has given an ultimatum to the alcoholic—one more time coming home drunk, and the partner will leave. The alcoholic again comes home drunk. The dilemma: What should the nonalcoholic spouse do?

This problem typifies those often used to study intellectual development in adulthood and is solved differently depending on the age of the respondent. The explanation for the different solutions also varies, creating two different pictures of why people's responses change (Lerner, 1986).

Age differences in solutions may reflect *quantitative* change, that is, a change in how much of something, such as knowledge, exists. Perhaps people give different solutions because they have learned more about marriages over the years and so are drawing on more experience. **In contrast, age differences in knowledge may reflect *qualitative change,* which involves a difference in the essence of what exists.** A qualitative change in knowledge means that the fundamental way in which people think has changed. Qualitative change is not a matter of more of the same, which characterizes quantitative change. Rather, qualitative change deals with a new quality in a person (Lerner, 1986). The notion of qualitative change has been adopted by many developmental psychologists. Writers such as Jean Piaget and Erik Erikson represent these qualitative changes as sequences of stages that individuals pass through on their way to maturity.

The Universal Versus Context-Specific Development Controversy

The controversy concerning whether there is only one pathway of development or several is the *universal versus context-specific development controversy.* One probably would not argue that all older adults are identical; rather one would likely point out that there are individual variations among them. Some theorists would explain that these differences are more apparent than real and that actually only one basic course of development exists for everyone. According to this view, what appear to be differences are really merely variations on the fundamental course of development, much like Hershey, Nestlé's, Godiva, and Neuchatel chocolates are all products of the same basic manufacturing process. This means that research conducted on one group of people, such as European Americans, can be generalized to all other groups.

The opposing view is that the differences one observes among people are not simply variations on a theme. Instead, this alternative view argues that human development has many pathways because development is inextricably linked with the context in which it occurs. Development is viewed as a process of dynamic interaction with the environment, and this interaction is *not* identical across all environments. Rather, each environment has its own unique aspects that shape development. This view would argue that differences observed among European American and African American older adults, for example, reflect fundamentally different courses of development that require separate sets of explanations. As any chocolate connoisseur will agree, there's a big difference between a Hershey's Kiss and a Godiva truffle.

Models of Adult Development and Aging

Understanding the underlying forces of development, as well as the three major controversies, provides the basis for creating various viewpoints on adult development and aging. Which of the forces theorists emphasize most and which side of each controversy they choose to highlight become critical when they begin to build models of development. As we will see, each model has its own combination of views on these topics, which in turn creates very different ways of accounting for development. Of the various models available for theorists (Pepper, 1942), we will focus on the three used most by developmentalists: the mechanistic, organismic, and contextual models.

The Mechanistic Model

Using a metaphor of a machine to explain how best to understand humans characterizes the *mechanistic model.* Machines are very complicated collections of interacting parts, which can be disassembled and studied separately. In short, the mechanistic model views the whole as the sum of the parts. Machines are also passive and reactive; they are incapable of doing anything on their own and rely on some environmental force to prompt them to action. We can clearly see that the mechanistic model's emphasis is on *nurture,* or the influence of the environment on behavior. The mechanistic model views people as passive organisms that react to their environment; they do not initiate actions.

Understanding human behavior from a mechanistic approach entails breaking down complex behaviors into less complex components. A good example of this is the psychometric approach to studying intelligence, the approach that is the basis for standardized intelligence tests. This approach proposes that intelligence consists of many discrete abilities, which are studied independently; a person's intelligence is conceived as the sum of the various abilities. The mechanistic model also emphasizes connections between environmental stimuli and observable behavior, rather than hypothetical concepts referring to internal processes. Finally, the mechanistic model focuses on *quantitative change.*

The Organismic Model

Viewing people as complex biological systems, and the whole as more than the sum of its parts, describes the *organismic model.* That is, something emerges from the interaction among the parts that is not predictable or understandable from focusing separately on the parts. For example, hydrogen is an extremely volatile substance that easily explodes, and oxygen provides a conducive atmosphere for fire. However, two parts hydrogen and one part oxygen, combined appropriately, provides a substance that is used to put fires out—water. So it is with people; one cannot know what a person is like simply by knowing his or her constituent parts.

The organismic model also postulates that people are active participants in their own development. People control aspects of their lives and in fact are responsible for initiating much of their intellectual and personal growth. Moreover, this development is headed to a particular goal or end state. Because the organismic model emphasizes *qualitative change,* it has provided the basis for stage theories of development, such as Piaget's theory of cognitive development. To continue our earlier example, organismic approaches to intelligence emphasize the general ways in which people think and how these ways of thinking change over time. Individual abilities are not studied independently, but rather they are thought to be reflections of an integrated mode of thought. Although such approaches are intuitively appealing, they are difficult to research because they require so many aspects of an individual to be considered simultaneously.

The Contextual Model

The model that views human development in terms of the historical event, that is, the specific point in history in which it is occurring, is the *contextual model.* How people in the late 20th century develop is different from the way people in the late 19th, or the 10th, or the 5th century B.C. developed. Each historical point has a unique combination of biological, psychological, sociocultural, and life-cycle forces that shape the way we develop. For example, our ability to protect ourselves from diseases such as polio means that we can focus our attention on other health problems, such as AIDS. In turn, each generation influences the forces that will shape future generations; development of an AIDS vaccine would lessen the need to fear this disease for our great-grandchildren.

The contextual model also proposes that the whole is greater than the sum of its parts and views people as active shapers of development. However, it is not known where human development is headed; there is no set goal or endpoint to development. *Multidirectionality* is strongly emphasized, meaning that there is more than one path to successful aging. The contextual model accepts both quantitative and qualitative change, depending on the domain in question. From this perspective, then, intelligence is the result of neither a specific combination of particular abilities nor an internally programmed holistic process. Rather, intelligence is the product of a unique combination of forces that operates on the individual within a specific context at a point in historical time. Research based on this approach is especially hard, as the possibility of identifying general principles of development is difficult because each individual's development could potentially be unique.

Research Implications of Developmental Models

How would the three developmental models influence the way developmentalists study a problem? To answer this question, let us consider three researchers studying job satisfaction across adulthood.

The mechanistic researcher would reduce job satisfaction to a few principles of learning that hold true for all people, regardless of age, and would search for the environmental contingencies that govern behavior. Understanding job satisfaction may consist of mapping the contingency between productivity and salary, for example, on the assumption that salary would be viewed as a reinforcer for good work.

In contrast, the organismic investigator would concentrate on discontinuities in job satisfaction across the life span by identifying the internal motivating factors for doing good work. This researcher might focus on a worker's desire to achieve or the thought processes that underlie self-concept at a given point in the life span. External contingencies, such as salary and working conditions, would be deemphasized.

Finally, the contextualist investigator would describe the relationship of current job satisfaction to job satisfaction earlier in life, to current sociocultural influences, and to future potentials. The contextualist researcher would also be interested in describing the reciprocal interactions among all of these factors. Job satisfaction might be explored by trying to discern the congruity, or fit, between the personal needs of the individual and the opportunities provided by the environment.

As you can see, scientists working within different models ask fundamentally different questions about the nature of development. They collect different data and may even come to very different conclusions. Some criterion other than "truth" must be used to evaluate theories based on different models, as what constitutes "truth" depends on the model in which one is working (Lerner, 1986). Because no one model is intrinsically better than another, Lerner (1986) suggests that the findings derived from research based on different models be evaluated in terms of how well they describe and explain development, as well as their utility in developing ways to optimize human behavior.

Practical Implications of Developmental Models

The model one adopts has important practical implications, too. Models are used to develop and implement everything from educational systems to social programs. Let's consider the Smith family. The Smiths live in the inner city of a large metropolitan area. Their income is barely above the poverty level, but it is enough to make them ineligible for most subsidy programs. Their outlook on life is not highly optimistic. How will we help the Smiths?

A mechanist will believe that environmental factors need to be changed. Consequently, the mechanist will suggest housing programs, income maintenance, and other interventions in which the Smiths are subjected to some externally driven change. Such an approach will ignore factors such as whether the Smiths want the programs in question and whether they like what is happening. In short, if the environment is changed, everything will fall into place.

In contrast, an organicist will be likely to do little or nothing. From this perspective the Smiths are responsible for their own development, and no outside intervention can change that. Attempts may be made to make the environment less of a hindrance, but the primary intervention will be to get them to become motivated to change. In other words, the family becomes responsible for its own behavior; the environment is innocent. This approach reflects a self-discovery, self-initiated, "pull yourself up by your own bootstraps" philosophy.

Finally, the contextualist will argue that the Smiths can be helped by changing the sociocultural context in which they live. Change will have to occur not only in the environment, but within the Smiths as well. For example, housing reform will be ineffective unless the Smiths take advantage of the opportunity. The contextual perspective will play down the quick fix in favor of a more broad-based social policy.

We see these different perspectives every day. Politicians debate the relative merits of intervention programs from each point of view. In the United States, many people believed that most of the mechanistic interventions instituted during the 1960s did not work, and these programs came under severe attack in the mid-1990s. In their place, many people opted for a more organismic approach, emphasizing that people must accept responsibility for their own situation and that government should do as little as possible. Nevertheless, irrespective of which model one adopts, complex social problems are not easily solved.

Concept Checks

1. What are some examples of the biological, psychological, sociocultural, and life-cycle forces of development?
2. Using test scores to describe changes in intelligence over time would be an example of which type of change (qualitative or quantitative)?
3. Which model of development (mechanistic, organismic, or contextual) would be most likely to support the view that one's experience of adulthood and aging is in part a function of the generation in which one lives?

THE MEANING OF AGE

Learning Objectives:

- What does the index variable chronological age mean?
- What do we mean by biological age, psychological age, and sociocultural age?
- How can we categorize developmental research based on how it uses the variable age? What is a surrogate variable?

We have seen that one of the basic forces of development are life-cycle forces, which reflect differences in the effects of events and so forth as a function of age. Consequently, one of the most important aspects of studying adult development and aging is understanding the concept of aging itself. Aging is not a single process. Rather, it consists of at least three distinct processes: primary, secondary, and tertiary aging (Birren & Cunningham, 1985). ***Primary aging*** **refers to the normal, disease-free development during adulthood.** Changes in biological, psychological, sociocultural, or life-cycle processes in primary aging are an inevitable part of the developmental process; examples include menopause, decline in reaction time, and the loss of family and friends. Most of the information in this book represents primary aging. ***Secondary aging*** **refers to developmental changes that are related to disease, lifestyle, and other environmentally induced changes that are not inevitable (e.g., pollution).** The progressive loss of intellectual abilities in Alzheimer's disease and related forms of dementia are examples of secondary aging. **Finally, *tertiary aging* refers to the rapid losses that occur shortly before death.** An example of tertiary aging is a phenomenon known as terminal drop, in which intellectual abilities show a marked decline in the last few years preceding death.

Increasingly, researchers are emphasizing that everyone does not grow old in the same way. Whereas most people tend to show *usual patterns of aging* that reflect the typical, or normative, changes with age, other people show *successful aging* in which few signs of change occur. For example, although most people tend to get chronic diseases as they get older, some people never do. What makes people who age successfully different? At this point, we do not really know for sure. It may be a unique combination of genetics, optimal environment, flexibility in dealing with life situations, a strong sense of personal control, and maybe even a bit of luck. For our present discussion, the main point to keep in mind throughout is that everyone's experience of growing old is somewhat different. Though many people develop arthritis, how each individual learns to cope will be unique.

Age as an Index

When most of us think about age, we usually think of how long we have been around since our birth; this way of defining age is known as *chronological age.* Chronological age provides a shorthand method to index time and to organize events and data by using a commonly understood standard, calendar time. Chronological age is not the only shorthand index variable used in adult development and aging. Gender, ethnicity, and socioeconomic status are others.

No index variable itself actually causes behavior. In the case of gender, for example, it is not whether a person is male or female per se that determines how long he or she will live on average, but rather the underlying forces, such as hormonal effects, that are the true causes. This point is often forgotten when age is the index variable, perhaps because it is so familiar to us and so widely used. However, age (or time) does not directly cause things to happen, either. Iron left out in the rain will rust, but rust is not caused simply by time. Rather, rust is a *time-dependent process* involving oxidation in which time is a measure of the rate by which rust is created. Similarly, human behavior is affected by experiences that occur with the passage of time, not by time itself. What we study in adult development and aging is the result of time- or age-dependent processes, not the result of age itself.

What do we need to do in order to know whether some behavior is actually time dependent? Birren and Renner (1977) argue that we need to understand the underlying biological, psychological, sociocultural, and life-cycle forces that are all intertwined in an index such as chronological age.

Definitions of Age

Age can be considered from each of the perspectives of the remaining basic forces of development (Birren & Cunningham, 1985): biological, psychological, and sociocultural.

Biological Age

Where people are relative to the maximum number of years they could possibly live is their *biological age.* Biological age is assessed by measuring the functioning of the various vital, or life-limiting, organ systems, such as the cardiovascular system. With increasing age the vital organ systems typically lose their capacity for self-regulation and adaptation, resulting in an increased probability of dying. Through a healthy lifestyle, one can slow some of the age-related change processes and be functionally younger biologically than a lifelong couch potato. In contrast, someone who has the disease progeria, in which the body ages abnormally rapidly, is biologically much older than his or her peers. In short, biological age accounts for many health-related aspects of functioning in assigning an age to an individual.

Psychological Age

The functional level of the psychological abilities that people use to adapt to changing environmental demands is their *psychological age.* These abilities include memory, intelligence, feelings, motivation, and other skills that foster and maintain self-esteem and personal control. For example, 15-year-old Michelle who attends college would be considered psychologically older in the intellectual domain, because the large majority of her classmates are 22 or older. On the other hand, Mildred, a 65-year-old English major, would be thought of as psychologically young in the intellectual area, because the majority of her classmates are chronologically younger.

Many myths about older adults stem from our misconceptions about the abilities that underlie definitions of psychological age. For example, many people believe that all types of memory and other cognitive abilities decline precipitously in later life. Many of these beliefs are wrong, meaning that we need to revise the standards by which we judge psychological aging in these domains.

Sociocultural Age

At some point, we all have probably been told to act our age. There seem to be unwritten expectations of how individuals of a certain chronological age should act. Such unwritten expectations are what is meant by sociocultural age. **More formally, *sociocultural age* refers to the specific set**

Although chronologically older than most of her classmates, the woman on the right is psychologically younger than most of her same-age peers.

of roles individuals adopt in relation to other members of the society and culture to which they belong. Sociocultural age is judged on the basis of many behaviors and habits, such as style of dress, customs, language, and interpersonal style. Most important is the extent to which a person shows the age-graded behavior expected by the society in which one lives; this forms the basis by which a person is judged to be socioculturally younger or older. If one is adopting new roles ahead of one's peers, then one is considered socioculturally older. For example, Loretta Lynn, who married at 14, would be considered socioculturally old in comparison with the typical age norm of the early- to mid-twenties for first marriage in U.S. society. In contrast, one who adopts roles later than one's peers would be considered socioculturally younger. Bette Midler, who had her first child when she was middle-aged, would be considered socioculturally young; most women have their first child during their twenties.

Sociocultural age is especially important in understanding many of the family and work roles we adopt. When to get married, have children, make career moves, retire, and so on are often influenced by what we think our sociocultural age is. Such decisions also play a role in determining our self-esteem and other aspects of personality. Many of the most damaging stereotypes about aging (such as that older people should not be having sex) are based on faulty assumptions about sociocultural age.

Issues in Studying Age

Developmental research can be categorized on the basis of how it uses the variable of age (Birren & Cunningham, 1985). **In the *developmentally static approach*, the major goal of the researcher is to describe individuals in particular age groups.** For instance, a researcher may be interested in how 21-year-olds and 30-year-olds behave on a date. In this case age is used mainly to define the boundaries of the investigation; the two groups would be studied at one point in time. **In contrast, the *developmentally dynamic approach* seeks to understand the processes of change.** The focus here is to understand how people develop, what characterizes change, and how change happens. In the developmentally dynamic approach, the researcher would be most interested in how 21-year-old daters evolve into 30-year-old daters. This would require following people for 9 years, periodically testing them along the way.

The need for precision in defining the role of age is more important in the developmentally dynamic approach. The ultimate interest of researchers in this approach is not the passage of time but rather the changes in behavior that emerge over time. These behavioral changes are only crudely indexed by chronological age (for example, not all 21-year-olds have the same amount of prior dating experience). Once this fact is recognized, however, there are two courses that could be followed.

In the first alternative, chronological age could be replaced by one of the definitions described earlier that focus on some specific process, such as psychological age. This would put the focus on a more specific ability, which could then be tracked over time. The advantage to this approach would be a more precise understanding of the developmental processes under investigation.

In the second alternative, chronological age is used as a *surrogate variable* to represent the very complex, interrelated influences on people over time. Use of a surrogate variable such as age does not allow a researcher to state the cause of some behavior precisely, because the surrogate variable represents so many different things (Birren & Cunningham, 1985). If we say that memory for details shows an age-related decrease, we do not know whether the difference stems from biological processes, psychological processes, sociocultural processes, or some combination of them. Even though chronological age is a crude index, it still may provide useful information that can be used to guide future, more precise research that could narrow the number of explanations.

To date, most researchers have chosen to use chronological age as a surrogate variable. However, the strategy adopted over the past decade is to combine this use of chronological age with the concepts of primary, secondary, and tertiary aging. In particular, most of the research reported in this book focuses on primary (disease-free) aging. Participants in most studies are described as "healthy, community-dwelling adults." Although this tie between age as a surrogate variable and primary aging is often not stated explicitly, it nevertheless offers an important way to document and understand the processes of aging that represent usual patterns of aging.

Concept Checks

1. What is a time-dependent process?
2. What are some examples of biological age, psychological age, and sociocultural age?
3. If a researcher follows a group of people over time to understand some phenomenon, is the person using a developmentally static or a developmentally dynamic approach?

RESEARCH METHODS

Learning Objectives:

- What do age, cohort, and time of measurement mean in the context of research designs?
- What are the basic developmental research designs?
- What alternative approaches to doing research are there?
- What are the special concerns about conducting research with adults?

The study of adult development and aging adheres to the principles of scientific inquiry. Information concerning adult development and aging is gathered in the same ways as in other social sciences, such as psychology, sociology, anthropology, and allied health and medical sciences. Gerontologists have the same problems as other scientists: finding appropriate control or comparison groups, limiting generalizations to the types of groups included in the research, and finding adequate means of measurement (Kausler, 1982).

What makes the study of adult development and aging a bit different from other areas of social science is the need to consider multiple influences on behavior. Explanations of development require consideration of all of the forces we considered earlier. This makes research on adult development

Events such as the Vietnam War that affect a particular generation are examples of normative history-graded influences, as well as experiences that create clear cohort effects.

and aging more difficult, if for no other reason than it requires examining more variables.

Age, Cohort, and Time of Measurement

Every study of adult development and aging is built on the combination of three fundamental effects: age, cohort, and time of measurement (Schaie, 1984). ***Age effects* reflect differences due to underlying processes, that is, biological, psychological, or sociocultural changes.** Although usually represented in research by chronological age, age effects refer to inherent changes within the person and are not caused by the passage of time per se. As we established earlier in this chapter, a better approach would be to use a more specific definition of age (such as biological, psychological, or sociocultural age).

***Cohort effects* are differences due to experiences and circumstances unique to the particular generation to which one belongs.** In general, cohort effects correspond to normative history-graded influences. However, in studying cohort effects, defining a cohort may not be easy. Cohorts can be specific, as in all people born in one particular year, or general, such as the baby-boom cohort. As described earlier, each generation is exposed to different sets of historical and personal events (such as World War II, home computers, opportunities to attend college). Later in this section we will consider evidence of just how profound cohort effects can be.

***Time-of-measurement effects* reflect differences stemming from sociocultural, environmental, historical, or other events at the time the data are obtained from the participants.** For example, data concerning wage increases given in a particular year may be influenced by the economic conditions of that year. If the economy is in a serious recession, pay increases would likely be small. In contrast, if the economy is booming, pay increases could be quite large. Clearly, whether a study is conducted during a recession or a boom will affect what is learned about pay changes. In short, when a researcher decides to do research could lead him or her to different conclusions about the phenomenon being studied.

In conducting adult development and aging research, investigators have attempted to identify and separate the three effects. This has not been easy, because all three influences are interrelated. If one is interested in studying 40-year-olds, one must necessarily select the cohort that was born 40 years ago. In this case age and cohort are *confounded,* because one cannot know whether the behaviors observed are because the participants are 40 years old or because of the specific life experiences they have had as a result of being born in a particular historical period. **In general, *confounding* refers to any situation in which one cannot determine which of two (or more) effects is responsible for the behaviors being observed.** Confounding of the three effects we are considering here represents the most serious problem in adult development and aging research.

Developmental Research Designs

What distinguishes developmental researchers from their colleagues in other areas of psychology is a fundamental interest in understanding how people change. Developmental researchers must look at the ways in which people differ across time. Doing so necessarily requires that they understand the distinction between age change and age difference. An *age change* occurs in an individual's behavior over time. A person's reaction time may not be as short at age 70 as it was at age 40. To discover an age change one must examine the same person at more than one point in time. An *age difference* is obtained when at least two different persons of different ages are compared. A person of 70 may have a longer reaction time than another person of age 40. Even though we may be able to document substantial age differences, we cannot assume that they imply an age change. We do not know whether the 70-year-old person has changed since he or she was 40, and of course we do not know whether the 40-year-old will be any different at age 70. In some cases age differences reflect age changes, and in some cases they do not.

If what we really want to understand in developmental research is age change (what happens as people grow older), we should strive to design our research with this goal in mind. Moreover, different research questions require different research designs. We will consider the most common ways in which researchers gather data concerning age differences and age changes: cross-sectional, longitudinal, time-lag, and sequential.

Figure 1.2 helps to keep these different research designs straight and shows how each of the designs relates to the others. The figure depicts a matrix containing each major effect (age, cohort, and time of measurement). Cohort is represented by the years down the left column. Time of measurement is represented by the years across the bottom. Age is represented by the numbers in the body of the table.

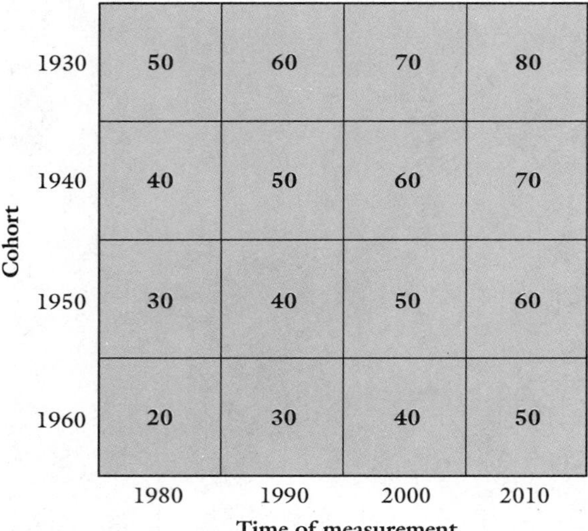

Figure 1.2 Matrix of time of measurement, cohort, and age (the cells in the body of the matrix), from which research designs can be constructed as described in the text.

Cross-Sectional Designs

To compare at least two groups of people varying in age (and cohort) at the same time of measurement, you can use *a cross-sectional design*. As such, it represents the developmentally static approach discussed earlier. Any single vertical column in Figure 1.2 represents a cross-sectional design. Cross-sectional designs allow researchers to examine age differences but not age change. The reason has to do with how many observed differences are explained.

Because all participants are measured at the same time, differences between the groups cannot be due to time-of-measurement effects. That leaves two possibilities: age change and cohort differences. Unfortunately, we cannot distinguish between them, which means that we do not know whether the differences we observe between groups stem from inherent developmental processes or from experiences peculiar to their cohort. To see this more clearly, take a careful look at Figure 1.2. Notice that the different age groups are automatically formed when particular cohorts are selected, and vice versa. Thus, if the researcher wants to study people of a certain age at a particular time, he or she has no choice in choosing a cohort.

This confounding of age and cohort is the major problem with cross-sectional studies.

Cross-sectional research tends to paint a bleak picture of aging. For example, as shown in Figure 1.3, early research on the development of intelligence across adulthood repeatedly showed large drops in performance with age. The problem is that we have no way of knowing whether most people show the same developmental progressions; that is, we cannot address the issue of individual differences over time.

Despite the confounding of age and cohort and the limitation of only being able to identify age differences, cross-sectional designs dominate the research literature in gerontology. The reason is a pragmatic one: Because all of the measurements are obtained at one time, cross-sectional research can be conducted relatively quickly and inexpensively compared with other designs. As long as their limits are recognized, cross-sectional studies can provide a snapshot view of age differences that may provide insight into issues that may be followed up with other designs that are sensitive to age change.

Longitudinal Designs

Testing a single cohort over multiple times of measurement defines a *longitudinal design.* Longitudinal designs represent the developmentally dynamic approach, as it provides information about age change. A longitudinal design is represented by any horizontal row in Figure 1.2. A major advantage of longitudinal designs is that age changes are identified because we are studying the same people over time. But if age changes are found, can we say why they occurred?

Because only one cohort is studied, cohort effects are eliminated as an explanation of change. However, the other two potential explanations, age and time of measurement, are confounded. For example, suppose that we wanted to follow the 1930 cohort over time. If we wanted to test these individuals when they were 70 years old, we would have to do so in 2000. Consequently, any changes we identify could be due to changes in underlying processes or factors that are related to the time we choose to conduct our measurement. For instance, if we conducted a longitudinal study of salary growth, the amount of salary change in any comparison could stem from real change in skills and worth of the person to the company or from the economic conditions of the times. In a longitudinal study we cannot tell which of these factors is more important.

Longitudinal studies have three additional potential problems. First, if the research measure requires some type of performance by the participants, we may have the problem of *practice effects.* Practice effects refer to the fact that performance may improve over time simply because people are being tested over and over again with the same measures. Repeatedly using the same measure on the same people may have significant effects on their behavior, may make the measure invalid, and may have a negative impact on the participants' perceptions of the research (Baltes, Reese, & Nesselroade, 1977).

Second, we may have a problem with *participant dropout.* Participant dropout refers to the fact that it is difficult to keep a group of research participants intact over the course of a longitudinal study. Participants may move, may lose interest, or may die. Suppose we want to examine the relationship between intelligence and health. Participant dropout can result in two different outcomes. We can end up with *positive selective survival* if the participants at the end of the study tend to be the ones who were initially higher on some variable; for example, the surviving participants are the ones who were the most healthy at the beginning of the study. In contrast, we could have *negative selective survival* if the participants at the conclusion of the study were initially lower on an important variable; for example, the surviving participants may have been those who initially weighed the least.

The extent to which the characteristics of the group change over time determines the degree of the problem. We may not know exactly what differences there are between those who return for every session and those who do not. What we do know is that the people who always return, in general, are more outgoing, are healthier, have higher self-esteem, and are more likely to be married than those who drop out (Schaie & Hertzog, 1985).

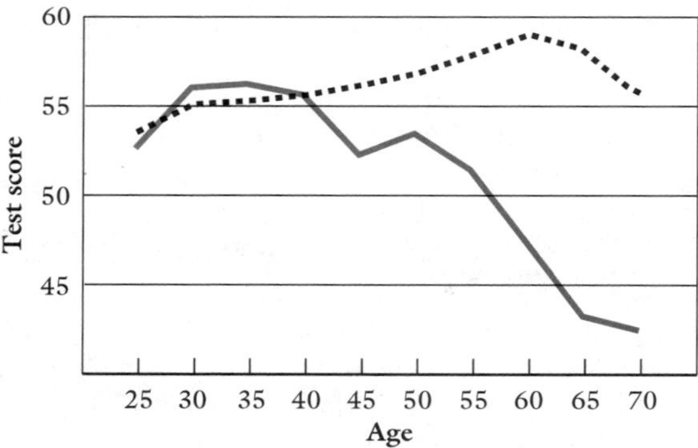

Figure 1.3 Cross-sectional (solid line) age differences and longitudinal (dashed line) age changes in intelligence for a verbal meaning test.
Source: "A Cross-Sequential Study of Age Changes in Cognitive Behavior," by K. W. Schaie and C. R. Strother, 1968, Psychological Bulletin, 70, *671–680. Copyright © 1968 by the American Psychological Association. Reprinted with permission.*

In any case, the result may be an overly optimistic picture of aging. Compare some typical results from longitudinal studies of intelligence, shown in Figure 1.3, with those gathered in cross-sectional studies. Clearly, the developmental trends represented are quite different.

The third problem with longitudinal designs is that our ability to apply the results to other groups is limited. The difficulty is that only one cohort is followed. Whether the pattern of results that is observed in one cohort can be generalized to another cohort is questionable. Thus, researchers using longitudinal designs run the risk of uncovering a developmental process that is unique to that cohort.

Because longitudinal designs necessarily take more time and are usually fairly expensive, they have not been used very frequently in the past. However, researchers now recognize that following individuals over time is badly needed to further our understanding of the aging process. Thus, longitudinal studies are becoming more common in the literature.

Time-Lag Designs

Measuring people of the same age at different times is a *time-lag design.* Time-lag designs are represented in Figure 1.2 by any top-left to bottom-right diagonal. Because only a single age is studied, there are no age-related differences. Because each cohort is associated with a unique time of measurement, however, these two effects are confounded. Time-lag designs are used to describe characteristics of people at a particular age. But because they provide no information on either age differences or age change, time-lag designs are not frequently used.

Sequential Designs

Thus far, we have considered three developmental designs, each of which has problems involving the confounding of two effects. These effects are age and cohort in cross-sectional designs, age and time of measurement in longitudinal designs, and cohort and time of measurement in time-lag designs. These confoundings create difficulties in interpreting behavioral differences between and within individuals, as illustrated in How Do We Know? Some of these interpretive dilemmas can be alleviated by using more complex designs called ***sequential designs***, which are shown in Figure 1.4 (Baltes et al., 1977; Schaie & Hertzog, 1985). Keep in mind, though, that sequential designs do not cure the confounding problems in the three basic designs.

Sequential designs build on the designs we have already considered. **As shown in the figure, a *cross-sequential design* consists of two or more cross-sectional studies that are conducted at two or more times of measurement.** These multiple cross-sectional designs each include the same age ranges; however, the participants are different in each wave of testing. For example, we might compare performances on intelligence tests for people between the ages of 20 and 50 in 1980 and then repeat the study in 1990 with a different group of people aged 30 to 60.

Figure 1.4 also depicts the longitudinal sequential design. **A *longitudinal sequential design* consists of two or more longitudinal designs that represent two or more cohorts.** Each longitudinal design in the sequence would begin with the same age range and follow people for the same length of time. For example, we may want to begin

HOW DO WE KNOW?

Conflicts Between Cross-Sectional and Longitudinal Data

As noted in the text, cross-sectional and longitudinal research designs have several limitations. What may not be clear, however, are the major implications that each has on drawing conclusions about age differences. Recall that in cross-sectional research we examine different groups of people of different ages at one point in time, thereby confounding age and cohort. In longitudinal research we examine one group of people at many points, thereby confounding age and time of measurement.

As an illustration of how using these two designs can result in opposite conclusions about age differences, let's examine the case of intellectual development. For many years a debate raged in the literature over whether intelligence increased, decreased, or remained the same across adulthood. This debate was fueled in large part by conflicting findings based on cross-sectional research and longitudinal research, reflected in Figure 1.3. Cross-sectional data documented clear age differences in intelligence with age. In contrast, longitudinal data showed no significant age differences. What conclusions could be drawn about each type of data? Which data are correct?

In the cross-sectional data, the age differences could reflect either true differences that occur with age or differences that are due to cohort, or generational, effects. For example, the fact that older people never learned computer skills in school whereas younger people did may make a difference in how well one performs on current tests of intelligence. The problem is that we cannot differentiate between these two equally plausible explanations.

In the longitudinal data, the lack of age effects could be a reflection of a true lack of change with age. However, it is also possible that only the brightest and healthiest people survived to be tested at the end of the study. This would mean that the characteristics of the sample at the end were significantly different from those of the sample at the beginning. In short, we ended up with a very different group of people. Moreover, we also do not know whether the lack of difference is due to other aspects of the environment that serve to support intellectual performance. Perhaps there are new discoveries about maintaining intellectual performance that assist older people. We cannot sort out all of these different explanations.

Neither type of data is entirely correct. It turns out that the confounding of age and cohort in the cross-sectional data was misinterpreted as showing *age* differences, when actually most of what are seen are differences due to *cohort*. The longitudinal data are problematic because of differential survival; that is, by the end of the research only the healthiest individuals remained. These survivors were not representative of the group that began the study.

This example illustrates the need for extreme caution in comparing the results of cross-sectional and longitudinal studies. We need to avoid making the same mistakes as researchers in the past. Fortunately, we have a viable solution: sequential designs.

---

a longitudinal study of intellectual development with a group of 50-year-olds in 1980, using the 1930 cohort. We would then follow this cohort for a period of years. In 1990 we would begin a second longitudinal study on 50-year-olds, using the 1940 cohort, and follow them for the same length of time as we do the first cohort.

Schaie (1965, 1977) has argued that combining cross-sequential sequences and longitudinal sequences yields a "most efficient design." The combined design yields data that can be used to address most of the major questions that interest developmental researchers. As an example, let us consider Schaie's own research on intellectual development in adulthood. The research began with a simple cross-sectional study in 1956 in which participants aged 22 to 67 years from four cohorts were given tests of intellectual abilities. In 1963 as many of these participants as possible were retested, providing longitudinal data on age changes in each of the four cohorts. At the same time, new groups of participants between 20 and 70 years old were recruited and tested. These new participants formed a second cross-sectional study

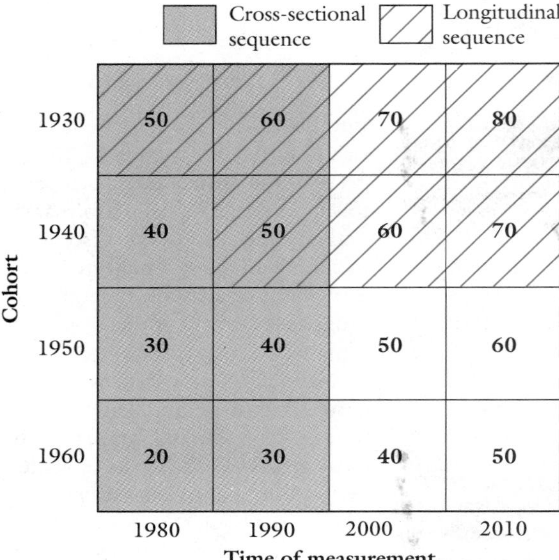

Figure 1.4 Matrix of time of measurement, cohort, and age, demonstrating sequential research designs. The first and second vertical columns illustrate cross-sectional sequences described in the text. The top two horizontal rows, likewise, illustrate longitudinal sequences mentioned in the text. (The three squares that are both shaded in green and striped are areas in the matrix where two sequences overlap.)

representing the same age groups that were tested in 1956. In 1970 both cross-sectional samples were retested, providing a second set of longitudinal data for the 1956 sample and the first for the 1963 sample. Finally, the 1963 sample was tested a third time in 1977, providing comparable 14-year spans for each of the two groups.

Although sequential designs are powerful and provide by far the richest source of information about developmental issues, few researchers use them because they are costly in terms of both money and time. Trying to follow many people over long periods of time, generating new samples, and conducting complex data analyses take considerable financial resources. Moreover, it took Schaie 21 years for all of the data to be gathered and an additional 5 years or so for the data to become widely published. Clearly, this type of commitment to one project is not possible for most researchers, especially those who are trying to establish themselves in the field. Additionally, in times of restricted research financing, the large sums needed for sequential designs may simply be unavailable.

Approaches to Doing Research

The specific design we choose for our research depends in large part on the question(s) we are trying to address in our study. Once we have made a decision, the next step involves choosing the approach we will use. Our choice at this point could limit what we may conclude from our data, especially the inferences we may draw concerning cause and effect. We will examine several approaches: experimentation, correlation, naturalistic inquiry, and observational and case studies.

Experimental Design

Suppose we are interested in learning whether having people study a word list in various ways makes a difference in how many items people will remember. What we could do is provide people of different ages with different types of instructions about how to study, and then see what happens when they are asked to remember the words. For example, we could tell one group each of younger and older adults to rehearse the words in the list we will show them three times each and not provide any special hints to a second group.

What we have done is an example of an *experiment*, which involves the manipulation of a key factor that the researcher believes is responsible for a particular behavior, as well as the random assignment of participants in the experimental and control groups. In our case, the key variable being manipulated is the instructions for how to study. More generally, in an experiment the researcher is most interested in identifying differences between groups of people. One group, the *experimental group*, receives the manipulation; another group, the *control group*, does not. This sets up a situation in which the level of the key variable of interest differs across groups.

Additionally, the investigator exerts precise control over all important aspects of the study, including the variable of interest, the setting, and the participants. Because the key variable is systematically manipulated in an experiment, researchers can infer cause-and-effect relationships about that variable. In our example, we can conclude that type of instruction (how people study) causes better or worse performance on a memory test. Discovering such cause-and-effect relationships is important if we are to understand the underlying processes of adult development and aging.

An important distinction is made between *independent variables,* which are the variables manipulated by the experimenter, and *dependent variables,* which are the behaviors or outcomes that are measured. In our example, the instructions that we give people would be the independent variable and the number of words people remember would be the dependent variable.

The results of experiments can come out in various ways. If everyone reacts the same way to the manipulation regardless of age, then we can conclude that the phenomenon under study may work in parallel ways across the age range examined. If younger and older adults improve their memory performance to equivalent degrees by rehearsing, then we could argue that rehearsal has the same benefit for both age groups. If one age group reacts very differently than the other to the manipulated variable, we obtain an *age-by-condition interaction.* Suppose the older adults benefited a great deal from rehearsing and the younger adults did not benefit at all. This age-by-condition interaction could mean that rehearsal instructions are only effective for older adults. In general, age-by-condition interactions are thought to imply that the underlying processes that produce the behavior being studied differ across age. By mapping out the conditions under which age-by-condition interactions are and are not present, we get a better picture of which psychological processes differ with age and which ones do not.

Finally, we must note that *age cannot be an independent variable because we cannot manipulate it.* Consequently, we cannot conduct true experiments to examine the effects of age on a particular person's behavior. At best, we can find *age-related effects* of an independent variable on dependent variables.

Correlational Design

In contrast to experiments, where the goal is to understand cause and effect, in *correlation* the goal is to uncover a relation between two or more observed variables. The strength and direction of a correlation is expressed by a *correlation coefficient,* abbreviated as r, which can range from -1.0 to 1.0. When $r = 0$, the two variables are unrelated. When r is greater than 0, the variables are positively related; when the value of one variable increases (or decreases), the other variable also increases (or decreases). When r is less than 0, the variables are inversely related; when one variable increases (or decreases), the other variable decreases (or increases).

An example of a correlational study is an investigation by Cavanaugh and Murphy (1986), who were interested in the relationship between anxiety and memory performance. They administered measures of anxiety and memory tests, and calculated the correlations between the two. Their results revealed a negative correlation between anxiety and memory performance, meaning that as people's anxiety increases, memory performance decreases.

Correlational studies do not give definitive information concerning cause-and-effect relationships; for example, the correlation between anxiety and memory performance in the Cavanaugh and Murphy (1986) study does not mean that one variable caused the other regardless of how large the relationship was. However, correlational studies do provide important information about the strength of relationship between variables, which is reflected in the absolute value of the correlation coefficient. Moreover, because developmental researchers are interested in how variables are related to factors that are very difficult, if not impossible, to manipulate, correlational techniques are used a great deal. In fact, most developmental research is, at some level, correlational because age cannot be manipulated within an individual. What this means is that we can *describe* a great many developmental phenomena, but we cannot *explain* very many of them.

Naturalistic Inquiry

Since the late 1970s psychologists have become increasingly concerned that experimental and correlational approaches greatly oversimplify human behavior. In particular, both of these techniques rely on the assumption that the important factors that determine human behavior can be isolated and studied independently (Hesse, 1980). One approach that does not make this assumption is naturalistic inquiry (Lincoln & Guba, 1985).

Naturalistic inquiry **is a research method that assumes human behavior is the result of complex, mutually dependent forces that cannot be studied in isolation.** This means human behavior must be studied in its natural environment and cannot be simulated in a laboratory. Naturalistic inquiry relies on carefully conducted interactions between an inquirer (the researcher) and a participant. The information to be learned from the investigation may not be clear at the outset, but it will emerge as the study progresses. A common technique used in naturalistic inquiry is the in-depth interview, which provides a very rich set of data. Lincoln and Guba (1985) provide 14 principles that guide naturalistic inquiry, covering everything from selecting the appropriate participants, to conducting interviews, to extracting the key information, to reporting one's findings to others.

Naturalistic inquiry seems especially appropriate for research involving social interactions and such psychological issues as self-concept. Because these topics involve dynamic interchange, naturalistic inquiry provides a closer approximation of the real world than either the experimental or the correlational approach (Cavanaugh & Morton, 1989).

Observational and Case Studies

Sometimes researchers may not be able to obtain measures directly from people and are only able to watch them carefully. ***Observational studies*** **are systematic investigations of people that provide detailed and useful information about particular behavior(s).** For example, a researcher may observe how efficiently people on an assembly line do their job by counting the number of tasks they perform each hour. Typically, observational studies are accomplished by a trained investigator who keeps a log book or structured record of the target behavior(s). The results of observational studies are used most often to construct descriptions of people's ongoing behavior in everyday settings.

In certain situations, researchers may be able to study a single individual in great detail, termed a *case study*. This technique is especially useful when researchers wish to investigate very rare phenomena, such as diseases that occur infrequently or unusual cases of extremely high ability. The identification of new diseases in medicine, for example, begin with a case study of one individual who has a pattern of symptoms that is different from any known syndrome. Case studies are also very valuable for opening new areas of study, which can be followed by larger studies using other methods (e.g., experiments).

Special Issues in Research on Adult Development and Aging

Conducting high-quality research is never easy, but several special problems exist in adult development and aging that make it especially challenging. Adults in general are much more sophisticated research participants than are children and adolescents. Most adults must be recruited into research and need a compelling reason to participate. This means that finding groups of adults who are representative of the gender, ethnic, racial, educational, cultural, socioeconomic, health, lifestyle, and other key characteristics of the population of all adults is very difficult. Indeed, one of the major limitations of research on adults is the bias in sampling of adults.

Sampling Bias and the Limitations of Research Data

Most of the research we will consider in this text has been conducted on middle-class, relatively well-educated European Americans. Additionally, much of the data on some specific issues, such as cardiovascular disease, come primarily from middle-class, European American men. Findings from such homogenous groups may have little to say about the experience of people from backgrounds different from those studied most frequently.

As we will see, ethnic, gender, and socioeconomic groups differ in important ways from each other. Based on the little data we have available, we already know that we cannot necessarily generalize our findings from research on European Americans to African Americans, Hispanic Americans, Native Americans, Asian Americans, the poor, the undereducated, and other groups whose values, needs, aspirations, and challenges may be completely different. When these other groups are included, explanations of developmental phenomena may need to be fundamentally altered (Stanford & Yee, 1991).

Adequate Measurement

To ensure that the data we obtain from a research project are sound, we must make sure that the measures we use are adequate. In particular, we must demonstrate that our measures are both reliable and valid. ***Reliability* concerns whether a technique measures a variable consistently.** For example, if we were to administer a self-esteem scale to a group of people on two occasions only a few days apart, we would need to find fairly consistent scores for both testing times to conclude that our measure is reliable. Reliability is an absolute must; data obtained from unreliable measures are worthless.

Whether a data gathering technique has *validity* refers to whether it measures what it is supposed to measure. For example, we must establish in fact that the self-esteem scale we are using indeed measures self-esteem. Validity may be established in several ways: comparing scores on this test of self-esteem to scores on other valid scales of self-esteem; evaluating how well this scale predicts scores on other related scales; seeing how well this scale corresponds to the true concept of self-esteem; or deciding how well this scale differentiates self-esteem from other personality traits and how well it agrees with similar notions such as self-concept. In general, the validity of a scale is harder to document than its reliability. And in adult development and aging, few scales, even those used frequently, have been shown to be valid measures with older adults. Data obtained with such measures should be interpreted cautiously.

Conducting Research Ethically

Conducting research on adults requires that investigators be very careful about what they are doing and treat their research participants with respect. To ensure that this happens, many professional organizations, such as the American Psychological Association, and governmental research funding agencies, such as the National Institutes of Health, have adopted strict guidelines for the protection of research participants.

In general, these ethical principles require investigators to submit their research proposals to ethics review panels prior to beginning the project. Review panels examine the proposal in detail. **One requirement is that researchers obtain *informed consent* from human participants before collecting data from them; that is, investigators must tell potential participants the purpose of the project, what they will be asked to do, whether there are any risks or potential harm that could happen during the project, any benefits they may receive, and any other relevant information the review panel deems appropriate.** Only when the review panel has given the investigator permission to proceed is the researcher able to begin the project.

The requirement for informed consent is very important. In the event that prospective participants cannot complete the informed consent procedure themselves, perhaps because they are incapacitated or because they have a condition, such as Alzheimer's disease, that causes intellectual impairment, someone else (usually a family member) must complete the process. However, researchers must take extra precautions to be sensitive to these individuals; for example, if it becomes apparent that the participant does not like the procedures, the researcher must stop collecting data from that individual.

These ethical principles provide important protections for participants and investigators alike. By treating research participants with respect, investigators are in a better position to make important discoveries about adult development and aging.

Concept Checks

1. What are the three basic effects examined in all developmental research?
2. A study in which an investigator follows two cohorts for several years each is an example of which type of developmental design?
3. Examining the relation between two variables is usually done with what approach?
4. What steps do researchers need to take prior to conducting a study involving human participants?

SUMMARY

Perspectives on Adult Development and Aging

Gerontology is the study of aging from maturity through old age, as well as the study of older adults as a special group. Myths and stereotypes about older adults may result in ageism, a form of discrimination against older adults simply because of their age.

The Life-Span Perspective

The life-span perspective divides human development into two phases: an early phase (childhood and adolescence) and a later phase (young adulthood, middle age, and old age). The life-span perspective emphasizes that in order to understand adult development and aging, we must employ multiple perspectives in an interdisciplinary fashion. Aging is a lifelong process that must be put into life time, social time, and historical time contexts. How one regards one's development is determined in part by one's social clock, which is a result of socialization and adaptation.

Forces, Controversies, and Models in Adult Development and Aging

The Forces of Development

Development is shaped by four forces. Biological forces include all genetic and health-related factors. Psychological forces include all internal perceptual, cognitive, emotional, and personality factors. Sociocultural forces include interpersonal, societal, cultural, and ethnic factors. Life-cycle forces reflect differences in how the same event or combination of biological, psychological, and sociocultural forces affects people at different points in their lives.

Normative age-graded influences are those life experiences that are highly related to chronological age. Normative history-graded influences are events that most people in a specific culture experience at the same point in time. Nonnormative influences are events that may be important for a specific individual but are not experienced by most people.

Controversies in Development

The nature-nurture controversy refers to the extent to which inborn, hereditary characteristics (nature) and experiential, or environmental, influences (nurture) determine who we are. The effects of any genetically linked trait depend on the environment in which the trait gets expressed; these effects vary from direct to indirect. Environmental effects occur within a range set by genetically linked traits. The focus on nature and nurture must be on how they interact.

The continuity-discontinuity controversy refers to competing views that adulthood is largely a matter of stability or that it is marked by significant and fundamental changes. Much of what we know about adult development and aging is description. We have few explanations for why or how these phenomena occur. Quantitative change focuses on differences in the amount of a characteristic; qualitative change emphasizes differences in the fundamental nature of the characteristic.

The universal versus context-specific development controversy concerns whether there is only one pathway of development or several. This issue becomes especially important in interpreting cultural and ethnic group differences.

Models of Adult Development and Aging

The mechanistic model views people as machines, that is, as passive, reactive collections of interacting parts controlled by external stimuli, with a focus on quantitative change. The organismic model views people as complex biological systems that are more than the sum of their parts. Emergence is a key idea, as are the notions that people are active shapers of their development, headed toward a goal, with an emphasis on qualitative change. The contextual model focuses on the historical context in which people develop. It also views people as active, as more than the sum of their parts, and as having many possible goals. Change can be both quantitative and qualitative. The various models lead to asking different research questions and to using different methodologies for addressing them. Developmental models are used to develop and implement many types of programs. Social policy is influenced differently by each of the models.

The Meaning of Age

Three types of aging are distinguished. Primary aging refers to the normal, disease-free development during adulthood. Secondary aging refers to developmental changes that are related to disease. Tertiary aging refers to the rapid losses that occur shortly before death.

Age as an Index

Chronological age is a poor descriptor of time-dependent processes, and serves only as a shorthand method to index the passage of calendar time. Time-dependent processes do not actually cause behavior.

Definitions of Age

Better definitions of age include biological age (where a person is relative to the maximum number of years he or she could possibly live), psychological age (where a person is in terms of the abilities that people use to adapt to changing environmental demands), and sociocultural age (where a person is in terms of the specific set of roles adopted in relation to other members of the society and culture).

Issues in Studying Age

Developmental research can be categorized in terms of whether it is static (focuses on description) or dynamic (focuses on processes of change). The best situation is when chronological age is replaced by a better definition of age. However, chronological age can be used as a surrogate variable if better measures are unavailable.

Research Methods

Age, Cohort, and Time of Measurement

Age effects reflect underlying biological, psychological, and sociocultural changes. Cohort effects are differences due to experiences and circumstances unique to the particular generation to which one belongs. Time-of-measurement effects reflect influences due to the specific point in historical time when one is obtaining information. Developmental research designs represent various combinations of age, cohort, and time-of-measurement effects. Confounding refers to any situation in which one cannot determine which of two (or more) effects is responsible for the behaviors being observed.

Developmental Research Designs

Cross-sectional designs examine multiple cohorts and age groups at a single point in time. They can only identify age differences and confound age and cohort. Longitudinal designs examine one cohort over two or more times of measurement. They can identify age change, but have several problems, including practice effects, dropout, and selective survival. Longitudinal designs confound age and time of measurement. Time-lag designs examine multiple cohorts of same-aged people. They confound cohort and time of measurement, and they are rarely used. Sequential designs involve more than one cross-sectional (cross-sequential) or longitudinal (longitudinal sequential) design. Although they are complex and expensive, they are important because they help disentangle age, cohort, and time-of-measurement effects.

Approaches to Doing Research

Experiments consist of manipulating one or more independent variables and measuring one or more dependent variables, and the random assignment of participants to the experimental and control groups. Experiments provide information about cause and effect. Correlational designs address relations among variables; they do not provide information about cause and effect. Naturalistic inquiry focuses on the complex, mutually dependent forces shaping development by studying it in its natural environment. Observational and case studies are systematic investigations of people that provide detailed descriptions of people's behavior in everyday situations.

Special Issues in Research on Adult Development and Aging

Most of the research on adults has focused on middle-class, relatively well-educated European Americans and in some cases on European American men. This creates serious problems for understanding the development experiences of other groups of people. Measures used in research must be reliable (measure things consistently) and valid (measure what they are supposed to measure). Investigators must obtain informed consent from their participants prior to their involvement in research.

REVIEW QUESTIONS

Perspectives on adult development and aging

- What are the premises of the life-span perspective?
- What is meant by life time, social time, and historical time, and how do they relate to the social clock?

Forces, controversies, and models in adult development and aging

- What are the four basic forces in human development?
- What are the major characteristics of normative age-graded, normative history-graded, and nonnormative influences?
- How do nature and nurture interact?
- What is the continuity-discontinuity controversy? What are the subissues in this controversy?
- What is the universal versus context-specific development controversy, and how does it relate to sociocultural forces?
- What are the three models used to study human development? What are their characteristics?

The meaning of age

- In what ways can age be defined? What are the advantages and disadvantages of each definition?
- What are the differences between developmentally static and developmentally dynamic research?

Research methods

- What are age, cohort, and time-of-measurement effects? How and why are they important for developmental research?
- What is a cross-sectional design? What are its advantages and disadvantages?
- What is a longitudinal design? What are its advantages and disadvantages?
- What differences are there between cross-sectional and longitudinal designs in terms of uncovering age differences and age changes?
- What is a time-lag design?
- What are sequential designs? What different types are there? What are their advantages and disadvantages?
- What is an experiment? What information does it provide?
- What is a correlational design? What information does it provide?
- What is naturalistic inquiry? What information does it provide?

- What are observational and case studies? What information do they provide?
- What are the major issues concerning bias in research on adult development and aging?
- What is meant by the reliability and validity of a measure?

INTEGRATING CONCEPTS IN DEVELOPMENT

1. Analyze each of the three major controversies in development in terms of the four developmental forces. Then consider how each of the three major models of development have different positions on each of the three controversies.
2. Using yourself as an example, figure out your age using chronological, biological, psychological, and sociocultural definitions.
3. Design a research project addressing a major social problem from the perspective of each of the three major developmental models using each of the various developmental designs and approaches to research.

KEY TERMS

adaptation The process of modifying behavior in response to changing physical and social environments.

age effects One of the three fundamental effects examined in developmental research, along with cohort and time-of-measurement effects, which reflects the influence of time-dependent processes on development.

ageism The untrue assumption that chronological age is the main determinant of human characteristics and that one age is better than another.

biological age A definition of age that focuses on the functional age of biological and physiological processes rather than on calendar time.

biological forces One of four basic forces of development that includes all genetic and health-related factors.

case studies An intensive investigation of individual people.

chronological age A definition of age that relies on the amount of calendar time that has passed since birth.

cohort effects One of the three basic influences examined in developmental research, along with age and time-of-measurement effects, which reflects differences due to experiences and circumstances unique to the historical time in which one lives.

confounding Any situation in which one cannot determine which of two (or more) effects is responsible for the behaviors being observed.

contextual model A model that views people as dynamic, active, not reducible to parts, and not headed toward a specific end point.

continuity-discontinuity controversy The debate over whether the same rules (continuity) or different rules (discontinuity) are used to explain change in human development.

correlation A relation or association between two variables.

cross-sectional design A developmental research design in which people of different ages and cohorts are observed at one time of measurement to obtain information about age differences.

cross-sequential design A developmental research design using more than one cross-sectional design.

dependent variable Behaviors or outcomes measured in an experiment.

developmentally dynamic approach A type of developmental research in which the goal is to understand the processes of change.

developmentally static approach A type of developmental research in which the goal is to describe individuals in a particular group.

experiment A study in which participants are randomly assigned to experimental and control groups and in which an independent variable is manipulated in order to observe its effects on a dependent variable so that cause-and-effect relationships can be established.

gerontology The study of aging from maturity to old age, as well as the study of older adults as a special group.

historical time A concept of time referring to the succession of social, political, economic, and environmental events through which people live.

independent variable Variable manipulated in an experiment.

informed consent Information given to potential research participants providing details about the purpose, procedures, and potential risks or benefits of the study.

life-cycle forces One of the four basic forces of development that reflects differences in how the same event or combination of biological, psychological, and sociocultural forces affects people at different points in their lives.

life-span perspective A view of the human life span that divides it into two phases, childhood/adolescence and young/middle/late adulthood.

life time A concept of time referring to the number of years a person has lived.

longitudinal design A developmental research design that measures one cohort over two or more times of measurement to examine age changes.

longitudinal sequential design A developmental research design using more than one longitudinal design.

mechanistic model A model that uses a machine metaphor to view people as the sum of their parts, as passive receptors of environmental input, and that focuses on quantitative change.

model A metaphorical representation of reality that allows very complex phenomena to become more understandable.

naturalistic inquiry An approach to doing research based on studying people in their natural environments.

nature-nurture controversy A debate concerning the relative influence of genetics and the environment on development.

nonnormative influences Random events that are important to an individual but do not happen to most people.

normative age-graded influences Those experiences caused by biological, psychological, and sociocultural forces that are closely related to a person's age.

normative history-graded influences Events experienced by most people in a culture at the same point in time.

observational studies Systematic investigations of people that provide detailed and useful information about particular behavior(s).

organismic model A view that people are complex organisms and active shapers of their environment, and that views change as qualitative.

primary aging The normal, disease-free development during adulthood.

psychological age A definition of age based on the functional level of psychological processes used to adapt to changing environments rather than on calendar time.

psychological forces One of the four basic forces of development that includes all internal perceptual, cognitive, emotional, and personality factors.

qualitative change A view of change emphasizing differences in kind rather than in amount.

quantitative change A view of change emphasizing differences in amount rather than in kind.

reliability The ability of a measure to produce the same value when used repeatedly to measure the identical phenomenon over time.

secondary aging Developmental changes that are related to disease, lifestyle, and other environmental changes that are not inevitable.

sequential designs Types of developmental research designs involving combination of cross-sectional and longitudinal designs.

social clock An internal set of developmental milestones used to mark one's progression through life.

socialization The ways in which people learn to function in society.

sociocultural age A definition of age emphasizing the functional level of social interaction skills rather than calendar time.

sociocultural forces One of the four basic forces of development that includes interpersonal, societal, cultural, and ethnic factors.

sociocultural time A concept of time referring to the ways that society determines the appropriate age for certain events to occur and sets the kinds of age-related expectations on behavior.

surrogate variable A variable which is used to represent the complex, interrelated influences on people over time, such as chronological age.

tertiary aging Rapid losses occurring shortly before death.

time-lag design A developmental research design examining same-aged people from different cohorts.

time-of-measurement effects One of the three fundamental effects examined in developmental research, along with age and cohort effects, which refers to effects resulting from the point in historical time when the data are collected.

universal versus context-specific development controversy A debate over whether there is a single pathway of development or several.

validity The degree to which an instrument measures what it is supposed to measure.

IF YOU'D LIKE TO LEARN MORE

Baltes, P. B. (1987). Theoretical propositions of life-span developmental psychology: On the dynamics between growth and decline. *Developmental Psychology, 23,* 611–626. A classic discussion of basic concepts underlying a life-span perspective; medium difficulty.

Baltes, P. B., Reese, H. W., & Nesselroade, J. R. (1977). *Life-span developmental psychology: Introduction to research methods.* Pacific Grove, CA: Brooks/Cole. Still the definitive introduction to developmental research methods; easy to medium.

Hagestad, G. O., & Neugarten, B. L. (1985). Age and the life course. In R. H. Binstock & E. Shanas (Eds.), *Handbook of aging and the social sciences* (2nd ed., pp. 35–61). New York: Van Nostrand Reinhold. An excellent discussion of the concepts of time and age; medium difficulty.

Lerner, R. M. (1986). *Concepts and theories of human development* (2nd ed.). New York: Random House. An excellent source for more information on the nature-nurture and continuity-discontinuity controversies, as well as the mechanistic, organismic, and contextual models; easy to medium difficulty.

CHAPTER 2

Diversity in Adulthood

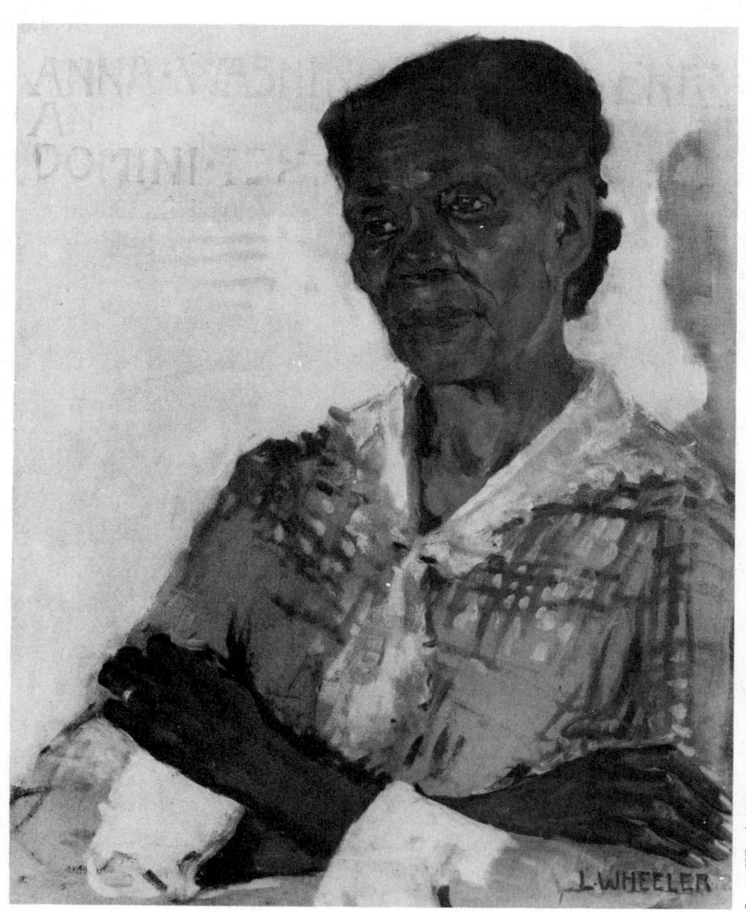

Laura Wheeler Waring, *Anna Washington Derry*, 1927. National Museum of American Art, Smithsonian Institution. Gift of the Harmon Foundation.

Mrs. Lottie Waters[1] is an African American 55-year-old great-grandmother born in a small town in southern Texas. She was delivered by her Aunt Elsie and Elsie's mother, Lucy. Like her own mother, Lottie had her first child at 15; she did the best she could at raising her five children. When Lottie was unable to care for them, she gave them to Elsie to "keep" for a time, a common practice in her community. When Lottie's second daughter had her own child, named Kermit, Lottie joined the ranks of wise women, meaning women who were grandmothers. At the time, Lottie was 32 years old. As a wise woman, Lottie was expected to care for children, her own and others. All children, biological or not, were treated similarly; Lottie's biological children treated them all as siblings. Wherever she came across misbehaving children (whether or not they were her own), she was expected to speak to them and correct them. Wise women do not need permission from the biological parents to discipline children. It is their duty to teach any child if the opportunity presents itself. When Lottie was 52 and Kermit's first child was born, Lottie celebrated a double transition: She became the mother of a wise woman (Kermit's mother), and she herself had "twice reached the age of wisdom." Lottie was wise because she had "raised" two generations and was now working on a third. And she was wise because she could recite the family history that had been taught to her by previous wise women.

Lottie Waters represents only one example of the

[1]This case is described in detail in Peterson (1990). Lottie Waters is not her real name.

rich diversity of adult development and aging. Her story drives home the point that what is expected or valued in one community (having children at a young chronological age) may not be valued in another (witness middle-class communities' fight against teenage pregnancy).

This chapter completes our introduction to adult development and aging by exploring it in broad social perspective, as we move from a personal level of analysis to a more encompassing level. First, we need to know who we are talking about: Who are older adults, and how diverse a group are they? Then we will consider the notions of status and role, two of the central ideas in understanding diversity in adulthood from a multidisciplinary framework. Next, we will see how societies organize themselves based on age, creating age stratification systems that help to define the status and roles we have. Finally, we will consider the rich diversity in the experience of aging by focusing on two topics: ethnicity and culture. Ethnicity is an important consideration in the United States, which is populated by a wide variety of people from many different backgrounds. We will conclude by seeing how cultures differ in their views of age and the aging process.

THE DEMOGRAPHICS OF AGING

Learning Objectives:

- What has the trend been in the median age of the U.S. population?
- How has the number and percentage of older adults in the U.S. population changed?
- How do the demographic changes in the United States compare with those in other countries?

As mentioned in Chapter 1, the population of the United States, along with most other industrialized countries, is "graying." Each year another group of roughly 2 million adults joins the more than 33 million U.S. citizens who have reached what society calls old age. The best way to begin our study of this population is to start with some basic questions: What is happening to the average age of the population? How many older people are there? How rapidly is this number growing now compared with a few years ago? Are there more older men or older women? What differences are there among the various ethnic and minority groups in the United States? What population trends exist in the rest of the world?

Answering these and related questions involves describing the population demographics (size, characteristics, growth, and other factors) of older adults in the United States. Most of our demographic information comes from large-scale surveys such as the census, and much of the information can be easily categorized (for example, gender of the respondent). However, a desire to understand the demographics of older adults forces us to confront a difficult question: What is old age?

The most common definition of old age refers to crossing the arbitrary boundary of 65 years. There is nothing magical about that particular age, any more than there is about a legal drinking age of 21. Age 65 was selected as the official marker of old age in the United States in the Social Security Act of 1935. Age 65 has subsequently been adopted by virtually everyone around the world as the arbitrary marker of old age. As we saw in Chapter 1, however, chronological age is a poor indicator of a person's physical, social, psychological, economic, or mental condition. Moreover, all people over age 65 are not the same. Some researchers argue that we should differentiate between the "young-old" (aged 65 to 84) and the "old-old" (aged 85 and over). Nevertheless, we will use the criterion of 65 in defining old age, keeping in mind the problems with using such an arbitrary index, and recognizing that researchers are moving away from a reliance on chronological age even for the distinction between young-old and old-old, arguing instead that physiological functioning is a better criterion.

The population of older adults is constantly changing as new members enter the group and other members leave through death. With each new member comes a personal history reflecting a combination of many developmental influences. For example, the newest entrants into old age were born in the early 1930s, meaning that they were born during the Great Depression, remember World War II, and had more education, better medical care, and different occupational experiences than their predecessors. As we saw in Chapter

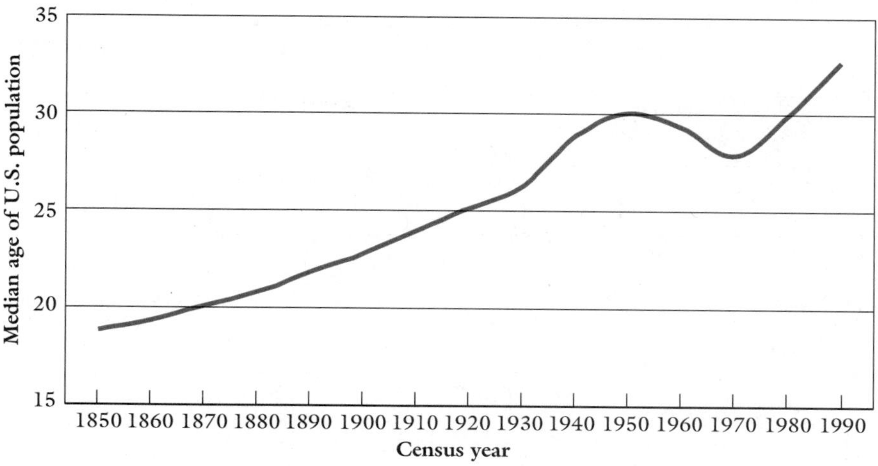

Figure 2.1 Median age of the U.S. population, 1850–1990
Source: U.S. Bureau of the Census, 1993

1, these cohort effects have important implications for interpreting developmental experiences.

What Is Happening to the Average Age of the Population?

What do people mean when they say that the population of the United States and other industrialized countries is "graying"? One way to answer this question is to examine the average age of the population using an index such as the median age. **The *median age* of the population is the age at which half of the people are younger and half are older.** The lower the median age, the more children and adolescents there are relative to the number of older adults; as the median age increases, the reverse is true. To see what has happened to the median age of the population of the United States over the past 140 years, look at Figure 2.1.

This graph shows three important things. First, the median age has increased nearly 14 years over the period, from 18.9 in 1850 to 32.7 in 1990. This means that in 1850, half of the country was composed of children and adolescents. In general, this increase in median age was gradual during the latter half of the 19th and the early 20th centuries. Second, the somewhat more rapid increase in median age between 1930 and 1950 occurred because people had fewer children during the Great Depression (the 1930s) and many young people (mostly men) were lost during World War II. Third, between 1950 and 1970 the median age *declined,* but since 1970 it has been increasing again. What happened?

The most important influence was the post-World War II baby boom. Compared with the immediately preceding decades, a huge number of children were born between the late 1940s and early 1960s. The result was a lowering of the median age of the country because so many people were younger than the median age. Once the baby boomers passed the median age and fewer children were being born, the median age began to increase. Indeed, the increase of 2.7 years between 1980 (30.0 years) to 1990 (32.7 years) is the largest change on the graph in one decade.

How Many Older Adults Are There?

Another way to answer the question about what people mean by the "graying" of the population is to examine the number of older adults in the population. As can be seen in Figure 2.2, the

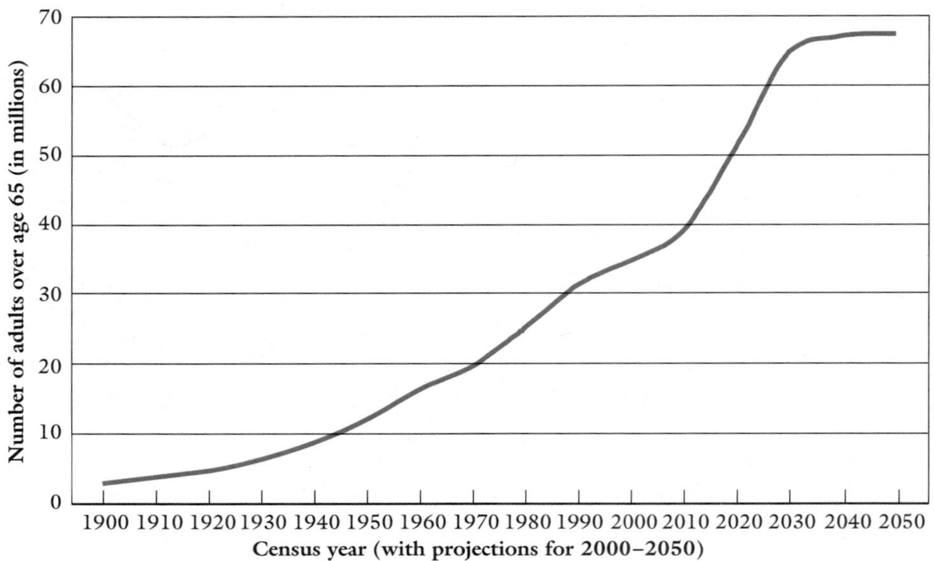

Figure 2.2 Number of adults over age 65, 1900–2050
Source: U.S. Bureau of the Census, 1993

number of older adults in the United States grew steadily during the 20th century. Between 1900 and 1990 there was a 10-fold increase in the number of older adults (from 3.1 million to roughly 31.7 million). Between 2010 and 2030 a major surge is expected as the members of the baby-boom generation reach old age, increasing the number by a whopping 25.5 million in just 20 years! Following the baby-boom surge, the rate of growth should slow and stabilize, with little increase through the year 2050.

Older adults were only 4% of the total population in 1900. By 1990 this proportion had increased to 12.7%, and it will increase to over 21% by 2030. Another way of looking at the proportion change is to look at how many older adults there are for every 100 children under age 18 in the population. In 1900 the population was truly young: There were only about 10 older adults for every 100 children (with the population median age of 22.7). By 1990 the population had matured, with nearly 50 older people for every 100 children (with the population median age of 32.7). By 2030, the U.S. Bureau of the Census projects, the number of older adults will actually exceed the number of children.

Not only is the population as a whole aging, but the older population itself has aged. Over the last 60 years, for example, the percentage of older adults who are over age 75 has increased from 29% in 1930 to nearly 50% in 1990. This trend reflects the fact that technological advances in health care, specifically the decreases in infant and childbirth mortality, have been largely responsible for the dramatic increases in overall average longevity.

What accounts for the differing rates of growth in the number of people in different age categories? The number of people entering old age in any one year depends on various combinations of three things: the number of people born 65 years earlier, the proportion of those born who survived to age 65, and the number of immigrants who joined this group over the years and are still living (Uhlenberg, 1987). For example, the proportion of men born during the early and mid-1920s who actually reached old age was lower than slightly older or younger groups because of the numbers of men killed during World War II. Likewise, the surge in older adults during the first three decades of the 21st century will be due to the very large number of babies born between 1946 and 1960 (the baby boom).

In addition, the proportion of the population that is over age 65 depends not only on the sheer number of older adults, but also on the number of babies born during the same period. As we saw when we considered trends in median age, whenever a large number of babies are born, there is a concomitant effect on the calculation of various demographic variables. Thus, whether 21% of the U.S. population in 2030 will be over age 65 will depend critically on the number of babies born between now and then.

Demographic projections are not always exact for other reasons, too. Many unpredictable factors intrude that demographers cannot build into their models. For example, in industrialized countries, the scope of the influence of AIDS on the population as a whole remains to be seen, although it has had and will continue to have a significant impact. Its effects in some countries, such as central Africa, are likely to be devastating, especially in regions where more than half of the adult population are infected with the HIV virus.

Clearly, these dramatic shifts in the composition of the population will have significant effects on daily life. From health care to city services and from wage scales to Social Security, the mechanisms of social support that all of us currently take for granted will undergo considerable stress and change as different groups vie for resources. Recognizing the problem and planning ahead for it may help us to avoid intergenerational competition for resources. Indeed, much of the most heated political debates about the U.S. budget in the mid-1990s focused on how to pay for programs for older adults (e.g., Medicare, Social Security).

Changes in the population demographics are not the same for all groups of people. One of the most important sources of these differences is ethnicity. The status and resources of many older members of minority ethnic groups reflect social and economic discrimination that they experienced earlier in life. As a result, many ethnic minority older adults are needy, are malnourished, and have poor access to medical care, little education, and substandard housing. This means that what may be true for European American older adults may not be true for the aged who are from an ethnic minority group.

Overall, older women outnumber older men, although the difference varies somewhat across racial and ethnic groups. These differences become more pronounced at higher age levels. Differences favoring women were not always the case, however. Until 1930 the gender ratio among the older population in the United States actually favored men. This situation was due in part to the predominance of male immigrants to the United States at the time, and the fact that many women died in young adulthood from complications of pregnancy and childbirth. Especially after mortality rates from childbearing declined, the gender ratio began to favor women (Uhlenberg, 1987). The current ratio is also partly explained by the fact that many more men than women died as a result of wars in this century, as well as from lifestyle factors (e.g., smoking), changes in immigration patterns, and better health habits. Finally, there are several health-related factors that tend to favor women.

Is the United States Alone in Changing Demographics?

The changing demographics in the United States are not unique, as displayed in Figure 2.3. Note that other industrialized nations such as France, Japan, and Sweden show similar trends. All of these countries have relatively low birthrates and death rates, as well as high standards of living. Although developed countries account for only one fourth of the world's population, they contain nearly one half of the world's older adults (Meyers, 1985). In terms of percentage of the population, Sweden leads the world, with roughly 23% of its population over age 65.

In contrast to the developed countries, other countries, such as Sri Lanka, have relatively young populations. On the average only 4% of the people living in nonindustrialized countries are over age 65. Nevertheless, these countries will experience explosive growth in the older adult population over the next several decades (Meyers, 1985). Between 1980 and 2025, the number of older adults living in less developed countries is expected to quadruple; in developed countries the number will only double.

DISCOVERING DEVELOPMENT

What Are the Demographics of Aging in Your Area?

The numbers are clear: The population of older adults is rising rapidly. However, the rate of growth is not the same in all parts of the United States, Canada, or other countries. To learn more about how demographic data are reported, and to discover how the number of older adults in your area has changed in the past few decades, complete the following exercise. Go to your library and obtain the official census data for your city, state, or province for the past 50 years. (In the United States, an official census is conducted every 10 years.) Construct graphs representing the number of men and women in as many different ethnic groups as possible as reported in each census. Compare your results with those for the entire United States as reported in the text.

Such a large and rapid increase in the number of older adults will severely strain the limited resources of nonindustrialized countries. This division of increasingly scarce resources across age groups will become a major issue in the decades ahead. How these issues are handled will have tremendous significance as we head into the 21st century.

Concept Checks

1. What does the concept *median age* mean?
2. What has been the relative increase in the percentage of older adults in the U.S. population since 1900?
3. How does the increase in the number of older adults in the United States compare with the increase in other countries?

AGE AS A DIMENSION OF DIVERSITY

Learning Objectives:

- How can age be viewed as a dimension of diversity?
- What is social identity theory? How do stereotypes of older adults affect our view of aging?
- What status and roles do older adults have?
- How does the experience of aging differ for men and women?

Think for a moment about your encounters with older adults. Some of them were undoubtedly pleasant; others were not. In either case, sometimes your judgment of the older adult's behavior was probably based on a stereotype (e.g., "oh, doesn't that older couple look *cute*"), or you put all older adults into one homogenous group (e.g., "don't you know all older people are nasty and self-centered"). Such descriptions indicate that older adults may be the targets of discrimination because they are "different." In this sense, older adults are different from younger adults in many ways, as we will see in this text. These differences, though, do *not* imply that older adults are inferior. On the contrary, in many respects older adults perform better than younger adults. Nevertheless, older adults are often the recipients of unpleasant acts from others.

In Chapter 1, we noted that ageism was a form of discrimination based on age. Being "different" from some reference group often means being disenfranchised by society. In modern Western society, the implicit reference group developmentally is younger adults. Thus, being older means being different. What is unusual about the case with age, though, is that attempting to disenfranchise older adults means that we are disenfranchising our future selves (Gatz & Cotton, 1994).

So why do people engage in ageism? According to Robert Butler (1975), the person who brought ageism to national awareness, ageism operates in both younger and older adults. For younger adults,

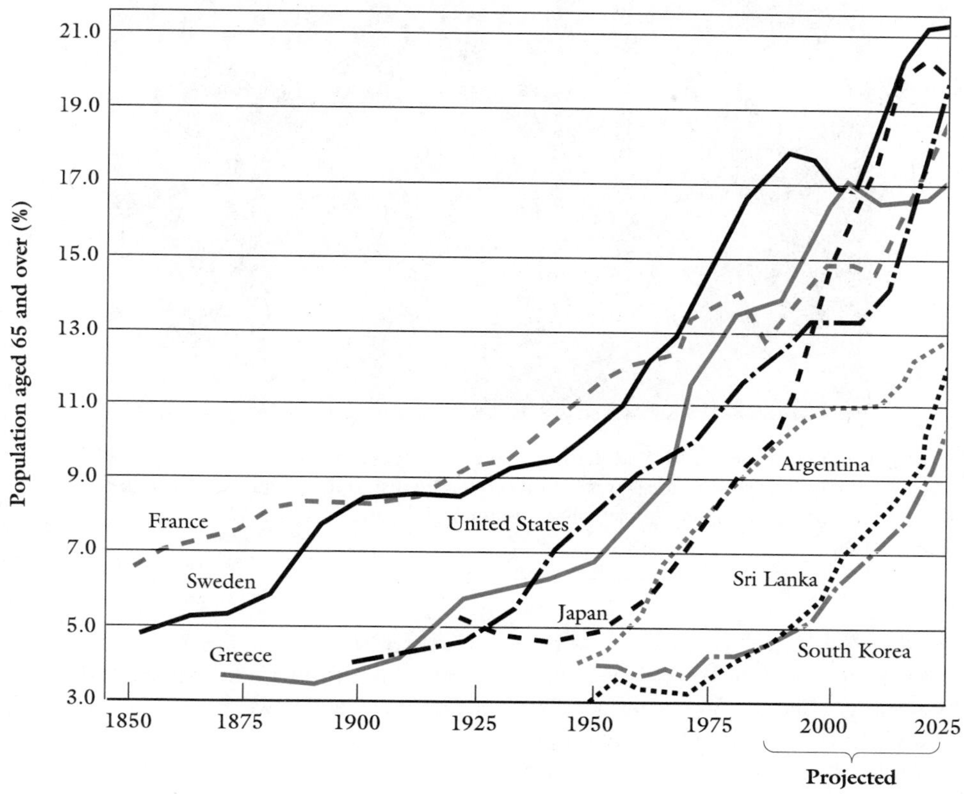

Figure 2.3 Trends in percentage of the population aged 65 and over in selected countries, 1850–2025 (projected).

Source: "Aging and Worldwide Population Change," (pp. 173–198), by G. C. Meyers, 1985. In R. H. Binstock and E. Shanas (Eds.), Handbook of Aging and the Social Sciences *Second Edition, p. 180, Van Nostrand Reinhold. Copyright ©1985 Duke University Center for Demographic Studies. Reprinted with permission from the author.*

ageism provides a way to protect oneself from the reality of growing old themselves, and to establish a way to indicate that older adults are a separate and different group for whom younger adults do not need to feel responsible. Butler also pointed out that older adults cooperate in ageism by hiding their age or not referring to themselves as older, partly due to their acceptance of negative stereotypes of aging.

Age and Diversity

Age is often overlooked as an important dimension of diversity despite the fact that along with gender and race, age is a basic cue used to put people in social categories (Gatz & Cotton, 1994). However, age is unique in several respects. First, age is both an ascribed identity (like race and gender) and an acquired identity (like educational level or

Ethnic minority older adults represent the fastest growing segment of the older adult population. This group of women also reflects the fact that there are proportionately more older women than men in the United States population.

occupation). Age is an ascribed identity when a person reaches an age, such as 65, that is considered old by society at large. Age is an acquired identity when a person joins a group such as the American Association of Retired Persons (AARP) or moves into a retirement community.

Second, age is different from most other dimensions of diversity in the degree to which people can move from one group to another (Gatz & Cotton, 1994). Most dimensions do not allow new members; that is, their membership is fixed by gender, ethnicity, or other factors. Only a few, such as the physically challenged or gays and lesbians, permit new members. Age is much more like the latter category; new members of the group of older adults are assured each year.

Third, the identity of "old" is simply added to the other identities a person already has (Gatz & Cotton, 1994). Provided they live long enough, everyone gets old. This creates multiple group memberships for people, such as older men, older Mexican Americans, and so forth. However, subcategories of older adults vary a great deal from each other; for example, only a relatively small minority of older adults have Alzheimer's disease or are extremely wealthy.

Ageism, Identity, and Stereotypes

Being a member of social groups is a very important source of one's identity, as is how the various groups interrelate. Indeed, social psychologists developed social identity theory as a way to explain the role of social group membership (Gatz & Cotton, 1994). ***Social identity theory*** **states that people define their identities along two dimensions: a social dimension based on ascribed and acquired social groups, as well as a standard against which to evaluate others when group membership is made important; and a personal dimension that includes the idiosyncracies that make a person unique.**

Social and personal dimensions of identity interact (Deaux, 1993). Age represents such an interaction, as it includes both social and personal identity because it includes both group membership and personal meaning (Gatz & Cotton, 1994). But group membership is only meaningful insofar as it provides a way to compare groups against each other. Thus, like "the poor" are contrasted with "the affluent," "older adults" are compared with "younger adults."

Group membership also serves as a way to provide status, power, and self-esteem to the members of a group (Gatz & Cotton, 1994). In general, people have a positive feeling about groups to which they belong, and they tend to discriminate against those groups that they perceive as threatening. One interesting way of maintaining self-esteem in groups is to believe that other group members have been discriminated against, but that they themselves have not been. An example would be older adults rating a "typical older adult" as more lonely, in poorer health, and more useless than they rate themselves (Harris & Associates, 1981).

We saw earlier that ageism is based in part on the stereotypes that people hold about older adults. ***Stereotypes* are generalizations of mostly negative attributes and behaviors to an entire group of people** (Gatz & Cotton, 1994). Are older adults subject to stereotyping?

An extensive meta-analytic literature review concluded that the answer was a qualified "yes" (Kite & Johnson, 1988). Differences between older and younger adults were greatest when older adults are rated for their "attractiveness" and "competence," rather than for their personality traits; in the latter case, differences were small or nonexistent. Additionally, differences are most obvious when the target is a "typical older adult"; when more individualized information was supplied, differences tended to disappear. Differences also were greater when the rater evaluated both a younger and an older adult; when different people rated each target, differences were smaller. Finally, in some areas such as seriousness of psychopathology, age is much less important than specific information (such as the type of psychological disorder). Taken together, the evidence suggests that stereotyping of older adults occurs, but it may not be as pervasive as some people think.

Other research has focused on the notion that negative views of old age reflect rejection of what we will become. From this perspective, stereotypes of older adults reflect a way of distancing oneself from the negative effects of physical aging, such as wrinkles and gray hair (Kite, Deaux, & Miele, 1991) and increased dependency (Hendricks & Leedham, 1989). Although the basis for these stereotypes is factually correct, what is misleading in many cases is the belief that all older adults have a given characteristic. Thus, although wrinkling of the skin is a universal change with age, becoming physically dependent is not.

As noted in social identity theory, people have multiple group memberships. Without question, stereotypes aimed at one group may have a multiplicative effect across group memberships. For example, older African American women are among the poorest people in society. People facing discrimination due to multiple "-isms" (racism, ageism) may have difficulty in establishing which social category is the most salient one for explaining how they are being treated. For example, an older African American woman may have difficulty figuring out whether she is being discriminated against primarily because she is old or because she is black.

The stereotypes that underlie ageism and the use of chronological age in research have much in common. In both cases, there is a basis of truth. However, both ignore important (and often sizable) differences among people. As we saw in Chapter 1, the use of such indices is done at considerable risk. We must be aware of ageism and recognize how it distorts our ability to understand and appreciate the diversity of aging.

Age, Status, and Roles

Status and role are two basic elements that help define who we are and that influence our self-concept and well-being. For those reasons, they underlie much of the research and theory in social-psychological approaches to adult development and aging. Two major theories are used to study the impact of status and role: the structural perspective and the interactionist perspective. They differ in several ways, most importantly in their view of the flexibility and activity of the individual.

The Structural Perspective

In classical sociological theory, the *structural perspective* concentrates on social structures and uses the concepts of status and role to define particular positions in society as well as the behavioral expectations associated with these positions. *Status* refers to a formal position in society that can be clearly and unambiguously specified and that may denote particular rights, privileges, prestige, and duties for the person. For example, traditional labels of "masculine," "older adult," and "minority" connote clusters of rights and privileges—such as senior citizen discounts or a seat on the subway—that may be independent of individual effort. People's statuses define the social contexts for evaluating others' behavior and serve to anchor people in the social structure. For example, a person having the status "older adult" who asks someone to give up his or her seat on the subway is evaluated differently from a person having the status "young adult" who makes the same request. Some U.S. mass transit systems even have signs in the vehicles making this distinction ("This seat reserved for older adults and handicapped passengers.").

The second important aspect of the structural perspective is role. ***Role* refers to the behaviors appropriate for any set of rights or duties.** For example, people with a particular status are expected to behave in certain prescribed, or normative, ways. Those with the status of parent are expected to care for their children; parents who fail to look after their children violate the normal parental role. Additionally, roles may be associated with specific ages, creating age norms for behavior.

Rosow (1985) applied the structural perspective to adult development and aging. His approach emphasized those roles that are essential to societal survival, such as parental roles and work roles. However, people also engage in many personally meaningful roles that are not included in Rosow's system. For example, many people assume nonstatus roles as hobbyists, weekend athletes, church workers, and the like that are viewed as important but not vital to societal survival. The most important implication of Rosow's approach is that *old age in the United States represents status without a role.* In Rosow's view old age is a time of loss of social identity that cannot be prepared for.

Rosow's structural perspective is useful in describing the ways in which social structures influence older adults through the predictable loss of certain social roles. Role loss is a major theme in psychosocial development; it is used to understand depression, changes in relationships, and changes in careers. For example, some of the adjustment problems experienced by some workers during retirement stem from the loss of meaningful work roles.

However, Rosow's argument has two problems. First, simply because people lose aspects of their social identity does not mean that their self-concept will suffer (Hagestad & Neugarten, 1985). The loss of the parental role when children leave home, for example, is hardly ever accompanied by serious psychological turmoil. Moreover, the opportunity to develop new informal roles through friendships could even bolster personal identity and counteract the effects of losses in societally essential social roles. Second, Rosow's view of older adults as victims of society does not fit well with the considerable evidence that most older people successfully meet their environmental demands.

In sum, Rosow concentrated on the influence of society, which is clearly important, but tended to ignore the active role of the individual in negotiating the developmental changes in status and roles. This latter point is the focus of the interactionist perspective.

The Interactionist Perspective

According to the structural perspective, status and role are bestowed on individuals by society; individuals have little if any influence on them (Passuth & Bengtson, 1988). **In contrast, the *interactionist perspective* emphasizes the individual's active interpretations of social structure as the main determinants of status and role** (George, 1980; Passuth & Bengtson, 1988). Interactionists maintain that people subjectively define their own relationships to social structures and are able to mold and alter those relationships if necessary.

The interactionist perspective is important for three reasons. First, we often choose the particular status we occupy and the specific role we act out. If we do not like them, we may have the option to make changes. Second, not all roles have narrowly defined behavioral expectations but, rather, offer a range of optional behaviors. Parenting is an example of a role with a wide range of acceptable behaviors, because there is considerable flexibility in how one can rear children effectively. Third, people create many informal roles in areas of interest to them. For example, people who become mediators in a debate or dispute voluntarily assume the informal role of peacemaker; when a truce is declared, their role is over.

The most important idea proposed in the interactionist perspective of status and role is that *people are able to create and modify social structures.* The individual's interpretations and perceptions are necessary elements in any attempt to understand human behavior. The interactionist perspective has influenced a great deal of work in adult development and aging, most importantly in theorizing about the interplay of heredity and environment. Some cognitive-developmental theories emphasize the active interaction with and interpretation of the environment, as well as perceptions of stress. Additionally, the interactionist perspective has led to several theories of how people interact with their environment.

Certainly, neither the structural perspective nor the interactionist perspective is sufficient by itself to explain adult development and aging. Both have merit. Society does define some roles, such as "parent," "child," "teacher," or "student." However, society does not often specify the behaviors appropriate to that role in detail. For example, the role of "student" carries only general behavioral proscriptions; subtle differences in how one should behave in different classes are not mentioned. In these more ambiguous situations, an interactionist perspective with a consideration of how the person perceives his or her situation, is more useful. Such a combined view helps us address the issue of how status is used to define a person's place in society.

Understanding How Older Adults Are Treated

To understand better our upcoming discussion of ethnic and cultural differences in adult development and aging, we must make a distinction between the status older people have and how they are treated (Keith, 1990). Sometimes, the two go hand in hand; older adults are treated very well in societies that highly value their older adults. In other cases, however, there is a big difference between the two. How does this occur?

Another important point about status and treatment is that many societies differentiate among older adults. For example, Glascock and Feinman (1981) found than most of the societies they studied had two different categories of older adults: "intact" and "decrepit." For example, Nepalese men who have vision or hearing impairments lose status compared with nonimpaired men (Beall & Goldstein, 1986).

Thus, we must be careful in jumping to conclusions about a society if we only notice the status afforded older adults, or only notice how they are treated. We must look deeper into each in order to gain insights into how older adults fit into the social structure.

Age and Gender

One of the most important dimensions of diversity in adult development and aging is gender. Men and women experience growing older differently. In most cultures, this is due in large part to different roles played by each throughout young adulthood and middle age that carry over to later life. In many cultures women, not men, are expected to assume kinship and caregiving roles. Such differing gender-based expectations has a profound effect on people's course of development.

Although in many societies men are often believed to have it better throughout much of the life span, most researchers agree that in most societies women age with less difficulty than men (Keith, 1990). However, there is much less agreement on why this is so. Some researchers argue that because women in many societies live out their lives mainly in domestic settings, they face fewer difficult transitions in late life (Keith, 1990). For example, the household tasks that women perform in many societies may be more easily adapted with age than the tasks men perform. Additionally, the caretaking roles women perform may help establish stronger bonds with children and grandchildren, who in turn may care for them in old age. The power positions men occupy may not engender such caring feelings (Harrell, 1981).

Other researchers emphasize women's experience with discontinuities during their lives (Cool & McCabe, 1983). For example, in many patrilineal societies, when a woman marries, she must leave her parental home for a potentially harsh initiation into a household controlled by her husband's mother. Women in such societies also have learned to adjust to abrupt physiological changes such as pregnancy, lactation, and menstruation, so that when changes related to aging occur they are viewed with less shock than they would be by men (Keith, 1990).

Finally, women in many societies are simply better off in old age than they were when they were young. For example, the shift from an obedient bride to a powerful, dominant older adult head of the household represents a clear increase in power and status (Keith, 1990). In many nonindustrialized societies, women in late middle age are freer and more powerful because they no longer have behavioral restrictions put on them, they have authority over other relatives, and they become eligible for special status and privileges outside the family (Brown & Kerns, 1985).

In sum, the basis for women's improving status within many societies appears to be the separation of the domestic and public spheres (Keith, 1990). That is, young women in these societies are greatly restricted in what they are allowed to do, with most of their duties focused on domestic tasks. With increasing age, however, these strictures dissipate and women are allowed to assume roles of authority and power similar to those held by men. In some cases, such as some Pacific societies, there may even be a blending or "muting" of gender differences in roles during late life (Counts & Counts, 1985a).

On a more basic level, men and women also differ dramatically on such things as income. In the United States, for example, older women's income is less than 60% that of older men (U.S. Bureau of the Census, 1995). This is due mainly to the fact that the majority of women who are currently over age 65 were not employed outside the home for most of their adult lives, thereby having little in the way of pensions or other income beyond what their husband's programs provide.

Concept Checks

1. What is the difference between ascribed and acquired group membership?
2. What is social identity theory?
3. What is meant by status and role?
4. Describe two gender differences in adult development and aging.

ETHNICITY AND ADULT DEVELOPMENT

Learning Objectives:

- What is meant by ethnicity? How does double jeopardy relate to aging? What is acculturation?
- How is ethnicity viewed in the life course?
- What is unique about the African American experience of aging?
- What is unique about the Hispanic American experience of aging?
- What is unique about the Asian and Pacific Island American experience of aging?
- What is unique about the Native American experience of aging?
- How important is ethnic identity in later life?

Before the mid-1960s research on adult development and aging was largely limited to the study of European American males. Racial and cultural diversity was ignored (Jackson, 1985). **The growing field of *ethnogerontology* seeks to draw attention to the influence that ethnicity has on the aging process.** One of the problems in examining ethnic variations in aging is a general lack of

Ethic identity is an important aspect of adult socialization from one generation to the next.

research (Jackson, 1985). This lack of data is apparent throughout this book; much of our knowledge about ethnic variations in aging is confined to demographics. We know some things about ethnic group differences in health and longevity. In contrast, we know very little about ethnic group differences in memory or cognitive development. Because examples of differences among ethnic groups on many psychological dimensions are discussed throughout the book, we will focus here on the importance of ethnicity in aging.

The Role of Ethnicity

What does it mean to talk about an ethnic group or ethnicity? On the surface we probably have an intuitive feel for what ethnicity is when we use labels such as Polish American or Korean American. However, providing a scientific definition of ethnicity is difficult. Several attempts have been made, with varying degrees of success.

An *ethnic group* can be defined as a collection of people within a larger society who have a common ancestry, memories of a shared historical past, and a cultural focus on one or more symbolic elements that they view as central to their identity as a people. According to Schermerhorn (1970), these shared elements could involve kinship patterns, living patterns, religious affiliation, language, nationality, tribal identity, common physical features, or any of a host of other variables.

Although Schermerhorn's definition provides some precision, it also creates problems. For example, "African American" would not qualify as an ethnic group because blacks from the southern United States, Jamaica, the Bahamas, and other locations do not share a common ancestry, nationality, or history. Moreover, ethnicity may not be easy to categorize. Children of an African American father and a European American mother would be difficult to classify in ethnic terms if the definition of ethnic group were based on biology.

An alternative view is that *ethnicity* reflects social differentiation based on cultural criteria,

such as a common language, customs, and voluntary associations, that foster ethnic identity and ethnic-specific social institutions and values (Holzberg, 1982). By this definition "African American" would qualify as an ethnic group because of shared values, language, customs, and so forth. An additional advantage of Holzberg's definition is that it distinguishes between ethnic group and minority group; for example, being Irish would reflect an ethnic identity, but not a minority group.

Finally, ethnicity is a dynamic concept (Barresi, 1990). That is, ethnicity is not a label that someone is born with. Rather, it is a rich heritage that sets the stage for a continually evolving and emerging identity. Ethnic groups are developing right along with the people in them.

Double Jeopardy

We saw earlier in this chapter that people can be members of more than one group simultaneously, such as being both old and African American. Moreover, most researchers agree that the experience of being old varies across ethnic groups. **A controversial extension of this argument concerns whether being old and being a member of an ethnic minority group creates a situation termed *double jeopardy.*** Talley and Kaplan (1956) originally used the term to refer to the situation of being simultaneously old and African American. At the time, older African Americans were perceived to be doubly jeopardized because they carried into old age "a whole lifetime of economic and social indignities" caused by racial prejudice and discrimination (National Urban League, 1964, p. 2). However, over the years the concept of double jeopardy has been expanded to include any individual, regardless of race, who has two or more traits that are socially undesirable, thereby subjecting him or her to prejudice and discrimination (Crandall, 1980).

Double jeopardy for older adult members of minority ethnic groups makes intuitive sense. For example, adults lose status in society as they grow older. Coupled with the already lowered social status of a minority ethnic group, becoming old would appear to put such individuals at a severe disadvantage. But as intuitively appealing as double jeopardy is, it turns out to be very difficult to document (Markides, Liang, & Jackson, 1990).

The problem appears to be twofold. First, researchers disagree on how to measure double jeopardy. M. Jackson and Wood (1976) operationalize it as existing whenever African Americans are more disadvantaged than European Americans in the same birth cohort. Jackson, Kolodny, and Wood (1982) define it as occurring when African Americans over age 65 are more disadvantaged than European Americans between 18 and 39 years old. Others (Cuellar & Weeks, 1980; Dowd & Bengtson, 1978) rely on subjective reports of members of minority ethnic groups concerning life satisfaction to define double jeopardy. Clearly, the lack of definitional consistency presents a problem: If researchers cannot agree on what double jeopardy is and how to measure it, then drawing conclusions from research is difficult.

Indeed, the second problem with the research literature on double jeopardy is inconsistent results. For one thing, cross-sectional research designs cannot address the notion that double jeopardy represents "a whole lifetime of economic and social indignities," as argued by the National Urban League (J. J. Jackson, 1985). Only longitudinal designs can address such questions, as pointed out in Chapter 1. Unfortunately, virtually all of the research on double jeopardy is cross-sectional. But even the cross-sectional studies yield conflicting results. Some report significant differences between older adult minority ethnic groups and older adult European Americans (M. Jackson et al., 1982; Register, 1981), whereas others find no differences (J. J. Jackson & Walls, 1978; Ward & Kilburn, 1983).

What are we to conclude? Perhaps the most reasonable position is to note that double jeopardy may not be the most important way to view older people who are members of ethnic minority groups because it focuses exclusively on social inequities without examining age changes in them, and tends to ignore underlying variables other than ethnicity that may be the real causal factors (J. J. Jackson, 1985; Markides et al., 1990). For example, it is true that the average older adult European American woman is better off financially than the average older adult African American woman. As J. J. Jackson points out, however, marital stability and occupational and wage histories also differ between the two. Thus, we may be asking the wrong question if we ask whether differences in life satisfaction between the groups is due to racial differences that led to double jeopardy. Rather, we need to learn how marital, occupational, wage history, and other variables are related to disadvantages in old age that happen to correlate with ethnicity (J. J. Jackson, 1985; Schaie, Orchowsky, & Parham, 1982).

Double jeopardy may yet prove to be an important part of the experience of aging for older ethnic minority individuals. What are needed, however, are (1) longitudinal investigations of the unique contributions of ethnicity to the experience of adulthood, (2) a stronger focus on variables other than race, and (3) work on how changes in society affect changes in the aging process of minority ethnic groups (Cool, 1987; J. J. Jackson, 1985; Markides et al., 1990). In this way, more and better data will be obtained that will allow a more appropriate examination of the double jeopardy hypothesis to occur.

Ethnicity and Acculturation

One of the challenges facing the United States is how to foster interaction among the various ethnic groups. Such interaction is always tricky, largely because the interacting groups may fear losing their ethnic identities in the process. **One way this happens is through a process called *acculturation,* "the sociocultural adjustment occurring when two or more 'cultures' interact"** (Roberts, 1987).

Societies in which one group is dominant are especially likely to pressure other groups to conform to their way of doing things. Language is a good example of how acculturation occurs. In the United States, a significant proportion of people speak a language other than English as their primary language; for most of these people, this language is Spanish. A heated debate is being waged over whether Spanish should be used in elementary schools to teach children who are native Spanish speakers. In contrast, Canada openly recognizes its French-speaking citizens and requires both English and French on all packages, official documents, and many scientific journals.

Whether or not it is official, acculturation is a stressful process. Acculturation resulted in increased health problems for Mexican Americans. Acculturation of young adults in this ethnic group also affects the well-being of Mexican American elders. Specifically, older Mexican Americans often report unhappiness over their adult children's failure to fulfill traditional parental care obligations (Markides & Martin, 1983) despite clear evidence of strong intergenerational ties (Markides, Boldt, & Ray, 1986). Older first-generation Japanese Americans' (Issei's) expectations about caregiving were tempered by the strong influence of American norms, which had been greatly adopted by their children (Nisei) (Masako & Liu, 1986).

A second area of research relating to acculturation focuses on feelings of alienation among recent immigrants. For example, Moon and Pearl (1991) found that recent Korean immigrants to the United States felt alienated. However, these feelings were related to age, length of time in the United States, and geographical location. Older Korean immigrants felt more alienated than their younger counterparts, and feelings of alienation decreased over time for both groups. Koreans who immigrated to locations with large Korean communities felt less alienated than immigrants moving to areas with small Korean communities. This latter finding emphasizes the importance of a supportive social network in helping people adjust to a new environment.

Although acculturation apparently has clear effects on the experience of aging, very few studies have examined the issue in detail. Moreover, we know even less about whether attempts at keeping ethnic traditions alive have any effect (positive or negative) on the stress associated with acculturation. As the population shifts in countries such as the United States toward the total number of individuals in minority ethnic groups outnumbering European Americans, we must begin to address these issues.

Ethnicity and the Life Course

Recall that one of the key aspects of the four basic forces of development is life-cycle forces, the notion that the meaning of events may change as people age. Although life-cycle forces are emphasized throughout this book, we have avoided an important question: How do the life-cycle forces that change the meaning of events vary across ethnic groups?

The answer to this question is that we derive our interpretations of events from our culture, and, more fundamentally, from our particular ethnic group or subgroup (Barresi, 1990). The attitudes and behaviors we learned when we were young shape our interpretations of events as adults, such as whether we are experiencing a life event "on time" or "off time" on our social clocks (see Chapter 1). For example, in some ethnic subgroups in the United States becoming a grandparent by age 30 is typical and considered on time. However, in other ethnic subgroups, having one's first child around age 30 is considered on time. The point is that whether behaviors are considered on or off time is heavily influenced by our particular ethnic heritage.

Of course, different perceptions of events could lead to differences of opinions or worse. One group may view another's perception as wrong and attempt to change it or to declare it unacceptable. On the other hand, perceptions may also change because of increased interaction among different groups. Teaching each other about our basic beliefs is important. Still, we need to keep in mind that people in ethnic groups different from our own may view the world in very different ways and may have different experiences of being an adult as a consequence.

But intergroup conflict is not the only potential problem. As subsequent generations become increasingly exposed to alternative viewpoints, intergenerational conflict may result (Barresi, 1990). For example, ethnic elders may resent the younger generation's rejection of the traditional ways of doing things. To older adults, traditions may represent more than a set of behavioral principles; these traditions may constitute a way of life that has helped them cope with a strange, sometimes hostile world and that ties them to their ancestral past (Barresi, 1990).

How various ethnic groups deal with age is fascinating. Some give increased status to older members of the group. Others make distinctions based on gender or other characteristics. Because of the complexity of this topic, the best we can do is to consider some snapshots, raising an important issue and discussing how a particular ethnic group deals with it. The first concerns the role that women play in the African American community. This picture raises an important point: The very definition of the life course varies across ethnic groups. The second portrait concerns gender-based behavioral norms in the Hispanic American community. Finally, we will look at how Korean Americans handle intergenerational relations.

As you consider each of these topics, keep in mind that many variations get played out within each community. Just as there are many important individual differences among European American communities, so there are differences within other ethnic groups.

African Americans

By far, older African Americans constitute the largest racial minority population of older adults in the United States, comprising roughly 8% of the total (U.S. Bureau of the Census, 1995). Most older African Americans live in metropolitan areas and tend to be very poor. The rampant poverty is a direct result of the systematic racism that older African Americans faced over their lives, which kept them from obtaining well-paying jobs (Atchley, 1994). For example, nearly 60% of older African American men and roughly 65% of older African American women could only find work as laborers, janitors, maids, nurses' aides, and other low-skilled jobs. In contrast, less than 30% of European American men and women worked in such jobs. The situation has improved for the next generation of African Americans, many more of whom are employed in professional careers such as teaching, social work, and management, as well as skilled factory jobs. However, the current generation of older African Americans are still paying for a lifetime of discrimination, especially in terms of their inability to obtain adequate retirement income.

African Americans differ from other ethnic groups on several dimensions pertaining to health as well. Older African Americans are at a much greater risk compared with older European Americans for several chronic diseases, such as coronary heart disease in African American women and many types of cancer in both men and women (Thorson, 1995).

We must certainly recognize that all older African Americans experienced the significant age-graded historical influence of systematic segregation, discrimination, and racism. Most apparent in the southern United States where Jim Crow laws forced African Americans to use separate (and usually inferior) facilities from drinking fountains to schools, and segregation, discrimination, and racism all shaped the lives of an entire group of people. Even though government-sponsored segregation is no longer legal, the problems of discrimination and racism persist and will continue to influence future generations of African Americans.

As an example of one of the unique aspects of the African American experience of aging, let's consider African American women. Their role in kinship and the importance of childbearing create a very different experience than that of most European American women.

African American Women

One of the most important roles that women in many ethnic groups play is to hold the various generations together. That is, the major kinship attachments tend to flow through mothers and grandmothers. Contact between generations tends to be fairly high and reasonably consistent across ethnic groups. However, factors such as average number of visits per month do not tell the whole story. There are very important and interesting differences among ethnic groups in what the visits mean and in how the notion of family itself is defined.

Older adult African American women offer an interesting case in point. They tend to have much more flexible definitions of kinship than do European American women, resulting in the absorption of grandchildren and "other relatives" into households headed by older women (Sokolovsky, 1990). In fact, older African American women are roughly four times more likely than European American women to live with dependent relatives under age 18. Tate (1983) finds that this makes a big difference in how younger people view older adults: "It appears that absorbed nonindependent younger blacks are more likely to accept their aged who become functionally impaired as a result of chronic conditions" (p. 99).

Many older African American women do not measure age on a fixed continuum of time but rather in terms of important life events that help a person mature (J. W. Peterson, 1990). For example, the phrase "You grew today" is used to reflect this view. For this group, the ethnically important phases of the life cycle are: having a child, a sign of procreation; raising a child, a sign of maturity; and becoming a grandparent, a sign of having reached the age of wisdom. The terms *old age* and *aging* are not part of the language of this community, although they understand these concepts as used by European Americans. Note that ties to chronological age are absent. Children, however, are highly valued, and wise women are the ones who pass on the cultural and ethnic heritage. Thus, it is knowledge, not possessions, that defines the importance of the role.

Status in this community is clearly attached to childbearing and not to chronological age. As a result, individuals who become mothers and grandmothers relatively young achieve the status; childless women, even those who are chronologically older, do not (J. W. Peterson, 1990). Most important is the experience that accrues with being a mother and grandmother. Life experience is what makes a woman wise.

Finally, African American women tend to have an especially strong relationship with their church. Whereas the family and the community offer African American women informal and relatively unstructured opportunities and positions of power, the church offers them access to more formal, structured positions of power, status, and respect (J. W. Peterson, 1990).

Hispanic Americans

Roughly 4% of the older population of the United States is of Spanish heritage, primarily Puerto Rican, Cuban, and Mexican. Thus, "Hispanic" is really a cluster, or an umbrella category, encompassing several different groups (Thorson, 1995). Indeed, this community recognizes alternative labels for itself (e.g., Latino/Latina) as well as differentiating various subgroups (e.g., Chicanos). Unlike African Americans, who are discriminated against mainly due to their skin color, Hispanic Americans are discriminated against mostly due to their language (Atchley, 1994). Because it is possible to adopt another language much more easily than it is to acquire another skin color, older Hispanic Americans have generally fared better, relatively speaking, than older African Americans. Still, Hispanic Americans lag considerably behind European Americans in terms of financial well-being (Thorson, 1995).

An important point when considering any ethnic group, but especially so with Hispanic Americans, is that length of time in the United States plays a major role in determining the degree to which they get along in society. For example, recent immigrants from Central America or Mexico face more obstacles than people from these same countries whose families immigrated several generations ago. Country of origin is sometimes less important than time and opportunity to be accepted into the society at large.

Within the Hispanic community, gender-typed age norms are important. Let's take a closer look at these norms as a way to learn more about one aspect of the experience of aging among Hispanic Americans.

Gender-Typed Age Norms Among Older Hispanic Americans

As we discovered earlier in this chapter, the aged in the United States tend to have few well-defined roles. However, a case can be made that certain activities are reserved for older people by each social or ethnic group (Ward, 1984a). Bastida (1987) examined such a set in older Hispanic Americans.

A more detailed summary of the results of Bastida's study can be found in How Do We Know? In general, she found that Mexican, Puerto Rican, and Cuban older adults living in the United States were fairly similar to one another. Her most important discovery was that older Hispanic Americans were quite realistic about their own aging: They knew that they were no longer able to do certain things. Sexual behaviors were not considered appropriate topics for conversation, and violators were sanctioned. Restrictions on behavior were generally more rigid for women than men; interestingly, women were usually the enforcers of the norms.

Asian and Pacific Island Americans

There are approximately 500,000 older Americans of Asian or Pacific Island descent, principally Japanese, Indian, Chinese, Korean, Filipino, Hawaiian, and Southeast Asian people. Although the U.S. government classifies all people from these geographic regions together, they actually differ considerably in culture, language, physical appearance, social class, and history of involvement in American society. For example, many Japanese and Chinese older adults have occupational backgrounds similar to many European Americans, whereas most Filipino older adults tended to work most of their lives in unskilled jobs. In general, there is as much variation within the Asian and Pacific Island American older adult population as there is among the European American older adult population. Still, as a group most Asian and Pacific Island American older adults tend to be better off financially than most African American older adults.

Older Asian and Pacific Island Americans who immigrated into the United States have unique problems with language, customs, and diet that do not mesh well with the range of services available to them in areas that do not have established communities of people from similar backgrounds. In many cases, pressures to adopt American customs conflicts with a desire to continue the ways of their country of origin. Moreover, immigration policies in the early part of the 20th century only permitted Asian and Pacific Island men to enter the United

HOW DO WE KNOW?

Gender-Typed Age Norms Among Older Hispanic Americans

Whether there are gender-related and age-related norms for behavior has been a topic of research in social gerontology for several decades (Thorson, 1995). Expectations that people should act their age are fairly common, from childhood through adulthood. An important issue for gerontologists is whether these age norms actually constrain behavior, and, if so, how they are enforced. Another important issue is whether these constraints can be documented in different ethnic groups.

To find out, Bastida (1987) conducted an investigation of age norms and their enforcement among older Hispanic Americans. She used three methods to examine the norms: extensive fieldwork, during which structured interviews were conducted; detailed content analyses of the responses; and a three-member panel to check the interpretation of the transcripts of the interviews. Bastida studied 160 older adults representing Mexican, Puerto Rican, and Cuban groups who lived in predominantly Hispanic American communities, or barrios, and whose dominant language was Spanish. Information was collected about age identification; aging; heterosexual relationships, including courtship, marriage, and sexual behavior; demographic characteristics; and observations from the field team, which spent at least 5 hours a day at the senior centers where the participants were interviewed.

Extensive content analyses revealed that around 70% of the men and nearly 85% of the women used realistic qualifiers concerning their age when responding to questions. For example, one 76-year-old woman explained: "What do these wrinkles tell you? Well, I'm old and must be realistic about it." Despite the fact that half of the sample was between 55 and 66, none of the participants labeled themselves middle-aged; the younger portion of the sample preferred the term *of advanced age,* whereas the oldest of the group preferred the expression *anciano,* or "very old." Participants openly admitted that age norms existed for grooming, courtship, marriage, and the ability to discuss sexuality. For example, there was a strong belief that one should dress according to his or her age, avoid flirting and courting, and never discuss his or her sexual practices.

It turned out that women were much harsher than men when it came to enforcement of the norms. More than 80% of the women expressed disapproval of other women who violated the norms, whereas only a third of the men expressed the same sentiment. Punishment was usually meted out by women in the same age group; thus, there was a strong tendency for each age group to police its own members concerning conformity to age norms. Gender differences were also noted in how men and women actively listened and in how they described their lovers.

Bastida's research is one of the best attempts at understanding how age norms operate naturalistically in a particular ethnic group. One important point that she noted was the general lack of differences among the three groups she studied, indicating that the age norms identified generalize across different Hispanic American groups. Considerably more work remains to be done, not only with Hispanic Americans but with other minority ethnic groups as well.

States; consequently, there are proportionately more older Asian and Pacific Island men than there is in any other ethnic group.

Older Asian and Pacific Island Americans also have important age-graded historical influences that must be recognized. Especially among the Japanese Americans who were placed in detention camps, those who lived during World War II experienced government-sponsored discrimination. As we noted in Chapter 1, such events can have profound effects on the course of people's development.

As an example of the kinds of issues older Asian and Pacific Island Americans face, let us consider relationships across generations among Korean Americans. Through this example, we will see how the pressures to blend into American society operate.

Intergenerational Relations Among Korean Americans

Korean Americans increased faster between 1970 and 1980 than any other ethnic group, with the exception of Mexicans and Filipinos (Kiefer et al.,

1985). Koh and Bell (1987) were concerned about the adjustment of these immigrants, especially about potential disruptions in family relationships for older adults. Older Koreans residing in the New York City area were asked about their relationships with children and grandchildren, living arrangements, and need for services.

Koh and Bell report that nearly 70% of the participants wanted to live independently, a figure comparable to that for European Americans. Moreover, older Koreans reported frequent contact with their children, at least by phone; this is also characteristic of other ethnic groups. Older Koreans faced many problems common to immigrants: language barriers, poor housing, loneliness, low income, and transportation difficulties. Two thirds of the older Koreans could not read or speak English, which created serious problems in dealing with the majority culture. In contrast to life in Korea, where one's children represented the only source of assistance, older immigrants were more likely to go to social service agencies for help.

In sum, Koh and Bell found that older Korean immigrants became similar to other ethnic groups in many respects in their living and relationship patterns. Their data suggest that these individuals accepted an intergenerational pattern more like that in the United States than that in their native Korea.

Native Americans

Older Native Americans comprise the smallest (less than 120,000 in the 1990 U.S. census) and poorest segment of the population of older adults in the United States. Over half of older Native Americans live in rural areas, double the percentage of European Americans. Most older Native Americans tended to not have paid jobs, resulting in very low incomes in later life due to the absence of pensions.

Native Americans are at much lower risk for many diseases compared with European Americans, such as heart disease, stroke, and cancer. However, the rates for alcoholism, cirrhosis of the liver, diabetes, and accidents are much higher in the Native American population (Thorson, 1995). Combined with serious poverty, these problems create a high rate of death in young adulthood and middle age; only 42% of Native Americans reach age 65, compared with roughly 70% in the rest of the population (Thorson, 1995).

Living on a reservation creates a fundamentally different situation for older Native Americans than is experienced by any other group. With a heritage as a conquered people, these individuals are confronted daily with highly paternalistic services, created by a government that views Native Americans as a group to be protected rather than as independent people, which are in many cases unsuited to their cultural needs (Atchley, 1994).

Living in cities is not much better. Like older African Americans, older Native Americans often have little education. Like older Asian and Pacific Island Americans, Native Americans may have language and customs difficulties. Unlike other ethnic groups, though, prospects for future generations of Native Americans are not improving significantly.

Less is known about older Native Americans than for any other group, making them an "invisible minority" in the United States. Partly this is due to their relatively small numbers. Due to the massive number of deaths from disease and systematic attempts at extermination, relatively few Native Americans survived into the 20th century. More important, though, is their heritage as a conquered people. This resulted in very low status in society, which in turn made it easier for researchers to ignore them. Although this situation is changing, it will take years to develop an extensive database of information about Native Americans' experience of aging.

The Importance of Ethnic Identity in Later Life

We have considered briefly how major ethnic groups in the United States experience aging. This discussion raises an important question: To what extent is it important or beneficial to maintain ethnic identity throughout adulthood? Cool (1987) provides an analysis of this point. **The pressure to maintain one's *ethnic identity,* or shared values and behaviors, is often pitted**

against the pressure to assimilate into the larger society. Many researchers have explored the notion that ethnic identity, in fact, serves as a source of support for older adults. For example, older Jewish residents of communities and nursing homes show a strong ethnic identity, whether or not Jewish traditions are supported (Hendel-Sebestyen, 1979; Holzberg, 1983; Meyerhoff, 1978). Royce (1982) argues that ethnic identity is important to older adults because it provides a source of solidarity for people who might otherwise be cut off from society.

Luborsky and Rubinstein (1987, 1990) argue that ethnic identity is a life-course phenomenon that gains in importance with age. They interviewed older Irish, Italian, and Jewish widowers and found that many of them had rediscovered their ethnic identities in old age. They identified four intertwined life-course concerns that were related to the meaning of ethnicity. First, the meaning of ethnic identity in later life is based on issues of life-span development and family history. These issues include the differentiation and separation of the self from the family and the simultaneous integration in, participation in, and attachment to the family.

Second, ethnic identity derives meaning from the historical settings and circumstances in which key events are experienced. For example, the currently popular ethnic festivals engender a feeling of pride in one's heritage and a desire to identify with one's ethnic group. In contrast, times of national conflict tend to lower the desire to identify with ethnic groups connected to the countries on the other side. During World War II many people of Japanese origin were sent to internment camps, and those of German heritage often tried to hide their background. The effect of timing and historical events on ethnic identity illustrates the point made in Chapter 1 about the importance of history-graded influences on development.

Third, Luborsky and Rubinstein found that current ethnic identity in these older men was situationally evoked depending on the needs and goals of the individuals. For example, many older men found themselves in the position of family historian after the death of their wives, who had fulfilled these roles earlier. Consequently, they became aware again of their family heritage and traditions, which fostered the reawakening of ethnicity.

Finally, past ethnic identity and experiences continue to be reworked as we consider our current ethnic identity. In other words, how we defined ourselves in the past is continually rethought and updated throughout adulthood. During old age as we move toward integrity, we are especially prone to rethinking our earlier definitions of who we are. It turns out that our sense of self includes a healthy dose of ethnicity.

The importance of Luborsky and Rubinstein's research is that the aspects of ethnic identity that they uncovered may be common to many ethnic groups. Moreover, ethnic identity is inextricably intertwined with other personal characteristics in our sense of self, which is reworked across the life span. Thus, ethnic identity itself is truly a developmental concept and is not fixed within any person at any point.

Concept Checks

1. What is meant by ethnicity, double jeopardy, and acculturation?
2. What is unique about older African American women?
3. What are some important gender differences among older Hispanic Americans?
4. What are some of the unique problems faced by older Asian and Pacific Island Americans?
5. How do older Native Americans differ from other ethnic groups?
6. How does ethnic identity increase in importance with age?

AGING AROUND THE WORLD

Learning Objectives:

- How is age defined across cultures?
- What is the importance of culture in the life course?
- How does the experience of aging differ across cultures?

• What are the consequences of inequality across cultures?

Suppose your instructor gave you the following assignment: You are to choose three different cultures around the world on three different continents and make arrangements to study older adults in each. Your task is to make whatever observations are necessary to determine similarities and differences with your own culture.

Your first inclination may be to pick destinations based on where you would like to vacation—a reasonable strategy on the face of it. But you may run into a snag. In choosing your sites, it may occur to you that you need to know what a culture *is* before you can book your tickets.

Writers use the word *culture* in many ways: as a focus of socialization, as a variable along which people differ, and as a way to organize behavior, to name a few. We have seen that whether a particular developmental theory holds up or whether a particular set of behaviors is observed across cultures is extremely important in evaluating its importance and generality. Even in our everyday speech we refer to people from different cultures, meaning that we do not expect them to be the same as us (although we may want them to become like us).

Culture, then, is an often-used concept, but it is not very well defined, nor is the term itself very old (Fry, 1988). The notion of culture dates only to the 19th century and the colonial expansion of Europe, when it was used as a way to convey obvious differences in the ways people did things in different parts of the world. However, culture rapidly became the most important concept in anthropological research (Fry, 1988). **Originally, it meant tradition or the complex set of customs that people are socialized into, but more recently *culture* has been used to mean the ways in which people go about daily life** (Fry, 1985; Ortner, 1984).

The study of aging in different cultures did not become a major area in anthropology until 1945 with the publication of Simmons's *Role of the Aged in Primitive Society.* Since the 1960s research in this area has grown considerably. Unfortunately, very little of this research has been conducted in a life-span developmental framework. Instead, the goal has been to describe the lives of older and younger members of societies. In this section we will consider how older adults fare in different cultures and how age itself is viewed.

Definitions of Age Across Cultures

Recall from Chapter 1 that the term *age* has many scientific meanings (chronological age, social age, psychological age, and so forth). It should come as no surprise that age also means different things across cultures. For example, the meaning of chronological age varies from nil to its formal incorporation into civil laws regulating behavior (Keith, 1990). In the United States, for instance, there are specific age requirements for obtaining a driver's license, becoming an elected official, and receiving retirement funds through Social Security. Usually, the need for explicit stipulation of age only occurs when citizenship principles go beyond direct kinship lines (Mayer & Müller, 1986). That is, only when social and civic laws involve more than regulating family behavior is there a need to specify age. Some authors (such as Mayer & Müller, 1986) point out that the emergence of nations created the "periodized" life course. Indeed, some types of crime, such as juvenile delinquency, exist only because societies create categories of crimes that refer to people with certain age status; such crimes are often termed *status offenses* as a result.

In most traditional societies, chronological age per se makes little difference. Rather, what matters is *generation* (Keith, 1990). In many, chronological age was not even counted until Western colonialization began. Still, many societies only render chronological age because they have to and disregard it in assigning seniority to its members. This is especially apparent when a person younger in chronological age is given more privileges associated with generational seniority than a person who is older in terms of time since birth (Fortes, 1984). For example, if greater status comes with becoming a grandparent, then the status is bestowed at the birth of the grandchild regardless of the chronological age of the grandparent. Chronologically old people who never have grandchildren never acquire the status.

Ignoring chronological age in favor of some other standard works well for these societies. The problem is that researchers tend to be ethnocentric and try to use a chronological age standard anyway. Although using this standard makes comparisons across cultures easier, it also masks important distinctions. One way around this problem would be for researchers to use both the custom of the society under study and a chronological standard for comparative purposes only.

Culture and the Life Course

If cultures vary in how they view chronological age, then it only stands to reason that they should also differ in how they structure the life course (Keith, 1990). When different cultures have alternative views of the various parts of the life span, these views will alter the interpretation of personal events. This will result in important differences in the experience of growing old. Consequently, whatever conclusions we draw from studying one culture may have little relevance to a culture that has a very different basis for defining the same events.

In some small societies, labels may be used to refer to different parts of the life span, such as "child," "young woman," "old man." However, these labels carry with them no status or specific roles. Other small societies have no labels; rather, when asked about a specific period during the life span they will list specific individuals as exemplars. Keith (1990) points out that societies in which the importance of specific periods of the life span is minimized tend to have several characteristics in common: small size, so that all members are known to each other; fluid social relations; and lack of personal property ownership. Societies without these characteristics, such as industrialized societies, tend to place far greater emphasis on periods in the life span.

Societies also differ in terms of the unit perceived as moving through the life course in the first place. Northern European ethnic groups, for example, think in terms of *individuals* moving through the life course. However, Meyer (1986) rightly notes that not only the individual as the unit of analysis but the life course itself are cultural creations that are not universal. For some cultures, life transitions are collective experiences shared, for instance, by entire families, not just one individual.

The notion of what it means to be a person also varies considerably across cultures. In middle-class communities in the United States, being a person means being independent (for example, heading a household) and having one's mental ability intact (Keith, Fry, & Ikels, 1990). But in some African cultures, full personhood is only attained if one has children and grandchildren (Sangree, 1989). And for followers of Confucianism, personhood is maintained after physical death as long as one's descendants tend the ancestral shrine.

With so many differences across cultures surrounding the life course, is there any common cultural perspective? The answer is a qualified yes. The common ground across cultures in views about the life course concerns reproductive status and responsibility (Keith, 1990). Cultures around the world make distinctions between people (usually women) who can and cannot have children and assign different tasks to people of different age status. But even here there are subtle cross-cultural differences; for example, some cultures do not allow women to hold positions of authority until after they can no longer have children, whereas other cultures bar them from such positions altogether. By the same token, transitions that many Westerners view as abrupt and irreversible, such as death, are viewed quite differently by other cultures. Melanesian societies view death as a lengthy, reversible, and negotiable stage of life (Counts & Counts, 1985b).

Finally, how people view the life course is not necessarily uniform, even in the same location. Take the Guatemalan village of Atchatlan, for instance. Natives believe life is a well-worn path that everyone should follow as closely as possible. But Mestizos in the same village hold the view of wider Guatemalan society and perceive many possible paths through life (Fry & Keith, 1982).

Formal rituals such as bar (or bat) mitzvahs and retirement parties are ways to mark transitions. This initiation rite among the Xavante in Brazil reflects the universal nature of such rituals.

Rituals and Life Transitions

Most cultures use rituals to mark changes over the life span. Typically, the most important rituals mark rites of passage. These rites are symbolic representations of the movement across the life span and ritualize the passage from one stage to another. Rites of passage traditionally include three phases (Keith, 1990): separation, marginality, and reincorporation. These phases may involve elaborate steps or may be collapsed to a few minutes. Initiates are typically dressed in different apparel to indicate their transition. (This is also true in many transitions as practiced in the United States; consider ritual garments used at baptisms, bar mitzvahs, and weddings, for example.)

Older adults play major roles in many cultural rites of passage. Because older people have successfully made these transitions themselves, they are seen as teachers or guides for the ritual passage. This is especially true in oral cultures, where, because there is no written language, older adults are the repositories of cultural wisdom and the keepers of the ritual itself.

Even in Western industrialized societies, the participation of older adults in rituals remains important. Although formal rites of passage may not occur on the broad societal level, rituals continue to be important at the religious, community, and family levels. For example, many religious groups have formal positions designated "elder," which are held by people perceived as having life experience and wisdom. Family rituals, such as Thanksgiving dinner, are often presided over by older members of the family, often in spite of declining health (Rosenthal & Marshall, 1988).

In general, rituals are important ways for older adults to maintain a feeling of being connected with other generations. Because rituals change very little over time, they also provide continuity across the life span; the rituals older adults assist in today are virtually the same as those they participated in as children and young adults. Family rituals are especially important in this regard in industrialized societies, as they offer one of the few formal opportunities for older adults to pass on important historical family practices and information to the younger generations.

Patterns of Aging Across Cultures

We noted earlier that all societies consider age as one component of their organization (Halperin, 1987). How age-based organization is accomplished varies considerably from one culture to another. We will consider three types of societies as examples: egalitarian societies, ranked horticultural societies, and age-set systems.

Egalitarian Societies

The oldest, smallest, and technologically simplest societies are egalitarian societies. They live by hunting and gathering in small, nomadic bands of extended families that come together or split apart according to seasonal variations in the availability of resources (Halperin, 1987). Some examples of egalitarian societies in the world today are the Eskimo, the Kalahari !Kung, and the Tiwi of Australia.

Egalitarian societies rule themselves by consensus, and no individual has differential access to resources (Leacock, 1978). Class differences do not exist. Reciprocity and sharing the wealth form the basis for interaction; in times of need, everyone does without.

Age is an important characteristic of egalitarian societies. Among the !Kung, older men and women assume the role of managers who control water, the most important resource (Biesele & Howell, 1981). Apparently, the !Kung reserve this most important task for those who have the most experience. Additionally, older !Kung are the keepers of essential technical information about the seasonal fluctuations in food supplies. This knowledge about plants and animals makes older adults a critical element in the survival of the !Kung in the Kalahari Desert. Because of their knowledge and their participation in decision making, older !Kung are cared for by their children and grandchildren (R. B. Lee, 1968). Because some degree of sophistication and expertise are needed for hunting and gathering, most of the physical labor is assigned to younger and middle-aged people; children and older adults live a relatively leisurely life.

Another interesting use of age grading concerns diet. The !Kung have strict age-graded norms concerning what foods may be eaten. For example, only children and older adults may eat ostrich eggs; the !Kung believe that ostrich eggs, if eaten by people of reproductive age, will cause insanity (Biesele & Howell, 1981). A more scientific explanation is that the !Kung reserve the eggs—a relatively scarce but excellent source of protein—for those who may have difficulty chewing the hard-shelled alternative, the more plentiful mongongo nuts.

In other egalitarian societies, expectations of people at different ages also vary with gender. For example, the Mundurucu of the Brazilian Amazon Basin have differing expectations of women at various points along the life span (Y. Murphy & Murphy, 1974). During their childbearing years women are to remain passive, retiring, and demure, are not to seek male company, and are to occupy separate physical and social domains. After menopause, however, women can sit anywhere, can speak freely and with authority, and are typically deferred to by men.

In general, egalitarian societies use age to organize roles that need to be performed. Older adults, to the extent that the society can provide for them, continue to fulfill important roles of teaching and socializing.

Ranked Horticultural Societies

The relationship between age and other aspects of society becomes more complicated in ranked horticultural societies. ***Ranked horticultural societies*** **are relatively permanent residents of a particular area and are much larger than egalitarian societies.** The most notable difference between the two is a clear ranking system in which "big men" and chiefs acquire a larger proportion of goods and power than other members of the society (Halperin, 1987). Big men are those who achieve power by creating a loyal following, whereas chiefs attain power by virtue of kinship connections. In most cases, such power is gained militarily; without this base, old men may be afforded status but little real power.

One example of a ranked horticultural society was that of the Coast Salish of the northwestern United States (Amoss, 1981). Among the Coast Salish generational position defined the most important roles; political and economic power were in the hands of the old. In combination with high kinship rank, age was the basis for redistribution of wealth. The older adults among the Coast Salish were valued for their knowledge and experience concerning such things as hunting, house building, and canoe making, as well as being the information source for rituals. Older members were also important in holding extended families together.

Holding older members of ranked horticultural societies in esteem for their experience and knowledge indicates that increased societal complexity does not necessarily bring with it devaluation of older adults (Foner, 1984). **This point argues**

SOMETHING TO THINK ABOUT

Modernization Theory and Respect for Older Adults

A major concern in studying aging in different cultures is to determine how older adults fare in different settings. One of the most influential theories that has guided this work is modernization theory. In brief, modernization theory provides a useful way of making comparisons between societies or within one society at different historical stages. It focuses on how a society is organized and differentiated in an attempt to explain why older adults are treated the way they are (Hendricks, 1982).

Modernization is a catch term closely associated with the Industrial Revolution of the 18th century, which began in Western Europe and continues to spread throughout the world today. The trend toward industrialization and subsequent urbanization, mass education, mass media, bureaucratization, wider dissemination of information, increased mobility, and rapid change brought about sweeping alterations in the traditional strata of society (Halperin, 1987; Silverman, 1987). As life got more complex, modernization had an enormous impact on the life course. Periods of the life span that were unimportant in nonindustrialized societies, such as adolescence, became well recognized and formalized. Age grades became ways to label obsolete skills, as older people fell behind technological innovations.

Anthropologists and sociologists who examined the effects of these widespread changes on societies came to believe that modernization was largely responsible for older adults' loss of prestige and power in industrialized societies (Cowgill & Holmes, 1972). Cowgill (1974) points to four major culprits: advances in health technology, which kept more people alive longer and led to the development of retirement; advances in economic technology, leading to new jobs that made the skills of older adults obsolete; urbanization, which led to young adults' migration away from the rural homes of older adults; and mass education, which gave the young an advantage over the old. Several researchers have presented data supporting modernization theory from a variety of countries such as Bangladesh, Chile, and Turkey (Bengtson, Dowd, Smith, & Inkles, 1975; Gilleard & Gurkan, 1987).

Although modernization theory is very popular, it has come under severe attack from some historians and anthropologists. Historians argue that there probably never was a time before the Industrial Revolution when older adults were uniformly treated with nothing but respect (Quadagno, 1982). Moreover, modernization theory tends to view all nonindustrialized societies alike in spite of their many differences. We have seen that these societies vary considerably in how they treat their older members, so to lump them all together is a serious oversimplification. Anthropologists point out that modernization of a society does not affect all cohorts similarly (Foner, 1984); thus, as initially younger cohorts age, the effects of modernization are extremely difficult to determine.

Although modernization theory fails to account for variations among different societies and how they treat their aged, it has illustrated that when societies undergo major and fundamental change, one of the hardest-hit groups is the old. Regardless of the adequacy of modernization theory in explaining how this happens, it still provides us with something to think about.

---

against *modernization theory,* which holds that devaluing of old age comes as a by-product of technological change and the growing obsolescence of older adults' skills. In ranked horticultural societies age represents valued experience, not obsolescence. As pointed out in Something to Think About, however, modernization theory controversially explains devaluation in old age in more technologically advanced countries.

Age-Set Systems

One of the clearest examples of age grading occurs in some African cultures, in which age is a formalized principle of social organization that explicitly regulates the allocation of social roles (Foner & Kertzer, 1978, 1979; Kertzer & Madison, 1981). ***Age-set systems* are groups of people who recognize common membership in a named grouping based on common age** (Kertzer & Madison, 1981).

Formal age-set systems appear to share several commonalities (Fry, 1988). Because they are predominantly male, they tend to involve the distribution of power; for example, they determine who has the most political clout (Fortes, 1984). Physiological age tends to be ignored; rather, age assumes a social-structural or organizational meaning (Bernardi, 1985). Status and rights tend to be uniquely assigned to each age set, such as novice, warrior, or elder. In contrast to inequality across age groups, there tends to be considerable equality among members of an age group (Fry, 1988), although in some cases this egalitarianism is more apparent than real.

Although formalized age grading exists in many forms (Bernardi, 1985), and in many locations (for example, North and South America, East Asia, and Western Europe; see Keith, 1990), it has been studied most in East African cultures (Kertzer & Madison, 1981). Among the Latuka, for example, both men and women past a certain age belong to an age set. The four age-set groupings in Latuka society are based solely on age; kinship and wealth are not considered. Within age sets there is no stratification for either gender. Labor is done by members of the two middle age sets; children and older adults are exempt. In the Gada society each age set constitutes an egalitarian group collectively progressing through the social grades (Fry, 1988).

Similar systems operate elsewhere in Africa. For example, the Masai have explicit and comprehensive age-based organization of their society (Keith, 1990). On the surface, Masai in younger age grades enjoy egalitarian relationships, and individuals in older age grades maintain social control. But there is more to it than that. The egalitarianism of the young appears to be a reaction to their limited access to power and wealth, rather than a true egalitarian spirit. As individuals get older and gain access to power and wealth, egalitarianism disappears. Thus, the age grades carry with them very important meanings that are manifested in different behaviors.

Some evidence suggests that age-set systems existed in North and South America, but with some differences. For example, age sets were important only in young adulthood among the Akwe-Shavante of Brazil (Maybury-Lewis, 1984). On the Great Plains age sets and their accompanying rights were bought and sold to others as a means of passing through the age grades (Fry, 1988).

As noted earlier, very few age-set systems refer to women. Several reasons have been offered for this gender difference (Keith, 1990). Women in these societies tend to be tightly tied to familial roles, which may override age commonalities (Kertzer & Madison, 1981). That is, women may be less likely to participate in same-age group activities than men because child rearing can occur across a wide age range. It may be that women's associations with their peers may be more activity based than age based. Additionally, major life transitions for women in these societies have more to do with reproduction than age. Because of large individual differences in age at onset of menopause, for example, it may be easier to allow nature to define status changes. Viewed this way, formal age-set systems may be a way that men compensate for the lack of such obvious biological markers (Keith, 1990).

Finally, the status bestowed on older members of age-set societies does not necessarily mean that all old people wield great power. On the contrary, the acquisition of power solely on the basis of age is quite rare (Keith, 1990). In most age-set societies, old men have power because they control the key societal resources, such as cattle, and have acquired many wives. Power simply takes many years to acquire, making it highly unlikely that a younger man could achieve it. That is, in some societies older adults are in power because they control key resources and have some special skill or knowledge. In the case of men, for example, one may have to prove oneself as a good hunter, warrior, father, and so forth in order to be eligible for a position of power.

Aging and Asian Cultures

Perhaps nowhere is the stereotype of revered older adults stronger in Americans' minds than in their view of how older people are treated in Asian cultures, especially in China and Japan. Americans envision a highly idealized image of honored elders who are greatly esteemed, veritably worshiped for their wisdom (Tobin, 1987), an image that has been bolstered in the scientific literature (Palmore, 1975; Palmore & Maeda, 1985). The image is false in many respects; we will consider Japan as an example.

Tobin (1987) explored American ideas about aging in Japan by asking students in Chicago and Hawaii to complete questionnaires and by interviewing 40 Americans living in Tokyo. All respondents pictured Japanese older adults to be highly respected, cared for, and happy with their lives. The actual state of affairs is quite different (Plath, 1980; Tobin, 1987). Older people in Japan are faced with a gamut of pressing issues: declining health, housing shortages, and economic and familial problems. Younger Japanese wonder if their children will care for them when they grow old. The belief by Westerners that Japanese culture fosters dependence (which contrasts sharply with Americans' strong belief in independence) has strongly influenced researchers' interpretation of observed behavior (for example, Doi, 1973). Tobin (1987) argues that Americans' belief in independence means that trying to get older adults in the United States to become dependent simply will not work; what one is like in old age reflects the values in the culture that one learned while young.

A growing problem in Asia is that Western views on aging are beginning to whittle away at time-honored cultural traditions (Martin, 1988). Although there are still public displays of respect for older adults (e.g., giving them seats on buses and trains), many Japanese families are no longer as willing to care for their older members, due to increased migration, industrialization, and participation of women in the workplace. These changes in traditions are more apparent in urban areas than in rural areas. In response to these changes China and Japan have both passed legislation mandating that family members must care for frail elders (Goldstein & Goldstein, 1986; Kii, 1981).

Freed's (1990) research is typical of recent findings. She reported a growing reluctance among middle-aged Japanese families to care for their older parents until they are unable to care for themselves. The Japanese families in Freed's study expressed ambivalence and conflict, and recognized that caregivers usually experience considerable stress. The families felt that the only way around this was to adopt a martyr stance. The families in Freed's study were typical of other middle-class Japanese who are placing increasing demands on the government for supportive services so that their parents can maintain their independence. Such feelings conflict with the long-held Japanese tradition that older parents should be cared for by their oldest son's wife.

Idealized images of honorable elders are damaging because they are merely one-dimensional pictures. The truth is that the problems faced in Western countries concerning health care and support for older adults are also pressing issues for countries around the world, including those in Asia.

Consequences of Inequality Across Cultures

Using age to divide societies into various strata is universal, as we have seen. An important consideration of such stratification is how age grading affects the members of each stratum. This issue is relevant only for societies that also have power differentiation through big men, chiefs, elected officials, and the like, because in these societies people in certain age groups control those in other age groups. In this section we will consider four consequences of the combination of age and unequal distribution of power (Foner, 1984): the presence of old men at the top, the presence of old women at the top, the losses of the old, and generational conflict.

Old Men at the Top

As we have noted earlier, in many societies older men are the leaders. They have an advantage over

Attitudes toward the elderly in Asian cultures may be changing as these countries become more urbanized and Westernized.

younger men in controlling material resources and other property, accumulating wives, and exercising authority both at home and in the wider community (Foner, 1984). They are also primary keepers of knowledge about rituals and other practices. This combination of factors typically leads to their being held in considerable esteem by other members of society.

Control of property and material resources is an important benefit of old age. Older men may be the only ones allowed to conduct property transfers, hold farming rights, and allocate resources. Younger men depend on senior relatives for approval of marriages, which are often arranged among the elders.

Control of resources may include control of people as well. Such power allows those in charge to command the labor and support of others, and it is considered by some to be the most important source of older men's wealth and status (Moore, 1978). Having many children is a sign of power in many nonindustrial societies, as is the number of wives one has. Indeed, Moore (1978) argues that wives are the most treasured possessions of all. Having many children also enables the older men to show more hospitality, an important source of prestige, and to gain more wealth by marrying off many daughters. It also guarantees that such old men will always have people around to care for them.

Old Women at the Top

Later life is when women in many societies gain freedom, prestige, power, and respect (Foner, 1984). While they are young, women are at the mercy of both men and older women, and they are burdened with many restrictions on behavior and even diet.

Although the opportunities available to older women in nonindustrialized societies are not as great as they are for men, they are considerably better than they are for younger women. In many societies aging brings a freedom to engage in previously prohibited behavior and to speak one's mind, some access to positions of political power, respect as a repository of wisdom and expertise, and ultimate authority over the household (Foner, 1984). For example, there is considerable documentation that among West African societies an older woman called the Queen Mother wielded considerable power, from selecting the new chief or king to running the affairs of the society when the king was away (Foner, 1984; Fortes, 1950; Wallace, 1971). Other patrilineal societies also give considerable power to dominating old mothers-in-law.

Most of the power held by older women involves the domestic arena (Foner, 1984; Fry, 1988). Older women have complete direction over younger adult women and children, with the senior wife in polygynous societies having the most authority. In many societies women gain prominence with age by becoming grandmothers. For example, LeVine (1978) notes that the most respected and powerful women in the Gusii culture were the oldest women with grandchildren, followed by other women with grandchildren, followed by women with married children. Married women with no children and unmarried adult women were at the bottom; they were at the mercy of everyone else. Similarly, in Chinese society older women who remained with the family could wield supreme authority over all other family members, even assuming control of the family's estate and affairs (Freedman, 1966).

With so much to gain, women in these societies eagerly anticipated growing old. Saddled with societal restrictions until after menopause, women greatly enjoyed their newfound freedom and respect. As Foner (1984) notes, the large discrepancy in power between men and women that is pointed out in sociological and psychological works diminishes significantly as women grow older.

Social Losses of Older Adults

The old are not always at the top in society. We know that well from observing our own culture, in which older adults do not have a great deal of power. Putting older people at or near the bottom is not unique to Western culture, however.

In some societies physically and mentally competent older adults are stripped of their power and prestige in well-established ways. Ortner (1978) writes that among the Sherpa, property was dispersed before death, beginning with the first child's marriage. Sons were given a share of the land and a house; daughters were provided with cash, jewels, and utensils. Parents would do anything they could to delay children's marriages, sometimes keeping them at home until they were in their thirties. However, eventually the youngest son married. According to custom, he inherited his parents' house. Parents became almost like servants, depending on the son for everything; they were left with virtually nothing. Property transfers before death also occurred in such diverse cultures as rural Ireland (Arensberg, 1968) and the Basque culture in Spain (Douglass, 1969).

Caring for physically or mentally incapacitated older adults was often difficult, especially in societies with few resources. In some cases frail older adults were cared for adequately, but in many they were not. Researchers have documented numerous societies that practiced abandonment or killing of incapacitated older adults (Glascock & Feinman, 1981; Maxwell, Silverman, & Maxwell, 1982; Simmons, 1945). In contrast, several reports have been made of societies like the !Kung who provide good care for their frail older adults (Goody, 1976; R. B. Lee, 1968; Simmons, 1945). Regardless of treatment, however, frail older adults were usually stripped of any real or ceremonial authority they had.

Intergenerational Conflict

One of the few universals in the study of aging in different cultures is the potential for intergenerational conflict. Young people the world over do not enjoy being subservient; they believe that older people are out of touch, and they want greater power for themselves (Foner, 1984). Yet these feelings are almost never expressed openly. Why do the strains between young and old so often remain hidden beneath the appearance of stable relationships?

There are logical reasons for suppressing the bad feelings between generations (Foner, 1984; Fry, 1985): Open conflict could lead to homicide, which is outlawed; open conflict is disruptive to society; young people begin to grow old themselves and gain a share of the power; old and young simply accept inequality as a fact of life; intergenerational kinship ties defuse much of the hostility; and the age groups may simply avoid each other.

What we see in virtually every culture studied is a balance between the impatience in the young and the need for continuity in the old. The balance works by channeling each generation's assets appropriately: the energy of youth into productive activities, such as hunting, and the wisdom and experience of age into decision-making activities. This balance is often precarious, but it illustrates that the tensions between generations that we see in our own culture are not unique.

Normative generational tension is not the only source of conflict, however. Sometimes intergenerational conflict comes from unwanted social changes. For example, older Sherpa live in a Buddhist society that highly values old age; they own their own homes, are usually in excellent physical shape, and have children nearby to care for them if necessary. However, many of them feel dissatisfied and dependent because they cannot live with their younger sons as prescribed by their tradition; many of the sons have gone to take jobs elsewhere (Beall & Goldstein, 1982). For some other cultures, coresidence with children due to economic necessity may disrupt traditional authority structures favoring older family members, which may actually promote conflict (Keith et al., 1990).

Clearly, intergenerational conflict is a part of the life cycle insofar as younger adults want to take over from older adults. But to the extent that industrialization and other social changes create unintended conflict, we should carefully consider whether those changes are worth the price.

Concept Checks

1. What is the most important basis for age in most traditional societies?
2. What rituals are practiced in Western society to mark the transition to old age?
3. How does modernization theory relate to aging?
4. What is intergenerational conflict, and how common is it across cultures?

SUMMARY

The Demographics of Aging

Defining old age as 65 years is an arbitrary criterion. The population of older adults is constantly changing.

What Is Happening to the Average Age of the Population?

The median age of the U.S. population has increased gradually for many decades, but is influenced by the number of babies born at a particular point in time.

How Many Older Adults Are There?

The number of older adults has increased greatly since 1900 and will continue to increase rapidly through the first part of the 21st century. There are more older women than men, mostly because of health factors that favor women. These changes in the population will have profound effects on the availability of services to older adults.

Is the United States Alone in Changing Demographics?

Other industrialized countries are also experiencing an increase in the number of older adults. However, the most rapid increases in older adults are occurring in less developed countries.

Age as a Dimension of Diversity

Age and Diversity

Age is both an ascribed and an acquired identity. Age differs from other sources of identity because people can move from one group to another. The identity "old" is simply added to other sources of identity.

Ageism, Identity, and Stereotypes

Social identity theory states that people define their identities along two dimensions: a social dimension based on ascribed and acquired social groups, as well as a standard against which to evaluate others when group membership is made important; and a personal dimension that includes the idiosyncracies that make a person unique. Stereotypes are usually negative generalizations, but may be positive. Negative stereotypes of aging are held only under specific circumstances.

Age, Status, and Roles

Status and roles are assigned by society and vary across age groups. Individuals' interpretations of their status and role are more important than societal definitions of them. Aspects of both the structural and interactionist perspectives are needed to understand the aging process. Social status of older people varies across cultures. However, high status does not guarantee good treatment, nor does low status always imply poor treatment.

Age and Gender

Women in most cultures have it better in old age than men partly due to life experience and partly due to societal structures, with the basis being the separation of the domestic and the public spheres of their lives. However, women are much worse off financially than are men.

Ethnicity and Adult Development

The Role of Ethnicity

Ethnicity is a social differentiation based on such things as a common language and customs that foster similar identity and values. The notion that older people in ethnic minority groups are at a double risk is not supported by research. Other variables, such as financial or marital status, are more important. Much of our identity across the life span comes from our ethnic background. The process of acculturation is stressful for immigrants and can cause physical health problems as well as negatively affect well-being.

African Americans

African Americans constitute the largest segment of the ethnic older adult minority population. Most are poor, and all suffered the effects of segregation, discrimination, and racism. Older African American women use different definitions of age than the majority European American population.

Hispanic Americans

Hispanic Americans are often discriminated against because of their language. Different groups of Hispanic Americans vary in terms of how well integrated they are into American society. Older Hispanic women tend to enforce gender-typed age norms for behavior.

Asian and Pacific Island Americans

This group has considerable variations among the various cultures represented. They have unique language, culture, and dietary problems, as well as important age-graded historical influences due to World War II. Pressure to conform to American society is great.

Native Americans

Less is known about this group than any other ethnic group. Many older Native Americans live on tribal lands, and as a group are the poorest segment of the population. They also have many unique problems dating to their conquest by European Americans.

The Importance of Ethnic Identity in Later Life

Older adults derive a considerable part of their well-being from their ethnic identity as it has evolved over the life course. However, the pressure to assimilate into the larger society is great. Still, ethnic identity tends to increase in importance with age.

Aging Around the World

Culture refers to the ways in which people go about daily life. The study of aging across cultures is a relatively new field of inquiry.

Definitions of Age Across Cultures

Age tends to take on different meanings across cultures. In many cultures, generation is more important than chronological age.

Culture and the Life Course

Different cultures vary in how they structure the life course. In some, there are specific labels for aspects of the life span (such as "old woman"). Some societies do not focus on individual development, but more on cohort and interdependence. All societies make distinctions based on reproductive status and responsibility. Many cultures use rituals or rites of passage to mark life transitions in status and role.

Patterns of Aging Across Cultures

Egalitarian societies rule by consensus and make no class distinctions. Age and gender are important characteristics, however. Ranked horticultural societies make distinctions based on power and wealth, which are somewhat related to age. Age-set systems make formal distinctions based on age, primarily among men. The stereotype of the wise elder in Asian cultures is changing as societies adopt Western culture. Middle-aged children are increasingly reluctant to care for frail parents in the children's home.

Consequences of Inequality Across Cultures

In some societies, old men are in the most powerful positions due to an accumulation of wealth, power, and women. In other societies, old women speak freely, gain power, and wield authority on an equal footing with men. In many societies, however, older adults lose power and prestige. Intergenerational conflict is a universal phenomenon.

REVIEW QUESTIONS

The demographics of aging

- What is the definition of old age? How was this criterion chosen?
- What trends have there been during the 20th century concerning the average age of the population?
- What trends have there been this century in the numbers of older adults in the population? What future trends are predicted?
- What trends exist in populations of older adults in various countries around the world?

Age as a dimension of diversity

- How does age differ from other aspects of identity?
- How does social identity theory relate to age and identity?
- What are some negative and positive stereotypes of aging?
- What are the structural and interactionist perspectives? How do they differ in terms of people's acquisition of status and role?
- How are status and the treatment of older adults related?
- How are status, role, and gender related in various societies?

Ethnicity and adult development

- How are ethnic group, ethnicity, and ethnic identity related?
- What is the double jeopardy hypothesis? Does it help us understand aging of people in ethnic groups?
- What are the effects of acculturation on older adults in ethnic groups?
- How does the experience of segregation, discrimination, and racism affect older African Americans?

- How are gender-typed age norms important to Hispanic Americans?
- What are some age-graded historical influences on older Asian and Pacific Island Americans?
- How does the experience of being a conquered people influence older Native Americans?
- How do older adults balance the pressure for ethnic identity with the pressure to assimilate into the larger society?

Aging around the world

- How do different cultures vary in terms of their use of chronological age to define status and roles?
- What role do rites of passage play in many cultures?
- What similarities and differences are there among egalitarian societies, ranked horticultural societies, and age-set systems?
- How are older adults treated in Asian cultures? Why are traditional values changing?
- What are the patterns of status and role in societies with old men at the top and old women at the top?
- How universal is intergenerational conflict? Why?

INTEGRATING CONCEPTS IN DEVELOPMENT

1. How will the dramatic demographic changes between now and 2030 likely affect stereotypes, status, and roles of aging?
2. How are the experiences of adult development and aging in various ethnic groups similar? How do they differ?
3. How do the experiences of adult development and aging in ethnic groups in the United States compare with people's experiences in other cultures?
4. What steps would you need to take in order to conduct good research comparing and contrasting aging among different ethnic groups or cultures?

KEY TERMS

acculturation Process by which immigrants to a country are brought into the dominant culture.

age-set systems People who recognize common membership in a particular group on the basis of age.

culture A term that describes the way in which people go about their daily lives.

double jeopardy The notion that being both old and from an ethnic minority group places one in an especially vulnerable position.

egalitarian societies Groups that live by hunting and gathering and that rule themselves by consensus.

ethnic group A socially identifiable group based on common language, customs, and voluntary association that fosters identity.

ethnic identity The personal integration of the shared values of an ethnic group.

ethnicity Social differentiation based on cultural criteria, such as common language, customs, and voluntary associations, that fosters ethnic identity and ethnic-specific social institutions and values.

ethnogerontology The study of ethnicity in an aging context.

interactionist perspective A sociological approach that emphasizes the individual's active interpretations of social structure as the main determinants of status and role.

median age The age at which half of the people are younger and half are older.

modernization theory A belief that the devaluation of age is an inevitable product of technological change.

ranked horticultural societies Relatively localized groups of people who have developed clear social ranking systems.

role A set of behaviors given to a person that one is expected to perform.

social identity theory A theory stating that people define their identities along two dimensions: a social dimension based on ascribed and acquired social groups, as well as a standard against which to evaluate others when group membership is made important; and a personal dimension that includes the idiosyncracies that make a person unique.

status A formal position in society that can be described unambiguously.

stereotypes Generalizations of mostly negative attributes and behaviors to an entire group of people.

structural perspective In classical sociological theory, an approach that concentrates on social structures and uses the concepts of status and role to define particular positions in society as well as the behavioral expectations associated with these positions.

IF YOU'D LIKE TO LEARN MORE

Delany, S., & Delany, E. A. (With A. H. Hearth). (1993). *Having our say: The Delany sisters' first 100 years.* New York: Kodansha International. A delightful and highly readable description of the experience of two African American sisters during the 20th century; easy reading.

Gelfand, D. E., & Barresi, C. M. (Eds.). (1987). *Ethnic dimensions of aging.* New York: Springer. Good summary of ethnic group differences in the experience of aging; medium difficulty.

Rossi, A. S. (Ed.). (1985). *Gender and the life course.* New York: Aldine-Atherton. One of the few books specifically on gender differences and aging; easy to medium difficulty.

Sokolovsky, J. (Ed.). (1990). *The cultural context of aging.* New York: Bergin & Garvey. A collection of articles about cultural differences in aging; easy to medium difficulty.

Stoller, E. P., & Gibson, R. C. (1994). *Worlds of difference: Inequality in the aging experience.* Thousand Oaks, CA: Pine Forge Press. An excellent collection of essays and reprints of classic articles on ethnic and cultural differences in aging; easy to medium difficulty.

CHAPTER 3

Physiological Changes

Rembrandt, *Self-Portrait as a Young Man* (left), *Self-Portrait as an Old Man* (right). Alinari/Art Resource, NY.

Old Age, this is Mr.[/Ms.] Professor; Mr.[/Ms.] Professor, this is Old Age.

Old Age.—Professor, I hope to see you well. I have known you for some time, though you think you did not know me. Shall we walk down the street together?

Professor (drawing back a little).—We can talk more quietly, perhaps, in my study. Will you tell me how it is you can seem to be acquainted with everybody you are introduced to, though [each] evidently considers you an entire stranger?

Old Age.—I make it a rule never to force myself upon a person's recognition until I have known him [or her] at least *five years.*

Professor.—Do you mean to say that you have known me so long as that?

Old Age.—I do. I left my card on you longer ago than that, but I am afraid you never read it; yet I see you have it with you.

Professor.—Where?

Old Age.—There, between your eyebrows,—three straight lines running up and down; all the probate courts know that token,—'Old Age, [its] mark.' Put your forefinger on the inner end of one eyebrow, and your middle finger on the inner end of the other eyebrow; now separate the fingers, and you will smooth out my sign-manual; that's the way you used to look before I left my card on you.

Professor.—What message do people generally send back when you first call on them?

Old Age.—*Not at home.* Then I leave a card and go. Next year I call; get the same answer; leave another card. So for five or six,—sometimes ten years or more. At last, if they don't let me in, I break in through the front door or the windows.

We talked in this way some time. Then Old Age said again,—Come, let us walk down the street together,—and offered me a cane, an eyeglass, a tippet, and a pair of overshoes.—No, much obliged to you, said I. I don't want those things, and I had a little rather talk with you here, privately, in my study. So I dressed myself up in a jaunty way and walked out alone;—got a fall, caught a cold, was laid up with a lumbago, and had time to think over this whole matter. (From the "Professor's Paper," in *The Autocrat of the Breakfast Table*)

Oliver Wendell Holmes wrote this story in 1858 when he was in his late 40s. No doubt he was trying to come to grips with his own realization that he was aging. Holmes's description of the denial that people go through has a lot of truth to it—How many people (including yourself) rejoice the day that they find their first wrinkle or gray hair? It's much more likely that one will find middle-aged adults whose arms are getting too short for them to read, or who try to cover up their growing bald spots, or who put a little extra foundation on to hide the crow's feet.

Biological and physical aging does bring certain inevitable changes like these. However, most of them will not force us to stop doing the things we enjoy now. In fact, there is little reason not to stay active well into old age. (Some of the best students in a ski class I took were in their mid-60s.) The good news is that the normative changes that we will consider do not mean that every organ system in our bodies is over the hill by age 30. Or ever. On the contrary, there is considerable variability in how rapidly our bodies age. Mounting evidence points to the fact that in many areas the aging process can be slowed significantly, as long as we take proper care of our bodies. Moderation and understanding age-related limits is the key.

Our goal in this chapter is to identify normal patterns of aging in body systems and to consider some deviations from these norms due to diseases in these systems. First, we will consider some of the major theories of biological aging. Next, we will consider some of the normal changes that occur in several systems in the body. The topics will be organized roughly from the ones that are least visible to those that are fairly obvious: the brain, the immune system, the cardiovascular system, the respiratory system, the senses, the reproductive system, and appearance and movement.

How do the basic developmental forces we examined in Chapter 1 relate to physiological changes people experience throughout adulthood? Clearly, biological forces are the most obvious, and will be the major focus of our discussions of changes in body systems in this chapter as well as our consideration of health in Chapter 4. In both

DISCOVERING DEVELOPMENT

Lay Theories of Aging

What does the average person believe about how and why we age physiologically? To find out, write down the topics in this chapter concerning the various organ and body systems. Ask some people you know of different ages two sets of questions. First, ask them what they think happens to each system as people grow older. Then ask them what they think causes these changes. Compile the results from your interviews and compare them to what you discover in this chapter. To what extent were your interviewees correct in their descriptions? Where were they off base? Does any of the misinformation match up with the stereotypes of aging we considered in Chapter 1? Why do you think this might be the case? How accurate are people? Discover for yourself.

---

chapters, we will be focusing primarily on normative changes and on biological and physical factors in disease. However, the other three forces (psychological, sociocultural, and life-cycle) must be kept in mind for a complete understanding of biological and physiological aging. For example, a person who becomes seriously ill for the very first time at age 70 may view the situation differently than someone else who has had several serious illnesses throughout life.

One commonly overlooked aspect of the outcomes of biological forces are the psychological consequences of physiological change. Whitbourne (1985) was one of the first to highlight this connection. She argued convincingly that only when physiological change is viewed in its proper psychological context (and vice versa) can we truly appreciate the impact of normative changes. Whitbourne's approach provides a way to highlight the importance of other forces on physiological change, and it will be an important aspect of this chapter. We will explicitly consider the psychological context for each of the physiological changes we examine.

The focus in this chapter is on age-related changes in major body systems. Thus, we will emphasize normative changes in those intrapersonal factors involving major organ systems. An important point to keep in mind throughout the chapter is that physiological changes do not necessarily imply functional changes. That is, just because a particular body system shows a statistically significant change over time does not mean that a person will necessarily be able to do less than before. Sometimes it takes substantial physiological change to affect behavior to a degree that a person actually notices it.

Before we examine some formal theories about biological aging, take the time to complete the Discovering Development exercise about people's beliefs about what happens to us physiologically as we grow old. Do people act like the professor in Holmes's story, or do they welcome aging with open arms? Do people believe that we maintain some degree of vigor, or do they think that it's all basically downhill? Compare and contrast your findings with the information in this chapter.

BIOLOGICAL THEORIES OF AGING

Learning Objectives:

- What does the wear and tear theory propose about the process of aging?
- What are the major hypotheses in cellular theories of aging?
- How do rate of living theories explain aging?
- How do programmed cell death theories propose that we age?
- How do the basic developmental forces interact in biological and physiological aging?

Why does everyone who lives long enough grow old physically and eventually die? What causes aging? These questions lie at the heart of adult development and aging, and represent an interface of science and philosophy. They are questions that have spurred researchers to come up with answers based on basic biological and physiological processes. Each answer, expressed as a theory, does a reasonable job at accounting for *some* of the normative changes we experience. (Hayflick, 1994). However, no one theory accounts for them all.

Wear and Tear Theory

In many respects, the human body is like a machine. It is kept alive by a pump, joints work similar to levers and pulleys, and most of our movements can be duplicated by robots. Thus, one way of speculating about aging is to think of how all machines eventually wear out. Indeed, this approach leads to a rather intuitively appealing theory. **The *wear and tear theory* suggests that the body is much like a machine that gradually deteriorates over time.**

There is some evidence that certain age-related problems are the result of lifelong use (such as osteoarthritis). However, such effects do not explain *why* we age. Hayflick (1994) suggests that if wear and tear is a fundamental cause of aging, then it probably operates at a molecular level. Yet even if such microscopic changes occur, they may not be the fundamental cause of aging but rather a sign of still another cause. Because it does not explain the process of aging very well, wear and tear theory is not an adequate explanation.

Cellular Theories

A second family of ideas points to cellular causes. Focusing on cells is reasonable, as they are a fundamental element in the body. Research findings have provided the basis for several cellular theories. One of them focuses on the number of times cells can divide, which presumably places limits on the life span of a complex organism. **Cells grown in laboratory culture dishes only undergo a fixed number of divisions at most before dying, with the number of possible divisions dropping depending on the age of the donor organism; this phenomenon is called the *Hayflick limit* after its discoverer, Leonard Hayflick** (Hayflick, 1994). For example, cells from human fetal tissue are capable of between 40 and 60 divisions; cells from a human adult are capable of only approximately 20. Originally, some researchers believed that the Hayflick limit could explain why cells inevitably die, but subsequent findings revealed that things were more complicated. For example, Harrison (1985) reported that cells from some older adults double as often as those from younger adults. Thus, the specific role of the Hayflick limit in human aging remains unclear beyond indicating that aging is probably genetically programmed.

Another cellular theory is based on a process called *cross-linking*, in which certain proteins in human cells interact randomly and produce molecules that get linked in such a way as to make the body stiffer. The proteins in question, which make up roughly one third of the protein in the body, are called *collagen*. Collagen serves a role in soft body tissue much like reinforcing rods in concrete. The more cross-links there are, the stiffer the tissue. For example, the tanning of leather involves using chemicals that create many cross-links to make the leather stiff enough for use in shoes and other products. As we age, the number of cross-links increases. This process may explain why muscles and arteries become stiffer with age. However, little adequate scientific data are available demonstrating that cross-linking actually impedes metabolic processes or causes the formation of faulty molecules that would create a fundamental cause of aging (Hayflick, 1994). Thus, even though cross-linking occurs, it probably is not an adequate explanation of aging.

A third type of cellular theory proposes that aging is due to unstable molecules called *free radicals,* which are highly reactive chemicals produced randomly in normal metabolism. When these free radicals interact with nearby molecules, problems may result. For example, free radicals may cause cellular damage, which in turn impairs the functioning of the organ, or may shut down the effects of important molecules (Hayflick, 1994). The most important evidence that free radicals may be involved in aging comes from research with substances that prevent the development of free radicals in the first place. These substances, called *antioxidants,* prevent oxygen from combining with susceptible molecules to form free radicals (Hayflick, 1994). There is a growing body of evidence that the ingestion of antioxidants results in postponing the appearance of age-related diseases such as cancer, cardiovascular disease, and declines in the immune system (Hayflick, 1994). Indirectly, the delay of disease may mean longer life. Whether free radicals explains aging, and not just age-related disease, though, remains to be seen (Hayflick, 1994).

Some evidence suggests that spontaneous changes occur in DNA, the hereditary building block of the cell. These changes underlie a fourth type of cellular theory. Some versions of this idea argue that the problem lies with the inability of DNA to replicate itself when cells divide, whereas others argue that the fault lies with DNA repair systems. Presumably, mistakes in DNA could trigger destructive processes that could seriously impair organ functioning. At present, though, how problems involving DNA relate to human aging remains a mystery (Tice, 1987).

Rate of Living Theories

***Rate of living theories* are based on the idea that people are born with a limited amount of some substance, potential energy, or physiological capacity that can be expended at some rate** (Hayflick, 1994). If it is used up early, one dies young; if used more slowly, one lives longer.

One variant of these theories concerns the rate of energy expenditure, or *metabolic capacity.* The notion is that people only have so much energy to expend in a lifetime. Although there is a relation among metabolic rate, body size, and longevity, there is little evidence that it is an underlying cause of aging (Hayflick, 1994).

Some researchers believe that how many calories one eats has a causal influence on aging. Evidence from experiments with rodents suggests that reducing calories lowers the risk of premature death, slows down a wide range of normative age-related changes, and results in some animals living twice as long as those on normal diets (Hayflick, 1994). Although controlled experimental evidence with humans is lacking, there are some suggestive cross-cultural findings. For example, Okinawans, who eat only 60% of the normal Japanese diet, have 40 times as many centenarians (people who are at least 100 years old) per capita as there are in Japan. Moreover, the Okinawan incidence of cardiovascular disease, diabetes, and cancer is half that of their Japanese counterparts (Monczunski, 1991).

A third variation of rate of living theories involves how readily one adapts to stress (Shock, 1977). Although stress per se does not cause aging, the body's ability to deal with changes in temperature and physical exertion declines with age. For example, elderly adults are more likely to die of exposure to cold and are more affected by hot weather than are younger adults. Later in this chapter, we will see that the cardiovascular and respiratory systems have lowered capacities to deal with physical exertion as we age.

Programmed Cell Death

A growing number of scientists believe that aging is a highly regulated process that is based on genetically programmed cell death (Lockshin & Zakeri, 1990; Vijg & Papaconstantinou, 1990). That is, even in cases where cell death appears random, researchers now believe that such losses are part of a master genetic program. ***Programmed cell death* appears to be a function of physiological processes, the innate ability to self-destruct, and the ability of dying cells to trigger key processes in other cells.** At present, we do not know how this self-destruct program gets activated, nor do we understand how it happens once underway. However, understanding programmed cell death may be the key to understanding how genes and physiological processes interact to produce aging. Currently, considerable research is being devoted to the role of programmed cell death in determining longevity.

Another variant of this theory is that natural selection has resulted in genes that are well-behaved until after reproductive maturation, at which point they begin to misbehave (Hayflick, 1994). These good-genes-gone-bad could explain why humans function well physiologically until midlife, at which point they begin to decline, a point in life corresponding to after most people have had children. Indeed, some fatal genetic disorders like Huntington's disease result in no noticeable symptoms until middle age. Unfortunately, the research evidence to support this intuitively appealing idea is meager at best (Hayflick, 1994).

Implications of the Developmental Forces

Although we do not yet have one unified theory of biological and physiological aging, the picture is becoming clearer. We know that there clearly are genetic components, that the body's chemistry lab produces incorrect products at times, and that there are errors in the operation and replication of DNA (Hayflick, 1994). From the perspective of the basic developmental forces, the biological theories provide ways to describe the biological forces. As we examine specific body systems in this chapter, and health-related processes in Chapter 4, we will begin to integrate the biological forces with the psychological, sociocultural, and life-cycle forces. In those discussions, notice how changes in body systems and diseases are influenced by these other factors.

The implication of this dynamic, interactive process is that the diagnosis and treatment of health-related concerns must also include many perspectives. It is not enough to have one's physical functioning checked to establish whether one is healthy. Rather, one needs not only a typical bodily physical, but also a checkup concerning psychological and sociocultural functioning. Finally, the results of all these examinations must be placed in the context of the overall life span by considering appropriate life-cycle factors. Although we do not yet have a unified theory of biological and physiological aging, and are not likely to in the near future (Hayflick, 1994), such a theory would have to account for a wide array of changes relating not only to biological forces, but to other forces as well.

Concept Checks

1. Which biological theory of aging proposes that the body is much like a machine that eventually breaks down?
2. What are the four types of cellular theories?
3. What is the basic premise of all rate of living theories?
4. What is the mechanism thought to underlie programmed cell death?
5. How might the four developmental forces interact in the context of biological and physiological aging?

THE BRAIN

Learning Objectives:

- What are the major structural changes that occur in neurons?
- How does neurons' ability to communicate with each other change with age?
- What imaging techniques are used to study the brain?
- What are the psychological effects of changes in the brain?

Star Trek fans may believe that space is the final frontier of discovery, but for many scientists it is the brain. Our knowledge of its secrets increases exponentially each year; so do our questions. Unlocking its functions and how they relate to specific behaviors is tough enough; understanding how these functions and their behavioral manifestations change over time is an additional and difficult challenge. Compared with changes in other organs, the specific changes that occur with age in the brain are difficult to see. There are few corollaries to the wrinkles we get on our skin or the shortness of breath we experience when we exercise. Observable evidence of brain changes is indirect—for example, forgetting someone's name or difficulty in solving a complex math problem. Yet concern about brain aging is high during adulthood due to the mistaken idea that dementia is inevitable and universal. In this section we will separate the myth from the reality of brain aging. Let us begin by taking a look at age-related changes in some key brain structures.

Age-Related Structural Changes in the Neuron

The age-related changes in the brain that we will consider occur mainly at the level of individual brain cells, called neurons. The changes often begin very subtly; they are often difficult to document because they are microscopic in nature and are hard to tie to specific behaviors. Still, our knowledge of normative changes in the brain is growing very rapidly due to major advances in technology. Much of what we have learned over the past decade has come from highly sophisticated computer-enhanced imaging techniques and from careful research in microbiology. In this section we will primarily consider changes that are currently viewed as normative. Abnormal brain aging, such as that which occurs in Alzheimer's disease, will be considered in more detail in Chapter 9.

The cells that are the building blocks of the brain are the *neurons* (see Figure 3.1). As shown in the figure, neurons have several parts that play specialized roles in receiving, conducting, and transmitting information. **At the left end of the neuron in the figure are the *dendrites,* which pick up the chemical signals coming in from other nearby neurons much like TV antennae pick up signals from nearby stations.** The signal is brought into the *cell body,* where it is converted into an electrochemical impulse and sent down the axon to the *terminal branches.* **The *terminal branches,* shown at the right end of the drawing, act like transmitter stations. Chemicals called *neurotransmitters* are released at the terminal branches and carry the information signal to the next neuron's dendrites.** The neurotransmitters are necessary for communication between neurons because neurons do not physically touch one another. **The gap between the terminal branches of one neuron and the dendrites of another, across which neurotransmitters travel, is called the *synapse.***

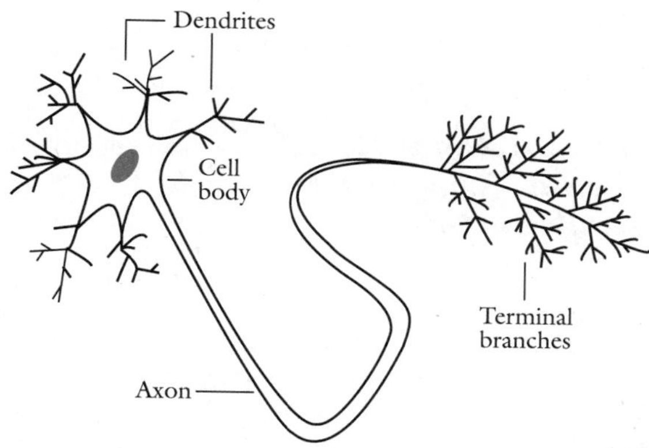

Figure 3.1 Example of a neuron. Major structures are the cell body, dendrites, axon, and terminal branches.

We are born with roughly 1 trillion neurons of different sizes and shapes, which constitute all the neurons we will ever have. Neurons grow in size and complexity across the life span but, like heart-muscle cells, cannot regenerate (Bondareff, 1985). Once a neuron dies it is lost forever.

Individual neurons undergo a wide variety of normative age-related changes. In most people, these changes produce little noticeable difference in behavior until very old age. However, when the changes are massive and occur more rapidly, disease is typically present. One problem in differentiating between normal and abnormal brain aging is that many of the same changes underlie both; for example, the defining characteristics of brain changes in Alzheimer's disease are also normative.

A second problem is that we have documented many neuronal changes, but we understand the implications of only a few. Tying specific brain changes to specific behaviors is very difficult. Much of this work relies on studies of people with brain injuries or disease, and is correlational. As we discussed in Chapter 1, this means that we cannot

HOW DO WE KNOW?

Brain Aging Is Not All Decline: Evidence for Dendritic Growth

One of the dominant views of brain aging is the neuronal fallout model, which pictures brain aging as characterized by loss and decline. Over the last decade, however, researchers have discovered strong evidence for neuronal *growth* across adulthood. This line of work was pioneered by Buell and Coleman (1979), who were among the first to describe this growth process. How did they find their evidence?

Buell and Coleman obtained samples of brain tissue from 15 individuals during autopsy. These individuals represented three groups: 5 were neurologically normal middle-aged adults averaging 51.2 years; 5 were normal older adults, averaging 79.6 years; and 5 were older adults who had brain diseases, averaging 76 years. The samples of brain tissue were from the area of the brain near the hippocampus (a structure in the middle of the brain).

The key measurement was the length of the average dendritic segment, which was obtained by dividing total length of the dendrite by the number of segments it contained. The researchers found that the average length of a dendritic segment was significantly longer in the normal elderly brains than in the normal middle-aged brains, and both were significantly longer than those in the brains of those with dementia.

The findings demonstrated clear evidence of continued growth of the dendrites in normal aging. Diseases such as Alzheimer's represent a failure of this process and actually involve a shrinking of the dendrites. Buell and Coleman were the first to definitively document growth in the brain during adulthood and aging. They speculate that there are two different populations of neurons in the normal older adult. One group consists of dying neurons, represented by the fallout model. The other group consists of surviving and growing neurons. Buell and Coleman argue that in normal aging the second group predominates until very late in life. How and when the shift from growth to decline occurs remains a mystery.

be certain that the brain changes found through imaging techniques, for example, actually caused the behaviors observed. Nevertheless, some consistent findings have been obtained, and we will consider them a bit later.

Cell Body and Axon

The most important change in the cell body and axon of neurons involves changes in the fibers contained there. **Sometimes, for reasons we do not understand, neurons in some parts of the brain develop *neurofibrillary tangles,* in which fibers in the axon become twisted together to form paired helical, or spiral, filaments** (Duara, London, & Rapoport, 1985). Large concentrations of neurofibrillary tangles are associated with behavioral abnormalities and are one defining characteristic of Alzheimer's disease (Bondareff, 1985). However, some degree of tangling occurs normally as we age. (This is an example of why it is sometimes difficult to tell the difference between normal and abnormal aging.)

Dendrites

When dendrites deteriorate, a person's ability to process information is impaired (Duara et al., 1985). Dendritic changes are complex. Scheibel (1982) maintains that dendrites of aging neurons are lost progressively, first from the outermost sections, but eventually from the entire dendritic structure. Ultimately the neuron is reduced to a stump with no dendrites, at which point it dies.

Buell and Coleman (1979) conducted a quantitative analysis in which they measured the length of the dendrites. Their results present a much different picture from Scheibel's. Buell and Coleman found that in normal aging, dendritic length of some neurons actually increases across adulthood. Only in abnormal aging, such as in Alzheimer's disease, do dendritic lengths decline. How Buell and Coleman drew this conclusion is examined in the How Do We Know feature.

What should we conclude from this discussion? Do dendrites typically shrivel up and die or do they continue to grow and proliferate? It appears that both descriptions may be correct (Duara et al., 1985). Curcio, Buell, and Coleman (1982) point out that in normal aging some neurons die whereas others, perhaps most, are prospering and continuing to grow. Thus, Scheibel's (1982) research provides a description of the degradation process, whereas Buell and Coleman's (1979) research describes the growth.

Plaques

Damaged and dying neurons sometimes collect around a core of protein and produce *neuritic plaques.* Neuritic plaques have been found in samples taken at autopsy from various parts of the brain (Kenney, 1982). Although the number of neuritic plaques increases with age, large numbers of them are not observed in normal brain aging until around age 90 (Adams, 1980). Until then high concentrations of neuritic plaques are considered characteristic of abnormal aging; for example, they are also indicative of Alzheimer's disease.

Because they are composed of degenerating neurons, neuritic plaques are believed to be a consequence, rather than a cause, of neural aging (Duara et al., 1985). As neuritic plaques become numerous, however, it is likely that they interfere with the normal functioning of healthy neurons (Bondareff, 1985).

Interpreting Neuronal Changes

Describing the effects of age-related processes on the brain is an enormous task. Individual experience and programmed physiological changes interact to produce an intricate set of changes in an already enormously complex system. Moreover, once a neuron dies, all the connections it made are lost, possibly along with the behaviors based on those connections.

Buell and Coleman's (1979) landmark research is an example of the complexity of age-related changes. They documented the coexistence of both dying and growing neurons in the same individuals in different parts of the brain. Both decline and growth were present in the brains of all adults between the ages of 44 and 92 who were studied. Consequently, a complete model of the aging brain requires an understanding of both why neurons die and why they continue to grow. It may be that the pattern of losses and gains represents an adaptive function. That is, we may be programmed to generate neuronal connections almost indiscriminately while we are young, thereby allowing as much learning to occur as possible. The normative losses accompanying aging would then represent judicious pruning of unused, redundant, unnecessary connections that can be removed without seriously compromising the person's ability to function.

The normative loss and growth pattern may also provide insight into abnormal brain aging. It could be that abnormal brain aging occurs when losses greatly outnumber gains before very old age. This is clearly the case in conditions such as Alzheimer's disease and related disorders, in which there is massive progressive loss of neurons in many areas of the brain.

Changes in Communication Among Neurons

Recall that because neurons do not physically touch one another, they communicate by releasing neurotransmitters into the synapse. Such communication is essential because behavior is governed by complex interconnections among many neurons. Understanding age-related changes in both the synapse and the neurotransmitters is also important for understanding changes in behavior (Bondareff, 1985).

Synapses

Establishing the pattern of age-related changes in synapses is difficult because two complex processes are occurring (Cotman & Holets, 1985). First, synapses are lost through neuronal degeneration and death. Second, new synapses are formed as a result of new learning and the continued growth of neurons. These two opposing processes result in no net change in the number of synapses, but they do produce changes in the configuration of synapses (Hoff, Scheff, Bernardo, & Cotman, 1982). In other words, the way in which neurons are organized and interconnected changes with age. Unfortunately, how these organizational changes affect human behavior is not clear (Cotman & Holets, 1985).

Neurotransmitters

Changes in the level of neurotransmitters affect the efficiency of information transmission among neurons. Age-related changes occur along several neurotransmitter pathways, which are groups of neurons that use the same neurotransmitter (Rogers & Bloom, 1985).

One pathway in the brain that is responsible for controlling motor movements uses the neurotransmitter ***dopamine.*** As we age, the level of dopamine decreases (McGeer & McGeer, 1980). If this decline is extreme, we develop Parkinson's disease. Parkinson's disease is characterized by tremors and a shuffling walking style, as well as serious depression (Fry, 1986). Although there is no cure, the symptoms of Parkinson's disease can be alleviated by medications; one drug, L-dopa, is converted into the neurotransmitter dopamine (Rogers & Bloom, 1985). The cause of the abnormal depletion of dopamine in Parkinson's disease is unknown (Dakof & Mendelsohn, 1986).

Age-related declines in the neurotransmitter ***acetylcholine*** are also well documented (Rogers & Bloom, 1985) and are linked with memory problems in old age (Drachman, Noffsinger, Sahakian, Kurdziel, & Fleming, 1980). Much current interest in acetylcholine is spurred by its link to both Alzheimer's disease and Huntington's disease. Some researchers speculate that there are causal connections between these diseases and abnormally low levels of choline acetyltransferase, an enzyme responsible for synthesizing acetylcholine (see Rogers & Bloom, 1985). Much of the search for drugs to alleviate the symptoms of Alzheimer's focuses on this and other enzymes related to acetylcholine.

Considerably less research has been conducted concerning age-related changes in levels of ***serotonin,*** a neurotransmitter that is involved in arousal and sleep (Rogers & Bloom, 1985). What little is known points to an age-related decline (Ponzio et al., 1982), which may underlie some of the age-related changes in sleep (Frolkis & Bezrukov, 1979).

Studying Brain-Behavior Relations: Imaging Techniques

If we could peek inside a living, working brain, what would we find? The answer to this question turns out to be one of the most exciting avenues of research on brain development. Investigators can now use computer-enhanced images to assist in diagnosing disease and even to study the thinking brain. Researchers mainly use three imaging techniques to do this: computed tomography (CT) scans, magnetic resonance imaging (MRI), and positron emission tomography (PET). The first two (CT and MRI) are widely used not only in research but also in the diagnosis of brain diseases such as tumors and strokes. All three have provided fascinating insights into brain functioning.

Computed Tomography (CT)

CT scans were the first of the high-tech imaging techniques, having been developed in the early 1970s by Hounsfield (1973). CT scans are created by passing highly focused X rays in various directions through a patient. The X rays are recorded by detectors, and computers are used to create a three-dimensional slice of the part of the body being studied. CT images produce shades of gray, which correspond to different types of tissue.

These days, CT scans of the brain are typically used only for medical diagnosis of tumors, strokes, and other conditions that produce brain lesions. For example, roughly 80% of strokes are detectable with CT scans within 24 hours after they occur (Wall, Brant-Zawadski, Jeffrey, & Barnes, 1981). CT scans also provide important information for recovery, as they can be used to monitor changes in the lesion. However, despite much excitement in the first few years after their development, CT scans were not highly useful in mapping cognitive functioning.

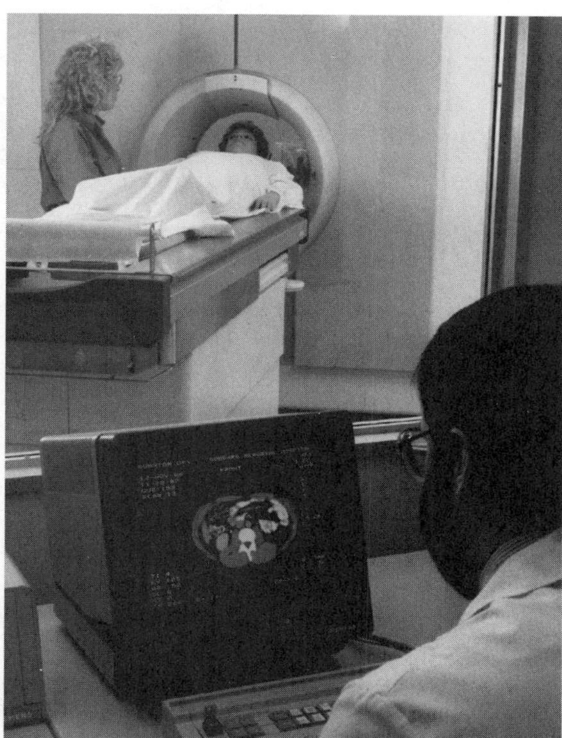

Brain imaging technology has become an essential tool in assessing and diagnosing health problems.

Magnetic Resonance Imaging (MRI)

MRI comes closer to science fiction perhaps than any other imaging technique. Based on principles of molecular structure and magnetic fields, the basic idea in MRI is that one's molecules are reoriented and then restored to their normal configuration (Brown & Bornstein, 1991). MRI devices are very large magnets and detectors that pick up radio frequencies that are shot through the body organ under study.

MRI scans are excellent tools for diagnosing brain diseases and are usually the imaging tool of choice. These scans are especially useful in assessing areas of damage due to hemorrhage and for evaluating damage to blood vessels and other soft tissues. MRI scans are typically better than CT scans in detecting small lesions and provide a more accurate assessment of a suspected disease. For these reasons, the use of MRI scans in routine diagnosis of suspected brain diseases has increased rapidly during the 1990s.

Positron Emission Tomography (PET)

PET scans work on principles similar to the other two imaging techniques. In this case, a radioactive isotope is injected into the brain, and positrons (a subatomic particle) are shot through from various directions. The positrons are detected and the information is processed by a computer. Two interesting aspects about PET scans make them especially useful for research. First, they measure glucose levels in the brain, thereby providing information about brain metabolism. Second, the computer-enhanced pictures are in color, making it relatively easy to see different levels of brain activity.

Measuring brain metabolism allows researchers to watch the brain at work. Individuals can be asked to think about something in particular, to solve a problem, or to learn a list of words while their brains are being monitored. This opportunity to observe a brain in action is currently not provided by CT or MRI scans (but scientists are trying with MRI). The fact that the pictures are in color enables researchers to know how active the brain is. For example, when the brain is hard at work, it uses more glucose; when it rests, it uses less. In PET scan pictures, high activity areas show up as red and low activity areas show up as blue.

PET scans have opened up many exciting avenues of research. For example, Caramazza and Hillis (1991) discovered what they think are separate areas in the brain for storing nouns and verbs. Other research has provided insights concerning basic information processing and memory. On the basis of these findings, some researchers are rethinking how the brain is organized. One recent idea is that the brain is organized into modules that control specific abilities and that these modules are related to each other in complex ways (Hooper, 1991). Research studies using PET scans are being conducted at a frenzied pace, with new data and new insights appearing weekly. Within the next few years, these data could revolutionize the assessment, treatment, and diagnosis of brain diseases, as well as help unlock the mystery of how the brain works.

Psychological Consequences of Brain Aging

Probably the worst stereotype about aging is that old people "get senile." Older adults may even consider an insignificant memory lapse as evidence of impending senility, even though memory lapses normally occur throughout life (Cavanaugh, Grady, & Perlmutter, 1983).

In fact, the term *senility* has no valid medical or psychological meaning, and its continued use simply perpetuates the myth that drastic mental decline is a product of normal aging (Whitbourne, 1985). It is not. The diseases involving considerable loss of memory, emotional response, and bodily functons are dementias. But dementia is not a part of normal aging; only 15% of people over age 65 have dementia (Katzman, 1987). People who develop dementia may show severe and progressive impairments of memory, judgment, comprehension, and motor functions (Huff, Growden, Corkin, & Rosen, 1987). It is fear of developing dementia that makes people interpret the slightest mental or physical mistake as symptomatic.

Nevertheless, several aspects of psychological functioning are affected by normal brain aging, which may, in turn, affect adults' adaptation to the environment (Whitbourne, 1985). For example, age-related declines in recent memory may be caused by neuronal losses. These changes make it more difficult for older adults to complete daily routines that demand remembering information over time, and the elderly become less efficient at learning new facts and skills (Whitbourne, 1985). On the other hand, continued growth in some areas may be one reason why there is little evidence of age-related changes in experience-based problem solving, reasoning, and judgment (Horn, 1982). This dual pattern of neuronal fallout and plasticity may be the underlying mechanism that explains why some intellectual functions decline with age and others do not.

Concept Checks

1. What structural changes occur in the cell body, axon, and dendrites of neurons?
2. What changes occur in neurotransmitters with age?
3. What are CT, MRI, and PET scans, and what is each used for?
4. What is the worst stereotype about the psychological effects of brain aging?

THE IMMUNE SYSTEM

Learning Objectives:
- What changes occur in immune system cells?
- How are antibodies and autoimmunity related?
- Is AIDS a significant problem for older adults?
- What are the psychological effects of age-related changes in the immune system?

One of the greatest milestones in medical history happened in this century: the conquering of many diseases. Illnesses that only a few generations ago were very serious problems, such as polio and diphtheria, are now rare in industrialized societies. Immunizations against these diseases were developed as a result of our increased knowledge of how the body's natural defense against disease works. This defense—the immune system—is a fascinating array of cells and processes: lymphocytes, antibodies, autoimmunity. Some of these exotic-sounding things (lymphocytes) help us fight infections by producing antibodies to invading viruses and germs. Other processes (autoimmunity) may provide the key to aging itself.

The study of the immune system has contributed greatly to the understanding of aging, primarily by describing the mechanisms that underlie changes in the susceptibility to disease. In particular, how immune system cells work and produce antibodies to invaders, how these cells are turned on and off, and what other body functions influence immune system functioning are a few of the discoveries that have been made in the last decade. Our knowledge has also been enhanced by studying immune system diseases such as acquired immune deficiency syndrome (AIDS) in terms of how the immune system is destroyed and how AIDS relates to other age-related disorders. In this section we will focus on the major changes seen with age that affect the body's ability to resist disease.

Changes in Immune System Cells

The human immune system is a highly advanced defense against invasion. It is composed of several types of cells that form a network of interacting parts: *cell-mediated immunity* (consisting of thymus-derived, or T lymphocytes), *humoral immunity* (B lymphocytes), and *nonspecific immunity* (monocytes and polymorphonuclear neutrophil leukocytes). Each of these components changes with age.

The primary job of the two types of *lymphocytes* is to defend against malignant (cancerous) cells, viral infection, fungal infection, and some bacteria (Berkow, 1987). Typically, the total number of T lymphocytes does not change with age, at least not until one is over 90 years old (Lehtonen, Eskola, Vainio, & Lehtonen, 1990). Likewise, the total concentration of indicators of B lymphocytes changes little with age (Abrams & Berkow, 1990).

But major changes occur in how well lymphocytes work. For one thing, older adults' immune systems take longer to build up defenses against specific diseases, even after an immunization injection. This could partially explain why older adults are more susceptible to bacterial and some viral infections (Abrams & Berkow, 1990; Terpenning & Bradley, 1991) and need to be immunized earlier against specific diseases such as influenza. One line of research in this area is investigating the possibility of administering substances such as growth hormones to older adults to stimulate the functioning of the lymphocytes; results thus far seem to indicate that when this is done, some specific lymphocyte functioning returns to normal (Nagel & Adler, 1988; Weksler, 1990).

Considerable interest arose during the 1980s over one type of lymphocyte, the natural killer cell. Natural killer cells are a subpopulation of lymphocytes that provide a broad surveillance system to prevent tumor growth, although how this happens is not yet fully understood (Kutza, Kaye, & Murasko, 1995). Natural killer cells have also been linked to resistance to infectious diseases and to a possible role in multiple sclerosis, a disease that typically manifests itself during young adulthood and early middle age (Nagel & Adler, 1988). However, the data concerning whether the activity of natural killer cells changes with age are contradictory (Kutza et al., 1995).

The general decline in responsiveness of the immune system is thought to be due to the loss of the body's ability to deal with multiple invaders at once, the toll of chronic diseases, and a domino effect of sorts among the lymphocytes (Abrams & Berkow, 1990). In the latter case, decline in the functioning of the T lymphocytes has negative consequences for the functioning of the B lymphocytes. In a sense, the T lymphocytes drive the system; when their functional ability declines, the rest of the system is hampered as a result.

Antibodies and Autoimmunity

When lymphocytes confront an invader, one of their responses is to produce an *antibody*, which protects the body from future invasions. Although longitudinal data on changes in the level of antibodies are lacking, cross-sectional research indicates that antibody levels for some specific invading organisms differ across age. For example, levels of antitetanus toxoid antibody decrease with age, especially in women (Nagel & Adler, 1988).

In normal, healthy adults the immune system is able to recognize organisms that are native to the individual; that is, the immune system does not produce antibodies to organisms that occur naturally. **One of the changes that occurs with age, however, is that this self-recognition ability begins to break down, and the immune system**

produces *autoantibodies* that attack the body itself (Weksler, 1990). **This process, termed *autoimmunity*, is thought to be partially responsible for tissue breakdown and perhaps for aging itself** (Nagel & Adler, 1988).

AIDS in Adult Development and Aging

Since first being detected in the United States in the early 1980s, AIDS has received an enormous amount of publicity and research. The disease has already claimed tens of thousands of lives in the United States alone. In fact, by the mid-1990s AIDS became the leading cause of death among young adult males aged 25 to 44 in the United States (Tanner, 1993). An increasing number of adults over age 40 are being diagnosed with AIDS, and many are over age 60. Most of these people will have gotten the disease through unsafe sexual activity.

As far as we know, there is no age difference in the symptoms of AIDS shown by older and younger adults. However, older adults' health tends to decline faster once symptoms begin. The reasons for this more rapid decline are not entirely clear, although it may be due in part to the age-related changes in the lymphocytes described above. Scientists know, for example, that the immune system attempts to fight the AIDS virus (Kendig & Adler, 1990); it may be that older adults' lowered ability to fight infection in general may contribute to the faster progress of the disease.

Of particular concern to developmentalists is the severe cognitive impairment in some AIDS patients. The impairment appears similar to the problems that develop in diseases such as Alzheimer's.

Psychological Consequences of Changes in the Immune System

At a practical level, changes in the immune system are manifested by increased frequency of illness. Psychologically, being ill more often could lead to lowered levels of self-esteem and the adoption of illness roles. Additionally, many people believe that there is little that can be done; poor health is simply a product of aging.

Clearly, such beliefs are unwarranted. Chapter 4 provides considerable detail on health promotion and disease prevention, actions that are successful with adults of all ages. Moreover, immunizations are available for many diseases and should be part of an older adult's health program (Nagel & Adler, 1988). Immunizations against tetanus and diphtheria should be given about every 10 years as a booster. Vaccination against pneumococcal pneumonia can be accomplished in one dose; boosters are not recommended. Yearly immunization against influenza is also a good preventive measure, but must be done with sufficient time to allow immunity to build up to effective levels.

As more older adults are diagnosed with AIDS, support systems specifically tailored for this group will be needed. AIDS conjures up different meanings for older adults than it does for younger people. Moreover, because there will be more older adults with AIDS, more education of older adults about the disease will be necessary.

Concept Checks

1. Which type of lymphocyte is the key to understanding changes with age in immune systems cells?
2. What is autoimmunity?
3. What are some specific concerns concerning AIDS and older adults?
4. What are some of the psychological consequences of the aging of the immune system?

THE CARDIOVASCULAR SYSTEM

Learning Objectives:

- What age-related changes occur in the structure and function of the cardiovascular system?
- What types of cardiovascular disease are common in adult development and aging?
- What are the psychological effects of age-related changes in the cardiovascular system?

Most of us can claim a relative who has (or perhaps has died from) cardiovascular disease. More people in industrialized countries die from cardiovascular disease than from any other cause. This is probably why more attention has been paid to cardiovascular fitness than to any other health issue.

Cardiovascular disease provides an excellent example of how the forces of development interact. On the biological front, we have established that cardiovascular disease has important genetic links. Psychologically, certain personality traits have been linked with increased risk of disease. Socioculturally, cardiovascular disease has been clearly tied to lifestyle. The impact of cardiovascular disease also differs as a function of the age of the individual. Let's explore in more detail how these various forces come together.

Age-Related Changes in Cardiovascular Structure and Function

The heart is an amazing organ. In a life span of 75 years, for example, the heart beats roughly 3 billion times, pumping the equivalent of about 900 million gallons of blood (Rockstein & Sussman, 1979). The heart itself consists of four chambers: the right and left atria and the right and left ventricles. Between each chamber and at each entrance and exit are the heart valves. These valves ensure that the blood flows in only one direction as the heart contracts during a beat.

Blood pressure is the ratio of the systolic pressure (the pressure during the contraction phase of a heartbeat) to the diastolic pressure (the pressure during the relaxation phase). This pressure is created by the ventricles, which are literally pushing the blood through the circulatory system. The numbers associated with blood pressure, such as 120/80, are based on measures of the force that keeps blood moving through the blood vessels. Definitions of normal blood pressure are somewhat arbitrary (Kannel, 1985) and can vary depending on who is doing the defining and the age of the person who is having his or her blood pressure checked.

Structural and Functional Changes

Two important age-related structural changes in the heart are the accumulation of fat deposits and the stiffening of the heart muscle due to tissue changes. By the late 40s and early 50s, the fat deposits in lining around the heart may form a continuous sheet. Meanwhile, healthy muscle tissue is being replaced by connective tissue, which causes a thickening and stiffening of the heart muscle and valves. This replacement is serious, because these changes reduce the amount of muscle tissue available to contract the heart. The net effect is that the remaining good muscle must work harder. To top it off, the amount of blood that the heart can pump declines from roughly 5 liters per minute at age 20 to about 3.5 liters per minute at age 70.

The most important changes in the circulatory system involve the stiffening ("hardening") in the walls of the arteries. These changes are caused by calcification of the arterial walls and by replacement of elastic fibers with less elastic ones.

The combination of changes in the heart and the circulatory system results in a significant decrease in a person's ability to cope with physical stress. This is one reason why older adults—in contrast with younger and middle-aged adults—are more likely to have heart attacks while performing moderately exerting tasks, such as shoveling snow.

Cardiovascular Disease

Incidence rates for some cardiovascular diseases in men and women between 35 and 84 years of age are listed in Table 3.1. Note that all diseases have a dramatic increase in rate with age and that for most of the diseases listed rates in men are higher than rates in women. The overall death rate in the United States from cardiovascular disease has dropped by more than one third since the early 1960s due to the improvement of lifestyle, lower overall rates of cigarette smoking, and improved treatment of cardiovascular disease through medication and surgical intervention (Timiras, 1994). However, the rate of death in some ethnic minority

TABLE 3.1 Incidence of major cardiovascular diseases per 10,000 people, as a function of age: United States, 1988

Age	Coronary Disease Men	Women	Cerebrovascular Accident Men	Women	Angina Men	Women	Myocardial Infarction Men	Women
35–44	42	7	2	4	8	5	21	2
45–54	108	33	20	12	30	21	54	9
55–64	202	99	40	26	74	54	91	25
65–74	227	136	92	80	52	51	119	51
75–84	247	236	196	112	25	94	168	90

Source: U.S. Department of Health and Human Services, 1988

groups such as African Americans remains nearly double that in European Americans (United States Department of Health and Human Services [USDHHS], 1988).

The clear gender difference in cardiovascular diseases has been the topic of much interest and debate (Nachtigall & Nachtigall, 1990). Premenopausal women appear somewhat protected from cardiovascular disease due to estrogen. Because estrogen production drops dramatically in postmenopausal women, their risk rises. However, not all premenopausal women have low risk. Women who have hypertension, who smoke, who have high levels of low-density lipoproteins (LDLs, or so-called bad cholesterol), who are obese, and who have diabetes are always at greater risk. Although estrogen replacement therapy for postmenopausal women is a popular but still controversial medical approach for lowering their risk, exercise and other behavioral approaches are considered better options by some physicians.

Ischemic Heart Disease

The most common heart disease in older adults is *ischemic heart disease,* which occurs in approximately 12% of women and 20% of men over 65 years of age (Lakatta, 1985). In this disorder the muscle cells of the heart receive insufficient oxygen because of poor circulation or partial blockages in the coronary arteries. Ischemic heart disease is a major contributing factor to congestive heart failure, a condition in which cardiac output and the ability of the heart to contract severely decline. In congestive heart failure, the heart enlarges, pressure in the veins increases, and there is swelling throughout the body.

Cardiac Arrhythmias

Irregularities in the heartbeat, termed *cardiac arrhythmias,* are fairly common in older adults (Lakatta, 1985). These disturbances include extra and uneven beats as well as fibrillation, in which the heart makes very rapid, irregular contractions. Why these changes occur is not entirely understood, but they may be related to the level of various salts (such as sodium and potassium) and minerals (such as calcium) in the bloodstream. Cardiac arrhythmias can be very dangerous, because they may alter the normal functioning of the heart. For example, arrhythmias involving the ventricles can cause sudden death.

Angina

Recall that one of the changes in the heart with age is a gradual reduction in blood flow. **When the reduction in blood flow becomes severe, the supply of oxygen to the heart muscle becomes insufficient, resulting in chest pain, called *angina.*** Angina may feel like chest pressure, a burning pain, or a squeezing that radiates from the chest to the back, neck, and arms (Berkow, 1987). In most cases the pain is induced by physical exertion and is relieved within 5 to 10 minutes by rest.

Treatment of angina is similar in adults of all ages; depending on when the angina occurs, patients are given nitroglycerine, beta-blocking agents, or calcium-blocking agents.

Myocardial Infarction

Perhaps the most dramatic age-related coronary disease is *myocardial infarction*, or heart attack. Myocardial infarction is especially serious for older adults; mortality following a heart attack is much higher for them (USDHHS, 1995). Heart attacks occur when the coronary blood flow drops below the level needed to nourish the heart muscle. If sustained, the interruption kills the heart muscle. The interruption in blood flow may result from a spasm, a progressive buildup of fatty plaques that clogs the coronary arteries, or some combination of factors. The initial symptoms of myocardial infarction are identical to those of angina but are typically more severe and prolonged. Additionally, there may be general symptoms such as nausea, vomiting, sweating, and severe weakness. In as many as 25% of patients, however, chest pain may be absent. These "silent" heart attacks are more common in older adults, especially those with diabetes (Berkow, 1987). Treatment of heart attack victims of all ages includes careful evaluation and a prescribed rehabilitation program consisting of lifestyle changes in diet and exercise.

Atherosclerosis

The age-related buildup of fat deposits on and the calcification of the arterial walls is called *atherosclerosis* (Berkow, 1987). Much like sandbars in a river or mineral deposits in pipes, the fat deposits interfere with blood flow through the arteries. These deposits begin very early in life and continue throughout the life span. Some amount of fat deposit inevitably occurs and is considered a normal part of aging. However, excess deposits may develop from poor nutrition, smoking, and other aspects of an unhealthy lifestyle.

Fat deposits sometimes provide points where a blood clot or other mass becomes stuck, completely blocking the blood flow. Such blockages are responsible for heart attacks and angina, and are one cause of cerebrovascular accidents (discussed next). Atherosclerosis may become so severe in the coronary arteries that they must be replaced surgically. This procedure, known as a coronary bypass, involves transplanting a blood vessel from another part of the body, usually the leg, to serve as a new coronary artery. Other techniques used to treat atherosclerosis in the coronary arteries include inserting a tiny catheter or a balloonlike device into the arteries and clearing the blockage, scraping deposits off artery walls, and using lasers to clear the arteries (Bierman, 1985). For reasons not yet understood, blocked coronary arteries do not always produce noticeable symptoms, so that periodic checkups are very important.

Cerebrovascular Disease

When severe atherosclerosis occurs in blood vessels that supply the brain, neurons may not receive proper nourishment, causing them to malfunction or die, a condition termed *cerebrovascular disease*. When the blood flow to a portion of the brain is completely cut off, a *cerebrovascular accident (CVA)*, or stroke, results (Berkow, 1987). **Causes of CVAs include clots that block blood flow in an artery, or the actual breaking of a blood vessel, which creates a *cerebral hemorrhage*.** The severity of a CVA and likelihood of recovery depend on the specific area of the brain involved, the extent of disruption in blood flow, and the duration of the disruption. Consequently, a CVA may affect such a small area that it goes virtually unnoticed, or it may be so severe as to cause death.

The risk of a CVA increases with age; in fact, CVAs are the third leading cause of death among the elderly in the United States (USDHHS, 1995). In addition to age, other risk factors include being male, being African American, and having high blood pressure, heart disease, or diabetes. The higher risk among African Americans appears to be due to a greater prevalence of hypertension in this population (USDHHS, 1988).

Recovery following a stroke must take into account not only the physical effects but also the psychological ones. For example, the sudden loss of the ability to move or speak can have profound effects on a person's self-esteem and sense of independence. Anger and frustration are very common reactions. The degree to which a person recovers functions affected by a stroke depend on the severity of the stroke, its location in the brain, the age of the person, the time between the stroke and the beginning of therapy, and the intensity of therapy. To set the stage for maximum recovery, both health care professionals and family members must provide support.

Hypertension

As we grow older, blood pressure tends to rise. Although parents of adolescents may claim otherwise, the main reason for this blood pressure rise is structural change in the cardiovascular system. **When blood pressure increases become severe, the disease *hypertension* results.** Roughly 35% of the population between the ages of 25 and 74 have some degree of hypertension. However, the rate is somewhat higher among African Americans; this difference may be due to a genetic mutation affecting enzymes that help control blood pressure (Haney, 1995). These differences may also explain why roughly twice as many African Americans die of strokes than European Americans.

Hypertension is a very serious matter. Older adults with hypertension have three times the risk of dying from cardiovascular disease. The long-term risk for young adults with hypertension may even be greater (Kannel, 1985). Because hypertension is a disease with no clear symptoms, most people with hypertension are not aware that they have a problem. Regular blood pressure monitoring is the only sure way to find out if one has hypertension.

Some of the causes of hypertension are not purely physiological. For example, stress and high sodium diets have been shown to cause hypertension in some people. Interestingly, differences in rates of hypertension in some ethnic groups support the causal roles of stress and diet. Espino and Maldonado (1990) report that the rate of hypertension was higher among Mexican Americans who were more acculturated into the American lifestyle. In fact, degree of acculturation was a better predictor of hypertension than socioeconomic variables such as income. They speculate that with acculturation comes higher levels of stress and the adoption of a less healthy diet that puts such people at risk. Poverty alone does not explain the difference. In short, the American lifestyle can be fatally hazardous to health.

Psychological Consequences of Changes in the Cardiovascular System

Clearly, the most important psychological consequences of cardiovascular system changes are reflected in the things people do to try to avoid cardiovascular disease. The past few decades have witnessed some remarkable changes in people's awareness of lifestyle factors as causes of heart attacks and heart disease. Many people have dramatically altered their diets (eating less red meat and saturated fat) and begun exercising. These changes, especially in exercise, significantly affect psychological functioning. We will also see how specific personality variables (such as hostility or anger) play key roles in cardiovascular disease. For many people, the specter of heart attacks is sufficient to get them to the health club or to the nearest park for a vigorous workout.

Concept Checks

1. What are the two most important structural changes in the heart and circulatory system?
2. What are the key types of cardiovascular disease in adulthood?
3. How does people's behavior reflect the psychological effects of cardiovascular change?

THE RESPIRATORY SYSTEM

Learning Objectives:

- What structural and functional changes occur with age in the respiratory system?
- What are the most common types of respiratory diseases in older adults?
- What are the psychological effects of age-related changes in the respiratory system?

Most of us only become aware of our breathing in the midst of physical exertion. But for many older adults, shortness of breath is a routine (and quite unpleasant) experience. How much of this age-related problem is due to a decline in the effectiveness of the respiratory system is hard to say. Air pollution, infections, smoking, and other factors all cause damage that could be mistaken for the effects of aging. Consequently, determining the strictly normative changes of aging on the pulmonary system is impossible (Kenney, 1982); the changes described in this section should be viewed as the combined effects of aging and living in a polluted and disease-bearing environment.

Age-Related Structural and Functional Changes

With increasing age, the rib cage and the air passageways become stiffer, making it harder to breathe. The lungs change in appearance over time, going gradually from their youthful pinkish color to a dreary gray, due mainly to breathing in carbon particles (from exhaust and smoke). The rate at which we can exchange oxygen for carbon dioxide drops significantly due to the destruction of the membranes of the air sacs in the lungs.

Changes in the maximum amount of air we can take into the lungs in a single breath begin in the 20s, decreasing by 40% by age 85 (Shephard, 1982). We also have a more difficult time dealing with increased need for oxygen during physical stress, as we cannot increase our air intake when we are old as much as we can when we are young. This further aggravates the shortness-of-breath problems older adults have (Kenney, 1982). However, there is some good news; these changes in capacity can be moderated by regular exercise, even in old age (Buskirk, 1985).

Respiratory Diseases

The most common and incapacitating respiratory disorder in older adults is *chronic obstructive pulmonary disease (COPD)*. Since the 1960s deaths directly attributed to COPD have tripled, due in part to better diagnosis but most importantly to increased long-term exposure to pollution (Burdman, 1986). In these diseases, the passage of air in the bronchial tubes becomes blocked and abnormalities develop in the lungs. Smoking, air pollution, infection, heredity, allergies, and pollutants are the major causes. COPD is a progressive disease in which the prognosis is usually very poor (Burdman, 1986).

***Emphysema* is the most serious type of COPD and is characterized by the destruction of the membranes around the air sacs in the lungs** (Lebowitz, 1988). This irreversible destruction creates "holes" in the lung, drastically reducing the ability to exchange oxygen and carbon dioxide. To make matters worse, the bronchial tubes collapse prematurely when the person exhales, thereby preventing the lungs from emptying completely. Emphysema is a very debilitating disease. In its later stages, even the smallest physical exertion causes a struggle for air. People with emphysema may have such poorly oxygenated blood that they become confused and disoriented. The sad part about emphysema is that in the vast majority of cases it is largely self-induced by smoking. The disease is rare in nonsmokers; most cases are caused by environmental pollutants, such as secondhand smoke or high levels of dust, and by genetic factors (Burdman, 1986).

Although upper respiratory infections decrease in frequency with age, lower respiratory infections such as pneumonia increase (Burdman, 1986). Consequently, older adults are more likely to die of pneumonia and related respiratory diseases. This age-related increase in frequency of pneumonia may be due in part to a lack of exercise (Burdman, 1986).

Psychological Consequences of Changes in the Respiratory System

The effects of age-related changes in the respiratory system that people notice most are shortness of breath and subsequent fatigue during physical exercise. It can be extremely frightening for a person to feel out of breath. The level of activity at which shortness of breath is experienced declines across adulthood. Increased concern over especially serious episodes of shortness of breath is understandable, and subsequent declines in physical activity may result (which in the long run only makes matters worse). In some cases people may become overly cautious and withdraw from any form of exercise. Such withdrawal can have a detrimental effect on other aspects of physiological functioning (for example, the cardiovascular system). Moreover, regular exercise has significant beneficial effects because it helps maintain higher levels of respiratory functioning.

Whitbourne (1985) hypothesized that reduced respiratory functioning has negative effects on sense of competence. Feeling that one is out of shape may follow experiences of shortness of breath, which may ultimately lower a person's sense of well-being. This lowered sense of self-esteem may further reduce activity. The bottom line is this: Keep exercising!

Concept Checks

1. What happens to the rib cage, air passages, and air sacs in the lungs as people age?
2. What is the most common form of chronic obstructive pulmonary disease?
3. What is the age-related change in the respiratory system that people notice the most?

THE SENSES

Learning Objectives:

- What age-related changes happen in vision?
- How does hearing change as people age?
- What happens to taste with increasing age?
- Does the ability to smell change as people grow older?
- What age-related changes occur in somesthesis and balance?

Have you ever watched middle-aged people try to read something that is right in front of them? If they do not already wear glasses or contact lenses, they typically move the material farther away so that they can see it clearly. This change in vision is one of the first noticeable signs of aging as we enter middle age. These changes in our sensory systems challenge our ability to interact with the world and to communicate with others. Some changes, such as those that impair our ability to smell, could even prove life threatening. In this section, we will consider changes in vision, hearing, taste, smell, somesthesis, and balance.

Vision

We rely extensively on sight in virtually every aspect of our waking life, from checking the time to combing our hair in the mirror. Perhaps because of our strong dependence on this sensory system, its age-related changes have profound and pervasive effects. Loss of vision is second only to cancer as the most feared consequence of aging (Verrillo & Verrillo, 1985). Although the extent of visual impairment varies across people, each one of us will eventually experience some form of visual impairment that requires treatment or that interferes with everyday life (Kline & Schieber, 1985).

The major changes in visual functioning can be grouped into two classes: changes in the structures of the eye and changes in the retina (Kline & Schieber, 1985). Structural changes begin to affect visual functioning during middle adulthood (around age 40). **The most important structural changes are decreases in the amount of light that passes through the eye (termed *transmissiveness*) and in the eye's ability to adjust and focus (termed *visual accommodation*).** Two diseases may result from structural changes. **First, opaque spots called *cataracts* may develop on the lens, which seriously limits the amount of light transmitted.** Cataracts are often treated by surgical removal and use of corrective lenses. **Second, the fluid in the eye may not drain properly, causing very high pressure; this condition, called *glaucoma*, can cause internal damage and loss of vision.** Glaucoma is a fairly common disease in middle and late adulthood.

The retina lines approximately two thirds of the interior of the eye. The specialized receptor cells in vision, the rods and the cones, are contained in the retina. They are most densely packed toward the rear and especially at the focal point of vision, a region called the macula. At the center of the macula is the fovea, where incoming light is focused for maximum acuity, as when one is reading.

Retinal changes usually begin in a person's 50s. With increasing age the probability of degeneration of the macula increases (Kline & Schieber, 1985). ***Macular degeneration* involves the progressive and irreversible destruction of receptors from any of a number of causes.** This disease results in the loss of the ability to see details; for example, reading is extremely difficult, and television is often reduced to a blur.

A second retinal disease that is related to age is actually a by-product of diabetes. Diabetes is accompanied by accelerated aging of the arteries, with blindness being one of the more serious side effects. *Diabetic retinopathy,* as this condition is called, can involve fluid retention in the macula, detachment of the retina, hemorrhage, and aneurysms. Because it takes many years to develop, diabetic retinopathy is more common among people who developed diabetes relatively early in life. Sadly, diabetic retinopathy is the leading cause of blindness in the United States (Lewis, 1979).

The structural and retinal changes in the visual system produce important changes in visual abilities. We will consider several changes: absolute and difference thresholds, sensitivity to glare, visual accommodation, acuity, and adaptation.

Absolute and Difference Thresholds

Research consistently demonstrates that older adults require a greater intensity of light than young adults to detect that something is out there (Kline & Schieber, 1985). The most important practical consequence of this change is that as we grow older, we tend to require higher levels of illumination to perform daily tasks. Older adults do not see as well in the dark, which may account in part for their reluctance to go places at night. Older adults also have more difficulty discriminating different levels of illumination, such as telling the difference between a 60-watt and a 75-watt lightbulb.

Sensitivity to Glare

One possible logical response to the need for more light would be to increase illumination levels. However, this solution may not work, because we also become increasingly sensitive to glare beginning around age 40 (Kline & Schieber, 1985). This change is especially important for older drivers, because reflected sunlight can pose a more serious problem for them. Consequently, the need for more illumination must be balanced with the need to avoid glare (Fozard & Popkin, 1978).

Visual Accommodation

Visual accommodation is the process by which the lens adjusts so that we can see nearby and faraway objects clearly. **Considerable research demonstrates an age-related decrease in the ability to focus on nearby objects, a condition termed *presbyopia*** (Kline & Schieber, 1985). Presbyopia is what makes middle-aged people hold reading material at increasing distances, and, once their arms become too short, forces them to get either reading glasses or bifocals.

As we age, the time we need to switch our focus from near to far (or vice versa) increases (Corso, 1981). This poses a major problem in driving. Because drivers are constantly alternating their focus from the instrument panel to other autos and signs on the highway, older drivers may miss important information because of their slower refocusing time (Panek & Rearden, 1986).

Acuity

The ability to see detail and to discriminate different visual patterns is termed *acuity.* The most common way of testing visual acuity is the Snellen test—the familiar eye chart—consisting of a standardized series of letters or symbols in different sizes that must be read at a distance of about 6 meters. Acuity shows a slight but steady decline between the ages of 20 and 60, with a more rapid decline thereafter (Richards, 1977). The consequences of decreases in visual acuity range from annoying, such as the print of this book looking fuzzy, to potentially serious, such as difficulty in reading medicine bottle labels.

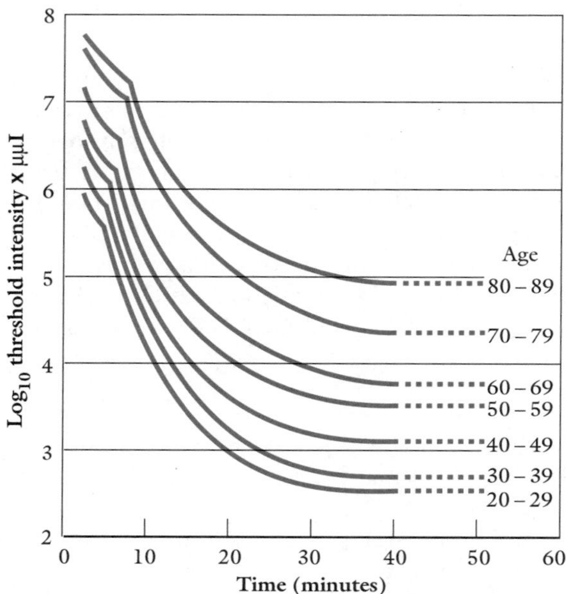

Figure 3.2 Dark adaptation as a function of age and time in the dark.

Source: "Dark Adaptation as a Function of Age: 1. A Statistical Analysis," by R. A. McFarland et al., 1960, Journal of Gerontology, 15, *149–154. Copyright © 1960 The Gerontological Society of America. Reprinted with permission.*

Adaptation

Adaptation is the change in sensitivity of the eye as a function of changes in illumination. **There are two types of adaptation: *dark adaptation,* the adjustment of the eye to dark environments, and *light adaptation,* the adjustment of the eye to bright environments.** Going from outside into a darkened movie theater involves dark adaptation; going back outside involves light adaptation. Research indicates that the time it takes for both types of adaptation increases with age (Kline & Schieber, 1985); the data for dark adaptation are depicted in Figure 3.2. In addition, the final level of dark adaptation is less in older adults (Wolf, 1960). This means that as we age, it takes us longer to adapt to changes in illumination, making us more susceptible to environmental hazards for the first few minutes following the change. For example, older drivers take longer to recover visually from the headlights of an oncoming car, making them less able to pick up critical information from the highway in the meantime.

Psychological Effects of Visual Changes

Evidence of visual changes in everyday life has been documented through surveys of over 400 adults ranging in age from 18 to 100 (Kosnik, Winslow, Kline, Rasinski, & Sekular, 1988). The responses indicated a two- to sixfold decline in visual ability in everyday situations, depending on the skill required. Imagine the problems people experience performing tasks that most of us take for granted, such as reading a book, watching television, reading grocery labels, driving a car, and so on. Simply making things brighter is not the answer. For increased illumination to work, surrounding surfaces must not increase glare. Use of flat paint rather than glossy enamel and avoiding highly polished floors are two steps that could be taken in designing environments. Details on dials, such as on stoves and radios, may be difficult to distinguish, as are some subtle facial features. As Whitbourne (1985) notes, these experiences may be especially difficult for people who always had good vision when young. Such people may simply avoid cooking or listening to their favorite music and become homebodies out of fear that they may not recognize a face.

People often do not recognize the extent of visual changes because these occur slowly over many years. Lack of awareness of these changes usually results in a failure to seek ways to compensate or correct for the problems. Most unfortunate are those individuals who believe that these decrements are simply a sign of aging and are untreatable. Many of the normal age-related changes in vision can be remediated. Periodic vision examinations can detect changes early, and correction of visual problems may help avert the internalization of these changes as potential threats to self-esteem.

Hearing

One of the most well-known changes in normal aging is the decline in hearing ability, which is quite

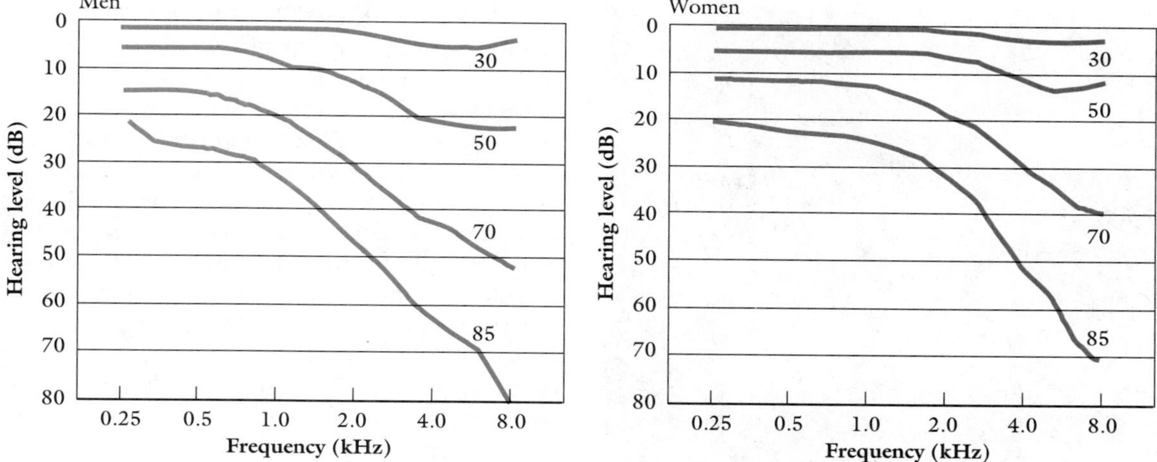

Figure 3.3 Amount of hearing loss in decibels for different pure tones in various age groups of men and women. Note higher frequencies and higher ages and more pronounced hearing loss in men.
Source: Meisami, 1994

dramatic across the life span (Olsho, Harkins, & Lenhardt, 1985). Age-related declines in hearing are progressive and may interfere with adaptation in later life. Significant hearing loss is widespread in older adults. If we visited a housing complex for the elderly, we would probably notice that television sets and radios are turned up fairly loud in most of the apartments. Research indicates that nearly half of normal older adults have a relatively serious hearing impairment. (P.D. Thomas et al., 1983). Men typically have greater loss than women, but this may be due to differential exposure to noisy environments (Olsho et al., 1985). Loss of hearing is gradual at first but accelerates during the 40s (Corso, 1984). This pattern can be seen quite clearly in Figure 3.3. **Note in the figure that hearing loss with age is greatest for high-pitched tones, a condition called *presbycusis*.**

Presbycusis

Presbycusis results from four types of changes in the inner ear (Olsho et al., 1985): (1) sensory, consisting of atrophy and degeneration of receptor cells; (2) neural, consisting of a loss of neurons in the auditory pathway in the brain; (3) metabolic, consisting of a diminished supply of nutrients to the cells in the receptor area; and (4) mechanical, consisting of atrophy and stiffening of the vibrating structures in the receptor area. Although the four types occur at different rates (12%, 31%, 35%, and 23%, respectively), rarely does an individual have only one of them (Schuknecht, 1974).

All of these types of presbycusis affect the ability to hear high-pitched tones. However, they differ in their effects on other aspects of hearing (Whitbourne, 1985). Sensory presbycusis has little effect on other hearing abilities. Neural presbycusis seriously affects the ability to understand speech. Metabolic presbycusis produces severe loss of sensitivity to all pitches. Finally, mechanical presbycusis produces loss across all pitches, but the loss is greatest for high pitches.

Hearing and Exposure to Noise

There is no doubt that lifelong exposure to noise has significant negative effects on hearing ability (Corso, 1981). Much of the research that established this relationship was conducted in industrial settings, but we now know that any source of sustained loud noise, whether from machinery or stereo headphones, produces damage.

An important question for developmentalists is

Hearing aids assist many people in maintaining communication. As this man knows, making sure that hearing aids are kept in working condition is important in this regard.

whether older people are more susceptible to hearing damage from noise. The results of several experiments demonstrate convincingly that the answer is no. People of all ages can lose their hearing from living in noisy environments. More important, noise causes more damage than aging (Corso, 1981). Cross-cultural evidence suggests that hearing loss is less in cultures that have lower exposure to noise. Corso (1981) refers to the damaging effect of repeated, sustained noise on adults' hearing as "premature presbycusis." Because of these effects workers in many industries are required to wear protective earplugs to guard against prolonged exposure. However, the use of stereo headphones, especially at high volume, can cause the same serious damage and should be avoided. It is especially easy to cause hearing loss with headphones if worn while exercising; the increased blood flow to the ear during exercise makes hearing receptors more vulnerable to damage.

Psychological Effects of Hearing Loss

Because hearing plays an almost irreplaceable role in social communication, its progressive loss could have an equally important effect on individuals' adjustment. Loss of hearing in later life can cause numerous adverse emotional reactions, such as feelings of loss of independence, social isolation, irritation, paranoia, and depression. Substantial research indicates that older people with hearing loss are generally not socially maladjusted or emotionally disturbed as a result of hearing loss per se (Norris & Cunningham, 1981). However, a strain on the quality of interpersonal relationships often exists due to friends' and relatives' tendency to attribute emotional changes to hearing loss and their failure to communicate properly with a hearing-impaired person (Thomas et al., 1983).

Thus, hearing loss may not directly affect older adults' self-concept or emotions, but it may negatively affect how they feel about interpersonal communication. Knowledge of hearing loss problems and of ways to overcome them on the part of non-hearing-impaired individuals can play a large part in minimizing the effects of hearing loss.

Taste

The expression "too old to cut the mustard" dates back to when people made mustard at home by grinding mustard seed and adding just the right amount of vinegar ("cutting the mustard") to balance the taste. If too much vinegar was added, the whole concoction tasted terrible, so the balance was critical. Many families found that elderly members tended to add too much vinegar, resulting in the saying.

Despite the everyday belief that taste ability changes with age, we do not have much data documenting what actually happens. What we know is that the ability to detect different tastes gradually declines and that these declines vary a great deal from flavor to flavor (Meisami, 1994). Whatever age differences we observe are not due to a decline in the sheer number of taste buds, however. Unlike other neural cells, the number of taste cells does not change appreciably across the life span (Engen, 1982). Moreover, many adults over age 60 have no apparent loss of taste sensitivity. And even for those who do, the decreases are typically slight (Spitzer, 1988). Likewise, age-related differences in taste preference are not substantial and may be due to a variety of factors including cultural experiences, the context in which the substances are consumed, or changes in the sensory areas in the brain. At present, however, it is impossible to distinguish among these possibilities. Finally, carefully conducted research shows no age differences in the ability to identify foods by taste alone (Murphy, 1985).

Psychological Effects of Changes in Taste

There is little question that older adults complain more about boring food (Schiffman & Covey, 1984; Whitbourne, 1985). The source of these complaints, however, cannot be predominantly physiological changes in taste. Age differences in taste are minimal; thus, the high incidence of food complaints among older adults is not based on changes in the ability to taste. The explanation appears to be that changes in the enjoyment of food are due to psychosocial issues (such as personal adjustment), to changes in smell (which we consider next), or to disease (Whitbourne, 1985). For instance, we are much more likely to eat a balanced diet and enjoy our food when we do not eat alone and when we get a whiff of the enticing aromas emanating from the kitchen.

Smell

"Stop and smell the roses." "OOOH! What's that perfume you're wearing?" "Yuk! What's that smell?" There is a great deal of truth in the saying "the nose knows." Smell is a major part of our everyday lives. How something smells can alert us that dinner is cooking, warn of a gas leak or a fire, let us know that we are clean, or be sexually arousing. A great many of our social interactions involve smell (or the lack of it). Billions of dollars are spent on making our bodies smell appealing to others. It is easy to see that any age-related change in sense of smell would have far-reaching consequences.

Researchers agree that the ability to detect odors remains fairly intact until the 60s, when it begins to decline fairly rapidly (Murphy, 1986). But people vary widely in the degree to which their abilities to detect odors are affected by age. Moreover, even within the same individual, the degree of change depends on the odors being tested (Stevens & Cain, 1987).

These variations could have important practical implications. A large survey conducted by the National Geographic Society indicated that older adults were not as able to identify particular odors as younger people. One of the odors tested was the substance added to natural gas that enables people to detect leaks, a potentially fatal problem. Changes in smell are greater than changes in taste (Stevens & Cain, 1985, 1986). Because much of the pleasure of eating comes from the odor of food, changes in smell are a major reason for the increase in food complaints with age.

Abnormal changes in the ability to smell are turning out to be important in the differential diagnosis of Alzheimer's disease (Meisami, 1994). According to several studies, individuals with Alzheimer's disease are able to identify only 60% of the odors identified by age-matched control participants; in more advanced stages of the disease, this was reduced to only 40% compared with controls. These changes provide clinicians another indicator for diagnosing suspected cases of Alzheimer's disease.

Psychological Effects of Olfactory Changes

The major psychological consequences of changes in olfactory ability concern eating, safety, and overall pleasurable experiences. Odors play an important role in enjoying food and in protecting us from harm. Socially, decreases in our ability to detect unpleasant odors may lead to embarrasing situations in which we are unaware that we have body odors or may need to brush our teeth. Social interactions could suffer as a result of these problems. Smells also play a key role in remembering past life experiences. Who can forget the smell of cookies baking in grandma's oven when we were little? Loss of odor cues may mean that our sense of the past suffers as well.

Somesthesis and Balance

Knowing our body's position right now, feeling our lover's soft touch, experiencing the pain of a paper cut, and sensing a chill in the evening air are only a few benefits of somesthesis and balance. These abilities convey information about touch, pressure, pain, kinesthesis, outside temperature, and body orientation. Unlike the other sensory systems we have considered, the somesthetic system has multiple types of receptors and neural pathways, most of which convey specific information about bodily stimulation.

Touch Sensitivity

The distribution of touch receptors is not consistent throughout the body; the greatest concentrations are in the lips, tongue, and fingertips. Although touch thresholds increase with age in the smooth (nonhairy) skin on the hand (Axelrod & Cohen, 1961), touch sensitivity in the hair-covered parts of the body is maintained into later life (Kenshalo, 1977). Sensitivity to vibration decreases in the lower but not the upper part of the body beginning around age 50 (Kenshalo, 1977).

Temperature Sensitivity

The complex way in which our thermal regulation and sensing system works makes it difficult to research. The few studies on aging and temperature sensitivity suggest a meaningful increase in the threshold for warmth (Clark & Mehl, 1971). Although a slight increase occurs in the cold threshold, this change appears minimal (Hensel, 1981; Kenshalo, 1979). These data appear to conflict with lowered tolerance of cold by older adults. However, the discrepancy may be due to different age effects between temperature sensitivity and temperature regulation (Whitbourne, 1985), but we do not know for certain.

Pain Sensitivity

Although there are many studies of age-related differences in sensitivity to pain, we still do not have a clear picture of what happens (Harkins & Kwentus, 1990). A major problem confronting researchers interested in pain threshold and pain tolerance (the highest level of pain that can be withstood) is that pain sensitivity varies across different locations on the body and with different types of stimulation. Moreover, experiencing pain is more than just a sensory experience; it involves cognitive, motivational, personality, and cultural factors as well.

Although older adults complain more about pain, the research evidence is conflicting. Data showing everything from decreased sensitivity to increased sensitivity can be found (Harkins & Kwentus, 1990). Corso (1987) notes that the problem is a lack of an appropriate definition of pain and a lack of understanding about how pain happens.

Kinesthesis

Knowing how our arms are positioned at any particular moment means that we have experienced our sense of body position, or kinesthesis. Kinesthesis involves sensory feedback concerning two kinds of movements. *Passive movements* are instigated by something (or someone) else, as, for example, when our lover picks up our hand. *Active movement* is voluntary, as in walking.

Age-related changes in passive movements depend on the part of the body in question. For example, differences are not observed for passive movement of the big toe but are found for several joints, including the knees and the hips (Ochs, Newberry, Lenhardt, & Harkins, 1985). However, age differences in active movements are not found. For example, judgments of muscle or tendon strain produced by picking up different weights do not differ with age (Ochs et al., 1985).

Balance

Information about balance is provided by the *vestibular system*, housed deep in the inner ear. The vestibular system is designed to respond to the forces of gravity as they act on the head and then to provide this information to the parts of the brain that initiate the appropriate movements so that we can maintain our balance.

Dizziness and vertigo are common experiences for older adults (Ochs et al., 1985). Dizziness is the vague feeling of being unsteady, floating, and lightheaded. Vertigo is the sensation that one or one's surroundings are spinning. These feelings are unpleasant by themselves, but they can also lead to serious injury from falls resulting from loss of balance.

The likelihood of falling increases with age. Falls may be life-threatening events, especially for those 75 and older (Ochs et al., 1985). Environmental hazards such as loose rugs and slippery floors are more likely to be a factor for healthy, community-dwelling older adults, whereas disease is more likely to play a role in institutionalized individuals. Increases in body sway, the natural movement of the body to maintain balance, occur with increasing age. Connections between the degree of body sway and likelihood of falling have been shown, with people who fall often having more body sway (Overstall, Johnson, & Exton-Smith, 1978).

Psychological Effects of Somesthesis and Balance

Sensations from the skin, internal organs, and joints serve critical functions. They keep us in contact with our environment, help us avoid falling, serve communication functions, and keep us safe. In terms of self-esteem, how well our body is functioning tells us something about how well we are doing. Losing bodily sensations could have major implications. Increased joint stiffness, loss of sexual sensitivity, and problems maintaining balance could result in increased cautiousness, loss of mobility, and decreased social interaction. How the individual views these changes is critical for maintaining self-esteem. Providing supportive environments that lead to successful compensatory behaviors can ameliorate the physical and social risks of lack of motor coordination.

Concept Checks

1. What are the major structural changes with age in the eye? What functional effects do these changes have?
2. What is presbycusis?
3. Does the ability to taste change with age?
4. When does the ability to detect odors begin to change?
5. What changes occur in the skin-based senses?

THE REPRODUCTIVE SYSTEM

Learning Objectives:

- What reproductive changes occur in women?
- What reproductive changes occur in men?
- What are the psychological effects of reproductive changes?

One of the most damaging stereotypes about older adults is that they have no desire for sexual contact. Nothing could be further from the truth. Many surveys show quite clearly that regardless of whether one is a grandparent or a newly married young adult, sexual desire still plays a major role in defining who we are. What is true is that human sexual behavior involves complex interactions among physiological and psychological factors. Age-related changes in these factors have important implications not only for sexual behavior but also for overall self-esteem and well-being.

Many of the major changes in our reproductive system begin during middle age. This has important psychological implications, as midlife is thought by many to be a key time for redefining ourselves. Such changes are most apparent in women, who undergo more dramatic physiological changes than men.

Reproductive Changes in Women

The major reproductive change in women during adulthood is the loss of the ability to bear children. This change begins in the 40s, as menstrual cycles become irregular, and by the age of 50 to 55 it is usually complete (Rykken, 1987). **This transition during which a woman's reproductive capacity ends and ovulation stops is referred to as the *climacteric. Menopause* refers specifically to the cessation of menstruation.** This end of monthly periods is accompanied by decreases in the levels of estrogen and progesterone, changes in the reproductive organs, and changes in sexual functioning (Solnick & Corby, 1983).

A variety of physical and psychological symptoms may accompany menopause due to decreases in hormonal levels (Solnick & Corby, 1983). These include hot flashes, chills, headaches, depression,

SOMETHING TO THINK ABOUT

Hormone Replacement Therapy

For many years, women have had the choice of taking medications to replace the female hormones that are not produced naturally by the body after menopause. These replacement hormones tend to reduce the physiological symptoms associated with the climacteric and may provide continued protection against cardiovascular disease. However, taking these drugs may not be risk free; some evidence of increased breast cancer risk in women taking replacement hormones had been reported based on combined analyses of small studies, but the extent of the risk for specific groups was unclear (Colditz et al., 1995). One of the main problems was the lack of large-scale epidemiological data examining different types of hormone therapies.

Controversy over the safety of hormone replacement therapy erupted in the summer of 1995. Within a one-month span, two large, well-designed studies published in two prestigious medical journals reported exactly opposite findings.

Colditz et al. (1995) began with a sample of 121,700 nurses who were between 30 and 55 years of age in 1976. Beginning in 1978, they had the nurses complete questionnaires every two years until they were diagnosed with breast cancer, died, or reached the end of the study in 1992. Based on their analysis of 725,550 person-years of follow-up, women who had been on hormone replacement therapy for 5 years or more were at significantly increased risk for breast cancer compared with women who had never been on hormone replacement therapy. The investigators noted that the risk was somewhat higher for women over age 60 and that the risk for all women was increased for estrogen-only and estrogen-plus-progestin therapies.

Stanford et al. (1995) studied 537 women diagnosed with breast cancer and 492 randomly selected control women without a history of breast cancer, all of whom were between ages 50 and 64. They worked backward from the case records to see whether more women who had been diagnosed with breast cancer had taken hormone replacement therapy. In direct opposition to Colditz et al.'s findings, Stanford et al. reported no increased risk in breast cancer from taking estrogen-progestin hormone replacement therapy.

What can we conclude? There are obvious differences in the research approaches in the two studies. Colditz et al. (1995) followed women prospectively; Stanford et al. (1995) worked backward from a specific point in time (the diagnosis of cancer in the one group). The ages of the samples differed, with Colditz et al. including younger women. Differences also existed in recruitment and in the data collection strategies. The vast difference in the ultimate sample sizes means that Colditz et al.'s study was more sensitive to potential differences. Do these factors explain why the data are contradictory? Perhaps, but probably not completely. It will take still more carefully controlled studies to sort out these issues. In any case, it is clear that the potential benefits of hormone replacement therapy must be weighed against the *potential* of increased risk for breast cancer. It's something to think about.

---

dizziness, nervousness, and a variety of aches and pains. Although many women report no symptoms at all, most women experience at least some due to their fluctuating hormones. The psychological consequences of menopause, which are often tied to the so-called empty-nest syndrome, will be explored more fully in Chapter 10.

There is some evidence of differences across ethnic groups in women's experiences before and after the climacteric (B. Jackson, Taylor, & Pyngolil, 1991). For example, studies of European American women reveal a decrease in reported physical symptoms following climacteric. In contrast, African American women reported more physical symptoms after climacteric than before. Although these differences could be due to the different age groups included in the various studies (B. Jackson et al., 1991), they also draw attention to the need to study the experiences of women from different ethnic and racial backgrounds.

One way that the symptoms associated with the climacteric can be addressed is through hormone replacement therapy. Many physicians also point out that having women take hormones after menopause may also provide some protection against cardiovascular disease, as described earlier in this chapter. However, as discussed in the Something to Think About feature, there is probably no other area of medical research that has resulted in more contradictory data about the potentially serious side effects (or lack thereof) than is the case with work on hormone replacement therapy.

Women's genital organs undergo progressive change after menopause (O'Donohue, 1987). The vaginal walls shrink and become thinner, the size of the vagina is reduced, the production of vaginal lubricant is reduced and delayed, and some shrinkage of the external genitalia occurs. These changes have important effects on sexual activity, such as an increased possibility of painful intercourse and a longer time as well as more stimulation needed to reach orgasm. More frequent failure to achieve orgasm also occurs compared with a woman's younger years. However, maintaining an active sex life throughout adulthood lowers the degree to which problems are encountered.

Despite the physical changes, there is no physiological reason why most women cannot continue sexual activity and enjoy it well into old age. Whether this happens depends more on the availability of a suitable partner than on a woman's desire for sexual relations. This is especially true for older women. The Duke Longitudinal Studies of Normal Aging (Busse & Maddox, 1985) found that older married women were far more likely to have an active sex life than unmarried women. Those married women whose sex life had ceased attributed their lack of activity to their husbands, who agreed with the judgment. In short, the primary reason for the decline in women's sexual activity with age is the lack of a willing or appropriate partner, not a lack of physical ability or desire (Robinson, 1983).

Reproductive Changes in Men

Unlike women, men do not have a physiological (and cultural) event to mark reproductive changes. Men do not experience a complete loss of the ability to have children. However, men do experience a normative decline in the quantity of sperm (Rykken, 1987). Sperm production declines by approximately 30% between age 25 and 60 (Solnick & Corby, 1983). However, even at age 80 a man is still half as fertile as he was at age 25 and is quite capable of fathering a child.

With increasing age the prostate gland enlarges, becomes stiffer, and may obstruct the urinary tract. Prostate cancer becomes a real threat during middle age (Harman & Talbert, 1985); annual examinations are extremely important. The majority of men show no reduction in testosterone comparable to the drop women experience in estrogen, but do demonstrate a gradual reduction in testosterone levels after the mid-20s (Davidson et al., 1983). However, some men who do experience an abnormally rapid decline in testosterone production during their late 60s report symptoms similar to those experienced by some menopausal women, such as hot flashes, chills, rapid heart rate, and nervousness (Harman & Talbert, 1985).

Men experience some physiological changes in sexual performance. By old age, men report less perceived demand to ejaculate, a need for longer time and more stimulation to achieve erection and orgasm, and a much longer resolution phase during which erection is impossible (Rykken, 1987). Older men also report more frequent failures to achieve orgasm and of losing their erection during intercourse. Because men's conception of masculinity is often linked to the ability to achieve erection and subsequently reach orgasm, these normative changes may result in psychological stress (Rykken, 1987). Sexual satisfaction for men in later life is directly related to the degree to which they believe these myths of male sexuality. Erectile failure can damage confidence and self-esteem and support the mistaken idea that erection equals manhood. Although erectile failure is most often due to diabetes or depression, external (and more easily treated) factors such as career issues, alcohol consumption, poor health, and boredom can also lead to decreased activity.

As with women, as long as men enjoy sex and have a willing partner, sexual activity is a lifelong option. Mutual sharing derived from sexual activity outweighs any negative feelings that may accompany normal declines in performance (Weg, 1983).

Psychological Consequences of Changes in the Reproductive System

Engaging in sexual behavior is an important aspect of human relationships throughout adulthood.

Healthy adults at any age are capable of having and enjoying sexual relationships. Moreover, the desire to do so normally does not diminish. Unfortunately, one of the myths in our society is that older adults cannot and should not be sexual. Many young adults find it difficult to think about their grandparents in this way.

Such stereotyping has important consequences. What comes to mind when we see an older couple being publicly affectionate? The reaction of many is that such behavior is cute. But observers tend not to refer to their own or their peers' relationships in this way. Many nursing homes and other institutions actively dissuade their residents from having sexual relationships and may even refuse to allow married couples to share the same room. Adult children may verbalize their opinion that their widowed parent does not have the right to establish a new sexual relationship. The message we are sending is that sexual activity is fine for the young but not for the old. The major reason why older women do not engage in sexual relations is the lack of a socially sanctioned partner. It is not that they have lost interest; rather, they believe that they are simply not permitted to express their sexuality any longer.

Concept Checks

1. What physical symptoms accompany age-related changes in women's reproductive system?
2. What are the major changes in men's reproductive system?
3. Does interest in sexual activity typically decline with age?

APPEARANCE AND MOVEMENT

Learning Objectives:

- How does people's appearance change with age?
- What age-related changes are there in our ability to move around in our environment?

We see the outward signs of aging first in the mirror: gray hair, wrinkled skin, and the bulge around our middle. These changes occur gradually and at different rates. How we perceive that person staring back at us in the mirror says a great deal about how we feel about aging; positive feelings about the signs of aging are related to positive self-esteem (Berscheid, Walster, & Bohrnstedt, 1973).

How easily we move our changing bodies in negotiating the physical environment is also a major component of adaptation and well-being in adulthood (Lawton & Nahemow, 1973). If we cannot get around we are forced to depend on others, which lowers our self-esteem and sense of competence. Having a body that moves effectively also allows us to enjoy physical activities such as walking, swimming, and skiing.

Appearance

To get a complete picture of age-related changes in appearance, we will consider the skin, hair, voice, and body build separately.

Skin

For many people, realization that they are aging comes with their first awareness of creases, furrows, and sagging in their skin (Whitbourne, 1985). On that day, it makes no difference that these changes are universal and inevitable. Or that they are due to a combination of changes in the structure of the skin and its connective and supportive tissue and to the cumulative effects of damage from exposure to sunlight (A. M. Kligman, Grove, & Balin, 1985). What matters on that day is that they have seen their first wrinkle up close and personally.

Wrinkles result from a complex process. It takes four steps to make a wrinkle (A. M. Kligman et al., 1985). First, the outer layer of skin becomes thinner through cell loss, causing the skin to become more fragile. Second, the collagen fibers that make up the connective tissue lose much of their flexibility, making the skin less able to regain its shape after a pinch, for example. Third, elastin fibers in the middle layer of skin lose their ability to

As this middle-aged man is discovering all too clearly, hair loss and facial wrinkles are sure signs of aging that many people find difficult to accept.

keep the skin stretched out, resulting in sagging. Finally, the underlying layer of fat, which helps provide padding to smooth out the contours, diminishes.

As much as people dislike wrinkles in American culture, it may come as a surprise to learn that much of the facial wrinkling experienced by adults is self-inflicted (A. M. Kligman et al., 1985). Facial wrinkles are not due solely (or perhaps even primarily) to age-related processes but also to chemical, physical, or other traumas. For example, many features of the "old" face including wrinkles are sunshine-induced: precancers, cancers, benign growths, blotches, saggy or stretchable skin, coarse skin, and yellow skin. Proper use of sunscreens and sunblocks slows the development of these problems (L. H. Kligman, Aiken, & Kligman, 1982). The message is clear: Young adults who are dedicated sun-worshippers will eventually pay a high price for their tans.

A lifetime of sun and of normative age-related processes makes older adults' skin thinner, gives it a leathery texture, makes it less effective at regulating heat or cold, and makes it more susceptible to cuts, bruises, and blisters (Fenske & Lober, 1990). The coloring of light-skinned people undergoes additional changes with age. The number of pigment-containing cells in the outer layer decreases, and those that remain have less pigment, resulting in somewhat lighter skin. In addition, age spots (areas of dark pigmentation that look like freckles) and moles (pigmented outgrowths) appear more often (A. M. Kligman et al., 1985). Some of the blood vessels in the skin may become dilated and create small, irregular red lines. Varicose veins may appear as knotty, bluish irregularities in blood vessels, especially on the legs (Bierman, 1985).

Hair

Gradual thinning and graying of the hair of both men and women occurs inevitably with age, although there are large individual differences in the rate of these changes (Kenney, 1982). Hair loss is caused by destruction of the germ centers that produce the hair follicles, whereas graying results from a cessation of pigment production. Men usually do not lose facial hair as they age; witness the number of balding men with thick bushy beards. In contrast, women often develop patches of hair on their face, especially on their chin. This hair growth is related to the hormonal changes of the climacteric (Kenney, 1982).

Voice

How one's voice sounds is one way we judge the age of a person. Younger adults' voices tend to be full and resonant, whereas older adults' voices tend to be thinner or weaker. Age-related changes in one's voice include lowering of pitch, increased breathlessness and trembling, slower and less precise pronunciation, and decreased volume. Some researchers (such as Benjamin, 1982) report that changes in the larynx (voice box), the respiratory system, and the muscles controlling speech cause these changes. However, other researchers contend that these changes result from poor health and are not part of normal aging (Ramig & Ringel, 1983). The question of whether changes in the voice are normative or mainly the product of disease remains unresolved.

Body Build

Two noticeable changes occur in body build during adulthood: a decrease in height and fluctuations in weight (Kenney, 1982). Height remains fairly stable until the 50s. Between the mid-50s and mid-70s men lose about 1¼ inches and women lose about 2 inches (Hayflick, 1994). Garn (1975) writes that this shortening is caused by compression of the spine from loss of bone strength, changes in the discs, and changes in posture. More details on changes in bone structure are provided below.

The experience of middle-age bulge is common. Typically, people gain weight between their 20s and their mid-50s, but lose weight throughout old age (Shephard, 1978). In old age the body loses muscle and bone, which weigh more than fat, in addition to some fat.

Psychological Consequences of Changes in Appearance

The appearance of wrinkles, gray hair, fat, and the like can have a major effect on an individual's self-concept (Sontag, 1972). Middle-aged adults may still think of themselves as young and may not appreciate others' references to them as old. Because our society places high value on looking young, middle-aged and older adults, especially women, may be regarded as less desirable on any number of dimensions, including intellectual capacity (Connor, Walsh, Lintzelman, & Alvarez, 1978). In contrast, middle-aged men with some gray hair are often considered distinguished, more experienced, and more knowledgeable than their younger counterparts.

Given social stereotypes, many women use any available means to compensate for these changes. Some age-related changes in facial appearance can be successfully disguised with cosmetics. Hair dyes can restore color. Surgical procedures such as facelifts can tighten sagging and wrinkled skin. But even plastic surgery only delays the inevitable; at some point everyone takes on a distinctly old appearance (A. M. Kligman et al., 1985).

Not everyone tries to hide the fact that he or she is aging. Many older people accept changes in their appearance without losing self-esteem. For example, Barbara Bush made an important statement about accepting aging by not dyeing her hair. These individuals powerfully counterbalance the dominant youth-oriented view in American society.

Movement

Muscles

As we grow older, the amount of muscle tissue in our bodies declines (Whitbourne, 1985). This loss is hardly noticeable in terms of strength and endurance; even at age 70 the loss is no more than 20% (deVries, 1983). After that, however, the rate of change increases. By age 80 the loss in strength is up to 40%, and it appears to be more severe in the legs than in the arms and hands (Grimby & Saltin, 1983; Shephard, 1981). However, some people retain their strength well into old age. In one study, 15% of people over age 60 showed no loss of grip strength over a 9-year period (Kallman, Plato, & Tobin, 1990). Research evidence suggests that muscle endurance also diminishes with age, but at a slower rate (Spirduso & MacCrae, 1990). Men and women show no differences in the rate of muscle change (Spirduso & MacCrae, 1990).

Losses in strength and endurance in old age have much the same psychological effect as changes in appearance (Whitbourne, 1985). In particular, these changes tell the person that he or she is not as capable of adapting effectively to the environment. Loss of muscle coordination (which may lead to walking more slowly, for example) may not be inevitable, but it can prove embarrassing and stressful. Exercise can improve muscle strength. Interestingly, the rate of improvement does not seem to differ with age; older adults get stronger at the same rate as younger adults (Moritani & deVries, 1980).

Bones and Joints

Normal aging is accompanied by the loss of bone tissue from the skeleton (Exton-Smith, 1985). Bone loss begins in the late 30s, accelerates in the 50s (particularly in women), and slows by the 70s (Avioli, 1982). The gender difference in bone loss is important. Once the process begins, women lose bone mass approximately twice as fast as men (Garn, 1975). The difference is due to two factors: Women have less bone than men in young adulthood, meaning that they start out with less ability to withstand bone loss before it causes problems; and the depletion of estrogen after menopause speeds up bone loss (Heaney, Gallagher, Johnston, Neer, Parfitt, & Wheden, 1982).

The age-related process involves a loss of internal bone mass, which makes bones more hollow. Note that there is also a small age-related gain due to bone growth; however, this gain is limited to the outer surface of the bone. In addition to these changes, bones tend to become porous with age. All of these bone changes cause an age-related increase in the likelihood of fractures (Currey, 1984). Broken bones in older people present more serious problems than in younger adults. When the bone of an older person breaks, it is more likely to snap and cause a "clean" fracture that is difficult to heal. Bones of younger adults fracture in such a way that there are many cracks and splinters to aid in healing. This is analogous to the difference in breaking a young, green tree branch and an old, dry twig.

Women are especially susceptible to severe bone degeneration, a disease called *osteoporosis* in which the loss of bone mass and increased porosity create bones that resemble laced honeycombs (Meier, 1988). Osteoporosis is the leading cause of broken bones in women (Exton-Smith, 1985). The disease appears more often in fair-skinned, European American, thin, and small-framed women than in other groups; for example, rates are substantially lower in African American women (Meier, 1988). Radiographic (such as X-ray) evidence suggests that at least 65% of all women over age 60 and virtually all women over age 90 are affected; in all, more than 20 million women in the United States have osteoporosis, with millions more at risk (Meier, 1988). Osteoporosis is also related to low bone mass at skeletal maturity, deficiencies of calcium and vitamin D, estrogen depletion, and lack of weight-bearing exercise (Meier, 1988). The gender, age, and race factors are probably related to differences on the other variables; for example, females tend to eat diets much lower in calcium than do males. Other risk factors include smoking, high-protein diets, and excessive alcohol, caffeine, and sodium intake (Exton-Smith, 1985).

The relationship of dietary calcium to osteoporosis is controversial (Meier, 1988). There is some evidence that dietary supplements of calcium after menopause do not slow the rate of bone loss; benefits appear to accrue when the supplements are provided before menopause. The reasons why estrogen depletion affects bone loss are also not understood, mainly because the effects must be indirect, as there are no estrogen receptors in bone tissue (Meier, 1988). Although estrogen replacement therapy may slow bone loss, this approach must be used cautiously because of potential side effects such as endometrial cancer. Additionally, estrogen therapy must be continued indefinitely, because bone loss speeds up as soon as the therapy is stopped. Finally, data showing that vitamin D metabolism plays a causative role in osteoporosis are clear; however, whether supplementary dietary vitamin D retards bone loss is less certain (Meier, 1988). Some research shows that vitamin D administered after menopause slows the loss of bone, whereas other research does not. However, the U.S. Food and Drug Administration endorses vitamin D supplements as a therapy for osteoporosis on the grounds that side effects are minimal and that there are some supportive data. Some evidence also supports the view that oral ingestion of magnesium, zinc, vitamin K, and special forms of fluoride may also be effective.

Age-related changes in the joints occur as a result of a degeneration of the protective cartilage (Exton-Smith, 1985). Beginning in the 20s cartilage shows signs of deterioration, such as thinning and becoming cracked and frayed. **Over time the bones underneath the cartilage become damaged, which, if this process occurs to a great**

extent, results in the disease *osteoarthritis.* Osteoarthritis is marked by gradual onset and progression of pain and disability, with minor signs of inflammation (Rogers & Levitin, 1987). The disease usually becomes noticeable in late middle age or old age, and it is especially common in people whose joints are subjected to routine overuse and abuse, such as athletes and manual laborers. Osteoarthritis is truly a wear-and-tear disease. Pain is typically worse when the joint is used, but redness, heat, and swelling are minimal or absent. Osteoarthritis usually affects the hands, spine, hips, and knees, sparing the wrists, elbows, shoulders, and ankles. Effective management approaches consist mainly of certain steroids and antiinflammatory drugs, rest and nonstressful exercises that focus on range of motion, diet, and a variety of homeopathic remedies.

A second and more common form of arthritis is *rheumatoid arthritis,* a more destructive disease of the joints (Rogers & Levitin, 1987). Rheumatoid arthritis also develops slowly and typically affects different joints and different types of pain than osteoarthritis. Most often, a pattern of morning stiffness and aching develops in the fingers, wrists, and ankles on both sides of the body. Joints appear swollen. The typical therapy for rheumatoid arthritis consists of aspirin or other nonsteroidal antiinflammatory drugs. Newer chemical therapies (such as methotrexate) and experimental drugs (such as cyclosporine) are showing promising results (Kremer, 1990). Rest and passive range-of-motion exercises are also helpful. Contrary to popular belief, rheumatoid arthritis is not contagious, hereditary, or self-induced by any known diet, habit, job, or exposure. Interestingly, the symptoms often come and go in repeating patterns.

Psychological Consequences of Changes in Movement

The changes in the joints, especially in arthritis, have profound psychological effects (Whitbourne, 1985). These changes can severely limit movement, thereby reducing independence and the ability to complete normal daily routines. Moreover, joint pain is very difficult to ignore or disguise, unlike changes in appearance. Consequently, the person who can use cosmetics to hide changes in appearance will not be able to use the same approach to deal with constant pain in the joints. However, participation in an exercise program appears to have some benefit. Older adults who suffer bone fractures face, in addition to the usual discomfort, several other consequences. For example, a hip fracture may force hospitalization or even a stay in a nursing home. For all fractures, the recovery period is considerably longer than that for a younger adult. Additionally, older people who witness friends or relatives struggling during rehabilitation may reduce their own activities as a precautionary measure (Costa & McCrae, 1980a).

Concept Checks

1. What changes occur in skin, hair, voice, and body build with age?
2. What happens to muscles, bones, and joints as we grow older?

SUMMARY

Biological Theories Of Aging

Wear and Tear Theory

Wear and tear theory suggests the body is much like a machine that gradually deteriorates over time. Although there is evidence that some organ systems do wear out, this theory does not explain why we age.

Cellular Theories

Cellular theories suggest that there may be limits on how often cells may divide before dying (termed the Hayflick limit), which may partially explain aging. A process called cross-linking results when certain proteins interact randomly and produce molecules that make the body stiffer. A third type of cellular theory proposes that free radicals, which are highly reactive chemicals produced randomly during normal cell metabolism, cause cellular damage. Spontaneous changes in DNA may also be responsible for aging.

Rate of Living Theories

Rate of living theories are based on the idea that people are born with a limited amount of some substance, potential energy, or physiological capacity that can be expended at some rate. Metabolic processes such as eating fewer calories or reducing stress may be related to living longer. The body's declining ability to adapt to stress with age may also be a partial cause of aging.

Programmed Cell Death

Programmed cell death is based on genetic hypotheses about aging. Specifically, there appears to be a genetic program that is triggered by physiological processes, the innate ability to self-destruct, and the ability of dying cells to trigger key processes in other cells.

Implications of the Developmental Forces

Although biological theories are the foundation of biological forces, the full picture of how and why we age cannot be understood without considering the other three forces (psychological, sociocultural, and life-cycle).

The Brain

Age-Related Structural Changes in the Neuron

Neurons are the basic cells in the brain. Some neurons develop neurofibrillary tangles, new fibers produced in the axon that are twisted. Large numbers of these are associated with Alzheimer's disease. Some neurons lose dendrites with age, whereas others gain dendrites. Damaged or dying neurons sometimes become surrounded by protein and form neuritic plaques. Large numbers of plaques are associated with Alzheimer's disease.

Changes in Communication Among Neurons

The ways in which neurons are interconnected change with age. Several neurotransmitter levels decrease with age, including dopamine, acetylcholine, and serotonin. These changes have important implications for drug interventions in older adults.

Studying Brain-Behavior Relations: Imaging Techniques

Three types of brain imaging are used in research: computed tomography (CT), magnetic resonance imaging (MRI), and positron emission tomography (PET). Each provides important information about brain structures. MRI scans are used most often in routine diagnosis of brain diseases. PET scans also provide information on brain metabolism.

Psychological Consequences of Brain Aging

The term *senility* no longer has medical meaning, nor do all (or even most) older adults become "senile." However, many people remain concerned about this issue. Brain changes underlie many behavioral changes, including memory.

The Immune System

Changes in Immune System Cells

The immune system is made of three parts. The number of lymphocytes (either T- or B-type) does not change with age. However, they do not work as quickly or as well in older adults, and the response time to build up lymphocytes is longer.

Antibodies and Autoimmunity

Some antibodies to specific diseases appear to decrease in number with age. In addition, people begin to develop autoimmunity, the development of antibodies that attack the body itself.

AIDS in Adult Development and Aging

AIDS is the leading killer of young adult males in some communities. The number of older adults with AIDS is increasing. Older adults' health declines faster once AIDS symptoms begin. Educational programs targeting older adults are needed.

Psychological Consequences of Changes in the Immune System

The belief that nothing can be done about illness in late life is often incorrect. Immunizations for many diseases exist, and are especially recommended for older adults.

The Cardiovascular System

Age-Related Changes in Cardiovascular Structure and Function

Some fat deposits in and around the heart, as well as inside arteries, is a normal part of aging. Heart muscle gradually is replaced with stiffer connective tissue. The most important change in the circulatory system is the stiffening ("hardening") of the walls of the arteries.

Cardiovascular Disease

Overall, men have a higher rate of cardiovascular disease than women. Several diseases increase in frequency with age: ischemic heart disease, cardiac arrhythmias, angina, heart attack, atherosclerosis (severe buildup of fat inside and the calcification of the arterial walls), cerebrovascular disease (cardiovascular disease in the brain), and hypertension (high blood pressure).

Psychological Consequences of Changes in the Cardiovascular System

The most important psychological effect of cardiovascular disease is the lifestyle changes people make to avoid cardiovascular disease. These changes include exercising, stopping smoking, and eating healthier diets.

The Respiratory System

Age-Related Structural and Functional Changes

The amount of air we can take into our lungs and how easily we can exchange oxygen and carbon dioxide decrease with age. Declines in the maximum amount of air we can take in also occur.

Respiratory Diseases

Chronic obstructive pulmonary disease (COPD), such as emphysema, increase with age. Emphysema is the most common form of age-related COPD; although most cases are caused from smoking, a few are caused from secondhand smoke, breathing polluted air, or genetic factors.

Psychological Consequences of Changes in the Respiratory System

Shortness of breath due to age-related changes may result in a reduction of activity in older adults. This may result in some people becoming overly cautious and socially withdrawn.

The Senses

Vision

Several age-related changes occur in the structure of the eye, including opaque spots on the lens (cataracts), glaucoma, macular degeneration, and diabetic retinopathy. Changes in visual functioning with age include the need for increased illumination, increased susceptibility to glare, difficulty seeing nearby objects (presbyopia), decreased acuity, and slower light and dark adaptation.

Hearing

Age-related declines in the ability to hear high-pitched tones (presbycusis) are universal. Exposure to noise speeds up and exacerbates hearing loss. Psychologically, losses in hearing can reduce the ability to have satisfactory communication with others.

Taste

Age-related changes in taste are minimal. Many older adults complain about boring food; however, these complaints appear to be largely unrelated to changes in taste ability.

Smell

The ability to detect odors declines rapidly after age 60 in most people. Changes in smell are primarily responsible for reported changes concerning food preference and enjoyment.

Somesthesis and Balance

Changes in sensitivity to touch, temperature, and pain are complex and not understood; age-related trends are unclear in most cases. Dizziness and vertigo are common in older adults and increase with age, as do falls. Changes in balance may result in increased caution in older adults when walking.

The Reproductive System

Reproductive Changes in Women

The transition from being able to have children to the cessation of ovulation is termed the climacteric; menopause refers to the end of menstruation. A variety of physical and psychological symptoms accompany menopause (e.g., hot flashes), including several in the genital organs. No changes occur in the desire to have sex; however, the availability of a suitable partner for women is a major barrier.

Reproductive Changes in Men

In men, sperm production declines gradually with age. Changes in the prostate gland occur and should be monitored by yearly examinations. Some changes in sexual performance, such as increased time to erection and ejaculation, and of the refractory period are typical.

Psychological Consequences of Changes in the Reproductive System

Healthy adults of any age are capable of engaging in sexual activity, and the desire to do so does not diminish with age. However, societal stereotyping creates barriers to free expression of such feelings.

Appearance and Movement

Appearance

Normative changes with age in appearance include: wrinkles, gray hair, thinner and weaker voice, decrease in height, and increase in weight in midlife followed by weight loss in late life. Cultural stereotypes have an enormous influence on the personal acceptance of age changes in appearance.

Movement

The amount of muscle decreases with age, but strength and endurance only change slightly. Loss of bone mass is normative; in severe cases, though, the disease osteoporosis may result in which bones become brittle and honeycombed. Osteoarthritis and rheumatoid arthritis are two diseases that impair a person's ability to get around and function in the environment.

REVIEW QUESTIONS

Biological theories of aging

- What biological theories have been proposed to explain aging? What are their similarities and differences?
- Why do some people argue that diets high in antioxidants can prolong life?
- What are some of the sociocultural forces that operate on the biological theories? What are some examples of these forces?

The brain

- What structural changes occur in the neuron with age? How are these changes related to diseases such as Alzheimer's?
- What happens to the interconnections among neurons with age?
- What changes occur in neurotransmitters with age?
- What types of brain imaging techniques are used and what structures and processes do they measure?
- What are the relationships between changes in the brain and changes in behavior?

The immune system

- What changes occur in the immune system with age?
- What happens in the development of antibodies as people grow older?
- How is AIDS affecting older adults?

The cardiovascular system

- What changes occur in the cardiovascular system with age? What gender differences have been noted? Which cardiovascular diseases increase in frequency with age?

The respiratory system

- What changes occur in the respiratory system with age? How are respiratory diseases related to age?

The senses

- What age-related changes occur in vision? What are the psychological effects of these changes?
- What age-related changes occur in hearing? What are the psychological effects of these changes?
- What age-related changes occur in taste and smell?
- What age-related changes occur in somesthesis, balance, and movement?

The reproductive system

- What age-related changes occur in women and men concerning their reproductive ability?
- How does interest in sexual activity change with age? What constraints operate on men and women?

Appearance and movement

- What age-related changes occur in appearance?
- What happens to muscle and bone tissue with age?

INTEGRATING CONCEPTS IN DEVELOPMENT

1. How do the various biological theories of aging match with the major age-related changes in body systems? Which theories do the best job? Why?
2. Why do you think that the rates of death from cardiovascular disease are so much higher in industrialized countries?
3. How might the age-related changes in the respiratory system be linked with societal policies on the environment?
4. Given what you now know about normative changes in appearance, what would you say about the stereotypes of aging you identified in the Discovering Development exercise you did in Chapter 1?

KEY TERMS

acuity Ability to see detail.

angina A painful condition caused by temporary constriction of blood flow to the heart.

antibody Type of immune system cell produced by lymphocytes that fights invading cells.

atherosclerosis A process by which fat is deposited on the walls of arteries.

autoantibodies Antibodies that attack the body itself.

autoimmunity The process by which autoantibodies are produced, which may be partially responsible for aging.

cardiac arrhythmias Irregularities in the heartbeat.

cataracts Opaque spots in the lens of the eye which seriously limit the amount of light transmitted.

cerebral hemorrhage The breaking of a blood vessel in the brain.

cerebrovascular accident (CVA) An interruption of the blood flow in the brain.

cerebrovascular disease A form of cardiovascular disease that involves the blood vessels in the brain.

chronic obstructive pulmonary disease (COPD) A family of age-related lung diseases that block the passage of air and cause abnormalities inside the lungs.

climacteric The transition during which a woman's reproductive capacity ends and ovulation stops.

cross-linking Random interaction among proteins that produce molecules that make the body stiffer.

dark adaptation A process by which the eye adapts from a bright environment to a dark one.

dendrites The part of a neuron that receives incoming information from other nearby neurons.

emphysema Severe lung disease that greatly reduces the ability to exchange carbon dioxide for oxygen.

free radicals Deleterious and short-lived chemicals that cause changes in cells that are thought to result in aging.

glaucoma Condition in which the fluid in the eye does not drain properly, causing very high pressure in the eyeball.

Hayflick limit The biological limit to the number of times a cell is able to reproduce itself, which is thought to be related to aging.

hypertension A disease in which one's blood pressure is too high.

ischemic heart disease The most common form of cardiovascular disease in older adults caused by decreased oxygen or poor circulation in the coronary arteries.

light adaptation The process by which the eye adapts from a dark environment to a bright environment.

lymphocytes Cells in the immune system responsible for fighting disease and other invading cells.

macular degeneration The progressive and irreversible destruction of receptors in the eye from any of a number of causes.

menopause The cessation of menstruation.

myocardial infarction A heart attack.

neuritic plaques A normative change in the brain involving amyloid protein collecting on dying or dead neurons. Large numbers of neuritic plaques is a defining characteristic of Alzheimer's disease.

neurofibrillary tangles A normative age-related change in the brain involving the production of new fibers in the neuron. Large numbers of neurofibrillary tangles is a defining characteristic of Alzheimer's disease.

neurons The basic cells in the brain.

neurotransmitters Chemicals released by neurons that are used for communicating between neurons.

osteoarthritis A form of arthritis marked by gradual onset and progression of pain and swelling, primarily due to overuse of a joint.

osteoporosis A degenerative bone disease more common in women in which bone tissue deteriorates severely to produce honeycomb-like bone tissue.

presbycusis A normative age-related loss of the ability to hear high-pitched tones.

presbyopia The normative age-related loss of the ability to focus on nearby objects, usually resulting in the need for glasses.

programmed cell death The idea that some cells are genetically programmed to die at particular points in the life span.

rate of living theories Biological theories of aging based on the idea that people are born with a limited amount of some substance, potential energy, or physiological capacity that can be expended at some rate.

rheumatoid arthritis A destructive form of arthritis involving more swelling and more joints than osteoarthritis.

synapse The gap between the terminal branches of one neuron and the dendrites of another neuron across which neurotransmitters travel.

terminal branches The transmitter-like parts of neurons that release neurotransmitters.

transmissiveness The degree to which light passes through the eye.

vestibular system Sensory system in the inner ear that allows us to keep our balance.

visual accommodation The eye's ability to adjust and focus.

wear and tear theory A biological theory of aging stating that aging is due to the body simply wearing itself out.

IF YOU'D LIKE TO LEARN MORE

Cart, C. S., Metress, E. K., & Metress, S. P. (1992). *Biological bases of human aging and disease.* Boston: Jones & Bartlett. A good basic overview of biological and physiological changes with age; easy reading.

Hayflick, L. (1994). *How and why we age.* New York: Ballantine Books. The best general overview to biological theories and research in print by one of the leading researchers in the field; easy to moderate.

Whitbourne, S. K. (1996). *The aging individual.* New York: Springer. A more advanced overview of biological and physiological changes, but with excellent discussions of the psychological effects of these changes; medium to difficult.

CHAPTER 4

Longevity, Health, and Prevention

Fairfield Porter, *The Tennis Game*, 1972. Lauren Rogers Museum of Art, Laurel, Mississippi.

Ought we to listen to the cry of humanity that life is too short and that it would be well to prolong it? Would it really be for the good of the human race to extend the duration of the life of [people] beyond its present limits? Already it is complained that the burden of supporting old people is too heavy, and [politicians] are perturbed by the enormous expense which will be entailed by State support of the aged. . . .

It has long been a charge against medicine and hygiene that they tend to weaken the human race. By scientific means unhealthy people, or those with inherited blemishes, have been preserved so that they can give birth to weak offspring. . . . It is clear that a valuable existence of great service to humanity is compatible with . . . precarious health. . . . It does not follow that we ought to cherish diseases and leave to natural selection the duty of preserving the individuals which can resist them. On the other hand, it is indispensable to try to blot out the diseases themselves, and, in particular, the evils of old age, by the methods of hygiene and therapeutics. . . . We must use all our endeavors to allow [people] to complete their normal course of life, and to make it possible for old [people] to play their parts as advisers and judges, endowed with their long experience of life.

Does this passage sound vaguely familiar, along the lines of contemporary debates over the quantity versus quality of life, the cost of health care for older adults, and calls for additional research on the causes and effective treatments for diseases such as cancer and Alzheimer's disease? If so, you may be surprised to learn that it appeared in 1908 in a collection of Élie Metchnikoff's works *The Prolongation of Life*. Metchnikoff, a Russian scientist who lived from 1845 to 1916, recognized the importance of separating the issues of disease and aging in order to focus scientific research efforts on eliminating disease so that older adults would be able to lead more productive lives and be viewed by society as having important contributions to make. The contemporary feel of Metchnikoff's writings shows that the current debates have a long history and that it is due to the kinds of research he and others championed that more people than ever are living to old age.

In this chapter we will see how longevity, health, and prevention have changed since Metchnikoff's era. We will see that all of these topics are linked through the basic developmental forces. To the extent that they all have some connection with lifestyle, we will consider how they may be at least partly under our control. At times, you may feel that many of the findings and recommendations appear to be little more than common sense. However, we must remember that many people in industrialized societies may not have the resources to live healthy lifestyles and that others choose not to follow even the most basic guidelines for a healthy lifestyle.

We will begin by considering the factors influencing how long people live. Next, we will focus on one of the most pervasive influences on health—stress—and discover what some of these effects are. Following that, we will consider several specific aspects of lifestyle: smoking, drinking, exercise, sleep, and nutrition. Each of these has important influences on the development of chronic conditions. Because it is often an outcome of an unhealthy lifestyle, cancer will be considered as an example of how these various influences may produce disease. Finally, we will conclude with a developmental perspective on health, disease, and prevention.

Throughout this discussion, we will relate the interactions among the basic developmental forces to the topics encountered here. For example, we will see how our genetic heritage interacts with lifestyle to affect how long we live.

HOW LONG WILL WE LIVE?

Learning Objectives:

- What are the average and maximum longevity for humans?
- What genetic and environmental factors influence longevity?
- What ethnic factors influence average longevity?

- What factors create gender differences in average longevity?

As we saw in Chapter 2, many more people are living to old age today than ever before. Young people today have already seen far more older adults than their great-great-grandparents did even if they themselves lived to old age. The tremendous increase in the number of older adults has focused renewed interest in life expectancy. Knowing how long we are likely to live is important not only for planning our lives, but also for government agencies, service programs, the business world, and insurance companies. Why? The length of life has an enormous impact on just about every aspect of life—from decisions about government health care programs (much higher costs to care for more chronically ill people) to retirement policy (debates over the age at which people may collect maximum retirement benefits) to premiums for life insurance (longer lives on average mean cheaper rates for young adults). Longer lives have forced change in all of these areas and will continue to do so into the next century.

Life expectancy can be examined from the perspective of the basic developmental forces, because how long we live depends on complex interactions among biological, psychological, socioeconomic, and life-cycle forces. For example, some people have many relatives who live to very old age, whereas others have relatives who die rather young. It is true that tendencies toward long lives (or short ones, for that matter) tend to run in families. As we will see, our "long-life genes" play a major role in governing how long we are likely to live.

But the world in which we live can affect how long we live, too. Environmental factors such as disease or toxic chemicals modify our genetic heritage and shorten our lifetime, sometimes drastically. By the same token, other environmental factors such as access to high-quality medical care can sometimes treat genetic defects that would have caused early death, thereby significantly altering our genetic heritage for the better. In short, no one developmental force can account for the length of life. Let's begin our exploration of how long we live with a discussion of different aspects of the concept of longevity.

Increasing the chances of living to celebrate one's 100th birthday, as this woman is doing, takes a combination of good genes and a healthy lifestyle.

Average and Maximum Longevity

The number of years one lives, as jointly determined by genetic and environmental factors, is called longevity. Researchers distinguish between two different types of longevity: average longevity and maximum longevity. ***Average longevity* is commonly called average life expectancy and refers to the age at which half of the individuals who are born in a particular year will have died.** Average longevity is affected by both genetic and

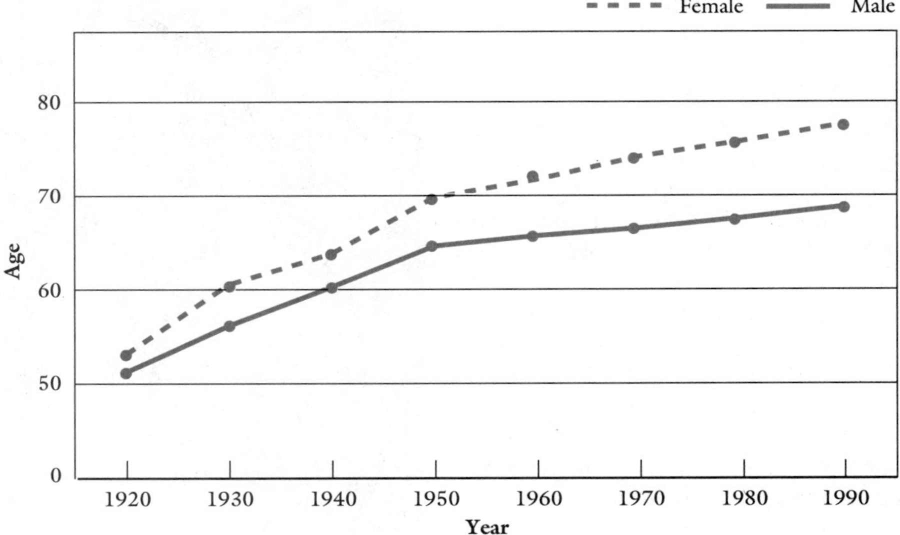

Figure 4.1 Life expectancy at birth, 1920–1990
Source: U.S. Bureau of the Census

environmental factors, as we will see in the next section. For people in the United States average longevity has been increasing steadily over this century; recent estimates are presented in Figure 4.1. Note in the figure that the most rapid increase in average longevity occurred in the first half of this century. These increases in average longevity were due mostly to declines in infant mortality rates through the elimination of diseases such as smallpox and polio and through better health care. Decrease in the number of women who died during childbirth was especially important in raising average life expectancies for females. All of these advances in medical technology and improvements in health care mean that more people survive to old age, thereby increasing average longevity in the general population.

Average longevity can be computed for people at any age. The most common method is to compute average longevity at birth, which is the projected age at which half of the people born in a certain year will have died. This computation takes into account people who die at any age, from infancy onward. When average longevity is computed at other points in the life span, the calculation is based on all of the people who are alive at that age; people who died earlier are not included. For example, computing the average longevity for people currently 40 years old would provide a predicted age at which half of those people will have died. People born into the same birth cohort but who died prior to age 40 would not be counted. The elimination of those who die at early ages from the computation of average longevity at a specific age explains why projected average longevity at age 65 is longer than it was at birth.

***Maximum longevity* refers to the oldest age to which any individual of a species lives.** Although the biblical character Methuselah is said to have lived to the ripe old age of 969 years, modern scientists are more conservative in their estimates of a human's maximum longevity. Most estimates place the limit somewhere around 120 years (Fry, 1985), arguing that the key body systems such as the cardiovascular system have limits on how long they can last. Whether this estimate of maximum longevity will change as new technologies produce better artificial organs remains to be seen. An important issue, of course, is whether extending the life span indefinitely would be a good idea.

Because maximum longevity of different animal species varies considerably, scientists have tried to understand these differences by considering important biological functions such as metabolic rate or relative brain size (Hayflick, 1994). Just as with biological theories of aging, none of these explanations has met with complete success (Hayflick, 1994). For example, why the giant tortoises of the Galapagos Islands typically live longer than we do remains a mystery.

Genetic and Environmental Factors in Longevity

What influences how long we will live on average? The general answer to this question is that one's average longevity is influenced by genetic, environmental, ethnic, and gender factors. Clearly, these factors interact; being from an ethnic minority group, for example, means that one has a higher risk of exposure to a harmful environment. But it is important to examine each of these and see how they influence our longevity. Let's begin with genetic and environmental factors.

Genetic Factors

A good way to increase one's chances of a long life is to come from a family with a history of long-lived individuals (Dublin, Lotka, & Spiegelman, 1946). For example, if your mother lives to at least age 80, roughly 4 years are added to your average longevity (Woodruff-Pak, 1988). Alexander Graham Bell (who also received the credit for inventing the telephone) was one of the first people to demonstrate systematically the benefits of coming from a long-lived family. Bell considered 8,797 of William Hyde's descendants and found that children of parents who had lived beyond 80 survived about 20 years longer than children whose parents had both died before they were 60. Evidence from research on twins also points toward the importance of genetics in determining longevity. Kallmann (1957) showed that even when identical twins lived in different environments, they died, on average, within about 3 years of each other, whereas fraternal twins died on the average of about 6 years apart.

Having long- or short-lived relatives is not the only genetic effect on longevity. Some diseases also have a known genetic component. Two of the best known of these are cardiovascular disease and Alzheimer's disease. The effects of these diseases on average longevity is significant. For example, for each parent, grandparent, or sibling who dies of cardiovascular disease before age 50, one typically loses 4 years from one's average longevity (Woodruff-Pak, 1988).

One exciting line of research, the human genome project, is attempting to map all of our genes. This research and its spin-offs in microbiology and behavior genetics has already produced some astounding results in terms of genetic linkages to disease. In the past few years, genetic links have been identified for cystic fibrosis, Alzheimer's disease, several forms of cancer, obesity, and some forms of alcoholism. Some attempts are even being made at treating genetic diseases by implanting "corrected" genes into young children in the hopes that the good genes will reproduce and eventually wipe out the defective genes. Perhaps these approaches may produce future cures for genetic diseases that do not make their appearance until adulthood, such as Huntington's disease.

Environmental Factors

Although heredity is a major determinant of longevity, environmental factors also affect the life span (Schneider & Reed, 1985). Some environmental factors are more obvious: diseases, toxins, lifestyle, and social class. Diseases, such as cardiovascular disease and Alzheimer's disease, receive a great deal of attention from researchers. Environmental toxins, mainly encountered as air and water pollution, are a continuing problem. For example, toxins in fish, bacteria and several cancer-causing chemicals in drinking water, and airborne pollutants are major agents in shortening longevity. Lifestyle factors such as stress, exercise, smoking, abusing alcohol or other drugs, and nutrition are also important. The impact of social class on longevity is due to the reduced access to goods and services, especially medical care, that characterizes most ethnic minority groups, the poor, and many elderly (American Association of Retired Persons [AARP], 1991). Most of these people have either no or badly inadequate health insurance, and many cannot afford the cost of a healthier lifestyle. For example, lead poisoning from old water pipes, air pollution, and poor drinking water are serious problems in large urban areas, but many people simply cannot afford to move. The sad part about most of these environmental factors is that we are responsible for them. Denying adequate health care to everyone, continuing to pollute our environment, and failing to address the underlying causes of poverty have undeniable consequences: They needlessly shorten lives and dramatically increase the cost of health care.

Other less obvious but equally important environmental factors affect how long we live. For example, marriage has a beneficial effect, as married people tend to live as much as 5 years longer than unmarried people (Woodruff-Pak, 1988). Apparently, having another person around to help take care of us, contribute to our financial stability, and help us regulate eating and sleeping habits can add years to our life. In fact, divorced men who live alone lose roughly 9 years from their average longevity (Woodruff-Pak, 1988).

The full impact of environmental factors is seen best when they are considered in combination. For instance, the American Cancer Society has estimated that a nonsmoking married person living in a rural area can expect on average to live 22 years longer than an unmarried smoker who lives alone in a large city. The cumulative effects of environmental factors can clearly be substantial.

Ethnic Differences in Average Longevity

We have known for a long time that people in different ethnic groups do not have the same average longevity at birth. For example, African Americans' average longevity at birth is roughly 6.5 years lower for men and about 5 years lower for women than it is for European Americans (National Center for Health Statistics, 1991). We might be tempted to conclude that these differences reflect genetic factors alone. However, we have seen that environmental factors play a major role in determining longevity. Because there are substantial differences on most environmental variables between the typical European American and the typical ethnic minority individual, we would be wrong to focus on genetic factors as the explanation.

In fact, ethnic differences in average longevity are quite complex (Go, Brustrom, Lynch, & Aldwin, 1995). Because individuals in ethnic minority groups are at greater risk for disease (e.g., sickle cell anemia) and accidents (e.g., homicide), have much less access to good health care, and live less healthy lifestyles for economic reasons, a greater proportion of ethnic minority individuals die relatively young compared with their European American counterparts. However, those individuals from ethnic minority groups who manage to survive to old age may live longer on average than European Americans. For example, African Americans who are currently 85 years old can expect to live on average 1 year longer than 85-year-old European Americans (Woodruff-Pak, 1988).

The reason for the switch in average longevity advantage has to do mainly with the kinds of people from ethnic minority groups who survive to old age. Such people tend to be healthier, as they typically have made it to old age without the assistance of high-quality medical care. To be sure, there is undoubtedly a genetic component among such people. However, until all people have equal access to health care and have equal opportunities to engage in healthy lifestyles, the degree to which genetic factors account for differences in average longevity will remain largely unknown.

Gender Differences in Average Longevity

A visit to a senior center or especially a long-term care facility might elicit a variation of the questions "Where are all the very old men? *Why* do women tend to live longer than men?" As Hayflick (1994) notes, the short (but accurate) answer to the question of why women live longer is that we do not know for sure. Surprisingly, this difference has resulted in relatively little research, despite the social, economic, and political effects that longer lives for women has.

If we consider average longevity from birth in the United States, females have roughly a 7-year edge over males. This difference closes during adolescence, increases in favor of females for much of adulthood, with the gap narrowing somewhat in very old age. The visible results of these differences is much more striking when considered in terms of the ratio of men to women at various ages. At birth, there are roughly 106 males for every 100 females; however, more male babies die in infancy or are stillborn. Increased vulnerability of males to disease continues throughout life. Between ages 65 and 69, the ratio has dropped to 81 males for every 100 females. The differential increases rapidly; between ages 80 and 84, the ratio is 53 to 100, and by age 100 it is down to 27 to 100.

These differences are fairly typical of most industrialized countries, but not of developing countries. Indeed, the female advantage in average longevity in the United States only became apparent in the early part of the 20th century (Hayflick, 1994). Why? Up until then so many women died in childbirth that their average longevity as a group was reduced to that of men. Death in childbirth still partially explains the lack of a female advantage in developing countries today; however, part of the reasons in some countries also relates to infanticide of female babies. Socioeconomic factors such as access to health care, work and educational opportunities, and athletics also help account for the emergence of the female advantage in industrialized countries (Hayflick, 1994).

Numerous ideas have been offered to explain the significant overall advantage women have over men in average longevity in industrialized countries (Hayflick, 1994). Overall, men's rates of dying from the top 15 causes of death are significantly higher than women's at nearly every age, and males are also more susceptible to infectious diseases. These differences have led some to speculate that perhaps there is no fundamental biological difference in longevity, but rather a greatly increased susceptibility in males of contracting certain fatal diseases (Hayflick, 1994).

Other researchers and theorists disagree; they argue that there are potential biological explanations. These include the fact that women have two X chromosomes compared with one in men; men have a higher metabolic rate; women have a higher brain-to-body weight ration; and women have lower levels of testosterone. However, none of these explanations has sufficient scientific support at this point to make them adequate explanations of why most women in industrialized countries can expect, on average, to outlive most men (Hayflick, 1994).

Concept Checks

1. What are some of the main reasons that average longevity increased during the 20th century?
2. What evidence is there that genetics influences average longevity?
3. What are some of the reasons for ethnic differences in average longevity?
4. What explanations have been offered to account for women's longer average longevity?

STRESS AND HEALTH

Learning Objectives:
- What is the stress and coping paradigm? What are its major components?
- How are stress and physical health related?
- What is the relation between stress and psychological functioning?
- How can people manage stress?

Stress is harmful to one's health. This belief is deeply held by most people and has resulted in entire industries based on the goal of reducing stress; even vitamin manufacturers market stress-formula preparations. Another widespread (and erroneous) belief is that stress-related health problems occur mainly in people who hold certain types of jobs, such as air traffic controllers or high-level business executives. Lower level employees are viewed as safe because they have little control over their working environment. Unfortunately, the relationships among job, stress, and health are not that simple. In fact, a carefully conducted study found that business executives had fewer stress-related health problems than waitresses, construction workers, secretaries, laboratory technicians, machine operators, farm workers, and painters (Smith, Colligan, Horning, & Hurrell, 1978). Stress occurs most when people must be extremely vigilant, perform complex work, and meet time demands placed on them by others. Responsibility and decision making alone seem not to matter.

Just as the belief that executives are more prone to stress-related illnesses than laborers is more myth than fact, many other aspects of stress and its relationship to health are not understood very well. Indeed, the relationship of stress to age, gender, and ethnic or racial status remains underresearched and poorly understood. For example, in the 1980s more women than men in all age groups reported that stress had a significant impact on their health in the previous year (USDHHS, 1988). The people between the ages of 30 and 44 reported the highest levels of stress, with those over age 65 reporting the lowest; the reasons underlying these differences are unknown. And we now know that the majority of ulcers are caused by bacteria, not by the overproduction of acids as a result of stress.

Despite literally thousands of scientific studies on stress and its effects on health, scientists still cannot agree on a definition. To some, stress is a property of events. In this approach, events vary in how stressful they are, but everyone who experiences a particular event comes under the same level of stress. To others, stress is a result of people's evaluation of events in the context of the various resources they have available to them. This approach emphasizes that no two people experience the same event in exactly the same way.

Because the second view is currently the most widely used approach for studying stress and the ways in which people deal with it, we will examine it in more detail. Although there are several variations of this approach, we will focus on Richard Lazarus's and Susan Folkman's framework as representative of the view that whether a person feels stressed depends on how he or she evaluates the situation at hand. Let's see how this decision occurs.

The Stress and Coping Paradigm

Perhaps the most influential approach to conceptualizing stress is the stress and coping paradigm, developed by Richard Lazarus and his colleagues (Lazarus, 1984; Lazarus, DeLongis, Folkman, & Gruen, 1985; Lazarus & Folkman, 1984). **The *stress and coping paradigm* views stress not as an environmental stimulus or as a response but, rather, as the interaction of a thinking person and an event.** How we *interpret* an event is what matters, not the event itself or what we do in response to it. Put more formally, stress is "a particular relationship between the person and the environment that is appraised by the person as taxing or exceeding his or her resources and endangering his or her well-being" (Lazarus & Folkman, 1984, p. 19). Note that this definition states that stress refers to a *transactional process* between a person and the environment, that it takes into account personal resources, that the person's *appraisal* of the situation is key, and that unless the situation is considered to be threatening, challenging, or harmful, stress does not result.

What exactly does this definition mean? Most important, there is no event that can be said to be equally and universally stressful. The transactional process between the person and the environment involves unique interactions of the basic developmental forces, if for no other reason than each person represents a unique combination of them. The resources a person has include such things as the cumulative experience of dealing with similar situations before, knowledge and/or access to information about the event, the financial ability to get help if necessary, and the time necessary to engage in any actions necessary to address the situation. Clearly, these resources vary a great deal from person to person and reflect the influence of biological (e.g., genetic), psychological (e.g., personality), sociocultural (e.g., ethnicity), and life-cycle (e.g., life stage) forces. These differences in resources are extremely important in understanding why some people apparently have little trouble dealing with very difficult events (e.g., a severe illness) whereas other people seem to have trouble with seemingly routine events (e.g., calming a crying child). Recognizing these differences, let's begin our closer look at the stress and coping paradigm with the concept of appraisal.

Appraisal

Lazarus and Folkman (1984) describe three types of appraisals of stress. ***Primary appraisal*** **serves to categorize events into three groups based on the significance they have for our well-being: irrelevant, benign-positive, and stressful.** Irrelevant events are ones that have no bearing on us personally; hearing about a typhoon nowhere near land in the South Pacific while sitting in our living room in Boston is an example. Benign-positive appraisals mean that an event has good effects, such as a long-anticipated pay increase. Finally, stressful appraisals mean that an event, such as failing a course or an upcoming operation, is perceived as harmful, threatening, or challenging.

Primary appraisals set a filter of sorts for events we experience. Specifically, any event that is appraised as either irrelevant or as benign-positive is not a stressful event in this framework. In a real sense, we decide which events are potentially stressful and which ones are not. This is an important point for two reasons. First, it means we can effectively sort out those events that may be problems and those that are not, allowing us to concentrate our efforts to deal with life's difficulties more effectively. Second, it also means that we could be wrong about our reading of an event. A situation that may appear at first blush to be irrelevant, for example, may actually be very important, or a situation deemed stressful initially may turn out not to be. Such mistakes in primary appraisal could set the stage for real (or imagined) crises later on.

If a person believes that an event is stressful, a second set of decisions, termed secondary appraisal, need to be made. ***Secondary appraisal*** **refers to our perceived ability to cope with harm, threat, or challenge.** Secondary appraisal is the equivalent of asking three questions: "What can I do?" "How likely is it that I can use one of my options successfully?" "Will this option reduce my stress?" How these questions are answered sets the stage for addressing them effectively. For example, if you believe that there is something that you can do in a situation that will make a difference, then your perceived stress may be reduced and you may be able to deal with the event successfully. In contrast, if you believe that there is little that you can do that would address the situation successfully or reduce your feelings of stress, then you may feel powerless and ineffective, *even if* others around you believe that there may be steps you could (or should) take. The important point is that what matters in secondary appraisals (and all other decisions in this framework) is what you think is true, not what others think.

After you make a decision about an event and reach some preliminary conclusion about what you should do about it (if anything), the situation continues to play itself out. As the event continues to unfold, you begin to get an idea as to whether your primary (and secondary, if necessary) appraisal was appropriate. If it was, then you would most likely stick with your original evaluation. However, sometimes you learn additional information or experience another situation that indicates you should reappraise the original event. ***Reappraisal*** **involves making a new primary or secondary appraisal resulting from changes in the situation.** For example, you may initially dismiss an accusation that your partner is "cheating" on you (i.e., make a primary appraisal that the event is irrelevant), but after being shown pictures of your partner in a romantic situation with another person, you reappraise the event as stressful. Reappraisal can either increase stress (if your partner had initially denied the encounter to you before) or lower stress (if, perhaps even later, you discovered that the photographs were fakes).

The three types of appraisals demonstrate that how people determine whether an event is stressful is a dynamic process. Initial decisions about events may be upheld over time, or they may change in the light of new information or personal experience.

Thus, different events may be appraised in the same way, and the same event may be appraised differently at any two points in time. This dynamic process helps explain why people react the way they do over the life span. For example, as our physiological abilities change with increasing age, we may have fewer physical resources to handle particular events. As a result, events that were appraised as not stressful in young adulthood may be appraised as stressful in late life.

Coping

During the secondary appraisal of an event labeled stressful in primary appraisal, we may believe that there is something we could do to deal with the event effectively. Collectively, these attempts at dealing with stressful events are called coping. **Lazarus and Folkman view *coping* more formally as a complex, evolving process of dealing with stress that is learned.** Much like appraisals, coping is seen as a dynamic, evolving process that is fine-tuned over time. Our first attempt might fail, but if we try again in a slightly different way we may succeed. ("If at first you don't succeed, try, try again" is a common way of saying this.) Second, it is learned, not automatic. That is why we often do not cope very well with stressful situations we are facing for the first time (such as the end of our first love relationship). The saying "practice makes perfect" applies to coping, too. Third, coping takes effort; it is something we work at that often is neither easy nor fast acting. Finally, coping requires only that we manage the situation; we are not *required* to overcome or control it. Indeed, many stressful events cannot be "fixed" or undone; many times the best we can do is to learn to live with the situation. It is in this sense that people say that we may cope with the death of a spouse.

The ways in which people cope can be classified in several different ways. At a general level we can distinguish between *problem-focused coping* and *emotion-focused coping*. Problem-focused coping involves attempts at tackling the stressful situation head-on in an attempt to eliminate the problem. Taking medication to treat a disease or spending more time studying for an examination are examples of problem-focused coping when faced with the stress of illness or failing a prior test. In general, problem-focused coping entails doing something directly about the problem at hand. Emotion-focused coping involves dealing with one's feelings about the stressful event. Allowing oneself to express anger or frustration over becoming ill or failing an exam is an example of this approach. The goal here is not necessarily to eliminate the problem, although this may happen. Rather, the purpose may be to help oneself deal with situations that may be difficult or impossible to tackle head-on.

Several other behaviors can also be viewed in the context of coping. Many people express that their relationship with God is an important aspect of coping (Ishler, Pargament, Kinney, & Cavanaugh, 1995). Psychoanalytic researchers point to Freud's notion of defense mechanisms as behaviors that may be used to reduce stress. In short, people use many different types of behaviors when they feel stressed.

How well we cope depends on several factors. For example, healthy, energetic people are better able to cope with an infection than frail, sick people. Psychologically, a positive attitude about oneself and one's abilities is also important. Good problem-solving skills put one at an advantage in having several options with which to manage the stress. Social skills and social support are important in helping one solicit suggestions and assistance from others. Finally, financial resources are important; having the money to pay a mechanic to fix one's car allows nonmechanically inclined individuals (like the author) to avoid the frustration of trying to do it oneself.

Aging and the Stress and Coping Paradigm

Two important areas of age differences in the stress and coping paradigm are the sources of stress and coping strategies. Age differences have been described for the kinds of things that people report as everyday stresses (Folkman, Lazarus, Pimley, & Novacek, 1987). Younger adults experience more stress in the areas of finance, work, home maintenance, personal life, family, and friends than do

Although restaurant servers must appear happy on the job, there is considerable stress associated with such occupations.

older adults. These differences are probably because the young adults are likely to be parents of small children and employed; parenting and work roles are less salient to retired older adults. The stresses reported frequently by older adults, coming mainly from the environment and social issues, may be more age related than role related. That is, environmental stress may be due to a decreased ability to get around rather than to a specific role.

Age differences in coping strategies are striking and consistent. For example, Blanchard-Fields and her colleagues have shown that younger adults tend to use defensive coping styles much of the time, whereas older adults choose coping strategies on the basis of whether they feel in control of the situation (Blanchard-Fields & Irion, 1988; Blanchard-Fields & Robinson, 1987; Irion & Blanchard-Fields, 1987). Even when people are faced with similar problems, age differences in coping style are apparent. For example, Felton and Revenson (1987) report that when trying to cope with their chronic illnesses, middle-aged adults were more likely to use interpersonal strategies such as information seeking than were older adults.

These age-related differences in coping strategies fit with developmental trends reported in personality research regarding some specific traits. In particular, there appears to be an age-related introversion that is reflected in increased passivity and more self-reflective behavior. It may be that these changes in personality are also reflected in the choice of a coping strategy.

Stress and Physical Illness

Considerable research has examined how stress causes physical illness. Zegans (1982) proposed numerous hypotheses about this connection. One of the most important of these involves the effects of stress on the immune system. V. Riley (1981) reports that increased levels of hormones called corticoids occur after prolonged stress and that they increase animals' vulnerability to viruses and possibly even cancer.

Research on humans has documented similar effects. Lower antibody levels and poorer functioning of some types of lymphocytes have been demonstrated in students who were under stress during examination periods (Jemmott et al., 1983; Kiecolt-Glaser, Speicher, Holliday, & Glaser, 1984). Interestingly, personality differences influenced the degree to which the immune system was affected. People who were motivated by power rather than friendship (Jemmott et al., 1983) and people who were lonely (Kiecolt-Glaser et al., 1984) were affected most.

This line of research suggests that stress lowers the ability of the immune system to fight infection. This may be why we sometimes get ill shortly after a relatively prolonged period of stress (for example, during vacation after a very stressful time at work). Although the relationship between stress and the immune system may help explain one mechanism of the stress-illness connection, it is not the only one. Additional connections between stress and illness can be seen in examining specific diseases.

Headaches

Nearly everyone gets an occasional tension headache that is ascribed to stress. For most of us, headaches are relatively minor problems. However, for the 10% to 12% of people who must seek medical attention, headaches present major difficulties (Holyroyd, Appel, & Andrasik, 1983). Those who go to physicians do not do so because they have different kinds of headaches. Rather, they suffer from more serious or frequent headaches than the rest of us. Holyroyd et al. (1983) differentiate two types of headache: tension headache and vascular headache. Research dating to the 1960s has demonstrated that stress causes tension headaches to a much greater extent than vascular headaches.

Cardiovascular Disease

Cardiovascular disease has several behavioral risk factors. One of the most provocative of these connections is between cardiovascular disease and self-imposed stress. Due to the work of M. Friedman and Rosenman (1974) we know that both personality and situational stress are related to cardiovascular disease. They identified two behavior patterns, which differ dramatically in terms of the risk of cardiovascular disease. Type A behavior pattern is associated with high rates of cardiovascular disease. An opposite style, Type B behavior pattern, is not associated with cardiovascular disease.

People exhibiting *Type A behavior pattern* are intensely competitive, angry, hostile, restless, aggressive, and impatient; individuals displaying *Type B behavior pattern* show nearly opposite tendencies. Type A people are at least twice as likely as Type B people to develop cardiovascular disease, even when other risk factors such as smoking, diabetes, hypertension, and high serum cholesterol are taken into account. Furthermore, serious heart disease rarely occurs before age 70 except among Type A people. It does not seem to matter how much junk food Type B people eat, how many cigarettes they smoke, or how little exercise they get. They will probably not die prematurely from cardiovascular disease (Eisdorfer & Wilkie, 1977).

These findings led researchers and those involved in rehabilitating cardiac patients to advocate major changes in lifestyle following heart attacks or other serious cardiovascular disease. The thinking was that if Type A behavior predisposed people to cardiovascular disease, then eliminating Type A traits would serve as a protective function. However, the relationship between Type A behavior and cardiovascular disease is more complex.

During the early and mid-1980s, researchers reported a reversal in the relationship between behavior type and cardiovascular disease when the risk for secondary cardiovascular disease was examined. That is, researchers began studying individuals who had already been diagnosed as having serious cardiovascular disease and investigated whether Type A or Type B people had a higher risk of developing additional heart diseases (such as having a second heart attack). The initial results were surprising and controversial, but were subsequently corroborated in other studies. Contrary to the finding concerning risk of initial heart disease,

HOW DO WE KNOW?

The Type A Controversy: Being Driven to Get Better

The controversy over whether Type A behavior is seriously detrimental to one's health has profound implications for treatment. It is a good idea, then, to take a closer look at one study that found an unexpected result.

Ragland and Brand (1988) examined the 22-year mortality of 257 men with heart disease. These men were part of the Western Collaborative Group Study, which uncovered the connection between Type A behavior pattern and coronary disease. Of these 257 men, 135 had symptomatic myocardial infarctions, 71 had silent myocardial infarctions, and 51 had angina; of those who had symptomatic myocardial infarctions, 26 died suddenly or within 24 hours of the onset of symptoms. A follow-up through 1983 showed that 128 of the men had died, and their cause of death was coded from death certificates by two independent raters; 91 died of heart disease and 37 from unrelated causes. For the 91 men who died of heart disease, whether they died within 24 hours of symptom onset was noted. The key analyses examined whether short-term and long-term outcomes were related differently to Type A and Type B patterns.

Results showed an almost identical mortality rate for Type A and Type B men who died within 24 hours of symptom onset. For long-term mortality, the fatality rate was 19.1 per 1,000 person-years for Type A and 31.7 per 1,000 person-years for Type B. Even when the data were examined in more detail, the Type A advantage never disappeared.

Although the results of the study point toward the conclusion that Type A men who survive their initial bout with heart disease are more likely to survive in the long run, Ragland and Brand suggest several caveats. First, we do not know how Type A and Type B people actually respond to coronary disease. For example, one group may change their lifestyle more completely than the other. Second, Type A men may be more likely to seek medical help for suspected heart disease. Finally, behavior patterns identified years before coronary disease is diagnosed may be meaningless; behavior patterns may have changed in the intervening years.

Still, the Ragland and Brand study points out that Type A and Type B behavior patterns have complex relationships with heart disease. The study also points out that we must be cautious in interpreting longitudinal data involving predictions over long periods.

Type A people actually recovered from their first heart attack better and had lower morbidity than Type B individuals (Case, Heller, Case, & Moss, 1985; Dimsdale, Gilbert, Hutter, Hackett, & Block, 1981; Shekelle, Gale, & Norusis, 1985). The strongest evidence for the reversal was reported by Ragland and Brand (1988), who examined 22-year follow-up data from the original Friedman and Rosenman study. Ragland and Brand (1988) also found lower morbidity following the first episode of serious cardiovascular disease in Type A people (see How Do We Know?).

Why do Type A people have a higher risk of first heart attack but a better chance to survive than Type B people? The answers are unclear. It may be that some of the characteristics of Type A people that make them movers and shakers also motivate them to overcome their disease. Indeed, researchers have noted that Type A people were much more likely to stick to diet and exercise regimens after heart attacks (Ragland & Brand, 1988) and have a more positive attitude about recovery (Ivancevich & Matteson, 1988). The laid-back approach of Type B people may actually work to their detriment during recovery.

Clearly, there is a need for caution in interpreting these findings. Type A and Type B patterns are just that—patterns. Only approximately 10% of the population is classified as a pure Type A or B. The rest of us fall somewhere in between. Additionally, the relationship between Type A behavior and cardiovascular functioning is obviously complex and varies between men and women of different ages (Harbin & Blumenthal, 1985). It is the hostility and anger component of Type A behavior that is the risk factor, rather than the entire behavioral cluster (Ivancevich & Matteson, 1988). Moreover, virtually nothing is known about how the relationship between Type A and cardiovascular disease is affected by increasing age, if at all. These issues need to be more thoroughly researched before we can gain a firm understanding of the relationship between behavior and cardiovascular disease, and how this relationship varies with age.

Stress and Psychological Functioning

It is commonly believed that stress causes psychological problems. Years of research, though, do not support that even an accumulation of stressful life events causes depression, schizophrenia, or anxiety disorders. Dohrenwend (1979, p.5) concluded that except for the death of a loved one or a very serious physical illness or injury, "it is difficult to find consistent evidence that other types of single life events can produce psychopathology in previously normal adults in societies free from war and other natural disasters." For stress to have a major influence on psychological functioning, Dohrenwend argues, three things must be present: (1) vulnerability from physical illness or injury, (2) undesirable life events, and (3) loss of social support. When all three factors occur simultaneously, psychopathology may result.

In contrast to the research on psychopathology, stress is related to other psychological processes. For example, Krause (1991) showed that certain kinds of stress, especially financial and fear of crime, promote social isolation in older adults. Moreover, chronic stressors of this sort foster a general distrust of other people, which in turn leads to additional isolation. This relationship is particularly strong in urban-dwelling older adults who are poor. Interestingly, Krause found that recent deaths were unrelated to distrust or to isolation. Death often brings one's family and friends together.

Krause's research brings out an important point: Stressors fluctuate in importance across adulthood. For example, the pressures from work are typically more salient to younger and middle-aged adults than to older adults, but stressors due to chronic conditions are often more important to older adults than to their younger counterparts. In other words, life-cycle forces must be taken into account when considering what kinds of stress adults of different ages are experiencing.

Managing Stress

The treatment of stress has been approached in many ways, based mainly on the various definitions of stress. Thus, if stress is seen as coming from environmental stimuli, treatment involves modifying, escaping, or ignoring these stimuli. Unfortunately, this approach is often impossible; for example, quitting a stressful job may be very difficult. Thus, most therapeutic efforts have focused on teaching people new ways to deal with the physical responses involved with stress or new ways to appraise the situation cognitively.

Managing the Response

Three methods have proven effective in dealing with the body's response to stress. Relaxation training is effective, particularly in controlling hypertension, insomnia, and tension headaches (Lavey & Taylor, 1985). Meditation or focusing attention so as not to dwell on negative thoughts is also effective. Shapiro (1985) concluded that meditation is as effective at reducing anxiety, phobias, and hypertension as relaxation training. Finally, biofeedback training also appears to be as effective as relaxation training at lowering muscle tension and skin temperature (Andrasik, Blanchard, & Edlund, 1985).

Changing the Appraisal

The best-researched cognitive approach to stress management is stress inoculation (Cameron & Meichenbaum, 1982; Meichenbaum, 1985; Meichenbaum & Cameron, 1983). Stress inoculation is similar to vaccination against disease. The process proceeds by identifying the source of the problem (conceptualization); learning new and practicing old coping skills (skills-acquisition rehearsal); and putting these skills into practice (application and follow-through). Several problems have been successfully treated with stress inoculation (Hamberger & Lohr, 1984), including test anxiety, public speaking anxiety, and social anxiety (Jaremko, 1983).

Other Approaches

Some effective stress management techniques hardly require any work at all. One that millions of people have used for centuries (probably without knowing it) is pet ownership. Pets help lower their owners' stress and, at least for older adults, is associated with fewer visits to physicians (Siegel, 1990). Pet therapy is a rapidly growing approach used in nursing homes to help raise residents' morale and health (Bustad, 1993). However, there may not be a general benefit of interacting with pets in the population at large; the positive effects may be limited to persons with special needs (Tucker, Friedman, Tsai, & Martin, 1995).

Concept Checks

1. What are the major components of the stress and coping paradigm?
2. What are the characteristics of behavior linked with cardiovascular disease?
3. What are the major connections between stress and psychological functioning?
4. What are the major ways that people manage stress?

HEALTH AND LIFESTYLE

Learning Objectives:

- What are the major hazards of cigarette smoking?
- What are the effects of alcohol dependence? What are the benefits of moderate drinking?
- What are the benefits of aerobic exercise?
- How does sleep change with age? What causes sleep disturbances?
- What are the nutritional requirements of older adults? How does diet affect health?

By this point in your life, you are undoubtedly aware of the consequences of behavior on your health. For example, you already know that smoking is bad for your health, as is long-term consumption of high quantities of alcohol. So it should not be surprising that these connections hold across adulthood and that in some cases the cumulative effects are what matter.

In this section, we will consider five lifestyle choices that have a considerable impact on health: smoking, drinking alcohol, exercise, sleep, and nutrition. We will examine how these behaviors create health problems, as well as how they affect people at different ages.

Smoking

If everyone who smoked would stop today, that would do more to improve health than any other single step. In the United States alone roughly 320,000 deaths each year are related to smoking, and 10 million more people have smoking-related chronic conditions (USDHHS, 1988). The American Cancer Society estimates that 75% of all cancers are due to either smoking or poor dietary habits.

These are sobering statistics. Although fewer older adults than younger or middle-aged adults smoke, the chronic conditions caused by smoking often are at their worst in old age. As we will see, this is because it usually takes years before the devastating effects become noticeable.

The rates of smoking vary not only with age but also with gender and ethnic status. Adult men tend to smoke more than adult women, although this difference is negligible in young adults. Among ethnic groups Native Americans tend to smoke much less than European Americans, African Americans tend to smoke more, and Hispanics and Asian Americans smoke about the same as European Americans (USDHHS, 1984). These differences in smoking rates result in different rates of smoking-related disease later in life; for example, lung cancer is relatively rare among elderly Native Americans.

The Hazards of Cigarette Smoking

The connection between cigarette smoking and cancer has been well documented since the 1960s. The United States Public Health Service notes that smokers have 10 times as much lung cancer, 3 to 10 times as much cancer of the mouth and tongue, 3 to 18 times as much cancer of the larynx, and 7 to 10 times as much bladder cancer as nonsmokers. Smoking plays a role in over half of all cancer deaths and is directly responsible for 75% of all lung cancer; 9 out of every 10 people who develop lung cancer are dead within 5 years.

Cancer is not the only disease caused by smoking; emphysema is mainly caused by smoking. The carbon monoxide and nicotine inhaled in cigarette smoke foster the development of atherosclerosis and angina (Wantz & Gay, 1981). Men and women smokers have roughly twice as much chance of dying of cardiovascular disease than nonsmokers (LaCroix et al., 1991). Women who smoke and take contraceptive pills for at least 5 years have an increased risk of heart attacks until menopause, even if they stop taking the pill (Layde, Ory, & Schlesselman, 1982). Smoking after the fourth month of pregnancy is linked with an increased risk of stillbirths, low birth weight, and perinatal death.

Clearly, smoking takes a frightening toll. But the prospect of lung cancer or other smoking-related disease has significantly lowered smoking rates only among men. The number of women smokers, especially among adolescents and young adults, is higher than ever. In fact, lung cancer has replaced breast cancer as the most common form of cancer among women. Among older women, lung cancer was the only major cause of death to show an increase during the 1980s, tripling in rate since the mid-1970s (USDHHS, 1991).

The Hazards of Secondhand Smoke

The hazards of cigarette smoke do not stop with the smoker. Nonsmokers who breathe secondhand smoke are also at higher risk for smoking-related diseases, including chronic lung disease (USDHHS, 1984), lung cancer (Pershagen, Hrubec, & Svensson, 1987; Sandler, Everson, & Wilcox, 1985), and heart disease (Garland, Barrett-Connor, Suarez, Criqui, & Wingard, 1985). Additionally, pregnant women who breathe secondhand smoke for as little as 2 hours a day at home or at work are more likely to give birth to infants who are below average in weight (Martin & Bracken, 1986). For these reasons many states and communities have passed stringent legislation severely restricting smoking in public areas, and smoking is not allowed at all on airplane flights within the United States.

Spouses of smokers appear to be especially vulnerable to the dangers of secondhand smoke. Nachtigall and Nachtigall (1990) report that wives of husbands who smoke are three times more likely to have heart attacks and other forms of cardiovascular disease. It is a sad legacy that smokers leave: They not only may die themselves of a smoking-related disease but also may kill their nonsmoking spouses the same way.

Quitting Smoking

If one smokes and wants to quit, how should one proceed? Many people successfully quit on their own, but others need formal programs. Whether a particular approach is effective depends on the individual; no one approach works with everyone.

Most stop-smoking programs are multimodal, in that they combine a number of aspects from different therapeutic approaches. For example, Lando (1977) used several behavior modification techniques as well as booster sessions after therapy was over. Lando reported a 76% success rate, which is much higher than the more typical 20% or 30% abstinence at 6- to 12-month follow-ups of other programs. The use of booster sessions is the key difference. Otherwise, the potential for relapse is quite high.

Because 70% to 80% of smokers who try to quit eventually relapse, Marlatt and Gordon (1980) investigated the relapse process itself. They concluded that for most people who have successfully quit smoking one cigarette is enough to create a full-blown relapse complete with feelings of utter failure. Marlatt and Gordon suggest that treatment programs take this into account and incorporate strategies to deal with these feelings caused by a slip.

Although some people may find formal programs helpful in their battle to stop smoking, as many as 95% of those who quit do so on their own, according to a survey by the United States Surgeon General's Office. Schachter (1982) speculates that people tend to go to clinics only after they have tried to quit on their own and failed. Thus, those who attend a clinic may not be a representative sample of smokers who try to quit; success rates at clinics of 20% to 30% may reflect success with the most difficult cases.

To date no one has convincingly demonstrated that one method of quitting smoking is more or less effective than another. What matters most are the person's commitment to quitting and being in an environment that fosters not smoking.

For those who have successfully stopped smoking, will their health ever return to normal? It takes considerable time, but eventually people who quit smoking return to a normal risk of disease. For example, within 10 to 15 years the risk of lung cancer has dropped to normal. Even in former smokers who did not quit until old age, the risk of death from cardiovascular disease returns to normal within a few years (LaCroix et al., 1991). The point is clear: If you don't smoke, don't start. If you do smoke, you're never too old to stop.

Drinking Alcohol

Having a beer while watching a sporting event, enjoying a fine wine with a gourmet meal, and celebrating a major life event with champagne represent some of the most common settings in which adults drink alcoholic beverages. Indeed, beer and wine consumption have been part of the human experience longer than the recorded history of it. Today, the majority of adults in many countries around the world continue to consume alcoholic beverages, although there have been downward trends in total consumption in industrialized countries over the past few decades (Wattis & Seymour, 1994). In part, this downward trend reflects increased concerns about living a healthy lifestyle, as well as increased concern about the dangers of drinking and driving and the association between alcohol and unwanted sexual activity.

The long association between social and life events and alcohol consumption brings with it several important societal issues. Some of the most important are the legal age at which people may drink and the attitudes toward alcohol that a society holds. In the United States, alcohol may not be consumed legally until age 21, which makes this particular birthday a significant one for many people. Among many college students, for example, the age 21 transition is treated as a rite of passage. Alcohol is also depicted as the means by which people have fun; many beer commercials show young adults engaged in social or fun activities. It is virtually impossible to escape being confronted with alcohol, either in person or through advertisements. By the time a person has reached 18 years of age, for example, he or she has already seen roughly 100,000 television commercials for beer alone!

By and large, most people who drink do so in moderation. Thus, it is important to differentiate normal drinking habits from alcohol abuse and alcohol dependence (Wattis & Seymour, 1994). ***Alcohol abuse*** **is defined broadly as consuming enough alcohol to cause physical, psychological, or social harm.** A common example of alcohol abuse would be someone becoming intoxicated and damaging another person's property or forcing another person to submit to unwanted sexual advances. ***Alcohol dependence*** **refers to a more severe form of abuse characterized by drinking behavior that becomes habitual and takes priority over other activities, increased tolerance of alcohol, repeated withdrawal symptoms that are relieved by further drinking, an awareness of feeling compelled to drink, and a reinstatement of this drinking pattern after abstinence. Alcohol dependence is a form of *addiction*, which means that it is a disease in which a physical dependence on alcohol develops with continued use and withdrawal symptoms appear when consumption stops.** Physical dependence occurs when a drug, such as alcohol, becomes so incorporated into the operation of the body's cells that it becomes necessary for normal functioning. If the drug is discontinued, the body's withdrawal reaction is manifested in ways that are opposite to the effects of the drug. Because alcohol is a central nervous system depressant, withdrawal symptoms include restlessness, irritability, and even trembling. (Withdrawal from cocaine, in contrast, involves feeling tired and lethargic.) Alcohol dependence results when a person becomes so dependent on alcohol that it interferes with personal relationships, health, occupation, and social functioning.

The term *alcoholism* is often used to refer to alcohol dependence, but sometimes refers to alcohol abuse as well. Statistics in the United States have for many years indicated that roughly 10% of drinkers show alcohol dependence (National Institute of Alcoholism and Alcohol Abuse [NIAAA], 1983). In fact, nearly half of all the alcohol consumed in the United States is drunk by only 10% of the drinkers. Alcohol presents a serious health problem when consumed in excess. For example, a blood alcohol level of .03, well below the legal limit in most states, significantly impairs driving skill (Wattis & Seymour, 1994). As we will also see, drinking excessively over a long period is associated with several serious health problems.

Alcohol Dependence

Research over the years has revealed that the incidence of alcohol dependence remains at a fairly constant rate of nearly 10% across adulthood (Cummings, 1993; NIAAA, 1983). Total alcohol consumption tends to decrease with age, with drinking peaking between ages 30 and 44 and declining steadily thereafter (USDHHS, 1988). Likewise, identification of individuals as alcohol dependent tends to peak by middle age. Two thirds of older adults who are alcohol dependent began drinking excessively earlier in life and persisted; only one third began abusing alcohol in old age (Scott & Mitchell, 1988). However, adults aged 65 and older have the highest rate (about 60%) of secondary hospital diagnoses that are alcohol related (Cummings, 1993). This means that a significant number of older adults who are admitted into hospitals for one ailment are subsequently found to have alcohol-related problems as well.

Men are more likely than women to be diagnosed as alcohol dependent. However, the extent to which this reflects a true gender difference or a diagnostic bias is unclear. For example, many people who are alcohol dependent are depressed, which has led some authors to speculate that women who are heavy drinkers are more likely to be labeled "depressed" rather than "alcohol dependent" (Kaplan, 1983). This diagnostic bias fits with the higher rate of women being labeled "depressed." Additionally, women tend to hide their problem drinking behavior more than men, making it harder to detect.

For many years the problem of alcohol dependence and aging was ignored, perhaps because surveys indicated a drop in the average level of alcohol consumption beyond midlife (NIAAA, 1983). However, a closer look at the data reveals that more recent cohorts drink more, perhaps because the current older generation was influenced by the ideas that led to Prohibition. This means that alcohol-related problems in older adults are likely to become more serious in future years as these heavier-drinking cohorts age (Wattis, 1983). Indeed, there is some evidence that a growing number of older adults actually increase their consumption of alcohol in late life (Cummings, 1993).

Negative Effects of Alcohol

Alcohol affects health both directly and indirectly. The primary direct health problem for long-term heavy drinkers is liver damage (Eckhardt et al., 1981). Drinking more than five or six drinks per day causes fat to accumulate in the liver, which, over time, restricts blood flow, kills liver cells, and causes a form of hepatitis. Continued heavy drinking results in cirrhosis, in which nonfunctional scar tissue accumulates. Cirrhosis is the leading cause of death in people who are alcohol dependent.

A serious indirect result of long-term heavy drinking is *Wernicke-Korsakoff syndrome*, which causes severe loss of memory for recent events, severe disorientation, confusion, and visual problems (Eckhardt et al., 1981). Wernicke-

Korsakoff syndrome is actually caused by thiamine (vitamin B_1) deficiency. Chronic thiamine deficiency causes, among other things, severe memory loss. Alcohol interferes with thiamine absorption (Thompson, 1978), and people who are alcohol dependent and continue drinking typically do not obtain all the nutrients they need. Although some individuals with Wernicke-Korsakoff syndrome make at least a partial recovery after they stop drinking, at least half show no improvement (Wattis & Seymour, 1994).

Women are especially vulnerable to the effects of alcohol dependence. Heavy alcohol consumption reduces fertility (Greenwood, Love, & Pratt, 1983) and can cause menstrual periods to stop. Alcohol's negative effects on two brain structures, the pituitary and hypothalamus, and on thiamine absorption, appear to be the culprits. Additionally, metabolism of alcohol in the stomach is especially lowered, meaning that more alcohol is available to circulate through the body and cause damage (Frezza, di Padova, Pozzato, Terpin, Baraona, & Lieber, 1990). Drinking during pregnancy increases the risk of fetal alcohol syndrome. Babies born with fetal alcohol syndrome have facial abnormalities, growth deficiencies, central nervous system disorders, and mental retardation (Pratt, 1980, 1982).

Although the rate of absorption of alcohol does not change with age (Wattis & Seymour, 1994), the effects of alcohol on the brain and liver and the level of blood alcohol following ingestion of a specific quantity of alcohol do (Scott & Mitchell, 1988). Older adults' cognitive functioning decreases more after a single drink than does that of younger adults (Jones & Jones, 1980).

Little research has been conducted on changes with age in the way in which the liver metabolizes alcohol. What is known suggests that the effects depend on the amount of alcohol consumed. Small amounts of alcohol in older adults slow the process by which other drugs may be cleared from the system; in contrast, high quantities of alcohol speed up this process (Scott & Mitchell, 1988). These effects have major implications for understanding older adults' higher susceptibility to drug interaction effects. The risk of interactions increases exponentially with the number of drugs taken (Wattis & Seymour, 1994). Because the typical effect of alcohol is to prolong the time that a drug is in the body, alcohol dramatically increases the likelihood that drug interactions will occur.

Another important difference between young and old drinkers concerns the level of alcohol in the blood. If the two groups are given equal doses of alcohol, older adults will have a higher blood-alcohol concentration (Scott & Mitchell, 1988). This age difference has important implications, as blood-alcohol levels provide an index of relative functional impairment; for example, an older adult has to drink less alcohol to be declared legally intoxicated than a younger adult does.

Benefits of Alcohol

Not all the effects of alcohol reported in the literature are negative. Results from several large longitudinal studies have also demonstrated some positive health effects from light drinking (*no more than* the equivalent of two glasses of beer per day). Findings from the Kaiser-Permanente study (Klatsky, Friedman, & Siegelaub, 1981), the Alameda County study (Berkman, Breslow, & Wingard, 1983), the Framingham study (L. A. Friedman & Kimball, 1986; Gordon & Kannel, 1984), and the Albany study (Gordon & Doyle, 1987) documented lower mortality rates among light drinkers. Additionally, light drinkers may have a much lower risk of stroke than abstainers or heavy drinkers even after controlling for hypertension, cigarette smoking, and medication (Gill, Zezulka, Shipley, Gill, & Beevers, 1986). Overall, the results reveal an inverted U-shaped relationship between the amount of alcohol consumed and the mortality rate, with light drinkers having a lower death rate than either abstainers or heavy drinkers. The relationship seems to be stronger for men than for women, especially for men under 60.

Why does light drinking appear to have benefits? No one knows for sure. Apparently, the findings are unrelated to such variables as group differences in personality, such as impatience and aggressiveness (Kaufman, Rosenberg, Helmrich, & Shapiro, 1985); protection against the effects of fat deposits (Haskell et al., 1984), or poor research designs

(Myers, 1983). These benefits of drinking must be interpreted carefully. Light drinking *does not* mean getting drunk. Drinking to the point of intoxication, even on a very occasional basis, is potentially dangerous.

Quitting Drinking

Several approaches have been used to help problem drinkers achieve abstinence. The most widely known of these is Alcoholics Anonymous (AA). Founded in 1935 by two former alcoholics, AA follows a strict disease model of alcoholism. The program itself is based on personal and spiritual growth, with the goal being total abstinence. AA is based on the notion that problem drinkers are addicted to alcohol and have no power to resist it. Moreover, abstaining alcoholics are in the process of recovering for the rest of their lives.

Even though AA has a long history, very little research has been done to document its effectiveness (Peele, 1984), primarily because AA is an anonymous fellowship, making it difficult to follow people over time. The little research that has been done suggests that AA may help as many as half of the people who remain in and effectively follow the AA program and may be especially effective for people with lower educational levels or higher needs for authoritarianism, dependency, and sociability (Miller & Hester,1980).

Many organizations provide Employee Assistance Programs (EAPs) to help workers with alcohol and other personal problems. EAPs provide a confidential way for people to discuss their problems and to receive the help they need. Additionally, if an employee seeks assistance through an EAP, he or she cannot be terminated for the problem as long as the treatment regimen is being followed.

Psychotherapy is widely used in a variety of treatment settings, including Veterans Administration hospitals, care units in other hospitals, private treatment centers, and private counseling. These approaches include psychoanalysis (Blum, 1966), behavior modification (Wallace, 1985), psychodrama (Blume, 1985), assertiveness training (Materi, 1977), and group therapy (Zimberg, 1985). For any of these approaches to be effective, the primary goal should be sobriety (Zimberg, 1985). Moreover, long-term sobriety may require combining psychotherapy with other programs such as AA. No research as been done specifically examining success rates in these various programs as a function of age. In general, however, long-term sobriety of at least 3 years is achieved by no more than 30% of individuals seeking treatment (Armor, Polich, & Stambul, 1976; Wiens & Menustik, 1983). These data clearly indicate that the relapse potential for recovering alcoholics is very high.

Exercise

Those who exercise regularly may be adding years to their life. As far back as Hippocrates, evidence exists that exercise affects longevity. There is no evidence that exercise actually affects the normal changes accompanying aging; however, considerable data point to the fact that exercise does modify the disease process, especially cardiovascular disease (Hayflick, 1994). Because cardiovascular disease is the leading cause of death in developed countries, delaying the disease has the effect of increasing longevity.

However, before you drop this book and head off to the gym in the hopes of a longer life, you may want to read the rest of this section. It turns out that the connection between exercise and longer life is more complicated than you might think. Let's see why.

Types of Exercise

Exercise can be grouped into two categories (Thomas & Rutledge, 1986): aerobic and nonaerobic. ***Aerobic exercise*** **places a moderate stress on the heart that is achieved by maintaining a pulse rate between 60% and 90% of the maximum.** Maximum heart rate can be estimated by subtracting your age from 220. Thus, if you are 40 years old, the target range would be between 108 and 162 beats per minute. The minimum time necessary to benefit from aerobic exercise depends on the intensity with which it is performed. For heart

Aerobic exercise is an important part of a healthy lifestyle throughout the life span.

rates near the low end of the range, sessions should last roughly 60 minutes, whereas for high heart rates, 15 minutes may suffice. Examples of aerobic exercise include jogging at a moderate to fast pace, rapid walking, step aerobics, swimming, and bicycling. Stretching before and after any aerobic exercise will help avoid injuries. Additionally, the best aerobic exercises are low impact, which place less stress on joints such as the knee and hip.

***Nonaerobic exercise* occurs when the heart rate does not exceed 60% of maximum for sustained periods.** Nonaerobic exercise does not have the positive health benefits of aerobic exercise, as discussed next. Examples of nonaerobic exercise are stretching, yoga, some forms of weightlifting, and range-of-motion exercises.

Aerobic Exercise and Aging

What happens to you when you exercise (besides becoming tired and sweaty)? Physiologically, adults of all ages show improved cardiovascular functioning and maximum oxygen consumption, lower blood pressure, better muscle strength and endurance, increased joint flexibility, and better neuromuscular coordination (Smith & Serfass, 1981). Psychologically, people who exercise regularly claim to have lower levels of stress (Blumenthal et al., 1988), better moods (Simons, McGowan, Epstein, Kupfer, & Robertson, 1985), and better cognitive functioning. These effects are found even with low-impact aerobics (Hopkins, Murrah, Hoeger, & Rhodes, 1990). Interestingly, the general effects of exercise are fairly consistent across age; older adults benefit from exercise and show patterns of improvement similar to those of younger and middle-aged adults. For example, the rate of heart disease is slowed in physically fit people even into the 80s (Posner et al., 1990).

The lack of significant age-related differences in the pattern of benefits from aerobic exercise is important. Recall from Chapter 3 that normative age changes in the cardiovascular, respiratory, skeletal, and muscular systems reduce the efficiency with which they work. Available evidence supports the idea that aerobic exercise tends to slow these changes (see Smith & Serfass, 1981). In physiological terms, then, older adults who exercise regularly could be in better condition than sedentary younger adults.

The optimal way to accrue the benefits of exercise, of course, is to maintain physical fitness across the life span. In planning an exercise program, however, three points must be remembered. First, one should always check with a physician before beginning a program of aerobic exercise. Second, moderation is extremely important; more is not better. Paffenbarger, Hyde, Wing, and Hsieh (1986) made this point clear in their study of 16,936 male Harvard graduates aged 35 to 74. They found that, compared with men who did not exercise at all, men who exercised moderately (walked 9 miles per week) had a 21% lower risk of mortality, and men who exercised strenuously (cycled for 6 to 8 hours per week) had a 50% lower mortality risk. However, men who engaged in extremely high levels of exercise (burning more than 3,500 kilocalories per week) had a *higher* mortality rate than the other two groups. Third, the reasons people exercise change across adulthood. Younger adults tend to exercise out of a concern for physical appearance, whereas older adults are more concerned with physical and psychological health (Trujillo, Walsh, & Brougham, 1991). This indicates that exercise programs may need to be marketed differently for adults of different ages.

Despite the many benefits of fitness and the increasing popularity of health spas, many adults simply do not exercise. For older adults, at least, the reason seems to be that they do not think they need to (USDHHS, 1988). Women become less active earlier than men, and people with lower education become inactive sooner than college graduates (Ostrow, 1980). The consequences of inactivity, however, can lead to premature death. Blair et al. (1989) documented that physically fit men and women live longer. They estimate that if everyone became fit, death rates could be reduced by 15% in women and 9% in men. There are role models for physical fitness, even for the elderly. Wiswell (1980) notes that the late King Gustav of Sweden still played tennis regularly at 80 and that older Olympic champions functioned better than 25-year-olds who had sedentary jobs.

Finally, getting people to exercise aerobically is not always easy. Emery and Gatz (1990) reported problems in getting older adults to comply with exercise routines. They point out that exercise programs will need to take individual differences in interest and ability into account in order to be successful. Indeed, social barriers and fears about the risks of exercising (for instance, falling down) keep many older women from participating in exercise programs (O'Brien & Vertinsky, 1991). Perhaps the best solution would be to educate older adults about the various types of exercise and to make several programs available to allow older adults to choose the one that is best for them.

The results from these studies must be placed into context, however. Despite considerable evidence that moderate exercise is associated with greater longevity, the real reason for the effects may be more complex (Hayflick, 1994). Specifically, the samples examined in these studies have differed in several ways other than simply the amount of exercise they do. For example, the participants usually differ in diet and amount of perceived stress. Additionally, the samples examined to date are not representative of the general population of the United States (or of any other country). Until the effects of these other factors combined with exercise are understood, and longitudinal studies with representative samples are undertaken, the real effects of exercise on longevity remain to be seen.

Sleep

How did you sleep last night? If you are elderly, chances are that you had some trouble. In fact, sleep complaints are quite common in older adults (Bootzin & Engle-Friedman, 1987). These complaints most often concern difficulty in falling asleep, frequent or prolonged awakenings during the night, early-morning awakenings, and a feeling of not sleeping very well. Effects of poor sleep are experienced the next day; moodiness, poorer performance on tasks involving sustained concentration, fatigue, and lack of motivation are some of the telltale signs. In this section we will consider the extent of sleep-related problems across adulthood and examine some of the reasons for them.

Results from national surveys and drug-use studies confirm that sleep disturbances increase with age. Mellinger, Balter, and Uhlenhuth (1985) reported that 45% of people between the ages of 65 and 79 had insomnia during the previous year. As we will see, many aspects of sleep decline with age. Interestingly, total sleep time over a 24-hour period does not change across adulthood (Webb & Swinburne, 1971), despite a significant drop with age in total sleep at night (Hauri, 1982). As you may have guessed, nap taking significantly increases with age (Zepelin, 1973).

Age-Related Changes in Sleep

The most consistent age-related difference in sleep is an increase in the frequency of awakenings as morning approaches (for example, Webb, 1982). Once awake, older adults have more difficulty getting back to sleep than younger adults. Webb and Campbell (1980) found that 50- to 60-year-olds took longer to fall back asleep after being awakened during the first 80 minutes of sleep than did 21- to 23-year-olds. Older adults also have more trouble falling asleep in the first place. Webb (1982) documented that it took women aged 50 to 60 twice as long to fall asleep initially as women aged 20 to 30.

Slight differences in REM (rapid eye movement) sleep have been noted between younger and older adults (Reynolds et al., 1985). Rather than increasing in duration over the course of the night as they do in younger adults, REM periods in older adults remain constant or decrease in length. Additionally, older adults spend more time in the light stages of sleep, which may account for the increase in frequency of awakenings.

We have all experienced the negative effects of all-nighters on next-day mood and performance. We tend to lose our temper more quickly, tire more easily, and have more problems paying attention. These negative effects increase with age. For example, Webb and Levy (1982) found that middle-aged adults (40 to 49 years old) showed significantly poorer performance on auditory vigilance, addition, and mood scales after two nights of sleep deprivation.

Although the data clearly show differences in sleep with age, these differences do not always result in complaints of sleep disturbance (Bootzin & Engle-Friedman, 1987). Differences in REM sleep, for example, may go unnoticed, whereas increased awakenings during the night will be reported. Thus, we need to be sensitive to the different levels of awareness that adults have of underlying changes in sleep.

Causes of Sleep Disturbance

Sleep is affected by numerous factors (Bootzin & Engle-Friedman, 1987): physical disorders, medication, alcohol, caffeine and nicotine, stress, and sleep habits and naps.

The most common physical disorders that affect sleep are sleep-related respiratory problems (Bootzin & Engle-Friedman, 1987). Among these are sleep apnea (a cessation of air flow for 10 seconds or longer occurring at least five times per night) and hypopnea (a 50% or greater reduction of air flow for 10 seconds or longer). Sleep apnea is the more common disorder, and it increases with age (Coleman et al., 1981). Physical illnesses can also disrupt sleep because of discomfort or pain. Pain associated with arthritis is one of the most frequent causes of sleep disturbance in the elderly (Prinz & Raskind, 1978).

Both prescription and over-the-counter medications can disrupt sleep regardless of age (Karacen & Williams, 1983). For example, asthma medication may contain epinephrine, which may interfere with sleep if taken at night. Tricyclic antidepressants suppress REM sleep and can cause involuntary leg twitches. Several medications used to treat seizures, Parkinson's disease, and hypertension can increase nighttime awakenings.

Serious drug-induced sleep disturbances can be caused by sleeping pills and tranquilizers. Sleeping pills have two dangers. First, they lose their effectiveness within two weeks of continued use (Kales,

Both prescription and over-the-counter medications can cause sleep disturbances.

Allen, Scharf, & Kales, 1970). Second, tolerance to them develops rapidly, so larger and larger doses are needed to produce an effect.

Sleeping pills and tranquilizers have several similar negative influences on sleep (Kales, Scharf, & Kales, 1978). They lower the amount of deep sleep and increase light sleep, decrease REM sleep on the night they are taken, and produce large REM rebound on subsequent nights. REM rebound is characterized by restless dreaming, nightmares, and fragmented sleep. Finally, they produce drug hangover effects and impaired motor and intellectual functioning as well as moodiness the next day. The carryover effects are probably due to the fact that many of these drugs remain in the bloodstream for days, resulting in the possibility that side effects could be observed for a relatively long period after the person has stopped taking the drug (Bootzin & Engle-Friedman, 1987).

The effects of alcohol on sleep are similar to those produced by sleeping pills and tranquilizers. In general, alcohol reduces REM sleep, and habitual heavy drinking produces fragmented sleep and several awakenings. Because alcohol is a depressant, it magnifies the effects of sleeping pills and tranquilizers, increasing the likelihood of fatal overdoses when they are combined.

Drinking a cup of regular coffee before bedtime is not usually a good idea for those who want to go to sleep. Smoking may have the same effect. The caffeine in the coffee and the nicotine in the cigarette produce insomnia or lighter and more fragmented sleep (Soldatos, Kales, Scharf, Bixler, & Kales, 1980). Reducing or eliminating excessive caffeine and nicotine can result in considerable improvement in sleep.

Stress is hazardous to your sleep. Even for people with no history of insomnia, worrying about exams, presentations, one's children, or one's spouse can cause sleep disturbances (Healey et al., 1981).

Sleep Habits and Naps

What do you do in your bedroom besides sleep? Do you read, talk on the telephone, watch television, snack, listen to music, or, worst of all, worry? All of these behaviors can be incompatible with falling asleep and are very common in insomniacs (Bootzin, 1977). The bed no longer is a cue for falling asleep; rather it becomes associated with arousal. The situation may become so bad that many insomniacs can seemingly sleep anywhere except in their own bed. In contrast, normal sleepers often have problems falling asleep anywhere else other than their own bed (Bootzin & Engle-Friedman, 1987). The solution to the problem is relatively easy. At the first sign of insomnia get out of bed and go somewhere else. By keeping the bed as a cue to go to sleep, many insomniacs quickly overcome their problem (Bootzin, 1977).

Another bad sleep habit is afternoon or evening naps (Webb, 1975). Such naps contain more deep sleep and less REM sleep. The night's sleep following one of these naps continues as if the nap were part of the night's sleep. That is, the entire night's sleep looks similar to the latter half of a normal night's sleep, containing more light and REM sleep and more awakenings (Webb, 1975). In contrast, morning naps have little effect on the subsequent night's sleep.

Taking naps whenever one feels tired has another, more serious effect. Adopting this strategy

TABLE 4.1 Typical stimulus-control instructions

1. Lie down intending to go to sleep only when you are sleepy.
2. Do not use your bed for anything except sleep; that is, do not read, watch television, worry, or eat in bed. Sexual activity is the only exception to this rule.
3. If you find yourself unable to fall asleep, get up and go into another room. Stay up as long as you wish, and then return to the bedroom to sleep. Although you should not watch the clock, get out of bed immediately if you still cannot fall asleep. The goal is to associate the bed with falling asleep *quickly*. If you are in bed more than 10 minutes without falling asleep and have not gotten up, you are not following instructions.
4. If you still cannot fall asleep, repeat Step 3. Do this as often as necessary throughout the night.
5. Set your alarm and get up at the same time every morning irrespective of how much sleep you got during the night. This will help your body acquire a constant sleep rhythm.
6. Do not nap during the day.

Source: "Sleep Disturbances" by R. R. Bootzin and M. Engle-Friedman, in L. L. Carstensen and B. A. Edelstein (Eds.), *Handbook of Clinical Gerontology*, pp. 238–251 Copyright ©1987. Pergamon Press. Reprinted with permission.

may cause disturbances in your *circadian rhythm*, or sleep-wake cycle. If such disturbances develop, an optimal sleeping time may never exist (Hauri, 1982), leading to chronic moodiness and fatigue. Disruptions of circadian rhythm are particularly common in hospital patients and the institutionalized elderly (Wessler, Rubin, & Sollberger, 1976). Additionally, excessive daytime sleepiness in the elderly may be indicative of an underlying disease and should be evaluated (Morewitz, 1988).

Treatment of Sleep Disorders

When most people have trouble sleeping, the first treatment they think of is medication. As we have seen, however, sleeping pills have little long-term effectiveness and several potentially serious side effects. Consequently, treatments other than medication have been the focus of considerable work (see Bootzin & Engle-Friedman, 1987; Borkovec, 1982). Two techniques that work well are stimulus-control instructions and progressive relaxation.

The goals of stimulus-control instructions are to help the insomniac acquire consistent sleeping rhythms, to ensure that the bed is a cue for sleeping, and to dissociate the bed from other competing activities (Bootzin, Engle-Friedman, & Hazelwood, 1983). A typical set of instructions is shown in Table 4.1. Notice that these instructions get the person to use the bed only for sleeping (an exception is made for sex) and do not allow the person to lie in bed if he or she does not fall right to sleep. In short, stimulus-control instructions seek to instill good sleeping habits.

Instructions for controlling stimuli are the most effective treatment for insomniacs of various ages (Bootzin, 1977; Borkovec, 1982; Lacks, Bertelson, Gans, & Kunkel, 1983; Puder, Lacks, Bertelson, & Storandt, 1983; Turner & Ascher, 1982). Simply restricting time in bed (a cornerstone of this approach) may do more to improve sleep habits in older adults than any other technique (Friedman, Bliwise, Yesavage, & Salom, 1991). Combining this approach with support and sleep-hygiene information appears to be even more effective (Bootzin et al., 1983).

Progressive relaxation includes several techniques, such as transcendental meditation, yoga, hypnosis, and biofeedback as well as traditional relaxation methods. The goal of all these approaches when used to treat sleep disturbances is to get people to relax at bedtime so that they will fall asleep faster. One widely used version of progressive relaxation involves the successive tightening and relaxing of the various muscle groups in the body. Since its development in the 1930s by Jacobson (1938), progressive relaxation has been the most widely prescribed and researched nonmedical therapy for sleep disturbances. There is now considerable evidence that it is effective in significantly shortening the time needed to get to sleep (Borkovec, 1982).

Recent evidence suggests that self-help approaches to treating sleep problems are not as effective as therapist-guided approaches (Riedel, Lichstein, & Dwyer, 1995). Only watching a self-help video about good sleep habits was not as effective as combining the video with therapist-guided sleep restrictions (e.g., restricting time in bed rather than increasing sleep time and keeping a sleep diary). When older adults have trouble falling asleep, they would be better off seeking help from a professional rather than trying to treat themselves.

Nutrition

How many times did your parents tell you to eat your vegetables? Or that you are what you eat? Most of us had many disagreements with our parents about food as we were growing up, but now, as adults, we realize that diet is important to good health. Experts agree that nutritional status directly affects one's mental, emotional, and physical functioning (McDonald & Sapone, 1993). With increasing age this relationship becomes even more important, as health is determined in part by the cumulative effects of dietary habits over the years.

Many believe that older adults as a group have poorer dietary habits than younger or middle-aged people and need to use vitamin and mineral supplements. This belief appears to be unfounded, at least until very old age. This is not to say, of course, that older adults do not have nutritional problems. For example, the institutionalized elderly often show significant weight loss and suffer various nutritional deficiencies, such as thiamine, vitamin B_{12}, and folic acid (Wallace & Schwartz, 1994). Economic factors often prevent the aged poor from eating adequate diets. Loss of one's partner, which causes many surviving spouses to eat alone, removes the important social component of sharing meals. Obtaining adequate nutrition is one of the most basic requirements for a health maintenance program; the poorer nutrition of many needy older people clearly contributes to their overall higher rate of chronic conditions.

Daily Dietary Requirements

Nutritional requirements, food and drink preferences, and eating habits change across the life span. Adolescents and young adults seemingly require huge quantities of junk food, whereas middle-aged adults require more meats and vegetables. Seriously, though, there are important developmental differences in some dietary requirements.

Several age-related changes in the body affect nutrition. Body metabolism and the digestive process slow down. Age-related changes in vision may hinder older adults' ability to read food labels, recipes, stove settings, or menus. Changes in smell diminish the potential enjoyment of food. Poor teeth may interfere with the ability to chew, thereby limiting the foods a person can eat. Nearly half of all older adults take medications that can adversely affect appetite or how the body extracts nutrients from food. All of these factors need to be considered when planning meals and making recommendations for older adults.

We will consider several major requirements briefly. Eating a good diet to maintain good health is a lifelong duty. A diet that provides adequate vitamins, minerals, protein, and complex carbohydrates needs to be maintained throughout life. Such a diet should be rich in fresh vegetables, fresh fruits, low-fat dairy products, legumes, and whole grains.

Practically speaking, the protein needs of older adults are no different from those of younger adults (McDonald & Sapone, 1993). However, some evidence suggests that protein metabolism in very old adults may be less efficient; if this is true, these individuals need more dietary protein (Munro & Young, 1978). People suffering from disease have greater protein needs at all ages (Isaksson, 1973).

Carbohydrates provide the energy necessary to maintain metabolic, physical, and mental activity. Although energy needs decrease across adulthood, the recommended sources of carbohydrates remain the same, namely, whole grains, fruits, vegetables, and naturally occurring sugars. The refining processes for white flour and table sugar decrease the amount of B vitamins (only three of which are restored by enriched flour), vitamin E, and trace minerals.

Old and young alike have the same needs for vitamins and minerals (McDonald & Sapone, 1993). Herbert (1988) reports that older adults do not need to adjust their vitamin intake and do not need vitamin supplements if they eat a well-balanced diet. Fads such as megavitamins should be avoided; the best advice is to get nutrition from food, not pills.

Diet and Health

Does what one eats affect how well one feels? The answer is a resounding yes. Considerable evidence shows beyond doubt that dietary habits strongly influence physical health. The strongest links have been established with cardiovascular disease and cancer.

The American Heart Association is quite clear in its recommendations concerning the amount of fat in our diet: Foods that are high in saturated fats—such as whole milk, butter, and processed foods containing coconut or palm oil—should be replaced with low-fat milk and vegetable oils (such as corn or olive oil). Eggs and red meat should be limited and replaced by fish, white-meat poultry (without the skin), and legumes. Egg substitutes should be used whenever possible. Additionally, the association recommends limiting sodium intake; high levels of sodium have been linked to hypertension.

The main goal of these recommendations is to lower the level of serum cholesterol. High cholesterol level is one risk factor for cardiovascular disease. Although this is true, two major types of cholesterol must be distinguished: low-density lipoproteins (LDL) and high-density lipoproteins (HDL). Low-density lipoproteins are thought to cause atherosclerosis. For this reason, LDL is sometimes referred to as "bad cholesterol" in the popular literature. High-density lipoproteins are thought to actually help keep arteries clear and may even help break down LDL. Consequently, HDL is sometimes referred to as "good cholesterol."

It is the ratio of LDL to HDL that is important in cholesterol screening. Relatively high levels of HDL are good; relatively high levels of LDL are bad. LDL levels have been linked to eating diets high in saturated fats; reducing these substances through diet modification is the easiest way to lower LDL levels. HDL levels can be raised through exercise, a diet high in fiber, and modest amounts of alcohol intake (such as one glass of beer per day). Finally, weight control is an important aspect in any overall diet plan.

Modifying one's diet to reduce LDL levels is effective in adults of all ages. For example, Löwik et al. (1991) found that older adults benefited just as much as younger adults from diet modification and weight reduction or control.

The American Cancer Society (1990) estimates that 35% of all cancers are caused by what we eat; as a result, they have issued extensive guidelines concerning diet. These recommendations include eating less fat and fewer salt-cured, smoked, and nitrite-cured foods; drinking less alcohol; and eating more fresh vegetables. The society points out that obesity greatly increases the risk for cancer. Excessive fat intake alone increases the chances of breast, colon, and prostate cancers. A high intake of commercially smoked meats (which contain nitrites and nitrates) is linked with stomach and esophageal cancers. Diets containing adequate levels of vitamin A may lower the risk of cancers of the larynx, esophagus, and lung. Similarly, high-fiber diets may reduce the risk of stomach and colon cancers.

As noted in Chapter 3, some researchers believe that diet can be used to prevent osteoporosis if it is begun in young adulthood. Because one of the causes of osteoporosis is a deficiency in calcium, diets should include foods that are high in calcium—for example, yogurt, broccoli, collards, turnip greens, salmon, sardines, oysters, and tofu. Interestingly, although protein is a daily requirement, too much protein can lead to loss of calcium through the urine.

Numerous studies over the past few decades confirm that calcium supplements in the diet of postmenopausal women helped slow the loss of bone mass (McDonald & Sapone, 1993). Although the amount of slowing depended on the source of the extra calcium and the age of the participants, ingesting an extra 1,000 to 1,400 mg of calcium per day appears to be the necessary amount to produce effects.

There is also some evidence that decreased levels of vitamin K may be linked to osteoporosis (Loeser, Wallin, & Sadowski, 1993). Although no prospective studies specifically examining this connection have been reported, the retrospective data currently available indicate that a connection between vitamin K and bone loss may exist.

Concept Checks

1. What are the primary hazards from smoking cigarettes and from secondhand smoke?
2. What are the effects of long-term alcohol dependence?
3. What are the benefits of aerobic exercise for older adults?
4. How does sleep change with age?
5. Compared with younger and middle-aged adults, what are the nutritional requirements of older adults?

CANCER

Learning Objectives:

- How does the risk of getting cancer change with age?
- What screening and prevention steps should people take?

Cancer is the second leading cause of death in the United States, behind cardiovascular disease. Every year roughly 1,000,000 people are diagnosed as having cancer, and roughly 500,000 die. Over the life span, nearly one in every three Americans will develop cancer (USDHHS, 1995). This ratio is likely to increase over the next few decades as a result of lifestyle (such as diet and smoking) and environmental (such as pollution) effects. Some researchers argue that as the rates of cardiovascular disease continue to decline, cancer will become the leading cause of death in the United States (Manton, Wrigley, Cohen, & Woodbury, 1991). There is already mounting evidence that cancer is present in many individuals whose cause of death is officially listed as due to some other cause such as pneumonia (Manton et al., 1991).

One truly unfortunate aspect of these statistics is that many current deaths due to cancer are preventable. Some forms of cancer, such as lung and colorectal cancer, are caused in large part by unhealthy lifestyles. Others, including breast and prostate cancer, have high probabilities for cure if they are detected early. In this section we will consider some of the issues pertaining to cancer and age, as well as screening strategies.

Cancer Risk and Age

The risk of getting cancer increases markedly with age (Young, Percy, & Asire, 1981). Figure 4.2 depicts the incidence rates for all forms of cancer as a function of age. As can be seen, the largest number of cases occurs in the age group 60 to 70. Notice that after age 40 the incidence rate increases sharply. For example, the incidence of cancer at age 50 is only about 400 cases per 100,000 people; by age 70, however, it has increased nearly fourfold to over 1,500 cases. Overall, half of all cancer occurs in individuals over age 65.

Estimates of the annual age-specific incidence rates of the most frequent types of cancer in older adults show that rates of lung cancer and bladder cancer are generally higher in men, with colorectal cancer occurring equally often. Death rates from various forms of cancer differ: lung cancer kills nearly twice as many as the next two highest, breast cancer (in women) and prostate cancer (in men), and roughly 2.5 times as many as colorectal cancer. According to American Cancer Society data, 5-year survival rates for these cancers differ

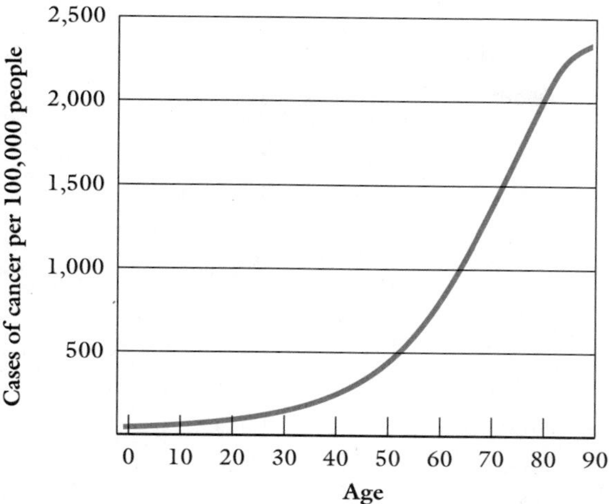

Figure 4.2 Age-related incidence of cancer
Source: National Cancer Institute

dramatically. Whereas only 13% of lung cancer patients are still living 5 years after diagnosis, an average of 80% of breast or prostate cancer patients are.

Why the incidence of cancer is much higher in the elderly is not entirely known. Part of the reason is poor health habits over a long period of time, such as cigarette smoking and poor diets. In addition, the cumulative effects of exposure to pollutants and cancer-causing chemicals are partly to blame. As noted in Chapter 3, some researchers believe that normative age-related changes in the immune system, resulting in a decreased ability to inhibit the growth of tumors, may also be responsible.

However, research in microbiology is increasingly pointing to some genetic links (Ershler, 1991). For example, in colorectal cancer there appears to be a complicated series of five to seven specific genetic events that come into play. These changes, which occur over time, eventually produce a cancerous tumor. Breast and prostate cancers have also been identified as having genetic links. Age-related tissue changes have been associated with the development of tumors, some of which become cancerous; some of these may be genetically linked as well. What remains to be seen is how these genetic events interact with environmental factors. Understanding this interaction process, predicted by the basic developmental forces, could explain why there are considerable individual differences across people in when and how cancer develops.

Screening and Prevention

The most effective way to address the problem of cancer is through increased use of screening techniques and making lifestyle changes as a preventive measure. The American Cancer Society strongly recommends these steps for people of all ages, but older adults need to be especially aware of what to do. Table 4.2 contains guidelines for the early detection of some common forms of cancer.

One problem in cancer screening and prevention in the elderly is a reluctance on the part of some physicians to tackle the problem aggressively (List, 1987, 1988; Samet, Hunt, & Key, 1986). Whether this failure stems from the myth that older patients have substantially lower survival rates (actually, the survival rates are quite similar) or from some other set of reasons is unclear. For their part, many older adults are reluctant to request the necessary tests, and in many cases may not be able to afford preventive care due to a lack of or insufficient insurance coverage (List, 1988). In any event, regular cancer screening should be part of all older adults' program of health promotion and disease prevention.

One of the biggest controversies in cancer prevention concerns the screening for prostate cancer. As discussed in the Something to Think About feature, the controversy demonstrates a combination of a lack of data concerning the causes and the course of the disease, as well as disagreement over treatment. This controversy mirrors similar debates concerning the treatment of breast cancer, in which the relative merits of radical mastectomy (removal of the breast and some surrounding tissue) versus lumpectomy (removal of the cancerous tumor only) as they relate to long-term survival are debated.

TABLE 4.2 Suggested screening steps for cancer

Test	Sex	Age	Frequency
Health counseling and cancer checkup	M&F	>20 >40	Every 3 years Every year
Breast self-examination	F	>20	Once a month
Physical examination		20–40	Every 3 years
		>40	Once a year
Mammography		35–40	Baseline
		40–50	Every 1–2 years
		>50	Once a year
Pelvic examination	F	20–40	Every 3 years
		>40	Once a year
Pap test	F	At onset of sexual activity to age 65	Yearly for 2 exams, then every 3 years
Endometrial biopsy	F	At menopause in women at high risk	
Prostate check	M	>40	Once a year
Rectal examination	M&F	>40	Once a year
Stool guaiac test	M&F	>40	Once a year

Source: American Cancer Society, 1980

Concept Checks

1. What happens to the rate of cancer as people grow older? What causes this change?
2. What are the most important steps people should take for cancer screening and prevention?

HEALTH, FUNCTIONING, AND PREVENTION

Learning Objectives:

- What factors are important to include in a model of disability in late life?
- What causes functional limitations and disability in older adults?
- What types of prevention are used? How do they relate to a model of disability?
- What factors must be considered in using medications with older adults?

Imagine that you are a time traveler and that you found yourself transported back to the year 1900. If you materialized as a health care worker, you would experience a world very different from the one you know in the present. People who became ill would have no antibiotics to help them fight infections, and there would be no immunizations against polio, measles, whooping cough, or any of a host of other diseases. No one fully understood the risks of a high-fat diet, the benefits of aerobic exercise, the dangers of cigarette smoking, or how to detect or treat cancer effectively. Coronary bypass surgery was not even the stuff of science fiction. Surviving childhood was a feat in itself; surviving to old age was unusual.

Your experience would undoubtedly make you

SOMETHING TO THINK ABOUT

The Prostate Cancer Dilemma

Roughly the size of a walnut and weighing about an ounce, the prostate gland is an unlikely candidate to create a major medical controversy. The prostate is located in front of the rectum and below the bladder, and wraps around the urethra (the tube carrying urine out through the penis). Its primary function is to produce fluid for semen, the liquid that transports sperm. In half of all men over age 60, the prostate tends to enlarge, which may produce such symptoms as difficulty in urinating and frequent nighttime urination.

Enlargement of the prostate can happen for three main reasons: prostatitis (an inflammation of the prostate that is usually caused by an infection), benign prostatic hyperplasia, and prostate cancer. Benign prostatic hyperplasia (BPH) is a noncancerous enlargement of the prostate that affects the innermost part of the prostate first. This often results in urination problems as the prostate gradually squeezes the urethra, but does not affect sexual functioning. Prostate cancer often begins on the outer portion of the prostate, which seldom causes symptoms in the early stages. Each year, more than 200,000 men in the United States are diagnosed with prostate cancer; 35,000 will die. For reasons we do not yet understand, African American men have a 40% higher chance of getting prostate cancer. Additionally, a genetic link is clear: A man whose brother has prostate cancer is four times more likely to get prostate cancer than a man with no brothers having the disease.

The controversy surrounding prostate cancer relates to whether early screening and detection reduces mortality from the disease. The American Cancer Society, the Prostate Health Council, and other groups have conducted aggressive campaigns to encourage men over age 50 (and at age 40 in high-risk groups) to undergo two diagnostic tests annually: the digital rectal examination (in which a physician examines the prostate by touch) and the prostate-specific antigen (PSA) blood test. In sharp contrast to clear evidence that early screening and detection of breast cancer in women reduces mortality by at least 30% among older women, no similar statistics exist yet for prostate cancer. This lack of data led the U.S. Preventive Services Task Force, the Canadian Task Force on the Periodic Health Examination, and others to recommend abandoning routine prostate cancer screening because of the cost and the uncertain benefits associated with treatment.

The sharp division among medical experts highlights the relation between carefully conducted research and public health policy. At present, there has not been a systematic comparison of various treatment options (which include surgery, radiation, hormones, and drugs), nor do we yet understand the natural course of prostate cancer in terms of which types of tumors spread to other organs and which ones do not (Calciano, Chodak, Garnick, Kuban, & Resnick, 1995). Given that some of the side effects of surgery include urinary incontinence and impotence, and that some of the other therapies may produce other unpleasant effects, there is debate on whether the disease should be treated at all in most patients (Calciano et al., 1995).

At present, men who experience prostate-related symptoms are left to decide for themselves what to do. Many men opt for immediate treatment and learn how to live with the subsequent side effects. Support groups for men with prostate cancer are becoming more common, and many encourage the patient's partner to participate. The controversy surrounding early screening and detection of prostate cancer is unlikely to subside soon, as the necessary research concerning effective treatment and survival will take years to conduct. Until then, if you or someone you know is over 50, or is in a high-risk group, the decision will still need to be made. What does one do? It's something to think about.

---

grateful that you live at the close of the 20th century rather than at its beginning. One of the most dramatic changes since 1900 has been the reduction in acute disease as a primary cause of death in industrialized countries (Fries & Crapo, 1986). Around 1900, acute diseases such as tuberculosis, polio, measles, diphtheria, typhoid fever, and syphilis claimed tens of thousands of lives in the United States each year. Today they claim relatively few. In fact, the risk of mortality from acute diseases has been reduced by at least 99% since 1900. Contrary to popular belief, the rate of acute disease actually drops across adulthood, as the immune system cumulatively builds defenses against invading organisms.

This means that during the 20th century we fundamentally changed our concepts of health and illness and how they relate to age. Now when we think of these connections, we focus on chronic conditions such as cardiovascular disease, cancer, and the like. Chronic conditions have a slower onset than acute diseases, but last much longer. They include progressive diseases and sensory or structural abnormalities, and their onset is usually in middle or old age. Some of the more common chronic conditions include: arthritis, ischemic heart disease, hypertension, Alzheimer's disease, hearing loss, vision loss, emphysema, persistent hemorrhoids, chronic back pain, and cancer. Developmental trends for chronic conditions are the opposite of those for acute diseases—the rate increases considerably with age. Indeed, many older adults who may have very low rates of acute diseases may have multiple chronic conditions.

The emergence of chronic conditions as a major factor in mortality in older adults has resulted in a growing emphasis on health and functioning in late life. In this section, we will examine a general theoretical model of functioning in late life, consider how chronic conditions relate to disability, and note some efforts at preventing functional decline in older adults.

A Model of Disability in Late Life

As we have noted, one of the defining characteristics of a chronic condition is that it lasts a long time. This means that for most adults, the time between the onset of a chronic condition and death is long, measured in years and even decades. Chronic diseases typically involve some level of discomfort, and physical limitations are common, everyday issues for most people. Over the course of the disease, these problems usually increase, resulting in more efforts by patients and health care workers alike to try to slow the progress of the disease. In many cases, these efforts allow people to resume such activities as daily walks and shopping and to feel optimistic about the future (Verbrugge, 1994).

In the context of chronic conditions, *disability* refers to the effects that chronic conditions have on people's ability to engage in activities that are necessary, expected, and personally desired in their society (Verbrugge, 1994). When people are disabled as a result of a chronic condition, they have difficulty doing daily tasks, such as household chores, personal care, job duties, active recreation, socializing with friends and family, doing errands, and so forth. One of the most important research efforts relating to health and aging is understanding how disability results from chronic conditions and what might be done to help prevent it.

Verbrugge and Jette (1994) have proposed an excellent and comprehensive model of disability resulting from chronic conditions, which is shown in Figure 4.3. The model consists of four main parts. The main pathway is an adaptation of frameworks proposed by the World Health Organization (1980) and the U.S. Academy of Science's Institute of Medicine (Pope & Tarlov, 1991), both of which were based on work by the sociologist Saad Nagi (1965, 1991). This pathway emphasizes the relations among *pathology* (the chronic conditions a person has), *impairments* of organ systems (such as muscular degeneration), *functional limitations* in the ability to perform activities (such as restrictions in one's mobility), and *disability*.

The model also includes *risk factors* and two types of intervention strategies: environmental and health care *(extra-individual factors)* and behavioral and personality *(intra-individual factors)*. Risk factors refer to long-standing behaviors or conditions that increase one's chances of functional limitation or disability. Examples of risk factors include low socioeconomic status, chronic health conditions, and health behaviors such as smoking. Extra-individual factors include interventions such as surgery, medication, social support services (e.g., meals-on-wheels), and physical environmental supports (e.g., ramps for a wheelchair). The presence of these factors often helps people maintain their independence and may make the difference between living at home and living in

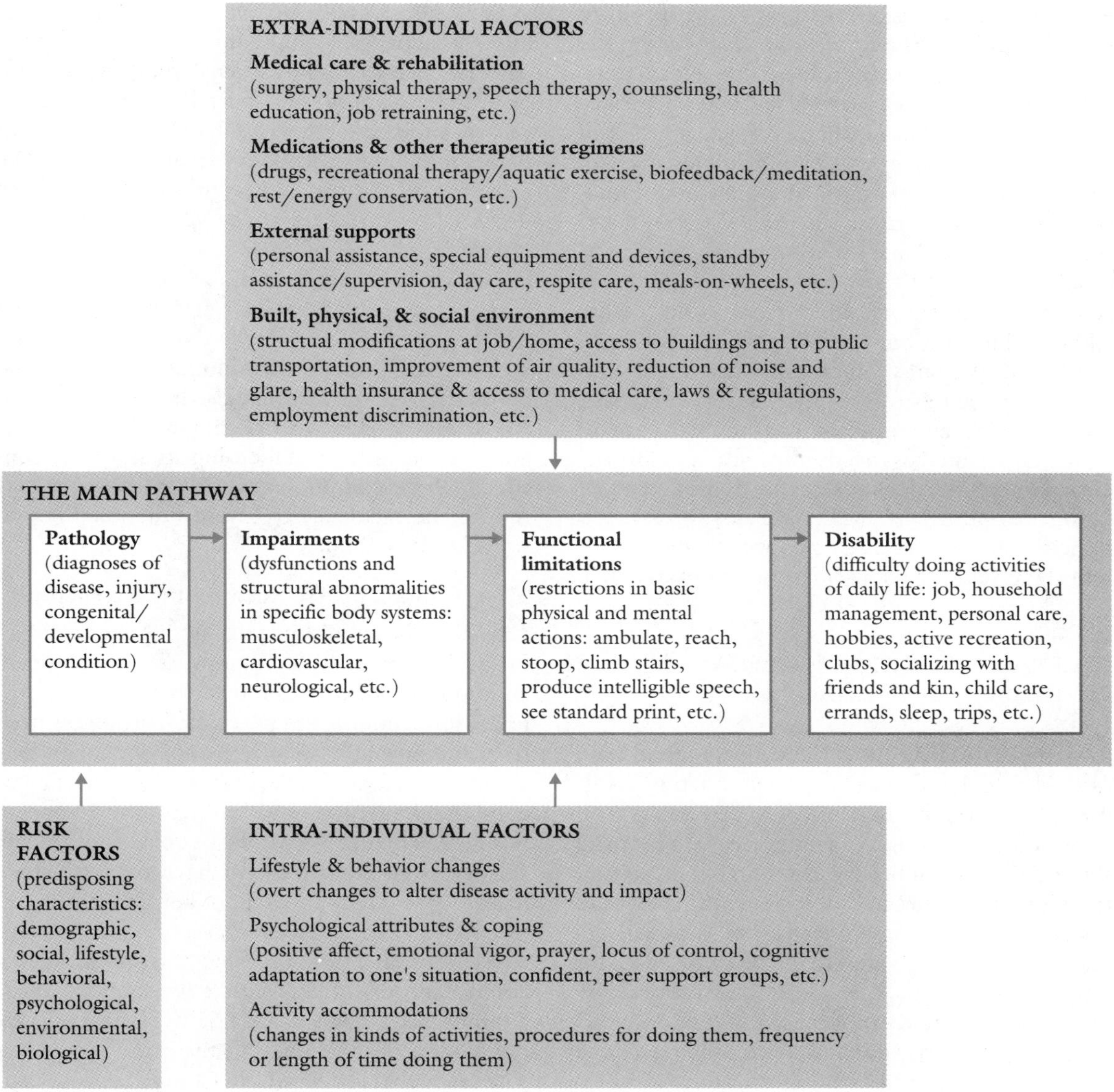

EXTRA-INDIVIDUAL FACTORS

Medical care & rehabilitation
(surgery, physical therapy, speech therapy, counseling, health education, job retraining, etc.)

Medications & other therapeutic regimens
(drugs, recreational therapy/aquatic exercise, biofeedback/meditation, rest/energy conservation, etc.)

External supports
(personal assistance, special equipment and devices, standby assistance/supervision, day care, respite care, meals-on-wheels, etc.)

Built, physical, & social environment
(structural modifications at job/home, access to buildings and to public transportation, improvement of air quality, reduction of noise and glare, health insurance & access to medical care, laws & regulations, employment discrimination, etc.)

↓

THE MAIN PATHWAY

Pathology (diagnoses of disease, injury, congenital/developmental condition) → **Impairments** (dysfunctions and structural abnormalities in specific body systems: musculoskeletal, cardiovascular, neurological, etc.) → **Functional limitations** (restrictions in basic physical and mental actions: ambulate, reach, stoop, climb stairs, produce intelligible speech, see standard print, etc.) → **Disability** (difficulty doing activities of daily life: job, household management, personal care, hobbies, active recreation, clubs, socializing with friends and kin, child care, errands, sleep, trips, etc.)

↑

RISK FACTORS
(predisposing characteristics: demographic, social, lifestyle, behavioral, psychological, environmental, biological)

↑

INTRA-INDIVIDUAL FACTORS

Lifestyle & behavior changes
(overt changes to alter disease activity and impact)

Psychological attributes & coping
(positive affect, emotional vigor, prayer, locus of control, cognitive adaptation to one's situation, confident, peer support groups, etc.)

Activity accommodations
(changes in kinds of activities, procedures for doing them, frequency or length of time doing them)

Figure 4.3 A model of the disablement process.
Source: Verbrugge and Jette, 1994

a long-term care facility. Intra-individual factors include such things as beginning an exercise program, keeping a positive outlook, and taking advantage of transportation programs to increase mobility.

Both extra-individual and intra-individual interventions are aimed at reducing the restrictions and difficulties resulting from chronic conditions. Unfortunately, sometimes they do not work as intended and may even create problems of their own.

For example, a prescribed medication may produce negative side effects that, instead of alleviating the condition, creates a new problem that in turn must be dealt with. Or social service agencies may have inflexible policies about when a particular program is available, which may make it difficult for a person who needs the program to participate in it. Situations such as these are termed *exacerbators* because they make the original situation worse than it was originally. Though they may be unintended, the results of exacerbators can be serious and require additional forms of intervention.

One of the most important aspects of Verbrugge and Jette's (1994) model is the emphasis on the fit between the person and the environment. When a person has needs that are met by the environment, the person's quality of life and adaptation are optimal. We will take a close look at this principle in Chapter 12, when we examine theoretical models of person-environment fit in detail.

What Causes Functional Limitations and Disability in Older Adults?

As you were reading about the Verbrugge and Jette (1994) model, you may have been thinking about various conditions that affect older adults you know. If you and your classmates created a list of all the conditions you believe cause functional limitations and disabilities in older adults, the list would undoubtedly be long. Indeed, over the years researchers have discovered the same thing and have reported numerous conditions that cause these problems (Boult, Kane, Louis, Boult, & McCaffrey, 1994). But by strategically combining a large representative sample with sophisticated statistical analyses, this list can be considerably shortened. If these steps are taken, what conditions best predict future problems in functioning?

One answer to this question comes from Boult et al. (1994) research, which was designed to identify chronic medical conditions that result in the development of severe functional limitations. They studied nearly 7,000 noninstitutionalized people over age 70 living in the United States at two points in time (1984 and 1988). At each point in time they classified people as being functionally intact, functionally limited due to their inability to perform at least one of seven target activities, or deceased. An important aspect of this investigation was that the researchers took exercise habits and demographic, socioeconomic, and psychosocial factors into account. Although the study was not designed as a direct test of the Verbrugge and Jette (1994) model, all of these factors are considered important in it. Boult et al. (1994) reported that two chronic conditions were strong predictors of functional limitations: cerebrovascular disease and arthritis. Additionally, the findings suggested that coronary artery disease may also be a predictor, but the statistical evidence for this was weaker. The authors concluded that focusing attention on identifying these conditions as early as possible may reduce the incidence of severe functional limitations in older adults.

How Important Are Socioeconomic Factors?

Once specific conditions that are highly predictive of future functional limitations can be identified, an important next question is whether the appropriate intervention and prevention programs need to be targeted at particular groups of people. One could argue, for example, that incidence of chronic conditions might vary as a function of socioeconomic level; that is, would people who are, on average, well educated and have relatively high incomes have the same rate of key chronic conditions as people in lower socioeconomic groups?

Reed et al. (1995) tackled this question in a comparison of roughly 2,000 residents of Marin County, California, over age 65 with the total U.S. population of individuals in the same age group. The researchers chose Marin County because of its status as the most affluent in California, and because residents there could be viewed as a model of a healthy community environment. Their findings came as a surprise. Not surprisingly, residents of Marin County lived on average longer than the typical American. However, despite their privileged status, the Marin Countians had the same prevalence of disease and disability as the U.S. population at large.

The implications of these findings, if further

research substantiates them, are sobering. Because of their longer average longevity, people from affluent communities can expect to spend a longer period of their later lives living with disabilities and in need of medical care (Reed et al., 1995). This would be especially true for women, due to their already greater average longevity. Chronic conditions do not appear to be postponed in affluent individuals; indeed, there may be a price to pay in terms of living with disabilities for a longer period of time.

Do Gender and Ethnicity Matter?

Throughout this and previous chapters, we have encountered important differences between men and women, and among various ethnic groups. Thus, one might expect that we would have considerable evidence on such differences in the area of health, especially in view of the discussion of them concerning average mortality earlier in this chapter. Unfortunately, this is not the case, particularly when it comes to cross-cultural comparisons involving developing countries that focus on adults' abilities to perform routine tasks, an important component in the model of health we examined earlier in this section.

In one of the few studies in this area, Rahman, Strauss, Gertler, Ashley, and Fox (1994) compared representative samples of men and women in the United States, Jamaica, Malaysia, and Bangladesh. In making their comparisons, Rahman et al. made corrections for gender differences in mortality and socioeconomic differences. Two of their findings, shown in Figure 4.4, are noteworthy. First, women's self-reported health was worse in all of the countries studied. Second, self-reported health problems were much more prevalent in the developing countries than they were in the United States.

Rahman et al.'s (1994) findings indicate that gender makes a difference in health and that the differences between men and women hold up across selected cultures. Of additional concern to researchers is whether ethnic groups differ from each other as well.

In a large study of over 5,100 older African American and European American men and women, Johnson and Wolinsky (1994) used the concepts of pathology, functional limitation, and disability to predict people's perceived health. Several of their findings are important. First, they discovered that the components of some scales used to measure such things as ability to care for oneself had different measurement properties for each group (e.g., African American men vs. women, European American men vs. women, African Americans vs. European Americans). This means that the scales may be measuring different things in different groups, making it very difficult to generalize findings from one group to another. Other scales (e.g., lower body disabilities) were equally valid across ethnic groups.

Second, Johnson and Wolinsky found several gender differences, especially in the European American group. For both ethnic groups, women's perceived health status was predicted by both the ability to perform several basic functions (e.g., personal care) and disability involving body mobility, whereas men's perceived health status was predicted mainly by ability to perform basic functions. In the European American group, ability to perform complex daily tasks, such as managing money, were more predictive of men's than of women's perceived health status.

Rahman et al.'s (1994) cross-cultural findings and Johnson and Wolinsky's (1994) results point to important gender, ethnic, and cultural differences in health, as well as in which specific aspects of chronic conditions, functional limitations, and disabilities predict what people perceive their health status to be. Such differences need to be taken into account in designing intervention programs; a one-size-fits-all approach will not be equally successful across these different groups of people. In the next section, we will explore different types of preventive interventions in more detail.

Issues in Prevention

As we have seen, Verbrugge and Jette's (1994) theoretical model offers a comprehensive account of disability resulting from chronic conditions and

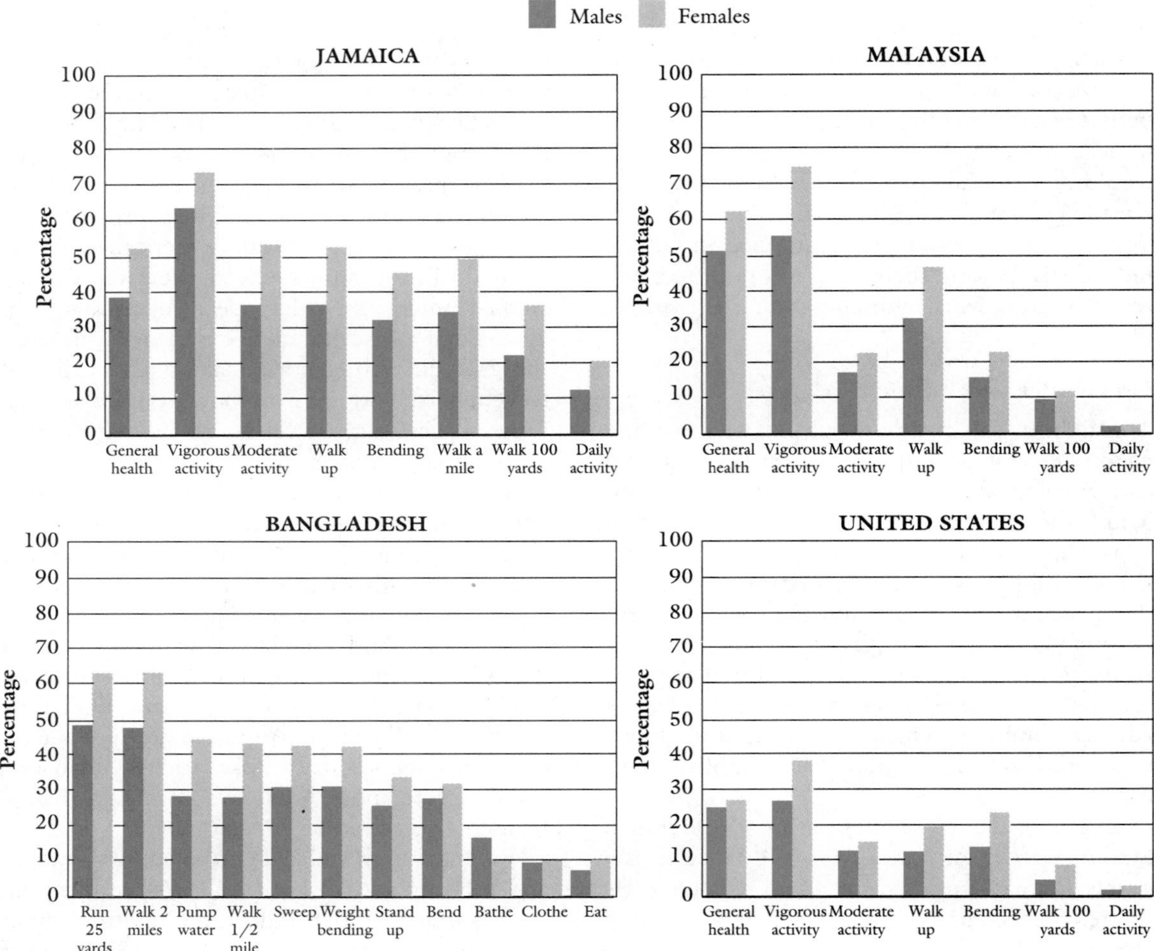

Figure 4.4 Percentage of men and women reporting difficulties in performing activities, in four countries.
Source: Rahman et al., 1994

provides considerable guidance for research. Another benefit of the model is that it also provides insight into ways to intervene so that disability might be prevented or its progress slowed. Prevention efforts can be implemented in many ways, from developing vaccines that immunize people against certain diseases to programs that transport people to supermarkets so that otherwise home-bound people can do their grocery shopping (German, 1995).

Traditionally, three types of prevention have been discussed: primary, secondary, and tertiary; more recently, the concept of quaternary prevention has been added (Verbrugge, 1994). ***Primary prevention* is any intervention that prevents a disease or condition from occurring.** Examples of primary prevention include immunizations against illnesses such as polio and influenza or controlling risk factors such as serum cholesterol levels and cigarette smoking in healthy individuals.

Secondary prevention **is instituted early after a condition has begun (but may not yet have been diagnosed) and before significant impairments have occurred.** Examples of secondary intervention include cancer and cardiovascular disease screening, as well as routine medical testing for other conditions. These steps help reduce the severity of the condition and may even reduce mortality from it. In terms of the main pathway in Verbrugge and Jette's (1994) model, secondary prevention occurs between pathology and impairments. ***Tertiary prevention*** **involves efforts to avoid the development of complications or secondary chronic conditions, managing the pain associated with the primary chronic condition, and sustaining life through medical intervention.** Some chronic conditions have a high risk of creating additional medical problems; for example, being bedridden as a result of a chronic disease is often associated with getting pneumonia. Tertiary prevention involves taking steps such as sitting the person up in bed to lower the risk of contracting additional diseases. In terms of the model, tertiary interventions are aimed at minimizing functional limitations and disability.

Historically, tertiary prevention efforts have not focused on functioning, but rather on avoiding additional medical conditions and on sustaining life (Verbrugge, 1994). Consequently, the notion of quaternary prevention has been developed to address functional issues. ***Quaternary prevention*** **refers to efforts specifically aimed at improving the functional capacities of people who have chronic conditions.** Like tertiary prevention, quaternary prevention focuses on the functional limitations and disability components of the model. Some examples of quaternary prevention are cognitive interventions to help people with Alzheimer's disease remember things or occupational therapy to help people maintain their independence.

Although prevention has a long and well-documented history with younger and middle-aged adults, it is a relatively new approach with older adults (German, 1995). Although most of the efforts with older adults to date have focused on primary prevention, increasing attention is being paid to secondary prevention through screening for early diagnosis of potential diseases such as cancer and cardiovascular disease. Consequently, few systematic studies of the benefits and outcomes of tertiary and quaternary prevention efforts have been done (German, 1995). Part of the reason for this is that older adults who have chronic conditions may perceive that tertiary and quaternary prevention programs are intended for younger adults and not participate in them (German, 1995). However, the numbers of such programs being conducted in local senior centers and other settings attractive to older adults is steadily increasing, which hopefully will result in higher participation rates. The stakes are high. Because tertiary and quaternary prevention programs are aimed at maintaining functional abilities and minimizing disability, the potential exists for effective, lower cost alternatives for addressing the needs of older adults with chronic conditions (German, 1995). With the information you gain from the Discovering Development exercise, you will be able to examine these trends in your own area.

Using Medication

One of the most important health issues for older adults is the use of both prescription and over-the-counter medications. In fact, older adults take roughly half of all drugs prescribed in the United States, and over one third take at least three prescribed drugs (Park, Morrell, Frieske, & Kincaid, 1992). When over-the-counter drugs are considered as well, most older adults take several medications every day. Most of these drugs are taken to relieve pain or related problems resulting from chronic conditions.

Because of their high rate of medication, older adults are also the group with the highest risk of adverse drug effects (Kane, Hasher, Stoltzfus, Zacks, & Connelly, 1994). These problems result from two major age-related changes. First, the physiological changes that occur with age change the way in which drugs are absorbed into the body, how long they remain, and how well they work. For example, changes in the stomach may slow

DISCOVERING DEVELOPMENT

The Changing Approach to Prevention

In our consideration of the four types of prevention, we noted that primary and secondary prevention typically receive more attention than either tertiary or quaternary prevention. This is especially true as health care in the United States and other countries moves more to a managed care approach built on health maintenance organizations (HMOs) that place more emphasis on avoiding disease. Under many of these models, health insurance will cover the costs of medical screening tests associated with primary and secondary prevention, but may not fully cover the need for rehabilitation or home care needed in tertiary or quaternary prevention to avoid the development of secondary problems.

Is this true for programs in your area? To find out, contact a local senior center and local HMOs to find out what types of prevention efforts for older adults are covered. Also inquire about how the coverage has changed (or not) over the past few years. Additionally, find out what programs may be available for individuals who can afford to pay. If you are employed, you may want to check into your own health care plan.

Share what you learn in class, and consider whether you think this approach is appropriate. This discussion will place you in the same position as legislators who need to evaluate and monitor publicly supported health care programs and balance the needs versus the costs.

---

down the rate at which drugs enter the body, meaning that achieving the effective level of the drug in the body may take longer to occur. Changes in liver and kidney functioning affect how rapidly the drug is removed and excreted from the body, meaning that levels of the drug may remain high for longer periods of time.

Second, age-related increases in the frequency of chronic conditions means that older adults are likely to have more than one medical problem for which medications are taken. **Treating multiple conditions results in *polypharmacy,* the use of multiple medications.** Polypharmacy is problematic, because many drugs do not interact well; the action of some drugs is enhanced when used in combination with others, whereas other drugs may not work at all compared to when they are used alone. Drug interaction effects can be serious. For example, they may create secondary medical problems that in turn need to be treated, and the primary condition may not be treated as effectively. Moreover, drug interaction effects can produce symptoms that appear to be caused by other diseases; in some cases they may cause confusion and memory loss that mimics Alzheimer's disease. Thus, including an analysis of a person's medication regimen, including both prescription and over-the-counter medications, is important indiagnosing health problems.

Given the high level of medication use among older adults, what can be done to minimize drug interaction effects? Physicians play a key role, but other health care professionals must also be alert, as older adults typically go to more than one physician. Accurate medication histories including all types of medicines are essential. Inappropriate use of drugs, such as antipsychotics to control behavior, must also be monitored.

The likelihood of adverse drug reactions increases as the number of medications increases. Taking more drugs also means that keeping track of each becomes more difficult. (Imagine if you had to keep track of six different medications, each of which has a different schedule.) Medication adherence (taking medications correctly) becomes less likely the more drugs people take and the more complicated each of the instructions are. Combined with sensory, physical, and cognitive changes in older adults, medication adherence is a significant problem in this age group (Park et al., 1992). The oldest old are especially at risk; the most common problem is that they simply forget to take the medication. Park et al. (1992) suggest using a grid type pillbox that has seven rows divided into several separate compartments corresponding to various times each day as a way to make it easier for people to remember which drugs to take.

The best approach, of course, is to keep the number of medications to a minimum (Monane, Gurwitz, & Avorn, 1993). If the use of drugs is determined to be essential, then periodic reevaluations should be conducted, and the medication discontinued when possible. Additionally, the lowest effective dosage should be used. In general, the use of medications with older adults should get the same careful consideration as with any other age group.

Concept Checks

1. What factors should be included in a model of adults' health?
2. What are the primary causes of disability in older adults?
3. What are the four major types of prevention?
4. What are some of the problems associated with medication use in older adults?

SUMMARY

How Long Will We Live?

Average and Maximum Longevity

Average longevity refers to the age at which half of the people born in a particular year will have died; maximum longevity refers to the longest time a member of a species lives. Average longevity increased dramatically in the first half of the 20th century, but maximum longevity remains at about 120 years. This increase was due mainly to the elimination of many diseases and a reduction in deaths during childbirth.

Genetic and Environmental Factors in Longevity

Having long- or short-lived parents is a good predictor of your own longevity (not counting accidents, of course). Living in a polluted environment can dramatically shorten longevity; being in a committed relationship lengthens it. Environmental effects need to be considered in combination.

Ethnic Differences in Average Longevity

Different ethnic groups in the United States have different average longevity. However, these differences are primarily due to differences in nutrition, health care, stress, and financial status. In late life, people in some ethnic minority groups live longer than European Americans.

Gender Differences in Average Longevity

Women tend to live longer than men, partly because males are more susceptible to disease and environmental influences. Numerous hypotheses have been offered for this difference, but none have been strongly supported.

Stress and Health

The Stress and Coping Paradigm

According to Lazarus, stress results from a perception of an event as taxing or exceeding one's resources and as endangering one's well-being. Primary and secondary appraisal involve making a decision about whether an event is stressful. Coping involves trying to do something about the stressful event; for example, some people try to change the event itself, whereas others focus more on their feelings about the event. The kinds of events that are stressful and the types of coping strategies people use differ with age.

Stress and Physical Illness

Stress lowers the immune system's ability to fight infection. Stress is believed to have a causal role in some types of headaches and cardiovascular disease, among others. Type A behavior pattern is associated with higher risk of first heart attack but with lower risk of subsequent heart attacks than Type B behavior pattern.

Stress and Psychological Functioning

Although stress is not directly related to psychopathology, it is related to certain behaviors such as social isolation. Stressors fluctuate in importance across adulthood.

Managing Stress

Several approaches to stress management are effective, including relaxation, biofeedback, stress inoculation, and pet ownership. Changing one's appraisal of the situation may also be an effective way to manage stress.

Health and Lifestyle

Smoking

Having people stop smoking would have a bigger impact on overall health than any other single step. Smoking cigarettes causes several health problems: cancer, emphysema, cardiovascular disease, and low birth weight babies. Breathing secondhand smoke can cause the same diseases as smoking. Pregnant women and spouses of smokers are especially susceptible to the effects of secondhand smoke. Most people who want to quit smoking need multiple attempts before they are successful. No one formal program is superior; most people quit on their own. Stopping smoking eventually allows one's risk of certain diseases to return to normal in most cases.

Drinking Alcohol

Alcohol abuse refers to drinking until one causes physical, psychological, or social harm; alcohol dependence refers to a severe form of abuse characterized by habitual drinking and other symptoms associated with addiction. Alcohol consumption peaks in middle age, but the incidence of alcohol dependence remains constant across adulthood. Gender bias is present in diagnosing alcohol dependence. The primary direct effect of long-term chronic alcohol dependence is liver damage. One serious indirect effect is Wernicke-Korsakoff syndrome, which is caused by a vitamin deficiency. The syndrome is a severe brain disorder affecting memory and awareness. Older adults are more affected than younger adults by the same amount of alcohol. Moderate drinking is associated with longer average longevity than abstinence or heavy drinking. Why this relation holds is unknown. Several methods are available to help people stop drinking: Alcoholics Anonymous (AA), psychotherapy, and treatment centers. Little is known about the relative effectiveness of these various programs, however.

Exercise

Aerobic exercise maintains a pulse rate between 60% and 90% of maximum; nonaerobic exercise does not. Aerobic exercise has several benefits, even for older adults: improved physiological functioning and lower stress. Moderate levels of exercise are more beneficial than high levels. Low motivation to exercise is a major barrier to participation in adults.

Sleep

Nearly half of older adults experience occasional insomnia. Waking up during the night is the most common age-related change. Slight changes in REM sleep also occur with age. The negative effects of sleep loss increase with age. Physical illness, sleep apnea, medications, alcohol, caffeine, nicotine, and stress can each cause problems with sleep. The bed should be used only for sleeping and not for reading, watching television, and the like. Afternoon and evening naps can disrupt that night's sleep. Stimulus-control instructions help insomniacs acquire consistent sleeping habits and help them associate the bed with sleeping only. Progressive relaxation involves a systematic program of steps to get a person to relax and fall asleep.

Nutrition

Needs for vitamins, minerals, and protein do not change across adulthood. Older adults need fewer carbohydrates. Eating high quantities of saturated fat is associated with atherosclerosis; eating lots of sodium is associated with hypertension. Eating foods high in saturated fat, sodium, and nitrites may cause cancers of the breast, colon, and prostate. High-fiber diets and foods containing vitamin A may lower the cancer risk. Obtaining enough calcium and vitamin D possibly could help prevent osteoporosis.

Cancer

Cancer Risk and Age

The risk of getting cancer increases markedly with age. The most common form of cancer is lung cancer. Lung cancer kills nearly twice as many people as any other form. The next most deadly are breast, prostate, and colorectal. Genetic links are being discovered for several types of cancer.

Screening and Prevention

There are several simple tests to detect cancer that should be taken regularly. Lifestyle changes are the best way to prevent cancer. However, there is controversy surrounding some screening procedures, such as for prostate cancer.

Health, Functioning, and Prevention

A Model of Disability in Late Life

Disability refers to the effects that chronic conditions have on people's ability to engage in activities in daily life. A model of disability includes pathology, impairments, functional limitations, disability, risk factors, extra-individual factors, and intra-individual factors. This model includes all of the four main developmental forces.

What Causes Functional Limitations and Disability in Older Adults?

The chronic conditions that best predict future disability are arthritis and cerebrovascular disease. Being wealthy helps increase average longevity, but does not protect one from developing chronic conditions, meaning that such people may experience longer periods of disability late in life. Women's health is generally poorer across cultures, especially in developing countries. Ethnic group differences are also important. Validity of measures of functioning sometimes differ across ethnicity and gender.

Issues in Prevention

There are four basic types of prevention: primary, secondary, tertiary, and quaternary. Most emphasis has been on primary and secondary. Less is known about prevention with older adults than for other age groups.

Using Medication

Older adults typically use multiple prescription and over-the-counter medications, termed polypharmacy. Physiological changes with age and drug interaction effects alter the effectiveness of medications. Drug interactions may cause additional medical problems and may mimic other conditions. Medication adherence is a problem, especially among the oldest old.

REVIEW QUESTIONS

How long will we live?

- What is the difference between average longevity and maximum longevity?
- What genetic and environmental factors influence average longevity?
- What ethnic and gender differences have been found?

Stress and health

- Describe what stress is in the stress and coping paradigm. What is the appraisal process? What is meant by coping?
- What are the major physical health consequences of stress?
- What are Type A and Type B behavior patterns? What is the controversy associated with them?
- What can be done to lower stress?

Health and lifestyle

- What are the health risks from smoking?
- What happens from extended exposure to secondhand smoke?
- How can people stop smoking?
- What is the difference between alcohol abuse and alcohol dependence?
- How does alcohol consumption vary with age?
- What happens to the rate of alcohol dependence with age?
- What are the negative effects of drinking?
- What benefits of moderate drinking have been noted?
- How can people stop drinking?
- What is the difference between aerobic and nonaerobic exercise?

- What are the benefits of aerobic exercise?
- Why don't older people exercise as much as they should?
- How does sleep change with age?
- What can cause sleep problems? How do these causes change with age?
- What are some ways to improve the quality of your sleep?
- How do nutritional needs change with age?
- What problems can result from a poor diet?

Cancer

- How does the risk of getting cancer vary with age?
- What are some of the known causes of lung and colon cancer?
- How can one prevent cancer?
- What is the controversy concerning prostate cancer?

Health, functioning, and prevention

- What is meant by disability?
- What are the key components in a model of disability in older adults?
- What conditions result in disability most often?
- How do socioeconomic status, ethnicity, and gender affect health and disability?
- What are the major types of prevention? How do they relate to the model of disability?
- What are the major problems associated with medications in older adults?

INTEGRATING CONCEPTS IN DEVELOPMENT

1. What physiological changes described in Chapter 3 are important in understanding health?
2. Based on information in Chapters 3 and 4, how might a primary prevention program be designed to avoid cardiovascular disease?
3. How do the ethnic differences in average longevity and in health relate to the diversity issues we examined in Chapter 2?
4. What physiological changes would be important to keep in mind in designing tertiary and quaternary prevention programs?

KEY TERMS

addiction A disease in which one develops a physiological need for a particular substance, such as drugs and alcohol.

aerobic exercise A form of exercise in which the pulse rate is 60% to 90% of the maximum, high enough so that the cardiovascular system benefits.

alcohol abuse Consuming enough alcohol to cause physical, psychological, or social harm.

alcohol dependence A more severe form of alcohol abuse characterized by drinking behavior that becomes habitual and takes priority over other activities, increased tolerance of alcohol, repeated withdrawal symptoms that are relieved by further drinking, an awareness of feeling compelled to drink, and a reinstatement of this drinking pattern after abstinence.

average longevity The length of time it takes for half of all individuals born in a certain year to die.

coping In the stress and coping paradigm, a complex, evolving process of dealing with stress that is learned.

disability The effects that chronic conditions have on people's ability to engage in activities that are necessary, expected, and personally desired in their society.

maximum longevity The maximum length of time an organism can live, roughly 120 years for humans.

nonaerobic exercise Exercise during which the heart rate does not exceed 60% of the maximum for sustained periods.

polypharmacy The use of multiple medications.

primary appraisal In the stress and coping paradigm, the process in which events are categorized into three groups based on the significance they have for well-being: irrelevant, benign-positive, or stressful.

primary prevention Any intervention that prevents a disease or condition from occurring.

quaternary prevention Efforts specifically aimed at improving the functional capacities of people with chronic conditions.

reappraisal In the stress and coping paradigm,

making a new primary or secondary appraisal resulting from changes in the situation.

secondary appraisal In the stress and coping paradigm, the perceived ability to cope with harm, threat, or challenge.

secondary prevention Interventions instituted early after a condition has begun (but may have not yet been diagnosed) and before significant impairments have occurred.

stress and coping paradigm An approach to stress emphasizing that it is people's perceptions of events rather than the events themselves that cause stress.

tertiary prevention Efforts to avoid the development of complications or secondary chronic conditions, managing the pain associated with the primary chronic condition, and sustaining life through medical intervention.

type A behavior pattern Behavior reflecting excessive competitiveness, time urgency, hostility, and aggressiveness.

type B behavior pattern Behavior reflecting relaxed, less preoccupied lifestyle in the absence of Type A behavior pattern.

Wernicke-Korsakoff syndrome A result of long-term chronic thiamine deficiency associated with chronic alcohol dependence that causes severe memory loss.

IF YOU'D LIKE TO LEARN MORE

Numerous well-written pamphlets on smoking, diet, and cancer can be obtained from your local chapter of the American Cancer Society. These pamphlets are easy to read, yet provide up-to-date information on technical topics.

Bond, L. A., Cutler, S. J., & Grams, A. (1995). *Promoting successful and productive aging*. Thousand Oaks, CA: Sage Publications. An excellent overview of research and theory on health promotion. Moderately difficult reading.

Kane, R. L., Evans, J. G., & Macfadyen, D. (1990). *Improving the health of older people: A world view*. Oxford, England: Oxford University Press. Presents a readable description of international perspectives on health promotion and aging. One of the few works in this area.

Kane, R. L., Ouslander, J. G., & Abrass, I. B. (1994). *Essentials of clinical geriatrics* (3rd ed.). New York: McGraw-Hill. A very comprehensive coverage of the complete range of topics in health and aging. Moderate difficulty, but it helps to have a working knowledge of anatomy and medicine.

Lieberman, F., & Collen, M. F. (1993). *Aging in good health: A quality lifestyle for the later years*. New York: Plenum.

CHAPTER 5

Information Processing

M. C. Escher, *Hand with Reflecting Sphere*, 1935.

Imagine that one day, just for the fun of it, you stroll into a Lamborghini dealership and are successful at getting the salesperson to let you take a Countach for a spin around the block. When you climb behind the wheel of the most expensive sports car you've ever seen in your life, your excitement almost gets the better of you. But as you start it up and ease into first gear, you are filled with utter terror. You suddenly realize that you must pay complete attention to what you're doing. After all, you wouldn't want to have an accident, would you? Now you are faced with the need to filter out everything—people's conversations, the radio, the sound of the wind whipping through your hair. How can you do it? More importantly, what abilities can you use to avoid an accident? If something happened on the road, how quickly could you respond? Would these abilities be any different in a younger adult than in an older adult? And, by the way, did you know that a Lamborghini Countach was a sports car before you read this? If so, how did you access this knowledge? If not, how did you incorporate this new knowledge?

These are the kinds of questions we will face in this chapter. This chapter begins a three-chapter sequence on cognition. In general, we will be examining how people process information from the world around them and make sense out of it. Although this material can be approached in several different ways, we will adopt the one that builds upward from basic processes, such as attention, through more complex ones, such as memory, to higher order thought. This "from-the-ground-up" approach should be viewed in context, though. Cognition is a highly dynamic thing; lower order processes such as attention help create higher order thought, and higher order thought helps determine where we focus our lower order processes. We need to notice things in order to build our knowledge, but what we know shapes what we notice.

In this chapter, we will see how people pay attention to things, and what paying attention consists of. We will consider researchers' studies of how fast people react to events, such as a car pulling into their lane on the highway. We will see how attention and other aspects of information processing are extremely important in understanding how accidents occur. Finally, we will consider some basic aspects of language processing. The remaining two chapters in the cognitive section will cover many aspects of memory (Chapter 6) and intelligence (Chapter 7). Together, these three chapters provide a broad view of cognition.

Research on how people process, store, and remember information, as well as how they think, tends to involve highly technical research methods and concepts. This means that we will need to consider research studies in more detail to understand and appreciate the findings. Another problem is that although we will begin our consideration of cognition with a prominent theoretical model, much of the research in the field makes only indirect contact with it. That is, much research on cognition and aging is conducted without an explicit connection to a specific theoretical framework. Nevertheless, a great deal of evidence has been amassed, some of it apparently contradictory, but all of it providing insight into how cognition works. Once all of the pieces have been considered, we will have a fairly detailed picture of how adults acquire, process, remember, and think.

Throughout this chapter, we will be considering results from experiments in which people made responses on computers. Although there is substantial evidence for age differences in some of the ways younger and older adults process information, part of the difference may be due to cohort effects. Specifically, older adults in general are much less used to working on computers than are younger adults, making the task relatively unfamiliar to older adults. Consequently, they may not perform up to their maximum. Whether this experiential difference accounts for much or only a small amount of the age differences researchers have uncovered remains to be seen; however, given that the research is cross-sectional, meaning that age and cohort effects are confounded, this explanation remains a possibility.

THE INFORMATION-PROCESSING MODEL

Learning Objectives:

- What are the primary aspects of the information-processing model?
- What evidence exists for age differences in early aspects of information processing?

How do we learn, remember, and think about things? Psychologists do not know for sure. About the best they can do is create models or analogues of how they believe our cognitive processes work. In this section, we will consider the most popular model—the information-processing model.

Overview of the Model

The information-processing model uses a computer metaphor to explain how people process stimuli. Just as with a computer, information enters the system (people's brains) and is transformed, coded, and stored in various ways. Information enters storage temporarily, as in a computer's buffer, until it is sometimes stored more permanently, as on a computer disk. At a later time, information can be retrieved in response to some cue, such as a command to retrieve a file. Let's see how this works more formally.

The *information-processing approach* is based on three assumptions (Neisser, 1976): (1) People are active participants in the process; (2) both quantitative (how much information is remembered) and qualitative (what kinds of information are remembered) aspects of performance can be examined; and (3) information is processed through a series of hypothetical stages, or stores. First, incoming information is transformed based on such things as what a person already knows about it. The more one knows, the more easily the information is incorporated. Second, researchers look for age differences in both how much information is processed and what types of information are remembered best under various conditions. Finally, researchers in adult development and aging focus on several specific aspects of information processing: early aspects, which include a very brief sensory memory; attention; psychomotor speed; a limited capacity primary memory (Poon, 1985); active processing of information in working memory (Hultsch & Dixon, 1990); a somewhat longer term but limited capacity secondary memory; and a relatively permanent and very large capacity tertiary memory (Poon, 1985).

Using the information-processing model poses three fundamental questions for adult development and aging: (1) Is there evidence of age differences in the storage aspects of information processing (e.g., early stages of processing, secondary memory, tertiary memory)? (2) What evidence is there for age differences in the process aspects of information processing (e.g., attention)? (3) Can the age differences in the storage aspects be explained through process aspects?

It will take us two chapters to answer these questions. In Chapter 5, we will focus on early aspects of processing, on attention, and on psychomotor speed and language processing. In Chapter 6, we will consider working memory, secondary memory, and tertiary memory, as well as address the reasons for age differences later in the system. By the end of these chapters, we will have a relatively complete picture of how we will have acquired, processed, stored, and be able to remember the information in these chapters.

Before we begin, we must place information processing in the broader perspective of the four basic forces in development. In Chapter 1, we saw that one of these was psychological forces, including sensory-perceptual functioning, motor functioning, and intellectual functioning. The information-processing model provides a fuller description of these and specifies the ways in which they operate. The information-processing model emphasizes the complexity of human thinking and the need to be aware of a vast array of influences on performance. We must also place all of these influences into larger contexts; biological forces such as changes in the brain, for example, could dramatically alter the effects of any particular influence. Life-cycle factors, such as why adults of different ages interpret instances of forgetting differently, may also influence how well people remember.

Among other important considerations for information processing are normative and disease-related biological, physiological, and lifestyle issues. For example, underlying neural changes, cardiovascular disease, Alzheimer's disease, and severe depression can all affect information-processing abilities as we age. These effects must be kept in mind as we examine the evidence for age differences in information processing. Although most of the research we will consider was conducted on apparently healthy people, our knowledge of the relation between normative changes in the brain and performance on information-processing tasks is still limited.

Early Aspects of Information Processing

All memories start as sensory stimuli—a song heard, a person seen, a hand felt. We need to experience these things for only a small fraction of a second in order to process the information. **This ability is due to the earliest step in information processing, *sensory memory,* where new, incoming information is first registered.** Sensory memory takes in very large amounts of information very rapidly. However, unless we pay attention to this information very quickly, it will be lost. For example, try drawing either side of a U.S. penny in detail. (Those who are not from the United States can try drawing a common coin in their own country.) Most of us find this task difficult despite seeing the coins every day. Much detailed information about pennies has passed through our sensory memory repeatedly, but because we failed to pay attention it was never processed to a longer lasting store.

One way of studying sensory memory is to measure how fast incoming information gets into the system for subsequent processing. *Encoding speed* refers to how rapidly this storage occurs. Encoding speed has been studied extensively, with the evidence clearly documenting age-related decrements. For example, Cerella, Poon, and Fozard (1982) showed age-related slowing of encoding speed in processing individual letters. These results mean that the amount of visual information that we can handle at one time, called perceptual span, declines with age. Practically speaking, this helps explain part of the reason older adults are slower and can only deal with smaller amounts of information compared with younger adults.

A second way of studying sensory memory is to look for age differences in how quickly information can be passed from sensory memory to later steps in processing, such as working memory. One way to test this is to see how efficiently information can be retrieved from sensory memory; in this case, there are no age differences (Poon & Fozard, 1980; A. D. Smith, 1975).

However, other aspects of sensory memory, such as susceptibility to backward masking, do show age differences. *Backward masking* involves presenting a target stimulus very briefly, followed by presenting another, or masking, stimulus that diminishes the distinctiveness of the target. For example, a person might be shown a letter (the target) very rapidly, followed quickly by a set of lines (the mask), and then asked to identify the target. By varying the interval between the target and the mask, researchers obtain an estimate of the degree to which the mask disrupts processing the target. Backward masking gives an estimate of how quickly information is moved out of sensory memory. Because sensory memory is continually being bombarded with information, getting the old information out so that new information can get in is essential; otherwise, a person may not be able to pick up essential incoming information. Susceptibility to backward masking indicates that this process is not working as quickly as it might.

Numerous researchers have documented that susceptibility to backward masking increases slightly with age (Kline & Schieber, 1985). That is, the interval between the target and the mask needed for people to still be able to identify the target stimulus is slightly longer for older adults. This may not seem like much. As we will see, however, even slightly slower processing can produce important differences in performance.

Concept Checks

1. What are the three assumptions underlying the information-processing approach?
2. What is the pattern of age differences in early aspects of information processing?

ATTENTION

Learning Objectives:

- What are the major aspects of feature integration theory?
- How is selective attention tested? What age differences are found?
- What is divided attention? Under what conditions are age differences observed?
- How is sustained attention assessed? When are age differences found?
- What are automatic processes? In what situations are age differences present?

Several times during my educational career, teachers would catch me gazing out the window. "Pay attention!" they would say sternly, and then invariably call on me next. Of course, I would not know the answer. "I expect you to pay better attention to class!" would typically be their next remark.

All of us probably have had similar experiences. Someone asks us a question and we continue to stare off into space. We are driving along a long, boring stretch of interstate highway and suddenly realize we have gone 20 miles with no awareness at all of anything that we saw along the way. The examples are quite varied but the outcome is the same: Somehow we come to realize that lots of information was available to us that we never processed. In short, we simply did not pay attention.

These everyday experiences are so vivid to us that we would expect psychologists to have a clear handle on what attention is. After all, it is one of the most important ways that information continues to get processed beyond the sensory memory stage. William James's (1890) view that "we all know what attention is" reflects this belief. It turns out that vivid experiences can be misleading. Attention is actually quite difficult to pin down. About the best researchers can do is describe three interdependent aspects of it (Posner & Boies, 1971): selectivity, attentional capacity, and vigilance.

***Selectivity* refers to how we choose the information we will process further.** As the word itself implies, selectivity in attention means that our ability to process information is limited. As we saw earlier during our spin in the Lamborghini, a great deal of information bombards sensory memory: telephone poles zipping past, other cars on the highway, dashboard information, passengers' conversations, scenery outside the car. However, this information remains there for only a very brief time. The next stop, working memory, can only handle a small amount of information at a time (see Chapter 6). This creates a problem: how to get information out of a large capacity store to a very small capacity store. This situation is similar to the problem created when a large capacity freeway (say, eight lanes in one direction) must use a small capacity tunnel (two lanes in one direction). The potential traffic jam could be enormous, with many drivers simply opting to exit the freeway. The problem in the information-processing system is similar: a traffic jam of information trying to get from sensory memory to working memory. Much of it simply exits the system and is lost before it can be passed along.

Several theories have been postulated to explain where and how the bottleneck in information flow occurs. All agree that somehow information gets selected out for further processing, and that this selection is part of attention. Although no one knows for sure how selectivity happens, there are several ideas. For example, some information is simply processed automatically, whereas other information takes effort. Also, we are more likely to process novel or unexpected information than information we have encountered numerous times before.

How do researchers studying aging and cognition investigate selectivity? Most do so by focusing on one type of task: comparing visual search performance with nonsearch performance (Plude & Doussard-Roosevelt, 1990). Visual search tasks require finding a specific target among several distractor stimuli; an example would be trying to find embedded figures of objects hidden in a large scene. Researchers use a more sterile version, typically involving finding specific letters from among a larger array of other letters. Nonsearch tasks make doing the task easier; for example, visual cues are given that provide prior information about where the target will be (Plude & Hoyer, 1985).

Attentional capacity **addresses the question of how much information can be processed at any given time.** Most researchers view capacity as the pool of resources available to support information-processing activity. Underlying this idea is the key assumption that some processing occurs automatically whereas other processing requires effort. Automatic processing places minimal demands on attentional capacity. Some automatic processes appear to be "prewired" in the sense that they require no attentional capacity and do not benefit from practice; others are learned through experience and practice (Plude & Doussard-Roosevelt, 1990). In either case, information that is processed automatically gets into the system largely without us being aware of it. For example, those who have been driving a car for many years are usually unaware of how hard they are pressing the accelerator pedal to make the car go forward from a stop.

In contrast, effortful processing requires some to all of the available attentional capacity. Most of the tasks involving deliberate memory, such as learning the words on a list, require effortful processing. In these cases, we are typically aware of what we are doing; for example, when we are first learning how to drive a car with a clutch, we are very aware of the information we are processing (e.g., how much to let up on the clutch versus how hard to press the accelerator pedal). Researchers who study aging and cognition investigate both automatic processing and effortful processing, and then often look at differences in performance across the two categories.

A second way of studying attentional capacity is to look at how well people perform multiple tasks simultaneously. For example, paying attention to a lecture in class while simultaneously taking notes requires us to monitor two things (lecture content and what we are writing) simultaneously. These divided-attention and dual-task studies provide interesting information about differences and similarities across adulthood.

Vigilance **or sustained attention refers to how well one is able to maintain attention in performing a task over a long period of time.** In general, these tasks involve monitoring a display (such as a radar screen) for the appearance of targets (such as airplane blips). Fewer studies of age differences in sustained attention have been conducted than on either of the other two topics (selectivity and capacity).

Our examination of age differences in selectivity, capacity, and sustained attention will focus on visual information processing for several reasons (Plude & Doussard-Roosevelt, 1990): (1) The great majority of the research has examined visual processing; (2) the potential loss of vision is of great concern to older adults; and (3) age differences in visual processing are believed to generalize to other sensory modalities. Let's see what the findings indicate.

Feature Integration Theory

Take a moment to look carefully at a picture in your room. Now that you have done that, close your eyes and describe to yourself what you saw. Your ability to do that required two basic processes. First, you had to extract key pieces of information from the picture. Second, you had to put these pieces together to figure out what was in the picture.

Feature integration theory is a formal way of expressing our experience (Treisman & Gelade, 1980). **According to *feature integration theory (FIT)*, visual processing consists of two main steps: feature extraction and feature integration.** Feature extraction involves paying attention to what we are seeing at each point and representing each dimension (color, shape, and so on) separately. Feature integration involves putting these separate dimensions together to make sense out of the visual stimulus. A key aspect of this process is that feature extraction and feature integration operate serially; that is, we can only process one part of the stimulus at a time.

FIT raises several interesting questions about aging and attention (Plude & Doussard-Roosevelt, 1990). Are there age differences in either or both aspects of processing? Do older people differ in the amount or kind of visual information they pick up? Are there differences in how quickly adults of various ages can perform feature extraction and feature integration? How do the age differences in vision discussed in Chapter 3 affect visual information processing? These are some of the questions we will address in the next three sections.

Selective Attention

As we have seen, a small proportion of information in sensory memory gets selected for further processing. In this section we will consider evidence concerning age differences in selectivity by examining three lines of research: visual search, spatial cuing, and attention switching. To preview a bit, age-related decrements are consistently found in visual search, but spatial cuing sometimes eliminates age differences (Plude & Doussard-Roosevelt, 1990). Age differences in the ability to shift attention appears to depend on the sensory modality being tested (McDowd & Birren, 1990).

Visual Search

Imagine yourself sitting at a computer terminal. You are told to push a key as fast as you can every time you see a red X, the target stimulus. "So far, so good," you say. To make things difficult, sometimes you will see other letters or colors (green Xs, green Os, and red Os)—the nontarget stimuli. The problem is that you have no idea where in the display the target will appear, so you must search for it among the nontargets.

This procedure is typical of visual search tasks and was actually used by Plude and Doussard-Roosevelt (1989). Visual search tasks always involve responding to a specific stimulus, the *target,* and ignoring everything else, the *nontargets.* Such tasks measure attention selectivity because the main data involve *nontarget interference effects;* that is, the degree to which the nontargets interfere with the ability to respond only to targets. Usually, nontarget interference effects are a matter of *display size;* that is, how many nontargets are presented with the target. In the example above, it would be harder to find 1 red X amid 50 red Os than amid 5 red Os.

Performance on visual search tasks is measured either in terms of how quickly people respond, termed *reaction time,* or in terms of the number and kinds of errors they make. When performance data on visual search tasks are plotted as a function of display size, the slope of the linear function provides information about attention selectivity. A flat horizontal line, indicating zero slope, means perfect selectivity; nontargets never interfere with processing of the target. Positive slopes indicate some degree of nontarget interference, with higher positive slopes indicating more interference. Research consistently demonstrates that older adults show larger positive slopes than younger adults (Plude & Hoyer, 1985).

At this point we need to bring in feature integration theory. Recall that FIT has two components, feature extraction and feature integration. Problems with either component (or both) could produce increased nontarget interference, which we know is age related. Is there a way to tell which aspect of FIT is the source of the difficulty?

By using techniques like those in the example (red and green Xs and Os), Plude (1986; Plude & Doussard-Roosevelt, 1989) isolated the source as the feature integration component. Younger and older adults were equally able to extract information about the target (such as color) automatically. However, when it came time to put the pieces of information together (that is, specific letter and specific color), older adults were at a significant disadvantage. Thus, older adults are slower on visual search tasks not because they have problems picking up the separate pieces of information, but because they are slower at putting the various pieces of information together.

Spatial Cuing

Imagine sitting at the same computer terminal as before. This time, though, things are a bit easier. You are now told to watch for an asterisk that will show up somewhere on the screen; shortly after it appears, either the target or a nontarget stimulus will be displayed in exactly the same spot.

This procedure, in which the location of a future stimulus is denoted on a screen, is known as *spatial cuing.* The idea behind using spatial cuing is to rule out certain other explanations for age differences in visual search tasks. For example, older adults may decline in their ability to find the location of a target embedded among many nontargets. If this is true, telling them ahead of time where it will appear solves this problem. Any remaining age differences would be due to reasons other than the person's ability to find the target.

When the spatial cue signals that a target will appear in that location, age differences disappear (Plude & Doussard-Roosevelt, 1990). As the actual locations of the targets move away from the locations of the cues, age differences reappear (Madden, 1990). In other words, when people know where to look, older and younger adults are equally able to identify targets. Hoyer (1987) extends this point by suggesting that some people accrue considerable experience and practice at looking for targets. These "expert lookers" are able to anticipate where a target is likely to appear and may even be able to compensate for normative, age-related sensory changes. For example, highly experienced bird-watchers find their feathered friends more quickly than novice bird-watchers because they know what to look for up in the trees.

Thus, age-related differences in feature integration are due in turn to age-related decrements in spatial localization ability. However, there are important qualifications. Age differences are eliminated only when the spatial cue provides unambiguous information about the target's subsequent position. When the cue is ambiguous (for instance, several asterisks appear and only one provides accurate information), age differences remain. This may suggest that other processes, such as generalized cognitive slowing (discussed later in this chapter), are also important for understanding age decrements in visual search. Additionally, experience and practice may play a role in eliminating age differences. The more experience one has, the better one performs the task.

Attention Switching

Once again, you are back at your computer terminal. This time, however, you are asked to do two different things. Some of the time you are told to focus your attention on the center character in a five-character string, which will be the target. Let's call this the narrow attention condition. At other times, you are told to widen your attention to include all five characters. In this case, the target will be one of the peripheral characters. Let's call this the broad attention condition. Thus, the task requires you to switch your attention from one character to five characters. Hartley and McKenzie (1991) used this task to demonstrate that under some circumstances older and younger adults switch their visual attentional focus similarly.

Interestingly, Hartley and McKenzie's data do not agree with findings from research on adults' ability to switch attention on auditory tasks. For example, Braune and Wickens (1985) reported age differences in pilots' ability to switch their attention when information was presented verbally rather than visually. Several factors may account for these discrepancies, such as possible differences in the rates of change in vision and hearing or different types of changes in visual and auditory sensory memory. At this point, the reasons for differences in age-related decrements between visual and auditory attention switching remain unknown.

Selectivity and Irrelevant Information

Thus far we have reached two major conclusions. Age decrements in selectivity appear to be greatest when tasks are complex and little information is available to assist performance. With advance information (such as spatial cuing), age differences are lessened. Why?

One popular hypothesis is that older adults have

reduced processing resources due to greater difficulty inhibiting the processing of irrelevant information (Hasher & Zacks, 1988). That is, older adults have more task-irrelevant thoughts during processing and have trouble keeping them out of their minds. This difference could explain why older people tend to be less accurate at finding targets; they have to contend with processing information about nontargets as well.

The inhibition idea has considerable support (Kane, Hasher, Stoltzfus, Zacks, & Connelly, 1994). For example, McDowd, Filion, and Oseas-Kreger (1991) showed that when relevant and irrelevant information are both presented in the same modality (e.g., visually), older adults distribute their attention more equally between the two types of information than younger adults. However, when relevant information was presented in one modality (say, visually) and irrelevant information in another (auditorially), older and younger adults both showed similar patterns of attention allocation. Thus, older adults apparently have more trouble selectively attending to relevant information when it and the irrelevant information are both presented in the same modality. One practical implication of this concerns driving, where lots of both relevant and irrelevant information occurs visually. Given these research findings, we would expect that older adults would have more difficulty in this situation, which could result in accidents. We will check our prediction a bit later in this chapter.

Additional research shows that the problem with inhibition is not universal across all aspects of stimuli (Connelly & Hasher, 1993). Age-related inhibitory deficits may be limited to an item's identity and not with other aspects of the stimulus such as its location. Moreover, attempts to get older adults to inhibit processing of key aspects of a distractor by creating the opportunity to do so do not appear to work (Kane et al., 1994). Such data provide support for Hasher and Zacks's (1988) inhibition hypothesis, but mean that inhibitory deficits are probably localized to specific aspects of stimuli. Additional support for this conclusion comes from data indicating that inhibitory deficits are specific to certain types of processing and do not provide a comprehensive explanation of age differences in cognitive performance (Kramer, Humphrey, Larish, Logan, & Strayer, 1994).

Dividing one's attention between driving and talking on the phone may be done better by young adults but may also not be the safest thing to do.

Divided Attention

Given that some evidence exists for age differences in *what* information is processed, do age differences also exist in *how much* information is processed? **This question is answered by studying attentional capacity, which is usually done by testing *divided attention*, which is the ability to successfully perform more than one task at the same time.**

Life is full of situations in which we need to do at least two things at once. Two common examples are listening to a lecture while writing in a notebook and driving a car while conversing with a passenger. Each of these situations requires monitoring what is going on in at least two different domains. How well we are able to perform these multiple simultaneous tasks depends on how much attentional capacity we have available for each. To

DISCOVERING DEVELOPMENT

How Good Are Your Notes?

At the beginning of this section we encountered several examples of divided-attention tasks. You are very familiar with one of them—writing notes while listening to a lecture. An interesting developmental question is whether the ability to take good notes differs with age. One way to find out informally is to compare the notes taken in the same class by young adult and older adult students. If there are no older adults in your class, there may be in other courses. Ask them if you can compare their notes with those of someone much younger. What predictions would you make based on the research evidence you have read thus far? What role would practice play in these differences? Whose notes are actually better? Why do you think this is?

---

the extent that any one task requires a great deal of our capacity, our ability to do other things may be impaired.

Older adults report that dividing attention among most combinations of activities becomes more difficult with increasing age, and, compared to younger adults, rate most combinations of activities as more difficult (Tun & Wingfield, 1995). However, ratings of one's ability to perform various types of activities vary a great deal across tasks. Keeping track of novel information in combinations of tasks is perceived as more difficult than those involving routine tasks or speech processing. These findings reflect the importance of self-evaluations of how well people think they can (or did) perform, which may have important implications for performance.

Experimental research on divided attention is a good example of how conclusions about age differences can change in the face of new evidence. At one time, researchers were convinced that age-related decrements in divided attention were inevitable (Craik, 1977). But Somberg and Salthouse's research in 1982 changed all that. By equalizing attentional performance on each of the two tasks used in this study, Somberg and Salthouse were able to eliminate age differences on the divided-attention task. Other researchers corroborated Somberg and Salthouse's findings (e.g., Wickens, Braune, & Stokes, 1987). Researchers had to go back to the lab to try and account for these new data.

Subsequent studies clarified things. It turns out that age differences are found on some divided-attention tasks and not others. The explanation involves task complexity and practice. When the divided-attention tasks are relatively easy, age differences are typically absent. However, when the tasks become more complicated, age differences emerge (McDowd & Craik, 1988; Plude, Murphy, & Gabriel-Byrne, 1989). In other words, adults of all ages can perform multiple easy tasks simultaneously, but older adults do not do as well as younger adults when they must perform multiple difficult tasks at the same time.

Age differences on divided-attention tasks can also be minimized if older adults are given extensive practice in performing the tasks. For example, when very large numbers of practice trials (from roughly 500 to over 11,000) are provided, age differences may disappear; with fewer practice trials (less than 300), age differences are often found (Rogers, Bertus, & Gilbert, 1994). These results imply that older adults may be able to learn through experience how to divide their attention effectively between tasks. Check out this idea by completing the Discovering Development feature.

The Processing Resources Hypothesis

Even though task complexity and high levels of practice provide conditions under which age differences on divided-attention tasks appear or are minimized, an important question remains: *Why* do older adults have more problems performing more difficult tasks, or tasks on which they have little practice, simultaneously? **Many theorists and researchers believe that with increasing age comes a decline in the amount of available *processing resources*, the amount of attention one has to apply to a particular situation.** The idea of declining processing resources was appealing, because it could account for poorer performance not only on attention tasks (Plude & Hoyer, 1985) but also on a host of others (Salthouse, 1991).

On the surface the notion of age-related decrements in processing resources offers a concise explanation of a wide range of age-related performance differences. But there is a nagging problem about the processing resource construct: It has never been clearly defined (Baddeley, 1981; Salthouse, 1988, 1991). In a carefully designed series of investigations, Salthouse and his colleagues set out to see what could be done (Salthouse, 1988; Salthouse, Kausler, & Saults, 1988). Their goal was to provide an empirical test of the processing resource explanation of age-related performance differences. Their results demonstrate that complete reliance on this idea is probably a mistake. Salthouse was able to show that although some kind of processing resource notion is a parsimonious explanation, the strong version of the resource decline idea that marks much current research has little empirical support. In other words, something besides a decline in processing resources is responsible for performance decrements with age.

Plude and Doussard-Roosevelt (1990) provide one possible answer. They argue that the problem stems back to age-related decrements in feature integration, at least when the multiple (and difficult) tasks are all visual. Complex tasks, they believe, require more features to be integrated, thereby differentially penalizing older adults.

In sum, divided-attention ability per se does not differ with age. Rather, task complexity is a primary determinant of age-related decrements; older adults are at a disadvantage when they must perform two or more complex tasks simultaneously (Plude & Doussard-Roosevelt, 1990). Thus, age differences on divided-attention tasks may actually reflect age differences on the components of each task (Hartley, 1992).

Sustained Attention

Did you ever think about the job that air traffic controllers have? They must sit in front of radar screens for hours keeping track of blips on the screen. Each blip represents an airplane, many of which have hundreds of people aboard. Air traffic controllers must sustain high levels of attention over long periods of time, as even the slightest error could have disastrous consequences.

Watching a radar screen is an excellent example of vigilance: the ability to sustain attention on a task for long periods of time. Researchers interested in studying age differences in vigilance use tasks very much like those performed by air traffic controllers. Investigators obtain two different measures of sustained attention: the number of targets correctly detected *(vigilance performance)* and the decrease in "hit" rate over time *(vigilance decrement)*.

Compared with work on other aspects of attention, relatively little research has focused on vigilance. What little there is suggests age-related decrements in vigilance performance but not in vigilance decrement (Parasuraman, 1987). This means that although older adults are not as accurate as younger adults in detecting targets, performance deteriorates at the same rate in both age groups. What causes this age difference in detection?

Parasuraman (1987) offers several suggestions. He points out that vigilance tasks are quite complex and require at least four different processes that could account for age differences: (1) alertness; (2) adaptation and expectancy; (3) sustained allocation of attentional capacity; and (4) development of automaticity. Parasuraman believes that only the first, alertness, is related to vigilance performance; the other three processes are related to vigilance decrement. We will consider the first three of these topics in this section, and the fourth in the next section.

Age-related differences in alertness on vigilance tasks have been well-established for many years. For example, Surwillo and Quilter (1964) demonstrated that older adults' poorer vigilance performance was correlated with lower physiological arousal. A longitudinal follow-up (Giambra & Quilter, 1988) verified this earlier finding. Thus, one good explanation of age differences in vigilance performance is age differences in arousal.

A second way of identifying sources of age differences in vigilance is by manipulating the predictability of how often or where a target will occur. First let's consider manipulation frequency of targets in a vigilance study involving monitoring a computer screen. The target is programmed to appear on the screen 10% of the time; the other 90% of the stimuli that appear will be nontargets. Prior to beginning, participants are told one of two things: either the true probability of a target appearing (10%) or an incorrect probability (50%). If a similar situation were presented to older and younger adults, would age differences emerge? Parasuraman (1987) provides the answer—no. Although vigilance decrements were greater for the incorrect probability condition, older and younger adults were affected equally. Thus, both groups were able to adapt their performance to reflect how often they expected to see a target. However, this only is true up to a point. At very high rates of target presentations in tasks that last a relatively long time, older adults' performance degrades compared with younger adults' performance (Mouloua & Parasuraman, 1995; Parasuraman & Giambra, 1991).

The other way of manipulating predictability is to vary the information given to people about where the target is likely to appear on the screen and to vary the context in which the target is presented. Mouloua and Parasuraman (1995) did this by creating three uncertainty conditions (low, medium, and high) in which the target was a lowercase letter: presenting letters one at a time in the center of the screen, presenting a lowercase letter in the middle of a string of uppercase letters in the middle of the screen, and presenting a lowercase letter in a string of uppercase letters randomly in one of the four corners of the screen. The researchers found no age differences for the low uncertainty condition (when single letters were presented at the center of the screen), but younger adults had significantly higher hit rates than did the older adults at both of the other conditions.

In a related series of studies, Madden, Connelly, and Pierce (1994) used a choice response task in which one of two targets could appear in one of four locations in a visual display. By manipulating the validity of the target cue and the presence of distractor stimuli, they showed that age differences depended on the situation. Age-related differences were minimal in shifting focused attention except when people were required to process nontarget information.

Taken together, the results from studies manipulating predictability show a clear pattern. As long as vigilance tasks involve a relatively low presentation rate of targets and the spatial location of targets is predictable, age differences are typically absent. However, when either the presentation rate is increased or the spatial predictability is decreased, older adults' performance begins to decline relative to younger adults' performance.

A third major way of examining vigilance performance is to focus on the complexity of the task. As we saw earlier, the amount of attentional capacity a task requires can be manipulated by changing the complexity of the task. One way to do this is to degrade the perceptual quality of the target, such as making the blip dimmer on a radar screen or making a target letter harder to discriminate from other letters. Parasuraman, Nestor, and Greenwood (1989) had younger and older adults perform a vigilance task under two conditions: normal and degraded. As might be expected, the degraded condition resulted in poorer vigilance performance and greater vigilance decrement than the normal condition. However, older and younger adults were affected similarly; no age differences as a function of condition were found.

Automatic Processes

A fourth way of studying vigilance involves investigating how responses become automatic. Because vigilance tasks tend to be highly repetitive (i.e., people make the same kinds of responses over and over, such as driving a car with a clutch every day for years), people's performance on them tends to improve for a while and then plateau. If this plateau corresponds to a high rate of accuracy that is maintained over time, then the response is considered to have become automatic. **In general, *automatic processes* are those that are fast, reliable, and insensitive to increased cognitive demands (e.g., performing other tasks).**

An interesting developmental question is whether age differences exist in the rates at which responses on vigilance tasks become automatic. This is often done by manipulating characteristics of new tasks and observing whether older and younger adults are equally adept at achieving a high level of performance with a great deal of practice. Most of these involve search tasks with two conditions (e.g., Rogers, Bertus, & Gilbert, 1994). In the consistent mapping (CM) practice condition, people are told to press one key if a target letter that is drawn from one set of letters appears and another key when the letters from a separate, nonoverlapping distractor set appear. A trial consists of a letter, the target, appearing on a screen followed by another display that either has or does not have the target in it. For example, the screen may show the target letter "N" followed by the display "B D F N P T." With practice, people learn which letters comprise the target set and which letters comprise the distractor set, so that eventually the search becomes automatic. In the varied mapping (VM) practice condition, target and distractor letters are chosen from the same set, meaning that people cannot learn to ignore any of the letters as they eventually do for the distractor letters in the CM practice condition. Thus, the VM practice condition is more difficult than the CM practice condition, and only the CM practice condition results in the development of automatic processing.

The search tasks used to study automatic processing can involve memory search or visual search. Memory search entails the presentation of a target in the center of a screen, followed by a letter at the center surrounded by a set of "placeholders," which are squares the same size as letters. The person must decide whether the letter in the second screen was the target letter. In visual search, a target letter is presented followed by a test consisting of a string of letters that may contain the target letter; the person must search the string to see if the target is among the distractors.

Using these search paradigms, numerous investigators have examined the development of automatic processes in older and younger adults. The general conclusion from these studies is that whether older adults will develop automatic processing depends on two major factors (Rogers et al., 1994). First, a sufficient amount of practice must be provided. Sufficient is an understatement; this practice sometimes consists of thousands of trials of consistent mapping (CM) over several sessions. Second, the type of search task matters. Automatic processing in older adults occurs with extensive CM practice on memory search tasks, but not on visual search tasks (e.g., Fisk, Cooper, Hertzog, Anderson-Garlach, & Lee, 1995; Fisk & Rogers, 1991). However, if the memory search task is difficult, age differences may emerge (Strayer & Kramer, 1994).

Why do these task differences occur? How do people learn automatic processing? **One possibility is that the processing of a specific and well-trained stimulus, such as a target letter, can automatically capture attention, making it an *automatic attention response*.** In this case, the process attracts attention even though attention was not required initially; an everyday example of this is when people respond to hearing their name being called by looking up even though they may have been engaged in another activity. In the context of a divided-attention paradigm, Rogers and colleagues (1994) found that older adults do not develop an automatic attention response in visual search situations; instead, older adults searched each display in looking for a target instead of responding only when a target was present.

Closer examination of how processes become automatic reveals a second set of possibilities. By varying the type of CM task, Fisk, Cooper, Hertzog, and Anderson-Garlach (1995) discovered that it is the components of tasks, and not the tasks themselves, that become automatized. For a task to appear automatized, all of its component processes must be automatic. Whether this happens depends on age and the learning processes involved. Thus, age and task differences may be the result of differences in the ease with which task components become automatized in people of different ages.

A final issue concerning automatic processing concerns whether people retain the process over time. Suppose an individual participated in several thousand CM practice trials in a memory search task. If that person came back to the laboratory 3, 6, or 16 months later, would he or she still process the stimuli automatically? In a series of studies, Fisk and colleagues (Fisk et al., 1994; Fisk, Cooper, Hertzog, Anderson-Garlach, & Lee, 1995) provide some insight. They provided standard CM training on a memory search task to older and younger adults. After a 3-, 6-, or 16-month retention interval, participants were retested. Fisk and colleagues observed that performance declines in both groups over 3 months, but remains stable between 3 and 6 months; even after a 16-month delay performance on the well-trained task-specific skill was equivalent between older and younger participants once the opportunity to use an automatic attention response was removed. However, older adults perform worse on moderately well-trained CM stimuli. These results support the role of practice in producing automatic processes in older adults. Interestingly, age-related retention differences can be increased if an incompatible task is inserted just before testing on the trained skill. Why this is the case will require more research (Fisk, Cooper, Hertzog, & Anderson-Garlach, 1995).

Research on age-related differences in attention point to two main conclusions. First, age differences are greatest when older adults are faced with having to perform complex tasks, especially more than one at a time. Second, these decrements appear to be localized in the feature integration process, where the various pieces of information picked up from a visual display are put together to figure out what the display is.

However, these conclusions do not answer an intriguing question: *Why* do these age-related decrements occur? At present, the leading possibility is a generalized cognitive slowing. It is to this possibility that we now turn.

Concept Checks

1. According to feature integration theory, what are the two main steps in visual processing?
2. Under what conditions do age differences disappear in selective attention tasks?
3. What are processing resources?
4. What are the effects of manipulating predictability in vigilance tasks?
5. What are automatic processes?

PSYCHOMOTOR SPEED

Learning Objectives:

- How is reaction time measured?
- What age differences are observed in reaction time?
- Why do people slow with age?
- How can age-related slowing be moderated?
- What do age differences in reaction time mean?

You are driving home from a friend's house and all seems to be going well. Suddenly, a car pulls out of a driveway right into your path. You must hit the brakes as fast as you can or you will have an accident. How quickly can you move your foot from the accelerator to the brakes?

This situation is a real-life example of psychomotor speed—making a quick motor movement in response to information that has been processed. In this case, the motor movement is switching your foot from one pedal to another, and the information is the visual stimulus of a car in your path.

Psychomotor speed is one of the most studied phenomena in adult development and aging research. Results from hundreds of studies point to a clear conclusion: People slow down as they get older. In fact, the slowing-with-age phenomenon is so well documented that many gerontologists accept it as the only universal behavioral change yet discovered. In this section we will examine some of the evidence for psychomotor slowing.

Psychomotor speed reflects the outcomes of sensory memory and attention, in that researchers are examining relatively early aspects of information processing. In fact, some of the ways in which psychomotor speed is measured, such as reaction time tasks, we have already encountered as indices of sensory memory functioning. Thus, psychomotor speed can be viewed to some extent as a reflection of how quickly and efficiently these early steps in information processing are completed.

Reaction Time Tasks

We have already encountered several situations in which rapid responding is essential. How is speed measured in a laboratory? Researchers use three types of reaction time tasks to study rapid responses to events: simple reaction time tasks, choice reaction time tasks, and complex reaction time tasks. In each task, the key measurement is the amount of time it takes to respond under the appropriate conditions. We will consider each briefly.

Simple Reaction Time

Simple reaction time involves responding to one stimulus, such as pressing a button as fast as possible every time a light comes on. Researchers typically study simple reaction time by breaking it down into two components: decision time and motor time. Decision time is the time it takes from the onset of the stimulus until the person begins to initiate a response. For example, it is the time it takes for the person to see the light, remember that a button is supposed to be pressed, and begin to make the correct response. Motor time is the time needed to complete the response. In our example, motor time would be the amount of time it takes the person to move and press the button.

Consistent age differences in overall simple reaction time and in each of its components have been reported (Borkan & Norris, 1980; Salthouse, 1985). Interestingly, the most noticeable difference between young and old is in the decision time component; differences in motor time tend to be smaller.

Choice Reaction Time

Tasks involving choice reaction time offer more than one stimulus and require a response to each in a different way. An example would be presenting a person with two lights—one red and one blue. That person's job is to press the left button every time the red light comes on and the right button when the blue light comes on. To perform well on such tasks the person needs to identify correctly the stimulus, decide which response goes with it, and make the response; moreover, he or she needs to do all of this as quickly as possible (Fozard, 1981). Several researchers have found that older adults are significantly slower on choice reaction tasks than younger adults (e.g., Salthouse & Somberg, 1982; Strayer, Wickens, & Braune, 1987).

Complex Reaction Time

The most difficult reaction time task involves complex reaction time, which requires making many decisions about when and how to respond. A good example of a complex reaction time task is driving a car: The number of stimuli is extremely large, and the range of possible responses is huge. For instance, suppose you are driving along the freeway when the car next to you begins to swerve into your lane right in front of you. Do you hit the brakes? (Or is there someone right behind you?) Swerve around it? (Or is there no place to go?) Blow your horn? (The other driver may not hear you.) Hit the car?

Researchers try to recreate these complex situations in the laboratory using computer tasks. When they do, the results are very consistent and are related to the complexity of the task. For example, Cerella, Poon, and Williams (1980) report that the magnitude of age differences in complex reaction time tasks increases as the task becomes more difficult. Thus, older adults become increasingly disadvantaged as situations demanding rapid response become more complex.

Longitudinal Evidence of Response Time Slowing

Much of the research reported thus far is based on cross-sectional studies. As we noted in Chapter 1, however, such research does not provide evidence of age changes; longitudinal research is needed to address this. How does longitudinal evidence of age changes compare with cross-sectional evidence? Data from the Baltimore Longitudinal Study of Aging indicates that the degree to which reaction time changes with age depends on gender and the type of task (Fozard, Vercruyssen, Reynolds, Hancock, & Quilter, 1994). Overall, reaction time declines significantly when examined within the same participants over time. However, men are consistently faster than women across the adult life span, a difference that is not explained by such demographic characteristics as education or health. Although practice may be a factor, more research is needed to provide an answer.

Age Differences in Components of Reaction Time

Although they may appear straightforward, reaction time tasks are actually quite complicated cognitively. In any reaction time task, three things are done. A person must: (1) perceive that an event has occurred, (2) decide what to do about it, and (3) carry out the decision (Welford, 1977). Successful performance in reaction time tasks involves many factors, including sensation, perception, attention, working memory, intelligence, decision making, and personality (Salthouse, 1985). Poor performance on reaction time tasks could be the result of a breakdown in any step in the process.

Because reaction time tasks involve complex mental activity, researchers must break reaction time down into components in order to discover which aspects show age differences (Goggin & Stelmach, 1990). Typically, this means that investigators must manipulate variables that are related to reaction time. Two of these variables are especially important: response preparation and response complexity.

Response Preparation

Many driver education programs emphasize what is known as defensive driving. That is, instructors stress that we must be prepared for the unexpected at all times; we never know when an emergency situation could arise. This means that we need to be on our toes all the time. But suppose things were a little different. Suppose that there were only a handful of dangerous intersections along our route, and everything in between was completely safe. Getting close to one of these intersections would provide advance warning that we may need to make a quick response. Moreover, having this advance warning may even help us respond faster.

Providing such advance information is what happens in studies of *response preparation*, which involves getting ready to make a particular response to a stimulus. Researchers typically study the effects of response preparation in simple reaction time tasks by varying the amount or type of information provided about the impending presentation of a stimulus. For example, investigators might flash an asterisk right before presenting the target. Measuring reaction times when advance information is either present or absent allows researchers to address an important developmental question about reaction time: Do age differences in speed on reaction time tasks occur because older adults prepare poorly to make a response?

The answer appears to be yes. Several investigators report that older adults are especially vulnerable to ambiguous advance information or long delays between the advance information and the time at which the response must be made (Gottsdanker, 1982; Stelmach, Goggin, & Garcia-Colera, 1987). An example of the typical findings is shown in Figure 5.1 (Stelmach et al., 1987). Younger, middle-aged, and older adults were presented with different kinds of preparatory information in advance of responding. This advance information varied in how much help it provided participants in knowing exactly what the response was to be, from very specific (level 0 uncertainty) to very nonspecific (level 3 uncertainty). The graph demonstrates two things. First, there is an orderly general slowing of responding, with a ranking of younger, middle-aged, and elderly adults from

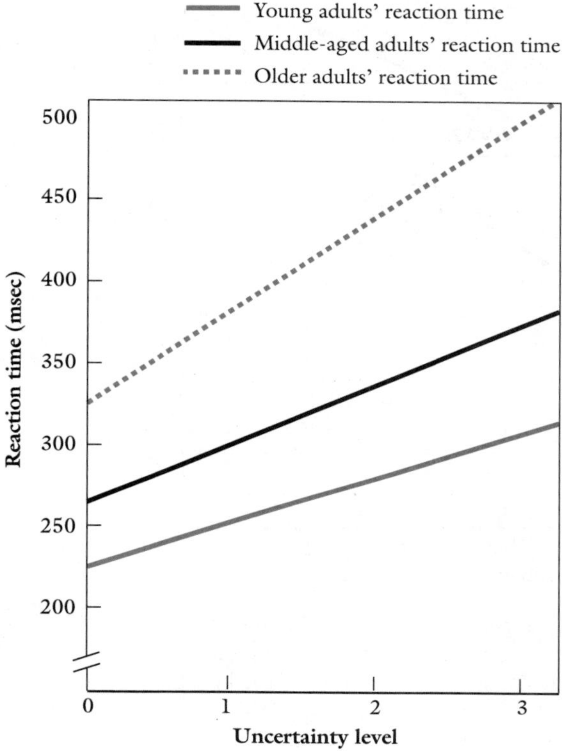

Figure 5.1 Reaction times in milliseconds for each age group plotted as a function of uncertainty. Notice that increased uncertainty slows older adults more than other groups.

Source: "Movement Specification Time with Age," by G. E. Stelmach, N. L. Goggin, and A. Garcia-Colera, 1987, Experimental Aging Research, 13, *p. 42. Copyright © 1987 by Beech Hill Enterprises, Inc. Reprinted with permission.*

least slow to slowest. Second, older adults are especially hurt by ambiguity; notice that the difference between them and the middle-aged adults *increases* as the uncertainty level goes up.

One way that ambiguity can be introduced is by giving incorrect information about the response. For example, a participant could be led to believe that he or she will need to make a specific hand movement (for example, turn hands palms up), only to find out at the time that he or she needs to make a different hand movement (turn hands palms down). Incorrect advance information forces the participant to reprogram his or her movements. When reprogramming is required, older adults are slowed down more than younger adults (Stelmach, Goggin, & Amrhein, 1988).

In sum, the research evidence shows that older adults are at a distinct disadvantage in reaction time tasks when they are not given specific advance information about the upcoming response. Such difficulties have many practical implications, the most important of which may be the effect on driving a car: Older people react more slowly to emergency situations.

Response Complexity

As we saw earlier, choice reaction time tasks and complex reaction time tasks involve decisions about which stimulus is present and which response needs to be made. These tasks make it possible to examine the effects of task complexity in several different ways. For example, the usual choice reaction time task involves using the same hand to push two different buttons. One way to complicate things is to require people to use both hands simultaneously. Another way would be not only to require simultaneous use of both hands, but also to have each hand move different distances to make the response.

Stelmach, Amrhein, and Goggin (1988) used these manipulations to study the effects of response complexity in younger and older adults. They found that older adults were more affected by increased complexity than younger adults. Older adults had difficulty coordinating movements of both hands across different distances so that the movements would end simultaneously. Light and Spirduso (1990) varied the complexity of response by having people make different movements with a microswitch. They also found that as response complexity increased, older adults proportionately slowed down more.

These findings fit well with the data from visual information-processing studies considered earlier. The results from both lines of research show that adults experience increasing difficulty dealing with complexity in a variety of settings as they get older.

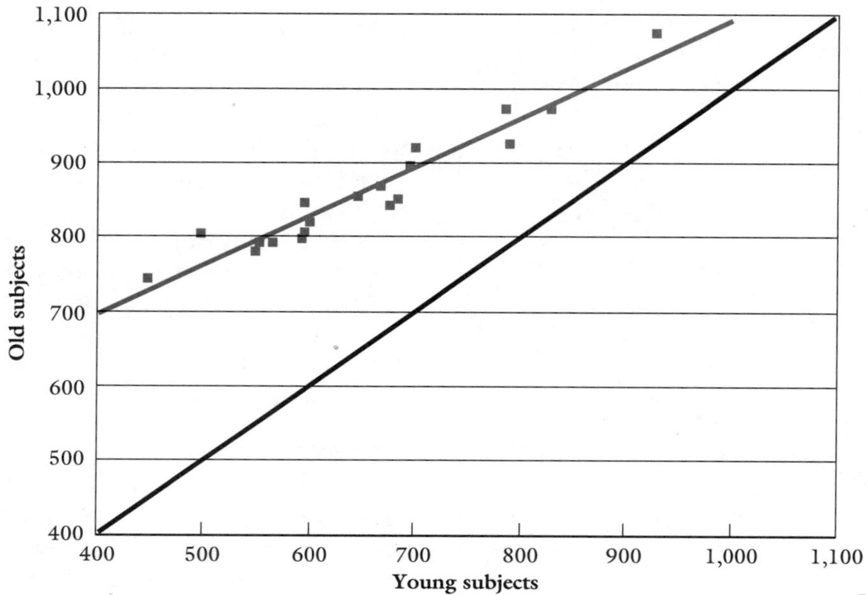

Figure 5.2 Brinley plot of old versus young reaction times (in msec) representing performance in "reversal" tasks. The black line represents the hypothetical points of equal performance between young and old. The green line represents the best fitting line through the data points.
Source: Fisk and Fisher, 1994

Interpreting Age Differences in Reaction Time

All of the data we have considered converge on a clear conclusion: People slow down as they grow older. A key question that researchers have asked for more than three decades is whether age-related slowing represents a simple mathematical function of psychomotor speed in young adulthood. The search for an answer began with Brinley's (1965) classic study in which he showed that if older adults' reaction times are plotted as a function of younger adults' reaction times, a linear (straight-line) function results. This technique, now known as Brinley plots, supports the notion that older adults are not poorer at responding in different tasks, they are only slower, and that the degree to which slowing occurs varies depending on the type of task. An example of a Brinley plot can be seen in Figure 5.2.

Since Brinley's pioneering study, researchers have been trying to show that Brinley's idea was correct. Many researchers point out that Brinley plots provide important insights into aging and cognition and are a way to examine underlying theories of cognition and aging (e.g., Maylor & Rabbitt, 1994; Myerson, Hale, Wagstaff, & Hale, 1994). To these researchers, Brinley plots provide evidence of a general linear model of age-related slowing, which can be used to explain a wide array of age-related differences.

Other researchers are not so sure. For example, Perfect (1994) raised several concerns about the use of Brinley plots. Most important, he argued that these plots fail to reflect data specifically created in computer models not to conform to a single linear function and that the mathematical parameters obtained from the plots differed significantly from the mathematical functions used to generate the data. These findings raise concerns about whether the plots accurately reflect the true state of affairs concerning reaction times. Cerella (1994) pointed out that the linear functions obtained in Brinley plots present a view of age-related slowing that is too simplistic. In his view, multidimensional models of information processing are needed.

Perhaps the most appropriate use of Brinley plots is to view them as one way to represent data as a way to assist in the evaluation of theories of age-related changes in cognition (Fisk & Fisher, 1994). However, rather than relying on plots of data as the primary way to test theories, Fisk and Fisher (1994) propose that models of performance and learning must play a more central role in evaluating theories. In the next section, we will examine some of the hypotheses underlying age-related slowing.

What Causes Age-Related Slowing?

The evidence documenting a normative decline with age in psychomotor speed is overwhelming, representing one of the most robust findings in gerontological research. What causes people to slow down? After many years of debate and several different ideas, researchers are zeroing in on an intriguing answer. Several theorists (such as Cerella, 1990; Myerson, Hale, Wagstaff, Poon, & Smith, 1990; Salthouse, 1985; Welford, 1988) argue that the reason people slow down has to do with age changes in neurons in the brain. Although there is disagreement about exactly what is happening, most researchers believe that physiological changes in the brain, rather than changes in higher level cognitive processes, are responsible for age-related slowing. We will consider two variations on this theme: neural networks and information loss.

Neural Networks

One way to conceptualize thinking is to consider it as a computational process occurring on a neural network (McClelland, Rumelhart, & the PDP Research Group, 1986). In this approach, thinking involves making connections among many neurons. Efficient thinking means making the fewest number of necessary connections between the point at which information comes in and the point at which an answer (or thought) comes out. Each connection requires a certain amount of time, so how quickly one thinks depends on the number of connections one needs to use.

For simplicity's sake, let's consider a simple reaction time task from this view of a neural network. The original neural network of Figure 5.3 shows that, hypothetically, eight links are the minimum number needed to get the information from the input side to the output side. Using only eight links would therefore be the most efficient (that is, the fastest) way to process the information. Suppose, though, that one of the neurons dies. The revised route of Figure 5.3 shows what happens. Notice that an extra (or a new) link is needed to bypass the break, bringing the minimum number up to nine links. Reaction time will be faster in the first case (using only eight links) than in the second (using nine).

Cerella (1990) builds a case that reaction times in older adults are slower because they must build many such bypasses. Based on sophisticated analyses of reaction time data, he constructed a set of mathematical equations that fit a neural network model and account for the research findings. His analyses show that reaction time data are extremely consistent with what would be expected in a brain undergoing systematic changes in how its neurons are interconnected.

Additional support for a neural network approach comes from simulation research on visual processing (Hannon & Hoyer, 1994). In a series of computer simulations, a specific model of age-related differences in figure completion performance was identified. Such simulations may provide insights into why older adults slow down with age.

Information Loss

Myerson and colleagues (1990) took a slightly different approach. They focused not so much on the links among neurons per se, but what happens during processing at each line. Their model is based on four assumptions:

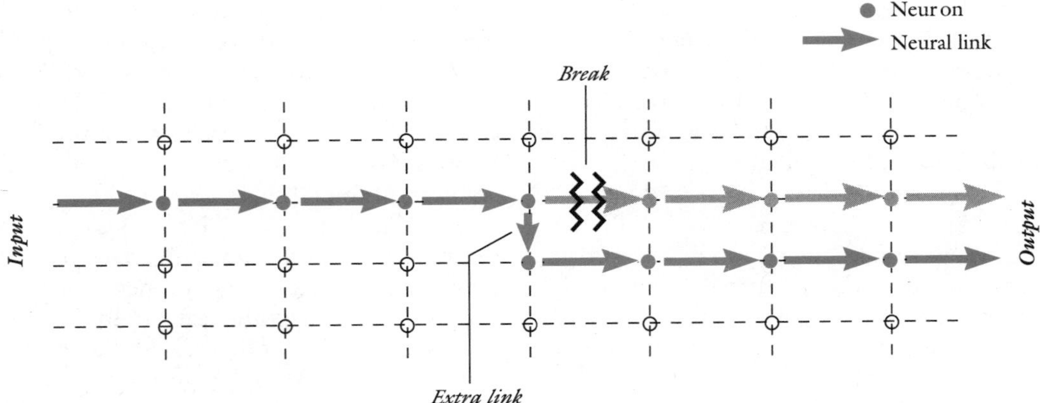

Figure 5.3 Schematic neural network. The network transmits signal from left to right. One link in the original, intact route is broken, forcing the signal to detour and adding one more link to the path for a total of nine.

Source: "Aging and Information Processing Rate," by J. Cerella. In J. E. Birren and K. W. Schaie (Eds.), Handbook of the Psychology of Aging, *Third Edition, p. 203. Copyright ©1990 Academic Press. Reprinted by permission.*

1. Information processing occurs in discrete steps, and overall processing speed is the total of how long it takes to accomplish each step. This assumption is based on the same neural network model as Cerella used.
2. How long each step takes depends on how much information is available at the beginning of the step. For example, if the task being done requires identification of particular letters, and if the quality of the printing is very poor, insufficient information may be available to make a rapid response. Additionally, as the task gets more complicated and more information is needed, processing speed slows down.
3. Information is lost during processing. This point is illustrated by thinking about photocopying a document. Each time the document is copied, there is a slight loss of quality. If the copy is then used to make a copy, more quality is lost. Continuing this process several times nicely demonstrates Myerson's theory of how information gets lost during information processing.
4. The most important effect of aging is an age-related increase in the rate at which information is lost. To continue our example, age differences in information loss would be analogous to the quality of the copy deteriorating faster in an old photocopy machine.

Like Cerella's neural network model, Myerson's information-loss model accounts for a wide range of data. Myerson and colleagues are able to predict with a high degree of accuracy older adults' reaction times from young adults' performance, irrespective of task. As a result, they view age-related slowing as a global process that is not localized in specific age-sensitive components. How they arrived at this theory is discussed in How Do We Know?

Together, these models provide powerful explanations of age-related slowing. They also provide strong support for working within the four basic developmental forces by explicitly connecting a psychological process (making quick responses) with underlying physiological processes. As noted in Chapter 3, rapid advances are being made in understanding how the brain works. These advances clearly benefit our understanding of psychomotor speed and aging. However, the question

HOW DO WE KNOW?

The Information-Loss Model

How do researchers come up with new explanatory models? One way is to combine the results of many studies with one's own research, look for consistencies, and derive explanations. That is what Myerson, Hale, Wagstaff, Poon, and Smith (1990) did. As noted in the text, they tried to explain why people slow with age using four basic assumptions: (1) processing occurs in steps; (2) the duration of the step depends on the information available; (3) information is lost during processing; and (4) an age-related increase occurs in the rate of information loss. Where did their final model come from?

First, Myerson and co-workers examined the results of over a dozen studies for trends in patterns of age differences. They then considered how well each of three possible explanations worked. The first alternative argues that even though older adults are slower, there are no real age differences in information-processing capabilities between older and younger adults. The second alternative was that the speed differences were due to age differences in some aspects of information processing but not others. The third alternative was that age differences in speed reflected age differences in all aspects of information processing.

Once the competing hypotheses were identified, the researchers set about systematically building a mathematical model to account for the data. Equations were derived for each alternative and used to try to predict the actual data. In only one case were the data adequately described, namely, the third alternative. Specifically, only the equations based on Myerson and colleagues' four assumptions, combined into one equation, provided a good description of the data. In fact, this equation accounted for 99% of the variance in the speed of older and younger adults on different types of information-processing tasks.

This systematic approach to model building is representative of how good theories are developed. Theory building takes a great deal of painstaking effort, but the investment is well worth it.

remains: Is there a way to slow these age-related decrements in psychomotor speed?

Slowing Down How Much We Slow Down

Consider for a moment what it takes to be a successful race car driver: a fast car, lots of driving knowledge, and lightning fast reactions. On the face of it, auto racing sounds tailor-made for young adults. But few drivers in their 20s win major races such as the Indianapolis 500. Many of the best drivers (for example, Al Unser, Jr.) reach the peak of their careers in their 30s. Or consider Paul Newman—the famous movie star and race car driver. He was racing successfully even in his late 50s. The data indicate that people in their 20s are faster than middle-aged adults, so how can older drivers still succeed?

At least two things make a difference: practice and experience. As we will see, both have been shown to make people respond faster. In addition, physical exercise also has a beneficial influence on reaction time.

Practice and Reaction Time

One way to see if age differences in psychomotor speed could be altered is by having people practice. Several studies over the years have examined this question (for example, Berg, Hertzog, & Hunt, 1982; Leonard & Newman, 1965; Madden & Nebes, 1980; Plude & Hoyer, 1981; Salthouse & Somberg, 1982). The dominant finding is that practice results in considerable improvement among all age groups. However, age differences in overall level of performance are seldom eliminated completely with practice.

Experience and Reaction Time

One reason that middle-aged race car drivers are able to win has to do with experience. They have driven in many races and have accumulated a

Although younger secretaries may type more characters within a specific time span than older secretaries, such differences are greatly reduced or eliminated when accuracy is taken into account.

wealth of information about driving in these events. Veteran drivers know that younger drivers have quicker reflexes to get themselves out of an emergency situation. But because of their experience, veterans are often able to avoid getting into trouble in the first place; they can anticipate what is likely to happen in front of them. This experience provides a way to compensate for slower psychomotor speed.

Researchers have studied real-world tasks to learn about the effects of experience on reaction time. Salthouse (1984) decided to examine performance in adults aged 19 to 72 on transcription typing. The typists in his study ranged in speed from 17 to 104 words per minute, with ability and age being unrelated. Salthouse examined several components of reaction time, including choice reaction time, speed of repetitive tapping, and the rate at which people can substitute specific digits for letters (for example, 3 for d). Results are shown in Figure 5.4.

As you can see in the graph, age-related slowing occurred on the choice reaction time task. Interestingly, however, no age effect occurred for typing. Why? Both tasks involved pressing keys, so what was the difference? One measure revealed a difference favoring older adults: span of anticipation. This measure was derived from a manipulation of the number of simultaneously visible to-be-typed characters, and it was interpreted as an indication of how far ahead of the currently typed character the typist was focusing his or her attention. Because a greater span of anticipation minimizes the importance of the speed of psychomotor processes as a major factor in skilled typing, the larger span on the part of the older typists can be considered an extremely effective compensatory mechanism. Thus, in some cases experience may allow older adults to compensate for psychomotor slowing.

Exercise and Reaction Time

As we noted in Chapter 4, one of the benefits claimed for aerobic exercise is improved cognitive performance. Most of this work is based on the effects of excercise on psychomotor speed. Several studies employing both simple and choice reaction time tasks document significant improvement in performance in older adults as a function of sustained exercise (Baylor & Spirduso, 1988; Rikli & Busch, 1986; Spirduso, 1980; Tomporowski & Ellis, 1986). That is, older adults who exercised regularly had significantly faster reaction times than sedentary older adults (Baylor & Spirduso, 1988).

These results do not mean that exercise affects all aspects of a reaction time task equally, however. Blumenthal and Madden (1988) demonstrated that the effects of exercise may be limited to the encoding and response components of a memory search task. In contrast, age appears to account for slower rates of memory search. Thus, the benefit of exercise for older adults' reaction time performance appears to stem from an enhancement of getting the information in and getting the response

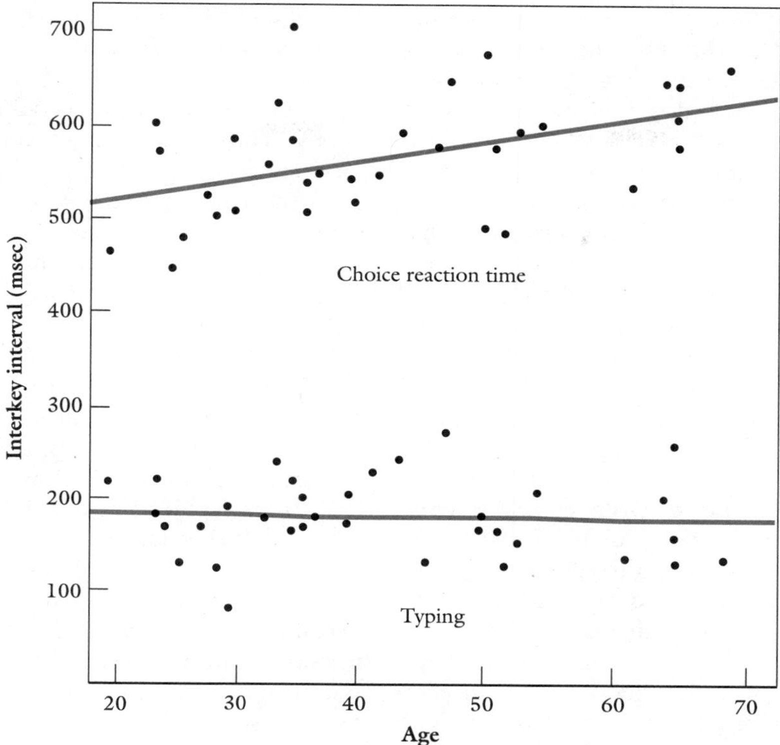

Figure 5.4 Comparison of speed in milliseconds of responding in choice reaction time task and typing as a function of age. Note how choice reaction time responses slow down with age whereas typing speed does not.

Source: "Effects of Age and Skill in Typing," by T. A. Salthouse, 1984, Journal of Experimental Psychology: General, 113, *345–371. Copyright ©1984 by the American Psychological Association. Reprinted with permission of the author.*

out. What happens in between may be relatively unchanged.

Concept Checks

1. What are the three types of reaction time tasks?
2. What age differences are observed in response preparation and response complexity?
3. What are Brinley plots?
4. What are the two major explanations of why people slow with age?
5. What effects do practice, experience, and exercise have on reaction time?

DRIVING AND ACCIDENT PREVENTION

Learning Objectives:

- What age-related differences are there in driving?
- How can home accidents be prevented?

To this point, we have concentrated on age differences in basic aspects of the information-processing system as found in laboratory settings. We have seen that in several areas older adults are at a disadvantage compared with younger (and often middle-aged) adults. However, most of the research we considered was based on esoteric tasks, such as finding the letter *X* in a visual display or pressing different keys for different color lights. If you are wondering what this work has to do with real life, you are not alone; many researchers wonder the same thing.

Early steps in information processing in fact have many important connections with everyday life, as we have noted from time to time throughout the chapter. For example, driving a car involves bombarding sensory memory with vast amounts of information, directing attention to some of it, and, when necessary, having excellent psychomotor speed. Thus, at this juncture in our consideration of cognition and aging we must consider these connections between basic information-processing skills and everyday situations.

Making connections between laboratory research findings and everyday life is one aspect of human factors research. **As a discipline, *human factors* tries to optimize the design of living and working environments** (Charness & Bosman, 1990b). Human factors professionals deal with interesting problems in just about every conceivable area. For example, they may be asked to design an easy-to-use computer keyboard, the layout of a cockpit for a jumbo jet, or a safe environment for nursing home residents. Although most human factors work focuses on designing working environments, increased interest is being paid to everyday situations. For example, many of the safety features built into modern appliances (such as irons that automatically shut off) and automobiles (brake lights mounted in the rear window, for example) are the result of human factors research.

To make the most effective designs, planners must know as much as possible about their clients. This in turn requires integrating information about people's basic sensory and information-processing abilities. In designs meant for older adults, planners need to understand changes in sensory abilities and those in basic information-processing abilities. Unfortunately, few human factors researchers have focused specifically on the needs of the elderly (Charness & Bosman, 1990b; D.B.D. Smith, 1990). Most of the previous work involves driving and other highway safety issues, as well as safety in the home.

Driving and Highway Safety as Information Processing

The vast majority of older adults live independently. Thus, access to workplaces, community services, leisure activities, and the like is an important consideration. Because roughly 80% of all trips made by older adults are in private automobiles (U.S. Department of Transportation, 1986), driving and highway safety are major issues for human factors research.

We have already noted that certain changes in vision, hearing, and information processing could cause problems for older drivers. For example, changes in light and dark adaptation and sensitivity to glare and changes in psychomotor speed present challenges to elderly drivers. Older drivers themselves report several difficulties (Yee, 1985), from trouble reading highway signs and the instrument panel to difficulty seeing the road to problems reaching the seatbelt. Difficulty with inhibiting irrelevant information could mean trouble sorting out benign situations from potentially dangerous ones. Observational and other objective data suggest additional problems: trouble with backing up, changing lanes, noting signs and warnings, turning properly, and yielding the right of way (National Highway Traffic Safety Administration, 1988; Yanik, 1988).

Many of these problems could be solved by redesigning vehicles with older adults in mind. For example, instrument panel luminance levels could be higher and made more glare-free (Mourant & Langolf, 1976), and headlights could be redesigned (Mortimer, 1989). Many other aspects of cars could be made more user-friendly for older adults (D.B.D. Smith, 1990): entry and egress, mechanical controls and locks, field of view, and safety features.

Why are these design issues unaddressed? Yanik (1994) argues that three barriers exist to designing automobiles for older drivers: (1) the designers tend to be young adults who lack experiential knowledge of the aging process; (2) young designers' notions of aging tend to be based on social stereotypes rather than on research; and (3) a general lack of applied research exists on how older adults interact with their cars. Removing these barriers would entail education (which would address the first two) and a systematic effort to conduct the appropriate research.

One area in which applied research has been conducted relates to visual processing. An important driving problem that could be affected by vision and information-processing changes is identifying signs, especially at dusk (Kline, 1994). For example, Sivak, Olson, and Pastalan (1981) found that older drivers needed to be considerably closer to text signs at night in order to read them, despite the fact that they had been equated with the younger drivers for daytime vision. A follow-up study in which older and younger drivers were equated for both daytime and nighttime vision revealed no performance differences, emphasizing that visual defects, not age, cause the problem (Sivak & Olson, 1982).

Kline, Ghali, Kline, and Brown (1990) examined how well younger, middle-aged, and older drivers could read text and icon highway signs. Text signs have various messages printed on them, such as "men working" and "divided highway." Icon signs are picture versions of text signs following international conventions; for example, a "men working" icon sign depicts a man using a shovel. Kline and colleagues showed that all age groups identified icon signs at greater distances than text signs. This effect was especially true at dusk. Most important, no age differences were found; older adults identified signs as well as younger adults. This finding is important, especially in view of the well-documented changes in vision and in visual information processing. Additionally, the distance at which older adults were able to identify the signs would provide enough time for them to prepare for any decisions, such as the need to exit or slow down.

Research on the visibility of signs indicates that when the visual abilities of older adults are used to guide the design of signs, their visibility can be greatly enhanced (Kline, 1994). Moreover, optical simulation and image-processing filters are newer techniques that also appear promising in designing signs and displays that are more effective for older drivers.

Highway Accidents

Many people believe that older drivers are unsafe. However, testing that theory is difficult, primarily because older adults have very different driving habits than younger and middle-aged adults. Older adults drive fewer total miles, less at night, less in bad weather, less in rush hour traffic, and less on freeways and the open highway (D.B.D. Smith, 1990). The consensus among researchers is that if older adults do have any elevated accident risk, it is compensated for by changes in driving habits, at least until late life (e.g., National Highway Traffic Safety Administration, 1988; Williams & Carsten, 1989).

Psychologists approach the study of age and highway accidents by focusing on the role of skills known to be relevant to driving. Age, per se, does not lead to accidents; rather, it is decreased skills that can cause them (Panek, Barrett, Sterns, & Alexander, 1977). Barrett, Alexander, and Forbes (1977) identified three information-processing variables that are especially important in understanding automobile accidents: perceptual strategies, selective attention, and reaction time.

Several researchers have studied the relationship between measures of basic skills and on-the-road behavior. Rackoff and Mourant (1979) found that older drivers (aged 60 to 70) who scored more poorly than younger drivers (aged 21 to 29) on tests of visual search, embedded figures, and reaction time also took longer to extract important information while driving. Shinar, McDowell, Rackoff, and Rockwell (1978) reported that older drivers who were not as able to filter irrelevant information were less effective in their visual search behavior on the road. Problems in selective attention are evident in accident victims' statements; "I never saw the other car" is a common example of a failure to detect important information. Moreover, older drivers have difficulty judging the speed of oncoming vehicles (Scialfa, Guzy, Leibowitz, Garvey, & Tyrrell, 1991).

An additional problem facing older drivers is that older adults tend to be taking more prescription and nonprescription medications than younger adults. Because many medications have side effects that could impair sensory, perceptual, and reaction time processes, all adults, but especially the elderly, need to be aware of these effects.

Given the number of potential problems facing older drivers, some researchers have emphasized a need for specialized training programs. A good example of this approach is the program created by Sterns and his colleagues (Sterns et al., 1978; Sterns, Barrett, Alexander, Valasek, and McIlvried, 1984; Sterns & Sanders, 1980). They developed an assessment and training program based on the sensory, perceptual, and reaction time processes involved in driving. Intensive and extensive retraining on deficient skills (such as looking down the road) were found to hold up 2 years after training. Importantly, short-term training was not effective.

In sum, many sensory and information-processing changes affect driving. However, human factors research on the use of icons on signs and training programs based on information-processing interventions effectively help older drivers compensate for these changes.

Age-related changes in sensory, motor, and physiological systems increase the likelihood that this woman may have an accident getting on or off the train.

Home Safety and Accident Prevention

By far, the most important home safety issue is falls. Changes in the vestibular system as well as combinations of changes in the muscular and skeletal systems place older adults at much greater risk of falling down. Additional risk factors include information-processing changes involving attention and focusing on relevant information such as cracks in the sidewalk. Much human factors research on falls has focused on the role of stair construction in falls (Pauls, 1985). This research has resulted in the incorporation of several safety standards into U.S. building codes concerning such things as handrails, ramps, and grab bars.

Unfortunately, little human factors research has been conducted on other home safety issues. Many important problems remain, such as legibility of dials and controls on stoves and ovens, and the design and ease of use of hot water faucets, door locks, and windows.

Accident Prevention

We are exposed to environmental risks every day; at any moment we could slip on a throw rug, trip on the stairs, or run a stop sign. Maintaining a safe environment, then, cannot be obtained through eliminating risk entirely. Rather, it must be based on a balanced approach to minimizing risk wherever possible, instituting better assessment and screening procedures, and educating people about hazards (Singleton, 1979).

The key to addressing the problem of safety is to remember that age alone does not cause accidents. Rather, it is the decline in sensory and information-processing skills that is responsible for age-related increases in some types of accidents. However, large differences exist across (and even within) individuals in the rate and extent of such changes. Consequently, accident prevention strategies must be sensitive to individual differences rather than simply focusing on age. As pointed out in Something to Think About, incorporating this knowledge is desirable, but it may be difficult to accomplish this goal.

Concept Checks

1. What age-related differences are observed in highway accidents?
2. What is the primary cause of older adults' accidents in the home?

LANGUAGE PROCESSING

Learning Objectives:

- What age differences are observed in understanding speech?
- What is the relation between language processing and information processing?
- What age differences are observed in implicit memory?

One of the most important information-processing abilities in everyday life is understanding and using language. Understanding what is said in a conversation, being able to read a note from a friend, and having the ability to respond allows us to interact with others and maintain social ties.

Once information has been registered in sensory memory and noticed by attentional processes, it is then transformed again based on its meaning. In language information, such as words or speech, this meaning is based on our ability to make a basic linguistic decision about it: Is the information being presented a word? Do we know what the information means? Thus, simple linguistic decisions represent the next step in information processing. Provided the information has linguistic meaning, is it processsed automatically or do we have to exert effort every time? These are the fundamental issues we will consider in this section. These basic language processing steps set the stage for research on the subsequent steps of working and other aspects of memory, which we will consider in Chapter 6.

Clearly, language processing is an important area of research in information processing. Like human factors, it is based on interactions between sensory systems and basic information-processing abilities. Language processing researchers distinguish between language comprehension and language production. ***Language comprehension*** involves handling words coming into the information-processing system and figuring out what they mean. Knowing the definition of words or that the person sitting across the table just asked you to pass the salt are two examples of language comprehension. In contrast, ***language production*** means being able to come up with an appropriate word or phrase when you are trying to say, or write, or think about something. A common example of language production is coming up with a person's name when you encounter them in a store.

Researchers have studied many aspects of both language comprehension and language production. Much of this work has been done in the context of memory or intelligence research. For example, having people learn and remember word lists or text passages is commonly examined in memory research, and testing people's vocabulary knowledge is typical in intelligence research. Both of these areas rely heavily on language production because people's scores are based on how often and how well they produce correct responses. In this section, we will focus on the basic processes of language comprehension.

Language Comprehension and Sensory Systems

Let's reflect a moment on some connections between language processing and what we know about age-related differences in information processing. Language comprehension is based initially on visual or auditory input. Many important changes in each of these sensory systems could

SOMETHING TO THINK ABOUT

Accidents and Older Adults

Accidents seldom "just happen," and many can be prevented. Accidental injuries become both more frequent and more serious in later life. Thus, attention to safety is especially important for older people.

Several factors make people in this age group prone to accidents. Poor eyesight and hearing can decrease awareness of hazards. Arthritis, neurological diseases, and impaired coordination and balance can make older people unsteady. Various diseases, medications, alcohol, and preoccupation with personal problems can result in drowsiness or distraction. Often mishaps are expressions of mental depression or of poor physical conditioning.

When accidents occur, older people are especially vulnerable to severe injury and tend to heal slowly. Particularly in women, bones often become thin and brittle with age, causing seemingly minor falls to result in broken hips.

Many accidents can be prevented by maintaining mental and physical health and conditioning and by cultivating good safety habits. *Falls* are the most common cause of fatal injury in the aged. Proper lighting can help prevent them. Here's what we can do:

- Illuminate all stairways and provide light switches at both the bottom and the top.
- Provide night-lights or bedside remote control light switches.
- Be sure *both* sides of stairways have sturdy handrails.
- Tack down carpeting on stairs, and use nonskid treads.
- Remove throw rugs that tend to slide.
- Arrange furniture and other objects so they are not obstacles.
- Use grab bars on bathroom walls and nonskid mats or strips in the bathtub.
- Keep outdoor steps and walkways in good repair.

Personal health practices are also important in preventing falls. Because older people tend to become faint or dizzy after standing too quickly, experts recommend rising slowly from sitting or lying positions. Both illness and the side effects of drugs increase the risk of falls.

Burns are especially disabling in the aged, who recover from such injuries more slowly. Here are some ways to avoid being burned:

- Never smoke in bed or when drowsy.
- When cooking, don't wear loosely fitting flammable clothing. Bathrobes, nightgowns, and pajamas catch fire.
- Set water heater thermostats or faucets so that water does not scald the skin.
- Plan which emergency exits to use in case of fire. Many older people trap themselves behind multiple door locks that are hard to open during an emergency. Install one good lock that can be opened from the inside quickly, rather than many inexpensive locks.

Motor vehicle accidents are the most common cause of accidental death among the 65–74 age group and the second most common cause among older people in general. The ability to drive may be impaired by such age-related changes as increased sensitivity to glare, poorer adaptation to dark, diminished coordination, and slower reaction time. Older adults can compensate for these changes by driving fewer miles; driving less often and more slowly; and driving less at night, during rush hour, and in the winter.

Older people who ride on public transportation should:

- Remain alert and brace themselves when a bus or subway train is slowing down or turning.
- Watch for slippery pavement and other hazards when entering or leaving a vehicle.
- Have the fare ready to prevent losing their balance while fumbling for change.
- Not carry too many packages, and leave one hand free to grasp railings.
- Allow extra time to cross streets, especially in bad weather.
- At night wear light-colored or fluorescent clothing and carry a flashlight.

Old people constitute about 11% of the population and suffer 23% of all accidental deaths. The National Safety Council reports that each year about 24,000 people over age 65 die from accidental injuries and at least 800,000 others sustain injuries severe enough to disable them for at least one day. Thus, attention to safety, especially in later life, can prevent much untimely death and disability. It's something to think about.

(Source: National Institute on Aging, 1980.)

influence how well or how easily we understand language. In vision, changes in light transmissiveness and accommodation could affect how clearly we see letters or words. In hearing, changes in pitch perception may alter how well we hear certain sounds. Earlier in this chapter we examined several changes in visual information processing that could also affect language comprehension. Most important, the data suggested that older adults have difficulty integrating different visual features. This could present problems when older adults read. One area we have not yet considered is understanding speech. It is to this topic we now turn.

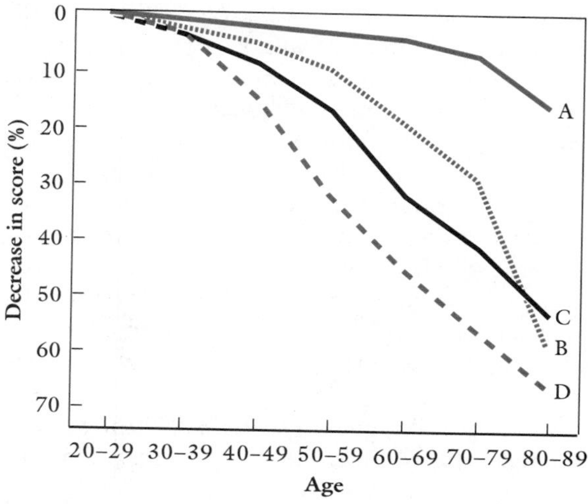

Figure 5.5 Decrease in percent intelligibility for speech as a function of age. Curves: **A**—unaltered speech; **B**—reverberated speech; **C**—overlapping speech with spondaic words; **D**—interrupted speech. For each curve, normal subjects 20–29 years served as zero reference.

Source: "Hearing and Aging: Implications of Recent Research Findings," by M. Bergman, 1971, Audiology, 10, *164–171. Copyright ©1971 S. Karger AG. Reprinted with permission.*

Understanding Speech

Have you ever tried to have a serious conversation at a noisy party? You may have had trouble understanding what the person you were with was saying. Or perhaps you have been in a quieter environment such as an art museum and couldn't quite pick up what the tour director was relating about the Monet masterpiece. Both of these situations can be annoying and embarrassing. Constantly saying, "I can't hear you; would you repeat what you said?" is no fun.

Obviously, being able to hear plays an important role in understanding speech. Given the normative decline in hearing due to presbycusis, does people's ability to understand speech decline as well? Fortunately, presbycusis normally does not affect the pitches used in most speech sounds until around age 80. As a result, speech understanding is usually not seriously impaired until late in life. However, a few sounds in English, such as *s, ch,* and *sh* involve pitches that are affected earlier. Consequently, middle-aged and young-old adults (ages 60 to 75) may have trouble understanding these sounds (Brant & Fozard, 1990).

How well people understand speech is tested in two ways. *Speech recognition* is measured by presenting the listener with a list of spondee words: Spondaic two-syllable words are pronounced with equal emphasis on both syllables (some English examples are *airplane, baseball, birthday,* and *headlight*). *Speech discrimination* is tested with monosyllabic words that include the various sounds in English.

Several studies have documented an age-related decrement in both speech recognition and speech discrimination abilities, especially after age 50 (Corso, 1981; Olsho et al., 1985). Typical results are shown in Figure 5.5. Notice that age differences become especially pronounced when the listening situation is made more difficult, such as when other voices are in the background or when speech is interrupted. Older adults also have difficulty understanding speech that is embedded in noise (Gordon-Salant, 1987).

How well people understand speech is also affected by how fast it is presented and whether the words are presented alone or in the context of regular speech. Stine, Wingfield, and colleagues examined these issues in a series of studies (see Stine & Wingfield, 1987; Stine, Wingfield, & Poon, 1986; Wingfield & Stine, 1986). They looked for age differences in speech understanding by using compressed speech, which allowed them to use presentation rates between 200 and 400 words per minute. In addition, they manipulated whether words were presented in sentences, with normal voice inflections, in meaningless but grammatically correct strings, or in random order. Results demonstrated the power of context. When words were presented normally in sentences, older adults performed at over 90% accuracy even at 400 or more words per minute. However, when words were presented in random strings or without normal vocal cues, older adults performed poorly even at slower rates (around 250 words per minute).

Stine and Wingfield's work clearly shows how context affects older adults' understanding of speech. On the one hand, context allows older adults to understand what is said even at very fast presentation rates. This finding is similar to the results from Salthouse's work on typing that we considered earlier. On the other hand, Stine and Wingfield's research also demonstrates how much older adults depend on context; their understanding of speech drops dramatically when contextual cues are not present. These effects get us into the realm of the role of information processing in language, to which we now turn.

Language Comprehension and Information Processing

How do words get processed beyond basic sensory systems so that we understand what they mean? This question has intrigued researchers for many years and continues to be one of the most active areas in cognitive psychology. Some argue that language processing is the key to understanding a host of other processes, including understanding memory. If this is true, then age-related changes in language processing may underlie the age-related differences in memory we will discuss in Chapter 6. For example, Craik and Byrd (1982) claimed that age-related differences in language processing result in less richly encoded information that makes information less memorable. Their claim is based on the belief that older adults' information-processing abilities are compromised—due to less attentional capacity, drops in processing speed, and changes in working memory.

Numerous investigators have examined aspects of Craik and Byrd's claim (Light, 1990). We will consider this research under two general headings: richness and extensiveness of encoding and encoding deficits.

Richness and Extensiveness of Encoding

Suppose you and a friend hear the name Martin Luther King, Jr., as part of a lecture in history class. Suppose further that you are very familiar with him but your friend is not. You will have a distinct advantage over your friend in remembering him. Why?

When linguistic information comes in, you look for ways to connect it to other information you already know. The more connections you can make, the better off you will be later when you need to remember the name. Because your friend can only make a few connections, getting the name to stick in memory will be more difficult.

The number of different connections created between incoming information and information already in a knowledge base is what is meant by rich and extensive encoding. If age differences in encoding occur, they could be manifested in two ways (Light, 1990). First, how knowledge is organized could change across adulthood, making it harder to keep connections intact. Second, the processes by which connections get made could change with age. However, neither appears to change substantially with age (Light, 1990).

Encoding Deficits

One school of thought is that extensive encoding underlies the ability to retrieve information. That is, information that is richly encoded is more easily retrieved. One way to test this is to ask people to judge whether a particular letter string is a word (called a lexical decision task). One variant of a lexical decision task, called *priming,* involves showing people related words prior to the letter string (for example, show the word *nurse* and ask people to judge whether the letter string *d-o-c-t-o-r* is a word). Researchers then focus on how quickly people make these decisions as the major variable of interest.

Performing well on lexical decision tasks requires a fairly rich knowledge base. Adults of all ages are equally adept at lexical decision tasks. For example, Stern, Prather, Swinney, and Zurif (1991) showed that older and younger adults had equal automatic lexical access. But what if people are then given a test to see if they can remember the words that they saw? In this case, older adults do worse than younger adults. This performance pattern of equivalent lexical access but poorer memory does not support the idea that poor encoding of lexical information underlies memory problems. Why? If encoding were the problem, people would not be able to make the lexical decisions, as they would not have processed the necessary information to make the judgment. Because adults of all ages perform this part very well, we know that the necessary information has been processed. Thus, the age differences that emerge in the memory task cannot be due to significant age differences in encoding of the basic lexical information.

A second issue concerning encoding deficits is that older adults do not take advantage of contextual cues when they encode information. Specifically, Rabinowitz, Craik, and Ackerman (1982) believed that older adults do not tend to create distinctive context-specific encoding, but rather have a tendency to use the same approach each time. Although there is some support for Rabinowitz's position, several investigators disagree. We have already seen that older adults use sentence context to process rapid speech. Additionally, researchers have shown that older adults often do use context-specific information at encoding (for example, Howard, Heisey, & Shaw, 1986) and in naming words (Nebes, Boller, & Holland, 1986).

In sum, there is no support for the contention that basic linguistic processing is the basis for age-related differences in memory. Knowledge is organized similarly in younger and older adults, and tests of immediate comprehension as measured by word naming and lexical decision tasks show no age differences. What, then, accounts for memory problems? As we will see in Chapter 6, the answer to this question is rather complex and involves the interaction of several factors.

Implicit Memory

Although age differences in language processing do not appear to underlie age differences in memory, one area in which the two overlap is implicit memory. ***Implicit memory*** **is a facilitation or change in task performance that is attributable to having been exposed to information at some earlier point in time, but which does not involve active, deliberate memory.** A good example of implicit memory is a language task such as stem completion. In a stem completion task, you would be required to complete a word stem with the first word that comes to mind (for instance, con _____). Previously, you may have been shown a list of words that contained a valid completion of the stem (such as con<u>tact</u>). If you have seen valid completions of the stems, you are more likely to use them later to complete the stems than you are to make up a different one (con<u>test</u>). This facilitation is called priming (Schacter, 1987). The memory aspect of the task is that you remember the stem completion you were shown; the implicit part is remembering it without being told to do so.

Early research on implicit memory focused on demonstrating that it was a separate process from deliberate memory. For example, whereas deliberate memory performance is affected by having people think about the meaning of the items, implicit memory is not (Graf & Mandler, 1984), and people with amnesia show severe problems on explicit memory tests but often perform similarly to normal people on implicit memory tests (Shimamura, 1986).

More recent research reveals some differences among various types of implicit memory tests. The most important distinction has been between perceptually based and conceptually based tests (Blaxton, 1989). Perceptually based implicit memory tasks rely on processing the physical features of a stimulus; an example would be to process whether a word appears in lowercase or uppercase letters. Conceptually based implicit memory tasks rely on the semantic meaning of the items, such as whether the word is a verb. Depending on what people are asked to process (i.e., physical features or semantic meaning), performance on the tests differ (Blaxton, 1989).

The difference between the types of tests has important implications for age differences (Small, Hultsch, & Masson, 1995). Results from several studies reveal a mixed patter of age differences in implicit memory; some studies find no differences (e.g., Mitchell, 1989; Russo & Parkin, 1993), whereas others demonstrate small differences in favor of young adults (e.g., Chiarello & Hoyer, 1988; Hultsch, Masson, & Small, 1991). To try to sort out these findings, Light and La Voie (1993) conducted a meta-analysis of the literature and examined age differences in studies using a variety of implicit memory tests. They found small, but reliable, age differences in performance on implicit memory tests.

Two reasons for the inconsistent findings have been noted (Small et al., 1995). First, because the effects are small, investigations with only 30 or so participants may not have sufficient statistical power to detect the differences (Small et al., 1995). Second, age differences in implicit memory depend on the type of test used. Age differences are evident on perceptually based tests, but not on conceptually based tests (Small et al., 1995). The reason for this different pattern may be related to the cognitive processes involved in performing each type of task. Hultsch and colleagues (1991; Small et al., 1995) believe that perceptually based implicit memory tests, such as stem completion, tap aspects early in information processing; conceptually based tests may tap aspects of semantic learning. Both of these are different from the processes involved in deliberate learning and remembering.

Intellectual ability may be another reason for the various patterns of age differences in implicit memory according to Cherry and Stadler's (1995) research. Using a spatial location task involving repeating sequences, they found no age differences in implicit memory between younger adults and higher ability older adults, but both of these groups performed more accurately than lower ability older adults. Combined with similar findings reported by Howard and Howard (1992), the data indicate that individual differences in ability should also be considered in interpreting the presence or absence of age differences in implicit memory.

Concept Checks

1. What is the effect of the rate of speech on older adults?
2. What evidence is there that linguistic processing underlies age differences in memory?
3. Why are the findings of age differences in implicit memory inconsistent?

SUMMARY

The Information-Processing Model

Overview of the Model

The information-processing model assumes an active participant, both quantitative and qualitative aspects of performance, and processing of information through a series of hypothetical stages.

Early Aspects of Information Processing

Sensory memory is the first level of processing incoming information from the environment. Sensory memory has a very large capacity, but information only lasts there a very short time. Age differences are found in two aspects of sensory memory: encoding speed and susceptibility to backward masking.

Attention

Feature Integration Theory

Three aspects of attention have been studied: selectivity, attentional capacity, and vigilance. Selectivity involves choosing which information gets passed from sensory memory to working memory. Attentional capacity refers to how much information can be processed at once. Some processes are automatic, placing little or no demand on attentional capacity; other processes require effort and put varying demands on capacity.

Vigilance or sustained attention refers to how long one can maintain attention while doing a task. Feature integration theory describes the process of encoding important aspects of a stimulus (feature extraction) and then putting those aspects together (feature integration).

Selective Attention

Age-related decrements are found in visual search, primarily due to differences in feature integration. Cuing spatial locations sharply reduces age differences when the cue provides unambiguous information. No age differences are found on visual attention switching tasks, but are found on auditory tasks. Older adults have more difficulty filtering out or inhibiting irrelevant information than younger adults, but this may be limited to the item's identity.

Divided Attention

Divided attention involves doing more than one task that demands attention. Age differences in divided attention depend on the degree of task complexity and practice. Some researchers claim that older adults have fewer processing resources than younger adults; however, this concept is ill defined.

Sustained Attention

Older adults are not as good as younger adults at detecting targets on vigilance tasks, but there are no age differences in the rate at which performance declines over time. As task complexity increases or predictability of the target decreases, age differences on vigilance tasks increase.

Automatic Processes

Automatic processes are those that are fast, reliable, and insensitive to increased cognitive demands. In general, age differences are not observed on consistent mapping practice but are found on variable mapping practice tasks.

Psychomotor Speed

Reaction Time Tasks

Simple reaction time involves responding as quickly as possible to a stimulus. Choice reaction time involves making separate responses to separate stimuli as quickly as possible. Complex reaction time involves making complicated decisions about how to respond based on the stimulus observed.

Age Differences in Components of Reaction Time

Two components of reaction time have been examined: response preparation and response complexity. Older adults do not prepare as well to make a response as younger adults. As task complexity increases, age differences increase.

Interpreting Age Differences in Reaction Time

One way that age differences in reaction time have been interpreted is through Brinley plots, which result in a linear function when older adults' reaction times are plotted as a function of younger adults' reaction times. However, this approach is controversial.

What Causes Age-Related Slowing?

One explanation of age differences, based on neural networks, is that older people need more neuronal connections to make the response. A second possibility, termed the information-loss model, is that older adults lose more information at each step of processing.

Slowing Down How Much We Slow Down

Although practice improves performance, age differences are not eliminated. However, experience allows older adults to compensate for loss of speed by anticipating what is likely to happen. The span of anticipation appears to be the reason that experience helps. Regular exercise also improves reaction time performance.

Driving and Accident Prevention

Driving and Highway Safety as Information Processing

Human factors tries to optimize the design of living and working environments. Older drivers have several problems, including reading highway signs, seeing at night, noting warnings, and performing various operating skills. Changes in information-processing abilities could make older adults more susceptible to accidents, although documenting the actual risk is difficult.

Home Safety and Accident Prevention

Older adults are more likely to hurt themselves by falling at home than younger adults. Age alone does not cause such accidents; rather, declines in physiological and sensory functioning are the reasons.

Language Processing

Language Comprehension and Sensory Systems

Language comprehension involves attaching meaning to incoming words. Language production involves coming up with an appropriate word or phrase. Speech comprehension is usually not affected by presbycusis until age 80. Speech recognition and speech discrimination begin to decline after age 50. The faster speech is presented, the greater the age differences in understanding it.

Language Comprehension and Information Processing

Age differences are usually not found on lexical decision tasks or on the number of connections people make to incoming information. Basic language processing deficits do not appear to be the cause of age differences in memory. Older adults do not take advantage of contextual cues when they encode information.

Implicit Memory

Implicit memory is the facilitation or change in task performance that is attributable to having been exposed to information at some earlier point in time, but which does not involve active, deliberate memory. Older adults are generally slightly worse on implicit memory tasks than younger adults.

REVIEW QUESTIONS

The information-processing model

- What assumptions does the information-processing model make?
- What are the early steps in information processing? What age differences have been noted?

Attention

- What aspects of attention have been studied? Define each of them.
- What is feature integration theory? How does it help researchers understand age differences in attention?
- What age differences have been reported in visual search? How can these age differences be reduced or eliminated?
- What age differences have been noted on divided-attention tasks? Why do these differences occur?
- What age differences occur on vigilance tasks? What variables affect the magnitude of age differences?

Psychomotor speed

- What different types of reaction time tasks are used to study psychomotor speed? What age differences have been found on each?
- How does task complexity affect age differences on reaction time tasks?
- Describe the neural networks approach to accounting for age differences in reaction time.
- How do practice and experience affect age differences in reaction time?
- What effect does exercise have on reaction time?

Driving and accident prevention

- What is human factors?
- What problems do older drivers have, and what interventions can be applied to help them?
- What accident risks do older adults face in their homes?

Language processing

- What is the difference between language comprehension and language production?
- How do speech comprehension, speech recognition, and speech discrimination change with age?
- What role do basic language processing deficits play in age differences in memory?
- What age differences have been found on implicit memory tasks?

INTEGRATING CONCEPTS IN DEVELOPMENT

1. How are changes in the sensory systems (discussed in Chapter 3) related to age differences in information processing?
2. Besides driving, what practical implications are there for slowing down with age?
3. How could a car's instrument panel be designed to help older drivers?
4. What connections are there between lifestyle factors in health and information processing?

KEY TERMS

attentional capacity A hypothetical construct referring to the amount of information that can be processed at a time.

automatic attention response Processing of a specific and well-trained stimulus, such as a target letter, that automatically captures attention.

automatic processes Processes that are fast, reliable, and insensitive to increased cognitive demands.

divided attention The ability to pay attention and successfully perform more than one task at a time.

feature integration theory (FIT) A theory of visual information processing consisting of two phases: feature extraction and feature integration. FIT explains a great deal of the age differences found in visual information processing.

human factors The study of how people interact with machines and other objects in their environment.

implicit memory A type of memory that occurs without one being aware that something has been remembered.

information-processing approach The study of how people take in stimuli from their environment and transform them into memories; the approach is based on a computer metaphor.

processing resources The amount of attention one has to apply to a particular situation.

reaction time The speed with which one makes a response.

response preparation Processes involved in getting ready to make a response in a reaction time task.

selectivity The process by which information is chosen for further processing in attention.

sensory memory The earliest step in information processing where new, incoming information is first registered.

spatial cuing A technique in visual processing research in which people are provided a hint concerning where the next target will appear.

vigilance Maintaining attention to the same task over an extended period of time.

IF YOU'D LIKE TO LEARN MORE

Cerella, J. (1990). Aging and information-processing rate. In J. E. Birren & K. W. Schaie (Eds.), *Handbook of the psychology of aging* (3rd ed., pp. 201–221). San Diego: Academic Press. Provides an overview of theories and data about processing resources and speed. Moderate to difficult reading.

Cerella, J., Rybash, J. M., Hoyer, W., & Commons, M. L. (Eds.). (1993). *Adult information processing: Limits on loss.* San Diego: Academic Press. One of the best single-volume accounts of age differences in information processing. Moderately difficult reading.

Hartley, A. A. (1992). Attention. In F. I. M. Craik & T. A. Salthouse (Eds.), *The handbook of aging and cognition* (pp. 3–49). Hillsdale, NJ: Erlbaum. Good review of research on attention. Moderately difficult reading.

Light, L. L., & Burke, D. M. (Eds.). (1988). *Language, memory, and aging.* New York: Cambridge University Press. A good introduction to the issues in this area. Moderately difficult reading.

CHAPTER 6

Memory

Andrew Wyeth, *Children's Doctor,* 1949. Collection of the Brandywine River Museum. Gift of Betsy James Wyeth ©1996 Andrew Wyeth.

Memory is a continuum ranging from vague, dim shadows to the brightest, most vivid totality. It may offer opportunity not merely to recall the past but to relive it, in all its original freshness, unaltered by intervening changes and reflections. . . . Simultaneity replaces sequence and a sense of oneness with one's past is achieved. Often such moments involve childhood memories, and then one experiences the self as it was originally, and knows beyond doubt that one is the same person as that child who still dwells within a time-altered body. Integration through memory with earlier states of being surely provides the sense of continuity and completeness that may be counted as an essential developmental task of old age.

Barbara Myerhoff's description of memory from her book *Re-membered Lives* (1980) points out that memory provides the basis for building a personal identity. With it, we can relive moments from our past and create our personal history. It is the remembering of these experiences that tells us who we are and where we came from.

Memory is such a pervasive aspect of our daily lives that we take it for granted. From remembering where we keep our toothbrush to tying our shoes to timing soft-boiled eggs—memory is always with us. Moreover, it gives us a sense of identity. Imagine how frightening it would be to wake up and have no memory whatsoever—no recollection of name, address, parents, or anything else.

Perhaps that is why we put so much value on maintaining a good memory in old age. Society uses memory as the yardstick with which to judge whether a person's mind is intact. Older adults are stereotyped as people whose memory is on the decline, people for whom forgetting is not to be taken lightly. Many people think that forgetting to buy a loaf of bread when one is 25 is all right, but forgetting it when one is 65 is cause for concern ("Do I have Alzheimer's disease?"). We will see that this belief is wrong. However, we undoubtedly have more at stake here than just another cognitive process. We are dealing with something that, as Myerhoff indicated, intimately involves our sense of self (Cavanaugh, Morton, & Tilse, 1989).

Most of the research described in this chapter views memory as an end in itself. That is, the goal is simply how well people perform the task of learning and remembering some material. Doing well on the memory test is the name of the game. Indeed, many situations in life present similar demands. We may need to have considerable information at our fingertips to do well at game shows such as *Jeopardy!*

But many other situations in everyday life call for the use of memory to serve some other function. That is, we use memory as a means to an end. For example, we use memory when we summarize the most recent episode of our favorite soap opera, tell other people about ourselves, or reminisce about our high school days. In these situations we *are* using memory, but the point is not just how much we remember. More often, the idea is to facilitate social exchange, to allow other people to get to know us, or to give ourselves a shared past with others.

These different uses of memory raise some intriguing questions about adult development and aging. Are there differences in the ways in which adults of different ages use memory? How would these differences affect performance on traditional memory tests? What should our criteria be for good versus poor memory? These questions are something to think about as we explore what has been discovered about aging and memory. We will attempt to answer them by looking at memory from different vantage points. First, we will continue applying the information-processing model introduced in Chapter 5 and see what happens to secondary and tertiary memory. Second, we will look at memory for discourse and see how people vary in the kinds of information they remember from such things as prose passages and television. Third, we will consider several ways in which adults remember things in everyday life and the differences between these settings and laboratory research. Fourth, we will examine how we use memory as a yardstick by which we judge our competence. In particular, we will consider the processes by which we evaluate our memory. Fifth, we will focus specifically on how we keep information stored in memory and how we get it back out.

An important aspect here will be how adults use different types of strategies to help themselves remember. Finally, we will see how memory problems are assessed and how some problems may be treated.

Memory researchers have long focused on three general steps in memory processing as potential sources of age differences: encoding, storage, and retrieval (Smith, 1996). ***Encoding*** **is the process of getting information into the memory system.** ***Storage*** **involves the manner in which information is represented and kept in memory. Getting information back out of memory is termed *retrieval*.** Because there is no evidence for age differences in how information is organized in storage, most research has examined encoding and retrieval as sources of age differences (Light, 1992).

More recently, researchers have looked to research on working memory as providing new insights into why age differences in memory occur. As we will see, working memory involves information that is being actively processed at any point in time, and it is an aspect of memory showing clear age differences.

INFORMATION PROCESSING REVISITED

Learning Objectives:

- What is working memory? What age differences have been found in working memory?
- How does secondary memory performance differ across age?
- What age differences have been found in the knowledge base and autobiographical aspects of tertiary memory?

Chapter 5 introduced us to the most widely used model of cognitive processes—the information-processing model. Recall that the information-processing model is based on a computer metaphor and that different aspects of the model have different jobs to perform. We focused on early steps in processing, psychomotor speed, attention, and language processing. Our focus in this section will be on three other main components: working memory, secondary memory, and tertiary memory.

Working Memory

When we left off in Chapter 5, we had followed the flow of information from its initial reception in sensory memory, through attention, to the initial steps of linguistic processing. We are now ready to consider how information is kept in one's mind either for additional processing into longer memory stores or is being held temporarily during retrieval. How this happens involves working memory.

Working memory **refers to the processes and structures involved in holding information in mind and simultaneously using that information, sometimes in conjunction with incoming information, to solve a problem, make a decision, or learn new information** (Craik & Jennings, 1992). Although some authors regard working memory as a specific store (Stine, 1990), others consider it an umbrella term for many similar short-term holding and computational processes relating to a wide range of cognitive skills and knowledge domains (Craik & Jennings, 1992). This places working memory right in the thick of things—it plays a critical and central role in encoding, storage, and retrieval.

Recall that sensory memory has a very large capacity to deal with incoming information. In contrast, researchers generally agree that working memory has a relatively small capacity. This capacity limitation of working memory operates like a juggler who can only keep a small number of items in the air simultaneously. Because working memory deals with information being processed right at this moment, it is also acts as a kind of mental scratchpad. This means that unless we take direct action to keep the information active, the page we are using will get used up quickly and tossed away. For this reason, we need to have some way to keep information in working memory.

The most important way in which information is held in working memory is through *rehearsal*, which involves either repeating items

Activities such as spinning involve retrieving elaborate memory representation for each aspect of the activity as well as accurately monitoring what one is doing.

over and over or making meaningful connections between the information in working memory and information already known (Craik & Lockhart, 1972; Kausler, 1985). Repeating items over and over works well if one only needs to keep information in mind for a relatively brief period of time, such as a phone number that will be dialed immediately. Making connections with information already in memory is much better if one needs to remember the number over a longer period of time, such as when it's one's lover's number.

Many researchers propose working memory as the basis for understanding language processing difficulties encountered in later life (for example, Kemper, 1988; Stine, 1990). This idea is based on the extremely important role that working memory is believed to play in information processing. For example, working memory is where all the action is during processing: It is where information obtains meaning and is transformed for longer storage. As a result, age differences here would have profound implications for just about all aspects of memory. The idea is that if information becomes degraded or is only partially integrated into one's knowledge base, it will be very difficult to remember it.

Evidence that the capacity of working memory declines somewhat with age is growing (Salthouse, 1991), although the extent of the decline is still in doubt. Foos (1995) found that younger and middle-aged adults can perform more than one memory task equivalently, but older adults performed the tasks more poorly, a finding consistent with the notion that the ability to allocate capacity in working memory to more than one task declines with age. Additionally, rehearsal ability declines, resulting in poorer quality information being passed along the system (Kausler, 1985). Salthouse (1991) believes that working memory is the key to understanding age differences in memory. He argues that the loss of some of the ability to hold items in working memory may limit older adults' overall cognitive functioning. Moreover, Salthouse points out that much of the apparent differences in working memory may in turn be related to speed of processing. That is, older adults' reduced working memory capacity may be due to their overall slower rate of processing.

However, some evidence suggests that age differences in working memory are not universal. For example, working memory appears to depend on the type of information being used and may even vary across different tasks (Daneman, 1987). Such differences complicate matters. The extent of age differences in working memory may depend more on one's degree of expertise in a particular area than on age per se. Could practice eliminate age differences in working memory?

Campbell and Charness (1990) decided to look into the matter. They had young, middle-aged, and older adults learn and practice an algorithm for squaring two-digit numbers (for example, learning how to calculate 57^2 in your head). Needless to say, this task is hard for the uninitiated; one not only needs many facts about multiplication at one's fingertips, but also needs to remember the results of all the intermediate calculations to get the correct answer.

Practicing the algorithm greatly reduced calculation errors for all age groups. However, the older group made more working memory errors (such as, leaving out steps in the calculation process). Moreover, practice did not substantially reduce age differences in the efficiency of working memory. These results imply two things. First, practice greatly enhances fact retrieval, as seen in the large reduction of calculation errors. Second, practice has only a minimal effect on improving working memory efficiency. Thus, although practice may help people retrieve information faster, it may not help them use it more efficiently. Age-related decrements in working memory efficiency appear to be normative.

Related evidence from a study of university professors provides additional support (Shimamura, Berry, Mangels, Rusting, & Jurica, 1995). Shimamura and colleagues found that professors showed less decline than most people do, probably because of their jobs, which require more efficient planning, organizational, and retrieval strategies. For example, giving a lecture places considerable demands on working memory, which, when practiced over many years, results in better efficiency in later life.

We noted at the beginning of this section that working memory is an umbrella term for several related processes. In an effort to understand the components of working memory, Salthouse and Babcock (1991) conducted a large-scale study of 400 adults. Salthouse and Babcock were able to separate working memory performance into storage, processing, and executive functions (which involve the coordination of storage and processing). Their results indicated that age differences in working memory were due mostly to the processing component of tasks, which in turn was mediated by reductions in simple speed of processing.

Because research on working memory is relatively new, a great deal more needs to be done. Salthouse and colleagues' attempt to link age differences in working memory with age differences in processing speed will open up new and exciting avenues for research. Campbell and Charness's differentiation between fact retrieval and working memory efficiency will help clarify the role of practice and expertise. There is little doubt at this point of the emerging importance of working memory as an important concept for understanding age-related differences in memory performance. For example, researchers have begun to show that working memory may be key to understanding the age differences in recall performance (discussed in the next section), especially in situations in which few cues for remembering exist (Park et al., 1994).

Secondary Memory

When most people think about memory, they think about having to remember something over time, whether a few minutes or many days. Everyday life is full of examples—remembering routines, performing on an exam, summarizing a book or movie, and remembering an appointment. These types of situations constitute what memory researchers call secondary memory (Poon, 1985;

Smith, 1996). ***Secondary memory* refers to the ability to remember rather extensive amounts of information from a few seconds to a few hours.** Memory researchers have created a wide variety of tasks requiring individuals to remember all sorts of information for varying lengths of time. Over a century of research has indicated that secondary memory represents a relatively large capacity store in which information can be kept for long periods.

The kind of information examined in research on secondary memory involves deliberately remembering information that is learned and remembered at a specific point in time. Thus, it reflects an aspect of *episodic memory,* the general class of memory having to do with time-dependent information processing. Examples of episodic memory include learning the material in this course so that you will be able to reproduce it on an examination in the future, remembering what you did on your summer vacation last year, and memorizing a speech for a play. A second major class of memory, termed *semantic memory,* concerns learning and remembering the meaning of words and concepts that are not tied to specific occurrences of events in time. Examples of semantic memory include knowing the definitions of words in order to complete crossword puzzles, being able to translate this paragraph from English into French, and understanding what the instructor is saying in a lecture. The distinction between episodic and semantic memory is important in understanding age differences in memory. For example, people with Alzheimer's disease show extreme deficits in episodic memory compared with older adults who do not have this disease, but these groups are more comparable on semantic memory performance (Cavanaugh & Nocera, 1994).

Because secondary memory includes so many of the day-to-day activities we adults perform, it has been the focus of more research than any other single topic in memory development (Poon, 1985). Typically, researchers study secondary memory by having people learn information, such as a list of words, and then asking them to recall or recognize the items. **In a *recall* test, people are asked to remember information without hints or cues.** Everyday examples of recall include telling everything that you can remember about a movie or taking an essay exam. ***Recognition,* on the other hand, involves selecting previously learned information from among several items.** Everyday examples of recognition include taking multiple-choice tests and picking out the names of your high school friends from a complete list of your classmates.

Memory researchers use several techniques to study the variables that influence secondary memory performance. For example, they may vary the way that the information to be learned is presented (such as in organized groups, with cues, or randomly); the speed at which it is presented; the familiarity of the material; and the conditions for remembering the items (for instance, giving recall cues or making a recognition test easy or hard).

The results from hundreds of studies on secondary memory point to several conclusions. Overall, older adults perform worse than younger adults on tests of secondary memory (Poon, 1985). These age differences are large; for example, more than 80% of a sample of adults in their 20s will do better than adults in their 70s (Verhaeghen, Marcoen, & Goossens, 1993). These differences are not reliably lowered either by providing slower presentation or by giving cues or reminders during recall. However, a recognition paradigm changes this picture. People of all ages perform better on recognition tests, and age differences between older and younger adults are reduced (Poon, 1985).

Older adults also tend to be less efficient at spontaneously using internal study strategies, such as using imagery or putting items into categories in one's mind to organize information during study. When older adults are instructed to use internal organizational strategies such as categorization, however, they not only can do so but also show significant improvement in performance. However, these improvements are not sufficient, in general, to substantially reduce age differences in recall performance (Verhaeghen et al., 1993). Additionally, the failure to use strategies such as association and repetition may be the result of age changes in speed of processing and associative memory (Verhaeghen & Marcoen, 1994). These findings suggest that older adults are not as successful in situations requiring them to devise an efficient way to acquire disorganized information, especially when they will be expected to recall it later.

Age differences between older and younger adults can be reduced in several ways. First, allowing older adults to practice or to perform a similar task before learning a new list improves performance. Knowing what one is expected to do usually makes it easier to perform well. Interestingly, better memory performance after practice parallels similar improvements following practice on tests of skills related to fluid intelligence (discussed in Chapter 7). Second, using material that is more familiar to older adults also improves their performance. For example, older adults do not remember words such as *byte* or *Walkman* as well as words such as *jitterbug* or *bobbysox*. Third, we will examine compensatory strategies that older adults may use to help themselves remember, as well as the influence of their beliefs about memory, a bit later in this chapter.

What, then, can we conclude about secondary memory? Older adults are apparently disadvantaged when left on their own to face relatively rapid-paced, disorganized information. However, secondary memory performance appears to be somewhat flexible and manipulable, with improvements coming from a variety of sources. In later sections we will consider some attempts to explain why age differences occur and several ways in which secondary memory problems can be corrected.

Tertiary Memory

Information that needs to be kept for a very long time (from a few hours to many years) is housed in *tertiary memory* (Poon, 1985). Such information includes facts learned earlier, the meaning of words, past life experiences, and the like. Very little research has been conducted on age differences in tertiary memory, for a variety of reasons. For one thing, designing an adequate test of very long-term memory so that we know how to interpret performance is difficult. For example, we often cannot know whether an incident that someone recalls from the past is what actually happened, because we cannot verify the facts. Additionally, if a person does not remember a fact from years past, it may be due either to an inability to retrieve the information or to a failure to have learned the information in the first place. This latter issue is especially important when older and younger adults are compared; we must make certain that both groups had the opportunity and learned the information. Some ingenious researchers, though, have managed to circumvent these problems and have studied two aspects of tertiary memory: knowledge base and autobiographical memory.

Knowledge Base

One way that researchers test tertiary memory is with questionnaires asking about events of public knowledge assumed to be available to everyone. A typical question would be to ask for the name of the spacecraft that exploded after launching in January 1986. Researchers who have examined adults' performance on tests of knowledge about historical events find little difference in performance across age groups (e.g., J. L. Lachman & Lachman, 1980; Perlmutter, Metzger, Miller, & Nezworski, 1980).

Camp (1989) conducted some interesting research on people's ability to combine pieces of information in tertiary memory to answer inference questions. The questions he asks are unlikely to have been encountered before, making this technique useful in exploring the kinds of information housed in tertiary memory. An example of one of Camp's questions might be: What horror movie character would want to avoid the Lone Ranger? Camp finds that older adults respond with the werewolf (who can be killed only with silver bullets, the Lone Ranger's trademark) as well as, and often better than, young adults. Camp argues that these findings indicate no age differences in tertiary memory and may be evidence for improvement.

The lack of age differences in the knowledge base aspects of tertiary memory is not really surprising. The information we keep in tertiary memory is very similar to the information that relates to crystallized intelligence, such as world knowledge and vocabulary. As pointed out in Chapter 7, crystallized intelligence undergoes little if any change with age. Thus, it may be that tertiary memory is also related to this set of abilities.

Autobiographical Memory

One very important type of tertiary memory involves remembering information and events from our own life. These recollections, or autobiographical memory, provide each of us with a personal history and help define who we are. As important as autobiographical memory is, though, very few studies have looked at how well people remember things over the course of their lives.

One kind of personal information we remember are the names of our high school classmates. Bahrick, Bahrick, and Wittlinger (1975) tested high school graduates aged 17 to 74 for recall of their classmates' names and recognition of their faces in yearbook pictures. Recognition of faces was consistently over 90% up to 15 years after graduation. Amazingly, adults in their 70s could still recognize 70% of their classmates' names 48 years after graduation! Clearly, tertiary memory remains fairly good. The study also demonstrates that in some areas we can assess the accuracy of very long-term memory. Being able to verify what individuals remember with some record of the true event is extremely important in evaluating our ability to remember over long periods of time.

The issue of verification is crucial in testing people's recollections of personally experienced events. Only in cases where records have been kept for many years is this usually possible. Coleman, Casey, and Dwyer (1991) examined records that were available from the Harvard Longitudinal Studies of Child Health and Development on individuals from birth to age 50. Detailed information was collected over the years on such things as which childhood diseases the participants had, whether they smoked cigarettes, and what kinds and how much food they ate. At age 50, participants completed a lengthy questionnaire about these issues, and their responses were compared with similar reports made 10 and 20 years earlier, as well as with the official records. Coleman and colleagues found amazing accuracy for information such as whether a person had ever been a smoker or had a particular disease such as chicken pox. In fact, half of the memories elicited at age 50 were *more* accurate than the memories for the same information elicited 10 years earlier at age 40! However, information about amounts of food consumed or about individual episodes was not remembered very well. Apparently, these events tend to get blended together and are not stored as separate incidents.

What distinguishes events that are memorable from those that are not? What makes a moment we will remember the rest of our lives? Many people think that highly traumatic events are ones that are indelibly etched in our memories. If so, then people who survived Nazi concentration camps should have vivid memories of their experiences. Wagenaar and Groeneweg (1990) examined the testimony of 78 survivors of Camp Erika, a Nazi concentration camp in the Netherlands during World War II. Dutch police initially interviewed the survivors about their experiences between 1943 and 1948. In 1984, during a war crimes trial for an accused Nazi collaborator, these witnesses gave sworn depositions about their experiences at Camp Erika.

As described in Something to Think About, the camp survivors' recollections were a mix of accurate and inaccurate information. In many cases memory was quite good; even 40 years later about half of the survivors remembered the exact date of their arrival at the camp and their entire identification number. They were able to recall the general conditions of the camp, overall treatment, and the like. However, they also had forgotten many important details, including in some cases their own brutal treatment. Wagenaar and Groeneweg point out that these forgotten details mean that even extreme trauma is no guarantee that an event will be remembered. Perhaps forgetting the horrors of being brutalized is even a type of self-protection.

Events do not always have to be personally

SOMETHING TO THINK ABOUT

The Memory of Concentration Camp Survivors

One of the most common beliefs about autobiographical memory is that we can remember vivid details about especially important events in our lives. Indeed, researchers have identified so-called flashbulb memories in which people report minute details about what they were doing when they heard about a particular event, such as the assassinations of John F. Kennedy and Martin Luther King, Jr., or when the war with Iraq began.

This belief is especially strong when it comes to remembering traumatic events. Personal, detailed accounts of these events are an essential part of the judicial process; the lack of well-remembered details may mean a failure to obtain a conviction. Juries often find it hard to believe that people who are victims of crime fail to remember key details of the event.

Recently, though, a provocative study on concentration camp survivors questions the assumption of detailed memories. As noted in the text, Wagenaar and Groeneweg report that many survivors of Camp Erika (a Nazi concentration camp) in the Netherlands could not remember basic details of their experience. Cognitive psychologists would argue that being in a concentration camp should have provided a classic flashbulb memory that should have lasted many years. Indeed, survivors reported remembering their experiences in vivid detail in their interviews with the Dutch press in the mid-1940s. After 40 years, though, the memories were gone for many people. Why?

For one thing, we know that information in tertiary memory changes over time. For example, as we have new experiences we integrate them into our memory base. Over time, it becomes increasingly difficult to remember just the initial event. Additionally, people tend to not want to remember highly traumatic events. Rather, people want to forget them in the sense of learning to live with them. For example, after the loss of a loved one, people try to focus on the good events they shared rather than on the negative ones (see Chapter 13). Getting on with one's life is a familiar approach to such issues.

Wagenaar and Groeneweg's findings make us think about our own personal past. Just because we do not remember events in detail does not mean we have faulty memories. But by the same token, remembering details does not mean the events happened exactly as we remember them. All our recollections are selective interpretations of the past. It's something to think about.

---

traumatic to be highly memorable, though. Some historical events that have considerable personal relevance, very unusual or novel events, and other events that are highly emotional are also remembered very well. Such memories are called *flashbulb memories* because they are so vivid that it seems as if we have a photograph of the event (Brown & Kulik, 1977). Although many events tend to be of major historical significance, such as the assassinations of John F. Kennedy and Martin Luther King, Jr., or the death of major movie or music stars, flashbulb memories may also involve personal autobiographical events (Rubin & Kozin, 1984). Such events tend to impress the circumstances in which the person first heard the news about the event and include information about the place, other people present at the time, what activities were occurring, and the source of the information (Cohen, Conway, & Maylor, 1994).

In general, research indicates that flashbulb memories are affected by aging. Studies of older adults' ability to remember the source of information consistently shows that they have more difficulty compared with young adults in remembering where, when, or from whom they learned information (Schachter, Harbluk, & McLachlan, 1987), as well as the context surrounding the event (Cohen et al., 1994). As a result, older adults experience fewer flashbulb memories than younger adults (Cohen et al., 1994).

Concept Checks

1. What major differences are there between older and younger adults' working memory?
2. How do age differences in recall and recognition compare?
3. What differences have been observed between older and younger adults in aspects of autobiographical memory?

MEMORY FOR DISCOURSE

Learning Objectives:

- What characteristics of individuals influence memory for discourse?
- How do task factors influence memory for discourse?
- What aspects of text materials affect memory?
- How does memory for discourse relate to secondary memory?

Adults of all ages spend a great deal of time reading books, magazines, and newspapers, and watching television programs and movies. Collectively, such material is termed ***discourse.*** Interest in whether there are age differences in how well people remember discourse is very strong. Indeed, how well adults remember prose, or text passages, is one of the fastest growing areas in memory research. In part, this rapid growth reflects the realization that prose (such as a newspaper story) is something people need to remember in everyday life; word lists typically are not.

To preview a bit, we will see that age differences in remembering discourse are minimized when tasks are made more naturalistic by providing unlimited study time, using long text passages, and requiring only a general summary rather than requiring details. However, younger adults appear to have a clear advantage in learning short passages and in remembering the details. These differences may become more important as we continue to move toward a society in which computerization makes rapid acquisition of large amounts of discourse mandatory (Meyer, 1987).

In this section we will mainly focus on adults' ability to remember information they have read. Our primary concern will be to understand the person, task, and text variables that affect learning and remembering prose.

Person Variables

Sometime in your educational career you probably had to read a rather lengthy novel for a literature class. Providing you opted for the book rather than the video or Cliff Notes version, you probably were surprised at how much different your recollections of the story were compared with your classmates'. Many of these differences were due to person variables—characteristics about individuals that affect how they learn and remember. These person variables include demographic characteristics, personal biases, and personal motivations for remembering certain bits of information while forgetting others.

One of the most researched person variables concerns education and verbal ability (Meyer & Rice, 1983). Most researchers agree that average- and low-verbal older adults (adults with mainly a high school education) perform significantly worse than younger adults (see Dixon & von Eye, 1984). The picture is less clear with high-verbal, college-educated older adults. Some researchers obtain age differences (Cohen, 1979; Light & Anderson, 1975) whereas others do not (Mandel & Johnson, 1984; Meyer & Rice, 1981). In related research examining memory for television programs, Cavanaugh (1983, 1984) also found no differences in high-verbal groups but significant differences in low-verbal groups. A representative set of results showing this differential connection between age and verbal ability is shown in Table 6.1.

Why is there such consistency regarding poor-verbal, lower educated groups and such disagreement concerning high-verbal, higher educated groups? B.J.F. Meyer (1987) provides an insightful discussion of this question. She points out that the pattern of results may be due to the use of tests of

TABLE 6.1 Proportion of statements correct for comprehension, probe recall, and recognition, as a function of age, vocabulary, and level of information

Measure	**Young** *High Verbal*	*Low Verbal*	**Old** *High Verbal*	*Low Verbal*
Comprehension				
Central	.98	.77	.99	.70
Plot-relevant	.81	.57	.79	.44
Plot-irrelevant	.61	.39	.59	.23
Probe recall				
Central	.95	.71	.92	.59
Plot-relevant	.74	.51	.80	.34
Plot-irrelevant	.29	.20	.26	.08
Recognition				
Central	.90	.81	1.00	.71
Plot-relevant	.77	.56	.89	.37
Plot-irrelevant	.38	.23	.34	.11

Source: "Comprehension and Retention of Television Programs by 20- and 60-year-olds," by J. C. Cavanaugh, 1983, *Journal of Gerontology, 38,* 190–196. Copyright ©1983 The Gerontological Society of America. Reprinted by permission.

verbal ability that are differentially sensitive to high ability levels. That is, some tests, such as the vocabulary subtest of the Wechsler Adult Intelligence Scale-Revised (WAIS-R), are poorer at discriminating people with high ability than other tests, such as the Quick Test (Borgatta & Corsini, 1964), which is a very difficult, 100-word vocabulary test. For example, adults who score in the 75th percentile on the vocabulary subtest of the WAIS-R score only at the 25th percentile of the Quick Test. Consequently, adults who score high on the vocabulary subtest may not be truly high on verbal ability. B.J.F. Meyer (1987) argues that many of the studies that found age differences in so-called high-verbal groups did not use sufficiently sensitive tests of verbal ability. Studies that included truly high-verbal adults found no age differences.

A second reason for the different patterns of age differences involves the strategies that readers use. Rice and Meyer (1985) asked young and older adults of both average- and high-verbal ability about the strategies they used while reading. Older, low-verbal ability adults reported using the fewest reading behaviors that foster good comprehension. B.J.F. Meyer (1987) argues that these data support the view that the lack of age differences between younger and older high-verbal adults is due to the older group's continued use of effective reading strategies. Meyer, Young, and Bartlett (1986) tested this hypothesis by training older average-verbal ability adults to use more effective reading strategies. Following five 90-minute training sessions, they used effective strategies more often and their text recall was substantially better.

How adults decide to retell a story is also important. Adams, Labouvie-Vief, Hobart, and Dorosz (1990) presented fables and nonfables to younger and older adults and examined their story recall styles. They found that older adults used a more integrative or interpretive style for nonfable passages, whereas younger adults used a more literal or text-based style. Age differences were not found for the fable passages. These findings mean that younger adults may spontaneously shift their recall style depending on the type of passage, whereas older adults may use a more consistently integrative style regardless of passage type.

Another person variable that affects performance is amount of prior knowledge. Hartley (1989) found that text recall varied in relation to how much people knew about the topic beforehand. One way to test this is to look for pieces of topic-relevant information that people remember in retelling the story but that were not actually in the passage. If prior knowledge is an important factor, then one should see a fair amount of this relevant, but not presented, information. Older adults appear especially likely to put pieces of prior knowledge into their recall of new information (Hultsch & Dixon, 1983). Interestingly, how prior knowledge affects text recall also appears to vary with age (S. W. Smith, Rebok, Smith, Hall, & Alvin, 1983). Smith and colleagues found that young adults added prior knowledge to make unorganized stories make more sense, whereas older adults added prior knowledge to make already well-organized stories more interesting.

Older and younger adults alike remember gist information from text, but younger adults tend to remember more low-level details.

Task Variables

Just as the way tasks are presented affects secondary memory performance, these same variables also affect prose memory. One of the most important task variables is speed of presentation. Studies show that older adults are differentially adversely affected by rapid presentation (Cohen, 1979; Stine, Wingfield, & Poon, 1986). Specifically, between 100 and 120 words per minute (wpm) appears to be the critical speed for exceeding older adults' processing capability. Meyer and Rice (1989) report that the average reading speed for older adults is 121 wpm, compared with 144 wpm for younger adults. They note, however, that nearly half of their older adults read more slowly than 120 wpm; few younger adults read as slowly. Thus, older adults may be at a disadvantage when presented with text at speeds geared to younger adults. Indeed, when the speed-of-presentation variable is removed and participants can pace themselves, age differences are eliminated (Harker, Hartley, & Walsh, 1982; Meyer & Rice, 1981; Meyer et al., 1986).

Few studies have compared varying reading speeds with memory for prose in the same study. Hartley, Stojack, Mushaney, Annon, and Lee (1994) examined different pacing conditions, determined by various measures of reading speed, with a self-paced reading condition. Hartley and colleagues found that age differences in recall of the material tended to increase as the length of reading time increased. Although measures of basic speed of processing explained much of the age differences, cognitive processes involved in the integration of information across sentences also appear to be involved.

Text Variables

All text material is not created equal. Some books or passages are very easy to read, comprehend, and remember, and others are not. Texts differ considerably in how all of the information they contain is organized. One way to think about text organization is to compare it to the outline form that is taught in composition classes. Some information is basic and is given prominence in the outline; other information simply expands the main points and is embedded in the outline. In a well-organized text the main ideas are all interrelated, and the passage is like a tightly woven tapestry. Such texts are more memorable, especially if one follows the built-in organizational structure.

Researchers have spent considerable effort examining whether there are age differences in memory for different kinds of information in texts. There appear to be no age differences in adults' memory for the major organizational elements of texts, such as the basic sequence of events or causal connections between events (Meyer & Rice, 1989; Meyer, Rice, Knight, & Jessen, 1979). However, remembering this kind of information does seem to be related to verbal ability; low- and average-ability adults are less able to use these organizational elements and remember fewer of them than high-ability adults (Meyer, 1983).

Because texts are constructed with information at different hierarchical levels of importance, a key question is whether there are age differences in memory for these different levels. Answering this question amounts to looking for age differences between memory for main ideas and memory for details. The literature on this issue is large and complex (Hultsch & Dixon, 1984; B.J.F. Meyer, 1987). In general, the data indicate two important points. First, when text is clearly organized, with emphasis on structure and the main ideas, older adults are just as good as younger adults in telling the difference between the main ideas and the details.

Second, verbal ability makes a big difference. Average-verbal older adults apparently do not benefit from advance signaling of important ideas, do not use the organizational structure to facilitate learning or retrieval as efficiently, and make fewer inferences about what they read. As a result, average-verbal older adults show a performance deficit compared with their younger average-verbal counterparts. In contrast, high-verbal older adults are very sensitive to the emphasis given to different pieces of information and to the overall structure of the text. In fact, they may be oversensitive to emphasis, because they tend to allocate more of their processing capacity to emphasized details than to the main ideas. Once again, verbal ability is apparently more important than age in understanding the patterns of performance.

Still, there may be more to it. Price (1991) reports that middle-aged women who were enrolled in a graduate-level gerontology course had different study strategies and motivation than younger students. The middle-aged women were more interested in learning concepts and how everything fits together; they were much less interested in learning facts. These findings are important, as they indicate that text structure and verbal ability may not be the only reasons for age differences in memory for text. Personal motivation may also be an important issue.

An important aspect of text variables is that they may interact with person variables to create differences in memory for discourse. An example of this interaction involves situations in which people hold opinions or have knowledge about a topic and are then presented additional written information. In terms of people's ability to remember this new information, does it matter whether the new information agrees or disagrees with what people already know?

To answer this question, Rice and Okun (1994) tested older adults' memory for accurate information about osteoarthritis that either contradicted their previously held false beliefs or affirmed their previously held accurate beliefs. All of the participants reported having osteoarthritis for at least 2 years. Rice and Okun found that older adults recall and recognize information that contradicts their previously held beliefs less accurately than they recall and recognize information that affirms their initial beliefs. The findings point out that individuals who educate older adults must be careful to identify misconceptions that they may bring into the situation. However, Rice and Okun also found that if the disconfirming material was stated explicitly, older adults were better at remembering the information later. Thus, explicitly stating that certain information is often misunderstood, then stating the correct information, may help older adults remember the accurate information.

In another important study that simulated actual interactions with physicians, McGuire (in press) also examined adults' memory for medical information, but in a different way. She presented either a well-organized or an unorganized videotaped simulated medical feedback session about osteoarthritis to older and younger adults. The information was provided by a geriatric physician. Recall was tested immediately following, one week after, or one month after the learning session. Younger adults initially recalled more information than older adults, but both age groups' performance declined equivalently over time.

This study indicates that none of the three classes of variables involved in memory for discourse operate in isolation. Understanding why age differences occur necessitates understanding how all of these variables interact.

Text Memory and Secondary Memory

The research we have considered in this section is actually another way to examine secondary memory, because it involves learning large amounts of information and remembering it over time (Poon, 1985). Thus, drawing parallels between the two literatures and comparing the important influences on memory for word lists and memory for text can be useful.

The most striking aspect about this comparison is that both are affected by a similar set of variables. Performance on word-list tasks and text-memory tasks are influenced by pacing, prior knowledge or familiarity, and verbal ability. Note that age is not one of these influential variables. Being old does not necessarily mean that one cannot remember, especially if the situation provides an optimal opportunity to do so.

Because of the parallels between influences on prose retention and memory for word lists, some researchers have tried to blend the two approaches. One tactic is to look at the processes underlying prose memory by using related secondary memory tasks. For example, Spilich (1985) obtained age differences for some steps leading up to the understanding of text. In particular, older and younger adults may have different definitions of words and use different classifications for words. For example, the word *rap* may be more likely to mean "to knock" to an older adult, whereas it more likely would mean "a form of music" to a younger adult. This may suggest that the associations formed in secondary memory for verbal material may differ for young and old. At a practical level, we should not assume that people of all ages understand the same meaning for a word or sentence.

Concept Checks

1. How do vocabulary ability and education influence memory for discourse?
2. How does pacing or reading speed influence memory for discourse?
3. How does the organization of text influence memory?
4. What similarities exist between memory for discourse and secondary memory performance?

MEMORY IN EVERYDAY LIFE

Learning Objectives:

- What age differences have been found in memory for location, recall of landmarks, learning routes, and configurational learning?
- What age differences are found in memory for activities, especially in prospective memory?

- How does memory for pictures compare with list learning?

As we noted at the beginning of this chapter, memory is so integral to our everyday life that we take it for granted. Only recently has there been substantial interest in examining age differences in memory in everyday life (West, 1986a). However, this research is extremely important for three reasons. First, it may shed some light on the generalizability of findings based on laboratory tasks such as word-list recall. Second, new or alternative variables that affect performance could be uncovered. Third, research on everyday memory may force us to reconceptualize memory itself. In this section we will focus on two aspects of everyday memory that have received the most attention: spatial memory and memory for activities.

Spatial Memory

Every time we remember where we left our keys, find our way by locating a prominent building, successfully return home from the grocery store, and remember where our car is parked after coming out a different door, we are using *spatial memory* (Kirasic & Allen, 1985). We will consider the developmental trends in each of these abilities.

Memory for Location

Researchers test people's memory for location in three ways (Kirasic & Allen, 1985). One way is based on the psychometric approach to intelligence described in Chapter 7, in which relevant primary mental abilities such as spatial ability are tested. Results from this approach indicate that performance peaks by midlife and decreases steadily thereafter.

The second and most common way to test people's memory for location is to present them with an array of objects, remove the objects, and ask the participants to reconstruct the array. Older adults do not perform this task as well as younger adults, regardless of whether the objects are household items (Attig, 1983; Pezdek, 1983; Waddell & Rogoff, 1981) or building locations on a map (Light & Zelinski, 1983; Ohta & Kirasic, 1983; Thomas, 1985). Charness (1981) found that younger chess players could reconstruct chess boards more accurately than older players, even though the two groups were matched for chess-playing ability.

In contrast to this consistent picture of age decrement, West and Walton (1985) found no decline when they conducted interviews of young and old participants about the exact location in their home of common personal items such as keys. West and Walton argue that familiarity and the fact that household locations are unlikely to change are the most likely reasons for the lack of age differences. The familiarity effect may be due to the additional contextual information available in home settings. Indeed, in a series of studies, Cherry (Cherry & Park, 1993; Cherry, Park, & Donaldson, 1993) found that providing contextual cues in laboratory-based studies of spatial memory clarified the issue. In these studies, the contextual cues consisted of locating objects in a three-dimensional array (rather than representing them in a three-dimensional drawing). Cherry found that contextual cues improve performance in both younger and older adults. The reason for the contextual enhancement effect may be related to working memory capacity (Dobson, Kirasic, & Allen, 1995). That is, contextual cues may reduce the demand on working memory, thereby helping people remember locations.

The third way to test spatial memory consists of actually carrying out tasks in real physical space. For example, Kirasic (1991) had older and younger adults plan the most efficient route possible in picking up items on a designated shopping list and then actually go get them. The manipulation was the shopper's familiarity with the supermarket; some shoppers were tested in their usual supermarket, and others were tested in a different one. Younger adults performed equivalently in the two settings, whereas older adults performed better in the familiar environment.

Recall of Landmarks

Most studies of landmark recall involve the ability to place landmarks correctly on a map or other

In familiar environments, older adults may do as well as younger adults in remembering locations. But when older adults like these women find themselves in unfamiliar places, they may have more difficulty remembering where they are going.

representation of a large-scale space. Young adults are more likely to organize their recall of a familiar downtown area based on spatial cues, which gives them an advantage in recalling correct location (Evans, Brennan, Skorpanich, & Held, 1984). In contrast, older adults' recall is influenced by frequency of usage, symbolic significance, natural landscaping, ease of finding the landmark, and uniqueness of architectural style (Lipman, 1991). In addition, some evidence suggests that older adults are less accurate at locating landmarks on a scale model (Ohta & Kirasic, 1983) and at learning locations when the information is presented sequentially, as is often done in a travelogue or tour (Walsh, Krauss, & Regnier, 1981).

These results suggest that older and younger adults use different strategies to learn and remember landmarks. Older adults may be more likely to use experiential or personal relevance as a way to remember location, whereas young adults may use physical space cues.

Route Learning

Only a handful of studies has considered how people remember the way from one place to another. Sinnott (1984a) asked participants to describe routes to and around the hospital where they were undergoing a battery of tests and to recognize specific pathways that occurred en route from one area of the hospital to another. She found no differences with age on any of these tasks. Ohta (1981) also found no age differences in adults' ability to find unknown routes to a specific room when the known route was blocked. However, he did report that older adults were less accurate in drawing sketch maps of routes inside buildings.

The research on learning and remembering routes raises a very practical question: What if people were provided with maps? Would they help people learn and remember the routes more effectively? Are some maps better than others? These are the questions that Caplan and Lipman (1995) addressed. They had younger and older adults learn a route through a neighborhood from a series of slides. The experiment had three main conditions: no learning aid, a sketch of the route labeled a "map," or the same sketch labeled a "diagram." The "map" and the "diagram" either did or did not have landmarks indicated on them. The findings were intriguing. Older men's performance was poorer than younger men's only when they had no learning aid. Including landmarks eliminated age-related decrements for scene memory. However, age differences for women were found only when the learning aid was labeled a "map." Moreover, including landmarks increased the age differences.

Caplan and Lipman (1995) interpreted this pattern of differences in terms of people's past history with spatial learning aids. They suggest that the findings reflect a cohort effect in that older women may not have had successful past experiences with using maps effectively. The fact that the same aid, when labeled a "diagram" did not produce similar effects argues in favor of this conclusion. Presumably, older women who have had successful past experiences with maps should not show such effects. As we have seen throughout this chapter, age differences in memory are quite complex; here we see that one's personal experience may have quite negative effects on performance. It also points out the importance of labels for memory aids in assessing their utility.

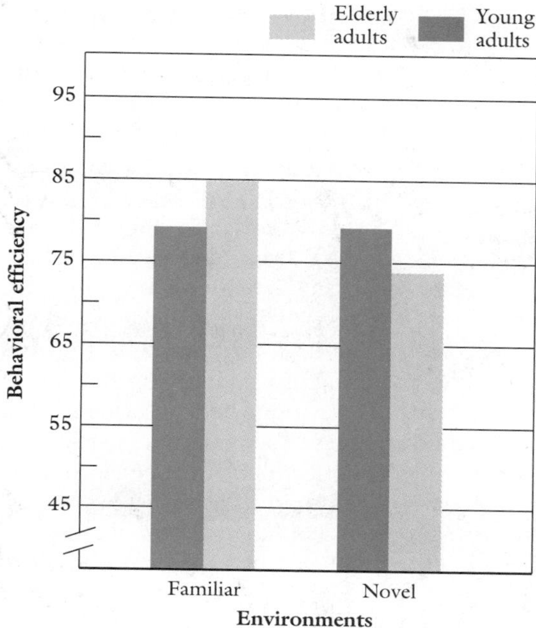

Figure 6.1 Differences in the behavioral efficiency of young and old adults while shopping in familiar and novel supermarkets

Source: "Aging, Spatial Performance, and Spatial Competence," by K. C. Kirasic and G. L. Allen, 1985, in N. Charness (Ed.), Aging in Human Performance. *Chichester, England: Wiley. Copyright © 1985 by John Wiley & Sons, Inc. Reprinted with permission of the publisher.*

Configurational Learning

Combining spatial and temporal information so that people can recognize a location when they view it from a different perspective requires *configurational learning*. Think about what people do when they go to a mall. They park their car and remember where it is based on the entrance they use. Suppose when they finish shopping they decide to leave the mall through a different door. Their ability to still remember where their car is requires configurational learning; they recognize the parking lot even though they are viewing it from a different position.

When configurational learning is tested with unfamiliar locations, young adults sometimes outperform older adults (Ohta, Walsh, & Krauss, 1981). In contrast, no age differences are found in distance and directional judgments or in efficient route planning when familiar locations are used, such as one's hometown or a familiar grocery store (Kirasic, 1980; Kirasic & Allen, 1985). The hometown advantage is depicted in Figure 6.1. Notice the lack of an age effect when the locations used were familiar to all participants.

Memory for Activities

How many times have you been asked, "What did you do today?" or "What have you been up to lately?" To answer these questions, you must use a second major type of everyday memory—memory for activities. Researchers test activity memory with a wide variety of tasks, including following instructions, recalling activities performed in a research laboratory, and remembering to perform actions.

One of the major issues in activity memory research is whether people must expend cognitive effort or whether remembering what we do happens automatically. Kausler (1985) attacked this problem by separating activity memory into two parts. First, he argued that *storing* activities and actions performed in a laboratory is probably automatic, requiring no cognitive effort or resources. His view is supported by evidence that rehearsing the names of activities that participants perform does not affect performance. Second, he argued that *remembering* the activities one has performed involves cognitive effort, because reliable age decrements are observed. Indeed, organization, which requires cognitive effort, facilitates recall of activities (Bäckman, 1985; Bäckman & Nilsson, 1984, 1985).

In essence, Kausler contends that the recall of activities performed in a laboratory is a direct analogue to everyday life. Many everyday memory situations involve the intentional, effortful retrieval of information learned by doing things (for example, we learn how to get around campus by walking around). In fact, activity memory may form the basis for acquiring much of our spatial memory.

A second major question in activity memory research is this: Does actually performing the actions help us remember them? It turns out that it does. Bäckman (1985) and Cohen and Faulkner (1989) found that performed actions were remembered more accurately than activities that had only been watched.

There is an interesting twist to Cohen and Faulkner's (1989) study. They also report age differences in the accuracy with which people remember whether they in fact performed the action. Older adults are more likely than younger adults to say that they performed tasks that they in reality only observed. Although more research on this issue is clearly needed, these findings have important implications. In situations where accuracy is crucial, such as in reporting one's recent activities to a physician or a police officer, older adults may be more likely to confuse what they saw with what they did.

A third focus of activity memory research involves examining whether the type of task performed has an effect on the likelihood that it will be remembered later. Kausler and Hakami (1983) found that older adults remembered doing problem-solving tests better than doing perceptual-motor, generic memory, and word lists. The reason for such differences remains to be uncovered. West (1986a) suggests that better-remembered tasks may be more familiar and, thereby, more memorable.

The fourth area of activity memory research is *prospective memory,* which involves remembering to remember (Harris, 1984b; Meacham, 1982). For example, when younger and older adults are asked to call a researcher at particular times, older adults are consistently better at remembering to do so (Moscovitch, 1982; Poon & Schaffer, 1982; West, 1984). Their secret is simple: They write down the number and message to be given. Younger adults rely on their own internal remembering strategies, which turns out to be less successful.

More recent research has examined different types of prospective memory. Einstein and McDaniel (1990) introduced a distinction between event-based and time-based prospective memory tasks. In event-based tasks, an action is to be performed when a certain external event happens, such as giving a certain person a message. A time-based task involves performing an action after a fixed amount of time, such as pressing a key every 8 minutes, or at a fixed point in time, such as remembering an appointment at 1 p.m. Einstein and McDaniel (1990) reasoned that time-based tasks should show more age differences as long as people use self-generated strategies to remember, as these tend to decline with age; the cues in event-based tasks may help reduce age differences. Do the data support this distinction?

The answer depends on the difficulty of the task.

If the task is complex and places high cognitive demands on people, older adults do not perform as well as younger adults when self-initiated retrieval was required (Mäntylä, 1994). These findings imply that like remembering events from the past, prospective memory involves a complex interaction of aspects of information processing. Additionally, the effects of task complexity fit well with data concerning similar effects in various types of attention tasks.

How accurately people perform prospective memory tasks may depend on the time of day. In an analysis of several studies, Leirer, Tanke, and Morrow (1994) found that older adults performed best in the early morning. In general, performance declines until midday, with either no further decline or some improvement later in the day depending on the type of task. Such time-of-day effects imply that attentional capacity required by prospective memory tasks is at its peak in the morning. However, little research has examined why this is the case, and the issue has not been systematically examined across all of adulthood.

Finally, a few researchers have tried to explain why age differences in memory for activities occurs. One view is that effort is required to retrieve the actions from memory and that older adults are less efficient at retrieval (Kausler & Lichty, 1988). One way to test this notion is to measure processing efficiency, which can be done by measuring processing speed in perceptual speed tests (Salthouse, 1992). Earles and Coon (1994) found that such measures of processing speed were an important predictor of adults' memory for activities they had performed in an experiment between 2 and 182 days later. Indeed, the amount of variance associated with age was reduced by 70% when processing speed was considered. However, processing speed could not account for all of the variance in adults' performance, meaning that other factors responsible for it remain to be discovered.

Thus, whether there are age differences in prospective memory is a complex issue. It appears to depend on the type of task, the cues used, and what is being measured.

Everyday Memory Versus List-Learning Performance

How does performance on everyday memory tests stack up to performance on traditional laboratory word-list tests? Overall, age decrements in performance on everyday memory tasks are smaller than on list-learning tasks (West, 1986a). Why? Unfortunately we do not know for certain. One thing is clear, however. Older adults perform consistently better when they are confronted with information that is familiar, which in turn enhances the motivation to perform the task in the first place (Perlmuter & Monty, 1989).

Memory for Pictures

One of the areas in which performance on list-learning tasks and tasks closer to everyday life can be compared is memory for pictures. Researchers use a variety of things to study picture memory: faces, abstract drawings, line drawings, and complex scenes. Overall, studies show that older adults perform worse than younger adults in remembering many types of pictorial stimuli (A. D. Smith & Park, 1990). For example, older adults do not remember faces (Mason, 1986) or where objects are placed in a colored three-dimensional array or on a distinctive map (Park, Cherry, Smith, & Lafronza, 1990) as well as younger adults.

Still, we must not be too hasty in concluding that age differences found in the laboratory automatically generalize to the real world. Park and her colleagues examined many of the traditional issues in laboratory research, including context effects, retention intervals, and stimulus complexity (Park, Puglisi, & Smith, 1986; Park, Puglisi, & Sovacool, 1983, 1984; Park, Royal, Dudley, & Morrell, 1988). Whereas older adults were clearly worse at remembering words, their immediate memory for pictures was about as good as young adults'. Age differences were observed only when delayed tests were given, and then only at certain time delay intervals. This research shows that we need to be cautious even in generalizing the findings from laboratory list-learning tasks using words to list-learning tasks using pictures.

Many factors influence what people remember from pictures. One of the most important of these concerns what people expect to see, termed *schemas.* For example, people who are told that they will be shown a picture of a kitchen immediately anticipate seeing a stove, refrigerator, sink, and other things commonly associated with a kitchen. Collectively, these items form a kitchen schema. Now suppose that these people were actually shown a picture of a kitchen for a brief time and asked to name the objects they saw. After recalling a few, they might realize that there were more objects there than they named. So, they might begin to guess what the others were, based on their kitchen schema.

Hess and Slaughter (1990) showed that older adults are more likely to use their schemas to fill in the blanks than younger adults. This appears especially likely when the scenes are not well organized, such as when a picture of a kitchen has the sink over the stove as opposed to beside it. These results fit with a wide body of literature suggesting that we tend to rely more on experience as we grow older to compensate for decrements in specific aspects of information processing (recall Salthouse's study of typing from Chapter 5) and memory. As we will see in Chapter 7, our knowledge base continues to improve into old age, giving us a good basis for using schemas.

Despite these innovative studies, the direct comparison between everyday memory and list learning is hampered by the lack of data establishing equivalent everyday tasks and list-learning tasks. We need a comprehensive analysis in which the memory demands of many everyday tasks and list-learning tasks are described. This analysis would provide a way to address the reasons for the presence or absence of age differences across different task domains.

Concept Checks

1. Under what conditions does a learning aid help people learn a route?
2. Why is task complexity important in prospective memory?
3. How are expectations related to memory for pictures?

SELF-EVALUATIONS OF MEMORY ABILITIES

Learning Objectives:

- What are the major types of memory self-evaluations?
- What age differences have been found in metamemory?
- How do younger and older adults compare on memory monitoring tasks? How is task experience important?

How good is your memory? Are you absent-minded? Or are you like the proverbial elephant who never forgets anything? Like most people, you probably tend to be your own harshest critic when it comes to evaluating your memory performance. We analyze, scrutinize, nitpick, and castigate ourselves for the times we forget; we rarely praise ourselves for all the things we do remember, and we continue to be on guard for more memory slips. The self-evaluations we make about memory may affect our daily life in ways that traditionally were unrecognized.

The self-evaluations we make about memory are complex (Cavanaugh, 1989; Cavanaugh et al., 1989). They are based not only on memory and performance per se but also on how we view ourselves in general, our theories about how memory works, what we remember from past evaluations, and our attributions and judgments of our effectiveness.

Aspects of Memory Self-Evaluations

Interest in what people know about or are aware of concerning memory, and how they evaluate it, is an old topic in both philosophy and psychology

(Cavanaugh & Perlmutter, 1982). Psychologists have dabbled with the topic for a century, studying everything from reports of children's awareness of problem-solving skills (Binet, 1903) to computer simulation of self-monitoring systems (Bobrow & Collins, 1975). In recent decades work on memory awareness has taken on a more developmental flavor. Researchers have focused primarily on two types of awareness about memory. **The first type involves knowledge about how memory works and what we believe to be true about it; this type of self-evaluation is referred to as *metamemory*.** For instance, we may know that recall is typically harder than recognition, that memory strategies are often helpful, and that working memory is not limitless. We may also believe that memory declines with age, that appointments are easier to remember than names, and that anxiety impairs performance. Metamemory is most often assessed with questionnaires that ask about these various facts and beliefs.

The second type of self-evaluation, called *memory monitoring*, refers to the awareness of what we are doing with our memory right now. We can be aware of the process of remembering in many ways. At times we know how we are studying, how we are searching for some particular fact, or how we are keeping track of time for an appointment. At other times we ask ourselves questions while doing a memory task. For example, when faced with having to remember an important appointment later in the day, we may consciously ask ourselves whether the steps we have taken (writing a note) are sufficient.

Age Differences in Metamemory

Researchers have explored age differences in metamemory mainly by using questionnaires (see Dixon, 1989, for a review). Many questionnaires have been developed over the years. Some of them, such as the Metamemory in Adulthood questionnaire (Dixon & Hultsch, 1983b) and the Cognitive Failures Questionnaire (Gilewski & Zelinski, 1986), tap several different areas of knowledge about memory, including knowledge about strategies, tasks, change with age, and capacity. Other questionnaires, such as the Memory Self-Efficacy Questionnaire (Berry, West, & Dennehey, 1989) and the Memory Controllability Inventory (Cavanaugh & Baskind, in press; Lachman, Bandura, Weaver, & Elliott, 1995), assess specific aspects of memory beliefs.

The pattern of age differences in metamemory is interesting. Older adults seem to know less than younger adults about the internal workings of memory and its capacity, view memory as less stable, expect that memory will deteriorate with age, and perceive that they have less control over memory (Cavanaugh & Poon, in press; Chaffin & Herrmann, 1983; Dixon & Hultsch, 1983b; Zelinski, Gilewski, & Thompson, 1980).

The belief in inevitable decline with age appears to be especially widespread. Williams, Denney, and Schadler (1983) found that none of their participants over age 65 expected memory to improve over time. Their participants also said that decline was related to expectations, less use of memory, lower levels of memory demands, and inactivity. This belief is potentially damaging. For example, people who think memory inevitably declines may also believe that strategy training is useless (Cavanaugh & Morton, 1988) and may think that there is little point in exerting effort to try and remember something that does not come to mind immediately (Cavanaugh & Green, 1990). We will take a closer look at these negative views a bit later.

Interestingly, the belief in inevitable decline does not apply equally to all aspects of memory. Older adults view memory capacity as declining more rapidly than the use of memory strategies (Dixon & Hultsch, 1983b). Similarly, adults report that different kinds of information present different likelihoods of being troublesome. For example, remembering names is universally problematic, but especially for older adults (Cavanaugh & Poon, 1989; Chaffin & Herrmann, 1983; Zarit, 1982). In contrast, remembering errands, appointments, and places appears to remain unchanged with age (Cavanaugh, Grady, & Perlmutter, 1983). You may find this to be the case yourself when you complete the exercise in the Discovering Development feature.

DISCOVERING DEVELOPMENT

How's Your Memory?

We have seen that metamemory refers to what people know and believe to be true about their memory. Recall that in Chapter 1, we discussed various stereotypes about older adults, one of which is the stereotype that all aspects of memory decline with age. Of course, we now know that this stereotype is false; although some aspects of memory differ with age, some do not.

Obtain a copy of one of the memory questionnaires described in the text. Examine it carefully and try to discern the different aspects of memory that are being assessed. Get your questionnaire approved by your human subjects research board and administer it to a broad range of adults of all ages. Gather your results and examine them for age differences relating to the different kinds of memory and types of questions.

The data you obtain will provide you with insights into the various ways that people view memory. Compare your findings to the results reported in the text. Do they agree? Why or why not?

Although questionnaire studies of metamemory provide important information, they must be interpreted carefully (Cavanaugh & Perlmutter, 1982). For example, Cavanaugh (1986–1987) discovered that how questions are worded makes a difference in how older adults respond. For example, when questions request a general overall rating of memory, older adults give more negative ratings than younger adults. But when the question pertains to a specific aspect of memory, such as memory for dates or errands, older adults' ratings are equivalent to those of younger adults.

Related work by Hertzog and his colleagues shows that how metamemory is organized may change across adulthood (Hertzog, Dixon, Schulenberg, & Hultsch, 1987; Hertzog, Hultsch, & Dixon, 1989). The facts people know about memory tend to form groups, or domains, of knowledge. As we age, the makeup of these domains may be a bit different. Because forgetting sometimes evokes strong emotional reactions in older adults, their memory knowledge may incorporate some of these feelings.

The Role of Memory Self-Efficacy

Belief in one's ability to accomplish things is a pervasive theme in literature, religion, psychotherapy, and many other diverse arenas (Cavanaugh & Green, 1990). **As it applies to memory, belief in oneself is referred to as *memory self-efficacy;* it is viewed as the belief that one will be able to perform a specific task and as an important construct in understanding how memory changes with age** (Cavanaugh, 1996). Memory self-efficacy is an important type of memory belief that is distinct from general knowledge about memory because, for example, one could know a great deal about how memory works, but believe that one's ability to perform in a specific situation is poor.

Since the late 1980s, memory self-efficacy has emerged as one of the key aspects of metamemory due to its importance in accounting for performance in several different types of situations, as well as helping to explain how people make performance predictions in the absence of direct experience with tasks (a topic considered in the next section) (Cavanaugh, 1996). Additionally, memory self-efficacy has been shown to be reliably distinct from general memory knowledge as assessed through questionnaires (Hertzog et al., 1989).

Welch and West (1995) propose that memory self-efficacy is also a key to understanding a broader array of phenomena, such as mastering the environment. Briefly, they propose that some older adults hold the assumption that memory inevitably declines with age and have experienced some age-related decreases in performance themselves. As people experience tasks or situations across adulthood that they complete successfully, their memory self-efficacy should remain strong; those who experience failure should show decrements in memory self-efficacy. These experiences should influence subsequent behavior; people who experience success may be more likely to seek out more challenging cognitive environments, whereas people experiencing failure may seek less cognitively demanding environments.

Age Differences in Memory Monitoring

Memory monitoring involves knowing what you are doing mentally right now. The most popular way researchers usually study memory monitoring is by having people predict how well they will do on a memory task. One variation of this technique requires that people predict how well they will do *before* they get a chance to see the task. For example, participants would be asked to predict how many words they think they could remember from a 20-item list before they see the list. The second variation requires people to make performance predictions after they have seen the task. This time, they get to see the list first and then would be asked to predict how many words they will remember.

Predictions Without Experience

Estimating our performance without having a chance to see what we are up against is hard. For example, guessing how well we will do on the first exam in a course is tough if we do not know anything about the exam style of the instructor. How well we think we will do depends on lots of test-related variables: item difficulty, fact versus concept questions, and the like.

When older adults are put in the position of having to estimate performance without seeing the task, they tend to overestimate how well they will do (for example, Bruce, Coyne, & Botwinick, 1982; Coyne, 1983; Mason, 1981; Murphy, Sanders, Gabriesheski, & Schmitt, 1981). For example, older adults typically predict that they will be able to remember more items than they actually can. Younger adults tend to be more accurate.

But older adults do not overestimate all the time. Camp, Markley, and Kramer (1983) asked older adults to predict recall of 15 words that were high in imagery, frequency, concreteness, and meaningfulness. When told to think about learning strategies, and then to make a prediction, older adults *under*estimated their performance. In this case, the need to think about strategies may have convinced older adults that the task was more difficult than it actually was. As a result, they gave lower estimates. Berry, West, and Scogin (1983) also found that older adults underestimated their performance when given everyday memory tasks.

Predictions After Experience

A much different picture of age differences emerges when participants have a chance to see the task before making a performance prediction. One way this is done is by asking people to rate their confidence that they will be able to remember each item on the list of words that will be learned. Results from several studies using this approach demonstrate that older adults are just as accurate in predicting their recall and recognition performances as younger adults (Lovelace, Marsh, & Oster, 1982; Perlmutter, 1978; Rabinowitz, Ackerman, Craik, & Hinchley, 1982). The usual finding is that, regardless of age, adults overestimate performance on recall tasks but underestimate performance on recognition tasks.

Comparing Prediction Types

Based on the research we have reviewed, older adults are at a disadvantage when asked to predict performance if they are given no information about the task. But when this information is forthcoming—either from direct experience, from instructions pertaining to important things to think about, or from a request for predictions on familiar everyday tasks—older adults do as well as younger adults. However, these studies do not address a very important question: What happens if people are given multiple trials with a task and are asked to predict performance on each trial?

Hertzog, Dixon, and Hultsch (1990) found that older and younger adults adjust their predictions across trials on a list-learning task. On the first trial, performance predictions tend to be inaccurate, and predictions are influenced by scores on memory questionnaires. On subsequent trials, though, predictions are more heavily influenced by actual performance on the preceding trial. Going one step further, Bieman-Copland and Charness (1994) had younger and older adults make predictions over trials on list-learning tasks in which they were given letter, rhyme, or meaning cues. Age differences were found in the ways younger and older adults adjusted their predictions from Trial 1 to Trial 2. Whereas younger adults raised or lowered their predictions across cue types based on their previous performance, older adults based their changed predictions on global differences between their previous prediction and performance.

These results indicate that the presence or absence of age differences on the first trial of a task, determined by whether people have experience in advance of doing the task, may be due to factors different from those responsible for age differences in how people change predictions over trials. Metamemory may be more important in understanding how people formulate initial predictions; analyzing one's previous performance may be more important for subsequent predictions.

Concept Checks

1. What is metamemory?
2. What is the difference between memory knowledge and memory self-efficacy?
3. What age differences are found in memory monitoring when predictions are made without any experience with the task?

SOURCES OF AGE DIFFERENCES IN MEMORY

Learning Objectives:

- What evidence is there for age differences in encoding?
- What age differences have been observed in retrieval?
- What are the relative contributions of encoding and retrieval in explaining age differences in performance?
- How is working memory a possible explanation of age differences in memory performance?

We have seen that older and younger adults differ in how well they perform on some memory tasks. Why do these age differences exist? Are older adults poorer at getting information into memory? Or do they get the information in just as well but have more difficulty getting it back out? Is it related to how efficiently they manipulate information in working memory?

For many years, most researchers examining age differences in memory performance had come to the conclusion that difficulties in retrieval were more important than those in encoding (Light, 1992). As we will see, however, more recent work based on brain metabolism and on working memory is raising questions about that conclusion.

Age Differences in Encoding

Results from years of research point to a clear age-related decrement in encoding processes (Craik, 1977; Kausler, 1982; Poon, 1985; Smith, 1996). Most of this work attempts to examine various components of encoding process. Additionally, considerable research points to a decline in the efficiency of encoding. We will examine the evidence for each.

Specific Components of Encoding

Recall that an important process in working memory is rehearsal, of which there are two kinds: rote rehearsal and elaborative, or meaning-based rehearsal. Elaborative rehearsal involves making connections between incoming information and information already known. For example, a person presented with the word *emu* and told that this is a bird that does not fly may try to think of other flightless birds. With some thought, *ostrich* may come to mind. Linking emu and ostrich would be an example of this type of rehearsal.

In a series of systematic studies, Howe (1988) examined this rehearsal process. He showed that the age-related decrement in encoding processes may be due to age differences in how easily people make connections between incoming information and information that was previously stored in memory. Older adults have more difficulty making these connections than younger adults. Interestingly, however, once these connections have been made, older and younger adults maintain them equivalently (which supports the conclusion that whereas encoding differences exist, storage differences do not). For example, older adults would be slower than younger adults at making the emu–ostrich connection, but once it is made both groups would remember it just as well.

Being slower at making connections with incoming information may reflect less elaborate processing by older adults (Smith, 1996). If this is true, then age differences should be reduced if elaborations are controlled by providing them at the outset. Unfortunately, the results from studies doing exactly this are confusing; some find that increased elaboration at encoding disproportionately benefits older adults (Park et al., 1990), whereas others find either no difference (Park, Puglisi, & Smith, 1986) or greater benefits for younger adults (Puglisi & Park, 1987). These findings point to a complex relation between elaboration at encoding and age (Craik & Jennings, 1992). Younger adults may benefit more quickly than older adults, who eventually improve to equivalent levels.

The complex nature of the data on elaboration raises an important issue. How people encode information is often a function of the memory strategies they use and how effective and efficient they are at producing quality representations in memory. Let's see how the use of strategies differs with age.

The Use of Strategies

When confronted with large amounts of information that we need to remember, we tend to use various techniques, called *strategies,* that make the task easier and increase the efficiency of storage. One extremely effective strategy for learning new information is to organize it. For example, consider a student's efforts to learn the information in college courses. Learning the necessary facts of chemistry, psychology, literature, and so forth is much easier if separate notebooks are kept for each class. Imagine the potential for confusion if all of the class notes were simply mixed together. Keeping them separate is an example of an organizational strategy.

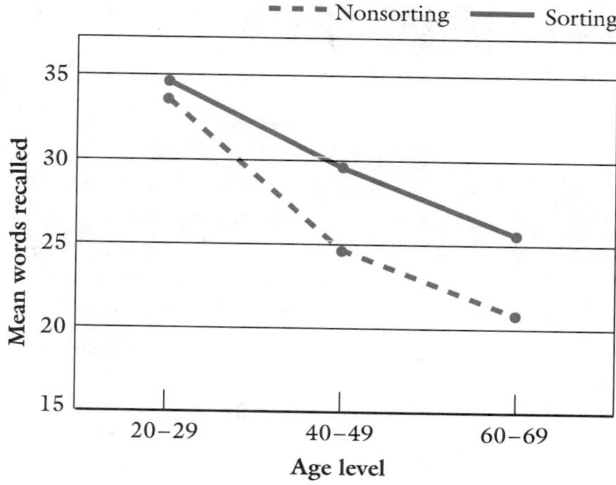

Figure 6.2 Mean number of words correctly recalled, as a function of age and sorting condition
Source: "Adult Age Differences in Free Classification and Free Recall," by D. F. Hultsch, 1971, Developmental Psychology, *4, 338–342. Copyright © 1971 by the American Psychological Association. Reprinted with permission of the author.*

Substantial evidence suggests that older adults do not spontaneously organize incoming information as often or as well as younger adults (Craik, 1977; Kausler, 1982; Smith, 1996). For example, older adults are less likely to take advantage of similarities in meaning among words (such as between *river* and *lake*) presented randomly in a list as a way to organize the items (Denney, 1974). Because the number of items remembered from such a list is highly related to the use of organization, younger adults outperform older adults on such tasks. Interestingly, older adults can use organization if they are told to do so (Schmitt, Murphy, & Sanders, 1981) or are experienced with sorting words into categories (Hultsch, 1971). This is clearly shown in Figure 6.2. However, the results of these manipulations are often short lived; older adults tend not to continue using organization over the long run if not required to do so.

The frequency of spontaneous use of other strategies also appears to decrease with age. For example, older adults are less likely to use imagery (forming pictures of items in one's mind) and other mnemonic memory devices (such as using the first letters of items to form a word, like *NASA*) (Kausler, 1982). When explicitly instructed to do so, however, older adults can use these and many other types of strategies. Moreover, their performance improves significantly compared with that of older adults who are not instructed.

Age Differences in Retrieval

Once we get information encoded and stored, we will at some point need to find it again and remember it. Researchers have agreed for many years that older adults have more difficulty retrieving information than do younger adults (Burke & Light, 1981; Craik, 1977; Kausler, 1982; Poon, 1985; Smith, 1996). This conclusion is based on research in three areas: (1) comparisons of performance using different types of retrieval; (2) comparisons of recall and recognition performances; and (3) studies of cued recall.

In considering the data on retrieval, we must remember that memory is not an exact reproduction of information that existed at an earlier time. Remembering is an active, dynamic process; recollections change over time to reflect an active construction process. In a real sense, the past is continually reconstructed every time we remember it.

Specific Components of Retrieval

Researchers distinguish two general retrieval processes. ***Heuristic retrieval*** **is any retrieval process that produces both successes and failures.** For example, when asked to give directions to a specific place, a person remembers some general steps ("I went south for a while"). These general steps may or may not help the person find the place again. Heuristic retrieval is used when information has been only partly learned, such as when someone has just moved to a new city and is unsure of street names. **In contrast, *algorithmic retrieval* is any retrieval process that produces error-free performance.** Remembering that the street one turns left on is three blocks south of the big red office building will provide a distinctive tag or cue to remember the key information. Algorithmic retrieval is used when information has been learned very well, such as when someone has lived in the same place a fairly long time and really knows his or her way around.

An important issue is whether age differences are equivalent for both kinds of retrieval. Apparently, they are not. Howe (1988) has documented that age differences are substantially greater for algorithmic retrieval than for heuristic retrieval. This indicates that younger adults may be better than older adults at retrieving a specific piece of information correctly, but both age groups are just as good at using general retrieval strategies that do not guarantee success. For example, older adults are typically worse than younger adults at remembering all of the detail steps needed to give precise directions to a specific location.

Recall Versus Recognition

As noted earlier, two types of retrieval tests are typically used in research. In free-recall tests no cues are given; a person is simply asked to remember all of the items on a list, for example. Recall tests are thought to place heavy demands on the retrieval process, because a person must generate all the cues for finding the correct information. In contrast, recognition involves picking the newly learned item from a list of both newly learned and distractor items. Because the testing environment provides cues, recognition tests are thought to place fewer demands on retrieval processes.

Studies consistently show substantial age differences on recall tests but small or nonexistent differences on recognition tests (Poon, 1985). These performance differences mean older adults have less effective retrieval processes when they must generate their own retrieval cues. However, when cues are provided, such as in recognition tests, older adults' performance improves.

Cued Recall

In addition to recognition tests, there are other means to reveal the ways in which retrieval cues help people remember. For example, researchers can provide cues in a recall task. *Cued recall* involves providing some hint, or aid, within the general constraints of a recall test. Examples would be asking a person to remember all of the fruits in a word list he or she studied or to recall the capital of Nepal after being told that its name begins with the letter *K*. Compared with their performances on free-recall tasks, older adults benefit more than younger adults when cues are provided, but age differences are not eliminated (A. D. Smith, 1977).

Relative Contributions of Encoding and Retrieval Differences

Younger adults find it easier than older adults to encode incoming information and organize it efficiently in order to retrieve it later. But this difference still leaves two questions unresolved: Are changes in memory with age primarily the result of decrements in storage, in retrieval, or in both? If both processes are responsible, then do both decline at the same rate? Based on the available evidence, the answers are that: (1) Changes in memory with aging are a consequence of decrements in both encoding and retrieval (Howe, 1988); and (2) recent evidence indicates that encoding difficulties may be especially important (Grady et al., 1995).

The first two points are evident in the research we considered earlier in this section. The third issue, concerning the possible fundamental importance of encoding, reveals how the brain imaging technique positron emission tomography (PET) can be brought to bear to help understand changes in memory. Grady and her research team (1995) examined cerebral blood flow in both younger and older adults during encoding and recognition of faces. Both age groups showed similar patterns of increased blood flow in specific areas of the brain during recognition, but differed significantly during encoding. Compared with older adults, younger adults showed significantly greater increases in blood flow to the left prefrontal and temporal areas of the brain. Grady and colleagues interpreted these differences as evidence that age-related memory differences may be due to older adults' failure to encode information adequately. Inadequate encoding could result in information not getting into memory at all, or being not as elaborately encoded, making retrieval more difficult at best.

The research on encoding and retrieval processes is important for three reasons. First, it emphasizes that age-related decrements in memory are complex; they are not due to changes in a single process. Second, intervention or training programs must consider both encoding and retrieval. Training people to use encoding strategies without also training them how to use retrieval strategies will not work. To the extent that only partial information is encoded, retrieval strategies need to focus on helping people find whatever aspects are available. Third, theories of how memory changes with age must take individual differences into account, especially differential rates of change in component processes. Theories of memory development must consider both those components of processes that change and those that do not.

The Emerging Role of Working Memory

As the concept of working memory has become more prominent in memory research, it has been increasingly implicated as a major source of the age differences in memory performance. For example, Hasher and Zacks (1988) postulate that the retrieval problems older adults experience are due to changes in working memory. Specifically, they show that older adults have more trouble keeping irrelevant information out of working memory than younger adults. This irrelevant information takes up valuable space in working memory, and prevents older adults from using it for relevant information. Gerard, Zacks, Hasher, and Radvansky (1991) report that older adults have increasing difficulty performing a speeded recognition test as the number of facts to be recognized goes up.

Numerous other researcher have also demonstrated that working memory is a key mediator variable between age and memory performance. This research has examined memory for menus, bus schedules, and maps (Kirasic & Allen, 1994; Kirasic, Dobson, Binder, & Allen, 1994); memory for discourse (Zabrucky & Moore, 1995); and free recall (Park et al., 1994). These conclusions are supported by research indicating that age differences in memory for discourse are substantially reduced when processing efficiency (a measure of working memory) is controlled (Zabrucky & Moore, 1994).

Some research implicating working memory as a key source of age differences in performance have gone a step further, and tried to identify even earlier components of information processing that may underlie the differences in working memory. At this point, it appears that age-related increases in basic processing speed may help account for age-related differences in working memory (Park et al., 1994; Salthouse, 1994). However, more research that includes measures of both working memory and processing speed need to be conducted.

Concept Checks

1. What age differences have been found in the use of memory strategies?
2. Are age differences in performance greatest for recall, cued recall, or recognition?
3. How has recent evidence from brain scans affected our understanding of the relative importance of encoding and retrieval?
4. Why is working memory important in understanding age differences in performance?

CLINICAL ISSUES AND MEMORY TESTING

Learning Objectives:

- What is the difference between normal and abnormal memory aging?
- What is the connection between memory and mental health?
- What are the major ways that clinicians assess memory?
- How is memory affected by nutrition and drugs?

To this point we have been trying to understand the changes that occur in normal memory with aging. But what about situations where people have serious memory problems that interfere with their daily lives? How do we tell the difference between normal and abnormal memory changes? These are but two of the issues that clinicians face. They are often confronted with clients who complain of serious memory difficulties. Clinicians must somehow differentiate the individuals who have no real reason to be concerned from those with some sort of disease. What criteria should be used to make this distinction? What diagnostic tests would be appropriate to evaluate adults of various ages?

Unfortunately, there are no easy answers to these questions (Erickson, Poon, & Walsh-Sweeney, 1980; Poon, 1986). As we have seen, the exact nature of normative changes in memory with aging is not yet understood completely. This means that we have few standards by which to compare people who may have problems. Second, there are few comprehensive batteries of memory tests that are specifically designed to tap a wide variety of memory functions (Mayes, 1995). Too often, clinicians are left with hit-or-miss approaches and often have little choice but to piece together their own assessment battery (Poon et al., 1986).

Fortunately, the situation is changing. Since the mid-1980s researchers and clinicians have begun to work closely to devise better assessments (Mayes, 1995). This collaboration is producing results that will help address the key questions in memory assessment: Has something gone wrong with memory? Is the loss normal? What is the prognosis? What can be done to help the client compensate or recover?

In this section we will consider some of the efforts being made to bridge the gap between laboratory and clinic. We will begin with a brief look at the distinction between normal and abnormal memory changes. Because abnormal memory changes could be the result of some other psychological or physical condition, we will consider links between memory and mental health. After that, we will consider some of the ways in which memory can be assessed in the clinical setting. Finally, we will discuss how memory is affected by nutrition and drugs.

Normal Versus Abnormal Memory Aging

As we have seen, there are many normative changes in memory as people grow old, such as in working memory and secondary memory. Still, many aspects of memory functioning do not change, such as the ability to remember the gist of a story. Increasingly forgetting names or what one needs at the supermarket, though annoying, appears to be part of aging. However, we also know that there are some people who experience far greater changes, such as forgetting where they live or their spouse's name. Where is the line dividing normative memory changes from abnormal ones?

From a functional perspective, one way to distinguish normal and abnormal changes is to ask whether the changes disrupt a person's ability to perform daily living tasks. The normative changes we have encountered in this chapter usually do not interfere with a person's ability to function in everyday life. When problems appear, however, it would be appropriate to find out what is the matter. For example, a person who repeatedly forgets to turn off the stove or forgets how to get home is clearly experiencing changes that affect personal safety and interfere with his or her daily life. Such changes should be brought to the attention of a physician or psychologist.

Recent advances in neuroscience, especially the study of brain-behavior relations, has led to an explosion in our knowledge of specific diseases or brain changes that can create abnormal memory performance. For example, researchers can test for specific problems in visual and verbal memory by examining glucose metabolism with PET scans (Berardi, Haxby, Grady, & Rapoport, 1991). Other brain imaging techniques such as CT scans and MRI allow researchers to find tumors, strokes, or other types of damage or disease that could account for poorer-than-expected memory performance. Certain changes in brain wave patterns are indicative of decrements in verbal memory (Rice, Buchsbaum, Hardy, & Burgwald, 1991). Finally, significantly poorer-than-normal performance on neuropsychological tests of memory are also useful in establishing for certain that the memory changes observed are indeed abnormal (Tuokko, Gallie, & Crockett, 1990).

Some diseases, especially the dementias, are marked by massive changes in memory. For example, Alzheimer's disease involves the progressive destruction of memory beginning with recent memory and eventually including the most personal—self-identity. Wernicke-Korsakoff syndrome involves major loss of recent memory and sometimes a total inability to form new memories after a certain point in time.

The most important point to keep in mind is that telling the difference between normal and abnormal memory aging, and in turn between memory and other cognitive problems, is often very difficult (Lezak, 1995). There is no magic number of times someone must forget something before getting concerned. Because serious memory problems can also be due to underlying mental or physical health problems, these must be thoroughly checked out in conjunction with obtaining a complete memory assessment.

Memory and Mental Health

Several psychological disorders involve distorted thought processes, which sometimes result in serious memory problems. The two disorders that have been the main focus of research are depression (Watts, 1995) and the dementias (Brandt & Rich, 1995); but other disorders, such as amnesia following a head injury or brain disease, are also important (O'Connor, Verfaellie, & Cermak, 1995). Depression is characterized by feelings of helplessness and hopelessness (American Psychiatric Association, 1994). Dementia, such as Alzheimer's disease, involves substantial declines in cognitive performance that may be irreversible and untreatable (American Psychiatric Association, 1994). Much of the research on clinical memory testing is on differentiating the changes in memory due to depression from those involved in Alzheimer's disease.

Serious depression impairs memory (Watts, 1995). For example, severely depressed people show a decreased ability to learn and recall new information (Cohen, Weingartner, Smallberg, Pickar, & Murphy, 1982); a tendency to leave out important information (McAllister, 1981); a decreased ability to organize (Breslow, Kocsis, & Belkin, 1981); less effective memory strategies (Weingartner, Cohen, & Bunney, 1982); an increased sensitivity to sad memories (Kelley, 1986); and decreased attention and reaction time (Breslow et al., 1981; Cohen et al., 1982).

Clinical models of depression emphasize its effects on cognition in everyday life (Beck, 1967, 1976; Garber & Seligman, 1980). In general, seriously depressed individuals develop negative expectations, decreased concentration, and attentional deficits that result in poorer memory. In contrast, mildly depressed individuals show little decrement. Unfortunately, few researchers have asked whether the effects of depression on memory vary with age. What data there are suggest that once normative age differences in secondary memory are eliminated statistically, few differences remain. Thus, at this point the memory impairments that accompany severe depression appear to be equivalent across adulthood. However, much more research needs to be done before we have a clear answer. Additionally, we need to know more about the possible effects of mild and moderate levels of depression.

Alzheimer's disease is characterized by severe and pervasive memory impairment that is progressive and irreversible (Cavanaugh & Nocera, 1994). The memory decrements in Alzheimer's disease involve the entire memory system, from sensory to tertiary memory. The changes that occur early in Alzheimer's disease are very similar to those that occur in depression. However, because depression is treatable and Alzheimer's disease is not, clinicians must differentiate the two. This differentiation is the underlying reason for the major effort to develop sensitive and comprehensive batteries of memory tests.

Clinical Memory Tests

Over the years, researchers and clinicians have devised several different ways of testing memory to determine whether a person is experiencing abnormal memory problems. We will consider three major types of tests: neuropsychological tests, behavioral and self-report measures, and rating scales.

Neuropsychological Tests

The traditional way to assess the degree of memory impairment someone has is to use all or part of large batteries of tests that were designed to assess several aspects of cognitive functioning, including attention, memory, and problem solving. Because these batteries of tests assess broad aspects of cognitive functioning and are used to assess possible psychological impairments due to abnormal brain (neurological) functioning, they are typically referred to as neuropsychological tests.

Ferris and Crook (1983) propose nine criteria for a comprehensive neuropsychological test, including that it samples a variety of cognitive functions, is sensitive to deficits, takes less than one hour to administer, has high reliability and validity, and is of appropriate difficulty for the population being studied. They recommend that all aspects of memory (primary, working, secondary, and tertiary) as well as attention and perceptual-motor speed be included in this battery. These suggestions have been supported and adopted by many of the leading clinicians involved in research on abnormal memory changes (Corkin, Growdon, Sullivan, Nissen, & Huff, 1986; Mohs, Kim, Johns, Dunn, & Davis, 1986).

The tests clinicians use to evaluate memory are one aspect of neuropsychological tests. These tests are designed to assess specific brain-behavior relations in a wide variety of domains, from general intelligence to particular aspects of memory. Although most comprehensive neuropsychological tests include several memory tests, some are designed to focus primarily on memory functioning. For example, the Wechsler Memory Scale - Revised is a fairly comprehensive test that examines many different aspects of verbal memory. It includes a variety of tasks, such as serial learning, paired associates, and short prose passages. Others, such as the Memory for Designs test, focus on visual memory. In these tests, people are typically shown a picture (such as an octagon) and asked to draw it from memory.

A neuropsychological assessment should always be coupled with complete health screening. A key aspect of the basic developmental forces is the interaction between physiology and behavior; memory performance is no exception. In any case, a systematic comprehensive approach is absolutely essential to sort out potentially treatable causes of memory problems from those that are untreatable. If real problems are suspected, one should search for a clinic specializing in comprehensive assessment. Having someone simply administer a short questionnaire or a mental status exam is not enough.

Behavioral and Self-Report Assessments of Memory Problems

People frequently complain or express concerns about their memory. Perhaps you have complained that you do not remember names or dates very well or often lose your keys. Rather than administering a battery of memory tests from a general neuropsychological test, many researchers and clinicians now recommend using behavioral assessments to diagnose memory problems (Knight & Godfrey, 1995). These tests involve having people actually perform everyday memory tasks using realistic material such as grocery lists or simulated situations in which they meet new people whose names they must remember (Crook & Larrabee, 1992). Such tests show great promise in assessing memory functioning and are much closer to the types of situations people actually face than are traditional memory batteries.

Another way to assess memory complaints is to use self-report scales. There are about a dozen questionnaires that assess memory complaints (Gilewski & Zelinski, 1986). These questionnaires assess a variety of memory situations, such as remembering people's names or remembering the time of year it is. Memory complaints assessed via questionnaires correlate moderately with performance on word-list and prose tasks and with standardized clinical memory tests (Zelinski, Gilewski, & Anthony-Bergstone, 1990). In addition, memory complaints show a stronger relation with depressed mood (Zarit, Cole, & Guider, 1981). These findings indicate that although memory complaints should not be considered an accurate account of a person's current memory ability, they may provide important information about performance problems related to how the person is feeling emotionally.

Gilewski and Zelinski (1986) state that memory questionnaires can be used in clinical practice, as long as they are not used as a substitute for memory tests and as long as they are multidimensional. For example, comprehensive questionnaires should tap such things as frequency of forgetting, perceptions of changes in memory over time, seriousness of memory failures, use of strategies, daily memory demands, memory for past events, and what efforts are made when forgetting occurs. The Memory Functioning Questionnaire (Gilewski, Zelinski, & Schaie, 1990) is one example of a comprehensive questionnaire that provides reliable and valid assessments of memory complaints.

Rating Scales

Instruments designed to assess memory from the viewpoint of an observer, usually a mental health professional are called *rating scales* (McDonald, 1986). This information is important as a means of providing an evaluation of the clinical significance of a memory impairment (Knight &

Godfrey, 1995). The most common behavior rating scales that tap memory are structured interviews and checklists.

Structured interviews vary in length from very short to extensive, which means that they also vary in how sensitive they are at picking up abnormal memory performance. Most structured interviews were developed with an eye toward diagnosing dementia. The most common of these are the various mental status examinations (Blessed, Tomlinson, & Roth, 1968; Folstein, Folstein, & McHugh, 1975; Kahn, Goldfarb, Pollack, & Peck, 1960). Mental status exams are used to screen people for serious problems. That is, mental status exams provide a very crude estimate of memory functioning, not nearly as good as one would get from an extensive battery of tests. However, mental status exams are very quick and easy to administer. Items on these scales focus on orientation to time and place and contain simple memory tests such as spelling *world* backwards. Mattis (1976) developed a more extensive mental status exam that provides a more complete view of cognitive processes. Mattis's scale examines primary memory and secondary memory more thoroughly than the other mental status exams.

Checklists provide a relatively easy way to obtain information from observers about the severity of a memory impairment. One very important source of diagnostic information is a person who is close to the client. Spouses or adult children can provide different perspectives than health care professionals and can usually complete a checklist relatively easily. Caregivers have known the person being assessed for a much longer time and may be in a better position to assess subtle changes in performance over time. They also provide important information about the severity of the problem that can be compared with information provided by the person being assessed. For example, the diagnosis of Alzheimer's disease is often furthered by examining the discrepancy between the client's assessment of memory functioning and the caregiver's assessment of the client's memory functioning (Reisberg et al., 1986). In the middle stages of the disease the clients' reports of memory problems drop, but caregiver's reports continue to increase.

Memory, Nutrition, and Drugs

Researchers and clinicians often overlook nutrition as a cause of memory failures in later life (Perlmutter et al., 1987). Unfortunately, we know very little about how specific nutrient deficiencies relate to specific aspects of memory. The available evidence links thiamine deficiency to memory problems in humans (Cherkin, 1984), and it links niacin and vitamin B_{12} deficiencies to diseases in which memory failure is a major symptom (Rosenthal & Goodwin, 1985).

Likewise, many drugs have been associated with memory problems. The most widely known of these is alcohol, which if abused over a long period is associated with severe memory loss. Less well known are the effects of other prescription and over-the-counter medications. For example, sedatives and tranquilizers have been found to impair memory performance (Block, DeVoe, Stanley, Stanley, & Pomara, 1985).

These data indicate that it is important to consider older adults' diets and medications when assessing their memory performance. What may appear to be serious decrements in functioning may, in fact, be induced by poor nutrition or specific medications. Too often, researchers and clinicians fail to inquire about eating habits and the medications people take. Adequate assessment is essential to avoid diagnostic errors.

Concept Checks

1. From a functional perspective, how does one tell the difference between normal and abnormal memory aging?
2. How does severe depression affect memory?
3. What are the major characteristics of neuropsychological tests, behavioral and self-report measures, and rating scales?
4. How does alcohol affect memory?

REMEDIATING MEMORY PROBLEMS

Learning Objectives:

- What are the major ways that memory skills are trained? How effective are these methods?
- What are the key individual difference variables in memory training?

Imagine that you have problems remembering where you left your keys. Or suppose that someone you love has gone through a comprehensive diagnostic process like that advocated in the previous section, and a memory problem was discovered. Is there anything that can be done to help people remember? In most cases, the answer is yes. Researchers have developed several different types of memory training programs, many of which are effective even with persons with severe memory impairments (Wilson & Moffat, 1984). In this section we will examine some of the attempts at remediating memory problems and some of the individual differences that affect the success of these programs.

Training Memory Skills

The notion that memory can be improved through acquiring skills and practicing them is very old, dating back to prehistory (Yates, 1966). For example, the story of the *Iliad* was told for generations through the use of mnemonic strategies before it was finally written down. Books that teach readers how to improve their own memory have also been around for a very long time (Grey, 1756). Interestingly, these old how-to books teach techniques that are virtually identical with those advocated in more recent books (Lorayne & Lucas, 1974; West, 1986b).

Training people how to remember information more effectively can be aimed not only at people with identifiable disorders, but also at people whose memory performance has declined as a result of normal, age-related changes (West, 1995). As you may have realized in our earlier discussion about memory strategies, most of them share several things in common. First, they require paying attention to the incoming information. Second, they rely on already stored information to facilitate making new connections with the new material. Finally, the best strategies are those that, in the process of encoding, provide the basis for future retrieval cues. In short, the very best memory strategies are the ones that practically guarantee that the appropriate cue will be available to access the stored information when it must be retrieved (West, 1995).

Memory aids or strategies can be organized into meaningful groups. Among the most useful of these classifications is Camp and colleagues' (1993) E-I-E-I-O framework. The E-I-E-I-O framework combines two types of memory, explicit memory and implicit memory, with two types of memory aids, external aids and internal aids. ***Explicit memory* involves the conscious and intentional recollection of information; remembering this definition on an exam is one example. *Implicit memory* involves effortless and unconscious recollection of information; knowing that stop signs are red octagons is usually not something that people need to exert effort to remember when they see one on the road. *External aids* are memory aids that rely on environmental resources, such as notebooks or calendars. *Internal aids* are memory aids that rely on mental processes, such as imagery.** The aha or *O!* experience in the framework is the one that comes with suddenly remembering something. As you can see in the table, the E-I-E-I-O framework helps organize how different types of memory can be combined with different types of memory aids to provide a broad range of intervention options to help people remember.

We can use Camp and colleagues' approach to examine research on external and internal memory aids. In addition, we will briefly review two alternatives, memory exercises and medications.

External Memory Aids

External memory aids are objects such as diaries, address books, calendars, notepads, microcomputers, and other devices commonly used to support

Type of Memory	Type of Memory Aid	
	External	*Internal*
Explicit	Appointment book Grocery list	Mental imagery Rote rehearsal
Implicit	Color-coded maps Sandpaper letters	Spaced retrieval Conditioning

memory in everyday situations (Cavanaugh et al., 1983; Harris, 1980). Some external aids involve actually using some external device to store information (such as computers and date books), whereas others involve the use of external aids to cue action (for instance, setting a book out so you won't forget it).

In general, explicit-external interventions are the most frequently used, probably because they are easy to use and widely available (Cavanaugh et al., 1983). For example, virtually everyone owns an address book, and small notepads are sold in hundreds of stores. But explicit-external interventions have other important applications, too. The problem of remembering one's medication schedule is best solved with an explicit-external intervention: a pillbox that is divided into compartments corresponding to days of the week and different times of the day. Research shows that this type of pillbox is the easiest to load and results in the fewest errors (Park, Morrell, Frieske, Blackburn, & Birchmore, 1991). Memory interventions like this can help older adults maintain their independence. Nursing homes also use explicit-external interventions, such as bulletin boards with the date and weather conditions, to help residents keep in touch with current events.

Advocating the use of external aids in memory rehabilitation is becoming increasingly popular. Zgola (1987) recommends external aids in working with Alzheimer's patients. For example, caregivers may label their kitchen cabinets to make it easier for the person with Alzheimer's disease to remember what is in them. Harris (1984a) suggests that for external cues to be most effective, they should (1) be given close to the time that action is required, (2) be active rather than passive, (3) be specific to the particular action, (4) be portable, (5) fit a wide range of situations, (6) store many cues for long periods, (7) be easy to use, and (8) not require a pen or pencil.

Countering this trend toward greater use of external strategies, West (1986b) cautions that overreliance on external aids can be a problem. She argues that memory is much like a muscle, which needs to be exercised to be kept in shape, an approach we will consider a bit later.

External-implicit combinations, more widely used with children, nevertheless have applicability with older adults in some situations. For example, many nursing homes use different color schemes to designate different wings or sections of the building. Because people process the color-coded aspects of the building automatically, the implicit nature of this external cue makes it ideal for people who may otherwise have difficulty learning and remembering new information.

Internal Memory Aids

Looking at Camp and colleagues' examples of internal memory aids may have triggered some personal experiences. For example, most people use rote rehearsal in preparing for an examination (repeating Camp—E-I-E-I-O over and over), or use mental imagery in remembering the location of their car in a parking lot (we're parked near the giraffe on the light post). Most research on memory training concerns improving people's use of these and other internal strategies that supply meaning and help organize incoming information (Bellezza, 1987). Classic examples of formal internal strategies include the method of loci (remembering items by mentally placing them in locations in a familiar environment), mental retracing (thinking about all the places you may have left your keys), turning letters into numbers, and forming acronyms out of initial letters (such as NASA from *N*ational *A*eronautic and *S*pace *A*dministration).

Most memory improvement courses train

A cookbook can be an effective and helpful memory aid, no matter how often one has made black bean soup.

people to become proficient at using one of these internal strategies. For example, Yesavage (1983) trained older adults to use images to help themselves remember people's names. As shown in Figure 6.3, this training was effective. Interestingly, certain personality traits may be associated with who benefits most from training. Gratzinger, Sheikh, Friedman, and Yesavage (1990) found that people who scored high on openness to experience (a dimension of personality) performed better with imagery than other people. In particular, the fantasy subfactor of the openness dimension was related to greater improvement as a result of imagery training. It may be that people who find it easy to fantasize may be better at coming up with the imagery that help them remember people's names.

Similar research has shown that training on most internal strategies improves memory significantly. For example, older adults have been successfully trained to use the method of loci as a way to help them remember items to be purchased at the grocery store (Anschutz, Camp, Markley, & Kramer, 1985). Unfortunately, these training programs have rarely been assessed over long intervals, so the degree of improvement after the course ends and how long this improvement lasts is largely unknown. One of the few exceptions was a 3-year follow-up to the grocery shopping study (Anschutz, Camp, Markley, & Kramer, 1987). Although Anschutz and her colleagues found that loci were readily available, older adults had abandoned their use of the locus method as a memory aid. Clearly, more research needs to be conducted to understand why adults stop using internal memory strategies that are effective in improving recall.

The internal strategies we have examined so far fall into the explicit-internal category in Camp and colleagues' system. One implicit-internal memory aid that has proven quite powerful is based on a technique called spaced retrieval. Camp (1989) relates that even in Alzheimer's disease people can learn new things with this technique. As described

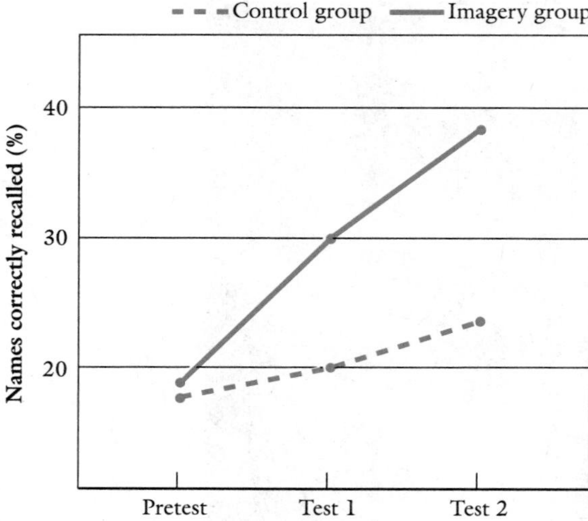

Figure 6.3 Proportion of names recalled at three points in the study. Pretest occurred in the first session before any training. Test 1 was after imagery training (in the imagery group) and after attitude training (in the control group). Test 2 was after both groups had received training in the face-name mnemonic.

Source: "Imagery Pretraining and Memory Training in the Elderly," by J. A. Yesavage, 1983, Gerontology, *29, 271–275. Copyright © 1983 by S. Karger. Reprinted with permission.*

in How Do We Know? he was able to teach people with Alzheimer's disease the names of the staff who worked with them.

Exercising Memory

Another approach to memory training is based on viewing memory as a mental muscle. This approach uses repetitive practice, which involves using specific memory exercises. Exercising memory on one type of task strengthens it, setting the stage for better memory in a variety of other tasks (Harris & Sunderland, 1981). For example, practicing how to organize a grocery list over and over will help one learn to organize other kinds of lists as well.

Exercising memory may have important benefits to a person during the rehabilitation process following an accident or stroke. For one thing, the person knows that something is being done about his or her memory problems. This may result in the belief that improvement is possible and that it is worth the effort. Second, evidence from both animal research (Wall, 1975) and human research (Black, Markowitz, & Cianci, 1975) indicates that early intervention with physical exercise promotes recovery after damage to the motor cortex. Harris and Sunderland (1981) suggest that the same benefit may accrue if memory practice is begun at the first sign of loss.

Memory Drugs

Although considerable research has focused on the underlying neurological mechanisms in memory, little definitive information is available that can be easily translated into treatment approaches. For example, we still are not sure which neurotransmitters are primarily involved with memory. This is not for lack of trying, though. Many attempts at enhancing memory through the use of drugs that affect the neurotransmitter acetylcholine, for example, have been made. However, attempts to improve memory by administering drugs that act on certain neurotransmitters produces only modest, short-term improvements with no long-term changes, and much of the work aimed at improving specific types of memory is also disappointing (Lombardi & Weingartner, 1995). This research is especially important for Alzheimer's disease and related disorders.

Combining Strategies

Which memory strategy is best clearly depends on the situation. For example, remembering names probably demands an internal strategy, whereas remembering appointments could most easily be helped by external strategies. For optimal improvement, the best approach is to tailor specific strategies to specific situations.

This is exactly what McEvoy and Moon (1988) did. They designed a comprehensive multiple strategy training program for improving older adults' memory in everyday situations. To remember names, older adults were taught an internal strategy emphasizing the need to associate new names with already known information. In contrast, use of external aids and how to review them was used for remembering appointments such as occasional physician visits. McEvoy and Moon found that after training, participants had fewer complaints

HOW DO WE KNOW?

What's My Name? Memory Training in Alzheimer's Disease

Memory intervention programs have been used with many different populations. However, one of the most interesting target groups consists of people with Alzheimer's disease. As noted in the text (and in Chapter 9), Alzheimer's disease is characterized by a severe and progressive deterioration in memory functioning. As a result, anything that could help people remember would be an important contribution.

In a series of studies, Camp (see Camp & McKitrick, 1991) showed that people with Alzheimer's disease can successfully be taught the names of staff people. His technique involves *spaced retrieval*, which consists of progressively increasing the amount of time between the recall of the target information (that is, a person's name). In the procedure, the trainer shows the client a photograph of a person and says that person's name. After an initial recall interval of 5 seconds, the trainer asks the client to remember the name. As long as the client remembers correctly, recall intervals are increased to 10, 20, 40, 60, 90, 120, 150, and so on. If the client forgets the target name, the correct answer is provided, and the next recall interval is decreased to the length of the last correct trial. During the interval, the trainer simply engages the client in conversation to prevent active rehearsal of the information.

Amazingly, even people who previously could not retain new information for more than 60 seconds can remember names taught via spaced retrieval for intervals up to 5 weeks. Although there are individual differences in how long people with Alzheimer's disease remember information learned this way, and how well they transfer new learning from photographs to the real people, these results are extremely encouraging. The intervention requires no drugs, can be done in any setting, and involves social activity. The training can even be inserted into everyday activities such as playing games or normal conversation, making it comfortable and uninterventionlike for the client. Although the technique needs to be refined, spaced retrieval seems to represent an easily applied intervention.

about their memory for names and faces, appointments, routine tasks, and spatial orientation.

McEvoy and Moon's study points out the importance of tailoring an intervention to fit the problem. What works best for one kind of information may not help us remember another. Moreover, their work also emphasizes the need for broad-based comprehensive intervention programs. Training people to only remember one kind of information is not helpful when their daily lives are filled with far more complicated demands.

Individual Difference Variables in Memory Training

As we have seen throughout this chapter, adults are a very heterogenous group when it comes to memory performance. For example, research reviewed earlier shows that verbal ability, prior knowledge, and familiarity influence how well one performs on memory tasks. Treat, Poon, Fozard, and Popkin (1978) argued that individual difference variables should be considered when designing memory training programs, especially for older adults. Moreover, training may be more effective when changes in emotional status (Popkin, Gallagher, Thompson, & Moore, 1982) and feelings of self-efficacy (Berry, 1986; Cavanaugh et al., 1989) are major goals of the program. Yesavage, Sheikh, Tanke, and Hill (1988) found that the benefits of memory training depend on the specific needs of the client. Older adults who were highly verbal benefited most from a training program emphasizing ways to connect incoming information with information they already knew. In contrast, older adults who were highly anxious benefited most from training that included a relaxation component.

An approach to memory training that includes both training on specific strategies with such relevant factors as relaxation (Stigsdotter Neely & Bäckman, 1993a, 1993b) and social support (Flynn & Storandt, 1990) has typically resulted in performance gains. However, whether the gains due to the combined approach are greater than those following traditional strategy training is unclear (Stigsdotter Neely & Bäckman, 1993a, 1993b). Moreover, although providing memory strategies improves performance for adults of all ages, surprisingly little research has been done to identify how broadly the effects of training generalize across tasks and individuals.

To examine these issues, Stigsdotter Neely and Bäckman (1995) compared performance in a control group and a group given composite training involving encoding operations, attentional functions, and relaxation. The training task involved learning a list of concrete words, and generalization of the strategy was tested on tasks involving recall of objects, recall of participant-performed tasks, and recall of abstract words. People who were trained on the combined strategy still outperformed the control group 6 months after training, but only generalized their strategy to the recall of objects task.

Additionally, age, education level, and level of general cognitive functioning did not predict performance after training; only performance on the pretraining task predicted future performance. These findings indicate that performance gains remain several months after strategy training on a specific task, but that people tend not to use the strategy in other situations very much.

In sum, the memory training literature is emerging as an important area for addressing questions about how memory performance differs with age. Although much more work on the issues of generalization and individual differences in the effectiveness of training remains to be done, the available research demonstrates that training may need to include not only a memory technique, but also memory-related components such as self-efficacy, relaxation, and so forth. Also remaining to be answered are the questions of how to predict who will benefit from memory training and why people differ in the degree to which they benefit from training.

Concept Checks

1. What is the E-I-E-I-O framework, and how does it help organize memory training?
2. What effect does combining approaches such as relaxation have on performance in memory training?

SUMMARY

Information Processing Revisited

Working Memory

Working memory refers to the processes and structures involved in holding information in mind and simultaneously using that information, sometimes in conjunction with incoming information, to solve a problem, make a decision, or learn. Information is kept active through rehearsal. In general, working memory capacity and rehearsal decline with age, although the extent of the decline is still in doubt. There is some evidence that age differences in working memory are not universal.

Secondary Memory

Secondary memory refers to the ability to remember extensive amounts of information over relatively long periods. In secondary memory, age-related decrements are typically found on recall tests but not on recognition tests. Older adults tend not to use memory strategies spontaneously as often or as well as younger adults. Age differences can be reduced in several ways.

Tertiary Memory

Tertiary memory involves remembering information over very long periods of time. In tertiary memory, age differences are typically not found in tests of the knowledge base. Some aspects of autobiographical memory remain intact for many years whereas other aspects do not. Verification of autobiographical memories is often difficult. Older adults have fewer flashbulb memories.

Memory for Discourse

Person Variables

Verbal ability is a major factor in determining age differences in discourse memory. Low-verbal older adults perform much worse than all younger adults; high-verbal older adults perform at least as well as high-verbal younger adults. Age differences in performance are also influenced by the use of effective reading strategies, how a story is retold, and prior knowledge. Older adults are especially likely to put pieces of prior knowledge in their recall of newly learned text.

Task Variables

Higher presentation speeds may put older adults at a disadvantage; age differences are reduced when self-pacing is used. Age differences in recall tend to increase as the length of reading time is increased. Age-related slowing in cognitive processing explains much of this difference.

Text Variables

Age differences are usually not found for the major organizational elements of text, but performance is related to verbal ability. With well-organized text, which emphasizes the structure and main ideas, age differences are typically not found. Older adults may be more interested in learning general points than in learning the details. Prior beliefs also make it difficult to learn and remember elements of text.

Text Memory and Secondary Memory

List learning and text memory are affected by similar variables, including pacing, prior knowledge, and verbal ability. Age per se is not a major cause of performance differences.

Memory in Everyday Life

Spatial Memory

Older adults do not reconstruct objects in a spatial array as accurately as do younger adults. However, with familiar objects or locations, or when contextual cues are provided, older adults' performance improves, and they may perform as well as younger adults. Older and younger adults use different strategies to learn the locations of landmarks, which sometimes results in performance differences. Older and younger adults appear equally able to learn a route, but complex differences (including gender differences) emerge when people use maps as a learning aid. Older and younger adults perform most configurational learning tasks equivalently, especially when the task involves familiar locations.

Memory for Activities

It is thought that processing of activities is automatic. Actually performing activities aids memory for older adults, but older adults are more likely to claim they performed actions they actually didn't. Some activities, such as problem-solving tasks, are remembered better than others, such as perceptual-motor tasks. Age differences are less likely on event-based prospective memory tasks than on time-based prospective memory tasks. How accurately prospective memory tasks are performed depends on the time of day. Processing speed may help explain these age differences.

Everyday Memory Versus List-Learning Performance

Older adults are worse at remembering some types of pictures, including faces, but sometimes these differences are only found on delayed tests involving particular delays. Older adults are more likely to rely on their experience, or schematic knowledge, to help them remember scenes, especially when the scenes depicted are not well organized.

Self-Evaluations of Memory Abilities

Aspects of Memory Self-Evaluations

There are two general categories of memory self-evaluations. Metamemory refers to knowledge about how memory works and what one believes to be true about it. Memory monitoring refers to the awareness of what we are doing with our memory right now.

Age Differences in Metamemory

Metamemory is typically assessed with questionnaires. Older adults seem to know less than younger adults about the workings of memory and its capacity, view memory as less stable, believe that their memory will decline with age, and feel that they have little control over these changes.

However, the belief in inevitable decline does not apply equally to all aspects of memory. How metamemory is organized may differ across adulthood. Memory self-efficacy is the belief in how well one will perform in a specific situation and is an important construct in understanding how people make judgments about performance before they have experience with a task.

Age Differences in Memory Monitoring

Older adults often overestimate how well they will do when making predictions without knowledge of or experience with the task. With task knowledge or experience, age differences are usually absent. These changes in pattern of predictions appears to be due to individuals being able to use performance on earlier trials to adjust their predictions in subsequent trials.

Sources of Age Differences in Memory

Age Differences in Encoding

Age-related decrements in encoding may be due to decrements in rehearsal in working memory and being slower at making connections with incoming information. Older adults do not spontaneously organize incoming information as well as younger adults, but they can use organizational helps when told to do so. However, the benefits of this approach are short-lived.

Age Differences in Retrieval

Age differences are greater for algorithmic retrieval than for heuristic retrieval. Age differences are greater on recall than on recognition tests. Older adults benefit more than younger adults from retrieval cues, but age differences in performance are not eliminated. The locus of retrieval problems seems to be working memory.

Relative Contributions of Encoding and Retrieval Differences

Changes in memory with age are due to both encoding and retrieval problems. Research involving brain imaging studies of blood flow in the brain show substantially less brain activity in older adults compared with younger adults during encoding.

The Emerging Role of Working Memory

Working memory is being discovered as a key to understanding age differences in memory performance. Possible explanations include difficulty in keeping interfering information out of working memory. More basic research implicates age-related slowing in information processing as an important precursor of working memory problems.

Clinical Issues and Memory Testing

Normal Versus Abnormal Memory Aging

Whether memory changes affect daily functioning is one way to separate normal from abnormal aging. Brain imaging techniques allow localization of problems with more precision. Some diseases are also marked by severe memory impairments. However, in many cases telling the difference between normal changes and those associated with disease or other abnormal events is difficult.

Memory and Mental Health

Dementia (such as Alzheimer's disease) and severe depression both involve memory impairment. In depression, negative belief systems may underlie these memory problems. Researchers and clinicians must learn to differentiate the various types of mental health problems.

Clinical Memory Tests

Neuropsychological tests assess broad aspects of cognitive functioning, including memory, attention, and problem solving. Such tests are designed to assess specific brain-behavior relations. Scores on memory self-evaluation questionnaires measuring memory complaints correlate with depression. Rating scales are completed by people other than the individual with the memory problems and are often used for diagnosing dementia. Two common types of rating scales are the mental status exam and checklists of specific memory problems.

Memory, Nutrition, and Drugs

Research evidence links niacin and vitamin B_{12} deficiencies to memory impairment. Drugs such as alcohol as well as some prescription and over-the-counter medications also have deleterious effects on memory.

Remediating Memory Problems

Training Memory Skills

The E-I-E-I-O framework, based on explicit-implicit aspects of memory and external-internal types of strategies is a useful way to organize ways of memory training. Older adults can learn new internal memory strategies, but like all adults will usually abandon them over time. External-explicit strategies (such as lists and calendars) are common, but internal-implicit strategies are effective even with persons who have Alzheimer's disease. Practicing remembering things helps to improve memory. Use of memory enhancing drugs does not work over the long run. Combining types of strategies may represent the best approach.

Individual Difference Variables in Memory Training

Memory training may be more effective when individual difference factors, such as emotional issues, are taken into account. Combining memory strategy training with relaxation training, for example, has been shown to be effective. However, older adults appear not to generalize the strategies across a range of different tasks.

REVIEW QUESTIONS

Information processing revisited

- What is working memory? What age differences have been found? What role does working memory play in understanding age differences in memory?
- What is secondary memory? How is it tested? What patterns of age differences have been found? What happens to the use of memory strategies with age?
- What is tertiary memory? How does tertiary memory differ with age in terms of the knowledge base and autobiographical memory?

Memory for discourse

- What factors influence memory for discourse? What age differences have been uncovered related to these influences?
- How do the patterns of age differences for discourse and list learning compare?
- What text and task variables are most important?

Memory in everyday life

- What age differences are there in memory for location? What factors influence performance? When do older and younger adults perform equivalently? Why?
- What difference does it make in accuracy in whether older and younger people actually performed the actions they need to remember?
- What types of prospective memory have been distinguished? What age differences are there in prospective memory?
- How do younger and older adults compare at remembering pictures?

Self-evaluations of memory abilities

- What major types of self-evaluations have been described?
- What age differences are there in memory knowledge and in beliefs about memory?
- What age differences have been found in making predictions about performance? What factors influence people's predictions?

Sources of age differences in memory

- What age differences have been found in encoding processes?
- What age differences have been found in retrieval processes?
- What is the relative contribution of encoding and retrieval in understanding age differences in memory?
- What is the emerging role of working memory in understanding age differences in memory?

Clinical issues and memory testing

- What criteria are used to determine the difference between normal and abnormal changes in a person's memory?

- What are the major mental health conditions that involve significant memory problems?
- What do neuropsychological tests assess? Of what use are self-report questionnaires?
- How are rating scales used to assess memory impairments?
- What effects do nutrition and drugs have on memory?

Remediating memory problems

- What is the E-I-E-I-O framework? How does it help organize memory training programs?
- How much do older adults benefit from each of the major types of memory training programs?
- What kinds of memory interventions work over time?

INTEGRATING CONCEPTS IN DEVELOPMENT

1. Based on material in Chapter 5 on attention and psychomotor speed, and the material in Chapter 6, what are the major factors involved in understanding age-related differences in memory?
2. What aspects of implicit memory, as discussed in Chapter 5, would be important to consider in designing memory training programs based on implicit memory?
3. How would you design an informational brochure for older adults to maximize their ability to remember it?

KEY TERMS

algorithmic retrieval Any retrieval process that produces error-free performance.

configurational learning Process requiring people to combine spatial and temporal information so that they can recognize a location when they view it from a different perspective.

encoding The process of getting information into the memory system.

explicit memory The conscious and intentional recollection of information.

external aids Memory aids that rely on environmental resources.

heuristic retrieval Any retrieval process that produces both successes and failures.

implicit memory The effortless and unconscious recollection of information.

internal aids Memory aids that rely on mental processes.

memory monitoring The awareness of what we are doing in memory right now.

memory self-efficacy The belief in one's ability to perform a specific memory task.

metamemory Memory about how memory works and what one believes to be true about it.

prospective memory Process involving remembering to remember something in the future.

rating scales Instruments designed to assess memory from the viewpoint of an observer, usually a mental health professional.

recall Process of remembering information without the help of hints or cues.

recognition Process of remembering information by selecting previously learned information from among several items.

rehearsal Process by which information is held in working memory, either by repeating items over and over or by making meaningful connections between the information in working memory and information already known.

retrieval The process of getting information back out of memory.

secondary memory The aspects of memory involved in remembering rather extensive amounts of information over relatively long periods of time.

storage The manner in which information is represented and kept in memory.

strategies Various techniques that make learning or remembering easier and that increase the efficiency of storage.

tertiary memory Aspect of memory involved with information kept over very long periods of time.

working memory Refers to the processes and structures involved in holding information in mind and simultaneously using that information, sometimes in conjunction with incoming information, to solve a problem, make a decision, or learn new information.

IF YOU'D LIKE TO LEARN MORE

Blanchard-Fields, F., & Hess, T. M. (Eds.). (1996). *Perspectives on cognitive changes in adulthood and aging*. New York: McGraw Hill. The best basic overview of age-related cognitive changes. Easy to moderate difficulty.

Craik, F. I. M., & Salthouse, T. A. (Eds.). (1992). *The handbook of aging and cognition*. Hillsdale, NJ: Erlbaum. One of the best overviews of memory and cognition in one volume. Moderate to difficult reading.

Poon, L. W. (Ed.). (1986). *Handbook for the clinical memory assessment of older adults*. Washington, DC: American Psychological Association. This edited book provides a broad discussion of how memory is evaluated and treated in clinical settings. Moderate to difficult reading.

Sinnott, J. D. (Ed.). (1994). *Interdisciplinary handbook of adult lifespan learning*. Westport, CT: Greenwood Press. A broad discussion of many different aspects of cognition, including cross-cultural studies. Moderate difficulty.

West, R. L., & Sinnott, J. D., (Eds.). (1991). *Everyday memory and aging: Current research and methodology*. New York: Springer-Verlag. Good overview of memory in everyday life. Moderate difficulty.

CHAPTER 7

Intelligence

Sydney and Frances Lewis by Jack Beal. Washington and Lee University, Lexington, VA.

DEFINING INTELLIGENCE

DEVELOPMENTAL TRENDS IN PSYCHOMETRIC INTELLIGENCE

QUALITATIVE DIFFERENCES IN ADULTS' THINKING

PROBLEM SOLVING, EXPERTISE, AND WISDOM

SUMMARY

REVIEW QUESTIONS

INTEGRATING CONCEPTS IN DEVELOPMENT

KEY TERMS

IF YOU'D LIKE TO LEARN MORE

Once upon a time, there lived an old man with his beautiful daughter. She fell in love with a handsome lad, and the two married with the old man's blessing. The young couple led a happy life, except for one problem: the husband spent his time working on alchemy, dreaming of a way to turn base elements into gold. Soon enough, he ran through his patrimony, and the young wife struggled to buy food each day. She finally asked her husband to find a job, but he protested. "I am on the verge of a breakthrough!" he insisted. "When I succeed, we will be rich beyond our dreams."

Finally the young wife told her father about the problem. He was surprised to learn that his son-in-law was an alchemist, but he promised to help his daughter and asked to see him the next day. The young man went reluctantly, expecting a reprimand. To his surprise, his father-in-law confided in him, "I, too, was an alchemist when I was young!" The father-in-law inquired about the young man's work, and the two spent the afternoon talking. Finally the old man stirred with excitement. "You have done everything I did!" he exclaimed. "You are surely on the verge of a breakthrough. But you need one more ingredient to change base elements into gold, and I have only recently discovered this secret." The old man paused and sighed. "But I am too old to undertake the task. It requires much work."

"I can do it, dear father!" the young man volunteered. The old man brightened. "Yes, perhaps you can." Then he leaned over and whispered, "The ingredient you need is the silver powder that grows on banana leaves. This powder becomes magic when you plant the bananas yourself, and cast certain spells upon it."

"How much powder do we need?" the young man asked. "Two pounds," the old man replied.

The son-in-law thought out loud, "That requires hundreds of banana plants!"

"Yes," the old man sighed, "and that is why I cannot complete the work myself." "Do not fear!" the young man said, "I will!" And so the old man taught his son-in-law the incantations and loaned him the money for the project.

The next day, the young man bought some land, and cleared it. He dug the ground himself, just as the old man had instructed him, planted the bananas, and murmured the magic spells over them. Each day he examined his plants, keeping weeds and pests away, and when the plants bore fruit, he collected the silver powder from the leaves. There was scarcely any on each plant, and so the young man bought more land, and cultivated more bananas. After several years, the young man collected two pounds of the magic dust. He rushed to his father-in-law's house.

"I have the magic powder!" the young man exclaimed. "Wonderful!" the old man rejoiced. "Now I can show you how to turn base elements into gold! But first you must bring your wife here. We need her help." The young man was puzzled, but obeyed. When she appeared, the old man asked his daughter, "While your husband was collecting the banana powder, what did you do with the fruits?"

"Why, I sold them," the daughter said, "and that is how we earned a living."

"Did you save the money?" the father asked.

"Yes," she replied.

"May I see it?" the old man asked. So his daughter hurried home and returned with several bags. The old man opened them, saw they were full of gold, and poured the coins on the floor. Then he took a handful of dirt, and put it next to the gold.

"See," he turned to his son-in-law, " you have changed base elements into gold!"

For a tense moment, the young man was silent. Then he laughed, seeing the wisdom in the old man's trick. And from that day on, the young man and his wife prospered greatly. He tended the plants while she went to the market, selling the bananas. And they both honored the old man as the wisest of alchemists. ("The Old Alchemist" is from *In the Ever After: Fairy Tales and the Second Half of Life* by Allan B. Chinen. Copyright ©1989 by Chiron Publications. Reprinted with permission.)

This old Burmese folktale drives home the point that wisdom has long been associated with age. Surprisingly, psychologists have only recently become interested in wisdom, perhaps because they have been busy studying a related topic—intelligence. Another reason for not researching wisdom was the widespread belief that it would be a waste of time. At one time researchers and theorists were convinced that all intellectual abilities inevitably declined as people aged, due to biological deterioration. For instance, Wechsler (1958) wrote that "nearly all studies . . . have shown that most human abilities . . . decline progressively after reaching a peak somewhere between ages 18 and 25" (p. 135).

In the decades since Wechsler's pessimistic view, many things changed. Researchers discovered that intellectual development is an extremely complex process. We cannot give a simple yes or no answer to the question "Does intelligence decline with age?" And we continue to move farther away, rather than closer to, a simple answer. Controversy is now quite common. For instance, Baltes and Schaie (1974) conclude that "general intellectual decline is largely a myth" (p. 35). Botwinick (1977) counters that "decline in intellectual ability is clearly a part of the aging picture" (p. 580).

Who is right? Does intelligence decline, or is that a myth? Does wisdom come with age? Answering these questions will be our goal in this chapter. Such widely divergent conclusions about age-related changes in intelligence reflect different sets of assumptions about the nature of intelligence, which are then translated into different theoretical and methodological approaches. We will examine three avenues of research on intelligence and age: the psychometric approach, the neofunctionalist approach, and the cognitive-process approaches.

Vocabulary ability, essential in solving crossword puzzles, is one example of an intellectual ability that shows improvement or stability across adulthood.

Along the way we will take a look at some attempts to modify intellectual abilities through training programs. But first, we need to consider the question of what intelligence is.

DEFINING INTELLIGENCE

Learning Objectives:

- How do people define intelligence in everyday life?
- What are the major components of the neofunctionalist approach?
- What are the major research approaches for studying intelligence?

What do we mean by intelligence? Is it being able to learn new things very quickly? Is it knowing a great deal of information? Is it the ability to adapt to new situations or to create new things or ideas? Or is it the ability to make the most of what we have and to enjoy life? Intelligence is all of these abilities and more. It is all of them in the sense that people who stand out on these dimensions are often considered smart, or intelligent. It is more than just these abilities because intelligence also involves the qualitative aspects of thinking style, or how one approaches and conceptualizes problems.

Intelligence in Everyday Life

Some intriguing work by Sternberg and his colleagues points out that intelligence involves more than just a particular fixed set of characteristics (Sternberg, Conway, Ketron, & Bernstein, 1981). They compiled a list of behaviors that laypeople at a train station, supermarket, or college library reported to be distinctly characteristic of either exceptionally intelligent, academically intelligent, everyday intelligent, or unintelligent people. This list of behaviors was then given to experts in the field of intelligence and to a new set of laypeople, who were asked to rate either how distinctively characteristic each behavior was of an ideally intelligent, academically intelligent, or everyday intelligent individual or how important each behavior was in defining these types of intelligent individuals. Ratings were analyzed separately for the experts and the laypeople.

Sternberg and his colleagues found extremely high agreement between experts and laypeople on ratings of the importance of particular behaviors in defining intelligence. The two groups agreed that intelligence consisted of three major clusters of related abilities: problem-solving ability, verbal ability, and social competence. Problem-solving ability consists of behaviors such as reasoning logically, identifying connections among ideas, seeing all aspects of a problem, and making good decisions. Verbal ability includes such things as speaking articulately, reading with high comprehension, and having a good vocabulary. Social competence includes behaviors such as accepting others for what they are, admitting mistakes, displaying interest in the world at large, and being on time for appointments.

Sternberg also wanted to know how these conceptions of intelligence differed across the adult life span. To find out, individuals aged 25 to 75 were asked to list behaviors that they viewed as characteristic of exceptionally intelligent 30-, 50-, or 70-year-olds. Behaviors such as motivation, how much intellectual effort people exert, and reading were said to be important indicators of intelligence for people of all ages. But other behaviors were specific to particular points in the life span. For example, planning for the future and being open-minded were listed most often for a 30-year-old. The intelligent 50-year-old was described as being willing to learn, having a well-established career, and being authoritative. At age 70, intelligent people were thought to be socially active, up on current events, and accepting of change.

The Big Picture: A Neofunctionalist View

One thing is clear about the ways people view intelligence—everyone considers it a complex construct. In the big picture, then, intelligence consists of many different types of skills. **Theories of intelligence, therefore, are *multidimensional;* that is, they specify many domains of intellectual abilities.** Although people disagree on the number of dimensions, they do agree that no single generic type of intelligence is responsible for all the different kinds of mental activities we perform.

Baltes (1993; Dittmann-Kohli & Baltes, 1990) took a broad view and concluded that intellectual development in adulthood is characterized by three main ideas in addition to multidimensionality: plasticity, multidirectionality, and interindividual variability. **Collectively, this view is termed the *neofunctionalist approach,* which asserts that some intellectual decline may be seen with age but that stability and growth in mental functioning also can be seen across adulthood.** It emphasizes the role of intelligence in human adaptation and daily activity.

The first concept, *plasticity,* refers to the range of functioning within an individual and the conditions under which a person's abilities can be modified within a specific age range. Plasticity implies that what may appear to be declines in some skills may in part represent a lack of practice in using them. The research on training cognitive abilities described later in this chapter (Project ADEPT, for example) supports this view. **The second concept, *multidirectionality,* refers to the distinct patterns of change in abilities over the life span, with these patterns being different for different abilities.** For example, developmental functions for specific abilities differ, meaning that the directional change in intelligence depends on the skills in question. **The last concept, *interindividual variability,* acknowledges that adults differ in the direction of their intellectual development** (Schaie, 1995). Schaie's sequential research indicates that within a given cohort some people show longitudinal decline in specific abilities, some show stability of functioning, and others show increments in performance (Schaie, 1995). Consequently, a curve representing typical or average changes with age may not really represent the various individuals in the group.

Using these four concepts of multidimensionality, plasticity, multidirectionality, and interindividual variability, Baltes and his colleagues proposed the neofunctionalist approach as a dual-process model. Two interrelated types of developmental processes are postulated. The first process, termed *cognition as basic processes,* concerns developmental changes in the basic forms of thinking associated with information processing and problem solving. Cognitive development in this first process is greatest during childhood and adolescence, as we acquire the requisite skills to handle complex cognitive tasks, such as those encountered in school. The second process, *pragmatic intelligence,* relates the basic cognitive skills in the first process to everyday cognitive performance and human adaptation. Pragmatic intellectual growth dominates adulthood. Indeed, later in this chapter we will see that such knowledge continues to increase until very late in life.

This broad view of intellectual development in adulthood provides the background for asking more specific questions about particular aspects of intelligence. As we will see, two primary research approaches have emerged.

Research Approaches to Intelligence

Sternberg's work points out that many different skills are involved in intelligence, depending on one's point of view. Interestingly, the behaviors listed by Sternberg's participants fit nicely with the more formal attempts at defining intelligence that we will encounter in this chapter. Researchers have studied these skills from many different perspectives, depending on their theoretical orientation. For example, some investigators approach these skills from a mechanistic worldview and study them as separate pieces that can be added together to form intelligence. Others take a more holistic view and think of intelligence as a way or mode of thinking. These various theoretical orientations result in very different means of studying intelligence.

Some investigators, such as Schaie and Horn, have concentrated on measuring intelligence as performance on standardized tests; this view represents the *psychometric approach.* For example, the problem-solving and verbal abilities in Sternberg and co-workers' study would be assessed by tests specifically designed to assess these skills. These tests focus on getting correct answers and tend to give less emphasis on the thought processes used to arrive at them. **Other researchers, such as Piaget, King, Kitchener, and Kramer, have been more concerned with the ways in which people conceptualize and solve problems rather than in scores on tests; they take a *cognitive-process approach* to intelligence, which emphasizes developmental changes in the modes and styles of thinking.** The age differences Sternberg found in which abilities their respondents believed were important correspond to the qualitative changes discussed by cognitive-process theorists.

In this chapter we will consider these theories and the research they stimulated. We will discover that each approach has its merits and that whether age-related changes in intelligence are found depends on how intelligence is defined and measured. But before you continue, complete the exercise in the Discovering Development feature. The information you uncover will be useful as you read the rest of the chapter.

Concept Checks

1. What three clusters of ability did Sternberg and colleagues identify in their study of people's everyday conceptualizations of intelligence?
2. What are the four major aspects of intelligence emphasized by the neofunctionalist approach?
3. What are the two major approaches for researching intelligence?

DEVELOPMENTAL TRENDS IN PSYCHOMETRIC INTELLIGENCE

Learning Objectives:

- What are primary mental abilities? How do they change across adulthood?
- What are secondary mental abilities? What are

DISCOVERING DEVELOPMENT

How Do People Show Intelligence?

Earlier in this section, we encountered Sternberg and colleagues' (1981) research on people's implicit theories of intelligence. However, that study only examined broad categories of behavior that could be considered intelligent. Moreover, it was not conducted in such a way as to permit comparisons with research-based approaches to intelligence.

You and your classmates could address these shortcomings in the following way. Ask adults of different ages what they think constitutes intelligent behavior, much the same as Sternberg and colleagues did. However, be careful to make sure people are specific about the abilities they nominate. Additionally, ask them about what makes adults' thinking different from adolescents' thinking and whether they believe there might be different stages of adults' thinking. Again, try to get your respondents to be as specific as possible.

Collate all the data from the class. Look for common themes in specific abilities, as well as in the qualitative aspects of thinking. As you read the rest of the chapter, see to what extent your data parallels that from more formal investigations.

---

the developmental trends for fluid and crystallized intelligence?
- What are the primary moderators of intellectual change?
- How successful are attempts at training primary mental abilities?

One way to define intelligence is to focus on individuals' performances on various tests of intellectual abilities and on how these performances are interrelated. This psychometric approach to intelligence has a long history; the ancient Chinese and Greeks used this method to select people for certain jobs, such as master horseman (Doyle, 1974; DuBois, 1968). It also served as the basis for Binet's (1903) pioneering work in developing standardized intelligence tests, as well as many modern theories of intelligence.

Because the psychometric approach focuses on the interrelationships among intellectual abilities, the major goal is to describe the ways in which these relationships are organized (Sternberg, 1985). This organization of interrelated intellectual abilities is termed the *structure* of intelligence. The most common way to describe the structure of intelligence is to picture it as a hierarchy (Cunningham, 1987).

Each higher level of this hierarchy represents an attempt to organize components of the level below in a smaller number of groups. The lowest level consists of individual test questions—the specific items that people answer on an intelligence test. These items can be organized into tests at the second level. The third level, primary mental abilities, reflects interrelationships among performances on intelligence tests. Interrelationships can also be uncovered among the primary mental abilities, which produce the secondary mental abilities at the fourth level. Third-order mental abilities in turn represent interrelationships among the secondary mental abilities. Finally, general intelligence at the top refers to the interrelationships among the third-order abilities.

Keep in mind that each time we move up the hierarchy we are moving away from people's actual performance. Each level above the first represents a theoretical description of how things fit together. Thus, there are no tests of primary abilities per se; primary abilities represent theoretical relationships among tests, which in turn represent theoretical relationships among actual performance.

So exactly how do researchers construct this theoretical hierarchy? The structure of intelligence is uncovered through sophisticated statistical detective work. First, researchers obtain people's performances on many types of problems. Next, the results are examined to determine whether performance on one type of problem—for example, filling in missing letters in a word—predicts performance on another type of problem—for example, unscrambling letters to form a word. **If the performance on one test is highly related to the performance on another, the abilities measured by the two tests are interrelated and are called a *factor*.**

Most psychometric theorists believe that intelligence consists of several factors. Although estimates of the exact number of factors vary from a few to over 100, most researchers and theorists believe the number to be relatively small. We will examine two types of factors: primary mental abilities and secondary mental abilities.

Primary Mental Abilities

Early in this century researchers discovered the existence of several independent intellectual abilities, each indicated by different combinations of intelligence tests (Thurstone, 1938). **The abilities identified in this way led to the proposition that intelligence is composed of several independent abilities, labeled *primary mental abilities*.** Thurstone initially examined seven primary mental abilities: number, word fluency, verbal meaning, associative memory, reasoning, spatial orientation, and perceptual speed. Over the years this list has been refined and expanded, resulting in a current list of 25 primary mental abilities that have been documented across many studies (Ekstrom, French, & Harman, 1979). Because it is difficult to measure all 25 primary abilities in the same study, researchers following in Thurstone's tradition concentrate on measuring only a subset. Typically, this subset consists of five primary mental abilities (Schaie, 1996):

- *number* or the basic skills underlying one's mathematical reasoning;
- *word fluency* or how easily one can produce verbal descriptions of things;
- *verbal meaning* or one's vocabulary ability;
- *inductive reasoning* or one's ability to extrapolate from particular facts to general concepts; and
- *spatial orientation* or one's ability to reason in the three-dimensional world in which we live.

How these five abilities fare with age will be considered next.

Age-Related Changes in Primary Abilities

One of the most important research projects on adult intellectual development is the longitudinal study being conducted by K. Warner Schaie and his colleagues in Seattle, Washington, which began in 1956 (Schaie, 1995). This study has not only uncovered most of what we know about how primary mental abilities change across adulthood, but also been the basis for creating new research methodologies, the sequential designs discussed in Chapter 1. Over the course of the study, more than 5,000 individuals have been tested over six testing cycles (1956, 1963, 1970, 1977, 1984, 1991). All the participants were recruited through a very large health maintenance organization in Seattle that is representative of the upper 75% of the socioeconomic spectrum. Like most longitudinal studies, though, Schaie's has encountered selectivity effects; that is, people who return over the years for retesting tend to do better than those who fail to return. However, an advantage of Schaie's sequential design is that by bringing in new groups of participants, he has been able to estimate the importance of selection effects, a major improvement over previous research.

Primary mental abilities underlie all meaningful activities of a person's daily life (Willis, Jay, Diehl, & Marsiske, 1992). Thus, the developmental trends uncovered in the Seattle Longitudinal Study provide important insights into the course of intellectual changes that affect people's work and daily living routines. Schaie (in press) summarizes the findings as follows. Based on analyzing the data collected through the most recent wave in 1991, people tend to improve on the primary abilities tested until their late 30s or early 40s. Scores then tend to stabilize until people reach their mid-50s or early 60s. But by their late 60s, people tend to show consistent declines in each testing. Although some people begin to show declines in their mid 50s, these decrements tend to be small until the mid-

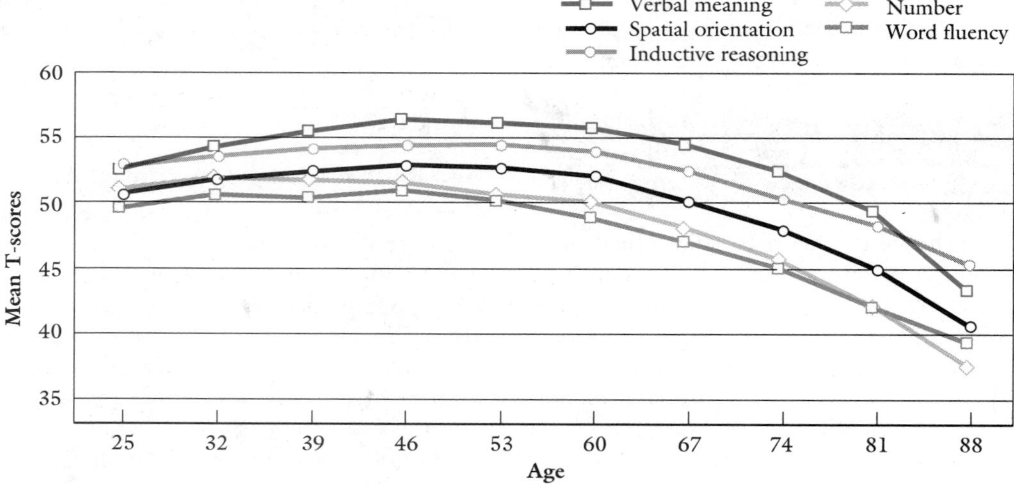

Figure 7.1 Longitudinal estimates of age changes on observed measures of five primary mental abilities
Source: Schaie, 1994

70s. Considering the modest improvements that most people make between young adulthood and middle age, scores are significantly lower than they were in young adulthood (roughly age 25) only by the mid-70s. These changes are depicted in Figure 7.1.

Do the general trends observed reflect global or specific changes in intelligence? That is, to what extent do people decline on all the primary abilities tested or only some of them? As you can see in Figure 7.2, even though by age 60 nearly everyone shows decline on one ability, very few people show decline on four or five abilities (Schaie, 1996). Even by age 88, only an extremely small number of people had declined significantly on all five abilities. This pattern may reflect a strategy of optimization of cognitive functioning in late life by selectively maintaining some abilities and not others (Baltes & Baltes, 1990). Even so, the evidence is clear that significant decrements in intellectual abilities occur by the time people are in their 80s, with most of the loss occurring in highly challenging, complex, and stressful situations that require activating cognitive reserves (Baltes, 1993).

Secondary Mental Abilities

Because so many primary mental abilities have been identified, some researchers think it may be easier to understand intellectual development by looking at interrelationships among them. **Careful consideration of the relationships among the primary mental abilities has resulted in the identification of *secondary mental abilities,* which are broad-ranging skills, each composed of several primary abilities** (Horn, 1982). At present, at least six secondary abilities have been found. Each of these is described in Table 7.1. Most of the developmental research and discussion of these abilities has been focused on two: fluid intelligence and crystallized intelligence.

Fluid and Crystallized Intelligence

Crystallized and fluid intelligence include many of the basic abilities that we associate with intelligence, such as verbal comprehension, reasoning, integration, and concept formation (Horn, 1978, 1982). Interestingly, they are associated with age differently, are influenced by different

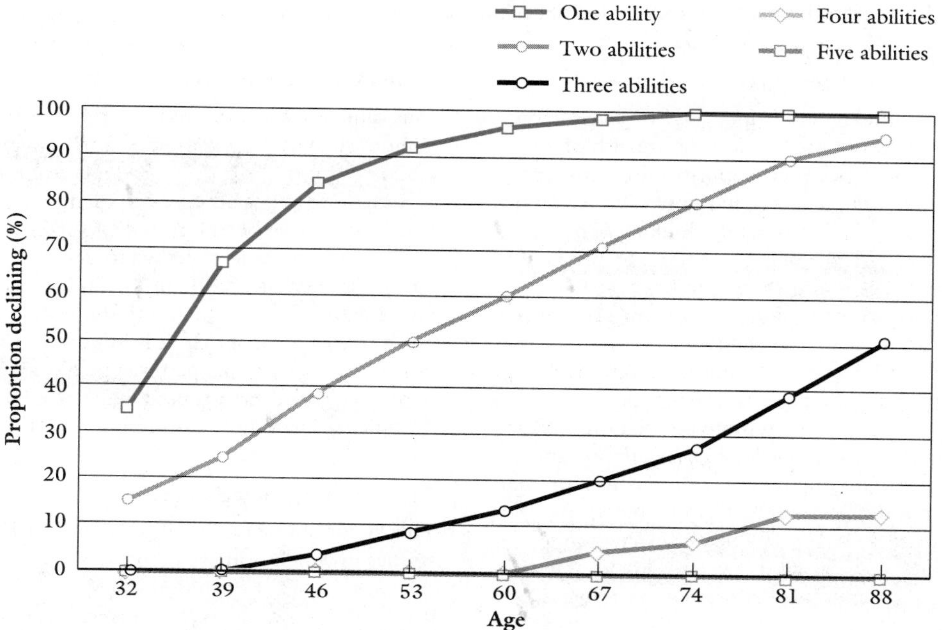

Figure 7.2 Cumulative proportion by age of individuals who show significant decline on one or more primary mental abilities
Source: Schaie, 1989.

underlying variables, and are measured in different ways.

***Fluid intelligence* consists of the abilities that make one a flexible and adaptive thinker, that allow one to draw inferences, and that allow one to understand the relations among concepts independent of acquired knowledge and experience.** It reflects the abilities one needs to understand and respond to any situation, but especially new ones: inductive reasoning, integration, abstract thinking, and the like (Horn, 1982). An example of a question that taps fluid abilities is:

> What letter comes next in the series *d f i m r x e* _____?[1]

Other typical ways of testing fluid intelligence include mazes, puzzles, and relations among shapes. Most of the time, these tests are timed, with higher scores associated with faster solutions.

***Crystallized intelligence* reflects knowledge that one has acquired through life experience and education in a particular culture.** Crystallized intelligence reflects one's breadth of knowledge, comprehension of communication, judgment, and sophistication with information (Horn, 1982). One's ability to remember historical facts, definitions of words, knowledge of literature, and sports trivia information are some examples. Many popular television game shows (such as "Jeopardy" and "Wheel of Fortune") are based on tests of contestants' crystallized intelligence. However, even though crystallized intelligence involves cultural knowledge, it is based partly on the quality of one's underlying fluid intelligence (Horn, 1982). For example, the breadth of one's vocabulary depends to some extent on how quickly one is able

[1]The next letter is *m*. The rule is to increase the difference between adjacent letters in the series by one each time. Thus, *f* is two letters from *d*, *i* is three letters away from *f*, and so on.

TABLE 7.1 Descriptions of major second-order mental abilities

Crystallized Intelligence (Gc)

This form of intelligence is indicated by a very large number of performances indicating breadth of knowledge and experience, sophistication, comprehension of communications, judgment, understanding conventions, and reasonable thinking. The factor that provides evidence of Gc is defined by primary abilities such as verbal comprehension, concept formation, logical reasoning, and general reasoning. Tests used to measure the ability include vocabulary (What is a word near in meaning to *temerity*?), esoteric analogies (Socrates is to Aristotle as Sophocles is to _____ ?), remote associations (What word is associated with *bathtub, prizefighting,* and *wedding*?), and judgment (Determine why a foreman is not getting the best results from workers). As measured, the factor is a fallible representation of the extent to which an individual has incorporated, through the systematic influences of acculturation, the knowledge and sophistication that constitutes the intelligence of a culture.

Fluid Intelligence (Gf)

The broad set of abilities of this intelligence include those of seeing relationships among stimulus patterns, drawing inferences from relationships, and comprehending implications. The primary abilities that best represent the factor, as identified in completed research, include induction, figural flexibility, integration, and, cooperatively with Gc, logical reasoning and general reasoning. Tasks that measure the factor include letter series (What letter comes next in the following series d f i m r x e?), matrices (Discern the relationships among elements of 3-by-3 matrices), and topology (From among a set of figures in which circles, squares, and triangles overlap in different ways, select a figure that will enable one to put a dot within a circle and square but outside a triangle). The factor is a fallible representation of such fundamental features of mature human intelligence as reasoning, abstracting, and problem solving. In Gf these features are not imparted through the systematic influences of acculturation but instead are obtained through learning that is unique to an individual or is in other ways not organized by the culture.

Visual Organization (Gv)

This dimension is indicated by primary mental abilities such as visualization, spatial orientation, speed of closure, and flexibility of closure, measured by tests such as gestalt closure (Identify a figure in which parts have been omitted), form board (Show how cut-out parts fit together to depict a particular figure), and embedded figures (Find a geometric figure within a set of intersecting lines). To distinguish this factor from Gf, it is important that relationships among visual patterns be clearly manifest so performances reflect primarily fluency in perception of these patterns, not reasoning in inferring the patterns.

Auditory Organization (Ga)

This factor has been identified on the basis of several studies in which primary mental abilities of temporal tracking, auditory cognition of relations, and speech perception under distraction-distortion were first defined among other primary abilities and then found to indicate a broad dimension at the second order. Tasks that measure Ga include repeated tones (Identify the first occurrence of a tone when it occurs several times), tonal series (Indicate which tone comes next in an orderly series of tones), and cafeteria noise (Identify a word amid a din of surrounding noise). As in the case of Gv, this ability is best indicated when the relationships among stimuli are not such that one needs to reason for understanding but instead are such that one can fluently perceive patterns among the stimuli.

Short-Term Acquisition and Retrieval

This ability comprises processes of becoming aware and processes of retaining information long enough to do something with it. Almost all tasks that involve short-term memory have variance in this factor. Span-memory, associative-memory, and meaningful-memory primary abilities define the factor, but measures of primary and secondary memory can also be used to indicate the dimension.

Long-Term Storage and Retrieval

Formerly this dimension was regarded as a broad factor among fluency tasks, such as those of the primary abilities labeled associational fluency,

(continued)

TABLE 7.1 (continued)

expressional fluency, and object flexibility. In recent work, however, these performances have been found to align with others indicating facility in storing information and retrieving information that was acquired in the distant past. It seems, therefore, that the dimension mainly represents processes for forming encoding associations for long-term storage and using these assocations, or forming new ones, at the time of retrieval. These assocations are not so much correct as they are possible and useful; to associate *tea kettle* with *mother* is not to arrive at a truth so much as it is to regard both concepts as sharing common attributes (e.g., warmth).

Source: Horn, 1982

to make connections between new words one reads and information already known, which is a component of fluid intelligence.

Any standardized intelligence test taps abilities underlying both fluid and crystallized intelligence. No single test of either ability exists, because each represents a cluster of underlying primary abilities. As a general rule tests that minimize the role of acquired, cultural knowledge involve mainly fluid intelligence; those that maximize the role of such knowledge involve mainly crystallized intelligence.

Developmentally, fluid and crystallized intelligence follow two very different paths, as depicted in Figure 7.3. Notice that fluid intelligence declines significantly as we grow older. Although our understanding of why this drop occurs is not yet complete, it may be related to changes in the underlying neurophysiological processes (i.e., structural changes in the brain, Horn & Hofer, 1992) and to lack of practice. In general, decline in fluid intelligence is associated primarily with decrements in the ability to organize information, ignore irrelevant information, focus or divide attention, and keep information in working memory (Horn & Hofer, 1992).

In contrast, crystallized intelligence does not normally decline with age; indeed, it may even increase as a result of continued experience and lifelong learning. This makes sense because one is continually adding to one's knowledge base by learning new words, acquiring new skills at home or work, and compiling information by reading, for example (Horn, 1982; Horn & Donaldson, 1980).

What do these different developmental trends imply? First, they indicate that although learning continues across adulthood, it becomes more difficult the older one gets. Consider what happens when Michele, age 27, and Margaret, age 70, try to learn a second language. Although Margaret's verbal skills in her native language (a component of crystallized intelligence) are probably better than Michele's verbal skills, Michele's probable superiority in the fluid abilities necessary to learn another language will usually make it easier for her to do so.

Second, these developmental trends point out once again that intellectual development varies a great deal from one set of skills to another. Beyond the differences in overall trends, individual differences in fluid and crystallized intelligence also vary. Whereas individual differences in fluid intelligence remain relatively uniform over time, individual differences in crystallized intelligence increase with age, largely because maintaining one's crystallized intelligence depends on being in situations that require one to use it (Horn & Hofer, 1992). For example, few adults get much practice in solving complex letter series tasks like the one we encountered earlier. But because people can improve their vocabulary skills by reading, and because people vary considerably in how much they read, differences are likely to emerge. In short, crystallized intelligence provides one with a rich knowledge base to draw on when material is somewhat familiar, whereas fluid intelligence provides the power to deal with learning in novel situations.

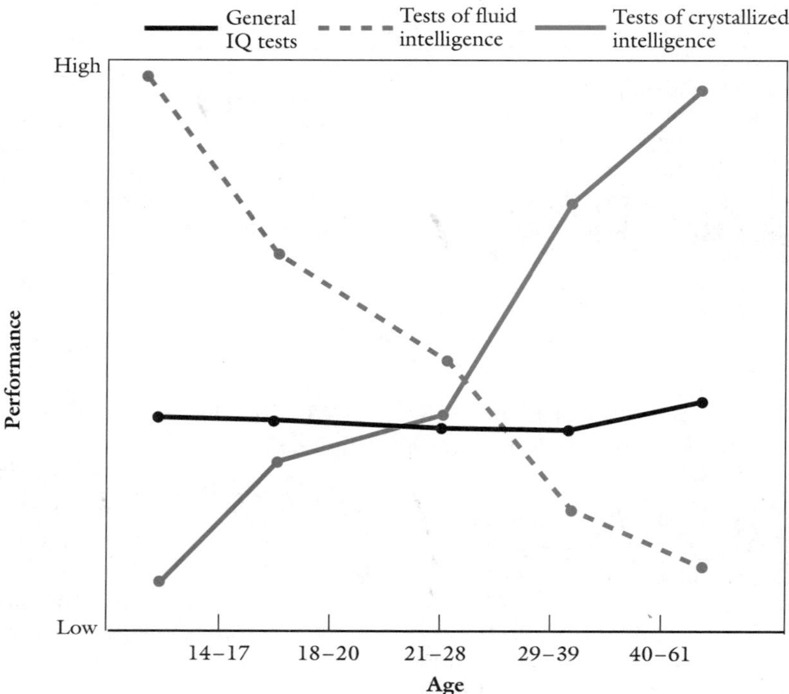

Figure 7.3 Performances on tests used to define fluid, crystallized, and general intelligence, as a function of age
Source: Ho,·n, 1970

Moderators of Intellectual Change

Based on the research we have considered thus far, two different developmental trends emerge: We see gains in experience-based processes, but losses in information-processing abilities. The continued growth in some areas is viewed as a product of lifelong learning. The losses are viewed as an inevitable result of the decline of physiological processes with age.

A number of researchers, though, disagree with the notion that intellectual aging necessarily involves an inevitable decline in fluid abilities (Labouvie-Vief, 1981). These researchers do not deny that some adults show intellectual decline. Based on large individual differences in intellectual performance over time, they simply suggest that these decrements may not happen to everyone to the same extent. They argue that there are many reasons besides age why performance differences occur. In this section we will explore some of the social and physiological factors that have been proposed as modifiers of intellectual development. These include cohort differences, educational level, social variables, personality, health and lifestyle, mindlessness, and relevancy and appropriateness of tasks.

Cohort Differences

Do the differences in intellectual performance obtained in some situations reflect true age-related change or mainly cohort, or generational, differences? This question gets right to the heart of the debate over interpreting developmental research

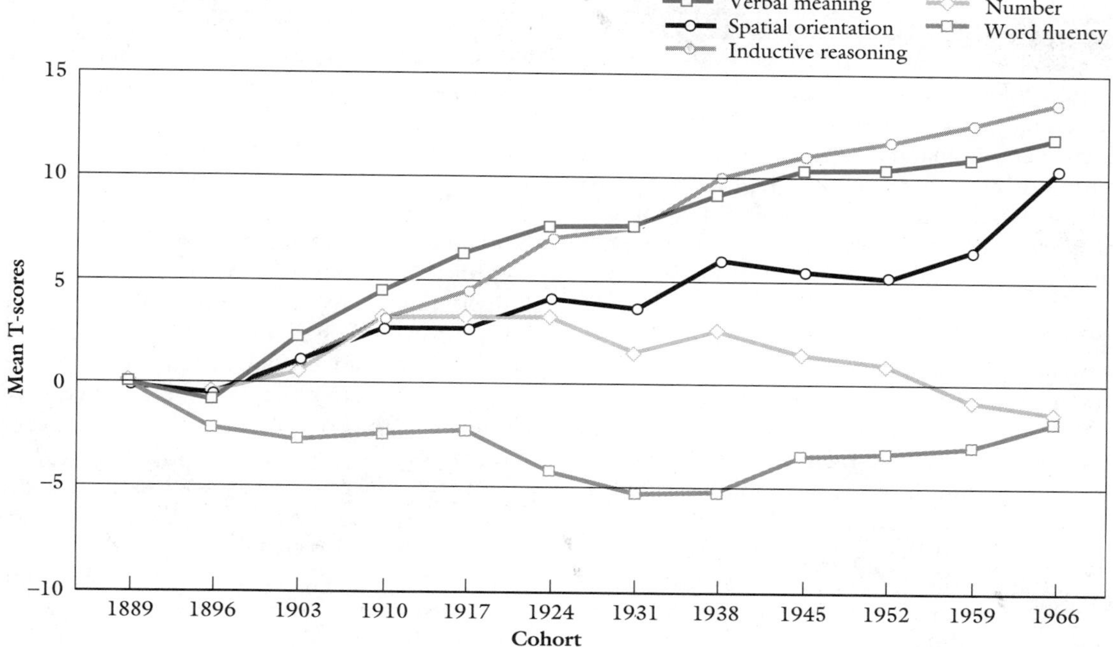

Figure 7.4 Cohort gradients showing cumulative cohort differences on five primary mental abilities for cohorts born from 1889 to 1966

Source: Schaie, 1994

on intelligence. On the one hand, dozens of cross-sectional studies document significant differences in intellectual performance with age. On the other hand, several longitudinal investigations show either no decrement or even an increase in performance (Labouvie-Vief, 1985).

The way to resolve the discrepancy between the two approaches involves comparing data collected over long periods of time from several samples and analyzed simultaneously in both cross-sectional and longitudinal designs. When this has been done, the results indicate that part of the apparent decline with age in performance on intelligence tests is due to generational differences rather than age differences (Schaie, 1996).

Marked generational changes in levels of performance on tests of primary abilities have been noted in the Seattle Longitudinal Study (Schaie, 1995). As you can see in Figure 7.4, more recent-born cohorts generally score better than earlier-born cohorts on verbal meaning, spatial orientation, and inductive reasoning. These trends reflect better educational opportunities, better lifestyles, better nutrition, and improved health care. Note that cohort differences on number ability show gradual declines over the middle 20th century and that word fluency is gradually increasing after showing declines earlier in this century.

The complex pattern of cohort differences indicates that interpreting data from cross-sectional studies is difficult. Recall that cross-sectional studies confound age and cohort; because there are both age- and cohort-related changes in intellectual abilities, drawing any meaningful conclusions is nearly impossible. Schaie (1996) argues that the trends indicate a leveling off of cohort differences, which may come to a halt by the end of this century. This conclusion is supported by a study of

531 adult parent-offspring pairs that indicated that generational (cohort) improvements were becoming smaller for more recently born pairs (Schaie, Plomin, Willis, Gruber-Baldini, & Dutta, 1992).

In sum, cohort differences provide important evidence about changes in intellectual abilities in adulthood. However, we must be careful not to read too much into these trends and recognize that they may not be sustained into the next century.

Educational Level

Even though researchers have known for many years that scores on intelligence tests are related to educational level (Miles & Miles, 1932), only since the late 1960s have investigators seriously considered the meaning of this relationship for intellectual development in adulthood. Several studies have documented that differences in educational level can account for some of the age differences that emerge (Blum & Jarvik, 1974; Gonda, 1980; Granick & Friedman, 1973; Green, 1969; Schaie & Strother, 1968).

Granick and Friedman (1973) took into account the fact that older adults had less formal education, on the average, than younger adults. Once this relationship between age and education had been controlled for, the age-related decline in intelligence was significantly reduced. Other researchers have compared people within a particular generation who differed in education. For example, Blum and Jarvik (1974) found better intellectual performance among older adult high school graduates than among older adults who had finished only elementary school.

The importance of education for intellectual development during adulthood may go beyond the absolute number of years spent in school (Gonda, 1980). For one thing, more highly educated individuals may adopt lifestyles that foster the maintenance of cognitive abilities. Highly educated older adults are also the exception in their generation; opportunities to go to college were not as prevalent 50 years ago as they are now.

Taken together, these factors indicate that one source of the cohort effect may be differences in the type and amount of education. The evidence points to the maintenance of intellectual abilities in well-educated adults at least into old age. As more well-educated cohorts grow old, education may also provide an explanation of why cohort differences on many measures are not increasing at the same rates as they did earlier in this century.

Social Variables

Numerous social demographic variables have been identified as important correlates of intellectual functioning. Think for a minute about the kind of job you currently have or would like to get. What kinds of intellectual skills does it demand? What similarities or differences are there between your chosen job (for example, school counselor) and a different one (say, accountant)? An interesting line of research concerns how the differences in cognitive skills needed in different occupations makes a difference in intellectual development (Labouvie-Vief, 1981). To the extent that a job requires you to use certain cognitive abilities a great deal, you may be less likely to show declines in them as you age.

Indirect support for this hypothesis comes from research showing that when older people are familiar with the tasks used in intelligence tests, they perform much better (Labouvie-Vief & Gonda, 1976). To the extent that people become practiced at thinking in a certain way, they may be less likely to show declines in that kind of thinking as they grow older.

Other social demographic variables implicated in slower rates of intellectual decline include a lengthy marriage to a well-educated and intelligent spouse (Schaie et al., 1992), exposure to stimulating environments, and the utilization of cultural and educational resources throughout adulthood (Schaie, 1984). Gold and her colleagues (1995) also found that a cognitively engaging lifestyle was a predictor of intellectual performance in a sample of Canadian men.

Personality

Several aspects of personality have been proposed as important for understanding intellectual change. Similar to research we examined in Chapter 6 on memory, one of these aspects concerns self-efficacy (Grover & Hertzog, 1991; Lachman & Leff, 1989). Lachman (1983) examined the causal relationship between perceptions of one's own cognitive abilities and performance on several measures of intelligence based on data collected on two occasions about two years apart. Most important, she found that people changed in their perceptions of their abilities over time. Interestingly, this change was related to people's initial level of fluid intelligence and sense of personal control over their life. High initial levels of fluid abilities and a high sense of internal control led to positive changes in people's perceptions of their abilities; low initial levels led to decreases in perceptions of ability. Thus, Lachman's results support the view that initial levels of cognitive ability affect changes in how abilities are perceived. How people perceive their abilities apparently has no effect on their actual intellectual abilities.

A related personality aspect concerns people's perceptions of changes in their intellectual performance (Schaie, Willis, & O'Hanlon, 1994). By comparing people's perceptions to actual test performance, Schaie and colleagues classified people as *realists* (people who accurately estimated changes in performance), *optimists* (people who overestimated positive change), and *pessimists* (people who overestimate negative change). Most people were classified as realists, although women were more likely than men to be pessimists on spatial abilities, and older people were more likely than younger people to be pessimists on verbal meaning and inductive reasoning.

Research also indicates that people who have flexible attitudes at midlife tend to experience less decline in intellectual competence than people who were more rigid in middle age (Schaie, 1995). Similarly, motor-cognitive flexibility in one's 60s is highly predictive of one's numerical and verbal abilities in late life (O'Hanlon, 1993).

Hayslip (1988) investigated relationships between personality and ability from an ego development perspective (see Chapter 8). He was interested in establishing connections between how people view themselves and their level of intellectual ability. He found that anxiety over the adequacy of one's ideational ability and feelings about bodily integrity were related to crystallized intelligence, whereas using cognitive resources to deal with reality and organizational ability related to fluid intelligence. These relationships suggest that individual differences in the maintenance of higher levels of intellectual functioning in later life may be motivated by the desire to protect oneself from feelings of worthlessness and loss of control over one's abilities.

Health and Lifestyle

One of the most difficult problems in any study of aging is the separation of normal processes from abnormal ones. So far our discussion of intellectual development has ignored this distinction; we have been concerned only with normal changes. However, not everyone is healthy, experiencing only normal cognitive aging. Moreover, disease is a hit-or-miss proposition, affecting some people primarily physically, as in arthritis, and others primarily cognitively, as in the early stages of dementia. Thus, we need to consider how specific aspects of health influence intellectual ability.

The most obvious relationship between health and intelligence concerns the functioning of the brain itself. We noted in Chapter 3 that several normative changes in brain structure with age affect functioning. Disorders such as Alzheimer's disease and head injuries may damage the brain and interfere with its functioning. In some cases these problems get worse as the individual ages. Obviously, the more extensive the damage, the more significant the impairment of intellectual ability.

The connection between disease and intelligence has been established fairly well in cardiovascular disease (Schaie, 1996). Schaie (1990) reports that people in the Seattle Longitudinal Study who declined in inductive reasoning ability (one aspect of fluid intelligence) had significantly more illness diagnoses and visits to physicians for cardiovascular disease. However, results concerning hypertension are more complex. Whereas severe hypertension has been associated with earlier-than-usual declines, mild hypertension may actually have positive effects on intellectual functioning (Sands & Meredith, 1992).

Mindlessness

Langer (1985) offers an interesting explanation of the apparent decline in intellectual abilities in adulthood. She argues that cognitive processing occurs at two levels: a mindful level, at which we are aware of what we are doing and are actively involved with the environment; and a mindless level, at which we are unaware of what we are doing and are only passively involved with the environment. Mindlessness occurs when we allow the situation to dictate our behavior, rather than stepping back and critically evaluating what we should be doing. Many times we go along with requests, for example, because everything seems to be correct: The con artist looks and acts like a bank executive, so we do not question his request to withdraw our savings. What we fail to do is ask ourselves whether the request is reasonable; we just go along because appearances say that we should.

Langer contends that mindlessness increases as we get older unless something is done to stop this rise. Moreover, older adults may engage in mindlessness at inappropriate times and appear incompetent. Unchecked increases in mindlessness may be part of the reason that institutionalized older adults seem less alert cognitively; that is, the institution may not foster mindfulness. In a provocative study Langer and Rodin (1976) demonstrated this point. When they increased mindfulness (in terms of personal control) in nursing home residents by encouraging them to make decisions and by giving them responsibilities for plants, the residents became happier, healthier, and more alert and did better on memory tests.

Although Langer's notion of mindlessness is still controversial, it fits well with the widely held belief and research evidence that people who remain cognitively active—mindful, in Langer's terms—are those who show the least decline (Blum & Jarvik, 1974).

Relevancy and Appropriateness of Tasks

All the psychometric tests used today trace their origin to Binet's (1903) original attempt to measure academic performance. Some researchers argue that the academic settings and skills that led to the development of these tests may not be equally important or relevant to adults. Consequently, they argue that we need new tests that are based on the problems adults typically face.

To build new tests requires understanding what skills adults use in everyday situations. Scheidt and Schaie (1978) tried doing just that. They interviewed older adults in parks, senior centers, and similar locations and asked them to name situations that involved using intelligence. In all, over 300 situations were described; looking for a place to live and figuring out how to pay a debt were two common examples. These responses provide a very different starting point for developing tasks for an intelligence test than trying to figure out how to measure classroom learning potential.

Willis, Schaie, and Lueers (1983) also looked at practical measures of intelligence, but from a different perspective. They examined the relationships between seven primary mental abilities, measured by traditional tests, and eight categories of everyday tasks, measured by the ETS Basic Skills Test. The categories of everyday tasks included understanding labels on medical or household articles, reading street maps, understanding charts or schedules, comprehending paragraphs, filling out forms, reading newspaper and phone directory ads, understanding technical documents, and comprehending news text. Three scores on the skills test were calculated; two scores reflected different levels of comprehension and information processing (literal and inference) and the third was the total score. Correlations between the scores for primary abilities and basic skills were very high for the older adults, indicating that the two tests were measuring similar things.

When Willis and colleagues examined their data to see which of the primary abilities best predicted each of the eight categories of everyday tasks, some interesting findings emerged. They had expected their measures of crystallized intelligence to be the best predictors, on the basis that these everyday skills reflect cultural knowledge and should not decline with age. Much to their surprise, the measures of fluid intelligence, especially figural relations, were the best predictors most of the time. Moreover, older adults did not always perform as well as the younger adults on the everyday skills test. In fact, the younger adults obtained near-perfect scores, whereas the older adults were significantly below ceiling, on average.

The Willis study is important for two reasons. First, it shows that traditional tests of primary mental abilities may predict performance on everyday tasks. For supporters of the psychometric approach, these data show that a total rejection of traditional tests on the ground that they are inadequate may be unwarranted. Second, the findings also show that tests consisting of what appear to be more relevant tasks may tap some of the same components of intelligence that the traditional tests are thought to measure. This suggests that we might develop new tests that consist of familiar tasks but that still tap the components of intelligence identified in psychometric research.

The issue of task relevancy is still far from being settled, however. As we will see later, many researchers and theorists argue quite strongly that only by abandoning a purely psychometric approach and moving to a focus on everyday uses of intelligence will we advance our understanding of intellectual aging. As with most controversies, there is something to be said for both sides.

Modifying Primary Abilities

As we have seen, older adults do not perform as well on tests of some primary abilities as younger adults, even after taking the moderators of performance into account (Schaie & Hertzog, 1983). In considering these results, investigators began asking whether there was a way to slow down or even reverse the declines. Are the age-related differences that remain after cohort and other effects are removed permanent? Or might these differences be reduced or even eliminated if older adults were given appropriate training? Can we modify adults' intelligence?

Attempts to answer these questions have appeared with increasing frequency since the mid-1970s. Several types of tasks have been examined, ranging from tests of skills underlying primary mental abilities (Willis & Schaie, in press) to the information-processing skills necessary to drive a car (Sterns & Sanders, 1980). Of these, perhaps the most interesting and important research area is the attempt to modify primary abilities that show early and substantial declines.

Primary abilities that are known to begin to decline relatively early in adulthood—such as inductive reasoning, spatial orientation, memory abilities, and figural abilities—have been examined most closely in intervention research (Willis & Schaie, in press). Labouvie-Vief and Gonda (1976) focused on inductive reasoning. They measured performance on the training task (the Letter Sets Test) and on a new transfer task that participants had not seen during training (Raven's Progressive Matrices). Training was given to three groups. Members of the first group were told to give themselves self-directional statements and feedback. The second group combined these with additional statements that were designed to help them cope with anxiety and to emphasize self-approval and success. Members of the third group received unspecific training; they simply practiced taking the Letter Sets Test with no instructions or feedback. Labouvie-Vief and Gonda found that inductive reasoning could be increased through training. They also found evidence for transfer of the training effects, because the performance of the trained groups was also better on the Raven's Progressive Matrices.

Project ADEPT

A much more comprehensive training study, involving a series of short longitudinal studies, was Pennsylvania State University's Adult Development and Enrichment Project (ADEPT) (Baltes & Willis, 1982). The training studies conducted as part of ADEPT included two levels of intervention in addition to a no-training control group. All groups were equivalent at the outset.

The first level of intervention involved minimal direct training and had test familiarity as its goal. Participants were given the same tests on several occasions to familiarize them with test taking, so that the researchers could learn about the effects of repeated testing alone.

The second type of training involved interventions tailored specifically for each of the primary abilities tested. Each training package was based on a thorough task analysis of the thinking processes involved in each ability. The resulting training programs varied a little in specific details, but in general they focused on teaching the relational rules associated with each test problem, over five sessions. Training on figural relations, for instance, involved practice with paper-and-pencil tests, oral feedback by the experimenter, group discussion, and review of the kinds of problems involving figural-relations ability.

Overall, the ability-specific training resulted in improvements in primary abilities. But the ability to maintain and to transfer the training effects varied. Evidence for long-term and broad transfer effects were strongest for figural relations. Training effects were found for inductive reasoning and attention/memory, but these effects did not transfer as well to new tasks.

These findings from the training studies are impressive when we consider their implications. The size of Baltes and Willis's improvements in fluid abilities were equivalent to the average 21-year longitudinal decline in these abilities reported by Schaie (1983). The implication of this comparison is that the decline in primary abilities can be slowed or even reversed by proper intervention strategies. The results are even more exciting given that the training packages in ADEPT were fairly short: an average of five 1-hour sessions. Although the reversal of age-related declines in all primary abilities and the duration of the effects of training remain to be seen, clearly we need to revise our view of pervasive, universal decline in primary abilities.

Other Attempts to Train Fluid Abilities

Schaie and Willis have extended the findings from Project ADEPT (Willis, 1990; Willis & Schaie, 1992, in press). This research involves the participants in Schaie's longitudinal study in Seattle. In one study (Schaie & Willis, 1986) participants were assigned to one of two groups based on their performance over a 14-year period (1970–1984). One group showed significant decline on either spatial ability or reasoning ability, and the other group remained stable on these measures. Schaie and Willis then provided a 5-hour training session on spatial ability and a similar session on reasoning ability for those who had declined. To examine the effects of training as a function of amount of decline, training was also provided to the individuals who had remained stable.

Schaie and Willis found that the cognitive training techniques could reverse declines that had been reliably documented over the 14-year period. However, the effects of cognitive training were largely ability specific. That is, gains were largest when the training matched the ability being tested; only modest gains in abilities were found that were not trained.

Most exciting, the improvements for both spatial and reasoning abilities essentially returned people who had declined to their earlier levels of functioning. In addition, the training procedures even enhanced the performance of many older people who had remained stable. This finding demonstrates that training is effective not only in raising the performance of decliners, but also in improving functioning in nondecliners beyond their initial levels (Willis, 1990).

Rather than simply training older adults on particular fluid abilities, Hayslip (1989) tried something different. He randomly assigned 358 community-dwelling older adults to one of four groups: inductive reasoning training (from Project ADEPT), stress inoculation training (to reduce people's feelings of anxiety), no training at all (a control group), or posttest only (a control group to examine the effects of just taking the final test). Several measures of inductive reasoning and other measures of intellectual abilities were given before training, one week after, and one month after training. Hayslip found that both training groups improved their performance, the effects of the stress inoculation training varied with the difficulty of the task and participants' willingness to apply the anxiety-reducing techniques they had learned to use with the tasks, and the degree to which training generalized to other tasks was limited. He concluded that at least part of the gain in performance was due to reductions in people's level of anxiety in taking tests of intellectual ability.

Considered together, the results from Project

ADEPT, the data from Schaie and Willis's research, and Hayslip's work allow us to conclude that declines in fluid abilities may be reversible. But how long do the improvements last?

Long-Term Effects of Training

Getting older adults to do better on skills underlying fluid intelligence is impressive. Having those benefits last over time would be even better, because it would provide a powerful argument in favor of providing intervention programs to more people.

Willis and Nesselroade (1990) report results from a 7-year follow-up to the original ADEPT study. Participants were initially trained in 1979 and received booster training sessions in 1981 and 1986. Significant training effects were found at each point, indicating that people continue to benefit from cognitive intervention as they move from young-old to old-old age. Even people in their late 70s and early 80s continued to perform at levels better than they had 7 years earlier prior to training. In fact, 64% of the training group's performance was above their pretraining baseline, compared with only 33% of the control group.

Similarly positive results were reported by Willis and Schiae (1992), who examined members of the Seattle Longitudinal Study 7 years after receiving training on either inductive reasoning or spatial orientation. The effects of training were not only substantial, but most impressive for people who had shown declines in the skills trained over the previous 14 years. However, the effects of booster sessions diminished as people grew older.

Hayslip, Maloy, and Kohl (1995) conducted a 3-year follow-up of Hayslip's (1989) original study involving training on inductive reasoning and on stress inoculation. Their findings provide strong support for the importance of booster sessions, especially for inductive reasoning training. Without subsequent retraining, performance levels nearly approached levels 3 years earlier prior to the original training.

These findings provide strong evidence that in the normal course of development no one is too old to benefit from training and that training slows down the rates of decline for those fluid abilities examined. However, unless people are somehow reminded of the training through booster sessions, gains demonstrated during training may well be lost. Whether the training designed in the original Project ADEPT or other approaches such as stress inoculation are more effective remains to be seen. In the end, which approach is superior may be less important than to train and maintain whatever strategy is selected for intervention.

Concept Checks

1. What five primary mental abilities have been studied most?
2. How do the developmental trajectories of fluid and crystallized intelligence differ?
3. What are the main moderators of intellectual change, and what influences do they have?
4. How effective are programs aimed at training primary mental abilities?

QUALITATIVE DIFFERENCES IN ADULTS' THINKING

Learning Objectives:

- What are the main points in Piaget's theory of cognitive development?
- What evidence is there for continued cognitive development beyond formal operations?
- What are the main points in Schaie's theory of adults' thinking?

When I was a student, I always thought it was unfair when instructors simply marked the answers to complex problems right or wrong. I always wanted partial credit for knowing how to set up the problem and being able to figure out some of the steps. Although I did not know it at the time, my argument paralleled one in the intelligence literature—the debate on whether we should pay attention mainly to whether an answer is right or wrong or to how the person reasons the problem through.

The psychometric approach we considered earlier does not focus on the thinking processes that underlie intelligence; rather, psychometrics concentrates on interrelationships among answers to test questions. In contrast, cognitive-process approaches focus on the ways in which people think; whether a particular answer is right or wrong is not very important.

We will consider two theories that represent cognitive-process approaches. First, we will examine Piaget's theory and the recent discussions concerning possible extensions of it. Second, we will consider Schaie's theory, which represents a very different way of viewing intelligence. Both theories postulate that intellectual changes are mainly qualitative, even though they differ on many points. Let us see what each has to say.

Piaget's Theory

According to Piaget (1970), intellectual development is adaptation through activity. We create the very ways in which our knowledge is organized and, ultimately, how we think. Piaget believed that the development of intelligence stems from the emergence of increasingly complex cognitive structures. He organized his ideas into a theory of cognitive development that changed the way psychologists conceptualize intellectual development.

Basic Concepts

For Piaget, thought is governed by the principles of adaptation and organization. *Adaptation* refers to the process of adjusting thinking to the environment. Just as animals living in a forest feed differently than animals living in a desert, how we think changes from one developmental context to another.

Because all biological systems adapt, the principle of adaptation is fundamental to Piaget's theory. Adaptation occurs through *organization,* which is how the organism is put together. Each component part has its own specialized function, which is coordinated into the whole. In Piaget's theory the organization of thought is reflected in *cognitive structures* that change over the life span. Cognitive structures determine how we think. It is the change in cognitive structures, the change in the fundamental ways in which we think, that Piaget tried to describe.

What are the processes that underlie intellectual adaptation? Piaget defined two: assimilation and accommodation. ***Assimilation* is the use of currently available knowledge to make sense out of incoming information.** It is the application of cognitive structures to the world of experience that makes the world understandable. For example, a child who only knows the word *dog* may use it for every animal she encounters. So, when the child sees a cat and calls it a dog, she is using available knowledge, the word *dog,* to make sense out of the world—in this case the cat that is walking across the living room. The process of assimilation sometimes leads to considerable distortion of incoming information, because we may have to force-fit it into our knowledge base. This is apparent in our tendency to forget information about a person that violates a stereotype.

***Accommodation* involves changing one's thought to make it a better approximation of the world of experience.** The child in our example who thought that cats were dogs eventually learns that cats are cats. When this happens, she has accommodated her knowledge to incorporate a new category of animal.

The processes of assimilation and accommodation serve to link the structure of thought to observable behavior. Piaget believed that most changes during development involved cognitive structures. His research led him to conclude that there were four structures (that is, four stages) in the development of mature thought: sensorimotor, preoperational, concrete operational, and formal operational. We will consider the major characteristics of each stage briefly. Because we are most interested in Piaget's description of adult thought, we will emphasize it.

Sensorimotor Period

In this first stage of cognitive development, intelligence is seen in infants' actions. Babies and infants gain knowledge by using their sensory and motor skills, beginning with basic reflexes (sucking and

How people reason on issues such as abortion is a good indicator of their cognitive developmental level.

grasping) and eventually moving to purposeful, planned sequences of behavior (such as looking for a hidden toy). The most important thing that infants learn during the sensorimotor period is that objects continue to exist even when they are out of sight; this ability is called *object permanence*.

Preoperational Period

Young children's thinking is best described as egocentric. This means that young children believe that all people and all inanimate objects experience the world just as they do. For example, young children believe that dolls feel pain. Although young children can sometimes reason through situations, their thinking is not based on logic. For example, a young child may believe that his father's shaving causes the tap water to be turned on because the two events always happen together.

Concrete Operational Period

Logical reasoning emerges in the concrete operational period. Children become capable of classifying objects into groups based on a logical principle, such as fruits or vegetables; mentally reversing a series of events; realizing that when changes occur in one perceptual dimension and they are compensated for in another, no net change occurs (termed *conservation*); and understanding the concept of transitivity (for instance, if $A > B$ and $B > C$, then $A > C$). However, children are still unable to deal with abstract concepts such as love; for example, love to children is a set of concrete actions and not an abstract ill-defined concept.

Formal Operational Period

For Piaget, the acquisition of formal operational thought during adolescence marks the end of cognitive development. Because he argues that formal operational thinking characterizes adult thought, we will consider this level in some detail. Several theorists have commented on the characteristics of formal operational thought (Basseches, 1984; Kramer, 1983; Labouvie-Vief, 1980, 1981, 1984; Sinnott, 1984b). We will use these commentaries to focus on four aspects of formal operational thought: (1) It takes a hypothesis-testing approach (termed hypothetico-deductive) to problem solving; (2) thinking is done in one framework at a time; (3) the goal is to arrive at one correct solution; and (4) it is unconstrained by reality.

Piaget describes the essence of formal operational thought as a way of conceiving abstract concepts and thinking about them in a very systematic, step-by-step way. Formal operational thought is governed by a generalized logical structure that provides solutions to problems that people have never seen and may never encounter. *Hypothetico-deductive* thought is similar to using the scientific method, in that it involves forming a hypothesis and testing it until it is either confirmed or rejected. Just as scientists are very systematic in testing experimental hypotheses, formal operational thinking allows people to approach problem solving in a logical, methodical way.

Consider the situation when one's car breaks down. When one takes it for repairs, the mechanic forms hypotheses about what may be wrong, based on a description of the trouble. The mechanic then begins to test each hypothesis systematically. For example, the compression of each cylinder may be checked, one cylinder at a time. It is this ability to hold other factors constant while testing a particular component that is one of the hallmarks of formal operational thought. By isolating potential causes of the problem, the mechanic arrives at a correct solution very efficiently.

When we use hypothetico-deductive thought, we do so to arrive at one unambiguous solution to the problem (Labouvie-Vief, 1980, 1981, 1984; Labouvie-Vief, Adams, Hakim-Larson, Hayden, & Devoe, 1985). Formal operational thought is aimed at resolving ambiguity; one and only one answer is the goal. When more than one solution occurs, there is a feeling of uneasiness, and people begin a search for clarification. This situation can be observed in high school classes when students press their teacher to identify the right theory (from among several equally good ones) or the right way to view a social issue (such as abortion). Moreover, when people arrive at an answer, they are quite certain about it, because it was arrived at through the use of logic. When answers are checked, the same logic and assumptions are typically used, which sometimes means that the same mistake is made several times in a row. For example, a person may repeat a simple subtraction error time after time when trying to figure out why his or her checkbook failed to balance.

Formal operational thinking knows no constraints (Labouvie-Vief, 1984; Piaget, 1970). It can be applied just as easily to real or to imaginary situations. It is not bound by the limits of reality (Labouvie-Vief, 1980). Whether one can implement a solution is irrelevant; what matters is that one can think about it. This is how people arrive at solutions to disarmament, for example, such as getting rid of all nuclear warheads tomorrow. To the formal operational thinker, the fact that this solution is logistically impossible is no excuse. The lack of reality constraints is not all bad, however. Reasoning from a Why not? perspective may lead to the discovery of completely new ways to approach a problem or even to the invention of new solutions.

Developmental Trends in Piagetian Thought

Considerable research has been conducted examining the developmental course of Piagetian abilities (Reese & Rodeheaver, 1985). Overall, the results are quite mixed and difficult to interpret, largely because the majority of studies are cross-sectional, the procedures used have strayed considerably from those described by Piaget, and the scoring criteria for performance are not systematized (Reese & Rodeheaver, 1985). Nevertheless, some general conclusions can be drawn (Papalia & Bielby, 1974; Rabbitt, 1977; Reese & Rodeheaver, 1985). We will consider the findings from research on formal operations and on concrete operations.

One serious problem for Piaget's theory is that many adults apparently do not attain formal operations. Several studies report that only 60% to 75% of American adolescents can solve any formal operational problems (Neimark, 1975), and some estimate that no more than 30% of adults ever complete the transition to the highest levels of formal operational thought (Kuhn, Langer, Kohlberg, & Haan, 1977; Tomlinson-Keasey, 1972). Piaget (1972) himself admitted that formal operations were probably not universal but, rather, tended to appear only in those areas in which individuals were highly trained or specialized.

Extreme pessimism may not be warranted, however. Kuhn and her colleagues showed that as many as 94% of the adolescents in her research demonstrated formal operational thought after being given appropriate background and practice (Kuhn & Angelev, 1976; Kuhn, Ho, & Adams, 1979). Chandler (1980) notes that the lack of evidence for formal operations in the elderly may be more indicative of their lack of interest in doing formal operational problems than a lack of ability; older adults "generally dislike bookish, abstract, or childish tasks of low meaningfulness"(p.82). Tomlinson-Keasey (1972) points out that attainment of the highest levels of formal operations may even depend on preference, as well as personal experience and the cognitive structures that are available. These results imply that the estimates of how many people attain formal operations may be misleading, that formal operational thought is used only in specialized situations, and that adults' thinking is not described very well by Piaget. We will develop this last alternative in more detail later.

Does the ability to use formal reasoning differ with age in people who achieve this level of thinking? The results are mixed. Some studies find that older adults do not perform as well as younger adults on formal operational tasks (Clayton & Overton, 1973). Clayton and Overton also found that performance on the formal operations tasks was correlated with measures of fluid intelligence, thereby linking formal operational abilities to normative decline. Other research, however, does not show evidence of age-related differences, at least not on all types of formal reasoning tasks. For example, no age differences were found in younger and older adults' use of deductive or formal reasoning, unless the task involved emotional aspects, in which case younger adults' performance was better than older adults' performance (Pollack, Overton, Rosenfeld, & Rosenfeld, 1995).

Because some cross-sectional studies of formal operations showed a lack of these abilities in some adults, researchers have also focused on the development of concrete operations. Two types of tasks have been used most frequently: classification tasks and conservation tasks. In general, the results from these investigations support Papalia and Bielby's (1974) conclusion that cognitive operations decline in the reverse order of their acquisition. That is, the highest, most complex abilities are the last to be acquired but the first to be lost. However, investigations of concrete operations are all cross-sectional and involve highly specialized tasks. Thus, conclusions about age differences must be made with extreme caution.

Some studies document significant age differences between older adults and middle-aged adults in performance on classification tasks, with older adults being worse (Denney & Cornelius, 1975; Storck, Looft, & Hooper, 1972).

A much larger number of investigators have examined conservation abilities. Conservation tasks involve judgments about whether the amount of a substance has been changed after a particular manipulation. For example, an investigator might show two clay balls of equal size, flatten one of them, and ask whether the lumps are still the same. Papalia (1972) found that conservation of substance, weight, and volume increased during childhood and declined in old age in the reverse order that they were acquired in childhood. Although some researchers confirmed her findings (Papalia, Salverson, & True, 1973; Storck et al., 1972), other researchers found little evidence for loss of conservation abilities (Chance, Overcast, & Dollinger, 1978; Eisner, 1973; Papalia-Finlay, Blackburn, Davis, Dellmann, & Roberts, 1980). Still other researchers have obtained very inconsistent results, with age differences not showing any particular pattern (Hornblum & Overton, 1976; Hughston & Protinsky, 1978; Protinsky & Hughston, 1978).

Clearly, whether conservation abilities change across adulthood remains an open question. Attempts to explain the results by gender differences, educational level, intelligence, and even institutionalization have not succeeded (Reese & Rodeheaver, 1985). It may be that traditional concrete operational tasks, like traditional formal operational tasks, may not be interesting or challenging to older adults (Chandler, 1980).

Going Beyond Piaget: Postformal Thought

Consider the following problem (Labouvie-Vief et al., 1985):

> John is known to be a heavy drinker, especially when he goes to parties. Mary, John's wife, warns him that if he gets drunk one more time, she will leave him and take the children. Tonight John is out late at an office party. John comes home drunk. Does Mary leave John? How certain are you of your answer? (p. 13)

When this and similar problems are presented to people of different ages, interesting differences emerge. Formal operational adolescents' responses clearly showed the ambiguity of the situation but also clearly reflected the need to search for the right answer. The ambiguity was considered a problem rather than an acceptable state of affairs. This is evident in the following answer (Labouvie-Vief et al., 1985):

> It's a good chance that she would leave him because she warns him that she will leave him and take the children, but warning isn't an absolute thing. . . . And, I'd be absolutely sure that, well let's see . . . I'm trying to go all the way. I'm trying to think of putting everything [together] so I can be absolutely certain of an answer. . . . It's hard to be absolutely certain. "If he gets drunk, then she'll leave and take the children." I want to say yes 'cause everything's in that favor, in that direction, but I don't know how I can conclude that she does leave John. (pp. 17–18)

When adults were given the same problem, they handled it differently, for the most part. Their responses showed a combination of logic, emotion, and tolerance for ambiguity, as can be seen in the following example (Labouvie-Vief et al., 1985):

> There was no right or wrong answer. You could get logically to both answers [yes or no] . . . It depends on the steps they take to their answer. If they base it on what they feel, what they know, and they have certain steps to get an answer, it can be logical. (p. 41)

Based on a strict interpretation of formal operational thought, the adults who made responses like the second example showed little evidence of formal operational thinking. Thus, it could be argued that Labouvie-Vief and colleagues' research supports the data described earlier that point to declines in formal operational thought across adulthood. But not everyone agrees that the research examining formal operational thinking across adulthood points to loss. Rather than concluding that differences in performance reflect declines in ability, the results are seen as indicative of another, qualitatively different, style of thinking. This latter interpretation implies that Piaget's theory may need modification. Specifically, some researchers have proposed that these performance differences on Piagetian tasks reflect cognitive development beyond formal operations.

Developmental Progressions in Adult Thought

By the 1970s, it was clear that Piaget's contention that formal operations was the end point of cognitive development had serious problems. One of the first to formally propose an alternative model was Riegel (1973, 1976), who argued that formal operations was quite limited in its applicability. By the mid-1980s many other authors agreed (Basseches, 1984; Cavanaugh, Kramer, Sinnott, Camp, & Markley, 1985; Commons, Richards, & Kuhn, 1982; Labouvie-Vief, 1980, 1981; Sinnott, 1984b).

Riegel and other writers point out that Piaget is concerned with describing logical, hypothetico-deductive thinking in his stage of formal operations but that this is not the only kind of thinking that adults do. In addition, they argue that Piaget's stage of formal operations is primarily limited to explaining how people arrive at one correct solution. How adults discover or generate new problems and how they sometimes appear to accept several possible solutions are not explained. Finally, the fact that adults often limit their thinking in response to social or other realistic constraints appears to be in conflict with the unconstrained generation of ideas characteristic of formal operations.

For these reasons some researchers have proposed that there is continued cognitive growth beyond formal operations (Commons, Richards, & Armon, 1984; Commons, Sinnott, Richards, & Armon, 1989). ***Postformal thought*, as it is called, is characterized by a recognition that truth (the correct answer) varies from situation to situation, that solutions must be realistic to be reasonable, that ambiguity and contradiction are the rule rather than the exception, and that emotion and subjective factors usually play a role in thinking.**

In one of the first investigations of cognitive growth beyond adolescence, Perry (1970) traced the development of thinking across the undergraduate years. He found that adolescents relied heavily on the expertise of authorities to determine what was right and wrong. At this point thinking is tightly bound by the rules of logic, and the only legitimate conclusions are those that are logically derived. For Perry, the continued development of thinking involves the development of increased cognitive flexibility. The first step in the process is a shift toward relativism. Relativism in thought refers to realizing that more than one explanation of a set of facts could be right, depending on one's point of view. Although relativism frees the individual from the constraints of a single framework, it also leads to skepticism. Because one can never be sure if one is right or wrong, the skeptic may not try to develop knowledge further, which may lead to feeling confused or adrift. Perry points out that the price of freeing oneself from the influence of authority is the loss of the certainty that came from relying on logic for all the answers.

To develop beyond skepticism, Perry showed, adults develop commitments to particular viewpoints. In Perry's later stages adults recognize that they are their own source of authority, that they must make a commitment to a position, and that others may hold different positions to which they will be equally committed. In other words mature thinkers are able to understand many perspectives on an issue, choose one, and still allow others the right to hold differing viewpoints. Thinking in this mature way is different from thinking in formal operational terms.

Reflective Judgment

Perry's landmark research opened the door to documenting systematic changes in thinking beyond formal operations. One of the best to emerge is King and Kitchener's (1994) refined descriptions of the development of reasoning in young adults. **On the basis of nearly two decades of research, they mapped the development of *reflective judgment*, which involves how people reason through dilemmas involving current affairs, religion, science, and the like.** On the basis of well-designed longitudinal studies of young adults, they identified a systematic progression of thinking, which is described in Table 7.2.

The first three stages in the model represent prereflective thought. Individuals do not acknowledge, and may not even perceive, that knowledge is uncertain. Consequently, they do not understand that some problems exist for which there is not a clearly and absolutely correct answer. Stages 4 and 5 represent quasi-reflective thinking, as people recognize that there are some problems that contain an element of uncertainty. However, although they use evidence, they are not adept at how to use evidence to draw a conclusion. Stages 6 and 7 represent true reflective judgment. People now realize that knowledge must be constructed and that claims about knowledge must be evaluated within the context in which they were generated, and that conclusions, though based on data, are open to reevaluation.

How does a person move from prereflective judgment to reflective judgment? Is the progression a gradual one or one involving qualitative shifts? Kitchener and Fischer (1990) argue that the progression involves both, depending on which aspect of development one emphasizes. Their view is based on the distinction between optimal level and skill acquisition aspects of development. **The *optimal level* of development is the highest level of information-processing capacity that a person is capable of doing.** The optimal level increases with age and is marked by relatively abrupt

TABLE 7.2 Description of the stages of reflective judgment

Stage 1

View of knowledge Knowlege is assumed to exist absolutely and concretely. It can be obtained with absolute certainty through direct observation

Concept of justification Beliefs need no justification since there is assumed to be an absolute correspondence between what is believed and what is true. There are no alternatives.

Stage 2

View of knowledge Knowledge is absolutely certain, or certain but not immediately available. Knowledge can be obtained via direct observation or via authorities.

Concept of justification Beliefs are justified via authority, such as a teacher or parent, or are unexamined and unjustified. Most issues are assumed to have a right answer, so there is little or no conflict in making decisions about disputed issues.

Stage 3

View of knowledge Knowledge is assumed to be absolutely certain or temporarily uncertain. In areas of temporary uncertainty, we can know only via intuition and bias until absolute knowledge is obtained.

Concept of justification In areas in which answers exist, beliefs are justified via authorities. In areas in which answers do not exist, since there is no rational way to justify beliefs, they are justified a-rationally or intuitively.

Stage 4

View of knowledge Knowledge is uncertain and idiosyncratic since situational variables (for example, incorrect reporting of data, data lost over time) dictate that we cannot know with certainty. Therefore, we can only know our own beliefs about the world.

Concept of justification Beliefs are often justified by reference to evidence, but still are based on idiosyncratic reasons, such as choosing evidence that fits an established belief.

Stage 5

View of knowledge Knowledge is contextual and subjective. Since what is known is known via perceptual filters, we cannot know directly. We may know only interpretations of the material world.

Concept of justification Beliefs are justified within a particular context via the rules of inquiry for that context. Justifications are assumed to be context-specific or are balanced against each other, delaying conclusions.

Stage 6

View of knowledge Knowledge is personally constructed via evaluations of evidence, opinions of others, and so forth across contexts. Thus we may know our own and other's personal constructions of issues.

Concept of justification Beliefs are justified by comparing evidence and opinion on different sides of an issue or across contexts, and by constructing solutions that are evaluated by personal criteria, such as one's personal values or the pragmatic need for action.

Stage 7

View of knowledge Knowledge is constructed via the process of reasonable inquiry into generalizable conjectures about the material world or solutions for the problem at hand, such as what is most probable based on the current evidence, or how far it is along the continuum of how things seem to be.

Concept of justification Beliefs are justified probabilistically via evidence and argument, or as the most complete or compelling understanding of an issue.

Source: Adapted from King and Kitchener, 1994

changes ("growth spurts") followed by periods of relative stability. Each spurt represents the emergence of a new developmental level ("stage") of thinking; the period of stability reflects the time needed by the individual to become proficient at using the newly acquired skills. ***Skill acquisition* describes the gradual, and somewhat haphazard, process by which people learn new abilities.** People progress through many small steps in acquiring skills before they are ready for the next growth spurt.

One's optimal level provides an indication of the highest stage a person has achieved in cognitive development, but probably does not indicate the level he or she will use most of the time (King & Kitchener, 1994). Why is this the case? Mostly, it is because the environment does not provide the supports necessary for high-level performance, especially for issues concerning knowledge. Consequently, people will, if pushed and if provided the necessary supports, demonstrate a level of thinking and performance far higher than they typically show on a daily basis. This discrepancy may provide an explanation of why fewer people are found at each successively more complex level of thinking who consistently use it.

Absolutist, Relativistic, and Dialectical Thinking

A growth in reflective judgment is not the only aspect of postformal thought that researchers have examined. For example, Kramer (1989) identified three distinct styles of thinking: absolutist, relativistic, and dialectical. Absolutist thinking involves firmly believing that there is only one correct solution to problems and that personal experience provides truth. Adolescents and young adults typically think this way. Relativistic thinking involves realizing that there are many sides to any issue, and that the right answer depends on the circumstances. Young and early middle-aged adults often think relativistically. One potential danger here is that relativistic thinking can lead to cynicism or an "I'll do my thing and you do yours" approach to life. Because relativistic thinkers reason things out on a case-by-case basis based on the situation, they are not likely to be strongly committed to any one position. The final step, dialectical thinking, clears up this problem. Dialectical thinkers see the merits in the different viewpoints, but are able to synthesize them into a workable solution. This synthesis often produces strong commitment and a definite plan of action.

Notice that there is considerable agreement between the first two styles in Kramer's model and the progression described in the reflective judgment model. Both talk about moving from an "I'm right because I've experienced it" position to an "I'm not so sure because your experience is different from mine" position. Both also provide insight into how young adults are likely to approach life problems. For example, Kramer (1989) shows how different thinking styles have major implications on how couples resolve conflict. She demonstrates that only those couples who think dialectically truly resolve conflict; other thinking styles tend to result in resentment, drifting apart, or even breaking up. We will examine these very interesting findings in more detail in Chapter 10.

The absolutist, relativistic, and dialectical framework has been adopted widely in the study of postformal thought. For example, Kramer and Kahlbaugh (1994) showed that what people remember from prose passages differs as a function of the kind of thinking people use. Sinnott (1994a, b) applied this framework to understanding how adults learn and how they should be taught. In this regard, teachers need to recognize that relativistic thought marks the point at which learning processes become inherently social.

Integrating Emotion and Logic

A theme in descriptions of the first set of qualitative changes in postformal thinking is a movement from "I'm right because I've experienced it" to an "I'm not so sure who's right because your experience is different than mine" position. These differences in thinking provide insights into how thinking styles have major implications for dealing with life problems. For example, couples who are able to understand and synthesize each other's point of view are much more likely to resolve conflicts; couples not able to do so are more likely to feel resentful, drift apart, or even break up

(Kramer, 1989). How can people avoid conflicts and become more able to deal with life problems?

Labouvie-Vief proposes that the answer lies in adults' gaining the ability to integrate emotion with logic in their thinking (Labouvie-Vief, 1980, 1981; Labouvie-Vief et al., 1985). She sees the main goal of adult thought as effectiveness in handling everyday life, rather than as the generation of all possible solutions. To her, adults make choices not so much on logical grounds but on pragmatic, emotional, and social grounds. Mature thinkers realize that thinking is a social phenomenon that demands making compromises and tolerating ambiguity and contradiction.

Consider the evidence that despite the possibility of pregnancy or of contracting AIDS or other sexually transmitted diseases, adolescents still tend not to use contraceptives when they have sexual relations. Why? Labouvie-Vief would argue that sexuality is too emotionally charged for adolescents to deal with intellectually. But is this a reasonable interpretation?

It may be. In a very provocative study, Blanchard-Fields (1986) asked high school students, college students, and middle-aged adults to resolve three dilemmas. One dilemma had low emotional involvement: conflicting accounts of a war between two fictitious countries, North and South Livia, each written by a supporter of one country. The other two dilemmas had high emotional involvement: a visit to the grandparents in which the parents and their adolescent son disagreed about going (the son did not want to go), and a pregnancy dilemma in which a man and a woman had to resolve an unintentional pregnancy (the man was anti-abortion, the woman was pro-choice).

Results are shown in Figure 7.5. Two important findings emerged. First, there were clear developmental trends in reasoning level, with the middle-aged adults scoring highest. Second, the high school and college students were equivalent on the fictitious war dilemma, but the high school students scored significantly lower on the grandparents and the pregnancy dilemmas. These findings suggest that high school students tend to think at a lower developmental level when confronted with

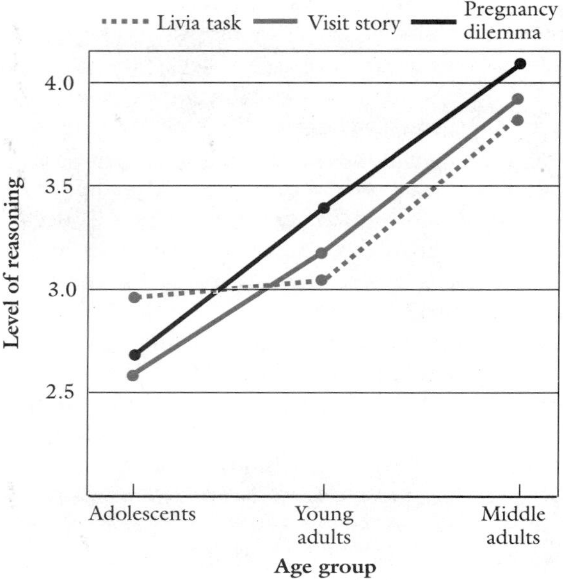

Figure 7.5 Level of reasoning as a function of age group and socioemotional task
Source: Blanchard-Fields, 1986

problems that are especially emotionally salient to them. Although more evidence is certainly needed, Blanchard-Fields's findings provide support for the idea that emotion and logic are brought together in adulthood.

Whether the findings from research examining relativistic or other forms of postformal thought document qualitative cognitive growth is a topic of debate. For example, Kramer (1983) argues that relativistic and related thinking can be interpreted within Piaget's original framework. Her main point is that formal operations include the kinds of thinking described in the postformal literature. For instance, constraining possible solutions to only those that are realistic is simply a subset of generating all possible solutions, a defining characteristic of formal operational thought. Consequently, adult thinking may be different from adolescent thinking, but arguing for additional stages is not necessary. Cavanaugh and Stafford (1989) point out that because the roles of experience and education are not understood and because the

Intellectual and creative abilities do not show across-the-board decline in adulthood. Like Henri Matisse, many individuals make great contributions in old age.

measures of postformal thought vary considerably from study to study, firm conclusions on the nature of adult cognitive development may be premature. Finally, Kramer and Woodruff (1986) showed that formal operations is not a prerequisite for relativistic thinking. On the contrary, it appears to be the other way around. However, it may be true that formal operations is a prerequisite for dialectical thinking (Cavanaugh et al., 1985).

Gender Issues and Postformal Thought

The evidence of differences between adolescents' and adults' thinking is clearly substantial. However, the research that has produced this evidence is typically grounded in the assumption that men and women think in essentially similar ways. Is this a reasonable assumption?

Some researchers do not think so; they argue that men and women use different thinking styles. Within this critique, researchers argue that the styles of thinking that we have discussed so far reflect a male bias and do not describe how women know the world. The most prominent of these critiques was Belenky, Clinchy, Goldberger, and Tarule's (1986) identification of five ways of knowing in women: silent, received, subjective, procedural, and constructed. *Silent knowing* reflects the passive acceptance of others' knowledge and one's own incompetence. *Received knowing* involves accepting from authorities ideas that are concrete, absolute, and dualistic (i.e., representing dichotomies such as good versus bad, with no gray areas). *Subjective knowing* involves using personal and private intuitions as the major source of understanding and authority. *Procedural knowing* involves adopting the dominant viewpoint and using a systematic and deliberate process of analysis in two ways. One way of accomplishing procedural knowing is using impersonal strategies based on the criteria of justice and fairness to establish what is "right." The second way is using interdependence and caring as the basis for establishing truth. Finally, *constructed knowing* includes being articulate about the self, reflecting one's own personal point of view, while tolerating contradiction and ambiguity.

These descriptions are certainly reminiscent of the styles of thinking considered earlier. For example, relativistic thinking has much in common with constructed knowing. Moreover, Belenky et al.'s description has an implicit developmental progression, in that each way of knowing appears to reflect a higher level of complexity. Thus, important questions are whether the proposed women's ways of knowing indeed reflect a developmental progression, are indeed more typical of women, and are related to other descriptions of postformal thinking.

Orr and Luszcz (1994) decided to address these issues by assessing the ways of knowing and relativistic thinking in a sample of male and female undergraduate and graduate students. They found that education, but not age, predicted relativistic thinking but not constructed knowing. Women used subjective knowing more than men, but men used procedural knowing more than women. No gender differences were observed for either constructed knowing or relativistic thinking, but the degree to which traditional notions of femininity was endorsed was positively related to both. Finally, procedural knowing decreased whereas constructed knowing increased with increasing evidence of relativistic thinking. Overall, these results point to minimal differences between men's and women's thinking; Belenky et al.'s (1986) ways of knowing do not appear to be unique to women. However, the ways of knowing do appear to reflect a developmental progression of increasingly complex thought. Still, differences do exist between constructed knowing and relativistic thinking that need to be pursued in additional studies.

The possibility of stages of cognitive development beyond formal operations is intriguing and has focused our attention on the existence of different styles of thinking across adulthood. It has certainly presented a counter to the stereotype of inevitable decline. The evidence supporting a separate stage of cognitive development beyond formal operations is growing, and its applicability has extended to solving practical problems, which we will explore a little later in this chapter. At this point, though, the existence of different styles of thinking in adulthood may help us understand why people sometimes have difficulty understanding each other. As explored in more detail in the Something to Think About feature, knowing the characteristics of each style is important in analyzing how people understand the world around them.

Schaie's Theory

Schaie (1977–1978) offers an alternative cognitive-process theory based on his research on adult intellectual development. He suggests that during childhood and adolescence the focus is on the acquisition of information and problem-solving skills. He contends that Piaget's theory is an example of a theory that explains this process. Schaie also thinks it is unlikely that we continue to develop more sophisticated ways to acquire new information beyond those described by Piaget. Therefore, if we are to understand what happens during adulthood, Schaie believes, we must shift our focus from how knowledge is acquired to how it is used.

As individuals move into young adulthood, they are no longer in a position to concentrate primarily on acquiring skills. As people begin careers and families, they concentrate more on achieving their goals. But to do so means that they must apply their knowledge to real-world problems, which involve social as well as abstract cognitive skills that are not measured well by most standardized intelligence tests. Schaie suggests that cognitive and social functioning begin to merge even more than in the past. Intellectual performance is likely to be best when tasks have, in his terms, "role-related achievement potential"; in other words, we do better on tasks when we are committed to them. Finally, a key theme in young adulthood is learning how to monitor oneself, keeping track of how things are going and how much progress is being made toward goals that may be years away.

During middle age, Schaie believes, the emphasis shifts again. Once people have become competent and independent, they are in a position to assume responsibility for others. Covering the time from the late 30s to the early 60s, this stage involves learning to appreciate the effects that one's own

SOMETHING TO THINK ABOUT

Practical Implications of Cognitive Strategies

One of the most important questions we can ask about qualitative aspects of intellectual development is whether the stage of thinking one is in makes a difference in human interaction. The answer to this question is yes. When two people who think at different cognitive developmental stages interact, there is a greater possibility of misunderstanding than when two people who are at the same cognitive developmental stage interact.

Let's consider a situation in which a couple is trying to work out a problem, such as whether one partner may continue to be friends with a former lover. Suppose that one partner thinks relativistically and the other partner thinks at an absolutist level, and that the relativistic thinker wants to maintain the friendship whereas the absolutist thinker believes such arrangements are inherently wrong. It will be impossible for the relativistic thinker to get the absolutist thinker to understand how such an arrangement could be possible. Due to the nature of each mode of thinking, the absolutist thinker is unlikely to give in. The relativistic thinker may need to capitalize on the ability to see situations from multiple perspectives and frame the situation in such a way as to reach a resolution. This approach would be most effective if the resolution relied on logic rather than emotion.

Think of situations in your own life when you have had sharp disagreements with another person. Was one reason for the disagreement a result of the way you both thought about the problem? How could you get around the limitations in thinking? How could you develop a strategy that would work with people of different levels of cognitive development? It's something to think about.

problem solutions have on one's family and friends. Part of this realization comes from the need for many people to develop what Neugarten (1969) calls "executive abilities." An example of executive abilities would be skills necessary for understanding how an organization works. When one is responsible for developing a solution to a marketing problem, for example, both subordinates and superiors need to be kept informed of the progress, because they are affected by the decisions. Finally, it is often during middle age that people become involved in socially responsible organizations at work (such as unions) and the community (for example, the PTA).

According to Schaie, later in life the need to acquire new skills or to monitor the effects of decisions decreases. The future seems shorter, and retirement eliminates the need to deal with these effects. What happens now is a reintegration of intellectual abilities into a simpler form. The emphasis is on remaining intellectually involved in meaningful situations. In Schaie's (1977–1978) words, this stage "completes the transition from 'what should I know?' through the 'how should I use what I know?' to the 'why should I know?' phase of life" (p. 135). Intellectual endeavors in later life are influenced by motivational and attitudinal considerations more than at any other time.

In sum, Schaie's model is a competency-based approach to adult intellectual development. Standardized intelligence tests do not measure his stages very well. Consequently, little research has been done on his framework. Still, Schaie's approach makes intuitive sense and stands as one of the few attempts to describe intellectual development from a life-span perspective. Once new assessment instruments are developed, it is likely that more work will be done on this framework.

Concept Checks

1. What are the four stages of cognitive development and their respective characteristics in Piaget's theory?
2. What are the major styles of thinking that have been identified beyond formal operations?

3. What are the stages in Schaie's theory of adult thought?

PROBLEM SOLVING, EXPERTISE, AND WISDOM

Learning Objectives:

- What are optimally exercised abilities and unexercised abilities? What age differences have been found in practical problem solving?
- What is encapsulation, and how does it relate to expertise? What is the role of experience in expertise?
- What is wisdom, and how does it relate to age and life experience?

So far, our consideration of intellectual abilities has included examinations of how people's performance on standardized tests and their modes of thinking differ with age. But what we have not considered in detail yet is how people actually use their intellectual abilities and demonstrate characteristics we associate with intelligent people: solving problems, gaining expertise, and becoming wise. What we have discovered in this chapter to this point is that people's crystallized intelligence, reflecting life experience, continues to grow (or at least not decline) until later in life, and that one hallmark of adults' thinking is the integration of emotion and logic. One might expect, then, that the ability to solve real-life problems would not decline until late adulthood, that expertise would increase, and that wisdom would be related to age. Are these expectations correct? Let's find out.

Problem Solving

One of the most important ways in which people use their intellectual abilities is to solve problems. Think for a minute about everyday life and the number of problem-solving situations one encounters in school, on the job, in relationships, driving a car, and so forth. Each of these settings requires one to analyze complex situations quickly, to apply knowledge, and to create solutions, sometimes in a matter of seconds.

Some people tend to be better at dealing with certain problems than with others. Why is that? One possible explanation has to do with the kinds of abilities we use regularly versus the abilities we use only occasionally. Nancy Denney has proposed a more formal version of this explanation, which we will consider next.

Denney's Model of Unexercised and Optimally Exercised Abilities

Denney developed a model of problem solving that is based on using intellectual abilities in everyday life. Denney (1982) postulates that intellectual abilities relating to problem solving follow two types of developmental functions. One of these functions represents unexercised, or unpracticed, ability, and the other represents optimally trained, or optimally exercised, ability. ***Unexercised ability*** **refers to the ability a normal, healthy adult would exhibit without practice or training.** Fluid intelligence is thought to be an example of untrained ability, because, by definition, it does not depend on experience and is unlikely to be formally trained (Horn, 1982). ***Optimally exercised ability*** **refers to the ability a normal, healthy adult would demonstrate under the best conditions of training or practice.** Crystallized intelligence is an example of optimally exercised ability, because the component skills (such as vocabulary ability) are used daily.

Denney argues that the overall developmental course of both abilities is the same: They tend to increase until late adolescence or early adulthood and slowly decline thereafter. These developmental functions are shown in Figure 7.6. At all age levels there is a difference in favor of optimally exercised ability, although this difference is less in early childhood and old age. As the developmental trends move away from the hypothetical ideal, Denney argues, the gains seen in training programs will increase. As we noted earlier in our discussion of attempts to train fluid intelligence, it appears that this increase occurs.

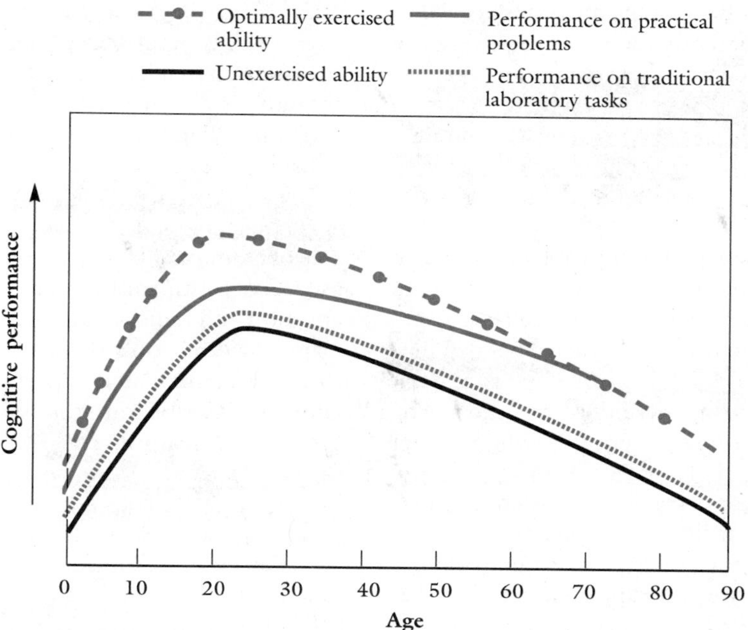

Figure 7.6 Developmental curves showing performance on practical problems and traditional laboratory tasks plotted against unexercised and optimally exercised abilities

Source: Adapted from Denney, 1982

Practical Problem Solving

Denney's model spurred considerable interest in how people solve practical problems. Based on the model, adults should perform better on practical problems than on abstract ones like those typically used on standardized intelligence tests. Tests of practical problem solving would use situations such as the following (Denney, Pearce, & Palmer, 1982):

> Let's say that a middle-aged woman is frying chicken in her home when, all of a sudden, a grease fire breaks out on top of the stove. Flames begin to shoot up. What should she do? (p. 116)

Findings from studies examining how well adults solve problems like this are mixed (Cornelius, 1990; Denney, 1990). Although most researchers find better performance on practical problems, how this performance differs with age is unclear. Some investigators (such as Denney & Pearce, 1989) find that performance peaks during midlife and decreases after that, as predicted by Denney's model. Other researchers (for example, Cornelius & Caspi, 1987) find continued improvement at least until around age 70.

What is clear is that performance on practical problems increases from early adulthood to middle age. Differences among studies occur in the age at which maximal performance is attained and in the direction and degree of change beyond midlife. However, some important differences among these studies could explain the differences in findings. One key difference is that several different measures are used in assessing practical problem-solving ability. Marsiske and Willis (1995) addressed this issue by using three separate measures of practical problem solving and seeing if they converged on a single set of abilities. Their results were enlightening. Each of the measures proved to be reliable and apparently valid, but they were not strongly interrelated and their relation to age also varied. Thus, competence in solving practical problems is a multidimensional construct, much like intelligence itself, calling into question whether a global construct of practical problem solving exists at all.

One way to assess practical problem solving in more focused terms is to create measures with clearly identifiable dimensions that relate to specific types of problems. This is what Diehl, Willis, and Schaie (1995) did by creating the Observed Tasks of Daily Living (OTDL) measure. The OTDL consists of three dimensions, which reflect three specific problems in everyday life: food preparation, medication intake, and telephone use. Each of these dimensions also reflects important aspects of assessing whether people can live independently, a topic we will explore in Chapter 12. Diehl et al. showed that performance on the OTDL is directly influenced by age, fluid intelligence, and crystallized intelligence, and indirectly by perceptual speed, memory, and several aspects of health. These results provide important links between practical problem solving and basic elements of psychometric intelligence and information processing.

Other research into the relation between practical problem solving and intellectual abilities provides more insight. Heidrich and Denney (1994) showed that different measures of problem solving relate differently to traditional measures of intelligence. Specifically, the ability to solve social problems (such as how an arguing couple might reconcile) and practical problems were related to each other and to measures of crystallized intelligence (vocabulary ability), whereas traditional problem-solving ability (scores on a Twenty Questions test) were related to measures of fluid intelligence (solving mazes). Thus, practical problem solving is a multidimensional construct, and which psychometric intellectual abilities are most influential depends on the type of problems to be solved.

The search for relations between psychometric intelligence and practical problem-solving abilities is only one way to examine the broader linkages with intellectual functioning. Recall that postformal thinking is grounded in the ways in which people conceptualize situations. Indeed, much of the research that led to the discovery of postformal thought involved presenting adults with lifelike problems; Blanchard-Fields's (1986) study that we considered earlier is an excellent example.

This close linkage between postformal thinking and solving practical problems also involves the role of emotionality. Remember that one of the key aspects of postformal thinking is the integration of emotion and logic. Blanchard-Fields, Jahnke, and Camp (1995) took this as a starting point and carefully manipulated the emotionality of problems. As described in more detail in the How Do We Know? feature, they found important age differences in problem-solving styles that were highly dependent on whether the problem situation was emotionally salient.

What can we conclude from the research on practical problem solving? First, practical problem-solving abilities are multidimensional and may not even interrelate strongly with each other. Second, the developmental functions of these abilities are complex and may differ somewhat across abilities. Third, the relations between practical problem-solving abilities and psychometric intelligence are equally complex. Finally, the close connection between solving practical problems and postformal thinking may prove fruitful in furthering our understanding of individual differences in abilities. In short, solving practical problems offers an excellent way to discover how all the topics we have considered in this chapter come together to produce behavior in everyday life.

Expertise

On many basic information-processing tasks, younger adults clearly outperform older adults. Yet, many people in their 60s and some in their 70s hold jobs that demand complex decision making, abstract reasoning, and memory for a lot of information. How do they do it?

The most popular answer is that older adults compensate for poorer performance through their expertise. That is, through years of experience and practice, adults build up a wealth of knowledge

HOW DO WE KNOW?

The Role of Emotionality in Solving Real-Life Problems

We have seen that the link between practical problem solving and postformal thinking is a close one indeed. This is especially true when problems that have an emotional aspect are examined, as was reported in Blanchard-Fields, Jahnke, and Camp's (1995) study. As they point out, most of the research on practical problem solving uses problems that have little emotional content in them. This may stack the deck against older adults, because of the connection between higher emotional intensity and demonstrating dialectical thinking (Kramer, 1990) and because they make more relativistic causal attributions in problem situations that are high in emotional salience (Blanchard-Fields & Norris, 1994). Age differences in problem-solving styles tend to be absent on problems low in emotional salience; however, on problems high in emotional salience, older adults showed more awareness of when to avoid or passively accept a situation within interpersonal, emotional domains, whereas younger adults tend to use a cognitive-analytic approach to all problems (Blanchard-Fields & Camp, 1990).

What would happen if the emotional salience of problems was carefully manipulated? Would it influence people's preferred mode of problem solving? Blanchard-Fields et al. studied 70 adolescents (aged 14–17), 69 young adults (aged 25–35), 74 middle-aged adults (aged 45–55), and 74 older adults (aged 65–75). Participants were given a total of 15 vignettes, with five rated in each of three categories as high (such as caring for an ill or aging parent), medium (such as moving to a new town), or low (such as returning defective merchandise) in emotional salience. Each solution was rated as reflecting one of four problem-solving styles: problem-focused action, involving overt behaviors that deal directly with the problem; cognitive problem analysis, involving cognitive efforts to solve the problem by thinking it through; passive-dependent behavior, involving attempts to withdraw from the situation in some way; and avoidant thinking and denial, involving attempts to manage the meaning of the problem.

Results showed that emotional salience has a clear affect on the problem-solving approaches people of different ages adopt. No age differences were found in relation to problem-focused strategies; they were found in all age groups with all types of problems. However, these strategies decrease as the emotional salience of the problem increases. In fact, passive-dependent and cognitive-analysis strategies increase with greater emotional salience of the problems. Young adults preferred cognitive-analysis strategies more than any other age group, which fits with their tendency to adopt formal operational or absolutist thinking. Although all age groups adopted avoidant-denial strategies as their second most preferred choice, older adults were especially likely to adopt this approach. Similarly, older adults used passive-dependent strategies more than younger adults in situations with high emotional saliency.

The tendencies of younger adults to use cognitive-analysis strategies and for older adults to use more avoidant-denial and passive-dependent strategies may reflect a combination of cognitive level and life experience. Other research has shown that older adults are better than younger adults at accepting uncontrollable events passively, an approach that is related to better adaptation (Rodin & Langer, 1977).

In sum, the degree to which emotionality is part of a problem, in conjunction with life experience and preferred modes of thinking, appears to influence the way one attempts to deal with the problem. One limitation of the Blanchard-Fields et al. study was the fact that the problems they used represented hypothetical situations. Future research should examine problems that participants actually face to get a more accurate picture of how people actually solve emotional problems in everyday life.

about alternative ways to solve problems or make decisions that enables them to bypass steps needed by younger adults (Ericsson & Smith, in press). In a way, this represents "the triumph of knowledge over reasoning" (Charness & Bosman, 1991); experience and age can defeat skill and youth. In research terms, older people are sometimes able to compensate for declines in some basic intellectual abilities (for example, the information-processing skills underlying fluid abilities).

Figuring out exactly what expertise is turns out to be difficult. Charness and Bosman (1990a) point out that experts are identified at times because they use novel approaches to solve difficult problems, because they have extensive knowledge about a particular topic, or because they are highly practiced. For example, expert physicians diagnose diseases differently than novice physicians (Patel & Groen, 1986), chess masters quickly evaluate very complex board positions (Charness & Bosman, 1990a), and typists look ahead to help avoid mistakes (see Chapter 5).

Little research has been done on age differences in expertise. What we know is that expert performance tends to peak in middle age and to drop off slightly after that (Charness & Bosman, 1990a). However, the developmental decrements observed here are nowhere near as great as they are for underlying information-processing skills, secondary memory, or fluid intelligence. Thus, older adults may be compensating for underlying decline by relying more on their experience.

Notice that the different developmental trajectories for expertise and basic information-processing abilities apparently means that the two are not strongly related. How can this be? Rybash, Hoyer, and Roodin (1986) proposed a process called encapsulation as the answer. ***Encapsulation* refers to the idea that the processes of thinking (such as attention, memory, logical reasoning) become connected to the products of thinking (such as knowledge about world history).** This process of encapsulation allows expertise to compensate for decrements in underlying processing ability, perhaps by making thinking in the particular domain more efficient.

Encapsulation reflects the fact that in adulthood knowledge becomes more and more specialized based on experience, which in turn reflects a lesser role of age-related neurological development and social demands for increased specialization of knowledge and expertise (Hoyer & Rybash, 1994). The emergence of encapsulated knowledge, unique to adulthood, becomes increasingly complex and resistant to change. Because it is experientially based, the development of cognition in adulthood is directed toward mastery and adaptive competency in specific domains, making it quite different from cognitive development during childhood, which is more genetically driven and uniform across content domains (Hoyer & Rybash, 1994). Knowledge encapsulation also implies that the notion of a general slowing of processing underlying cognitive changes in later life may be wrong. Research examining processing in different domains indicates that speed of processing differs across knowledge domains (Clancy & Hoyer, 1993). These findings indicate that the efficiency of the underlying mechanics (e.g., neural pathways), procedures, or computations required to carry out cognitive tasks depends on the amount of experientially acquired knowledge a person has in that domain.

Knowledge encapsulation has important implications for studying intellectual development in adulthood. Encapsulated knowledge cannot be decomposed to study its constituent parts, meaning that mechanistic approaches (such as the one used in the psychometric research we examined earlier in this chapter) or ones predicating across-the-board declines are inappropriate. Rather, approaches that take a more holistic view and that stress developing formal models of computational processes with a specific domain in particular contexts are more appropriate (Hoyer & Rybash, 1994).

In the next section, we will also see how the role of experience in cognitive development is changing the way we conceptualize wisdom. As we will see, wisdom is more closely associated with having certain types of experiences than it is with age per se.

Wisdom

We began this chapter with a tale about an old man's wisdom. Seemingly caught in a no-win situation with his son-in-law, the old alchemist comes up with an insightful and clever solution on how to turn base elements (dirt) into gold. Chinen (1989) points out that this tale highlights several aspects of wisdom: It involves *practical knowledge,* it is *given altruistically,* it involves *psychological insights,* and it is *based on life experience.*

Research tends to support Chinen's conclusions. From a psychological perspective, wisdom has been viewed as involving three cognitive processes (Kramer, 1990): practical and social intelligence, such as the ability to solve real-world problems; insight into the deeper meanings underlying a given situation; and awareness of the relative, uncertain, and paradoxical nature of human problems, reflected in postformal thinking. A growing body of research has been examining these aspects.

Based on years of research using in-depth think-aloud interviews with young, middle-aged, and older adults about normal and unusual problems that people face, Baltes and Staudinger (1993) describe four characteristics of wisdom:

- Wisdom deals with important and/or difficult matters of life and the human condition.
- Wisdom is truly "superior" knowledge, judgment, and advice.
- Wisdom is knowledge with extraordinary scope, depth, and balance applicable to specific situations.
- Wisdom, when used, is well intended and combines mind and virtue (character).

Baltes and Staudinger used this framework to develop five specific criteria for determining whether a person demonstrates wisdom: expertise in the practical aspects of daily living; breadth of ability to define and solve problems; understanding of how life problems differ across the life span; understanding that the "right thing to do" depends on the values, goals, and priorities one has; and recognition of the complexity, difficulty, and uncertainty in problems one faces in life. Both the general framework and the specific criteria point out that people who are wise are experts in the basic issues in life (Baltes & Staudinger, 1993). Wise people know a great deal about how to conduct their life, how to interpret life events, and what life means.

One important issue with Baltes and Staudinger's approach to wisdom is whether it has a psychological bias. That is, the framework and criteria may not capture the "true" essence of wisdom, if one were to examine the characteristics of what people in everyday life define as wise behavior. To examine this possibility, Baltes, Staudinger, Maercker, and Smith (1995) compared people who were nominated as wise to groups of clinical psychologists and highly educated older and younger groups. Their results indicated that the wise nominees performed as well on the five criteria of wisdom as did the clinical psychologists, who in other studies had outperformed other groups. The wisdom nominees also scored extremely well in tasks involving life management and on the criterion of recognizing that the "right thing to do" varies across people. Based on these findings, Baltes et al. concluded that their framework and criteria are not biased in such a way as to differentially favor psychologists.

Two important aspects of wisdom have been demonstrated fairly clearly. First, wisdom is not the same thing as creativity; wisdom is the growth of expertise and insight, whereas creativity is the generation of a new solution to a problem (Simonton, 1990).

Second, the relationship between age and wisdom is complex. Certainly, wisdom has long been characterized as the province of older adults. For example, studies of people's implicit theories of wisdom, in which people are asked to nominate the wisest person they know, indicate that people of all ages tend to nominate someone who is older than they are (Denney, Dew, & Kroupa, 1995). However, when the criteria for wisdom discussed earlier are applied to people's knowledge and actions, a different picture emerges. An example of this alternative view is provided in Smith and Baltes's (1990) research. They had adults respond to hypothetical life-planning problems, such as whether to accept a promotion or whether to retire. The problems were presented as dilemmas facing fictitious people, and participants had to reason out a solution. For example, one study had people respond to life-planning problems such as this: A 15-year-old girl wants to get married right away. What should she consider and do? Answers were then analyzed in terms of the degree to which they reflect wisdom. Contrary to the stereotype, Smith and Baltes found no association between age and wise answers. Instead, they found evidence of wisdom in adults of all ages. The key variable appears to be having extensive life experience with the type of problem given, not just life experience in general. Thus, given the right circumstances, a 35-year-old and a 75-year-old could give equally wise solutions to a life problem.

Research based on cognitive developmental

changes in adulthood such as those discussed earlier concerning postformal thinking has uncovered other aspects in the growth of wisdom. Several investigators point out that a wise person is one who is able to integrate thinking, feeling, and acting into a coherent approach to a problem (Kramer, 1990; Orwoll and Perlmutter, 1990). This research implies that *empathy* or *compassion* is an important characteristic of wise people, due to their ability to overcome automatic responses to show concern for core human experiences and values (Pascual-Leone, 1990). Thus, wise people are able to see through situations and get to the heart of the matter, rather than be caught in the superficial aspects of the situation. Indeed, some evidence suggests that, compared with young- and middle-aged adults, older adults are more generous in donating their time and money to charity and express greater social concern (Haan, Millsap, & Hartka, 1986).

So what specific factors help one become wise? Baltes (1993) identifies three factors: (1) *general personal conditions,* such as mental ability; (2) *specific expertise conditions,* such as mentoring or practice; and (3) *facilitative life contexts,* such as education or leadership experience. Other researchers point to additional criteria. For example, Kramer (1990) argues that the *integration of affect and cognition* that occurs during adulthood results in the ability to act wisely. Personal growth across adulthood, reflecting Erikson's concepts of generativity and integrity, helps foster the process as well. All of these factors take time. Thus, although growing old is no guarantee that wisdom will develop, it provides one with the time that, if used well, will provide a supportive context for it.

The picture of wisdom that is emerging appears to support the opening tale. Just as the old alchemist's response was based on his own specific experience with trying to make gold, so too our own wisdom comes from becoming experts at dealing with particular kinds of problems.

Concept Checks

1. What do optimally exercised abilities and unexercised abilities mean?
2. How does the process of encapsulation occur?
3. What are the five criteria of determining whether someone is wise according to Baltes and colleagues?

SUMMARY

Defining Intelligence

Intelligence in Everyday Life

Experts and laypeople agree that intelligence consists of problem-solving ability, verbal ability, and social competence. Motivation, exertion of effort, and reading are important behaviors for people of all ages; however, some age-related behaviors are also apparent.

The Big Picture: A Neofunctionalist View

The neofunctionalist view emphasizes that there is some intellectual decline with age, but there is also stability and growth. Four points are central. Plasticity refers to the range within which one's abilities are modifiable. Multidimensionality refers to the many abilities that underlie intelligence. Multidirectionality refers to the many possible ways individuals may develop. Interindividual variability acknowledges that people differ from each other.

Research Approaches to Intelligence

Two main approaches are used to study intelligence. The psychometric approach focuses on performance on standardized tests. The cognitive-process approach emphasizes the quality and style of thought.

Developmental Trends in Psychometric Intelligence

Primary Mental Abilities

Primary abilities comprise the several independent abilities that form factors on standardized intelligence tests. Five have been studied most: number, word fluency, verbal meaning, inductive reasoning, and spatial orientation. Primary mental abilities show normative declines with age that may affect performance in everyday life after around age 60, although declines tend to be small until the mid-70s. However, within-individual differences show that very few people decline equally in all areas.

Secondary Mental Abilities

Fluid intelligence refers to innate abilities that make people flexible and adaptive thinkers and that underlie the acquisition of knowledge and experience. Fluid intelligence normally declines with age. Crystallized intelligence refers to knowledge acquired through life experience and education. Crystallized intelligence does not normally decline with age until very late life. As age increases, individual differences remain stable with fluid intelligence, but increase with crystallized intelligence.

Moderators of Intellectual Change

Age-related declines in fluid abilities have been shown to be moderated by cohort, education, social variables, personality, health, lifestyle, mindlessness, and task familiarity. Cohort effects and familiarity have been studied most. Cohort differences are complex and depend on the specific ability. Age differences in performance on familiar tasks are similar to those on standardized tests. Although taking both into account reduces age differences, they are not eliminated.

Modifying Primary Abilities

Several studies show that fluid intelligence abilities improve after direct training and after anxiety reduction. Improvements in performance match or exceed individuals' level of decline. Training effects appear to last for several years regardless of the nature of the training, but generalization of training to new tasks is rare.

Qualitative Differences in Adults' Thinking

Piaget's Theory

Key concepts in Piaget's theory include adaptation to the environment, organization of thought, and the structure of thought. The processes of thought are assimilation (using previously learned knowledge to make sense of incoming information) and accommodation (making the knowledge base conform to the environment). According to Piaget, thought develops through four stages: sensorimotor, preoperations, concrete operations, and formal operations. Older adults do not perform as well on tests of formal operations as younger adults, but results on tests of concrete operations are mixed.

Going Beyond Piaget: Postformal Thought

Considerable evidence shows that the style of thinking changes across adulthood. The development of reflective judgment in young adulthood occurs as a result of seven stages. Other research has identified a progression from absolutist thinking to relativistic thinking to dialectical thinking. A key characteristic of postformal thought is the integration of emotion and logic. Much of this research is based on people's solutions to real-world problems. Although there has been suggestions that women's ways of knowing differ from men's, research evidence does not provide strong support for this view.

Schaie's Theory

Schaie suggests that thinking in adulthood moves from a focus on acquiring information to executive abilities and teaching others to remain cognitively active.

Problem Solving, Expertise, and Wisdom

Problem Solving

In Denney's model, both unexercised and optimally exercised abilities increase through early adulthood and slowly decline thereafter. Performance on practical problem solving increases through middle age. Research indicates that sound measures of practical problem solving can be constructed, but these measures do not tend to relate to each other, indicating that problem solving is multidimensional. The emotional salience of problems is an important feature that influences problem-solving style.

Expertise

Older adults can often compensate for declines in some abilities by becoming experts, which allows them to anticipate what is going to be required on a task. Knowledge encapsulation occurs with age, in which the processes of thinking become connected with the products of thinking. Encapsulated knowledge cannot be decomposed and studied in a componential fashion.

Wisdom

Wisdom involves four general characteristics: it deals with important matters of life; it consists of superior knowledge, judgment, and advice; it is knowledge of exceptional depth; and it is well intentioned. Five specific behavioral criteria are used to judge wisdom: expertise, broad abilities, understanding how life problems change, fitting the response with the problem, and realizing that life problems are often ambiguous. Wisdom also entails integrating thought and emotion to show empathy or compassion. Wisdom may be more strongly related to experience than to age.

REVIEW QUESTIONS

Defining intelligence

- How do laypeople and researchers define intelligence?
- What are the two main ways that intelligence has been studied? Define each.

Developmental trends in psychometric intelligence

- What are primary mental abilities? Which ones have been studied most? How do they change with age?
- Define fluid and crystallized intelligence. How does each change with age?
- What factors moderate age changes in fluid intelligence? What role does cohort play?
- What benefits do older people get from intervention programs aimed at improving fluid abilities? What training approaches have been used? How well do trained skills generalize?

Qualitative differences in adults' thinking

- What are the key concepts in Piaget's theory?
- What stages of cognitive development did Piaget identify? What age differences have been found in them? Do adults use formal operations?
- What is reflective judgment? What are the stages in its development? What are absolutist, relativistic, and dialectical thinking? How do emotion and logic become integrated? What evidence is there for gender differences in postformal thinking?
- Describe Schaie's theory of cognitive development.

Problem solving, expertise, and wisdom

- What are unexercised and optimally exercised abilities? How do their developmental paths differ from each other?
- What are the developmental trends in solving practical problems? How does emotional salience of problems influence problem-solving style?
- What is an expert? How is expertise related to age?
- What is knowledge encapsulation?
- What criteria are used to define wisdom? How is wisdom related to age?

INTEGRATING CONCEPTS IN DEVELOPMENT

1. How are the primary and secondary mental abilities related to the aspects of information processing considered in Chapters 5 and 6?
2. What do you think an integrated theory linking postformal thinking, practical problem solving, expertise, and wisdom would look like?
3. What aspects of secondary mental abilities do you think would be most closely linked to expertise? Why?

KEY TERMS

accommodation Changing one's thought to make it a better approximation of the world of experience.

assimilation The use of currently available knowledge to make sense out of incoming information.

cognitive-process approach An approach to intelligence that emphasizes the ways in which people conceptualize problems and focuses on modes or styles of thinking.

crystallized intelligence Knowledge that is acquired through life experience and education in a particular culture.

encapsulation The idea that the processes of thinking become connected to the products of thinking.

factor The interrelations among performances on similar tests of psychometric intelligence.

fluid intelligence Abilities that make one a flexible and adaptive thinker, that allow one to draw inferences, and that allow one to understand the relations among concepts independent of acquired knowledge and experience.

interindividual variability An acknowledgment that adults differ in the direction of their intellectual development.

multidimensional The notion that intelligence consists of many dimensions.

multidirectionality The distinct patterns of change in abilities over the life span, with these patterns being different for different abilities.

neofunctionalist approach A view asserting that some intellectual decline may be seen with age but that stability and growth in mental functioning also can be seen across adulthood.

optimal level In the reflective judgment framework, the highest level of information-processing capacity that a person is capable of doing.

optimally exercised ability The ability a normal, healthy adult would demonstrate under the best conditions of training or practice.

plasticity The range of functioning within an individual and the conditions under which a person's abilities can be modified within a specific age range.

postformal thought Thinking characterized by a recognition that truth varies across situations, that solutions must be realistic to be reasonable, that ambiguity and contradiction are the rule rather than the exception, and that emotion and subjective factors play a role in thinking.

primary mental abilities Independent abilities within psychometric intelligence based on different combinations of standardized intelligence tests.

psychometric approach An approach to intelligence involving difining it as performance on standardized tests.

reflective judgment Thinking that involves how people reason through dilemmas involving current affairs, religion, science, and the like.

secondary mental abilities Broad-ranging skills composed of several primary mental abilities.

skill acquisition In the reflective judgment framework, the gradual, and somewhat haphazard, process by which people learn new abilities.

unexercised ability The ability a normal, healthy adult would exhibit without practice or training.

IF YOU'D LIKE TO LEARN MORE

Commons, M. L., Richards, F. A., & Armon, C. (Eds.). (1984). *Beyond formal operations: Late adolescent and adult cognitive development.* New York: Praeger. Commons, M. L., Sinnott, J. D., Richards, F. A., & Armon, C. (Eds.). (1989). *Adult development: Vol. 1. Comparisons and applications of adolescent and adult developmental models.* New York: Praeger. Two of the best collections of research and theory on postformal thinking. Easy to difficult reading.

King, P. M., & Kitchener, K. S. (1994). *Developing reflective judgment: Understanding and promoting intellectual growth and critical thinking in adolescents and adults.* San Francisco: Jossey-Bass. The most thorough description of the reflective judgment framework, including excellent discussions on the longitudinal data on which it is based. Easy reading.

Schaie, K. W. (1995). *Intellectual development in adulthood: The Seattle Longitudinal Study.* New York: Cambridge University Press. The most complete review of the Seattle Longitudinal Study in a single volume. A must read not only for the information about psychometric intelligence, but also for the information on research methodology. Moderately difficult reading.

Sinnott, J. D. (Ed.). (1994). *Interdisciplinary handbook of adult lifespan learning.* Westport, CT: Greenwood Press. An excellent eclectic collection of chapters on various topics pertaining to intellectual development in adulthood. Easy to moderately difficult reading.

Sternberg, R. J. (Ed.). (1990). *Wisdom: Its nature, origins, and development* (pp. 279–313). Cambridge, UK: Cambridge University Press. One of the few collections of articles on wisdom that provides a broad survey of the topic. Moderately difficult reading.

CHAPTER 8

Personality and Social Cognition

Giovanni Costetti, *Pensive Woman.* Alinari/Art Resource, NY.

Already at the age of twenty-five you see the professional mannerism settling down on the young commercial traveller, on the young doctor, on the young minister, on the young counselor-at-law. You see the little lines of cleavage running through the character, the treks of thought, the prejudices, the ways of the "shop" in a word, from which the man can by-and-by no more escape than his coat sleeve can suddenly fall into a new set of folds. On the whole, it is best he should not escape. It is well for the world that in most of us, by the age of thirty, the character has set like plaster, and will never soften again. (James, 1890, p. 121)

One of the oldest debates in psychology concerns whether personality development continues across the life span. From the earliest days, prominent people argued both sides. William James and Sigmund Freud, for example, believed that personality was set by the time adulthood rolled around. Indeed, Freud thought that development was essentially complete in childhood. On the other hand, Carl Jung asserted the viewpoint that personality was continually shaped throughout our lives. Aspects of personality come and go as people's experiences and life issues change.

A century of research has done little to clarify the issue. We still have two main theoretical camps, one arguing for stability and the other for change. There is far less agreement on the developmental course of personality than for any other topic in adult development and aging. Theories and concepts abound. Data are contradictory, and results often depend on which specific measures researchers use. Perhaps the best way to achieve one's own resolution of the controversy is through one's own research project.

Most of us will eventually attend a high school reunion. It is amusing, so it is said, to see how our classmates have changed over the years. In addition to noticing gray or missing hair and a few wrinkles, we should pay attention to personality characteristics. For example, will Jackie be the same outgoing person she was as captain of the cheerleaders? Will Shawn still be as concerned about social issues at 48 as he was at 18? To learn as much about our friends as possible, we could make careful observations of our classmates' personalities over the course of several reunions. Then, at the gathering marking 60 years since graduation, we could examine the trends we observed. Did our classmates' personalities change substantially? Or did they remain essentially the same as they were 60 years earlier?

How we think these questions will be answered provides clues to our personal biases concerning personality stability or change across adulthood. As we will see, biases about continuity and discontinuity are more obvious in personality research than in any other area of adult development.

Why should the area of personality be so controversial? The answer lies in the paradoxical beliefs we hold about personality itself. At one level we all believe that people have complex personalities that remain relatively constant over time. A person with a stable personality is easier to deal with in different situations; when a person behaves in ways that violate our expectations, we act surprised. Imagine the chaos that would result if every week or so everyone woke up with a brand new personality: The once easygoing husband is now a real tyrant, trusted friends are now completely unpredictable, and our patterns of social interaction are in a shambles. Clearly, we must rely on consistency of personality to survive in day-to-day life.

Still, we like to believe that we can change undesirable aspects of our personalities. Imagine what it would be like, for example, if we could never overcome shyness; if anxiety were a lifelong, incurable curse; or if our idiosyncratic tendencies that cause others to tear their hair out could not be eliminated. Our assumption of the modifiability of personality is very strong indeed. The field of psychotherapy is a formal verification of that.

Thinking about personality from the perspective of the basic developmental forces provides a very helpful way to understand the arguments in personality theory and research. As pointed out throughout this book, the forces emphasize the complexity of influences on any specific issue; personality is no exception. Genetic factors and physical health exert important influences on personality and how it is expressed. Socialization influences which aspects of personality may be learned as we grow up and age. Life-course factors are especially important for theorists who emphasize that the issues people face change over time. Although few attempts have been made at integrating these influences in personality research, we need to keep them in mind when drawing our own conclusions on the matter.

Levels of Analysis and Personality Research

The debate over the degree to which personality in adulthood remains stable or changes is one that has generated numerous studies and theoretical perspectives. Consequently, sorting out the various approaches helps us understand what aspects of personality the various researchers are describing. Drawing on the work of several theorists and researchers, McAdams (1994) describes three parallel levels of personality structure and function. Each level contains a wide range of personality constructs. McAdams refers to the levels with rather generic names: ***dispositional traits, personal concerns,*** and ***life narrative.***

***Dispositional traits* consist of aspects of personality that are consistent across different contexts and can be compared across a group along a continuum representing high and low degrees of the characteristic.** This is the level of personality most people think of first, and it includes commonly used descriptors such as shy, talkative, authoritarian, and the like. ***Personal concerns* consist of things that are important to people, their goals, and their major concerns in life.** Personal concerns are usually described in motivational, developmental, or strategic terms; they reflect the stage of life a person is in at the time. ***Life narrative* consists of the aspects of personality that pull everything together, those integrative aspects that give a person an identity or sense of self.** The creation of an identity is the goal of this level.

McAdams (1994) points out that as one moves from dispositional traits to personal concerns to life narrative, the more likely it is that change will be observed. In a sense, the level of dispositional traits can be viewed as the "raw stuff" of personality, whereas each successive level must be constructed to a greater extent. In the following sections, we will use McAdams's levels to organize our discussion of personality in adulthood. Let's begin with the "raw stuff" and see how dispositional traits are structured in adulthood.

DISPOSITIONAL TRAITS ACROSS ADULTHOOD

Learning Objectives:

- What is the five-factor model of dispositional traits?
- What other evidence is there for long-term stability in dispositional traits?
- What criticisms have been leveled at the five-factor model?
- What can we conclude from theory and research on dispositional traits?

Consider the following anecdote:

> Over the course of numerous encounters you notice that Michelle is always surrounded by a group of people. On closer observation you see why this is so. She walks up to people and initiates conversations, is at ease with strangers, is pleasant, and is often described as the "life of the party."

What can we say about Michelle? One conclusion could be that she is an outgoing, or extroverted, person. How did we arrive at this judgment? We probably combined several aspects of her behavior into a concept that describes her rather concisely. What we have done is to use the notion of a personality trait. Extending this same reasoning to many areas of behavior is the basis for trait theories of personality. More formally, people's characteristic behaviors can be understood through attributes that reflect underlying dispositional traits, which are relatively enduring aspects of personality. We use the basic tenets of trait theory when we describe ourselves and others with such terms as *calm, aggressive, independent, friendly,* and so on.

Three assumptions are made about traits (McCrae & Costa, 1984). First, traits are based on comparisons of individuals, because there are no absolute quantitative standards for concepts such as friendliness. Second, the qualities or behaviors making up a particular trait must be distinctive enough to avoid confusion. Imagine the chaos that would result if friendliness and aggressiveness had many behaviors in common yet some that were vastly different. Finally, the traits attributed to a specific person are assumed to be stable characteristics. We normally assume that people who are friendly in several situations are going to be friendly the next time we see them. These three assumptions are all captured in the definition of a trait: a trait is any distinguishable, relatively enduring way in which one individual differs from others (Guilford, 1959, p. 6). Based on this definition, trait theories assume that little change in personality will occur across adulthood.

Most trait theories have several guiding principles in common. An important one for our present discussion concerns the structure of traits. Structure refers to the way in which traits are thought to be organized within the individual. This organization is usually inferred from the pattern of related and unrelated traits and is generally expressed in terms of dimensions. Personality structures can be examined over time to see whether they change with age.

The Five-Factor Model

Although many different trait theories of personality have been proposed over the years, few have been concerned with or have been based on adults of different ages. A major exception to this is the five-factor model proposed by McCrae and Costa (1990). Their model is strongly grounded in cross-sectional, longitudinal, and sequential research. **The *five-factor model* consists of five independent dimensions of personality: neuroticism, extraversion, openness to experience, agreeableness-antagonism, and conscientiousness-undirectedness.**

The first three dimensions of Costa and McCrae's model—neuroticism, extraversion, and openness to experience—have been the ones most heavily researched. Each of these dimensions is represented by six facets that reflect the main characteristics associated with it. The remaining two dimensions were added to the original three in the late 1980s to account for more data and to bring the theory closer to other trait theories. In the following sections we will consider each of the five dimensions briefly.

Neuroticism

The six facets of neuroticism are anxiety, hostility, self-consciousness, depression, impulsiveness, and vulnerability. Anxiety and hostility form underlying traits for two fundamental emotions: fear and anger. Although we all experience these emotions at times, the frequency and intensity with which they are felt vary from one person to another. People who are high in trait anxiety are nervous, high-strung, tense, worried, and pessimistic. Besides being prone to anger, hostile people are irritable and tend to be hard to get along with.

The traits of self-consciousness and depression relate to the emotions shame and sorrow. Being high in self-consciousness is associated with being sensitive to criticism and teasing and to feelings of inferiority. Trait depression refers to feelings of sadness, hopelessness, loneliness, guilt, and low self-worth.

The final two facets of neuroticism—impulsiveness and vulnerability—are most often manifested as behaviors rather than as emotions. Impulsiveness is the tendency to give in to temptation and desires due to a lack of willpower and self-control. Consequently, impulsive people often do things in excess, such as overeating and overspending, and they are more likely to smoke, gamble, and use drugs. Vulnerability refers to a lowered ability to deal effectively with stress. Vulnerable people tend to panic in a crisis or emergency and to be highly dependent on others for help.

McCrae and Costa (1984) note that, in general, people who are high in neuroticism tend to be high in each of the traits. High neuroticism typically results in violent and negative emotions that interfere with people's ability to handle problems or to

Continuity in dispositional traits is important for maintaining relationships.

get along with other people. We can see how this cluster of traits would operate: a person gets anxious and embarrassed in a social situation such as our class reunion, the frustration in dealing with others makes the person hostile, which may lead to excessive drinking at the party, which may result in subsequent depression for making a fool of oneself, and so on.

Extraversion

The six facets of extraversion can be grouped into three interpersonal traits (warmth, gregariousness, and assertiveness) and three temperamental traits (activity, excitement seeking, and positive emotions). Warmth, or attachment, refers to a friendly, compassionate, intimately involved style of interacting with other people. Warmth and gregariousness (a desire to be with other people) make up what is sometimes called sociability. Gregarious people thrive on crowds; the more social interaction, the better. Assertive people make natural leaders, take charge easily, make up their own minds, and readily express their thoughts and feelings.

Temperamentally, extraverts like to keep busy; they are the people who seem to have endless energy, talk fast, and want to be on the go. They prefer to be in stimulating, exciting environments and will often go searching for a challenging situation. This active, exciting lifestyle is evident in the extravert's positive emotion; these people are walking examples of zest, delight, and fun.

An interesting aspect of extraversion is that this dimension relates well to occupational interests and values. People high in extraversion tend to have people-oriented jobs, such as social work, business administration, and sales. They value humanitarian goals and a person-oriented use of power. Individuals low in extraversion tend to prefer task-oriented jobs, such as architecture or accounting.

Openness to Experience

The six facets of openness to experience represent six different areas. In the area of fantasy, openness means having a vivid imagination and active dream life. In aesthetics, openness is seen in the appreciation of art and beauty, a sensitivity to pure experience for its own sake. Openness to action refers to a willingness to try something new, whether it be a new kind of cuisine, a new movie, or a new travel destination. People who are open to ideas and values are curious and value knowledge for the sake of knowing. Open people also tend to be open minded in their values, often admitting that what may be right for one person may not be right for everyone. This outlook is a direct outgrowth of open individuals' willingness to think of different possibilities and their tendency to empathize with others in different circumstances. Open people also experience their own feelings strongly and see them as a major source of meaning in life.

Not surprisingly, openness to experience is also related to occupational choice. Open people are likely to be found in occupations that place a high value on thinking theoretically or philosophically and less emphasis on economic values. They are typically intelligent and tend to subject themselves to stressful situations. Occupations such as psychologist or minister, for example, appeal to open people.

Agreeableness-Antagonism

The easiest way to understand the agreeableness-antagonism dimension is to consider the traits that characterize antagonism. Antagonistic people tend to set themselves against others; they are skeptical, mistrustful, callous, unsympathetic, stubborn, and rude; and they have a defective sense of attachment. Antagonism may be manifested in ways other than overt hostility. For example, some antagonistic people are skillful manipulators or aggressive go-getters with little patience. In some respects these individuals have characteristics similar to the Type A behavior pattern (see Chapter 4).

Scoring high on agreeableness, the opposite of antagonism, may not always be adaptive either, however. These people may tend to be overly dependent and self-effacing, traits that often prove annoying to others.

Conscientiousness-Undirectedness

Scoring high on conscientiousness indicates that one is hardworking, ambitious, energetic, scrupulous, and persevering. Such people have the will to achieve (Dignam & Takemoto-Chock, 1981), that is, to work hard and make something of oneself. Undirectedness is viewed primarily as being lazy, careless, late, unenergetic, and aimless.

Research Evidence

Costa and McCrae have investigated whether the traits that make up their model remain stable across adulthood (e.g., Costa & McCrae, 1980b, 1988; Costa, McCrae, & Arenberg, 1980). Because their results are very consistent from study to study, we will consider the findings from the Costa, McCrae, and Arenberg study as representative. The data came from the Baltimore Longitudinal Study of Aging for the 114 men who took the Guilford-Zimmerman Temperament Survey (GZTS) on three occasions, with each of the two follow-up testings about 6 years apart.

What Costa and colleagues found was surprising. Even over a 12-year period, the 10 traits measured by the GZTS remained highly stable; the correlations ranged from .68 to .85. In much of personality research we might expect to find this degree of stability over a week or two, but to see it over 12 years is noteworthy. Even when the researchers looked at individual scores, they found that people had changed very little.

We would normally be skeptical of such consistency over a long period. But similar findings were obtained in other studies conducted over a 10-year span by Costa and McCrae (1977) in Boston, an 8-year span by Siegler, George, and Okun (1979) at Duke University, and a 30-year span by Leon, Gillum, Gillum, and Gouze (1979) in Minnesota. Even more amazing was the finding that personality ratings by spouses of each other showed no systematic changes over a 6-year period (Costa & McCrae, 1988). Thus, it appears that individuals change very little in self-reported personality traits over periods of up to 30 years and over the age range of 20 to 90. As described in How Do We Know? these stable traits also relate to such things as being happy.

This is a truly exciting and important conclusion. Clearly, lots of things change in people's lives over 30 years. They marry, divorce, have children, change jobs, face stressful situations, move, and maybe even retire. Social networks and friendships

HOW DO WE KNOW?

Happy and Unhappy People

We all know what it feels like to be happy, and we also know what it feels like to be unhappy. But for researchers in personality, feelings are not enough. They want to identify the parts of our personalities that underlie being happy and being unhappy.

Costa and McCrae (1980b) examined the relationships between personality and happiness in three studies. Their participants were a subsample of 1,100 men who were members of the Normative Aging Study. The participants came from a variety of socioeconomic groups, and most were veterans. They were asked to complete a series of four questionnaires over a 3-month interval. These questionnaires measured personality traits and subjective well-being.

Results from the first investigation showed that similar relationships held between personality and well-being across a number of different scales. Moreover, different clusters of traits seemed to relate to happiness and unhappiness. Fear, anger, and poor impulse control were related to unhappiness, whereas sociability, tempo, and vigor related to happiness. Thus, it appears that happiness and unhappiness represent different aspects of personality; they are not two sides of the same coin.

In the second study Costa and McCrae tested this idea. Specifically, they examined whether neuroticism was differentially related to unhappiness and whether extraversion was differentially related to happiness. Their suspicions were confirmed.

Having documented that different dimensions of personality influenced happiness and unhappiness, Costa and McCrae asked another question: Does this relationship hold over long periods of time, or is it limited to short-term mood changes? In the third study they compared scores on the personality tests administered 10 years earlier to current measures of happiness. They found that scores on the earlier personality tests accurately predicted current happiness or unhappiness.

This series of studies is representative of the careful research done by Costa and McCrae, which shows that personality is relatively stable over very long periods of time. It also should serve as a model of carefully thought-out, programmatic scientific inquiry.

---

come and go. Society changes, and economic ups and downs have important effects. Personal changes in appearance and health occur. People read volumes, see dozens of movies, and watch thousands of hours of television. But their underlying personality dispositions hardly change at all. Or do they?

Additional Longitudinal Studies of Dispositional Traits

Active to Passive Mastery

Neugarten and her colleagues (1964) provided some of the earliest findings based on interviews, projective tests, and questionnaires administered to a large, representative sample of adults between the ages of 40 and 80 over a 10-year span. They found that adaptational processes such as coping styles, life satisfaction, and strength of goal-oriented behavior remained stable. However, they also discovered a shift from *active mastery* to *passive mastery* among the men in their sample. Men at age 40 felt in control of their lives; they viewed risk taking positively and believed that they had considerable energy to tackle problems head-on. By age 60, however, men viewed their environment as harmful and threatening and themselves as accommodating.

The shift from active to passive mastery has been observed in several cultures, including the Navajo and the Lowland and the Highland Mayans of Mexico. Increasing age produces a tendency to accommodate the self to outside influences and a tendency for men and women to become more preoccupied with inner feelings, experiences, and cognitive processes. Gutmann (1978) argues that this increasing *interiority* reflects a normative shift in personality, and Neugarten (1973) points out that it is one of the best documented changes in personality across adulthood. Although interiority reflects many of the characteristics of introversion, it also indicates that older adults tend to decrease their attachments to the external world.

The Berkeley Studies

Researchers in Berkeley, California, conducted one of the largest longitudinal studies on personality development. In this investigation the parents of participants being studied in research on intellectual development were followed for roughly 30 years between ages 40 and 70 (Maas, 1985; Maas & Kuypers, 1974; Mussen, 1985). From the enormous amount of data gathered over the years, researchers were able to categorize men and women into subgroups based on their lifestyles (for instance, whether mothers were employed) and personality type. Based on the longitudinal follow-up data, gender differences were identified in terms of the best predictors of life satisfaction in old age. The data suggest that lifestyle during young adulthood is the better predictor of life satisfaction in old age for women but that personality is the better predictor for men (Mussen, 1985).

Additional analyses of the Berkeley data provide other insights into personality development. Haan examined data from Q-sorts, a technique in which an individual arranges descriptors of personality into piles varying in the extent to which they reflect oneself (Haan, 1976, 1981, 1985; Haan, Millsap, & Hartka, 1986). Six dimensions of personality were derived from the Q-sort approach: self-confident-victimized (degree of feeling comfortable with oneself and certain of acceptance by others); assertive-submissive (degree of direct and aggressive style of living); cognitively committed (degree of intellectual and achievement orientation); outgoing-aloof (degree of social enjoyment of others); dependable (degree of controlled productivity); and warm-hostile (degree of interpersonal giving and support) (Haan et al., 1986).

Haan and her colleagues found that orderly, positive progressions over time were observed for all the personality components except assertive-submissive. When Haan tried to explain these developmental patterns, however, she ran into difficulty. Accounts based on theories that examine other aspects of personality, such as those discussed later in this chapter, could not account for the results. Personality did not change in all areas simultaneously, nor was there evidence of change only during times of transitions. The observation of several gender differences, the nonlinear trends over time, and the lack of equal improvement in all components indicate that personality development is a complicated process. Haan and her colleagues argue that changes in personality probably stem from life-cycle experiences that may force a person to change. We will consider a stronger version of this view later in the chapter.

Critiques of the Five-Factor Model

Despite the impressive collection of research findings based on it, the five-factor model has its share of critics. Alwin (1994) points out that the evidence for stability reported by Costa and McCrae could be due to several quite different statistical functions other than an essentially flat line across adulthood that would allow for change in parts of the life span not studied by trait researchers. In a major review of the literature, Block (1995) raises several concerns with the Costa and McCrae approach. Most of Block's criticisms are based on perceived methodological problems, such as the way the dimensions were identified statistically and the way the questionnaire assessment was developed and used. This critique is based on the view that the statistical and empirical grounds on which the five-factor model is built is shaky. For example, Block argues that using laypeople to specify personality descriptors, the approach used to create the terms used in the five-factor model, is fraught with risk, chiefly due to the lack of any compelling scientific data to support such labeling. Thus, Block argues that the wide acceptance of the five-factor model is premature and that considerably more research needs to be done.

Additional limitations of the five-factor model were raised by McAdams (1992). He points out that any model of dispositional traits says nothing about the core or essential aspects of human nature. In contrast, theorists we will consider later, such as Erikson and Loevinger, do discuss such core aspects, which cannot be translated into the language of dispositional traits. Second, dispositional traits rarely provide enough information about people so that accurate predictions can be made about how they will behave in a particular situation. Third, the assessment of dispositional traits generally fails to provide causal explanations of human behavior. Fourth, dispositional traits ignore the sociocultural context of human development. Fifth, the assessment of dispositional traits reduces a person to a set of scores on a series of linear continua anchored by terms that are assumed to be both meaningful and opposite. Finally, the assessment of dispositional traits through questionnaires assumes that the respondent is able to take an objective, evaluative stance regarding his or her personal characteristics. McAdams's criticisms nevertheless reflect the view that assessing dispositional traits has its place in personality research; his point is simply that dispositional traits should not be viewed as reflecting one's entire personality.

As we might expect, the critiques themselves are controversial. For example, Costa and McCrae (1995) and Goldberg and Saucier (1995) point to flaws in Block's argument, such as his overlooking of research favorable to the five-factor model. Arguments about the place for assessing dispositional traits within the study of personality reflect the biases of the authors. The controversy surrounding Costa and McCrae's basic claim that dispositional traits typically remain stable in adulthood will continue, and it is likely to result in more, and even better, research.

Conclusions About Dispositional Traits

What can we conclude from the research on the development of personality traits across adulthood? On the surface it appears that we have conflicting evidence. On the one hand, we have a definition of traits that requires stability. Costa and McCrae, among others, argue strongly for this position; they report that there is little evidence (and perhaps possibility) of change. On the other hand, Neugarten and the Berkeley group argue for both change and stability. They say that at least some traits change, opening the door to personality development in adulthood. One partial resolution can be found if we consider how the research was done. Clearly, the overwhelming evidence supports the view that personality traits remain stable throughout adulthood when data are averaged across many different kinds of people. However, if we ask about specific aspects of personality in very specific kinds of people, we are more likely to find some evidence of both change and stability.

The recent critiques of the five-factor model have created a climate in which more careful scrutiny of research on dispositional traits is likely to occur. More sophisticated statistical techniques are likely to be applied in the future, which should help address many of the criticisms.

An important issue for future research is the role of life experiences. If a person experiences few events that induce him or her to change, then change is unlikely. In this view a person will be at 60 very much the same as he or she is at 30, all other factors being held constant. As we will see later, this idea has been incorporated formally into other theories of personality. On the basis of dispositional traits, then, we should have little difficulty knowing our high school classmates many years later.

Concept Checks

1. What are the five dimensions of the five-factor model?
2. What were the main findings from the active to passive mastery and the Berkeley studies?
3. What are the criticisms aimed at the five-factor model?
4. Are dispositional traits stable over time?

PERSONAL CONCERNS AND QUALITATIVE STAGES IN ADULTHOOD

Learning Objectives:

- What are personal concerns?
- What are the main elements of Jung's theory?
- What are the stages in Erikson's theory? What types of clarifications and extensions of it have

been offered? What research evidence is there to support his stages?
- What are the stages in Loevinger's theory? What evidence is there to support her stages?
- What are the main points and problems with theories based on life transitions?
- What can we conclude about personal concerns?

What does it mean to know another person well? McAdams (1994) believes that to know another person well takes more than just knowing where he or she falls on the dimensions of dispositional traits. Rather, it also means knowing what issues are important to a person, what the person wants, how the person goes about getting what he or she wants, what the person's plans for the future are, how the person interacts with others who provide key personal relationships, and so forth. In short, we need to know something about a person's personal concerns. Personal concerns reflect what people want during particular times of their lives and within specific domains; they are the strategies, plans, and defenses people use to get what they want and avoid getting what they don't want.

What's Different About Personal Concerns?

Recently, many researchers have begun analyzing personality in ways that are explicitly contextual, in contrast to work on dispositional traits, which ignores context. This recent work emphasizes the importance of sociocultural influences on development that shape people's wants and behaviors. For example, Thorne (1989; Thorne & Klohnen, 1993) showed that when people talk about themselves, they go well beyond speaking in dispositional trait terms. Rather, people provide more narrative descriptions that rely heavily on their life circumstances, that is, the sociocultural experiences they have had that shape their lives. Moreover, people are highly likely to describe developmentally linked concerns that change over time. Cantor (1990; Cantor & Harlow, 1994) highlighted this aspect of self-descriptions in differentiating between "having" traits and "doing" everyday behaviors that address the strivings, tasks, and goals that are important in everyday life. This latter aspect of personality emphasizes the importance of understanding culturally mandated, developmentally linked "life tasks" that reflect these changing concerns.

Although relatively little research has been conducted on the personal concerns level of personality, a few things are clear (McAdams, 1994). Personality constructs at this level are not reducible to traits. Rather, such constructs need to be viewed as conscious descriptions of what a person is trying to accomplish during a given period of life and what goals and goal-based concerns the person has. As Cantor (1990) notes, these constructs speak directly to the question of what people actually do in life. Moreover, we would expect that considerable change would be seen at this level of personality, given the importance of sociocultural influences and the changing nature of life tasks as people mature.

In contrast to the limited empirical data on the development of personal concerns, the theoretical base is arguably the richest. For the better part of a century, the notion that people's personality changes throughout the life span has been described in numerous ways, typically in theories that postulate qualitative stages that reflect the central concern of that period of life. In this section, we will consider several of these theories and evaluate the available evidence for each. Let's begin with the theory that got people thinking about personality change in midlife—Carl Jung's theory.

Jung's Theory

Jung represents a turning point in the history of psychoanalytic thought. Initially allied with Freud, he soon severed the tie and developed his own ideas, which have elements of both Freudian theory and humanistic psychology. He was one of the very first theorists to believe in personality development in adulthood; this marked a major break with Freudian thought, which argued that personality development ended in adolescence.

Jung's theory emphasizes that each aspect of a person's personality must be in balance with all of the others. This means that each part of the personality will be expressed in some way, whether through normal means or through neurotic symptoms or in dreams. Jung asserts that the parts of the personality are organized in such a way as to produce two basic orientations of the ego. One of these orientations is concerned with the external world; Jung labels it extraversion. The opposite orientation, toward the inner world of subjective experiences, is labeled introversion. To be psychologically healthy, both of these orientations must be present, and they must be balanced. Individuals must be able to deal with the external world effectively and also be able to evaluate their inner feelings and values. It is when people overemphasize one orientation or the other that they are classified as extraverts or introverts.

Jung advocates two important age-related trends in personality development. The first relates to the introversion-extraversion distinction. Young adults are more extraverted than older adults, perhaps because of younger people's needs to find a mate, have a career, and so forth. With increasing age, however, the need for balance creates a need to focus inward and explore personal feelings about aging and mortality. Thus, Jung argued that with age comes an increase in introversion.

The second age-related trend in Jung's theory involves the feminine and masculine aspects of our personalities. Each of us has elements of both masculinity and femininity. In young adulthood, however, most of us express only one of them while usually working hard to suppress the other. In other words, young adults most often act in accordance with gender-role stereotypes appropriate to their culture. As they grow older, people begin to allow the suppressed parts of their personality out. This means that men begin to behave in ways that earlier in life they would have considered feminine, and women behave in ways that they formerly would have thought masculine. These changes achieve a better balance that allows men and women to deal more effectively with their individual needs rather than being driven by socially defined stereotypes. This balance, however, does not mean a reversal of sex roles. On the contrary, it represents the expression of aspects of ourselves that have been there all along but that we have simply not allowed to be shown. We will return to this issue at the end of the chapter when we consider gender-role development.

Jung stretched traditional psychoanalytic theory to new limits by postulating continued development across adulthood. Other theorists took Jung's lead and argued not only that personality development occurred in adulthood but also that it did so in an orderly sequential fashion. We will consider the sequences developed by two theorists, Erik Erikson and Jane Loevinger.

Erikson's Stages of Psychosocial Development

The best-known life-span theorist is Erik Erikson (1982). According to him, personality is determined by the interaction between an inner maturational plan and external societal demands. He proposes that the life cycle comprises eight stages of development, summarized in Table 8.1. The sequence of stages is thought to be biologically fixed.

Each stage in Erikson's theory is marked by a struggle between two opposing tendencies, both of which are experienced by the person. The names of the stages reflect the issues that form the struggles. The struggles are resolved through an interactive process involving both the inner psychological and the outer social influences. Successful resolutions establish the basic areas of psychosocial strength; unsuccessful resolutions impair ego development in a particular area and adversely affect the resolution of future struggles. Thus, each stage in Erikson's theory represents a kind of crisis.

The sequence of stages in Erikson's theory is based on the *epigenetic principle*, which means that each psychosocial strength has its own special time of ascendancy, or period of particular importance. The eight stages represent the order of this ascendancy. Because the stages extend across the whole life span, it takes a lifetime to acquire all of the psychosocial strengths. Moreover, Erikson realizes that present and future behavior must have its roots in the past, because later stages build on the foundation laid in previous ones.

TABLE 8.1 Summary of Erikson's theory of psychosocial development, with important relationships and psychosocial strengths acquired at each stage

Stage	Psychosocial Crisis	Significant Relations	Basic Strengths
1 Infancy	Basic trust versus basic mistrust	Maternal person	Hope
2 Early childhood	Autonomy versus shame and doubt	Parental persons	Will
3 Play age	Initiative versus guilt	Basic family	Purpose
4 School age	Industry versus inferiority	"Neighborhood," school	Competence
5 Adolescence	Indentity versus identity confusion	Peer groups and outgroups; models of leadership	Fidelity
6 Young adulthood	Intimacy versus isolation	Partners in friendship, sex, competition, cooperation	Love
7 Adulthood	Generativity versus stagnation	Divided labor and shared household	Care
8 Old age	Integrity versus despair	"Mankind," "my kind"	Wisdom

Source: Erikson, 1982

Erikson argues that the basic aspect of a healthy personality is a sense of trust toward oneself and others. Thus, the first stage in his theory involves *trust versus mistrust,* representing the conflict that an infant faces in developing trust in a world it knows little about. With trust come feelings of security and comfort.

The second stage, *autonomy versus shame and doubt,* reflects children's budding understanding that they are in charge of their own actions. This understanding changes them from totally reactive beings to ones who can act on the world intentionally. Their autonomy is threatened, however, by their inclinations to avoid responsibility for their actions and to go back to the security of the first stage.

In the third stage the conflict is *initiative versus guilt.* Once children realize that they can act on the world and are somebody, they begin to discover who they are. They take advantage of wider experience to explore the environment on their own, to ask many questions about the world, and to imagine possibilities about themselves.

The fourth stage is marked by children's increasing interest in interacting with peers, their need for acceptance, and their need to develop competencies. Erikson views these needs as representing *industry versus inferiority,* which is manifested behaviorally in children's desire to accomplish tasks by working hard. Failure to succeed in developing self-perceived competencies results in feelings of inferiority.

During adolescence, Erikson believes, we deal with the issue of *identity versus identity confusion.* The choice we make, that is, the identity we form, is not so much who we are but, rather, whom we can become. The struggle in adolescence is choosing from among a multitude of possible selves the one we will become. Identity confusion results when we are torn over the possibilities. The struggle involves trying to balance our need to choose a possible self and the desire to try out many possible selves.

During young adulthood the major developmental task, *intimacy versus isolation,* involves establishing a fully intimate relationship with another. Erikson (1968) argues that intimacy means the sharing of all aspects of oneself without fearing the loss of identity. If intimacy is not achieved, isolation results. One way to assist the development of intimacy is to choose a mate who represents the ideal of all one's past experiences. The

Reminiscing with the help of photographs from one's past is one way that people review their lives.

psychosocial strength that emerges from the intimacy-isolation struggle is love.

With the advent of middle age the focus shifts from intimacy to concern for the next generation, expressed as *generativity versus stagnation*. The struggle occurs between a sense of generativity (the feeling that people must maintain and perpetuate society) and a sense of stagnation (the feeling of self-absorption). Generativity is seen in such things as parenthood, teaching, or providing goods and services for the benefit of society. If the challenge of generativity is accepted, the development of trust in the next generation is facilitated, and the psychosocial strength of care is obtained.

In old age individuals must resolve the struggle between *ego integrity and despair*. This last stage begins with a growing awareness of the nearness of the end of life, but it is actually completed by only a small number of people (Erikson, 1982). The task is to examine and evaluate one's life and accomplishments and to verify that it has meaning. This process often involves reminiscing with others and actively seeking reassurance that one has accomplished something in life. People who have progressed successfully through earlier stages of life face old age enthusiastically and feel that their life has been full. Those feeling a sense of meaninglessness do not anxiously anticipate old age, and they experience despair. The psychosocial strength achieved from a successful resolution of this struggle is wisdom. Integrity is not the only issue facing older adults; Erikson points out that they have many opportunities for generativity as well. Older people often play an active role as grandparents, for example, and many maintain part-time jobs.

Clarifications and Expansions of Erikson's Theory

Erikson's theory has had a major impact on thinking about life-span development. However, some aspects of his theory are unclear, poorly defined, or unspecified. Traditionally, these problems have led critics to dismiss the theory as untestable and incomplete. The situation is changing, however. Other theorists have tried to address these problems by identifying common themes, specifying underlying mental processes, and reinterpreting and integrating the theory with other ideas. These ideas are leading researchers to reassess the utility of Erikson's theory as a guide for research on adult personality development.

Logan (1986) points out that Erikson's theory can be considered as a cycle that repeats: from basic trust to identity and from identity to integrity. In this approach the developmental progression is trust → achievement → wholeness. Throughout life we first establish that we can trust ourselves and other people. Initially, trust involves learning about ourselves and others, represented by the first two stages (trust versus mistrust and autonomy versus shame and doubt). The recapitulation of this idea in the second cycle is seen in our struggle to find a person with whom we can form a very close relationship yet not lose our own sense of self (intimacy versus isolation). Additionally, Logan shows how achievement—our need to accomplish and to be recognized for it—is a theme throughout Erikson's theory. During childhood this idea is reflected in the two stages initiative versus guilt and industry versus inferiority, whereas in adulthood it is represented by generativity versus stagnation. Finally, Logan points out that the issue of understanding ourselves as worthwhile and whole is first encountered during adolescence (identity versus identity confusion) and is reexperienced during old age (integrity versus despair). Logan's analysis emphasizes that psychosocial development, although complicated on the surface, may actually reflect only a small number of issues. Moreover, he points out that we do not come to a single resolution of these issues of trust, achievement, and wholeness. Rather, they are issues that we struggle with our entire lives.

One aspect of Erikson's theory that is not specified is the rules that govern the sequence in which issues are faced. That is, Erikson does not make clear why certain issues are dealt with early in development and others are delayed. Moreover, how transitions from one stage to the next happen is also not fully explained. Van Geert (1987) proposes a set of rules that fills in these gaps. He argues that the sequence of stages is guided by three developmental trends. First, an inward orientation to the self gradually replaces an outward orientation to the world. This trend is similar to Jung's increase in introversion with age. Second, we move from using very general categories in understanding the world to using more specific ones. This trend is reflected in cognitive development, in that our earliest categories do not allow the separation of individual differences (for example, we use *dog* to mean all sorts of animals). Third, we move from operating with limited ideas of social and emotional experiences to more inclusive ideas. During childhood we may love only those people we believe are deserving, for example, whereas in adulthood we may love all people as representatives of humanity. By combining these three developmental trends, van Geert constructs rules for moving from one stage to another.

Although van Geert's approach has not been tested completely, his ideas fit with Erikson's theory and with other related data. For example, Neugarten (1977) points to an increase in interiority with age across adulthood, an idea very similar to van Geert's inward orientation. Cognitive developmental research (see Chapter 7) supports the development of more refined conceptual categories. Thus, van Geert's approach may be quite useful in understanding psychosocial development as well as in providing a way to identify the cyclic progression described by Logan.

Viney (1987) shows how other approaches to human development can add to Erikson's theory. As an example, she points to the sociophenomenological approach, which emphasizes that people change in how they interpret and reinterpret events. That is, the meaning of major life events changes from earlier to later in the life span. In a study that examined individuals between the ages of 6 and 86, she documented that the positive and negative descriptors that people used to characterize their lives changed considerably. Interestingly, these shifts in descriptors appear to parallel Erikson's stages. For example, adults over age 65 are more likely to talk about trying to get their lives in order or feeling completely alone than are adults under age 65. Although Viney's research was not intended to be a direct test of Erikson's theory, her results indicate that we may be able to document his stages in research based on different approaches to development. Additionally, Viney's research may indicate that the themes identified by Erikson are applicable to many situations, including the way in which we view events.

Finally, some critics argue that Erikson's stage of generativity is much too broad to capture the essence of adulthood. For example, Kotre (1984) contends that adults experience many opportunities to express generativity that are not equivalent and do not lead to a general state. Rather, he sees generativity more as a set of impulses felt at different times in different settings, such as at work or in grandparenting. More formally, Kotre describes five types of generativity: ***biological and parental generativity,*** which concerns raising children; ***technical generativity,*** which relates to the passing of specific skills from one generation to another; ***cultural generativity,*** which refers to being a mentor (as discussed in more detail in Chapter 11); *agentic generativity,* which refers to the desire to be or to do something that transcends death; and *communal generativity,* which represents a person's participation in a mutual, interpersonal reality. Only rarely, Kotre contends, is there a continuous state of generativity in adulthood. He asserts that the struggles identified by Erikson are not fought constantly; rather, they probably come and go. We will examine this idea in more detail a bit later in the next section.

Finally, Hamachek (1990) provided behavioral and attitudinal descriptors of Erikson's last three stages. These descriptors are meant to create a series of continua of possibilities for individual development. This reflects the fact that few people have an exclusive orientation to either intimacy or isolation, for example, but more commonly show some combination of the two. These behavioral and attitudinal descriptors provide a framework for researchers who need to operationalize Erikson's concepts.

Research on Generativity

Perhaps the central period in adulthood from an Eriksonian perspective is the stage of generativity versus stagnation. Most research on adults based on Erikson's theory has focused on this stage, as have many of the expansions of the theory (e.g., Kotre, 1984). One recent empirically based effort to describe generativity in more precise terms is the work by McAdams and de St. Aubin (1992; de St. Aubin & McAdams, 1995). They view generativity as a multidimensional construct involving seven interrelated components: social demand, belief in self and species, generative concerns, desires, commitments, behaviors, and personal narration. These seven aspects are uniquely organized in each person. Although they can be expressed by adults of all ages, certain types of generativity are more common at some ages than others. For example, middle-aged and older adults show a greater preoccupation with generativity themes than do younger adults in their accounts of personally meaningful life experiences, and middle-aged adults have made more generative commitments (e.g., "save enough money for my daughter to go to medical school"), reflecting a major difference in the inner and outer worlds of middle-aged and older adults as opposed to younger adults (McAdams, de St. Aubin, & Logan, 1993).

McAdams and de St. Aubin (1992; de St. Aubin & McAdams, 1995) showed that generative concern, defined as a general personality tendency of interest in caring for younger individuals, and generative action, defined as the actual behaviors that promote the well-being of the next generation, related differently to dispositional traits. For example, generative concern is consistently related to life satisfaction and overall happiness, whereas generative action, which sometimes entails getting immersed in the messiness of interpersonal relationships, is not directly connected with life satisfaction or happiness. The difference is that generative concern has to do with the *meaning* one derives from caring for younger individuals, whereas generative action concerns dealing with the hassles of caring. For example, new parents may derive considerable meaning from the birth of a child and show high generative concern; they are less enthusiastic about the lack of sleep they get when performing the necessary nighttime feedings as a generative action.

Similar research focusing specifically on middle-aged women yields comparable results. Peterson and Klohnen (1995) examined generativity from the viewpoint of personality characteristics, work productivity, parental involvement, health concerns, and political interests in separate samples of Mills College and Radcliffe College alumnae who were in their early to mid-40s. They found that generative women have prosocial personality characteristics, express generative attitudes through their work, are personally invested in being a parent, and exhibit caring behaviors toward others outside of their immediate families.

These data demonstrate that the personal concerns of middle-aged adults are fundamentally different than those of younger adults. Moreover, these concerns are not consistently or uniformly related to dispositional traits. Considered together, these findings provide considerable support for Erikson's contention that the central concerns for adults change with age. However, the

TABLE 8.2 Summary of Loevinger's stages of ego development in adulthood

Stage	Description
Conformist	Obedience to external social rules
Conscientious-conformist	Separation of norms and goals; realization that acts affect others
Conscientious	Beginning of self-evaluated standards
Individualistic	Recognition that the process of acting is more important than the outcome
Autonomous	Respect for each person's individuality; tolerance for ambiguity
Integrated	Resolution of inner conflicts

data also indicate that generativity is much more complex than Erikson originally proposed and may not diminish in late life.

Loevinger's Theory

Loevinger (1976) saw a need to extend the groundwork laid by Erikson both theoretically and empirically. For her, the ego is the chief organizer: the integrator of our morals, values, goals, and thought processes. Because this integration performed by the ego is so complex and is influenced by personal experiences, it is the primary source of individual differences at all ages beyond infancy. Ego development is the result of dynamic interaction between the person and the environment. Consequently, it consists of fundamental changes in the ways in which our thoughts, values, morals, and goals are organized. Transitions from one stage to another depend on both internal biological changes and external social changes to which the person must adapt.

Although Loevinger proposes eight stages of ego development, beginning in infancy, we will focus on the six that are observed in adults (see Table 8.2). An important aspect of her theory is that most people never go through all of them; indeed, the last level is achieved by only a handful of individuals. There is growing cross-sectional and longitudinal evidence that these stages are age related (Cook-Greuter, 1990; Redmore & Loevinger, 1979). At each stage Loevinger identifies four areas that she considers important to the developmental progression: character development (reflecting a person's standards and goals); interpersonal style (representing the person's pattern of relations with others); conscious preoccupations (reflecting the most important things on the person's mind); and cognitive style (reflecting the characteristic way in which the person thinks). As we consider the ego levels important for adults, we will examine them in terms of these four areas.

A few adults operate at the *conformist* level. Character development at this stage is marked by absolute conformity to social rules. If these rules are broken, feelings of shame and guilt result. Interpersonally, conformists need to belong and show a superficial niceness. Of central importance is appearance and social acceptability. Conformists see the world only in terms of external tangibles, such as how one looks and if one behaves according to group standards. Thinking is dominated by stereotypes and clichés and is relatively simplistic.

Most adults in American society operate at the *conscientious-conformist* level. At this stage character development is marked by a differentiation of norms and goals; in other words, people learn to separate what they want for themselves from what social norms may dictate. People deal with others by recognizing that they have an impact on them and on the group as a whole. People at this level begin to be concerned with issues of personal adjustment and coping with problems; they need reasons for actions and recognize that life presents many opportunities from which they may choose. They are still concerned with group standards, and the desire for personal adjustment is sometimes suppressed if it conflicts with the needs of the group.

The next level, the *conscientious* stage, is marked by a cognitive style in which individuals begin to understand the true complexity of the world. People at this stage focus on understanding the role that the self plays; character development involves self-evaluated standards, self-critical thinking, self-determined ideals, and self-set goals. This level represents a shift away from letting other people or society set their goals and standards for them. Interpersonal relations are characterized by intensity, responsibility, and mutual sharing. People evaluate behavior using internalized standards developed over the years. They come to realize that they control their own future. Although more complex, conscientious people still think in terms of polarities, such as love versus lust or inner life versus outer appearance. But they recognize responsibility and obligation in addition to rights and privileges.

Loevinger postulates that the *individualistic* level builds on the previous (conscientious) level. A major acquisition at the individualistic level is a respect for individuality. Immature dependency is seen as an emotional problem, rather than as something to be expected. Concern for broad social problems and differentiating one's inner life from one's outer life become the main preoccupations. People begin to differentiate process (the way things are done) from outcome (the answer); for example, people realize that sometimes the solution to a problem is right but the way of getting there involves hurting someone. The flavor of the individualistic person is an increased tolerance for oneself and others. Key conflicts are recognized as complex problems: dependence as constraining versus dependence as emotionally rewarding, and morality and responsibility versus achievement for oneself. The way of resolving these conflicts, however, usually involves projecting the cause onto the environment rather than acknowledging their internal sources.

Being committed to broad social concerns is the essence of Loevinger's individualist phase of ego development.

At Loevinger's *autonomous* level comes a high tolerance for ambiguity with conflicting needs both within oneself and others. Autonomous individuals' interpersonal style is characterized by a respect for each person's independence but also by an understanding that people are interdependent. The preoccupations at this level are vividly conveyed feelings, self-fulfillment, and understanding of the self in a social context. Autonomous people have the courage to acknowledge and face conflict head-on rather than projecting it onto the environment. They see reality as complex and multifaceted and no longer view it in the polarities of the conscientious stage. Autonomous individuals recognize that problems can be viewed in multiple ways and are comfortable with the fact that other people's viewpoints may differ from their own. They recognize the need for others' self-sufficiency and take a broad view of life.

The final level in Loevinger's theory is termed

the *integrated* stage. Inner conflicts are not only faced but also reconciled and laid to rest. Goals that are recognized to be unattainable are renounced. People at the integrated level cherish an individuality that comes from a consolidated sense of identity. They are very much like Maslow's (1968) self-actualized person; that is, they are at peace with themselves and have realized their maximum potential. They recognize that they could have chosen other paths in life but are content with and make the most out of the one that they picked. Such people are always open to further growth-enhancing opportunities and make the most out of integrating new experiences into their lives.

Loevinger has spent decades developing the Sentence Completion Test, which provides a measure of ego development. The measure consists of sentence fragments (similar to "When I think of myself I ______") that respondents complete. Responses are then scored in terms of the ego developmental level they represent. Although it is a difficult instrument to learn how to use, the Sentence Completion Test has very good reliability. Trained coders have high rates of agreement in rating responses, often over 90% of the time.

Loevinger's theory is having an increasing impact on adult developmental research. One of its advantages is that because of the Sentence Completion Test it is more empirically based than Erikson's theory, so that researchers can document the stages more precisely. Loevinger's theory is the major framework for research examining relationships between cognitive development and ego development (King, Kitchener, Wood, & Davison, 1989). For example, Blanchard-Fields (1986) found ego level was the best predictor of young and middle-aged adults' reasoning on social dilemma tasks, such as what to do about an unwanted pregnancy. Likewise, Labouvie-Vief, Hakim-Larson, and Hobart (1987) reported that ego level was a strong predictor of the coping strategies used across the life span from childhood to old age. Both studies documented age-related increases in ego level that were associated with higher levels of problem-solving ability or with more mature coping styles.

Theories Based on Life Transitions

Jung's belief in a midlife crisis, Erikson's belief that personality development proceeds in stages, and Loevinger's notion that cognitive and ego development are mutually interactive laid the foundation for other theorists' efforts. To get a flavor of what these theorists did, take a moment to think about your own life, as suggested in Something to Think About.

For many laypeople, the idea that adults go through an orderly sequence of stages that includes both crises and stability reflects their own experience. This is probably why books such as Sheehy's *Passages* (1976), *Pathfinders* (1981), and *New Passages* (1995) are met with instant acceptance, or why Levinson's (Levinson, Darrow, Kline, Levinson, & McKee, 1978) and Vaillant's work (Vaillant, 1977; Vaillant & Vaillant, 1990) has been applied to everything from basic personality development to understanding how men's occupational careers change. A universal assumption of these theories is that people go through predictable crises that are age related. Some life transition theories (e.g., Levinson's) also propose that these crises are followed by periods of relative stability. The overall view is that adulthood consists of a series of alternating periods of stability and change.

Compared with the theories we have considered to this point, however, theories based on life transitions are built on shakier ground. For example, some are based on small, highly selective samples (such as men who attended Harvard) or surveys completed by readers of particular magazines. This is in contrast, for example, to Loevinger's large database obtained with well-researched, psychometrically sound measures. Thus, the research methods used in studies of life transitions lead one to question the validity of their findings.

An important question about life transition theories is the extent to which they are real and actually occur to everyone. Life transition theories typically present stages as if they are universally experienced by everyone. Moreover, many have specific ages tied to specific stages (such as, age 30

SOMETHING TO THINK ABOUT

The Personal Side of Stage Theories

Studying stage theories generally makes us wonder how we stand. Evaluating our own ego development and other aspects of personality can be both fun and humbling. It can be fun in the sense that learning something about oneself is enjoyable and enlightening; it can be humbling in the sense that we may have overestimated how advanced we really are. There is another side to this personal evaluation, though, that is equally important.

Take a few moments and think back perhaps 5 or 10 years. What things were important to you? How well did you know yourself? What were your priorities? What did you see yourself becoming in the future? What were your relationships with other people based on? Now answer these questions from your perspective today.

If you are like most people, answering these questions will make you see the ways in which you have changed. Many times we are in the worst position to see this change, because we are embedded in it. We also find ourselves reinterpreting the past based on the experiences we have had in the meantime.

The focus of the stage theories we have considered is the change in the ways that we see ourselves. We do look at the world differently as we grow older. Our priorities do change. Take a few moments now and jot down how you have changed over the years since high school. Then write down how you see yourself now. Finally, write down how you would like to see your life go in the future. These ideas will give you something to think about now and again later when we consider Whitbourne's ideas about scenarios and life stories.

---

or age 50 transitions). As we know from cognitive developmental research in Chapter 7, however, this is a very tenuous assumption. Individual variation is the rule, not the exception. What actually happens may be a combination of expectations and socialization. For example, Dunn and Merriam (1995) examined data from a large, diverse national sample and found that less than 20% of people in their early 30s experienced the Age Thirty Transition that forms a cornerstone of Levinson and colleagues' (1978) theory. The experience of a midlife crisis, discussed next, is an excellent case in point.

In Search of the Midlife Crisis

One of the most important ideas in theories based on life transitions is that middle-aged adults experience a personal crisis that results in major changes in how they view themselves. During a midlife crisis, people are supposed to take a good hard look at themselves and, they hope, attain a much better understanding of who they are. Difficult issues such as one's own mortality and inevitable aging are supposed to be faced. Behavioral changes are supposed to occur; we even have stereotypic images of the middle-aged male running off with a much younger female as a result of his midlife crisis.

Some research seems to document the crisis. Jaques (1965) reported that male artists went through a crisis precipitated by the recognition of their own mortality. Time since birth was replaced by time left to live in the minds of these middle-aged men. Levinson and his colleagues (1978) write that middle-aged men in his study reported intense internal struggles that were much like depression.

However, far more research fails to document the existence of a particularly difficult time in midlife. Baruch (1984) summarizes a series of retrospective interview studies of American women between the ages of 35 and 55. The results showed that women in their 20s were more likely to be uncertain and dissatisfied than were women at midlife. Middle-aged women only rarely mentioned normative developmental milestones such as marriage, childbirth, or menopause as major turning points in their lives. Rather, unexpected events such as divorce and job transfers were more likely to cause crises. Studies extending Levinson's theory to women have not found strong evidence of a traumatic midlife crisis either (Harris, Ellicott, & Holmes, 1986; Reinke, Holmes, & Harris, 1985; Roberts & Newton, 1987).

The midlife crisis was also missing in data obtained as part of the Berkeley studies of personality traits. Most middle-aged men said that their careers were satisfying (Clausen, 1981), and both men and women appeared more self-confident, insightful, introspective, open, and better equipped to handle stressful situations (Haan, 1985; Haan et al., 1986). Even direct attempts to find the midlife crisis failed. In two studies Costa and McCrae (1978) could identify only a handful of men who fit the profile, and even then the crisis came anytime between 30 and 60. A replication and extension of this work, conducted by Farrell and Rosenberg (1981), confirmed the initial results.

McCrae and Costa (1984) point out that the idea of a midlife crisis became widely accepted as fact due to the mass media. People take it for granted that they will go through a period of intense psychological turmoil in their 40s. The problem is that there is little hard scientific evidence of it. The data suggest that midlife is no more or no less traumatic for most people than any other period in life. Perhaps the most convincing support for this conclusion comes from Farrell and Rosenberg's (1981) research. These investigators initially set out to prove the existence of a midlife crisis, as they were firm believers in it. After extensive testing and interviewing, however, they emerged as nonbelievers.

Perhaps the best way to view midlife is as a time of both gains and losses (Lachman, Lewkowicz, Marcus, & Peng, 1994). That is, the changes people perceive in midlife can be viewed as representing both gains and losses—competence, ability to handle stress, sense of personal control, purpose in life, and social responsibility are all at their peak, whereas physical abilities, women's ability to bear children, and physical appearance are examples of changes many view as negative. This gain-loss view emphasizes two things. First, the exact timing of change is not fixed but occurs over an extended period of time. Second, change can be both positive and negative at the same time. Thus, rather than seeing midlife as a time of crisis, one may want to view it as a period during which several aspects of one's life acquire new meanings.

Conclusions About Personal Concerns

Based on the theories and research evidence we have considered, substantive change in adults' personal concerns definitely occurs as people age. This conclusion is in sharp contrast to the stability observed in dispositional traits, but does support McAdams's (1994) contention that this middle level of personality should show some change. What is also clear, however, is that a tight connection between such change and specific ages is not supported by the bulk of the data. Rather, change appears to occur in wide windows of time depending on many factors, including one's sociocultural context. Finally, more research is needed in this area, especially investigations that provide longitudinal evidence of change within individuals.

Concept Checks

1. What do we mean by the term *personal concerns*?
2. What happens in midlife according to Jung?
3. What are Erikson's eight stages?
4. What are the main points in Loevinger's theory?
5. What is the principal problem with theories based on life transitions?
6. Do personal concerns change across adulthood?

LIFE NARRATIVES, IDENTITY, AND THE SELF

Learning Objectives:

- What are the main aspects of McAdams's life-story model?
- What are the main points of Whitbourne's identity theory?

- What developmental aspects are there in self-concept and possible selves?
- How does religiosity factor into adult development?
- How does gender-role identity develop in adulthood?
- What conclusions can be drawn from research using life narratives?

Who are you? What kind of person are you trying to become? Answering these questions requires concepts of personality that go beyond dispositional traits and personal concerns. The aspects of personality we have discussed thus far are important, but they lack a sense of integration, unity, coherence, and overall purpose (McAdams, 1994). For example, understanding a person's goals (from the level of personal concerns) does not reveal who a person is trying to be, or what kind of person the person is trying to create. What is lacking in other levels of analysis is a sense of the person's identity or sense of self.

In contrast to Erikson's (1982) proposition that identity formation is the central task of adolescence, many researchers are now coming to understand the important ways in which identity and the creation of the self continue to develop throughout adulthood (e.g., Hermans, Kempen, & Van Loon, 1992). This emerging field of how adults continue constructing identity and the self relies on life narratives, or the internalized and evolving story that integrates a person's reconstructed past, perceived present, and anticipated future into a coherent and vitalizing life myth (McAdams, 1994). Careful analysis of people's life narratives provides insight into their identity.

In this section, we will consider two evolving theories of identity. Dan McAdams is concerned with understanding how people see themselves and how they fit into the adult world. Susan Krauss Whitbourne investigated people's own conceptions of the life course and how they differ from age norms and the expectations for society as a whole. To round out our understanding of identity and the self, we will also examine related constructs. Before beginning, though, take time to complete the exercise in the Discovering Development feature. It will give you a sense of what a life narrative is and how it might be used to gain insight into identity and the sense of self.

McAdams's Life-Story Model

McAdams (1993, 1994) argues that a person's sense of identity cannot be understood using the language of dispositional traits or personal concerns. It is not just a collection of traits, nor is it a collection of plans, strategies, or goals. Instead, it is based on a story of how the person came into being, where the person has been, where he or she is going, and who he or she will become. McAdams argues that people create a *life story* that is an internalized narrative with a beginning, a middle, and an anticipated ending. The life story is created and revised throughout adulthood as people change and the changing environment places different demands on them.

McAdams's (1993) research indicates that people in Western society begin forming their life story in late adolescence and early adulthood, but it has its roots in the development of one's earliest attachments in infancy. According to McAdams, each life story contains seven essential features: narrative tone, image, theme, ideological setting, nuclear episodes, character, and ending.

The *narrative tone* of a person's identity is the emotional feel of the story, ranging from bleak pessimism, conveyed through tragedy and irony, to blithe optimism, conveyed through comic and romantic descriptions. A life story's unique *imagery* consists of the characteristic sights, sounds, emotionally charged pictures, symbols, metaphors, and the like that a person incorporates. The *themes* are recurrent patterns of motivational content, reflected in terms of the person repeatedly trying to attain his or her goals over time. The two most common themes are agency (reflecting power, achievement, and autonomy) and communion (reflecting love, intimacy, and belongingness). The life story's *ideological setting* is the backdrop of beliefs and values, or the ideology, a person uses to set the context for his or her actions.

Every life story contains certain *nuclear episodes*

DISCOVERING DEVELOPMENT

Who Do You Want to Be When You "Grow Up"?

From the time you were a child, people have posed this question to you. In childhood, you probably answered by indicating some specific career, such as firefighter or teacher. But now that you are an adult, the question takes on new meaning. Rather than simply a matter of picking a profession, the question goes much deeper to the kinds of values and the essence of the person you would like to become.

Take a few minutes and think about who you would like to be in another decade or two (or maybe even 50 years hence). What things will matter to you? What will you be doing? What experiences will you have had? What lies ahead?

This exercise will give you a sense of the way in which researchers try to understand people's sense of identity and self through the use of personal narrative. You might even keep what you have written, and check it when the appropriate number of years have elapsed.

---

of key scenes involving symbolic high points, low points, and turning points. These episodes provide insight into scenes involving perceived change and continuity in life. People prove to themselves and others that they have either changed or remained the same by pointing to specific events that support the appropriate claim. The main *characters* in people's lives represent idealizations of the self, such as "the dutiful mother" or "the reliable worker." Integrating these various aspects of the self is a major challenge of midlife and later adulthood. Finally, all life stories need an *ending* through which the self is able to leave a legacy that creates new beginnings. Life stories in middle-aged and older adults have a clear quality of "giving birth to" a new generation, a notion essentially identical to generativity.

McAdams (1994) believes that the model for change in identity over time is a process of fashioning and refashioning one's life story. This process appears to be strongly influenced by culture. At times, the reformulation may be at a conscious level, such as when people make explicit decisions about changing careers. At other times, the revision process is unconscious and implicit, growing out of everyday activities. The goal is to create a life story that is coherent, credible, open to new possibilities, richly differentiated, reconciling of opposite aspects of oneself, and integrated within one's sociocultural context (McAdams, 1993, 1994).

Whitbourne's Identity Theory

A second and related approach to understanding identity formation in adulthood is Whitbourne's (1987) idea that people build their own conceptions of how their lives should proceed. **The result of this process is the *life-span construct,* the person's unified sense of the past, present, and future.**

There are many influences on the development of a life-span construct: identity, values, and social context are a few. Together, they shape the life-span construct and the ways in which it is manifested. The life-span construct has two structural components, which in turn are the ways in which it is manifested. The first of these components is the *scenario,* which consists of expectations about the future. The scenario translates aspects of our identity that are particularly important at a specific point into a plan for the future. The scenario is strongly influenced by age norms that define key transition points; for example, graduating from college is a transition that is normally associated with the early 20s. In short, a scenario is a game plan for how we want our lives to go.

Joan, a typical college sophomore, may have the following scenario: She expects that her course of study in nursing will be difficult but that she will finish on time. She hopes to meet a nice guy along the way whom she will marry shortly after gradu-

Young adulthood is a time when one's life story is first constructed. These new doctoral degree recipients are likely in the midst of this process.

ation. She imagines that she will get a good job at a major medical center that will offer her good opportunities for advancement. She and her husband will probably have a child, but she expects to keep working. Because she feels that she will want to advance, she assumes that at some point she will obtain a master's degree. In the more distant future she hopes to be a department head and to be well-respected for her administrative skills.

Tagging certain expected events with a particular age or time by which we expect to complete them creates a social clock (see Chapter 1). Joan will use her scenario to evaluate her progress toward her goals. With each major transition she will check how she is doing against where her scenario says she should be. If it turns out that she has achieved her goals earlier than she expected, she will be proud of being ahead of the game. If things work out more slowly than she planned, she may chastise herself for being slow. If she begins to criticize herself a great deal, she may end up changing her scenario altogether; for example, if she does not get a good job and makes no progress, she may change her scenario to one that says she should stay home with her child.

As Joan starts moving into the positions laid out in her scenario, she begins to create the second component of her life-span construct, her *life story*. The life story is a personal narrative history that organizes past events into a coherent sequence. The life story gives events personal meaning and a sense of continuity; it becomes our autobiography. Because the life story is what we tell others when they ask about our past, it eventually becomes somewhat overrehearsed and stylized. An interesting aspect of the life story, and autobiographical memory in general, is that distortions will occur with time and retelling (Neisser & Winograd, 1988). In life stories, distortions allow the person to feel that he or she was on time, rather than off time, in terms of past events in the scenario. In this way people feel better about their plans and goals and are less likely to feel a sense of failure.

Whitbourne (1986) conducted a fascinating cross-sectional study of 94 adults ranging in age from 24 to 61. They came from all walks of life and

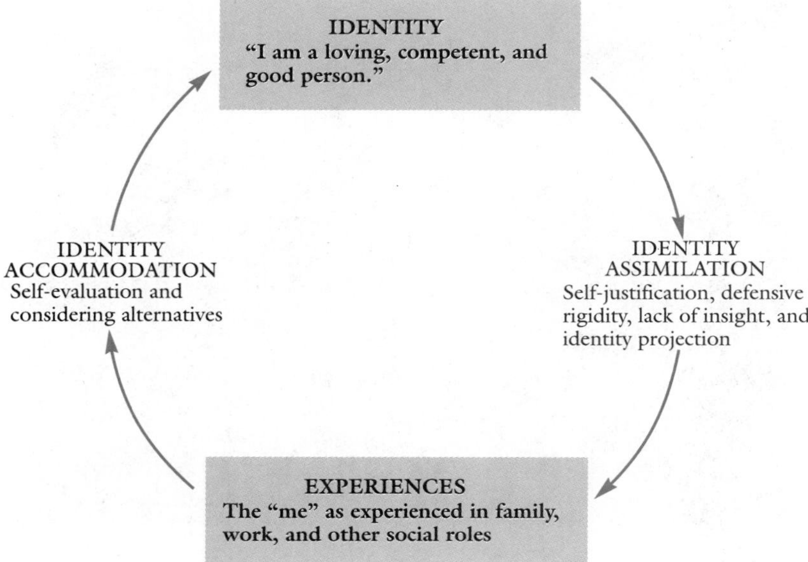

Figure 8.1 Whitbourne's model of adult identity processes
Source: Whitbourne, 1986

represented a wide range of occupations and life situations. Using data from very detailed interviews, Whitbourne was able to identify what she believes is the process of adult identity development based on an equilibrium between identity and experience. Her model is presented in Figure 8.1.

As can be seen, the processes of equilibrium are based on Piaget's concepts of assimilation and accommodation (see Chapter 7). Whitbourne has explicitly attempted to integrate concepts from cognitive development with identity development to understand how identity is formed and revised across adulthood. The assimilation process involves using already existing aspects of identity to handle present situations. Overreliance on assimilation makes the person resistant to change. Accommodation, on the other hand, reflects the willingness of the individual to let the situation determine what he or she will do. This often occurs when the person does not have a well-developed identity around a certain issue.

Not surprisingly, Whitbourne (1986) found that the vast majority of adults listed family as the most important aspect of their lives. Clearly, adults' identity as loving constitutes the major part of the answer to the question "Who am I?" Consequently, a major theme in adults' identity development is trying to refine their belief that "I am a loving person." Much of this development is in acquiring and refining deep, emotional relationships.

A second major source of identity for Whitbourne's participants was work. In this case the key seemed to be keeping work interesting. As long as individuals had an interesting occupation that enabled them to become personally invested, their work identity was more central to their overall personal identity. This is a topic we will pursue in Chapter 11.

Although Whitbourne found evidence of life transitions, she found no evidence that these transitions occurred in a stagelike fashion or were tied to specific ages. Rather, she found that people tended to experience transitions when they felt they needed to and to do so on their own time line. More recently, Whitbourne (1996a) has developed the Identity and Experiences Scale–General to measure identity processes in adults. Her model has been expanded to incorporate how people adapt more generally to the aging process (Whitbourne, 1996b). This scale assesses an individual's use of assimilation and accommodation in forming identity in a general sense, and is based on her earlier work (Whitbourne, 1986). Results thus far are promising, in that the scale reliably differentiates individuals with an assimilative style from those with an accommodative style. Additionally, identity style appears to be different than one's coping style, indicating that both are necessary in order to understand how adults deal with events in their lives.

Self-Concept and Possible Selves

As we have seen, two important aspects of identity in adulthood is how one integrates various aspects of the self and how one sees oneself in the future. Self-perceptions and how they differ with age have been examined in a wide variety of studies and have been shown to be related to many behaviors. Changes in self-perceptions are often manifested in changed beliefs, concerns, and expectations. ***Self-concept* is the organized, coherent, integrated pattern of self-perceptions.** It includes the notions of self-esteem and self-image.

Kegan (1982) attempted to integrate the development of self-concept and cognitive development. He postulated six stages of the development of self, corresponding to stages of cognitive development described in Chapter 7. Kegan's first three stages—which he calls incorporative, impulsive, and imperial—correspond to Piaget's sensorimotor, preoperational, and concrete operational stages (see Chapter 7). During this time, he believes, children move from knowing themselves on the basis of reflexes to knowing themselves through needs and interests. At the beginning of formal operational thought during early adolescence (see Chapter 7), he argues, a sense of interpersonal mutuality begins to develop; he terms this period the interpersonal stage. By late adolescence or young adulthood, individuals move to a mature sense of identity based on taking control of their own life and developing an ideology; Kegan calls this period the institutional stage. Finally, with the acquisition of postformal thought (see Chapter 7) comes an understanding that the self is a very complex system that takes into account other people; Kegan terms this period the interindividual stage. Kegan's (1982) work emphasizes the fact that personality development does not occur in a vacuum. Rather, we must not forget that the person is a complex integrated whole. Consequently, an understanding of the development of self-concept or any other aspect of personality is enhanced by an understanding of how it relates to other dimensions of development.

This point was clearly demonstrated by Labouvie-Vief and colleagues (Labouvie-Vief, Chiodo, Goguen, Diehl, & Orwoll, 1995). Working within a cognitive-developmental framework, they documented age differences in self-representation in people ranging in age from 11 to 85 years. Specifically, they found that mature adults move from representations of the self in young adulthood that are relatively poorly differentiated from others or from social conventions and expectations to representations in middle age that were highly differentiated to representations in old age that were less differentiated. An important finding was that the degree of differentiation in self-representation was related to the level of cognitive development, providing support for Kegan's position.

In one of the few longitudinal studies of self-concept, Mortimer, Finch, and Kumka (1982) followed a group of men for 14 years, beginning when the participants were college freshmen. They found that self-image consisted of four dimensions: well-being, interpersonal qualities, activity, and unconventionality. Well-being included self-perceptions concerning happiness, lack of tension, and confidence. Interpersonal qualities referred to self-perceptions concerning sociability, interest in others, openness, and warmth. The activity component consisted of self-perceptions of strength, competence, success, and activity. The unconventionality dimension indicated that men saw themselves as impulsive, unconventional, and dreamy. Clearly, what Mortimer and colleagues found concerning self-image is very closely related to Costa and McCrae's model of personality, described earlier in this chapter.

Over the 14-year period the men in the Mortimer study showed little change as a group. The structure of self-concept remained stable. Some fluctuation at the level of self-image was noted, though. Both well-being and competence declined during college but rebounded after graduation. Self-perceptions of unconventionality declined after college. Sociability showed a steady decline across the entire study.

At the intraindividual level, the data indicated that self-perceptions of confidence were related to life events. The course of a man's career, his satisfaction with career and marriage, his relationship with his parents, and his overall life satisfaction followed patterns that could be predicted by competence. For example, men whose competence scores remained above the group average experienced few problems related to their jobs and had higher marital and life satisfaction than men whose competence scores were below the group average.

Interestingly, a man's degree of confidence as a college senior influenced his later evaluation of life events, and it may have even set the stage for a self-fulfilling prophecy. Mortimer and colleagues suggest that these men may actively seek and create experiences that fit their personality structure. This hypothesis is supported by longitudinal research on gifted women, whose high self-confidence in early adulthood becomes manifested as a high life satisfaction during their 60s (Sears & Barbee, 1978).

The results from the Mortimer, Finch, and Kumka (1982) study are strikingly similar to the data from the Berkeley studies described earlier in this chapter. Recall that data from these studies also support the idea that life events are important influences on personality development. In the present case, life events clearly influence one's self-concept. We will consider in the next section how adults explain why certain things or certain events happen to them.

Possible Selves

One important aspect of self-concept consists of ideas about different people we could become. **In particular, we have aspects of self-concept representing what we could become, what we would like to become, and what we are afraid of becoming; together, these aspects are called *possible selves*** (Markus & Nurius, 1986). What we could or would like to become often reflects personal goals; we may see ourself as a leader, as rich and famous, or as in shape. What we are afraid of becoming may show up in our fear of being undervalued, or overweight, or lonely. Our possible selves are very powerful motivators; indeed, much of our behavior can be viewed as efforts to approach or avoid these various possible selves and to protect the current view of self (Markus & Nurius, 1986).

The topic of possible selves offers a way to understand how both stability and change operate in adults' personality. On the one hand, possible selves tend to remain stable for at least some period of time and are measurable with psychometrically sound scales (for example, Ryff, 1991). On the other hand, possible selves may change in response to efforts at personal growth (Cross & Markus, 1991), which would be expected from ego development theory. In particular, possible selves facilitate adaptation to new roles across the life span. For example, a full-time mother who pictures herself as an executive once her child goes to school may begin to take evening courses to acquire new skills. Thus, possible selves offer a way to bridge the experience of the current self and our imagined future self.

Researchers have begun studying age differences in the construction of possible selves. Cross and Markus (1991) asked people aged 18 to 86 to describe their hoped-for and feared possible selves. Responses were grouped into categories (such as family, personal, material). Several interesting age differences emerged. In terms of hoped-for selves,

18- to 24-year-olds listed family concerns most often (for instance, marrying the right person). In contrast, 25- to 39-year-olds listed family concerns last; their main issues concerned personal things (such as being a more loving and caring person). By ages 40 to 59, family issues again became most common (such as being a parent who can "let go" of his or her children). For 60- to 86-year-olds, personal issues were most prominent (for example, being able to be active and healthy for another decade at least).

All age groups listed physical issues as their most frequent feared self. For the two younger groups, being overweight and, for women, becoming wrinkled and unattractive when old were commonly mentioned. For the middle-aged and older adult groups, fear of having Alzheimer's disease or being unable to care for oneself were frequent responses.

Overall, adolescents and young adults were far more likely to have multiple possible selves and to believe more strongly that they could actually become the hoped-for self and successfully avoid the feared self. By old age, though, both the number and strength of belief had diminished. Older adults were more likely to believe that both the hoped-for and feared selves were not under their personal control. These findings may reflect differences with age in personal motivation, beliefs in personal control, and the need to explore new options.

In a fascinating series of studies, Ryff (1991) adopted the notion of possible selves as a way to redefine the meaning of well-being in adulthood and showed how adults' views of themselves are different at various points in adulthood. Based on the responses of hundreds of adults, Ryff (1989, 1991) identified six dimensions of psychological well-being for adults and discovered many important age and gender differences in well-being based on these components:

- *Self-acceptance:* having a positive view of oneself; acknowledging and accepting the multiple parts of oneself; and feeling positive about one's past;
- *Positive relation with others:* having warm, satisfying relationships with people; being concerned with their welfare; being empathic, affectionate, and intimate with them; and understanding the reciprocity of relationships;
- *Autonomy:* being independent and determining one's own life; being able to resist social pressures to think or behave in a particular way; evaluating one's life by internal standards;
- *Environmental mastery:* being able to manipulate, control, and effectively use resources and opportunities;
- *Purpose in life:* having goals in life and a sense of direction in one's life; feeling that one's present and past life has meaning; having a reason for living;
- *Personal growth:* feeling a need for continued personal improvement; seeing oneself as getting better and being open to new experiences; growing in self-knowledge and personal effectiveness.

One important discovery from Ryff's research is that young, middle-aged, and older adults have very different views of themselves depending on whether they are describing their present, past, future, or ideal self-perceptions. Examples of these differences for self-acceptance and autonomy are shown in Figure 8.2. As can be seen, young and middle-aged adults are much more accepting of their ideal and future selves than they are of their present and past selves. For older adults, the differences are smaller. As Ryff (1991) notes, only by including all of these self-ratings will we understand people's sense of personal progress or decline over time from their goal of ideal functioning. Clearly, people judge themselves by many standards, and these differ with age.

But perhaps the most interesting findings concern the difference between people's ideal vision of themselves and what they thought they were really like. A careful look at the graphs will show that the differences between the ideal-self ratings and the present-self ratings diminish with age. This finding implies that older adults see themselves as closer to really being the person they wanted to become than does any other age group. Ryff's data fit well with Erikson's (1982) idea of integrity. As people

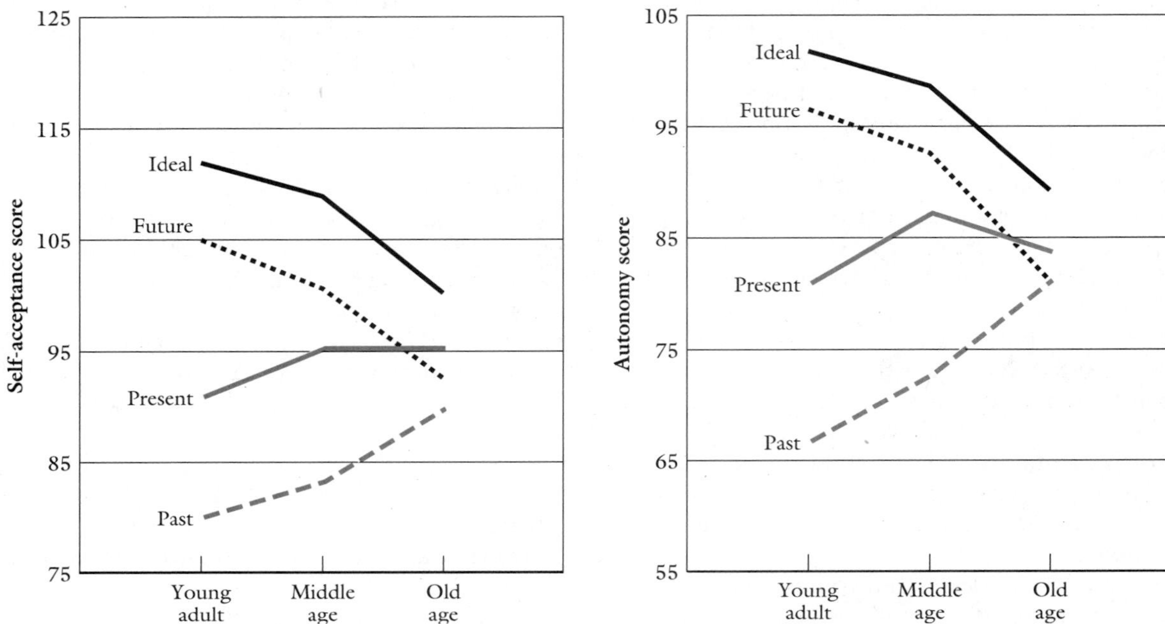

Figure 8.2 Age differences in self-acceptance scores and autonomy scores in young, middle-aged, and older adults.
Source: Ryff, 1991

achieve integrity, they view their past less critically and become content with how they have lived their lives.

Taken together, the work on possible selves is opening new and exciting avenues for personality research. Possible selves offers a way to examine the importance of personal perception in determining motivation to achieve and change, as well as a way to study personality systematically with sound research methods. Because it provides an interesting bridge between different approaches to personality theory, it will likely be the focus of much research in the future.

Religiosity

For many adults, the relationship they have with God is a key aspect of their identity. For example, Krause (1995) reports that feelings of self-worth are lowest for those older adults with very little religious commitment. Research consistently finds that in many cases older adults use their religious faith more than anything else, including reliance on family or friends, when they must deal with problems. When asked to describe their most frequent ways of dealing with problems in life, nearly half of the people surveyed (45%) in one study listed coping strategies associated with religion (Koenig, George, & Siegler, 1988). Of these, the most frequently used were placing trust in God, praying, and getting strength and help from God.

Reliance on religion in times of stress appears especially important for African Americans, who as a group are intensely involved in religious activities (Levin & Taylor, 1993). Churches offer considerable social support for the African American community and serve an important function for the advocacy of social justice (Roberts, 1980). For example, the civil rights movement in the 1950s and 1960s was led by Dr. Martin Luther King, Jr., a Baptist minister, and contemporary congregations advocate for equal rights for all. The role of the church in African Americans' lives is central; indeed, one of the key predictors of life satisfaction among African Americans is regular church attendance (Coke, 1992).

Within the African American community, religion is especially important to women. The greater importance of the church in the lives of older African American women is supported by results from four national surveys of African American adults (Levin, Taylor, & Chatters, 1994). They are more active in church groups and attend services more frequently than African American men or either European American men or women. However, the gender differences diminish in the people over age 70, indicating that religion becomes more important for older African American men.

Older persons of Mexican heritage adopt a different approach. Research indicates that they use *la fé de la gente* ("the faith of the people") as a coping strategy (Villa & Jaime, 1993). The notion of *fé* incorporates varying degrees of faith, spirituality, hope, cultural values, and beliefs. *Fé* does not necessarily imply that people identify with a specific religious community. Rather, they identify with a cultural value or ideology.

Among Native Americans, the spiritual elders are the wisdomkeepers, the repositories of the scared ways and natural world philosophies that extend indefinitely back in time (Wall & Arden, 1990). The wisdomkeepers also share dreams and visions, perform healing ceremonies, and may make apocalyptic prophecies. The place of the wisdomkeepers in the tribe is much more central than religious leaders in Western society.

Service providers would be well advised to keep the self-reported importance of religion in the lives of many older adults in mind when designing interventions to help them adapt to life stressors. For example, older adults may be more willing to talk with their minister about a personal problem than they would be to talk with a psychotherapist; when they seek help from a professional, it is more often with their family physician. However, when working with people of Mexican heritage, providers need to realize that a major source of distress for this group is lack of familial interaction and support. Overall, many churches offer a wide range of programs to assist poor or homebound older adults in the community. Such programs may be more palatable to recipients than ones based in social service agencies. Nevertheless, to be successful service providers need to view life as their clients see it.

Gender-Role Identity

Another critical aspect of identity concerns people's gender-role identity. What we consider to be appropriate personality characteristics for women and men reflect shared cultural beliefs of what is considered prototypically masculine and feminine styles (Williams & Best, 1990). In U.S. society, women are traditionally described as weaker, less active, and more concerned with affiliation, nurturance, and deference. Men are regarded as stronger, more active, and higher in autonomy, achievement, and aggression (Huyck, 1990). In addition, there are also gender-age stereotypes (Gutmann, 1987). Old men are seen as less stereotypically masculine or warriorlike and more as powerful elderly men striving for peace. Old women tend to be viewed as matriarchs overseeing extended families or as evil witches who use power malevolently. Some cultures view older adults as genderless, having lost the need for differentiated gender-role identity after they concluded their child-rearing duties (Gailey, 1987).

Evidence from several studies indicates that changes occur in the statements adults of different ages endorse about masculinity and femininity. In general, these findings show a tendency for older men and women to endorse similar self-descriptions. For example, data from the Berkeley studies document a move toward greater similarity between older men and older women. Haan (1985; Haan et al., 1986) and Livson (1981) found that both men and women described themselves as more nurturant, intimate, and tender with age. Gutmann (1987), Sinnott (1986), and Turner (1982) reported similar findings. Overall, the data from these studies indicate that men and women appear most different in late adolescence and young adulthood and become increasingly similar in late-middle and old age (Huyck, 1990).

Longitudinal data on individual development is largely lacking. What evidence is available suggests that a majority (54%) of people remain in the same gender-role category over a 10-year period (Hyde, Krajnik, & Skuldt-Niederberger, 1991). However, this still means that a substantial number of people demonstrate change. As Hyde and co-workers (1991) note, however, we currently have no way of predicting who will change and who will not.

The move toward gender-role identity similarity may not always be apparent at the behavioral level. Although older men often indicate a greater willingness to develop close relationships, for example, few actually have the skills to do so (Turner, 1982). Troll and Bengtson (1982) argue that the change is more internal than external and tends to involve feelings about dependence and autonomy. Moreover, they point out that much of the change may be due to the failing health of elderly men. Because older wives tend to be healthier than their husbands, the balance of power may shift out of necessity to wives, and men may be forced to accept a more dependent role.

Whether the changes in self-assessments of gender-role identity reflect true changes in underlying personality traits is debatable. The lack of consistent behavioral evidence and the statistically small differences in some of the self-assessment data lead some authors to argue that no changes in personality occur (for example, Costa & McCrae, 1980b). In contrast, others see the convergence in self-assessments as evidence that older men and women transcend stereotypes to become essentially gender free (Sinnott, 1986). Still others view any change in self-assessment, no matter how small, as at least personally relevant (Gutmann, 1987).

It will be interesting to see whether the trend toward similarity continues over the next few generations. Changes in how younger men and women view themselves as a result of women's new roles in society may shift the trend downward in age or may make it disappear altogether. As noted in Chapters 1 and 10, gender is one way that societies stratify themselves. Whether changes in self-report have any bearing on true behavioral change is something that only time will tell.

Conclusions About Narratives, Identity, and the Self

We have seen that to fully understand a person, we must consider how the individual integrates his or her life into a coherent structure. The life-narrative approach provides a way to learn how people accomplish this integration. The theoretical frameworks developed by McAdams and by Whitbourne offer excellent avenues for research. One of the most promising new areas of inquiry, possible selves, is already providing major insights into how people construct future elements of their life stories.

When combined with the data from the dispositional trait and personal concerns literatures, research findings on identity and the self provide the capstone knowledge needed to understand what people are like. The complexity of personality is clear from this discussion; perhaps that is why it takes a lifetime to complete.

Concept Checks

1. What is a life story as defined in McAdams's theory?
2. What connection is there between Whitbourne's theory of identity and Piaget's theory of cognitive development?
3. What are possible selves?
4. How does religiosity factor into identity?
5. How does gender-role identity develop in adulthood?
6. Does the sense of identity and self change in adulthood?

SOCIAL COGNITION

Learning Objectives:

- What are causal attributions and what age differences have been noted?
- What is personal control and what age differences have been found?

Throughout this book we have emphasized that all aspects of human development take place within particular sociocultural contexts; indeed, the sociocultural factor is one of the basic influences on development. Personality is no exception. As mentioned earlier in this chapter, sociocultural influences on personality are important. Equally important is the level of intellectual development one has achieved, especially for understanding how one thinks of oneself. For example, we considered Kegan's theory, which takes context into account by integrating personality development with cognitive development. McAdams' and Whitbourne's work on life stories also makes clear the importance of one's social context. The projections one makes are clearly influenced by one's earlier experiences, and cognitive developmental level, as how one constructs a life story, should vary across levels. With these discussions serving as background, the stage is set for us to consider in more detail how thinking and personality intersect.

One of the fastest growing areas of research in adult development and aging is *social cognition,* which focuses on the linkages between life-tasks and goals, representations of the self and others, cognitive strategies, and outcomes related to adjustment and functioning (Blanchard-Fields & Abeles, 1996). The majority of the research has examined the content and structure of people's understanding of social reality and the cognitive processes involved in accessing such social information. Social cognition research also focuses on the functional importance of social representations for actual behaviors and on how and to what end people access and use information under particular kinds of social situational demands.

Our discussion will focus on two specific aspects of social cognition: causal attributions and personal control. Each has a relatively long history of research in nondevelopmental domains, and each provides insights into the interface between cognition and personality.

Causal Attributions

Suppose a student performs extremely well on the exam covering this chapter. What caused his or her good performance? Was it something the student did? Or was it due to some other reason, such as luck or chance? **Answers to these questions provide insights into the explanations people construct to explain their behavior, which are referred to as *causal attributions.***

For many years, we have known that college students typically produce informational distortions when making causal attributions about problem solving (e.g., Nisbett & Ross, 1980). However, the life experience accumulated by middle-aged and older adults may result in such people reaching different conclusions about why things happen the way they do.

In a series of creative investigations, Blanchard-Fields (1994; Blanchard-Fields & Norris, 1994) studied the differences in causal attributions across the adult life span. Blanchard-Fields (1994) presented participants with different situations having positive or negative outcomes and asked them to decide whether the main character in the story (dispositional attributions), the situation (situational attributions), or a combination of both (interactive attributions) was responsible for the event. When the target events were ambiguous, all adults tended to make interactive attributions, but older adults did so at a higher rate. However, older adults blamed the main character more than younger groups, especially in negative relationship situations. When the main character was more involved, all adults made more dispositional attributions. Older adults made more interactive attributions when the events involved interpersonal relationships, whereas younger adults made more interactive attributions for ambiguous events involving personal achievement.

In a subsequent study, Blanchard-Fields and Norris (1994) examined the connection between cognitive level (e.g., absolutist, relativistic, and dialectical thinking) and attributions. They found that middle-aged adults scored higher on dialectical attributional reasoning (considering dispositional and situational factors in relation to each other, mutually determined, and co-defined) than adolescents, young adults, or older adults. Blanchard-Fields and Norris took a sociocultural perspective in explaining why older adults were more predisposed to making dispositional attributions and engaged in less dialectical reasoning in negative relationship situations. Thus, older adults appeared to apply specific social schemas to the task that were particularly salient, apparently due to their stage in life and the cohort in which they were socialized.

These findings indicate that the explanations people create to account for behavior vary depending on the type of situation and the age of the person. What is also emerging is the importance of the sociocultural context in which people are socialized, as this appears to create different social schemas that are then used to make causal attributions. More research is needed to shed additional light on how these age differences are created and under what circumstances they appear.

Personal Control

Suppose a student does not perform on the exam as well as he or she thought. Was it the student's own fault? Or was the exam too picky? How we answer such questions sheds light on how we tend to explain, or attribute, our behavior. The study of attributions is one of the major areas in social psychology and is the topic of numerous theories. Among the most important ways in which we analyze the cause of events is in terms of who or what is in control in a specific situation. ***Personal control* is the degree to which one believes that one's performance in a situation depends on something that one personally does.** A high sense of personal control implies a belief that performance is up to you, whereas a low sense of personal control implies that your performance is under the influence of forces other than your own.

Personal control has become an extremely important idea in a wide variety of settings (Baltes & Baltes, 1986). For example, it is thought to play a role in memory performance (see Chapter 6), in intelligence (see Chapter 7), in depression (see Chapter 9), and in adjustment to and survival in institutions (see Chapter 12). Despite this range of research, however, we do not have a clear picture of developmental trends in people's sense of personal control.

Most of the research on personal control has been conducted using a locus-of-control framework. Locus of control refers to who or what one thinks is responsible for performance. Traditionally, researchers use the label *internal* to describe people who take personal responsibility and the label *external* to describe people who believe that others (or chance) are responsible. Evidence from both cross-sectional studies (Gatz & Siegler, 1981; Ryckman & Malikioski, 1975) and longitudinal studies (Lachman, 1985; Siegler & Gatz, 1985) is contradictory. Some find that older adults are more likely to be internal than younger adults, whereas others find older adults more likely to be external than younger adults.

Lachman (1986) argues that a major reason for the conflicting findings is the multidimensionality of personal control. Specifically, she shows that one's sense of control depends on which domain, such as intelligence or health, is being assessed. Moreover, she demonstrates that older adults often acknowledge the importance of outside influences on their behavior but still believe that what they do matters.

Indeed, Brandtstädter (1989) clearly showed that the developmental patterns of personal control vary considerably from one domain to another. For example, perceived control over one's development shows an overall age-related decrease. However, perceived marital support shows an age-related increase. In a subsequent study, Brandtstädter and Rothermund (1994) found a high degree of stability over 8 years in middle-aged adults' general sense of control. They also examined the effects of perceptions of control within 17 specific life goal domains (e.g., family security, emotional stability, and self-development) on general perceptions of control. The degree to which self-perceptions of control within a particular goal domain affects general sense of control depends on the personal importance of that domain. Additionally, losses of control within a goal domain affect general perceptions of control to a lesser degree if the importance of the goal declines over time.

Based on this research, Brandtstädter and Greve (1994) propose that the preservation and stabilization of a positive view of the self and personal development in later life involve three interdependent processes. First, people engage in activities that prevent or alleviate losses in domains that are personally relevant for self-esteem and identity. For example, people might use memory aids more if having a good memory is an important aspect of self-esteem and identity. Second, people make accommodative changes and readjust their goals and aspirations as a way to lessen or neutralize the effects of negative self-evaluations in key domains. For instance, if a person notices that the time it takes to walk a mile at a brisk pace has increased, then the target time could be increased to help lessen the impact of feelings of failure. Third, people use immunizing mechanisms that alter the effects of self-discrepant evidence. In this case, a person who is confronted with evidence that his or her memory performance has declined could look for alternative explanations or simply deny the evidence.

Brandtstädter and Greve (1994) are not without their critics, however. For example, Carstensen and Freund (1994) question whether the losses people experience, though real, actually threaten the *self*. Additionally, these authors argue that age-related changes in goals could also be the result of movement through the life cycle, and not simply due to coping with blocked goals.

One's sense of personal control is a complex, multidimensional aspect of personality. Consequently, general normative age-related trends may not be found. Rather, changes in personal control may well depend on one's experiences in different domains and may differ widely from one domain to another.

Concept Checks

1. How do causal attributions differ with age?
2. What is personal control?

SUMMARY

Dispositional Traits Across Adulthood

The Five-Factor Model

Costa and McCrae's model has five components: neuroticism, extraversion, openness to experience, agreeableness-antagonism, and conscientiousness-undirectedness. Each of these dimensions has several descriptors. Research consistently shows little change on these dimensions across adulthood.

Additional Longitudinal Studies of Dispositional Traits

There appears to be a shift from active to passive mastery during adulthood. Evidence from the Berkeley studies shows that lifestyle is a better predictor of life satisfaction for women, but personality is a better predictor for men. Additional evidence found no support for a life crisis model or for a continual change model of personality development. Gender differences were also apparent.

Critiques of the Five-Factor Model

Several criticisms of the five-factor model have been made: several different statistical functions could account for the stability observed; the research may have methodological problems; dispositional traits do not describe the core aspects of human nature and do not provide good predictors of behavior; and dispositional traits do not consider the contextual aspects of development.

Conclusions About Dispositional Traits

The bulk of the evidence suggests that dispositional traits are relatively stable across adulthood, but there may be a few exceptions. Criticisms of the research point to the need for better statistical analyses and a determination of the role of life experiences.

Personal Concerns and Qualitative Stages in Adulthood

What's Different About Personal Concerns?

Personal concerns take into account a person's developmental context and distinguish between "having" traits and "doing" everyday behaviors. Personal concerns refer to descriptions of what people are trying to accomplish and the goals they create.

Jung's Theory

Jung emphasized various dimensions of personality (masculinity-femininity; extraversion-introversion). Jung argues that people move toward integrating these dimensions as they age, with midlife being an especially important period.

Erikson's Stages of Psychosocial Development

The sequence of Erikson's stages is trust versus mistrust, autonomy versus shame and doubt, initiative versus guilt, industry versus inferiority, identity versus identity confusion, intimacy versus isolation, generativity versus stagnation, and ego integrity versus despair. Erikson's theory can be seen as a trust-achievement-wholeness cycle repeating twice, although the exact transition mechanisms have not been clearly defined. Generativity has received more attention than other adult stages; Kotre described five types. Research indicates that generative concern and generative action can be found in all age groups of adults, but they are particularly apparent among middle-aged adults.

Loevinger's Theory

Loevinger proposed eight stages of ego development, six of which can occur in adulthood: conformist, conscientious-conformist, conscientious, individualistic, autonomous, and integrated. Most adults are at the conscientious-conformist level. Linkages to cognitive development are apparent.

Theories Based on Life Transitions

In general, life transition theories postulate periods of transition that alternate with periods of stability. These theories tend to overestimate the commonality of age-linked transitions. Research evidence suggests that crises tied to age 30 and to midlife do not occur to most people. However, most middle-aged people do point to both gains and losses, which could be viewed as change.

Conclusions About Personal Concerns

Theory and research both provide support for change in the personal concerns people report at various times in adulthood.

Life Narratives, Identity, and the Self

McAdams's Life-Story Model

McAdams argues that people create a life story that is an internalized narrative with a beginning, middle, and anticipated ending. He also describes seven essential features of a life story: narrative tone, image, theme, ideological setting, nuclear episodes, character, and ending. Adults reformulate their life stories throughout adulthood.

Whitbourne's Identity Theory

Whitbourne believes that people have a life-span construct: a unified sense of their past, present, and future. The components of the life-span construct are the scenario (expectations of the future) and the life story (a personal narrative history). She integrates the concepts of assimilation and accommodation from Piaget's theory to explain how people's identity changes over time. Family and work are two major sources of identity.

Self-Concept and Possible Selves

Self-concept is the organized, coherent, integrated pattern of self-perception. The events people experience help shape their self-concept. Self-presentation across adulthood is related to cognitive-developmental level. Self-concept tends to stay stable at the group mean level. Age differences in possible selves are more apparent in terms of hoped-for self than feared self. Although younger and middle-aged adults view themselves as improving, older adults view themselves as declining. The standards by which people judge themselves change over time.

Religiosity

Older adults use religion more often than any other strategy to help them cope with problems in life. This provides a strong influence on identity. Use of religion is especially true for African American women, who are more active in their church groups and attend services more frequently. Other ethnic groups also gain important aspects of identity from religion.

Gender-Role Identity

Evidence from several studies shows changes in the statements adults of different ages endorse about masculinity and femininity. The tendency is for older men and women to endorse similar statements, but whether this reflects underlying personality change is debatable.

Conclusions About Narratives, Identity, and the Self

The life narrative approach provides a way to learn how people integrate the various aspects of their personality. Possible selves, religiosity, and gender-role identity are important areas in need of additional research.

Social Cognition

Causal Attributions

Causal attributions are explanations people construct to explain their behavior. Age differences have been found in the conditions under which adults of various ages make dispositional attributions, situational attributions, and interactive attributions.

Personal Control

Personal control is the degree to which one believes that performance depends on something one does. Age differences in the degree of personal control depend on the domain being studied. Some evidence suggests that people develop several strategies concerning personal control to protect a positive self-image.

REVIEW QUESTIONS

Dispositional traits across adulthood

- What is a dispositional trait?
- Describe Costa and McCrae's five-factor model of personality. What are the descriptors in each dimension? How do these dimensions change across adulthood?
- What evidence is there in other longitudinal research for change in personality traits in adulthood? Under what conditions is there stability or change?
- What are the specific criticisms that have been raised concerning the five-factor model?
- What does most of the evidence say about the stability of dispositional traits across adulthood?

Personal concerns and qualitative stages in adulthood

- What is meant by a personal concern? How does it differ from a dispositional trait?
- Describe Jung's theory. What important developmental changes did he describe?
- Describe Erikson's eight stages of psychosocial development. What cycles have been identified? How has his theory been clarified and expanded? What types of generativity have been proposed? What evidence is there for generativity? What modifications to Erikson's theory has this research suggested?
- Describe Loevinger's theory of ego develop-

ment, with particular emphasis on the stages seen in adults.
- What are the major assumptions of theories based on life transitions? What evidence is there that a midlife crisis really exists? How can midlife be viewed from a gain-loss perspective?
- Overall, what evidence is there for change in personal concerns across adulthood?

Life narratives, identity, and the self
- What are the basic tenets of McAdams's life-story theory? What are the seven elements of a life story?
- What is Whitbourne's life-span construct? How does it relate to a scenario and a life story? How did Whitbourne incorporate Piagetian concepts into her theory of identity?
- What is self-concept? What shapes it?
- What are possible selves? What developmental trends have been found in possible selves?
- How is religiosity an important aspect of identity in older adults?
- How does gender-role identity develop across adulthood?

Social cognition
- What is a causal attribution? What types of attributions have been studied? How do attributions differ across age and type of event?
- What is meant by personal control? How does it differ over age?

INTEGRATING CONCEPTS IN DEVELOPMENT

1. What relations can be found among dispositional traits, personal concerns, and life narratives?
2. How does personality development reflect the four basic forces of development discussed in Chapter 1?
3. How does social cognition relate to postformal thought (Chapter 7)?
4. How does personal control relate to concepts such as memory self-efficacy discussed in Chapter 6?

KEY TERMS

causal attributions Explanations people construct to explain their behavior, which can be situational, dispositional, or interactive.

dispositional trait A relatively stable, enduring aspect of personality.

epigenetic principle In Erikson's theory, the notion that development is guided by an underlying plan in which certain issues have their own particular times of importance.

five-factor model A model of dispositional traits with the dimensions of neuroticism, extraversion, openness to experience, agreeableness-antagonism, and conscientiousness-undirectedness.

life narrative The aspects of personality that pull everything together, those integrative aspects that give a person an identity or sense of self.

life-span construct In Whitbourne's theory of identity, the way in which people build a view of who they are.

personal concerns Things that are important to people, their goals, and their major concerns in life.

personal control The belief that what one does has an influence on the outcome of an event.

possible selves Aspects of the self-concept involving oneself in the future in both positive and negative ways.

self-concept The organized, coherent, integrated pattern of self-perceptions.

IF YOU'D LIKE TO LEARN MORE

Erikson, E.H. (1982). *The life cycle completed: Review:* New York: Norton. Erikson's own summary of his theory that highlights adulthood. Moderately difficult reading.

McAdams, D.P. (1993). *The stories we live by: Personal myths and the making of the self.* New York: William Morrow. Fascinating reading that lays the groundwork for McAdams's theory of life narratives. Easy to moderate reading.

Whitbourne, S.K. (1986). *The me I know: A study of adult identity.* New York: Springer-Verlag. The general overview of Whitbourne's theory of identity from a cognitive perspective. Interesting reading that is easy to moderately difficult.

Wrightsman, L.S. (1988). *Personality development in adulthood.* Beverly Hills, CA: Sage Publications. General overviews of personality research and theories in adulthood. Easy to moderate reading.

CHAPTER 9

Mental Health and Intervention

Alberto Giacometti, *The Artist's Mother.* 1950. Oil on canvas, 35⅜″ × 24″. The Museum of Modern Art, New York. Acquired through the Lillie P. Bliss Bequest. Photograph © 1996 The Museum of Modern Art, New York.

Mary lived by herself for 30 years after her husband died.[1] For all but at last 5 years or so of this period, she managed very well. Her children, who live in various parts of the country, visited her occasionally. Friends down the street looked in on her and cooked meals on occasion. Little by little, though, family members began noticing that Mary wasn't quite right; for example, her memory slipped, she sounded confused sometimes, and her moods changed without warning. Some family members attributed these changes to the fact that she was in her 80s. But when they discovered that she sometimes forgot about things in the refrigerator and then ate them even though they had become moldy and that she occasionally ate other strange things, they began to think differently. The family ultimately realized that she could no longer care for herself and that help had to be found. She moved to a type of group home but continued to deteriorate. She started having trouble remembering things from even a few minutes before. Names of family members became mixed up at first, and later were forgotten. She began to wander. Finally, Mary had to leave the group home and be placed in a nursing home. The times when she was living in the present became fewer. Her physical abilities continued to deteriorate, until eventually she could not feed herself. Toward the end of her life she could not eat solid food and had to be force-fed. Mary died of Alzheimer's disease after more than 15 years of slow, agonizing decline.

Situations like this happen to families every day. Certainly, behavior like Mary's is not part of normal aging. But for families and even for professionals, realization does not occur until something very strange happens, and this realization often results in tumultuous family upheaval. Depending on the particular problem, it may mean deciding whether to institutionalize a spouse or a parent, another very difficult process.

This chapter is about the people who do not make it through adulthood to old age in the usual way. This minority of adults develop mental health difficulties that cause them problems in their daily lives and that sometimes rob them of their dignity. Two sets of disorders have received the most attention: depression and acute and chronic organic syndromes. However, increased attention is being paid to other problems, such as anxiety, personality disorders, and psychoses.

As we consider different types of mental disorders, we will note how each is diagnosed, what is known about causes, and what effective treatments are available. In the final section we will consider some therapeutic techniques used in community outpatient clinics, nursing homes, and other settings to try to provide the most supportive environment possible.

[1]This case is true, but the names have been changed to protect confidentiality.

MENTAL HEALTH AND THE ADULT LIFE COURSE

Learning Objectives:

- How are mental health and psychopathology defined?
- What are the key dimensions used for categorizing psychopathology?
- Why are ethnicity and aging important variables to consider in understanding mental health?

Problems like the ones just described are considered to be sufficiently different to most people to warrant the label "mental illness" or "mental disorder." **What distinguishes the study of mental disorders, or *psychopathology,* in adulthood and aging is not so much the content of the behavior as its context, that is, whether it interferes with daily functioning.** To understand psychopathology as it is manifested in adults of different ages, we must see how it fits into the life span developmental perspective outlined in Chapter 1.

Defining Mental Health and Psychopathology

The first issue confronting us in understanding psychopathology is how to define it. This is not easy. Most scholars avoid the issue entirely or try simply to say what mental health or psychopathology is not. What constitutes "normal" or "abnormal" behavior is hard to define precisely, because expectations and standards for behavior change over time, over situations, and across age groups (Birren & Renner, 1980). Thus, what is considered mental health depends on the circumstances under consideration. Birren and Renner (1980) summarize several arguments concerning the nature of mental health and argue that mentally healthy people have the following characteristics: (1) a positive attitude toward self, (2) an accurate perception of reality, (3) a mastery of the environment, (4) autonomy, (5) personality balance, and (6) growth and self-actualization.

Alternatively, we could consider behaviors that are harmful to oneself or others, that lower one's well-being, and that are perceived as distressing, disrupting, abnormal, or maladaptive (Fry, 1986). Although this approach is used frequently with younger or middle-aged adults, it presents problems when applied to older adults. Some behaviors that would be considered abnormal under this definition may actually be adaptive under some circumstances for many older people (such as isolation, passivity, aggressiveness) (Birren & Renner, 1979). Consequently, an approach to defining abnormal behavior that emphasizes the consideration of behaviors in isolation and from the perspective of younger or middle-aged adults is inadequate for defining abnormal behaviors in the elderly (Gurland, 1973). For example, because of physical, financial, social, health, or other reasons, some older adults do not have the opportunity to master their environment. Depression or hostility may be an appropriate and justified response to such limitations. Moreover, such responses may actually help them deal with their situation more effectively and adaptively.

The important point in differentiating normal from abnormal behavior (or mental health from mental illness) is that behaviors must be interpreted in context. In other words, we must consider what else is happening and how the behavior fits the situation in addition to such factors as the age and other personal characteristics of the individual.

A Multidimensional Approach to Psychopathology

Suppose two persons, one young and one old, came into your clinic, each complaining about a lack of sleep, changes in appetite, a lack of energy, and feeling down. What would you say to them?

If you evaluate them in identical ways, you might be headed for trouble. Just as we have seen in other chapters that older and younger adults may think differently or view themselves differently, the meaning of their symptoms and complaints may also differ, even though they appear to be the same. This point is not always incorporated into views of psychopathology. For example, some approaches assume that the same underlying cause is responsible for abnormal or maladaptive behavior regardless of age and that the symptoms of the mental disease are fairly constant across age. Although such models are often used in clinical diagnosis, they are inadequate for understanding psychopathology in old age. Viewing adults' behavior from a developmental forces perspective makes a big difference in how we approach psychopathology. Let's see why.

Interpersonal Factors

The nature of a person's relationships with other people, especially family members and friends, is a key dimension in understanding how psychopathology is manifested in adults of different ages. Important developmental differences occur in the interpersonal realm; for example, younger adults are more likely to be expanding their network of friends, whereas older adults are more likely to be experiencing losses. Thus, feelings of grief or sadness would be considered normal in older adults but might not be in younger adults (Parkes, 1972). Chapter 10 summarizes developmental changes in key relationships that may influence adults' interpretation of symptoms.

Intrapersonal Factors

Intrapersonal factors include variables such as age, gender, personality, and cognitive abilities. All of these variables influence the behaviors that people exhibit and affect our interpretation of them. For example, an older African American female who lives in a high-crime area may be highly suspicious of other people. To label her behavior paranoid may be inappropriate. In short, we must ask whether the behavior we see is appropriate for a person of this age, sex, personality type, ability level, and so forth in this specific context.

Biological and Physical Factors

Various chronic diseases, limitations on functioning, and other ailments can provide an explanation of behavior. Because health problems increase with age (see Chapters 3 and 4), we must be increasingly sensitive to them when dealing with older adults. In addition, genetic factors often underlie important problems in old age. For example, the evidence is growing that Alzheimer's disease has a genetic component. Physical problems may provide clues about underlying psychological difficulties; marked changes in appetite, for example, may be a symptom of depression. Moreover, some physical problems may even present themselves as psychological ones. For example, extreme irritability can be caused by thyroid problems, and memory loss can result from certain vitamin deficiencies. In any case, physical health and genetic factors are extremely important dimensions to take into account in diagnosing psychopathology in adults and should be among the first avenues explored.

Life-Cycle Factors

How one behaves at any point in adulthood is strongly affected by one's past experiences and the issues one is facing. These life-cycle factors must be taken into account in evaluating adults' behaviors. For example, a middle-aged woman who wants to go back to school may not have an adjustment disorder; she may simply want to develop a new aspect of herself. Likewise, an older man who provides vague answers to personal questions may not be resistant; he may simply be reflecting his generation's reluctance to disclose one's inner self to a stranger. Most important, the meaning of particular symptoms may change with age. For example, problems with early morning awakenings may indicate depression in a young adult, but may simply be a result of normal aging in an older adult (see Chapter 4).

Issues in Clinical Assessment

Identification of mental disorders rests on accurate evaluation and assessment. Psychologists have a myriad of tests and measures at their disposal for assessing adults' functioning. Such assessment is a major problem if the person is elderly, because virtually all of the tests and measures were developed for use with young and middle-aged adults (Fry, 1986; Zarit, Eiler & Hassinger, 1985). Very few tests have been standardized with the elderly, which means that we have little idea what a typical older adult would score, let alone one who is experiencing some problem.

Although the primary diagnostic guide—the *Diagnostic and Statistical Manual of Mental Disorders, Fourth Edition Revised (DSM-IV)* published by the American Psychiatric Association (1994)—does not provide different lists of symptoms for each disorder based on the age of the individual, it does view mental disorders as multidimensional. Specifically, *DSM-IV* is built on five axes that reflect the heterogeneity among people with the same disorder (LaBruzza, 1994). The first three "diagnostic" axes reflect traditional forms of psychopathology (Axis I), such as depression; personality disorders (Axis II); and general medical conditions that are relevant to the case (Axis III), such as cardiovascular disease. The remaining two "nondiagnostic" axes relate to psychosocial and environmental problems (Axis IV), such as economic or occupational problems, and a global assessment of the person's functioning (Axis V). Despite this approach, however, insufficient attention is paid to important age, gender, and ethnic group differences.

Allowances need to be made when assessing older adults. For example, they tend to report their problems in more global terms than younger adults, and they may tire more easily during the assessment session (Fry, 1986). Consequently, adhering to rigid time schedules, limited standardized instructions, and specific wordings of questions may be inappropriate and result in incorrect decisions.

Ethnicity, Aging, and Mental Health

As we encountered first in Chapter 1, and have seen elsewhere in the text, sociocultural influences are a major and typically overlooked factor in understanding people's behavior and developmental history. Mental health is no exception; in fact, it is vitally important that sociocultural influences be considered in evaluating people's behavior in this domain of functioning and in designing effective means of treating problems (Jackson, Antonucci, & Gibson, 1995). For example, by the time most people of color reach old age in the United States, they have experienced a lifetime of inadequate health care, greater exposure to environmental risks, and the stress of prejudice and discrimination (Jackson, 1993). Let's look more closely at the key issues.

In neither the general nor the ethnic populations do most people have mental disorders (Jackson et al., 1995). Still, very little is known about the nature and extent of the difficulties people do face in ethnic populations, especially for groups other than African Americans. Neither positive mental health nor psychopathology has been adequately defined in any group, and no current approach takes social context into account in such a way as to be sensitive to contextual differences in ethnic communities. For example, although many explanations of deviant and antisocial behavior are grounded in the oppressive life conditions that characterize many ethnic communities, the conceptualization of positive mental health for older ethnic individuals does not take the lifetime accumulation of such effects into account (Jackson et al., 1995). However, such sensitivity to conditions does not preclude the possibility of commonalities across ethnic groups in how people respond; indeed, identifying such commonalities would be an excellent place to start.

What little data we have suggest both similarities and differences in the incidence of specific types of psychopathology across different ethnic groups. Most epidemiological studies on the prevalence and incidence of mental disorders in young adults show little difference across ethnic groups (Jackson et al., 1995). However, a much more complex picture emerges when older adults are studied (Stanford and DuBois, 1992). For example, among Hispanic older adults, males show higher rates of alcohol abuse, whereas females have higher rates of phobia and panic disorders. Native American males also have high rates of alcohol abuse.

The complicated relations among age, ethnicity, and risk of developing a mental disorder merely emphasize the importance of including age and ethnicity in studies of psychopathology. Clearly, a life-course perspective that includes ethnicity would be the approach of choice. But even if such a framework were adopted, we would still be faced with another problem—appropriate assessment of functioning.

People have different ways of describing how they feel. Such differences are amplified by ethnic and cultural differences in what one is supposed to reveal to strangers about one's inner self. Placed in a context of important differences in social stressors, physical health, and age, assessment of mental health in older ethnic adults is a daunting task. Currently, there is disagreement in the literature over some key issues in this regard. For example, do ethnicity and social class alter the relation between chronic stressors and mental health? To what extent do social support, religiosity, and the family support system buffer people against stress differently across ethnic groups? Answers to these questions are difficult, as the few studies that address them provide inconclusive results (Jackson et al., 1995).

What can be done to determine the ways in which ethnicity influences mental health? Jackson et al. (1995) argue that researchers should adopt an ethnic research matrix that takes as its defining elements ethnicity, national origin, racial group membership, gender, social and economic statuses, age, acculturation, coping reactions, and mental health outcomes (e.g., psychopathology, positive

DISCOVERING DEVELOPMENT

Sociocultural Factors in Mental Health

In the text, we have seen the complex relations among age, ethnicity, economic status, and mental health. Despite the importance of these variables in understanding how people view mental health, surprisingly little research has been done on the topic.

To get a sense of the differences across various groups in the ways in which mental health is viewed, take the time to conduct the following project. Get several classmates to team up and talk with people from many different ethnic and economic class backgrounds. Ask them what they consider to be mentally healthy and mentally unhealthy behaviors in their environments. Focus especially on suspiciousness, fear, dependence, and other behaviors that could be viewed as either mentally healthy or indicative of a disorder, depending on the context. Make sure you talk with both men and women.

Bring your findings to class, where you should share them with your classmates. See if you can come up with a consensus view of different approaches to mental health. How would you go about assessing the various groups for mental disorders? What intervention or treatments would you create?

---

adjustment). Only by adopting this comprehensive approach will we be able to understand what, how, and when aspects of race, ethnicity, age, and the life course influence mental health. You can begin the process yourself by completing the exercise in the Discovering Development feature.

Concept Checks

1. How is psychopathology defined?
2. What are axes used in diagnosing psychopathology?
3. What is known about the role of ethnicity and aging in mental health?

DEPRESSION

Learning Objectives:
- What are the most common characteristics of people with depression?
- How is depression diagnosed?
- What causes depression?
- How is depression treated?
- What is the relation between suicide and age?

Depression is one of the most common mental disorders and one of the most treatable (LaRue, Dessonville, & Jarvik, 1985). Estimates are that at any one point between 2% and 5% of all adults have a clinical depressive disorder and that roughly 15% of community residents have some depressive symptoms; the odds across adulthood of ever having a depressive disorder are between 20% and 25% (Schneider, 1995). There is increasing evidence that depression is a major mental health problem among older adults that has been badly underdiagnosed and undertreated (Friedhoff, 1994). In part, this is due to important differences in symptoms between younger and older adults.

More research has been conducted on depression than on any other form of mental disorder, partly because it is relatively common (and probably more so than previously believed), and partly because it often is a secondary problem in other forms of disorders, such as dementia and chronic illness. For these reasons, we will consider depression in detail.

Characteristics of Older People with Depression

Although the primary risk factors for depression in older adults are similar to those for young adults, some important differences include being female, unmarried, widowed, or recently bereaved; experiencing stressful life events; and lacking an adequate social support network (Zisook & Schucter, 1994). Subgroups of older adults who are at greater risk include those with chronic illnesses (of whom up to half may have major depression), nursing home residents, and family caregivers (of whom up to 40% may have major depression) (Schneider, 1995).

Women who are diagnosed as having a severe depressive disorder outnumber men in young adulthood and old age, but men outnumber women during the latter part of midlife (ages 55 to 64) (Leaf et al., 1988). This difference may reflect a gender bias on the part of clinicians, however, who may simply be more willing to diagnose depression in women (Feinson, 1987; Rodeheaver & Datan, 1988). For example, the much higher rate of diagnosed alcoholism in men during young adulthood and early middle age and a connection between alcoholism and depression suggest that depression in men is a common but undiagnosed problem (Turner, 1987). Other factors that reflect possible gender bias are also associated with the higher rates of clinical depression: being widowed (Vernon & Roberts, 1982); having lower economic resources (Hirschfield & Cross, 1982); and being in poorer health (Salzman & Shader, 1979). These data argue strongly that we need to be cautious in interpreting differential rates of depression in men and women.

Smallegan (1989) found higher rates of depressive symptoms in European Americans than in African Americans. In fact, upper-class African Americans reported the lowest level of symptoms of all the groups she studied. Because so few studies have included these individuals, however, Smallegan was unable to offer any explanation of this finding. Clearly, much more research is needed in examining ethnic group differences.

Simply because a person lives alone does not necessarily mean that they have strong feelings of loneliness, which may be a symptom of depression.

Diagnosis of Depression

The major criteria for diagnosing depressive disorders are described in two classification systems: the *DSM-IV* (American Psychiatric Association, 1994) and the Research Diagnostic Criteria (RDC) (Spitzer, Endicott, & Robins, 1978). Although these two sets of criteria differ somewhat in their specificity, they are similar in viewing depression as a multidimensional disturbance in biological, social, and psychological functioning.

An important aspect about the diagnosis of depression is that the relative importance of specific symptoms, and the ways in which people describe them, differ markedly with age. As we consider the symptoms that characterize depression and the ways in which it is assessed, these differences will be noted.

General Symptoms

The most prominent feature of clinical depression is *dysphoria*, that is, feeling down or blue. Importantly, older adults may not label their down feelings as depression but, rather, as "pessimistic" or "helpless" (Fry, 1986). Indeed, a large community study of over 6,500 adults revealed that older adults were much less likely to endorse statements relating to dysphoria (Gallo, Anthony, & Muthén, 1994). Additionally, older adults are also more likely to show signs of apathy, subdued self-deprecation, expressionlessness, and changes in arousal than are younger people (Epstein, 1976). It is common for older depressed individuals to withdraw, not speak to anyone, confine themselves to bed, and not take care of bodily functions. Younger adults may engage in some of these behaviors but to a much lesser extent.

The second major component of clinical depression is the accompanying physical symptoms. These include insomnia, changes in appetite, diffuse pain, troubled breathing, headaches, fatigue, and sensory loss (Lehmann, 1981). The presence of these physical symptoms in the elderly must be evaluated carefully. As noted in Chapter 4, some sleep disturbances may reflect normative changes that are unrelated to depression; however, regular early morning awakening is consistently related to depression, even in the elderly (Rodin, McAvay, & Timko, 1988). Alternatively, the physical symptoms may reflect an underlying physical disease that is manifested as depression. Indeed, many older adults admitted to the hospital with depressive symptoms turn out to have previously undiagnosed medical problems that are uncovered only after thorough blood and metabolic tests (Sweer, Martin, Ladd, Miller, & Karpf, 1988). Because the incidence of hypochondriasis (being overly concerned with one's health) increases with age, care must be taken to make sure that complaints about health are really related to depression (Gallagher & Thompson, 1983). Thoughts about suicide are particularly important, especially in the elderly, and should be considered a serious symptom (Osgood, 1985). Note that feelings one might expect to be evaluated, such as excessive worry or self-pity, are not included in the diagnostic criteria. This is because they are not unique to depression and do not help clinicians discriminate depression from other disorders (Spitzer et al., 1978).

The third characteristic is that the symptoms described must last at least two weeks. This criterion is used to rule out the transient symptoms that are common to all adults, especially after a negative experience such as receiving a rejection letter from a potential employer or getting a speeding ticket.

Fourth, other causes for the observed symptoms must be ruled out. For example, other health problems, neurological disorders, medications, metabolic conditions, alcoholism, or other forms of psychopathology can cause depressive symptoms. These must be considered in order to know how to treat the problem.

Finally, the clinician must determine how the person's symptoms are affecting his or her daily life. Is the ability to interact with other people impaired? Can he or she carry out domestic responsibilities? What about effects on work or school? Is the person taking any medication? Clinical depression involves significant impairment in daily living.

Women and Depressive Symptoms

As noted earlier, women tend to be diagnosed as being depressed more often than men. This has led some researchers to focus specifically on women's experience of depression to identify the kinds of symptoms they have. In a series of studies, Newmann, Engel, and Jensen (1990, 1991) looked at the patterns of symptoms women report and how these symptoms change over time. They found two different depressive syndromes and four different but related forms of psychological distress.

The two depressive syndromes differ on whether two key symptoms are present: dysphoria and feelings of guilt or self-blame. They are present in classic clinical depression, but appear to be absent in a version of depression called the depletion syndrome of the elderly (Fogel & Fretwell, 1985). Several other symptoms described above are common to the two different types (such as feeling worthless, losing interest in things, and having various physical symptoms). Interestingly, four limited forms of psychological distress were found, each being independent of the others: sleep disturbances, loss of energy, loneliness, and self-deprecating attitude. These results clearly show that the symptoms of depression, as well as the syndrome itself, are far more complicated than most people imagine.

In their second study, Newmann and colleagues (1991) showed that the classic depressive syndrome declines in frequency with age whereas the depletion syndrome increases. These findings imply that the age-related declines in the frequency of severe depression discussed earlier probably reflect classic depression. Moreover, these results point to the need for very careful diagnosis of depression in women.

Assessment Scales

Numerous scales are used to assess depression, but because most were developed on younger and middle-aged adults, they are most appropriate for these age groups. The most important difficulty in using these scales with older adults is that they all include several items assessing physical symptoms. Although the presence of such symptoms is usually indicative of depression in younger adults, as we noted earlier such symptoms may not be related to depression at all in the elderly. More recently, scales aimed specifically at older adults have been developed.

An important point to keep in mind about these scales is that the diagnosis of depression should never be made on the basis of a test score alone. As we have seen, the symptoms observed in clinical depression could be indicative of other problems, and symptom patterns are very complex. Moreover, there is some evidence of gender bias; in one study, both the Geriatric Depression Scale and the Beck Depression Inventory were more accurate in diagnosing depression in older women than in older men (Allen-Burge, Storandt, Kinscherf, & Rubin, 1994). Only by a thorough assessment of many aspects of physical and psychological functioning can a clinician make an accurate assessment.

Causes of Depression

Several theories about the causes of depression have been proposed. They can be grouped into two main categories: biological (or physiological) theories and psychosocial theories.

Biological and Physiological Theories

The most popular of the biological and physiological theories links depression to imbalances in or insufficient supplies of particular neurotransmitters (Maas, 1978; see Chapter 3). As we noted in Chapter 3, neurotransmitters are chemicals that provide the communication links between the neurons, or brain cells. Because most neurotransmitter levels decline with age, some researchers postulate that depression in the elderly is more likely to be a biochemical problem (Gerner & Jarvik, 1984). However, the link between neurotransmitter levels and depression is still unclear. The problem is that response to drug therapies has not yet been shown to be directly related to changes in neurotransmitter levels.

Other researchers argue that depression may be due to abnormal functioning of the hemispheres in the brain (Weingartner & Silberman, 1982). Neuropsychological tests, that is, tests that measure brain function, and electroencephalograms (EEGs) document abnormalities and impairments in the right hemisphere of persons diagnosed as having depression (Davidson, Schwartz, Saron, Bennett, & Goleman, 1979).

Depression is also linked to physical illness, especially in the elderly. Salzman and Shader (1979) and Verwoerdt (1980, 1981) note that there is considerable evidence that worsening physical health in the elderly often goes hand in hand with worsening symptoms of depression; expressions of guilt, crying, irritability, anxiety, and dependency are common. Among the physical diseases that often include obvious symptoms of depression are dementia, brain tumors, cerebrovascular disease, hypothyroidism, and cardiovascular disease (Fry, 1986). Given the connection between physical diseases and depressive symptoms, it is clearly important for the diagnostic process to include a complete physical examination.

Psychosocial Theories

By far, the most widely held belief is that depression is due to some psychologically traumatic event. Several themes emerge in this literature: loss, negative life events, internalization, and internal belief systems.

The most common theme of psychosocial theories of depression is *loss* (Butler & Lewis, 1982). Bereavement has been the type of loss receiving the most attention, but the loss of anything considered personally important could also be a trigger. Gaylord and Zung (1987) identified eight types of loss that may result in dysphoria or depression: loss of a loved one; loss of health or physical attractiveness; loss of job or caretaking roles; loss of personal possessions; loss of lifestyle; failure of plans or ventures; loss of group membership or status; and loss of a pet. Moreover, these losses may be real and irrevocable, threatened and potential, or imaginary and fantasized. The likelihood that these losses will occur varies with age. Middle-aged adults are more likely to experience the loss of physical attractiveness, for example, whereas older adults are more likely to experience the loss of a loved one.

The belief that *negative life events* cause depression is widely held. Indeed, major negative life events often trigger feelings of sadness and dysphoria. Additionally, some theorists view depression as resulting from a search for the self that uncovers negative or missing aspects of identity. These issues are especially important in understanding depression in midlife. It may be that events surrounding changes in employment and family result in a questioning of self, which in turn may result in dysphoria.

However, the research evidence suggests that specific events probably do not cause cases of severe depression (Fry, 1986; Gaylord & Zung, (1987). The lack of evidence for an event trigger for severe depression despite popular belief to the contrary probably reflects a difference of perspective. That is, feeling down is extremely common after experiencing a traumatic event; as noted in Chapter 13, it is a universal experience during the grieving process. When people experience these feelings, they may have a tendency to label themselves as "depressed." But as we have seen, feelings alone are not enough to indicate severe clinical depression. What happens following a significant loss is a much milder form of depression, which may in fact be a normal response to the situation (Blazer & Williams, 1980).

Internalization is a theme expressed in psychoanalytic theory. Freud viewed depression (or melancholia, in his terminology) as a profoundly painful dejection, cessation of interest in the outside world, loss of the capacity to love, and lowering of self-regarding feelings that resulted in severe self-reproaches (Mendelson, 1982). For Freud, this loss becomes internalized, and the displeasure felt toward someone else becomes focused on oneself. Thus, in psychoanalytic terms, depression is hostility turned inward. The loss of self-esteem is also an important part of psychoanalytic theories of depression. In general, this loss comes from faulty aspects of how one presents oneself, the superego, the ideal self, and self-critical ego functions (Mendelson, 1982).

An alternative approach is taken in behavioral and cognitive theories of depression. **This approach emphasizes *internal belief systems*, which focuses on how people interpret uncontrollable events** (Beck, 1967). The idea behind these theories is that experiencing unpredictable and uncontrollable events instills a feeling of helplessness, which results in depression. Additionally, perceiving the cause of negative events as some inherent aspect of the self that is permanent and pervasive also plays an important role in causing feelings of helplessness and hopelessness. In short, according to this approach people who are depressed believe that they are personally responsible for their plight, that things are unlikely to get better, and that their whole life is a shambles.

Despite numerous studies attempting to find a psychological cause of depression, no definitive links have yet been established. What we know at this point is that certain experiences of loss and certain belief systems are often found in people with depression. However, we cannot conclude that such things actually caused the person to become depressed. To establish those connections we will need carefully conducted longitudinal research. Finally, we need to remember from a multidimensional model that psychological events are not independent of biological ones. That is, experiencing loss could have implications for our neurotransmitter balance, which in turn could be a cause of depression.

Treatment of Depression

As we have seen, depression is a complex problem that can result from a wide variety of causes. We

TABLE 9.1 Summary of acute treatments for major depression in older persons

Treatment	Efficacy	Comments
Antidepressant medications	Numerous (more than 30) randomized, placebo-controlled trials of several tricyclics, buproprion, trazodone, and others. Trial results are for acute treatment responses.	Adequate doses, plasma levels, and treatment duration are essential in order to maximize response. Response may take 6 to 12 weeks, somewhat longer than in younger patients. Side effects may limit use.
Augmentation of antidepressants with lithium, thyroid medications, carbamazepine	Patients nonresponsive to several weeks of treatment with standard antidepressant medications may respond rapidly after these medications are added. Evidence is based on case series and reports.	May be useful in patients who are not responding or only partially responding to standard antidepressant medications. Constitutes acceptable clinical practice.
Electroconvulsive therapy	Clearly effective in severe depression; depression with melancholia, and depression with delusions and when antidepressants are not fully effective. Sometimes combined with antidepressants.	In medication-resistant patients, acue response rate is approximately 50%. Relapse rate is high requiring attention to maintenance antidepressant treatment. Effects are more favorable with increasing age.
Psychotherapy	More effective treatment than waiting list, no treatment, or placebo; equivalent to antidepressant medications in geriatric outpatient populations generally, with both major or minor depression. About half of studies are group interventions. Therapy orientations were cognitive, interpersonal, reminiscence, psychodynamic, and eclectic.	Studies have been in elderly outpatients who were not significantly suicidal and for whom hospitalization was not indicated. There is no evidence of efficacy in severe depression. Distribution of responses may be different from the response to medication.
Combined antidepressant medication and psychotherapy	Effective in outpatients using manual-based therapies; the relative contributions of each component are not well understood.	Combined therapy has not been adequately studied in elderly people.

Source: U.S. Public Health Service, 1993

have also noted that depression can vary in severity, from fairly normal responses to traumatic events to very serious, life-threatening lack of concern for oneself. However, an extremely crucial point is that all forms of depression benefit from some form of therapy (Thompson & Gallagher, 1986). For the severe forms, medications may be needed. In some cases of severe, long-term depression, electroconvulsive therapy may be required. For the less severe forms of depression, and usually in conjunction with medication for severe depression, there are various forms of psychotherapy. A summary of the various treatment options is presented in Table 9.1.

Drug Therapy

Two families of drugs are used to combat severe depression. **The most commonly used medications are the *heterocyclic antidepressants***

(HCAs). HCAs were formerly known as tricyclic antidepressants, but the recent marketing of monocyclic, bicyclic, and tetracyclic antidepressants led to the change in terminology (Berkow, 1987). Although HCAs are effective in at least 70% of cases, they are most effective with younger and middle-aged individuals (Berkow, 1987; Epstein, 1978). The main problem with HCAs in older age groups is that the elderly are more likely to have medical conditions or to be taking other medications that inhibit their use. For example, people who are taking antihypertensive medication or who have any of a number of metabolic problems should not take the tricyclic HCAs (Baldessarini, 1978). Moreover, the risk for side effects beyond the typical one of dry mouth are much greater in the elderly (Epstein, 1978), although some of the newer HCAs have significantly lower risk. Because HCAs must be taken for roughly a week before the person feels relief, compliance with the therapy is sometimes difficult.

A second group of drugs that relieves depression is the *monoamine oxidase (MAO) inhibitors,* so named because they inhibit MAO, a substance that interferes with the transmission of signals between neurons. MAO inhibitors are generally less effective than the tricyclics and can produce deadly side effects (Walker & Brodie, 1980). Specifically, they interact with foods that contain tyramine or dopamine—mainly cheddar cheese but also others, such as wine and chicken liver—to create dangerously, and sometimes fatally, high blood pressure. MAO inhibitors are used with extreme caution in the United States, usually only after HCAs have proved ineffective. Research on other MAO inhibitors that have reduced risk is under way (Berkow, 1987).

The newest form of medication to treat depression is called *selective serotonin reuptake inhibitors (SSRIs).* SSRIs gained wide popularity beginning in the late 1980s because they have the lowest overall rate of side effects of any other antidepressant. SSRIs work by boosting the level of serotonin, which is a neurotransmitter involved in regulating moods. One of the SSRIs, Prozac, has been the subject of controversy, as it has been linked in a small number of cases with the serious side effect of high levels of agitation. Drugs like Prozac make people "not sad," which is different than making people happy. Other SSRIs, such as Zoloft and Serzone, appear to have fewer adverse reactions.

If periods of depression alternate with periods of mania or extremely high levels of activity, a diagnosis of *bipolar disorder* is made (American Psychiatric Association, 1994). Bipolar disorder is characterized by unpredictable, often explosive mood swings as the person cycles between extreme depression and extreme activity. The drug therapy of choice for bipolar disorder is lithium (Berkow, 1987), which came into widespread use in the early 1970s. Lithium is extremely effective in controlling the mood swings, although we do not completely understand why it works. The use of lithium *must* be monitored very closely, because the difference between an effective dose and a toxic dose is extremely small (Mahoney, 1980). Because lithium is a salt, it raises blood pressure, making it dangerous to use with individuals who have hypertension or kidney disease. The effective dosage level for lithium decreases with age; physicians unaware of this change run the risk of inducing an overdose, especially in the elderly (Maletta, 1984). Compliance is also a problem, because no improvement is seen for between 4 and 10 days after the initial dose (Berkow, 1987) and because it turns out that many individuals with bipolar disorder do not like having their moods controlled by medication (Jamison, Gerner, & Goodwin, 1979).

Electroconvulsive Therapy

Electroconvulsive therapy (ECT) is viewed by many people as an extreme and even cruel form of therapy. This perspective was probably justified in the past, when ECT was used as depicted in books and movies such as *One Flew Over the Cuckoo's Nest.* The popular perception is that ECT is used only for the most extreme mentally disturbed individuals; it was this view that forced Thomas Eagleton to withdraw his candidacy for the vice-presidency of the United States in 1972.

In fact, ECT is an extremely effective treatment for severe depression, especially in people whose depression has lasted a long time, who are suicidal, who have serious physical problems caused by their depression, and who do not respond to medications (Salzman, 1975; Weiner, 1979). ECT is now tightly regulated, and it can be used only after review of each individual case (Walker & Brodie, 1980). ECT involves passing a current of 70 to 150 volts from one of the person's temples to the other for less than 1 second (Weiner, 1979). This results in a seizure similar to that experienced in severe forms of epilepsy. To prevent the person from injury, he or she is given a strong muscle relaxant. The effective voltage appears to increase with age, which means that treatments need to be spaced further apart and the person monitored more closely (Weiner, 1979).

Although we do not understand how it works, ECT has some advantages (Salzman, 1975). Unlike antidepressant medications, it has immediate effects. Usually, only a few treatments are required, compared with long-term maintenance schedules for drugs. But ECT also has some side effects. Memory of the ECT treatment itself is lost. Memory of other recent events is temporarily disrupted, but it usually returns within a week or two (Salzman, 1975).

At one time, ECT was thought to be a safe and effective method of treatment for severe depression in older adults with heart disease. Recent evidence, however, indicates that the risk of heart attacks in older adults following ECT treatment has been underestimated (Rice, Sombrotto, Markowitz, & Leon, 1994).

Psychotherapy

Psychotherapy is an approach to treatment based on the idea that talking to a therapist about one's problems can help. Often, psychotherapy can be very effective by itself in treating depression. In cases of severe depression, psychotherapy may be combined with drug or ECT therapy. Of the more than 100 different types of psychotherapy, three general approaches seem to work best with depressed people: behavior therapy, cognitive therapy, and psychoanalytic therapy.

The fundamental idea in *behavior therapy* is that depressed people receive too few rewards or reinforcements from their environment (Lewinsohn, 1975). Thus, the goal of behavior therapy is to get them to increase the good things that happen to them. Often, this can be accomplished by having people increase their activities; if they do more, the likelihood is that more good things will happen. Additionally, behavior therapy seeks to get people to decrease the number of negative thoughts they have, because depressed people tend to look at the world pessimistically. They get little pleasure out of activities that nondepressed people enjoy a great deal: seeing a funny movie, playing a friendly game of volleyball, or being with a lover.

To get activity levels up and negative thoughts down, behavior therapists usually assign homework—tasks that force clients to practice the principles they are learning during the therapy sessions (Gallagher & Thompson, 1983; Lewinsohn, 1975). This may involve going out more to meet people, joining new clubs, or just learning how to enjoy life. Family members are instructed to ignore negative statements made by the depressed person and to reward positive self-statements with attention, praise, or even money.

An effective approach that incorporates Lewinsohn's (1975) behavioral approach but is presented in a less traditional therapeutic setting is the *Coping with Depression Course* (Lewinsohn, Steinmetz, Antonuccio, & Teri, 1984). The course adopts a psychoeducational approach, in that the principles of behavior therapy are embedded in an educational program. The advantage of a psychoeducational approach is that the stigma of receiving traditional psychotherapy is removed, because classes are held in a workshop setting. However, research indicates that the course is as effective as traditional behavior therapy for mildly and moderately depressed adults of all ages (Gallagher & Thompson, 1983).

***Cognitive therapy* for depression is based on the idea that depression results from maladaptive beliefs or cognitions about oneself.** From this perspective, a depressed individual views the self as inadequate and unworthy, the world as insensitive and ungratifying, and the future as bleak and unpromising (Beck, Rush, Shaw, & Emery, 1979). In cognitive therapy the person is taught how to recognize these thoughts, which have become so automatic and ingrained that other perspectives are not seen. Once this awareness has been achieved, the person learns how to evaluate the self, world, and future more realistically. These goals may be accomplished through homework assignments similar to those used in behavior therapy. These often involve reattributing the causes of events, examining the evidence before drawing conclusions, listing the pros and cons of maintaining an idea, and examining the consequences of that idea. Finally, individuals are taught to change the basic beliefs that are responsible for their negative thoughts. For example, people who believe that they have been failures all their lives or that they are unlovable are taught how to use their newfound knowledge to achieve more realistic appraisals of themselves (Gallagher & Thompson, 1983).

Cognitive therapy alone is also an effective treatment for mildly and moderately depressed adults of all ages. However, the process of change may take longer in older adults, who may also need more encouragement along the way. Despite the need for extra support, older adults are able to maintain the gains made during therapy as well as younger and middle-aged adults (Gallagher & Thompson, 1983).

The goal of *psychoanalytic therapy* is to alter the personality structure so that the individual can function more adaptively. Because the underlying cause of psychopathology is thought to lie in relationships earlier in life, much of psychoanalytic therapy deals with feelings about conflicts in past events and relationships. To achieve the goal of adaptive functioning, one of two approaches is used. In the first, *insight therapy,* the therapist helps the client gain insight into the maladaptive defenses and character defects causing the problem. Feelings about events and relationships earlier in life are discussed, and potential solutions are explored. In the second approach the goal is not insight but, rather, support of existing coping mechanisms to better face current problems. In *supportive therapy,* the strengthening of adaptive defenses and the replacement of maladaptive defenses is of primary concern. Both insight and supportive therapies are effective with adults of all ages.

Two versions of psychoanalytic therapy particularly useful with older adults are *life review therapy* and *reminiscence*. The goal of both therapies is to use the memories of previous events and relationships as ways to confront and resolve conflicts. Life review therapy and reminiscence can be done individually or in groups, and they can be unstructured or structured (by using particular topics as triggers). Although both approaches have become very popular and are claimed to be effective (Kaminsky, 1978; Lesser, Lazarus, Frankel, & Havasy, 1981), why they work and how remembering the past relates to specific cognitive and emotional processes are unknown (Merriam, 1980).

Concept Checks

1. Who is most likely to be depressed?
2. What are the major symptoms of depression?
3. What are the major biological and psychological causes of depression?
4. What are the chief ways in which depression is treated?

ANXIETY, PERSONALITY, AND PSYCHOTIC DISORDERS

Learning Objectives:

- What are the symptoms of anxiety disorders? How are they treated?
- What are the major types of personality disorders? How do the symptoms change over time?
- What are the characteristics of people with psychotic disorders?

Although depression is the most common mental disorder, several other problems also occur. In this section, we will examine three types of disorders that are receiving increased attention: anxiety disorders, personality disorders, and psychotic disorders. The first two are being recognized as important, and often undiagnosed, disorders. The increased attention being paid to psychotic disorders is due mainly to the fact that psychotic symptoms are very common in diseases such as Alzheimer's disease.

Anxiety Disorders

Imagine that you are about to give a speech before an audience of 500 people. In the last few minutes before your address, you begin to feel nervous, your heart starts to pound, and your palms get sweaty. These feelings, common even to veteran speakers, are similar to those experienced by individuals with anxiety disorders: a group of conditions that are based on fear or uneasiness. Anxiety disorders include anxiety states, in which feelings of severe anxiety occur with no specific trigger; phobic disorders, characterized by irrational fears of objects or circumstances; and obsessive-compulsive disorders, in which thoughts or actions are repeatedly performed for no apparent reason to lower anxiety. Anxiety disorders are diagnosed in as many as 10% of elderly women and 5% of elderly men, which is somewhat higher than in younger adults (Cohen, 1990).

Symptoms and Diagnosis of Anxiety Disorders

Common to all the anxiety disorders are physical changes that interfere with social functioning, personal relationships, or work. These physical changes include dry mouth, sweating, dizziness, upset stomach, diarrhea, insomnia, hyperventilation, chest pain, choking, frequent urination, headaches, and a sensation of a lump in the throat (Fry, 1986). These symptoms occur in adults of all ages, but they are particularly common in older adults due to loss of health, relocation stress, isolation, fear of losing control over their lives, or guilt resulting from feelings of hostility toward family and friends (Fry, 1986). Himmelfarb (1984) demonstrated the importance of these factors in understanding anxiety disorders in the elderly. After Himmelfarb statistically controlled the relationship between age and anxiety for such factors as health, quality of housing, and social support, the relationship was substantially reduced. Thus, we must be cautious in interpreting reports that the frequency of anxiety disorders increases with age. Such reports may be indicative of other, more important, factors.

Another important issue concerning anxiety disorders in older adults is that anxiety may be an appropriate response to the situation. For example, helplessness anxiety is generated by a potential or actual loss of control or mastery (Verwoerdt, 1981). Additionally, a series of severe negative life experiences may result in a person's reaching the breaking point and appearing highly anxious. Many older adults who show symptoms of anxiety disorder have underlying health problems that may be responsible for the symptoms. In all cases the anxious behavior should be investigated first as an appropriate response that may not require intervention. The important point is to evaluate the older adult's behavior in context.

These issues make it difficult to diagnose anxiety disorders, especially in older adults (Tice & Perkins, 1996). The problem is because there usually is nothing specific that a person can point to as the specific trigger or cause. Additionally, anxiety in older adults often accompanies an underlying physical disorder or illness. These secondary causes of anxiety need to be disentangled from the anxiety symptoms so that each may be dealt with appropriately.

Treatment of Anxiety Disorders

Both drug therapy and psychotherapy are used to treat anxiety disorders. ***Benzodiazepines* are the most widely prescribed medications for anxiety, and include such drugs as Valium, Librium, Serax, and Ativan** (Fry, 1986). Although benzodiazepines are effective with adults of all ages, they must be used very carefully with older adults. Effective dosage levels are lower in the elderly, and the potential for side effects is much greater. Most important, these drugs can cause decreased cognitive functioning, which may be mistaken for early dementia. In general, the benzodiazepines may cause drowsiness, loss of coordination, headaches, and lower energy levels. Moreover, because of the potential for addiction, the long-term use of these drugs should be avoided.

In most cases the treatment of choice for anxiety disorders is psychotherapy. A broad range of approaches is effective with adults of all ages. Of particular note are the relaxation techniques described in Chapter 4. These procedures help the anxious person learn to relax and to control the feelings of anxiety before they get out of hand. Other behavioral techniques such as systematic desensitization are especially effective with phobias. The advantage of these psychotherapeutic techniques is that they usually only involve a few sessions, have high rates of success, and offer clients procedures that they can take with them. Best of all, they have no long-term side effects, unlike their medical counterparts.

Personality Disorders

The study of personality disorders is full of difficulties. As we saw in Chapter 8, the very definition of personality is controversial, making it very hard for clinicians to figure out what they are supposed to be noticing. Merely referring to maladaptive personality traits that result in impaired functioning or personal distress does not help. Fortunately, all is not utterly chaotic.

What little evidence there is on the rate of personality disorders across the adult life span indicates that personality disorder is the primary diagnosis in the primary care setting in roughly 5% to 8% of clients (Sadavoy & Fogel, 1992). A major problem in this research is that few studies of noninstitutionalized populations include individuals over age 65. More data are available concerning nursing home residents, psychiatric outpatients, and psychiatric inpatients; in these cases, incidence rates range from 30% to 60% (Agronin, 1994).

Classification, Diagnosis, and Treatment of Personality Disorders

Personality disorders are described in terms of three general clusters (Sadavoy & Fogel, 1992): the odd or eccentric group (which includes paranoid, schizoid, and schizotypal personality disorders); the dramatic, emotional, and erratic group (which includes antisocial, borderline, histrionic, and narcissistic personality disorders); and the anxious, fearful group (which includes avoidant, dependent, obsessive-compulsive, and passive-aggressive personality disorders). Most clinicians believe that the underlying characteristics of personality disorders can be traced to early life and remain relatively stable or perhaps become somewhat less apparent across the life span (Agronin, 1994). However, a significant number of cases apparently do not appear until late life.

Which type of personality disorder a person develops is a result of a complex set of interacting influences: environmental, interpersonal, stress, loss, energy, coping styles, health, and personality traits (Sadavoy & Fogel, 1992). It is largely unknown how these factors differ across the life span in determining how a personality disorder will be manifested. In any case, the major way that personality disorders manifest themselves is through problems with interpersonal relationships. For example, when people are forced to live together (such as in nursing homes or residence halls), the stress of the situation may precipitate the manifestation of maladaptive behaviors such as claiming that one's roommate steals things. Personality disorders may also come to light through excessive concern with one's physical health and functioning. Although this may be a sign of an underlying disease, excessive concern with no evidence of an illness is cause for concern. In older adults especially, another warning sign is depressive withdrawal from social contact, which often accompanies the loss of a significant personal relationship (e.g., the death of a spouse).

One barrier to understanding personality disorders is the general lack of longitudinal data on the actual progression of symptoms. The available evidence suggests that some types of personality disorders (e.g., paranoid, schizoid) change very little over time and may even worsen with age, whereas other types (e.g., passive-aggressive, antisocial, narcissistic) improve over time (Agronin, 1994; Sadavoy & Fogel, 1992). Indeed, some evidence suggests that the latter types are relatively rare in older adults, which tends to corroborate the view that these problems lessen over time.

Treatment of personality disorders is difficult in general, and little information is available specifically addressing the needs of older adults. The situation with older adults is complicated by the difficulty in disentangling physical health issues from the observed behavior and in obtaining reliable histories of the person's behavioral past (Sadavoy & Fogel, 1992). One approach is to treat the other identified problems to determine the extent to which the problem behaviors may be eliminated. Concomitantly, behavior management programs can be initiated that target specific troublesome behaviors; some evidence shows that as long as formal, written behavioral contracts are developed that some improvements are possible (Sadavoy & Fogel, 1992).

Clearly, a great deal of additional research on personality disorders is needed, especially in older adults (Agronin, 1994). In particular, we need additional information about which problem behaviors characterize which personality disorders over time, how to take age differences into account in the diagnostic process, how symptoms improve or worsen with age, how personality disorders interact with other mental health problems (especially with depression and organic mental disorder), and what types of interventions work best.

Psychotic Disorders

Some forms of psychopathology, referred to as psychoses, involve losing touch with reality and the disintegration of personality. Two behaviors that occur in these disorders are *delusions,* which are belief systems not based on reality, and *hallucinations,* which are distortions in perception.

Although the development of psychotic disorders as the primary problem in late life is rare, occurring in roughly 1% of the population, understanding these disorders is important for other reasons (Jeste, Naimark, Halpain, & Lindamer, 1995). The behaviors present in psychotic disorders are commonly manifested as secondary problems in other disorders, especially in organic mental disorders such as Alzheimer's disease (Rabins, 1992). Indeed, psychotic symptoms are an important aspect of the diagnosis of some of these other disorders and can be managed in the same way. This linkage has resulted in late-life psychoses being divided into two major categories based on the presumed cause of the symptoms: those associated with organic mental disorders (e.g., dementia), and those associated with syndromes in which the cause is unclear (e.g., schizophrenia) (Jeste et al., 1995). Because the basic symptoms are similar in both categories, we will focus on the latter one here.

Schizophrenia

Schizophrenia is characterized by the severe impairment of thought processes, including the content and style of thinking; distorted perceptions; loss of touch with reality; a distorted sense of self; and abnormal motor behavior (American Psychiatric Association, 1994). Individuals with schizophrenia may show these abnormal behaviors in several ways: loose associations (such as saying that they have a secret meeting with the president of the United States in the local bowling alley); hearing voices that tell them what to do; believing that they can read other people's minds; believing that their body is changing into something else; or sometimes through bizarre delusions (for example, that they are Jesus or that they are being spied on). Additionally, schizophrenic individuals tend to show very little or highly inappropriate emotionality (laughing hysterically at the news of a major tragedy, for instance). They are often confused about their own identity, have difficulty working toward a goal, and tend to withdraw from social contact.

The second hallmark symptom of schizophrenia is delusions, or well-formed beliefs not based in reality. Most often, these delusions involve persecution ("People are out to get me"). The distinction between paranoid disorders and schizophrenia is fuzzy; indeed, one type of schizophrenia is termed paranoid type. In general, hallucinations, loose associations, and absent or inappropriate emotions do not occur in paranoid disorders (American Psychiatric Association, 1994).

The beliefs underlying delusions can result in anger, resentment, or even violent acts. Because individuals with psychoses are extremely suspicious and rarely seek help on their own, such people tend to come to the attention of authorities after having repeated run-ins with the police or neighbors, starting legal proceedings against others on mysterious grounds, or registering complaints about fictitious or distorted events.

Most researchers believe that schizophrenia occurs most often before age 45 (Post, 1987). These researchers assert that older adults tend to show different symptoms than younger or middle-aged adults; for example, older adults show less thought disorder and less flattening of their emotions than younger adults (Rabins, 1992). Some researchers disagree, however, maintaining that there are few differences with age in the numbers of individuals who experience schizophrenic symptoms and no differences in the nature of the symptoms (Blazer, George, & Hughes, 1988). More research is needed to clarify the issue.

What is clear is that over the long haul people with schizophrenia tend to show one of three outcomes. Some experience only one episode and are hospitalized for a brief period. Others show a gradual decrease in symptoms over time, perhaps as a result of living in institutions. Still others have symptoms that remain constant over their entire adult life span. In general, most older schizophrenic adults need some sort of structured care. The trend toward deinstitutionalization in the United States over the past few decades has resulted in many older adults with schizophrenia ending up either in nursing homes, where the staff may have neither the training nor the time to respond effectively, or, unfortunately, as homeless street people.

Treatment of Schizophrenia

Traditionally, treatment of schizophrenia has emphasized medication. Drug therapy consists of *antipsychotics,* medications that are believed to work on the dopamine system (see Chapter 4). Some of the more commonly used antipsychotics are Haldol, Thorazine, and Mellaril. These medications must be used with extreme caution in adults of all ages due to the risk of serious toxic side effects, especially the loss of motor control. Despite these risks antipsychotics are often used in nursing homes and other institutions as tranquilizing agents to control problem patients.

In general, individuals with schizophrenia are difficult to treat in psychotherapy. The severe thought disturbances characteristic of schizophrenia make it difficult for therapists to work with clients. Because of their extreme suspiciousness, paranoid individuals may be reluctant to cooperate in psychotherapy. If these barriers can be overcome, however, there is some evidence that supportive therapy may be effective (Fry, 1986). The goals of therapy for such individuals tend to be adaptive rather than curative, that is, helping these people adapt to daily living rather than attempting to cure them.

Concept Checks

1. What are the major treatment options for anxiety disorders?
2. What are the major categories of personality disorders?
3. What are the primary characteristics of psychoses?

ORGANIC MENTAL DISORDERS

Learning Objectives:

- What is dementia? How do dementias differ from delirium?
- What are the major symptoms of Alzheimer's disease? How is it diagnosed? What causes it? What intervention options are there?
- What are some other major forms of dementia?
- What do family members caring for dementia patients experience?

As the title of this section implies, we are about to consider several forms of mental disorders that are caused by changes in the brain. At several points in this and other chapters, we have encountered references to a set of disorders termed dementia; this is one form of organic mental disorder.

Probably no other condition associated with aging is more feared than dementia, a family of disorders. In dementia people may literally lose their mind, being reduced from complex, thinking, feeling human beings to confused, vegetative victims unable even to recognize their spouse and children. Approximately 4.4 million older Americans, or roughly 15% of people over age 65, have some type of dementing disorder (Davies, 1988). Estimates are that the number may double in the next 50 years due to the increase in very old adults (Crook, 1987). Fewer than 1% of the people are afflicted at age 65, but the incidence rises sharply to 20% of those over 80.

Although there is a real basis for fearing dementia, the vast majority of older adults are not demented. For many people, it is the fear of dementia that is the most serious problem, leading them to label every time that they misplace their keys a symptom. It is hard to know how many older adults have unstated fears because they can no longer remember things in the same ways they did when they were younger. But as noted in Chapter 6, memory abilities show some normative changes with age. Consequently, what many people believe are signs that they are becoming demented are actually quite normal.

The Family of Dementias

The term *dementia* does not refer to a specific disease but, rather, to a family of diseases that are characterized by cognitive and behavioral deficits involving some form of permanent damage to the brain. About a dozen forms of dementia have been identified. Because dementia involves identifiable damage to the brain, it is also one of the diseases termed *organic mental disorders*. These criteria mean that dementia involves severe cognitive and behavioral decline and is not caused by a rapid onset of a toxic substance or by infection (American Psychiatric Association, 1994).

Dementias can be classified in several ways. For many years the age of the patient at diagnosis was used as the basis for classification. Dementias diagnosed in people younger than 60 to 65 years old were termed *presenile,* and those diagnosed in people older than 60 to 65 were termed *senile dementia.* Over the past two decades, however, this terminology has been declining in popularity and meaning, largely because new discoveries are revealing that age makes little difference in the types of underlying neurological changes (Crook, 1987). Thus, the trend is to refer to the various diseases by name rather than by the terms *presenile* and *senile.*

A second way to group dementias is more useful and important. Some dementias can be treated effectively, and a few can even be reversed. This distinction between reversible and irreversible dementias has profound implications for the patient.

Reversible dementia refers to a loosely defined set of disorders that are characterized by cognitive difficulties but that are treatable (Zarit & Zarit, 1983). ***Delirium* is characterized by impaired awareness of self and surroundings, attention deficits, tendencies toward hallucinations and delusions, disorientation, changes in alertness, disturbed sleep patterns, and rapid changes in symptoms and their severity; memory may be affected** (Lipowski, 1980). The common underlying factor is a disruption of cerebral metabolism; susceptibility to such metabolic disruptions increases with age. Indeed, the National Institute on Aging (1980) emphasizes that almost any internal disturbance can lead to cognitive symptoms in older adults.

Common causes of delirium include the toxic effects of medications (see Table 9.2) or drug interactions, infections, electrolyte imbalances, malnutrition, and potassium deficits. Symptoms may also appear following surgery, fractures, head injuries, changes in the environment, or the death of a close relative. Depression may manifest itself as cognitive impairment (Wells, 1979). The important point is that cognitive symptoms, especially in an older adult, do not necessarily indicate an untreatable, irreversible disease; careful diagnosis is an absolute must. Unfortunately, such careful diagnoses are often unavailable because of the lack

TABLE 9.2 Drugs that may cause cognitive deficits as side effects

Antidepressants used to treat depression
Benzodiazepines used to treat anxiety disorders
Bromocriptine used to treat Parkinson's disease
Carbamazepine used to treat seizure disorders
Cimetidine used to treat ulcers
Digoxin used to treat congestive heart failure and cardiac arrhythmias
Lithium used to treat bipolar disorders
Meclizine used to prevent dizziness or motion sickness
Neuroleptics used to treat psychotic disorders or severe behavior problems
Phenobarbitol used to treat seizure disorders
Phenytoin used to treat seizure disorders
Ranitidine used to treat ulcers
Scopolamine often used before surgery

of physicians who specialize in geriatric medicine. As a result many older adults are misdiagnosed as having Alzheimer's disease when they actually have a treatable disorder such as delirium or depression. Additionally, physicians who are not geriatric specialists often dismiss serious cognitive or behavioral symptoms as part of normal aging, which they clearly are not.

In the next two sections we will focus on dementias that are irreversible and degenerative. The most common and widely known of these is Alzheimer's disease, but others are important as well: multi-infarct dementia, Parkinson's disease, Pick's disease, Creutzfeld-Jakob disease, Huntington's disease, normal-pressure hydrocephalus, and alcoholic dementia.

Alzheimer's Disease

***Alzheimer's disease* is the most common form of progressive, degenerative, and fatal dementia, accounting for perhaps as many as 70% of all cases of dementia** (Davies, 1988). We have only recently realized how common Alzheimer's disease is, however. When Alois Alzheimer first described the sequence of changes in 1907, he was referring to a person 51 years old. For the next 60 years physicians believed that the disease was very rare and that it was a form of presenile dementia. It was not until Tomlinson, Blessed, and Roth (1970) showed that the same kinds of changes occurred in both early onset and late onset of the disease that physicians realized that age was not a factor. As a result virtually all that we know about Alzheimer's disease has been learned since 1970, with new discoveries coming almost daily.

The rapid growth in awareness that Alzheimer's disease is a major health problem resulted in the formation of the Alzheimer's Association in 1980. The association serves as a national advocacy group, sponsors workshops and research into the causes and treatment of the disease, and provides support groups for family caregivers. Nearly 200 chapters have been formed in communities throughout the United States, with roughly 1,000 family support groups (Lombardo, 1988). Another important function of the association is to provide information; its book *Understanding Alzheimer's Disease* (Aronson, 1988) provides a nontechnical summary of the disease and the complex family, ethical, and legal issues involved in it.

Neurological Changes in Alzheimer's Disease

The changes in the brain that characterize Alzheimer's disease are microscopic. This means that definitive diagnosis of the disease can be done only at autopsy; brain biopsies are an alternative, but the risks are so high that they are rarely performed (Crook, 1987). These progressive changes eventually cause so much destruction of the brain that the person dies. The microscopic changes that define Alzheimer's disease are neurofibrillary tangles, neuritic plaques, and granulovacuolar degeneration.

Neurofibrillary tangles (see Chapter 3) are accumulations of pairs of filaments in the neuron that become wrapped around each other; when examined under a microscope, these paired filaments look like intertwined spirals. Neurofibrillary tangles occur in several areas of the brain, and the number of tangles is directly related to the severity of symptoms (Farmer, Peck, & Terry, 1976). **Neuritic plaques (see Chapter 3) are spherical structures consisting of a core of *amyloid,* a protein, surrounded by degenerated fragments of dying or dead neurons.** The plaques are also found in various parts of the brain and are related to the severity of the disease (Blessed et al., 1968). Degeneration of neurons in some areas of the brain results in the formation of vacuoles, or spaces that become filled with fluid and granular material. Although *granulovacuolar degeneration* is a defining characteristic of Alzheimer's disease, its relationship to the severity of the disease is still unknown.

In addition to these three changes, atrophy of various parts of the brain has been found in Alzheimer's disease. However, brain atrophy is not a reliable indicator, because it is associated not only with Alzheimer's disease but also with many other diseases as well as normal aging (Crook, 1987).

Considerable research has uncovered specific neurotransmitter deficits associated with Alzheimer's disease. Most notable is a marked decrease in the enzyme *choline acetyltransferase,* a marker for acetylcholine, a neurotransmitter involved in learning and memory (Davies & Maloney, 1976). The decline in acetylcholine appears to be caused mainly by the degeneration of the *nucleus basalis of Meynert* and surrounding structures in the base of the brain (Dekker, Connor, & Thal, 1991). These changes may be the cause of the drastic declines in cognitive functions associated with Alzheimer's disease. Other studies have revealed decreases in other neurotransmitters, including noradrenaline (Bondareff, Mountjoy, & Roth, 1982), serotonin (Gottfries, Roos, & Winblad, 1976), and dopamine (Gottfries, Gottfries, & Roos, 1969). Changes in these neurotransmitters may be related to other symptoms, such as agitation, sleep disturbances, and perceptual difficulties.

Although the changes occurring in the brains of Alzheimer's victims are substantial, we must use caution in assuming that they represent qualitative differences from normal aging. They may not. Gottfries (1985) notes that all of the changes seen in Alzheimer's disease, including the structural and neurotransmitter changes, are also found in normal elderly people. To be sure, the changes in Alzheimer's disease are much greater. But the important point is that Alzheimer's disease may be merely an exaggeration of normal aging and not something qualitatively different from it.

Symptoms and Diagnosis

The major symptoms of Alzheimer's disease are gradual changes in cognitive functioning: declines in memory, learning, attention, and judgment; disorientation in time and space; difficulties in word finding and communication; declines in personal hygiene and self-care skills; inappropriate social behavior; and changes in personality (Crystal, 1988; Davies, 1988). These symptoms tend to be vague in the beginning, and they mimic other psychological problems such as depression or stress reactions. For example, an executive may not be managing as well as she once did and may be missing deadlines more often. Slowly, the symptoms get worse. This executive, who once could easily handle millions of dollars, cannot now add two small numbers. A housewife cannot set the table. A person who was previously outgoing is now quiet and withdrawn; a gentle person is now hostile and aggressive. Emotional problems become increasingly apparent, including depression, paranoia, and agitation. Wandering becomes a serious problem, especially because the person may have no idea where he or she is or how to get home, thus posing a genuine safety concern. As the disease progresses, the patient becomes incontinent and more and more dependent on others for care, eventually becoming completely incapable of even such simple tasks as dressing and eating. **In general, the symptoms associated with Alzheimer's disease are worse in the evening than in the morning, a phenomenon that is referred to as *sundowning* among caregivers.**

The rate of deterioration in Alzheimer's disease is highly variable from one victim to the next, although progression is usually faster when onset occurs earlier in life (Bondareff, 1983). However, we can identify a series of stages that the patient goes through (Reisberg, Ferris, de Leon, & Crook, 1982). Many diseases cause problems similar to those observed in the early stages of Alzheimer's disease. In fact, fewer than 10% of those individuals who show mild cognitive impairment will go on to develop more serious cognitive impairment within several years of the clinical evaluation (Reisberg et al., 1985).

Although a definitive diagnosis of Alzheimer's disease depends on an autopsy, the number and severity of behavioral changes allows clinicians to make increasingly accurate early diagnosis (Crook, 1987). For this earlier diagnosis to be relatively accurate, however, it must be comprehensive and broad. Table 9.3 provides the set of guidelines developed by a work group convened by the National Institute of Neurological and Communicative Diseases and Stroke (McKhann et al., 1984). Note that a great deal of the diagnostic effort goes into ruling out other possible causes for the observed cognitive deficits. This point emphasizes the fact that all possible treatable causes for the symptoms must be eliminated before a diagnosis of Alzheimer's disease may be made. Unfortunately, many clinicians do not conduct such thorough diagnoses.

As noted in Table 9.3, the clinical diagnosis of Alzheimer's disease consists of noting the history of the symptoms, documenting the cognitive impairments, conducting a general physical exam and neurological exam, performing laboratory tests to rule out other diseases, obtaining a psychiatric evaluation, performing neuropsychological tests, and assessing functional abilities (Crystal, 1988). The history or progress of the disease should be obtained from both the patient, if possible, and a family member. The questions asked must cover when the problems began, how they have changed, what the patient is capable of doing, and other medical problems.

The cognitive impairments are typically documented through a *mental status exam* (see Chapter 6), which is a brief series of questions tapping orientation ("What day is this? Where are you?"), memory, arithmetic ability (counting backwards), ability to follow directions, motor skills (copying a design), and general information ("Who is the president now?"). The general physical exam and neurological exam help rule out other causes such as cardiovascular disease, nutritional problems, or strokes.

The use of brain imaging techniques, described in Chapter 3, are also important. For example, a magnetic resonance imaging (MRI) assessment can help determine whether there is any evidence of a series of small strokes, a tumor, or other physiological explanation for the cognitive impairment and other symptoms the person may be experiencing.

A series of laboratory tests must be conducted to rule out additional causes of the observed behaviors. Blood tests look for evidence of chronic infections and for abnormal levels of vitamin B_{12}, folic acid, and thyroid hormone. An EEG should be performed to rule out subtle seizures and to verify that the characteristic diffusely slow EEG pattern in Alzheimer's disease is present. Brain imaging techniques such as MRI may be used (see Chapter 3). However, none of these imaging techniques provides conclusive evidence; at best they can rule out the presence of tumors, strokes, or other abnormalities (Crystal, 1988).

A psychiatric evaluation must be done to rule out any serious emotional problems that may be causing the observed deficits. A battery of neuropsychological tests should be administered to document the extent of the cognitive deficits and to provide additional information concerning the possibility of tumors or strokes. The functional abilities of the patient must be evaluated as well; these include instrumental daily activities, such as cooking and cleaning, and personal self-care skills, such as dressing and bathing.

Searching for a Cause

We do not know what causes Alzheimer's disease. One notion is that a viral infection causes the changes in the brain (Davies, 1988). The viral idea is credible, because a virus appears to be involved in Creutzfeld-Jakob disease, another form of dementia. If a virus turns out to be responsible, though, it is probably slow acting. Unfortunately, scientists have not yet been able to detect a specific virus in the brains of people with Alzheimer's disease.

A second idea about a cause that has been widely reported is aluminum toxicity (Thal, 1988). The

TABLE 9.3 Criteria for the diagnosis of probable Alzheimer's disease

1. Criteria for clinical diagnosis of *probable* Alzheimer's disease include
   - Dementia established by clinical examination and documented by Mini-Mental State Test (Folstein, Folstein, & McHugh, 1975), Blessed Dementia Scale (Blessed, Tomlinson, Roth, 1968), or some similar examination and confirmed by neuropsychological tests
   - Deficits in two or more areas of cognition
   - Progressive worsening of memory and other cognitive functions
   - No disturbance of consciousness
   - Onset between ages 40 and 90, most often after age 65
   - Absence of systemic disorders or other brain diseases that in and of themselves could account for progressive deficits in memory and cognition
2. Diagnosis of *probable* Alzheimer's disease is supported by
   - Progressive deterioration of specific cognitive functions, such as language (aphasia), motor skills (apraxia), and perception (agnosia)
   - Impaired activities of daily living and altered patterns of behavior
   - Family history of similar disorders, particularly if confirmed neuropathologically
   - Laboratory results of normal lumbar puncture as evaluated by standard techniques, normal pattern or nonspecific changes in EEG, such as increased slow-wave activity, and evidence of cerebral atrophy on CT with progression documented by serial observation
3. Other clinical features consistent with diagnosis of *probable* Alzheimer's disease, after exclusion of causes of dementia other than Alzheimer's disease, include
   - Plateaus in course of progression of illness
   - Associated symptoms of depression; insomnia; incontinence; delusions; illusions; hallucinations; catastrophic verbal, emotional, or physical outbursts; sexual disorders; and weight loss
   - Other neurological abnormalities in some patients, especially with more advaned disease and including motor signs, such as increased muscle tone, myoclonus, or gait disorder
   - Seizures in advance disease
   - CT normal for age
4. Features that make diagnosis of *probable* Alzheimer's disease uncertain or unlikely include
   - Sudden, apoplectic onset
   - Focal neurological findings such as hemiparesis, sensory loss, visual field deficits, and uncoordination early in the course of the illness
   - Seizures or gait disturbance at onset or very early in course of illness
5. Clinical diagnosis of *probable* Alzheimer's disease
   - May be made on basis of dementia syndrome, in absence of other neurological, psychiatric, or systemic disorders sufficient to cause dementia and in the presence of variations in onset, in presentation, or in clinical course
   - May be made in presence of second systemic or brain disorder sufficient to produce dementia, which is not considered to be cause of dementia
   - Should be used in research studies when single, gradually progressive severe cognitive deficit is identified in absence of other identifiable cause
6. Criteria for diagnosis of *definite* Alzheimer's disease are
   - Clinical criteria for probable Alzheimer's disease
   - Histopathological evidence obtained from biopsy or at autopsy
7. Classification of Alzheimer's disease for research purposes should specify features that may differentiate subtypes of the disorder, such as
   - Familial occurrence
   - Onset before age of 65
   - Presence of trisomy-21
   - Coexistence of other relevant conditions, such as Parkinson's disease

Source: National Institute of Neurological and Communicative Diseases and Stroke

idea is that aluminum, which is deadly to brain cells, starts the chain of events leading to Alzheimer's disease. Although high concentrations of aluminum have been reported in some Alzheimer's disease victims, there is no evidence that links the use of aluminum in daily life, such as in cookware or deodorant, to Alzheimer's disease.

At present, the main focus of research is on a genetic link (Sherrington et al., 1995). The strong possibility that at least some forms of Alzheimer's disease are inherited is a major concern of families of disease victims. The research evidence to date strongly indicates that genetic factors may be a powerful determinant of Alzheimer's disease, and possible markers on chromosomes have been found (e.g., Sherrington et al., 1995). The most promising of this work has noted links between the genetic markers and the production of amyloid protein, the major component of neuritic plaques (Raeburn, 1995).

Although doing genetics research poses several methodological difficulties, it appears from some family trees and studies of relatives and twins that Alzheimer's disease shows an autosomal dominant inheritance pattern. **An *autosomal dominant* pattern is one in which only one gene from one parent is necessary to produce the disease; this means that there is a 50% chance that the child of an affected parent will have the disorder.** An autosomal dominant pattern for Alzheimer's disease makes sense, because we know that at least two other forms of dementia, Pick's disease and Huntington's disease, are autosomal dominant.

Another exciting finding has linked a genetic mutation associated with amyloid protein to Alzheimer's disease. Goate and colleagues (1991) found that two families with early-onset Alzheimer's disease also had one altered amino acid in amyloid protein, a molecule associated with the formation of neuritic plaques. If this finding holds up, it may be the clue that will unlock the mystery of Alzheimer's disease.

Some genetics research has also linked Alzheimer's disease with Down syndrome, a genetic form of mental retardation (Breitner, 1988). Almost all people with Down syndrome over age 40 develop severe cognitive impairments and brain changes like those in Alzheimer's disease, leading some researchers to hypothesize a linkage between the two diseases. However, subsequent evidence showed this was not likely to be the case. The genetic evidence concerning amyloid is considerably stronger than that concerning a general link with chromosome 21, the chromosome involved with Down syndrome (Raeburn, 1995; Sherrington et al., 1995).

Even if a specific gene is identified, many questions about the cause of Alzheimer's disease will remain. Why does it take so long for the genetic defect to appear? What mechanism starts it? Why is there so much variation when it appears? Answers to these questions will help considerably in understanding how Alzheimer's disease develops.

Supposing that an autosomal dominant pattern were responsible, what would this mean for the relatives of Alzheimer's disease victims? Actually, it would depend on the relative's age. Even though the risk would always be greater, even at age 65 this increased risk would have little practical significance, because the overall incidence of Alzheimer's disease at this age is low. But by age 80 the risk to first-degree relatives would be roughly 25%, compared with 6% in the general population (Breitner, 1988). Although these numbers are not reassuring, they are considerably lower than the risk for many other autosomal dominant genetic diseases, such as Huntington's disease.

Tests can be developed to detect genes that transmit diseases via an autosomal dominant pattern. Such a test already exists for Huntington's disease. As discussed in Something to Think About, however, taking the test is not an easy decision, even when there is a high risk of passing the disease on to one's children.

Intervention Strategies

Alzheimer's disease is incurable. However, much research has been done looking for ways to alleviate the cognitive deficits and behavioral problems that characterize the disease. These strategies are summarized in Table 9.4.

Much of the research has focused on various drugs that could improve memory (Raskind & Peskind, 1992; Schneider, 1995). These drugs

SOMETHING TO THINK ABOUT

Genetic Tests for Dementia—Difficult Choices

When scientists discovered that they could determine whether someone was carrying the gene for Huntington's disease, they thought it would be a welcome relief to thousands of families. After all, Huntington's disease is a terrible scourge of adults in their 30s, 40s, or 50s, eventually institutionalizing most and killing them all. As noted in the text, those who have one parent with the disease run a 50-50 chance of having it themselves and, if they have children, of passing it on to them. So it seemed likely that the ability to determine in advance who would develop or escape the disease would be welcomed by affected families—allowing them to plan more practically about having children, choosing jobs, obtaining insurance, organizing finances, and pursuing social and leisure interests.

But the scientists were wrong. Only a small fraction of those at risk and close enough to obtain the test have done so. Why?

The answer is not with the test, which involves a genetic analysis of blood samples taken from the person being tested and from six or so family members. At present the test is administered at government expense on a trial basis at five medical centers: Columbia University, Johns Hopkins University, Massachusetts General Hospital, the University of Michigan, and the University of Minnesota.

Perhaps the answer lies in the fact that a positive result on the test means a high probability of developing the disease. In short, one learns that one faces a long, terrible death. The test is 99% accurate.

Samuel L. Baily, former chairman of the National Huntington's Disease Association, chose not to have the test even though his mother died from Huntington's disease at age 58, 8 years after she was diagnosed. Baily, symptom-free at age 52, said that he would rather just take his chances with the disease, which had also killed his maternal grandfather. He prefers to live with the hope of not getting it than with the knowledge that he will.

Others choose a different course. Karen Sweeney, 28, who is married and has four children, told interviewers that she had to know (J. Brody, 1988a). The stress of knowing that her mother and grandfather both died from the disease had taken its toll on her and on her marriage. After moving to Baltimore to be eligible for the Johns Hopkins testing program, Karen and her husband went through extensive counseling before the test. For Karen, the news was good: no Huntington's.

Certainly, Huntington's disease and all other forms of dementia are terrible, killer diseases. With research rapidly advancing on Alzheimer's disease, it is likely that a test for a genetic marker for it will be developed in the next decade. It is also likely that a test will be available before there is a cure. If you had relatives who had died from Alzheimer's disease or Huntington's disease, if you were planning to have a family, and if a test were available, what would you do? It's something to think about.

---

have included a wide variety of compounds aimed at improving cerebral blood flow or levels of various neurotransmitters. Although some drugs, such as tacrine, have been reported to improve cognitive functioning, these successes have often been achieved with carefully selected patients on carefully selected tests, and none of the drugs has shown reliable improvements in a wide variety of patients (Schneider, 1995).

In contrast to the poor picture for improving cognitive performance, improving other behavioral problems is possible. Drugs that are used primarily in younger patients for the treatment of schizophrenia, such as thioridazine and haloperidol, are effective in lowering the severe psychiatric symptoms that develop during the course of Alzheimer's disease (Schneider, 1995). Similarly, antidepressants are effective in alleviating the depressive symptoms that typically accompany the early stages of the disease (Crook & Cohen, 1983), and sedatives may be effective for sleep disturbances. However, these medications should be used with considerable caution, because dosage levels for older adults may be far lower than those for younger patients, and side effects may be much more serious (Salzman, 1984).

TABLE 9.4 Overview of treatments for symptoms of dementia

Symptoms	Treatment Considerations	Comments
Cognitive or memory impairments	Reversal or prevention of cognitive deterioration is the treatment goal. This is currently an area of active pharmacologic investigation. There is no evidence that social interventions, "retraining," or education is meaningfully effective in improving cognitive function per se.	One cholinesterase inhibitor, tacrine, is available by prescription. Other cholinergic drugs are under investigation. Such drugs are likely to confer modest improvements in memory in a minority of Alzheimer's patients. Long-term efficacy is not known. Use in other dementias is not tested.
Impaired social function and activities of daily living	Environmental manipulations to allow patients with dementia to function better may be helpful. Experimental medications that seem effective for cognitive symptoms may affect daily activities and social function also. Psychosocial interventions directed toward caregivers may postpone nursing home placement.	There are no drugs currently available. Drugs that improve cognition would be expected to improve cognition-dependent social function. Drugs that limit further deterioration would be expected to preserve basic activities of daily living.
Behavioral symptoms (depression and mood-related symptoms)	Depressive symptoms may occur in 10% to 20% of dementia patients with Alzheimer's, usually earlier in the course than psychotic symptoms appear. Antidepressant medication may be helpful.	A randomized trial of imipramine showed no significant advantage over placebo. A trial of moclobemide (not available in the United States), however, suggested more efficacy than placebo.
Behavioral symptoms (hallucinations, delusions, agitation, aggression)	These symptoms, which most patients have during the illness course, influence quality of life and institutionalization. Environmental manipulations may be helpful in reducing symptoms. Various medications may be effective; neuroleptics are best studied.	Several placebo-controlled trials with neuroleptics, usually haloperidol or thioridazine, indicate efficacy for an acute treatment period of 8 weeks or less. There have been many case reports, but there have been very few controlled trials with other medications such as antidepressants, anticonvulsants, β-blockers, or serotonin uptake blockers.

Source: U.S. Public Health Service, 1993

Several interventions that do not involve drugs are also available. Cognitive problems can be addressed by creating a supportive environment, such as labeling the contents of cupboards, and by using behavioral techniques to teach new strategies (see Chapter 6). Depression, irritability, wandering, and emotional problems can also be effectively dealt with through behavioral techniques. Most important in this regard is the introduction of a straightforward daily schedule in which meals, medications, and naps always come at the same time. Environmental interventions—such as control of lighting, noise, and temperature in bedrooms—may also help alleviate sleep disturbances. Reality orientation therapy, discussed in detail later in this chapter, may also be effective.

In the long run most Alzheimer's disease patients become completely dependent on others, leaving caregivers few intervention options. We will consider the burden on the family members in a later section.

Other Forms of Dementia

As we have noted, dementia represents a family of different diseases. In this section, we will consider several of them briefly.

Multi-Infarct Dementia

Until Tomlinson and colleagues' (1970) discovery that Alzheimer's disease was not rare, most physicians and researchers believed that most cases of dementia resulted from cerebral arteriosclerosis and its consequent restriction of oxygen to the brain. As described in Chapter 3, arteriosclerosis is a family of diseases that, if untreated, may result in heart attacks or strokes. For the present discussion it is the stroke, or *cerebrovascular accident (CVA)*, that concerns us. CVAs (see Chapter 3) result from a disruption of the blood flow, termed an *infarct*, which may be caused by a blockage or hemorrhage.

A large CVA may produce severe cognitive decline, but this loss is almost always limited to specific abilities. This pattern is different from the classic, global deterioration seen in dementia. **However, a series of small CVAs can produce this global pattern, which results in a condition termed *multi-infarct dementia*** (Hachinski, Lassen, & Marshall, 1974). Multi-infarct dementia accounts for 10% to 15% of all cases of dementia (Crook, 1987).

The course of multi-infarct dementia is very different from that seen in Alzheimer's disease (Crook, 1987). Multi-infarct dementia has a sudden onset, and its progression is described as stepwise, or stuttering. This is in contrast to the insidious onset and gradual progression of Alzheimer's disease. The symptom pattern in multi-infarct dementia is highly variable, especially early in the disease. Again, this is in contrast to the similar cluster of cognitive problems shown by Alzheimer's disease patients.

Blass and Barclay (1985) report that the median survival of multi-infarct dementia patients is only 2 to 3 years, much shorter than that of Alzheimer's disease patients. They argue that the diagnosis of multi-infarct dementia should be reconsidered if the patient survives longer than 2 years without any evidence of additional CVAs.

The steps in diagnosing multi-infarct dementia are similar to Alzheimer's disease. Evidence of CVAs from diagnostic imaging (CT or MRI) and a history of cerebrovascular disease are usually the key factors (Davies, 1988). In a small percentage of cases, however, evidence of both Alzheimer's disease and multi-infarct dementia is found.

Multi-infarct dementia is especially tragic compared with Alzheimer's disease, in that there are known risk factors that can be controlled. Among these are hypertension and others noted in Chapters 3 and 4. Attention to these factors earlier in life may well lower the risk of multi-infarct dementia considerably.

Parkinson's Disease

A form of dementia known primarily for its characteristic cluster of motor problems defines *Parkinson's disease:* very slow walking, stiffness, difficulty getting in and out of chairs, and a slow tremor. These behavioral symptoms are caused by a deterioration of the neurons in the midbrain that produce the neurotransmitter dopamine (Lieberman, 1974). Administration of the drug L-dopa greatly alleviates these behavioral problems.

Recent research evidence established a link between Parkinson's-like symptoms and a soil-dwelling bacterium (*Discover,* Oct. 1990). The bacterium, *Nocardia,* is easily breathed in when one inhales dust. When laboratory mice were injected with the bacterium, they developed the motor symptoms associated with Parkinson's disease. Interestingly, when they were given L-dopa, the symptoms disappeared; when the drug wore off the symptoms returned. It is too early to tell whether a cause for Parkinson's disease has been discovered, but the link is intriguing.

The connection between Parkinson's disease and dementia was not generally recognized until the late 1970s. Researchers now estimate, however, that between 14% and 40% of people with Parkinson's disease will develop dementia (Raskind & Peskind, 1992). Although early research proposed that the dementia associated with Parkinson's disease was the same as in Alzheimer's disease, more recent research indicates that the two are different. In particular, examination of brain tissue at autopsy reveals that a structural change called Lewy bodies occurs with much more frequency in dementia associated with Parkinson's disease (Raskind & Peskind, 1992).

Pick's Disease

Pick's disease is a very rare form of dementia that is clinically very hard to discriminate from Alzheimer's disease. Nevertheless, it is quite distinct neuropathologically, that is, in terms of the structural changes in the brain. Some researchers and clinicians note that patients in the early stages of Pick's disease show little memory impairment but marked behavioral changes, such as social inappropriateness, loss of modesty, and uninhibited sexual behavior (Lishman, 1978). Neuropathological changes include striking atrophy of the frontal and temporal lobes, the absence of both senile plaques and neurofibrillary tangles, but the presence of so-called Pick's bodies in neurons (Davies, 1988). An interesting research question is why the cognitive changes in Pick's disease so closely resemble those in Alzheimer's disease even though the structural changes in the neurons are quite different. Perhaps a partial explanation is that the nucleus basalis of Meynert, a major source of acetylcholine, is destroyed in both diseases (Price et al., 1982). An additional interesting parallel is that Pick's disease appears to be determined by a single autosomal dominant gene (Sjogren, Sjogren, & Lindgren, 1952), the same genetic mechanism being investigated as a factor in Alzheimer's disease.

Creutzfeld-Jakob Disease

Creutzfeld-Jakob disease is another very rare form of dementia that is characterized by a relatively early onset, very rapid course (rarely more than 2 years from diagnosis to death), and severe changes in EEG patterns (Siedler & Malamud, 1963). These changes appear to be caused by severe neuronal degeneration, a very marked proliferation of *astrocytes* (star-shaped cells in the brain), and a spongy appearance of the gray matter in the brain. There are no senile plaques or neurofibrillary tangles (as in Alzheimer's disease), no massive atrophy (as seen in Pick's disease), and no vascular damage (as in multi-infarct dementia) (Lishman, 1978).

The most important aspect of Creutzfeld-Jakob disease is that it appears to be transmitted by a slow-acting virus. Moreover, the disease is clinically and neuropathologically related to kuru, a transmissible form of dementia found in the Fore linguistic tribe in New Guinea (Gajdusek, 1977). Gajdusek's research shows that the virus responsible is transmitted through the practice of cannibalism and has an incubation of many years. The research documenting that these forms of dementia are communicable earned these investigators a Nobel Prize and opened research to the possibility that Alzheimer's disease may also be caused by a virus.

Huntington's Disease

Huntington's disease is an autosomal dominant disorder that usually begins between the ages of 35 and 50. The disease generally manifests itself through involuntary flicking movements of the arms and legs; the inability to sustain a motor act such as sticking out one's tongue; prominent psychiatric disturbances such as hallucinations, paranoia, and depression; and clear personality changes, such as swings from apathy to manic behavior (Berkow, 1987). Cognitive impairments typically do not appear until late in the disease. The onset of these symptoms is very gradual. The course of Huntington's disease is progressive; patients ultimately lose the ability to care for themselves physically and mentally. Walking becomes impossible, swallowing is difficult, and cognitive loss becomes profound (Berkow, 1987). Changes in the brain thought to underlie the behavioral losses include degeneration of the caudate nucleus and the small-cell population, as well as substantial decreases in the neurotransmitters GABA and substance P. Although antipsychotic medications are sometimes used to control the psychiatric disturbances and agitated behaviors, they are only partially effective (Berkow, 1987). As noted earlier, a test is available to determine whether one has the marker for the Huntington's disease gene.

Normal-Pressure Hydrocephalus

Normal-pressure hydrocephalus is another rare form of dementia that is characterized by enlarged cerebral ventricles but normal cerebrospinal fluid pressure (Crook, 1987). The ventricles are the chambers in the brain that contain cerebrospinal fluid. This condition is caused most often by a head injury or hemorrhage deep in the brain (Hakim & Adams, 1965). The early symptoms are usually general cognitive deficits, hesitancy or shuffling during walking, and urinary incontinence (Berkow, 1987). The diagnosis can be confirmed through CT or MRI, which document the enlarged ventricles, but clinical observation of these three problems is usually sufficient (Mulrow, Feussner, Williams, & Vokaty, 1987). Treatment of the disease is usually through shunting, a procedure that helps drain the cerebrospinal fluid to lower the pressure. Many patients do not respond to this procedure, however, especially if the disease has been present a long time (Berkow, 1987).

Alcoholic Dementia

In Chapter 4, we noted that one of the consequences of long-term chronic alcoholism was Wernicke-Korsakoff's syndrome. This disease, caused by a chronic deficiency of thiamine, causes major losses of memory and other cognitive functioning. The condition is treatable if the vitamin deficiency is detected early in the process, and cessation of excessive alcohol consumption is usually associated with improved cognitive functioning as well.

Caring for Dementia Patients at Home

The changes that happen to a person who has a form of dementia are devastating, not only to the patient but also to the the whole family (Aneshensel, Pearlin, Mullan, Zarit, & Whitlach, 1995). Watching a spouse, parent, or sibling go from being an independent, mature adult to being a helpless shell who is oblivious to his or her surroundings is extremely difficult.

Despite these formidable emotional issues, the vast majority of dementia patients are cared for by their family members at home. Until the mid-1970s little was known about their experience, and little information was available on effective home-care strategies. The appearance of Mace and Rabin's *The 36-Hour Day* in 1981 marked a major turning point; their book remains one of the best guides for families caring for a dementia patient. Throughout the 1980s and early 1990s, researchers have focused on two main lines of investigation concerning caregiving: identifying effective strategies of care and documenting the stress and burden felt by the family.

One useful way of conceptualizing family caregiving is as an unexpected career (Aneshensel et al., 1995). As shown in Figure 9.1, the caregiving career begins with the onset of the illness and moves through a number of separate steps. Note that the process does not end with the placement of the affected family member in a nursing home, or even with that person's death. Rather, Aneshensel et al. (1995) point out that the career continues through the bereavement and social readjustment period, at which point one may continue on with life. Note also that the kind of caregiving also changes, from the comprehensive caregiving, which covers all aspects of the process, to sustained caregiving in the home to foreshortened caregiving in the nursing home to withdrawal from caregiving.

Because the majority of people with dementia have Alzheimer's disease, most of the research focuses on caregivers of these patients. The advice offered, however, applies to caregivers of all dementia patients.

Effective Caregiving Strategies

Aronson (1988) provides an excellent summary of the interventions and decisions that caregivers can make that will make the care of Alzheimer's patients as successful as possible. Key steps to be taken

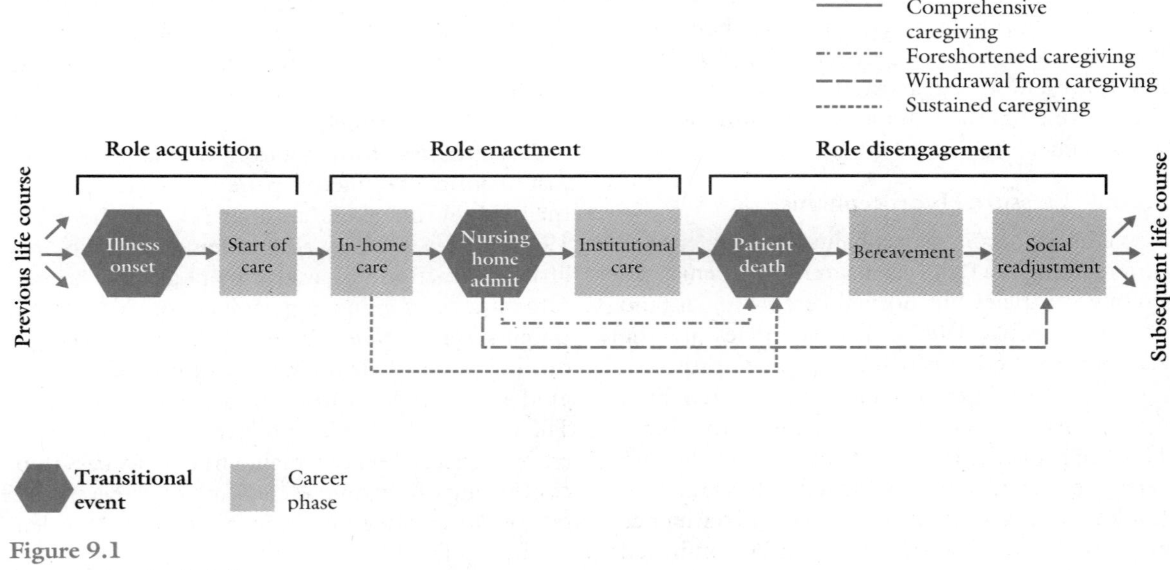

Figure 9.1
Source: Aneshensel et al., 1995

once a diagnosis is made include obtaining accurate information about the disease; involving the patient as much as possible in decisions; identifying the primary caregiver; reassessing the patient's living situation; setting realistic goals; making realistic financial plans; identifying a source of regular medical care; maximizing the patient's opportunity to function at his or her optimal level; making realistic demands of the patient; and using outside services as needed. The goal of these early steps is to build a broad support network of relatives, medical personnel, and service providers that may be needed later. The new responsibilities of family members require changes in daily routines; people adjust to these roles at different rates.

Many behaviors and situations that we take for granted need to be rethought when we find ourselves caring for an Alzheimer's disease patient. Dressing, bathing, and grooming become more difficult or even aversive to the patient. Use of Velcro fasteners, joining the patient during a bath or shower, and other such changes may be necessary. Nutritional needs have to be monitored, because patients may forget that they have just eaten or may forget to eat. Medications must be used with considerable caution. Changes in personality and sexual behavior need to be viewed as part of the disease. Sleeplessness can be addressed by establishing consistent bedtimes, giving warm milk or tryptophan, and limiting caffeine intake. Wandering is an especially troublesome problem because it is difficult to control; making sure that the patient has an identification bracelet with the nature of the problem on it and making the house accident-proof are two preventive steps. In severe cases of wandering it may be necessary to use restraints, but only under the direction of a health care professional. Incontinence, which usually occurs late in the disease, is a troubling and embarrassing issue for the patient; use of special undergarments or diapers or medications to treat the problem are two of the available options. Incontinence is not necessarily related to Alzheimer's disease; for example, stress incontinence, which is

Keeping persons with Alzheimer's disease involved in everyday activities is an important aspect of good caregiving.

fairly common among older women, is unrelated to dementia.

One of the most difficult issues faced by caregivers concerns taking things away from the patient and restricting activity. Relatively early in the disease the patient will experience problems handling finances. It is not uncommon for patients to spend hundreds or even thousands of dollars on strange items, to leave the checkbook unbalanced and bills unpaid, and to lose money. Although the patient can be given some money to keep, someone else must handle the day-to-day accounts. Traveling alone is another sticky issue. Families of dementia patients often wait until a major calamity occurs before recognizing their loved one's deteriorating condition. Instead, families should limit solo excursions to places within walking distance; all other trips should be made with at least one family member along. Driving is often a contentious issue, especially if the patient does not recognize his or her limitations. Once it is clear that the patient cannot drive, the family must take whatever steps are necessary. In some cases this entails simply taking the car keys, but in others it becomes necessary to disable the car. Suggesting that the patient could be chauffeured is another alternative.

Two rapidly growing options for caregivers are respite care and adult day care. ***Respite care* is designed to allow family members to get away for a time.** It can consist of in-home care provided by professionals or temporary placement in a residential facility. In-home care is typically used to allow caregivers to do errands or to have a few hours free, whereas temporary residential placement is reserved for a more extended respite, such as a weekend. Respite care is a tremendous help to caregivers. In one study there was marked improvement in family members' reports of problems after a two-week respite (Burdz, Eaton, & Bond,

1988). ***Adult day care*** **provides placement and programming for frail elderly people during the day.** This option is used most often by adult children who are employed. The demand for respite and adult day care far exceeds their availability, making them limited options. An additional problem is that many insurance programs will not pay for these services, making them too expensive for caregivers with limited finances. Even when services are available, however, many families do not use them until their informal support system begins to break down (Caserta, Lund, Wright, & Redburn, 1987).

In general, family members must change their entire daily routines to care for a dementia patient. Such complete alterations in habits, coupled with watching the deterioration in their loved one, create an extremely stressful situation.

Family Stress and Burden

Taking care of a person with dementia is an extremely stressful, time-consuming job. For many caregivers it becomes a full-time job, going from a situation that they control to one that controls them. In her book *Another Name for Madness,* Marion Roach (1985) vividly describes what the process is like. She relates the range of feelings she experienced caring for her mother (who was in her early 50s when she was diagnosed with Alzheimer's disease): anger, frustration, worry, pity, guilt, and a host of others.

Researchers have documented what Roach and all other caregivers go through. The most commonly used concept to describe the experience is burden (Teri, Truax, Logsdon, Uomoto, & Zarit, 1990). Burden relates to the experience of psychological stress and distress as the result of caring for a frail elder. Most of the research on burden has been focused on caregivers of Alzheimer's disease patients, although some work has documented similar experiences in those caring for stroke patients and head-injured patients as well (Schulz, Tompkins, & Rau, 1988).

Caregivers experience considerable negative effects: chronic fatigue, anger, depression, loss of friends, loss of time to themselves, dissatisfaction with other family members, physical and mental strain, stress symptoms, less life satisfaction, and lower well-being (Cavanaugh & Kinney, 1994; Kinney & Stephens, 1989). Men tend to report higher levels of morale than women (Gilhooly, 1984), perhaps because women become more emotionally involved in caregiving and care for more severely impaired patients. Married daughters caring for their parents often are forced to quit their jobs (Brody, Kleban, Johnsen, Hoffman, & Schoonover, 1987), whereas married sons often are not. Spouses who care for their partner report lower levels of physical health, mental health, and financial resources than spouses without such a burden (George & Gwyther, 1986; Gilhooly, 1984).

We must be careful, however, not to overgeneralize these findings. Most of the research on caregivers has been conducted on middle-class European American adults; how they view caring for relatives may not be the same for other ethnic groups. Research to date indicates that there are both similarities and differences among different ethnic groups. For example, Hennessy and John (1995) found that Pueblo Indian caregivers report similar experiences of role strain, interpersonal tensions and conflict within the family, feelings of uncertainty about managing care, and perceptions of detrimental effects of caregiving on personal health as do European American caregivers. However, the Pueblo Indian caregivers do not indicate that they experience social constraints, limits on personal freedom, or embarrassment.

One important finding is that it is far more likely that daughters rather than sons will care for their parents (Brody, 1985). Moreover, daughters may have to deal not only with the problems of caregiving but also with resentments at having to assume a form of child-rearing responsibilities in midlife. Compared with spouse caregivers, daughters have many more competing pressures such as career and family, adding to their burden (Brody, 1985; Quayhagen & Quayhagen, 1988).

Considerable research documents that it is not a specific aspect of Alzheimer's disease or related disorders—such as wandering or incontinence—

HOW DO WE KNOW?

Caregiver Burden—A Stress and Coping Approach

Caring for a dementia patient is a highly demanding and stressful job. Some researchers have begun to study the effects of caregiving by turning to the model of stress and coping proposed by Lazarus and Folkman (1984). Briefly, this model postulates that stress is the perception that one's resources are being taxed and that one is being threatened. To measure stress in this way, Lazarus and his colleagues developed the Hassles Scale, which measures whether stressful events have happened recently, and, if so, to what extent they were perceived as troublesome.

Kinney and Stephens (1989) adapted this idea to the caregiving situation. They believed that the amount of burden experienced by caregivers of Alzheimer's disease patients could be understood in Lazarus and Folkman's framework. Kinney and Stephens developed the 42-item Caregiving Hassles Scale. Each item on the scale is a commonly encountered situation, such as giving the patient a bath. Respondents indicate whether each event has occurred in the previous week and to what extent it represents a difficulty (on a four-point scale).

Caregivers of Alzheimer's disease patients reported many hassles. The most common ones involved assisting the patient with daily living (bathing, dressing) and dealing with cognitive limitations and behavior problems. The severity of perceived problems correlated with poor caregiver-patient relations and higher levels of anxiety, hostility, and depression in caregivers. Hassles that were related to patients' behavior problems proved most troublesome; apparently, dealing with emotional outbursts and the like presented serious problems for coping.

A key aspect of the Kinney and Stephens data is that the specific behaviors that were perceived as hassles varied a great deal across caregivers. This finding is in keeping with Lazarus and Folkman's notion that it is not what happens, but how you perceive what happens, that matters. Kinney and Stephens have provided a useful approach to the study of caregiving and have made use of a general model of stress and coping to do so. It demonstrates that the study of adult development and aging does involve the application of concepts and models developed in different contexts to many other settings.

---

that cause these problems (Cavanaugh & Kinney, 1994; Kinney & Cavanaugh, 1993). Rather, it is the caregiver's perception of the situation that matters. For example, the perception that one's social support system is gone is a powerful predictor of the decision to institutionalize the patient, whereas the actual physical condition of the patient is not (George & Gwyther, 1986).

Some investigators of caregiver burden (Haley, Levine, Brown, Berry, and Hughes, 1987; Kinney & Stephens, 1989) have adopted a stress and coping approach based on Lazarus and Folkman's (1984) model, described in Chapter 4. In this approach it is the perception that one's resources are being taxed by the present situation that causes the burden, not the objective real situation. This approach, described in more detail in How Do We Know?, fits well with the data and should provide a useful framework for future research.

Concept Checks

1. What is delirium?
2. What are the defining neurological characteristics of Alzheimer's disease?
3. What are the major characteristics of multi-infarct dementia?
4. What are the major feelings experienced by family caregivers?

FAMILY INTERVENTION AND FAMILY THERAPY

Learning Objectives:

- What are the characteristics of family therapy?

- What are the most common conflicts experienced by older adults?
- What approaches are used in family therapy?

Although many problems encountered during adulthood are best resolved at an individual level, other problems involve family factors and home relationships. These latter difficulties are best handled by working with the family as a whole. If adults are able to receive adequate help from family members and have a positive, collaborative relationship with them, their whole mental outlook, behavioral functioning, and adaptation to life is enhanced (Fry, 1986). Because family ties remain important throughout adulthood (see Chapter 10), family intervention is an important topic for adults of all ages. As we will see, because family therapy is effective for families confronting Alzheimer's disease, it is likely that this approach will continue to grow in popularity.

This section looks at the goals of family intervention and family therapy and discusses some important aspects of evaluating family dynamics. We will also consider some age-related issues pertaining to family dynamics that are important considerations in designing effective interventions.

What Is Family Therapy?

Family therapy **views the family as an independent system of members who mutually influence one another** (Haley, 1971). Consequently, changing the behavior of one family member means changing the whole family system. In addition, we must understand what particular roles are played by each member (parent, child, nurturer, martyr, and so forth) and how these roles are interrelated. Families also have certain rules that govern the communication among their members; these must be identified as well.

An assumption in family therapy is that functional families work toward the growth and development of their members, whereas dysfunctional families produce the distress or destruction of their members. These ends are achieved by implementing the roles and rules of the family.

The role of the family therapist is to identify the roles played by each member and the rules by which they play. Although there are several different ways in which these identifications are made and the therapy is carried out, all agree on the importance of improving the communication skills among family members as the first step.

Common Issues in Family Therapy with Older Adults

Issues addressed in family therapy reflect the myriad of problems that occur in family relationships. When these problems involve older adults, however, they tend to focus on three themes (Fry, 1986): conflicts between spouses, conflicts between adult children and their elderly parents, and conflicts in communications and expectations.

Conflicts Between Spouses

One common problem confronting spouses of all ages is change in life circumstances. For middle-aged adults, these changes may include children's leaving home or a new job. For older spouses, these changes include retirement, loss of income, or physical incapacitation. In all of these cases such changes may reactivate earlier problems in the marriage. Despite feeling unhappy, many of these couples continue to live together out of fear of change or economic necessity. Conflict between the spouses may arise out of each party's resistance to change, inability to meet the other's needs, or feelings of being forced to adopt new and unwanted roles (such as a caregiver).

Conflicts Between Adult Children and Their Elderly Parents

When adult children become caregivers to their parents, conflict may result from the stress. Assuming additional responsibility for the management of an elderly parent often takes a high toll, as discussed earlier in this chapter. Elderly parents may try to assume control of the household, the spouses of the adult children may resent the extra duties put on their partners, or the adult children may resent their parents for disrupting the household. Additionally, older parents may be unfairly blamed for marital problems between adult children and their spouses. The results of such conflicts can be devastating to the family.

Conflicts in Communications and Expectations

Many families cannot maintain open communication with all of their members, especially during times of conflict. Such open communication is clearly needed between adult children and their parents. What is often overlooked is that adult children need to be able to openly discuss matters with their parents but may not feel comfortable in doing so. For example, middle-aged adults may feel the urge to talk about their feelings with their parents, who have experienced middle-age firsthand, but the adult children may be reluctant to actually open up to their parents. Additionally, one generation may place excessive role demands on the other, such as the oldest generation expecting the middle generation to be perfect parents and perfect achievers in the workplace.

Techniques for Family Therapy

Herr and Weakland (1979) discuss several techniques for family intervention. Most important is ***communication skills training,*** in which family members learn how to listen to other family members and to express their own feelings more clearly. Early in the family therapy process, the therapist must determine what the problems confronting the family really are and uncover any hidden agendas a particular member has. Additionally, realistic goals for recovery must be set. The therapist also must ascertain how the family dealt with similar problems in the past and determine which solution strategies worked and which ones failed. New alternatives are offered as needed. Also important is determining and explicitly stating the family rules for interaction and pointing out when these rules need to be changed. Finally, the family members must all agree on the nature and direction of change.

Several studies have documented that family therapy is effective in dealing with problems involving older adult family members (such as Cicirelli, 1986; Zarit & Anthony, 1986). Family therapy is often the approach of choice in addressing problems stemming from caregiving. For example, the increased ability to communicate feelings of guilt, anger, closeness, and love allows family members to deal with their feelings more adaptively.

Concept Checks

1. What is family therapy?
2. What conflicts do older adults experience that are important in family therapy?
3. What is communication skills training?

WORKING WITH THE INSTITUTIONALIZED ELDERLY

Learning Objectives:

- What is the goal of sensory training?
- What is reality orientation?
- What is involved in validation therapy?
- How does remotivation therapy work?
- What other approaches to therapy are used in institutions?

Traditionally, one of the most underserved groups of older adults has been residents of nursing homes. However, these individuals can benefit significantly from a wide variety of intervention programs targeted for different levels of ability (Weiner, Brok, & Snadowsky, 1987). Indeed, nursing homes are one of the fastest growing areas of mental health intervention in developing strategies and programs. The ability of cognitively impaired individuals to benefit from such intervention has been sadly underestimated in the past; we now know that even people with moderately severe impairment can benefit. In this section we will consider some of the major techniques that are used with institutionalized elderly people to optimize their abilities.

A word of caution is needed before we begin

Group activities such as coloring Easter eggs play an important role in fostering a sense of personal control and identity among the institutionalized elderly.

our survey. These techniques have been widely adopted, but there is very little research evidence that they are effective. Although future research may demonstrate that these programs work, for the time being we must be careful not to assume that they will result in improvements in functioning.

Sensory Training

Sensory training is aimed at bringing a person back in touch with the environment (Weiner et al., 1987). This technique is effective in getting highly regressed residents who have psychomotor, sensory, verbal, or cognitive deficits to reexperience their surroundings and remake social contacts. Sensory training begins with social introductions among group members, followed by body-awareness exercises and sensory stimulation. These activities stimulate social participation and sensory experience through the use of common objects. Having participants talk or think about their experiences also enhances cognitive activity.

Sensory training works best when groups are not too large, five to seven persons, and when they are conducted every morning, seven days a week. The meeting place and time should always be the same, to eliminate confusion. Any materials that can be used to stimulate the senses—from cotton balls to sandpaper to different-colored objects—are appropriate.

The major advantage of sensory training is that individuals who are usually excluded from other groups because of the sensory or cognitive impairments can benefit. And because no special equipment needs to be purchased, sensory training is inexpensive as well.

Reality Orientation

Reality orientation—based on repetition and relearning—is a technique that was developed for the moderately confused resident (Stephens, 1975). The key to reality orientation is that it is a 24-hour program that is integrated in the entire environment. The goal is to keep the resident in touch with what is going on in the world in every way possible.

Implementing a reality orientation program involves several things. Residents are addressed by a title such as Mr. or Mrs. unless they specify otherwise. Plenty of clocks and bulletin boards with calendars are placed in prominent locations. Name cards are used at meals. Activities are interesting and diversified and are announced on the public address system. Birthdays are recognized individually, and special meals are served on holidays. Visiting hours are liberal, and volunteers are encouraged to visit. Color-coded rooms and hallways are used. Independence is encouraged as much as possible. In short, everything that occurs in the institution is geared to keeping residents in touch with reality.

Research findings on the effects of reality orientation are mixed. It appears to be most beneficial for mildly disoriented individuals (Spayd & Smyer, 1988). Overall, reality orientation appears to improve individuals' knowledge of basic orienting facts (such as day, month, time) rather than providing them with a set of transferrable skills for dealing with different environments (Hart & Fleming, 1985).

Attitude therapy is usually used in conjunction with reality orientation. Basically, attitude therapy aims at identifying each resident's primary interactive style, which is then dealt with by the staff in certain specified and consistent ways. For example, active friendliness is used with apathetic, withdrawn residents; passive friendliness, with frightened, suspicious residents; matter-of-factness, with manipulative residents; kind firmness, with depressed residents; and a no-demands approach, with angry, hostile residents. Attitude therapy is designed to reinforce adaptive behaviors and not to reinforce maladaptive behaviors.

Validation Therapy

In sharp contrast to reality orientation, validation therapy does not involve correcting a person's disorientation (Wetzler & Feil, 1979). For example, Anne believed that her son was a young infant, when in fact he was a middle-aged adult. Gentle attempts at reorienting her failed, partly because Anne could not remember the correct information over time. When Anne began to address a doll as her son, the staff was encouraged to talk to her about her son, such as how she cared for him and about his favorite foods or toys. The staff's acceptance of Anne's disorientation *validated* Anne's feelings. Such validation may keep residents from becoming agitated, as well as provide things for staff and residents to talk about. Note that the goal of validation therapy is not to correct disoriented statements, or to confirm them. Rather, the goal is to validate the *emotions* incorporated in the disoriented belief to relieve distress (Spayd & Smyer, 1988).

Remotivation Therapy

Remotivation therapy is a structured program based on a set of standard topics intended to reawaken the interest of apathetic residents (Weiner et al., 1987). The program works by getting a group of 10 to 15 residents to discuss a topic such as clothing or food in a five-step process: (1) creating a climate of acceptance by welcoming each member; (2) creating a bridge to reality by selecting a topic for discussion; (3) sharing the world of reality by asking the group members about the topic; (4) appreciating the world of reality by getting members to share their ideas or by stimulating reminiscence; and (5) creating a climate of appreciation by noting the good contributions made by each member. Remotivation therapy should be conducted once or twice a week for between 30 and 60 minutes. The structured program lasts 12 weeks. Group leaders for remotivation therapy should have completed a 30-hour course in the technique at a training center, primarily because the program adheres to a rigid, precise format and requires preparation.

Additional Therapeutic Approaches

In addition to sensory training, reality therapy, validation therapy, and remotivation therapy, a host of other interventions are used in institutions. Four of the more popular ones are activities and recreation therapy, milieu therapy, supportive group therapy, and pet therapy.

Activities and recreation therapy helps to optimize residents' functioning and improve their quality of life by getting them involved in physical and mental activities (Haun, 1965). A comprehensive program should include a wide variety of voluntary activities that can be performed individually, in small groups, and in large groups. The ability to choose activities is the key; whether it is playing solitaire or watching movies in a group, the benefits of participation are greater if it is the resident's choice (Weiner et al., 1987). Being able to make decisions fosters independence and self-esteem.

Milieu therapy takes a different approach. Rather than a staff member designing the program, the resident designs the environment so that it most closely reflects the kind of setting that he or she was used to before entering the nursing home (Weiner et al., 1987). This enables the resident to sustain social roles and puts responsibility for these roles on the resident rather than the staff. Residents in a milieu therapy program are placed together based on similarities in their primary needs, degree of independence, and degree of disability.

Many nursing homes and other residential facilities are beginning *supportive group therapy* for their residents. These groups serve many functions, but mainly they focus on promoting better human relationships, dealing with feelings of loneliness or inferiority, and encouraging coping (Hartford, 1980). These groups have been shown to increase residents' sense of personal control, life satisfaction, and trust (Moran & Gatz, 1987).

Pet therapy is one of the fastest growing techniques with institutionalized older adults (Brickel, 1984). Pets are used to enhance feelings of responsibility and control, trigger reminiscence, and promote social interaction. Short-term gains in positive feelings about oneself, well-being, and cognitive functioning have been reported, but few detailed studies of pet therapy have been conducted. For individuals who are not institutionalized, playing with pets has no effect on longevity.

Concept Checks

1. What is the goal of sensory training?
2. What is the basic approach used in reality orientation?
3. What is the goal of validation therapy?
4. What is the five-step process in remotivation therapy?
5. What are some other therapies used in institutions?

SUMMARY

Mental Health and the Adult Life Course

Defining Mental Health and Psychopathology

Definitions of mental health need to reflect appropriate age-related criteria. Behaviors need to be interpreted in context. Mentally healthy people have positive attitudes, accurate perceptions, environmental mastery, autonomy, personality balance, and personal growth.

A Multidimensional Approach to Psychopathology

Consideration of key interpersonal, intrapersonal, biological and physiological, and life-cycle factors is essential for accurate diagnosis of mental disorders. Diagnostic criteria need to reflect age differences in symptomatology. *DSM-IV* uses five axes to diagnose mental disorders.

Ethnicity, Aging, and Mental Health

Little research has been done to examine ethnic differences in the definition of mental health and psychopathology in older adults. There is some evidence of different incidence rates across groups. A multidimensional research approach is needed to address the lack of data.

Depression

Characteristics of Older People with Depression

Recent research indicates that depression may be underdiagnosed and undertreated. Depression is the most common mental disorder in adults. Gender differences are noted, but may be due in part to bias. Some ethnic differences have been noted.

Diagnosis of Depression

Common features of depression include dysphoria, apathy, self-deprecation, expressionlessness, changes in arousal, withdrawal, and several physical symptoms. Additionally, the problems must last at least 2 weeks, not be caused by another disease, and negatively affect daily living. Clear age differences exist in the reporting of symptoms. Many assessment scales are not sensitive to age differences in symptoms.

Causes of Depression

Possible biological causes of severe depression are neurotransmitter imbalance, abnormal brain functioning, or physical illness. Loss is the main psychosocial cause of depression. Research evidence shows negative life events per se are unrelated to depression. Internal belief systems are also important.

Treatment of Depression

Three families of drugs (HCAs, MAO inhibitors, and SSRIs), electroconvulsive therapy, and various forms of psychotherapy are all used to treat depression. All therapies have an appropriate use. Older adults benefit most from behavior and cognitive therapies.

Anxiety, Personality, and Psychotic Disorders

Anxiety Disorders

Anxiety disorders include panic, phobia, and obsessive-compulsive problems. Symptoms include a variety of physical changes that interfere with normal functioning. Context is important in understanding symptoms. Both drugs and psychotherapy are used to treat anxiety disorders.

Personality Disorders

Personality disorders can be classified into three broad categories. Most clinicians believe that personality disorders begin early in life. Evidence suggests that depending on the type, personality disorders either remain the same or improve somewhat across adulthood, although good longitudinal data are scarce. Treatment is difficult.

Psychotic Disorders

Psychotic disorders are classified as being caused by organic mental disorders or by syndromes in which the cause is unclear; the latter group includes schizophrenia. Hallucinations and delusions are the primary symptoms of psychoses. Schizophrenia is a severe thought disorder with an onset usually before age 45. Treatment usually consists of using drugs; psychotherapy is not often effective alone.

Organic Mental Disorders

The Family of Dementias

Dementia is a family of disorders. Reversible dementias such as delirium can be treated. Irreversible dementias such as Alzheimer's disease cannot. Common causes of delirium include toxic effects of drugs, infections, electrolyte imbalances, malnutrition, and potassium deficits.

Alzheimer's Disease

Alzheimer's disease is a progressive, fatal disease that is diagnosed at autopsy through three neurological changes: neurofibrillary tangles, neuritic plaques, and granulovacuolar bodies. Major symptoms of Alzheimer's disease include gradual and eventually pervasive memory loss, emotional changes, and eventual loss of motor functions. Diagnosis of Alzheimer's disease consists of ruling out all other possible causes of the symptoms. This involves thorough physical, neurological, and neuropsychological exams. Current research suggests that Alzheimer's disease may be genetic, perhaps with an autosomal dominant inheritance pattern, although other theories have been proposed. Although no cure for Alzheimer's disease is available, interventions to relieve symptoms are advisable and possible, including various drug and behavioral interventions.

Other Forms of Dementia

Multi-infarct dementia is caused by several small strokes. Changes in behavior depend on where in the brain the strokes occur. Characteristic symptoms of Parkinson's disease include tremor and problems with walking. Treatment is done with drugs. Some people with Parkinson's disease will develop dementia. Symptoms of Pick's disease show up early as behavioral, rather than memory, problems. The disease appears to be genetic. Creutzfeld-Jakob disease is caused by a virus. It has an early onset, has a very rapid course, and causes severe brain changes. Huntington's disease is a genetic disorder that usually begins in middle age with motor and behavioral problems. Normal-pressure hydrocephalus is a rare disorder caused by enlarged ventricles in the brain. Alcoholic dementia (Wernicke-Korsakoff's syndrome) is caused by a thiamine deficiency.

Caring for Dementia Patients at Home

Caring for dementia patients at home can cause significant stress and disrupts relationships. Respite care and adult day care help caregivers deal with the stress and burden. Daughters and daughters-in-law do most of the caregiving.

Family Intervention and Family Therapy

What is Family Therapy?

Family therapy views the family as an independent system of members who mutually influence each other. All members participate in therapy on the notion that changing behavior in one family member influences everyone.

Common Issues in Family Therapy with Older Adults

Several issues are typically dealt with in family therapy: spousal conflict, parent-child conflict, and communication problems. Each of these needs to be identified and dealt with in therapy.

Techniques for Family Therapy

Communication skills training is the most important technique. The therapist must assist in identifying hidden agendas and in setting goals for recovery.

Working with the Institutionalized Elderly

Sensory Training

Sensory training aims at getting a person back in touch with the environment. This technique is effective in getting highly regressed residents to reexperience their surroundings.

Reality Orientation

Reality orientation is a technique based on repetition and relearning in an attempt to treat disoriented residents. The technique works best with mildly disoriented persons. Attitude therapy is often used in conjunction with reality orientation.

Validation Therapy

Validation therapy aims at dealing with the person's disorientation in an accepting, nonthreatening way. The goal is to validate the person's emotions.

Remotivation Therapy

Remotivation therapy seeks to get apathetic residents interested in activities. It involves a five-step process and is part of a structured program.

Additional Therapeutic Approaches

Other techniques include activities and recreation therapy, milieu therapy, supportive group therapy, and pet therapy.

REVIEW QUESTIONS

Mental health and the adult life course
- How do definitions of mental health vary with age?
- What are the implications of adopting a multidimensional model for interpreting and diagnosing mental disorders?
- What are the five axes of *DSM-IV*?
- Why is ethnicity an important consideration in understanding mental health?

Depression
- How does the rate of depression vary with age?
- What symptoms are associated with depression? How do they vary with age?
- What biological causes of depression have been offered?
- How is loss associated with depression?
- What treatments of depression have been developed? How well do they work with older adults?

Anxiety, personality, and psychotic disorders
- What symptoms are associated with anxiety disorders?
- How are anxiety disorders treated?
- What are personality disorders? How can they be categorized?
- What evidence is there about changes in symptoms with age and time in personality disorders?
- What are psychoses? What are their major symptoms?
- What treatments are most effective for schizophrenia?

Organic mental disorders
- What is the difference between reversible and irreversible dementia?
- What is delirium? What causes it?
- What is Alzheimer's disease? How is it diagnosed?
- What causes Alzheimer's disease? What interventions are available?
- What other types of dementia have been identified? What are their characteristics?
- What happens when people care for dementia victims at home?

Family intervention and family therapy
- What is family therapy? How does it differ from individual psychotherapy?
- What issues are typically dealt with in family therapy? How are they addressed?

Working with the institutionalized elderly
- What are the main therapies used with institutionalized elderly?
- What evidence is there that any of these techniques are effective?

INTEGRATING CONCEPTS IN DEVELOPMENT

1. Why do you think there may be cases of hallucinations and delusions in people with Alzheimer's disease?
2. Why is there a connection between depression and dementia?
3. Why might family therapy be a good intervention for Alzheimer's disease?
4. What would studying people with Alzheimer's disease tell us about normal memory changes with age?

KEY TERMS

adult day care A program in which older adults are housed during the day when they cannot care for themselves. Adult day care is often used with persons who have Alzheimer's disease.

Alzheimer's disease An irreversible form of dementia characterized by progressive declines in cognitive and bodily functions, eventually resulting in death.

amyloid A type of protein involved in the formation of neuritic plaques both in normal aging and in Alzheimer's disease.

autosomal dominant A type of genetic transmission in which only one gene from one parent is necessary for a person to acquire a trait or a disease.

behavior therapy A type of psychotherapy that focuses on and attempts to alter current behavior. Underlying causes of the problem may not be addressed.

benzodiazepines A type of medication used to treat anxiety disorders.

bipolar disorder A type of psychopathology characterized by both depression and mania.

cognitive therapy A type of psychotherapy aimed at altering the way people think as a cure for some forms of psychopathology, especially depression.

delirium A form of organic mental disorder characterized by impaired awareness of self and surroundings, attention deficits, tendencies toward hallucinations and delusions, disorientation, changes in alertness, disturbed sleep patterns, and rapid changes in symptoms and their severity; memory may be affected.

dementia A family of diseases characterized by cognitive decline. Some forms are treatable, whereas others are not.

dysphoria Feeling down or blue, marked by extreme sadness; the major symptom of depression.

family therapy A type of psychotherapy that views the family as a dynamic system, with a focus on working with all family members.

heterocyclic antidepressants (HCAs) The most common form of drugs given to treat depression.

internal belief systems An aspect of personality having to do with personal control, which is thought to be a key factor in psychosocial theories of depression.

mental status exam A short screening test that assesses mental competence, usually used as a brief indicator of dementia or other serious cognitive impairment.

monoamine oxidase (MAO) inhibitors A type of drug used to treat depression that has potentially serious side effects.

multi-infarct dementia A form of dementia caused by a series of small strokes.

Parkinson's disease A form of dementia marked by tremor and difficulty in walking.

psychoanalytic therapy Psychotherapy based on Freudian theory.

psychopathology Another term for mental disorder.

respite care Providing relief to caregivers for some period of time.

selective serotonin reuptake inhibitors (SSRIs) A type of drug used to treat depression that works by altering the functional level of serotonin in the brain.

sundowning The phenomenon in which persons with Alzheimer's disease show an increase in symptoms later in the day.

IF YOU'D LIKE TO LEARN MORE

Aronson, M.K. (Ed.). (1988). *Understanding Alzheimer's disease.* New York: Scribner's. This book remains the most readable comprehensive resource on Alzheimer's disease, developed in conjunction with the Alzheimer's Association. Easy reading.

Birren, J.E., Sloane, R.B., & Cohen, G.D. (Eds.). (1992). *Handbook of mental health and aging* (2nd ed.). San Diego: Academic Press. A comprehensive handbook covering all the major topics in mental health, assessment, and specific disorders. Moderately difficult to difficult.

Hunt, T., & Lindley, C.J. (Eds.). (1989). *Testing older adults.* Austin, TX: Pro-Ed. Provides an overview of assessment in a wide variety of situations with many different types of older adults. Moderately difficult.

McGowin, D.F. (1994). *Living in the labyrinth: A personal journey through the maze of Alzheimer's.* Cambridge, MA: Mainsail. A personal account of Alzheimer's disease, which makes fascinating reading. Easy.

Weiner, M.B., Brok, A.J., & Snadowsky, A.M. (1987). *Working with the aged* (2nd ed.). Norwalk, CT: Appleton-Century-Crofts. An easy, readable overview of therapeutic interventions with people in nursing homes.

CHAPTER 10

Relationships

Pierre Auguste Renoir, *Luncheon of the Boating Party.* Phillips Collections, Washington, DC/Superstock.

Imagine yourself many decades from now. Your children are all adults, with children and grandchildren of their own. In honor of your birthday, they have all gathered, along with your friends. As a present to you, they have assembled hundreds of photographs and dozens of videos from your life. As you begin looking at them, you realize for the first time how lucky you have been to have so many wonderful people in your life. You realize that it has been your relationships that has made your life fun and worthwhile. As you look around, especially at the younger generations, you recall one of the sayings of Muhammad: "To all young people who honor the old, on account of their age, may God appoint those who shall honor them in their years." And you realize that relationships are truly a key to happiness.

Could you picture what it would be like going through life totally alone? Think of all the wonderful experiences you would miss—never knowing what friendship is all about, never being in love, never dreaming about children and becoming a grandparent someday, never being able to wish on a star that you and someone special could be together. In truth, our journey through life is not made alone. We are accompanied by many friends and relatives who love us and make us feel important. The same point was made years ago by the songwriter who said that people who need people are the luckiest people in the world. The bonds we form with friends and family get us through the good and bad times. The good times are so much better and the bad times are so much easier to take if we have someone to share them with.

How we express our mutual interdependence with other people differs according to the situation—whether it be a family interaction, a love and sexual relationship, or a friendship. Relations that reflect love and attachment are especially important, because they are essential to survival and well-being throughout the life span. Although the nature of love in relationships is different at different ages, there is no doubt that men and women strive to attain it regardless of age (Reedy, Birren, & Schaie, 1981).

In this chapter we will explore some of the forms that our personal relationships take. First, we will consider friendships and love relationships and how they change across adulthood. Because love relationships usually involve a couple, we will explore how it is that two persons find each other and marry and how marriages develop. We will also consider singlehood, divorce, remarriage, and widowhood. Finally, we will take up some of the important roles associated with personal relationships, including parenting, family roles, and grandparenting.

RELATIONSHIPS

Learning Objectives:

- What role do friends play across the adult life span?
- How are siblings important, especially in late life?
- What characterizes love relationships? How do these vary across cultures?
- What are abusive relationships? What are elder abuse and neglect?

Some of the most important people in our lives are our friends. Indeed, a popular television show in the mid-1990s, called *Friends,* was based on the relationships among young adults and the need to have people around who really care about you. Sometimes, friendships turn into something more. Love blossoms, and relationships become more intimate and intense. In this section, we will examine friendships and love relationships in adulthood, and see why and how they are central to our lives.

Friendships

What is a friend? Someone who is there when you need to share? Someone not afraid to tell you the truth? Someone to have fun with? The question is surely difficult to answer. But we all have an intuitive understanding that friendships are necessary, that they take work and time to develop, and that they play an important role in our daily lives.

Creating Friendships

A friendship, like any other intimate relationship, needs time to grow. Friendships develop in three stages that reflect different levels of involvement. During the first phase there is only mutual awareness; people notice each other and make some judgment. This phase quickly passes to the second, termed surface contact, in which little self-disclosure occurs and the two persons' behavior is governed by existing social norms. In these first two stages the people become what most of us call acquaintances. For a true friendship a third stage is necessary. As self-disclosure begins, the acquaintanceship moves into the mutuality stage, marking the transition to friendship. At this point the individuals probably start feeling a sense of commitment to each other and begin to develop private norms to guide their relationship. It is during this last stage that characteristics typically associated with close friendships—such as honesty, sincerity, and emotional support—emerge (Newman, 1982).

Developmental Aspects of Friendships

On the average, people tend to have more friends and acquaintances during young adulthood than at any subsequent period (Antonucci, 1985). Although their numbers decline, friendships are still important in later life. Even when faced with constraints to maintaining friendships such as increased disability, most people over age 85 still actively maintain friendships (Johnson & Troll, 1994).

Surprisingly, older adults' life satisfaction is largely unrelated to the quantity or quality of contact with the younger members of their own family but is substantially related to the quantity

Friendships remain important throughout adulthood.

and quality of contacts with friends (Antonucci, 1985; Essex & Nam, 1987; Lee & Ellithorpe, 1982). The importance of maintaining contacts with friends cuts across ethnic lines as well. Ellison (1990) showed that happiness among African Americans is strongly related to the number of friends.

Why are friends so important to older adults? Some researchers believe that one reason may be older adults' concern that they not become burdens to their families (Roberto & Scott, 1986). As a result they help their friends foster independence. This reciprocity is a crucial aspect of friendship in later life, because it allows the paying back of indebtedness over time. Also important, though, is that friends are fun for people of all ages. The relationships we have with family members are not always positive, but we choose our friends for their pleasure value (Larson, Mannell, & Zuzanek, 1986).

In general, older adults tend to have fewer relationships with people in general and to develop fewer new relationships than people do in midlife and particularly in young adulthood (Carstensen, 1995). For many years, researchers tended to view this phenomenon as merely a reflection of the loss of relationships in late life through death and other means. However, Carstensen (1993, 1995) has shown that the changes in social behavior seen in late life reflect a much more complicated and important process. **She proposes a life-span theory of *socioemotional selectivity*, which argues that social contact is motivated by a variety of goals, including information seeking, self-concept, and emotional regulation.**

Each of these goals is differentially salient at different points of the adult life span and results in very different social behaviors. For example, when information seeking is the goal, such as when a person is exploring the world, trying to figure out how he or she fits, what others are like, and so forth, meeting many new people is an essential part of the process. However, when emotional regulation is the goal, people tend to become highly selective in their choice of social partners and nearly always prefer people who are familiar to them.

Carstensen (1993, 1995) believes that information seeking is the predominant goal for young adults, that emotional regulation is the major goal for older people, and that the three goals are in relative balance in midlife. Her research supports this view; people become increasingly selective in their choice of who they want to have contact with. Carstensen's theory provides a more complete explanation of why older adults tend not to replace the relationships they lose to any great extent.

Gender Differences in Friendships

Men's and women's friendships tend to differ in adulthood (Rawlins, 1992; Tannen, 1990). These differences originate in childhood and are most apparent during young adulthood (Fox, Gibbs, & Auerbach, 1985). Women tend to base their friendships on more intimate and emotional sharing; they use friendship as a means to confide in others. For women, getting together with friends often takes the form of asking them over for coffee to discuss personal matters. In contrast, men tend to base friendships on shared activities or interests; they are more likely to go bowling, go fishing, or talk sports with their friends. For men, confiding in others is inconsistent with the need to compete and may be a reason for men's reluctance to do so (Huyck, 1982). Indeed, competition is often a part of men's friendships, as evidenced in pick-up basketball games; however, the competition is usually set up so that the social interaction is the most important element, not who wins or who loses (Rawlins, 1992). Interestingly, the act of confiding, which is essential for intimacy as we will see later in this chapter, is a basis of the female approach to friendship. Compared with men, women have much more experience with such intimate sharing from early childhood and are more comfortable with vulnerability. Social pressure on men to be brave and strong may actually inhibit their ability to form close friendships (Rawlins, 1992). Indeed, Hacker (1981) found that 25% of the women surveyed said that they revealed only their weaknesses to friends, whereas 20% of the men revealed only their strengths.

Male-Female Friendships

Such differences in friendship formation create interesting opportunities and difficulties when men and women want to be friends with each other. Cross-gender friendships offer an opportunity to explore tasks or skills that are more commonly associated with the other gender, such as mowing the lawn, sewing, home repair, and cooking. But women may not understand why men want to set up minicompetitions all the time, and men may be baffled at why women keep wanting to talk about their problems (Tannen, 1990). Men also have a tendency to sexualize cross-gender friendships more often than women, who may be offended at such overtures and would prefer to remain just friends (Rawlins, 1992).

Sibling Relationships

The longest-term relationships we typically have in our lives are with our siblings, because siblings usually outlive parents. For people over age 60, 83% report that they feel close to at least one brother or sister (Dunn, 1984). This closeness dates to childhood and adolescence and is based on shared family experiences. Besides closeness, other dimensions of sibling friendships include involvement with each other, frequency of contact, envy, and resentment. Based on these dimensions, Gold, Woodbury, and George (1990) identified five different types of sibling interactions:

- *Congenial sibling relationships,* characterized by high levels of closeness and involvement, average levels of contact, and relatively low levels of envy and resentment
- *Loyal sibling relationships,* characterized by average levels of closeness, involvement, and contact, and relatively low levels of envy and resentment
- *Intimate sibling relationships,* characterized by high levels of closeness and involvement, but low levels of envy and resentment
- *Apathetic sibling relationships,* characterized by low levels on all dimensions
- *Hostile sibling relationships,* characterized by relatively high levels of involvement and resentment, and relatively low levels on all other dimensions

When combined across different possible sibling pairs, the relative frequencies of these five types of sibling relationships differ. Loyal and congenial relationships describe nearly two-thirds of all older sibling pairs. Additionally, older African American siblings have apathetic or hostile relationships with their siblings nearly five times less often than older European Americans do (4.5% for African Americans versus 22% for European Americans; Gold, 1990). Sometimes, hostile sibling relationships in late life date back to sibling rivalries that began in childhood (Greer, 1992).

When different combinations of sibling pairs are considered separately, ties between sisters are typically the strongest, most frequent, and most intimate (Cicirelli, 1980; Lee, Mancini, & Maxwell, 1990). In contrast, brothers tend to maintain less frequent contact (Connidis, 1988). Little is known about brother-sister relationships.

Some older adults end up providing care for or

living with one of their siblings, especially when one sibling has no other family members to provide care. Research indicates that siblings who receive help from their brothers or sisters tend to be younger, live alone (never-married, divorced, or single), have few children, and live in small cities (Cicirelli, Coward, & Dwyer, 1992). Most people with two or more siblings believe that their brothers or sisters would provide help in a crisis and would share their home if necessary (Connidis, 1994).

Cross-cultural research reveals more information about the sibling bond in adulthood. The degree to which siblings' roles are substitutable (for example, a father or his brother could serve as a male role model) or complementary (for example, it takes a male and a female to form a father-mother couple) is important in many cultures. For example, in some Oceanic cultures, a gender-based division of labor results in complementary roles in the economic system (brothers are responsible for managing coconut palms whereas their sisters manage taro plots, for instance) (Feinberg, 1983). Some Irish American men continue to farm land for their brother's widow, an example of substitutability (Salamon, 1982). The Ibaloi and Kankana-ey people in the Philippine highlands even have terms in their languages to distinguish both gender and relative age (J. T. Peterson, 1990). These distinctions suggest a complex kinship structure that assigns specific tasks to specific genders at specific ages. Such practices occur in Western families (young girls may be given different tasks to perform than their older sisters), but we have no systematic data on them.

Clearly, there are major gaps in our understanding of sibling relationships. This is truly unfortunate, as our brothers and sisters play an important and meaningful role throughout our lives.

Love Relationships

Love is one of those things that everybody can feel but nobody can define adequately or completely. (Test yourself: How would you explain what you mean when you look at someone and say, "I love you"?) Despite the difficulty in defining it, love underlies our most important relationships in life. In this section we will consider the components of love and how it develops across adulthood.

The Components of Love

There is little consensus about the nature of love. What most researchers do is identify important concepts of love and then use them to create different categories of love. Sternberg (1986) conducted a series of detailed studies on people's conceptions of love and how love is manifested in different ways. Based on this research, Sternberg developed a theory of love based on three components: (1) *passion,* an intense physiological desire for someone; (2) *intimacy,* the feeling that one can share all one's thoughts and actions with another; and (3) *commitment,* the willingness to stay with a person through good and bad times. Based on different combinations of these three components, Sternberg identified seven forms of love:

1. *Liking:* Intimacy is present, as are closeness, understanding, support, and affection, but there is no commitment or passion. This form describes most of our friendships.
2. *Infatuation:* There is lots of passion here, based on strong physical attraction. This form is what people call "love at first sight." But infatuation can end just as quickly as it starts, as there is no intimacy or commitment.
3. *Empty love:* Sometimes, relationships lose their passion and intimacy and are only based on commitment. An example is couples who no longer "love" each other, but who do not divorce because of children.
4. *Romantic love:* When couples connect both intimately and passionately, romance is born. But there is no commitment to complement their physical and emotional bonds.
5. *Fatuous love:* Once in a while, couples are "swept off their feet" into a rapid courtship and marriage. Their commitment is based on passion, because they have not given themselves time to let intimacy develop. Such relationships often fail as a result.
6. *Companionate love:* In this case, intimacy and

commitment are both present. This type characterizes long-term friendships, as well as long-term marriages in which passion has diminished.

7. *Consummate love:* The goal of all love relationships is to have commitment, intimacy, and passion all present. Such complete love is very difficult to maintain without devoting a great deal of energy to working at it.

Ideally, a true love relationship such as marriage has passion, intimacy, and commitment, although the balance shifts as time passes. Let's take a look at how these balances shift.

Love Across Adulthood

The different combinations of love that Sternberg identifies can be used to understand how relationships develop. Early in a relationship passion is usually high, but intimacy and commitment tend to be low. This results in infatuation: an intense, physically based relationship in which the two persons have little understanding of each other and a high risk of misunderstanding and jealousy. Interestingly, this pattern seems to characterize all kinds of couples—married, unmarried, heterosexual, and homosexual (Kurdek & Schmitt, 1986).

As the relationship continues, companionate love develops, a style characterized by greater intimacy and commitment but no passion. As Hatfield and Walster (1978) put it, "Passionate love is a fragile flower—it wilts in time. Companionate love is a sturdy evergreen; it thrives with contact." Sternberg (1986) compares infatuation to a drug addiction; in the beginning, even a small touch is enough to drive each partner into ecstasy. Gradually, though, one needs more and more stimulation to get the same feeling. Lovers eventually get used to the pleasures of passion with the same person, and passion fades. The wild passion of youth gives way to the deeper, committed love of adulthood.

Although the styles of love appear to differ with age, some important aspects of love relationships appear to maintain their same relative importance over time. Reedy, Birren, and Schaie (1981) examined 6 aspects of love relationships in 102 happily married couples: communication, sexual intimacy, respect, help and play behaviors, emotional security, and loyalty. As can be seen in Figure 10.1, the importance of some of love's aspects in satisfying relationships differs as a function of age. Overall, the findings support the idea that passion is relatively more important to younger couples, whereas tenderness and loyalty are relatively more important to older couples. Interestingly, sexual intimacy is equally important for young and middle-aged couples, and communication is more important to young couples than to any other group. Notice, however, that the relative rankings of the different components of love are the same for all age groups. Thus, although the particular weights may vary, there are remarkable similarities across age in the nature of love relationships.

These results make intuitive sense. It is reasonable that young couples should focus more on communication, because they are still in the process of getting to know each other. Once this has occurred, and people begin to anticipate their partner's reactions, they move to a love based more on security, commitment, and loyalty. Of course, all of this assumes that one has a partner to love in the first place. How we find one of these is the topic of the next section.

Falling in Love

Everybody wants to be loved by somebody, but actually having it happen is fraught with difficulties. In his book *The Prophet,* Kahlil Gibran points out that love is a two-sided issue: just as it can give one the greatest ecstasy, so can it cause one the greatest pain. Yet, most of us are willing to take the risk.

As you may have experienced, taking the risk is fun (at times) and trying (at other times). Making a connection can be ritualized, such as when people use pick-up lines in a bar, or can happen almost by accident, such as when two people literally run into each other in a crowded corridor. Because nearly all of the research that has examined the process by which people meet and fall in love has been done with heterosexual couples, we will focus on them. The question that confronts us is, How do men and women fall in love?

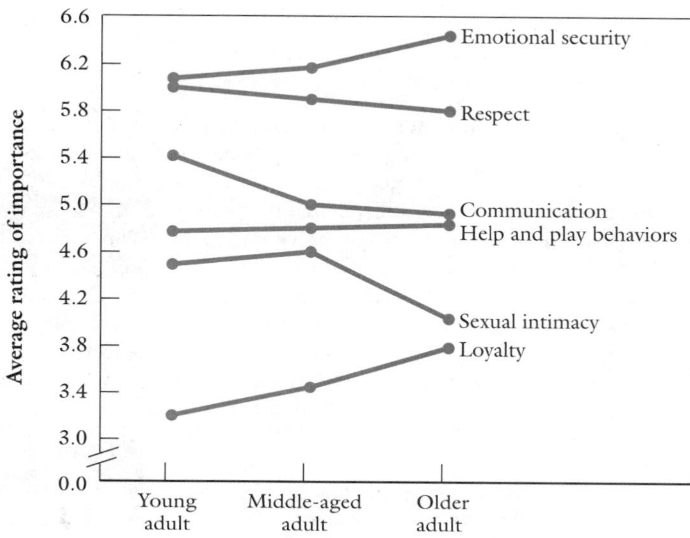

Figure 10.1 Developmental differences in components of love. Note that there are differences across age in the ratings of the different components but that the rank orders of the components are the same.

Source: Reedy et al., 1981

The answer is that they do it quite differently. Men tend to be more romantic: believing in love at first sight, feeling that there is only one true love destined for them, regarding love as magical and impossible to understand, and believing rather quickly that they are compatible with their partner. Women tend to be cautious pragmatists who believe that financial security is as important as passion in a relationship, that there are many people whom a person could learn to love, and that love does not conquer all differences (Peplau and Gordon, 1985). These differences even carry over into views about the best way to make up after a fight: Most men believe that the best way for a woman to apologize is through passionate sex, whereas most women believe that the best way for a man to apologize is through a personal, heartfelt discussion (Peplau and Gordon, 1985). Finally, a man's dissatisfaction with a heterosexual relationship is a much better predictor of the relationship's demise than a woman's dissatisfaction, in part because women's approach to love includes a stronger desire to try to make the relationships work (Cowan & Cowan, 1992).

How do these dimensions based on U.S. samples compare with cross-cultural evidence? In an extraordinary study grounded in sociobiological theory, Buss and a large team of researchers (1990) identified the effects of culture and gender on mate preferences in 37 cultures worldwide. They had people rate and rank each of 18 characteristics (such as mutual attraction, chastity, dependable character, good health) on how important or desirable it would be in choosing a mate. These characteristics were based on ones used in U.S. research since the 1940s.

Buss found strong cultural effects, with each culture producing somewhat different preferences. A more detailed discussion of these is in How Do We Know? Chastity proved to be the characteristic showing the most variability across cultures; in some cultures it is highly desired, whereas in others

HOW DO WE KNOW?

Choosing Mates Around the World

If you were a male living in India, how would the woman of your dreams differ from the ideal woman of a male living in Finland? Likewise, how do the desired men differ for women living in Nigeria and Great Britain? Buss and his colleagues (1990) decided to find out. They specifically examined the effects of culture and gender on mate preferences on a truly worldwide sample. Participants in the 37 samples (N equals 9,474) represented 33 countries from 6 continents and 5 islands.

Participants were asked to complete measures concerning important factors in choosing a mate (such as, rating desired characteristics of potential mates) and preferences concerning potential mates (for example, ranking characteristics of potential mates from highest to lowest). Data were gathered by individuals in each country. In some cases, the survey items had to be modified to reflect the local culture. For example, many couples in Sweden, Finland, and Norway do not get married, opting instead simply to live together. In Nigeria, items had to reflect the possibility of many wives due to the practice of polygyny. Data collection in South Africa was described as "a rather frightening experience" due to the difficulty in collecting data from both white and Zulu samples. Finally, in some cases data were never received due to government interference or the lack of official approval to conduct the study. Such problems highlight the difficulty in doing cross-cultural research and the need to take local culture into account in designing research instruments.

As noted in the text, statistical analyses showed that each culture displayed a unique ordering of preferences concerning ideal characteristics. Despite the diversity, some common themes emerged. First, cultures tend to vary along a dimension referred to as *traditional-modern.* Countries such as China, India, Iran, and Nigeria represent the traditional end, whereas the Netherlands, Great Britain, Finland, and Sweden represent the modern end. In addition, the relative importance of education, intelligence, and refinement in choosing a mate is an important dimension along which countries vary.

Overall, Buss and his colleagues' results clearly demonstrate that mate selection is a complex process no matter where one lives. The study also shows that socialization plays a key role in attractiveness; characteristics that are highly desirable in one culture may be highly undesirable in another. It must be recognized, however, that the sociobiological and evolutionary psychological approach which framed Buss's study is controversial. Rather than mating patterns being a product of natural selection processes, they could also be the result of cultural influences that define "appropriate" and "inappropriate" potential mates. What is clear is that the question of how and why people choose the partners they do is a very complex and controversial issue, and that Buss et al.'s research has provided a major stimulus for discussion and additional research.

---

it matters little. Interestingly, consistent gender differences emerged across cultures on the characteristics of earning potential (endorsed consistently more often by women) and physical attractiveness (endorsed consistently more often by men). Buss and colleagues argue that the consistency of these gender differences across cultures supports evolution-based speculation about the importance of resources and reproductive value in mates. That is, in their respective search for mates, men around the world value physical attractiveness in women whereas women around the world look for men who will be good providers.

Violence in Relationships

Up to this point, we have been considering relationships that are relatively healthy and positive. Sadly, this is not always the case. **Sometimes relationships become violent; one person becomes aggressive toward the partner, creating an *abusive relationship.*** Such relationships have received increasing attention over the past few decades. Indeed, some authors believe, as does the U.S. criminal justice system under some circumstances, that abusive relationships can be used as an explanation for one's behavior (Walker, 1984). **For**

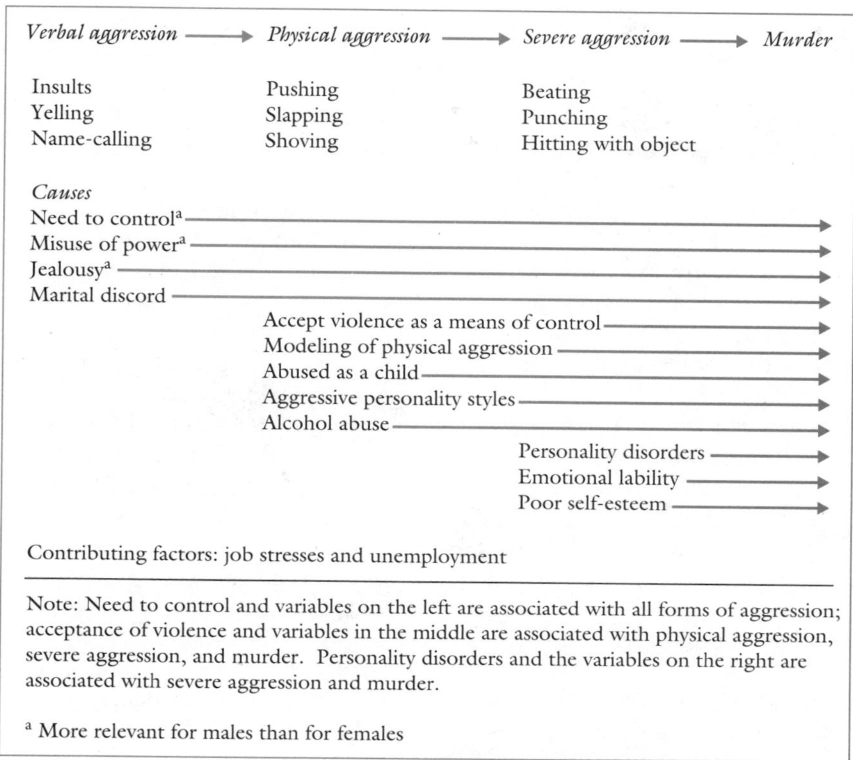

Figure 10.2 Framework for understanding violence in relationships.
Source: O'Leary, 1993

example, *battered woman syndrome* represents the situation in which a woman believes that she cannot leave the abusive situation and may even go so far as to kill her abuser.

What kind of aggressive behaviors occur in abusive relationships? What causes such abuse? Researchers are beginning to find answers to these and related questions. Based on a decade of research on abusive partners, O'Leary (1993) argues that there is a continuum of aggressive behaviors toward a spouse, which progresses as follows: verbally aggressive behaviors, physically aggressive behaviors, severe physically aggressive behaviors, and murder of the partner. The causes of the abuse also vary with the type of abusive behavior being expressed. O'Leary's approach is shown in Figure 10.2.

Two points are interesting concerning the continuum of violent behaviors. The first point is that there may be fundamental differences in the types of aggression that go beyond level of severity. Lower levels of physically aggressive behavior, such as pushing or slapping, are relatively common; 25% to 40% of men and women who are in committed relationships display such behaviors on occasion (Riggs and O'Leary, 1992; Straus, Gelles, & Steinmetz, 1980). In contrast, some men are extremely abusive from the outset of the relationship; they are thought to comprise the subset of batterers who seriously physically injure their partner and create coercive control over their lives (Stark, 1992).

The second interesting point, depicted in the figure, is that the suspected underlying causes of aggressive behaviors differ as the type of aggressive behaviors change (O'Leary, 1993). As can be seen, the number of suspected causes of aggressive behavior increases as the level of aggression increases. Thus, the causes of aggressive behavior become more complex as the level of aggression worsens. Such differences in cause imply that the approaches to treating abusers should vary with the nature of the aggressive behavior (O'Leary, 1993). Situational factors that contribute to all levels of aggression are alcoholism, job stressors, and unemployment; the presence of these factors increases the likelihood that violence will occur in the relationship (O'Leary, 1993).

Gender differences in some of the underlying causes of aggressive behavior in relationships have been reported (O'Leary, 1993). Most important, the triad of need to control, misuse of power, and jealousy are more pertinent causes for men than for women. For example, men are more likely than women to act aggressively because they want to make sure their partner knows "who the boss is" and who makes the rules.

Two additional, and controversial, causes of aggressive or abusive behaviors have been widely discussed: attitudes held by a patriarchal society and being abused as a child. Feminist critiques of the causes of family violence argue that male aggression toward their female partner results in part from the inequality of women in a patriarchal society (Dobash & Dobash, 1992; Yllö, 1993). From this perspective, abuse is considered to be a "normal" result of male socialization, in which domination of women is strongly reinforced in society. Indeed, the pattern of gender differences discussed above support this view, in that men are more likely than women to act aggressively out of a need to exert control or power. And there is some cross-cultural evidence showing that when women and men are treated more equally, men are unlikely to abuse women (Levinson, 1988). Thus, male violence against women is thought to be one of the means for men to dominate women (Yllö, 1993).

The second controversial cause of aggressive behavior in relationships concerns the widely held belief that people who are abusers were probably abused themselves as children (O'Leary, 1993). But is there evidence to support this view? It certainly looks that way when people who are in therapy for abusing their partners are examined. In this case, 60% of men had been victims of child abuse themselves, and 44% had witnessed violence between parents (O'Leary, 1993). Because few women are in therapy as abusers, similar statistics for them are unavailable.

But if abusive individuals in the general population are examined, including those who are not in therapy, the picture changes dramatically. In general community samples, 13% of men and 12% of women who were physically aggressive toward their partners had been exposed to violence in their families of origin, either by being abused themselves or witnessing their parents be violent toward each other (O'Leary, 1993).

These statistics underscore the complexity of the causes of aggressive behaviors toward one's partner. At least in community samples, the majority of aggressive partners were not victims of abuse themselves as children. Having experienced or witnessed violence as a child may be more predictive of the subset of people who may end up in therapy for abusive behavior than of who is likely to become abusive in the first place.

Researchers are also beginning to document differences in how aggressive behaviors are viewed by the men and women who display them. For example, partners in relatively new relationships who display lower levels of physical aggression (pushing, shoving) tend not to view them as abusive and claim not to have done them in self-defense (Cascardi, Vivian, & Meyer, 1991; O'Leary et al., 1989). However, women in longer-term relationships view their aggressive acts as self-defense; men still tend not to see them as either abusive or self-defense (Cascardi et al., 1991). And the reasons why men and women kill their partners also differ (Browne & Williams, 1993; Cascardi & O'Leary, 1992). Men tend to murder their partners on the basis of jealousy and need for control. In contrast, women usually have contacted law enforcement agencies repeatedly asking for protection prior to murdering their partner, indicating that women kill mainly in self-defense.

Many people wonder why people stay in abusive relationships. One reason is that many abused individuals have low self-esteem and do not believe that they can do anything about their situation; indeed, many believe that they deserve their abuse (Walker, 1984). Fear also plays a major role, especially with abused women, as some who leave the relationship are tracked down and killed by (ex-)boyfriends and (ex-)husbands. Many women are financially dependent on their partners and would have no means of supporting themselves and their children. Other victims may minimize the abuse, saying that it only happens when their lover is drunk or high, or when stressed, or even that it is a sign of love for them. Surprisingly, some abused women who are beaten regularly do not consider their relationships unhappy (O'Leary et al., 1989).

Many communities have realized the seriousness of abuse and have established shelters for women and their children. Programs have also been established to treat abusive men. However, the legal system in many localities is not set up to deal with domestic violence; women in some locations cannot sue their husbands for assault, and restraining orders may offer little real protection from additional violence. Much remains to be done to protect women and their children from the fear and the reality of continued abuse.

Elder Abuse and Neglect

In addition to the types of abuse that occur in couple relationships, abuse is unfortunately a part of some relationships involving older parents and their adult children. In this section, we will consider what elder abuse and neglect are, how often they happen, and what victims and abusers are like.

Elder abuse is difficult to define precisely in practice. In general, researchers and public policy advocates alike describe several different categories of *elder abuse* (National Aging Resource Center on Elder Abuse [NARCEA], 1990): physical (such as beating or withholding care), psychological/emotional (such as verbal assaults and social isolation), sexual, material or financial exploitation (such as illegal or improper use of funds), and the violation of rights (such as being forced out of one's house or denying privacy).

In addition to abuse, *neglect* of older adults is also a growing problem (NARCEA, 1990). Neglecting older adults can be either intended, such as refusing to fulfill basic caregiving obligations with the intention of inflicting harm, or unintended, such as not providing adequate medical care because of a lack of knowledge on the caregiver's part (Wolf, Godkin, & Pillemer, 1986).

Part of the problem in agreeing on a common definition of elder abuse and neglect is that perceptions differ across ethnic groups. For examples, African American, Korean American, and European American older females used different criteria in deciding whether scenarios they read represented abuse (Moon & Williams, 1993). Specifically, older Korean American women were much less likely to judge a particular scenario as abusive and to indicate that help should be sought than older women in either of the other two groups. These ethnic differences may result in conflicts between social service workers, who may be using one set of definitions, and clients, who may be using another, in deciding who should receive protective services.

Official estimates suggest that 3% to 4% of older adults in the United States are the victims of abuse or neglect. However, as is the case with child and spousal abuse, most researchers believe these estimates to be low (NARCEA, 1990). The most common are neglect, physical abuse, and financial or material exploitation.

Older adults living in the community are not the only ones who are abused and neglected. In a study of 577 randomly selected nurses and nurses aides who worked in intermediate care and skilled nursing facilities, Pillemer and Moore (1989) asked respondents to report about actions they had either performed themselves or had witnessed other staff commit. They reported that 10% of the respondents admitted to physically abusing a resident, and 40% admitted to psychologically abusing a resident at least once over the past year. Additionally, 36% reported seeing acts of physical abuse, and 81% reported observing acts of psychological abuse over the same time period.

One of the most hotly contested issues in adulthood and aging is trying to understand which older adults are at greatest risk for abuse and neglect. This issue must be sorted out to provide the most appropriate services to victims and to develop effective prevention strategies. At present there are two competing views of who is at risk. At the heart of the debate is a deceptively simple question: Are abuse victims dependent on perpetrators, or are perpetrators dependent on abuse victims?

Most researchers and policy makers assume that abuse victims are dependent. Indeed, the typical picture is one of a victim who has been abused by his or her caregiver, who in turn is under considerable stress from having to provide care (Steinmetz, 1993). The stress, frustration, and feelings of burden caregivers experience are too much for some to take; they lash out and turn their emotions into abusive behavior. In this view, abuse and neglect of older adults have much in common with child abuse and neglect; both involve victims who are highly dependent on their perpetrators for basic care. This view is easy for people to understand, which is probably the reason most prevention programs are based on a dependent-victim model.

Other researchers strongly disagree. Rather than victims being dependent on caregiver-perpetrators, they see it differently: It's the perpetrators who are dependent on the victims (Pillemer, 1993). These perpetrators are not acting out their frustration; they are seen as deviant and suffering from mental disorders. In this approach, perpetrators depend on their victims for basic necessities, such as a place to live and financial assistance. Perpetrators also tend to be more violent in general, to have been arrested for other crimes, and to have been hospitalized for psychiatric disorders (Pillemer, 1993).

Which of these views is correct has profound implications for prevention and treatment. If victims are dependent, then programs are needed to provide basic services to caregivers to lower their stress. If perpetrators are deviant and have mental disorders, then programs need to identify individuals who are at risk for abusing older adults. Clearly, additional research is needed to provide the appropriate direction for policy makers and to settle the controversy.

Much more attention has been paid to identifying characteristics of abusers. Adult children are generally more likely to abuse older adults than are other people (NARCEA, 1990). In general, people who abuse or neglect older adults show higher rates of substance abuse and mental health problems, are inexperienced caregivers, have more economic problems, receive little help from other family members for caregiving, are hypercritical and unsensitive of others, and are more likely to have been abused themselves (NARCEA, 1990; Pillemer, 1993).

An important exception to these general patterns concerns abuse of persons with dementia. Research has shown that in this case, spouses are much more likely to actually become violent with the care-recipient, especially when the spousal caregiver had experienced violent or aggressive behavior from the care-recipient (Pillemer & Suitor, 1992). There is some reason for hope, however. Additional data suggest that spousal caregivers who have violent feelings report a greater likelihood that they will place the care-recipient in a nursing home in the near future (Pillemer & Suitor, 1992).

These characteristics fit within the family violence model as an explanation of other forms of abuse. Some authors argue that elder abuse and neglect can be viewed as similar to cases of spousal abuse when the perpetrator is a spouse, and to child abuse when the perpetrator is a family caregiver (Steinmetz, 1993). Other writers (Pillemer, 1993) deny any similarity between abuse of older adults and children, except in cases where mental disorders are present in both types of abusers. Although more research is needed to sort out these possible connections, they nevertheless demonstrate that abuse and neglect of older adults could have aspects in common with other types of family violence. These connections could provide the basis for more research on a general theoretical model of spousal and intergenerational abuse that would allow us to know the circumstances most likely to give rise to abuse and neglect.

Concept Checks

1. What gender differences have been found in friendships?
2. What type of sibling relationship is the strongest?

3. What are the three fundamental components of love relationships?
4. What are the types of violent behavior in abusive relationships and their associated causes?

LIFESTYLES AND LOVE RELATIONSHIPS

Learning Objectives:

- What are the challenges and advantages of being single?
- What are the characteristics of cohabiting people?
- What are gay male and lesbian relationships like?
- What is marriage like across adulthood?
- Why do people divorce and remarry?
- What are the experiences of widows and widowers?

Developing relationships is only part of the picture in understanding how adults live their lives with other people. Putting relationships in context is the goal of the following sections, as we explore the major lifestyles of adults. First, we will consider people who never get married. Next, we will look at those who cohabitate and those who are in same-sex relationships. We will also consider those who get married and those who divorce and remarry. Finally, we will discuss people who are widowed.

Singlehood

During the early years of adulthood, most Americans are single. Current estimates are that 75% of men and 60% of women between the ages of 20 and 25 are unmarried. These percentages have been rising over the past few decades with the rise in median age of first marriage and are similar in all industrialized countries (Burns, 1992). Most single men and women enjoy this part of their lives, during which they have few responsibilities. For women, being single has the advantage of increasing the likelihood that they will go to college (Haggstrom, Kanouse, & Morrison, 1986).

Surprisingly, information about single people is very scarce. Beyond the contradictory popular images of them as swingers on cruise ships and getaway weekends or as lonely people existing in quiet desperation, few scientific data are available. Perhaps the lack of research is due to the fact that relatively few adults never marry, so singlehood is treated as a transient state of little inherent interest. This situation may change as more people in recent cohorts remain single.

Deciding Not to Marry

Evidence drawn from several sources indicates that men and women typically decide whether to remain single between 25 and 30 (Phillis & Stein, 1983). One of the few consistent trends that emerges is a tendency for people with very little formal education (less than 5 years) and women with graduate training to remain single. Some speculate that some highly intelligent women choose career and personal freedom over marriage or that these women stay single because they intimidate men with their superior earning power and career success (Doudna & McBride, 1981; Unger, 1979).

How the decision to remain single occurs has been the subject of much speculation. Various explanations have been offered for delayed marriage, including changes in sexual standards, the increased financial independence of women, various liberation movements, changing economic conditions, and changing conceptions of marriage (Safilios-Rothschild, 1977; Stein, 1978). However, some adults may simply postpone indefinitely the decision about whether to marry and slide into singlehood.

Because they spend a lifetime without a spouse, single adults develop long-standing alternative social patterns based on friendships. Women, especially, are highly involved with relatives—caring for an aged parent, living with a sibling, or actively helping nieces and nephews. Loneliness is typically not present; one study found that never-married women were comparable to married ones (Essex & Nam, 1987), and other evidence argues that they are not socially isolated (Rubinstein, 1987).

The Single Role

Scientifically, we know very little about what it is like to be a single adult. Some evidence suggests that many never-married adults have more androgynous gender identities, have high achievement needs, are more autonomous, and want to maintain close relationships with others (Phillis & Stein, 1983). Many singles are acutely aware of their ambivalent feelings concerning their desires to have a successful career and their equally strong desires for intimacy. For many, this ambivalence is the reason they choose not to risk marriage.

Perhaps the two most difficult issues for single people are how to handle dating and others' expectations that they should marry. Both men and women experience role constrictions while dating: how sex should be handled, how to date without getting too serious too fast, and how to initiate a close friendship without coming on too strong. In addition, other people often assume that everyone gets married and sometimes force a single person to defend his or her status. This pressure to marry is especially strong for women as they near 30; frequent questions such as "Any good prospects yet?" may leave women feeling conspicuous or left out as many of their friends marry.

Although attitudes are changing, people (especially women) who choose not to marry are often ostracized. Americans are extremely couple oriented, and as their friends marry, single people find their friendship networks shrinking accordingly. Moreover, such social behaviors as feeling sorry for never-married people compound our basic lack of understanding of them. Still, many never-married people report that they are quite happy. For many, the satisfaction derived from careers and friendships is more than enough (Alwin, Converse, & Martin, 1985).

Cohabitation

Not being married does not mean having to live alone. Many unmarried adults live with other people who are not family members. Such living arrangements include sharing apartments and houses with other same-gender occupants. **In the present context, however, we will define *cohabitation* as referring to two members of the opposite gender who live together and who are not married but are in a relationship.**

Over the last 25 years cohabitation has increased almost 60-fold. Proponents argue that it is a preparation for marriage; opponents may view it as living in sin. In this section we will consider who cohabits and why.

Who Cohabits?

Although most attention is focused on college-age cohabitants, living together is certainly not confined to this age group. Research shows that cohabitants come from all socioeconomic backgrounds and represent all age groups. For instance, older couples sometimes choose cohabitation rather than marriage for financial reasons, and men who have less than a high school education or who are not attending college are more likely to cohabit (Glick & Norton, 1979). Other research shows that by the mid-1980s almost one third of all women between 20 and 29 had lived with an unrelated man (Tanfer, 1987).

Another group likely to cohabit is recent immigrants. For example, Muschkin and Myers (1989) report that cohabitation among second-generation Puerto Rican immigrants to the United States is higher than for first-generation individuals.

Attitudes Toward Cohabitation

In general, young adults consider cohabitation more as a relevant step toward marriage than as a permanent alternative to it (Bumpass, Sweet, & Cherlin, 1991). This is especially true of women, who are much more eager to marry their partners than are men (Blumstein & Schwartz, 1983). Cohabitation seems acceptable to students in a strong, affectionate, monogamous relationship that, they believe, will eventually lead to marriage. Partners emphasize the educational and socializing value of cohabitation and describe it as a valuable learning experience that aids in personal growth and helps the couple evaluate their degree of commitment to each other (Macklin, 1988).

Gender differences in attitudes toward cohabitation have been noted. Men appear somewhat more open to cohabiting and do not feel the need for as strong an emotional commitment before living together. Women generally expect a deeper commitment and may feel exploited if it is absent (Macklin, 1988). Men are more likely to take it for granted that their partner will want to marry them, but, as noted earlier, women tend to be more eager to get married in order to achieve commitment (Blumstein & Schwartz, 1983).

Cohabitation Versus Marriage

For many, choosing whether to cohabit or to marry is a difficult and emotionally charged decision. Indeed, most cohabiting couples either marry or end the relationship in a relatively short period (Macklin, 1988). Cohabitants who do marry are very different from those who continue living together. Blumstein and Schwartz (1983) found that cohabitants who married held much more traditional views about the roles of men and women in society, were not avant-garde about their relationships, were more likely to pool their money and resources from the start, and saw each other in more flattering ways.

Considerable research has been aimed at uncovering differences between cohabiting and married couples. At first glance one might expect cohabiting couples to be more egalitarian than their married counterparts on the ground that they must be more liberal and open minded. However, this does not seem to be the case. Decision making, division of labor, communication, and satisfaction with the relationship do not appear to distinguish cohabiting and married couples (Yllo, 1978). Cohabiting couples are not more liberated in making financial decisions than married couples; when women have more power over the finances, cohabiting couples tend to fight as well (Blumstein & Schwartz, 1983). Finally, cohabitants do not engage in sex outside of their relationship any more often than do married couples (Phillis & Stein, 1983). Differences in the rate of nonmonogamous relationships are more related to cohort than to type of relationship, with younger couples more likely to engage in sex outside of their primary relationship (Blumstein & Schwartz, 1983).

Interestingly, cohabitation does not seem to make marriages any better; in fact, it may do more harm than good, resulting in marriages that are less happy (Booth and Johnson, 1988). Why is this the case? Part of the answer may be that cohabiting couples tend to be less conventional, be less religious, and come from lower socioeconomic backgrounds, which may put them at higher risk for divorce (DeMaris and Rao, 1992). And part of the reason may be that marrying after already living with someone represents much less of a change in the relationship than when a couple marry who had not been cohabiting prior to their wedding; such couples lack the newly wedded bliss seen in couples who had not cohabited (Thompson and Colella, 1992). Although there are many good reasons for cohabiting, preparing a couple for marriage apparently is not one of them.

Gay Male and Lesbian Couples

Less is known about the developmental course of gay male and lesbian relationships than about any other type. Perhaps this is because these relationships are not widely viewed as an acceptable alternative to traditional marriage. Besides the usual problems of instability and guilt that sometimes accompany other forms of cohabitation, gay male and lesbian couples experience several additional problems resulting from the disapproval of much of society for such relationships. For example, the loss of one's mate cannot be mourned as easily, because in many situations revealing one's gay or lesbian relationship may put one's job in jeopardy (Kimmel, 1978).

Gay male and lesbian relationships are similar to traditional marriages in many ways; financial problems and decisions, household chores, and power differentials are issues for all couples. Schneider (1986) reports that lesbian partners tend to divide household chores more equitably than cohabiting heterosexual couples. Moreover, gay male and lesbian parents do not differ substantially on these dimensions from heterosexual parents (Kimmel & Sang, 1995; Kurdek, 1995b). Like heterosexual couples, at midlife gay male and lesbian partners must deal with career development issues, how to create social networks as a couple and as individuals, planning for retirement, and the like (Kimmel & Sang, 1995).

Few longitudinal studies of gay male and lesbian couples have been conducted. Kurdek (1995a, b) summarizes his own work, which focused on specific relationship issues that are important over time. In interpersonal intimacy, Kurdek found that compared with gay male couples, lesbian partners attributed greater importance to equality in their notion of an ideal relationship. Additionally, the value attributed to attachment (i.e., doing things together as a couple) in the ideal relationship declined for both types of relationships, reflecting increased feelings of trust and security. This pattern is essentially the same for heterosexual couples as well. The balance between changes in current levels of both equality and attachment predicted the degree of commitment in the relationship for both gay male and lesbian couples.

Despite the general lack of research on gay male and lesbian relationships, several general conclusions can be drawn (Kurdek, 1995b). At the most basic level, gay men and lesbians see themselves as part of a couple. However, lesbian couples are more likely to view themselves as sexually exclusive. Compared with heterosexual couples, gay couples and especially lesbian partners are more likely to practice an ethic of equality. Gay male and lesbian couples show much the same types of changes over time, general patterns of satisfaction with the relationship, and similar predictors of relationship success as do heterosexual couples.

Marriage

Without question the vast majority of adults want their love relationships to result in marriage, although Americans are again taking longer to get there. As can be seen in Figure 10.3, the median age at first marriage for adults in the United States has been rising for several decades. From 1960 to 1990 the median age for men rose about 3 years, from roughly 23 to 26, and the age for women rose nearly 4 years, from roughly 20 to 24 (U.S. Bureau of the Census, 1991). Also note that this increase follows a decline over the first half of the century; in fact, the current averages are roughly comparable to what they were in 1890.

As anyone who has tried it knows, marriage is hard work. Most of us also have an intuitive sense that certain factors—such as similarity of interests and values, age of the couple, and so forth—make a difference in the probability that a marriage will succeed. But we may not be aware of other important determinants. What is it, exactly, that keeps marriages going strong over time?

Factors Influencing Marital Success

Although marriages, like other relationships, differ from one another, some important predictors of future success can be identified. One key factor in enduring marriages is the relative maturity of the two partners at the time they are married. In general, the younger the partners are, the lower the odds that the marriage will last, especially when the individuals are in their teens or early 20s (Kelly, 1982). In part, the age issue relates to Erikson's (1982) belief that intimacy cannot be achieved until after one's identity is established (see Chapter 8). Other reasons that marriages may or may not last include the degree of financial security (low security is related to high risk of failure) and pregnancy at the time of the marriage (being a pregnant bride is related to high risk of failure, especially in very young couples) (Kelly, 1982).

A second important point is that marriages based on similarity of values and interests are the most likely to succeed (Diamond, 1986). **The importance of *homogamy,* marriage based on similarity, cannot be overlooked.** To the extent the couple shares similar values, goals, attitudes, socioeconomic status, ethnic background, and religious beliefs, their relationship is more likely to succeed. Homogamy is an important predictor across a wide variety of cultures and societies, as diverse as Americans in Michigan and Africans in Chad (Diamond, 1986).

A third factor in predicting marital success is a feeling that the relationship is equal. **According to *exchange theory,* marriage is based on each partner contributing something to the relationship that the other would be hard pressed to provide.** Satisfying and happy marriages result when both partners perceive a fair exchange across all the dimensions of the relationship. Couples often

Figure 10.3 Median age at first marriage.
Source: U.S. Bureau of the Census, 1991

experience problems achieving equity because of competing demands between work and family, an issue we will take up again in Chapter 11.

The Developmental Course of Marital Satisfaction

Considerable research has been conducted on marital satisfaction across adulthood. Most research shows that overall marital satisfaction is highest at the beginning of the marriage, falls until the children begin leaving home, and rises again in later life (Berry & Williams, 1987). However, no one pattern is true for all couples; in fact, several patterns are true of marriages at any point in time.

In its early days marriage is at its most intense. During this honeymoon phase, the couple spend considerable time together—talking, going out, establishing their marital roles, arguing, making up, and making love. In good marriages, in which husband and wife share many activities and are open to new experiences together, this honeymoon phase results in bliss and high satisfaction (Olson & McCubbin, 1983). When the marriage is troubled, the intensity of the honeymoon phase creates considerable unhappiness (Swenson, Eskew, & Kohlhepp, 1981).

During the honeymoon phase the couple must learn to adjust to the different perceptions and expectations each person has for the other. Many wives tend to be more concerned than their husbands with keeping close ties with their friends. Many women are also more likely to identify problems in the marriage and want to talk about them (Peplau & Gordon, 1985). The couple must also learn to handle confrontation. Indeed, learning effective conflict resolution strategies may be the most important thing a newly married couple can do for their marriage.

As the bliss of the honeymoon phase becomes a memory, marital satisfaction tends to decline, especially for many women. The decline in satisfaction holds for couples of diverse educational, religious, employment, age, and racial backgrounds (Glenn & McLanahan, 1981, 1982). The most common reason given for this drop is the birth of children. For most couples, having children means having substantially less time to devote to the marriage. As we will see in our discussion of parenthood, taking care of children is hard work, stealing energy that used to be spent on keeping the marriage alive and well (Glenn & Weaver, 1978). The fact that even childless couples experience a modest decline in marital satisfaction means that the drop is not totally due to having children. For example, Kurdek (1991a) found that declines in marital satisfaction over the first 3 years of marriage were related to lower education and failure to pool financial resources. However, whether being childless is a voluntary decision or due to infertility may make a big difference in marital satisfaction, with the latter group experiencing considerable stress (Matthews & Matthews, 1986).

By midlife, marital satisfaction hits rock bottom, and some differences between husbands and wives emerge (Turner, 1982). Husbands at all stages of the marriage tend to describe it in positive terms, whereas middle-aged wives tend to be more critical. For example, Lowenthal, Thurnher, and Chiriboga (1975) found that 80% of husbands, but only 40% of wives, rated their marriages favorably in midlife. Wives' chief complaint about their husbands was that they were too dependent and clingy; interestingly, this difference in feelings is sometimes noted in newlyweds, but then it is husbands who describe their wives in such terms.

Marital satisfaction usually begins to rebound, at least temporarily, following the launching of adult children (Rhyne, 1981). The improvement is especially noteworthy in women, and it stems partly from the increased financial security after children leave, the relief from the day-to-day duties of parenting, and the additional time that wives have with their husbands.

For some middle-aged couples, however, marital satisfaction continues to be low. These couples tend to be ones who have grown apart but who continue to live together. In essence, they have become emotionally divorced (Fitzpatrick, 1984). For these couples, more time together is not a welcome change. Additionally, the physical appearance of one's partner is a contributor to marital satisfaction, particularly for men (Margolin & White, 1987). Because age-related changes in women's appearance are viewed more negatively by society (see Chapter 3), some middle-aged men become increasingly disenchanted with their marriage.

Several studies report that marital satisfaction tends to be fairly high in older couples (Anderson, Russell, & Schumm, 1983; Lee, 1988; Maas & Kuypers, 1974). This level of satisfaction appears to be unrelated to the amount of past or present sexual interest or sexual activity (Bullock & Dunn, 1988) but is positively related to the degree of interaction with friends (Lee, 1988).

However, some researchers observe inconsistencies in satisfaction in long-term marriages (Ade-Ridder & Brubaker, 1983; Sporakowski & Axelson, 1984; Swensen & Trahaug, 1985). For example, Gilford (1984) reports that marital satisfaction among older couples increases shortly after retirement but decreases as health problems and age rise. Sporakowski and Axelson (1984) found that 80% of couples married at least 50 years recollected their marriages as being happy from their wedding day to the present. Surprisingly, however, only 28% of these couples named their spouse as being one of their closest friends.

The discrepant data concerning marital satisfaction in long-term marriages may be due to several factors. For one thing couples in this cohort were less likely to have divorced due to disagreement than those in more recent cohorts and may have simply developed detached, contented styles (Norton & Moorman, 1987). Older couples may also have different criteria for marital satisfaction than younger couples. Or they may simply not see the point in arguing anymore. Moreover, many older couples do not need to have their spouses be

DISCOVERING DEVELOPMENT

What Keeps Married People Together?

Most newspapers have a section devoted to weddings and anniversaries. Each week or so, papers publish the names (and often the pictures) of couples celebrating their golden (50th) or higher anniversary. Occasionally, there may even be a couple celebrating their diamond (75th) anniversary!

Most of us marvel at the longevity such couples demonstrate not just in years lived, but in the fact that they managed to keep a relationship together for so long. How do they do it? To find out, talk to couples who have been married at least 40 years. Ask them what initially got them together, how their relationship changed (and perhaps remained the same) over the years. Find out what things are most different now, what happened that they least expected, and what their happiest and most difficult times were. Make sure you get their "advice" for young couples on how to ensure a long and happy marriage.

Bring your interview results to class and pool them. See if you can create a "prescription" for marital success. Compare your findings to those reported in the text.

their best friends to be satisfied with their marriage. Indeed, Lee (1988) found lower marital satisfaction among older couples with working wives and retired husbands than among couples where both spouses were working or were retired. Unfortunately, our understanding of the dynamics of long-term marriages is extremely limited, so sorting out these possibilities must await further research.

Overall, marital satisfaction ebbs and flows over time. The pattern of a particular marriage over the years is determined by the nature of the dependence of each spouse on the other. When dependence is mutual and about equal, the marriage is strong and close. When the dependence of one partner is much higher than that of the other, however, the marriage is likely to be characterized by stress and conflict. Changes in individual lives over adulthood shift the balance of dependence from one partner to the other; for example, one partner may go back to school, become ill, or lose status. Learning how to deal with these changes is the secret to long and happy marriages.

The fact that marital satisfaction has a general downward trend, but varies considerably across couples, led Karney and Bradbury (1995) to propose a vulnerability-stress-adaptation model of marriage. This model sees marital quality as a dynamic process resulting from the couples' ability to handle stressful events in the context of their particular vulnerabilities and resources. As couples' ability to adapt changes over time, the quality of the marriage will change as well.

What Are Long-Term Marriages Like?

Maybe you know couples who have celebrated their golden wedding anniversary. Perhaps you have even participated in such a celebration for your grandparents. You may have wondered how these couples managed to stay together for so long. If so, you would probably find the exercise in the Discovering Development feature an interesting one.

The answer to this question lies in considering types of marriages. Over the years several attempts have been made at describing types of marriages. For example, Cuber and Harroff (1965) asked middle-aged couples to describe what their marriages had been like. This approach yields different categories, but such descriptions are static; that is, they simply describe what couples are like at one point. Although point-in-time models are helpful, they do not capture the dynamics of marriage over the long haul. To do this requires longitudinal research.

Weishaus and Field (1988) conducted a longitudinal study of 17 couples married between 50 and 69 years that included measures of relationship quality over virtually the entire length of the couples' years together. The results of their research show that long-term marriages vary in their developmental trajectories. Moreover, couples show a real ability to roll with the punches and adapt to changing circumstances. For example, a serious illness to one spouse may not be detrimental to the relationship and may even make the bond stronger. Likewise, couples' expectations about marriage change over time, gradually becoming more congruent.

What specific characteristics differentiate middle-aged and older married couples? To answer this question, Levenson, Carstensen, and Gottman (1993, 1994; Carstensen, Gottman, & Levenson, 1995) conducted a series of studies. They found that compared with middle-aged married couples, older married couples showed reduced potential for conflict and more potential for pleasure in several areas (including interacting with their children), equivalent levels of overall physical and mental health, fewer gender differences in sources of pleasure, and more positive emotions. When discussing a problem, older couples were less emotionally negative and more positive emotions. When discussing a problem, older couples were less emotionally negative and more affectionate than middle-aged couples. Not surprisingly, older unhappy couples acted like unhappy couples of all ages; they showed more negative emotions, and when discussing a problem, engaged in more negative exchanges with their spouse.

In sum, people who have been happily married for a long time act much like Bobbie and Jack, a couple married nearly 50 years, who point to "open and honest communication with each other, a desire to support each other no matter what, and an undying commitment to each other." Their advice to couples on how to help ensure their own golden anniversary? "Never go to sleep angry at your partner." Excellent advice.

Caring for a Spouse

When most couples pledge their love to each other "in sickness and in health," most envision the sickness part to be no worse than an illness lasting a few weeks. And for most couples that may be the case. But for some couples, this pledge may be severely tested.

Caring for a chronically ill spouse presents different challenges than caring for a chronically ill parent (a topic we will consider later in this chapter). Spousal caregivers assume their role usually after decades of shared responsibilities in the marriage. Without warning, the division of labor that had worked for years must be readjusted. Such change inevitably stresses the relationship. This is especially true in cases involving Alzheimer's disease or other dementias because of the cognitive and behavioral consequences of the disease (see Chapter 9).

Studies of caregivers of persons with Alzheimer's disease typically show that marital satisfaction is much lower than for healthy couples (Cavanaugh & Kinney, 1994). Spousal caregivers report a loss of companionship and intimacy over the course of caregiving (Williamson & Schulz, 1990; Wright, 1991). Marital satisfaction is also an important predictor of spousal caregivers' reports of depressive symptoms; the better the perceived quality of the marriage, the fewer symptoms caregivers report (Cavanaugh & Kinney, 1994).

Most spousal caregivers are forced to respond to an environmental challenge that they did not choose, their partner's illness, and adopt the caregiver role out of necessity. Once they adopt the role, though, caregivers assess their ability to carry out the duties required. Longitudinal research indicates that how caregivers perceive their ability to provide care at the outset of caregiving may be key (Kinney & Cavanaugh, 1993). Caregivers who perceive themselves as competent try to rise to the occasion; data indicate that they report fewer and less intense caregiving hassles than spousal caregivers who see themselves as less competent (Kinney & Cavanaugh, 1993). In addition to trying at times to tackle problems head-on and dealing with one's feelings about caregiving, spousal caregivers also use religion as a means of coping with their situation (Ishler, Pargament, Kinney, & Cavanaugh, 1995).

All things considered, though, providing full-time care for a spouse is very stressful (Kinney & Cavanaugh, 1993). Coping with a spouse who may not remember your name, who may act aggressively toward you, and who has a chronic and fatal disease presents serious challenges even to the happiest of couples.

Divorce and Remarriage

Through separation, divorce, and desertion, many adults make the transition from being married back to being single each year. (Later we will consider people who return to singlehood as the result of the death of their spouse.) These transitions are always stressful and difficult. The transition from being married to being single again brings with it important changes in both status and role expectations. For example, holidays may be difficult for individuals now unable to be with their children. In this section we will consider several important issues in dealing with divorce and the decision to remarry.

Divorce

Most adults enter marriage with the idea that the relationship will be permanent. Unfortunately, this permanence is becoming less attainable for more and more couples. Their early intimacy fails to grow. Rather than growing together, they grow apart.

Many factors may disrupt a relationship to the extent that a couple seeks divorce. We will consider attitudes toward divorce, changing expectations of marriage, gender differences, and demographic factors. We will also look at some of the problems faced by divorced adults and the odds that they will enter into new relationships or marriages. But first it would be helpful to consider the facts: What are the odds of getting divorced?

Since reaching a post–World War II low during the 1950s, divorce rates for first marriages have been rising consistently at about 10% per year. (From 1960 to 1988 the actual increase was nearly 250%.) During the late 1980s the increase in the divorce rate slowed, although it is still too early to tell whether that trend will continue. Presently, at least one in every three households is affected by divorce. Based on current trends, couples who have recently married have no better than a 50-50 chance of remaining married for life (Fisher, 1987).

Statistics worldwide and from different periods indicate that marriages fail relatively quickly. Internationally, the peak time for divorce is 3 or 4 years after the wedding, or when the couple are in their late 20s. The United States reflects that trend, with half of all divorces occurring within the first 7 years of marriage (Fisher, 1987).

Another way to approach the question of who is likely to get divorced is to examine personal demographic factors. One consistent factor related to divorce is ethnicity. African Americans are more likely than European Americans to divorce or separate (Glenn & Supancic, 1984). Hispanic groups show considerable variability; Mexican Americans and Cuban Americans have divorce rates similar to European Americans; the rate for Puerto Ricans is much higher (Bean & Tienda, 1987). Age is also important. The divorce rate for those who marry before age 20 is substantially higher than for those who marry after age 20 (Glenn & Supancic, 1984). This difference is due in large part to the negative effects of premarital pregnancy on teenage couples. Higher frequency of attendance at religious services is related to lower divorce rates. Interestingly, conservative Protestant denominations (for example, Nazarene, Pentecostal, Baptist) show relatively high divorce rates; rates for Protestants in general are higher than for either Catholics or Jews (Glenn & Supancic, 1984).

The factors that are good predictors of divorce are many of the same ones that argue against getting married in the first place (Udry, 1971). Differences on such dimensions as educational level, race, religion, or socioeconomic status produce marital discord more easily than do similarities.

One prominent reason given for the increase in divorce is that it is not perceived as negatively as it once was. Previous generations considered divorce the solution of last resort and held divorced adults

TABLE 10.1 Main reasons men and women give for divorcing

Reasons Women Give		Reasons Men Give	
1. Communication problems	70%	1. Communication problems	59%
2. Basic unhappiness	60%	2. Basic unhappiness	47%
3. Incompatibility	56%	3. Incompatibility	45%
4. Emotional abuse	56%	4. Sexual problems	30%
5. Financial problems	33%	5. Financial problems	29%
6. Sexual problems	32%	6. Emotional abuse	25%
7. Alcohol abuse by spouse	30%	7. Women's liberation	15%
8. Infidelity by spouse	25%	8. In-laws	12%
9. Physical abuse	22%	9. Infidelity by spouse	11%
10. In-laws	11%	10. Alcohol abuse by self	9%

Source: Cleek and Pearson, 1985

in low regard, sometimes not allowing them to remarry. Even today, divorce is seen as a sign of failure—a pronouncement that the couple wish to end a relationship that they originally intended to last for a lifetime (Crosby, 1980). Still, divorced adults are not subjected to as many overt discriminations as they once were. So in some ways divorce has become a more acceptable, if not respectable, status.

Closely related to this change in attitude toward divorce is a shift in expectations for marriage. More people now expect marriage to be a positive experience and to be personally fulfilling. When a marriage fails to produce bliss, divorce is often pursued as the way to a new and better partner. In the past husbands and wives did not expect to understand each other, because the other gender was a natural mystery. Today, middle-class marriage partners have a more flexible view and expect each other to be a friend, lover, wage earner, and caregiver (Blumstein & Schwartz, 1983).

These changes are evident in the reasons that people give for divorcing. In 1948 recently divorced women cited cruelty, excessive drinking, and nonsupport as the most common reasons (Goode, 1956). By 1985 the reasons had shifted to communication problems, basic unhappiness, and incompatibility (Cleek & Pearson, 1985). Although women usually cite more reasons than men, as can be seen in Table 10.1 there is considerable agreement between the genders. The differences are interesting: Whereas 22% of women cite physical abuse as a significant cause of their divorce, only 3% of men do; and whereas 15% of men cite women's liberation as a cause, only 3% of women do.

These changes in reasons reflect a major shift toward no-fault divorce laws in the United States. In 1948, blame—such as infidelity or nonsupport—had to be established and was legally required for divorce. Today, blame is not a prerequisite, and reasons such as incompatibility are acceptable.

Although the changes in attitudes toward divorce have eased the social trauma associated with it, divorce still takes a high toll on the psyche of the couple. A nationwide survey in the United States revealed that divorce could impair individuals' well-being for at least 5 years after the event, producing a greater variety of long-lasting negative effects than even the death of a spouse (Nock, 1981). A longitudinal study of divorced people showed that they were more depressed than they had been when they were married (Menaghan & Lieberman, 1986). Divorced people living alone tend to be less happy than either married or cohabiting couples, with degree of unhappiness also related to the number of divorces one has had (Kurdek, 1991b).

Even though the psychological cost of divorce is high, divorced people do not wish they were still married. An intensive longitudinal study found that 5 years after the divorce only 20% of former partners thought that the divorce had been a mistake. Most approved of it, even if they had been initially opposed to it. However, most of the people said that they had underestimated the pain that the divorce would cause (Wallerstein & Kelly, 1980).

The effects of divorce change over time. In the initial phase shortly after the breakup, the partners often become even angrier and more bitter toward each other than they were before the separation. These feelings are often fostered by lawyers, who encourage partners to fight over property and custody of the children. Additionally, many partners underestimate their attachment to each other and may be overly sensitive to criticism from them. The increased hostility is often accompanied by periods of depression and disequilibrium, as patterns of eating, sleeping, drug and alcohol use, work, and residence change (Kelly, 1982).

Men have a more difficult time in the short run (Chiriboga, 1982). Most men report being shocked by the break, because it is usually the wife who files for divorce (Kelly, 1982). Husbands are more likely to be blamed for the problems, to accept the blame, to move out, and thereby to find their social life disrupted (Kitson & Sussman, 1982). Thus, although women are typically more distressed before the separation, men have more psychological and physical stress immediately after it (Bloom & Caldwell, 1981).

In the long run, however, women are much more seriously affected by divorce. The reasons are both social and economic. Women have fewer marriage prospects, find it more difficult to establish new relationships if they have custody of the children, and are at a major disadvantage financially. The financial problems of divorced women received considerable attention in the late 1980s as states passed laws to enforce child support payments. Additionally, an ex-wife is not legally entitled to any of her former husband's Social Security benefits unless the divorce occurs after he has stopped working, nor does she share in pension or health benefits (Cain, 1982). These problems are especially important for middle-aged divorcees, who may have spent years as a homemaker and have few job skills.

Divorced mothers with children are much more likely to feel serious financial strains than are their ex-husbands.

Divorce in middle age or late life has some special characteristics. In general, the older the individuals are, the greater the trauma (Chiriboga, 1982), largely because of the long period of investment in each other's emotional and practical lives. Longtime friends often turn away or take sides, causing additional disruption to the social network. Middle-aged and elderly women are at a significant disadvantage for remarriage—an especially traumatic situation for women who obtained much of their identity from their roles as wife and mother. An additional problem for elderly divorced people is that even if the divorce occurred many years earlier, children and other relatives may still blame them for breaking apart the family (Hennon, 1983).

The difficulty in adjusting to divorce often depends on whether there are children. Childless couples tend to adjust more readily, probably because they can make a clean break and a fresh start. For divorced people with children, the trouble typically begins during the custody battle. Despite much public discussion of joint custody, it is far more typical that one parent gains custody and assumes the role of two parents, whereas the other is reduced to an occasional visitor. Over 90% of the time the mother receives custody. The price she pays is very high. At the same time that her responsibilities as a parent are increasing, her financial resources are decreasing. On average, divorced mothers experience a 73% decline in their standard of living within the first year following divorce. In contrast, their ex-husbands typically enjoy a 42% rise (Weitzman, 1985). Child care is expensive, and most divorced fathers contribute less than before the separation. In fact, only about one third of all child support payments are actually made.

Divorced fathers pay a psychological price (Furstenberg & Nord, 1985). Although many divorced fathers would like to remain active in their children's lives, few actually are. Within 3 years after the divorce, fewer than half of noncustodial fathers are involved in decisions regarding their children, and less than 60% of children on average see their fathers even once a month (Seltzer, 1991). The fact that about one quarter of divorced couples end up as bitter enemies (Ahrons & Wallisch, 1987) only makes matters worse for all concerned.

The problems between divorced people with young children can be overcome (Ahrons & Rodgers, 1987; Wallerstein & Kelly, 1980). Some former couples are able to get over their anger and cooperate with each other. This is especially true if the couple had no children (Masheter, 1991). Adjustment is also helped if both or neither remarries. Interestingly, it is easier for a new husband to accept his wife's friendly relationship with her former husband than it is for a new wife to accept her husband's friendly relationship with his ex-wife.

But the issues concerning divorce and children do not disappear if the children are young adults. Research indicates that young adults whose parents divorce experience a great deal of emotional vulnerability and stress (Cooney & Uhlenberg, 1990). Anger, conflicting loyalties, and worry about their parent's future are common reactions. Relationships with parents may be irreparably harmed. Even many years later, divorced fathers are less likely than mothers to experience positive relationships with their adult children. Fathers also do not believe they will be able to rely on their children for support in times of need (Cooney & Uhlenberg, 1990).

Remarriage

Although divorce is a traumatic event, it does not seem to deter people from eventually beginning new relationships that typically lead into another marriage. Nearly 80% of divorced people remarry within the first 3 years (Glick & Lin, 1986). However, rates vary across ethnic groups. African Americans remarry more slowly than European Americans, and Hispanics remarry more slowly than either of these other two groups (Coleman & Ganong, 1990). Remarriage is much more likely if the divorced people are young, mainly because there are more partners available. Partner availability favors men at all ages, because men tend to marry women younger than themselves. For this reason the probability that a divorced woman will remarry declines with increasing age. Older divorced women with higher educational levels are the least likely to remarry (Glick & Lin, 1986), probably because of a shortage of eligible unmarried older men and a lower need for the financial security provided by a man. However, several studies indicate higher well-being among widows who remarried than among those who remained single (Burks, Lund, Gregg, & Bluhm, 1988; Gentry & Schulman, 1988).

Very little research has been conducted on second (or third or more) marriages. Remarried people report that they experience their second marriage differently. They claim to enjoy much better communication, to resolve disagreements with greater goodwill, to arrive at decisions more equitably, and to divide chores more fairly (Furstenberg, 1982). Indeed, most couples believe that they will be more likely to succeed the second time around (Furstenberg, 1982). For African Americans, this appears to be true; divorce rates for remarriages are lower than for first marriages (Teachman, 1986). However, second marriages in general have a slightly higher risk of dissolution than first marriages if one spouse has custody of children from a previous marriage. Perhaps this optimism is the only way that people can overcome the feelings of vulnerability that usually accompany the breakup of the first marriage.

Adapting to new relationships in remarriage can be difficult. Hobart (1988) reports differences between remarried men and women in this regard. For remarried men, the preeminent relationship is with his new wife; other relationships, especially those with his children from his first marriage, take a back seat. For remarried women, the relationship with their new husband remains more marginal than their relationship with their children from the first marriage. Thus, the higher failure rate for second marriages involving stepchildren may stem from differences in the centrality of particular relationships between husbands and wives.

Remarriage late in life tends to be happier than remarriage in young adulthood (Campbell, 1981), especially if the couple are widowed rather than divorced. The biggest problem faced by older remarried individuals is resistance from adult children, who may think that the new spouse is an intruder and who may be concerned about an inheritance.

Because roughly 60% of all divorces involve children and because most divorced people remarry, most second-marriage families face the problems of integrating stepchildren. Unfortunately, we have almost no information about how stepparents interact with their new families. For example, we lack such basic information as the extent to which the factors that influence parent-child relationships in first marriages are modified in subsequent marriages.

What little information we have suggests that stepparents are more readily accepted by very young or adult children and by families that were split by divorce rather than by death. Male children tend to accept a stepparent more readily, especially when the new parent is a man. However, children often feel that an opposite-gender stepparent "plays favorites" (Hetherington, Cox, & Cox, 1982). Adolescent stepchildren are especially difficult to deal with, and many second marriages fail because of this problem (White & Booth, 1985). To the extent that children still admire their absent biological parent, the stepparent may have feelings of inadequacy. Finally, stepparents and stepchildren alike often have unrealistic expectations for the relationship. Both parties need time to adjust to the new marriage (Hetherington et al., 1982).

There is essentially no socializing mechanism for becoming a stepparent. No consensus exists for how stepparents are supposed to behave, how stepparenting is to be similar or different from biological parenting, or how one's duties, obligations, and rights should be meshed with those of the absent biological parent. In many cases stepparents adopt their partner's children to surmount some of these problems. However, emotionally charged issues remain. Much more needs to be learned about the experience of stepparenting, and the status, rights, and obligations of stepparents need to be clarified.

Widowhood

Traditional marriage vows proclaim that the union will last "till death us do part." Experiencing the death of a spouse is certainly a traumatic event (see

Chapter 13), and it is one that is experienced by couples of all ages. Widowhood is more common for women; over half of all women over age 65 are widows, but only 15% of the same-aged men are widowers. The reasons for this discrepancy are related to biological and social forces: Women have longer life expectancies and typically marry men older than themselves. Consequently, the average American married woman can expect to live 10 to 12 years as a widow.

The impact of widowhood goes far beyond the ending of a partnership. Because they have been touched by death, widowed people are often left alone by family and friends who do not know how to deal with a bereaved person. As a result, widows and widowers often lose not only a spouse but also those friends and family who feel uncomfortable including a single person rather than a couple in social functions. Additionally, widowed individuals may feel awkward as the third party or may even view themselves as a threat to married friends (Field & Minkler, 1988). Going to a movie or a restaurant by oneself may be unpleasant or unsatisfying to widows or widowers, so they may just stay home. Unfortunately, others may assume that they simply wish or need to be alone.

For both widows and widowers, the first few months alone can be very difficult. Both are at risk for increased physical illness and report more symptoms of depression, lost status, economic hardship, and lower social support (Stroebe & Stroebe, 1983). But feelings of loss do not dissipate quickly. As we will see in Chapter 13, feeling sad on important dates is a common experience, even many years after a loved one has died.

Unlike some other cultures, U.S. society does not have well-defined social roles for widowed people. We even tend to show disapproval toward those who continue to grieve for too long. Because widowhood is most often associated with older women, the few social supports are largely organized for them.

Considerable research supports the notion that widowhood has different meanings for men and women. But the evidence is much less clear on the question of whether widowhood is harder for men or women. To appreciate the controversy, let us consider what we know about these effects and meanings.

In general, a woman's reaction to widowhood depends on the kind of relationship she had with her husband. To the extent that women derived their identities from their husbands and did things as a couple, serious disruptions will result (Lopata, 1975). But women whose lives are centered in individual interactions will experience far less loss of identity and typically make only small changes in their lifestyle.

In a study of over 300 widows in Chicago, Lopata (1973, 1975) found six ways in which women dealt with the death of their spouse: (1) "Liberated" women had worked through their loss and moved on to lead complex, well-rounded lives; (2) "merry widows" had lifestyles filled with fun, dating, and entertainment; (3) working women were either still career oriented or had simply taken any available job; (4) "widow's widows" lived alone, valued their independence, and preferred the company of other widows; (5) traditional widows lived with their children and took an active role in their children's and grandchildren's lives; and (6) grieving women were willingly isolated and could not work through their husbands' deaths or were isolated because they lacked interpersonal or job skills, but they wished to become more involved.

Gentry and Schulman (1988) studied remarriage as a coping response in older widows. They interviewed 39 widows who had remarried, 192 who had considered remarriage, and 420 who had not considered it. They found that women who had remarried reported significantly fewer concerns than either of the other groups. Interestingly, the remarried widows were also the ones who recalled the most concerns immediately after the death of their spouse. Apparently, remarriage helped these widows deal with the loss of their husband by alleviating loneliness and emotional distress.

Many people feel that the loss of one's wife presents a more serious problem than the loss of one's husband. Perhaps this is because a wife is often a man's only close friend and confidant or because men are usually unprepared to live out their lives alone (Glick, Weiss, & Parkes, 1974). Men are often ill equipped to handle such routine and necessary tasks as cooking, shopping, and keeping house, and they become emotionally isolated from family members. As more men become facile at housekeeping tasks, it remains to be seen whether these patterns will characterize future generations of widowers. It may be the social isolation of widowers that becomes the most important factor in poor adjustment (Turner, 1982).

Men are generally older when they are widowed than are women. Thus, to some extent the greater overall difficulties reported by widowers may be due to this age difference. Indeed, if age is held constant, widows report higher anxiety than widowers (Atchley, 1975). Regardless of age, men have a clear advantage over women in the opportunity to form new heterosexual relationships; interestingly, though, older widowers are actually less likely to form new, close friendships than are widows. Perhaps this is simply a continuation of men's lifelong tendency to have few close friendships.

Concept Checks

1. What are the two most difficult issues for single people?
2. What is the connection between cohabitation and marriage?
3. What differences are there between gay male and lesbian couples and heterosexual couples?
4. How does marital satisfaction change across the length of the marriage?
5. What are the main reasons people get divorced?
6. What gender differences have been reported concerning people who are widowed?

PARENTHOOD

Learning Objectives:

- Why do people decide to have children?
- What is it like to be a mother or father? What special issues confront single parents?
- What does child rearing involve?
- How do people cope with children leaving home?

Most Americans believe that having children is normal, natural, and necessary. We also tend to think that having children will be a joyful and fulfilling experience and that good parents are guided by their natural love for their children. These notions are applied especially to the mother, and belief in a maternal instinct is widespread. Unfortunately, no one is likely to possess the innate ability to be a good parent. Perhaps this is the reason adults often feel considerable anxiety over having children. "When are you going to start a family?" is a question commonly asked of young couples. But once the child is present, adults often feel inadequate. In the words of one new parent, "It's scary being totally responsible for another person."

Scary as it might be, the birth of a child transforms a couple (or a single parent) into a family. **Although the most common form of family in Western societies is the *nuclear family,* consisting of parent(s) and child(ren), the most common form around the world is the *extended family,* in which grandparents and other relatives live with parents and children.** In this section we will explore some of the aspects of parenthood, including the decision process itself and the joys and pains of having children.

Deciding Whether to Have Children

At some point during an intimate relationship, couples discuss whether to have children. This decision is more complicated than most people think, because a couple must weigh the many benefits with the many drawbacks. On the plus side children provide a source of personal satisfaction and love, fulfill the need for generativity, provide a potential source of companionship, and serve as a source of vicarious experience (Frieze, Parsons, Johnson, Ruble, & Zellman, 1978). Children also present problems. In addition to the financial burden, children also change established interaction patterns. For instance, they disrupt a couple's sexual relationship and decrease the amount of time for shared activities by up to half. Moreover, having children is stressful. Some of the most important sources of stress accompanying parenthood have been known for many years (Rossi, 1980): cultural pressure to have children, possible involuntary or unplanned parenthood, irrevocability of having a child, lack of formal education for parenting, and lack of consensus about how to be a good parent.

Although most couples still opt to have children even when they recognize the stresses and strains, an increasing number of couples are remaining childless. These couples have several advantages over those who choose to have children. Child-free couples report having happier marriages, more freedom, and higher standards of living. But they must also face social criticism from the larger child-oriented society and may run the risk of feeling more lonely in old age (Van Hoose & Worth, 1982).

For many couples, having children of their own is not an option: One or both partners may be infertile. About one in six couples experiences fertility problems, and experts believe the problem is increasing. Both psychological factors (such as anxiety or stress) and physical factors (such as disease) may cause infertility. In women physical problems that can cause infertility include the failure to ovulate, fallopian tube blockage, endometriosis, abnormalities in the vaginal mucus, and untreated gonorrhea or chlamydia. In men they include faulty or insufficient sperm, varicoceles (a varicose enlargement of the veins of the spermatic cord), and blockages of the sperm ducts.

The Parental Role

Today, couples have fewer children and have their first child later than in the past. Indeed, until 1993 couples in which mothers were over age 30 when they had their first child had been increasing. The slight decline since then is due mainly to fewer numbers of women of childbearing age in cohorts following the baby boomers. Delaying first children has important benefits. Traditionally, mothers have been thought to be crucial for the normal development of the child (Fields & Widmayer, 1982). Older mothers are more at ease being parents, spend more time with their babies, and are more affectionate and sensitive to them (Ragozin, Basham, Crnic, Greenberg, & Robinson, 1982).

Timing of fatherhood also makes a difference in the ways in which fathers interact with their children. Compared with men who become fathers in their 20s, men who become fathers in their 30s are generally more invested in their paternal role and spend up to three times as much time in caring for preschool children as younger fathers (Cooney, Pedersen, Indelicato, & Palkovitz, 1993). However, men who become fathers in their 30s are also more likely to feel ambivalent and resentful about time lost to their careers (Cooney et al., 1993).

Parenting is full of rewards, but also takes a great deal of work. Caring for young children is demanding and may create difficulties over division of labor, especially if both parents are employed outside the home. Mothers appear equally divided among those who love taking care of their children and working, those who don't, and those who are neutral about it (Thompson & Walker, 1989). Fathers largely report that they like taking care of their children; however, they are also less involved in direct child care (LaRossa, 1988).

Being a middle-aged parent with adolescent and adult children has special issues. As we will see later in this chapter, parent-child relationships change during this period, going from clearly hierarchical to more egalitarian as both children and parents mature.

In general, parents manage to deal with the many challenges of child rearing reasonably well. They learn when to compromise and when to apply firm but fair discipline. And if given the choice, most parents do not regret their decision to have children.

Single Parents

One of the fastest growing groups of adults is single parents, most of whom are women. The increasing divorce rate, the large number of women who keep children born out of wedlock, and the desire of many single adults to have or adopt children are all contributing factors to this phenomenon. Being a single parent raises important questions: What happens when only one adult is responsible for child care? How do single parents meet their own needs for emotional support and intimacy? Certainly, how one feels about being single also has important effects.

Some of the personal and social situations of single parents have been studied with these issues in mind. Many divorced single parents report feelings of frustration, failure, guilt, and ambivalence about the parent-child relationship (Van Hoose & Worth, 1982). Frustration usually results from a lack of companionship and from loneliness, often in response to the fact that most social activities are typically reserved for couples. Feelings of guilt may lead to attempts to make up for the child's lack of a father or mother, or they may result when the parent indulges himself or herself. Because children are sometimes seen as hindrances to developing new relationships, parents may experience ambivalence toward them. These feelings may also arise if children serve as a reminder of a former failure.

Single parents, regardless of gender, face considerable obstacles. Financially, they are usually much less well-off than their married counterparts. Integrating the roles of work and parenthood are difficult enough for two persons; for the single parent the hardships are compounded. Financially, single mothers are hardest hit. Emotionally, single fathers may have the worst of it; according to some research, their sleep, eating, play, work, and peer relations are badly affected, and they are more depressed than any other group of men (Pearlin & Johnson, 1977). Moreover, because most men are not socialized for child rearing, the lack of basic skills necessary to care for children may compound these problems.

One long-standing concern of particular importance to single parents is dating (Phillis & Stein, 1983). Indeed, the three most popular questions asked by single parents are "How do I become available again?" "How will my children react?" and "How do I cope with my own sexuality?" Clearly, initiating a new relationship is difficult for many single parents, especially those with older children. They may be hesitant to express this side of themselves in front of their children or may strongly dislike their children's questioning about or resentment of their dates. Moreover, access to social activities is more difficult for single parents; in response, organizations such as Parents Without Partners have been established to provide social outlets.

Overall, single parents seeking new relationships typically do so discreetly. Both mothers and fathers express concern about having dates stay overnight, although women feel more strongly about this (Greenberg, 1979). Single parents share the same needs as other adults; it is fulfilling them that is the problem. Of course, many single parents learn how to deal with the problem and find fulfilling relationships.

Alternative Forms of Parenting

Not all parents raise their own biological children. In fact, roughly one third of North American couples become stepparents, foster parents, or adoptive parents sometime during their lives. To be sure, the parenting issues we have discussed thus far are just as important in these situations as when people raise their own biological children. However, some special problems arise as well.

A big issue for foster, adoptive, and stepparents is how strongly the child will bond with his or her new parent. Although infants less than one year old will probably bond well, children who are old enough to have formed attachments with their biological parents may have competing loyalties. For example, some stepchildren remain strongly attached to the noncustodial parent, actively resist attempts to integrate them into a new family ("My real mother wouldn't make me do that"), or exhibit behavioral problems such as drinking or continually invading the stepparent's privacy (Pasley & Ihinger-Tallman, 1987). Additionally, stepparents usually must deal with continued visitation by the noncustodial parent, which may exacerbate any difficulties. These problems are often the basis for second divorce and are a major reason why second marriages are at high risk for dissolution as discussed earlier in this chapter.

Still, many stepparents and stepchildren ultimately develop good relationships with each other. Stepparents must be sensitive to and understanding of the relationship between the stepchild and his or her biological, noncustodial parent. Allowing stepchildren to develop the relationship with the stepparent at their own pace also helps.

Adoptive parents also contend with attachment to birth parents, but in different ways. In addition to attachments that may predate the adoption, adopted children may wish to locate and meet their birth parents. Wanting to know one's origins is understandable, but such searches can strain the relationships between these children and their adoptive parents, who may interpret these actions as a form of rejection (Rosenberg, 1992). In general, though, recent research indicates that, compared with nonadopted children, adopted children are more confident, have a more positive view of the world, feel more in control of their lives, and view their adoptive parents as more nurturing (Marquis & Detweiler, 1985).

Foster parents tend to have the most tenuous relationship with their children because the bond can be broken for any of a number of reasons having nothing to do with the quality of the care being provided, such as courts awarding custody back to birth parents or another couple legally adopting the child. Dealing with attachment is difficult; parents want to provide secure homes but may not have children long enough to establish continuity. Furthermore, because many children in foster care have been unable to form attachments at all, they may not be willing or able to form ones that will inevitably be broken. As a result, foster parents must be willing to tolerate considerable ambiguity in the relationship and have few expectations about the future.

Finally, many gay men and lesbian women also desire to be parents. Some have biological children themselves, whereas others choose adoption or foster parenting. Although gay men and lesbian women make good parents, they often experience resistance to having children. Actually, research indicates that children reared by gay or lesbian parents do not experience any more problems than children reared by heterosexual parents.

On the contrary, substantial evidence exists that children raised by gay or lesbian parents do not develop sexual identity or any other problems any more than children raised by heterosexual parents (Flaks, Ficher, Masterpasqua, & Joseph, 1995; Patterson, 1995). In fact, some evidence suggests that children raised by gay and lesbian parents may even have some advantages over children raised by heterosexual parents. Gay men are often especially concerned about being good and nurturing fathers and try hard to raise their children with nonsexist, egalitarian attitudes (Bozett, 1988). And lesbian mothers exhibit more parenting awareness skills than do heterosexual parents (Flaks et al., 1995).

The Child-Rearing Years

Raising children is a difficult job that is best described as a juggling act. One has to not only tend to the children's needs, but also maintain an intimate relationship with one's spouse, help maintain a home, and probably maintain a career. Child rearing alone involves nurturing, socializing, and providing opportunities for intellectual and emotional growth. Throughout this process, parents need to develop their own style of parenting. Ideally, this should be a mutually interactive process between the parents and the children. All these duties demand considerable attention, so it is no wonder why many parents get tired!

All the issues discussed earlier concerning moth-

Married couples are usually happier and more satisfied with their relationship after their children have left home.

ers and fathers and single parents come into play in child rearing. Initially, parents are often most concerned with doing things right, but this concern gradually gives way as parents gain experience. Indeed, most parents successfully figure out how to raise their children, helped in no small measure by the fact that children themselves are fairly resilient. Although parents tend to differ in style when children are very young, they tend to become more similar in dealing with them as they become adolescents (Turner, 1982).

As we noted earlier, it is during the child-rearing years that marital satisfaction reaches its ebb. This finding is more understandable given the number of demands placed on parents.

When the Children Leave

One of the biggest events in a family occurs when one's children leave home to establish their own careers and families. For most parents, children's departures are gradual; contact is still fairly frequent, and most ties are not cut. **Eventually, the youngest child departs, creating a new situation for the middle-aged parents: the empty nest, or *postparental family.***

The departure of the youngest child can be a traumatic time. This is especially true for mothers who had defined their identity mainly in terms of their children. The psychological effects of the empty nest can be important, as one mother complained: "My daughter was 21 when she married. It's not that I wanted her to stay with me, but I missed her terribly. I just felt so alone."

For many years this kind of reaction was thought to be universal in women. Children were thought to be a central source of satisfaction for mothers. This belief has not been supported by contemporary research (Turner, 1982). For most parents, the departure of the youngest child is not a particularly distressing event. Many people even perceive it as a change for the better (Nock, 1982). Adolescents can be difficult to live with, so to be rid of conflict and challenges to parental authority can be a relief. As one parent said: "It's fantastic. I have more free time, less laundry, lower expenses, and my husband and I can do what we want when we want."

This mother described another important aspect of the postparental period. For the first time in many years, a couple are living by themselves. They must learn about each other again and adjust to a different lifestyle without children. Most couples feel contentment over the successful completion of child rearing. They may now have the time to continue developing the intimacy in their relationship that brought them together years earlier. Research on marital satisfaction and personal happiness supports these notions (Turner, 1982).

Marital satisfaction typically rises from the low point when one's children are teenagers to a high during the postparental period that is second only to the period of newlywedded bliss. The opportunity to re-create the interpersonal relationship that originally led the couple to marry accounts for this upswing. Thus, for most couples, an empty nest is a happy nest.

But what if the nest does not become empty? When children refuse to leave home or repeatedly return after nominally moving out, parental distress is likely (Troll, 1975). This is especially true if the child is perceived to be delaying the transition to adulthood longer than the parents believe is reasonable. Additionally, more adult children are returning home because they have difficulty finding employment and cannot afford housing, or they experience financial problems following divorce. To the extent that these issues result in parent-child conflict, parents tend to be highly dissatisfied with the living arrangements and wish their child would leave (Aquilino & Supple, 1991). The outcome in this case is severely strained parent-child relationships. Empty nests are not only happy nests; they are also the nests that parents expect to have.

Concept Checks

1. What are the major factors people consider when they think about having children?
2. How does age relate to parenting?
3. What are new parents typically concerned with initially?
4. How do most parents deal with children leaving?

FAMILY DYNAMICS AND MIDDLE AGE

Learning Objectives:

- How does the relationship between middle-aged parents and their adult children change?
- How do middle-aged adults deal with their aging parents?

Family ties across generations provide the basis for socialization and for continuity in the family's identity. These ties are particularly salient for members of the middle-aged generation, precisely because they are the link between their aging parents and their young adult children. **The pressure on this generation is considerable; in fact, middle-agers are often referred to as the *sandwich generation* to reflect their position between two generations (their parents and their children) that puts demands and pressures on them.**

Being a middle-aged parent also affords the opportunity to assume new roles (Green & Boxer, 1986). **Mothers (more so than fathers) tend to take on the role of *kinkeepers*, the people who gather the family together for celebrations and keep family members in touch with each other.** Studies of African American families, for example, have shown that kinship ties provide a wide variety of support, from financial aid and role models for young parents to caregiving for the older generation (Stanford & Lockery, 1984). Kinkeeping becomes especially important once grandchildren arrive, which we will discuss in more detail later in this chapter. Mothers may also go to college or begin new careers because their children encourage them. Unfortunately, much less is known about new roles for middle-aged fathers.

Part of being "sandwiched" between two generations means dealing with paradoxes in relationships. As explored in the Something to Think About feature, these paradoxes entail both positive and negative aspects of role conflicts and rewards.

In this section we will examine some of the dynamics between the middle-aged and their aging parents and between them and their young adult children. Along the way we will clear up some popular misconceptions about neglect of elderly parents and war between the generations.

Becoming Friends with Adult Children

Sometime during middle age, most parents experience two positive developments with their chil-

SOMETHING TO THINK ABOUT

The Paradoxes of the "Sandwich Generation"

Being caught between two generations brings with it some interesting paradoxes. Looking downward in terms of generations, one is still a parent, yet one does not (nor should) have the same degree of control over an adult child's behavior that was the case years earlier. Nevertheless, a parent still cares and loves an adult child very much. Nearly all middle-aged parents understand the paradox of feeling parental but recognizing that one's child is now an independent adult.

A second and even more complex paradox involves caring for one's aging parent. This problem is especially an issue for women, who end up doing most of the family caregiving. Caring for a parent involves several paradoxes (Bengston, Rosenthal, & Burton, 1995): between the degrees to which one is truly "sandwiched"; between the burdens and benefits of providing care; and between objective and subjective realities.

Without question, having to care for a parent adds a role to one's life. However, emerging evidence suggests that people who have a number of roles they must fulfill may actually have more opportunities for greater social support, better access to resources, and greater personal competence (Lopata, 1993).

Some people believe that caring for a parent always brings more burdens than benefits. Such beliefs belie a bias that caring involves a one-directional flow of help. Actually, most adult child–older parent interactions are highly reciprocal. Only when a parent is in extremely poor health does the relationship become more burdensome for the adult child.

This latter point is related to the third paradox. Any relationship may be perceived as burdensome or rewarding, or both. Thus, we must take a careful look at individuals' situation to understand how the relationship is being perceived. We must look at not only what adult children give, but also what they get back in the form of satisfaction, meaning, and feelings of continuity (Marshall, Matthews, & Rosenthal, 1993).

In sum, understanding how middle-aged adults feel "sandwiched" by the pressures of parenting and caring for their own parents entails understanding the complexities of reciprocal family relationships. There are both plusses and minuses that must be considered. It's something to think about.

---

dren: suddenly their children see them in a new light, and their children leave home. After the strain of raising adolescents (imagine being the parent of someone exactly like you during your teenage years), parents often rejoice in a transformation that occurs when their children head into young adulthood. In general, parent-child relationships improve considerably when children become young adults (Troll & Bengtson, 1982). The difference can be dramatic, as it was in Deb's case. "When Sacha was 15, she acted as if I was the dumbest person on the planet. But," she said with a wry smile, "now that she's 21 she acts as if I got smart all of a sudden. I like being around her; she's a great kid and we're really becoming friends."

One of the secrets of making this transition as smoothly as possible is the extent to which parents foster and approve of their children's attempts at being independent. Most parents eventually achieve an *empty nest* successfully, as we noted in the previous section. Only those people who derive a major source of their identity through being a parent tend to have difficulties.

Even though their children leave home, middle-aged parents do not abandon them. Parents still provide considerable financial help (such as paying college tuition) when possible. And most help in other ways ranging from mundane (making the washer and dryer available to their college-age children) to the extraordinary (providing the down payment for their child's house). Young adults and their middle-aged parents typically believe that they have strong, positive relationships and that they can count on each other for help when necessary (Troll & Bengtson, 1982). And some evidence suggests that continuing to care for adult children enhances older mothers' well-being (Spitze, Logan, Joseph, & Lee, 1994).

Of course, all this help doesn't mean that everything is perfect. Conflicts still arise. One study found that about one third of middle-class fathers surveyed complained about their sons' lack of achievement or about their daughters' poor choice of husbands (Nydegger, 1986).

Once children have gone, parents typically take stock and ask themselves what kind of job they did as parents. Ryff, Lee, Essex, and Schmutte (1994) argue that this parental evaluation is an important part of parents' midlife evaluation of themselves. Moreover, because parents *are* the major influence on children, the stakes for this self-evaluation are high; how one's child turns out is a powerful statement about one's success or failure as a parent (Ryff et al., 1994).

To test this idea, Ryff and colleagues (1994) assessed a random sample of 114 middle-aged mothers and 101 middle-aged fathers, all from different middle-class families in the U.S. Midwest, who had at least one child aged 21 or over. The researchers asked parents to rate their child's adjustment and educational and occupational attainment, to compare their child to other children that age, and to rate their psychological well-being.

Overall, results showed that positive views of children's personal and social adjustment predicted nearly all of the measures of parental well-being. This means that parents' sense of self-acceptance, purpose in life, and environmental mastery were strongly related to how well they thought their children were adjusted. Similar, but somewhat weaker, relations were found between children's accomplishments and parental well-being. No differences between mothers and fathers were found.

Parents were also asked to rate how well they thought their children were doing compared with themselves when they were the same age. These data were intriguing. Parents who thought their children were better adjusted (that is, were more self-confident, happy, and interpersonally skilled) than they themselves were in early adulthood had *lower* levels of well-being. Why? Shouldn't parents be pleased that their children are well adjusted? Ryff and colleagues (1994) suggest that this finding, though seemingly counterintuitive, is really understandable in terms of social comparison. That is, in many domains people suffer negative consequences (such as having lower self-esteem) when they perceive other people are doing better than they are (Suls & Wills, 1991). Even though parents by and large want their children to be happy, they may have difficulty accepting it if they turn out to be *too* happy.

In contrast, parents who rated their children as having attained better educational and occupational levels felt more positive about themselves compared with parents who rated their children lower on these dimensions. In this case, parents may feel that they have achieved the American Dream of the next generation doing better than they did.

Ryff and colleagues showed that midlife parents' self-evaluations are clearly influenced by their perceptions of how their children turned out. Perhaps this is one way that parents validate the time and energy that they devoted to their children.

Middle-Aged Adults and Their Aging Parents

You probably have had little trouble so far in this section seeing yourself in the role of adult child. Try now to imagine your middle-aged parents in the same role in relation to their parents (your grandparents). Of course, if you are already middle-aged, this exercise is a lot easier! Being a child is a role that people are increasingly still playing well into adulthood and in many cases into their 60s or 70s. How do middle-aged adults relate to their parents? What happens when their parents become frail? We will consider these issues in this section.

Keeping in Touch

According to a widespread myth, older parents are largely neglected by their middle-aged children. The myth is sustained by the belief that sometime in the past (the "good old days"), middle-aged children were more devoted to their parents than they are today, and that today's children just don't care for their parents like they used to (Lee, 1985).

These beliefs are wrong. True, proportionately fewer older adults live with their children today than a century ago, but this is mainly because older adults today are far more financially independent (Lee, 1985). A century ago there were no Social Security or other pension plans, so older adults had to live with other family members to make ends meet, not necessarily because they wanted to. Today, most older adults live within a 30-minute drive of one of their children. (Of course, their other children may be scattered across the country.)

Middle-aged children and their parents remain in fairly frequent contact. Roughly 80% of older parents have seen one of their children in the past two weeks, a rate that does not differ between urban and rural dwellers (Krout, 1988b). Middle-aged children report that they enjoy visiting their parents. Some use these visits to reevaluate the meaning of the relationship as their parents continue to age and grow closer to death (Helson & Moane, 1987).

Caring for Aging Parents

Most middle-aged adults have parents who are in reasonably good health. For a growing number of people, however, being a middle-aged child of aging parents involves providing some level of care. More often than not the job of caring for older parents falls to a daughter or daughter-in-law. This gender difference is striking. Even after ruling out all other demographic characteristics of adult child caregivers and their care-recipients, daughters are over three times more likely to provide care than are sons (Dwyer & Coward, 1991). This gender difference is also found in other cultures. For example, even though in Japanese culture the oldest son is responsible for parental care, it is his wife who actually does the day-to-day caregiving.

In some situations, older parents must move in with one of their children. Such moves usually occur after decades of both generations living independently. This history of independent living sets the stage for adjustment difficulties following the move, as both parties must accommodate their lifestyles. Most of the time, adult children provide care for their mothers, who may in turn have provided care for their husbands before they died.

Caring for one's parent presents a dilemma (Wolfson, Handfield-Jones, Glass, McClaran, & Keyserlingk, 1993). **Most adult children feel a sense of responsibility, termed *filial obligation*, to care for their parent if necessary.** For example, adult child caregivers sometimes express the feeling that they "owe it to mom or dad" to care for them; after all, their parent provided for them for many years and now one has the chance to give something back.

But caring for an older parent is not without its price. Living with one's parent after decades on one's own is usually not done by choice; each party would just as soon live apart. The potential for conflict over daily routines and lifestyles is high. Overall, stress in adult caregiving results primarily from two sources (Robinson & Thurnher, 1979):

- Adult children may have trouble coping with declines in their parents' functioning, especially when the declines involve cognitive abilities. If caregivers do not know why their parents are declining, such lack of knowledge may result in feelings of ambivalence and antagonism toward their parents.
- When the caregiving situation is perceived as confining, or seriously infringes on the adult child's other responsibilities (such as spouse, parent, employee, and so forth), the situation is likely to be perceived negatively. This is likely to lead to mixed feelings of anger and guilt.

Much research over the past few decades clearly documents that middle-aged adults expend a great deal of energy, time, and money helping their older parents (Brody, 1990). In fact, nearly 90% of the daily help older people receive comes from adult children and other relatives (Morris & Sherwood, 1984). These efforts pay off. Family care helps prevent or at least delay institutionalization (Brody, 1981).

Caring for one's parent comes at some psychological cost. Even the most devoted adult child caregiver feels depressed, resentful, angry, and guilty at times (Halpern, 1987). Many middle-aged caregivers are pressed financially, as they may still be paying child care or college tuition expenses and may not be able to save adequately for retirement. Financial pressures are especially serious for those caring for parents with chronic conditions, such as Alzheimer's disease, that require services that are not covered by medical insurance. In some cases, adult children may even need to quit their jobs to provide care because adequate alternatives, such as adult day care, are unavailable. Although caring for parents is stressful for all adult children, adult daughters' level of stress is especially affected (Mui, 1995).

From the parent's perspective things are not always rosy either. Independence and autonomy are important traditional values in American culture, and their loss is not taken lightly. Older adults are more likely than their children to express the desire to pay a professional for assistance rather than ask a family member for help, and they are more likely to find it demeaning to live with their children (Brody, Johnson, Fulcomer, & Lang, 1983; Hamon & Blieszner, 1990). Most only move in as a last resort.

Determining whether older parents are satisfied with the help their children provide is difficult (Thomas, 1988). Those who are satisfied tend to be in somewhat better health, do not mind living with relatives, and believe that families should help. In contrast, those who are frail, who have little desire to live with relatives, and who prefer help from nonfamily sources are least satisfied.

Caring for an older parent is becoming increasingly common. But it is a situation that is often difficult for both caregiver and care-recipient alike. In the absence of appropriate alternatives, though, many families have little choice.

Concept Checks

1. What factors influence parents' evaluations of how their children turned out?
2. What is filial obligation?

GRANDPARENTING

Learning Objectives:

- What styles of grandparenting have been identified?
- What meanings do people derive from being grandparents?
- What characterizes relationships between grandparents and grandchildren?
- What are the important aspects of great-grandparenthood?

Becoming a grandparent is an exciting time for most people and represents the acquisition of new roles (Robertson, 1977). Many grandmothers see their role as easier than mothering, affording pleasure and gratification without requiring them to assume major responsibility for the care and socialization of the child (Robertson, 1977). These days, becoming a grandparent usually happens while one is middle-aged rather than elderly, and it is frequently occurring as early as age 40 (Kivnick, 1982). Moreover, many younger grandparents have living parents themselves, making for truly multigenerational families.

Overall, surprisingly little research has been conducted on grandparents and their relationships with their grandchildren. We know that grandparents differ considerably in how they interact with grandchildren and in the meanings they derive from these interactions. We also know a little about how each group perceives the other and about the benefits of these relationships.

Styles of Grandparenting

Because grandparents, like all other groups, are diverse, how they interact with their grandchildren, termed their *grandparenting style,* differs (Neugarten & Weinstein, 1964). The most common style, characterizing about one third of grandparents, is called *formal.* These grandparents see their role in fairly traditional terms, occasionally indulging the grandchild, occasionally babysitting, expressing a strong interest in the grandchild, but maintaining a hands-off attitude toward child rearing—leaving that aspect to the parents. A second common style is used by the *fun seeker,* whose relationship is characterized by informal playfulness. The *distant* grandparent appears mainly on holidays, birthdays, or other formal occasions with ritual gifts for the grandchild but otherwise has little contact with him or her. A few grandmothers are *surrogate parents,* filling in for working mothers. Finally, a few grandfathers play the role of *dispenser of family wisdom,* assuming an authoritarian position and offering information and advice.

Little research has examined how grandparents develop different styles. It appears that grandparents under age 65 are more likely to be fun seeking, whereas those over 65 tend to be more formal. Whether this difference is due to the age of the grandparent, the age of the grandchild, or generational differences between younger and older grandparents is unclear. Some evidence points to a combination of factors. Grandparents tend to be more playful with younger grandchildren, but as both groups age, a more formal relationship emerges (Kahana & Kahana, 1970; Kalish, 1975).

Robertson (1977) offers an alternative description of grandparenting styles based on her study of 125 grandmothers. She identifies a social and a personal dimension of grandparenting. The social dimension emphasizes societal needs and expectations, whereas the personal dimension focuses on personal factors and individual needs. Four combinations of these dimensions are possible. The *appointed* type is high on both dimensions of grandmothering. These grandmothers are very involved with their grandchildren and are equally concerned with indulging them and with doing what is morally right for them. The *remote* type is detached and has low social and personal expectations about the grandmothering role. *Symbolic* grandmothers emphasize the normative and moral aspects of the grandmothering role, and they have few personal expectations. *Individualized* grandmothers emphasize the personal aspects of grandmothering and ignore the social or moral side of the relationship.

Additional support for Robertson's social and personal dimensions comes from investigations of how grandparents influence their grandchildren's attitudes and lifestyle. Many grandparents recommend religious, social, and vocational values through storytelling, giving friendly advice, or working together on special projects (Cherlin & Furstenberg, 1986). In return, grandchildren keep grandparents updated on current cultural trends.

The Meaning of Grandparenthood

Research has shown that people derive several positive meanings from grandparenthood. Kivnick (1982) administered a lengthy questionnaire to 286 grandparents. Based on the statistical procedure of factor analysis, Kivnick identified five meanings of grandparenting: centrality, or the degree to which grandparenting is a primary role in one's life; value as an elder, or being perceived as a wise, helpful person; immortality through clan, in that the grandparent leaves behind not one but two generations; reinvolvement with one's personal past, by recalling relationships with one's own grandparents; and indulgence, or getting satisfaction from having fun with and spoiling one's grandchildren.

Comparing the meanings derived by grandparents with the styles of grandparenting provides several similarities. For example, the notion that grandparents have a tendency to spoil or indulge their grandchildren appears as both a style and a meaning. Because of these apparent similarities, S. S. Miller and Cavanaugh (1990) decided to investigate whether there were any systematic relationships. They reported two major findings. First, most grandparents find several sources of meaning in being a grandparent. Second, there are few consistent relationships between the style of grandparenting and the various sources of meaning. J. L. Thomas, Bence, and Meyer (1988) also found that the symbolic meaning of grandparenthood was of little importance to the satisfaction derived from being a grandparent. Thomas (1986a, 1986b) reports that satisfaction with grandparenthood is higher in grandmothers and that the opportunity to nurture and support grandchildren is an important source of satisfaction.

What these results imply is that we may not be able to describe specific standardized styles or meanings of grandparenthood. This is not that surprising, because grandparents are so diverse. Moreover, to expect that there should be consistencies between how a 50-year-old grandfather interacts with a 2-year-old grandson and how an 80-year-old grandmother interacts with her 18-year-old grandson may be ridiculous. Grandparent-grandchild relationships may well be too idiosyncratic to be described in general terms (Bengtson & Robertson, 1985).

Grandparents and Grandchildren

The relationships between grandparents and grandchildren vary with the age of the child. Younger children (up to age 10 or so) tend to be closer to their grandparents than older children. Grandparents also tend to enjoy younger grandchildren more because they are so responsive (Kahana & Kahana, 1970). Still, many adolescents and young adults view their grandparents as a special resource and value their relationships with them. Most young adults think that adult grandchildren have a responsibility to help their grandparents when necessary and without pay (Robertson, 1976).

Relationships between grandparents and grandchildren may also vary with the gender of the child. Some authors have suggested that grandmothers and granddaughters have better relationships than do grandfathers and grandsons (Atchley, 1977; Hagestad, 1978). According to these writers, this may be because the relationships are along the maternal kinkeeping line, supporting the speculation made in the previous section about middle-aged women and their role as kinkeepers.

When the grandparent-grandchild relationship is viewed from the child's perspective, another set of interesting findings emerges. When asked to provide written descriptions of their grandparents, children use a greater variety of descriptors for the grandparent with whom they have the more reciprocal relationship (Schultz, 1980). Children also attribute more perspective-taking ability and more feelings of attachment to their favorite grandparent.

A growing concern among grandparents is maintaining contact with grandchildren after a divorce of the parents (Johnson, 1988; Johnson & Barer, 1987). Indeed, in 1990 only half of the states in the United States had laws dealing with grandparental rights following divorce (Edelstein, 1990). In some cases contact is broken by the former in-laws. In other cases paternal grandmothers actually expand their family network by maintaining contact with their grandchildren from their sons' first marriage as well as subsequent ones (Johnson & Barer, 1987). Overall, however, maternal grandmothers whose daughters have custody have more contact with grandchildren following their daughters' divorces, and paternal grandmothers have less contact following their sons' divorces if their son does not have custody of the grandchildren (Cherlin & Furstenberg, 1986; Johnson, 1983).

Ethnic Differences

Grandparenting styles and interaction patterns differ somewhat among ethnic groups. In the United States, for example, African Americans, Asian Americans, Italian Americans, and Hispanic Americans are more likely to be involved in the lives of their grandchildren than are members of other

Interactions between grandparents and grandchildren vary among individuals and across age and cultures.

groups. Differences within these ethnic groups are also apparent. Italian American grandmothers tend to be much more satisfied and involved with grandparenting than Italian American grandfathers, who tend to be more distant. Among Hispanic groups, Cuban Americans are least likely and Mexican Americans most likely to be involved with the daily lives of their descendants (Bengtson, 1985). African American grandmothers under age 40 feel pressured to provide care for a grandchild that they were not eager for, whereas those over age 60 tend to feel that they are fulfilling an important role. African American men, though, perceive grandparenthood as a central role, and do so more strongly than European American grandfathers (Kivett, 1991).

Kornhaber (1985) notes that styles of grandparenting vary with ethnic background. This fact is highlighted by the case of an 18-month-old girl who had grandparents from two very different ethnic backgrounds: one pair Latino and one pair Nordic. Her Latino grandparents tickled, frolicked with, and doted over her. Her Nordic grandparents let her be but loved her no less. Her Latino mother thought the Nordic grandparents were "cold and hard," and her Nordic father thought his in-laws were "driving her crazy." The child, though, was perfectly content with both sets of grandparents.

Weibel-Orlando (1990) also reports variations between Native Americans and other groups. Among Native Americans, grandmothers tend to take a more active role than grandfathers. She also identified four main styles: distant, custodial, fictive, and cultural conservator. The first two parallel styles found in other ethnic groups, whereas the latter two are particularly Native American. Fictive grandparents are ones who fill in for missing or dead biological grandparents; cultural conservator grandparents actively solicit their children to allow the grandchildren to live with them in order to expose them to the Native American way of life.

The Changing Role of Grandparents

Grandparenting is not what it used to be. Detachment rather than involvement seems increasingly to characterize grandparent-grandchild relations (Bengtson & Robertson, 1985; Kornhaber & Woodward, 1981; Rodeheaver & Thomas, 1986). There are many complex reasons for a more detached style. Increased geographic mobility often means that grandparents live far away from their grandchildren, making visits less frequent and the relationship less intimate. Grandparents today are more likely to live independent lives apart from their children and grandchildren. Grandmothers are more likely to be employed themselves, thereby having less time to devote to caring for their grandchildren. Because of the rising divorce rate, some grandparents rarely see grandchildren who are living with a former son- or daughter-in-law. Finally, grandparents are not seen as the dispensers of child-rearing advice that they once were, so they tend to take a background role to maintain family harmony.

Most grandparents are comfortable with their reduced role and are quite happy to leave child rearing to the parents. In fact, those who feel responsible for advising their grandchildren tend to be less satisfied with the grandparenting role than those who feel that their role is mainly to enjoy their grandchildren (Thomas, 1986a).

Great-Grandparenthood

With increasing numbers of people, especially women, living to a very old age, the number of great-grandparents is rising rapidly. However, cohort trends in age at first marriage and age at parenthood also play a role. When these factors are combined, we find that most great-grandparents are women who married relatively young and had children and grandchildren who also married and had children relatively early.

The little research that has been conducted on this group indicates that their sources of satisfaction and meaning differ somewhat from those of grandparents (Doka & Mertz, 1988; Wentkowski, 1985). Three aspects of great-grandparenthood appear to be most important (Doka & Mertz, 1988).

First, being a great-grandparent provides a sense of personal and family renewal. Their grandchildren have produced new life, renewing their own excitement for life and reaffirming the continuance of their lineage. Seeing their families stretch across four generations may also provide psychological support through feelings of symbolic immortality that help them face death. That is, they know that their families will live many years beyond their own lifetime. Second, great-grandchildren provide diversion in great-grandparents' lives. There are now new things to do, places to go, and new people to share them with. Third, becoming a great-grandparent is a milestone, a mark of longevity. The sense that one has lived long enough to see the fourth generation is perceived very positively.

For many reasons, such as geographic distance and health, most great-grandparents maintain a distant relationship with their great-grandchildren. Still, the vast majority (over 90%) are proud of their new status (Wentkowski, 1985). As we enter the 21st century and the number of elderly people increases, four-generation families may become the norm.

Concept Checks

1. What are the major styles of grandparenting?
2. What five meanings of grandparenthood have been identified?
3. What ethnic differences have been noted in grandparent-grandchild relationships?
4. What are the three main aspects of great-grandparenthood?

SUMMARY

Relationships

Friendships

People tend to have more friendships during young adulthood than during any other period. Friendships in old age are especially important for maintaining life satisfaction. Men tend to have fewer close friends and base them on shared activities. Women tend to have more close friends and base them on emotional sharing. Cross-gender friendships tend to be difficult.

Sibling Relationships

Sibling relationships are important, especially in late life. Five types of sibling relationships have been identified: congenial, loyal, intimate, apathetic, and hostile. Ties tend to be strongest between sisters.

Love Relationships

Passion, intimacy, and commitment are the key components of love, which form seven types of love relationships. Although styles of love change with age, the priorities within relationships do not. Men tend to be more romantic; women tend to be pragmatic. Selecting a mate works best when there are shared values, goals, and interests. There are cross-cultural differences in which specific aspects of these are most important.

Violence in Relationships

Levels of aggressive behavior range from verbal aggression to physical aggression to murdering one's partner. The causes of aggression become more complex as the level of aggression increases. People remain in abusive relationships for many reasons, including low self-esteem and the belief that they cannot leave. Abuse and neglect of older adults is an increasing problem. Most perpetrators are adult children. It is unclear whether older victims are dependent on their caregivers or the caregivers are dependent on the victims.

Lifestyles and Love Relationships

Singlehood

Most adults decide by age 30 whether they plan on getting married. Never-married adults often develop a strong network of close friends. Dealing with other people's expectations that they should marry is often difficult for single people.

Cohabitation

Young adults usually cohabit as a step toward marriage, whereas older adults tend to cohabit for financial reasons. Cohabitation is only rarely seen as an alternative to marriage. Overall, more similarities than differences exist between cohabiting and married couples.

Gay Male and Lesbian Couples

Gay male and lesbian couples are similar to married heterosexual couples in terms of relationship issues. Lesbian couples tend to be more egalitarian.

Marriage

The most important factors in creating stable marriages are similarity, maturity, and conflict resolution skills. For couples with children, marital satisfaction tends to decline until the children leave home, although individual differences are apparent, especially in long-term marriages. Most long-term marriages tend to be happy, and partners in them express fewer negative emotions.

Divorce and Remarriage

Currently, odds are 50-50 that a new marriage will end in divorce. Reasons for divorce show a lack of the qualities that make a strong marriage. Also, societal attitudes about divorce have eased and expectations about marriage have increased. Recovery from divorce is different for men and women. Men tend to have a tougher time in the short run. Women clearly have a harder time in the long run, often for financial reasons. Difficulties between divorced partners usually involve visitation and child support. Most divorced couples remarry. Second marriages are especially vulnerable to stress if stepchildren are involved. Remarriage in later life tends to be very happy.

Widowhood

Widowhood is more common among women because they tend to marry men older than they are, but widowed men are typically older. Reactions to widowhood depend on the quality of the marriage. Men generally have problems in social relationships and in household tasks; women tend to have more financial problems.

Parenthood

Deciding Whether to Have Children

Although having children is stressful, most people do it anyway. A substantial minority of couples have fertility problems.

The Parental Role

The timing of parenthood is important in how involved parents are in their families as opposed to their careers. Single parents are faced with many problems, especially if they are women and are divorced. The main problem is reduced financial resources. A major issue for adoptive parents, foster parents, and stepparents is how strongly the child will bond with them. Each of these relationships has some special characteristics. Gay and lesbian parents also face numerous obstacles, but they usually are good parents.

The Child-Rearing Years

Raising children demands considerable flexibility in juggling the competing time demands. Parents need to develop their own style of parenting. Initial concern with doing the right thing subsides with experience.

When the Children Leave

Most parents do not report severe negative emotions when their children leave. Difficulties emerge to the extent that children were a major source of a parent's identity. However, parents typically report distress if adult children move back.

Family Dynamics and Middle Age

Becoming Friends with Adult Children

Most parent-child relationships move toward friendship. Middle-aged women often assume the role of kinkeeper to the family. Middle-aged parents may get squeezed by competing demands of their children, who want to gain independence, and their elderly parents, who want to maintain independence.

Middle-Aged Adults and Their Aging Parents

Middle-aged adults do not abandon their par-ents. Contact is frequent and generally positive. The vast majority of help older adults get is from their children. Parental care usually falls to a daughter or daughter-in-law. Caring for a frail parent is costly both financially and emotionally. Most elderly parents in the United States would prefer not to live with their children, however.

Grandparenting

Styles of Grandparenting

Grandparents vary considerably in how they interact with their grandchildren, both in style and in frequency. Overall, grandparents tend to be more playful with children than the children's parents are.

The Meaning of Grandparenthood

People derive positive meaning from being a grandparent, and it is related to self-esteem. However, meaning derived is not strongly related to interactive style.

Grandparents and Grandchildren

Relationship characteristics vary with the age of the child. With younger children the emphasis is more on fun, but with young adults it is on common issues and a desire to learn about each other. Maintaining contact with grandchildren following the parents' divorce is an important issue to many grandparents. Ethnic differences in grandparent-grandchild relationships are apparent, especially in terms of child care.

Great-Grandparenthood

Increased life expectancies make it more likely that children will have great-grandparents. Being a great-grandparent is an important source of personal and family renewal and provides diversion.

REVIEW QUESTIONS

Relationships

- How does the number and importance of friendships vary across adulthood?
- What gender differences are there in the number and type of friends?
- What are the major types of sibling relationships?
- What are the components of love? How do styles of love differ with age?
- What characteristics make the best matches between adults? How do these characteristics differ across cultures?
- What is the relation between type of abusive behavior and its cause?
- What are the current explanations of elder abuse in terms of characteristics of the victim and of the abuser?

Lifestyles and love relationships

- How do adults who never marry deal with the need to have relationships?
- What are the reasons that people cohabit? How are cohabiting people and married people alike and different?
- What are the relationship characteristics of gay male and lesbian couples?
- What are the most important factors in creating stable marriages?
- What are the developmental trends in marital satisfaction? How do these trends relate to having children?
- What factors are responsible for long-term marriages?
- What are the major reasons people get divorced? How are these related to societal expectations about marriage and attitudes about divorce?
- What characteristics about remarriage make it similar and different from first marriage? How does satisfaction in remarriage vary as a function of age?
- What are the characteristics of widowed people? How do men and women differ in their experience of widowhood?

Parenthood

- Why do couples decide to have children? What effects do children have on relationships?
- What is known about parenting and the age of the parent when the first child is born?
- What are the important issues in being an adoptive parent, foster parent, or stepparent? What special challenges are there for gay and lesbian parents?
- What impact does children leaving home have on parents? Why do adult children return?

Family dynamics and middle age

- How do middle-aged parents relate to their children?
- What roles do middle-aged mothers assume in the family?
- What are the important issues facing middle-aged adults who care for their elderly parents?
- How does independence relate to children, their middle-aged parents, and elderly parents?

Grandparenting

- What styles and meanings of grandparenting do people demonstrate?
- How do grandparents and grandchildren relate?

How do these relationships change with the age of the grandchild?
- What ethnic differences have been noted in grandparenting?
- What are the important issues and meanings of being a great-grandparent?

INTEGRATING CONCEPTS IN DEVELOPMENT

1. What components would a theory of adult relationships need to have?
2. What are some examples of each of the four developmental forces as they influence adult relationships?
3. What role do the changes in sexual functioning discussed in Chapter 3 have on love relationships?

KEY TERMS

abusive relationship A relationship in which one partner displays aggressive behavior toward the other partner.

battered woman syndrome A situation in which a woman believes that she cannot leave an abusive relationship and may even go so far as to kill her abuser.

cohabitation Two members of the opposite gender living together who are not married but who are in a relationship.

exchange theory A theory of relationships based on the idea that each partner contributes something to the relationship that the other would be hard pressed to provide.

extended family A family consisting of parents, children, grandparents, and other relatives all living together.

filial obligation The feeling that, as an adult child, one must care for one's parents.

homogamy The notion that similar interests and values are important in forming strong, lasting interpersonal relationships.

kinkeepers Members of the family, predominantly women, who maintain contacts with other family members across generational lines.

nuclear family A family consisting of parents and children.

postparental family A family in which the children have grown and left.

sandwich generation A term referring to the middle-aged generation, which has both elderly parents and adult children.

socioemotional selectivity A theory of relationships that argues that social contact is motivated by a variety of goals, including information seeking, self-concept, and emotional regulation.

IF YOU'D LIKE TO LEARN MORE

Blieszner, R., & Bedford, V. H. (Eds.). (1995). *Handbood of aging and the family.* Westport, CT: Greenwood. An excellent collection of chapters covering all aspects of the aging family from basic characteristics to social policy issues. Easy to moderate reading.

Blumstein, P., & Schwartz, P. (1983). *American couples.* New York: Morrow. One of the classics and one of the most complete and readable studies of all types of couple relationships (marriage, cohabitation, and gay male and lesbian relationships). Easy reading.

Boss, P.G., Doherty, W. J., LaRossa, R., Schumm, W. R., & Steinmetz, S. K. (1993). *Sourcebook of family theories and methods.* New York: Plenum. A superb book that covers all the major theories and methods used in family research in one volume. Easy to moderate reading.

Brody, E. M. (1990). *Women in the middle: Their parent-care years.* New York: Springer. A solid, research-based description of women's experiences as middle-aged parents and caregivers. Easy to moderate reading.

Katchadourian, H. (1987). *Fifty: Midlife in perspective.* New York: W. H. Freeman. Good source for family issues in midlife. Easy reading.

Sussman, M. B. (1985). The family life of old people. In R. H. Binstock & E. Shanas (Eds.), *Handbook of aging and the social sciences* (2nd ed., pp. 415–449). New York: Van Nostrand Reinhold. Good summary of relationships in later life by one of the people who helped found this line of research. Moderately difficult.

CHAPTER 11

Work, Leisure, and Retirement

Jacob Lawrence, *Builders*, 1980. Courtesy of Francine Selders Gallery, Seattle, WA and SAFECO Insurance Companies, Seattle, Washington.

OCCUPATIONAL CHOICE AND DEVELOPMENT

Occupations and Careers / Occupational Choice / Occupational Priorities and Expectations / The Role of Mentors / Job Satisfaction / *How Do We Know?: Periodicity and Job Satisfaction*

GENDER, ETHNICITY, BIAS, AND DISCRIMINATION

Gender Differences in Occupational Choice / Women and Occupational Development / Ethnicity and Occupational Development / Bias and Discrimination

OCCUPATIONAL TRANSITIONS

Factors Influencing Occupational Transitions / Retraining Workers / Loss of One's Job

DUAL-EARNER COUPLES

Balancing Multiple Roles / The Child Care Dilemma / *Something to Think About: Division of Labor and Role Conflict in Dual-Earner Couples* / Impact on Occupational Development

LEISURE ACTIVITIES

Leisure in the Life Cycle / Types of Leisure Activities / Developmental Changes in Leisure / Correlates and Consequences of Leisure Activities

RETIREMENT

Defining Retirement / *Discovering Development: Are You "Retired"?* / Deciding to Retire / Planning for Retirement / Adjustment to Retirement / Family, Friends, and Community

SUMMARY

REVIEW QUESTIONS

INTEGRATING CONCEPTS IN DEVELOPMENT

KEY TERMS

IF YOU'D LIKE TO LEARN MORE

One of the most interesting undergraduates I ever met was Earl. Earl was not a typical student. He was obviously older than the average undergraduate, but that's not why he stood out. What made Earl different was that he was preparing to embark on his third occupation. For 24 years he was in the Air Force, first as a pilot and later as a staff officer. His military experiences were often exciting but scary, especially when bullets ripped through his cockpit as he was flying missions over Vietnam. On returning to the United States, he taught some members of Congress and the Senate how to fly. He transferred to the staff of NATO, but dealing with politicians became so frustrating that he retired. At age 44 he began his second occupation, as an insurance salesman. Although he was promoted and did well, he became disenchanted and resigned after 5 years. At age 50 he went back to college to prepare for a third occupation, in physical therapy.

Earl has worked for all of his adult life. None of us should find that terribly exciting or unusual by itself. It is hard to imagine what adulthood would be like if we did not work. In fact, Sigmund Freud once wrote that love and work were the two defining aspects of adulthood. Work is such an important part of our lives that many people view themselves in terms of their occupation and judge others by theirs. What makes Earl such a good example of modern conceptions of work is that he pursued more than one career. The fundamental changes that have occurred in the corporate world since the 1970s have created a situation in which it is no longer expected that most people will work for the same company throughout adulthood until they retire. Indeed, even what it means to retire is undergoing a redefinition.

In this chapter we will seek answers to several questions: Why do people work? How do people choose occupations? How do occupations develop? What factors produce individual differences in occupational patterns? How do people spend time when they are not working? What happens to them after they retire?

As will become clear, research addressing these questions about work has focused primarily on middle-class European American men; far less is known about women or about other ethnic groups. Although more research on women and on other ethnic groups is being conducted, we must be careful in applying existing research and theory to these other groups until data have been compiled.

OCCUPATIONAL CHOICE AND DEVELOPMENT

Learning Objectives:

- What types of occupational categories are there? What is the social status of each?
- What factors influence occupational choice?
- What priorities and expectations do people have about occupations?
- What role do mentors play in occupational development?
- What factors influence job satisfaction? What causes alienation and burnout?

In the 1960s the phrase "different strokes for different folks" was used to get across the point that people's motives and needs differ. Thus, work has different meanings for different people. Studs Terkel, the author of the fascinating book *Working* (1974), writes that work is "a search for daily meaning as well as daily bread, for recognition as well as cash, for astonishment rather than torpor; in short, for a sort of life rather than a Monday through Friday sort of dying. Perhaps immortality, too, is part of the quest" (p. xiii).

Most people work because they have to earn a living somehow. This does not mean, of course, that money is the only reward for working. For most of us, things such as friendships, the chance to exercise skills, and feeling useful are also important. Occupational prestige and the social recognition that results are important influences on one's feelings of self-worth. Occupations that provide some satisfaction because one likes the activities they call for, that allow for some degree of autonomy, and that make room for one's creative potential generally make for greater job involvement. These occupations also tend to be more prestigious.

Regardless of what they do for a living, people view their job as a key element in their sense of identity. This feeling can be readily observed when people introduce themselves socially: "Hi, I'm Kevin. I'm an accountant. What do you do?" One's job affects one's life in a whole host of ways, from living place to friends to clothes to how one talks. In short, the impact of work cuts across all aspects of life. Work, then, is a major social role of adult life. This role—one's occupation—provides an important anchor that complements our other anchor—love relationships.

Occupations and Careers

In understanding work roles, terminology is important. The term *occupation* is applied to all forms of work, but the term *career* is sometimes reserved for prestigious occupations. In this view a career is an elite institution in Western society (Stevens-Long, 1988). Ritzer (1977) argues that people who have careers stay in one occupational field and progress through a series of stages to achieve upward mobility, greater responsibility, mastery, and financial compensation. From this perspective, university professors and lawyers in a large firm have careers; assembly line workers and secretaries do not.

Other authors disagree, viewing career as any organized path an individual takes across time and space—that is, any consistent, organized involvement in any role (Van Maanen & Schein, 1977). In this perspective physicians, carpenters, and homemakers have several careers simultaneously: as workers, spouses, citizens, and so forth.

In this chapter we will use the term *occupation* rather than career to refer to work roles. As we will see, occupations are highly developmental. Even young children are in the midst of the social preparation for work, as evidenced by pretend play and prodding questions from adults such as "What do you want to be when you grow up?" School curricula, especially in high school and college, are geared toward preparing people for particular occupations. We develop our interests in various occupations over time, and the changes that occur in occupations represent some of the most important events in the life cycle. Before we explore occupations as developmental phenomena, however, we need to consider how different occupations are associated with different levels of social status.

Social Status and Occupations

Workers in the United States are not all viewed as equally valuable. How people are treated is, in part, a function of the kind of work they do, which is given a particular status in society. Occupational status is correlated with intellectual ability and achievement, although not perfectly.

Five general levels of workers can be identified: marginal workers, blue-collar workers, pink-collar workers, white-collar workers, and executives and professionals. Where one falls in this hierarchy influences lifestyle, well-being, and social recognition. We will consider the characteristics of each level briefly.

Marginal workers work occasionally, but never long enough with one employer to establish a continuous occupational history. Their unstable working patterns are due to several factors, such as the lack of necessary language or other abilities, discrimination, a criminal record, or physical or mental disorders. The lack of steady employment has serious negative effects on most other aspects of their lives, such as increased marital distress.

Blue-collar occupations are those that do not require formal education past high school and may be based more on physical than intellectual skills. Blue-collar occupations vary tremendously, however, from unskilled labor to the highly complex trades of electricians and pipe fitters, for example. In general, blue-collar occupations offer little mobility; moves typically reflect changes for better pay or job security or result from unemployment. One problem faced by blue-collar workers is being looked down on by supervisors and upper-middle-class professionals, and many express inferiority feelings (Terkel, 1974).

Pink-collar occupations are held primarily by women. These positions include office and clerical worker, bank teller, receptionist, and the like. Typically, these occupations do not pay high wages. Although men may hold some of these positions, such as bank teller, they do so only for short periods before they are promoted.

White-collar occupations are in offices rather than in factories or outdoors. Although the skills required are thought to be more intellectual than those needed for blue-collar occupations, white-collar workers are not always paid better. What they do get, however, is higher status. Many white-collar jobs require formal education beyond high school, although there is very little evidence that this education is always directly related to job performance. Unhappiness among white-collar workers comes mostly from their feeling that the extra time and expense for more education is not sufficiently rewarded and from middle-level managers' feelings that they have little real effect on corporate decision making.

Executives and professionals have the highest status as well as the highest education. They are in the optimal position to control their own occupational development and to obtain the rewards that most other workers cannot. Comparisons among executives and professionals are usually not in terms of salaries but in how far and how quickly they progress.

The Changing Nature of Work

The research we will encounter in this chapter is predicated on conceptions of work like those we have just discussed. This traditional view of work assumes that one's job consists of a certain set of tasks that need to be performed (Cascio, 1995). But this view is rapidly becoming outmoded. Global competition means that workers in the United States are competing for jobs with workers in the same industries in France, Russia, Taiwan, China, Poland, Argentina, and the rest of the world.

The globalization of work has also resulted in massive changes in both the number and type of jobs available to U.S. workers and the skills these jobs require. For example, between 1987 and 1994, more than 7 million permanent layoffs were announced in the United States (Cascio, 1995). These layoffs were not due to companies losing money; indeed, 81% of the companies that downsized during this period were profitable during that year. Rather, layoffs occur mostly because of competition, productivity, relocation of operations, mergers and acquisitions, infusion of new technology, or plant obsolescence. Even though many laid off workers find new jobs, the new positions invariably involve drastic pay cuts, resulting in downward mobility.

What do these changes mean? In short, a fundamental redefinition of work is occurring. Organizations must respond rapidly to market conditions that change quickly. Managers must use flexible styles of leadership depending on the situation, with an emphasis on being able to bring out employees' creativity and best efforts. Workers must assume more autonomy and decision-making authority and must have a variety of technical skills. Everyone must learn continually to stay current with the latest technology and newest skills.

As we head into the 21st century, the increasingly complex, technologically based workplace is here to stay. We must change the way we think about organizations and about our basic conceptions of what a job entails.

Occupational Choice

Our work life serves as a major source of our identity, provides us with an official position, and influences our lifestyle and social interactions; therefore, choosing an occupation is a serious matter. Although most people think that occupational choice is something that is largely the province of young adults, much of what we will consider also holds true for middle-aged and older workers who are looking to change occupations either voluntarily or because they lost their jobs. As we will see later, more adults are changing occupations than ever before and are having to rethink the kinds of jobs they want to have. Moreover, as the downsizing trend in corporations continues, many adults may be forced to look for new employment in different fields.

From a developmental perspective, the decisions people make about occupations may change over time. As people face different life issues or achieve new insights about themselves, they may well decide that their best bet would be to change occupations. Additionally, occupational choices may reflect personal or social clocks (see Chapter 1); individuals of different ages may feel different degrees of pressure to make a certain occupational choice.

Regardless of age, two issues in deciding on an occupation are important: personality and interests, and self-efficacy. Let's consider each in turn.

Personality and Interests

Although we tend to think of occupational choice as something done during adolescence or young adulthood, recent theories and research have increasingly adopted a life-course perspective (Adler & Aranya, 1984). The main theoretical frameworks for occupational choice have focused on aspects of one's personality (see Chapter 8).

Holland (1973, 1985) developed a theory based on the intuitively appealing idea that people choose occupations to optimize the fit between their individual traits—such as personality, intelligence, skills, and abilities—and their occupational interests. He categorizes occupations in two ways: by the interpersonal settings in which people must function and by their associated lifestyle. He identifies six personality types that combine these factors; they are summarized in Table 11.1.

Support for Holland's personality types comes from other research examining the relationship between personality and occupational choice. Research comparing his types with Costa and McCrae's five dimensions of personality (see Chapter 8) suggests considerable overlap (Costa, McCrae, & Holland, 1984). For instance, his social and enterprising types fell into Costa and McCrae's extraversion dimension. In a study of 171 African American nursing personnel, Day and Bedeian (1995) found that personality traits significantly predicted job performance and how long employees remain with the same organization.

The congruence between traits and occupational selection in Holland's theory exists at the level of interest, not at the level of performance requirements per se. He predicts that people will choose the occupation that has the greatest similarity to their personality type. By doing this, they optimize their ability to express themselves, apply their skills, and take on new roles. Occupational satisfaction, for Holland, is maximized by having a good match between personality and occupation. Indeed, Spokane (1985) documented the relationship between such a congruence and occupational persistence, occupational choice, occupational stability, and work satisfaction.

Holland's theory does not mean that personality completely determines what occupation one chooses. The connection is that certain occupations are typically chosen by people who act or feel a certain way. Most of us would rather do something that we like to do than something we are forced to do. Thus, unless we have little choice due to financial or other constraints, we typically choose occupations on that basis. When mismatches occur, people usually adapt by changing jobs, changing interests, or adapting the job to provide a better match.

Although the relationships between personality and occupational choice are important, we must recognize that there are limits. Men and women are differentially represented in Holland's types (Costa et al., 1984). Regardless of age, women are more likely than men to be in the social, artistic, and conventional types. Additionally, Holland's theory ignores the context in which the decision is made. For example, he overlooks the fact that many people may not have much choice in the kind of job they can get because of external factors such as family, financial pressures, or ethnicity. There are also documented changes in congruence between personality type and occupation across adulthood (Adler & Aranya, 1984). In short, we must recognize that what occupation we choose is related not only to what we are like but also to the dynamic interplay between us and the social situation we are in.

Self-Efficacy

Occupational choice is strongly influenced by what we think of ourselves. Regardless of age, we evalu-

TABLE 11.1 Summary of Holland's personality types and their relationship to occupational choices

Investigative

The model type is task-oriented, intraceptive, asocial; prefers to think through rather than act out problems; needs to understand; enjoys ambiguous work tasks; has unconventional values and attitudes. Vocational preferences include aeronautical design engineer, anthropologist, astronomer, biologist, botanist, chemist, editor of a scientific journal, geologist, independent research scientist, meteorologist, physicist, scientific research worker, writer of scientific or technical articles, zoologist.

Social

The model type is sociable, responsible, feminine, humanistic, religious; needs attention; has verbal and interpersonal skills; avoids intellectual problem solving, physical activity, and highly ordered activities; prefers to solve problems through feelings and interpersonal manipulations of others. Vocational preferences include assistant city school superintendent, clinical psychologist, director of welfare agency, foreign missionary, high school teacher, juvenile delinquency expert, marriage counselor, personal counselor, physical education teacher, playground director, psychiatric case worker, social science teacher, speech therapist, vocational counselor.

Realistic

The model type is masculine, physically strong, unsociable, aggressive; has good motor coordination and skill; lacks verbal and interpersonal skills; prefers concrete to abstract problems; conceives of self as being aggressive and masculine and as having conventional political and economic values. Persons who choose or prefer the following occupations resemble this type: airplane mechanic, construction inspector, electrician, filling station attendant, fish and wildlife specialist, locomotive engineer, master plumber, photoengraver, power shovel operator, power station operator, radio operator, surveyor, tree surgeon, tool designer.

Artistic

The model type is asocial; avoids problems that are highly structured or require gross physical skills; resembles the investigative type in being intraceptive and asocial; but differs from that type in that the person has a need for individualistic expression, has less ego strength, is more feminine, and suffers more frequently from emotional disturbances; prefers dealing with environmental problems through self-expression in artistic media. Vocational preferences include art dealer, author, cartoonist, commercial artist, composer, concert singer, dramatic coach, free-lance writer, musical arranger, musician, playwright, poet, stage director, symphony conductor.

Conventional

The model type prefers structured verbal and numerical activities and subordinate roles; is conforming (extraceptive); avoids ambiguous situations and problems involving interpersonal relationships and physical skills; is effective at well-structured tasks; identifies with power; values material possessions and status. Vocational preferences include bank examiner, bank teller, bookkeeper, budget reviewer, cost estimator, court stenographer, financial analyst, computer equipment operator, inventory controller, payroll clerk, quality control expert, statistician, tax expert, traffic manager.

Enterprising

The model type has verbal skills for selling, dominating, leading; conceives of self as a strong, masculine leader; avoids well-defined language or work situations requiring long periods of intellectual effort; is extraceptive; differs from the conventional type in that the person prefers ambiguous social tasks and has a greater concern with power, status, and leadership; is orally aggressive. Vocational preferences include business executive, buyer, hotel manager, industrial relations consultant, manufacturer's representative, master of ceremonies, political campaign manager, real-estate salesperson, restaurant worker, speculator, sports promoter, stock and bond salesperson, television producer, traveling salesperson.

Source: Holland, 1985

ate our abilities in terms of our strengths and weaknesses. Because we are likely to shy away from doing things that we think we have little ability to do, we tend to choose occupations that match what we think we may be able to do. Bandura (1986) terms this self-evaluation process self-efficacy.

It is what we think we are good at that influences occupational choice, not what we are actually good at. In fact, the two are often completely unrelated (Panek & Sterns, 1985). Typically, the more efficacious that people judge themselves to be, the wider the range of occupational options they consider appropriate and the better they prepare themselves educationally for different occupational pursuits. People who have less confidence in themselves tend to limit their options, even when they have the true ability to engage in a wide range of occupations (Betz & Hackett, 1986; Lent & Hackett, 1987).

Self-efficacy theory also helps us understand differences between men and women and between European Americans and minorities in occupational choices (Bandura, 1990). Cultural practices that convey lower expectations for women, stereotypic gender roles, gender-typed behaviors, and structural barriers to advancement eventually lower one's self-efficacy. Consequently, women and minorities may limit their interests and range of occupational options by the belief that they lack the ability for occupations traditionally occupied by European American men, even though they do not differ from European American men in actual ability.

Occupational Priorities and Expectations

For most of us, getting a job is not enough; we would also like to move up the ladder. How quickly occupational advancement occurs (or does not) may lead to such labels as "fast-tracker" or "dead-ender" (Kanter, 1976). People who want to advance learn quickly how long to stay at one level and how to seize opportunities as they occur; others soon learn the frustration of remaining in the same job with no chance for promotion.

How we advance through our occupation seems to be related to several factors beyond those important in choosing an occupation. Among these are expectations, support from co-workers, priorities, and job satisfaction. All of these help us face what psychologists call early professional socialization, in other words, what we are expected to do in our occupation.

What does one want from an occupation? Money? Fame? Glory? One's answers to this question are a function of one's *occupational priorities.* Such things as fame, money, and helping others may motivate a person to run for public office, work at a second job, or enter social work. Knowing a worker's priorities, what he or she values most, helps us understand what things about an occupation are probably satisfying or unsatisfying.

Differences in occupational priorities in workers of all ages were made clear in a longitudinal study conducted by American Telephone and Telegraph (AT&T) begun in 1977, which was designed to parallel a study started in 1956 (Howard & Bray, 1980). In the 1970s managers at AT&T were more diverse than they were in prior decades; almost half were women, and one third were ethnic minorities. No differences between the younger and older groups were found in intellectual ability (although the younger group was better educated), need for achievement, or personal work standards.

Key differences emerged in motivation for upward mobility, leadership, and desire for emotional support. The younger managers' expectations of rewards from work were much lower; they did not see most of their major rewards of life satisfactions coming from work. This view contrasted sharply with the older managers' high work motivation and early desire for promotion. The younger managers also had a lower desire to be responsible for subordinates and to direct others. Finally, they had a much stronger desire to provide emotional support to co-workers.

The findings at AT&T, depicted in Figure 11.1, are not unique. Other research has for several decades documented the move away from materi-

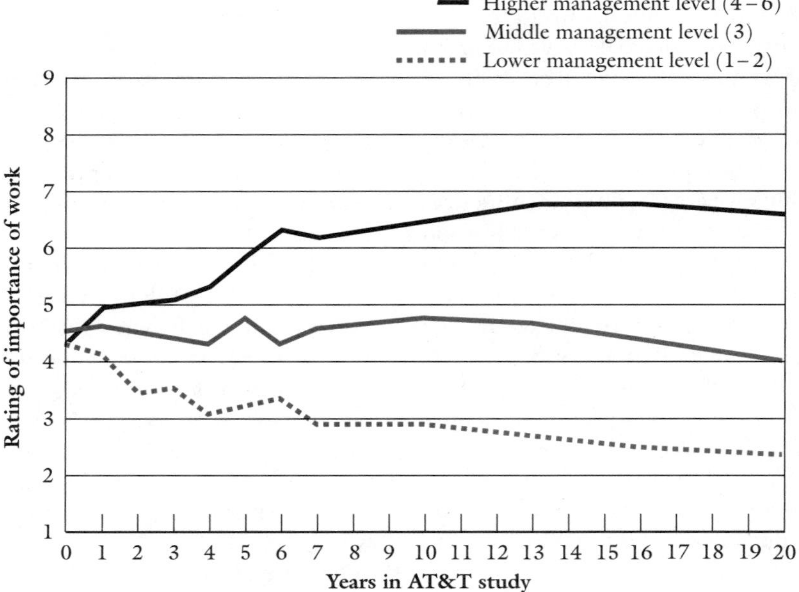

Figure 11.1 Changes in the relative importance of work at different levels of management in the AT&T study
Source: Howard and Bray, 1980

alism, power seeking, upward mobility, and competition toward an emphasis on individual freedom, personal growth, and cooperation (Jones, 1980; Yankelovich, 1981). Howard and Bray (1980) note that changes in workers' priorities may have significant implications for the effectiveness of our work socialization systems.

Expectation of a financially and personally rewarding occupation is praiseworthy. It may also be asking for trouble after reality shock hits, because very few jobs offer perfect combinations of material and personal rewards. As a result many people become disenchanted with their jobs. Terkel (1974) documented many of these reactions: "I'm a machine" (a spot-welder). "A monkey could do what I do" (a receptionist). "I'm an object" (a model). Disillusionment occurs in all types of occupations, from the assembly line worker who feels like a robot to the high-level corporate executive who feels like a small piece of a giant machine. Such shattered expectations must have an effect on another important factor in occupational development: job satisfaction.

Individuals form opinions about what it will be like to work in a particular occupation based on what they learn in school and from their parents. People tend to set goals regarding what they want to become and when they hope to get there. This tendency is so common, in fact, that in their theory of adult male development Levinson and his colleagues (1978) maintain that forming a *dream,* as they put it, is one of the young adult's chief tasks.

As young adults head toward middle and old age, a major task is to refine and update occupational expectations. Refining one's dream typically involves trying to achieve a goal, monitoring progress toward the goal, and changing or even abandoning the goal as necessary. For some, modifying goals comes as a result of failure (such as changing from a business major because one is flunking economics courses), racial or sexual discrimination, lack of opportunity, obsolescence of skills, economic reasons, or changing interests. In some cases one's initial choice may have simply been unrealistic; for example, nearly half of all young adults would like to become professionals (such as lawyers or physicians), but only one person in seven actually makes it (Cosby, 1974).

Typically, by the time one reaches midlife it is relatively clear whether one's occupational goals are realistic and achievable. Indeed, we saw in Chapter 8 that midlife development involves assessing what one has achieved and what one can accomplish, especially in view of how one helps the next generation (Erikson's notion of generativity). Whenever one finds the need to modify occupational goals, stress usually results. And even though some goal modification is essential from time to time, one usually is surprised that one could be wrong about what seemed to be a logical choice in the past. As Gina put it, "I really thought I wanted to be a flight attendant; the travel sounded really interesting. But it just wasn't what I expected."

Perhaps the rudest jolt for most of us, called *reality shock*, comes during the transition from school to the real world, where things just never seem to happen the way the textbooks say that they are supposed to. Reality shock (Van Maanen & Schein, 1977) befalls everyone, from the young mother who discovers that newborns demand an incredible amount of time to the accountant who learns that the financial forecast that took days to prepare may simply end up in a file cabinet. Although reality shock is typically associated with young adults, as more adults return to school to change occupations, reality shock is becoming an increasingly important issue for them, too. The visionary aspects of the dream may not disappear altogether, but a good hearty dose of reality goes a long way toward bringing one down to earth and comes to play an increasingly important role in one's occupation and self-concept. For example, the woman who thought that she would receive the same rewards as her male counterparts for comparable work is likely to become increasingly angry and disillusioned when her successes result in smaller raises and fewer promotions.

A longitudinal study begun in 1956 by AT&T provides some of the best evidence available about one's dream and reality shock. In general, the research examined the variables related to personality and ability that could predict occupational success and satisfaction (Bray, Campbell, & Grant, 1974). The initial sample consisted of 422 European American males in a pool of lower level managers from which future upper level managers would be chosen. Some participants were college graduates hired at the manager level, and the remainder were men without a college degree who had been promoted through the ranks.

The findings revealed considerable support for both Levinson's dream and a period of reality shock (Howard & Bray, 1980). Young managers began their occupations full of expectations but rapidly became more realistic. On average, by the time the college-educated men were 29 years old and the noncollege men were 34, the strong desire to seek additional promotions had decreased markedly. Two reasons for the decline were given. First, workers were concerned about disruption to the family due to the need to move following a promotion. Second, workers reported a lack of desire to devote more time to work, which would be required on entering upper level management. Interestingly, these men were satisfied with their jobs. In fact, they found them challenging, and their intrinsic motivation levels did not drop despite their reluctance to advance.

Although the AT&T study provided important insights, its limitations must be recognized. The inclusion of only European American males means that the developmental trends for other groups is largely unknown. Second, only white-collar workers with the potential of moving up the corporate ladder were studied. People in service, unskilled, and blue-collar jobs probably differ in important ways, because their potential for upward mobility is limited.

The Role of Mentors

Imagine how hard learning a new occupation would be with no support from other (usually older) people. Being socialized into an occupation goes well beyond the relatively short formal train-

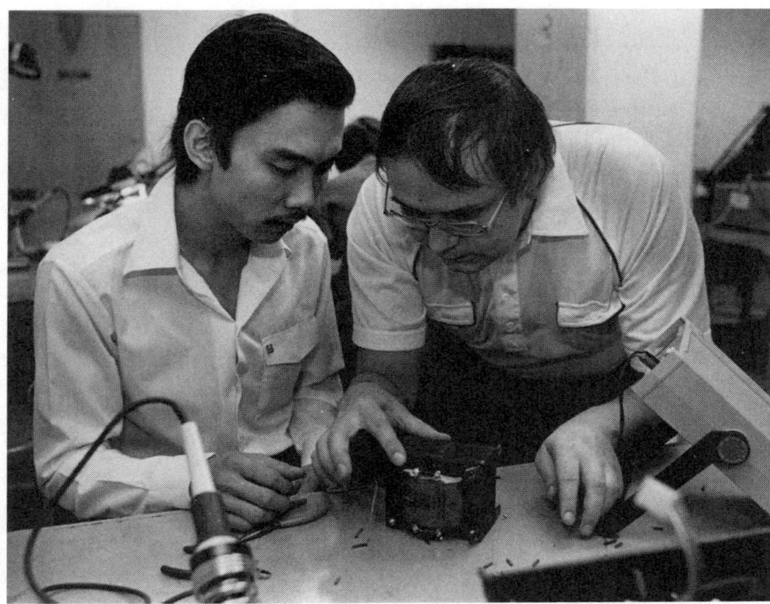

Mentoring of young workers by older, more experienced ones is an important aspect of generativity in Erikson's theory.

ing one receives. Indeed, much of the most critical information one needs to know is usually not taught in training seminars. Instead, most people are shown the ropes by more experienced coworkers. **In many cases, an older, more experienced person, called a *mentor*, makes a specific effort to do this** (Levinson et al., 1978). Although mentors by no means provide the only specific source of guidance in the workplace, they have been studied fairly closely.

A mentor is part teacher, part sponsor, part model, and part counselor. The mentor helps a young worker avoid trouble ("Beware of what you say around Bentley") and provides invaluable information about the many unwritten rules that govern day-to-day activities in the workplace (not working too fast on the assembly line, wearing the right clothes, and so on). As part of the relationship, a mentor makes sure that his or her protégé is noticed and receives credit for good work from supervisors. As a result, occupational success often depends on the quality of the mentor-protégé relationship. Consequently, mentors fulfill two main functions: improving the protégé's chances for advancement and promoting his or her psychological and social well-being (Kram, 1980, 1985; Kram & Isabella, 1985; Noe, 1987).

Playing the role of a mentor is also a developmental phase in one's occupation. Helping a younger employee learn the job fulfills aspects of Erikson's (1982) phase of generativity. In particular, the mentor is making sure that there is some continuity in the field by passing on the accumulated knowledge and experience he or she has gained by being in it for a while. This function of the mentor is part of middle-aged adults' attempts at ensuring the continuity of society and accomplishing or producing something worthwhile (Erikson, 1982). In this sense, mentoring is clearly an example of intergenerational exchange in the workplace.

The mentor-protégé relationship develops over

time. Based on her in-depth study, Kram (1985) proposes a four-stage sequence. The first stage, *initiation,* constitutes the 6- to 12-month period during which the protégé selects a mentor and they begin to develop their relationship. The second stage, *cultivation,* lasts from 2 to 5 years and is the most active phase of the mentoring relationship. This is the period when the mentor provides considerable occupational assistance and serves as a confidant. The third stage, *separation,* is the most difficult. It begins when the protégé receives a promotion, often to the level of the mentor. The protégé must emerge from the protection of the mentor to demonstrate his or her own competence. Both parties experience feelings of loneliness and separation. The final period is *redefinition.* In this period the protégé and mentor reestablish their relationship but with a new set of rules based more on friendship between peers.

Research on the selection of mentors by young adults reveals that potential mentors' interpersonal skills are the single most important factor (Olian, Carroll, Giannantonio, & Feren, 1988). Additionally, protégé are attracted to mentors who are connected in the organization and who are older than themselves.

Some authors think that women have a greater need for a mentor than men (Busch, 1985). However, women seem to have a more difficult time finding an adequate mentor. One reason is that female role models who could serve a mentoring function are scarce, especially in upper level management. Only 7% of the women in the workforce are in administrative, executive, or managerial jobs, compared with 12% of men (U.S. Department of Labor, 1988). This is an unfortunate situation, especially in view of the fact that women who have female mentors are significantly more productive than women with male mentors (Goldstein, 1979). Although many young women report that they would feel comfortable with a male mentor (Olian et al., 1988), there are additional problems beyond productivity. Several researchers note that cross-gender mentor-protégé relationships produce conflict and tension resulting from possible sexual overtones, even when there has been no overtly sexual behavior on anyone's part (Kram, 1985).

Job Satisfaction

What does it mean to be satisfied with one's job or occupation? **In a general sense *job satisfaction* is the positive feeling that results from an appraisal of one's work** (Locke, 1976). In research, specific aspects such as satisfaction with working conditions, pay, and co-workers are considered. In practice, American workers actually have a multidimensional conceptualization of job satisfaction.

Due to the complex nature of job satisfaction, most jobs end up being satisfying in some ways (such as achievement and power) and not in others (such as pay and working conditions). Factors that make jobs satisfying at one time may become less important the longer one is in an occupation or as new concerns are raised in society. For example, concern over health and safety problems played a much more important role in job satisfaction in the late 1970s than they did a decade earlier (Quinn & Staines, 1979). Additionally, occupational values change over time; military personnel and politicians have lost some of the prestige that they once had, whereas environmentally oriented jobs have increased in social worth. Given that the structural elements of a job (such as working conditions) affect satisfaction, an important question is whether the age of the worker is also related to his or her job satisfaction.

Almost all the studies that have investigated the relationship between overall job satisfaction and age have found a low to moderate increase in satisfaction with increasing age (see James & Jones, 1980; Schwab & Heneman, 1977). However, several important qualifications need to be made in relation to this finding.

First, the results could be due to self-selection factors. That is, people who truly like their jobs may tend to stay in them, whereas people who do not may tend to leave. To the extent that this is the case, age differences in job satisfaction may simply

HOW DO WE KNOW?

Periodicity and Job Satisfaction

Considerable evidence shows that job satisfaction tends to increase with age. Why this is true has been the subject of much debate. One hypothesis is that changes in job satisfaction are actually related to job seniority, or job tenure. The idea is that satisfaction tends to be high in the beginning of a job, to stabilize or drop during the middle phase, and to rise again later. Each time a person changes jobs, the cycle repeats.

Shirom and Mazeh (1988) decided to study the cyclical nature of job satisfaction systematically. They collected questionnaire data from a representative sample of 900 Israeli junior high school teachers with up to 23 years of seniority. The questionnaire contained items concerning teachers' satisfaction with salary, working hours, social status, contacts with pupils, autonomy, opportunities for professional growth, and opportunities for carrying out educational goals. The focus of analysis was on year-to-year changes in satisfaction.

Using a statistical technique called spectral analysis, Shirom and Mazeh were able to show that teachers' job satisfaction followed systematic 5-year cycles that were strongly related to seniority but unrelated to age. They noted that a major work-related change, a sabbatical leave, or a change in school characterized teachers' work approximately every 5 years. They concluded that each of these changes reinstated the cycle of high-lowered-high job satisfaction, which, when tracked over long periods, appears to show a linear increase in overall job satisfaction.

An important implication of Shirom and Mazeh's data is that change may be necessary for long-term job satisfaction. Although the teaching profession has change built into it, such as sabbatical leaves, many occupations do not (Latack, 1984). This option of changes in job structure and other areas should be explored for more occupations.

---

reflect the fact that with sufficient time, many people eventually find a job in which they are reasonably happy.

Second, the relationship between worker age and job satisfaction is complex. Satisfaction does not increase in all areas with age. Older workers are more satisfied with the intrinsic personal aspects of their jobs than they are with the extrinsic aspects, such as pay (Morrow & McElroy, 1987).

Third, increases in job satisfaction may not be due to age alone but, rather, to the degree to which there is a good fit between the worker and the job (Holland, 1985). From this perspective, increasing age should be related to increased job satisfaction: Older workers have had more time to find a job that they like or may have resigned themselves to the fact that things are unlikely to improve, resulting in a better congruence between worker desires and job attributes (Barrett, 1978). A. T. White and Spector (1987) showed that the relationship between age and job satisfaction was due mainly to congruence and having an appropriate sense of control over one's job. Older workers also may have revised their expectations over the years to better reflect the actual state of affairs. Because expectations become more realistic and are therefore more likely to be fulfilled, job satisfaction increases over time (Hulin & Smith, 1965).

Fourth, work becomes less of a focus in men's lives as they age and achieve occupational success (Bray & Howard, 1983). This process of disengagement from work can begin as early as the 30s for men who are not advancing rapidly in their occupations, but it comes somewhat later for men who achieve some degree of success. Consequently, for many men it takes less to keep them satisfied due to lower work motivation.

Fifth, men may discover different sources of satisfaction. As men stay in an occupation longer, they begin to find satisfaction in different ways. For example, they derive pleasure from accomplishing tasks and from becoming independent in their work. Interestingly, lower level managers become more nurturant as time goes on, but the men at the top of the hierarchy become progressively more remote and detached and less sympathetic and helpful (Howard, 1984).

Finally, job satisfaction may be cyclical. That is, it may show periodic fluctuations that are not related to age per se but, rather, to changes that people intentionally make in their occupations (Shirom & Mazeh, 1988). The idea is that job satisfaction increases over time because people change jobs or responsibilities on a regular basis, thereby keeping their occupation interesting and challenging. This provocative idea of periodicity in job satisfaction is explored further in How Do We Know?

Alienation and Burnout

No job is perfect. There is always something about it that is not as good as it could be; perhaps the hours are not optimal, the pay is lower than one would like, or the boss does not have a pleasant personality. For most workers, these negatives are merely annoyances. But for others, they create extremely stressful situations that result in deeply rooted unhappiness with work: alienation and burnout.

When workers feel that what they are doing is meaningless and that their efforts are devalued, or when they do not see the connection between what they do and the final product, a sense of *alienation* is likely to result. Studs Terkel (1974) interviewed several alienated workers for his book *Working* and found that each of them expressed feeling as though they were merely a nameless, faceless cog in a large machine.

Employees are most likely to feel alienated when they perform routine, repetitive actions such as those on an assembly line (Terkel, 1974). Interestingly, many of these functions are being automated and performed by robots. Especially since the beginning of corporate downsizing in the 1980s, many middle level managers do not feel that they have the same level of job security that they once had. Consequently, their feelings toward their employers have become more negative in many cases (Roth, 1991).

How can employers avoid creating alienated workers? Research indicates that involving employees in the decision-making process, creating flexible work schedules, and instituting employee development and enhancement programs help (Roth, 1991). Indeed, many organizations have instituted new practices such as total quality management (TQM), partly as a way to address worker alienation. TQM and related approaches make a concerted effort to get employees involved in the operation and administration of their plant or office. Such programs work; absenteeism drops and the quality of work improves in organizations that implement them (Offerman & Growing, 1990).

Sometimes the pace and pressure of one's occupation becomes more than one can bear, resulting in *burnout*, a depletion of a person's energy and motivation. Burnout is a unique type of stress syndrome, characterized by emotional exhaustion, depersonalization, and diminished personal accomplishment (Cordes and Dougherty, 1993). Burnout is most common among people in the helping professions, such as teaching, social work, and health care (Cordes & Dougherty, 1993). People in these professions are dedicated to helping people face problems and must constantly deal with complex problems, usually under difficult time pressures. Added to the pressures of bureaucratic paperwork, dealing with these pressures on a daily basis may become too much for workers to bear. Ideals are abandoned, frustration builds, and disillusionment and exhaustion set in. In short, the worker is burned out.

The best defenses against burnout are getting workers to lower their expectations of themselves and enhancing communication within organizations. No one in the helping professions can resolve all problems perfectly; lowering expectations of what workers can realistically accomplish will help them deal with real-world constraints. Similarly, improving communication across different aspects of organizations to keep workers informed of the outcome of their efforts will help give them a sense that what they do matters in the long run. Finally, research evidence also suggests that lack of support from one's co-workers may cause depersonalization; improving such support through teamwork may be an effective intervention (Corrigan et al., 1994).

In short, making sure that workers feel that they are important to the organization by involving them in decisions, keeping expectations realistic, ensuring good communication, and promoting teamwork may help employees avoid alienation and burnout. As organizations adopt different management styles, perhaps these goals can be achieved.

Concept Checks

1. What are the five major categories of occupations?
2. What is Holland's theory?
3. What is reality shock?
4. What are the stages in the development of the mentor-protégé relationship?
5. What factors are associated with job satisfaction in older workers?

GENDER, ETHNICITY, BIAS, AND DISCRIMINATION

Learning Objectives:

- What gender differences are there in occupational choice? How are women in nontraditional occupations viewed?
- What issues are related to women's occupational development?
- What factors result in ethnic differences in occupational development?
- What are the various ways in which bias and discrimination occur in the workplace?

People differ a great deal in how they choose and develop their occupations. Even though they may be in the same jobs, men and women differ in their experiences regarding the role of work in their lives. Similarly, people from different ethnic groups vary in their experiences, too. Unfortunately, gender and ethnicity may result in discriminatory practices that interfere with adults' occupational development. Although these issues have not received the research attention they deserve, they are important, as we will see.

Gender Differences in Occupational Choice

As we noted at the beginning of the chapter, most of the research over the years on occupational choice and development focused on men. Over the past few decades, though, some researchers have discovered important differences between men and women in how they experience work.

Men and women differ on many dimensions when it comes to choosing occupations. Boys and girls are often steered in different directions, and some occupations reflect clear gender differences (e.g., nursing, longshore workers). Men are groomed for future employment. Most boys learn at an early age that men are known by the work they do, and they receive strong encouragement for thinking about what occupation they would like to have. Occupational achievement is stressed as a core element of masculinity. Important social skills are taught through team games, in which they learn how to play by the rules, to accept setbacks without taking defeat personally, to follow the guidance of the leader, and to move up the leadership hierarchy by demonstrating qualities that are valued by others.

Women have traditionally not been so well trained. The skills that they have been taught are quite different—how to be accommodative and supportive—and they have received little in the way of occupation-related skills (Shainess, 1984). However, the women's movement has stressed the importance of providing girls the necessary skills for occupations outside the home. Given that more than half of women are now employed and that this trend will probably continue, it is especially important that women be exposed to the same occupational socialization opportunities as men.

Attention to women's occupational choices is relatively recent (Betz & Fitzgerald, 1987), due mainly to the assumptions that women's primary roles were homemaker and mother and that occupations were important only to single women.

Perhaps as a result of the influence of these stereotypes, occupational choices and developmental patterns differ between men and women. For example, one study found that male college seniors with a C+ average believed they were capable of earning a Ph.D. but that women with a B+ average thought they were incapable of doing so (Baird, 1973). Even a year after graduation women with an A average were no more likely to be attending graduate or professional schools than were men with a B average (Barnett & Baruch, 1978). These findings fit with self-efficacy influences on occupational selection discussed earlier, and they indicate the strength of the effects that early differences in socialization can have on subsequent occupational achievement.

Although it is still too early to tell, as women continue to move into the workforce, the ways in which they choose occupations are likely to become more similar to the processes that men use. Whereas research on occupational choice before the 1970s tended to focus on men, more recent research routinely includes women. Over the next decade we will likely see even fewer differences between men and women in the ways in which they decide to pursue occupations.

Traditional and Nontraditional Occupations

As more women enter the workforce, a growing number of them work in occupations that are considered traditionally male-dominated, such as construction or engineering. This research has focused on three issues (Swanson, 1992): selection of nontraditional occupations, characteristics of women in nontraditional occupations, and perceptions of nontraditional occupations.

Why some women choose nontraditional occupations appears to be related to personal feelings and experiences, as well as expectations about the occupation (Brooks and Betz, 1990). Concerning personal experiences, women who attend single-sex high schools and who have both brothers and sisters chose the least traditional occupations, apparently because they are exposed to more options and fewer gender-role stereotypes (Rubenfeld & Gilroy, 1991). Personal feelings are important; a study of Japanese students found that women had significantly lower confidence in their ability to perform in male-dominated occupations than in female-dominated occupations (Matsui, Ikeda, & Ohnishi, 1989).

The characteristics of women in nontraditional occupations have been studied as well. Betz, Heesacker, and Shuttleworth (1990) found that women who scored high on femininity, as defined by endorsing traditional feminine gender roles, and those in female-dominated occupations had the poorest match between their abilities and their occupational choices. These findings mean that women who score high on traditional measures of femininity have difficulty finding occupations that allow them to take advantage of their abilities. Additionally, women in female-dominated occupations also find that in general their jobs do not allow them to use their abilities to the fullest. In sum, many women have difficulty finding occupations that match their skills.

Despite the attempts by the women's movement to remove gender stereotyping of occupations, women who choose nontraditional occupations are still viewed more poorly by their peers of either sex, even though they have high job satisfaction themselves (Brabeck & Weisgerber, 1989; Pfost & Fiore, 1990). This finding holds up in cross-cultural research as well. In a study conducted in India, both women and men gave higher "respectability" ratings to males than to females in the same occupation (Kanekar, Kolsawalla, & Nazareth, 1989). People even make inferences about working conditions based on their perception of an occupation as traditionally masculine or feminine. Scozarro and Subich (1990) report that female-dominated occupations were perceived as offering nice working conditions, whereas male-dominated occupations were perceived as offering good pay and promotion potential.

Taken together, these studies show that we still have a long way to go before people can choose any occupation they want without having to contend with gender-related stereotypes. Although differences between women in traditional and nontraditional occupations are narrowing, key differences in opportunities remain. Finally, virtually no research has examined differences between males in traditional and nontraditional occupations (Swanson, 1992). This absence of data is troubling, for we cannot uncover reasons why men choose traditional or nontraditional occupations, or why some men still perpetuate gender stereotypes about particular occupations.

Women and Occupational Development

For many years research on women's occupational development was based on the assumption that most women saw their primary roles as homemaker and mother (Betz & Fitzgerald, 1987). Consequently, descriptions of women's occupational development were predicated on this assumption, and continuous employment outside the home was viewed as nontraditional. This assumption is clearly wrong. Researchers' descriptions now reflect the fact that most women in the United States work outside the home, many because of financial reasons.

Betz (1984) examined the occupational histories of 500 college women 10 years after graduation. Two thirds of these women were highly committed to their occupations, which for 70% were traditionally female ones. Most had worked continuously since graduation. Only 1% had been full-time homemakers during the entire 10-year period; 79% reported that they had successfully combined occupations with homemaking. Concerning occupational development, women in traditional female occupations were less likely to change occupations. If they did change, the move was more likely to be downward than were the changes made by women in nontraditional occupations.

An intriguing question is why highly educated women leave what appear to be well-paid occupations. Studies of women MBAs with children have identified a cluster of family and workplace issues (Rosin & Korabik, 1990, 1991). Family obligations, such as child care, appear to be most important for women working part-time. For these women, adequate child care arrangements or having the flexibility to be at home when children arrive back from school often make the difference between being able to accept a job or remaining at home. In contrast, women who have made the decision to work full-time have resolved the problem of child care. Workplace issues that appear most important for these women are gender related, such as unsupportive or insensitive work environments, organizational politics, and the lack of occupational development opportunities. In this case, women are focusing on issues that could create barriers to their occupational development and are looking for ways to avoid them.

Ethnicity and Occupational Development

What factors are related to occupational selection and development of people from ethnic minorities? Unfortunately, not much research has been conducted from a developmental perspective; rather, most researchers have focused on the limited opportunities ethnic minorities have and structural barriers such as discrimination that they face. Most of the developmental research to date focuses on occupational selection issues and variables that foster occupational development.

In terms of occupational selection, three topics examined in recent studies include nontraditional occupations, vocational identity (the degree to which one views one's occupation as a key element of identity), and issues pertaining to occupational aspirations.

African American women and European American women do not differ in plans to enter nontraditional occupations (Murrell, Frieze, & Frost, 1991). However, African American women who choose nontraditional occupations tend to plan for more formal education than necessary to achieve their goal. This may lead to a situation in which these women are actually overqualified for the jobs that they are in; for example, a woman may have a college degree but be working in a job that does not require that level of education.

Vocational identity varies with both ethnicity and gender. Compared with European American women and Hispanic men, African American and

European American men have higher vocational identity when they graduate from college (Steward & Krieshok, 1991). Lower vocational identity means that people define themselves primarily in terms of things in life other than work.

Occupational aspirations refer to the goals one has for the kind of occupation one would like to have, whereas occupational expectations refers to the occupation one believes one will actually get. Hispanics differ from European Americans in several ways on these variables. They have high occupational aspirations but low expectations, and they differ in their educational attainment as a function of national origin, generational status, and social class (Arbona, 1990). However, Hispanics are similar to European Americans in occupational development and work values.

Research on occupational development of ethnic minority workers is clear on one point: Whether an organization is responsive to the needs of ethnic minorities makes a big difference for employees. Both European American and ethnic minority managers who perceive their organizations as responsive and positive for ethnic minority employees are more satisfied with and committed to the organization (Burke, 1991a, 1991b). But much still remains to be accomplished. African American managers, report less choice of jobs, less acceptance, more career dissatisfaction, lower performance evaluations and promotability ratings, and more rapid attainment of plateaus in their careers than European American managers (Greenhaus, Parasuraman, & Wormley, 1990). Over 60% of African American protégés have European American mentors, which is problematic because same-ethnicity mentors provide more psychosocial support than cross-ethnicity mentors (Thomas, 1990).

Bias and Discrimination

Since the 1960s, organizations in the United States have been sensitized to the issues of bias and discrimination in the workplace. Hiring, promotion, and termination procedures have come under close scrutiny in numerous court cases, resulting in a host of laws to govern these processes.

Gender Bias and the Glass Ceiling

Even though the majority of women work outside the home, women in high-status jobs are unusual. Not until 1981 was a woman, Sandra Day O'Connor, appointed to the U.S. Supreme Court; it took another 12 years before a second woman, Ruth Bader Ginsburg, was appointed associate justice. Few women serve in the highest ranks of major corporations, and women are substantially outnumbered at the senior faculty level of most universities and colleges.

One intuitively appealing reason for the scarcity of women in top-level jobs is work overload when women with occupations outside the home are also expected to perform most of the day-to-day housekeeping chores and child care. Contrary to intuition, however, work overload is usually not a factor (we will come back to this topic later in this chapter). **Far more important is *sex discrimination*, denying a job to someone solely on the basis of whether the person is a man or a woman.**

Baron and Bielby (1985) pull no punches in discussing sex discrimination: "Our analyses portray [sex] discrimination as pervasive, almost omnipresent, sustained by diverse organizational structures and processes. Moreover, this segregation drastically restricts women's career opportunities, by blocking access to internal labor markets and their benefits" (p. 245). Women are being kept out of high-status jobs by the men at the top.

Women themselves refer to a *glass ceiling*, the level to which they may rise in a company but beyond which they may not go. This problem is most obvious in companies that classify jobs at various levels (as does the civil service). The greatest disadvantage facing women occurred near the boundary between lower tier and upper tier job grades. Women tend to move to the top of the lower tier and remain there, whereas men are typically promoted to the upper tier, even when other factors, such as personal attributes and qualifications, are controlled (DiPrete and Soule,

1988). The U.S. government admitted in 1991 that the glass ceiling was not only real, but pervades the workplace. Indeed, some surveys indicate that over 90% of women believe that there is a glass ceiling in the workplace.

Beyond discrimination in hiring and promotion, women are also the victims of pay discrimination. According the U.S. Department of Labor (1995), in many occupations men are paid substantially more than women in the same positions; indeed, on the average, women are paid only about three-fourths or less of what men are paid. And the situation has gotten worse; the pay gap actually widened from the 1980s to the early 1990s. In the early 1980s, the pay gap was 21%, whereas by the early 1990s it had widened to 35%. Over the long run, such lower pay will mean significantly lower pensions for women in lower paying occupations.

Several ideas have been promoted as solutions to pay discrimination. **One of these is *comparable worth,* which refers to equating pay in occupations that are determined to be equivalent in importance but differ in terms of the gender distribution of the people in them.** Determining which male-dominated occupations should be considered equivalent to which female-dominated occupations for pay purposes can be difficult and controversial.

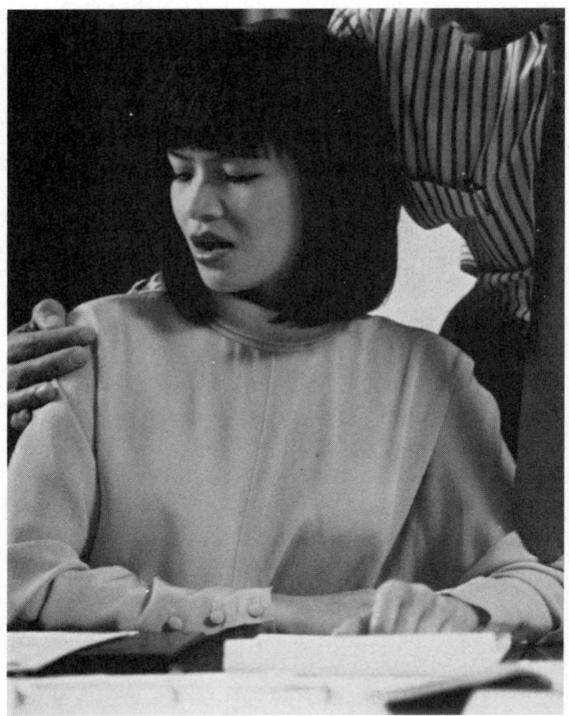

Sexual harassment is a complex topic. Touching someone, as this man is doing, may be potentially harassing behavior if it is unwanted or inappropriate.

Sexual Harassment

Although the sexual harassment of women in the workplace has been documented for centuries, only recently has it received much attention from researchers (Fitzgerald & Shullman, 1993). Interest among U.S. researchers increased dramatically after the 1991 Senate hearings involving Supreme Court nominee Clarence Thomas and Anita Hill, who accused him of sexual harassment, the U.S. Navy "Tailhook" scandal involving the mistreatment of women by Navy personnel with the knowledge of their commanders, and charges that led to the resignation of Bob Packwood from the U.S. Senate in 1995.

How many people have been sexually harassed and what do people think sexual harassment entails? These are two areas researchers are investigating, but neither topic is straightforward. Reliable statistics on the number of victims are extremely difficult to obtain, in part due to the unwillingness of many victims to report harassment and to the differences involving reporting procedures. Indeed, estimates are that less than 5% of victims ever report their experiences to anyone in authority (Fitzgerald et al., 1988). Even given these difficulties, several studies document that over 40% of women report having been sexually harassed in the workplace at least once (Fitzgerald & Shullman, 1993).

Of course, the crux of the matter is what constitutes harassment. The complexity of sexual harassment has led to the use of research designs that allow this complexity to be examined. Using ambiguous situations is a technique that many researchers use. In fact, research on perceptions of what constitutes harassing behavior usually requires people to read vignettes of hypothetical incidents involving sexually suggestive touching, sexual remarks, and the like and decide if it was harassment. Research on sexual harassment can be organized into three general areas (Gelfand, Fitzgerald, & Drasgow, in press): so-called quid pro quo situations in which sex is used in exchange for promotions and the like; gender harassment, such as commenting on body parts; and unwanted sexual attention, such as kissing and fondling.

In general, women are more likely to view such behaviors as offensive than are men (Fitzgerald & Ormerod, 1991). **This gender gap in perceptions resulted in the institution in the case of *Ellison v. Brady* (U.S. 9th Circuit Court) of the so-called *reasonable woman standard* as the appropriate legal criterion for determining whether sexual harassment has occurred.** If a reasonable woman would view a behavior as offensive, the court held, then it is offensive even if the man did not consider it to be offensive.

Several other factors also influence whether a behavior is considered offensive besides the gender of the perceiver (Fitzgerald & Ormerod, 1991). These include the degree to which the behavior is explicit or extreme (such as rape versus a friendly kiss), victim behavior (such as whether the victim was at all responsible for what happened), supervisory status (whether the perpetrator was a direct supervisor of the victim), harasser's intentions (whether the perpetrator knew that the victim found the behavior offensive), and frequency of occurrence (such as a one-time occurrence versus a regular event). Unfortunately, little research has been done to identify what aspects of organizations foster harassment or the impact of educational and training programs aimed at addressing the problem.

Cultural Bias

Racial discrimination and cultural bias in the workplace are reflected in many different ways (Marsella, 1994). Ethnic minority workers are disproportionately in low-paying, low-status jobs and often lack the necessary education to advance. They must often take high-risk jobs that no one else will accept.

Cultural bias is reflected in many ways. Among the most common are insensitivity to the values, language, customs, dress, food, and personal styles of ethnocultural groups. More blatantly, bias is displayed in outright prejudice and racism, expressed in the form of humor directed at minorities, jokes made at their expense, and, in some cases, actual physical violence.

The most problematic aspect of cultural bias is racial discrimination, in which employment or promotion is decided on the basis of race or ethnicity. Affirmative action programs, begun in the United States during the 1960s, were aimed at addressing this problem. Considerable debate about the merits of such programs began in earnest during the mid-1990s, resulting in some programs being eliminated or modified. Regardless of the outcome of these debates, racism and cultural bias in the workplace remains a major problem.

Age Discrimination

Mature workers over age 40 face several special issues concerning employment. Although they are less likely overall to be unemployed, when they are they encounter more difficulty in finding another job than people under age 40. This means that unemployed mature workers are more likely to exhaust their unemployment benefits and to become discouraged at finding another job. Older workers (those over age 55) are most likely to become discouraged (U.S. Senate Special Committee on Aging, 1989).

Two major barriers to older workers involve age discrimination and labor market issues. The first involves deliberately passing over someone for a job due to age. The second concerns issues about reasons for employment problems facing older workers. Let's consider each of these.

One structural barrier to occupational development is *age discrimination*, which involves denying a job or promotion to someone solely

on the basis of age. The U.S. Age Discrimination in Employment Act of 1967 made illegal the use of age as a criterion in hiring, firing, layoff, working conditions, and referral by employment agencies. This law protects all workers over age 40 and stipulates that people must be hired based on their ability, not their age. Also not allowed under the law are job advertisements reflecting age preferences, age discriminatory pressures by labor unions, and retaliation against workers who assert their rights under the law. Additionally, employers cannot segregate or classify workers or otherwise denote their status on the basis of age. As amended in 1986, the act also prohibits mandatory retirement from most jobs.

Age discrimination occurs in several ways (Snyder & Barrett, 1988). For example, employers can make certain types of physical or mental performance a job requirement and argue that older workers are incapable of it, or they can make cuts in the number of employees in an attempt to get rid of older workers by using mandatory retirement. Supervisors sometimes will use age as a factor in performance evaluations for raises or promotions or in decisions about which employees are eligible for additional training.

Perceptions of age discrimination are widespread; nearly 700 federal court cases have been filed since 1970. Snyder and Barrett (1988) reviewed these cases and found that the employer had been favored about 65% of the time. Job-performance information was crucial in all cases; however, this information was usually presented in terms of general differences between young and old. Surprisingly, many courts did not question inaccurate information or stereotypic views of aging presented by employers, despite the lack of scientific data documenting age differences in actual job performance. In addition, prosecutors and the courts have treated age discrimination more leniently than racial discrimination (Eglit, 1989). Thus, despite the dramatic increase since 1980 in the number of cases reported to the Equal Employment Opportunity Commission, the proportion of cases actually prosecuted has dropped significantly, indicating a less-than-enthusiastic attitude toward enforcement of the law against age discrimination.

Although the extent of age discrimination is unknown, most adults think it is widespread. For example, 80% of Americans polled agreed with the statement that "most employers discriminate against older people and make it difficult for them to find work." Even more telling, the same survey found that more than one third of employers believed that age discrimination is common (U.S. Senate Special Committee on Aging, 1989). As we will see in the next section, older workers are especially likely to be offered buyouts in situations involving corporate downsizing, raising the issue of whether such practices involve age discrimination.

Mature workers must face several labor market barriers to employment: job dislocation, displacement of homemakers into the labor force, declines in seniority protection, costs of benefits for older workers, lack of opportunity for part-time employment, and problems of job reentry for retirees who desire to return to employment.

As we will see later in this chapter, job dislocations can occur for many reasons, such as plant closings, company downsizing, mergers, and the like. Most seriously affected in the United States have been manufacturing jobs, which dropped from 30% of all jobs in the 1960s to only 17% in 1990 (Barlett & Steele, 1992). Of the manufacturing workers over age 55 who were displaced, only 40% were able to find new jobs, compared with over 70% of those in their 20s. Moreover, older manufacturing workers tend to be laid off first.

Women who were homemakers are sometimes thrust into the labor market in midlife through divorce or widowhood. Many of these women have few marketable job skills. Consequently, they often encounter considerable difficulty in finding a job that pays enough to make ends meet. Indeed, the fact that many displaced homemakers have severe employment problems was recognized by the U.S. Congress in 1978 when displaced homemakers were categorized as "hard to employ" under the Comprehensive Employment Training Act.

In the past, older workers were protected from layoffs and similar problems through job seniority. Job seniority meant that workers with the longest service would be the last to be laid off, the first called back, and given first choice on promotions. Because the workers with the most seniority tended to be older, job seniority was a protection for older workers. However, this protection is eroding as labor unions become less of a factor, and because the courts' and the National Labor Relations Board's growing tendency to rule in favor of employers in labor disputes (Gersuny, 1987).

The costs of benefits for older workers is another structural problem. Although there is little evidence that older workers as a group actually cost more than younger workers, changes in the way health care is financed had major effects on older workers. In 1982, the U.S. Congress enacted several changes designed to reduce the amount of funds required by Medicare, which directly increased the costs of hiring older workers. The problem was that if employers provided health insurance to workers, this insurance was required to be the primary insurance for everyone, even those workers who were otherwise eligible for Medicare because they were over age 65. Private health insurance for people over 65 is much more expensive than for younger people. Additionally, the employer's insurance was required to cover a worker's spouse if he or she were over age 65, adding even more costs. These changes provided companies a major disincentive for hiring older workers.

The lack of alternatives to traditional retirement for all those who would like them is another barrier to employment for older adults. Many individuals would like to retire partially and to keep working in a reduced capacity. However, fewer than 10% of employers offer a phased or partial retirement option (Quinn & Burkhauser, 1990). In fact, many employers have been moving in the opposite direction, that is, offering retirement buyouts as part of their downsizing. These buyouts are offered nearly exclusively to older workers, partly in an effort to reduce the size of management, but also partly from the mistaken notion that eliminating older workers is good for the organization (Seltzer & Karnes, 1988).

In sum, numerous structural barriers exist that make it difficult for many older adults to either find a job or to remain employed as long as they would like. Clearly, efforts to protect older workers have not worked very well, and more education about the value of older workers is needed.

Concept Checks

1. What factors lead some women to choose nontraditional occupations?
2. What is the primary reason women in full-time high-status jobs quit after having children?
3. How do ethnic groups differ in terms of choosing nontraditional occupations, vocational identity, occupational aspirations, and occupational development?
4. Define glass ceiling, comparable worth, sexual harassment, and age discrimination.

OCCUPATIONAL TRANSITIONS

Learning Objectives:

- Why do people change occupations?
- Why is worker retraining necessary and important?
- What happens to people when they lose their jobs?

In the past people quite often chose an occupation during young adulthood and stayed in it throughout their working years. Today, many people take a job with the expectation that they will not be in it forever. Changing jobs is almost taken for granted; the average American will change jobs between 5 and 10 times during adulthood (Toffler,

1970). Some authors view occupational changes as positive; Havighurst (1982), for example, strongly advocates such flexibility. According to his view, building change into the occupational life cycle may help to avoid disillusionment with one's initial choice. Changing occupations may be one way to guarantee challenging and satisfying work, and it may be the best option for those in a position to exercise it (Shirom & Mazeh, 1988).

Factors Influencing Occupational Transitions

Several factors have been identified as important in determining who will remain in an occupation and who will change. Some of these factors—such as personality—lead to self-initiated occupation changes. Others—such as obsolescence and economic factors—cause forced occupational changes.

Personality

Personality is important in self-initiated occupational change. Recall that Holland (1985) postulates that people with certain personality characteristics are suited to particular jobs. If a worker makes an initial selection and later comes to dislike an occupation, it may be because his or her personality does not match the job.

Several researchers have documented that personality factors and situational pressure combine to determine whether a person will remain in an occupation (for example, Clopton, 1973; Wiener & Vaitenas, 1977). For example, Wiener and Vaitenas found that lack of interest, incongruity with one's occupation, lack of consistent and diversified interests, fear of failure, or a history of emotional problems predicted occupational change. Age was not a predictor. Such findings support our earlier point that similar factors influence occupational choice throughout adulthood.

Obsolescence and Economic Factors

Sometimes people cannot choose whether they want to change occupations; they are forced to do so. For example, people may be forced to look for new occupations as a result of technological change (such as assembly line workers being replaced by robots) or economic factors (such as economic recessions).

Technological change is occurring at an ever-increasing rate, such that the skills that one learns today may be obsolete in only a few years. When this occurs, individuals may find that they are forced into making occupational changes. As an example, many Americans with skills important in heavy manufacturing, such as making steel, were displaced in the late 1970s and 1980s as domestic plants closed. Thus, workers are being forced to retrain themselves as never before—either just to keep up with change or to learn about new employment opportunities. The latter reason is especially important; in 25 years at least one quarter of the readers of this book will hold jobs in fields or specializations that currently do not exist.

Layoffs are one primary impetus to change occupations. Layoffs occur most often during large economic recessions, such as the one during the early 1990s. Unlike most previous recessions in the United States, this time people in all types of occupations were affected, from blue-collar laborers to high-level corporate executives. In addition, some workers decide to seek new occupations because of personal economic factors, such as insufficient pay. For example, recently divorced women may need to find higher paying occupations, especially if child support payments are not received.

Retraining Workers

A person hired into a specific job is selected because the employer believes that person offers the best fit between abilities he or she already has and those needed to perform the job. As most people can attest, though, the skills needed to perform a job typically change over time. Such changes may be due to the introduction of new technology, additional responsibilities, or promotion.

Unless one is able to keep one's skills up to date, the outcome is likely to be either job loss or career plateauing (Froman, 1994). ***Career plateauing***

involves either a lack of promotional opportunity from the organization or a person's decision not to seek advancement. In either job loss or career plateauing, retraining may be an appropriate response, either to improve technical skills, such as new computer skills, or for midcareer or older employees to learn how to find new career opportunities, such as résumé preparation and career counseling.

Many corporations as well as community and technical colleges offer retraining programs in a variety of fields. Organizations that promote employee development typically promote in-house courses to improve one's skills or may offer tuition reimbursement programs for individuals who successfully complete courses at colleges or universities.

The retraining of midcareer and older workers points to the need for lifelong learning (Sinnott, 1994c). For corporations to meet the challenges of a global economy, they must include retraining in their employee development programs. Such programs will help people not only improve their chances of advancement in their chosen occupations, but also make successful transitions from one occupation to another.

Loss of One's Job

As noted earlier in this chapter, changing economic conditions in the United States over the past few decades (such as increased competition from foreign companies), as well as changing demographics, have forced many people out of their jobs. Heavy manufacturing and support businesses (such as the steel, oil, and automotive industries) and farming were the hardest hit during the 1970s and 1980s. But no one is immune. Indeed, the corporate takeover frenzy of the 1980s, the recession of the early 1990s, and continuing corporate downsizing put many middle and upper level corporate executives out of work as well.

Losing one's job can have enormous personal impact (DeFrank & Ivancevich, 1986). Declines in physical health and self-esteem, depression, anxiety, and suicide are common (Lajer, 1982). Few gender differences in these effects are found (Leana & Feldman, 1991). Although the loss of one's job means the loss of income and status, these effects vary with age. Some middle-aged men are more vulnerable to negative effects than older or younger men (DeFrank & Ivancevich, 1986). However, workers in their 50s who lose their jobs do not always report negative outcomes (Leana & Feldman, 1992). Some may have been planning to retire in the near future and see this as an opportunity to do so, others are hired back as consultants, and still others use their situation to try doing something new.

Studies over the years are clear on one point, though. The extent of the effects of losing one's job is related to the degree of financial stress one is under and the timing of the loss (Estes & Wilensky, 1978). Childless couples and couples with young children suffer the most; couples whose children have left home or are independent fare better. Lajer (1982) reports that admission to a psychiatric unit following job loss is more likely for people who are over age 45 or have been unemployed for a long period.

What happens to the mental health of people who remain unemployed for relatively long periods of time? Wanberg (1995) assessed 129 people over a period of 9 months following the loss of a job. Only those people who were satisfied with their new jobs showed significant improvements in mental health; people who were unhappy in their new jobs and people who were still unemployed showed no change.

People who are unemployed show considerable variability among themselves. For example, Wanberg and Marchese (1994) showed that four clusters of unemployed people could be identified, varying along the dimensions of financial concerns, employment commitment, job-seeking confidence level, degree of time structure, and adaptation to unemployment. These clusters can be identified as follows: confident, but concerned about getting another job; distressed about being unemployed; unconcerned and indifferent about being unemployed; and optimistic about the future and coping with unemployment. The differing characteristics of these clusters means that interventions with unemployed individuals must take these differences into account.

The effects of losing one's job emphasize the central role that occupations play in forming a sense of identity in adulthood. How one perceives the loss of a job plays a major role in determining what the long-term effects will be.

Concept Checks

1. What are the major factors that predict occupational transition?
2. What is career plateauing? How can it be avoided?
3. What effects do people experience when they lose their jobs?

DUAL-EARNER COUPLES

Learning Objectives:

- What gender differences exist in the division of household tasks? How is role conflict handled?
- What factors make a difference for employees who have children?
- What effects on occupational development are there for dual-earner couples?

At one time, most people in the United States pictured a two-parent home in which the father had an occupation and the mother stayed at home to raise the children. What 30 years will do! Today, only a clear minority of families fit this view. The vast majority consist of both parents working outside the home, largely because families need the dual income to pay the bills and maintain a moderate standard of living. As we will see, dual-earner couples experience both benefits and costs to this arrangement.

The experiences of most dual-earner couples are similar to those of Jan (a cashier at a local supermarket) and Tom (a worker at the nearby auto assembly plant). Jan and Tom are in their late 20s and have a 3-year-old daughter, Terri. Although they like the fact that their combined income lets them own a modest house, they also feel that there are many strains.

"You know, at times I feel overwhelmed," Jan related. "It's not that Tom doesn't help around the house. But it's not as much as he could. Most days after work I have to pick up Terri from Mom's and then come home and prepare dinner. After a hard day, that's about the last thing I want to do. I guess I'm not very good at being a superwoman, or whatever they call it. I also still feel a little guilty leaving Terri with Mom; there are times when I think I ought to be home with her rather than out working."

"But look at what we've got now," Tom responded. "You used to complain about things a lot more. You should think about all the things we wouldn't have if you didn't work."

Jan and Tom's experiences point out the major gains and stresses reported by dual-earner couples. On the benefit side, their standard of living is higher, which allows them to have more material goods and provide better for their children. However, as Jan indicated, there are several stresses as well. For most dual-earner couples, the biggest problem is the division of housework duties.

Balancing Multiple Roles

When both members of a couple are employed, who cleans the house, cooks the meals, and takes care of the children when they are ill? Despite much media attention and claims of increased sharing in the duties, women still assume the lion's share of housework regardless of employment status. Wives spend about twice as many hours per week as their husbands in family work and bear the greatest responsibility for household and child care tasks (Benin & Agostinelli, 1988). Indeed, it is this unequal division of labor that creates most arguments and causes the most unhappiness for dual-earner couples.

A great deal of evidence indicates that women have decreased the amount of time they spend on housework since the 1970s, especially when they are employed, and that men have increased the amount of time they spend on such tasks (Swanson, 1992). The increased participation of men in these tasks is not all that it seems, however. Most of the increase is on weekends, with specific tasks that they agree to perform, and is largely unrelated to women's employment status (Zick & McCullough, 1991). In short, this increase in men's participation has not done much to lower women's burdens around the house.

Husbands and wives view the division of labor in very different terms. Benin and Agostinelli (1988) found that husbands were most satisfied with an equitable division of labor based on the number of hours spent, especially if the amount of time needed to perform household tasks was relatively small. Wives, on the other hand, were most satisfied if the division favored them; their satisfaction was unaffected by the total number of hours spent, but it was affected by the husband's willingness to perform women's traditional chores. Broman (1988) reports similar results with African American dual-earner couples. In this study women were twice as likely as men to feel overworked by housework and to be dissatisfied with their family life.

Ethnic differences in the division of household labor are also apparent. In a study of European American, African American, and Hispanic men, several interesting patterns emerged (Shelton & John, 1993). African American and Hispanic men tend to spend more time doing household tasks than do European American men. This finding supports the view that African American households are more egalitarian than European American households. Moreover, the increased participation of African American men was primarily true of employed, as opposed to unemployed, men and reflected a greater participation in traditionally female tasks, such as washing dishes and cooking. Similarly, Hispanic men's participation also tended to reflect increased participation in these tasks. Overall, European American men spent the least time helping with traditionally female tasks. These data clearly indicate that the degree to which men and women divide household tasks varies not only with gender, but with ethnicity as well.

Role conflict **is another problem expressed by many dual-earner couples; figuring out how to balance time at work and time with family confronts everyone.** Many women were raised with motherhood as a major goal and feel torn between raising their children and continuing their occupation (Shainess, 1984). Guilt feelings may be exacerbated by others who feel that a woman who places her children in day care is not a good mother. Her partner may also have his own views that do not agree with hers, further compounding the problem.

However, most employed women and men manage to resolve the apparent tension between work and parenting. Women in one study were clear in their commitment to their careers, marriage, and children, and they were successfully combining them without high levels of distress (Guelzow, Bird, & Koball, 1991). Contrary to popular belief, age of children was not a factor in stress level; only the number of children was important. Guilt was not an issue for these women. Men in the same study reported sharing more of the child care tasks as a way of dealing with multiple role pressures. Additionally, low stress in men was associated with having a flexible work schedule that would allow them to care for sick children and other family matters. Similarly, a study of Japanese dual-earner couples indicated that support of the husband buffered the relationship between parental demands and work-family conflict (Matsui, Ohsawa, & Onglatco, 1995). Together these findings are encouraging, as they indicate that more dual-earner couples are learning how to adaptively balance work and family.

Dual-earner couples often have difficulty finding time to be alone with each other, especially if both work long hours (Kingston & Nock, 1987). The amount of time together is not necessarily the most important issue; as long as the time is spent in shared activities such as eating, playing, and conversing, couples tend to be happy.

Issues concerning balancing work and family are extremely important in couples' everyday lives. Learning how to deal with multiple roles is an important process in current industrial societies. We are creating patterns that will provide the anticipatory socialization for our children. Even

SOMETHING TO THINK ABOUT

Division of Labor and Role Conflict in Dual-Earner Couples

One of the largest issues facing American society in the 1990s is how dual-earner couples can balance their occupational and family roles. With the majority of couples now consisting of two wage earners, issues such as who does the household chores and how child care is arranged will become increasingly important.

Many people believe that work and family roles mutually influence each other. That is, when things go bad at work, family suffers, and when problems occur at home, work suffers. As noted in the text, such role conflicts and mutual interaction appear not to be the case. It is more of a one-way street. For the most part, problems at home have little effect on job performance, whereas trouble at work could spill over to home life.

Negotiating agreeable arrangements of household and child care tasks are critical. But as noted in the text, truly equitable divisions of labor are clearly the exception. Most American households with dual-earner couples still operate under a gender-segregated system: There are wives' chores and husbands' chores. Without question, all these tasks are important and must be performed to ensure domestic sanitation. However, these tasks take time. The important point for women is that it is not how much time is spent in performing household chores that matters but which tasks are performed. The research cited in the text indicates that what bothers wives the most is not that their husbands are lazy but that their husbands will not perform some "women's work." Men may mow the lawn, wash the car, and even cook, but they rarely run the vacuum, scrub the toilet, or change the baby's diaper.

Husbands would be viewed much more positively by their wives if they performed more of the traditionally female tasks. Marital satisfaction would be likely to improve as a result. Moreover, the role modeling provided to children in these households would be a major step in breaking the transmission of age-old stereotypes. It's something to think about.

---

now, most dual-earner couples feel that the benefits, especially the extra income, are worth the costs. Many dual-earner couples, however, have no choice but to try to deal with the situation as best they can: Both partners must work simply to pay the bills.

But what effects do family matters have on work performance and vice versa? Recent evidence suggests our work and family lives do not have equal influences on the other. Work stress has a far bigger impact on family life than family stress has on work performance. In general, women feel the work-to-family spillover to a greater extent than men, but both men and women feel the pressure (Gutek, Searle, & Klepa, 1991). Single mothers have an especially hard time if they have more than one child (Polit, 1984). And cross-cultural data from a study of dual-earner couples in Singapore showed that wives are more likely to suffer from burnout than husbands; wives' burnout resulted from both work and nonwork stress, whereas husbands' burnout resulted only from work stress (Aryee, 1993). As discussed in Something to Think About, this means that couples need to take seriously the job of deciding how to divide up tasks.

The Child Care Dilemma

Many mothers grapple with the difficult decision of whether to return to work after having children. Surveys of mothers with preschool-aged children reveal that the motivation for returning to work tends to be related to how attached mothers are to their work. For example, in one survey of Australian mothers, those with high work attachment cited more intrinsic personal achievement reasons for returning. Those with low work attachment cited pressing financial needs. Those with moderate work attachment were divided between intrinsic and financial reasons (Cotton, Antill, & Cunningham, 1989). Apparently, the reasons women return (or do not return) to work following the birth of a child are complex and go well beyond simply trying to work out child care arrangements.

Recent evidence demonstrates some surprising findings when single parents are compared with nonsingle parents. Regardless of gender, single parents report less difficulty concentrating on work and less stress because of child care problems (Tetrick, Miles, Marcil, & Van Dosen, 1994). Though contrary to popular perception, these findings may indicate that single parents may be better at adapting to the dual roles of parenthood and employee.

Child Care and Worker Behavior

Employed parents with small children are confronted with the difficult act of leaving their children in the care of others. In response to mounting pressure from parents, most industrialized countries (but not the United States) provide government-supported child care centers for employees as one way to help ease this burden. Does providing a center make a difference in an employee's feelings about work, absenteeism, or productivity?

The answer is that it's not as simple as opening a center. Just making a child care center available at work to employees does not necessarily reduce parents' work-family conflict or absenteeism (Goff, Mount, & Jamison, 1990). What is key is how one's supervisor acts. Irrespective of where the child care center is located, when supervisors are sympathetic and supportive regarding family issues and child care, parents report lower work-family conflict and had lower absenteeism.

How these issues play out in the United States over the next several years will be interesting to watch. The passage in early 1993 of the Parental Leave Act means that for the first time new parents will be able to take unpaid time off to care for their children and return to their jobs. Experience from other countries indicates that parental leave has different effects on each parent. For example, a large-scale study in Sweden showed that fathers who took parental leave were more likely to be involved in child care and to reduce their work involvement. Regardless of fathers' participation, mothers still retained primary responsibility for child care and stayed less involved in and received fewer rewards in the labor market (Haas, 1990).

Impact on Occupational Development

Besides the impact on their personal lives, dual-earner couples sometimes report negative effects on occupational development. The most obvious influence occurs when one partner decides to interrupt his or her occupation while the children are young and later reenters the labor force. Skills may have to be learned or relearned, and such returnees may find themselves competing with younger workers for the same positions.

What about people who do not interrupt their careers? For example, suppose you and your spouse have occupations in which you are both extremely happy. One day, your spouse comes home and tells you about an incredible opportunity for advancement. The problem is that the position is in another city 1,000 miles away. To remain together, you would have to quit your job and move. What would you do? It turns out that whether you are a husband or a wife makes an enormous difference; husbands' careers are clearly given higher priority. One survey showed that 77% of women and 68% of men said that a wife should quit her job if her husband were offered a good position in another city. In contrast, only 10% of the women and 18% of the men said that the husband should refuse the offer so that his wife could continue with her job (Roper Organization, 1980).

Research indicates that both working mothers and fathers both benefit from job flexibility that allows them to balance work and family obligations (Marshall & Barnett, 1994). These family-friendly organizations typically allow employees to set their own schedules and have generous sick and family leave policies. Such flexibility and benefits results in higher job satisfaction and reduced work-family strain.

Some couples avoid making the decision as to whether both partners should work. Rather than trying to decide whether the other partner should quit and move, an increasing number of people are living apart. Such living arrangements are common in some occupations—such as acting, politics, sports, and the military—and are becoming more popular among professional couples. (Other reasons for couples to live apart are less glamorous; spending time in prison is one example). Although this arrangement may work for people who can afford to visit each other often, for many people the stress of long-distance relationships can be severe. Some couples eventually decide that the costs of separation are higher than the benefits of maintaining both occupations, and they reunite. Others decide to make the separation permanent, and they break up. Indeed, Rindfuss and Stephen (1990) found that married couples living apart are roughly twice as likely to get divorced compared with married couples living together. In this case, absence does not make the heart grow fonder.

Concept Checks

1. What differences are there in how husbands and wives divide household tasks?
2. What is the most important thing an organization can do for employees with children?
3. What helps both working fathers and mothers balance work and family obligations?

LEISURE ACTIVITIES

Learning Objectives:

- What life-cycle factors are important in understanding leisure?
- What types of leisure activities do adults exhibit?
- What developmental differences are there in leisure activities?
- What factors predict leisure activities?

Leisure is something that is important to each of us and is something we intuitively understand. For researchers, though, leisure is hard to define. Many authors take the easy way out and define it as the opposite of work. In this case, leisure is any time not spent doing what one is employed to do. But this definition ignores time spent with family and friends, as well as time spent sleeping. Leisure can also be viewed as a state of mind, like relaxation. In this case, only you know if you are being leisurely or not. This, too, is inadequate for research.

In the end, researchers often opt for the definition that leisure is time that one has to do things for pleasure. More formally, we can define leisure as any way in which people express themselves in discretionary activities (Gordon, Gaitz, & Scott, 1976). However, important differences can be seen in how men and women, as well as people in different ethnic groups, view leisure (Henderson, 1990). For example, one study of African American women revealed that they viewed leisure as both freedom from the constraint of needing to work and as a form of self-expression (Allen & Chin-Sang, 1990).

Gerontologists have recognized the importance of leisure in maintaining positive well-being for many years (Cutler & Hendricks, 1990). Without question, leisure plays a major role in people's lives in terms of how they spend their time and the benefits derived from it. In this section we will examine how leisure fits in the life cycle, the types of leisure activities people do, and how leisure activities change over adulthood.

Leisure in the Life Cycle

To make sense of what adults of all ages do when they are not working, we must consider how leisure fits into various parts of the life cycle. Leisure is influenced by many factors, and its meaning depends heavily on the person involved. Which leisure activities one engages in are a result of things such as personal preferences, what one's friends like to do, health, physical ability, and past experiences. Only when leisure is viewed in this broader perspective can we understand age differences in adults' leisure activities.

One important constant across adulthood appears to be the importance of the quality of leisure activities rather than their quantity (Kelly, Steinkamp, & Kelly, 1987). That is, it is not how many leisure activities one engages in that matters; rather, it is how much one enjoys them. For example, people with severe physical limitations may derive more benefit from leisure activities than very healthy adults if benefit is based on the quality of social interaction (Kelly et al., 1987).

A second important factor is that one's sense of self changes with age (see Chapter 8), which is accompanied by changes in what people do to seek affirmation. Lawton (1985a) suggests that personal expectations may affect what older adults do for leisure activities. For example, older adults may not think that physical leisure activities (such as aerobics) are appropriate and may refuse to participate in them. Others may feel entirely differently. Still, if people of certain ages are made to feel uncomfortable in some activities, it is unlikely they will continue to participate.

Finally, we must look at the broad context in which leisure occurs. Individuals with spouses and families tend to engage in more communal or group activities than single adults. Moreover, leisure activities are also one way to meet new people. Many adults join clubs or health spas not only for the leisure and health benefits, but also because they present opportunities to make new friends.

Types of Leisure Activities

Virtually any activity that one engages in could be considered a leisure activity. To help organize the options, researchers have generally classified leisure activities into four categories: cultural—such as attending sporting events, concerts, church services, or meetings; physical—such as golf, hiking, aerobics, or gardening; social—such as visiting with friends or going to parties; and solitary—such as reading, listening to music, or watching television (Bossé & Ekerdt, 1981; Glamser & Hayslip, 1985). Leisure activities can also be considered in terms of degree of personal involvement; examples of leisure activities organized along this dimension are listed in Table 11.2

TABLE 11.2 Forms of leisure activity and how they vary in intensity of cognitive, emotional, or physical involvement

Very high intensity	Sexual activity
	Highly competitive games or sports
	Dancing
Moderately high intensity	Creative activities (art, literature, music)
	Nurturance or teaching (children's arts and crafts)
	Serious discussion and analysis
Medium intensity	Attending cultural events
	Participating in clubs
	Sightseeing or travel
Moderately low intensity	Socializing
	Reading for pleasure
	Light conversation
Low intensity	Solitude
	Quiet resting
	Taking a nap

Given the wide range of options, how do people pick the leisure activities they want to do? Apparently, each of us has a leisure repertoire, a personal library of intrinsically motivated activities that we do regularly (Mobily, Lemke, & Gisin, 1991). The activities comprising our repertoire are determined by two things: perceived competence (how good we think we are at the activity compared with other people our age) and psychological comfort (how well we meet our personal goals for performance). Other factors are important as well: income, interest, health, abilities, transportation, education, and social characteristics. How these factors influence leisure activities probably changes across adulthood, although exactly how this happens is currently unknown (Burrus-Bammel & Bammel, 1985).

Developmental Changes in Leisure

A national survey found age and cohort differences in leisure activities (L. Harris & Associates, 1975). As age increased, fewer of the activities that adults considered leisure involved strenuous physical exertion, whereas sedentary activities—such as reading and watching television—became more common.

Age differences have also been reported concerning the variety of leisure activities (Bray & Howard, 1983; Elder, 1974; Lowenthal et al., 1975). These studies indicate that young adults participate in a greater range of activities than for middle-aged people. Gordon and colleagues (1976) report that young adults prefer intense leisure activities, that middle-aged adults focus more on home- and family-oriented activities that are less intense, and that the elderly further narrow the range of activities and lower their intensity. Additionally, few older African American men participate in outdoor recreational activities, a rate that is somewhat lower than for other ethnic groups (Brown & Tedrick, 1993).

Longitudinal studies of changes in leisure activities show considerable stability over reasonably long periods (Cutler & Hendricks, 1990). In general, frequent participation in leisure activities during childhood continues into adulthood. Similar findings hold for the pre- and postretirement years.

Correlates and Consequences of Leisure Activities

Several variables are related to the kinds of leisure activities people choose. Adults may face barriers to leisure participation such as health problems and lack of transportation. These barriers are especially important for understanding participation of older adults and various ethnic groups. Indeed, health problems are the primary reason given when older adults explain their lack of participation in leisure activities (McGuire, Dottavio, & O'Leary, 1986).

Gender differences occur along several lines. For example, men are much more likely to participate in outdoor leisure activities such as hunting and fishing, whereas women are more likely to engage in cultural and home-based leisure activities (Lawton, Moss, & Fulcomer, 1986–87).

Type of residence also appears to matter. People who live in retirement housing participate more frequently in leisure activities than people living in typical neighborhoods (Moss & Lawton, 1982). Part of the reason for this finding is that retirement communities often provide structured activities for residents whereas many age-integrated neighborhoods and communities do not.

What benefits do people get for participating in leisure activities? Researchers agree that being involved in leisure activities is related to positive well-being (for example, Kelly et al., 1987). The key aspect of this relationship is not the level of participation. Instead, how much satisfaction one derives from leisure activities is more important in promoting well-being (Lawton et al., 1986–87). Indeed, an Israeli study showed that satisfaction with leisure activities is the crucial variable in the relationship between participation and well-being (Lomranz, Bergman, Eyal, & Shmotkin, 1988).

Leisure activities represent a major aspect of people's lives. Leisure is an important source of well-being across adulthood and offers ways of meeting new people. At the same time, we need to learn much more about how people spend their discretionary time. For example, we need to know how leisure activities vary across ethnic groups, how activity patterns may change with changing population demographics, and how economic factors influence which activities are realistically possible for people to pursue.

Concept Checks

1. What are the important life-cycle factors in understanding leisure?
2. How can leisure activities be classified?
3. What age differences have been noted in leisure activities?
4. What benefits do people derive from leisure activities?

Retiring from one's occupation is an opportunity for celebration with one's co-workers of all ages, which is one reason it serves as a marker event in people's lives.

RETIREMENT

Learning Objectives:

- How is retirement defined?
- What influences people's decisions to retire?
- How should people prepare for retirement?
- How well do most people adjust to retirement?
- How does retirement affect relationships with family, friends, and community?

Most people probably take it for granted that someday, after working for many productive years, they will retire. But until 1935, when Social Security was inaugurated, retirement was rarely even considered by most Americans. Only since World War II have there been a substantial number of retired people in the United States. Today, the number is increasing rapidly, and the notion that people work a specified time and then retire is built into our expectations about work.

The enactment of Social Security and the advent of various pension and savings plans have been accompanied by profound changes in attitudes toward retirement. Most people now view it as a right—a rather interesting view considering that work has long been considered virtually a moral obligation. It is this curious juxtaposition that makes retirement a very interesting topic.

As the number of retirees increases, several issues will be thrust to the forefront. Among them are early retirement, retirement planning, educational and work options for retirees, and health care for these individuals. We will explore many of these issues, as well as attitudes toward retirement and adjustment to it. But the first step in reaching these insights is to achieve a reasonably clear definition of it.

Defining Retirement

Like leisure, retirement is difficult to define. One way to look at retirement is to equate it with complete withdrawal from the workforce. But this definition is inadequate; many retired people continue to work part time. Another possibility would be to define retirement as a self-described state. However, this definition will not work either, because some African Americans never define themselves as "retired" (Gibson, 1987, 1991).

The most useful way to view retirement is as a complex process by which people withdraw from full-time participation in an occupation (Elder & Pavalko, 1993). The complexity of the retirement process must be acknowledged for us to understand what retirement means to people in different ethnic groups. For example, although middle-class European Americans often use a criterion of full-time employment to define themselves as retired or not, Mexican Americans use any of several different criteria depending on how the question is asked (Zsembik & Singer, 1990). We can approach our definition of retirement in three ways: as a process, as a paradox, and as a change.

Retirement as a Process

The process of retirement begins as soon as one thinks about what life after employment might be like. More thinking usually leads to some sort of planning, even if it is only to check with one's employer about available financial benefits such as Social Security or pension funds. (We will discuss the planning process in a later section).

Retirement as a Paradox

Retirement involves the loss of two very important things that we derive from work: income and status. We might assume that losing these key aspects of one's life would be reflected in poor adjustment. The paradox of retirement is that despite these losses the majority of retirees say that they are satisfied; they like and enjoy being retired.

Retirement as a Change

Retirement involves change in almost every aspect of life. On the surface, such monumental change may appear overwhelming. But retirees have an advantage that is often overlooked. By the time they retire, they have already experienced several disruptive life transitions such as marriage, children leaving home, or moving; what they have learned from previous events provides the basis for adjusting to retirement. Clearly, retirement is complex.

The Changing Nature of Retirement

Although these three ways of defining retirement provide considerable insight into its complexity, we must also recognize that things concerning retirement are changing rapidly. Just as there is fundamental change occurring in the definition of work, so too are similar changes occurring in the definition of retirement. More individuals in their post-retirement years are working in part-time jobs, primarily to supplement their incomes, but also to maintain adequate levels of activity. Many older adults are also involved in volunteering their time to many different organizations.

The need for some older adults to continue working is becoming more formally recognized. For example, one senior center in Wilmington, Delaware, offers job-training programs for older workers. These programs prepare workers for a variety of jobs that provide a way for them to earn a living. Some corporations, such as McDonald's, actively recruit older workers because of their reputation for reliability and responsibility. Indeed, roughly a third of recent retirees report being partially retired (or partially employed) at some point, but their employment is usually in low-paying jobs taken out of economic necessity (Quinn & Burkhauser, 1990).

As more people anticipate longer periods of retirement, and with the virtual removal of all mandatory retirement, one interesting research question will be whether more individuals will choose to continue working if possible. The numbers of employed older adults may also increase if people's financial status is insufficient to support them if they retire. Indeed, much debate occurred in the mid-1990s about the long-term viability of the Social Security system; if this system changes dramatically, it would have a major effect on decisions to retire. As the baby-boom generation approaches retirement age, examination of such programs will increase, as will debates about the proper time to retire. As you consider the issues in

DISCOVERING DEVELOPMENT

Are You "Retired"?

We noted in the text that retirement can be defined from at least three main perspectives and that the changing nature of work is also creating changes in how retirement is viewed. Try finding evidence of these changes in your own community. Pay a visit to a local senior center and talk with some of the older members who worked their entire adult lives for the same company. See how well they fit into the aspects of work and retirement discussed in the chapter. Then talk with some people who accepted "early retirement" buyouts from corporations as part of a downsizing effort. See how their work careers differed from the older individuals' careers. Try to get a sense of how these people view themselves—as retirees, or as something else. Share your results with the class and discuss their implications for future generations of workers.

the following sections, you should recognize that new views on the role and nature of retirement are emerging that may force us to reconsider issues that had previously been thought to be settled. You can see this for yourself by doing the Discovering Development exercise.

Deciding to Retire

The decision to retire is an intensely personal one that involves carefully weighing several factors. Overall, more workers retire by choice than for any other reason (Henretta, Chan, & O'Rand, 1992). Usually, these individuals retire when, considering projected income from Social Security, pension plans, and personal savings, they feel financially secure.

Of course, other people do not retire by choice. For some, this is due to corporate downsizing and involves accepting a buyout package (Henretta et al., 1992). For the rest of the people who do not retire on their own terms, the major predictors of the decision to retire—such as health, financial status, and attitudes toward retirement—have remained relatively constant for several decades. However, there are some important differences involving gender and ethnicity.

Health and Financial Security

One of the most important influences on retirement decisions is health, regardless of whether one is approaching mandatory retirement. Clark and Spengler (1980) report that poor health is one of the two main reasons that people retire early; financial security is the other (Ward, 1984a, 1984b). The importance of health cuts across ethnic group lines, especially in terms of early retirement. For example, health problems causing functional impairment is the main reason European Americans, African Americans, and Mexican Americans retire early (Stanford, Happersett, Morton, Molgaard, & Peddecord, 1991).

Feeling secure financially is another extremely important factor in deciding to retire. Many people have plans that involve money, such as traveling, and most would like to maintain their lifestyle. Many corporations offer preretirement planning programs that provide advice about this topic.

Attitudes Toward Retirement

People with rewarding jobs typically do not look forward to retirement as much as do people with unrewarding jobs. For example, blue-collar workers tend to desire retirement (as long as they have enough money) but professionals and self-employed people may not. Being autonomous and having responsibility in a job is associated with more negative attitudes toward retirement (Barfield & Morgan, 1978; Streib & Schneider, 1971).

Attitudes toward retirement for those in middle level jobs, including clerical and service personnel, are best predicted by income. Workers with high incomes and those who have good pension plans are most favorable about retirement. This relationship is so strong and holds for such a wide range of middle level jobs that some writers believe that it is the relationship between workers and money, not that between people and work, that should be researched (Shanas, 1972).

Educational level is another important predictor of attitudes, but the connection is complex. For men, it appears that more education is accompanied by more negative feelings, but this could be due to the likelihood that such men are in more autonomous jobs (Sheppard, 1976). The evidence is contradictory for women. Sheppard (1976) reports that the most highly educated women are positive about retiring and do so earlier. On the contrary, Streib and Schneider (1971) found that women with higher incomes, better education, and higher status jobs tended to continue working longer. Clearly, more research is needed to sort out the relationship between education and retirement attitudes, especially for women.

Age and cohort differences also influence attitudes. At one time many believed that younger workers were more favorably disposed to retirement than older workers (Atchley, 1976). Contradictory evidence has been reported, however; Barfield and Morgan (1978) found that older cohorts were more favorably disposed to retire. These differences may reflect two changes in attitudes about retirement. First, workers may be becoming more receptive to the idea that employment does not last forever. It should be remembered that retirees who participated in earlier studies had largely begun working before retirement was commonplace. Second, many researchers have changed their assumption that retirement is "a major disruption of an adult's role and would tend to have deleterious consequences for the individual" (Streib & Schneider, 1971, p. 5). Rather, many investigators are viewing retirement simply as another normative life transition to which most people adjust positively.

Gender

Although most research on retirement decisions has focused on men, some work has examined women. George, Fillenbaum, and Palmore (1984) found that a married woman's decision to retire is predicted by her age and her husband's working, not by characteristics of her occupation. Campione (1987) found that a woman's decision to retire was related not only to her husband's wages but also to her own financial status independent of her husband. These discrepant findings may be due to changing demographics. That is, only in the past few years have women remained in the workforce long enough to make the decision to retire based on their own wage history and financial security.

Ethnicity

Little research has been conducted on retirement decisions as a function of ethnicity. Important differences among ethnic groups about retirement are being uncovered, however, which emphasize the need for more research. As pointed out earlier, African Americans may not label themselves as "retired" for many reasons—from socialization to the need to adopt the disability role in order to maximize their benefits (Gibson, 1987, 1991). Because many African Americans do not have the financial or other resources to retire and must continue to work into old age, researchers have often excluded them.

A few investigators have examined the characteristics of retired African Americans (Gibson, 1986, 1987; Irelan & Bell, 1972; J. S. Jackson & Gibson, 1985; Murray, 1979). These studies show that African Americans often do not decide to retire, because many may not have an occupation to retire from. Instead, they appear to label themselves as either "retired" or "unretired" based on subjective disability, work history, and source of income. An important finding is that gender differences appear to be absent among African Americans; men and women base their self-labels on the same variables. Thus, findings based on European American samples must not be generalized to African Americans, and separate theoretical models for African Americans may be needed (Gibson, 1987). The same is undoubtedly true for other ethnic groups as well.

Planning for Retirement

What do people need to do to plan for retirement? Is it just a matter of saving money? Or do people need to take psychological factors into account as well? Can prospective retirees anticipate and avoid some of the difficulties? For example, one common problem in adjusting to the retirement role is the abruptness of the transition from employment to unemployment. What processes might minimize the difficulties of this change?

One key element to successful retirement is preparation (Kamouri & Cavanaugh, 1986). Getting ready can take several forms: conscious or unconscious planning, informal or formal steps, and so on. **One formal way to prepare for retirement is to participate in a *preretirement education program.*** Such programs cover a wide variety of topics, from financial planning to adjustment; a typical content list is contained in Table 11.3. Campione (1988) found that men who do some preparing on their own, who are married and have families to plan for, who are healthy, and who have high occupational status are more likely to participate in formal preretirement programs. This profile reflects a strong bias in program participants; lower income, minority individuals are not represented.

Every comprehensive planning program for retirement focuses on two key aspects: finances and attitudes. We will consider some of the ramifications of each.

TABLE 11.3 Topics in a typical preretirement education program

I. Deciding to retire: When is the right time?
II. Psychological aspects of aging
   A. Work roles and retirement
   B. Personal identity issues
   C. Retirement as a process, paradox, and change
   D. Effects on relationships with family and friends
III. Finances
   A. Social Security
   B. Pension
   C. Insurance
   D. Employment
IV. Legal aspects
   A. Wills
   B. Personal rights as senior citizens
V. Health
   A. Normal aging
   B. Medicare and Medicaid
   C. Issues in health insurance
VI. Where to live: the pros and cons of moving
VII. Leisure time activities
   A. Travel
   B. Hobbies
   C. Clubs and organizations
   D. Educational opportunities
   E. Volunteering

Finances

Retirement, on average, involves a 50% reduction in income (Foner & Schwab, 1981). Obviously, if one is not prepared for this degree of income loss, financial pressures will be severe. Financial planning is necessary on several levels. First, most people are part of mandatory retirement plans such as Social Security. Although planning ends here for the majority of people, it is not enough. Many people also draw on pension plans provided by their employer. If possible, individuals should also save funds in anticipation of income loss, such as in individual retirement accounts. However, the majority of American workers cannot set aside sufficient funds to carry them through their retirement years in the lifestyle they enjoyed before retirement.

Professionals who have the ability to plan for retirement tend to do it similarly, even across some ethnic groups. For example, African American professionals tend to use financial planning strategies very similar to European American professionals (Richardson & Kilty, 1989).

Attitudes

Aside from finances, one's attitudes about retirement probably have the most important effect on satisfaction (Foner & Schwab, 1981). Even if it only involves thinking about when to retire and looking forward to it, developing a positive attitude is central to more rapid adjustment to and enjoyment of retirement (Barfield & Morgan, 1978; Kimmel, Price, & Walker, 1978). More formal preparation, such as participation in preretirement programs, is associated with more positive attitudes (Friedman & Orbach, 1974), but this relationship may be due to the fact that people who already hold favorable attitudes are the most likely to plan.

The relationship between attitudes and participation in preretirement programs has been addressed by Kamouri and Cavanaugh (1986). They compared four groups of workers: retired workers who had participated in a preretirement program, retired workers who had not participated, employees in a preretirement program, and employees on the waiting list for a program. Kamouri and Cavanaugh found that workers who had the benefit of a program had a more realistic view of retirement than those who had not participated. The main benefit of participating in a preretirement program seemed to be realistic expectations that could be translated into a more positive attitude in the first few years of retirement. After about 3 years of retirement people who had not participated in the program were comparable in their attitudes to those who had, but they did note that their initial experiences had not been what they had expected.

Adjustment to Retirement

Everyone agrees on one point about retirement: It is a life transition that produces stress. Successful retirement requires responding to the challenges it presents and having a supportive network of relatives and friends. New patterns of involvement must be developed in the context of changing roles and lifestyles (Antonovsky & Sagy, 1990). Before considering the research on whether people usually find retirement satisfying, we will look at three theoretical frameworks that help put the literature into perspective: work styles, values, and continuity.

Work Styles

One way to conceptualize adjustment to retirement is by examining different combinations of work styles and lifestyles. Lowenthal (1972) suggests that past behavior and attitudes during their employment years influence people's adjustment to retirement. Thus, individuals who have always been strongly work oriented—viewing work as an end in itself—will be most likely to consider retirement traumatic. Lowenthal argues that unless highly work-oriented people find a substitute for work, retirement may be an unpleasant experience for them.

People who are less strongly oriented toward work as a means to social acceptance may view retirement as a crisis, but they will eventually adjust. Lowenthal suggests that these instrumental, other-directed people may need to find a substitute for work, but usually this need is only temporary.

Three other groups complete Lowenthal's classification: the receptive-nurturant type, the autonomous type, and the self-protective type. Receptive-nurturant people are typically women who have lifelong commitments to emotional goals and intimacy. For them, the quality of the relationship with their partners is the key to adjustment in retirement. Provided the relationship is perceived as solid, retirement should present little difficulty.

Many autonomous individuals are in occupations that allow them to decide when to retire. These people present a complex pattern of creativity, varied goals, and self-generativity. If retirement is voluntary, little disruption should be expected; however, mandatory retirement may lead to depression until reorientation is achieved.

Finally, the self-protective person often sees nothing special about retirement; it is simply another chapter in a life full of struggles. Dependency on or responsibility for others is not allowed. These individuals have always been detached or disengaged. As long as retirement does not require radical change, it does not produce a crisis.

Lowenthal's approach clearly allows for a wide variety of possibilities. One common theme across the different types is that a redistribution of energy may be needed for successful adjustment to retirement; this change is reminiscent of the reevaluations that occurred earlier in development. Indeed, enduring aspects of personality and lifestyle are useful in predicting adjustment to retirement (Maas & Kuypers, 1974; Neugarten, 1977).

Values

A second theoretical framework, suggested by Atchley (1976), is compatible with Lowenthal's. Atchley proposes that how the individual views the role of the job in his or her life determines the extent to which retirement is a crisis. If the job fulfills goals not achieved by other activities and if it is considered important throughout adulthood, retirement will demand a major reorganization of one's values. However, if one's goals have been attained or if one's job was never considered of primary importance, little reorganization will be necessary. Atchley agrees with Lowenthal in concluding that strongly job-oriented people seek substitutes for work or even second occupations after retiring; these individuals are not able to reorganize their lives enough otherwise.

Continuity

As we have seen, retirement involves important decisions. Atchley (1989) argues that any time middle-aged and older adults make adaptive choices, they attempt to build on the past. In other words, adults try to maintain continuity. Atchley believes this continuity occurs in two domains: internal and external. Internal continuity occurs when one wants to preserve some aspect of oneself from the past, such as a specific personality trait or a skill, so that one's past is sustaining and supporting one's new self. External continuity involves maintaining social relationships, roles, and environments, such as living in the same neighborhood. To the extent that internal and external continuity are maintained, satisfaction with retirement is likely to be high.

Satisfaction

Once people retire, do they like it? The evidence suggests that they do. However, an interesting and important historical shift has been seen in the research findings. Numerous national cross-sectional surveys conducted from the 1950s to the late 1970s documented that as long as income and health were maintained adequately, satisfaction with retirement was high (for example, Barfield & Morgan, 1978; Streib & Schneider, 1971).

By 1980, however, retirees' responses had begun to change; a significantly higher proportion of them, although generally satisfied with retirement, felt that they would prefer to work. These findings reflect retirees' increased concern over financial security. Indeed, two findings support this conclusion. First, the increase during the 1970s in the proportion of retirees preferring to work paralleled the increase in the inflation rate in the United States. Second, retirees not collecting pensions were more likely to want to work than retirees on pensions.

In sum, little evidence supports the stereotypical view of retirement as leading inevitably to poor adjustment. On the contrary, research since the 1950s has shown consistently that most people are satisfied with retirement living. Although an increasing number of people express a desire to work, this response comes largely from financial pressures and not from a fundamental dislike for retirement. Positive adjustment outcomes do not imply, however, that reorganization and change are unnecessary. Such changes are vital to maintaining one's psychological well-being. Reorientation occurs in most aspects of one's life; we will examine three contexts in the next section: family, friends, and community.

Family, Friends, and Community

Retirement rarely affects only a single individual. No matter how personal the joys and sorrows of retirement may be, retirees' reactions are influenced by the social environment of their family, friends, and community. These social ties help us deal with the stresses of retirement, as they do in other life transitions. A long history of research verifies that social relationships help cushion the effect of life stress throughout adulthood. This support takes many forms: letting people know that they are loved; offering help if needed; providing advice; taking care of others' needs; just being there to listen. We should expect retirees who have close and strong social ties to have an advantage in dealing with change.

Family

Much attention has been focused on the role of intimate and family relationships in adjusting to retirement. Marriage has provided the framework for almost all of this work. Ideally, marital partners provide mutual support during the transition to retirement. Whether marriage actually serves this function is unclear. The few studies specifically dealing with the connection between marital status and satisfaction with retirement provide conflicting results. Some evidence suggests that never-married retirees are as satisfied as married retirees, whereas divorced, separated, or widowed retirees are much less happy (Barfield & Morgan, 1978). Perhaps never-married people prefer singlehood and become accustomed to it long before retirement. Additionally, the difficulties encountered by those whose marriages were disrupted indirectly emphasize the stabilizing effects of marriage. But it seems that whatever relationship exists holds mainly for men; marital status alone has little effect on older women's satisfaction (Fox, 1979). Furthermore, we know almost nothing about the link between the quality of retirees' marriages and satisfaction with retirement.

Possible benefits aside, retirement undoubtedly has profound effects on intimate relationships. It often disrupts long-established patterns of family interaction, forcing both partners (and others living in the house) to adjust. Simply being together more puts strain on the relationship. Daily routines need rearrangement, which may be stressful.

One common change that confronts most retired couples is the division of household chores. Although retired men tend to do more work around the home than they did before retirement, this situation does not always lead to desirable outcomes (Ingraham, 1974). For example, an employed husband may compliment his wife on her domestic skills; after retirement, however, he may suddenly want to teach her to do it correctly. Part of the problem may be that such men are not used to taking orders about how chores are supposed to be done. One former executive told interviewers that before he retired, when he said "Jump!" highly paid employees wanted to know how high. "Now, I go home, I walk in the door and my wife says, 'Milton, take out the garbage.' I never saw so much garbage" (Quigley, 1979, p. 9). Finally, part of the problem may be in the perception of one's turf; after retirement men feel that they are thrust into doing things that they, and their partners, may have traditionally thought of as "women's work" (Troll, 1971).

Retirees maintain and may sometimes increase contact with their children, grandchildren, and other relatives. These contacts are viewed as an important component in retirees' lives. Still, independence between generations is associated with high satisfaction among retirees (Riley & Foner, 1968). This need for independence is underscored by the fact that visits with children sometimes have a depressing rather than a positive effect on older (65+) male retirees. Apparently, changing power relationships within the family are responsible; visiting children may serve to emphasize the father's loss of control over them.

Frequency of contact with other relatives does not appear to be related to life satisfaction among middle- and upper-middle-class retirees. That is, visiting relatives does not have negative effects, but it does not add to a retiree's overall satisfaction either (Lemon, Bengtson, & Peterson, 1972).

Friends

Intimate and family relationships are clearly important sources of support for retirees. However, they are not the only ones; friendship networks also provide support that often complements family networks. Friends sometimes provide types of

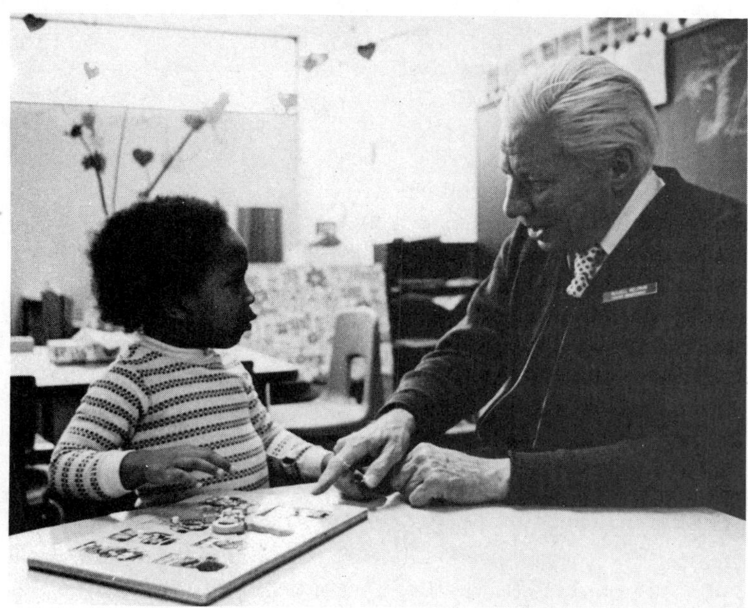

The Foster Grandparent Program, among others, provides a way for older adults to maintain meaningful personal roles.

support that, because of the strong emotional ties, families may be less able to offer: a compassionate, but objective listener; a companion for social and leisure activities; or a source of advice, transportation, and other assistance. The extent to which friends contribute to retirees' overall satisfaction is unclear, but seeing friends and having a confidant appears to be important (Lemon et al., 1972).

In general, neither the number nor the quality of friendships declines as a result of retirement (Bossé, Aldwin, Levenson, Spiro, & Mroczek, 1993). When friendships change during retirement, it is usually due to some other reason, such as very serious health problems, that interferes with people's ability to maintain friendships. We do need to bear in mind the gender differences in friendships we discussed in Chapter 10, though. Older men have fewer close personal friends for support than older women. This difference may help explain the gender difference between marital status and satisfaction discussed earlier. Men, because of their fewer close relationships, may be forced to rely more on their wives for support.

Community

Because social ties are generally related to retirees' satisfaction, an important consideration is whether the social environment facilitates continuing old ties and forming new ones. The past few decades have witnessed the rapid growth of organizations devoted to providing these opportunities to retirees. National associations such as the American Association of Retired Persons provide the chance to learn about what other retirees are doing and about services such as insurance and discounts. Numerous smaller groups exist at the community level; these include senior centers and clubs. Many trade unions also have programs for their retired members.

Another common way that retired adults maintain community ties is by volunteering. Older adults report that they volunteer to help them deal with life transitions (Adlersberg & Thorne, 1990), to maintain social interactions, and to better their communities (Morrow-Howell & Mui, 1989). There are many opportunities for retirees to help others. One federal agency, ACTION, administers four programs that have hundreds of local chapters: Foster Grandparents, Senior Companions, the Retired Senior Volunteer Program, and the Service Corps of Retired Executives. Nearly half of older adults aged 65 to 74 volunteer their services in some way, with substantial participation rates even among people over age 80 (Chambré, 1993). These rates represent more than a 400% increase since the mid-1960s, when only about 1 in 10 older adults did volunteer work. What accounts for this tremendous increase?

Several factors are responsible (Chambré, 1993): improved public perception of the skills and wisdom older adults have to offer, a redefinition of the nature and merits of volunteer work, a more highly educated population of older adults, and greatly expanded opportunities for people to become involved in volunteer work that they enjoy. Given the demographic trends of increased numbers and educational levels of older adults discussed in Chapter 13, even higher rates of voluntarism are expected during the next few decades (Chambré, 1993). These opportunities may be a way for society to tap into the vast resources that older adults offer as well as provide additional meaningful roles for older adults.

Concept Checks

1. What are the three main ways of defining retirement?
2. What are the major predictors of the decision to retire?
3. What is included in a preretirement education program?
4. Why are work styles, values, and continuity important in understanding how people adjust to retirement?
5. How do retirees interact with their communities?

SUMMARY

Occupational Choice and Development

Occupations and Careers

Occupations are a reflection of socialization into the work role. Five general levels of occupations can be distinguished: marginal, blue-collar, pink-collar, white-collar, and executives and professionals. The rise of a global economy is changing the nature of work, as organizations try to meet changing market factors rapidly and managers and workers must adopt different leadership styles and assume more autonomy.

Occupational Choice

Holland's theory is based on the idea that people choose occupations to optimize the fit between their individual traits and their occupational interests. Six personality types that represent different combinations of these have been identified; research supports the validity of this approach, although some gender differences have been found. Occupational choice is strongly influenced by what we think we would be good at, a variation of self-efficacy, and not necessarily what we actually are good at.

Occupational Priorities and Expectations

The things people want from their occupations are termed occupational priorities. Differences in occupational priorities have been noted over the past several decades. Periodic updating of occupational priorities is important. Reality shock is the realization that one's expectations about an occupation are different than the reality one experiences. Reality shock can occur in people of all ages.

The Role of Mentors

A mentor is a co-worker who teaches a new employee the unwritten rules and fosters occupational development. Being a mentor helps middle-aged workers achieve generativity. Mentor-protégé relationships develop over time through four stages, much like other relationships. Gender differences in the need for mentors and how the relationships develop have been noted.

Job Satisfaction

Older workers report higher job satisfaction than younger workers, but this may be partly due to self-selection; unhappy workers may quit. Other reasons include intrinsic satisfaction, good fit, lower importance of work, finding nonwork diversions, and life-cycle factors. Feeling that what one is doing is meaningless results in alienation; too much stress in one's occupation can lead to burnout. Providing more autonomy and flexibility addresses alienation; more appropriate expectations and communication addresses burnout.

Gender, Ethnicity, Bias, and Discrimination

Gender Differences in Occupational Choice

Men and women are socialized differently into occupational roles; men's socialization tends to be broader and more complete. Men may tend to overestimate their ability, whereas women may tend to downplay theirs and may sometimes be reluctant to pursue high-status occupations. Why some women choose nontraditional occupations appears to be related to personal feelings and experiences and to occupational expectations. Many women have difficulty finding occupations that match their level of skill. Women in nontraditional occupations are viewed more poorly by both men and women.

Women and Occupational Development

Traditionally, research on occupational development assumed that women did not have careers. Women in traditionally female careers tend not to change occupations. Women who leave well-paid occupations do so for many reasons, including family obligations (for women working part-time) and workplace issues (for women working full-time).

Ethnicity and Occupational Development

African American and European American women do not differ in plans to enter nontraditional occupations, but African American women plan for more education. Vocational identity varies with both gender and ethnicity; occupational aspirations vary across ethnic groups. Whether an organization is responsive to the needs of ethnic minorities makes a big difference for employees.

Bias and Discrimination

Sex discrimination remains the chief barrier to women's occupational development. Women and ethnic minorities face a glass ceiling, which limits how high they can rise in an organization. Pay inequity, expressed as comparable worth, is also a problem; women get paid a fraction of what men in similar jobs earn. Sexual harassment is a problem in many situations; the reasonable woman standard is used to decide whether an act constitutes harassment. Cultural bias operates in many ways, such as insensitivity to the values, language, customs, dress, food, and personal styles of different groups. Sometimes cultural bias is expressed as racism and discrimination. Making employment decisions only on the basis of age or denying employment or promotion is age discrimination if the worker is over age 40. Age discrimination occurs in many ways, such as differential layoff patterns and stereotypic views of older workers. Several other labor market barriers also exist for older workers.

Occupational Transitions

Factors Influencing Occupational Transitions

Important reasons people change occupations include personality, obsolescence, and economic factors. Layoffs are the primary impetus to change occupations.

Retraining Workers

Learning new skills is essential to maximizing one's opportunities. Career plateauing may result if one does not stay current. Retraining of midcareer and older workers is an example of the need for lifelong learning.

Loss of One's Job

Losing one's job is a traumatic event that can affect every aspect of a person's life, resulting in declines in physical health and self-esteem, depression, anxiety, and suicide. These effects are related to the degree of financial stress one is under and the timing of the job loss. Finding a new job one is satisfied with reverses these declines.

Dual-Earner Couples

Balancing Multiple Roles

Although men have increased the amount of time they spend on household tasks, women still do much more. Husbands and wives view the division of labor in very different terms. Ethnic differences are also apparent. Although many couples report feeling role conflict, most manage to solve the problem. However, time together as a couple often suffers. Work stress has a much bigger impact on family life than vice versa.

The Child Care Dilemma

The mere availability of a workplace child care center does not solve the dilemma. Sympathetic supervisors are essential to lowering the stress of how child care issues can be resolved.

Impact on Occupational Development

Wives are far more likely to interrupt their occupational development for their husbands than husbands are for their wives. Both mothers and fathers benefit from job flexibility that allows them to balance work and family obligations.

Leisure Activities

Leisure in the Life Cycle

Quality of activity rather than quantity is a key to understanding why people engage in particular leisure activities. Other important factors include changing sense of self and family interests.

Types of Leisure Activities

Leisure activities can be categorized in terms of cultural, physical, and social dimensions. People develop a repertoire of preferred leisure activities. Each activity has a different meaning and importance to every individual.

Developmental Changes in Leisure

The main reasons leisure activities change over adulthood are health or ability changes and self-perceptions. The variety of leisure activities also differs with age.

Correlates and Consequences of Leisure Activities

Men are more likely to engage in outdoor and sports activities whereas women are more likely to engage in cultural or home-based activities. People in retirement communities engage in more leisure activities. Leisure activities produce positive well-being.

Retirement

Defining Retirement

Retirement can be viewed as a process, as a paradox, and as change. Overall, it is a way in which people withdraw from full-time employment. Changing conceptions of work are resulting in changing conceptions of retirement.

Deciding to Retire

Most people retire by choice. For those who do not, the major predictors of retirement are health, financial status, attitudes toward retirement, gender, and ethnicity.

A growing number of people retire due to corporate downsizing. Attitudes toward retirement are influenced by income, education, age, and cohort.

Planning for Retirement

Preretirement education programs cover a variety of topics, including finances, attitudes, health, and expectations. Financial planning for retirement is essential. Realistic expectations toward retirement are important predictors of future satisfaction.

Adjustment to Retirement

People who are highly work oriented usually have a more difficult time with retirement than people who are less work oriented. Retirement can also be understood in terms of a reorientation of values and a need for continuity. Most people are satisfied with retirement.

Family, Friends, and Community

Retirement affects all types of relationships. It may disrupt long-term friendships and produce stress. However, contacts are maintained with children and may even increase. Friendship networks provide support that complements that received from family. Community participation options are increasing for retirees as more people do volunteer work and are employed part-time.

REVIEW QUESTIONS

Occupational choice and development

- What different types of occupations have been distinguished? What are the characteristics and status of each?
- How is work changing as a result of the global economy?
- Briefly describe Holland's theory linking personality and occupational choice. What personality types did Holland identify? How are they related to occupational fit?
- How is self-efficacy linked to occupational choice?
- What are occupational priorities and how do they change over time? How are these related to reality shock?
- What is a mentor? What role does a mentor play in occupational development?
- How does the mentor-protégé relationship change over time?
- What is the developmental course of job satisfaction? What factors influence job satisfaction?
- What are alienation and burnout? How are they related to job satisfaction?

Gender, ethnicity, bias, and discrimination

- What gender differences have been identified that relate to occupational choice? How do men and women differ in terms of rating their own abilities and skills?
- How are women in nontraditional occupations perceived?
- What are the major barriers to women's occupational development?
- What are the major barriers to occupational development related to ethnicity?
- How are sex discrimination and the glass ceiling related?
- What is comparable worth?
- How is sexual harassment defined?
- What is age discrimination and how does it operate?
- What are the main labor market barriers to older workers?

Occupational transitions

- What are the major reasons that people change occupations?
- Why is retraining workers important?
- What effects do people report after losing their jobs?

Dual-earner couples

- How do dual-earner couples balance multiple roles and deal with role conflict?
- What factors are important in child care for employees?
- What happens in dual-earner relationships when one partner is offered a promotion that involves a move? What other occupational development effects occur?

Leisure activities

- What are the major reasons people engage in leisure activities? What benefits occur?

- What kinds of leisure activities do people perform?
- How do leisure activities change over the life span?
- What gender differences are there in leisure activities?

Retirement

- In what ways can retirement be viewed? What changes in the definition of retirement may occur in the next several years?
- What are the main predictors of the decision to retire? What predicts attitudes toward retirement?
- What steps should people take to prepare for retirement?
- How do people adjust to being retired?
- What effects does retirement have on relationships with family, friends, and community?

INTEGRATING CONCEPTS IN DEVELOPMENT

1. What role do personal relationships play in one's work, leisure, and retirement?
2. How does cognitive development and personality influence work roles?
3. What implications are there for the removal of mandatory retirement in terms of normal cognitive changes with age?

KEY TERMS

age discrimination Denying employment or promotion to someone on the basis of age. Age discrimination is illegal in the United States.

alienation The feeling that results when workers feel that what they are doing is worthless and that their efforts are devalued, or when they do not see the connection between what they do and the final product.

burnout The feeling that results when the pace and the pressure of one's occupation becomes more than one can bear, causing a depletion of a person's energy and motivation.

career plateauing The lack of promotional opportunity from the organization or the person's decision not to seek advancement.

comparable worth The notion that people should be paid equally for similar work regardless of gender.

glass ceiling An invisible but real barrier to the occupational development of women and minorities that allows them to advance to a certain level in an organization and no higher.

job satisfaction How happy one is with one's job.

mentor A person who teaches the informal rules of an organization.

occupational priorities The reasons why one works, and how they are viewed by an individual.

preretirement education program A program aimed at educating workers about the broad range of issues they will face in retirement, including health, adjustment, and finances.

reality shock A term representing the realization that the real world does not work like a textbook.

reasonable woman standard The appropriate basis for defining sexual harassment; defined as the standard by which a reasonable woman would consider a behavior as offensive.

role conflict A clash between competing or incompatible sets of roles, most often seen in work versus family settings.

sex discrimination Denying a person a position or a promotion solely on the basis of gender.

IF YOU'D LIKE TO LEARN MORE

Crosby, F. (1991). *Juggling: The unexpected advantages of balancing career and home for women, their families and society.* New York: Free Press. Intriguing discussion of balancing multiple roles of work and family. Moderately difficult.

Feather, N.T. (1990). *The psychological impact of unemployment.* New York: Springer-Verlag. One of the best scholarly discussions of unemployment. Moderately difficult.

Gerson, K. (1993). *No man's land: Men's changing commitments to family and work.* New York: Basic Books. Based on a series of life history interviews, this book gives a male perspective on balancing work and family. Easy reading.

Keita, G.P., & Hurrell, J.J., Jr. (Eds.). (1994). *Job stress in a changing workforce.* Washington, DC: American Psychological Association. A wide-ranging discussion of issues including diversity, culture, ethnicity, age, and role conflict. Easy to moderately difficult depending on the chapter.

Palmore, E. (Ed.). (1986). *Retirement: Causes and consequences.* New York: Springer. An overview of the issues relating to retirement. Moderate to difficult.

CHAPTER 12

Where We Live

Grandma Moses, *Moving Day on the Farm*, 1951. Copyright ©1987, Grandma Moses Properties Co., New York.

Let me introduce you to Henry. Henry, or as his friends call him, Hank, has lived in the same neighborhood all of his 75 years. He grew up only a block or so from where he lives now, which is where he moved 53 years ago when he married Marilyn. Hank and Marilyn raised five children in their modest three bedroom rowhouse; two still live across the city but the other three are scattered across the country. Hank has been living alone for the past several months, ever since Marilyn suffered a stroke and had to be placed in a nursing home. Hank's oldest daughter has been concerned about her father and has been pressing him to move in with her. Hank is reluctant—he likes knowing his neighbors, shopping in familiar stores, and being able to do what he wants. And he wonders how well he could adapt to living in a new neighborhood after all these years. He realizes that it might be easier for him to cope if he lived with his daughter, but it's a tough decision.

Hank's dilemma drives home an important point. People do not live in a vacuum; they live in environments. As perfectly obvious as this statement seems, it has only been in the last few decades that the living environments in which people operate have been studied systematically. And it is only more recently that researchers in adult development have given them much thought. **The principle concern in the field of *environmental psychology* has been the interaction of people with the communities or other settings in which they live.** The basic assumption is that "a person's behavioral and psychological state can be better understood with knowledge of the context in which the person behaves" (Lawton, 1980, p. 2). In other words, Hank's problem and the decision he needs to make can be understood better if we do not isolate his cognitive processes from the context and neighborhood in which his decision making takes place.

In this chapter we will see how differences in the interaction between personal characteristics and the living environment can have profound effects on our behavior and our feelings about ourselves. Several theoretical frameworks will be described that can help us understand how to interpret person-environment interactions in a developmental context. We will consider the communities and neighborhoods that influence us and that partially determine whether we will be happy. Similarly, there are several aspects of housing that play important roles in our lives. Because some people do not live in the community, we will take a close look at long-term care facilities, especially nursing homes. Finally, we will look at people on the move and examine the effects of community-based and institutional relocation. Even though we must sometimes consider the person separately from the environment, keep in mind throughout the chapter that in the end it is the interaction of the two that we want to understand.

Examining person-environment interactions highlights several important aspects of the basic forces of development. Where one lives is influenced by a host of variables: age, gender, ethnicity, physical health, mental health, finances, and availability of social support or a caregiver, to mention only a few. Many of these factors (such as gender) are ones we tend to overlook. Over the course of the chapter, we will specifically examine these influences in detail.

THEORIES OF PERSON-ENVIRONMENT INTERACTIONS

Learning Objectives:

- What is the competence and environmental press model?
- What is the congruence model?
- What are the major aspects of stress and coping theory relating to person-environment interactions?
- What is the loss-continuum concept?
- What are the common themes in the theories of person-environment interactions?

To appreciate the roles that different environments play in our lives, we need a framework for interpreting how people interact with them. Theories of person-environment interactions help us understand how individuals view their environments and how these views may change as people age. Because the field of environmental psychology has only recently been approached from a developmental perspective, few theories are well thought out (Scheidt & Windley, 1985). We will consider four that have received the most attention: competence and environmental press, congruence, stress and coping, and the loss-continuum concept.

All these theories can be traced to a common beginning. Many years ago Kurt Lewin (1936) conceptualized person-environment interactions in the equation B equals $f(P, E)$. **This relationship defining *person-environment interactions* means that behavior (*B*) is a function of both the person (*P*) and the environment (*E*).** Recent theorists have taken Lewin's equation and described the components in the equation in more detail. Specifically, their speculations concern what it is about people and about environments that combine to form behavior.

Most of these models emphasize the importance of people's perceptions of their environments. That is, although objective aspects of environments (for example, crime, housing quality) are important, personal choice plays a major role. For example, many people deliberately choose to live in New York or Atlanta, even though crime rates in those cities are higher than in Selma or Walla Walla, and they have an opportunity to live in any of these locations. The importance of personal perception in environments is similar to the role of personal perception in cognitive theories of personality (see Chapter 8) and in concepts such as personal control. As we will see, these ideas, especially the notion of personal control, have been included in many approaches to understanding person-environment interactions.

Competence and Environmental Press

One way to express the person-environment interaction is by focusing on competence and environmental press (Lawton, 1982; Lawton & Nahemow, 1973). ***Competence* is defined as the theoretical upper limit of an individual's capacity to function.** Lawton and Nahemow (1973) believe that competence involves five domains: biological health, sensory-perceptual functioning, motor skills, cognitive skills, and ego strength. These domains are thought to underlie all other abilities, and they are lifelong. Unfortunately, the components of competence are not easy to measure. The problem is that most measures of the components involve the environment in some way. As noted in Chapter 3, for example, biological health is strongly related to the type of environment in which we live. Thus, in most research one must settle for a rough approximation of a person's true competence.

Environments can be classified on the basis of the varying demands that they place on the individual, a notion termed *environmental press.* Lawton borrowed the concept of environmental press from Murray (1938). The demands that environments put on people (environmental press) can be any combination of three types: physical, interpersonal, or social. Physical demands include such things as having to walk three flights of stairs to one's apartment. Interpersonal demands include the various pressures we feel to get along with other people. Social demands include such things as the local laws or social customs that affect our lives.

Lawton and Nahemow's (1973) model is a combination of these ideas. They assert that behavior is a result of a person of a particular competence level acting in an environment of a specific press level. Furthermore, behavior is placed on a continuum from positive to negative and is thought to be manifested at two levels—as observable behavior and as affect, or feelings. Each of these elements is represented schematically in Figure 12.1.

Low to high competence is represented in the figure on the vertical axis, and the horizontal axis represents weak to strong press level. Points in the graph show various combinations of person-environment interactions. Most important, the shaded areas demonstrate that adaptive behavior and positive affect result from many different combinations of competence and press levels, not just one. As one moves farther away from these areas—due to a change in press level, for example—behavior becomes increasingly maladaptive, and affect becomes more negative. Notice that maladaptive behavior and negative affect also result from many combinations of competence and press levels. **Finally, the darkly shaded area labeled *adaptation level* represents points where press is average for particular levels of competence.** The adaptation level is where behavior and affect are normal, so we are usually unaware of them. Awareness increases as we move away from adaptation level.

As an example of Lawton and Nahemow's model, consider Rick. Rick works in a store in an area of Omaha, Nebraska, where the crime rate is moderately high, representing a moderate level of environmental press. Because he is very good at self-defense, he has high competence; thus, he manages to cope. Because the Omaha police chief wants to lower the crime rate in that area, he increases patrols, thereby lowering the press level. If Rick maintains his high competence, maladaptive behavior may result because he has more competence than is optimal for the new environment. But if instead of the police a street gang moved in, he would have to increase his competence and be more prepared in order to maintain his adaptation level. Other changes in the environment (such as arson threats) or in his competence (such as a broken arm) would create other combinations.

Before leaving Lawton and Nahemow's model, we need to note an important implication that it has for aging. The less competent the individual is, the greater the impact of environmental factors. To the extent that individuals experience declines in health, sensory processes, motor skills, cognitive

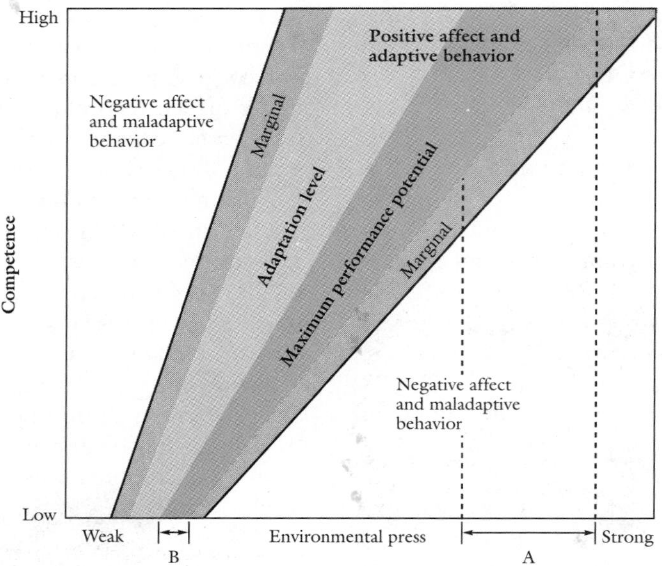

Figure 12.1 Behavioral and affective outcomes of person-environment interactions based on the competence–environmental press model. This figure indicates that an individual of high competence will show maximum performance over a larger range of environmental situations than will a less competent person. The range of optimal environments occurs at a higher level of environmental press (A) for the most competent person than it does for the least competent person (B).

Source: "Ecology and the Aging Process," by M. P. Lawton and L. Nahemow. In C. Eisdorfer and M. P. Lawton (Eds.), The Psychology of Adult Development and Aging, p. 661. *Copyright ©1973 by the American Psychological Association. Reprinted with permission.*

skills, or ego strength, they will be less able to cope with environmental demands. Thus, for older adults to maintain good adaptational levels, either changes to lower environmental press or interventions to raise competence would need to be undertaken. This point is made clearer in the Discovering Development feature. Take some time and complete it.

The Congruence Model

Kahana's (1982) congruence model includes the ideas of competence and environmental press, but it applies to them differently. In Kahana's view people vary in their needs, and environments differ in their ability to satisfy them. **According to the *congruence model,* people with particular needs search for the environments that will meet them best.** To the extent that a match exists, the individual feels content and satisfied; when a mismatch occurs, stress and discomfort result.

Congruence between the person and the environment is especially important when either individual or environmental options are limited. Limitations can occur for three reasons: (1) environmental characteristics are restricted, such as when public transportation is unavailable for going

DISCOVERING DEVELOPMENT

What's Your Adaptation Level?

Lawton and Nahemow's competence and environmental press model has wide applicability, as the example of Rick in the text indicates. It provides an excellent introduction to the importance of considering both people's capabilities and the environmental demands made of them. To understand the way the model works, consider yourself. Make a list of the different aspects of your life, such as school, social activities, work, and so forth. Think about each of these areas, and rate yourself in terms of your abilities. For example, in the case of school, consider each course you are taking and rate how capable you are in each. Then consider the number and kinds of demands made on you in each area. For instance, in the case of school, think about the many demands put on you in each course. Now look at how your rating of your competence intersects with the kinds and number of demands. Does it place you in the position of feeling bored? In this case, you would fall in the left side of the depiction of the model. Are you feeling stressed out and under pressure? Then you would fall on the right side of the figure. Feeling just about right? You've experienced your adaptation level. Doing this analysis on the various aspects of your life may help you understand why you feel more competent in some areas than in others.

shopping; (2) an individual's freedom is limited, such as when he or she must always eat at the same time every day; and (3) one believes that one has limited freedom, such as when one thinks that there is no way to get around despite a reliable bus system. Restricted environments are exemplified most clearly by long-term care facilities such as nursing homes and hospitals. Limits on individual freedom can result from age-related declines in competence. Self-perceptions of limited freedom reflect the belief that one's life is controlled by external forces, in the ways described in Chapter 9.

When applied specifically to the older adult, Kahana's congruence model shows that several points should be considered for optimizing the person-environment fit (Kahana & Kahana, 1983). One must consider not only the kind of situation, such as whether the person is in a single-family, congregate, or institutional living arrangement, but personal factors as well. Personal factors are very important because people vary in their needs. Some of us value autonomy and independence highly, for example, whereas others place less importance on them. We must be careful when designing programs and interventions for adults to take these individual differences into account. Otherwise, we may unintentionally increase the discrepancy between the person and the environment, resulting in increases in stress for the people we intended to help.

Kahana's model is especially useful when considering issues in institutional settings such as nursing homes and hospitals. Indeed, most of the research that has examined issues such as autonomy has been done in long-term care facilities (Collopy, 1988; Hofland, 1988). This makes sense when one realizes that it is in these settings that difficult decisions are most often made that involve trade-offs between personal freedom and institutional requirements (Collopy, 1988). We will return to Kahana's congruence model later when we focus on nursing homes.

Stress and Coping Theory

Schooler (1982) has applied Lazarus's cognitive theory of stress and coping, described in Chapter 4, to the understanding of the older person's interaction with the environment. The basic premise of Lazarus's theory is that people evaluate situations to assess their potential threat value. Situations may be evaluated as harmful, beneficial, or irrelevant. When situations are viewed as harmful or threatening, people also establish the range of coping responses that they have at their disposal for removing the harmful situation. This process results in making a coping response. Outcomes of coping may be positive or negative depending on many contextual factors.

Schooler (1982) argues that this perspective is especially helpful in understanding older adults because of their increased vulnerability to social and physical hazards. To test his ideas, Schooler evaluated retest data on a sample of 521 people drawn from a national sample of 4,000 older adults living in long-term care facilities. In particular, he examined the impact of three potential stressors (environmental change, residential mobility, and major life events) on health or morale. He also examined the buffering, or protective, effects of social support systems and ecological factors on the relationships among the stressors and outcomes. Consistent with the theory, Schooler showed that the presence of social support systems affected the likelihood that particular situations would be defined as threatening. For example, living alone is more likely to be viewed as stressful when one has little social support than when one has many friends who live nearby.

Schooler's work provides an important theoretical addition because it deals with the relation between everyday environmental stressors and the adaptive responding of community-dwelling individuals. However, he admits that more research needs to be done, especially in the area of understanding how the threat-appraisal process varies with age across different environmental contexts.

The Loss-Continuum Concept

Pastalan (1982) views aging as a progressive series of losses that reduce one's social participation. **This *loss continuum* includes children leaving, loss of social roles, loss of income, death of spouse or close friends and relatives, loss of sensory acuity, and loss of mobility due to poorer health.** Because these losses reduce people's ability to partake fully in community resources, their own home and immediate neighborhood take on far greater importance. This increase in importance means that older adults are especially sensitive to even small environmental changes (Regnier, 1983; Rowles & Ohta, 1983).

The importance of the immediate neighborhood in the loss-continuum concept is illustrated by the fact that a one-block radius around homes in cities is critical. Beyond this radius the rate at which older people make trips for shopping or other purposes drops sharply (Silverman, 1987). Consequently, well-planned environmental changes, even those on a small scale, can have significant payoffs for older adults. Pastalan (1982) himself views his approach as less a theory than a guide to practical change to facilitate the maintenance of competence and independence of older adults.

Common Theoretical Themes

The four theories we have considered have much in common. Most important, all of them agree that the focus must be on the interaction between the person and the environment, not on one or the other. Another important common theme is that no one environment will meet everyone's needs. Rather, a range of potential environments may be optimal.

As noted earlier, however, the study of person-environment interactions is very new and is not well systematized. Researchers do not agree on the set of environmental factors that must be accounted for or on which set of personal needs must be met for optimal satisfaction. They are also not sure whether developmental changes occur in person-environment interactions (Rowles & Ohta, 1983). Such transitions would be expected based on life-cycle forces, but this approach has generally not been used in person-environment research (Silverman, 1987). However, one thing is clear: Older people require a broad range of living environments to satisfy their personal needs.

Concept Checks

1. Define the following terms: competence, environmental press, and adaptation level.
2. What are the basic components of the congruence model?

3. What are the main aspects of Schooler's stress and coping theory?
4. What is the loss-continuum concept?
5. What common themes can be identified in the various theories of person-environment interaction?

COMMUNITIES, NEIGHBORHOODS, AND HOUSING

Learning Objectives:

- What aspects of community size are important?
- What aspects of neighborhoods matter most to older adults?
- What are the major settings in which older adults live?
- What are the most important aspects of communities, neighborhoods, and housing?

The most general levels at which we can examine person-environment interactions are communities and neighborhoods. Communities are usually defined as geographic or political units, such as cities and towns. Neighborhoods are the parts of the larger community that groups of people identify with and often label; Flatbush in Brooklyn, Buckhead in Atlanta, and South Central Los Angeles are some examples. In this section we will examine several aspects of communities and neighborhoods that have an impact on us and some personal factors that are important in considering the composition of the environment. We will also take a brief look at some crucial aspects of housing for older adults.

Community Size

Among the most important dimensions of a community that affect the life satisfaction of the residents is community size, conveniently represented along the rural-urban continuum. Hundreds of studies have examined the effects of size on all kinds of personal characteristics, from overall life satisfaction to knowledge about the availability of services (for example, Krout, 1988a, 1988b; Silverman, 1987). Some marked differences have emerged that are important for understanding person-environment interactions, especially among older adults. In interpreting differences between rural and urban communities, keep in mind that size alone does not tell us why the differences emerge. Other factors such as economic or ethnic differences that were not or could not be measured may also be responsible.

Overall Satisfaction

In overall life satisfaction the effects of community size are complex. No clear trends emerge for young adults, but both direct and indirect effects have been documented for older adults. Liang and Warfel (1983) used the results of surveys done nationally and in three states to study urban-rural differences in life satisfaction. They found that the large size of a community had a negative impact on the degree of actual and perceived integration into the community; in other words, people in large cities were less integrated than people in smaller communities. However, feeling that one is a part of the community does not affect the life satisfaction of people living in large cities as much as it does that of people in small communities. In large cities health factors are more important. The importance of health as a predictor of satisfaction is highlighted by Lawton's (1980) finding that when health factors are controlled, no differences in satisfaction as a function of community size are observed.

Liang and Warfel's findings support results from several other studies and generations of folk wisdom concerning the informal social network (Lawton, 1985b). Rural communities often lack sufficient health care facilities, shopping centers, and so on. **However, friends, neighbors, and family, collectively termed the *informal social network*, often make up for these shortcomings by providing some of the missing services, such as by visiting sick friends** (Davis, 1980; Rowles, 1983). The more one feels like part of the community, the larger one's informal network is and the higher one's life satisfaction (Rowles, 1983).

Still, many older people prefer to live in large

The spirit of community among the Amish is especially evident when someone in the area needs a new barn.

cities because of greater opportunities for social interaction. In contrast to small towns, large cities have better public transportation, which greatly facilitates older adults' ability to maintain contact with their families, friends, and ethnic group (Rudzitis, 1984).

Complexity

A second way to examine urban-rural differences is to look at the complexity of the community (Taietz, 1975). *Complexity* refers to the degree of differentiation among the services available to a community. Taietz (1975; Taietz & Milton, 1979) and Krout (1988a) examined complexity in rural and urban communities in New York State by determining older adults' knowledge of locally available social services, housing, retail trade, community planning, and medical specialties. Taietz found that higher complexity was associated with accurate information about facilities only in urban areas. As complexity increased in smaller communities, accuracy of knowledge about available facilities decreased. Krout extended these findings by demonstrating that residents of smaller communities were less aware of services on average but that this relationship might vary with a particular personal need for a specific service. Krout's results are explored in more detail in How Do We Know?

Because accurate information is essential for appropriate use of community services, an accompanying decline in resource utilization would be expected in complex small communities. The end result is that individuals' life satisfaction may decline because they perceive needs that are not being adequately met. That is, even if services are available, as long as people think that they are not, their overall satisfaction may be adversely affected.

Ideal Communities

Finally, some studies have examined people's notions of what the ideal community ought to have. In a comprehensive investigation Blake and Law-

HOW DO WE KNOW?

Awareness of Services and Community Size

Lack of awareness of public services among older adults has been cited as a major reason many services are underutilized. However, few studies have examined the awareness levels of rural and urban elderly residents at the community level. One exception to this lack of research is a study conducted by Krout (1988a).

Krout surveyed a random sample of 600 elderly residents of a metropolitan county and a nonmetropolitan county in western New York. He was interested in how aware people were of various services as a function of three types of factors: predisposing, enabling, and need. Predisposing factors affect the likelihood that people become aware of services; they include such things as age, gender, race, marital status, education, home ownership, and contact with children. Enabling factors facilitate or inhibit the use of services; household income and car ownership are two common ones. The need factor reflects various conditions, such as health problems, that affect the degree to which people seek out services.

Krout collected data in personal interviews. He asked respondents what they knew about eight types of services in their community: elderly visitors, home health, home help, home meals, hot luncheon sites, information referral services, legal aid, and transportation. The greatest awareness was shown for transportation, home meals, and hot luncheon sites, all of which were familiar to at least 75% of the respondents. However, people living in the metropolitan county were more aware of services, in general, than were the nonmetropolitan residents.

When Krout subjected his data to further statistical analyses, he found that community size was the best predictor of awareness. However, additional characteristics related to the personal factors were also important. For predisposing factors, young-old, non-European American, better educated, married homeowners were more aware of services. For enabling factors, income was related to awareness. Finally, people with health problems or those who needed help with the activities of daily living were more aware of services.

Krout's research shows that awareness of available services in one's community is more than a function of community size. Those who have specific reasons to know about services are also the ones who are aware of them. Krout's results must be interpreted with some caution, however, because he studied only elderly residents of two counties in New York. Whether the factors he found would generalize to other parts of the United States or to other Western countries remains to be seen.

---

ton (1980) found that younger and older adults living in both rural and urban communities agreed that high-quality medical care, good schools, adequate numbers of good jobs, and a variety of stores should be available. However, several age and community differences emerged when comparisons were made of the absolute level of importance of these factors. Younger adults were most concerned about jobs and schools, and urbanites were more concerned about social facilities. Overall, older adults were more satisfied with the facilities available in their community than were younger adults.

For many older adults, smaller rural towns in which they have lived most or all of their lives provided these amenities. However, many such towns in the United States have experienced difficult economic times, resulting in the outward migration of many young people to larger cities. The decline of such towns hits older residents especially hard, as they have substantial economic and personal investment in their homes and communities (Norris-Baker & Scheidt, 1994). For some, age-related changes in health may mean relocation regardless of the town's situation. For those who remain, the environmental stressors experienced in declining towns is significant and should be viewed in the broader context of loss.

Neighborhoods

Neighborhoods provide a setting for social interaction as well as a convenient location for obtaining goods and services. Most research on neighborhoods from a developmental perspective concerns people's perceptions of their neighborhood as a good place to live and the utilization of local services. One general finding from this work is that as people age, they become more dependent on their local environment (Regnier, 1983). With this in mind, we will focus on the factors of the neighborhood that are particularly important to older adults.

People's perceptions of their neighborhoods not only affect how they behave there but also have an impact on their overall psychological well-being. The important point here is that it is often the perception of the environment that matters, not necessarily the way things really are. The relationship between objective neighborhood characteristics, such as the actual number of stores, and well-being is modest at best (Lawton & Nahemow, 1979). This lack of relationship between objective indicators and subjective perception fits with the cognitive theories of personality (see Chapter 8) in which the emphasis is on what people believe to be true about themselves and not their scores on personality tests.

Crime

Crime is one important dimension related to individuals' perceptions of their neighborhoods. More than anything else, it is the fear of crime, rather than actually being a victim of crime, that affects overall well-being (Lawton & Yaffe, 1980). Moreover, a survey of middle-aged and older residents of Los Angeles showed that concern about being a victim of crime was more related to neighborhood crime rate than it was to age. However, this positive relationship between concern and crime rate was not constant for African Americans, Mexican Americans, and European Americans. That is, African Americans and Mexican Americans are less easily influenced by neighborhood crime rates than are European Americans (Janson & Ryder, 1983). In general, the data suggest that there is little evidence to support the view that most older adults live like prisoners in their homes out of fear (Lawton, 1985b). The perception of safety is the important consideration in satisfaction with one's neighborhood (Jirovec, Jirovec, & Bossé, 1985).

Structural Features

The age structure of neighborhoods as a factor in well-being has been examined in several studies. Lawton and Nahemow (1979) conducted an extensive examination of 31 characteristics of neighborhoods as factors in the well-being of 2,400 older tenants of planned housing projects. They found that living in a neighborhood with a high proportion of older adults was related to greater participation in activities, higher satisfaction with housing, and more interpersonal interactions with other tenants. Although these findings support the idea that there are benefits of living in a neighborhood with many similarly aged people, Lawton and Nahemow point out that the size of the benefits is small. Indeed, some older adults are more satisfied living where they have few age peers. The benefits of living near age peers depend on the particular person; individual differences are large.

A study conducted by the Veterans Administration of 100 older men in Boston showed that perceived safety was by far the most important consideration in choosing a neighborhood (Jirovec et al., 1985). Interestingly, the other major characteristics listed—such as beauty, space, and antiquity—were aesthetic ones reflecting subjective, personal perceptions of the environment. Absent from this list were more traditional factors such as accessibility of resources or concentration of age peers.

When Lawton and Nahemow (1979) examined ethnic factors and neighborhood structure, they found parallel results. Specifically, friendship and activity patterns were highest for African American older people when they lived in neighborhoods that had higher concentrations of African Americans. Overall, though, the results indicated that European Americans and African Americans were affected similarly by structural factors in the neighborhood.

Finally, people sometimes become attached to their neighborhoods. This may be especially true for older adults who have lived in the same place for decades and have become dependent on local services. This attachment may feed into one's general well-being by providing opportunities to reminisce about the past. Rowles (1980) suggests that reminiscing about the neighborhood may complement and accompany age-related increases in spatial constriction and dependence on the local area. As our society continues to be increasingly mobile, however, fewer of us will live in the same neighborhood all of our lives. Thus, it will be interesting to see whether our feelings of attachment to where we live change over the next few decades.

Ethnicity

Only a few researchers have considered race or ethnicity as important aspects of neighborhoods. Biegel and Farkas (1990) found that African American older adults were less likely than European American ethnic older adults to visit or borrow things from their neighbors. However, there were no differences in perceptions of how much help one's neighbors would provide if needed. Reasons for the differences in social visiting focus on neighborhood security; urban African Americans are more likely to live in neighborhoods with poor street lighting, higher crime rates, poor sidewalks, and inaccessible stairs.

One major resource available in the African American community is the church. Indeed, the church in these communities is considered a frame of reference, a mediating institution, and a catalyst for economic, political, and social change (Eng, Hatch, & Callan, 1985). The church also serves as a primary means for social activity and interaction among its older members and provides considerable support for older members and nonmembers alike who reside in the community (Taylor & Chatters, 1986).

Among European American ethnic groups, attachment to neighborhood in older residents is uniformly high. For example, the clear majority of residents living in either single ethnic group or mixed ethnic group neighborhoods really liked their neighborhoods (Biegel & Farkas, 1990).

A positive aspect of living in age-segregated housing is the opportunity to socialize with one's peers.

Housing

Over 20% of the households in the United States are headed by an adult over age 65, and the number of such households is growing more rapidly than the proportion of older adults in the general population (Silverman, 1987). Of these households headed by older adults, roughly 70% are owner occupied. Unfortunately, these homes are often older, in poorer condition, and in less desirable neighborhoods than housing for younger and middle-aged adults. However, older homeowners have some clear advantages over renters; 86% of the homeowners have paid off their mortgage, whereas the renters spend an average of 30% of their income on housing. Older renters also tend to live in poorer quality apartments than their younger counterparts.

Golant (1984) points out an important consideration about housing that is often overlooked. Most older homeowners and renters live in homes designed for younger cohorts that are inappropriate for the changing needs of older adults. For example, most housing is too large, built on multiple levels, and designed with few fixtures to compensate for changing perceptual and motor skills.

Despite the range of housing options, little developmental research has been conducted to examine the effects of these different arrangements on adults of various ages. Instead, gerontologists have primarily focused on age-segregated versus age-integrated housing. This research has been conducted in five main settings: apartment complexes for older adults, retirement communities, congregate housing, single-room-occupancy (SRO) hotels, and continuing care retirement communities.

Age-Segregated Versus Age-Integrated Housing

Most older adults live in *age-integrated* communities, where there are people of all ages. Increasingly, however, older adults are opting for communities that are *age-segregated*, that is, exclusively for older adults. In the United States federally assisted age-segregated housing projects began in 1956. Although roughly 6% of older adults live in age-segregated housing, this number is still well below that in some European countries such as the Netherlands, Sweden, France, and West Germany (Silverman, 1987). Since the 1960s the impact of age-segregated housing on older adults has been the topic of considerable research.

Early studies by Rosow (1967) on middle- and working-class elderly people in Cleveland and by Messer (1968) on public housing residents in Chicago showed that high concentrations of older adults resulted in higher levels of social contacts and morale, especially for women. Later research supported these findings, but added some important cautions. For example, Lawton confirmed that age-segregated housing resulted in increased social participation, interaction with other tenants, and satisfaction with housing (Lawton, 1980; Lawton, Moss, & Moles, 1984). However, Lawton (1980) and Carp (1976) both point out that these findings may be a function of the kind of housing and the particular neighborhood studied. For example, the people whom Rosow studied lived in an old, established neighborhood with long-term friendship patterns already in place. Whether the benefits of age-segregated housing extend to newer neighborhoods is a topic we will explore in the next few sections.

Apartment Complexes for Older Adults

Several researchers have conducted excellent studies of people living in apartment complexes for older adults. Two research methods have been used: interviews and participant observation.

The classic interview study of apartment residents was done by Carp (1966, 1976) at Victoria Plaza in San Antonio. Carp not only collected baseline data but also conducted follow-up interviews for 8 years following initial occupancy. In general, Carp found that the move to Victoria Plaza was associated with improved social and psychological well-being, lower mortality, a lower rate of nursing home placement, improved health, and increased social participation as compared with remaining in one's original home. Although the people who moved to Victoria Plaza chose to do so and may not represent older people in general, they received many benefits.

Although the findings from other interview studies have not always been as impressive, they do tend to agree with Carp's overall conclusions that age-segregated apartments produce many benefits. For example, Lawton and Cohen (1974) and Messer (1967) found improved well-being following a move to an age-segregated housing complex.

In contrast to interview studies, the investigator in participant observation research actually lives in the housing project. One of the best examples of such research was done by Hochschild (1973), who studied 46 low-income elderly residents, mostly widows, in San Francisco. An important characteristic of this project was the development of a *subculture,* or a strong positive feeling distinctive to the occupants. That is, although they did not have a great awareness of what was happening in the community around them, they were well informed on the events that were relevant to their lives. They celebrated birthdays together; looked in on one another; shared information, shopping, and costs; and communicated with one another extensively. Hochschild viewed these new shared roles as replacements for roles lost in their former communities; these new roles protected the residents against loneliness.

In a much larger study Jacobs (1975) examined a high-rise apartment building for working-class elderly people on a college campus in Syracuse, New York. Unlike the complex studied by Hochschild, the one in Syracuse was large (over 400 residents) and ethnically diverse, with obvious tensions between the majority European Americans and the small number of African Americans. Additionally, the fact that some of the residents were frail was resented by others, who feared that the project would turn into a nursing home. Jacobs found that many residents were apathetic, passive, and isolated. Consequently, Jacobs concluded that a cohesive subculture would not result from simply putting people of the same age together. Rather, the emergence of a subculture depends on such factors as number, ethnicity, and health status.

In short, what we have learned from research on apartment complexes is that it takes much more than a collection of same-aged people to make a coherent, satisfying community. From a life-cycle perspective, past experiences, attitudes, and needs must be considered and taken into account. When these factors are considered and a subculture emerges, the positive impact of living in such settings is substantial (Longino, 1982).

Retirement Communities

Another rapidly growing form of age-segregated housing is retirement communities. In retirement communities not only is housing restricted to people of a given age, but the whole community is designed to cater to the needs of older adults. For example, housing units are often one story, electric golf carts are a preferred mode of transportation, and activities are planned with the older adult in mind. From their beginning in the Sun Belt states, retirement communities are now appearing across the United States.

Despite the considerable publicity that retirement communities have received, surprisingly little research has been done on their effects on residents. What little there is points to two opposite conclusions. Survey studies show that retirement communities tend to have overwhelmingly European American, relatively affluent, better educated, healthier, married older adults (for example, Heintz, 1976). Life satisfaction among residents is high; few wish to move out, and social participation is high.

In sharp contrast, participant observation research paints a very different picture. Jacobs (1974, 1975) studied the geographically isolated community of Fun City southeast of Los Angeles. The typical resident there was lonely, unhappy, and in despair. Social participation was low; only around 500 of the nearly 6,000 residents were active in a club or organization. In terms of Lawton and Nahemow's environmental press model, an imbalance existed between high personal competence and low environmental demands, resulting in poor adaptation. Jacobs also reported strong racist attitudes toward African Americans, Hispanics, and Native Americans, which was thought to be responsible for the lack of minority residents.

It is unclear why the findings in the survey and participant observation studies were so discrepant. It may be that residents want to highlight only the good aspects on a survey and that the negative aspects must be uncovered by personal observations. Geographic location could also be a factor, as well as how good the match is between competence and environmental demands. Further research is clearly needed to resolve these issues.

Congregate Housing

Congregate housing represents an intermediate step between living independently and living in a long-term care setting. Congregate housing includes what is sometimes called intermediate, communal, or community housing. The importance of congregate housing is that it provides a viable alternative to placement in long-term care facilities for people who need supportive services to maintain their independence.

Great Britain has led the way in developing congregate housing. The complex usually has self-contained apartments that are linked to a central office for emergencies. A medical clinic with a full-time nursing staff is on the premises. Planned social activities are organized by a trained staff. Heumann and Boldy (1982) surveyed several British facilities and concluded that residents remained functionally independent longer and were more likely to avoid placement in long-term care facilities than elderly residents of conventional housing.

Congregate housing in the United States has adopted the British model. Carlin and Mansberg (1984) showed that residents of a congregate facility in the northeastern United States were remarkably active in organizing and participating in activities. Their strong sense of cohesiveness was demonstrated by their sense of pride and mutual concern for the home and the residents. Ross (1977) also noted a strong sense of cohesiveness in her study of a congregate home for the working-class elderly in Paris.

The need for increased congregate facilities was identified as one of the most pressing housing needs in the United States a decade ago (U.S. Office of Technology Assessment, 1984). Estimates are that 3 million elderly people in the United States need some sort of assisted housing, with the number expected to increase dramatically over the next few decades. Because little is known about the optimal design of congregate facilities and the type of resident who will benefit most, however, social policy awaits more research on these issues. Such research would benefit from the theoretical perspectives outlined at the outset, with special attention on the relationship between competence and demands and the congruence between needs and services.

SRO Hotels

Rather than living in congregate facilities, some elderly want to maintain their independence. The single-room-occupancy (SRO) hotel offers an alternative for people who desire a high degree of autonomy. SRO hotels are usually located in dangerous and dilapidated areas of inner cities (Lawton, 1980).

Erickson and Ekert (1977) classify SROs into three types: skid row hotels, the most deteriorated type, with mainly male, low-income occupants; working-class hotels, relatively clean, with housekeeping services and mostly male occupants; and middle-class hotels, more comfortable and expensive, with equal numbers of male and female occupants and some activities. Several participant observation studies have shown that residents of skid row and working-class hotels are fiercely independent, have large social networks, have marginal relationships with family, show high mutual support, and are usually poor (Ekert, 1980; Sokolovsky & Cohen, 1983; Stephens, 1976; Teski, 1981). Survey research has documented similar findings; men living in SROs and on the street are in generally poorer health than their community-dwelling counterparts, and these health problems are related to stress, unfulfilled needs, relative youth, and contacts with agencies (Cohen, Teresi, & Holmes, 1988). Unfortunately, almost none of these data have been analyzed from a developmental perspective.

Most researchers agree that SROs play an important role in serving poor, independently minded elderly people. However, the number of SROs is rapidly diminishing, often because of urban renewal. For example, 89% of the SROs in New York City disappeared between 1970 and 1983 and were replaced with luxury housing (Sanjek, 1984). This substantial loss of SROs may be partially responsible for the increase in the homeless elderly, a connection that needs to be explored.

Continuing Care Retirement Communities

Continuing care retirement communities (CCRCs) offer a range of housing from independent housing through full nursing care (Sherwood, Ruchlin, & Sherwood, 1989). Financially, many CCRCs work differently than other housing options. Individuals pay a substantial lump sum when they move in and a monthly fee for as long as they remain there. Payments do not vary with the level of care. Because CCRCs are typically very expensive, residents tend to be wealthier, better educated, more involved, and unmarried and childless than the average older adult (Sherwood et al., 1989).

Homelessness among older adults is a growing problem in urban areas. However, few programs are aimed specifically at addressing their special needs.

One emerging trend in CCRCs is to design them in a way that integrates the physical, social, psychological, medical, and operational requirements of older adults to provide a setting in which people of all functional abilities can enjoy a dignified lifestyle (Thompson, 1994). Such communities incorporate design features such as barrier-free environments, a choice of paths from one location to another, single-story construction, and user-friendly apartments. Such designs promote independence and safety for older residents, thereby allowing them to remain in independent living situations as long as possible and reducing medical and social problems.

Little research has been conducted on CCRCs other than on the financial considerations (Parmelee & Lawton, 1990). Sherwood and colleagues (1989) showed that CCRC residents waited until late in life (usually their late 70s) before entering. They also showed that CCRC residents wanted the security of knowing that their future needs would be met.

Homeless Elderly

Although older adults have many housing options, the unfortunate truth is that some older people have nowhere to call home. No one knows for certain how many homeless people there are in the United States (estimates range from 250,000 to 2.5 million). Virtually every U.S. city of any size has an identifiable population of homeless people.

Between 25% and 30% of all homeless people are thought to be over age 60 (Cohen, Teresi, Holmes, & Roth, 1988). Moreover, homeless elderly represent every ethnic group and are heterogenous on many other dimensions as well (such as education, past occupation, gender). Reasons for homelessness vary (Martin, 1990). Some people lost their jobs and income and could not find affordable housing. Some are battered women. Some have serious mental health problems or drug or alcohol problems. Because most programs to aid homeless people are targeted at younger people and families, older homeless adults are often overlooked (Martin, 1990).

Living on the street requires many survival strategies. Just figuring out how to get something to eat or how to get a shower may require considerable skill. Maintenance strategies include denial, fantasy, and self-entertainment, and survival skills range from learning how to carefully pick through discarded food to sleeping sitting up to living totally in public view. Some cities have shelters, but these are often too small to meet the demand. Overall, life on the street is extremely difficult, dangerous, and stressful (Cohen, Teresi, Holmes, & Roth, 1988).

At present, we know so little about the homeless elderly that it is even difficult to know what kinds of intervention programs might work. Although providing adequate nutrition and a decent place to stay are clearly important, many other needs, such as physical and mental health, must also be met. Clearly, much more emphasis on the plight of homeless older adults is urgently needed.

Conclusions

Although most of the research on communities, neighborhoods, and housing reviewed here focuses on how old people make out in various communities, living arrangements in old age come from many decisions over the life span. Decisions about family size, kinship pattern, health care, occupational choices, and personal priorities all contribute to housing decisions in later life. Disruptions in these areas earlier in adulthood may have long-term carryover effects in old age.

The most important point to remember about communities, neighborhoods, and housing is that optimizing the person-environment fit is the goal. Wiseman (1981) argues that the first step should be changing the person's level of competence or personal resources through such interventions as better health care and economic security. The second step would be to change the environment through relocation. The final strategy is to facilitate environmental interactions for older adults, such as by instituting better transportation. What we need to know most of all is whether the success of these suggestions is related to normative developmental changes.

Concept Checks

1. What are the key aspects of community size?
2. What are the most important aspects of neighborhoods for older adults?
3. What are the different settings in which older people live?
4. What is the most important thing to keep in mind about communities, neighborhoods, and housing?

LIVING IN LONG-TERM CARE FACILITIES

Learning Objectives:

- What are the major types of long-term care facilities?
- What are the characteristics of the typical nursing home resident?
- What are the main ways of understanding the key characteristics of nursing homes?
- How can a nursing home be a "home"?
- How should people communicate with nursing home residents?

The last place that Maria thought she would end up was a bed in one of the local nursing homes. "That's a place where old people go to die," she used to say. "It's not gonna be for me." But here she was. Maria, 84 and living alone, had fallen and broken her hip. She needed to stay for a few weeks while she recovered. She hated the food; "tasteless goo" she calls it. Her roommate, Arnetta, refers to the place as "jail" to her daughter. Arnetta, 79 and essentially blind, has Alzheimer's disease.

Maria and Arnetta may be the kind of people you think of when you conjure up images of nursing homes. To be sure, you will probably find some people like them there. But for each Maria or Arnetta, there are many more who come to terms with their situation and struggle to make sense of their lives. Nursing homes are indeed places where people who have very serious health problems go, and for many it is their final address. Yet if you take the time to go into a nursing home, you will find many inspiring people who have quite a story to tell.

Nursing homes suffer from many misconceptions. The first is that most older people end up in one. That perception is clearly not true. At any moment approximately 5% of the population over 65 is living in a facility of this type. This may seem to be a small number of people, especially in view of the dominant stereotype of disability and sickness in old age. Before we feel too relieved, however, we must also recognize that the probability that someone who lives past age 85 will spend at least some time in a long-term care facility is much higher than 1 in 20—it is more like 1 in 4 (Johnson, 1987). Thus, the number of people who are potentially affected by long-term care facilities is rather large.

Long-term care settings are very different environments from those we have considered so far. As we will see, the residents of such facilities differ on many dimensions from their community-dwelling counterparts. Likewise, the environment itself is markedly different from neighborhood and community contexts. But because many aspects of the environment in these facilities are controlled, it offers a unique opportunity to examine person-environment interactions in more detail.

In this section we will examine types of long-term care settings, the typical resident, and the psychosocial environment in the facilities. Because virtually all of the adult developmental research in this field focuses on older adults, we will concentrate on their experiences.

Maintaining a social network is important, especially when living in a nursing home.

Types of Long-Term Care Facilities

The main types of long-term care facilities for elderly residents are nursing homes, personal-care and boarding homes, and psychiatric hospitals. Nursing homes house the largest number of older residents of long-term care facilities. They are governed by state and federal regulations that establish minimum standards for care. Two levels of care in nursing homes are defined in the federal regulations (Johnson & Grant, 1985). ***Skilled nursing care*** consists of 24-hour care requiring skilled medical and other health services, usually from nurses. *Intermediate care* is also 24-hour care necessitating nursing supervision, but at a less intense level. In actual practice the major differences between the two are the types and numbers of health care workers on the staff. Perhaps for this reason, the distinction between skilled and intermediate care is often blurred.

Personal-care homes and boarding homes may also be regulated by states; however, no federal guidelines for these types of facilities exist. These facilities are usually very small, and they house people who need assistance with daily needs because of disabilities or chronic disorders such as arthritis but who otherwise are in fairly good health. The quality of care in these facilities varies widely.

In the past, psychiatric hospitals housed many more older adults than they do now. Older adult patients who are admitted to psychiatric hospitals due to serious psychological disorders such as paranoia or severe depression stay there for a much shorter period than even 20 years ago. Since the mid-1960s older psychiatric patients have been increasingly dismissed and relocated in the community or in other settings. Unfortunately, little research has been conducted to measure the adjustment of these individuals after relocation. Sometimes, older adults who suffer severe emotional or cognitive deficits are often placed in nursing homes rather than psychiatric hospitals. However, some states have begun to stop this practice as well, arguing that nursing home placements are inappropriate for these individuals. Again, we have essentially no information on how such people fare after being told they must leave or are denied entrance into a nursing home.

Because they contain the majority of older adults who live in long-term care facilities, nursing homes have been the setting for almost all the research on the effects of placement in these settings. For this reason nursing homes will be the focus of the remainder of this section. Caution should be exercised in generalizing the results from nursing home research to other types of facilities. Differences in structure, staffs, and residents' characteristics make comparisons of different types of facilities difficult. As a result we need more research on the experience of older residents of other types of facilities and on how these experiences compare with those of nursing home residents. Additionally, as noted in Something to Think About, funding for nursing homes will be an increasingly important issue in the coming decades.

Who Is Likely to Live in Nursing Homes?

Who is the typical resident of a nursing home? She is very old, European American, financially disadvantaged, probably widowed or divorced, and possibly without living children. These characteristics are not similar to the population at large, as discussed in Chapter 1. For example, men are underrepresented in nursing homes, as are minorities. At least some of the ethnic differences may be a matter of personal choice rather than institutional policy. For example, some older Mexican Americans remain in the community to be cared for by family and friends regardless of their degree of impairment (Eribes & Bradley-Rawls, 1978). However, Burr (1990) reports that the rates for placing older unmarried adults are converging for African Americans and European Americans, and the reasons for doing so are essentially the same (for example, poor health).

What are the problems of typical nursing home residents? For the most part, the average nursing home resident is clearly impaired, both mentally and physically. Indeed, the main reason for placing almost 80% of nursing home residents is health. Still, placement in a nursing home is usually done only as a last resort; over half of the residents come from other facilities such as general hospitals (Lawton, 1980).

Clearly, frail older people and their relatives alike do not see nursing homes as an option until other avenues have been explored. This may account for the numbers of truly impaired individuals who live in nursing homes; the kinds and amount of problems make life outside the nursing home very difficult on them and their families. In fact, if all other things are equal, the best predictor of who will be placed in a nursing home is the absence of a viable social support system (George, 1980).

The fact that older adults and their families do not see nursing homes as the placement of choice means that the decision was probably made reluctantly. In some cases individuals other than family members enter the decision process. One common situation involves older adults living in age-segregated housing projects, most of which have some type of policy concerning the level of functioning that residents must have to remain. In actual practice most housing projects have explicit policies in areas concerning safety and liability; for example, some have regulations that tenants who need constant monitoring or who are nonambula-

SOMETHING TO THINK ABOUT

Financing Long-Term Care

The current system of financing long-term care in the United States is in very serious trouble. Nursing home costs in 1995 averaged about $30,000 per year and were far and away the leading catastrophic health care expense. Contrary to popular belief, Medicare pays only 2% of nursing home expenses, and the typical private insurance plan pays only an additional 1%. Most often, the typical nursing home resident must deplete his or her life savings to pay for care. Once residents become totally impoverished, they become dependent on Medicaid. This public subsidy for nursing home care cost over $20 billion in 1990 and is increasing rapidly. For example, governmental support of long-term care, which represented 0.45% of the gross national product in 1988, is expected to grow to 1.42% by 2050 (Wiener, 1988). How will we be able to finance the long-term health care system?

One option is through the private sector. This approach includes long-term care insurance, individual retirement accounts for long-term care, health maintenance organizations, and alternative housing arrangements such as congregate housing. Many of these options place the burden on individuals to come up with ways of financing their own care. The Brookings Institution estimates that by 2018 private long-term care insurance will be affordable by as many as 45% of older adults. However, these projections also indicate that at best, private insurance will lower Medicaid expenditures by only 2% to 5%. Such modest reductions in public support would also accompany individual retirement accounts, alternative housing, health maintenance organizations, and other options. Consequently, large subsidies from government will still be needed for long-term care regardless of what the private sector does.

Given that government subsidies for long-term care will be required for the foreseeable future, the question becomes how to finance them. Under the current Medicaid system older adults are not protected from becoming impoverished. Moreover, the way that the system is designed, the substantial majority of people needing care will ultimately qualify for the program once their savings are depleted. With the aging of the baby-boom generation, Medicaid costs will skyrocket. If we want to continue the program in its current form, additional revenues will be needed, perhaps in the form of taxes.

The questions facing us are whether we want to continue forcing older adults to become totally impoverished when they need long-term care, whether we want the government to continue subsidy programs, and whether we would be willing to pay higher taxes for this subsidy. How we answer these questions will have a profound impact on the status of long-term care over the next few decades. It's something to think about.

---

tory must move out. However, most of these regulations are deliberately vague concerning basic skills needed for daily living, such as the ability to maintain one's own apartment, and about areas of personal behavior involving mental confusion, emotional instability, and drinking problems (Bernstein, 1982).

Bernstein surveyed the managers of 136 housing projects concerning their criteria for asking tenants to leave. She found substantial agreement across policies, which are summarized in Table 12.1. As can be seen, the most frequent reason for asking tenants to leave involved psychological functioning (mental ability, emotional stability, and so on). Tenants most often left voluntarily because they needed constant supervision. Notice that these reasons (and most of the other criteria listed) are similar to the characteristics of the typical nursing home resident.

Characteristics of Nursing Homes

We can examine nursing homes on two dimensions: physical and psychosocial. Physical characteristics include factors such as size, staff-to-resident ratio, numbers and types of activities, and certification requirements. Unfortunately, very

TABLE 12.1 Most frequently mentioned reasons for asking tenants to leave housing projects or for their leaving voluntarily

	Projects Asked Tenants to Leave (%)	Projects' Tenants Left Voluntarily (%)
Tenant showed mental decline (senility, not mentally alert) or had problems such as emotional imbalance, aggressive behavior, paranoia, depression, etc.	61	27
Tenant was a potential health or safety hazard to self or others (accidents, fire, flooding, etc.).	32	10
Tenant needed daily supervision of activities, medication, and personal well-being.	30	67
Tenant had an alcohol abuse problem.	29	6
Tenant was bedridden and/or needed skilled nursing care facility (24-hour).	25	55
Tenant was a major disturbance or had a difficult personality.	22	0
Tenant had severe illness (stroke, heart, cancer, etc.).	18	39
Tenant had a general decline in health (frailty, deterioration, going downhill).	16	30
Tenant left to be with family members.	0	60
Tenant needed to have meals cooked or provided (if meals were on site, they were not frequent enough or tenant was unable to get to them).	0	20

Source: "Who Leaves—Who Stays: Residency Policy in Housing for the Elderly" by J. Bernstein, 1982, *Gerontologist, 22,* 305–313.

little research has been done comparing facilities on these dimensions. As a result we do not have a good idea of how much variance exists on these dimensions across nursing homes and when differences become important.

More is known about the effects of these dimensions on residents' psychosocial well-being. The combination of the physical, personal, staff-related, and service-related aspects of the nursing home makes up a milieu, a higher order abstraction of the environmental context (Lawton, 1980).

Over the last decade several researchers have been conceptualizing the effects of the institutional milieu on residents. We are already familiar with Kahana's ideas; an expansion of the previous discussion will be presented here. A second investigator, Moos, has taken a somewhat different approach that emphasizes measurement; we will also consider his views in detail. Finally, we will consider some work by Langer from a social-psychological perspective.

The Congruence Approach

In describing her congruence theory, Kahana (1982) also discusses several dimensions along which person-environment congruence can be classified (see Table 12.2). She is especially interested in describing facilities, so most of her research is aimed at documenting her dimensions in these settings.

Kahana's approach emphasizes that personal well-being is the product not just of the character-

TABLE 12.2 Environmental and individual dimensions of Kahana's congruence model with descriptions of important aspects of each

Environment	Individual
Segregate Dimension	
a. Homogeneity of composition of environment. Segregation based on similarity of resident characteristics (sex, age, physical functioning and mental status).	a. Preference for homogeneity, i.e., for associating with like individuals. Being with people similar to oneself.
b. Change vs. sameness. Presence of daily and other routines, frequency of changes in staff and other environmental characteristics.	b. Preference for change vs. sameness in daily routines, activities.
c. Continuity of similarity with previous environment of resident.	c. Need for continuity with the past.
Congregate Dimension	
a. Extent to which privacy is available in setting.	a. Need for privacy.
b. Collective vs. individual treatment. The extent to which residents are treated alike. Availability of choices in food, clothing, etc. Opportunity to express unique individual characteristics.	b. Need for individual expression and idiosyncracy. Choosing individualized treatment whether that is socially defined as "good" treatment or not.
c. The extent to which residents do things alone or with others.	c. Preference for doing things alone vs. with others.
Institutional Control	
a. Control over behavior and resources. The extent to which staff exercises control over resources.	a. Preference for (individual) autonomy vs. being controlled.
b. Amount of deviance tolerated. Sanctions for deviance.	b. Need to conform.
c. Degree to which dependency is encouraged and dependency needs are met.	c. Dependence on others. Seeks support or nurturance vs. feeling self-sufficient.
Structure	
a. Ambiguity vs. specification of expectations. Role ambiguity or role clarity (e.g., rules learned from other residents).	a. Tolerance of ambiguity vs. need for structure.
b. Order vs. disorder.	b. Need for order and organization.

continued

TABLE 12.2 continued

Stimulation-Engagement *Environment*	*Individual*
a. Environmental input (stimulus properties of physical and social environment).	a. Tolerances and preference for environmental stimulation.
b. The extent to which resident is actually stimulated and encouraged to be active.	b. Preference for activities vs. disengagement.

Affect *Environment*	*Individual*
a. Tolerance for or encouragement of affective expression. Provision of ritualized show of emotion (e.g., funerals).	a. Need for emotion expression. Display of feelings, whether positive or negative.
b. Amount of affective stimulation. Excitement vs. peacefulness in environment.	b. Intensity of affect, for example, need for vs. avoidance of conflict and excitement (shallow affect).

Impulse Control *Environment*	*Individual*
a. Acceptance of impulsive life vs. sanctions against it. The extent to which the environment gratifies need immediately vs. postponed need gratification. Gratification-deprivation ratio.	a. Ability to delay need gratification. Preference for immediate vs. delayed reward. Degree of impulse need.
b. Tolerance of motor expression—restlessness, walking around in activities or at night.	b. Motor control; psychomotor inhibition.
c. Premium placed by environment on levelheadedness and deliberation.	c. Impulsive closure vs. deliberate closure.

Source: "A Congruence Model of Person-Environment Interaction" by E. Kahana, 1982, in M.P. Lawton et al. (Eds.), *Aging and the Environment: Theoretical Approaches*. New York: Springer. Reprinted by permission of Dr. Eva Kahana.

istics of the facility and of the individual but also of the congruence between the individual's needs and the ability of the facility to meet them. People whose needs are congruent with the control provided by the facility should have the highest well-being. However, any number of factors could potentially be important in determining congruence, as is demonstrated by the large number of subdimensions in the congruence model.

Harel (1981) investigated which of these many factors in determining congruence was the most important in predicting well-being. Based on 125 interviews in 14 nursing homes, Harel found that continuing ties with preferred members of the resident's social network was the most important variable. Meeting social needs, then, should constitute a major goal for facilities. Harel suggested that a resident services department be established in nursing homes as well as policies allowing greater opportunities for choice in socializing.

Attempting to establish congruence in the social domain may have direct benefits. Greene and

Monahan (1982) demonstrated that the frequency of family visitation affected residents' level of impairment. Specifically, those residents who were visited often by their families had significantly higher levels of psychosocial functioning. This suggests that meeting social needs through visitation has a positive and direct effect on residents' well-being.

Moos's Approach

A second way to examine the person-environment interaction in long-term care facilities has been offered by Moos and his colleagues (Moos & Lemke, 1984, 1985). Moos believes that facilities can be evaluated in physical, organizational, supportive, and social climate terms. Each of these areas is thought to have an effect on the well-being of the residents.

Several scales have been developed to assess facilities on these dimensions. The Multiphasic Environmental Assessment Procedure (MEAP), one of the most comprehensive, assesses four aspects of the facility: physical and architectural features; administrative and staff policies and programs; resident and staff characteristics; and social climate. Each area is measured by separate multidimensional scales. Together, information from the MEAP provides a complete picture that allows a judgment to be made about how well the facility meets residents' needs.

Moos's approach has the advantage that separate dimensions of the person-environment interaction can be measured and examined independently. For one thing, it establishes areas of strength and weakness so that appropriate programs can be devised. But perhaps more important it may provide a basis for future efforts at developing rating systems for evaluating the overall quality of a facility. At present, such questions as what really distinguishes good and bad nursing homes, for example, are unanswerable. Only further refinement of measures like those developed by Moos will give us a clue.

Social-Psychological Perspectives

Langer approaches the issue of person-environment interactions quite differently from either Kahana or Moos. She believes that the important factor in residents' well-being is the degree to which they perceive that they are in control of their lives (Langer, 1985).

To demonstrate her point, she conducted an ingenious experiment. One group of nursing home residents were told that staff members were there to care for them and to make decisions for them about their daily lives. In contrast, a second group of residents were encouraged to make their own decisions concerning meals, recreational activities, and so forth. This second group showed marked improvements in well-being and activity level compared with the first group (Langer & Rodin, 1976). These improvements were still seen 18 months later; in fact, the second group also seemed to have lower mortality rates (Rodin & Langer, 1977).

Based on her findings, Langer became convinced that making residents feel competent and in control were key factors in promoting positive person-environment interactions in nursing homes. Langer (1985) points to several aspects of the nursing home environment that fail in this regard. First, the decision to place a person in a nursing home is often made by persons other than the individual involved. Staff members may communicate their belief that the resident is simply incapable of making any decision or may treat him or her like a child, rather than like an adult who is moving to a new home.

Second, the label "nursing home resident" may have strong negative connotations. This is especially true if as a younger adult the person had negative preconceived ideas about why people go to nursing homes. A long history of social-psychological research shows that the individual may begin to internalize these stereotypical beliefs, even if they are unwarranted (Kelley, 1967). Other labels such as "patient" may have similar effects.

Third, the demonstration of tender loving care may serve mainly to reinforce the belief in one's incompetence. That is, in helping people perform basic tasks such as getting dressed, we run the risk of increasing their level of incompetence and dependence on others. Again, providing assistance where none is needed may be a way in which the staff communicates its belief that the individual cannot fend for himself or herself at all.

The physical aspects of the environment may also reinforce the belief of no control. To the extent that the environment is unfamiliar or is difficult to negotiate, persons living in it may feel incompetent. Mastering the environment increases feelings of control, but if this process is either not allowed or made too easy, the outcome may be negative.

Finally, Langer (1985) argues that routine is also detrimental to well-being. If the environment is too predictable, there is little for people to think about; in Langer's terms we become mindless. In this state we are typically not aware of what we do; we behave as if we were on automatic pilot. If nursing home environments promote mindlessness, then individuals behave automatically and have difficulty remembering what happened even a short time before. When this occurs, the staff may view the person as incompetent. But because we all engage in mindless activity (for example, performing a series of complex but automatic functions while driving) about which we have no recollection (one often cannot recall anything about driving the last several miles), we cannot justify this same mindlessness as indicative of incompetence in older adults.

Other researchers have replicated Langer's basic findings in nursing homes (Schulz & Hanusa, 1979) and retirement communities (Slivinske & Fitch, 1987). Even though some researchers have failed to replicate Langer's research when nursing home residents are reexamined over longer periods (Schulz & Hanusa, 1978), the points raised concerning how nursing home residents should be treated are still very important. Indeed, Buschman and Hollinger (1994) found that providing affective social support through touching is an effective substitute for residents' inability to control their environment. Still, whether the benefits of increased control last over the long run is still an open issue. Whether we should treat nursing home residents with respect is not.

Can a Nursing Home Be a "Home"?

One key aspect of nursing homes has been largely overlooked: To what extent do residents consider a nursing home takes on the meaning of "home"? This gets to the heart of what makes people feel that the place in which they live is more than just a dwelling. On the surface, it would appear that nursing homes are full of barriers to this feeling. After all, they may have regulations about the extent to which residents may bring their own furnishings and other personal effects with them, and residents are in an environment that has plenty of structural reminders that this is not a house in suburbia. Not having one's own refrigerator, for example, means that one can no longer invite friends over for a home-cooked meal (Shield, 1988).

Can nursing home residents move beyond these barriers and reminders and achieve a sense of "home"? Apparently so, but with some very important qualifications. Groger (1995) interviewed 20 older African American adults, 10 who lived in nursing homes and 10 who were home-care clients. Groger's analysis of her interviews revealed that nursing home residents can indeed feel "at home." The circumstances that foster this feeling include having the time to think about and participate in the placement decision, even if only minimally; having prior knowledge of, and positive experience with, a specific facility; defining "home" predominantly in terms of family and social relationships rather than in terms of place, objects, or total autonomy; and being able to establish some kind of continuity between home and nursing home either through activities or through similarities in living arrangements.

Groger (1995) also reports that getting nursing home residents to reminisce about home may actually facilitate adjustment. Some residents only concluded that the nursing home was "home" after long and detailed reflection on their prior home. Additionally, it may be easier for nursing home residents to feel "at home" on some days than others, and from one situation to another, depending on the events or stimuli at the time.

Helping nursing home residents feel "at home" is an important issue that needs to be explored in more detail. Perhaps having people think about what constitutes a "home" before and after placement may make the otherwise difficult transition from community to the facility easier to face. For those who need the care provided in a nursing home, anything that can be done to ease the transition would be a major benefit.

Communicating with Residents

One of the things many people find difficult is talking with nursing home residents. This problem is especially difficult when interacting with residents who are cognitively impaired. Unfortunately, this uneasiness often results in people relying on stereotypes of older adults in general and nursing home residents in particular in speaking to them, which results in inappropriate communication styles.

Ryan, Giles, Bartolucci, and Henwood (1986) described a general "communication predicament" of older adults in which younger adults overaccommodate their speech based on their stereotyped expectations of dependence and incompetence. Such speech conveys a sense of declining abilities, loss of control, and helplessness, which, if continued, may cause older adults to lose self-esteem and withdraw from social interactions. As time goes on, older adults who are talked to in this way may even begin behaving in ways that reinforce the stereotypes.

Inappropriate speech to older adults that is based on stereotypes of incompetence and dependence is referred to as *patronizing speech.* Patronizing speech is marked by slower speech, exaggerated intonation, higher pitch, increased volume, repetitions, tag and closed-end questions, and simplification of vocabulary and grammar. Speaking in this way can be conceptualized as "secondary baby talk," which is baby talk inappropriately used with adults (Ryan, Hamilton, & See, 1993). **Secondary baby talk, sometimes referred to as *infantilization,* also involves the use of a person's first name when it is not warranted, terms of endearment, simplified expressions, short imperatives, an assumption that the recipient has no memory, and cajoling as a means of demanding compliance** (Whitbourne, Culgin, & Cassidy, 1995).

Whitbourne and colleagues (1995) showed that infantilizing speech is viewed extremely negatively by some older adults. They found that community-dwelling older adults rated infantilizing speech especially negatively and were particularly resentful of its intonation aspects as indicative of a lack of respect. Nursing home residents were less harsh in their judgments, giving support to the idea that being exposed to infantilizing speech lowers one's awareness of its demeaning qualities. Whitbourne and colleagues also found no evidence that infantilizing speech is high in nurturance, as some previous authors had suggested.

How should people talk to older adults, especially those living in nursing homes? Ryan, Meredith, MacLean, and Orange (1995) propose the communication enhancement model as a framework for appropriate exchange. This model is based on a health promotion model, which seeks opportunities for health care providers to optimize outcomes for older adults through more appropriate and effective communication. As you can see in Figure 12.2, this model emphasizes that communication with older adults must be based on recognizing individualized cues, modifying communication to suit individual needs and situations, appropriately assessing health and social problems, and empowering both older adults and health care providers.

Although the Ryan and colleagues' model has not yet been tested extensively, it can be readily applied to communication situations involving interactions with older adults from different ethnic groups and with older adults who have cognitive impairments. This approach promotes mental, social, and physical well-being among older adults. But most important, it reminds us that we must speak to all older adults in a way that conveys the respect they deserve.

Concept Checks

1. What are the various types of long-term care facilities?
2. What are the characteristics of the typical nursing home resident?
3. What are the major points of the various approaches to describing the characteristics of nursing homes?

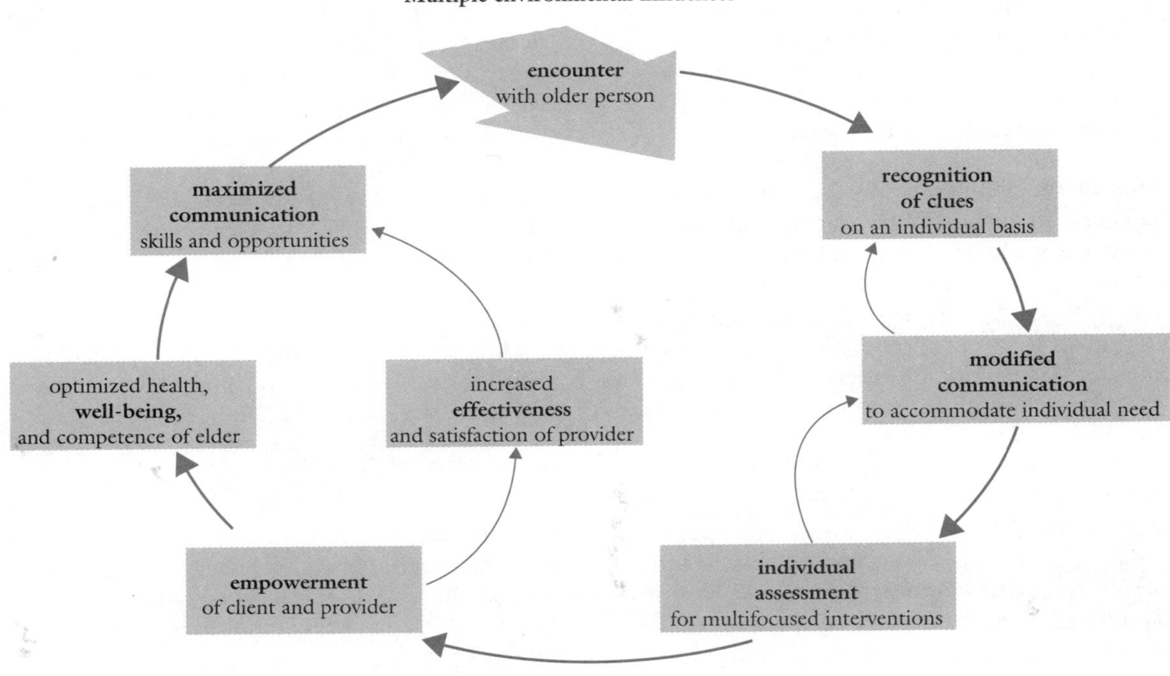

Figure 12.2 Communication enhancement model.
Source: Ryan, Meredith, MacLean, & Orange (1995)

4. Under what conditions can a nursing home be a "home" for its residents?
5. What is the communication enhancement model?

RELOCATION

Learning Objectives:

- What are the most important variables in understanding community-based relocation?
- What are the most important issues in relocation to and relocations within long-term care facilities?

The United States is a highly mobile society. The time when people lived their entire lives in the same neighborhood has largely passed. Adults of all ages relocate, and many are already veterans by the time they reach 21. Regardless of one's age or previous experience, relocation is a challenge. Whether it is moving to a different floor in the dorm or across the country, moving disrupts our physical and social environments and tests our coping skills. Living in a house full of boxes and moving cartons is a hassle; leaving friends and family for a strange city hundreds of miles away is emotionally traumatic. But lots of things determine whether a move will be psychologically tolerable or a nightmare. Exactly what impact does moving have on psychological well-being? Does the type of relocation make a difference? What factors make adjustment after moving easier or more difficult?

To answer these questions, we will examine two types of relocation: community based and institutional. Community-based moves involve moving from one residence to another, regardless of whether the two are in the same neighborhood or a great distance apart. The key ingredient is that the person maintains an independent residence. In contrast, institutional relocations involve moving either from a community-based residence to a long-term care facility or from one facility to another. The major factor here is that the individual is not able to live independently in the community.

Community-Based Relocation

Community-based relocations are fairly common. Although younger adults are the most likely to move, middle-aged and older adults do relocate. Indeed, roughly one third of adults over age 45 in the United States have moved within the previous 5 years. Clearly, community-based relocation is fairly common.

This pattern of mobility is not limited to the United States. Rogers, Watkins, and Woodward (1990) examined mobility patterns in the United States, Great Britain, Italy, and Japan. They found that the United States and Great Britain both show clear patterns of elderly migration to specific locations having high concentrations of older adults. This pattern is less well defined in Italy, and hardly occurs at all in Japan. Family ties—strong in both these countries—along with few identifiable retirement regions combine to keep migration rates down.

Why People Move

Although many older adults head to the Sun Belt, many do not. In fact, recent trends indicate that the flight to warmer climates is slowing, and many elderly people choose to relocate to retirement communities in the North (J. W. Meyer, 1987). Regardless of where they go, why do they move in the first place?

In one of the few developmental studies on mobility, Speare and Meyer (1988) identified four reasons for moving mentioned by movers 55 and older that corresponded to changes in later life: amenity, kinship, retirement, and widowhood. *Amenity mobility* is based on a primary or secondary reason of climate change. *Kinship mobility* occurs because the person wants to be closer to relatives. *Retirement mobility* takes place in response to retirement, with climate and distance from relatives not a factor. *Widowhood mobility* occurs when a person desires to be closer to important members of the social support system other than the immediate family.

The characteristics of elderly movers differ somewhat based on the reason for moving. As summarized in Table 12.3, amenity and retirement movers are similar in that both groups are richer and better educated, own their own home, and are married. Kinship movers tend to be older than other types but in other respects are similar to other groups. Widowhood movers have significantly lower income, are older, but are also well educated and own homes. Additionally, amenity and retirement movers head to the South and West more often than other types, who relocate to all regions.

These findings were extended in a study of the motives for relocation in a nationally representative of older Americans over age 70 (De Jong, Wilmoth, Angel, & Cornwell, 1995). Six primary motives were identified: health, affiliation, economic security, comfort, functional independence, and getting on with life after a family crisis. Importantly, health was not the dominant motive; the remaining five motives were mentioned roughly equally.

As older adults begin to have trouble performing tasks of daily living or when their health begins to fail, they are also likely to move (Longino, Jackson, Zimmerman, & Bradsher, 1991; Speare, Avery, & Lawton, 1991). For example, Longino and co-workers (1991) found that in adults over age 70, a move between an amenity relocation and an institutional relocation was often precipitated by declines in one's ability to take care of daily tasks without assistance. Similarly, De Jong and colleagues (1995) found that change in the level of disability was an important factor in relocation only for those older adults who list health as their primary motive for moving.

TABLE 12.3 Percentages of movers and nonmovers aged 55 and older who fall into various descriptive categories

Movers, by Reason Independent Variables	*Amenity*	*Kinship*	*Retirement*	*Widowed*	*Other*	**Nonmovers**
Age groups						
55 to 64	53.6	41.4	59.2	35.4	57.8	41.3
65 to 74	25.5	33.8	29.4	32.1	26.9	34.9
75 and over	21.0	24.8	11.5	32.5	15.3	23.8
Total	100.1*	100.0	100.1	100.0	100.0	100.0
Household types						
Single person	32.9	48.4	18.5	89.5	45.8	33.0
2+ persons	8.7	9.9	0.0	10.5	13.1	11.0
Married couple	58.4	41.7	81.5	0.0	41.1	56.0
Total	100.0	100.0	100.0	100.0	100.0	100.0
Previous tenure						
Homeowner	70.8	48.7	78.6	62.8	29.7	78.2
Renter	29.2	51.3	21.4	37.2	70.3	21.8
Total	100.0	100.0	100.0	100.0	100.0	100.0
Education (in years)						
0 to 7	8.7	13.2	6.9	17.4	20.2	14.5
8 to 11	27.1	39.6	25.2	25.2	28.3	30.9
12 to 15	50.3	34.8	55.7	33.7	39.5	41.8
16+	13.9	12.3	12.2	23.7	12.0	12.9
Total	100.0	99.9	100.0	100.0	100.0	100.1
Income/poverty						
Below poverty	13.1	20.9	8.7	39.8	28.9	16.3
Below 2 × poverty	21.8	32.5	27.6	28.7	27.0	28.1
Above 2 × poverty	65.1	46.6	63.6	31.5	44.1	55.6
Total	100.0	100.0	99.9	100.0	100.0	100.0

Source: "Types of Elderly Residential Mobility and Their Determinants," by A. Speare, Jr., and J. W. Meyer, 1988, *Journal of Gerontology, 43,* 574–581. Copyright © 1988 by The Gerontological Society of America. Reprinted with permission.
*Totals may not equal 100 due to rounding off.

Factors Affecting Adjustment

Simply because relocation happens frequently does not diminish its psychological impact. One way to think about this aspect of relocation is to consider the psychological stress moving introduces and the effects that stress has on a person's adjustment. When relocation is viewed this way, an important question comes to mind. Given that any relocation is potentially stressful, what variables influence an individual's perception of stress in community-based relocations?

Four variables appear to be important. Obviously, the degree to which familiar behavior patterns are disrupted is a consideration. Second, the sense of personal loss at leaving one's former residence also affects subsequent adjustment. To the extent that one was very attached to one's old home, adjustment to one's new home may be harder. A third variable is the distance involved in the move; the farther one moves, the greater the disruption of routines is likely to be. Finally, the reason for the move is very important. It is generally true that people who make voluntary moves perceive the relocation more positively than people who make involuntary moves.

Although the four variables of disruption, loss, distance, and reason are good predictors of stress in community-based moves, people show substantial individual differences in adjustment even for identical levels of loss. How well one adjusts to relocation, then, is a function not only of disruption and so forth but also of several personal factors involving social status, social support, environmental variables, and perception of the move. These personal factors affect the perception of stress and facilitate or hinder the adjustment process. Because they are important factors in understanding how individuals cope with relocation, we will consider them more thoroughly in the following sections.

Social status factors such as occupation, education, and socioeconomic status provide an indication of where a person fits in the community and an index of life experience. Of the many social status variables that could influence adjustment to community-based relocation, only two have been studied systematically. Higher levels of education lead to better adjustment (Storandt, Wittels, & Botwinick, 1975), as does higher socioeconomic status, reflected in occupation and income (Rosow, 1967; Storandt et al., 1975). Because more highly educated people tend to have higher socioeconomic status, the two factors may operate together.

One thing is clear from this work. Our understanding of the influence of social status on adjustment to relocation is quite limited. Important factors such as marital status, race, and gender have not been examined very thoroughly as potential influences. Until such multivariate research is done, we will not know whether the influence of education and socioeconomic status holds independent of these other factors.

Social support systems provide both emotional and other types of assistance during relocation. We have already seen that maintaining friendships is an important factor in nursing home residents' well-being; the same is true for people who move. Research shows that good relationships with family and friends facilitate adjustment to relocation (George, 1980; Lawton, 1980).

Some research has examined changes in social support systems following relocation. Interestingly, it appears that people do not substitute relationships with one group for missing relationships with another. For instance, older adults whose children or other close relatives move away do not substitute friendships with age peers for the missing familial ties (Hochschild, 1973). The best possible situation is one in which old friendship and family bonds can be maintained and new ones developed.

Environmental variables such as the physical characteristics of the new residence and the nature of the new community affect adjustment. In particular, the issues of space, privacy, and convenience are important physical factors. Improvements on these dimensions will lead to better adjustment (Lawton, 1980). Additionally, people who move to communities having high proportions of same-age peers tend to adjust better (Rosow, 1967; Teaff, Lawton, Nahemow, & Carlson, 1978). This effect is probably due to the greater ease of forming new friendships when one is surrounded by people of similar age and background, thereby helping to build a new social support system.

People's *perception of the move,* such as what they believe to be their degree of control, has a direct bearing on how well they adjust, independent of the true situation. In general, if people think that they are being forced to move, adjustment problems are more likely to result (George, 1980).

If perception is viewed as a function of advance knowledge of the move, a contrasting picture emerges. Schooler (1982) found that when moves were expected, the outcomes were worse than when they were unexpected. He speculated that advance knowledge of an impending relocation might induce anxiety, which might be exacerbated by the trauma of the move itself. Interestingly, when expected relocations resulted in a better environment or when a confidant was available, the negative impact was reduced. However, Schooler did not take into account why people were moving or their attitudes about it, so the overall meaning of his results is somewhat unclear. Still, we should not dismiss his results; they point out that even when individuals know that they are going to move, some people may suffer from the anxiety induced by this knowledge.

How well do these variables predict adjustment when examined simultaneously? Ryff and Essex (1992) examined 120 older women who had experienced community relocation. They found that their reasons for moving (which they termed push factors), reasons for selecting the new setting (termed pull factors), how they compared with others in their new setting, how they were viewed following the move by people important to them, how their behaviors changed after the move, and whether these evaluations occurred in aspects of their lives central to their sense of self provided strong predictions of psychological well-being after the move. This was especially true for feelings of environmental mastery, purpose in life, and positive relations with others. Thus, how well people adjust to community-based relocation depends on the degree to which people's evaluations of their move are connected to key aspects of the self.

Long-Term Effects

Most studies of adjustment to community-based relocation have followed the participants for only a short time after they move. Because short-term effects may differ from long-term effects, longitudinal investigations are required to address this possibility. All of the psychological consequences of moving that we have considered thus far are based on short-term assessments. In this section we will consider what we know about the long-term effects of moving in the community.

Two projects have examined adjustment of movers approximately a year after their voluntary relocation. Both involved older adults moving from independent community residences to housing projects designed specifically for older adults, and both involved comparisons between movers and people who were on the waiting list for admission to the housing complex (termed *nonmovers* in this study).

In the first project participants were all eligible for low-income housing and had limited financial assets. They were tested on four areas relating to psychological adjustment: cognitive and psychomotor performance, health, activity level, and morale and well-being. Testing was done twice, 5 months before the move and 9 months after. The results showed no differences between movers and nonmovers on any of the measures, so the investigators concluded that moving had no long-term adverse effects (Storandt & Wittels, 1975; Storandt et al., 1975; Wittels & Botwinick, 1974).

The second project involved individuals who wanted to move to Victoria Plaza in San Antonio. For those people who succeeded at getting into the project, the new residences offered considerably improved surroundings than had been available in the previous residence. Movers and nonmovers were tested three times: 6 months before the move and 1 and 8 years after the move. Health, mortality rates, and well-being were measured. Results showed that on each test the movers were significantly better off than the nonmovers on every measure. Thus, when relocation involves significant improvements in one's physical surroundings, the benefits of moving or the costs of not moving are potentially very long-lasting (Carp, 1966, 1975, 1977).

Relocation to and Within Long-Term Care Facilities

We saw in earlier discussion that although only about 5% of the people over age 65 reside in long-term care facilities at any one time, many more people spend at least part of their lives there. This means that many people face the transition from living in the community to living in a long-term care facility each year. As in community-based relocation, these people experience disruption in routines and in social relationships and a sense of loss from leaving the previous home.

From the previous discussion, and perhaps from personal experience, we might expect institutional relocation to be more difficult to deal with psychologically. After all, older and younger people view placement in a long-term care facility with dread and see it as an admission that they are no longer competent enough to care for themselves. Admission to a long-term care facility also involves giving up a great deal of personal freedom and privacy. But do these factors necessarily imply that all institutional relocations result in negative outcomes?

Personal Factors Affecting Adjustment

To answer this question, we must consider many of the same personal factors affecting adjustment that are important in community-based moves: social status, social support, and involuntary versus voluntary relocation. Moreover, several other variables must be considered in institutional relocation: physical and cognitive resources, personality factors, and preparation experiences.

Relocation to a nursing home is not random. As noted earlier, very old European American women who are widowed or unmarried and who have minimal financial resources are the most likely to be placed when they face serious health problems. Although these *social status* variables accurately predict who the typical relocator will be, they do not appear to predict level of adjustment in the nursing home.

Physical health and cognitive abilities facilitate institutional relocation (Tobin & Lieberman, 1976). Specifically, people in poor health and those who have experienced severe cognitive declines are more likely to have adjustment problems. Although inadequate physical and cognitive resources predict maladjustment, adequate resources do not guarantee successful relocation.

The importance of *social support* as a factor in adjustment to institutional relocation cannot be overemphasized. As indicated earlier, lack of a viable social support system is the best predictor of placement in a nursing home (George, 1980). The maintenance of old support systems and the development of new ones after relocation to a nursing home eases adjustment (Greene & Monahan, 1982; Harel, 1981). Furthermore, close primary relationships are associated with better adjustment following relocation from one facility to another (Wells & Macdonald, 1981). These relationships provide residents with a source of continuity that enable them to deal better with an emotionally stressful event.

A cluster of *personality traits* appears to be related to survival among nursing home residents: aggression, hostility, assertiveness, and narcissism (Tobin & Lieberman, 1976). Because people with these traits are not usually the easiest to get along with, it may seem surprising that such unpleasant characteristics are related to at least one aspect of adjustment. However, these traits may represent the only means by which a person can assert his or her individuality and dislike for the lack of personal freedom in the facility. In this sense these characteristics may represent a more adaptive response than passive acceptance, even though the latter behavior will win more friends among the staff.

Preparation for institutional relocation involves not only formal programs but also informal ones through friendship networks. A number of studies have shown that adjustment following relocation from one facility to another is better if residents are given a formal preparation program (for instance, Pino, Rosica, & Carter, 1978). Borup (1981) concluded that the major objective of these programs should be to help reduce the stress and anxiety associated with the relocation.

Whether relocation is *voluntary or involuntary* predicts adjustment in community-based relocation; involuntary moves are more stressful. Thus, we would expect that involuntary moves to long-term care facilities would also be more stressful. Unfortunately, almost no research has examined this issue. The problem is that most institutional relocations are involuntary, so researchers have not considered this factor.

Type of Relocation and Adjustment

We have seen that many personal factors influence adjustment following institutional relocation. To understand the adjustment process itself, however, we must consider two types of institutional relocation: relocation from the community to a long-term care facility and relocation from one facility to another. We have alluded to these different types in our discussion of personal factors; we will now examine them in more detail. Almost all the relevant studies have concentrated on nursing homes as the setting, so our survey will focus on this type of facility.

Three issues that are important in the adjustment process following relocations from the community to a nursing home have been investigated fairly intensely: person-environment fit, short-term versus long-term adjustment patterns, and factors immediately before placement.

The appropriateness of the nursing home and of the services it provides is related to level of residents' morale 1 year after their relocation (Morris, 1975). People who are placed in inappropriate nursing homes have significantly lower morale than those who are appropriately placed. These findings once again show the importance of Kahana's (1982) notion of congruence, or person-environment fit.

In examining adjustment after a move from the community to a nursing home, a researcher must be careful to follow the residents long enough. This point was nicely demonstrated by Spasoff and his colleagues (1978). They found that life satisfaction was consistently high at 1 month and 1 year after relocation. However, 25% of the original sample had died, and 15% had been moved to other nursing homes during the first year. Clearly, the sample that was tested after 1 year was different from the one tested initially. Spasoff and his colleagues (1978) demonstrated that investigators need to be sensitive to these changes in sample characteristics to avoid incorrect conclusions about long-term adjustment.

Tobin and Lieberman conducted a major longitudinal investigation of adjustment to moves from the community to nursing homes (Tobin & Lieberman, 1976). They were able to isolate the effects of relocation itself by examining three groups of people: a group that was waiting for admission to a nursing home, a group that had been in a nursing home for 1 to 3 years, and a sample that stayed in the community throughout the study. Five factors in adjustment (physical health, cognitive functioning, emotional states, emotional responsiveness, and self-perception) were measured at three times: before the placement of the relocation group, 2 months after relocation, and 1 year after.

Most important, Tobin and Lieberman found that even before placement the relocation group resembled the nursing home group more than the community group. Moreover, the main influences on adjustment and identity after placement are those that lead to placement in the first place. Following relocation, the first few months seem to be the most difficult, although some people experience relocation stress up to a year later. Thus, Tobin and Lieberman's results show that it is older adults with the fewest personal resources to handle stress who are most likely to be involved in the stress of relocation from the community to a nursing home.

Few studies have examined the psychological adjustment process following relocation from one facility to another. Rather, investigators have looked at mortality rates as the measure of successful relocation. A highly controversial series of studies by Borup and his associates in the late 1970s and early 1980s spurred a heated debate over the connection between interfacility relocation and mortality (Borup, 1981, 1982, 1983; Borup & Gallego, 1981; Borup, Gallego, & Heffernan, 1979, 1980).

Borup concluded from his own and others' research that relocation alone had no effect on residents' mortality. He argues that in some cases a moderate environmental change can even have a positive effect, for reasons similar to Langer's concerning mindlessness. Finally, Borup attributes most of the apparent negative consequences of relocation to the length of time spent in the nursing home. That is, he feels that the same observations of decline would be made if residents remained in the same nursing home for the same period.

Borup's conclusions have been attacked by several authors (Bourestom & Pastalan, 1981; Horowitz & Schulz, 1983). Criticisms of Borup's research design and interpretations of his own and others' findings have been the main focus of these debates. These authors are also concerned that nursing homes will misapply Borup's results and abandon all attempts to make relocation less stressful. These critics force us to evaluate the evidence carefully, and they stimulate discussion on a very important topic.

The weight of the evidence points to the conclusion that interfacility relocation per se has little if any direct effect on mortality. Future researchers will be focusing on the question of psychological adjustment following such moves. It remains to be seen whether the findings from this research will prove as controversial as those from mortality research.

Relocation within the same facility occurs relatively frequently. Surprisingly, though, very little research has been done examining routine room changes within the same nursing home. On the basis of an intensive investigation of room changes in four nursing homes over one year using a wide variety of methods, Everard, Rowles, and High (1994) developed a decision-making model of how room changes occur. Their model consists of five phases. The *precursor phase* includes the period during which residents or their families voice concerns about the room, financial concerns about rooms occur (such as the need to move from a private room to a shared room), a change in care is required, or the bed is needed for another resident. The *initiation phase* follows, at which point the resident, family, staff, or facility makes a formal request for a room change. The *decision phase* includes evaluating the request, informing the appropriate parties, and consulting with the resident, family, and staff. The *action phase* involves the decision as to whether an established resident moves, a new resident moves, there are multiple moves, or no change is warranted. Finally, the *outcomes phase* reflects new tensions that may occur among the resident, his or her new roommate, and the staff; resident morbidity and well-being; and new opportunities for the relocated resident, new roommate, and staff to create relationships.

In one of the few studies that addresses these phases, Pruchno and Resch (1988) examined one-year outcomes, defined as mortality rates, in one group following room changes for reasons other than health and in a nonmover group matched for competence. Through advanced statistical analyses, Pruchno and Resch showed that the connection between mortality after relocation and initial competence was complex. Mortality rates for movers who had high or low initial competence were lower than for the nonmover group. However, movers with moderate initial competence showed higher mortality levels. Pruchno and Resch argue that moving represented a positive and stimulating experience for residents with high or low competence, whereas those with moderate competence viewed the move as disruptive and confusing. The important point from this research is that mortality effects following a move may be related to the environmental cues that are most salient to the residents. That is, residents who notice the negative features of the move may be more at risk than those who focus on the positive aspects.

Concept Checks

1. What are the major variables affecting adjustment to community-based relocation?
2. What factors facilitate adjustment to relocation to and within long-term care facilities?

SUMMARY

Theories of Person-Environment Interactions

Environmental psychology focuses on the interactions between people and communities or other settings in which they live. Behavior is viewed as a function of both the person and the environment.

Competence and Environmental Press

Person-environment interaction refers to the fact that behavior is a function of both the person and the environment. Competence is the upper limit on one's capacity to function. Environmental press reflects the demands placed on a person. Lawton and Nahemow's model establishes points of balance between the two, called adaptation level. One implication of the model is that the less competent a person is, the more impact the environment has.

The Congruence Model

Kahana's congruence model proposes that people search for environments that best meet their needs. Congruence between the person and the environment is especially important when either individual or environmental options are limited. The congruence model helps focus on individual differences and on understanding adaptation in nursing homes and other long-term care facilities.

Stress and Coping Theory

Schooler applied Lazarus' model of stress and coping to person-environment interactions. Schooler claims that older adults' adaptation depends on their perception of environmental stress and their attempts to cope. Social systems and institutions may buffer the effects of stress.

The Loss-Continuum Concept

The loss-continuum concept is based on the view of aging as a progressive series of losses that reduces one's social participation. Thus, home and neighborhood take on more importance. This approach is a guide to helping older adults maintain competence and independence.

Common Theoretical Themes

All theories agree that the focus must be on interactions between the person and the environment. No single environment will meet everyone's needs.

Communities, Neighborhoods, and Housing

Community Size

Satisfaction with where one lives varies as a function of the quality of one's informal social network, degree of differentiation of services, and residents' expectations of what the community should be like. The informal social network is especially important in rural communities. Knowledge of services is key to their utilization. The decline of rural towns is hardest on older residents.

Neighborhoods

People's perception of their neighborhood affects their overall well-being, and people are influenced by perceptions (and not necessarily the reality) concerning crime and structural features. Personal preference concerning the age structure of neighborhoods is an important individual difference variable. Ethnic differences are widespread in terms of what a neighborhood is and the role it plays in people's lives.

Housing

Older adults live in a wide variety of housing: age segregated, age integrated, apartment complexes, retirement communities, congregate housing, SRO hotels, and continuing care retirement communities. Participant observation research has revealed subcultures that emerge in many types of housing. Satisfaction with different types of housing varies a great deal across individuals and research methods. Continuous care retirement communities incorporate many design aspects based on research on older adults. A growing number of older adults are homeless.

Conclusions

The most important point to remember about communities, neighborhoods, and housing is that optimizing the person-environment fit is the goal. Interventions should be based on this principle.

Living in Long-Term Care Facilities

At any given point in time, only about 5% of older adults are in long-term care facilities. Such facilities offer excellent examples of the importance of person-environment fit.

Types of Long-Term Care Facilities

Nursing homes, personal care and boarding homes, and psychiatric hospitals are the main types of facilities in which older adults live. A distinction within nursing homes is between skilled nursing care and intermediate care. The number of older adults in psychiatric hospitals has declined rapidly in the past few decades.

Who Is Likely to Live in Nursing Homes?

The typical resident is European American, very old, financially disadvantaged, widowed or divorced, and possibly without living children. Placement in nursing homes is seen as a last resort and is often based on the lack of other alternatives, lack of other caregivers, or policies in the level of functioning needed to remain in one's present housing.

Characteristics of Nursing Homes

Kahana's congruence model emphasizes the importance of fit between the person and the nursing home. This model discusses seven environmental and individual dimensions. Members of residents' social network are especially important. Moos's approach emphasizes evaluation of physical, organizational, supportive, and social climate aspects. Langer emphasizes the importance of a sense of personal control in maintaining well-being and even staying alive. Control interventions can also help address depression.

Can a Nursing Home Be "Home"?

Residents of nursing homes can come to the conclusion that this can be "home." This concept refers to the fact that "home" is more than simply a place to live. Coming to the feeling that one is "at home" sometimes requires reflection on what one's previous "home" was like and recognizing that a nursing home can have some of the same characteristics.

Communicating with Residents

Inappropriate speech to older adults is based on stereotypes of dependence and lack of abilities. Patronizing and infantilizing speech are examples of demeaning speech, which are rated extremely negatively by older adults. The communication enhancement model has been proposed as a framework for appropriate exchange. This model is based on a health promotion model that seeks opportunities for health care providers to optimize outcomes for older adults through more appropriate and effective communication.

Relocation

Community-Based Relocation

People move for many reasons, such as better climate, being closer to relatives, in response to retirement, or to be closer to friends. Adjustment to relocation depends on the degree of disruption to familiar behavior patterns, sense of loss of residence, distance of the move, and whether the move is voluntary. Individual difference variables affecting adjustment include social status, social support systems, environmental variables, and the perception of the move. Important predictors of who will relocate include health, cognitive abilities, social support, and personality traits.

Relocation to and Within Long-Term Care Facilities

Preparation for relocation and voluntary relocation facilitate adjustment. Physical health, cognitive abilities, social support, and personality traits are also important predictors of adjustment. Person-environment fit is key to overall adjustment. Changing facilities does not significantly increase mortality rates. Moving from one room to another is a common occurrence.

REVIEW QUESTIONS

Theories of person-environment interactions

- What is environmental psychology?
- What are person-environment interactions?
- Describe Lawton and Nahemow's theory of environmental press. In their theory, what is adaptation level?
- Describe Kahana's congruence model. In what settings is this model especially appropriate?
- Describe the application of the stress and coping

model to person-environment interactions. What kinds of things buffer stress?
- Describe the loss-continuum concept.
- What are the common themes expressed by the various theories of person-environment interactions?

Communities, neighborhoods, and housing
- What factors affect satisfaction with where one lives?
- What factors influence the perceptions of neighborhoods? What ethnic differences have been noted in neighborhood perceptions?
- What kinds of housing do older adults live in?

Living in long-term care facilities
- How many older adults live in long-term care facilities at any given point?
- What types of facilities house older adults?
- Who is most likely to live in a nursing home? Why?
- How have the characteristics of nursing homes been studied? How do Kahana's approach, Moos's approach, and Langer's approach differ?
- How does a resident of a nursing home come to view it as a "home"?
- What are the characteristics of inappropriate speech aimed at older adults? What is an alternative approach?

Relocation
- Why do people move?
- What factors influence adjustment to relocation?
- What factors predict who is likely to relocate to a nursing home?
- How do preparation and the degree to which the move is voluntary affect adjustment?

INTEGRATING CONCEPTS IN DEVELOPMENT

1. What do the demographics about the aging of the population imply about the need for long-term care through the first few decades of the 21st century?
2. How do the theories of person-environment interaction include the basic developmental forces?
3. What housing needs are likely over the next few decades?

KEY TERMS

adaptation level In person-environment interactions, the point at which competence and environmental press are in balance.

age-integrated Communities in which people of all ages live.

age-segregated Communities that are exclusively for older adults.

competence In person-environment interactions, the theoretical upper limit of a person's ability to function.

congruence model In person-environment interactions, the notion that people need to find the environment in which they fit and that meets their needs the best.

environmental press In person-environment interactions, the demands put on a person by the environment.

environmental psychology The study of person-environment interactions.

infantilization Also termed *secondary baby talk,* a type of speech that is inappropriate and demeaning to older adults.

informal social network The friends, neighbors, and family who provide support but who are not connected with any formal social service agency.

loss continuum A theory of person-environment interactions based on the notion that social participation declines as personal losses increase.

patronizing speech Inappropriate speech to older adults that is based on stereotypes of incompetence and dependence.

person-environment interactions The interface between people and the world in which they live that forms the basis for development.

IF YOU'D LIKE TO LEARN MORE

Johnson, C.L. (1987). The institutional segregation of the aged. In P. Silverman (Ed.), *The elderly as modern pioneers.* Bloomington: Indiana University Press. Good summary of the major issues in nursing homes. Moderately difficult.

Lawton, M.P., Windley, P.G., & Byerts, T.O. (1982). *Aging and the environment: Theoretical approaches.* New York: Springer. A good overview of person-environment interactions. Moderately difficult.

Silverman, P. (1987). Community settings. In P. Silverman (Ed.), *The elderly as modern pioneers.* Bloomington: Indiana University Press. Good summary of the major issues in housing. Moderately difficult.

CHAPTER 13

Dying and Bereavement

Andrew Wyeth, *Beckie King*, 1946. Dallas Museum of Art, Gift of Everett L. DeGolyer.

There is an ancient Buddhist story called the Parable of the Mustard Seed. The parable tells of Kisa Gotami, a woman born in poverty, who got married and, as was the custom, went to live with her husband's family. Because she was poor, his family treated her with contempt, until she gave birth to a son, when she was treated with respect. Sadly, when the son was only a few years old, he died. Kisa was overcome with grief. She had liked the respect she received since her son's birth so much that she wanted to try anything and everything to bring him back. She went from house to house, carrying her son, asking people for medicine for him. But everywhere she went people laughed and made fun of her, saying where did anyone ever find medicine for the dead. Kisa had no idea what they meant.

Now a certain wise man heard of this, and thought that Kisa must have been driven out of her mind with sorrow to set out on such a quest. He sent word to her that only the Teacher would know about medicine for her son. So, Kisa set out for a nearby monastery where the Teacher lived. When she arrived, she asked him for medicine for her son. Seeing that she was sincere, the Teacher told her to go into the city, and, starting at the first house, knock on every door, and, in whatever house no one has ever died, fetch tiny grains of mustard seed for medicine.

Delighted at the prospect of finding medicine, she set off. Coming to the first house, she asked for the mustard seed. But when the seed was brought, Kisa realized she could not accept it because someone had died there. So she gave it back. On arriving at the second, and the third, and the fourth houses, Kisa encountered the same problem. Someone had died in each, and she could not accept the mustard seed. In fact, it would have been impossible to count the number of people who had died in the families she met.

Suddenly, she realized the truth. No family ever escapes the reality of death. She understood that this was what the Teacher wanted her to learn for herself. She now fully comprehended that all life is impermanent. Her grief for her son became easier to bear.

Kisa Gotami's lesson about grief is one that each of us must learn for ourselves. Death is not something we particularly like to think about, let alone face. Intellectually, we understand that all life is impermanent. Emotionally, we often try and shield ourselves from the truth, as Kisa did.

Indeed, Americans have a paradoxical relationship with death. On the one hand, we are fascinated by it. The popularity of news stories about murders or wars and the crowds of onlookers at accidents testify to that. Tourists often visit the places where famous people died or are buried. People around the world watch CNN broadcasts that show the horrors of war and genocide in which tens of thousands of people are killed. But when it comes to pondering our own death or that of people close to us, we have considerable problems, as La Rochefoucauld wrote over 300 years ago when he said that it is easier to look in to the sun than to contemplate death. When death is personal, we become uneasy. We may not be as willing to watch CNN if we knew their coverage would concern our own death. It is hard indeed to look at the sun.

For most people in the United States, death is no longer a personal experience until middle age. We typically do not experience death up close as children; indeed, many Americans believe it is important to shield children from death. But just a few generations ago in America, and still in most of the world, death is part of people's everyday life experience. Children are present when family members die. Viewings and wakes are held in the home, and children are active participants in funeral services. In our technological times, perhaps we should consider what these changes in personal experience with death mean for life-span development.

In this chapter we will consider death from many perspectives. We will examine some of the issues surrounding how it is defined legally and medically. We will address several questions: Why do most of us avoid thinking about death? What it is like to die? How are dying people cared for? How do survivors grieve and cope with the loss of a loved one? Finally, we will consider two issues that transcend science: the possibility of an afterlife and the near-death experience.

DEFINITIONS AND ETHICAL ISSUES

Learning Objectives:

- How is death viewed in sociocultural terms?
- How is death defined legally and medically?
- What is euthanasia? How does one make decisions about medical care known to others?
- What are the costs of life-sustaining interventions?
- What are the major issues concerning suicide? Who is most likely to commit suicide?

From the viewpoint of a dictionary, death is very simple—it is the transition between being alive and being dead. Similarly, dying is the process of making this transition. It all seems clear enough, doesn't it? But, as has been true with many other concepts in this book, death and dying are far more complicated and in fact are very hard to define.

The notions of death and dying are much like the notions of youth (or middle age or old age) and aging. We saw in Chapter 1 that it is extremely difficult to give precise definitions of these terms because age itself has many different meanings. Issues such as when middle age ends and old age begins have no easy answers. The same is true for death. What is death? When does death occur? The dictionary notwithstanding, it is very difficult in practice to give precise answers. As we will see, it depends on one's perspective.

Sociocultural Definitions of Death

What comes to mind when you hear the word *death*? Black crepe paper or a cemetery? A driver killed in a traffic accident? Old people in nursing homes? A gathering of family and friends? A transition to an eternal reward? A car battery that doesn't work anymore? An unknowable mystery? Each of these possibilities represents one of the ways in which death can be considered in Western culture (Kalish, 1987). People in other cultures and traditions may view death differently. People around the world may use the same words or concepts that we do, but they may not mean the same things.

For example, Westerners tend to divide people into groups based on chronological age, even though we recognize the limitations of this concept (see Chapter 1). Although we would like to divide people along more functional grounds, practicality dictates that chronological age will have to do. However, other cultures divide people differently. Among the Melanesians the term *mate* includes the very sick, the very old, and the dead; the term *toa* refers to all other living people. This distinction is the most important one, not the one between all the living and all the dead as in our culture (Counts & Counts, 1985b). Other South Pacific cultures believe that the life force may leave the body during sleep or illness, suggesting that sleep, illness, and death are considered together. In this way people "die" several times before experiencing "final death" (Counts & Counts, 1985b). For example, among the Kaliai, "the people . . . are prepared to diagnose as potentially fatal any fever or internal pain or illness that does not respond readily to treatment" (p. 150). Mourning rituals and definitions of states of bereavement also vary across cultures (Simmons, 1945). Some cultures have formalized periods of time during which certain prayers or rituals are performed. For example, Orthodox Jews recite the *Kaddish* after the death of a close relative, cover the mirrors in the house, and the men slash their ties as a symbol of loss. Family members may be prohibited from doing certain things (such as refraining from all social activities) for a specific period of time. Thus, in considering death, dying, and bereavement, we must keep in mind that the experiences of our culture may not generalize to others.

Meanings of Death

Kalish (1987) and Kastenbaum (1975) thought that death can be viewed in at least 10 ways: as an image, a statistic, an event, a state of being, an

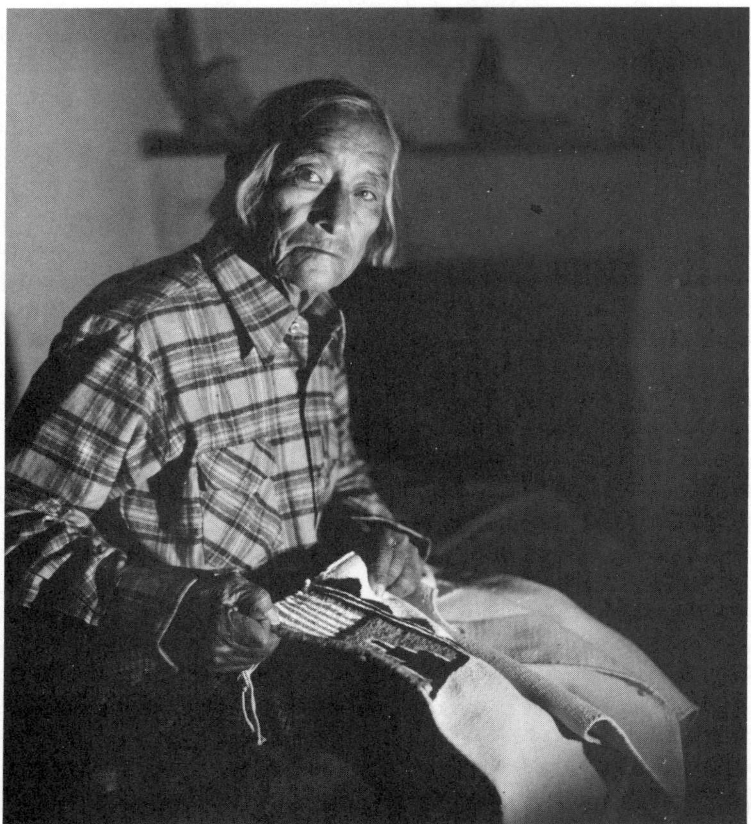

Among the Hopi, the length of life is believed to be tied to good deeds.

analogy, a mystery, a boundary, a thief of meaning, a basis for fear and anxiety, and a reward or punishment. These different ways of viewing death are a reflection of the diverse ways in which society deals with death. Kalish agrees with Kastenbaum's ideas: "Death means different things to the same person at different times; and it means different things to the same person at the same time" (Kalish, 1976, p. 483). Let's consider what these "different things" are.

Every culture has *particular images or objects* that serve as reminders of death. For instance, a flag at half staff, sympathy cards, and tombstones all bring death to mind. People may try to avoid thinking about or viewing these reminders. Others may see these images and feel uneasy or may simply think about their own inevitable death.

Each year, numerous reports summarize death-related information: how many people died from certain diseases, traffic accidents, or murders, for example. These *mortality statistics* are vital to many organizations such as insurance companies (which use them to set premium rates for health and life insurance) and community planners (who use them to project needs for various services). But they also tend to sanitize and depersonalize death by removing the personal context and presenting death as a set of numbers.

Whenever someone dies, it is an *event*. The legal community marks it with official certificates and procedures. Family and friends gather to mourn and comfort one another. Funerals or memorial services are held. Memorial funds may be established. All of these actions serve to mark a person's death and illustrate how death brings people together. The gathering is sometimes seen on a societal level; the national mourning following the Challenger tragedy is an example.

What is it like to be dead? All answers to this question are examples of our belief in death as a *state of being*. Individual differences are the rule here, and particular beliefs are mainly a product of personal experiences and religious beliefs. Death may be thought of as a state of perpetual being, a state of nothingness, a time of waiting or of renewal, an experience that is much like this life, or an existence that involves a transformation of being. While we are alive, each of these views is equally valid; perhaps we will learn more when we make the transition ourselves.

In our language we have many sayings that use the notion of death as an *analogy* to convey the uselessness of people or objects: "That's a dead battery" or "you're a deadhead." In addition, some animals, such as opossums, use playing dead as a defense against predators. Finally, a person who is considered totally unimportant by family or acquaintances may be disowned and treated as if he or she were dead, and may even be referred to in conversations in the past tense.

Even though we know that death is inevitable, it is rarely a major topic for discussion or consideration. More important, because we have so little scientifically valid information about death, it remains an unanswered question, the ultimate *mystery* in our lives. Try as we might, death is one life event (like the moment that life begins) that is understood only when it is experienced. It is also one life event in which doing any advance work is impossible; one cannot even watch a daytime talk show to find out exactly what it is like to die and really be dead. Which, of course, is a major reason that we are typically afraid to die.

Regardless of how one views the state of death, it is seen as an end, or *boundary,* of one's earthly existence. When the end of a period of time is approaching, we tend to pay greater attention to it and to use the time remaining more effectively. For example, as students near the end of a term, they typically change the way in which they spend the remaining time, based on their priorities (more studying and less partying in order to do well on their final exams and pass their courses). Consider how your use of time would change if you could assume 400 more years of life rather than 50 or 60. Would you continue doing what you are right now? Or would you do something different?

By the same token, as people's death becomes more imminent, how they use their remaining time becomes more important. For example, Kalish and Reynolds (1981) found that 29% of people over 60 thought about their death every day, compared with 15% under 40 and 11% between 40 and 60.

Interestingly, people allot themselves a certain number of years to which they feel entitled. Although the exact number of years varies across the life span, most people feel that this amount of time is only fair; this view is termed the *just world view* by social psychologists (Kalish, 1987). If death becomes imminent many years before this perceived entitled length of life, the person is liable to feel cheated. If the number of expected years of life is exceeded, then death is seen to be playing by the rules; it is now all right to die.

Intellectually, we all know that we may die at any time, but in modern society the probability of death before old age is relatively low. This was not always true. In earlier centuries death occurred almost randomly across the life cycle, with many deaths among infants, young children, and women in childbirth. Aries (1974) believes that people in earlier times lived each day to the fullest because they knew firsthand that death really did occur to people of all ages.

Today, we are so convinced that we will live a long life that we let many days simply slip by. We delay fulfillment of dreams or ambitions until the later years, when illness or limited finances may restrict our ability to do what we had planned. In this sense death has *robbed us of the meaning of life.* We no longer take each day and use it for everything it is worth. As a result the conflicts of the later years (Erikson, 1982; see Chapter 8) involve questions of what life means, such as why we should bother learning new things since death is so close (Kalish, 1987).

Thinking about death may bring about feelings of *fear and anxiety.* Because so much research has examined this topic, we will consider it in detail later. At this point, though, it is important to realize that older adults are more likely to express acceptance and acquiescence at the inevitability of death.

Many people believe that the length of life is a *reward or punishment* for how righteously or sinfully one lives. For example, the Hopi Indians believe that kindness, good thoughts, and peace of mind lead to a long life (Simmons, 1945). Similarly, a study of four ethnic communities in Los Angeles (African American, Hispanic, Japanese American, and white) found that over half of the respondents over 65 and about 30% of younger respondents agreed with the statement, "Most people who live to be 90 years old or older must have been morally good people" (Kalish & Reynolds, 1981). Finally, the Managalase, an Oceanic society, believe that simply remaining alive into old age is a sign of strength of soul, and their elderly are treated with more respect than in most societies (McKellin, 1985).

Legal and Medical Definitions

Sociocultural approaches help us understand the different ways in which people view death. But these views do not address a very fundamental question: How do we determine that someone has died? To answer this question, we must turn our attention to the medical and legal definitions of death.

Determining when death occurs has always been a judgment. Just as there is considerable debate over when life begins, so there is over when life ends. The solution typically has been for experts to propose a set of criteria, which are then adopted by society (Jeffko, 1979). **For thousands of years people accepted and applied the criteria known today as those defining *clinical death,* a lack of heartbeat and respiration. Today, however, the most widely accepted criteria are the eight listed below, which constitute *brain death:***

1. No spontaneous movement in response to any stimuli
2. No spontaneous respirations for at least one hour
3. Total lack of responsiveness to even the most painful stimuli
4. No eye movements, blinking, or pupil responses
5. No postural activity, swallowing, yawning, or vocalizing
6. No motor reflexes
7. A flat electroencephalogram (EEG) for at least 10 minutes
8. No change in any of these criteria when they are tested again 24 hours later

For a person to be declared brain dead, all of these eight criteria must be met. Moreover, other conditions that might mimic death—such as deep coma, hypothermia, or drug overdose—must be ruled out.

According to most hospitals, the lack of brain activity must be true of both the cortex (which involves higher processes such as thinking) and the brainstem (which involves vegetative functions such as heartbeat and respiration). **It is possible for a person's cortical functioning to cease while brainstem activity continues; this is a *persistent vegetative state,* from which the person does not recover.** This distinction between cortical and brainstem activity is important, as the famous case of Karen Ann Quinlan demonstrated. Quinlan's cortical functioning had stopped as the result of a deadly mixture of alcohol and barbiturates. Her family wished to remove her from life support; however, in the mid-1970s this was a very controversial decision; it eventually required a decision by the U.S. Supreme Court, which established a family's right to do so. However, once Quinlan was disconnected, her brainstem continued to function, and she continued to survive on her own for several years.

Based on this and similar cases, some professionals began to argue that the criteria for death should include only cortical functioning. **This approach,**

termed *cortical death,* would allow physicians to declare an individual who had no cortical functioning dead even when brainstem functioning continued. Under a definition of cortical death, Quinlan would have been declared legally dead years before she actually died. Proponents of a cortical death definition point out that those functions that we typically use to define humanness, such as thinking and personality, are located in the cortex. When these functions are destroyed, it is argued, the person no longer exists. Although the idea of cortical death as a definition has many adherents, it is not used as a legal definition anywhere in the United States.

Ethical Issues

Imagine the following situation. Betty is working in a health care facility when a woman who is not breathing and has no pulse is rushed into the facility. About 6 months ago, this woman was diagnosed as having ovarian cancer, a very aggressive form of the disease that is typically fatal in a relatively short period of time. Should Betty attempt to revive her knowing that she is terminally ill and would be in a great deal of pain? Or should she let her die without any intervention?

This is an example of the kinds of problems faced in the field of *bioethics,* the study of the interface between human values and technological advances in health and life sciences. Specific issues range from whether to conduct research involving genetic engineering to whether someone should be kept alive by forced feeding or by a machine. In the arena of death and dying, the most important bioethical issue is euthanasia.

Derived from the Greek word meaning good death, *euthanasia* refers to the act or practice of ending a life for reasons of mercy. The moral dilemma posed by euthanasia becomes apparent when we try to decide the circumstances under which a person's life should be ended. In our society this dilemma occurs most often when individuals are being kept alive by machines or when someone is suffering from a terminal illness.

Euthanasia can be carried out in two very different ways. ***Active euthanasia* involves the deliberate ending of someone's life.** This can be done by the patient or someone else administering a drug overdose or using other means; by making it known that no extraordinary measures are to be applied to keep the person alive, through, for example, a living will; or through ending a person's life without his or her permission, by so-called mercy killing. For example, Dr. Jack Kevorkian, a physician in Michigan, created a "suicide machine" that allows people to administer lethal doses of medication to themselves. Dr. Kevorkian has also provided the means for people to breathe carbon monoxide through a mask. All of the people whom Dr. Kevorkian has assisted in their suicides have been terminally ill or in pain.

Cases of active euthanasia often provoke considerable debate (Cutter, 1991). For example, physicians and family members who assist in suicides are sometimes prosecuted. Dr. Kevorkian started a heated national debate with his efforts. Books such as *Final Exit* that describe various types of lethal drug overdoses create controversy. In general, Western societies tend to view many forms of active euthanasia as objectionable if there is no clear evidence that the person in question wanted the action taken.

The second form of euthanasia, *passive euthanasia,* involves allowing a person to die by withholding an available treatment. For example, chemotherapy might be withheld from a cancer patient, a surgical procedure might not be performed, or food could be withdrawn. Again, these approaches can cause controversy. On the one hand, few would argue with a decision not to treat a newly discovered cancer in a person in the late stages of Alzheimer's disease, if treatment would do nothing but prolong and make even more agonizing an already certain death. On the other hand, many people might argue with a decision to withhold nourishment from a terminally ill person; indeed, such cases often end up in court. For example, in 1990 the U.S. Supreme Court took up the case of Nancy Cruzan, whose family wanted to end her forced feeding. The Court ruled in *Cruzan v. Director, Missouri Department of Health* that unless clear and incontrovertible evidence is presented that an individual desires to have nourishment stopped (such as through a durable power of attorney or living will), a third party (such as a parent or spouse) may not decide to end it.

Most people find it difficult to decide how they feel about euthanasia. They opt for making case-by-case decisions that could vary with the circumstances. Active euthanasia is not generally supported, usually out of fear that it might be used against people who were not terminally ill or who were defenseless against such movements, such as the cognitively impaired (Kieffer, 1979). Physicians report that they would usually agree with passive euthanasia but only if authorized by the family. The belief that one person should not kill another is deeply rooted in our society; for that reason euthanasia is likely to be a much-debated topic for many years to come.

Clearly, euthanasia is a complex legal and ethical issue. In most jurisdictions, euthanasia is legal only when a person has made known his or her wishes concerning medical intervention. Unfortunately, many people do not take this step, perhaps because they do not know the options available to them. But without clear directions, medical personnel may be unable or unwilling to take a patient's preferences into account.

Two ways exist to make such intentions known: living wills and durable power of attorney. The purpose of both is to make one's wishes about the use of life support known in the event one is unconscious or otherwise incapable of expressing them. A durable power of attorney has an additional advantage: It names a specific person who has the legal authority to speak for another person if necessary. Although both of these documents have considerable support (many states in the United States have laws concerning these documents), several problems exist as well. Foremost among these is that many people fail to inform their relatives about their living will, do not make their wishes known, or do not tell the person named in a durable power of attorney where the document is kept. Obviously, this puts relatives at a serious disadvantage if decisions concerning the use of life-support systems need to be made.

Some countries, such as the Netherlands, have taken a different route (Cutter, 1991). In 1984, the Dutch Supreme Court eliminated prosecution for physicians who assist in suicide if five criteria are met: (1) The patient's condition is intolerable with no hope for improvement; (2) no relief is available; (3) the patient is competent; (4) the patient makes the request repeatedly over time; and (5) two physicians agree with the patient's request.

How many other countries will follow the Netherlands' example and permit physician-assisted suicides remains to be seen. Bioethicists must make the dilemmas clear, and we must make ourselves aware of the issues. Given that the last days of life for older adults are often complicated by the lack of advance directives concerning the types of care they really want, helping older adults prepare either a living will or a durable power of attorney is very important. (Foley, Miles, Brock, & Phillips, 1995). What is at stake is literally a matter of life and death. Take a minute and reflect more on these issues in the Something to Think About feature.

The Price of Life-Sustaining Care

A growing debate in Western society concerns the financial, personal, and moral costs of keeping people alive on life-support machines. For example, many people argue that treating secondary diseases in terminally ill older adults or keeping them alive on life support makes little sense. They argue that such treatment is extremely expensive, that these individuals will soon die anyway, and needlessly prolonging their lives will be a burden on society. In these cases, it is argued, both the individual and society would be better off simply allowing the person to die.

In contrast, many people—including many physicians—go to extraordinary lengths to keep very premature infants alive, despite high risks of permanent brain damage or physical disability from the intervention. Some people point out that not only is the medical care at the time often more expensive for infants (an average of several thousand dollars per day for neonatal intensive care),

SOMETHING TO THINK ABOUT

Dying with Dignity and Euthanasia

The publicity given to Dr. Jack Kevorkian and his insistence of his right to assist people who want to die has served to focus attention on the controversial issue of euthanasia. His actions have resulted in legal and legislative actions to ban physician-assisted suicide. Regardless of what one personally believes about Kevorkian's tactics, it is certain that his actions have provoked an important discourse in bioethics.

As noted in the text, people have the option of choosing not to have their lives extended through artificial means such as life-support technology. Whether there is a moral distinction between assisting people who want to die and allowing them to die by withholding some sort of intervention continues to be debated by ethicists, physicians, and the public (Markson, 1995). This controversy reflects the confusion about the appropriate norms for dying in the United States and in other industrialized countries. Proponents of euthanasia argue that people should be allowed to choose the time and method of their death, a view that is often called the "right to die with dignity." Opponents claim that no one has the right to "play God" with people's lives. The controversy is even played out in elections and bookstores. Voters in the United States have typically defeated referenda to allow physician-assisted suicide, yet Derek Humphry's (1991) book *Final Exit: The Practicalities of Self-Deliverance and Assisted Suicide for the Dying* was a best-seller.

Public resistance to keeping terminally ill individuals alive on life-support equipment encouraged the U.S. Congress to pass the Patient Self-Determination Act of 1990, which requires health care facilities receiving Medicare funds to inform patients about their right to prepare advance directives stating their preferences for terminal care (Markson, 1995). Although there is widespread belief that such directives, either through a living will or a durable power of attorney, are a good idea, relatively few people have actually prepared documents indicating their preferences for life-sustaining treatment (Markson, Fanale, Steel, Kern & Annas, 1995). Moreover, most physicians do not explain the relative success of various types of medical interventions; for example, only 15% of people under 70 and nearly none of those older who suffer cardiac arrest leave the hospital even if cardiopulmonary resuscitation (CPR) is used (Nuland, 1993). Clearly, the decision as to whether such interventions should be used may be affected by the knowledge family members have about the effectiveness of the intervention.

Without doubt, the issues surrounding euthanasia will continue to provoke debate for many years to come. If this debate is used to help sort out the ethics and morality of issues concerning people's right to die, then perhaps Dr. Kevorkian's controversial actions may have a beneficial effect after all. It's something to think about.

---

but the potential cost to families and society if the person should need constant care could be enormous. Additionally, the emotional costs can be devastating to many families. But many such children are not affected negatively by the intervention and grow up to be normal in all respects.

There are no easy solutions to these dilemmas. At present, there is no way to predict which premature infant will develop normally or which seriously ill older person will recover. But as the tensions among high-tech medicine, spiraling health care costs, and people's ability to afford to pay continue to escalate, confronting these issues will become increasingly more common.

Suicide

One of the hardest things for many people to understand is why someone would end his or her own life. People commit suicide in all manner of ways, mostly in solitude but sometimes in highly dramatic ways, such as when Bantcho Bantchevsky leapt from the balcony to his death during intermission of the Metropolitan Opera's performance of Verdi's *Macbeth.* Occasionally, a suicide casts a sense of mystery on events; attempts to link the suicide of Vincent Foster to the Whitewater affair in the mid-1990s is a recent example.

Every year, roughly 30,000 people in the

United States commit suicide (USDHHS, 1996). For many years, researchers have believed that the true rate is much higher (Osgood, 1985), because most officials will rule that a death is accidental if at all possible to save the family from the social stigma associated with suicide. Drug overdoses are often considered to be accidental, for example, as are most single-car accidents. The number of actual suicides could possibly be as high as 100,000 per year (Stenback, 1980).

Suicide and Age

The relationship between suicide rates and age changed considerably between the mid-1930s and the early 1990s. Although the overall rate has remained reasonably constant, the rate for older adults dropped from roughly 40 per 100,000 to 20 per 100,000. This drop had been much greater, but during the 1980s the rate of suicide among older adults increased over 20%. In contrast, the rate for young people aged 15 to 24 roughly doubled between the mid-1930s and the early 1990s from 8 per 100,000 to nearly 15 per 100,000 (Conwell, 1994). Reasons for the changes are unclear.

Overall, older adults in the United States commit suicide at a much higher rate than any other group, at least twice as high as that in the general population (26.5 per 100,000 in 80- to 84-year-olds versus 12.4 per 100,000 overall) (Conwell, 1994). Comparable statistics in other countries reveal an even wider gap in some countries (La Vecchia, Lucchini, & Levi, 1994). In China, for example, people over age 65 commit suicide about 3 times more often. Relative to many other countries, the suicide rate in the United States is moderate, as shown in Figure 13.1.

In understanding these age differences, we must keep several important points in mind. Many more young people attempt suicide than actually succeed, with the ratio of unsuccessful attempts to successes about 7:1 (Stenback, 1980). Around midlife, however, the ratio switches, so that by old age successes outnumber unsuccessful attempts by nearly 8:1 (Sendbeuhler & Goldstein, 1977). This switch has led many theorists to believe that suicide attempts by younger people are more often cries for help or acts of hostility directed at others, such as parents or lovers. In contrast, older adults seldom attempt suicide as a means of getting attention; rather, they are clearly interested in killing themselves and are far more deadly in their methods (Osgood, 1985).

Although severe depression is a major factor in suicide in people of all ages, older adults who commit suicide are also much more likely to be physically ill than are younger suicide victims. About half of the older men and about one third of older women who commit suicide are seriously ill, many with cancer or a disease that affects the brain (Whitlock, 1986). Indeed, more than three-fourths of older adults who commit suicide had visited their primary care physician within the month prior to their suicide (Conwell, 1994). Sadly, most also have moderately severe, but undiagnosed, symptoms of depression.

Suicide, Ethnicity, and Gender

Overall, European American males have the highest rate of successful suicide (USDHHS, 1996). For European American males, late adolescence and the first few years of adulthood show a relatively high rate, falling slightly through midlife and rising dramatically in late life. African American and Hispanic males also show an early peak, but their rate stays substantially lower than European American males in old age. Asian American males show peak suicide rates in old age but at a lower level than European Americans. White women show a slight increase in suicide rate in midlife, followed by a decrease through old age. Finally, women in other ethnic groups have a low rate of suicide throughout adulthood.

Recent trends, however, indicate that changes may be occurring in the African American community (Alston, Rankin, & Harris, 1995). During the 1980s, for example, suicide rates among older African American males nearly doubled. Why this increase occurred is unknown.

The substantial difference in overall suicide rates between men and women may be misleading (Williams, 1977). More women than men *attempt* suicide, but more men than women *succeed* in killing themselves, primarily because men tend to

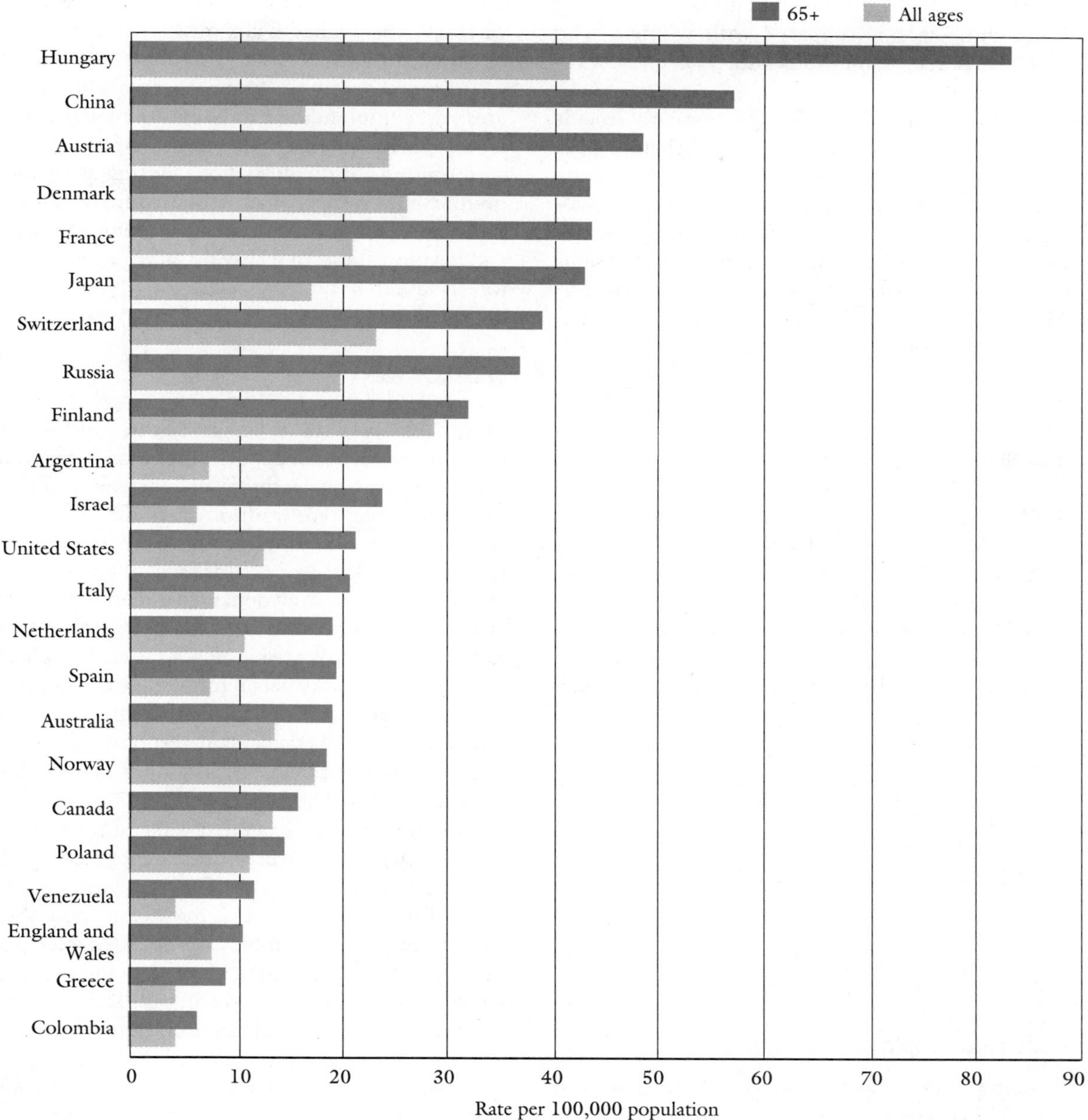

Figure 13.1 Suicide rates for all ages and for older adults in selected countries.
Source: World Health Organization

use more lethal means (such as guns and jumping from high places) compared with women, who prefer less lethal methods (such as poison or sleeping pills).

No adequate explanation of women's suicide statistics has been offered. The notion that the peak in European American women's rate during midlife reflects the empty nest syndrome is inadequate, because it fails to explain why women in other ethnic groups are able to experience the same event with no corresponding increase in suicide. Much more research needs to be done to understand these issues.

Concept Checks

1. What are the 10 ways that death can be viewed socioculturally?
2. What are the criteria for determining brain death versus clinical death?
3. What is the difference between active and passive euthanasia?
4. What are the costs of life-sustaining interventions?
5. What is the relation between suicide and age?

THINKING ABOUT DEATH: PERSONAL COMPONENTS

Learning Objectives:

- What is death anxiety, and to what is it related?
- What are some behavioral manifestations of death anxiety?
- How do people cope with death anxiety?

Being afraid to die is considered normal by most people. As one research participant put it, "You are *nuts* if you aren't afraid of death" (Kalish & Reynolds, 1976). Still, most authors agree that death is a paradox (Schulz, 1978). That is, we are afraid of or anxious about death, but it is this same fear or anxiety that directly or indirectly causes much of our behavior. We will examine this paradox in the following sections. Specifically, we will focus on two questions: What is it about death that we fear or that makes us anxious? How do we show our fear or anxiety?

Before proceeding, however, take a few minutes and complete the exercise in the Discovering Development feature. Although it may be a bit daunting and difficult at first, writing your own obituary is a way to gain insight into what you think are your most important accomplishments and relationships. In a way, it serves as a process for conducting a life review.

Death Anxiety

Death anxiety is tough to pin down. Indeed, it is the ethereal nature of death, rather than something about it in particular, that usually makes us feel so uncomfortable. We cannot put our finger on something specific about death that is causing us to feel uneasy. Because of this, we must look for indirect behavioral evidence to document death anxiety. Techniques have varied considerably: projective personality tests, such as the Rorschach Inkblots; paper-and-pencil tests, such as Templer's Death Anxiety Scale; and measures of physiological arousal, such as galvanic skin response. Research findings suggest that death anxiety is a complex, multidimensional construct.

On the basis of several diverse studies using many different measures, researchers conclude that death anxiety consists of several components. Each of these components is most easily described with terms that resemble examples of fear but cannot be tied to anything specific. Schulz (1978) concluded that the components of death anxiety included pain, body malfunction, humiliation, rejection, nonbeing, punishment, interruption of goals, and negative impact on survivors. To complicate matters further, any of these components can be assessed at any of three levels: public, private, and nonconscious. That is, what we admit feeling about death in public may differ considerably from what we feel when we are alone with our own thoughts. In short, the measurement of death anxiety is complex, and researchers need to specify which aspect(s) they are assessing.

DISCOVERING DEVELOPMENT

How Do You Describe a Life?

If you have ever looked carefully at a newspaper, you know that everyone who dies has a brief summary of his or her life published in an obituary. Obituaries serve several purposes, including telling the world the important aspects of one's life as well as listing one's surviving family members. If you have ever read an obituary, you also realize that they tend to be fairly short, usually less than 200 words in most cases.

Imagine that unlike most people, you have the opportunity to write your own obituary. Imagine further that you can create the obituary based on the life you hope to have. Take a moment to reflect on this, and then compose a 150- to 200-word obituary that includes your age at the time of your death, the cause of death, your major life accomplishments, and your family survivors. When finished, read it over carefully. You may want to keep it for future reference to see how closely your life really does turn out in relation to your dreams.

Considerable research has been conducted to learn what demographic and personality variables are related to death anxiety. Although the results are often ambiguous, some patterns have emerged.

Gender differences in death anxiety have been inconsistent. Some researchers find that women score higher than men on questionnaire measures of death anxiety (such as Iammarino, 1975; Templer, Ruff, & Franks, 1971), but others do not (Dickstein, 1972; Nehrke, Bellucci, & Gabriel, 1977). When differences are observed, women tend to view death in more emotional terms, whereas men tend to view it in more cognitive terms (Degner, 1974; Krieger, Epsting, & Leitner, 1974; Wittkowski, 1981). Acceptance and anxiety had always been thought to be antithetical, but they may not be (Kalish, 1985). Keith (1979) offers perhaps the best way of understanding the controversy. Keith's questionnaire combines items that measure death anxiety, perceptions of life after death, and general acceptance. Women apparently find the prospect of their own death more anxiety producing than men do, but they simultaneously have a greater acceptance of their own death.

Several studies have demonstrated a complex relationship between death anxiety and religiosity, defined as being a churchgoing, denomination-affiliated person or as adhering to a traditional belief system (Feifel & Nagy, 1981; Templer, 1972). Although studies have documented the link between belief in an afterlife and degree of religiosity, the relationship between belief in an afterlife and death anxiety independent of religiosity needs further exploration (Kalish, 1985).

Few investigators have examined death anxiety in relation to ethnicity. Myers, Wass, and Murphey (1980) found that elderly African American respondents in the American South expressed higher death anxiety than their European American counterparts. Bengtson, Cuellar, and Raga (1977) observed declines in death anxiety with age among three ethnic communities (African Americans, Mexican Americans, and European Americans) but did not find differences across the ethnic groups. Bengtson and colleagues (1977) also found that elderly African Americans were much more likely to expect a long life than either Mexican Americans or European Americans, confirming results obtained earlier by Reynolds and Kalish (1974).

Although the elderly think more about death than any other age group, they are less fearful and more accepting of it (Bengtson et al., 1977; Kalish & Reynolds, 1981; Keller, Sherry, & Piotrowski, 1984). Several reasons have been offered for this consistent finding (Kalish, 1987): Older adults have more chronic diseases, and they realistically know that these health problems are unlikely to improve over time; the probabilities are high that many members of their family and friendship network have died already; the most important tasks of life have been completed; and they have thought a great deal about their death. Kalish

(1987) also suggests that a major reason for reduced death anxiety in later life is that the value and satisfaction of living are not as great.

Death anxiety may also be related to the occupation one has, the experiences one has had with the death of others, and how one views aging. Vickio and Cavanaugh (1985) found that among nursing home employees those who had positive outlooks on older adults and on their own aging tended to have lower death anxiety. They also found that level of death anxiety was related to job; cooks and housekeepers tended to have higher anxiety than nurses and social service workers. The level of death anxiety was unrelated to the number of deaths among friends or relatives of the employee, but it was inversely related to the number of deaths among residents known by the employee.

Strange as it may seem, death anxiety may have a beneficial side. For one thing being afraid to die means that we often go to great lengths to make sure we stay alive. Because staying alive helps to ensure the continuation and socialization of the species, fear of death may serve as a motivation to have children and raise them properly.

Clearly, death anxiety is complex. We are uncertain on many of its aspects. Yet, we can see death anxiety and fear in action all the time in the many behaviors that we show.

How Do We Show Death Anxiety?

When we are afraid or anxious, our behavior changes in some way. One of the most common ways in which this occurs in relation to death is through avoidance (Kastenbaum, 1975). Avoiding situations that remind us of death occurs at both the unconscious and conscious levels. People who refuse to go to funerals because they find them depressing or who will not visit dying friends or relatives may be consciously avoiding death. Unconscious avoidance may take the form of being too busy to help out a dying person. Society provides several safeguards to help us avoid the reality of death, from isolating dying people in institutions to providing euphemisms for referring to death, such as saying that a person has "passed away."

A second way of showing fear or anxiety is the opposite of the first; rather than avoiding death, we challenge it (Kalish, 1984). In this case people deliberately and repeatedly put themselves in dangerous, life-threatening situations such as skydiving, auto racing, rock climbing, war, and so forth. These people have not been studied sufficiently to know whether they feel a need to assert their superiority over death. But interestingly enough, a study of pedestrian behavior at a busy intersection in Detroit revealed that people who took chances in crossing the street (for example, not looking before crossing, walking against the light, and jaywalking) were more likely to have thought about suicide and expected to live a significantly shorter time than more cautious pedestrians (Kastenbaum & Briscoe, 1975).

Death anxiety can be exhibited in numerous other ways. Some of the more common include changing lifestyles, dreaming and fantasizing, using humor, displacing fear or anxiety onto something else such as work, and becoming a professional who deals with death (Kalish, 1984). Such behaviors are indicative of large individual variations in how we handle our feelings about death. Still, each of us must come to grips with death and learn how to deal with it on our own terms.

Learning to Deal with Death Anxiety

Although some degree of death anxiety may be appropriate, we must guard against letting it become powerful enough to interfere with our normal daily routines. Several ways exist to help us in this endeavor. Perhaps the one most often used is to live life to the fullest. Kalish (1984, 1987) argues that people who do this enjoy what they have; although they may still fear death and feel cheated, they have few regrets. In a sense they "realize that [they] might die any moment, and yet live as though [they] were never going to die" (Lepp, 1968, p. 77).

Koestenbaum (1976) proposes several exercises and questions to increase one's death awareness. Some of these are to write your own obituary and plan your own death and funeral services. You can also ask yourself: "What circumstances would help make my death acceptable?" "Is death the sort of thing that could happen to me right now?"

These questions serve as a basis for an increasingly popular way to reduce anxiety: death education. Most death education programs combine factual information about death with issues aimed at reducing anxiety and fear in order to increase sensitivity to others' feelings. These programs vary widely in orientation; they can include such topics as philosophy, ethics, psychology, drama, religion, medicine, art, and many others. Additionally, they can focus on death, the process of dying, grief and bereavement, or any combination of them. In general, death education programs help primarily by increasing our awareness of the complex emotions that are felt and expressed by dying individuals and their families.

Concept Checks

1. What gender differences have been observed concerning death anxiety?
2. What are two major ways people show death anxiety?
3. How does death education help people deal with death anxiety?

THINKING ABOUT DEATH: THEORIES OF DYING

Learning Objectives:

- What are the five stages in Kübler-Ross' theory?
- What are the phases in the phase theory of dying?
- What components are needed for a contextual theory of dying?
- How does the dying process differ for older adults?

What is it like to die? How do terminally ill people feel about dying? Are people more concerned about dying as they grow older? To answer these questions, a few scholars have developed theories of dying that are based on interviews and other methods. The point of these theories is to show that dying is a complex process and that our thoughts, concerns, and feelings change as we move closer to death. We will examine three ways of conceptualizing the dying process: a stage approach, a phase approach, and a contextual approach. We will also consider how the thoughts and feelings of dying people vary as a function of age.

The Stage Theory of Dying

Elisabeth Kübler-Ross became interested in the experience of dying as an instructor in psychiatry at the University of Chicago in the early 1960s. When she began her investigations into the dying process, such research was quite controversial; her physician colleagues were initially outraged, and some even denied that their patients were terminally ill. Still, she persisted. Over 200 interviews with terminally ill people convinced her that most people followed a sequence of emotional reactions. Using her experiences, she developed a sequence of five stages that described the process of an appropriate death: denial, anger, bargaining, depression, and acceptance (Kübler-Ross, 1969).

When people are told that they have a terminal illness, their first reaction is likely to be shock and disbelief. *Denial* is a normal part of getting ready to die. Some want to shop around for a more favorable diagnosis, and most feel that a mistake has been made. Others try to find assurance in religion. Eventually, though, most people accept the diagnosis and begin to feel angry.

In the *anger* stage, people express hostility, resentment, and envy toward health care workers, family, and friends. Individuals ask, "Why me?" and express a great deal of frustration. The fact that they are going to die when so many others will live seems so unfair. As these feelings begin to be dealt with and to diminish, the person may begin to bargain.

In the *bargaining* stage, people look for a way out. Maybe a deal can be struck with someone, perhaps God, that would allow survival. For example, a woman might promise to be a better mother if only she could live. Or a person sets a timetable, such as "just let me live until my

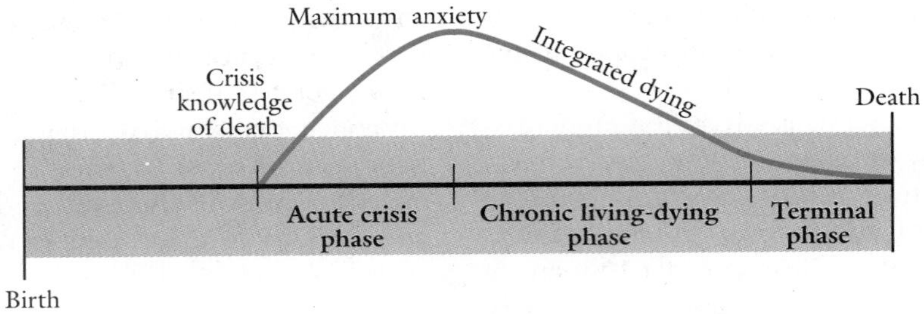

Figure 13.2 The phase theory of dying.

daughter graduates from college." Eventually, the individual becomes aware that these deals will not work.

When one can no longer deny the illness, perhaps due to surgery or pain, feelings of *depression* are very common. People report feeling deep loss, sorrow, guilt, and shame over their illness and its consequences. Kübler-Ross believes that allowing people to discuss their feelings with others helps move them to an acceptance of death.

In the *acceptance* stage, the person accepts the inevitability of death and often seems detached from the world and at complete peace. "It is as if the pain is gone, the struggle is over, and there comes a time for the 'final rest before the journey' as one patient phrased it" (Kübler-Ross, 1969, p. 100).

Although she believes that these five stages represent the typical course of emotional development in the dying, Kübler-Ross (1974) cautions that not everyone goes through all of them or progresses through them at the same rate or in the same order. In fact, we could actually harm dying individuals by considering these stages as fixed and universal. Individual differences are great, as Kübler-Ross points out. Emotional responses may vary in intensity throughout the dying process. Thus, the goal in applying Kübler-Ross's theory to real-world settings would be to help people achieve an appropriate death. An appropriate death is one that meets the needs of the dying person, allowing him or her to work out each problem as it comes.

The Phase Theory of Dying

Instead of offering a series of stages, some writers view dying as a process with three phases: an acute phase, a chronic living-dying phase, and a terminal phase (Pattison, 1977a; Weisman, 1972). These phases are represented in Figure 13.2.

The acute phase begins when the individual becomes aware that his or her condition is terminal. This phase is marked by a high level of anxiety, denial, anger, and even bargaining. In time, the person adjusts to the idea of being terminally ill, and anxiety gradually declines. During this chronic living-dying phase, a person generally has many contradictory feelings that must be integrated. These include fear of loneliness, fear of the unknown, and anticipatory grief over the loss of friends, of body, of self-control, and of identity (Pattison, 1977b). These feelings of fear and grief exist simultaneously or alternate with feelings of hope, determination, and acceptance (Shneidman, 1973). Finally, the terminal phase begins when the individual begins withdrawing from the world. This last phase is the shortest, and it ends with death.

The notion of a *dying trajectory* was introduced to describe these three phases more clearly by describing the length and the form of one's dying process. Four dying trajectories have been suggested, differing mainly in whether death is certain or uncertain (Glaser & Strauss, 1965, 1968; Strauss & Glaser, 1970):

1. Certain death is expected at a known time, such as when one is told that one has 6 months to live.
2. Certain death is expected but at an unknown time, such as when one is told that one has between 6 months and 5 years.
3. It is uncertain whether one will die, but the answer will be clear in a known period of time; for example, exploratory surgery will resolve the issue.
4. It is uncertain whether one will die, and there is no known time when the question will be answered; for example, one has a heart problem that may or may not be fatal and could cause problems at some point in the future.

The last two trajectories are thought to produce the most anxiety due to their higher degrees of ambiguity and uncertainty. The acute phase is lengthened, and the overall trajectory is more difficult. It seems that knowing whether one is going to die plays an important role in the ability to deal with the problem and the degree of overall adjustment.

Although stages and phases of dying have not been researched very thoroughly, it seems that how people deal with their own death is a complicated process. Denial and acceptance can take many forms and may even occur simultaneously. People take a last vacation and update their will at the same time. It is becoming increasingly clear that it is not the task of health care workers or mental health workers to force someone to die in a particular way. There is no such thing as one right way to die. The best we can do is to make sure that we stay in touch with the dying person's (and our own) feelings and are available for support. In this way we may avoid contributing to what could be considered a wrong way to die: being abandoned and left to die alone.

Moving Toward a Contextual Approach to Dying

One of the difficulties with both the stage theory and phase theory of dying is a general lack of research evaluating them in a wide variety of contexts (Kastenbaum & Thuell, 1995). By their very nature, both of these theories imply a particular sequentiality and directionality. Stage theories, in particular, emphasize qualitative differences among the various stages. However, the duration of a particular stage, or a specific phase, varies considerably from individual to individual. Both of these theories assume some sort of underlying process for moving through the stages or phases but do not clearly state what *causes* a person to move from one to another.

One reason for these problems is the realization that there is no one right way to die, though there may be better or worse ways of coping (Corr, 1991–92). A perspective that recognizes this would approach the issue from the perspective of the dying person and the issues, or tasks, they must face. Corr (1991–92) identified four dimensions of such tasks: bodily needs, psychological security, interpersonal attachments, and spiritual energy and hope. This holistic approach acknowledges individual differences and rejects broad generalizations. Corr's task-work approach also recognizes the importance of the coping efforts of family members, friends, and caregivers as well as those of the dying person.

Kastenbaum and Thuell (1995) argue that what is needed is an even broader, contextual approach that takes a more inclusive view of the dying process. They point out that theories must be able to handle people who have a wide variety of terminal illnesses and be sensitive to dying people's own perspectives and values related to death. The socioenvironmental context within which dying occurs, which often changes over time, must be recognized. For example, a person may begin the dying process living independently but end up in a long-term care facility. Such moves may have profound implications for how the individual copes with dying. A contextual approach would also provide guidance for health care professionals, families, and others in terms of how to protect the quality of life, provide better care, better prepare caregivers, and provide research questions.

We do not yet have such a comprehensive theory of dying. But as Kastenbaum and Thuell point out, we can move in that direction by rejecting a reductionistic approach for a truly holistic one. One way to accomplish this is to examine people's experiences as a narrative that can be written from many points of view (e.g., the patient, family members, caregivers). What would emerge would be a rich description of a dynamically changing process.

An Adult Developmental Perspective on Dying

Dying is not something that happens only to one age group. Most of us tend not to think about it, because we associate dying with old age. But babies die of sudden infant death syndrome, children die in accidents, and adolescents and young adults die from cancer. Death knows no age limits. Yet one person's death often seems more acceptable than another's (Kastenbaum, 1985). The death of a 95-year-old woman is considered natural; she had lived a long, full life. But the death of an infant is considered to be a tragedy. Whether or not such feelings are justified, they point to the fact that death is experienced differently depending on age: Treatment differs, and responses to others' losses differ. In this section we will briefly examine the personal side of how the age of a dying person (young adults and older adults) changes how death is viewed.

The old die mainly from chronic diseases, such as heart disease and cancer; young adults die mainly from accidents (Kalish, 1987). The diseases of older adults typically incapacitate before they kill, resulting in a dying trajectory of slow decline and eventual death. Because older adults and younger adults die in different ways, their dying processes differ (Kalish, 1985):

1. Financial costs for the elderly are higher due to the need for long-term care.
2. The elderly's need for health and human care is greater.
3. The elderly have more potential for leading a normal life during the early part of the dying process.
4. The elderly have a longer period to contemplate and plan for their death.
5. The elderly have more opportunity to see old friends or visit important places.
6. The elderly are more likely to die in institutions and are more likely to be confused or comatose immediately before their death.
7. More elderly women die without a spouse or sibling to participate in care, making them more dependent on adult children.

In short, the elderly take longer to die and are more likely to die in isolation than any other age group.

Many of the concerns of dying individuals seem to be specific to how old they are (Kalish, 1987). The most obvious difference comes in the extent to which people feel cheated. Younger adults are more likely to feel deprived of the opportunity to experience a full life than are middle-aged or older adults. Younger adults feel that they are losing what they might attain; older adults feel that they are losing what they have. Beyond these general differences, however, not much is known about how adults of various ages differ in how they face death. Most of the literature focuses on older adults. Clearly, we need more information about what it is like to be young or middle-aged and to be dying.

One important factor that affects dying older adults is that their deaths are viewed by the community as less tragic than the deaths of younger people (Kalish & Reynolds, 1976; Kastenbaum, 1985). Consequently, older adults receive less intense life-saving treatment and are perceived as less valuable and not as worthy of a large investment of time, money, or energy: "The terminally aged may be as helpless as a child, but they seldom arouse tenderness" (Weisman, 1972, p. 144). Many dying older adults reside in long-term care facilities where contacts with family and friends are fewer. Kalish (1987) writes that the elderly, especially the ill and those with diminished functional competence, offer less to their communities. Consequently, when their death occurs the emotional pain is not as great because the resulting losses are viewed as less significant and meaningful.

Concept Checks

1. What are the five stages in Kübler-Ross' theory?
2. What are the four dying trajectories?
3. What would a contextual theory of dying include?
4. What are some of the differences in the dying process for older adults?

WHERE WILL WE DIE?

Learning Objectives:

- What determines where most people will die?
- What is the purpose and function of a hospice?

Where do most of us want to die? Surveys indicate that most older people would rather die at home but that this wish is not as important to middle-aged people (Kalish & Reynolds, 1976). Family members who had cared for relatives who died at home usually feel glad that it happened that way, even though about one third wonder whether home care was the right decision (Cartwright, Hockey, & Anderson, 1973).

Despite the expressed wishes of most people, the vast majority of us will not die at home among family and friends. Rather, approximately 75% of deaths occur in institutions such as hospitals and nursing homes (Lerner, 1970; Marshall, 1980). This increasing institutionalization of death has two major consequences (Schulz, 1978). First, health care professionals are playing a more important role in dying people's lives. This means that the medical staff is being forced to provide emotional support in situations largely antithetical to their main mission of healing and curing. This dilemma presents health care workers with problems that we will consider later.

A second important result of the institutionalization of death is that dying is being removed from our everyday experience. Not long ago, each of us would have known what it was like to interact with a dying person and to be present when someone died. Institutions isolate us from death, and some argue that the institutions are largely to blame for our increasing avoidance of death and dying people. Unfortunately, we cannot evaluate this opinion because we cannot randomly have some people die at home and others die at hospitals to compare the effects of each in an experiment.

Dying in a Hospital Versus Dying at Home

As indicated earlier, the trend during the 20th century has been away from dying at home. What implications does this trend have? Certainly, some people still die at home either because their deaths occur unexpectedly or because they have chosen to remain at home. Yet even in these cases some people are still taken to a hospital where the official declaration is made (Marshall, 1980). In a technical sense, then, most people die at a hospital or other health care facility.

Perhaps the best explanation for this change relates to advances in health care itself. As health care became more effective, efficient, and technologically advanced, people needed to take advantage of hospital facilities to make certain that everything possible had been done. Even when a person's illness is terminal, there is a good chance that a lengthy hospital stay will result. Hospitals offer another major advantage compared to home: continuous care. Caring for a dying person is often time consuming and draining and may require special medical expertise. Hospitals are typically better equipped to handle these demands.

All is not on the hospital's side, however. Autonomy and personal relationships usually suffer when people are in a hospital (Kalish, 1984). People remaining at home have less difficulty on these dimensions; rigid visitation hours are the exception at home.

What, then, determines where we will die? Kalish (1984) offers six factors: physical condition, availability of care, finances, competence of institutions, age, and personal preference. Clearly, the particular health problem that a person has may dictate the context for dying. If it demands intensive or sophisticated medical treatment or if the degree of incapacitation is great, a medical facility is likely to be chosen.

Kalish notes that the availability of caregivers outside the health care institution plays a very important role. If an individual has several people who can provide care at home, an institution is a less likely choice. Overall, then, the best predictor of nursing home admission is the degree of social support available (George & Gwyther, 1986). However, caregivers must be more than just available; they must be willing to make the necessary sacrifices as well.

Finally, personal preference plays a role. Some people simply prefer to be at home in familiar surroundings with their family and friends when they die. Others, who fear that they will burden their loved ones or that emergency medical assistance may be unavailable, choose a hospital or nursing home. Kalish (1985) writes that dying at home is most appropriate when the person is reasonably alert and capable of interaction with others, when his or her health condition is beyond treatment, when dying at home would provide something meaningful to the person, and when death is imminent.

The Hospice Alternative

As we have seen, most people would like to die at home among family and friends. An important barrier to this choice is the availability of support systems when the individual has a terminal disease. In this case most people believe that they have no choice but to go to a hospital or nursing home. However, another alternative exists. **A *hospice* is an approach to assisting dying people that emphasizes pain management and death with dignity** (Koff, 1981). The emphasis in a hospice is on the quality of life. This approach grows out of an important distinction between the prolongation of life and the prolongation of death. In a hospice the concern is to make the person as peaceful and comfortable as possible, not to delay an inevitable death. Although medical care is available at a hospice, it is aimed primarily at controlling pain and restoring normal functioning. This orientation places hospices between hospitals and homes in terms of contexts for dying.

Modern hospices are modeled after St. Christopher's Hospice in England, founded in 1967 by Dr. Cicely Saunders. The services offered by a hospice are requested only after the person or physician believes that no treatment or cure is possible, making the hospice program markedly different from hospital or home care. The differences are evident in the principles that underlie hospice care: Clients and their families are viewed as a unit; clients should be kept free of pain; emotional and social impoverishment must be minimal; clients must be encouraged to maintain competencies; conflict resolution and fulfillment of realistic desires must be assisted; clients must be free to begin or end relationships; and staff members must seek to alleviate pain and fear (Saunders, 1977).

Two types of hospices exist: inpatient and outpatient. Inpatient hospices provide all care for clients; outpatient hospices provide services to clients who remain in their own homes. This latter variation is becoming increasingly popular, largely because more clients can be served at a lower cost.

Hospices do not follow a hospital model of care. The role of the staff in a hospice is not so much to do *for* the client as it is just to be *with* the client. A client's dignity is always maintained; often more attention is paid to appearance and personal grooming than to medical tests. Hospice staff members also provide a great deal of support to the client's family. At inpatient hospices visiting hours are unrestricted, and families are strongly encouraged to take part in the client's care (VandenBos, DeLeon, & Pallack, 1982).

Researchers have documented important differences between inpatient hospices and hospitals (Hinton, 1967; Parkes, 1975; VandenBos et al., 1982). Hospice clients were more mobile, less anxious, and less depressed; spouses visited hospice clients more often and participated more in their care; and hospice staff members were perceived as more accessible. In addition, E. K. Walsh and Cavanaugh (1984) showed that most hospice clients who had been in hospitals before coming to a hospice strongly preferred the care at the hospice.

Although the hospice is a valuable alternative for many people, it may not be appropriate for everyone. Some disorders require treatments or equipment not available at inpatient hospices, and some people may find that a hospice does not meet their needs or fit with their personal beliefs. Walsh and Cavanaugh found that the perceived needs of hospice clients, their families, and the staff did not always coincide. In particular, the staff and family members emphasized pain management, whereas many of the clients wanted more attention paid to personal issues. The important point from this study is that the staff and family members may need to ask clients what they need more often, rather than making assumptions about what they need.

Although a hospice offers an important alternative to a hospital or other institution as a place to die, it is not always available. For example, older adults who are slowly dying but whose time of death is uncertain may not be eligible. Meeting the needs of these individuals will be a challenge for future health care providers.

Concept Checks

1. What are the major predictors of where someone will die?
2. What are the primary characteristics of a hospice?

CARING AND HELPING RELATIONSHIPS

Learning Objectives:
- What are the major needs of dying people?
- What are the attitudes of health care workers about working with dying clients?
- What are the major ways that mental health workers assist the dying?

The growing awareness that death is a developmental process and the fact that death no longer occurs as frequently at home have led to a substantial increase in the number of people who work with the dying. The contexts may vary (hospitals, hospices, nursing homes), but the skills that are required and the kinds of relationships that develop are similar. With this in mind, we will focus on the helping done by health care and mental health workers. As a prelude to this discussion, let us consider what it is like to work with the dying and the basic needs that must be met.

Working with Dying People

Most people think that working with individuals who are dying must be hard. They serve as reminders that we, too, will die someday. As indicated earlier, this is a scary proposition. The realization that we will die makes us question the value of things, because dying people are proof that we cannot control all aspects of our lives. Few of us really control when or how we die. Many dying people experience pain, are unpleasant to look at or be near, and have a limited future. Most of us do not like to be reminded of these things. Finally, dying involves loss, and most of us do not seek out relationships with people when we know they are going to end painfully.

Despite these issues, many people work with the dying and have extremely positive experiences. Most of these individuals chose their occupation because of their interests. Yet they still experience stress and psychologically withdraw from their work. Although common, this withdrawal is not an inevitable part of working with people who are dying.

One way to help dying people is to understand their needs. Dying people have three especially important needs: the need to control pain, the need to retain dignity and feelings of self-worth, and the need for love and affection (Schulz, 1978). The mission of the people who work with the dying is meeting these needs.

When a terminal disease is painful, an important need is pain management. Several approaches are available, such as surgery, drugs, hypnosis, and biofeedback. Particularly in the case of chemotherapy for cancer, the management of pain can sometimes become the major focus of intervention. In such cases, considering additional issues such as compliance with the treatment is especially important.

The need for dignity and self-worth is extremely important. Recall that this was one of the needs stated most often by hospice clients in the Walsh and Cavanaugh (1984) study. Dignity can be enhanced by involving the dying person in all decisions that affect him or her, including control over the end of life. Loss of a sense of control can create serious psychological stress, which can have physical implications as well.

Showing love and affection to the dying can help reduce the fear of abandonment that many of us have. Love and affection can be communicated by touching or other physical contact, but it can also be shown by simply being present and listening, supporting, and reassuring the person that he or she is not alone.

How are these needs met? In addition to the family, health care and mental health workers share the responsibility. Let us consider how well they treat dying people.

Helping the Dying: Health Care Workers

How do health care workers deal with dying people? Do they confront the issues? What do they tell dying people about their condition? How do their clients feel about it? These are some of the questions that will concern us in this section. Although there is little research on these important topics, we can get some feel for the ways in which health care professionals handle death and dying.

Attitudes and Behaviors

Because the medical profession is oriented toward helping people and saving lives, death could be seen as a failure. Several researchers have shown that this was the perspective taken by many physicians and nurses in the past (Glaser & Strauss, 1965; Kastenbaum & Aisenberg, 1976; Pearlman, Stotsky, & Dominick, 1969). Most of this research documented that medical personnel in hospitals tended to avoid patients once it was known that they were dying. Indeed, one study found that nurses were slower to respond to the call lights of terminally ill patients than to those of other patients (Le Shan, in Kastenbaum & Aisenberg, 1976). Furthermore, when dying patients confront doctors or nurses with statements about death, such as "I think I'm going to die soon," the most common responses are fatalism ("We all die sometime"), denial ("You don't really mean that"), and changing the subject. These responses represent ways of not dealing with death.

How comfortable health care workers are in discussing death with dying people seems to be related to the amount of experience they have had with death, although the nature of the relationship is unclear. For example, some studies find that nurses' uneasiness increases with experience (Pearlman et al., 1969), whereas others find that experience makes it easier (Vickio & Cavanaugh, 1985). These discrepancies may stem from using interviews as opposed to questionnaires or from the general trend toward being open, honest, and supportive with people who want to talk about death. Indeed, there have been many calls in the medical literature for better communication with dying people (Kalish, 1985).

Changes in attitudes and behavior toward the dying may well reflect the spirit of the times (Kalish, 1987). During the 1980s there was a movement away from viewing science and technology as producing the ultimate in health care. Instead, the emphasis was increasingly on the relationship between health care workers and the dying person. At the same time the basic rights of the dying were being demanded, including the right to die with dignity. These changes at the societal level are probably the most important reasons for the shift in attitudes and behaviors over the past few decades.

Informing the Client

Should a patient be told that he or she is going to die? In the past this was only rarely done; most patients remained uninformed. The reasoning seemed to be that admitting the truth might accelerate the patient's decline, although it is also likely that it was done to protect the health care workers from facing death. This policy was typically followed regardless of the patient's wishes. For example, one comprehensive survey revealed that even though 75% to 90% of terminally ill patients indicated that they wanted to be told if they were dying, 70% to 90% of the physicians withheld that information (Feifel, 1965).

The majority practice today among medical personnel is to tell the patient the truth. Still, deciding whether to confront a person with the news that he or she is dying is a complex decision. For instance, sometimes it is just not known for certain whether a person will live or die. Full disclosure often depends on the physical and mental health of the patient. However, most investigators believe that the physician or nurse can help the client achieve a good death by being honest, by letting clients take the initiative in requesting information, and by being available for support (Hinton, 1967).

Most terminally ill people understand that there is something seriously wrong with them even before they are officially informed. With this growing awareness comes the additional recognition that others know as well. If others are unwilling to talk about it, patients may engage in a *mutual pretense* with family, friends, and professionals. In mutual pretense everyone knows that death is coming soon, but everyone acts as if nothing serious is the matter. Mutual pretense is difficult to carry out over a long period, however, because it is likely that someone will break the rules and talk about the disease. Providing a supportive context in which the impending death can be discussed avoids the problem altogether.

When death occurs in a health care setting, it is often hidden from public view. In some cases extreme measures are taken, such as disguising bodies or hiding them to protect other patients. Such actions are interpreted by some as additional examples of health care workers' denial of death. Although the therapeutic valve of protecting other patients has never been demonstrated, these practices continue in some places.

Helping the Dying: Mental Health Workers

Not all of the concerns of dying people involve their medical problems. Caring for the dying also entails meeting the psychological needs described by Kübler-Ross and others. We can separate the work done by mental health workers into two types: psychotherapy and paraprofessional counseling.

Psychotherapy

Dying people seek psychotherapy for many reasons. Sometimes, confronting our fears and anxieties is too difficult to handle on our own, and some professional help is needed. Concerns about work, conflicts with family, and financial matters may interfere with the ability to resolve the difficult psychological issues.

Conducting psychotherapy with the dying is often difficult. Use of the traditional hour-long session may be stressful if the client cannot sit that long or inconvenient if medical treatment needs to be continuous. Moreover, many psychotherapists have the same problems in dealing with death as medical personnel. When the therapist is forced to confront his or her own death anxiety and fear, it may hinder the psychotherapeutic process. And because many therapists use a medical model of pathology, dying people may not fit with their particular viewpoint. Most psychotherapists tend to focus on current problems and functioning rather than probing the distant past. Perhaps the best idea is to use the therapy to foster personal growth (Le Shan, 1969).

Paraprofessional Counseling

Working through anxieties and fears when one is dying does not always require a psychotherapist. In fact, most of the time it is accomplished by talking to relatives, friends, clergy, social workers, and medical personnel. The issues that are discussed are for the most part the same as those discussed with psychotherapists, and the feelings that are expressed are just as intense. Many people believe that having friends and family who are willing to listen and provide support is a key factor in resolving problems, although there is little research dealing with dying people.

Concept Checks

1. What are the three most important needs of dying people?

2. Should most people be told the truth about dying? Why?
3. What mental health approaches have been used with dying people?

SURVIVORS: THE GRIEVING PROCESS

Learning Objectives:

- What differences are there between expected and unexpected deaths?
- What are the three general stages of grief?
- What are the normal reactions people have to loss?
- What age differences have been observed in the effects of normal grief on health?
- What are the characteristics of abnormal grief?
- What effects do different types of loss have on grief?

Each of us suffers many losses over a lifetime. Whenever we lose someone close to us through death or other separation, we experience both grief and mourning. *Grief* refers to the sorrow, hurt, anger, guilt, confusion, and other feelings that arise after suffering a loss. *Mourning* concerns the ways in which we express our grief. These expressions are highly influenced by culture; for some mourning may involve wearing black, attending funerals, and observing an official period of grief, whereas for others it means drinking, wearing white, and marrying the deceased spouse's sibling. Thus, grief corresponds to the emotional reactions following loss, whereas mourning refers to the culturally approved behavioral manifestations of our feelings.

In this section we will examine how people deal with loss. Because the grieving process is affected by the circumstances surrounding the death, we must first differentiate between expected and unexpected loss. Next, because grief can be expressed in many ways, the differences between normal and abnormal reactions will be explored. Finally, how well we cope with the death of a loved one is related to the kind of relationship that existed. Thus, we will compare grieving following different kinds of loss.

Expected Versus Unexpected Death

For many years people believed that the intensity and course of grief depended on whether the death was expected or occurred suddenly and unexpectedly (Shand, 1920). Fulton (1970) labeled the two situations as "high-grief death" and "low-grief death." A high-grief death is one that is unexpected; for example, an accidental death. Low-grief deaths are expected; an example would be the death of a spouse following a long illness. According to Fulton, the main difference is not that people in one situation necessarily grieve more (or less) than those in another situation. Rather, when death is anticipated, people go through a period of anticipatory grief before the death that serves to buffer the impact of the loss when it comes.

Research on grief following expected versus unexpected deaths supports Fulton's basic point. The opportunity for anticipatory grieving has been shown to result in a lower likelihood of psychological problems one year after the death of a spouse (Ball, 1976–77; Parkes, 1975), greater acceptance by parents following the death of a child (Binger et al., 1969), and more rapid recovery of effective functioning and subsequent happiness (Glick et al., 1974). However, anticipating the death of someone close does produce considerable stress in itself (Norris & Murrell, 1987).

However, that does not mean that people who experience the anticipated death of a loved one do not grieve. Indeed, Hill, Thompson, and Gallagher (1988) found that the intensity of feelings per se do not differentiate widows whose husbands had been ill for at least one month prior to their deaths from widows whose husbands died unexpectedly.

The reasons anticipated deaths result in quicker recovery are not yet fully understood. We know that the long-term effects of stressful events, in general, are less problematic if they are expected, so that the same principles probably hold for death. Perhaps it is the opportunity to rehearse what it

The memory of those who have died from AIDS is kept alive through the Name Project. The AIDS Quilt, a section of which is shown here, is an especially moving experience for those who view it.

would be like without the dying person and the chance to make appropriate arrangements that helps. In practicing, we may realize that we need support, may feel lonely and scared, and may take steps to get ourselves ready. Moreover, if we recognize that we are likely to have certain feelings, they may be easier to understand and deal with when they come.

Another difference between expected and unexpected deaths is that an anticipated death is often less mysterious. Most of the time we know why the person died. A sudden death from an accident is not as easy to comprehend, as there does not seem to be a good explanation for it. There is no disease to blame, and survivors may fear that it could just as easily happen to them. Knowing the real reason why someone dies makes adjustment easier.

Stages of Grief

How do people grieve? What do they experience? The process of grieving is a complicated and personal one. Just as there is no right way to die, there is no right way to grieve. Recognizing that there are plenty of individual differences, we will consider these patterns in this section.

Writers have found it convenient to describe the grieving process as consisting of several phases. Like the stages and phases of dying, the phases of grieving are not clearly demarcated, nor does one pass from one to another cleanly. The goal of this approach is simply to describe the major steps of recovery following a death. The phases reflect the fact that when someone close to us dies, we must reorganize our lives, establish new patterns of behavior, and redefine relationships with family and friends. Although the phases have an implied sequence, we must keep in mind that some people reexperience them over time and that progress through them is not always even or predictable.

The grieving process can be divided into three main phases: initial phase, intermediate phase, and recovery phase (Averill, 1968; Parkes, 1972; Pincus, 1976). Each phase has certain characteristics, and particular issues are more important at some points than others.

When the death occurs, and usually for a few weeks afterward, the survivor's reaction is shock, disbelief, and numbness. People often report feeling empty, cold, and confused, which serves to protect them from the pain of bereavement. The shock and disbelief typically continue for several days following the death and then give way to several weeks of sorrow and sadness, which are expressed mainly through crying.

Over time, one is expected to begin recovering from these feelings. As a result of this pressure survivors may suppress emotions. Unfortunately, suppression of feelings is often interpreted as a sign of recovery, which it certainly is not. Along with learning how to deal with sorrow, survivors must handle feelings of not being able to go on with life. Fortunately, most people eventually realize that these anxieties are not well founded and that they are actually hindering their own recovery.

Several weeks after the death, people begin to realize what life without the deceased person means. Researchers point to three behavior patterns that characterize this second, or intermediate, phase. First, the bereaved person thinks about the death a great deal; feelings of guilt or responsibility are common. Second, survivors try to understand why the person died. They search for some reason for the death, to try to put it in a meaningful context. Finally, people search for the deceased. They feel the person's presence and dream or even converse with him or her. Such behavior demonstrates a longing to be with the deceased, and it is often a reaction to feelings of loneliness and despair. Eventually, these feelings and behaviors diminish, and the bereaved person moves to the final phase.

Entry into the recovery phase of grief often results from a conscious decision that continued dwelling on the past is pointless and that one's life needs to move forward. Once this is recognized, recovery can begin. Behaviorally, the process takes many forms, with increased socializing one common example. It is not unusual to see marked improvement in the survivor's self-confidence. Emerging from a bereavement experience is an achievement. People are often more capable and stronger as a result of coping with such a tragic event. New skills may be developed, whether they be cooking, balancing a checkbook, or home repair.

In considering these phases of grief, we must avoid making several mistakes. First, grieving ultimately is an individual experience. The optimal process for one person may not be the best for someone else. Second, we must not underestimate the amount of time it takes to progress from the initial shock to recovery. To a casual observer, this may seem to occur over a few weeks. Actually, it takes much longer to resolve the complex emotional issues that we face during bereavement. Researchers and therapists alike agree that it takes at least a year for a person to be reasonably recovered, and 2 years is not uncommon. Interestingly, Weiss (1975) proposed a 2-year period as the time needed for most people to recover from divorce. Finally, *recovery* may be a misleading term. It is probably more accurate to say that we learn to live with our loss, rather than that we recover. The impact of the loss of a loved one lasts a very long time, perhaps for the rest of one's life.

Normal Grief Reactions

The feelings experienced during grieving are intense, which not only makes it difficult to cope but also may cause one to wonder whether he or she is normal. A summary of college students' perceptions of normal responses is presented in Table 13.1. **Many authors refer to the psychological side of coming to terms with bereavement as *grief work*.** Vickio, Cavanaugh, and Attig (1990) found that college students were well aware of the need for grief work, correctly recognized the need for at least a year to do it, and were very sensitive to the range of emotions and behaviors demonstrated by the bereaved. In the following sections we will consider some of the most common reactions to bereavement.

Sorrow and Sadness

All the evidence we have suggests that intense feelings are the most common ones experienced during the grieving process (Kalish, 1985). Some studies have even found that these feelings of sadness can be so intense that they make the individual appear clinically depressed. For ex-

TABLE 13.1 Perceptions of typical grief reactions following the death of a loved one

Type of Reaction	Occurs During Initial Period of Grieving (Percent Citing the Reaction)	Occurs During Intermediate or Long-Term Grieving (Percent Citing the Reaction)	Sign That Grieving Is Abnormal if Occurring Long After Loss (Percent Citing the Reaction)
Disbelief	32.5%	0.8%	2.7%
Denial	24.4	8.1	5.5
Shock	48.0	1.6	8.2
Sadness	80.5	80.5	0
Anger	52.8	39.0	10.0
Hatred	8.1	5.7	9.1
Guilt	12.2	10.6	0
Fear	8.9	1.6	0.9
Anxiety	4.9	4.9	0.9
Confusion	9.8	6.5	0
Helplessness	4.9	0.8	0
Emptiness	10.6	6.5	0
Loneliness	13.0	16.3	0
Acceptance	2.4	2.4	1.8
Relief	3.3	0.8	5.5
Happiness that person died	4.1	0.8	66.4
Lack of enthusiasm	0	3.3	0
Absence of emotions	1.6	1.6	4.5

Source: *Perceptions of Grief Among University Students* by C.J. Vickio, J.C. Cavanaugh, and T. Attig, 1990, *Death Studies,* p. 236

ample, in the month following the death of their spouse, many widows display symptoms similar to those of depressed psychiatric clients. Many of these women lack a strong support system of family and friends (Kalish, 1981).

Denial and Disbelief

When death happens unexpectedly, a very common response is denial. Usually this response involves an intellectual recognition that the person has died but an inability or unwillingness to believe it. Sometimes denial is seen when a family starts to make plans that would normally have included the deceased person and then realizes the problem. At other times denial is shown when parents refuse to change the room of their deceased child or a widower continues to say "we." We must recognize that denial is sometimes adaptive and protective. Without denial during the first few days after the death, the pain might be overwhelming. Taken to extremes, however, denial can become very maladaptive.

Guilt

Guilt is probably the most complex reaction to death. Sometimes guilt arises because we have

The assassination of Israeli Prime Minister Itzak Rabin in 1995 was accompanied by national mourning, illustrating how death as a historical event can be felt at an individual level.

mixed feelings toward the person who died. We may be angry that he or she died yet relieved that we are not burdened with caretaking duties any longer. Perhaps the most common source of guilt is what Kalish (1981) calls the "If only I had . . ." syndrome: "If only I had gotten home in time"; "If only I had made him go to the doctor earlier"; "If only I had expressed my feelings toward Mom while she was still alive." Guilt most often results from feeling that there was something one could have done to prevent the death, that one should have treated the person better while he or she was still alive, or that one is actually relieved that the person died. Such feelings are commonplace in normal grief, but they must be monitored so that they do not become overwhelming.

Religious Beliefs

Many people find strength in their religious beliefs after experiencing the death of a loved one. For example, Pargament (1990; Pargament et al., 1990, 1991) has found that people often look to God as a way to deal with negative, traumatic life events. Death is one of the most common of these events that people cite as an example. Mainstream Christians in the United States, for instance, tend to view death as an event externally caused by God, as a loss, and as unchangeable. They look to their religion as a way to express their feelings of closeness to each other and as a way to understand what is happening to them (Pargament et al., 1991). However, unexpected or untimely death may cause people to question the "goodness" or "fairness" of a God who "allows" such things to occur.

Parents whose children die may find comfort in their religious beliefs. For example, Cook and Wimberley (1983) report that parents who use religious coping tend to report three reasons for their beliefs: (1) reunion with the child in an afterlife; (2) the child's death as serving a noble purpose; (3) the death as punishment for parental wrongdoing. For these parents, religion serves as a compensatory mechanism that helps them work through their grief.

Anniversary Reactions

Resolving grief takes time, as we have seen. During that time, and for many years to come, certain dates that have personal significance may reintroduce feelings of grief. For example, holidays such as Thanksgiving that were spent with the deceased person may be difficult times. The actual anniversary of the death can be especially troublesome. **The term *anniversary reaction* itself refers to changes in behavior related to feelings of sadness on important personal dates relating to the deceased person.** Personal experience and research show that recurring feelings of sadness or other examples of the anniversary reaction are very common in normal grief (Bornstein & Clayton, 1972).

Longitudinal Research Findings

Most research on how people react to the death of a loved one is cross-sectional. Norris and Murrell (1987) conducted a longitudinal study of older adults' grief work in which three interviews were conducted before the death and one after. The results of their research are described in more detail in the How Do We Know? feature. Briefly, Norris and Murrell reported that bereavement did not affect physical health; family stress increased as the death approached but diminished afterwards; before the death, family stress was associated with worsening health; after the death, health worsened only if there had been no family stress before the death; and after the death, psychological stress always increased. The results of this study have important implications for interventions. That is, interventions aimed at reducing stress or promoting health may be more effective if done before the death. Additionally, because health problems increased only among those who felt no stress before the death, it may be that the stress felt before the death is a product of anticipating it. Lundin (1984) also found this to be the case, in that health problems increased only for those experiencing sudden death.

Age Differences in Effects of Normal Grief on Health

Norris and Murrell's finding that bereavement per se has little direct effect on physical health caught some people by surprise. Most people assumed that losing a close loved one would have an obvious negative effect on the health of the survivor, especially if the survivor were elderly. After all, older adults are more vulnerable to stress (see Chapters 3 and 4), and the loss of a loved one was assumed to be stressful.

Perkins and Harris (1990) decided to look at this issue carefully. In a cross-sectional study, they compared younger, middle-aged, and older adults who had experienced the loss of a spouse, sibling, or sibling-in-law in the previous 5 years. Surprisingly, they found that middle-aged adults were most likely to report negative physical health problems following bereavement, with younger and older adults reporting few health problems. Perkins and Harris argue that younger adults are able to deal with their losses because they are better equipped overall to handle stress. Because older adults have more experience with and anticipate such losses, they draw on their background in order to cope physically. In contrast, middle-aged adults have less experience and are also in the midst of dealing with their own mortality (see Chapter 8). As a result, the loss of a close family member is an emotionally unsettling reminder of their own fate.

Abnormal Grief Reactions

Not everyone is able to move through the phases of grief and begin rebuilding his or her life. Sometimes the feelings of hurt, loneliness, or guilt are so overwhelming that they become the focus of the survivor's life. Thus, what distinguishes normal from abnormal grief is not the kind of reaction but, rather, its intensity and duration (Schulz, 1985). For example, statements such as "I really feel that if I had gotten home from the store even 5 minutes earlier my husband would be alive" would be considered normal if made a month or so after the death. When made 3 years afterward, however, they would be considered abnormal. Likewise, intense feelings are normal early in the process, but if they never diminish they are classified as abnormal.

Elderly people who had difficulty coping with a death 2 years later were found to be different from good copers (Lund et al., 1985–86). Poor copers expressed lower self-esteem before bereavement, were more confused, had a greater desire to die, cried more, and were less able to keep busy shortly after the death.

Overall, the most common manifestation of abnormal grief is excessive guilt and self-blame. In some people guilt results in a disruption of everyday routines and a diminished ability to function. People begin to make judgment errors, may reach a state of agitated depression, may experience

HOW DO WE KNOW?

Family Stress and Adaptation Before and After Bereavement

What happens to a family that experiences the death of a loved one? Norris and Murrell (1987) sought to answer this question by tracking families before and after bereavement. As part of a very large normative longitudinal study, they conducted detailed interviews approximately every 6 months. The data concerning grief reactions constitute a subset of this larger study, in which 63 older adults in families experiencing the death of an immediate family member were compared with 387 older adults in families who had not been bereaved.

The measures obtained extensive information on physical health, including functional abilities and specific ailments, psychological distress, and family stress. The psychological distress measure tapped symptoms of depression. The family stress measure assessed such things as new serious illness of a family member, having a family member move in, additional family responsibilities, new family conflict, or new marital conflict.

The results were enlightening. Among bereaved families, overall family stress increased before the death and then decreased. The level of stress experienced by these families was highest in the period right around the death. Moreover, bereavement was the only significant predictor of family stress, meaning that it was the anticipation and experience of bereavement that caused stress. Even more interesting were the findings concerning the relationship between health and stress. Bereaved individuals who reported stress before the death were in poorer health before the death than were bereaved persons who were not experiencing stress. However, bereaved individuals reporting prior

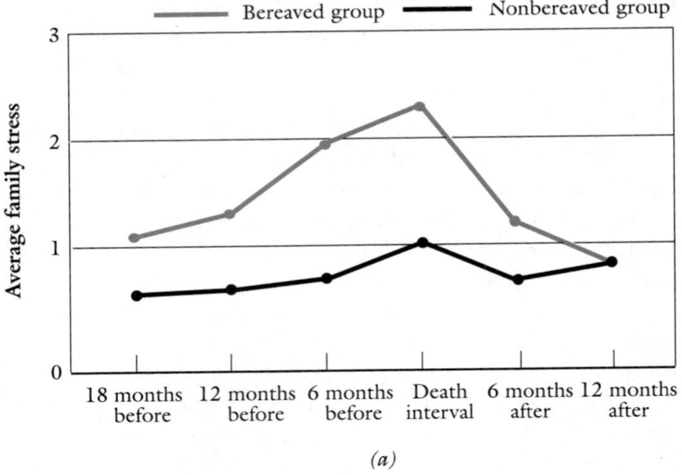

Figure 13.3 Family stress experienced by bereaved and nonbereaved groups. Part *a* shows stress over a 30-month period. Part *b* shows the relationship between health and stress before and after bereavement.

Source: "Older Adult Family Stress and Adaptation Before and After Bereavement," by F. N. Norris and S. A. Murrell, 1987, Journal of Gerontology, 42, *609, 610. Copyright © 1987 by the Gerontological Society of America. Reprinted by permission of the publisher and author.*

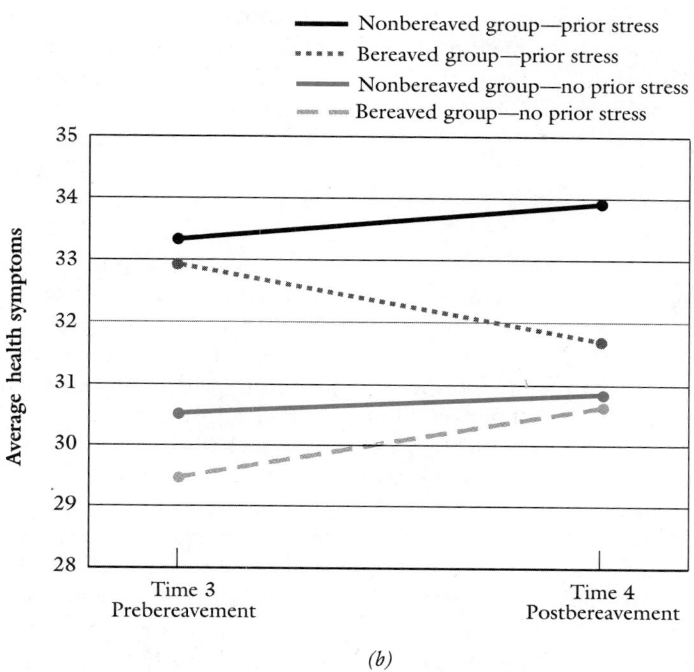

(b)

stress showed a significant *drop* in physical symptoms 6 months after the death; bereaved persons reporting no prior stress reported no change. The net result was that both groups ended up with about the same level of physical symptoms 6 months after bereavement. Both sets of results are depicted in Figure 13.3.

The Norris and Murrell study has two major implications. First, bereavement does not appear to cause poor health; the bereaved groups were not much different from the group of nonbereaved people in nonstressful families. Second, bereavement appears to result in a marked increase in psychological distress. In sum, marked changes in psychological distress following bereavement are normal, but marked changes in physical health are not.

problems sleeping or eating, and may have intense recurring thoughts about the deceased person. Many of these individuals either seek professional help voluntarily or are referred by concerned family members or friends. Unfortunately, the long-term prognosis for people suffering abnormal grief responses is not good (Schulz, 1985).

Types of Loss and Grieving

Consider the following deaths from cancer: an adolescent, a middle-aged mother, and an elderly man. Our reaction to each of them is different, even though all of them died from the same disease. The way we feel when someone dies is partially determined by the age of that person. Our society tends to view some deaths as more tragic or as easier to accept than others. Even though we really know that this approach has no research support, people nevertheless act as if it did. For example, people typically consider the death of a child as extremely traumatic, unless it occurred at birth. Or if one's parent dies when one is young, the loss is considered greater than if one is middle-aged and the parent is old.

The point is that our society in a sense makes judgments about how much grief one should have following different types of loss. We have noted that death is always a traumatic event for survivors. But unfortunately the survivors are not always allowed to express their grief over a period of time or even to talk about their feelings. These judgments that society makes serve to impose arbitrary time limits on the grieving process, despite the fact that virtually all the evidence we have indicates that we should not do that.

We must also recognize that the customs and traditions we observe in American society do not reflect the views of cultures earlier in history or other cultures around the world (Jecker & Schneiderman, 1994). For example, some cultures throughout history have practiced infanticide when they have been unable to provide support for their children. Keeping these cultural differences in mind, let's consider three types of loss and see how these judgments occur.

Death of One's Parent

Most parents die after their children have grown. But whenever it occurs, parental death hurts. We lose not only a key relationship but also an important psychological buffer between us and death. We, the children, are now next in line. Indeed, when one's parent dies, it often leads the surviving children to redefine the meaning of parenthood and the importance of time together (Malinak, Hoyt, & Patterson, 1979).

For most people, the death of a parent deprives them of many important things: a source of guidance and advice, a source of love, and a model for their own parenting style. It may also deny them the opportunity to improve aspects of their relationship with a parent. The loss of a parent is perceived as a very significant one; society allows us to grieve for a reasonable length of time.

In the context of our earlier discussion of anticipated and unanticipated deaths, how do people grieve when their parents die after a stay in a long-term care facility? In a study of 84 adult children whose parents had died during a stay in a nursing home, Pruchno, Moss, Burant, and Schinfeld (1995) found that the majority of the people were upset about their parent's death, even though it was anticipated. Even though all the participants experienced partial grief during the length of their parent's stay in the nursing home, these researchers found that the greater the stress experienced by the adult child prior to his or her parent's death, the more difficult the bereavement process. This is especially true for adult children who viewed the nursing home placement as negative; these individuals are sadder and take less comfort in memories of their deceased parent than people who view the nursing home placement as the right thing to do. Not surprisingly, the greater the mental impairment of the parent prior to death, the more relief the adult children felt after the death. Thus, even for adult children for whom the death of a parent is anticipated, the breaking of the tie between parent and child inevitably results in emotional sadness and upset, as well as feelings of separation, relief, and a loss of a buffer against death. Nevertheless, after one's parent has died, the memories of the relationship serve as a comfort for many people.

Death of One's Child

The death of a child is generally perceived as a great tragedy, because children are not supposed to die before their parents. It is as if the natural order of things has been violated. The loss is especially traumatic if it occurs suddenly, such as in sudden infant death syndrome or an automobile accident. But parents of terminally ill children still suffer a great deal, even with the benefit of anticipatory grieving. Mourning is always intense, and some parents never recover or attempt to reconcile the death of their child.

One of the most overlooked losses is the loss of a child through stillbirth, miscarriage, abortion, or neonatal death (Borg & Lasker, 1981). Attachment to one's child begins prenatally. His or her death hurts deeply, so to contend that the loss of a child before or at birth is not as tragic as the loss of an older child makes little sense. Yet parents who experience this type of loss are expected to recover very quickly and are often the recipients of unfeeling comments if these societal expectations are not met. Research indicates, though, that parents experience considerable grief. For example, Thomas and Striegel (1994–95) found that because both mothers and fathers bond with the fetus or baby during the early stages of pregnancy, they both grieve for their loss, but in different ways. Mothers grieve most for their lost child, whereas fathers grieve more for their wives. The most important factor in coping with the loss was the couple's support and reliance on each other.

Finally, grandparents' feelings can easily be overlooked. They, too, feel the loss when their grandchild dies. Moreover, they grieve not only for the grandchild but also for their own child's loss (Hamilton, 1978). Grandparents must also be included in whatever rituals or support groups the family chooses.

Death of One's Spouse

More has been written about the death of a spouse than about any other type of loss. It clearly represents a deep personal loss, especially when the couple had a very long and close relationship. In a very real way when one's spouse dies, a part of oneself dies, too.

The death of a spouse is different from other losses. There is pressure from society to mourn for a period of time. Typically, this pressure is manifested if the survivor begins to show interest in finding another mate before an acceptable period of mourning has passed. Although Americans no longer define the length of such periods, many feel that about a year is appropriate. That such pressure and negative commentary usually do not accompany other losses is another indication of the seriousness with which most people take the death of a spouse.

Another important point concerning the loss of one's spouse involves the age of the survivor. Young adult spouses tend to show more intense grief reactions immediately following the death than do older spouses. However, the situation 18 months later is reversed. At that time older spouses report more grief than do younger spouses (Sanders, 1980–81). Indeed, older bereaved spouses may grieve for at least 30 months (Thompson, Gallagher-Thompson, Futterman, Gilewski, & Peterson, 1991). The differences seem to be related to four factors: The death of a young spouse is more unexpected, there are fewer same-aged role models for young widows or widowers, the dimensions of grief vary with age, and the opportunities for remarriage are greater for younger survivors. Older widows anticipate fewer years of life and prefer to cherish the memory of their deceased spouse rather than to attempt a new marriage (Raphael, 1983).

Some longitudinal studies have examined the grief process in reaction to the death of a spouse. Dimond, Lund, and Caserta (1987) found that social support played a significant role in the outcome of the grieving process during the first 2 years after the death of a spouse. In particular, it is the quality of the support system, rather than the number of friends, that is particularly important.

One interesting aspect of spousal bereavement concerns how the surviving spouse rates the marriage. Futterman, Gallagher, Thompson, Lovett, and Gilewski (1990) had bereaved older adults rate their relationships at 2, 12, and 30 months after the death of their spouses. Nonbereaved older adults were also studied as a comparison group. Bereaved widows and widowers rated their marriage more positively than nonbereaved older adults, indicating a positive bias in remembering a marriage lost through death. However, bereaved spouses' ratings were related to depression in an interesting way. The more depressed the bereaved spouse, the more positively the marriage was rated. In contrast, depressed nonbereaved spouses rated their marriage negatively. This result suggests that the loss of a positive relationship through death, as well as its consequences (for instance, loss of other social contacts), is viewed as a negative outcome.

Comparing Types of Loss

Little research has been done comparing people's grief reactions from different types of loss. In general, bereaved parents are the most depressed and have more grief reactions in general than either bereaved spouses or adult children (Owen, Fulton, & Markusen, 1982). Other research shows that the intensity of depression in a bereaved person following loss is related to the perceived importance of the relationship with the deceased person (Murphy, 1988). Survivors are more often and more seriously depressed following the death of someone particularly important to them.

One study compared the grief reactions of 255 middle-aged women who had experienced the loss of a spouse, a parent, or a child within the preceding 2 years. Bereaved mothers reported significantly higher levels of depression than widows, who in turn reported significantly greater depression than adult children. In fact, over 60% of the bereaved mothers had depression scores in the moderate to severe depression range (Leahy, 1993).

Care must be exercised in interpreting these data. As noted earlier, there are many aspects of grief other than depression. Until researchers study these other aspects, it is premature to conclude that some types of loss always result in greater grief than others. All we can say in the meantime is that following some types of loss, some people report more symptoms of depression, at more serious levels.

Concept Checks

1. What are the principal differences between expected and unexpected death?
2. What are the major stages of grief?
3. What is grief work?
4. What age group appears most vulnerable to health effects of loss?
5. What are main symptoms of abnormal grief?
6. How do people cope with different types of loss?

NEAR-DEATH EXPERIENCES

Learning Objective:

- What are the major aspects of near-death experience?

Most people believe that death does not mark the end of being. Although the exact nature of this belief in an afterlife varies widely across individuals and cultures, the themes are the same. We can examine these themes with two questions in mind. Is the belief in an afterlife just wishful thinking? Do we have any scientific indication that there may be reason to suspect another life or type of existence?

These were the questions that prompted Moody (1975, 1988) to interview children and adults who had had close calls with death. **His research led to the labeling of these close calls as *near-death experiences*, phenomena that have several aspects in common.** In many cases these people had been clinically dead, and in other cases they had come very close to dying. On the basis of these interviews Moody was able to identify several common reports for people of all ages, although individual experiences differed somewhat. The common aspects of the experiences include the following:

1. An awareness of a buzzing or drumming sound or possibly hearing oneself declared dead

2. Feeling oneself moving out of one's body and then quickly down a tunnel, funnel, or cave toward an intense light
3. Seeing or feeling the presence of dead relatives who are present to help one make the transition from this life
4. Sensing the light as a power or presence, sometimes interpreted or experienced as love, that makes one review one's own life rather than be judged
5. "Seeing" one's life pass in front of one's eyes as a kaleidoscopic view of one's own thoughts and deeds
6. Being instantly able to tap into knowledge of any sort
7. Being aware or being told that the time for one's death has not yet come and that one must return to finish the normal life span

Some of the people whom Moody interviewed resented having survived. For them, the near-death experience was extraordinarily pleasant, and they felt cheated. For most people, the close encounter with death gave them a new and more positive outlook on life. Many people changed their lifestyles, and some acquired a deep spiritual commitment. Most no longer feared death, because they felt that the knowledge of what it would be like had removed the mystery and doubt.

Moody makes no claims that these experiences prove that there is life after death. Nevertheless, he does believe that these data are significant, if for no other reason than that the experiences reported by his participants were remarkably similar. Subsequent verification of these reports have been offered (Moody, 1977; Siegel, 1980). As a result many people see the themes and consistency of the reports as evidence that there is life after death. Because belief in an afterlife is so common, this is not very surprising.

The believers in the evidence are not without their critics, however. Siegel (1980) uses evidence from biology, psychology, and anthropology to dismiss claims that the reports reflect experiences of an afterlife. Siegel tries to show how each of the common themes in these reports can be explained by known processes (such as hallucinations similar to those induced by drugs). He argues that because we know so little about the workings of the brain, it is more likely that the experiences reflect neurological processes than actual experiences of an afterlife.

Whose interpretation is correct? Unfortunately, the question is presently unanswerable and is likely to stay that way. But even if the claims of an afterlife are exaggerated, the belief in its potential existence is probably adaptive in this life. Many people are more likely to use death as a stimulus for personal growth if they think that something might follow it. Additionally, without the concept of an afterlife, death could result for some people in a devastating fear of total nonbeing. A belief in an afterlife may be nothing more than a way of denying the reality and the finality of death. But for some people, the adaptive value of this belief is truly great. For them, it provides a rationale for living life to the fullest.

Concept Checks

1. What are the most common aspects of near-death experiences?

SUMMARY

Definitions and Ethical Issues

Sociocultural Definitions of Death

Different cultures have different meanings for death. Some of the meanings in Western culture include images, statistics, events, state of being, analogy, mystery, a boundary, a thief of meaning, a basis for fear and anxiety, and a reward or punishment.

Legal and Medical Definitions

Three legal criteria of death have been proposed: clinical death, brain death, and cortical death. Brain death, which includes eight specific criteria, is the definition used most often in the United States and other industrialized societies. If brainstem functioning continues after cortical function stops, the person is said to be in a persistent vegetative state.

Ethical Issues

Bioethics examines the interface between values and technological advances. Two types of euthanasia are distinguished. Active euthanasia means deliberately ending someone's life through some sort of intervention or action. Passive euthanasia means ending someone's life by withholding treatment. Personal preferences for medical intervention can be communicated through a living will or a durable power of attorney.

The Price of Life-Sustaining Care

Keeping individuals alive with life support not only is financially costly, but also can take an emotional toll. Adults should make their wishes known.

Suicide

Suicide rates for older adults overall are much higher than that for other age groups. Ethnic differences are also apparent; European American men are the most likely to commit suicide. Suicide is related to having serious physical illness, as well as to depression.

Thinking About Death: Personal Components

Death Anxiety

Most people exhibit some degree of anxiety about death, even though it is difficult to both define and measure. Individual difference variables include gender, religiosity, age, ethnicity, and occupation. Death anxiety may have some benefits.

How Do We Show Death Anxiety?

The main ways death anxiety is shown is by avoidance (e.g., refusing to go to funerals) and by deliberately challenging it (e.g., engaging in extreme sports). Other ways of showing it include changing lifestyles, dreaming and fantasizing, using humor, displacing fears, and becoming a death professional.

Learning to Deal with Death Anxiety

Several ways to deal with anxiety exist: living life to the fullest, personal reflection, and education. Death education has been shown to be extremely effective.

Thinking About Death: Theories of Dying

The Stage Theory of Dying

Kübler-Ross's theory includes five stages: denial, anger, bargaining, depression, and acceptance. Some people do not progress through all of these stages, and some people move through them at different rates. People may be in more than one stage at a time and do not necessarily go through them in order.

The Phase Theory of Dying

An alternative view states that dying occurs in three phases: an acute phase, a chronic living-dying phase, and a terminal phase. A dying trajectory describes a person's passage through the phases. Four primary trajectories have been identified, differing mainly in whether death is certain or uncertain.

Moving Toward a Contextual Theory of Dying

A contextual theory of dying emphasizes the tasks that a dying person must face. Four dimensions of these tasks have been identified: bodily needs, psychological security, interpersonal attachments, and spiritual energy and hope. A contextual theory would be able to incorporate differences in reasons people die and the places people die.

An Adult Developmental Perspective on Dying

Older adults take longer to die and are more likely to die alone than any other group. Most concerns of dying individuals are specific to age. The social view of the degree to which a death is considered tragic is an important aspect of the dying process.

Where Will We Die?

Dying in a Hospital Versus Dying at Home

Most people want to die at home but actually die at a hospital. This is a reflection of professional and technological changes in health care. Six factors predict where a person will die: physical condition, availability of care, finances, competence of institutions, age, and personal preference.

The Hospice Alternative

The goal of a hospice is to maintain the quality of life and to manage the pain of terminal patients. Hospice clients are typically in better psychological status than hospital patients but are also less mobile. Family members tend to stay more involved in the care of hospice clients.

Caring and Helping Relationships

Working with Dying People

Many people have positive experiences working with dying people. The most important things many dying people need are pain management, dignity, and self-worth.

Helping the Dying: Health Care Workers

Many physicians have difficulty dealing with terminal patients. Comfort in this regard depends on the amount of personal experience one has in dealing with death. Most health care workers believe that terminal patients should be told that they are dying. However, some patients engage in mutual pretense and do not accept their condition. Likewise, death is often hidden in health care settings.

Helping the Dying: Mental Health Workers

Psychotherapy and paraprofessional counseling often help terminal patients deal with their condition.

Survivors: The Grieving Process

Expected Versus Unexpected Death

Grief is equally intense in both expected and unexpected death, but may begin before the actual death when the patient has a terminal illness. Unexpected death is often termed high-anxiety death; expected death is often termed low-anxiety death. Expected deaths are usually less mysterious than unexpected deaths.

Stages of Grief

Three main phases of grief have been identified: initial phase, intermediate phase, and recovery phase. Dealing with grief usually takes at least 1 to 2 years. Individual differences are very large.

Normal Grief Reactions

Normal grief reactions include sorrow, sadness, denial, guilt, and religious beliefs. Grief often returns around the anniversary of the death. Longitudinal findings indicate that interventions to reduce stress and promote health relating to loss would be more effective if done prior to the death.

Age Differences in Effects of Normal Grief on Health

In general, experiencing the death of a loved one does not directly influence physical health. Middle-aged adults have the most difficult time dealing with grief. Poor copers tend to have low self-esteem before losing a loved one.

Abnormal Grief Reactions

Excessive guilt and self-blame are common signs of abnormal grief. Abnormal grief reactions are typically determined by how long feelings of grief last.

Types of Loss and Grieving

The death of a parent serves to remind people of their own mortality and deprives them of a very important person in their lives. The death of a child (including miscarriage and perinatal death) is thought to be the most traumatic type of loss. Loss of a spouse is a great loss of a lover and companion. Bereaved spouses tend to have a positive bias about their marriage.

Near-Death Experiences

Many people report near-death experiences having several similar components. Whether these experiences reflect life after death is open to debate.

REVIEW QUESTIONS

Definitions and ethical issues
- What are the various sociocultural meanings for death?
- What are the three legal criteria for death?
- What are the criteria necessary for brain death?
- What is bioethics and what kinds of issues does it deal with?
- What are the two types of euthanasia? How do they differ?
- What are the costs, both financial and psychological, of keeping someone on life support?
- Who is most likely to commit suicide? What are some reasons why people commit suicide?

Thinking about death: personal components
- What is death anxiety? What factors influence death anxiety?
- How do people demonstrate death anxiety?
- How do people learn to deal with death anxiety?

Thinking about death: theories of dying
- Describe Kübler-Ross's stage theory of dying. How do people progress through the stages?
- Describe the phase theory of dying. What is a dying trajectory?
- What is necessary for creating a contextual theory of dying?
- How is age related to dying?

Where will we die?
- Where do most people want to die? Where do they actually die?
- What is a hospice? How does hospice care differ from hospital care?

Caring and helping relationships
- What is it like to work with dying people?
- What needs do dying people have?
- How do physicians and other health care workers deal with dying people?
- How do mental health workers deal with dying people?

Survivors: the grieving process
- What effects does an expected versus an unexpected death have on the grieving process?
- What are the stages of grief? How long does grief usually last?
- What are the differences between normal and abnormal grief reactions? What age differences are there in grief reactions?
- How does the type of loss affect grief?

Near-death experiences
- What is the near-death experience?

INTEGRATING CONCEPTS IN DEVELOPMENT

1. What effect do you think being at different levels of cognitive development has on people's thinking about death?
2. What parallels are there between the stages of dying and the experience of grief? Why do you think they may be similar?
3. How can we use the study of death, dying, bereavement, and grief to provide insights into the psychological development of people across adulthood?

KEY TERMS

active euthanasia Deliberately ending a person's life through an intervention or action.

anniversary reaction Feelings of sadness and loneliness on holidays, birthdays, and the anniversary of a loved one's death.

bioethics The study of the interface between

human values and technological advances in health and life sciences.

brain death A definition of death that relies on eight criteria including the lack of an EEG for 24 hours.

clinical death A definition of death based on the lack of a spontaneous pulse and respiration.

cortical death A definition of death based on the lack of brain activity in the cortex.

dying trajectory The pattern exhibited by a dying person in terms of the phase theory of dying.

euthanasia Meaning "good death," the practice of allowing people who have a terminal illness to die.

grief work The psychological side of coming to terms with bereavement.

hospice An approach to assisting dying people that emphasizes pain management and death with dignity.

near-death experiences Experiences related by people who have been near death or clinically dead involving feelings of floating, peace, and meeting deceased loved ones.

passive euthanasia Allowing a person to die by withholding an available treatment.

persistent vegetative state A state in which a person's brainstem is the only part of the brain that is functioning, a state from which the person does not recover.

IF YOU'D LIKE TO LEARN MORE

Fulton, R., & Bendiksen, R. (Eds.). (1994). *Death and identity* (3rd ed.). Philadelphia: Charles Press. A collection of classic and original articles that take a life-span perspective. Easy to moderately difficult depending on the article.

Kalish, R. A. (1987). Death and dying. In P. Silverman (Ed.), *The elderly as modern pioneers* (pp. 320–334). Bloomington: Indiana University Press. Relatively easy.

Kushner, H. S. (1981). *When bad things happen to good people.* New York: Schocken. A classic book that is very thought provoking. This book was written by a rabbi after the death of his son. Easy reading, but take it slowly.

Nuland, S. B. (1994). *How we die: Reflections on life's final chapter.* New York: Knopf. A very important and informative book that provides an excellent discussion of what happens when people die. Great for dispelling myths about dying. Easy reading.

Stephenson, J. S. (1985). *Death, grief, and mourning: Individual and social realities.* New York: Free Press. A discussion of death from an interdisciplinary view that includes historical and philosophical perspectives. Mainly, the book presents a historical and philosophical discussion. Easy to moderately difficult depending on the topic.

Taylor, N. (1993). *A necessary end.* New York: Nan A. Talese. A personal story of the author's coping with the death of his parents and his search for meaning. Easy reading.

CHAPTER 14

Looking Toward the 21st Century

Marc Chagall, *Foward!*, 1917. Art Gallery of Ontario, Toronto. Gift of Sam and Ayala Zacks.

By the time you reach old age, the 21st century will be well along. Technical advances will make commonplace what is only science fiction today. Our daily lives may be vastly different than they are right now. Life will undoubtedly be more complicated. You will probably have experienced first-hand many of the things discussed in this book: marriage, children, career changes, relocation, personal development, physical and cognitive changes, and so on.

For now, though, we must be content with gazing into a crystal ball. We know many things about adult development and aging to guide us, but there are many unknowns, too. Throughout this book we have made predictions about this future and guessed how older people may fare. Some of these predictions are positive; for example, it is likely that more people will live to advanced ages. Other forecasts are not so rosy; as more people live to a very old age, there will be more need for long-term care. These predictions represent our best guess about what life will be like in 40 years or so, based on what we know now and what is likely to happen if we continue the way we are going.

The purpose of this chapter is to pull together several crucial issues facing gerontologists as we enter the 21st century. This survey will not be exhaustive; rather, we will focus on two things: points that have been singled out for special concern, and areas where major advances may have a dramatic impact on our own development.

Three issues have been identified as trouble spots for the future. The first is the need for better research, a problem that underlies all others. Second, we will examine the growing crisis in health care and health policy. Third, we will consider the need for creating productive roles for older adults.

Other issues concern areas of ongoing research that have the potential to revolutionize our own developmental course. Chief among these is research on biological and physiological aspects of aging. Also important are discoveries that are being made in the cognitive domain that challenge age-old stereotypes of aging.

CHANGING DEMOGRAPHICS

Learning Objective:

- How will the demographic profile of the United States change by 2030?

In Chapter 2 we noted several trends in the population of the United States during this century. These trends are not likely to change in the foreseeable future. Changes in the composition of the older adult population contribute to potentially critical issues that will emerge over the next few decades. One especially important area concerns the potential for intergenerational conflict.

Because the resources and roles in a society are never divided equally among different age groups, the potential for conflict always exists. One well-known intergenerational conflict is that between adolescents and their parents. Less well known is the potential for conflict between middle-aged adults and older adults (Uhlenberg, 1987). This type of conflict has not traditionally been a source of serious problems in society for several reasons: Older adults made up a small proportion of the population, family ties between adult children and their parents worked against conflict, and middle-aged people were hesitant to withdraw support from programs for the elderly. Despite these potent forces protecting against conflict, the situation is changing. For example, the debate over the rate of growth of Medicare that created very heated political debates in the mid-1990s would have been unthinkable just a few years earlier.

To see more clearly how these changing demographics could have an enormous effect on society at large and on the programs that target older adults, let us project forward to the year 2030, when the last of the baby-boom generation will have reached age 65. Between now and 2030

- The proportion of older adults will nearly double.
- Older adults will be much more politically sophisticated and organized. They will be very well educated and will be familiar with life in a highly complex society in which one must learn to deal with bureaucracies.
- Older adults will expect to keep their more affluent lifestyle, Social Security benefits, health care, and other benefits accrued through their adult life. A comfortable retirement will be viewed as something that everyone is entitled to.
- The ratio of workers to retirees will fall from its current level of roughly 3.5:1 to 2:1. This means that to maintain the same level of benefits in programs such as Social Security, the working members of society will have to pay significantly higher taxes than workers do now.
- The increase in divorce that has occurred over the past two decades may result in a lowered sense of obligation on the part of middle-aged adults toward their absent parents. For example, will adult children feel obliged to care for an elderly father who left the family when they were very young? Should a lowered sense of obligation result, it is likely that many fewer older adults will have family members available to care for them, placing significantly greater burden on society for their care.
- The more rapid increase in ethnic minority elderly will force a reconsideration of issues such as discrimination and access to goods and services, as well as provide a much richer and broader understanding of the aging process.

No one knows for certain what society will be like by 2030. However, the changes we have noted in demographic trends suggest the need for taking action now. The information contained in this book will provide a basis for this action.

Concept Checks

1. What are some of the effects of changing demographics on society?

THE NEED FOR RESEARCH

Learning Objectives:

- What are the major types of research that will be needed in the near future?
- What are some of the emerging fields?

Throughout this book we have seen that adult development and aging are complex processes that we are far from understanding. Because the number of older people is rising and because we need more and better information, three issues need to be addressed in the near future if we are to optimize our own development into the next century. These are better research, health care, and productive roles.

In Chapter 1 we considered various methods for conducting research on adult development and aging. Recall that of the major methods (cross-sectional, longitudinal, time lag, and sequential), longitudinal and sequential designs are the ones that tell us what we really want to know: whether a particular process or behavior changes over time. Cross-sectional research identifies only differences that are related to age; they may reflect true age change or merely cohort differences. But the vast majority of research we have considered in this book is cross-sectional. Longitudinal and sequential work is confined mainly to topics in cognitive and personality development. Where does this leave us?

The problem we are faced with is the possibility that much of what we know about adult development and aging may not reflect true age changes. Rather, it may largely reflect cohort differences that are, in turn, a reflection of the changes that have occurred in society over this century. Recall from Chapter 2 that the modernization of society has a strong influence that may differ across generations. This may mean that differences in intellectual skills or memory performance are due to changes in the skills needed by each succeeding generation to survive and adapt in daily life.

Cross-sectional research will never solve the problem, because age and cohort are always confounded. Longitudinal research addresses the issue of age change, but it is severely limited because the results may not generalize across cohorts. Sequential research appears to be our best, and only, way out. We must have reliable data on whether the differences we observe between age groups are something innate in humans or whether they are due more to historical experiential factors.

But improved research does not only mean using a different, more sophisticated design. It also means cutting across disciplines and incorporating findings from one field to interpret data from another. A good example is the need for truly interdisciplinary biopsychosocial research. The search for the genetic link in Alzheimer's disease, for instance, may also yield the key to why cognitive processes fail (see Chapter 9). Cognitive scientists and neurological scientists working together will make substantially more progress than either group working alone. Likewise, a connection may exist between changing levels of neurotransmitters and aspects of personality, mainly studied through psychopathology (see the discussion on depression in Chapter 9).

Improved research also means including broader, more representative samples that reflect the diversity of the population. We saw in Chapter 2 that the U.S. population is becoming increasingly diverse and that the fastest growing segments of the older adult population are among ethnic minorities. If we are to understand the richness of the aging experience in all groups, we *must* include *all* groups in research.

The point is that we need better research not only to understand more about adult development and aging but also to know how better to commit resources for the future. As we will see, the most serious problem facing the United States concerning the elderly is health care; the lack of data collected over time from multiple cohorts seriously impairs our ability to plan for the future. Getting better information also means changing our research priorities from a system that rewards quantity (which promotes more cross-sectional research) to one that rewards high quality (which would promote more longitudinal and sequential research). Perhaps changing our priorities should be the place to start; otherwise, the future will arrive and we will still not have a database. Two areas of research make this point clearly: research on the causes of aging and research on the brain.

The Causes of Aging

As we noted in Chapters 3 and 4, we have learned a great deal about the biology and physiology of aging. Our knowledge is increasing even more through research on diseases of aging, especially Alzheimer's disease. As noted in Chapter 9, Alzheimer's disease is thought by many to be qualitatively similar to normal aging. By combining research on both normal and abnormal aging, we may unlock the genetic basis of human aging in our own lifetime. Not even Ponce de León, the conquistador who searched for the fountain of youth, could have imagined that.

We already have the technology to greatly prolong life by curing diseases that only a few decades ago were major killers. High-tech surgical techniques make cataract operations routine. Open-heart surgery and cancer treatments that were only dreams in the 1960s are commonplace. Diagnostic techniques through computer-enhanced imaging allow physicians to detect problems even before they are manifested. Artificial joints make greater mobility a reality for many.

What might these changes mean to us? For one thing, they almost ensure that, barring accidents, virtually everyone will have the chance to live to a very old age. But more important is the prospect that in our lifetime we may have the ability to reverse the aging process itself. The implications of this possibility are mind-boggling. Bioethicists (see Chapter 13) would have to deal with the question of whose aging process could be reversed and under what circumstances it would be done. Would genetic engineering be routinely performed on victims of Alzheimer's disease or other genetic disorders? Could the average person have his or her aging process slowed? Who would decide? What impact would the significant slowing of aging have on society? How would we deal with the population increase?

These and other questions bring home the sobering fact that understanding the biological-physiological process of aging may create more problems than it solves. As pointed out many times in the text, we need to approach the problem from the point of view that aging is the result of a complex set of four interacting forces, and, in this context, to ask what outcome is in our best interest.

Interestingly, unlocking the secrets of aging would tend to exacerbate the health care problems facing the United States. Larger numbers of people living to unprecedented old age might completely overburden the system. This problem emphasizes the point that progress in one area may create additional dilemmas elsewhere. It also points out the need for careful planning and policy making in the years ahead.

The Emergence of Neuroscience

Perhaps no other area of research in adult development and aging has forced more rethinking of stereotypes than work on intellectual and memory skills. From the earliest descriptions of older people to the present, the belief has been that with old age comes a marked diminution of cognitive ability. As we learned in Chapters 5, 6, and 7, however, researchers over the past two decades have discovered that this stereotype is only partially true.

In fact, aging does bring changes in cognitive abilities. Some people do decline, but others do not. Moreover, it is beginning to appear that even cognitive skills that we thought declined may actually be amenable to remediation. The discovery that one's predominant mode or style of thinking may change as one ages and that thought becomes reunited with emotion are revolutionizing the way in which psychologists view older adults. The effects are dramatic. We have gone from questioning whether we even needed to document the decline because we were so certain of it, in the 1950s, to being very cautious in discussing the developmental trends in relatively

Preventive health care and living a healthy lifestyle will continue to be important issues as we head into the 21st century.

specific abilities, because we accept the fact that not all abilities change.

This reconceptualization has had a dramatic effect on research on information processing, memory, and intelligence over the past decade. **We are witnessing a transformation in experimental paradigms from examining the behavioral level to examining the underlying neurological processes that cause the behavior in the first place; this emerging field of *neuroscience* has seen an explosion of growth in only a few years.** Generally speaking, neuroscience research on aging and cognition has as its goal the discovery of not only *what* happens, but *why* it happens. This approach does not fit neatly within traditional theories, and well-tested theories based on neuroscience have not yet been developed, making it difficult to make sense of the cognition literature. But in the not-too-distant future, theories and evidence grounded in neuroscience will be the mainstream. When this happens, then psychological phenomena will be placed on a research continuum with basic biological and physiological processes, an exciting prospect indeed.

Concept Checks

1. What are some of the primary needs in terms of research design?
2. What are some emerging issues for research?

HEALTH CARE

Learning Objective:

- What are the primary issues likely to be concerning health care?

No problem in the world, especially in the United States, will be more pressing in the coming years than the need for health care for older adults (Bond, Cutler, & Grams, 1995; J. A. Brody, 1988b; Ferraro & Sterns, 1990). The number of elderly will increase dramatically over the next 30 to 40 years, most rapidly in the over-80 age group, who will constitute the largest, single federal entitlement group. Health care costs for adults over age 65 will soar as the expenses for chronic and debilitating diseases mount due to the increased numbers of people in this age group. Long-term care is already in crisis; beds are in short supply, and the cost of the average nursing home is beyond the means of many (see Chapter 12). Information is also scarce, and statistical tools for analyzing it are often inadequate (National Research Council [NRC], 1988).

The growing concern over health care for the elderly prompted the National Research Council (NRC) to study the situation and to make several recommendations concerning future health care policy (NRC, 1988). These recommendations address several areas of special concern, as well as general issues. This study was responsible, in part, for the debates over health care policy in the United States during the mid-1990s.

The NRC identified the financing of medical care for older adults as the most important health policy issue facing the United States. The cost of care, who will pay for it, and how it will be financed are issues that *must* be addressed. The changes in Medicare and Medicaid during the 1980s and the growing realization that private insurance will need to become more heavily involved have had a significant impact on how health care is financed. Indeed, the cost projections for long-term care were so high that it was largely ignored in the attempts to reform health care in the early 1990s and was also largely ignored in the public debates over Medicare and Medicaid in the mid-1990s. We noted in Chapters 9 and 12 that many public and private insurance programs do not adequately cover the cost of quality long-term care. The trend toward increased reliance on individuals to either have their own health coverage or pay for care themselves has profound implications for people facing chronic debilitating conditions such as Alzheimer's disease. It has also created a significant new avenue for the insurance industry, which now markets numerous long-term care insurance policies. The NRC also pointed to a lack of adequate data on the cost burden of such care, and it placed high priority on obtaining this information.

How health care is delivered is a second issue facing American society. The diminishing number of physicians in rural areas and in some specialties, the closing of inner-city hospitals, and the lack of transportation to health care centers present significant problems to older adults, especially minority groups and the frail. The growth of for-profit care and business-oriented approaches to health care, not recognizing age differences in recovery time from illness, and increased competition also create barriers to quality health care for the elderly.

The NRC identified the need for and cost of long-term care as major factors in the overall financing picture. Many nursing homes do not take Medicaid clients, for example, forcing many of the poor to settle for lower quality care or no care. There is no consistent program of data collection to determine how many people are likely to need long-term care in the future. Surveys also need to include facilities other than nursing homes, such as chronic disease hospitals, mental health facilities, rehabilitation centers, group homes, halfway houses, and residential facilities.

A smart investment strategy, according to the NRC, would be to spend health care dollars on health promotion and disease prevention. This approach would emphasize keeping oneself in good health thereby avoiding the more expensive treatment programs. Generally speaking, paying for checkups and needed treatment early in the disease process is markedly less expensive than waiting until the disease has spread. Important intervention goals include promoting healthy activities and lifestyle among older adults. Whether the federal government should finance prevention and promotion is an important policy decision.

Monitoring health care systems to ensure that people get the best care for their money and that care quality meets high standards are also important. Simply solving the financing problem is only half the battle. The health care industry must be held accountable for its actions.

Carrying out the NRC's recommendations will be expensive. By its own estimate, data collection alone may cost $15 billion to $20 billion or more. Such a high price tag makes one wonder whether the benefits would justify the expense. The answer is a resounding yes today, as it was a decade ago. At that time, there was too little information available to address the coming crisis in health care adequately (Hollander & Becker, 1988); the situation now is not much better. Policy makers need reliable data on which to base decisions about where to allocate federal dollars to do the most good for the most people. Not collecting adequate information and not making appropriate policy decisions would be far more expensive, both in dollars and in the quality of life of older people. Our goals should be to enable the elderly to stay healthy and functionally independent as long as possible, to provide access to quality health care of whatever type is appropriate, and to provide care in the least restrictive and most cost-effective environment (Somers, 1987). The issue facing us is whether we are willing to assume the cost burden. If not, the alternatives are not pleasant to think about.

Concept Checks

1. What were the major recommendations on health care in the National Research Council study?

PRODUCTIVE ROLES FOR OLDER ADULTS

Learning Objectives:

- What psychological aspects are important for creating productive roles?
- What societal issues will help develop productive roles?

What will older adults be doing in the 21st century? Some researchers see new roles as inevitable, if for no other reason than that there will be so many of them. Golant (1988) envisions that "the beginning decades of the 21st century will be known as the Golden Era for Older People. While our attention as this century closes is on the population we now refer to as Yuppies, in the 21st century the spotlight will be on the Yeepies that is, Youthful Energetic Elderly People Involved in Everything" (p. 13). Whether or not Yeepies come to pass remains to be seen. Nevertheless, there will certainly be an emphasis on productive roles for older adults.

Creating productive roles for older adults will require consideration of general psychological functioning as well as a consideration of several important societal issues. As has been pointed out by several authors (e.g., Grams & Albee, 1995), adopting a prevention approach is a good way to approach this issue, because it emphasizes what needs to be done to maximize each person's developmental potential. Studies of people over age 90 (Bury & Holme, 1991) and of centenarians (e.g., Beard, 1991) have supported this view and emphasized that only when psychological functioning occurs within an appropriately supportive social context will optimal outcomes be realized. We will briefly consider each of these two major aspects.

Psychological Components

The single most important contribution of psychology to the study of adult development and aging is its demonstration that much of the decline in psychological functioning is not an inevitable outcome of aging. Although by now such information is hardly surprising to you, society has yet to fully appreciate its implications. American society retains a fairly negative view of age despite much data showing that such a view is wrong. In part, the problem stems from a general lack of appreciation for the diversity of aging; pick any two of your older relatives and you probably have two different models of what aging is all about. Until recently, even scientists failed to acknowledge the enormous human variations in the ways in which people traverse adulthood.

With an appreciation of diversity and individual differences comes a realization that some people may even excel in old age. Rowe and Kahn (1987) understood this and distinguished between "usual" and "successful" aging. **In *usual aging*, external factors heighten the effects of biologi-**

cal and physiological processes. In *successful aging,* external factors play either a neutral or positive role. For example, consider the role of education in maintaining cognitive performance (see Chapter 7). Low levels of education are associated with significantly greater decrements; high levels of education are associated with maintenance of intellectual ability even into late life.

Other researchers have uncovered ways in which older adults clearly excel well beyond the range of younger adults. Smith and Baltes (1990) describe people who become experts in living, and in some cases greatly outperform younger adults at cognitive tasks. The point is that we simply do not know the absolute maximum that older adults can do. Perhaps it is time we found out.

Another critical area of psychological functioning for creating productive roles is well-being in the context of longer life. People living in advanced technological societies potentially have access to several ways of extending their lives through material goods and high-quality health care. But in the drive to extend average longevity, an essential question has been ignored: Is it a good idea to blanketly extend life?

Researchers have yet to focus much attention on the issue of the quality of the extra years that technology buys. For example, are the years we add onto people's lives with improved medical care good, productive years? Or are they years in which one's health deteriorates and chronic diseases are numerous? Related to this issue is the notion that one could outlive one's *expected* longevity, that is, how long you *think* you will live. For example, if you think you will not live past 75, perhaps because no other relative in your family ever has, you may map out your life based on this assumption. But what do you do when you turn 76? This birthday wasn't planned, and you may feel confused as to what you should be doing with yourself.

These issues raise important questions that psychologists need to address for life in the 21st century. The degree to which old age brings well-being is vitally important; many times in this book we have seen the importance of maintaining well-being and feeling that you have some control over your life. Finding personal meaning in growing old will surely be an important topic for aging individuals and researchers alike.

Societal Components

One of the key issues currently facing older adults is the lack of formal social roles. Adults now relinquish many of the major roles of adulthood by the time they reach old age. We have noted that older cohorts experience major declines in societal significance as a result of these role losses. One of the most important of these relinquished roles is work. As more people enter retirement over the coming decades, the issue of how to keep older adults connected with society will become more critical.

At present, older adults do the best they can to create productive roles (Herzog, Kahn, Morgan, Jackson, & Antonucci, 1989). Herzog and colleagues (1989) found that older adults participate in many unpaid productive activities at levels comparable to their younger and middle-aged counterparts. These activities range from volunteering in organizations to providing informal help to others to home repair and housework. Few older Americans currently get paid for what they do, although this is true for older women than it is for older men.

In an effort to develop guidelines for addressing the need to develop productive roles for older adults, the Committee on an Aging Society (CAS) of the Institute of Medicine and the National Research Council explored unpaid productive roles as one alternative (CAS, 1986). Unpaid productive roles are ones in which individuals make a significant contribution to society but are not given wages. The difference between paid and unpaid productive roles is sometimes arbitrary, and the work is often similar.

Voluntarism has a long, distinguished tradition in the United States. From Boy Scout troop leaders to friendly visitors in hospitals and nursing homes, millions of people donate their time freely each year. The CAS argues that we should look to older adults as a major source of volunteers in social and health services. It proposes that a systematic effort at providing unpaid productive roles for older

Having older adults share their experiences and wisdom is one way of providing productive roles for them in society.

adults would accomplish two things. First, it would increase the availability of some social and health services that could be provided by nonprofessionals. For example, existing programs such as Foster Grandparents could be enhanced, and new programs such as home visitation for the frail elderly could be started in many communities. Second, unpaid productive roles would give older people a formal way to maintain self-esteem and identity after retirement without having to be employed. Unpaid productive roles would enable them to retain societal significance by using their accumulated years of experience and expertise.

An important issue not directly addressed by the CAS is that volunteers often end up in clerical or social tasks, with little opportunity to have a direct say in the operation of the program. This is not an optimal situation, of course, because volunteers often come into the program with years of experience. This is especially true for older adults, who may view volunteer positions as low-status roles that do not take advantage of their experience.

The CAS gives most attention to the prospect of older volunteers (providing, of course, that the status and menial nature of volunteer work are addressed). It points out that declining federal and state support of social service programs through the 1980s has led to a serious shortage of people to provide these much needed services. The growing number of older people could be a resource in easing the impact of personnel cuts that have been made as a result of fewer dollars. Estimates are that between 35% and 40% of older adults already perform some sort of volunteer work, and projections are that this figure will increase (Kieffer, 1986). Thus, the potential pool is relatively large.

If a concerted effort is to be made to provide older adults with formalized roles through unpaid productive activities, several impediments to participation need to be addressed (CAS, 1986). Older people are often not actively recruited by organizations or are not encouraged to remain. Individuals are often expected to cover expenses such as transportation, with little hope for tax deductions to help defray such costs. Unions are often reluctant to accept volunteers, viewing them as a way to displace paid employees. Some older adults themselves view voluntarism as a form of exploitation, feeling that volunteers are considered second-class citizens in organizations. The lack of adequate transportation for elderly people who do not drive means that people who might otherwise volunteer will not do so because they cannot get there.

How can we eliminate these barriers? First, we need to explicitly recognize that older adults have a wealth of experience and expertise that should not be allowed to go to waste. Kieffer (1986) notes that this expertise of the elderly has been systematically and increasingly thrown away since the 1940s. We need to begin to draw on older adults as experts in much the same way as members of some nonindustrialized societies do. Second, we need to make positive appeals to older adults to become volunteers and share their knowledge. Third, we need to provide incentives for volunteers, including increased recognition. Fourth, we need improved supervision, development, and management of volunteer programs. Providing services takes coordination of both government and business. Careful planning needs to be done, and programs have to be monitored to ensure that they provide optimal services. Finally, the impediments outlined earlier need to be removed. Most important, transportation to and from the volunteer site should be provided to those who want to participate.

Well-planned and well-managed volunteer programs could become extremely cost effective, both in terms of the services they provide and the benefits to the volunteers. Social and health services that are currently unavailable could be provided at a fraction of the cost of identical programs using only a paid staff. Volunteers benefit by feeling more useful in society and regaining aspects of identity lost after retirement.

Volunteer programs are not a panacea, however. The CAS notes that volunteer programs should never be used as a way to cut corners or to eliminate needed professionals. Such programs should be viewed as a way to supplement existing services, not as a replacement for them. Used appropriately, however, voluntarism could be an effective way to reconnect older adults to society.

Concept Checks

1. What two major areas of psychological functioning are important for creating productive roles?
2. What societal components are important for creating productive roles?

SOME FINAL THOUGHTS

In this book you have seen a snapshot of what adult development and aging are like today. You have learned about their complexities, myths, and realities. But more than anything else, you have seen what we really know about the pioneers who have blazed the trail ahead of us.

In a short time it will be your turn to lead the journey. The decisions you make will have an enormous impact on those who will be old: your parents, grandparents, and the people who taught you. The decisions will not be easy ones. But you have an advantage that the pioneers did not. You have the collected knowledge of gerontologists to help. With a continued concerted effort you will be able to address the problems and meet the challenges that lie ahead. Then, when you yourself are old, you will be able to look back on your life and say, "I lived long—and I prospered."

SUMMARY

Changing Demographics

The rapid increase in the number of older adults between now and 2030 means that social policy must take the aging of the population into account. Changing demographics will affect every aspect of life in the United States, including health care and all social services programs.

The Need For Research

To answer the most important questions about adult development and aging, we need more longitudinal and sequential research that is multidisciplinary. Better research will help us make better decisions about resource allocation in the future. Research on the causes of aging and in the emerging field of neuroscience will be of special importance.

Health Care

The most pressing need in the United States is a comprehensive health care program that takes into account the high cost of caring for large numbers of people with chronic diseases, especially in long-term care. A cost-effective approach would be to emphasize health promotion, especially in the elderly.

Productive Roles for Older Adults

Psychological Components

A distinction that is becoming more important is that between usual and successful aging. We need to learn more about how and why some people appear not to be affected very much by normative aging processes. An important issue is the quality of life that people accrue through healthier lifestyles.

Societal Components

At a societal level, we need to develop productive roles for older adults. Current impediments to active participation need to be removed. Recommendations on how to create productive roles need to be implemented.

REVIEW QUESTIONS

Changing demographics

- What will the population in the United States look like in 2030?
- What impact will these demographic characteristics have on social policy?

The need for research

- What kinds of research are needed the most? Why?
- What effect would unlocking the secrets of aging have on society?
- What is the focus of neuroscience research?

Health care

- Why is health care considered to be the most important issue facing the United States?
- What kind of health care policy is needed? Why?

Productive roles for older adults

- What is the difference between usual and successful aging?
- What issues concerning older adults' well-being will be important in the years ahead?
- What possible sources are there for productive roles for older adults?
- What barriers currently exist to participation?

INTEGRATING CONCEPTS IN DEVELOPMENT

1. Suppose you were brought in as a consultant on aging policy issues to the U.S. Congress. Based on the demographic information presented in this chapter and in Chapter 2, what recommendations would you make on health care, Social Security, and social service programs?
2. Now that you have been introduced to the new field of neuroscience, what areas of integration in Chapters 3, 5, 6, and 7 do you think might emerge in the next few years?
3. Taking the many topics discussed in Chapters 10 and 11 into account, what are some possible productive roles for older adults?

KEY TERMS

neuroscience An emerging field of research that examines the connection between underlying neurological processes and behavior.

successful aging The process of aging in which external factors play either a neutral or a positive role.

usual aging The process of aging in which external factors heighten the effects of biological and physiological processes.

IF YOU'D LIKE TO LEARN MORE

Beard, B. B. (1991). *Centenarians: The new generation.* Westport, CT: Greenwood Press. A fascinating and partly personal account of the contributions made by people who have lived to be at least 100 years old. Easy reading.

Bond, L. A., Cutler, S. J., & Grams, A. (Eds.). (1995). *Promoting successful and productive aging.* Thousand Oaks, CA: Sage Publications. A good overview of the prevention approach to living a productive and healthy life. Easy to moderately difficult.

REFERENCES

Abrams, W. B., & Berkow, R. (Eds.). (1990). *The Merck manual of geriatrics.* Rahway, NJ: Merck Sharp & Dohme Research Laboratories.

Adams, C., Labouvie-Vief, G., Hobart, C. J., & Dorosz, M. (1990). Adult age group differences in story recall style. *Journal of Gerontology: Psychological Sciences, 45,* P17–P27.

Adams, R. D. (1980). Morphological aspects of aging in the human nervous system. In J. E. Birren & R. B. Sloane (Eds.), *Handbook of mental health and aging* (pp. 149–160). Englewood Cliffs, NJ: Prentice-Hall.

Ade-Ridder, L., & Brubaker, T. H. (1983). The quality of long-term marriages. In T. H. Brubaker (Ed.), *Family relationships in later life* (pp. 21–30). Beverly Hills, CA: Sage Publications.

Adler, S., & Aranya, N. (1984). A comparison of the work needs, attitudes, and preferences of professional accountants at different career stages. *Journal of Vocational Behavior, 25,* 574–580.

Adlersberg, M., & Thorne, S. (1990). Emerging from the chrysalis: Older women in transition. *Journal of Gerontological Social Work, 16,* 4–8.

Agronin, M. E. (1994). Personality disorders in the elderly: An overview. *Journal of Geriatric Psychiatry, 27,* 151–191.

Ahrons, C., & Rodgers, R. H. (1987). *Divorced families: A multidisciplinary view.* New York: Norton.

Ahrons, C., & Wallisch, L. (1987). The relationship between former spouses. In D. Perlman & S. Duck (Eds.), *Intimate relationships: Development, dynamics, and deterioration* (pp. 269–296). Beverly Hills, CA: Sage Publications.

Allen, K. R., & Chin-Sang, V. (1990). A lifetime of work: The context and meanings of leisure for aging black women. *The Gerontologist, 30,* 734–740.

Allen-Burge, R., Storandt, M., Kinscherf, D. A., & Rubin, E. H. (1994). Sex differences in the sensitivity of two self-report depression scales in older depressed inpatients. *Psychology and Aging, 9,* 443–445.

Alston, M. H., Rankin, S. H., & Harris, C. A. (1995). Suicide in African American elderly. *Journal of Black Studies, 26,* 31–35.

Alwin, D. F. (1994). Aging, personality, and social change: The stability of individual differences over the adult life span. In D. L. Featherman, R. M. Lerner, & M. Perlmutter (Eds.), *Life-span development and behavior* (Vol. 12, pp. 135–185). Hillsdale, NJ: Erlbaum.

Alwin, D. F., Converse, P. E., & Martin, S. S. (1985). Living arrangements and social integration. *Journal of Marriage and the Family, 47,* 319–334.

American Association of Retired Persons. (1988). *A portrait of older minorities.* Washington, DC: Author.

American Association of Retired Persons. (1991). *A profile of older Americans.* Washington, DC: Author.

American Cancer Society. (1990). *1990 Facts and figures.* Atlanta: Author.

American Psychiatric Association. (1994). *Diagnostic and statistical manual of mental disorders* (4th ed.). Washington, DC: Author.

Amoss, P. T. (1981). Coast Salish elders. In P. T. Amoss & S. Harrell (Eds.), *Other ways of growing old* (pp. 227–238). Stanford, CA: Stanford University Press.

Anastasi, A. (1958). Heredity, environment, and the question "how?" *Psychological Review, 65,* 197–208.

Anderson, S. A., Russell, C. S., & Schumm, W. R. (1983). Perceived marital quality and family life-cycle categories: A further analysis. *Journal of Marriage and the Family, 45,* 127–139.

Andrasik, F., Blanchard, E. B., & Edlund, S. R. (1985). Physiological responding during biofeedback. In S. R. Burchfield (Ed.), *Stress: Psychological and physiological interactions* (pp. 282–306). Washington, DC: Hemisphere.

Aneshensel, C. S., Pearlin, L. I., Mullan, J. T., Zarit, S. H., & Whitlach, C. J. (1995). *Profiles in caregiving: The unexpected career.* San Diego: Academic Press.

Anschutz, L., Camp, C. J., Markley, R. P., & Kramer, J. J. (1985). Maintenance and generalization of mnemonics for grocery shopping by older adults. *Experimental Aging Research, 11,* 157–160.

Anschutz, L., Camp, C. J., Markley, R. P., & Kramer, J. J. (1987). Remembering mnemonics: A three-year follow-up on the effects of mnemonic training in elderly adults. *Experimental Aging Research, 13,* 141–143.

Antonovsky, A., & Sagy, S. (1990). Confronting developmental tasks in the retirement transition. *The Gerontologist, 30,* 362–368.

Antonucci, T. C. (1985). Personal characteristics, social support, and social behavior. In R. H. Binstock & E. Shanas (Eds.), *Handbook of aging and the social sciences* (2nd ed., pp. 94–128). New York: Van Nostrand Reinhold.

Aquilino, W. S., & Supple, K. R. (1991). Parent-child relations and parent's satisfaction with living arrangements when adult children live at home. *Journal of Marriage and the Family, 53,* 13–27.

Arbona, C. (1990). Career counseling research and Hispanics: A review of the literature. *The Counseling Psychologist, 18,* 300–323.

Arensberg, C. (1968). *The Irish countryman: An anthropological study.* New York: Peter Smith.

Aries, P. (1974). *Western attitudes toward death: From the Middle Ages to the present* (P. N. Ranum, Trans.). Baltimore: Johns Hopkins University Press.

Armor, D. J., Polich, J. M., & Stambul, H. B. (1976). *Alcoholism and treatment.* Santa Monica, CA: Rand.

Aronson, M. K. (Ed). (1988). *Understanding Alzheimer's disease.* New York: Scribner's.

Aryee, S. (1993). Dual-earner couples in Singapore: An examination of work and nonwork sources of their experienced burnout. *Human Relations, 46,* 1441–1468.

Atchley, R. C. (1975). The life course, age grading, and age-linked demands for decision making. In N. Datan & L. H. Ginsberg (Eds.), *Life-span developmental psychology: Normative life crises* (pp. 261–278). New York: Academic Press.

Atchley, R. C. (1976). *The sociology of retirement.* Cambridge, MA: Schenkman.

Atchley, R. C. (1977). *The social forces in later life.* Belmont, CA: Wadsworth.

Atchley, R. C. (1989). A continuity theory of normal aging. *The Gerontologist, 29,* 183–190.

Attig, M. S. (1983, November). *The processing of spatial information by adults.* Paper presented at the meeting of the Gerontological Society of America, San Francisco.

Averill, J. R. (1968). Grief: Its nature and significance. *Psychological Bulletin, 70,* 721–748.

Avioli, L. V. (1982). Aging, bone, and osteoporosis. In S. G. Korenman (Ed.), *Endocrine aspects of aging* (pp. 199–230). New York: Elsevier Biomedical.

Avolio, B. J., & Waldman, D. A. (1987). Personnel aptitude-test scores as a function of age, education, and job type. *Experimental Aging Research, 13,* 109–113.

Axelrod, S., & Cohen, L. D. (1961). Senescence and embedded-figure performance in vision and touch. *Perceptual and Motor Skills, 12,* 283–288.

Bäckman, L. (1985). Further evidence for the lack of adult age differences on free recall of subject performed tasks: The importance of motor action. *Human Learning, 4,* 79–87.

Bäckman, L., & Nilsson, L.-G. (1984). Aging effects in free recall: An exception to the rule. *Human Learning, 3,* 53–69.

Bäckman, L., & Nilsson, L.-G. (1985). Prerequisites for the lack of age differences in memory performance. *Experimental Aging Research, 11,* 67–73.

Baddeley, A. (1981). The cognitive psychology of everyday life. *British Journal of Psychology, 72,* 257–269.

Bahrick, H. P., Bahrick, P. P., & Wittlinger, R. P. (1975). Fifty years of memory for names and faces: A cross-sectional approach. *Journal of Experimental Psychology, 104,* 54–75.

Baird, L. (1973). *The graduates.* Princeton, NJ: Educational Testing Service.

Baldessarini, R. J. (1978). Chemotherapy. In A. M. Nicholi (Ed.), *The Harvard guide to modern psychiatry* (pp. 387–432). New York: Belknap.

Ball, J. F. (1976–77). Widow's grief: The impact of age and mode of death. *Omega: Journal of Death and Dying, 7,* 307–333.

Baltes, M. M., & Baltes, P. B. (Eds.). (1986). *The psychology of control and aging.* Hillsdale, NJ: Erlbaum.

Baltes, P. B. (1979). Life-span developmental psychology: Some converging observations on history and theory. In P. B. Baltes & O. G. Brim, Jr. (Eds.), *Life-span development and behavior* (Vol. 2, pp. 255–279). New York: Academic Press.

Baltes, P. B. (1993). The aging mind: Potential and limits. *The Gerontologist, 33,* 580–594.

Baltes, P. B., & Baltes, M. M. (1990). Psychological perspectives on successful aging: The model of selective optimization with compensation. In P. B. Baltes & M. M. Baltes (Eds.), *Successful aging: Perspectives from the behavioral sciences* (pp. 1–34). Cambridge, UK: Cambridge University Press.

Baltes, P. B., Reese, H. W., & Nesselroade, J. R. (1977). *Life-span developmental psychology: Introduction to research methods.* Pacific Grove, CA: Brooks/Cole.

Baltes, P. B., & Schaie, K. W. (1974). Aging and IQ: The myth of the twilight years. *Psychology Today, 7,* 35–40.

Baltes, P. B., & Staudinger, U. M. (1993). The search for a psychology of wisdom. *Current Directions in Psychological Science, 2,* 75–80.

Baltes, P. B., Staudinger, U. M., Maercker, A., & Smith, J. (1995). People nominated as wise: A comparative study of wisdom-related knowledge. *Psychology and Aging, 10,* 155–166.

Baltes, P. B., & Willis, S. L. (1982). Enhancement (plasticity) of intellectual functioning: Penn State's Adult Development and Enrichment Project (ADEPT). In F. I. M. Craik & S. Trehub (Eds.), *Aging and cognitive processes* (pp. 353–389). New York: Plenum.

Bandura, A. (1986). *Social foundations of thought and action: A social cognitive theory.* Englewood Cliffs, NJ: Prentice-Hall.

Bandura, A. (1990). Reflections on non-ability determinants of competence. In J. Kolligan, Jr., & R. J. Sternberg (Eds.), *Competence considered: Perceptions of competence and incompetence across the lifespan.* New Haven, CT: Yale University Press.

Barfield, R. E., & Morgan, J. N. (1978). Trends in satisfaction with retirement. *The Gerontologist, 18,* 19–23.

Barlett, D. L., & Steele, J. B. (1992). *America: What went wrong?* Kansas City: Andrews and McMeel.

Barnett, R. C., & Baruch, G. K. (1978). *The competent woman: Perspectives on development.* New York: Halstead/Wiley.

Baron, J. N., & Bielby, W. T. (1985). Organizational barriers to gender equality: Sex segregation of jobs and opportunities. In A. S. Rossi (Ed.), *Gender and the life course* (pp. 233–251). New York: Aldine.

Barresi, C. M. (1990). Ethnogerontology: Social aging in national, racial, and cultural groups. In K. F. Ferraro (Ed.), *Gerontology: Perspectives and issues* (pp. 247–265). New York: Springer.

Barrett, G. V. (1978). Task design, individual attributes, work satisfaction, and productivity. In A. Negandhi & B. Wilpert (Eds.), *Current research in work organizations.* Kent, OH: Kent State University Press.

Barrett, G. V., Alexander, R. A., & Forbes, J. B. (1977). Analysis of performance measurement and training requirements for driving decision making in emergency situations. *JSAS Catalogue of Selected Documents in Psychology, 7,* 126 (Ms. No. 1623).

Baruch, G. K. (1984). The psychological well-being of women in the middle years. In G. K. Baruch & J. Brooks-Gunn (Eds.), *Women in midlife* (pp. 161–180). New York: Plenum.

Basseches, M. (1984). *Dialectical thinking and adult development.* Norwood, NJ: Ablex.

Bastida, E. (1987). Sex-typed age norms among older Hispanics. *The Gerontologist, 27,* 59–65.

Baylor, A. M., & Spirduso, W. W. (1988). Systemic aerobic exercise and components of reaction time in older women. *Journal of Gerontology, 43,* P121–P126.

Beall, C., & Goldstein, M. C. (1982). Work, aging, and dependency in a Sherpa population in Nepal. *Social Science and Medicine, 16,* 141–147.

Beall, C., & Goldstein, M. C. (1986). Age differences in sensory and cognitive function in elderly Nepalese. *Journal of Gerontology, 41,* 387–389.

Bean, F., & Tienda, M. (1987). *The Hispanic population in the United States.* New York: Russell Sage Foundation.

Beard, B. B. (1991). *Centenarians: The new generation.* Westport, CT: Greenwood Press.

Beck, A. T. (1967). *Depression: Clinical, experimental, and theoretical aspects.* New York: Harper & Row.

Beck, A. T. (1976). *Cognitive therapy and the emotional disorders.* New York: International Universities Press.

Beck, A. T., Rush, J., Shaw, B., & Emery, G. (1979). *Cognitive therapy of depression.* New York: Guilford.

Belenky, M. F., Clinchy, B. M., Goldberger, N. R., & Tarule, J. M. (1986). *Women's ways of knowing: The development of self, voice, and mind.* New York: Basic Books.

Bellezza, F. S. (1987). Mnemonic devices and memory schemas. In M. A. McDaniel & M. Pressley (Eds.), *Imagery and related mnemonic processes: Theories, individual differences, and applications* (pp. 34–55). New York: Springer-Verlag.

Bengtson, V. L. (1985). Diversity and symbolism in grandparental roles. In V. L. Bengtson & J. F. Robertson (Eds.), *Grandparenthood* (pp. 11–25). Beverly Hills, CA: Sage Publications.

Bengtson, V. L., Cuellar, J. B., & Raga, P. K. (1977). Stratum contrasts and similarities in attitudes toward death. *Journal of Gerontology, 32,* 76–88.

Bengtson, V. L., Dowd, J. J., Smith, D. H., & Inkles, A. (1975). Modernization, modernity and perceptions of aging: A cross-cultural study. *Journal of Gerontology, 30,* 688–695.

Bengtson, V. L., & Robertson, J. F. (Eds.). (1985). *Grandparenthood.* Beverly Hills, CA: Sage Publications.

Bengtson, V. L., Rosenthal, C., & Burton, L. (1995). Paradoxes of families and aging. In R. H. Binstock & L. K. George (Eds.), *Handbook of aging and the social sciences* (4th ed., pp. 253–282). San Diego: Academic Press.

Benin, M. H., & Agostinelli, J. (1988). Husbands' and wives' satisfaction with the division of labor. *Journal of Marriage and the Family, 50,* 349–361.

Benjamin, B. J. (1982). Phonological performance in gerontological speech. *Journal of Psycholinguistic Research, 11,* 159–167.

Berardi, A., Haxby, J. V., Grady, C. L., & Rapoport, S. I. (1991). Asymmetries of brain glucose metabolism and memory in healthy elderly. *Developmental Neuropsychology, 7,* 87–97.

Berg, C., Hertzog, C., & Hunt, E. (1982). Age differences in the speed of mental rotation. *Developmental Psychology, 18,* 95–107.

Berkman, L. F., Breslow, L., & Wingard, D. L. (1983). Health practices and mortality risk. In L. F. Berkman & L. Breslow (Eds.), *Health and ways of living: The Alameda County study* (pp. 61–112). New York: Oxford University Press.

Berkow, R. (Ed.). (1987). *The Merck manual of diagnosis and therapy* (15th ed.). Rahway, NJ: Merck, Sharp, & Dohme Research Laboratories.

Bernardi, B. (1985). *Age class systems: Social institutions and politics based on age.* Cambridge: Cambridge University Press.

Bernstein, J. (1982). Who leaves—who stays: Residency policy in housing for the elderly. *The Gerontologist, 22,* 305–313.

Berry, J. M. (1986). *Memory complaints and performance in older women: A self-efficacy and causal attribution model.* Unpublished doctoral dissertation, Washington University, St. Louis.

Berry, J. M., West, R. L., & Dennehey, D. M. (1989). Reliability and validity of the Memory Self-Efficacy Questionnaire. *Developmental Psychology, 25,* 701–713.

Berry, J. M., West, R. L., & Scogin, F. (1983, November). *Predicting everyday and laboratory memory skill.* Paper presented at the meeting of the Gerontological Society of America, San Francisco.

Berry, R. E., & Williams, F. L. (1987). Assessing the relationship between quality of life and marital and income satisfaction: A path analytic approach. *Journal of Marriage and the Family, 49,* 107–116.

Berscheid, E., Walster, E., & Bohrnstedt, G. (1973). Body image. The happy American body: A survey report. *Psychology Today, 7*(6), 119–131.

Betz, E. L. (1984). A study of career patterns of women college graduates. *Journal of Vocational Behavior, 24,* 249–263.

Betz, N., & Fitzgerald, L. F. (1987). *The career psychology of women.* New York: Academic Press.

Betz, N. E., & Hackett, G. (1986). Applications of self-efficacy theory to understanding career choice behavior. *Journal of Social and Clinical Psychology, 4,* 279–289.

Betz, N. E., Heesacker, R. S., & Shuttleworth, C. (1990). Moderators of the congruence and realism of major and occupational plans in college students: A replication and extension. *Journal of Counseling Psychology, 37,* 269–276.

Biegel, D. E., & Farkas, K. J. (1990). The impact of neighborhoods and ethnicity on black and white vulnerable elderly. In Z. Harel, P. Ehrlich, & R. Hubbard (Eds.), *The vulnerable aged* (pp. 116–136). New York: Springer.

Bielby, D. D., & Bielby, W. T. (1988). She works hard for the money: Household responsibilities and the allocation of work effort. *American Journal of Sociology, 93,* 1031–1059.

Bieman-Copland, S., & Charness, N. (1994). Memory knowledge and memory monitoring in adulthood. *Psychology and Aging, 9,* 287–302.

Bierman, E. L. (1985). Arteriosclerosis and aging. In C. E. Finch & E. L. Schneider (Eds.), *Handbook of the biology of aging* (2nd ed., pp. 842–858). New York: Van Nostrand Reinhold.

Biesele, M., & Howell, N. (1981). The old people give you life: Aging among !Kung hunter-gatherers. In P. T. Amoss & S. Harrell (Eds.), *Other ways of growing old* (pp. 77–98). Stanford, CA: Stanford University Press.

Binet, H. (1903). *L'étude experimentale de l'intelligence.* Paris: Schleicher.

Binger, C. M., Ablin, A. R., Feuerstein, R. C., Kushner, J. H., Zoger, S., & Mikkelson, C. (1969). Childhood leukemia—Emotional impact on patient and family. *New England Journal of Medicine, 280,* 414.

Birren, J. E., & Cunningham, W. (1985). Research on the psychology of aging: Principles, concepts, and theory. In J. E. Birren & K. W. Schaie (Eds.), *Handbook of the psychology of aging* (2nd ed., pp. 3–34). New York: Van Nostrand Reinhold.

Birren, J. E., & Renner, V. J. (1977). Research on the psychology of aging. In J. E. Birren & K. W. Schaie (Eds.), *Handbook of the psychology of aging* (pp. 3–38). New York: Van Nostrand Reinhold.

Birren, J. E., & Renner, V. J. (1979). A brief history of mental health and aging. In *Issues in mental health and aging: Vol. 1. Research* (pp. 1–26). Washington, DC: National Institute of Mental Health.

Birren, J. E., & Renner, V. J. (1980). Concepts and issues of mental health and aging. In J. E. Birren & R. B. Sloane (Eds.), *Handbook of mental health and aging* (pp. 3–33). Englewood Cliffs, NJ: Prentice-Hall.

Black, P., Markowitz, R. S., & Cianci, S. (1975). Recovery of motor function after lesions in motor cortex of monkey. In R. Porter & D. W. Fitzsimmons (Eds.), *Outcome of severe damage to the central nervous system* (pp. 65–70). Amsterdam: Elsevier.

Blair, S. N., Kohl, H. W., Paffenbarger, R. S., Clark, D. G., Cooper, K. H., & Gibbons, L. W. (1989) Physical fitness and all-cause mortality: A prospective study of healthy men and women. *Journal of the American Medical Association, 262,* 2395–2401.

Blake, B. F., & Lawton, M. P. (1980). Perceived community functions and the rural elderly. *Educational Gerontology, 5,* 375–386.

Blanchard-Fields, F. (1986). Reasoning on social dilemmas varying in emotional saliency: An adult developmental study. *Psychology and Aging, 1,* 325–333.

Blanchard-Fields, F. (1994). Age differences in causal attributions from an adult development perspective. *Journal of Gerontology: Psychological Sciences, 49,* P43–P51.

Blanchard-Fields, F., & Abeles, R. P. (1996). Social cognition and aging. In J. E. Birren & K. W. Schaie (Eds.), *Handbook of the psychology of aging* (4th ed., pp. 150–161). San Diego: Academic Press.

Blanchard-Fields, F., & Camp, C. J. (1990). Affect, individual differences, and real world problem solving across the adult life span. In T. Hess (Ed.), *Aging and cognition: Knowledge organization and utilization* (pp. 461–497). Amsterdam: North-Holland.

Blanchard-Fields, F., & Irion, J. C. (1988). The relation between locus of control and coping in two contexts: Age as a moderator variable. *Psychology and Aging, 3,* 197–203.

Blanchard-Fields, F., Jahnke, H. C., & Camp, C. (1995). Age differences in problem-solving style: The role of emotional salience. *Psychology and Aging, 10,* 173–180.

Blanchard-Fields, F., & Norris, L. (1994). Causal attributions from adolescence through adulthood: Age differences, ego level, and generalized response style. *Aging and Cognition, 1,* 67–86.

Blanchard-Fields, F., & Robinson, S. L. (1987). Age differences in the relation between controllability and coping. *Journal of Gerontology, 42,* 497–501.

Blass, J. P., & Barclay, L. L. (1985). New developments in the diagnosis of dementia. *Drug Development Research, 5,* 39–58.

Blaxton, T. A. (1989). Investigating dissociations among memory measures: Support for transfer appropriate processing framework. *Journal of Experimental Psychology: Learning, Memory, and Cognition, 15,* 657–668.

Blazer, D., George, L. K., & Hughes, D. C. (1988). Schizophrenic symptoms in an elderly community population. In J. A. Brody & G. L. Maddox (Eds.), *Epidemiology and aging: An international perspective* (pp. 134–149). New York: Springer.

Blazer, D., & Williams, C. D. (1980). Epidemiology of dysphoria and depression in the elderly populations. *American Journal of Psychiatry, 137,* 439–444.

Blessed, G., Tomlinson, B. E., & Roth, M. (1968). The association between quantitative measures of dementia and of senile changes in the cerebral grey matter of elderly subjects. *British Journal of Psychiatry, 114,* 797–811.

Block, J. (1995). A contrarian view of the five-factor approach to personality description. *Psychological Bulletin, 117,* 187–215.

Block, R., DeVoe, M., Stanley, B., Stanley, M., & Pomara, N. (1985). Memory performance in individuals with primary degenerative dementia:Its similarity to diazepam-induced impairments. *Experimental Aging Research, 11,* 151–155.

Bloom, B. L., & Caldwell, R. A. (1981). Sex differences in adjustment during the process of marital separation. *Journal of Marriage and the Family, 43,* 693–701.

Blum, E. M. (1966). Psychoanalytic views of alcoholism: A review. *Quarterly Journal of Studies of Alcohol, 27,* 259–299.

Blum, J. E., & Jarvik, L. F. (1974). Intellectual performance of octogenarians as a function of education and initial ability. *Human Development, 17,* 364–375.

Blume, S. B. (1985). Psychodrama and the treatment of alcoholism. In S. Zimberg, J. Wallace, & S. B. Blume (Eds.), *Practical approaches to alcoholism psychotherapy* (pp. 87–108). New York: Plenum.

Blumenthal, J. A., Emery, C. F., Cox, D. R., Walsh, M. A., Kuhn, C. M., Williams, R. B., & Williams, R. S. (1988). Exercise training in healthy Type A middle-aged men: Effects on behavioral and cardiovascular responses. *Psychosomatic Medicine, 50,* 418–433.

Blumenthal, J. A., & Madden, D. J. (1988). Effects of aerobic exercise training, age, and physical fitness on memory-search performance. *Psychology and Aging, 3,* 280–285.

Blumstein, P., & Schwartz, P. (1983). *American couples.* New York: Morrow.

Bobrow, D. G., & Collins, A. (1975). *Representation and understanding: Studies in cognitive science.* New York: Academic Press.

Bond, L. A., Cutler, S. J., & Grams, A. (Eds.). (1995). *Promoting successful and productive aging.* Thousand Oaks, CA: Sage Publications.

Bondareff, W. (1983). Age and Alzheimer's disease. *Lancet, 1,* 1447.

Bondareff, W. (1985). The neural basis of aging. In J. E. Birren & K. W. Schaie (Eds.), *Handbook of the psychology of aging* (2nd ed., pp. 95–112). New York: Van Nostrand Reinhold.

Bondareff, W., Mountjoy, C. Q., & Roth, M. (1982). Loss of neurons or origin of the adrenergic projection to cerebral cortex (nucleus locus ceruleus) in senile dementia. *Neurology, 32,* 164–168.

Booth, A., & Johnson, E. (1988). Premarital cohabitation and marital success. *Journal of Family Issues, 9,* 387–394.

Bootzin, R. R. (1977). Effects of self-control procedures for insomnia. In R. B. Stuart (Ed.), *Behavioral self-management: Strategies, techniques, and outcomes* (pp. 176–195). New York: Brunner/Mazel.

Bootzin, R. R., & Engle-Friedman, M. (1987). Sleep disturbances. In L. L. Carstensen & B. A. Edelstein (Eds.), *Handbook of clinical gerontology* (pp. 238–251). New York: Pergamon Press.

Bootzin, R. R., Engle-Friedman, M., & Hazelwood, L. (1983). Insomnia. In P. M. Lewinsohn & L. Teri (Eds.), *Clinical geropsychology: New directions in assessment and treatment* (pp. 81–115). New York: Pergamon Press.

Borg, S., & Lasker, J. (1981). *When pregnancy fails.* Boston: Beacon.

Borgatta, E. F., & Corsini, R. J. (1964). *Manual for the Quick Word Test.* New York: Harcourt, Brace, & World.

Borkan, G. A., & Norris, A. H. (1980). Assessment of biological age using a profile of physiological parameters. *Journal of Gerontology, 35,* 177–184.

Borkovec, T. D. (1982). Insomnia. *Journal of Consulting and Clinical Psychology, 50,* 880–895.

Bornstein, P. E., & Clayton, P. J. (1972). The anniversary reaction. *Diseases of the Nervous System, 33,* 470–472.

Borup, J. H. (1981). Relocation: Attitudes, information network, and problems encountered. *The Gerontologist, 21,* 501–511.

Borup, J. H. (1982). The effects of varying degrees of interinstitutional environmental change on long-term care of patients. *The Gerontologist, 22,* 409–417.

Borup, J. H. (1983). Relocation and mortality research: Assessment, reply, and the need to refocus the issues. *The Gerontologist, 23,* 235–242.

Borup, J. H. & Gallego, D. T. (1981). Mortality as affected by interinstitutional relocation: Update and assessment. *The Gerontologist, 21,* 8–16.

Borup, J. H. & Gallego, D. T., & Heffernan, P. G. (1979). Relocation and its effect on mortality. *The Gerontologist, 19,* 135–140.

Borup, J. H., & Gallego, D. T., & Heffernan, P. G. (1980). Relocation: Its effect on health, functioning, and mortality. *The Gerontologist, 20,* 468–479.

Bossé, R., Aldwin, C. M., Levenson, M. R., Spiro, A., III, & Mroczek, D. K. (1993). Change in social support after retirement: Longitudinal findings from the Normative Aging Study. *Journal of Gerontology: Psychological Sciences, 48,* P210–P217.

Bossé, R., & Ekerdt, D. J. (1981). Change in self-perception of leisure activities with retirement. *The Gerontologist, 21,* 650–653.

Botwinick, J. (1977). Intellectual abilities. In J. E. Birren & K. W. Schaie (Eds.), *Handbook of the psychology of aging* (pp. 580–605). New York: Van Nostrand Reinhold.

Boult, C., Kane, R. L., Louis, T. A., Boult, L., & McCaffrey, D. (1994). Chronic conditions that lead to functional limitation in the elderly. *Journal of Gerontology: Medical Sciences, 49,* M28–M36.

Bourestom, N., & Pastalan, L. (1981). The effects of relocation on the elderly: A reply. *The Gerontologist, 21,* 4–7.

Bozett, F. W. (1988). Gay fatherhood. In P. Bronstein & C. P. Cowan (Eds.), *Fatherhood today: Men's changing role in the family* (pp. 214–235). New York: Wiley.

Brabeck, M. M., & Weisgerber, K. (1989). College students' perceptions of men and women choosing teaching and management: The effects of gender and sex role egalitarianism. *Sex Roles, 21,* 841.

Brandt, J., & Rich, J. B. (1995). Memory disorders in the dementias. In A. D. Baddeley, B. A. Wilson, & F. N. Watts (Eds.), *Handbook of memory disorders* (pp. 243–270). Chichester, England: Wiley.

Brandtstädter, J. (1989). Personal self-regulation of development: Cross-sequential analyses of development-related control beliefs and emotions. *Developmental Psychology, 25,* 96–108.

Brandtstädter, J., & Greve, W. (1994). The aging self: Stabilizing and protective processes. *Developmental Review, 14,* 52–80.

Brandtstädter, J., & Rothermund, K. (1994). Self-percepts of control in middle and later adulthood: Buffering losses by rescaling goals. *Psychology and Aging, 9,* 265–273.

Brant, L. J., & Fozard, J. L. (1990). Age changes in pure tone thresholds in a longitudinal study of normal aging. *Journal of the Acoustical Society of America, 88,* 813–820.

Braune, R., & Wickens, C. D. (1985). The functional age profile: An objective decision criterion for the assessment of pilot performance capacities and capabilities. *Human Factors, 27,* 681–693.

Bray, D. W., Campbell, R. J., & Grant, D. L. (1974). *Formative years in business.* New York: Wiley.

Bray, D. W., & Howard, A. (1983). The AT&T longitudinal studies of managers. In K. W. Schaie (Ed.), *Longitudinal studies on adult psychological development* (pp. 266–312). New York: Guilford.

Breitner, J. C. S. (1988). Alzheimer's disease: Possible evidence for genetic causes. In M. K. Aronson (Ed.), *Understanding Alzheimer's disease* (pp. 34–49). New York: Scribner's.

Breslow, R., Kocsis, J., & Belkin, B. (1981). Contribution of the depressive perspective to memory function in depression. *American Journal of Psychiatry, 138,* 227–230.

Brickel, C. M. (1984). The clinical use of pets with the aged. *The Gerontologist, 2,* 72–74.

Brinley, J. F. (1965). Cognitive sets, speed, and accuracy of performance in the elderly. In A. T. Welford & J. E. Birren (Eds.), *Behavior, aging, and the nervous system* (pp. 1–36). Springfield, IL: Charles Thomas.

Brody, E. M. (1981). Women in the middle and family help to older people. *The Gerontologist, 21,* 471–480.

Brody, E. M. (1985). Parent care as a normative family stress. *The Gerontologist, 25,* 19–29.

Brody, E. M. (1990). *Women in the middle: Their parent-care years.* New York: Springer.

Brody, E. M., Johnsen, P. T., Fulcomer, M. C., & Lang, A. M. (1983). Women's changing roles and help to elderly parents: Attitudes of three generations of women. *Journal of Gerontology, 38,* 597–607.

Brody, E. M., Kleban, M. H., Johnsen, P. T., Hoffman, C., & Schoonover, C. B. (1987). Work status and parent care: A comparison of four groups of women. *The Gerontologist, 27,* 201–208.

Brody, J. (1988a, August 29). New test for Huntington's creates difficult choices. *Atlanta Journal,* p. 2B.

Brody, J. A. (1988b). Changing health needs of the ageing population. In D. Evered & J. Whelan (Eds.), *Symposium on research and the ageing population* (pp. 208–215). Chichester, England: Wiley.

Broman, C. L. (1988). Household work and family life satisfaction of Blacks. *Journal of Marriage and the Family, 50,* 743–748.

Brooks, L., & Betz, N. E. (1990). Utility of expectancy theory in predicting occupational choices in college students. *Journal of Counseling Psychology, 37,* 57–64.

Brown, G. C., & Bornstein, R. A. (1991). Anatomical imaging methods for neurobehavioral studies. In R. A. Bornstein & G. G. Brown (Eds.), *Neurobehavioral aspects of cerebrovascular disease.* New York: Oxford University Press.

Brown, J. K., & Kerns, V. (Eds.). (1985). *In her prime: A new view of middle-aged women.* South Hadley, MA: Bergin & Garvey.

Brown, M. B., & Tedrick, T. (1993). Outdoor leisure involvements of Black older Americans: An exploration of ethnicity and marginality. *Activities, Adaptation, and Aging, 17,* 55–65.

Brown, R., & Kulik, J. (1977). Flashbulb memories. *Cognition, 5,* 73–99.

Browne, A., & Williams, K. R. (1993). Gender, intimacy, and lethal violence: Trends from 1976 to 1987. *Gender and Society, 7,* 78–98.

Bruce, P. R., Coyne, A. C., & Botwinick, J. (1982). Adult age differences in metamemory. *Journal of Gerontology, 37,* 354–357.

Buell, S. J., & Coleman, P. D. (1979). Dendritic growth in the aged human brain and failure of growth in senile dementia. *Science, 206,* 854–856.

Bullock, W. A., & Dunn, N. J. (1988, August). *Aging, sex, and marital satisfaction.* Paper presented at the meeting of the American Psychological Association, Atlanta.

Bumpass, L. L., Sweet, J. A., & Cherlin, A. (1991). The role of cohabitation in declining rates of marriage. *Journal of Marriage and the Family, 53,* 913–927.

Burdman, G. M. (1986). *Healthful aging.* Englewood Cliffs, NJ: Prentice-Hall.

Burdz, M. P., Eaton, W. D., & Bond, J. B. (1988). Effect of respite care on dementia and nondementia patients and their caregivers. *Psychology and Aging, 3,* 38–42.

Burke, D. M., & Light, L. L. (1981). Memory and aging: The role of retrieval processes. *Psychological Bulletin, 90,* 513–546.

Burke, R. J. (1991a). Organizational treatment of minority managers and professionals: Costs to the majority? *Psychological Reports, 68,* 439–449.

Burke, R. J. (1991b). Work experiences of minority managers and professionals: Individual and organizational costs of perceived bias. *Psychological Reports, 69,* 1011–1023.

Burks, V., Lund, D., Gregg, C., & Bluhm, H. (1988). Bereavement and remarriage for older adults. *Death Studies, 12,* 51–60.

Burns, A. (1992). Mother-headed families: An international perspective and the case of Australia. *Society for Research in Child Development: Social Policy Report, 6,* 1–22.

Burr, J. A. (1990). Race/sex comparisons of elderly living arrangements. *Research on Aging, 12,* 507–530.

Burrus-Bammel, L. L., & Bammel, G. (1985). Leisure and recreation. In J. E. Birren & K. W. Schaie (Eds.), *Handbook of the psychology of aging* (2nd ed., (pp. 848–889). New York: Van Nostrand Reinhold.

Bury, M., & Holme, A. (1991). *Life after ninety.* London: Routledge.

Busch, J. W. (1985). Mentoring in graduate schools of education: Mentors' perceptions. *American Educational Research Journal, 22,* 257–265.

Buschmann, M. T., & Hollinger, L. M. (1994). Influence of social support and control on depression in the elderly. *Clinical Gerontologist, 14,* 13–28.

Buskirk, E. R. (1985). Health maintenance and longevity: Exercise. In C. E. Finch & E. L. Schneider (Eds.), *Handbook of the biology of aging* (2nd ed., pp. 894–931). New York: Van Nostrand Reinhold.

Buss, D. M., Abbott, M., Angeleitner, A., Asherian, A., Biaggio, A., Blanco-Villasenor, A., Bruchon-Schweitzer, M., Chu'u, H-Y., Czapinski, J., Deraad, B., Ekehammar, B., El Lohamy, N., Fioravanti, M., Georgas, J., Gjerde, P., Guttman, R., Hazan, F., Iwawaki, S., Janakiramaiah, N., Khosroshani, F., Kreitler, S., Lachenicht, L., Lee, M., Liik, K., Little, B., Mika, S., Moadel-Shahid, M., Moane, G., Montero, M., Mundy-Castle, A. C., Niit, T., Nsenduluka, E., Pienkowski, R., Pirttila-Backman, A-M., Pone de Leon, J., Rousseau, J., Runco, M. A., Safir, M. P., Samuels, C., Sanitioso, R., Serpell, R., Smid, N., Spencer, C., Tadinac, M., Todoreva, E. N., Troland, K., Van Den Brande, L., Van Heck, G., Van Langenhove, Yang, K-S. (1990). International preferences in selecting mates: A study of 37 cultures. *Journal of Cross-Cultural Psychology, 21,* 5–47.

Busse, E. W., & Maddox, G. L. (1985). *The Duke longitudinal studies of normal aging: 1955–1980.* New York: Springer.

Bustad, L. K. (1993). Health benefits of human-animal interaction. In F. Lieberman & M. F. Collen (Eds.), *Aging in good health: A quality lifestyle for the later years* (pp. 165–188). New York: Plenum.

Butler, R. M. (1975). *Why survive? Being old in America.* New York: Harper & Row.

Butler, R. N., & Lewis, M. I. (1982). *Aging and mental health* (3rd ed.). St. Louis: C. V. Mosby.

Cain, B. S. (1982, December 12). Plight of the grey divorcee. *New York Times Magazine,* pp. 89–90, 92, 95.

Calciano, R., Chodak, G. W., Garnick, M. B., Kuban, D. A., & Resnick, M. I. (1995, April 15). The prostate cancer conundrum. *Patient Care,* pp. 84–88, 91–95, 99–102, 104.

Cameron, R., & Meichenbaum, D. (1982). The nature of effective coping and the treatment of stress related problems: A cognitive-behavioral perspective. In L. Goldberger & S. Breznitz (Eds.), *Handbook of stress: Theoretical and clinical aspects* (pp. 695–710). New York: Free Press.

Camp, C. J. (1989). World knowledge systems. In L. W. Poon, D. C. Rubin, & B. Wilson (Eds.), *Everyday cognition in adulthood and late life* (pp. 457–482). New York: Cambridge University Press.

Camp, C. J., Foss, J. W., Stevens, A. B., Reichard, C. C., McKitrick, L. A., & O'Hanlon, A.M. (1993). Memory training in normal and demented elderly populations: The E-I-E-I-O model. *Experimental Aging Research, 19,* 277–290.

Camp, C. J., Markley, R. P., & Kramer, J. J. (1983). Spontaneous use of mnemonics by elderly individuals. *Educational Gerontology, 9,* 57–71.

Camp, C. J., & McKitrick, L. A. (1991). Memory interventions in Alzheimer's-type dementia populations: Methodological and theoretical issues. In R. L. West & J. D. Sinnott (Eds.), *Everyday memory and aging: Current research and methodology* (pp. 155–172). New York: Springer-Verlag.

Campbell, A. (1981). *The sense of well-being in America: Recent patterns and trends.* New York: McGraw-Hill.

Campbell, J. I. D., & Charness, N. (1990). Age-related declines in working-memory skills: Evidence from a complex calculation task. *Developmental Psychology, 26,* 879–888.

Campione, W. A. (1987). The married woman's retirement decision: A methodological comparison. *Journal of Gerontology, 42,* 381–386.

Campione, W. A. (1988). Predicting participation in retirement preparation programs. *Journal of Gerontology, 43,* S91–S95.

Cantor, N. (1990). From thought to behavior: "Having" and "doing" in the study of personality and cognition. *American Psychologist, 45,* 735–750.

Cantor, N., & Harlow, R. E. (1994). Personality, strategic behavior, and daily-life problem solving. *Current Directions in Psychological Science, 3,* 169–172.

Caplan, L. J., & Lipman, P. D. (1995). Age and gender differences in the effectiveness of maplike learning aids in memory for routes. *Journal of Gerontology: Psychological Sciences, 50B,* P126–P133.

Caramazza, A., & Hillis, A. E. (1991). Lexical organization of nouns and verbs in the brain. *Nature, 349,* 788–790.

Carlin, V. F., & Mansberg, R. (1984). *If I live to be 100. . . . Congregate housing for later life.* West Nyack, NY: Parker.

Carp, F. M. (1966). *A future for the aged.* Austin: University of Texas Press.

Carp, F. M. (1975). User evaluation of housing for the elderly. *The Gerontologist, 16,* 102–111.

Carp, F. M. (1976). Housing and living environments of older people. In R. H. Binstock & E. Shanas (Eds.), *Handbook of aging and the social sciences* (pp. 244–271). New York: Van Nostrand Reinhold.

Carp, F. M. (1977). Impact of improved living environment on health and life expectancy. *The Gerontologist, 17,* 242–249.

Carstensen, L. L. (1993). Motivation for social contact across the life span: A theory of socioemotional selectivity. In J. E. Jacobs (Ed.), *Nebraska symposium on motivation: Vol 40. Developmental perspectives on motivation* (pp. 209–254). Lincoln: University of Nebraska Press.

Carstensen, L. L. (1995). Evidence for a life-span theory of socioemotional selectivity. *Current Directions in Psychological Science, 4,* 151–156.

Carstensen, L. L., & Freund, A. M. (1994). The resilience of the aging self. *Developmental Review, 14,* 81–92.

Carstensen, L. L., Gottman, J. M., & Levenson, R. W. (1995). Emotional behavior in long-term marriage. *Psychology and Aging, 10,* 140–149.

Cartwright, A., Hockey, L., & Anderson, J. L. (1973). *Life before death.* London: Routledge & Kegan Paul.

Cascardi, M., & O'Leary, K. D. (1992). *Gender specific trends in spousal homicide across a decade.* Unpublished manuscript, State University of New York, Stony Brook.

Cascardi, M., Vivian, D., & Meyer, S. (1991). *Context and attributions for marital violence in discordant couples.* Paper presented at the annual meeting of the Association for the Advancement of Behavior Therapy, New York.

Cascio, W. F. (1995). Whither industrial and organizational psychology in a changing world of work? *American Psychologist, 50,* 928–939.

Case, R. B., Heller, S. S., Case, N. B., & Moss, A. J. (1985). Type A behavior and survival after acute myocardial infarction. *New England Journal of Medicine, 312,* 737–741.

Caserta, M. S., Lund, D. A., Wright, S. D., & Redburn, D. E. (1987). Caregivers to dementia patients: The utilization of community services. *The Gerontologist, 27,* 209–214.

Cavanaugh, J. C. (1983). Comprehension and retention of television programs by 20- and 60-year-olds. *Journal of Gerontology, 38,* 190–196.

Cavanaugh, J. C. (1984). Effects of presentation format on adults' retention of television programs. *Experimental Aging Research, 10,* 51–53.

Cavanaugh, J. C. (1986–1987). Age differences in adults' self-reports of memory ability: It depends on how and what you ask. *International Journal of Aging and Human Development, 24,* 241–277.

Cavanaugh, J. C. (1989). The importance of awareness in memory aging. In L. W. Poon, D. C. Rubin, & B. Wilson (Eds.), *Everyday cognition in adulthood and late life* (pp. 416–436). New York: Cambridge University Press.

Cavanaugh, J. C. (1996). Memory self-efficacy as a key to understanding memory change. In F. Blanchard-Fields & T. M. Hess (Eds.). *Perspectives on cognitive changes in adulthood and aging* (pp. 488–507). New York: McGraw Hill.

Cavanaugh, J. C., & Baskind, D. (in press). Relations among basic processes, beliefs, and performance: A lifespan perspective. In D. Herrmann, M. Johnson, C. McEvoy, C. Hertzog, & P. Hertel (Eds.), *Basic and applied memory: Research on practical aspects of memory.* Hillsdale, NJ: Erlbaum.

Cavanaugh, J. C., Grady, J. G., & Perlmutter, M. (1983). Forgetting and use of memory aids in 20 to 70 year olds' everyday life. *International Journal of Aging and Human Development, 17,* 113–122.

Cavanaugh, J. C., & Green, E. E. (1990). I believe, therefore I can: Self-efficacy beliefs in memory aging. In E. A. Lovelace (Ed.), *Aging and cognition: Mental processes, self-awareness, and interventions* (pp. 189–230). Amsterdam: North-Holland.

Cavanaugh, J. C., Kinney, J. M. (1994, July). *Marital satisfaction as an important contextual factor in spousal caregiving.* 7th International Conference on Personal Relationships, Groningen, The Netherlands.

Cavanaugh, J. C., Kramer, D. A., Sinnott, J. D., Camp, C. J., & Markley, R. J. (1985). On missing links and such: Interfaces between cognitive research and everyday problem solving. *Human Development, 28,* 146–168.

Cavanaugh, J. C., & Morton, K. R. (1988). Older adults' attributions about everyday memory. In M. M. Gruenberg & P. Morris (Eds.), *Practical aspects of memory: Vol. 1. Current research and issues* (pp. 209–214). Chichester, England: Wiley.

Cavanaugh, J. C., & Morton, K. R. (1989). Contextualism, naturalistic inquiry, and the need for new science: A rethinking of everyday memory aging and childhood sexual abuse. In D. A. Kramer & M. Bopp (Eds.), *Transformation in clinical and developmental psychology* (pp. 89–114). New York: Springer-Verlag.

Cavanaugh, J. C., Morton, K. R., & Tilse, C. R. (1989). A self-evaluation framework for understanding everyday memory aging. In J. D. Sinnott (Ed.), *Everyday problem solving: Theory and application* (pp. 266–284). New York: Praeger.

Cavanaugh, J. C., & Murphy, N. Z. (1986). Personality and metamemory correlates of memory performance in younger and older adults. *Educational Gerontology, 12,* 387–396.

Cavanaugh, J. C., & Nocera, R. (1994). Cognitive aspects and interventions in Alzheimer's disease. In J. D. Sinnott (Ed.), *Interdisciplinary handbook of adult lifespan learning* (pp. 389–407). New York: Greenwood Press.

Cavanaugh, J. C., & Perlmutter, M. (1982). Metamemory: A critical examination. *Child Development, 53,* 11–28.

Cavanaugh, J. C., & Poon, L. W. (1989). Metamemorial predictors of memory performance in young and old adults. *Psychology and Aging, 4,* 365–368.

Cavanaugh, J. C., & Stafford, H. (1989). Being aware of issues and biases: Directions for research on post-formal thought. In M. L. Commons, J. D. Sinnott, F. A. Richards, & C. Armon (Eds.), *Adult development: Vol. 1. Comparisons and applications of adolescent and adult development models* (pp. 272–292). New York: Praeger.

Cerella, J. (1990). Aging and information-processing rate. In J. E. Birren & K. W. Schaie (Eds.), *Handbook of the psychology of aging* (3rd ed., pp. 201–221). San Diego: Academic Press.

Cerella, J. (1994). Generalized slowing in Brinley plots. *Journal of Gerontology: Psychological Sciences, 49,* P65–P71.

Cerella, J., Poon, L. W., & Fozard, J. L. (1982). Age and iconic read-out. *Journal of Gerontology, 37,* 197–202.

Cerella, J., Poon L. W., & Williams, D. M. (1980). Age and the complexity hypothesis. In L. W. Poon (Ed.), *Aging in the 1980s* (pp. 332–340). Washington, DC: American Psychological Association.

Chaffin, R., & Herrmann, D. J. (1983). Self reports of memory abilities by old and young adults. *Human Learning, 2,* 17–28.

Chambré, S. M. (1993). Voluntarism by elders: Past trends and future prospects. *The Gerontologist, 33,* 221–228.

Chance, J., Overcast, T., & Dollinger, S. J. (1978). Aging and cognitive regression: Contrary findings. *Journal of Psychology, 98,* 177–183.

Chandler, M. J. (1980). Life-span intervention as a symptom of conversion hysteria. In R. R. Turner & H. W. Reese (Eds.), *Life-span developmental psychology: Intervention* (pp. 79–91). New York: Academic Press.

Charness, N. (1981). Aging and skilled problem solving. *Journal of Experimental Psychology, 110,* 21–38.

Charness, N., & Bosman, E. A. (1990a). Expertise and aging: Life in the lab. In T. M. Hess (Ed.), *Aging and cognition: Knowledge organization and utilization* (pp. 343–385). Amsterdam: North-Holland.

Charness, N., & Bosman, E. A. (1990b). Human factors and design for older adults. In J. E. Birren & K. W. Schaie (Eds.), *Handbook of the psychology of aging* (3rd ed., pp. 446–463). San Diego: Academic Press.

Cherkin, A. (1984). Effects of nutritional status on memory function. In H. J. Armbrecht, J. M. Prendergast, & R. M. Coe (Eds.), *Nutritional intervention in the aging process* (pp. 229–249). New York: Springer-Verlag.

Cherlin, A. J., & Furstenberg, F. F., Jr. (1986). *The new American grandparent: A place in the family, a life apart.* New York: Basic Books.

Cherry, K. E., & Park, D. C. (1993). Individual difference and contextual variables influence spatial memory in younger and older adults. *Psychology and Aging, 8,* 517–526.

Cherry, K. E., Park, D. C., & Donaldson, H. (1993). Adult age differences in spatial memory: Effects of structural context and practice. *Experimental Aging Research, 19,* 333–350.

Cherry, K. E., & Stadler, M. A. (1995). Implicit learning of a nonverbal sequence in younger and older adults. *Psychology and Aging, 10,* 379–394.

Chiarello, C., & Hoyer, W. J. (1988). Adult age differences in implicit and explicit memory: Time course and encoding effects. *Psychology and Aging, 3,* 358–366.

Chinen, A. B. (1989). *In the ever after.* Willmette, IL: Chiron.

Chiriboga, D. A. (1982). Adaptation to marital separation in later and earlier life. *Journal of Gerontology, 37,* 109–114.

Cicirelli, V. G. (1980). Sibling relationships in adulthood: A life-span perspective. In L. W. Poon (Ed.), *Aging in the 1980s* (pp. 455–474). Washington, DC: American Psychological Association.

Cicirelli, V. G. (1986). Family relationships and care/management of the dementing elderly. In M. Gilhooly, S. Zarit, & J. E. Birren (Eds.), *The dementias: Policy and management* (pp. 89–103). Englewood Cliffs, NJ: Prentice-Hall.

Cicirelli, V. G., Coward, R. T., & Dwyer, J. W. (1992). Siblings as caregivers for impaired elders. *Research on Aging, 14,* 331–350.

Clancy, S. M., & Hoyer, W. J. (1993). Skill and hemispheric specialization in detecting disparity in visual images. *Brain and Cognition, 21,* 192–202.

Clark, R. L., & Spengler, J. J. (1980). *The economics of individual and population aging.* New York: Cambridge University Press.

Clark, W. C., & Mehl, L. (1971). Thermal pain: A sensory decision theory analysis of the effect of age and sex on d′, various response criteria, and 50 percent pain threshold. *Journal of Abnormal Psychology, 78,* 202–212.

Clausen, J. A. (1981). Men's occupational careers in the middle years. In D. H. Eichorn, N. Haan, J. Clausen, M. Honzik, & P. Mussen (Eds.), *Present and past in middle life* (pp. 321–351). New York: Academic Press.

Clayton, V. P., & Overton, W. F. (1973, November). *The role of formal operational thought in the aging process.* Paper presented at the meeting of the Gerontological Society of America, Miami.

Cleek, M. B., & Pearson, T. A. (1985). Perceived causes of divorce: An analysis of interrelationships *Journal of Marriage and the Family, 47,* 179–191.

Clopton, W. (1973). Personality and career change. *Industrial Gerontology, 17,* 9–17.

Cohen, C. I., Teresi, J. A., & Holmes, D. (1988). The physical well-being of old homeless men. *Journal of Gerontology, 43,* S121–S128.

Cohen, C., Teresi, J., Holmes, D., & Roth, E. (1988). Survival strategies of older homeless men. *The Gerontologist, 28,* 58–65.

Cohen, G. (1979). Language comprehension in old age. *Cognitive Psychology, 11,* 412–429.

Cohen, G., & Faulkner, D. (1989). The effects of aging on perceived and generated memories. In L. W. Poon, D. C. Rubin, & B. Wilson (Eds.), *Everyday cognition in adulthood and late life* (pp. 222–243). New York: Cambridge University Press.

Cohen, R. M., Weingartner, H., Smallberg, S. A., Pickar, D., & Murphy, D. L. (1982). Effort and cognition in depression. *Archives of General Psychiatry, 39,* 593–597.

Cohen, G. D. (1990). Psychopathology and mental health in the mature and elderly adult. In J. E. Birren & K. W. Schaie (Eds.), *Handbook of the psychology of aging* (3rd ed., pp. 359–371). San Diego: Academic Press.

Cohen, G. D., Conway, M. A., & Maylor, E. A. (1994). Flashbulb memories in older adults. *Psychology and Aging, 9,* 454–463.

Coke, M. M. (1992). Correlates of life satisfaction among elderly African Americans. *Journal of Gerontology: Psychological Sciences, 47,* 316–320.

Colditz, G. A., Hankinson, S. E., Hunter, D. J., Willett, W. C., Manson, J. E., Stampfer, M. J., Hennekens, C., Rosner, B., & Speizer, F. E. (1995). The use of estrogens and progestins and the risk of breast cancer in postmenopausal women. *New England Journal of Medicine, 332,* 1589–1593.

Coleman, K. A., Casey, V. A., & Dwyer, J. T. (1991, June). *Stability of autobiographical memories over four decades.* Paper presented at the meeting of the American Psychological Society, Washington.

Coleman, M., & Ganong, L. H. (1990). Remarriage and stepfamily research in the 1980s: Increased interest in an old family form. *Journal of Marriage and the Family, 52,* 925–940.

Coleman, R. M., Miles, L. E., Guilleminault, C. C., Zarcone, V. P., van den Hoed, J., & Dement, W.C. (1981). Sleep wake disorders in the elderly: A polysomnographic analysis. *Journal of the American Geriatrics Association, 29,* 289–296.

Collopy, B. J. (1988). Autonomy in long term care: Some crucial distinctions. *The Gerontologist, 28(Suppl.),* 10–17.

Committee on an Aging Society. (1986). *Productive roles in an older society.* Washington, DC: National Academy Press.

Commons, M. L., Richards, F. A., & Armon, C. (Eds.). (1984). *Beyond formal operations: Late adolescent and adult cognitive development.* New York: Praeger.

Commons, M. L., Richards, F. A., & Kuhn, D. (1982). Systematic and metasystematic reasoning: A case for levels of reasoning beyond Piaget's stage of formal operations. *Child Development, 53,* 1058–1069.

Commons, M. L., Sinnott, J. D., Richards, F. A., & Armon, C. (Eds.). (1989). *Adult development: Vol. 1. Comparisons and applications of adolescent and adult developmental models.* New York: Praeger.

Connelly, S. L., & Hasher, L. (1993). Aging and the inhibition of spatial location. *Journal of Experimental Psychology: Human Perception and Performance, 19,* 1238–1250.

Connidis, I. (1988, November). *Sibling ties and aging.* Paper presented at the Gerontological Society of America, San Francisco.

Connidis, I. (1994). Sibling support in older age. *Journal of Gerontology: Social Sciences, 49,* S309–S317.

Connor, C. L., Walsh, R. P., Lintzelman, D. K., & Alvarez, M. G. (1978). Evaluation of job applicants: The effects of age versus success. *Journal of Gerontology, 33,* 246–252.

Conwell, Y. (1994). Suicide in the elderly. In L. S. Schneider, C. F. Reynolds, B. D. Lebowitz, & A. J. Friedhoff (Eds.), *Diagnosis and treatment of depression in late life: Results of the NIH Consensus Development Conference.* Washington, DC: American Psychiatric Press.

Cook-Greuter, S. (1990). Maps for living: Ego development theory from symbiosis to conscious universal embeddedness. In M. L. Commons, J. D. Sinnott, F. A. Richards, & C. Armon (Eds.), *Adult development: Vol. 1. Comparisons and application of adolescent and adult developmental models.* New York: Praeger.

Cook, J. A., & Wimberley, D. W. (1983). If I should die before I wake: Religious commitment and adjustment to the death of a child. *Journal for the Scientific Study of Religion, 22,* 222–238.

Cool, L., & McCabe, J. (1983). The "scheming hag" and the "dear old thing": The anthropology of aging women. In J. Sokolovsky (Ed.), *Growing old in different cultures.* Belmont, CA: Wadsworth.

Cool, L. E., (1987). The effects of social class and ethnicity on the aging process. In P. Silverman (Ed.), *The elderly as modern pioneers* (pp. 211–227). Bloomington: Indiana University Press.

Cooney, T. M., Pedersen, F. A., Indelicato, S., & Palkovitz, R. (1993). Timing of fatherhood: Is "on-time" optimal? *Journal of Marriage and the Family, 55,* 205–215.

Cooney, T. M., & Uhlenberg, P. (1990). The role of divorce in men's relations with their adult children after mid-life. *Journal of Marriage and the Family, 52,* 677–688.

Cordes, C. L., & Dougherty, T. W. (1993). A review and integration of research on job burnout. *Academy of Management Review, 18,* 621–656.

Corkin, S., Growdon J. H., Sullivan, E. V., Nissen, M. J., & Huff, F. J. (1986). Assessing treatment effects: A neuropsychological battery. In L. W. Poon (Ed.), *Handbook for clinical memory assessment of older adults* (pp. 156–167). Washington, DC: American Psychological Association.

Cornelius, S. W. (1990). Aging and everyday cognitive abilities. In T. M. Hess (Ed.), *Aging and cognition: Knowledge organization and utilization* (pp. 411–459). Amsterdam: North-Holland.

Cornelius, S. W., & Caspi, A. (1987). Everyday problem solving in adulthood and old age. *Psychology and Aging, 2,* 144–153.

Corr, C. A. (1991–92). A task-based approach to coping with dying. *Omega, 24,* 81–94.

Corrigan, P. W., Holmes, E. P., Luchins, D., Buichan, B., Basit, A., & Parks, J. J. (1994). Staff burnout in a psychiatric hospital: A cross-lagged panel design. *Journal of Organizational Behavior, 15,* 65–74.

Corso, J. F. (1981). *Aging sensory systems and perception.* New York: Praeger.

Corso, J. F. (1984). Auditory processes and age: Significant problems for research. *Experimental Aging Research, 10,* 171–174.

Corso, J. F. (1987). Sensory-perceptual processes and aging. In K. W. Schaie (Ed.), *Annual review of gerontology and geriatrics* (Vol. 7, pp. 29–55). New York: Springer.

Cosby, A. (1974). Occupational expectations and the hypothesis of increasing realism of choice. *Journal of Vocational Behavior, 5,* 53-65.

Costa, P. T., Jr., & McCrae R. R. (1977). Cross-sectional differences in masculinity-femininity in adult men. *The Gerontologist, 17,* 50.

Costa, P. T., Jr., & McCrae, R. R. (1978). Objective personality assessment. In M. Storandt, I. C. Siegler, & M. F. Elias (Eds.), *The clinical psychology of aging* (pp. 119–143). New York: Plenum.

Costa, P. T., Jr., & McCrae, R. R. (1980a). Somatic complaints in males as a function of age and neuroticism: A longitudinal analysis. *Journal of Behavioral Medicine, 3,* 245–258.

Costa, P. T., Jr., & McCrae, R. R. (1980b). Still stable after all these years: Personality as a key to some issues in adulthood and old age. In P. B. Baltes & O. G. Brim, Jr. (Eds.), *Life-span development and behavior* (Vol. 3, pp. 65–102). New York: Academic Press.

Costa, P. T., Jr., & McCrae, R. R. (1988). Personality in adulthood: A six-year longitudinal study of self-reports and spouse ratings on the NEO Personality Inventory. *Journal of Personality and Social Psychology, 54,* 853–863.

Costa, P. T., Jr., & McCrae, R. R. (1995). Solid ground in the wetlands of personality: A reply to Block. *Psychological Bulletin, 117,* 216–220.

Costa, P. T., Jr., McCrae, R. R., & Arenberg, D. (1980). Enduring dispositions in adult males. *Journal of Personality and Social Psychology, 38,* 793–800.

Costa, P. T., Jr., McCrae, R. R., & Holland, J. L. (1984). Personality and vocational interests in an adult sample. *Journal of Applied Psychology, 42,* 390–400.

Cotman, C. W., & Holets, V. R. (1985). Structural changes at synapses with age: Plasticity and regeneration. In C. E. Finch & E. L. Schneider (Eds.), *Handbook of the biology of aging* (2nd ed., pp. 617–644). New York: Van Nostrand Reinhold.

Cotton, S., Anthill, J. K., & Cunningham, J. D. (1989). The work motivations of mothers with preschool children. *Journal of Family Issues, 10,* 189–210.

Counts, D., & Counts, D. (Eds.). (1985a). *Aging and its transformations: Moving toward death in Pacific societies.* Lanham, MD: University Press of America.

Counts, D. A., & Counts, D. R. (1985b). I'm not dead yet! Aging and death: Processes and experiences in Kalia. In D. A. Counts & D. R. Counts (Eds.), *Aging and its transformations* (pp. 131–156). Langham, MD: University of America Press.

Cowan, C. P., & Cowan, P. A. (1992). *When partners become parents.* New York: Basic Books.

Cowgill, D. (1974). Aging and modernization: A revision of the theory. In J. Gubrium (Ed.), *Late life: Communities and environmental policy* (pp. 123–146). Springfield, IL: Charles C. Thomas.

Cowgill, D., & Holmes, L. D. (1972). *Aging and modernization.* New York: Appleton-Century-Crofts.

Coyne, A. C. (1983, November). *Age, task variables, and memory knowledge.* Paper presented at the meeting of the Gerontological Society of America, San Francisco.

Craik, F. I. M. (1977). Age differences in human memory. In J. E. Birren & K. W. Schaie (Eds.), *Handbook of the psychology of aging* (pp. 384–420). New York: Van Nostrand Reinhold.

Craik, F. I. M., & Byrd, M. (1982). Aging and cognitive deficits: The role of attentional sources. In F. I. M. Craik & S. Trehub (Eds.), *Aging and cognitive processes* (pp. 191–211). New York: Plenum.

Craik, F. I. M., & Jennings, J. M. (1992). Human memory. In F. I. M. Craik & T. A. Salthouse (Eds.), *The handbook of aging and cognition* (pp. 51–110). Hillsdale, NJ: Erlbaum.

Craik, F. I. M., & Lockhart, R. S. (1972). Levels of processing: A framework for memory research. *Journal of Verbal Learning and Verbal Behavior, 11,* 671–684.

Crandall, R. C. (1980). *Gerontology: A behavioral science approach.* Reading, MA: Addison-Wesley.

Crook, T. H. (1987). Dementia. In L. L. Carstensen & B. A. Edelstein (Eds.), *Handbook of clinical gerontology* (pp. 96–111). New York: Pergamon Press.

Crook, T. H., & Cohen, G. (1983). *Physician's guide to the diagnosis and treatment of depression in the elderly.* New Canaan, CT: Mark Powley Associates.

Crook, T. H., & Larrabee, G. J. (1992). Normative data on a self-rating scale for evaluating memory in everyday life. *Archives of Clinical Neuropsychology, 7,* 41–51.

Crosby, J. F. (1980). Critique of divorce statistics and their interpretation. *Family Relations, 29,* 51–58.

Cross, S., & Markus, H. (1991). Possible selves across the life span. *Human Development, 34,* 230–255.

Crystal, H. A. (1988). The diagnosis of Alzheimer's disease and other dementing disorders. In M. K. Aronson (Ed.), *Understanding Alzheimer's disease* (pp. 15–33). New York: Scribner's.

Cuber, J. F., & Harroff, P. B. (1965). *Sex and the significant Americans.* Baltimore: Penguin.

Cuellar, J. B., & Weeks, J. R. (1980). *Minority elderly Americans: A prototype for area offices on aging (executive summary).* San Diego: Allied Home Health Association.

Cummings, N. A. (1993). Chemical dependency among older adults. In F. Lieberman & M. F. Collen (Eds.), *Aging in good health: A quality lifestyle for the later years* (pp. 107–113). New York: Plenum.

Cunningham, W. R. (1987). Intellectual abilities and age. In K. W. Schaie (Ed.), *Annual review of gerontology and geriatrics* (Vol. 7, pp. 117–134). New York: Springer.

Curcio, C. A., Buell, S. J., & Coleman, P. D. (1982). Morphology of the aging central nervous system: Not all downhill. In J. A. Mortimer, F. J. Pirozzola, & G. I. Maletta (Eds.), *Advances in neurogerontology: Vol. 3. The aging motor system* (pp. 7–35). New York: Praeger.

Currey, J. D. (1984). Effects of differences in mineralization on the mechanical properties of bone. *Philosophical Transactions of the Royal Society of London (Biology), 304(1121),* 509–518.

Cutler, S. J., & Hendricks, J. (1990). Leisure and time use across the life course. In R. H. Binstock & L. K. George (Eds.), *Handbook of aging and the social sciences* (3rd ed., pp. 169–185). San Diego: Academic Press.

Cutter, M. A. G. (1991). Euthanasia: Reassessing the boundaries. *Journal of NIH Research, 3*(5), 59–61.

Dakof, G. A., & Mendelsohn, G. A. (1986). Parkinson's disease: The psychological aspects of a chronic illness. *Psychological Bulletin, 99,* 375–387.

Daneman, M. (1987). Reading and working memory. In J. R. Beech & A. M. Colley (Eds.), *Cognitive approaches to reading* (pp. 57–86). New York: Wiley.

Davidson, J. M., Chen, J. J., Crapo, L., Gray, G. D., Greenleaf, W. J., & Catania, J. A.

(1983). Hormonal changes and sexual function in aging men. *Journal of Clinical Endocrinology and Metabolism, 57,* 71–77.

Davidson, R. J., Schwartz, G. E., Saron, C., Bennett, J., & Goleman, D. J. (1979). Frontal vs. parietal EEG asymmetry during positive and negative affect. *Psychophysiology, 16,* 202–203.

Davies, P. (1988). Alzheimer's disease and related disorders: An overview. In M. K. Aronson (Ed.), *Understanding Alzheimer's disease* (pp. 3–14). New York: Scribner's.

Davies, P., & Maloney, A. J. F. (1976). Selective loss of central cholinergic neurons in Alzheimer's disease. *Lancet, 2,* 1403.

Davis, K. C. (1980). The position and status of Black and White aged in rural Baptist churches in Missouri. *Journal of Minority Aging, 5,* 242–248.

Day, D. V., & Bedeian, A. G. (1995). Personality similarity and work-related outcomes among African-American nursing personnel: A test of the supplementary model of person-environment congruence. *Journal of Vocational Behavior, 46,* 55–70.

Deaux, K. (1993). Reconstructing social identity. *Personality and Social Psychology Bulletin, 19,* 4–12.

DeFrank, R., & Ivancevich, J. M. (1986). Job loss: An individual level review and model. *Journal of Vocational Behavior, 19,* 1–20.

Degner, L. (1974). The relationship between some beliefs held by physicians and their life-prolonging decisions. *Omega: Journal of Death and Dying, 5,* 223.

De Jong, G. F., Wilmoth, J. M., Angel, J. L., & Cornwell, G. T. (1995). Motives and the geographical mobility of very old Americans. *Journal of Gerontology: Social Sciences, 50B,* S395–S404.

Dekker, J. A. M., Connor, D. J., & Thal, L. J. (1991). The role of cholinergic projections from the nucleus basalis in memory. *Neuroscience and Biobehavioral Reviews, 15,* 299–317.

DeMaris, A., & Rao, K. V. (1992). Premarital cohabitation and subsequent marital stability in the United States: A reassessment. *Journal of Marriage and the Family, 54,* 178–190.

Denney, N. W. (1974). Classification abilities in the elderly. *Journal of Gerontology, 29,* 309–314.

Denney, N. W. (1982). Aging and cognitive changes. In B. B. Wolman (Ed.), *Handbook of developmental psychology* (pp. 807–827). Englewood Cliffs, NJ: Prentice-Hall.

Denney, N. W. (1990). Adult age differences in traditional and practical problem solving. In E. A. Lovelace (Ed.), *Aging and cognition: Mental processes, self-awareness, and interventions* (pp. 329–349). Amsterdam: North-Holland.

Denney, N. W., & Cornelius, S. W. (1975). Class inclusion and multiple classification in middle and old age. *Developmental Psychology, 11,* 521–522.

Denney, N. W., Dew, J. R., & Kroupa, S. L. (1995). Perceptions of wisdom: What is it and who has it? *Journal of Adult Development, 2,* 37–47.

Denney, N. W., & Pearce, K. A. (1989). A developmental study of practical problem solving in adults. *Psychology and Aging, 4,* 438–442.

Denney, N. W., Pearce, K. A., & Palmer, A. M. (1982). A developmental study of adults' performance on traditional and practical problem-solving tasks. *Experimental Aging Research, 8,* 115–118.

de St. Aubin, E., & McAdams, D. P. (1995). The relations of generative concern and generative action to personality traits, satisfaction/happiness with life, and ego development. *Journal of Adult Development, 2,* 99–112.

deVries, H. A. (1983). Physiology of exercise and aging. In D. W. Woodruff & J. E. Birren (Eds.), *Aging: Scientific perspectives and social issues* (pp. 285–304). Pacific Grove, CA: Brooks/Cole.

Diamond, J. (1986). I want a girl just like the girl. . . . *Discover, 7*(11), 65–68.

Dickstein, L. S. (1972). Death concern: Measurement and correlates. *Psychological Reports, 30,* 563–571.

Diehl, M., Willis, S. L., & Schaie, K. W. (1995). Everyday problem solving in older adults: Observational assessment and cognitive correlates. *Psychology and Aging, 10,* 478–491.

Dignam, J. M., & Takemoto-Chock, N. K. (1981). Factors in the natural language of personality: Re-analysis, comparison, and interpretation of six major studies. *Multivariate Behavioral Research, 16,* 149–170.

Dimond, M., Lund, D. A., & Caserta, M. S. (1987). The role of social support in the first two years of bereavement in an elderly sample. *The Gerontologist, 27,* 599–604.

Dimsdale, J. E., Gilbert, J., Hutter, A. M., Hackett, T. P., & Block, P. C. (1981). Predicting cardiac morbidity based on risk factors and coronary angiographic findings. *American Journal of Cardiology, 47,* 73–76.

DiPrete, T. A., & Soule, W. T. (1988). Gender and promotion in segmented job ladder systems. *American Sociological Review, 53,* 26–40.

Discover. (1990, October). Parkinson's bug. 18.

Dittmann-Kohli, F., & Baltes, P. B. (1990). Toward a neofunctionalist conception of adult intellectual development: Wisdom as a prototypical case of intellectual growth. In C. Alexander & E. Langer (Eds.), *Beyond formal operations: Alternative endpoints to human development* (pp. 54–78). New York: Oxford University Press.

Dixon, R. A. (1989). Questionnaire research on metamemory and aging: Issues of structure and function. In L. W. Poon, D. C. Rubin, & B. A. Wilson (Eds.), *Everyday cognition in adulthood and late life* (pp. 394–415). New York: Cambridge University Press.

Dixon, R. A., & Hultsch, D. F. (1983). Structure and development of metamemory in adulthood. *Journal of Gerontology, 38,* 682–688.

Dixon, R. A., & von Eye, A. (1984). Depth processing and text recall in adulthood. *Journal of Reading Behavior, 26,* 109–117.

Dobash, R. P., & Dobash, R. E. (1992). *Women, violence, and social change.* New York: Routledge.

Dobson, S. H., Kirasic, K. C., & Allen, G. L. (1995). Age-related differences in adults' spatial task performance: Influences of task complexity and perceptual speed. *Aging and Cognition, 2,* 19–38.

Dohrenwend, B. P. (1979). Stressful life events and psychopathology: Some issues of theory and method. In J. E. Barrett, B. M. Rose, & G. L. Klerman (Eds.), *Stress and mental disorder* (pp. 1–15). New York: Raven.

Doi, T. (1973). *The anatomy of dependence.* Tokyo: Kodansha.

Doka, K. J., & Mertz, M. E. (1988). The meaning and significance of great-grandparenthood. *The Gerontologist, 28,* 192–197.

Doudna, C., & McBride, F. (1981). Where are the men for the women at the top? In P. Stein (Ed.), *Single life: Unmarried adults in social context.* New York: St. Martin's.

Douglass, W. A. (1969). *Death in Murelaga: Funerary ritual in a Spanish Basque village.* Seattle: University of Washington Press.

Dowd, J. J., & Bengtson, V. L. (1978). Aging in minority populations: An examination of the double jeopardy hypothesis. *Journal of Gerontology, 33,* 427–436.

Doyle, K. O., Jr. (1974). Theory and practice of ability testing in ancient Greece. *Journal of the History of the Behavioral Sciences, 10,* 202–212.

Drachman, D. A., Noffsinger, D., Sahakian, B. J., Kurdziel, S., & Fleming, P. (1980). Aging, memory, and the cholinergic system: A study of dichotic listening. *Neurobiology of Aging, 1,* 39–43.

Duara, R., London, E. D., & Rapoport, S. I. (1985). Changes in structure and energy metabolism of the aging brain. In C. E. Finch & E. L. Schneider (Eds.), *Handbook of the biology of aging* (2nd ed., pp. 595–616). New York: Van Nostrand Reinhold.

Dublin, L. I., Lotka, A. J., & Spiegelman, M. (1946). *The money value of a man.* New York: Ronald.

DuBois, P. H. (1968). A test dominated society: China 1115 B.C.–1905 A.D. In J. L. Barnette (Ed.), *Readings in psychological tests and measurements* (pp. 249–255). Homewood, IL: Dorsey Press.

Dunn, J. (1984). Sibling studies and the developmental impact of critical incidents. In P. B. Baltes & O. G. Brim, Jr. (Eds.), *Life-span development and behavior* (Vol. 6). New York: Academic Press.

Dunn, T. R., & Merriam, S. B. (1995). Levinson's age thirty transition: Does it exist? *Journal of Adult Development, 2,* 113–124.

Dwyer, J. W., & Coward, R. T. (1991). A multivariate comparison of the involvement of adult sons versus daughters in the care of impaired parents. *Journal of Gerontology: Social Sciences, 46,* S259–S269.

Earles, J. L., & Coon, V. E. (1994). Adult age differences in long-term memory for performed activities. *Journal of Gerontology: Psychological Sciences, 49,* P32–P34.

Eckhardt, M. J., Harford, T. C., Kaelber, C. T., Parker, E. S., Rosenthal, L. S., Ryback, R. S., Salmoiraghi, G. C., Vanderveen, E., & Warren, K. R. (1981). Health hazards associated with alcohol consumption. *Journal of the American Medical Association, 246,* 648–666.

Edelstein, S. (1990–91, December–January). Do grandparents have rights? *Modern Maturity,* 40-42.

Eglit, H. (1989). Ageism in the workplace: An elusive quarry. *Generations, 13,* 31–35.

Einstein, G. O., & McDaniel, M. A. (1990). Normal aging and prospective memory. *Journal of Experimental Psychology: Learning, Memory, and Cognition, 16,* 717–726.

Eisdorfer, C., & Wilkie, F. (1977). Stress, disease, aging, and behavior. In J. E. Birren & K. W. Schaie (Eds.), *Handbook of the psychology of aging* (pp. 251–275). New York: Van Nostrand Reinhold.

Eisner, D. A. (1973). *The effect of chronic brain syndrome upon concrete and formal operations in elderly men.* Unpublished manuscript cited in Papalia & Bielby (1974).

Ekert, J. K. (1980). *The unseen elderly: A study of marginally subsistent hotel dwellers.* San Diego: Campanile.

Ekstrom, R. K., French, J. W., & Harman, H. H. (1979). Cognitive factors: Their identification and replication. *Multivariate Behavioral Research Monographs,* No. 79, 2.

Elder, G. H., Jr. (1974). *Children of the great depression.* Chicago: University of Chicago Press.

Elder, G. H., Jr., & Pavalko, E. K. (1993). Work careers in men's later years: Transitions, trajectories, and historical change. *Journal of Gerontology: Social Sciences, 48,* S180–S191.

Ellison, C. G. (1990). Family ties, friendships, and subjective well-being among Black Americans. *Journal of Marriage and the Family, 52,* 298–310.

Emery, C. F., & Gatz, M. (1990). Psychological and cognitive effects of an exercise program for community-residing older adults. *The Gerontologist, 30,* 184–188.

Eng, E., Hatch, J., & Callan, A. (1985). Institutionalizing social support through the church and into the community. *Health Education Quarterly, 12,* 81–92.

Engen, T. (1982). *The perception of odors.* New York: Academic Press.

Epstein, L. J. (1976). Depression in the elderly. *Journal of Gerontology, 31,* 278–282.

Epstein, L. J. (1978). Anxiolytics, anti-depressants and neuroleptics in the treatment of geriatric patients. In M. A. Lipton, A. D. Mascio, & K. F. Killam (Eds.), *Psychopharmacology: A generation of progress* (pp. 1517–1523). New York: Raven.

Eribes, R. A., & Bradley-Rawls, M. (1978). Underutilization of nursing home facilities by Mexican American elderly in the Southwest. *The Gerontologist, 18,* 363–371.

Erickson, R., & Ekert, K. (1977). The elderly poor in downtown San Diego hotels. *The Gerontologist, 17,* 440–446.

Erickson, R. C., Poon, L. W., & Walsh-Sweeney, L. (1980). Clinical memory testing of the elderly. In L. W. Poon, J. L. Fozard, L. S. Cermak, D. Arenberg, & L. W. Thompson (Eds.), *New directions in memory aging* (pp. 379–402). Hillsdale, NJ: Erlbaum.

Ericsson, K. A., & Smith, J. (Eds.). (1991). *Toward a general theory of expertise: Prospects and limits.* New York: Cambridge University Press.

Erikson, E. H. (1968). *Identity: Youth and crisis.* New York: Norton.

Erikson, E. H. (1982). *The life cycle completed: Review.* New York: Norton.

Ershler, W. B. (1991). Cancer biology and aging. *Journal of NIH Research, 3*(1), 50–52.

Espino, D. V., & Maldonado, D. (1990). Hypertension and acculturation in elderly Mexican Americans: Results from 1982–84 Hispanic HANES. *Journal of Gerontology: Medical Sciences, 45,* M209–M213.

Essex, M. J., & Nam, S. (1987). Marital status and loneliness among older women. *Journal of Marriage and the Family, 49,* 93–106.

Estes, R. J., & Wilensky, H. L. (1978). Life cycle squeeze and the morale curve. *Social Problems, 25,* 277–292.

Evans, G. W., Brennan, P. L., Skorpanich, M. A., & Held, D. (1984). Cognitive mapping and elderly adults: Verbal and location memory for urban landmarks. *Journal of Gerontology, 39,* 452–457.

Everard, K., Rowles, G. D., & High, D. M. (1994). Nursing home room changes: Toward a decision-making model. *The Gerontologist, 34,* 520–527.

Exton-Smith, A. N. (1985). Mineral metabolism. In C. E. Finch & E. L. Schneider (Eds.), *Handbook of the biology of aging* (2nd ed., pp. 511–539). New York: Van Nostrand Reinhold.

Farmer, P. M., Peck, A., & Terry, R. D. (1976). Correlations among neuritic plaques, neurofibrillary tangles, and the severity of senile dementia. *Journal of Neuropathology and Experimental Neurology, 35,* 367–376.

Farrell, M. P., & Rosenberg, S. D. (1981). *Men at midlife.* Boston: Auburn House.

Featherman, D. L. (1981). The life-span perspective in social science research. In American Association for the Advancement of Science (Ed.), *Policy outlook: Science, technology, and the issues of the eighties Vol. 2: Sources.* Washington, DC: U. S. Government Printing Office.

Feifel, H. (1965). The function of attitudes toward death. In Group for the Advancement of Psychiatry (Eds.), *Death and dying: Attitudes of patient and doctor* (pp. 632–641). New York: Mental Health Materials Center.

Feifel, H., & Nagy, V. T. (1981). Another look at fear of death. *Journal of Consulting and Clinical Psychology, 49,* 278–286.

Feinberg, R. (1983). The meaning of sibling on Anata. In M. Marshall (Ed.), *Siblingship in Oceania: Studies in the meaning of kin relations* (pp. 105–148). New York: University Press of America.

Feinson, M. C. (1987). Mental health and aging: Are there gender differences? *The Gerontologist, 27,* 703–711.

Felton, B. J., & Revenson, T. A. (1987). Age differences in coping with chronic illness. *Psychology and Aging, 2,* 164–170.

Fenske, N. A., & Lober, C. W. (1990). Skin changes of aging: Pathological implications. *Geriatrics, 45(3),* 27–35.

Ferraro, K. F., & Sterns, H. L. (1990). Epilogue: "2020 vision" and beyond. In K. F. Ferraro (Ed.), *Gerontology: Perspectives and issues* (pp. 357–360). New York: Springer.

Ferris, S. H., & Crook, T. H. (1983). Cognitive assessment in mild to moderately severe dementia. In T. H. Crook, S. Ferris, & R. Bartus (Eds.), *Assessment in geriatric psychopharmacology.* New Canaan, CT: Mark Powley Associates.

Field, D., & Minkler, M. (1988). Continuity and change in social support between young-old and old-old or very-old age. *Journal of Gerontology: Psychological Sciences, 43,* P100–P106.

Fields, T. M., & Widmayer, S. M. (1982). Motherhood. In B. B. Wolman (Ed.), *Handbook of developmental psychology* (pp. 681–701). Englewood Cliffs, NJ: Prentice-Hall.

Fisher, H. E. (1987). The four-year itch. *Natural History, 96*(10), 22–33.

Fisk, A. D., Cooper, B. P., Hertzog, C., & Anderson-Garlach, M. M. (1995). Age-related retention of skilled memory search: Examination of associative learning, interference, and task-specific skills. *Journal of Gerontology: Psychological Sciences, 50B,* P150–P161.

Fisk, A. D., Cooper, B. P., Hertzog, C., Anderson-Garlach, M. M., & Lee, M. D. (1995). Understanding performance and learning in consistent memory search: An age-related perspective. *Psychology and Aging, 10,* 255–268.

Fisk, A. D., & Fisher, D. L. (1994). Brinley plots and theories of aging: The explicit, muddled, and implicit debates. *Journal of Gerontology: Psychological Sciences, 49,* P81–P89.

Fisk, A. D., Hertzog, C., Lee, M. D., Rogers, W. A., & Anderson-Garlach, M. M. (1994). Long-term retention of skilled visual search: Do young adults retain more than old adults? *Psychology and Aging, 9,* 206–215.

Fisk, A. D., & Rogers, W. A. (1987, November). *Associative and priority learning in memory and visual search: A theoretical view of age-dependent practice effects.* Paper presented at the National Institute on Aging Conference on Aging and Attention, Washington, DC.

Fisk, A. D., & Rogers, W. A. (1991). Toward an understanding of age-related memory and visual search effects. *Journal of Experimental Psychology: General, 120,* 131–149.

Fitzgerald, L. F., & Ormerod, A. J. (1991). Perceptions of sexual harassment: The influence of gender and academic context. *Psychology of Women Quarterly, 15,* 281–294.

Fitzgerald, L. F., & Shullman, S. L. (1993). Sexual harassment: A research analysis and agenda for the 1990s. *Journal of Vocational Behavior, 42,* 5–27.

Fitzgerald, L. F., Shullman, S. L., Bailey, N., Richards, M., Swecker, J., Gold, Y., Ormerod, A. J., & Weitzman, L. (1988). The incidence and dimensions of sexual harassment in academia and the workplace. *Journal of Vocational Behavior, 32,* 152–175.

Fitzpatrick, M. A. (1984). A topological approach to marital interaction—Recent theory and research. *Advances in Experimental Sociology, 18,* 1–47.

Flaks, D. K., Ficher, I., Masterpasqua, F., & Joseph, G. (1995). Lesbians choosing motherhood: A comparative study of lesbian and heterosexual parents and their children. *Developmental Psychology, 31,* 105–114.

Flynn, T. M., & Storandt, M. (1990). Supplemental group discussions in memory training for older adults. *Psychology and Aging, 5,* 178–181.

Fogel, B. S., & Fretwell, M. (1985). Reclassification of depression in the medically ill elderly. *Journal of the American Geriatrics Society, 42,* 446–448.

Foley, D. J., Miles, T. P., Brock, D. B., & Phillips, C. (1995). Recounts of elderly deaths: Endorsements for the Patient Self-Determination Act. *The Gerontologist, 35,* 119–121.

Folkman, S., Lazarus, R. S., Pimley, S., & Novacek, J. (1987). Age differences in stress and coping processes. *Psychology and Aging, 2,* 171–184.

Folstein, M. F., Folstein, S. E., & McHugh, P. R. (1975). Mini-mental state: A practical method for grading the cognitive state of patients for the clinician. *Journal of Psychiatric Research, 12,* 189–198.

Foner, A., & Kertzer, D. I. (1978). Transitions over the life course: Lessons from age-set societies. *American Journal of Sociology, 83,* 1081–1104.

Foner, A., & Kertzer, D. I. (1979). Intrinsic and extrinsic sources of change in life course transitions. In M. W. Riley (Ed.), *Aging from birth to death: Interdisciplinary perspectives* (pp. 121–136). Boulder, CO: Westview.

Foner, A., & Schwab, K. (1981). *Aging and retirement.* Pacific Grove, CA: Brooks/Cole.

Foner, N. (1984). *Ages in conflict: A cross-cultural perspective on inequality between old and young.* New York: Columbia University Press.

Foos, P. W. (1995). Working memory resource allocation by young, middle-aged, and old adults. *Experimental Aging Research, 21,* 239–250.

Fortes, M. (1950). Kinship and marriage among the Ashanti. In A. R. Radcliffe-Brown & D. Forde (Eds.), *African systems of kinship and marriage* (pp. 252–284). London: Oxford University Press.

Fortes, M. (1984). Age, generation and social structure. In D. Kertzer & J. Keith (Eds.), *Age and anthropological theory* (pp. 99–122). Ithaca, NY: Cornell University Press.

Fox, A. (1979, January). Earnings replacement rates of retired couples: Findings from the Retirement History Study. *Social Security Bulletin, 42,* 17–39.

Fox, M., Gibbs, M., & Auerbach, D. (1985). Age and gender dimensions of friendship. *Psychology of Women Quarterly, 9,* 489–502.

Fozard, J. L. (1981). Speed of mental performance and aging: Costs of age and benefits of wisdom. In F. J. Piorzzolo & G. J. Maletta (Eds.), *Behavioral assessment and psychopharmacology* (pp. 59–94). New York: Praeger.

Fozard, J. L., & Popkin, S. J. (1978). Optimizing adult development: Ends and means of an applied psychology of aging. *American Psychologist, 33,* 975–989.

Fozard, J. L., Vercruyssen, M., Reynolds, S. L., Hancock, P. A., & Quilter, R. E. (1994). Age differences and changes in reaction time: The Baltimore longitudinal study of aging. *Journal of Gerontology: Psychological Sciences, 49,* P179–P189.

Freed, A. O. (1990). How Japanese families cope with fragile elderly. *Journal of Gerontological Social Work, 15,* 39–56.

Freedman, M. (1966). *Chinese lineage and society: Fukien and Kwangtung.* London: Athlone.

Freeman, J. T. (1979). *Aging: Its history and literature.* New York: Human Sciences Press.

Frezza, M., Di Padava, C., Pozzato, G., Terpin, M., Baraona, E., & Lieber, C. S. (1990). High blood alcohol level in women: The role of decreased gastric alcohol dehydrogenase activity and first-pass metabolism. *New England Journal of Medicine, 322,* 95–99.

Friedhoff, A. J. (1994). Consensus panel report. In L. S. Schneider, C. F. Reynolds,

B. D. Lebowitz, & A. J. Friedhoff (Eds.), *Diagnosis and treatment of depression in late life: Results of the NIH Consensus Development Conference.* Washington, DC: American Psychiatric Press.

Friedman, E. A., & Orbach, H. L. (1974). Adjustment to retirement. In S. Arieti (Ed.), *American handbook of psychiatry: Vol. 1* (2nd ed., pp. 609–645). New York: Basic Books.

Friedman, L. A., & Kimball, A. W. (1986). Coronary heart disease mortality and alcohol consumption in Framingham. *American Journal of Epidemiology, 124,* 481–489.

Friedman, L., Bliwise, D. L., Yesavage, J. A., & Salom, S. R. (1991). A preliminary study comparing sleep restriction and relaxation treatments for insomnia in older adults. *Journal of Gerontology: Psychological Sciences, 46,* P1–P8.

Friedman, M., & Rosenman, R. H. (1974). *Type A behavior and your heart.* New York: Random House.

Fries, J. F., & Crapo, L. M. (1986). The elimination of premature disease. In K. Dychtwald (Ed.), *Wellness and health promotion for the elderly* (pp. 19–38). Rockville, MD: Aspen.

Frieze, I. H., Parsons, J. E., Johnson, P. B., Ruble, D. N., & Zellman, G. L. (1978). *Women and sex roles: A social psychological perspective.* New York: Norton.

Frolkis, V. V., & Bezrukov, V. V. (Eds.). (1979). *Aging of the central nervous system: Vol. 11. Interdisciplinary topics in human aging.* New York: Karger.

Froman, L. (1994). Adult learning in the workplace. In J. D. Sinnott (Ed.), *Interdisciplinary handbook of adult lifespan learning* (pp. 203–217). Westport, CT: Greenwood Press.

Fry, C. L. (1985). Culture, behavior, and aging in the comparative perspective. In J. E. Birren & K. W. Schaie (Eds.), *Handbook of the psychology of aging* (2nd ed., pp. 216–244). New York: Van Nostrand Reinhold.

Fry, C. L. (1988). Theories of age and culture. In J. E. Birren & V. L. Bengtson (Eds.), *Emergent theories of aging* (pp. 447–481). New York: Springer.

Fry, C. L., & Keith, J. (1982). The life course as a cultural unit. In M. W. Riley, R. P. Abeles, & M. S. Teitelbaum (Eds.), *Aging from birth to death. Vol. II: Sociotemporal perspectives* (pp. 51–70). Boulder, CO: Westview.

Fry, P. S. (1986). *Depression, stress, and adaptation in the elderly.* Rockville, MD: Aspen.

Fulton, R. (1970). Death, grief, and social recuperation. *Omega: Journal of Death and Dying, 1,* 23–28.

Furstenberg, F. F., Jr. (1982). Conjugal succession: Reentering marriage after divorce. In P. B. Baltes & O. G. Brim, Jr. (Eds.), *Life-span development and behavior* (Vol. 5, pp. 108–146). New York: Academic Press.

Furstenberg, F. F., Jr., & Nord, C. W. (1985). Parenting apart: Patterns of childbearing after marital disruption. *Journal of Marriage and the Family, 47,* 893–912.

Futterman, A., Gallagher, D., Thompson, L. W., Lovett, S., & Gilewski, M. (1990). Retrospective assessment of marital adjustment and depression during the first two years of spousal bereavement. *Psychology and Aging, 5,* 277–283.

Gailey, C. W. (1987). Evolutionary perspectives on gender hierarchy. In B. B. Hess & M. M. Feree (Eds.), *Analyzing gender* (pp. 32–67). Beverly Hills, CA: Sage.

Gajdusek, D. C. (1977). Unconventional viruses and the origin and disappearance of kuru. *Science, 197,* 943–960.

Gallagher, D., & Thompson, L. W. (1983). Depression. In P. M. Lewinsohn & L. Teri (Eds.), *Clinical geropsychology* (pp. 7–37). New York: Pergamon Press.

Gallo, J. J., Anthony, J. C., & Muthén, B. O. (1994). Age differences in the symptoms of depression: A latent trait analysis. *Journal of Gerontology: Psychological Sciences, 49,* P251–P264.

Garber, J., & Seligman, M. E. P. (Eds.). (1980). *Human helplessness: Theory and applications.* New York: Academic Press.

Garland, C., Barrett-Connor, E., Suarez, L., Criqui, M. H., & Wingard, D. L. (1985). Effects of passive smoking on ischemic heart disease mortality of nonsmokers: A prospective study. *American Journal of Epidemiology, 121,* 645–650.

Garn, S. M. (1975). Bone loss and aging. In R. Goldman & M. Rockstein (Eds.), *The physiology and pathology of aging* (pp. 39–57). New York: Academic Press.

Gatz, M., & Cotton, B. (1994). Age as a dimension of diversity: The experience of being old. In E. J. Trickett, R. J. Watts, & D. Birman (Eds.), *Human diversity: Perspectives on people in context* (pp. 334–355). San Francisco: Jossey-Bass.

Gatz, M., & Siegler, I. C. (1981, August). *Locus of control: A retrospective.* Paper presented at the meeting of the American Psychological Association, Los Angeles.

Gaylord, S. A., & Zung, W. W. K. (1987). Affective disorders among the aging. In L. L. Carstensen & B. A. Edelstein (Eds.), *Handbook of clinical gerontology* (pp. 76–95). New York: Pergamon Press.

Gelfand, M., Fitzgerald, L. F., & Drasgow, F. (in press). The latent structure of sexual harassment: A cross-cultural confirmatory analysis. *Journal of Vocational Behavior.*

Gentry, M., & Schulman, A. D. (1988). Remarriage as a coping response for widowhood. *Psychology and Aging, 3,* 191–196.

George, L. K. (1980). *Role transitions in later life.* Pacific Grove, CA: Brooks/Cole.

George, L. K., Fillenbaum, G., & Palmore, E. (1984). Sex differences in the antecedents and consequences of retirement. *Journal of Gerontology, 39,* 364–371.

George, L. K., & Gwyther, L. P. (1986). Caregiver well-being: A multidimensional examination of family caregivers of demented adults. *The Gerontologist, 26,* 253–259.

Gerard, L., Zacks, R. T., Hasher, L., & Radvansky, G. A. (1991). Age deficits in retrieval: The fan effect. *Journal of Gerontology: Psychological Sciences, 46,* P131–P136.

German, P. S. (1995). Prevention and chronic disease in older individuals. In L. A. Bond, S. J. Cutler, & A. Grams (Eds.), *Promoting successful and productive aging* (pp. 95–108). Thousand Oaks, CA: Sage Publications.

Gerner, R. (1980). Depression in the elderly. In O. Kaplan (Ed.), *Psychopathology of aging* (pp. 97–148). New York: Academic Press.

Gerner, R. H., & Jarvik, L. F. (1984). Antidepressant drug treatment in the elderly. In E. Friedman, F. Mann, & S. Gerson (Eds.), *Depression and anti-depressants: Implications for consideration and treatment.* New York: Raven.

Gersuny, C. (1987). Employment seniority and senior citizens. *The Gerontologist, 27,* 458–463.

Giambra, L. M., & Quilter, R. E. (1988). Sustained attention in adulthood: A unique, large-sample, longitudinal and multicohort analysis using the Mackworth Clock Test. *Psychology and Aging, 3,* 75–83.

Gibson, R. C. (1986). *Blacks in an aging society.* New York: Carnegie Corporation.

Gibson, R. C. (1987). Reconceptualizing retirement for Black Americans. *The Gerontologist, 27,* 691–698.

Gibson, R. C. (1991). The subjective retirement of black Americans. *Journal of Gerontology: Social Sciences, 46,* S204–S209.

Gilewski, M. J., & Zelinski, E. M. (1986). Questionnaire assessments of memory complaints. In L. W. Poon (Ed.), *Handbook for clinical memory assessment of older adults* (pp. 93–107). Washington, DC: American Psychological Association.

Gilewski, M. J., Zelinski, E. M., & Schaie, K. W. (1990). The Memory Functioning

Questionnaire for assessment of memory complaints in adulthood and old age. *Psychology and Aging, 5,* 482–490.

Gilford, R. (1984). Contrasts in marital satisfaction throughout old age: An exchange theory analysis. *Journal of Gerontology, 39,* 325–333.

Gilhooly, M. L. M. (1984). The impact of caregiving on caregivers: Factors associated with the psychological well-being of people supporting a demented relative in the community. *British Journal of Medical Psychology, 57,* 35–44.

Gilhooly, M. L. M. (1986). Senile dementia: Factors associated with caregivers' preference for institutional care. *British Journal of Medical Psychology, 59,* 165–171.

Gill, J. S., Zezulka, A. V., Shipley, M. J., Gill, S. K., & Beevers, D. G. (1986). Stroke and alcohol consumption. *New England Journal of Medicine, 315,* 1041–1046.

Gilleard, C. J., & Gurkan, A. A. (1987). Socioeconomic development and the status of elderly men in Turkey: A test of modernization theory. *Journal of Gerontology, 42,* 353–357.

Glamser, F., & Hayslip, B., Jr. (1985). The impact of retirement on participation in leisure activities. *Therapeutic Recreation Journal, 19,* 28–38.

Glascock, A. P., & Feinman, S. (1981). Social asset of social burden: Treatment of the aged in non-industrial societies. In C. L. Fry (Ed.), *Dimensions: Aging, culture, and health* (pp. 13–32). New York: Praeger.

Glaser, B. G., & Strauss, A. L. (1965). *Awareness of dying.* Chicago: Aldine-Atherton.

Glaser, B. G., & Strauss, A. L. (1968). *Time for dying.* Chicago: Aldine-Atherton.

Glenn, N. D., & McLanahan, S. (1981). The effects of offspring on the psychological well-being of older adults. *Journal of Marriage and the Family, 43,* 409–421.

Glenn, N. D., & McLanahan, S. (1982). Children and marital happiness: A further specification of the relationship. *Journal of Marriage and the Family, 44,* 63–72.

Glenn, N. D., & Supancic, M. (1984). The social and demographic correlates of divorce and separation in the United States: An update and reconsideration. *Journal of Marriage and the Family, 46,* 563–575.

Glenn, N. D., & Weaver, C. N. (1978). The marital happiness of remarried divorced persons. *Journal of Marriage and the Family, 40,* 269–282.

Glick, I. O., Weiss, R. S., & Parkes, C. M. (1974). *The first year of bereavement.* New York: Wiley.

Glick, P. C., & Lin, S.-L. (1986). Recent changes in divorce and remarriage. *Journal of Marriage and the Family, 48,* 737–748.

Glick, P. C., & Norton, A. J. (1979). Marrying, divorcing, and living together in the U.S. today. *Population Bulletin, 32,* 1–41.

Go, C. G., Brustrom, J. E., Lynch, M. F., & Aldwin, C. M. (1995). Ethnic trends in survival curves and mortality. *The Gerontologist, 35,* 318–326.

Goate, A., Chartier-Harlin, M.-C., Mullan, M., Brown, J., Crawford, F., Fidani, L., Guiffra, L., Haynes, A., Irving, N., James, L., Mant, R., Newton, P., Rooke, K., Roques, P., Talbot, C., Williamson, R., Rossor, M., Owen, M., & Hardy, J. (1991). Segregation of a missense mutation in the amyloid precursor protein gene with familial Alzheimer's disease. *Nature, 349,* 704–706.

Goff, S. J., Mount, M. K., & Jamison, R. L. (1990). Employer supported child care, work/family conflict, and absenteeism: A field study. *Personnel Psychology, 43,* 793–809.

Goggin, N. L., & Stelmach, G. E. (1990). Age-related deficits in cognitive-motor skills. In E. A. Lovelace (Ed.), *Aging and cognition: Mental processes, self-awareness, and interventions* (pp. 135–155). Amsterdam: North-Holland.

Golant, S. M. (1984). The effects of residential and activity behaviors on old people's environmental experiences. In I. Altman, J. Wohlwill, & M. P. Lawton (Eds.), *Human behavior and the environment: Elderly people and the environment* (pp. 239–278). New York: Plenum.

Golant, S. M. (1988). Housing in the year 2020: What does the future hold? In S. M. Golant, D. L. Gutmann, B. L. Neugarten, & S. S. Tobin (Eds.), *The aging society: A look toward the year 2020* (pp. 8–28). Chicago: Center for Applied Gerontology.

Gold, D. T. (1988, November). *Late-life sibling relationships: Does race affect typological distribution?* Paper presented at the meeting of the Gerontological Society of America, San Francisco.

Gold, D. T. (1990). Late-life sibling relationships: Does race affect typological distribution? *The Gerontologist, 30,* 741–748.

Gold, D. T., Woodbury, M. A., & George, L. K. (1990). Relationship classification using grade of membership analysis: A typology of sibling relationships in later life. *Journal of Gerontology: Social Sciences, 45,* S43–S51.

Goldberg, L. R., & Saucier, G. (1995). So what do you propose we use instead? A reply to Block. *Psychological Bulletin, 117,* 221–225.

Goldstein, A., & Goldstein, S. (1986). The challenge of an aging population in the People's Republic of China. *Research on Aging, 8,* 179–199.

Goldstein, E. (1979). Effect of same-sex and cross-sex role models on the subsequent academic productivity of scholars. *American Psychologist, 34,* 407–410.

Gonda, J. (1980). Relationship between formal education and cognitive functioning: A historical perspective. *Educational Gerontology, 5,* 283–291.

Goode, W. J. (1956). *After divorce.* Glencoe, IL: Free Press.

Goody, J. (1976). Aging in non-industrial societies. In R. H. Binstock & E. Shanas (Eds.), *Handbook of aging and the social sciences* (2nd ed., pp. 117–129). New York: Van Nostrand Reinhold.

Gordon, C., Gaitz, C. M., & Scott, J. (1976). Leisure and lives: Personal expressivity across the life span. In R. H. Binstock & E. Shanas (Eds.), *Handbook of aging and the social sciences* (2nd ed., pp. 310–341). New York: Van Nostrand Reinhold.

Gordon, T., & Doyle, J. T. (1987). Drinking and mortality: The Albany study. *American Journal of Epidemiology, 125,* 263–270.

Gordon, T., & Kannel, W. B. (1984). Drinking and mortality: The Framingham study. *American Journal of Epidemiology, 120,* 97–107.

Gordon-Salant, S. (1987). Age-related differences in speech recognition performance as a function of test format and paradigm. *Ear and Hearing, 8,* 277–282.

Gottfries, C. G. (1985). Alzheimer's disease and senile dementia: Biochemical characteristics and aspects of treatment. *Psychopharmacology, 86,* 245–252.

Gottfries, C. G., Gottfries, I., & Roos, B. E. (1969). The investigation of homovanillic acid in the human brain and its correlation to senile dementia. *British Journal of Psychiatry, 115,* 563–574.

Gottfries, C. G., Roos, B. E., & Winblad, B. (1976). Monoamine and monoamine metabolites in the human brain post mortem in senile dementia. *Aktuelle Gerontologie, 6,* 429–435.

Gottsdanker, R. (1982). Age and simple reaction time. *Journal of Gerontology, 37,* 342–348.

Grady, C. L., McIntosh, A. R., Horwitz, B., Maisong, J. M., Ungerleider, L. G., Mentis, M. J., Pietrini, P., Schapiro, M. B., & Haxby, J. V. (1995). Age-related reductions in human recognition memory due to impaired encoding. *Science, 269,* 218–221.

Graf, P., & Mandler, G. (1984). Activation makes words more accessible but not necessarily more retrievable. *Journal of Verbal Learning and Verbal Behavior, 23,* 553–568.

Grams, A., & Albee, G. W. (1995). Primary prevention in the service of aging. In L. A. Bond, S. J. Cutler, & A. Grams (Eds.), *Promoting successful and productive aging* (pp. 5–35). Thousand Oaks, CA: Sage Publications.

Granick, S., & Friedman, A. S. (1973). Effect of education on decline of psychometric test performance with age. *Journal of Gerontology, 22,* 191.

Gratzinger, P., Sheikh, J. I., Friedman, L., & Yesavage, J. A. (1990). Cognitive interventions to improve face-name recall: The role of personality trait differences. *Developmental Psychology, 26,* 889–893.

Green, A. L., & Boxer, A. M. (1986). Daughters and sons as young adults. In N. Datan, A. L. Green, & H. W. Reese (Eds.), *Life-span developmental psychology: Intergenerational relations* (pp. 125–150). Hillsdale, NJ: Erlbaum.

Green, R. F. (1969). Age-intelligence relationships between ages sixteen and sixty-four: A rising trend. *Developmental Psychology, 1,* 618–627.

Greenberg, J. B. (1979). Single parenting and intimacy: A comparison of mothers and fathers. *Alternative Lifestyles, 2,* 308–330.

Greene, V. L., & Monahan, D. J. (1982). The impact of visitation on patient well-being in nursing homes. *The Gerontologist, 22,* 418–423.

Greenhaus, J. H., Parasuraman, S., & Wormley, W. M. (1990). Effects of race on organizational experiences, job performance evaluations, and career outcomes. *Academy of Management Journal, 33,* 64–86.

Greenwood, J., Love, E. R., & Pratt, O. E. (1983). The effects of alcohol or of thiamine deficiency upon reproduction in the female rat and fetal development. *Alcohol and Alcoholism, 18,* 45–51.

Greer, J. (1992). *Adult sibling rivalries.* New York: Crown.

Grey, R. (1756). *Memoria technica* (4th ed.). London: Hinton.

Grimby, G., & Saltin, B. (1983). The aging muscle. *Clinical Physiology, 3,* 209–218.

Groger, L. (1995). A nursing home can be a home. *Journal of Aging Studies, 9,* 137–153.

Grover, D. R., & Hertzog, C. (1991). Relationships between intellectual control beliefs and psychometric intelligence in adulthood. *Journal of Gerontology: Psychological Sciences, 46,* P109–P115.

Guelzow, M. G., Bird, G. W., & Koball, E. H. (1991). An exploratory path analysis of the stress process for dual-career men and women. *Journal of Marriage and the Family, 53,* 151–164.

Guilford, J. P. (1959). *Personality.* New York: McGraw-Hill.

Gurland, B. J. (1973). A broad clinical assessment of psychopathology in the aged. In C. Eisdorfer & M. P. Lawton (Eds.), *The psychology of adult development and aging* (pp. 343–377). Washington, DC: American Psychological Association.

Gutek, B. A., Searle, S., & Klepa, L. (1991). Rational versus gender role explanations for work-family conflict. *Journal of Applied Psychology, 76,* 560–568.

Gutmann, D. (1978). *Personal transformation in the post-parental period: A cross-cultural view.* Washington, DC: American Association for the Advancement of Science.

Gutmann, D. L. (1987). *Reclaimed powers: Toward a new psychology of men and women in later life.* New York: Basic Books.

Haan, N. (1976). Personality organization of well-functioning younger people and older adults. *International Journal of Aging and Human Development, 7,* 117–127.

Haan, N. (1981). Common dimensions of personality: Early adolescence to middle life. In D. H. Eichorn, N. Haan, J. Clausen, M. Honzik, & P. Mussen (Eds.), *Present and past in middle life* (pp. 117–151). New York: Academic Press.

Haan, N. (1985). Common personality dimensions or common organization across the life span. In J. M. Munnichs, P. Mussen, E. Olbrich, & P. G. Coleman (Eds.), *Life-span and change in gerontological perspective* (pp. 17–44). New York: Academic Press.

Haan, N., Millsap, R., & Hartka, E. (1986). As time goes by: Change and stability in personality over fifty years. *Psychology and Aging, 1,* 220–232.

Haas, L. (1990). Gender equality and social policy: Implications of a study of parental leave in Sweden. *Journal of Family Issues, 11,* 401–423.

Hachinski, V. C., Lassen, N. A., & Marshall, J. (1974). Multi-infarct dementia—A cause of mental deterioration in the elderly. *Lancet, 2,* 207–210.

Hacker, H. M. (1981). Blabbermouths and clams—Sex differences in self-disclosure in same-sex and cross-sex friendship dyads. *Psychology of Women Quarterly, 5,* 385–401.

Hagestad, G. (1978). *Patterns of communication and influence between grandparents and grandchildren.* Paper presented at the World Conference on Sociology, Helsinki, Finland.

Hagestad, G. O., & Neugarten, B. L. (1985). Age and the life course. In R. H. Binstock & E. Shanas (Eds.), *Handbook of aging and the social sciences* (2nd ed., pp. 35–61). New York: Van Nostrand Reinhold.

Haggstrom, G. W., Kanouse, D. E., & Morrison, P. A. (1986). Accounting for education shortfalls of mothers. *Journal of Marriage and the Family, 48,* 175–186.

Hakim, S., & Adams, R. D. (1965). The special clinical problem of symptomatic hydrocephalus with normal cerebrospinal fluid pressure: Observations on cerebrospinal fluid hydrodynamics. *Journal of the Neurological Sciences, 2,* 307–327.

Haley, J. (1971). Family therapy. *International Journal of Psychiatry, 9,* 233–242.

Haley, W. E., Levine, E. G., Brown, S. L., Berry, J. W., & Hughes, G. H. (1987). Psychological, social, and health consequences of caring for a relative with senile dementia. *Journal of the American Geriatrics Society, 35,* 405–411.

Halperin, R. H. (1987). Age in cross-cultural perspective: An evolutionary approach. In P. Silverman (Ed.), *The elderly as modern pioneers* (pp. 228–252). Bloomington: Indiana University Press.

Halpern, J. (1987). *Helping your aging parents.* New York: McGraw-Hill.

Hamachek, D. (1990). Evaluating self-concept and ego status in Erikson's last three psychosocial stages. *Journal of Counseling and Development, 68,* 677–683.

Hamberger, K., & Lohr, J. (1984). *Stress and stress management: Research and applications.* New York: Springer.

Hamilton, J. (1978). Grandparents as grievers. In J. O. Sahler (Ed.), *The child and death.* St. Louis: C. V. Mosby.

Hamon, R. R., & Blieszner, R. (1990). Filial responsibility expectations among adult child–older parent pairs. *Journal of Gerontology: Psychological Sciences, 45,* P110–P112.

Haney, D. Q. (1995, February 12). Mutation linked to blacks' stroke risk. *Indianapolis Star.*

Hannon, D. J., & Hoyer, W. J. (1994). Mechanisms of visual-cognitive aging: A neural network account. *Aging and Cognition, 1,* 105–119.

Harbin, T. J., & Blumenthal, J. A. (1985). Relationship among age, sex, the Type A behavior pattern, and cardiovascular reactivity. *Journal of Gerontology, 40,* 714–720.

Harel, Z. (1981). Quality of care, congruence, and well-being among institutionalized aged. *The Gerontologist, 21,* 523–531.

Harker, J. O., Hartley, J. T., & Walsh, D. A. (1982). Understanding discourse: A life-span approach. In B. A. Hutson (Ed.),

Advances in reading/language research (Vol. 1, pp. 155–202). Greenwich, CT: JAI.

Harkins, S. W., & Kwentus, J. (1990). Pain, discomfort, and suffering in the elderly. In J. J. Bonica (Ed.), *Clinical management of pain*. Philadelphia: Lea & Febinger.

Harman, S. M., & Talbert, G. B. (1985). Reproductive aging. In C. E. Finch & E. L. Schneider (Eds.), *Handbook of the biology of aging* (2nd ed., pp. 457–510). New York: Van Nostrand Reinhold.

Harrell, S. (1981). Growing old in rural Taiwan. In P. Amoss & S. Harrell (Eds.), *Other ways of growing old* (pp. 193–210). Palo Alto, CA: Stanford University Press.

Harris, J. E. (1980). Memory aids people use: Two interview studies. *Memory and Cognition, 8,* 31–38.

Harris, J. E. (1984a). Methods of improving memory. In B. Wilson & N. Moffat (Eds.), *Clinical management of memory problems* (pp. 46–62). Rockville, MD: Aspen.

Harris, J. E., (1984b). Remembering to do things: A forgotten topic. In J. E. Harris & P. E. Morris (Eds.), *Everyday memory, actions, and absentmindedness* (pp. 71–92). London: Academic Press.

Harris, J. E., & Sunderland, A. (1981). A brief survey of the management of memory disorders in rehabilitation units in Britain. *International Rehabilitation Medicine 3,* 206–209.

Harris, L., & Associates (1975). *The myth and reality of aging in America.* Washington, DC: National Council on the Aging.

Harris, L., & Associates. (1981). *Aging in the 80s: America in transition.* Washington, DC: National Council on Aging.

Harris, R. L., Ellicott, A. M., & Holmes, D. S. (1986). The timing of psychosocial transitions and changes in women's lives: An examination of women aged 45 to 60. *Journal of Personality and Social Psychology, 51,* 409–416.

Harrison, D. E. (1985). Cell and tissue transplantation: A means of studying the aging process. In C. E. Finch & E. L. Schneider (Eds.), *Handbook of the biology of aging* (2nd ed., pp. 322–356). New York: Van Nostrand Reinhold.

Hart, J., & Fleming, R. (1985). An experimental evaluation of reality orientation therapy with geriatric patients in a state mental hospital. *Clinical Gerontologist, 1,* 45–52.

Hartford, M. E. (1980). The use of group methods for work with the aged. In J. E. Birren & R. B. Sloane (Eds.), *Handbook of mental health and aging* (pp. 806–826). Englewood Cliffs, NJ: Prentice-Hall.

Hartley, A. A. (1992). Attention. In F. I. M. Craik & T. A. Salthouse (Eds.), *The handbook of aging and cognition* (pp. 3–50). Hillsdale, NJ: Erlbaum.

Hartley, A. A., & McKenzie, C. R. M. (1991). Attentional and perceptual contributions to the identification of extrafoveal stimuli: Adult age comparisons. *Journal of Gerontology: Psychological Sciences, 46,* P202–P206.

Hartley, J. T. (1989). Memory for prose: Perspectives on the reader. In L. W. Poon, D. C. Rubin, & A. Wilson (Eds.), *Everyday cognition in adult and late life* (pp. 135–156). New York: Cambridge University Press.

Hartley, J. T., Stojack, C. C., Mushaney, T. J., Annon, T. A. K., & Lee, D. W. (1994). Reading speed and prose memory in older and younger adults. *Psychology and Aging, 9,* 216–223.

Hasher, L., & Zacks, R. T. (1988). Working memory, comprehension, and aging: A review and new view. In G. T. Bower (Ed.), *The psychology of learning and motivation* (Vol. 22, pp. 193–225). New York: Academic Press.

Haskell, W. L., Camargo, C., Jr., Williams, P. T., Vranizan, K. M., Krauss, R. M., Lindgren, F. T., & Wood, P. D. (1984). The effect of cessation and resumption of moderate alcohol intake on serum high-density lipoprotein subfractions. *New England Journal of Medicine, 310,* 805–810.

Hatfield, E., & Walster, E. (1978). *A new look at love.* Reading, MA: Addison-Wesley.

Haun, P. (1965). *Recreation: A medical viewpoint.* New York: Teachers College, Columbia University Press.

Hauri, P. (1982). *The sleep disorders.* Kalamazoo, MI: Upjohn.

Havighurst, R. J. (1982). The world of work. In B. B. Wolman (Ed.), *Handbook of developmental psychology* (pp. 771–787). Englewood Cliffs, NJ: Prentice Hall.

Hayflick, L. (1994). *How and why we age.* New York: Ballantine Books.

Hayslip, B., Jr. (1988). Personality-ability relationships in aged adults. *Journal of Gerontology, 43,* P79–P84.

Hayslip, B., Jr. (1989). Alternative mechanisms for improvements in fluid ability performance among older adults. *Psychology and Aging, 4,* 122–124.

Hayslip, B., Jr., Maloy, R. M., & Kohl, R. (1995). Long-term efficacy of fluid ability interventions with older adults. *Journal of Gerontologys,: Psychological Sciences, 50B,* P141–P149.

Healey, E. S., Kales, A., Monroe, L. J., Bixler, E. O., Chamberlin, K., & Soldatos, C. R. (1981). Onset of insomnia: Role of life-stress events. *Psychosomatic Medicine, 43,* 439–451.

Heaney, R. P., Gallagher, J. C., Johnston, C. C., Neer, R., Parfitt, A. M., & Whedon, G. D. (1982). Calcium nutrition and bone health in the elderly. *American Journal of Clinical Nutrition, 36,* 987–1013.

Heidrich, S. M., & Denney, N. W. (1994). Does social problem solving differ from other types of problem solving during the adult years? *Experimental Aging Research, 20,* 105–126.

Heintz, K. M. (1976). *Retirement communities.* New Brunswick, NJ: Rutgers University Center for Urban Policy Research.

Helson, R., & Moane, G. (1987). Personality change in women from college to midlife. *Journal of Personality and Social Psychology, 52,* 1176–1186.

Hendel-Sebestyen, G. (1979). Role diversity: Toward the development of community in a total institutional setting. *Anthropological Quarterly, 52,* 19–28.

Henderson, K. A. (1990). The meaning of leisure for women: An integrative review of the research. *Journal of Leisure Research, 22,* 228–243.

Hendricks, J. (1982). The elderly in society: Beyond modernization. *Social Science History, 6,* 321–345.

Hendricks, J., & Leedham, C. A. (1989). Creating psychological and societal perspectives in old age. In P. S. Fry (Ed.), *Psychological perspectives on helplessness and control in the elderly* (pp. 369–394). Amsterdam: Elsevier North-Holland.

Hennessy, C. H., & John, R. (1995). The interpretation of burden among Pueblo Indian caregivers. *Journal of Aging Studies, 9,* 215–229.

Hennon, C. B. (1983). Divorce and the elderly: A neglected area of research. In T. H. Brubaker (Ed.), *Family relationships in later life* (pp. 149–172). Beverly Hills, CA: Sage Publications.

Henretta, J. C., Chan, C. G., & O'Rand, A. M. (1992). Retirement reasons versus retirement process: Examining the reasons for retirement typology. *Journal of Gerontology: Social Sciences, 47,* S1–S7.

Hensel, H. (1981). *Thermoreception and temperature regulation.* New York: Academic Press.

Herbert, V. (1988). Megavitamins, food fads, and quack nutrition in health promotion: Myths and risks. In R. Chernoff & D. A. Lipschitz (Eds.), *Health promotion and disease prevention in the elderly* (pp. 45–66). New York: Raven Press.

Hermans, H. J. M., Kempen, H. J. G., & van Loon, R. J. P. (1992). The dialogic self: Beyond individualism and rationalism. *American Psychologist, 47,* 23–33.

Herr, J., & Weakland, J. (1979). *Counseling elders and their families: Practical tech-*

niques for applied gerontology. New York: Springer.

Hertzog, C., Dixon, R. A., & Hultsch, D. F. (1990). Relationships between metamemory, memory predictions, and memory task performances. *Psychology and Aging, 5,* 215–223.

Hertzog, C., Dixon, R. A., Schulenberg, J., & Hultsch, D. F. (1987). On the differentiation of memory beliefs from memory knowledge: The factor structure of the Metamemory in Adulthood scale. *Experimental Aging Research, 13,* 101–107.

Hertzog, C., Hultsch, D. F., & Dixon, R. A. (1989). Evidence for the convergent validity of two self-report metamemory questionnaires. *Developmental Psychology, 25,* 687–700.

Herzog, A. R., Kahn, R. L., Morgan, J. N., Jackson, J. S., & Antonucci, T. C. (1989). Age differences in productive activities. *Journal of Gerontology: Social Sciences, 44,* S129–S138.

Hess, T. M., & Slaughter, S. J. (1990). Schematic knowledge influences on memory for scene information in young and older adults. *Developmental Psychology, 26,* 855–865.

Hesse, M. (1980). *Revolutions and reconstructions in the philosophy of science.* Bloomington: Indiana University Press.

Hetherington, E. M., Cox, M., & Cox, R. (1982). Effects of divorce on parents and children. In M. E. Lamb (Ed.), *Nontraditional families: Parenting and child development* (pp. 233–288). Hillsdale, NJ: Erlbaum.

Heumann, L., & Boldy, D. (1982). *Housing for the elderly: Policy and planning formulation in Western Europe and North America.* London: Croom Helm.

Hill, C. D., Thompson, L. W., & Gallagher, D. (1988). The role of anticipatory bereavement in older women's adjustment to widowhood. *The Gerontologist, 28,* 792–796.

Himmelfarb, S. (1984). Age and sex differences in the mental health of older persons. *Journal of Consulting and Clinical Psychology, 52,* 844–856.

Hinton, J. M. (1967). *Dying.* Harmondsworth, England: Penguin.

Hirschfield, R. M. A., & Cross, C. K. (1982). Epidemiology of affective disorders: Psychosocial risk factors. *Archives of General Psychiatry, 39,* 35–46.

Hobart, C. (1988). The family system in remarriage: An exploratory study. *Journal of Marriage and the Family, 50,* 649–661.

Hochschild, A. R. (1973). *The unexpected community.* Englewood Cliffs, NJ: Prentice-Hall.

Hoff, S. F., Scheff, S. W., Bernardo, L. S., & Cotman, C. W. (1982). Lesion-induced synaptogenesis in the dentate gyrus of aged rats. 1: Loss and reacquisition of an impaired degeneration clearing response. *Journal of Comparative Neurology, 205,* 252–259.

Hofland, B. F. (1988). Autonomy in long term care: Background issues and a programmatic response. *The Gerontologist, 28(Suppl.),* 3–9.

Holland, J. L. (1973). *Making vocational choices: A theory of careers.* Englewood Cliffs, NJ: Prentice-Hall.

Holland, J. L. (1985). *Making vocational choices: A theory of vocational personalities and work environments.* Englewood Cliffs, NJ: Prentice-Hall.

Hollander, C. F., & Becker, H. A. (1988). Planning for health services for the elderly. In D. Evered & J. Whelan (Eds.), *Symposium on research and the ageing population* (pp. 221–228). Chichester, England: Wiley.

Holyroyd, K. A., Appel, M. A., & Andrasik, F. (1983). A cognitive-behavioral approach to psychophysiological disorders. In D. Meichenbaum & M. E. Jarenko (Eds.), *Stress reduction and prevention* (pp. 219–259). New York: Plenum.

Holzberg, C. S. (1982). Ethnicity and aging: Anthropological perspectives on more than just the minority elderly. *The Gerontologist, 22,* 249–257.

Holzberg, C. S. (1983). Anthropology, life histories, and the aged: The Toronto Baycrest Center. *International Journal of Aging and Human Development, 18,* 255–275.

Hooper, C. (1991). To be or not two bees: Verbs, nouns and the brain. *Journal of NIH Research, 3*(6), 49–54.

Hopkins, D. R., Murrah, B., Hoeger, W. W. K., & Rhodes, R. C. (1990). Effect of low-impact aerobic dance on the functional fitness of elderly women. *The Gerontologist, 30,* 189–192.

Horn, J. L. (1978). Human ability systems. In P. B. Baltes & O. G. Brim, Jr. (Eds.), *Life-span development and behavior* (Vol. 1, pp. 211–256). New York: Academic Press.

Horn, J. L. (1982). The aging of human abilities. In B. B. Wolman (Ed.), *Handbook of developmental psychology* (pp. 847–870). Englewood Cliffs, NJ: Prentice-Hall.

Horn, J. L., & Donaldson, G. (1980). Cognitive development in adulthood. In O. G. Brim, Jr., & J. Kagan (Eds.), *Constancy and change in human development* (pp. 445–529). Cambridge, MA: Harvard University Press.

Horn, J. L., & Hofer, S. M. (1992). Major abilities and development in the adult period. In R. J. Sternberg & C. A. Berg (Eds.), *Intellectual development* (pp. 44–99). Cambridge, UK: Cambridge University Press.

Hornblum, J. N., & Overton, W. F. (1976). Area and volume conservation among the elderly: Assessment and training. *Developmental Psychology, 12,* 68–74.

Horowitz, M. J., & Schulz, R. (1983). The relocation controversy: Criticism and commentary on five recent studies. *The Gerontologist, 23,* 229–234.

Hounsfield, G. N. (1973). Computerized transverse axial scanning (tomography). *British Journal of Radiology, 46,* 1016–1022.

Howard, A. (1984, August). *Cool at the top: Personality characteristics of successful executives.* Paper presented at the meeting of the American Psychological Association, Toronto.

Howard, A., & Bray, D. W. (1980, August). *Career motivation in mid-life managers.* Paper presented at the meeting of the American Psychological Association, Montreal.

Howard, D. V., Heisey, J. G., & Shaw, R. J. (1986). Aging and the priming of newly learned associations. *Developmental Psychology, 22,* 78–85.

Howard, D. V., & Howard, J. H. (1992). Adult age differences in the rate of learning serial patterns: Evidence from direct and indirect tests. *Psychology and Aging, 7,* 232–241.

Howe, M. L. (1988). Measuring memory development in adulthood: A model-based approach to disentangling storage-retrieval contributions. In M. L. Howe & C. J. Brainerd (Eds.), *Cognitive development in adulthood* (pp. 39–64). New York: Springer-Verlag.

Hoyer, W. J. (1987, November). *Domains of attention.* Paper presented at the National Institute on Aging Conference on Aging and Attention, Washington, DC.

Hoyer, W. J., & Rybash, J. M. (1994). Characterizing adult cognitive development. *Journal of Adult Development, 1,* 7–12.

Huff, F. J., Growden, J. H., Corkin, S., & Rosen, T. J. (1987). Age at onset and rate of progression of Alzheimer's disease. *Journal of the American Geriatrics Society, 35,* 27–30.

Hughston, G. A., & Protinsky, H. W. (1978). Conservation abilities of elderly men and women: A comparative investigation. *Journal of Psychology, 98,* 23–26.

Hulin, C. L., & Smith, P. C. (1965). A linear model of job satisfaction. *Journal of Applied Psychology, 49,* 209–216.

Hultsch, D. F., (1971). Adult age differences in free classification and free recall. *Developmental Psychology, 4,* 338–342.

Hultsch, D. F., & Dixon, R. A. (1983). The role of pre-experimental knowledge in text processing in adulthood. *Experimental Aging Research, 9,* 17–22.

Hultsch, D. F., & Dixon, R. A. (1984). Memory for text materials in adulthood. In P. B. Baltes & O. G. Brim, Jr. (Eds.), *Life-span development and behavior* (Vol. 6, pp. 77–108). New York: Academic Press.

Hultsch, D. F., & Dixon, R. A. (1990). Learning and memory in aging. In J. E. Birren & K. W. Schaie (Eds.), *Handbook of the psychology of aging* (3rd ed., pp. 258–274). San Diego: Academic Press.

Hultsch, D. F., Masson, M. E. J., & Small, B. J. (1991). Adult age differences in direct and indirect tests of memory. *Journal of Gerontology: Psychological Sciences, 46,* P22–P30.

Hultsch, D. F., & Plemons, J. K. (1979). Life events and life-span development. In P. B. Baltes & O. G. Brim, Jr. (Eds.), *Life-span development and behavior* (Vol. 2, pp. 1–36). New York: Academic Press.

Humphry, D. (1991). *Final Exit: The practicalities of self-deliverance and assisted suicide for the dying.* Eugene, OR: Hemlock Society.

Huyck, M. H. (1982). From gregariousness to intimacy: Marriage and friendship over the adult years. In T. M. Field, A. Huston, H. C. Quay, L. Troll., & G. E. Finley (Eds.), *Review of human development* (pp. 471–484). New York: Wiley.

Huyck, M. H. (1990). Gender differences in aging. In J. E. Birren & K. W. Schaie (Eds.), *Handbook of the psychology of aging* (3rd ed., pp. 124–132). San Diego: Academic Press.

Hyde, J. S., Krajnik, M., & Skuldt-Niederberger, K. (1991). Androgyny across the life span: A replication and longitudinal follow-up. *Developmental Psychology, 27,* 516–519.

Iammarino, N. K. (1975). Relationship between death anxiety and demographic variables. *Psychological Reports, 17,* 262.

Ingraham, M. (1974). *My purpose holds: Reactions and experiences in retirement of TIAA-CREF annuitants.* New York: Educational Research Division, Teachers Insurance and Annuity Association College Retirement Equities Fund.

Irelan, L. M., & Bell, D. B. (1972). Understanding subjectively defined retirement: A pilot analysis. *The Gerontologist, 12,* 354–356.

Irion, J. C., & Blanchard-Fields, F. (1987). A cross-sectional comparison of adaptive coping in adulthood. *Journal of Gerontology, 42,* 502–504.

Isaksson, B. (1973). Clinical nutrition: Requirements of energy and nutrients in diseases. *Bibliography of Nutrition and Dietetics, 19,* 1.

Ishler, K., Pargament, K. I., Kinney, J. M., & Cavanaugh, J. C. (1995, November). *Religious coping, general coping, and controllability: Testing the hypothesis of fit.* Paper presented at the meeting of the Gerontological Society of America, Los Angeles.

Ivancevich, J. M., & Matteson, M. T. (1988). Type A behavior and the healthy individual. *British Journal of Medical Psychology, 61,* 37–56.

Jackson, B., Taylor, J., & Pyngolil, M. (1991). How age conditions the relationship between climacteric status and health symptoms in African American women. *Research in Nursing and Health, 14,* 1–9.

Jackson, J. J. (1985). Race, national origin, ethnicity, and aging. In R. H. Binstock & E. Shanas (Eds.), *Handbook of aging and the social sciences* (2nd ed., pp. 264–303). New York: Van Nostrand Reinhold.

Jackson, J. J., & Walls, B. E. (1978). Myths and realities about aged Blacks. In M. R. Brown (Ed.), *Readings in gerontology* (2nd ed., pp. 95–113). St. Louis: C. V. Mosby.

Jackson, J. S. (1993). Racial influences on adult development and aging. In R. Kastenbaum (Ed.), *The encyclopedia of adult development* (pp. 18–26). Phoenix, AZ: Oryx Press.

Jackson, J. S., Antonucci, T. C., & Gibson, R. C. (1995). Ethnic and cultural factors in research on aging and mental health: A life-course perspective. In D. K. Padgett (Ed.), *Handbook on ethnicity, aging, and mental health* (pp. 22–46). Westport, CT: Greenwood Press.

Jackson, J. S., & Gibson, R. C. (1985). Work and retirement among the black elderly. In Z. Blau (Ed.), *Current perspectives on aging and the life cycle* (pp. 193–222). Greenwich, CT: JAI.

Jackson, M., Kolodny, B., & Wood, J. L. (1982). To be old and Black: The case for double jeopardy on income and health. In R. C. Manuel (Ed.), *Minority aging, sociological and social psychological issues* (pp. 161–170). Westport, CT: Greenwood.

Jackson, M., & Wood, J. L. (1976). *Aging in America: Implications for the Black aged.* Washington, DC: National Council on the Aging.

Jacobs, J. (1974). *Fun city: An ethnographic study of a retirement community.* New York: Holt, Rinehart, & Winston.

Jacobs, J. (1975). *Older persons and retirement communities.* Springfield, IL: Charles C Thomas.

Jacobson, E. (1938). *Progressive relaxation.* Chicago: University of Chicago Press.

James, L. R., & Jones, A. P. (1980). Perceived job characteristics and job satisfaction: An examination of reciprocal causation. *Personnel Psychology, 33,* 97–135.

James, W. (1890). *The principles of psychology.* New York: Holt.

Jamison, K. R., Gerner, R. H., & Goodwin, F. K. (1979). Patient and physician attitudes toward lithium: Relationships to compliance. *Archives of General Psychiatry, 36,* 866–869.

Janson, P., & Ryder, L. K. (1983). Crime and the elderly: The relationship between risk and fear. *The Gerontologist, 23,* 207–212.

Jaques, E. (1965). Death and the mid-life crisis. *International Journal of Psychoanalysis, 46,* 502–514.

Jaremko, M. E. (1983). Stress inoculation training for social anxiety with emphasis on dating anxiety. In D. Meichenbaum & M. E. Jaremko (Eds.), *Stress reduction and prevention* (pp. 419–450). New York: Plenum.

Jecker, N. S., & Schneiderman, L. J. (1994). Is dying young worse than dying old? *The Gerontologist, 34,* 66–72.

Jeffko, W. G. (1979, July 6). Redefining death. *Commonweal,* 394–397.

Jemmott, J. B., Borysenko, J. Z., Borysenko, M., McClelland, D. C., Chapman, R., Meyer, D., & Benson, H. (1983). Academic stress, power motivation, and decrease in secretion rate of salivary secretory immunoglobulin A. *Lancet, 1,* 1400–1402.

Jeste, D. V., Naimark, D., Halpain, M. C., & Lindamer, L. A. (1995). Strengths and limitations of research on late-life psychoses. In M. Gatz (Ed.), *Emerging issues in mental health and aging* (pp. 72–96). Washington, DC: American Psychological Association.

Jirovec, R. L., Jirovec, M. M., & Bossé, R. (1985). Environmental determinants of neighborhood satisfaction among urban elderly men. *The Gerontologist, 24,* 261–265.

Johnson, C. L. (1983). A cultural analysis of the grandmother. *Research on Aging, 5,* 547–567.

Johnson, C. L. (1987). The institutional segregation of the elderly. In P. Silverman (Ed.), *The elderly as modern pioneers* (pp. 307–319). Bloomington: Indiana University Press.

Johnson, C. L. (1988). Active and latent functions of grandparenting during the divorce process. *The Gerontologist, 28,* 185–191.

Johnson, C. L., & Barer, B. (1987). Marital instability and the changing kinship networks of grandparents. *The Gerontologist, 27,* 330–335.

Johnson, C. L., & Grant, L. (1985). *The nursing home in American society.* Baltimore: Johns Hopkins University Press.

Johnson, C. L., & Troll, L. E. (1994). Constraints and facilitators to friendships in late late life. *The Gerontologist, 34,* 79–87.

Johnson, R. J., & Wolinsky, F. D. (1994). Gender, race, and health: The structure of health status among older adults. *The Gerontologist, 34,* 24–35.

Jones, L. Y. (1980). *Great expectations: America and the baby boom generation.* New York: Coward, McCann, & Geoghegan.

Jones, M. K., & Jones, B. M. (1980). The relationship of age and drinking habits to the effects of alcohol on memory in women. *Journal of Studies on Alcohol, 41,* 179–186.

Kahana, B., & Kahana, E. (1970). Grandparenthood from the perspective of the developing grandchild. *Developmental Psychology, 3,* 98–105.

Kahana, E. (1982). A congruence model of person-environment interaction. In M. P. Lawton, P. G. Windley, & T. O. Byerts (Eds.), *Aging and the environment: Theoretical approaches* (pp. 97–121). New York: Springer.

Kahana, E., & Kahana, B. (1983). Environmental continuity, futurity, and adaptation of the aged. In G. D. Rowles & R. J. Ohta (Eds.), *Aging and milieu: Environmental perspectives on growing old* (pp. 205–230). New York: Academic Press.

Kahn, R. L., Goldfarb, A. I., Pollack, M., & Peck, A. (1960). Brief objective measures for the determination of mental status in the aged. *American Journal of Psychiatry, 117,* 326–328.

Kales, A., Allen W. C., Scharf, M. B., & Kales, J. D. (1970). Hypnotic drugs and effectiveness: All-night EEG studies of insomniac subjects. *Archives of General Psychiatry, 23,* 226–232.

Kales, A., Scharf, M. B., & Kales, J. D. (1978). Rebound insomnia: A new clinical syndrome. *Science, 201,* 1039–1040.

Kalish, R. A. (1975). *Late adulthood.* Pacific Grove, CA: Brooks/Cole.

Kalish, R. A. (1976). Death in a social context. In R. H. Binstock & E. Shanas (Eds.), *Handbook of aging and the social sciences* (pp. 483–507). New York: Van Nostrand Reinhold.

Kalish, R. A. (1981). *Death, grief, and caring relationships.* Pacific Grove, CA: Brooks/Cole.

Kalish, R. A. (1984). *Death, grief, and caring relationships* (2nd ed.). Pacific Grove, CA: Brooks/Cole.

Kalish, R. A. (1985). The social context of death and dying. In R. H. Binstock & E. Shanas (Eds.), *Handbook of aging and the social sciences* (2nd ed., pp. 149–170). New York: Van Nostrand Reinhold.

Kalish, R. A. (1987). Death and dying. In P. Silverman (Ed.), *The elderly as modern pioneers* (pp. 320–334). Bloomington: Indiana University Press.

Kalish, R. A., & Reynolds, D. (1976). *Death and ethnicity: A psychocultural study.* Los Angeles: University of Southern California Press.

Kalish, R. A., & Reynolds, D. K. (1981). *Death and ethnicity: A psychocultural study.* Farmingdale, NY: Baywood.

Kallman, D. A., Plato, C. C., & Tobin, J. D. (1990). The role of muscle loss in the age-related decline of grip strength: Cross-sectional and longitudinal perspectives. *Journal of Gerontology: Medical Sciences, 45,* M82–M88.

Kallmann, F. J. (1957). Twin data on the genetics of aging. In G. E. Wolstenhoime & C. M. O'Connor (Eds.), *Methodology of the study of ageing* (pp. 131–143). London: Churchill.

Kaminsky, M. (1978). Pictures from the past: The use of reminiscence in casework with the elderly. *Journal of Gerontological Social Work, 1,* 19–31.

Kamouri, A., & Cavanaugh, J. C. (1986). The impact of pre-retirement education programs on workers' pre-retirement socialization. *Journal of Occupational Behavior, 7,* 245–256.

Kane, M. J., Hasher, L., Stoltzfus, E. R., Zacks, R. T., & Connelly, S. L. (1994). Inhibitory attentional mechanisms and aging. *Psychology and Aging, 9,* 103–112.

Kanekar, S., Kolsawalla, M. B., & Nazareth, T. (1989). Occupational prestige as a function of occupant's gender. *Journal of Applied Social Psychology, 19,* 681–688.

Kannel, W. B. (1985). Hypertension and aging. In C. E. Finch & E. L. Schneider (Eds.), *Handbook of the biology of aging* (2nd ed., pp. 859–877). New York: Van Nostrand Reinhold.

Kanter, R. M. (1976, May). Why bosses turn bitchy. *Psychology Today,* 56–59.

Kaplan, M. (1983). The issue of sex bias in DSM III: Comments on articles by Spitzer, Williams, and Kass. *American Psychologist, 38,* 802–803.

Karacen, I., & Williams, R. L. (1983). Sleep disorders in the elderly. *American Family Physicians, 27,* 143–152.

Karney, B. R., & Bradbury, T. N. (1995). The longitudinal course of marital quality and stability: A review of theory, method, and research. *Psychological Bulletin, 118,* 3–34.

Kastenbaum, R. (1975). Is death a life crisis? On the confrontation with death in theory and practice. In N. Datan & L. Ginsberg (Eds.), *Life-span developmental psychology: Normative life crises* (pp. 19–50). New York: Academic Press.

Kastenbaum, R. (1985). Dying and death: A life-span approach. In J. E. Birren & K. W. Schaie (Eds.), *Handbook of the psychology of aging* (2nd ed., pp. 619–643). New York: Van Nostrand Reinhold.

Kastenbaum, R., & Aisenberg, R. B. (1976). *The psychology of death* (rev. ed.). New York: Springer.

Kastenbaum, R., & Briscoe, L. (1975). The street corner: Laboratory for the study of life-threatening behavior. *Omega: Journal of Death and Dying, 6,* 33–44.

Kastenbaum, R., & Thuell, S. (1995). Cookies baking, coffee brewing: Toward a contextual theory of dying. *Omega, 31,* 175–187.

Katzman, R. (1987). Alzheimer's disease: Advances and opportunities. *Journal of the American Geriatrics Society, 35,* 69–73.

Kaufman, D. W., Rosenberg, L., Helmrich, S. P., & Shapiro, S. (1985). Alcohol beverages and myocardial infarction in young men. *American Journal of Epidemiology, 121,* 548–554.

Kausler, D. H. (1982). *Experimental psychology and human aging.* New York: Wiley.

Kausler, D. H. (1985). Episodic memory: Memorizing performance. In N. Charness (Ed.), *Aging and human performance* (pp. 101–141). Chichester, England: Wiley.

Kausler, D. H., & Hakami, M. K. (1983). Memory for activities: Adult age differences and intentionality. *Developmental Psychology, 19,* 889–894.

Kausler, D. H., & Lichty, W. (1988). Memory for activities: Rehearsal independence and aging. In M. L. Howe & C. J. Brainerd (Eds.), *Cognitive development in adulthood: Progress in cognitive development research* (pp. 93–131). New York: Springer-Verlag.

Kegan, R. (1982). *The evolving self.* Cambridge, MA: Harvard University Press.

Keith, J. (1990). Age in social and cultural context: Anthropological perspectives. In R. H. Binstock & L. K. George (Eds.), *Handbook of aging and the social sciences*

(3rd ed., pp. 91–111). San Diego: Academic Press.

Keith, J., Fry, C. L., & Ikels, C. (1990). Community as context for successful aging. In J. Sokolovsky (Ed.), *The cultural context of aging* (pp. 245–261). New York: Bergin & Garvey.

Keith, P. M. (1979). Life changes and perceptions of life and death among older men and women. *Journal of Gerontology, 34,* 870–878.

Keller, J. W., Sherry, D., & Piotrowski, C. (1984). Perspectives on death: A developmental study. *Journal of Psychology, 116,* 137–142.

Kelley, C. M. (1986). Depressive mood effects on memory and attention. In L. W. Poon (Ed.), *Handbook for the clinical memory assessment of older adults* (pp. 238–243). Washington, DC: American Psychological Association.

Kelley, H. H. (1967). Attribution theory in social psychology. *Nebraska Symposium on Motivation, 15,* 192–241.

Kelly, J. B. (1982). Divorce: The adult perspective. In B. B. Wolman (Ed.), *Handbook of developmental psychology* (pp. 734–750). Englewood Cliffs, NJ: Prentice-Hall.

Kelly, J. R., Steinkamp, M. W., & Kelly, J. R. (1987). Later-life satisfaction: Does leisure contribute? *Leisure Sciences, 9,* 189–200.

Kemper, S. (1988). Geriatric psycholinguistics: Syntactic limitations of oral and written language. In L. L. Light & D. M. Burke (Eds.), *Language, memory, and aging* (pp. 58–76). New York: Cambridge University Press.

Kendig, N. E., & Adler, W. H. (1990). The implications of acquired immunodeficiency syndrome for gerontology research and geriatric medicine. *Journal of Gerontology: Medical Sciences, 45,* M77–M81.

Kenney, R. A. (1982). *Physiology of aging: A synopsis.* Chicago: Yearbook Medical.

Kenshalo, D. R. (1977). Age changes in touch, vibration, temperature, kinesthesis, and pain sensitivity. In J. E. Birren & K. W. Schaie (Eds.), *Handbook of the psychology of aging* (pp. 562–579). New York: Van Nostrand Reinhold.

Kenshalo, D. R. (1979). Changes in the vestibular and somasthetic systems as a function of age. In J. M. Ordy & K. Brizzee (Eds.), *Aging: Vol. 10. Sensory systems and communication in the elderly* (pp. 269–282). New York: Raven.

Kertzer, D. I., & Madison, O. B. B. (1981). Women's age-set systems in Africa: The Latuka of southern Sudan. In C. L. Fry (Ed.), *Dimensions: Aging, culture, and health* (pp. 109–130). New York: Praeger.

Kiecolt-Glaser, J. K., Speicher, C. E., Holliday, J. E., & Glaser, R. (1984). Stress and the transformation of lymphocytes in Epstein-Barr virus. *Journal of Behavioral Medicine, 7,* 1–12.

Kiefer, C. W., Kim, S., Choi, K., Kim, L., Kim, B.-L., Shon, S., & Kim, T. (1985). Adjustment problems of Korean-American elderly. *The Gerontologist, 25,* 477–482.

Kieffer, G. H. (1979). *Bioethics: A textbook of issues.* Reading, MA: Addison-Wesley.

Kieffer, J. A. (1986). The older volunteer resource. In Committee on an Aging Society (Ed.), *Productive roles in an older society* (pp. 51–72). Washington, DC: National Academy Press.

Kii, T. (1981). Status changes of the elderly in Japan's legal, family, and economic institutions. In C. Nusberg & M. M. Osako (Eds.), *The situation of the Asian/Pacific elderly.* Washington, DC: International Federation on Aging.

Kimmel, D. C. (1978). Adult development and aging: A gay perspective. *Journal of Social Issues, 34,* 113–130.

Kimmel, D. C., Price, K. F., & Walker, J. W. (1978). Retirement choice and retirement satisfaction. *Journal of Gerontology, 33,* 575–585.

Kimmel, D. C., & Sang, B. E. (1995). Lesbians and gay men in midlife. In A. R. D'Augelli & C. J. Patterson (Eds.), *Lesbian, gay, and bisexual identities over the lifespan* (pp. 190–214). New York: Oxford University Press.

King, P. M., & Kitchener, K. S. (1994). *Developing reflective judgment: Understanding and promoting intellectual growth and critical thinking in adolescents and adults.* San Francisco: Jossey-Bass.

King, P. M., Kitchener, K. S., Wood, P. K., & Davison, M. L. (1989). Relationships across developmental domains: A longitudinal study of intellectual, moral, and ego development. In M. L. Commons, J. D. Sinnott, F. A. Richards, & C. Armon (Eds.), *Adult development: Vol. 1. Comparisons and applications of adolescent and adult developmental models* (pp. 57–72). New York: Praeger.

Kingston, P. W., & Nock, S. L. (1987). Time together among dual-earner couples. *American Sociological Review, 52,* 391–400.

Kinney, J. M., & Cavanaugh, J. C. (1993, November). *Until death do us part: Striving to find meaning while caring for a spouse with dementia.* Paper presented at the meeting of the Gerontological Society of America, New Orleans.

Kinney, J. M., & Stephens, M. A. P. (1989). Hassles and uplifts of giving care to a family member with dementia. *Psychology and Aging, 4,* 402–408.

Kirasic, K. C. (1980, November). *Spatial problem solving in elderly adults: A hometown advantage.* Paper presented at the meeting of the Gerontological Society of America, San Diego.

Kirasic, K. C. (1991). Spatial cognition and behavior in young and elderly adults: Implications for learning new environments. *Psychology and Aging, 6,* 10–18.

Kirasic, K. C., & Allen, G. L. (1985). Aging, spatial performance, and spatial competence. In N. Charness (Ed.), *Aging and human performance* (pp. 191–223). Chichester, England: Wiley.

Kirasic, K. C., & Allen, G. L. (1994, July). *Aging, working memory, and declarative learning.* Paper presented at the International Working Memory Conference, Cambridge, England.

Kirasic, K. C., Dobson, S. H., Binder, K. S., & Allen, G. L. (1994, April). *A model of cognitive aging: The effect of age and processing resources on learning in adulthood.* Paper presented at the Cognitive Aging Conference, Atlanta.

Kitchener, K. S., & Fischer, K. W. (1990). A skill approach to the development of reflective thinking. In D. Kuhn (Ed.), *Contributions to human development: Developmental perspectives on teaching and learning* (Vol. 21, pp. 48–62). Basel, Switzerland: Karger.

Kite, M. E., Deaux, K., & Miele, M. (1991). Stereotypes of young and old: Does age outweigh gender? *Psychology and Aging, 6,* 19–27.

Kite, M. E., & Johnson, B. T. (1988). Attitudes toward older and younger adults: A meta-analysis. *Psychology and Aging, 3,* 233–244.

Kitson, G. L., & Sussman, M. B. (1982). Marital complaints, demographic characteristics, and symptoms of mental distress in divorce. *Journal of Marriage and the Family, 44,* 87–101.

Kivett, V. R. (1991). Centrality of the grandfather role among older rural black and white men. *Journal of Gerontology: Social Sciences, 46,* S250–S258.

Kivnick, H. Q. (1982). *The meaning of grandparenthood.* Ann Arbor, MI: UMI Research.

Klatsky, A. L., Friedman, G. D., & Siegelaub, A. B. (1981). Alcohol and mortality: A ten-year Kaiser-Permanente experience. *Annals of Internal Medicine, 95,* 139–145.

Kline, D. W. (1994). Optimizing the visibility of displays for older observers. *Experimental Aging Research, 20,* 11–23.

Kline, D. W., & Schieber, F. (1985). Vision and aging. In J. E. Birren & K. W. Schaie (Eds.), *Handbook of the psychology of aging* (2nd ed., pp. 296–331). New York: Van Nostrand Reinhold.

Kline, T. J. B., Ghali, L. M., Kline, D. W., & Brown, S. (1990). Visibility distance of highway signs among young, middle-aged, and older observers: Icons are better than text. *Human Factors, 32,* 609–619.

Kligman, A. M., Grove, G. L., & Balin, A. K. (1985). Aging of human skin. In C. E. Finch & E. L. Schneider (Eds.), *Handbook of the biology of aging* (2nd ed., pp. 820–841). New York: Van Nostrand Reinhold.

Kligman, L. H., Aiken, F. J., & Kligman, A. M. (1982). Prevention of ultraviolet damage to the dermis of hairless mice by sunscreens. *Journal of Investigative Dermatology, 78,* 181–189.

Knight, R. G., & Godfrey, H. P. D. (1995). Behavioural and self-report methods. In A. D. Baddeley, B. A. Wilson, & F. N. Watts (Eds.), *Handbook of memory disorders* (pp. 393–410). Chichester, England: Wiley.

Koenig, H. G., George, L. K., & Siegler, I. C. (1988). The use of religion and other emotion-regulating coping strategies among older adults. *The Gerontologist, 28,* 303–310.

Koestenbaum, P. (1976). *Is there an answer to death?* Englewood Cliffs, NJ: Prentice-Hall.

Koff, T. H. (1981). *Hospice: A caring community.* Cambridge, MA: Winthrop.

Koh, J. Y., & Bell, W. G. (1987). Korean elderly in the United States: Intergenerational relations and living arrangements. *The Gerontologist, 27,* 66–71.

Kornhaber, A. (1985). Grandparenthood and the "new social contract." In V. L. Bengtson & J. F. Robertson (Eds.), *Grandparenthood* (pp. 159–172). Beverly Hills, CA: Sage Publications.

Kornhaber, A., & Woodward, K. L. (1981). *Grandparent/grandchildren: The vital connection.* Garden City, NJ: Anchor.

Kosnik, W., Winslow, L., Kline, D. W., Rasinski, & Sekular, R. (1988). Visual changes in everyday life throughout adulthood. *Journal of Gerontology, 43,* P63–P70.

Kotre, J. (1984). *Outliving the self: Generativity and the interpretation of lives.* Baltimore: Johns Hopkins University Press.

Kram, K. E. (1980). *Mentoring processes at work: Developmental relationships in managerial careers.* Unpublished doctoral dissertation, Yale University, New Haven, CT.

Kram, K. E. (1985). *Mentoring at work: Developmental relationships in organizational life.* Glenview, IL: Scott, Foresman.

Kram, K. E., & Isabella, L. (1985). Mentoring alternatives: The role of peer relationships in career development. *Academy of Management Journal, 21,* 110–132.

Kramer, A. F., Humphrey, D. G., Larish, J. F., Logan, G. D., & Strayer, D. L. (1994). Aging and inhibition: Beyond a unitary view of inhibitory processing in attention. *Psychology and Aging, 9,* 491–512.

Kramer, D. A. (1983). Post-formal operations? A need for further conceptualization. *Human Development, 26,* 91–105.

Kramer, D. A. (1989). A developmental framework for understanding conflict resolution processes. In J. D. Sinnott (Ed.), *Everyday problem solving: Theory and applications* (pp. 138–152). New York: Praeger.

Kramer, D. A. (1990). Conceptualizing wisdom: The primacy of affect-cognition relations. In R. J. Sternberg (Ed.), *Wisdom: Its nature, origins, and development* (pp. 279–313). Cambridge, UK: Cambridge University Press.

Kramer, D. A., Angiuld, N., Crisafi, L., & Levine, C. (1991, August). *Cognitive processes in real-life conflict resolution.* Paper presented at the annual meeting of the American Psychological Association, San Francisco.

Kramer, D. A., & Kahlbaugh, P. E. (1994). Memory for a dialectical and a nondialectical prose passage in young and older adults. *Journal of Adult Development, 1,* 13–26.

Kramer, D. A., & Woodruff, D. S. (1986). Relativistic and dialectical thought in three adult age-groups. *Human Development, 29,* 280–290.

Krause, N. (1991). Stress and isolation from close ties in later life. *Journal of Gerontology: Social Sciences, 46,* S183–S194.

Krause, N. (1995). Religiosity and self-esteem among older adults. *Journal of Gerontology: Psychological Sciences, 50B,* P236–P246.

Kremer, J. M. (1990). Severe rheumatoid arthritis: Current options in drug therapy. *Geriatrics, 45*(12), 43–48.

Krieger, S., Epsting, F., & Leitner, L. M. (1974). Personal constructs, threat, and attitudes toward death. *Omega: Journal of Death and Dying, 5,* 289.

Krout, J. A. (1988a). Community size differences in service awareness among elderly adults. *Journal of Gerontology, 43,* 528–530.

Krout, J. A. (1988b). Rural versus urban differences in elderly parents' contacts with their children. *The Gerontologist, 28,* 198–203.

Kübler-Ross, E. (1969). *On death and dying.* New York: Macmillan.

Kübler-Ross, E. (1974). *Questions and answers on death and dying.* New York: Macmillan.

Kuhn, D., & Angelev, J. (1976). An experimental study of the development of formal operational thought. *Child Development, 47,* 697–706.

Kuhn, D., Ho, V., & Adams, C. (1979). Formal reasoning among pre- and late adolescents. *Child Development, 50,* 1128–1135.

Kuhn, D., Langer, J., Kohlberg, L., & Haan, N. (1977). The development of formal operations in logical and moral judgment. *Genetic Psychology Monographs, 95,* 97–188.

Kurdek, L. A. (1991a). Predictors of increases in marital distress in newlywed couples: A 3-year prospective longitudinal study. *Developmental Psychology, 27,* 627–636.

Kurdek, L. A. (1991b). The relations between reported well-being and divorce history, availability of a proximate adult, and gender. *Journal of Marriage and the Family, 53,* 71–78.

Kurdek, L. A. (1995a). Developmental changes in relationship quality in gay male and lesbian cohabiting couples. *Developmental Psychology, 31,* 86–94.

Kurdek, L. A. (1995b). Lesbian and gay couples. In A. R. D'Augelli & C. J. Patterson (Eds.), *Lesbian, gay, and bisexual identities over the lifespan* (pp. 243–261). New York: Oxford University Press.

Kurdek, L. A., & Schmitt, J. P. (1986). Early development of relationship quality in heterosexual married, heterosexual cohabiting, gay, and lesbian couples. *Developmental Psychology, 22,* 305–309.

Kutza, J., Kaye, D., & Murasko, D. M. (1995). Basal natural killer cell activity of young versus elderly humans. *Journal of Gerontology: Biological Sciences, 50A,* B110–B116.

Labouvie-Vief, G. (1980). Beyond formal operations: Uses and limits of pure logic in life-span development. *Human Development, 23,* 141–161.

Labouvie-Vief, G. (1981). Proactive and reactive aspects of constructivism: Growth and aging in life-span perspective. In R. M. Lerner & N. A. Busch-Rossnagel (Eds.), *Individuals as producers of their development* (pp. 197–230). New York: Academic Press.

Labouvie-Vief, G. (1984). Logic and self-regulation from youth to maturity: A model. In M. L. Commons, F. A. Richards, & C. Armon (Eds.), *Beyond formal operations: Late adolescent and adult cognitive development* (pp. 158–179). New York: Praeger.

Labouvie-Vief, G. (1985). Intelligence and cognition. In J. E. Birren & K. W. Schaie (Eds.), *Handbook of the psychology of aging* (2nd ed., pp. 500–530). New York: Van Nostrand Reinhold.

Labouvie-Vief, G., Adams, C., Hakim-Larson, J., Hayden, M., & Devoe, M. (1985). *Logical problem solving and metalogical knowledge from preadolescence to adulthood.* Unpublished manuscript, Wayne State University, Detroit.

Labouvie-Vief, G., Chiodo, L. M., Goguen, L. A., Diehl, M., & Orwoll, L. (1995). Representations of self across the life span. *Psychology and Aging, 10,* 404–415.

Labouvie-Vief, G., & Gonda, J. N. (1976). Cognitive strategy training and intellectual performances in the elderly. *Journal of Gerontology, 31,* 327–332.

Labouvie-Vief, G., Hakim-Larson, J., & Hobart, C. J. (1987). Age, ego level, and the life-span development of coping and defense processes. *Psychology and Aging, 2,* 286–293.

LaBruzza, A. L. (1994). *Using DSM-IV: A clinician's guide to psychiatric diagnosis.* Northvale, NJ: Jason Aronson.

Lachman, J. L., & Lachman, R. (1980). Age and the actualization of world knowledge. In L. W. Poon, J. L. Fozard, L. S. Cermak, D. Arenberg, & L. W. Thompson (Eds.), *New directions in memory and aging* (pp. 285–311). Hillsdale, NJ: Erlbaum.

Lachman, M. E. (1983). Perceptions of intellectual aging: Antecedent or consequence of intellectual functioning? *Developmental Psychology, 19,* 482–498.

Lachman, M. E. (1985). Personal efficacy in middle and old age: Differential and normative patterns of change. In G. H. Elder, Jr. (Ed.), *Life-course dynamics: Trajectories and transitions, 1968–1980* (pp. 188–213). Ithaca, NY: Cornell University Press.

Lachman, M. E. (1986). Locus of control in aging research: A case for multidimensional and domain-specific assessment. *Psychology and Aging, 1,* 34–40.

Lachman, M. E., Bandura, M., Weaver, S. L., & Elliott, E. (1995). Assessing memory control beliefs: The Memory Controllability Inventory. *Aging and Cognition, 2,* 67–84.

Lachman, M. E., & Leff, R. (1989). Perceived control and intellectual functioning in the elderly: A 5-year longitudinal study. *Developmental Psychology, 25,* 722–728.

Lachman, M. E., Lewkowicz, C., Marcus, A., & Peng, Y. (1994). Images of midlife development among young, middle-aged, and older adults. *Journal of Adult Development, 1,* 201–211.

Lacks, P., Bertelson, A. D., Gans, L., & Kunkel, J. (1983). The effectiveness of three behavioral treatments for different degrees of sleep onset insomnia. *Behavior Therapy, 14,* 593–605.

LaCroix, A. Z., Lang, J., Scherr, P., Wallace, R. B., Cornoni-Huntley, J., Berkman, L., Curb, J. D., Evans, D., & Hennekens, C. H. (1991). Smoking and mortality among older men and women in three communities. *New England Journal of Medicine, 324,* 1619–1625.

Lajer, M. (1982). Unemployment and hospitalization among bricklayers. *Scandinavian Journal of Social Medicine, 10,* 3–10.

Lakatta, E. G. (1985). Heart and circulation. In C. E. Finch & E. L. Schneider (Eds.), *Handbook of the biology of aging* (2nd ed., pp. 377–413). New York: Van Nostrand Reinhold.

Lando, H. A. (1977). Successful treatment of smokers with a broad-spectrum behavioral approach. *Journal of Consulting and Clinical Psychology, 45,* 361–366.

Langer, E. J. (1985). Playing the middle against both ends: The usefulness of older adult cognitive activity as a model for cognitive activity in childhood and old age. In S. Yussen (Ed.), *The growth of reflection in children* (pp. 267–285). New York: Academic Press.

Langer, E. J., & Rodin, J. (1976). The effects of choice and enhanced personal responsibility for the aged: A field experiment in an institutional setting. *Journal of Personality and Social Psychology, 34,* 191–198.

LaRossa, R. (1988). Fatherhood and social change. *Family Relations, 34,* 451–457.

Larson, R., Mannell, R., & Zuzanek, J. (1986). Daily well-being of older adults with friends and family. *Psychology and Aging, 1,* 117–126.

LaRue, A., Dessonville, C., & Jarvik, L. F. (1985). Aging and mental disorders. In J. E. Birren & K. W. Schaie (Eds.), *Handbook of the psychology of aging* (2nd ed., pp. 664–702). New York: Van Nostrand Reinhold.

Latack, J. C. (1984). Career transitions within organizations: An exploratory study of work, nonwork, and coping strategies. *Organizational Behavior and Human Performance, 34,* 296–322.

Lavey, R. S., & Taylor, C. B. (1985). The nature of relaxation therapy. In S. R. Burchfield (Ed.), *Stress: Psychological and physiological interactions* (pp. 329–358). Washington, DC: Hemisphere.

La Vecchia, C., Lucchini, F., & Levi, F. (1994). Worldwide trends in suicide mortality. *Acta Psychiatrica Scandinavica, 90,* 53-64.

Lawton, M. P. (1980). *Environment and aging.* Pacific Grove, CA: Brooks/Cole.

Lawton, M. P. (1982). Competence, environmental press, and the adaptation of old people. In M. P. Lawton, P. G. Windley, & T. O. Byerts (Eds.), *Aging and the environment: Theoretical approaches* (pp. 33–59). New York: Springer.

Lawton, M. P. (1985a). Activities and leisure. In M. P. Lawton & G. L. Maddox (Eds.), *Annual review of gerontology and geriatrics* (Vol. 5, pp. 127–164). New York: Springer.

Lawton, M. P. (1985b). Housing and living environments of older people. In R. H. Binstock & E. Shanas (Eds.), *Handbook of aging and the social sciences* (2nd ed., pp. 450–478). New York: Van Nostrand Reinhold.

Lawton, M. P., & Cohen, J. (1974). The generality of housing impact on the well-being of older people. *Journal of Gerontology, 29,* 194–204.

Lawton, M. P., Moss, M., & Fulcomer, M. (1986–87). Objective and subjective uses of time by older people. *International Journal of Aging and Human Development, 24,* 171–188.

Lawton, M. P., Moss, M., & Moles, E. (1984). The supra-personal neighborhood context of older people: Age heterogeneity and well-being. *Environment and Behavior, 16,* 89–109.

Lawton, M. P., & Nahemow, L. (1973). Ecology of the aging process. In C. Eisdorfer & M. P. Lawton (Eds.), *The psychology of adult development and aging* (pp. 619–674). Washington, DC: American Psychological Association.

Lawton, M. P., & Nahemow, L. (1979). Social areas and the well-being of tenants in housing for the elderly. *Multivariate Behavior Research, 14,* 463–484.

Lawton, M. P., & Yaffe, S. (1980). Victimization and fear of crime in elderly public housing tenants. *Journal of Gerontology, 35,* 768–779.

Layde, P. M., Ory, H. W., & Schlesselman, J. J. (1982). The risk of myocardial infarction in former users of oral contraceptives. *Family Planning Perspectives, 14,* 78–80.

Lazarus, R. S. (1984). Puzzles in the study of daily hassles. *Journal of Behavioral Medicine, 7,* 375–389.

Lazarus, R. S., DeLongis, A., Folkman, S., & Gruen, R. (1985). Stress and adaptational outcomes. *American Psychologist, 40,* 770–779.

Lazarus, R. S., & Folkman, S. (1984). *Stress, appraisal, and coping.* New York: Springer.

Le Shan, L. (1969). Psychotherapy and the dying patient. In L. Pearson (Ed.), *Death and dying* (pp. 28–48). Cleveland: Case Western Reserve University Press.

Leacock, E. (1978). Women's status in egalitarian society: Implications for social evolution. *Current Anthropology, 19,* 247–275.

Leaf, P. J., Berkman, C. S., Weissman, M. M., Holzer, C. E., Tischler, G. L., & Myers, J. K. (1988). The epidemiology of late-life depression. In J. A. Brody & G. L. Maddox (Eds.), *Epidemiology and aging: An international perspective* (pp. 117–133). New York: Springer.

Leahy, J. M. (1993). A comparison of depression in women bereaved of a spouse, a child, or a parent. *Omega, 26,* 207–217.

Leana, C. R., & Feldman, D. C. (1991). Gender differences in responses to unemployment. *Journal of Vocational Behavior, 38,* 65–77.

Leana, C. R., & Feldman, D. C. (1992). *Coping with job loss.* New York: Lexington Books.

Lebowitz, M. D. (1988). Respiratory changes of aging. In B. Kent & R. Butler (Eds.), *Human aging research: Concepts and techniques* (pp. 263–276). New York: Raven.

Lee, G. R. (1985). Kinship and social support of the elderly: The case of the United States. *Aging and Society, 5,* 19–38.

Lee, G. R. (1988). Marital satisfaction in later life: The effects of nonmarital roles. *Journal of Marriage and the Family, 50,* 775–783.

Lee, G. R., & Ellithorpe, E. (1982). Intergenerational exchange and subjective well-being among the elderly. *Journal of Marriage and the Family, 44,* 217–224.

Lee, R. B. (1968). What hunters do for a living, or how to make out on scarce resources. In R. B. Lee and I. DeVore (Eds.), *Man the hunter.* Chicago: Aldine-Atherton.

Lee, T. R., Mancini, J. A., & Maxwell, J. W. (1990). Sibling relationships in adulthood: Contact patterns and motivation. *Journal of Marriage and the Family, 52,* 431–440.

Lehmann, H. E. (1981). Classification of depressive disorders. In T. A. Ban, R. Gonzalez, A. S. Jablensky, N. A. Sartorius, & F. E. Vartanian (Eds.), *Prevention and treatment of depression* (pp. 3–17). Baltimore: University Park Press.

Lehtonen, L., Esola, J., Vainio, O., & Lehtonen, A. (1990). Changes in lymphocyte subsets and immune competence in very advanced age. *Journal of Gerontology: Medical Sciences, 45,* M108–M112.

Leirer, V. O., Tanke, E. D., & Morrow, D. G. (1994). Time of day and naturalistic prospective memory. *Experimental Aging Research, 20,* 127–134.

Lemon, B. W., Bengtson, V. L., & Peterson, J. A. (1972). An exploration of the activity theory of aging: Activity types and life satisfactions among in-movers to a retirement community. *Journal of Gerontology, 27,* 511–523.

Lent, R. W., & Hackett, G. (1987). Career self-efficacy: Empirical status and future directions. *Journal of Vocational Behavior, 30,* 347–382.

Leon, G. R., Gillum, B., Gillum, R., & Gouze, M. (1979). Personality stability and change over a 30-year period: Middle to old age. *Journal of Consulting and Clinical Psychology, 47,* 517–524.

Leonard, J. A., & Newman, R. C. (1965). On the acquisition and maintenance of high speed and high accuracy on a keyboard task. *Ergonomics, 8,* 281–304.

Lepp, I. (1968). *Death and its mysteries.* New York: Macmillan.

Lerner, M. (1970). When, why, and where people die. In O. G. Brim, Jr., H. E. Freeman, S. Levine & N. A. Scotch (Eds.), *The dying patient* (pp. 5–29). New York: Russell Sage Foundation.

Lerner, R. M. (1986). *Concepts and theories of human development* (2nd ed.). New York: Random House.

Le Shan, L. (1969). Psychotherapy and the dying patient. In L. Pearson (Ed.), *Death and dying.* Cleveland: Case Western Reserve University Press.

Lesser, J., Lazarus, L. W., Frankel, R., & Havasy, S. (1981). Reminiscence group therapy with psychotic geriatric inpatients. *The Gerontologist, 21,* 291–296.

Levenson, R. W., Carstensen, L. L., & Gottman, J. M. (1993). Long-term marriage: Age, gender, and satisfaction. *Psychology and Aging, 8,* 301–313.

Levenson, R. W., Carstensen, L. L., & Gottman, J. M. (1994). The influence of age and gender on affect, physiology, and their interrelations: A study of long-term marriages. *Journal of Personality and Social Psychology, 67,* 56–68.

Levin, J. S., & Taylor, R. J. (1993). Gender and age differences in religiosity among Black Americans. *The Gerontologist, 33,* 16–23.

Levin, J. S., Taylor, R. J., & Chatters, L. M. (1994). Race and gender differences in religiosity among older adults: Findings from four national surveys. *Journal of Gerontology: Social Sciences, 49,* S137–S145.

LeVine, R. (1978). Adulthood and aging in cross-cultural perspective. *Items, 31/32,* 1–5.

Levinson, D. (1988). Family violence in cross cultural perspective. In V. B. Van Hasselt, R. L. Morrison, A. S. Bellack, & M. Hersen (Eds.), *Handbook of family violence* (pp. 435–456). New York: Plenum.

Levinson, D. J., Darrow, C., Kline, E., Levinson, M., & McKee, B. (1978). *The seasons of a man's life.* New York: Knopf.

Lewin, K. (1936). *Principles of topological psychology.* New York: McGraw-Hill.

Lewinsohn, P. M. (1975). The behavioral study and treatment of depression. In M. Hersen, R. M. Eisler, & P. M. Miller (Eds.), *Progress in behavior modification* (Vol. 1, pp. 19–64). New York: Academic Press.

Lewinsohn, P. M., Steinmetz, J. L., Antonuccio, D. O., & Teri, L. (1984). *The coping with depression course.* Eugene, OR: Castalia.

Lewis, R. A. (1979). Macular degeneration in the aged. In S. S. Han & D. H. Coons (Eds.), *Special senses and aging.* Ann Arbor, MI: Institute of Gerontology, University of Michigan.

Lezak, M. D. (1995). *Neuropsychological assessment* (3rd ed.). New York: Oxford University Press.

Liang, J., & Warfel, B. L. (1983). Urbanism and life satisfaction among the aged. *Journal of Gerontology, 38,* 97–106.

Lieberman, A. (1974). Parkinson's disease: A clinical review. *American Journal of Medical Science, 267,* 66–80.

Light, K. E., & Spirduso, W. W. (1990). Effects of aging on the movement complexity factor of response programming. *Journal of Gerontology: Psychological Sciences, 45,* P107–P109.

Light, L. L. (1990). Interactions between memory and language in old age. In J. E. Birren & K. W. Schaie (Eds.), *Handbook of the psychology of aging* (3rd ed., pp. 275–290). San Diego: Academic Press.

Light, L. L. (1992). The organization of memory in old age. In F. I. M. Craik & T. A. Salthouse (Eds.), *The handbook of aging and cognition* (pp. 111–165). Hillsdale, NJ: Erlbaum.

Light, L. L., & Anderson, P. A. (1975). Working-memory capacity, age, and memory for discourse. *Journal of Gerontology, 45,* 737–747.

Light, L. L., & La Voie, D. (1993). Direct and indirect measures of memory in old age. In P. Graf & M. E. J. Masson (Eds.), *New directions in cognition, development, and neuropsychology* (pp. 207–230). Hillsdale, NJ: Erlbaum.

Light, L. L., & Zelinski, E. M. (1983). Memory for spatial information in young and old adults. *Developmental Psychology, 19,* 901–906.

Lincoln, Y. S., & Guba, E. G. (1985). *Naturalistic inquiry.* Beverly Hills, CA: Sage Publications.

Lipman, P. D. (1991). Age and exposure differences in acquisition of route information. *Psychology and Aging, 6,* 128–133.

Lipowski, Z. J. (1980). *Delirium.* Springfield, IL: Charles C. Thomas.

Lishman, W. A. (1978). *Organic psychiatry: The psychological consequences of cerebral disorder.* Oxford, England: Blackwell Scientific.

List, N. (1987). Perspectives in cancer screening in the elderly. *Geriatric Clinic, 3,* 433–445.

List, N. D. (1988). Cancer screening in the elderly. In R. Chernoff & D. A. Lipschitz (Eds.), *Health promotion and disease prevention in the elderly* (pp. 113–129). New York: Raven.

Livson, F. B. (1981). Paths to psychological health in the middle years: Sex differences. In D. Eichorn, N. Haan, J. Clausen, M. Honzik, & P. Mussen (Eds.), *Past and present in middle life* (pp. 183–194). New York: Academic Press.

Locke, E. A. (1976). The natures and causes of job satisfaction. In M. Dunnette (Ed.), *Handbook of industrial/organizational psychology* (pp. 1297–1349). Chicago: Rand McNally.

Lockshin, R. A., & Zakeri, Z. F. (1990). MINIREVIEW: Programmed cell death: New thoughts and relevance to aging. *Journal of Gerontology: Biological Sciences, 45,* B135–B140.

Loeser, R. F., Wallin, R., & Sadowski, J. (1993). Vitamin K and vitamin K-dependent proteins in the elderly: Implications for bone and cartilage biology. In R. R. Watson (Ed.), *Handbook of nutrition in the aged* (2nd ed., pp. 263–280). Boca Raton, FL: CRC Press.

Loevinger, J. (1976). *Ego development.* San Francisco: Jossey-Bass.

Logan, R. D. (1986). A reconceptualization of Erikson's theory: The repetition of existential and instrumental themes. *Human Development, 29,* 125–136.

Lombardi, W. J., & Weingartner, H. (1995). Pharmacological treatment of impaired memory function. In A. D. Baddeley, B. A. Wilson, & F. N. Watts (Eds.), *Handbook of memory disorders* (pp. 577–601). Chichester, England: Wiley.

Lombardo, N. E. (1988). ADRDA: Birth and evolution of a major voluntary health association. In M. K. Aronson (Ed.), *Understanding Alzheimer's disease* (pp. 323–326). New York: Scribner's.

Lomranz, J., Bergman, S., Eyal, N., & Shmotkin, D. (1988). Indoor and outdoor activities of aged women and men as related to depression and well-being. *International Journal of Aging and Human Development, 26,* 303–314.

Longino, C. F. (1982). American retirement communities and residential relocation. In M. A. Warnes (Ed.), *Geographical perspectives on the elderly* (pp. 239–262). London: Wiley.

Longino, C. F., Jr., Jackson, D. J., Zimmerman, R. S., & Bradsher, J. E. (1991). The second move: Health and geographical mobility. *Journal of Gerontology: Social Sciences, 46,* S218–S224.

Lopata, H. Z. (1973). *Widowhood in an American city.* Cambridge, MA: Schenkman.

Lopata, H. Z. (1975). Widowhood: Societal factors in life-span disruptions and alternatives. In N. Datan & L. H. Ginsberg (Eds.), *Life-span developmental psychology: Normative life crises* (pp. 217–234). New York: Academic Press.

Lopata, H. Z. (1993). The interweave of public and private: Women's challenge to American society. *Journal of Marriage and the Family, 55,* 176–190.

Lorayne, H., & Lucas, J. (1974). *The memory book.* New York: Ballantine.

Lovelace, E. A., Marsh, G. R., & Oster, O. J. (1982). *Prediction and evaluation of memory performance by young and old adults.* Paper presented at the meeting of the Gerontological Society of America, Boston.

Lowenthal, M. F. (1972). Some potentialities of a life-cycle approach to the study of retirement. In F. M. Carp (Ed.), *Retirement* (pp. 307–338). New York: Behavioral Publications.

Lowenthal, M., Thurnher, M., & Chiriboga, D. (1975). *Four stages of life.* San Francisco: Jossey-Bass.

Löwik, M. R. H., Wedel, M., Kok, F. J., Odink, J., Westenbrink, S., & Meulmeester, J. F. (1991). Nutrition and serum cholesterol levels among elderly men and women (Dutch nutrition surveillance system). *Journal of Gerontology: Medical Sciences, 46,* M23–M28.

Luborsky, M., & Rubinstein, R. L. (1987). Ethnicity and lifetimes: Self-concepts and situational contexts of ethnic identity in late life. In D. E. Gelfand & C. M. Barresi (Eds.), *Ethnic dimensions of aging* (pp. 35–50). New York: Springer.

Luborsky, M. R., & Rubenstein, R. L. (1990). Ethnic identity and bereavement in later life: The case of older widowers. In J. Sokolovsky (Ed.), *The cultural context of aging* (pp. 229–240). New York: Bergin & Garvey.

Lund, D. A., Dimond, M. S., Caserta, M. F., Johnson, R. J., Poulton, J. L., & Connelly, J. R. (1985–86). Identifying elderly with coping difficulties after two years of bereavement. *Omega: Journal of Death and Dying, 16,* 213–224.

Lundin, T. (1984). Morbidity following sudden and unexpected bereavement. *British Journal of Psychiatry, 144,* 84–88.

Maas, H. S. (1985). The development of adult development: Recollections and reflections. In J. M. A. Munnichs, P. Mussen, E. Olbrich, & P. G. Coleman (Eds.), *Life-span and change in a gerontological perspective* (pp. 161–175). New York: Academic Press.

Maas, H. S., & Kuypers, J. A. (1974). *From thirty to seventy.* San Francisco: Jossey-Bass.

Maas, J. W. (1978). Clinical and biochemical heterogeneity of depressive disorders. *Annals of Internal Medicine, 88,* 556–563.

Mace, N. L., & Rabins, P. V. (1981). *The 36-hour day.* Baltimore: Johns Hopkins University Press.

Macklin, E. D. (1988). Heterosexual couples who cohabit nonmaritally: Some common problems and issues. In C. S. Chilman, E. W. Nunnally, & F. M. Cox (Eds.), *Variant family forms* (pp. 56–72). Beverly Hills: Sage.

Madden, D. J. (1990). Adult age differences in the time course of visual attention. *Journal of Gerontology: Psychological Sciences, 45,* P9–P16.

Madden, D. J., Connelly, S. L., & Pierce, T. W. (1994). Adult age differences in shifting focused attention. *Psychology and Aging, 9,* 528–538.

Madden, D. J., & Nebes, R. D. (1980). Aging and the development of automaticity in visual search. *Developmental Psychology, 16,* 377–384.

Mahoney, M. J. (1980). *Abnormal psychology.* New York: Harper & Row.

Maletta, G. J. (1984). Use of antipsychotic medication in the elderly. In C. Eisdorfer (Ed.), *Annual review of gerontology and geriatrics* (Vol. 4, pp. 174–220). New York: Springer.

Malinak, D. P., Hoyt, M. F., & Patterson, V. (1979). Adults' reaction to the death of a parent: A preliminary study. *American Journal of Psychiatry, 136,* 1152–1156.

Mandel, R. G., & Johnson, N. S. (1984). A developmental analysis of story recall and comprehension in adulthood. *Journal of Verbal Learning and Verbal Behavior, 23,* 643–659.

Manton, K. G., Wrigley, J. M., Cohen, H. J., & Woodbury, M. A. (1991). Cancer mortality, aging, and patterns of comorbidity in the United States: 1968 to 1986. *Journal of Gerontology: Social Sciences, 46,* S225–S234.

Mäntylä, T. (1994). Remembering to remember: Adult age differences in prospective memory. *Journal of Gerontology: Psychological Sciences, 49,* P276–P282.

Margolin, L., & White, J. (1987). The continuing role of physical attractiveness in marriage. *Journal of Marriage and the Family, 49,* 21–27.

Markides, K., Boldt, J. S., & Ray, L. A. (1986). Sources of helping and intergenerational solidarity: A three generations study of Mexican Americans. *Journal of Gerontology, 41,* 506–511.

Markides, K., Liang, J., & Jackson, J. S. (1990). Race, ethnicity, and aging: Conceptual and methodological issues. In R. H. Binstock & L. K. George (Eds.), *Handbook of aging and the social sciences* (3rd ed., pp. 112–129). San Diego: Academic Press.

Markides, K., & Martin, H. W. (1983). *Older Mexican Americans: A study in an urban barrio.* Austin: University of Texas Press.

Markson, E. W. (1995). To be or not to be: Assisted suicide revisited. *Omega, 31,* 221–235.

Markson, L. J., Fanale, J., Steel, K., Kern, D., & Annas, G. (1995). Implementing advance directives in the primary care setting. *Archives of Internal Medicine, 154,* 2321–2327.

Markus, H., & Nurius, P. (1986). Possible selves. *American Psychologist, 41,* 954–969.

Marlatt, G. A., & Gordon, J. R. (1980). Determinants of relapse: Implication for the maintenance of behavior change. In P. O. Davidson & S. M. Davidson (Eds.), *Behavioral medicine: Changing health lifestyles* (pp. 410–452). New York: Brunner/Mazel.

Marquis, K. S., & Detweiler, R. A. (1985). Does adopted mean different? An attributional analysis. *Journal of Personality and Social Psychology, 48,* 1054–1066.

Marsella, A. J. (1994). Work and well-being in an ethnoculturally pluralistic society: Conceptual and methodological issues. In G. P. Keita & J. J. Hurrell, Jr. (Eds.), *Job stress in a changing workforce* (pp. 147–160). Washington, DC: American Psychological Association.

Marshall, N. L., & Barnett, R. C. (1994). Family-friendly workplaces, work-family interface, and worker health. In G. P. Keita & J. J. Hurrell, Jr. (Eds.), *Job stress in a changing workforce* (pp. 253–264). Washington, DC: American Psychological Association.

Marshall, V. (1980). *Last chapters: A sociology of aging and dying.* Pacific Grove, CA: Brooks/Cole.

Marshall, V., Matthews, S., & Rosenthal, C. (1993). Elusiveness of family life: A challenge for the sociology of aging. In G. Maddox & M. P. Lawton (Eds.), *Annual review of gerontology and geriatrics, Vol. 13: Kinship, aging, and social change* (pp. 39–72). New York: Springer.

Marsiske, M., & Willis, S. L. (1995). Dimensionality of everyday problem solving in older adults. *Psychology and Aging, 10,* 269–283.

Martin, L. G. (1988). The aging of Asia. *Journal of Gerontology, 43,* S99–S113.

Martin, M. A. (1990). The homeless elderly: No room at the end. In Z. Harel, P. Ehrlich, & R. Hubbard (Eds.), *The vulnerable aged* (pp. 149–166). New York: Springer.

Martin, T. R., & Bracken, M. B. (1986). Association of low birth weight with passive smoke exposure in pregnancy. *American Journal of Epidemiology, 124,* 633–642.

Masako, O., & Liu, W. T. (1986). Intergenerational relations and the aged Japanese Americans. *Research on Aging, 8,* 125–155.

Masheter, C. (1991). Postdivorce relationships between ex-spouses: The roles of attachment and interpersonal conflict. *Journal of Marriage and the Family, 53,* 103–110.

Maslow, A. H. (1968). *Toward a psychology of being* (2nd ed.). New York: Van Nostrand Reinhold.

Mason, S. E. (1981, November). *Age group comparisons of memory ratings, predictions, and performance.* Paper presented at the meeting of the Gerontological Society of America, Toronto.

Mason, S. E. (1986). Age and gender as factors in facial recognition. *Experimental Aging Research, 12,* 151–154.

Materi, M. (1977). Assertiveness training: A catalyst for behavior change. *Alcohol Health and Research World, 1,* 23–26.

Matsui, T., Ikeda, H., & Ohnishi, R. (1989). Relation of sex-typed socializations to career self-efficacy expectations of college students. *Journal of Vocational Behavior, 35,* 1–16.

Matsui, T., Ohsawa, T., & Onglatco, M-L. (1995). Work-family conflict and the stress-buffering effects of husband support and coping behavior among Japanese married working women. *Journal of Vocational Behavior, 47,* 178–192.

Matthews, R., & Matthews, A. M. (1986). Infertility and involuntary childlessness: The transition to nonparenthood. *Journal of Marriage and the Family, 48,* 641–649.

Mattis, S. (1976). Mental status examination for organic mental syndrome in the elderly patient. In L. Bellak & T. B. Karasu (Eds.), *Geriatric psychiatry: A handbook for psychiatrists and primary health care physicians* (pp. 79–121). New York: Grune & Stratton.

Maxwell, R. J., Silverman, P., & Maxwell, E. K. (1982). The motive for gerontocide. In J. Sokolovsky (Ed.), *Aging and the aged* (Part 1, pp. 67–84). Williamsburg, VA: Studies in Third World Societies (Public No. 22).

Maybury-Lewis, D. (1984). Age and kinship: A structural view. In D. I. Kertzer & J. Keith (Eds.), *Age and anthropological theory* (pp. 123–140). Ithaca, NY: Cornell University Press.

Mayer, K. U., & Müller, W. (1986). The state and the structure of the life course. In A. B. Sorenson, F. W. Weinert, & L. R. Sherrod (Eds.), *Human development and the life course: Multidisciplinary perspectives* (pp. 217–245). Hillsdale, NJ: Erlbaum.

Mayes, A. R. (1995). The assessment of memory disorders. In A. D. Baddeley, B. A. Wilson, & F. N. Watts (Eds.), *Handbook of memory disorders* (pp. 367–391). Chichester, England: Wiley.

Maylor, E. A., & Rabbitt, P. M. A. (1994). Applying Brinley plots to individuals: Effects of aging on performance distributions in two speeded tasks. *Psychology and Aging, 9,* 224–230.

McAdams, D. P. (1992). The five-factor model in personality: A critical appraisal. *Journal of Personality, 60,* 329–361.

McAdams, D. P. (1993). *The stories we live by: Personal myths and the making of the self.* New York: William Morrow.

McAdams, D. P. (1994). Can personality change? Levels of stability and growth in personality across the life span. In T. F. Heatherton & J. L. Weinberger (Eds.), *Can personality change?* (pp. 299–313). Washington, DC: American Psychological Association.

McAdams, D. P., & de St. Aubin, E. (1992). A theory of generativity and its assessment through self-report, behavioral acts, and narrative themes in autobiography. *Journal of Personality and Social Psychology, 62,* 1003–1015.

McAdams, D. P., de St. Aubin, E., & Logan, R. (1993). Generativity in young, midlife, and older adults. *Psychology and Aging, 8,* 221–230.

McAllister, T. W. (1981). Cognitive functioning in the affective disorders. *Comprehensive Psychiatry, 22,* 572–586.

McClelland, J. L., Rumelhart, D. E., & the PDP Research Group. (1986). *Parallel distributed processing: Explorations in the microstructure of cognition.* Cambridge, MA: MIT Press.

McCrae, R. R., & Costa, P. T., Jr. (1984). *Emerging lives, enduring dispositions.* Boston: Little, Brown.

McCrae, R. R., & Costa, P. T., Jr. (1990). *Personality in adulthood.* New York: Guilford.

McDonald, H. J., & Sapone, F. M. (1993). *Nutrition for the prime of life.* New York: Plenum.

McDonald, R. S. (1986). Assessing treatment effects: Behavior rating scales. In L. W. Poon (Ed.), *Handbook for the clinical memory assessment of older adults* (pp. 129–138). Washington, DC: American Psychological Association.

McDowd, J. M., & Birren, J. E. (1990). Aging and attentional processes. In J. E. Birren & K. W. Schaie (Eds.), *Handbook of the psychology of aging* (3rd ed., pp. 222–233). San Diego: Academic Press.

McDowd, J. M., & Craik, F. I. M. (1988). Effects of aging and task difficulty on divided attention performance. *Journal of Experimental Psychology: Human Perception and Performance, 14,* 267–280.

McDowd, J. M., Filion, D. L., & Oseas-Kreger, D. M. (1991, June) *Inhibitory deficits in selective attention and aging.* Paper presented at the meeting of the American Psychological Society, Washington, DC.

McEvoy, C. L., & Moon, J. R. (1988). Assessment and treatment of everyday memory problems in the elderly. In M. M. Gruneberg, P. E. Morris, & R. N. Sykes (Eds.), *Practical aspects of memory: Current research and issues* (Vol. 2, pp. 155–160). Chichester, England: Wiley.

McGeer, E., & McGeer, P. L. (1980). Aging and neurotransmitter systems. In M. Goldstein, D. B. Caine, A. Liegerman, & M. O. Thorner (Eds.), *Advances in biochemical psychopharmacology: Vol. 23. Ergot compounds and brain function: Neuroendocrine and neuropsychiatric aspects* (pp. 305–314). New York: Raven.

McGuire, F. A., Dottavio, D., & O'Leary, J. T. (1986). Constraints to participation in outdoor recreation across the life span: A nationwide study of limitors and prohibitors. *The Gerontologist, 26,* 538–544.

McGuire, L. C. (in press). Remembering what the doctor said: Organization and adults' memory for medical information. *Experimental Aging Research.*

McKellin, W. H. (1985). Passing away and loss of life: Aging and death among the Managalese of Papua New Guinea. In D. A. Counts & D. R. Counts (Eds.), *Aging and its transformations* (pp. 181–202). Lanham, MD: University Press of America.

McKhann, G., Drachman, D., Folstein, M., Katzman, R., Prince, D., & Stadlam, E. M. (1984). Clinical diagnosis of Alzheimer's disease: Report of the NINCDS-ADRDA Work Group under the auspices of the Department of Health and Human Services Task Force on Alzheimer's disease. *Neurology, 34,* 939–944.

Meacham, J. A. (1982). A note on remembering to execute planned actions. *Journal of Applied Developmental Psychology, 3,* 121–133.

Meichenbaum, D. (1985). *Stress inoculation training.* New York: Pergamon Press.

Meichenbaum, D., & Cameron, R. (1983). Stress inoculation training: Toward a general paradigm for training coping skills. In D. Meichenbaum & M. E. Jaremko (Eds.), *Stress reduction and prevention* (pp. 115–154). New York: Plenum.

Meier, D. E. (1988). Skeletal aging. In B. Kent & R. Butler (Eds.), *Human aging research: Concepts and techniques* (pp. 221–244). New York: Raven.

Meisami, E. (1994). Aging of the sensory systems. In P. Timiras (Ed.), *Physiological basis of aging and geriatrics* (2nd ed., pp. 115–131). Boca Raton, FL: CRC Press.

Mellinger, G. D., Balter, M. B., & Uhlenhuth, E. H. (1985). Insomnia and its treatment. *Archives of General Psychiatry, 42,* 225–232.

Menaghan, E. G., & Lieberman, M. A. (1986). Changes in depression following divorce: A panel study. *Journal of Marriage and the Family, 48,* 319–328.

Mendelson, M. (1982). Psychodynamics of depression. In E. S. Paykel (Ed.), *Handbook of affective disorders* (pp. 162–174). New York: Guilford.

Merriam, S. (1979). Middle age: A review of the research. *New Directions for Continuing Education, 2,* 7–15.

Merriam, S. (1980). The concept and function of reminiscence: A review of research. *The Gerontologist, 20,* 604–609.

Messer, M. (1967). The possibility of an age-concentrated environment becoming a normative system. *The Gerontologist, 7,* 247–251.

Messer, M. (1968). Age grouping and social status of the elderly. *Sociologist and Social Research, 52,* 271–279.

Meyer, B. J. F. (1983). Text structure and its use in studying comprehension across the adult life span. In B. A. Huston (Ed.), *Advances in reading/language research* (Vol. 2, pp. 9–54). Greenwich, CT: JAI.

Meyer, B. J. F. (1987). Reading comprehension and aging. In K. W. Schaie (Ed.), *Annual review of gerontology and geriatrics* (Vol. 7, pp. 93–115). New York: Springer.

Meyer, B. J. F., & Rice, G. E. (1981). Information recalled from prose by young, middle, and old adults. *Experimental Aging Research, 7,* 253–268.

Meyer, B. J. F., & Rice, G. E. (1983). Learning and memory from text across the adult life span. In J. Fine & R. O. Freedle (Eds.), *Developmental studies in discourse* (pp. 291–306). Norwood, NJ: Ablex.

Meyer, B. J. F., & Rice, G. E. (1989). Prose processing in adulthood: The text, the reader, and the task. In L. W. Poon, D. C. Rubin, & B. Wilson (Eds.), *Everyday cognition in adulthood and late life* (pp. 157–194). Cambridge: Cambridge University Press.

Meyer, B. J. F., Rice, G. E., Knight, C. C., & Jessen, J. L. (1979). *Effects of comparative and descriptive discourse types on the reading performance of young, middle, and old adults* (Prose Learning Series No. 7). Tempe, AZ: Department of Educational Psychology, Arizona State University Press.

Meyer, B. J. F., Young, C. J., & Bartlett, B. J. (1986, August). *A prose learning strategy: Effects on young and old adults.* Paper presented at the meeting of the American Psychological Association, Washington, DC.

Meyer, J. W. (1986). The self and the life course: Institutionalization and its effects. In A. B. Sorenson, F. W. Weinert, & L. R. Sherrod (Eds.), *Human development and the life course: Multidisciplinary perspectives* (pp. 199–216). Hillsdale, NJ: Erlbaum.

Meyer, J. W. (1987). A regional scale temporal analysis of the net migration patterns of elderly persons over time. *Journal of Gerontology, 42,* 366–375.

Meyerhoff, B. (1978). *Number our days.* New York: Simon & Schuster.

Meyers, G. C. (1985). Aging and worldwide population change. In R. H. Binstock & E. Shanas (Eds.), *Handbook of aging and the social sciences* (2nd ed., pp. 173–198). New York: Van Nostrand Reinhold.

Miles, C. C., & Miles, W. R. (1932). The correlation of intelligence scores and chronological age from early to late maturity. *American Journal of Psychology, 44,* 44–78.

Miller, S. S., & Cavanaugh, J. C. (1990). The meaning of grandparenthood and its relationship to demographic, relationship, and social participation variables. *Journal of Gerontology: Psychological Sciences, 45,* P244–P246.

Miller, W. R., & Hester, R. K. (1980). Treating the problem drinker: Modern approaches. In W. R. Miller (Ed.), *The addictive behaviors* (pp. 11–142). Oxford: Pergamon Press.

Mitchell, D. B. (1989). How many memory systems are there? *Journal of Experimental Psychology: Learning, Memory, and Cognition, 15,* 31–49.

Mobily, K. E., Lemke, J. H., & Gisin, G. J. (1991). The idea of leisure repertoire. *Journal of Applied Gerontology, 10,* 208–223.

Mohs, R. C., Kim, Y., Johns, C. A., Dunn, D. D., & Davis, K. I. (1986). Assessing changes in Alzheimer's disease: Memory and language. In L. W. Poon (Ed.), *Handbook for the clinical memory assessment of older adults* (pp. 149–155). Washington, DC: American Psychological Association.

Monane, M., Gurwitz, J. H., & Avorn, J. (1993). Pharmacotherapy with psychoactive medications in the long-term-care setting: Challenges, management, and future directions. *Generations, 17,* 57–60.

Monczunski, J. (1991). That incurable disease. *Notre Dame Magazine, 20 (1),* 37.

Moody, R. A., Jr. (1975). *Life after life.* Atlanta: Mockingbird.

Moody, R. A., Jr. (1977). *Reflections on life after life.* New York: Bantam Books.

Moody, R. A., Jr. (1988). *The light beyond.* New York: Bantam.

Moon, A., & Williams, O. (1993). Perceptions of elder abuse and help-seeking patterns among African-American, Caucasian American, and Korean-American elderly women. *The Gerontologist, 33,* 386–395.

Moon, J-H., & Pearl, J. H. (1991). Alienation of elderly Korean American immigrants as related to place of residence, gender, age, years of education, time in the U.S., living with or without children, and living with or without a spouse. *International Journal of Aging and Human Development, 32,* 115–124.

Moore, S. F. (1978). Old age in a life-term social arena: Some Chagga in Killimanjaro in 1974. In B. G. Meyerhoff & A. Simic (Eds.), *Life's career: Aging* (pp. 23–76). Beverly Hills, CA: Sage Publications.

Moos, R. H., & Lemke, S. (1984). *Multiphasic environmental assessment procedure: Manual.* Palo Alto, CA: Social Ecology Laboratory, Stanford University Press.

Moos, R. H., & Lemke, S. (1985). Specialized living environments for older people. In J. E. Birren & K. W. Schaie (Eds.), *Handbook of the psychology of aging* (2nd ed., pp. 864–889). New York: Van Nostrand Reinhold.

Moran, J. A., & Gatz, M. (1987). Group therapies for nursing home adults: An evaluation of two treatment approaches. *The Gerontologist, 27,* 588–591.

Morewitz, J. (1988). Evaluation of excessive daytime sleepiness in the elderly. *Journal of the American Geriatrics Society, 36,* 324–330.

Moritani, T., & deVries, H. A. (1980). Potential for gross muscle hypertrophy in older men. *Journal of Gerontology, 35,* 672–682.

Morris, J. N. (1975). Changes in morale experienced by elderly institutional applicants along the institutional path. *The Gerontologist, 15,* 345–349.

Morris, J. N., & Sherwood, S. (1984). Informal support resources for vulnerable elderly persons: Can they be counted on, why do they work? *International Journal of Aging and Human Development, 18,* 1–17.

Morrow, P. C., & McElroy, J. C. (1987). Work commitment and job satisfaction over three career stages. *Journal of Vocational Behavior, 30,* 330–346.

Morrow-Howell, N., & Mui, A. (1989). Elderly volunteers: Reasons for initiating and terminating service. *Journal of Gerontological Social Work, 13,* 21–34.

Mortimer, J. T., Finch, M. D., & Kumka, D. (1982). Persistence and change in development: The multidimensional self-concept. In P. B. Baltes & O. G. Brim, Jr. (Eds.), *Life-span development and behavior* (Vol. 4, pp. 263–313). New York: Academic Press.

Mortimer, R. G. (1989). Older drivers' visibility and comfort in night driving: Vehicle safety factors. In *Proceedings of the Human Factors Society 33rd Annual Meeting* (pp. 154–158). Santa Monica, CA: Human Factors Society.

Moscovitch, M. C. (1982). A neuropsychological approach to perception and memory in normal and pathological aging. In F. I. M. Craik & S. Trehub (Eds.), *Aging and cognitive processes* (pp. 55–78). New York: Plenum.

Moss, M. S., & Lawton, M. P. (1982). Time budgets of older people: A window on four lifestyles. *Journal of Gerontology, 37,* 115–123.

Mouloua, M., & Parasuraman, R. (1995). Aging and cognitive vigilance: Effects of spatial uncertainty and event rate. *Experimental Aging Research, 21,* 17–32.

Mourant, R. R., & Langolf, G. D. (1976). Luminance specifications for automobile instrument panels. *Human Factors, 18,* 71–84.

Mui, A. C. (1995). Caring for frail elderly parents: A comparison of adult sons and daughters. *The Gerontologist, 35,* 86–93.

Mulrow, C. D., Feussner, J. R., Williams, B. C., & Vokaty, K. A. (1987). The value of clinical findings in the detection of normal pressure hydrocephalus. *Journal of Gerontology, 42,* 277–279.

Munro, H. N., & Young, V. R. (1978). New approaches to the assessment of protein status in man. In A. N. Howard & I. M. Baird (Eds.), *Recent advances in clinical nutrition* (pp. 33–41). London: Libby.

Murphy, C. (1985). Cognitive and chemosensory influences in age-related changes in the ability to identify blended foods. *Journal of Gerontology, 40,* 47–52.

Murphy, C. (1986). Taste and smell in the elderly. In H. L. Meiselman & R. S. Rivlin (Eds.), *Clinical measurement of taste and smell* (pp. 343–371). New York: Macmillan.

Murphy, M. D., Sanders, R. E., Gabriesheski, A. S., & Schmitt, F. A. (1981). Metamemory in the aged. *Journal of Gerontology, 36,* 185–193.

Murphy, S. (1988). Mental distress and recovery in a high-risk bereavement sample three years after untimely death. *Nursing Research, 37,* 30–35.

Murphy, Y., & Murphy, R. F. (1974). *Women of the forest.* New York: Columbia University Press.

Murray, H. A. (1938). *Explorations in personality.* New York: Oxford University Press.

Murray, J. (1979). Subjective retirement. *Social Security Bulletin, 42,* 20–25, 43.

Murrell, A. J., Frieze, I. H., & Frost, J. L. (1991). Aspiring to careers in male- and female-dominated professions: A study of Black and White college women. *Psychology of Women Quarterly, 15,* 103–126.

Muschkin, C., & Myers, G. C. (1989). Migration and household family structure: Puerto Ricans in the United States. *International Migration Review, 23,* 495–501.

Mussen, P. (1985). Early adult antecedents of life satisfaction at age 70. In J. M. A. Munnichs, P. Mussen, E. Olbrich, & P. G. Coleman (Eds.), *Life-span and change in a gerontological perspective* (pp. 45–61). New York: Academic Press.

Myerhoff, B. G. (1980). Re-membered lives—Memory and survival: The importance of our own life stories. *Parabola: Myth and the Quest for Meaning, 5,* 74–77.

Myers, J. E., Wass, H., & Murphey, M. (1980). Ethnic differences in death anxiety among the elderly. *Death Education, 4,* 237–244.

Myers, T. (1983). Corroboration of self-reported alcohol consumption—A comparison of the accounts of a group of male prisoners and those of their wives/cohabitees. *Alcohol and Alcoholism, 18,* 67–74.

Myerson, J., Hale, S., Wagstaff, D., Poon, L. W., & Smith, G. A. (1990). The information-loss model: A mathematical theory of age-related cognitive slowing. *Psychological Review, 97,* 475–487.

Myerson, J., Wagstaff, D., & Hale, S. (1994). Brinley plots, explained variance, and the analysis of age differences in response latencies. *Journal of Gerontology: Psychological Sciences, 49,* P72–P80.

Nachtigall, L. E., & Nachtigall, L. B. (1990). Protecting older women from their growing risk of cardiac disease. *Geriatrics, 45*(5), 24–34.

Nagel, J. E., & Adler, W. H. (1988). Immunology. In B. Kent & R. Butler (Eds.), *Human aging research: Concepts and techniques* (pp. 299–310). New York: Raven.

Nagi, S. Z. (1965). Some conceptual issues in disability and rehabilitation. In M. B. Sussman (Ed.), *Sociology and rehabilitation* (pp. 100–113). Washington, DC: American Sociological Association.

Nagi, S. Z. (1991). Disability concepts revisited: Implications for prevention. In A. M. Pope & A. R. Tarlov (Eds.), *Disability in America: Toward a national agenda for prevention* (pp. 309–327). Washington, DC: National Academy Press.

National Aging Resource Center of Elder Abuse. (1990). *Elder abuse and neglect: A synthesis of research.* Washington, DC: Author.

National Center for Health Statistics. (1988). *Annual survey of births, marriages, divorces, and deaths: United States, 1987.* Hyattsville, MD: U.S. Public Health Service.

National Center for Health Statistics. (1991). *Annual survey of births, marriages, divorces, and deaths: United States, 1990.* Hyattsville, MD: U.S. Public Health Service.

National Highway Traffic Safety Administration. (1988). *Traffic safety plan for older drivers.* Washington, DC: U.S. Department of Transportation.

National Institute of Aging. (1980). Senility reconsidered. *Journal of the American Medical Association, 244,* 259–263.

National Institute of Alcoholism and Alcohol Abuse (NIAAA). (1983). *Fifth special report to the U.S. Congress on alcohol and health* (DHHS Publication No. ADM 84-1291). Washington, DC: U.S. Government Printing Office.

National Research Council. (1988). *The emerging population in the twenty-first century: Statistics for health policy.* Washington, DC: National Academy Press.

National Urban League. (1964). *Double-jeopardy—The older Negro in America today.* New York: Author.

Nebes, R. D., Boller, F., & Holland, A. (1986). Use of semantic context by patients with Alzheimer's disease. *Psychology and Aging, 1,* 261–269.

Nehrke, M. F., Bellucci, G., & Gabriel, S. J. (1977). Death anxiety, locus of control, and life satisfaction in the elderly. *Omega: Journal of Death and Dying, 8,* 359–368.

Neimark, E. D. (1975). Longitudinal development of formal operational thought. *Genetic Psychology Monographs, 91,* 171–225.

Neisser, U. (1976). *Cognition and reality.* San Francisco: W. H. Freeman.

Neisser, U., & Winograd, E. (Eds.). (1988). *Remembering reconsidered.* New York: Cambridge University Press.

Neugarten, B. L. (1969). Continuities and discontinuities of psychological issues into adult life. *Human Development, 12,* 121–130.

Neugarten, B. L. (1973). Personality change in later life: A developmental perspective. In C. Eisdorfer & M. P. Lawton (Eds.), *The psychology of adult development and aging* (pp. 311–335). Washington, DC: American Psychological Association.

Neugarten, B. L. (1977). Personality and aging. In J. E. Birren & K. W. Schaie (Eds.), *Handbook of the psychology of aging* (pp. 626–649). New York: Van Nostrand Reinhold.

Neugarten, B. L., & Associates (Eds.). (1964). *Personality in middle and late life.* New York: Atherton.

Neugarten, B. L., & Datan, N. (1973). Sociological perspectives on the life cycle. In P. B. Baltes & K. W. Schaie (Eds.), *Life-span developmental psychology: Personality and socialization* (pp. 53–69). New York: Academic Press.

Neugarten, B. L., & Hagestad, G. O. (1976). Age and the life course. In R. H. Binstock & E. Shanas (Eds.), *Handbook of aging and the social sciences* (pp. 35–55). New York: Van Nostrand Reinhold.

Neugarten, B. L., & Weinstein, K. K. (1964). The changing American grandparent. *Journal of Marriage and the Family, 26,* 299–304.

Newman, B. M. (1982). Mid-life development. In B. B. Wolman (Ed.), *Handbook of developmental psychology* (pp. 617–635). Englewood Cliffs, NJ: Prentice-Hall.

Newmann, J. P., Engel, R. J., & Jensen, J. E. (1990). Depressive symptom patterns among older women. *Psychology and Aging, 5,* 101–118.

Newmann, J. P., Engel, R. J., & Jensen, J. E. (1991). Changes in depressive-symptom experiences among older women. *Psychology and Aging, 6,* 212–222.

Nisbett, R., & Ross, L. (1980). *Human inference: Strategies and shortcomings of social judgment.* Englewood Cliffs: Prentice-Hall.

Nock, S. L. (1981). Family life transitions: Longitudinal effects on family members. *Journal of Marriage and the Family, 43,* 703–714.

Nock, S. L. (1982). The life-cycle approach to family analysis. In B. B. Wolman (Ed.), *Handbook of developmental psychology* (pp. 636–651). Englewood Cliffs, NJ: Prentice-Hall.

Noe, R. A. (1987). *An exploratory investigation of the antecedents and consequences of mentoring.* Unpublished manuscript, University of Minnesota, Minneapolis.

Norris, F. N., & Murrell, S. A. (1987). Older adult family stress and adaptation before and after bereavement. *Journal of Gerontology, 42,* 606–612.

Norris, M. L., & Cunningham, D. R. (1981). Social impact of hearing loss in the aged. *Journal of Gerontology, 36,* 727–729.

Norris-Baker, C., & Scheidt, R. J. (1994). From "Our Town" to "Ghost Town"? The changing context of home for rural elders. *International Journal of Aging and Human Development, 38,* 181–202.

Norton, A. J., & Moorman, J. E. (1987). Current trends in marriage and divorce among American women. *Journal of Marriage and the Family, 49,* 3–14.

Nuland, S. B. (1993). *How we die: Reflections on life's final chapter.* New York: Knopf.

Nydegger, C. N. (1986). Asymmetrical kin and the problematic son-in-law. In N. Datan, A. L. Greene, & H. W. Reese (Eds.), *Life-span developmental psychology: Intergenerational relations* (pp. 99–124). Hillsdale, NJ: Erlbaum.

O'Brien, S. J., & Vertinsky, P. A. (1991). Unfit survivors: Exercise as a resource for aging women. *The Gerontologist, 31,* 347–357.

Ochs, A. L., Newberry, J., Lenhardt, M. L., & Harkins, S. W. (1985). Neural and vestibular aging associated with falls. In J. E. Birren & K. W. Schaie (Eds.), *Handbook of the psychology of aging* (2nd ed., pp. 378–399). New York: Van Nostrand Reinhold.

O'Connor, M., Verfaellie, M., & Cermak, L. S. (1995). Clinical differentiation of amnesic subtypes. In A. D. Baddeley, B. A. Wilson, & F. N. Watts (Eds.), *Handbook of memory disorders* (pp. 53–80). Chichester, England: Wiley.

O'Donohue, W. T. (1987). The sexual behavior and problems of the elderly. In L. L. Carstensen & B. A. Edelstein (Eds.), *Handbook of clinical gerontology* (pp. 66–75). New York: Pergamon Press.

Offerman, L. R., & Growing, M. K. (1990). Organizations of the future: Changes and challenges. *American Psychologist, 45,* 95–108.

O'Hanlon, A. M. (1993). *Inter-individual patterns of intellectual change: The influence of environmental factors.* Unpublished doctoral dissertation, The Pennsylvania State University.

Ohta, R. J. (1981). Spatial problem-solving: The response selection tendencies of young and elderly adults. *Experimental Aging Research, 7,* 81–84.

Ohta, R. J., & Kirasic, K. C. (1983). The investigation of environmental learning in the elderly. In G. Rowles & R. J. Ohta (Eds.), *Aging and milieu* (pp. 83–95). New York: Academic Press.

Ohta, R. J., Walsh, D. A., & Krauss, I. K. (1981). Spatial perspective-taking ability in young and elderly adults. *Experimental Aging Research, 7,* 45–63.

O'Leary, K. D. (1993). Through a psychological lens: Personality traits, personality disorders, and levels of violence. In R. J. Gelles & D. R. Loseke (Eds.), *Current controversies on family violence* (pp. 7–30). Newbury Park, CA: Sage Publications.

O'Leary, K. D., Barling, J., Arias, I., Rosenbaum, A., Malone, J., & Tyree, A. (1989). Prevalence and stability of physical aggression between spouses: A longitudinal analysis. *Journal of Consulting and Clinical Psychology, 57,* 263–268.

Olian, J. D., Carroll, S. J., Giannantonia, C. M., & Feren, D. B. (1988). What do proteges look for in a mentor? Results from three experimental studies. *Journal of Vocational Behavior, 33,* 15–37.

Olsho, L. W., Harkins, S. W., & Lenhardt, M. L. (1985). Aging and the auditory system. In J. E. Birren & K. W. Schaie (Eds.), *Handbook of the psychology of aging* (2nd ed., pp. 332–377). New York: Van Nostrand Reinhold.

Olson, D. H., & McCubbin, H. (1983). *Families: What makes them work.* Beverly Hills, CA: Sage Publications.

Orr, R., & Luszcz, M. (1994). Rethinking women's ways of knowing: Gender commonalities and intersections with postformal thought. *Journal of Adult Development, 1,* 225–233.

Ortner, S. (1984). Is female to male as nature is to culture? In M. Z. Rosaldo & L. Lamphere (Eds.), *Women, culture, and society* (pp. 67–88). Stanford, CA: Stanford University Press.

Ortner, S. B. (1978). *Sherpas through their rituals.* New York: Cambridge University Press.

Orwoll, L., & Perlmutter, M. (1990). The study of wise persons: Integrating a personality perspective. In R. J. Sternberg (Ed.), *Wisdom: Its nature, origins, and development* (pp. 160–177). Cambridge, UK: Cambridge University Press.

Osgood, N. J. (1985). *Suicide in the elderly.* Rockville, MD: Aspen.

Ostrow, A. C. (1980). Physical activity as it relates to the health of the aged. In N. Datan & N. Lohman (Eds.), *Transitions of aging* (pp. 41–56). New York: Academic Press.

Overstall, P. W., Johnson, A. L., & Exton-Smith, A. N. (1978). Instability and falls in the elderly. *Age and Ageing, 7 (Supplement 6),* 92–96.

Owen, G., Fulton, R., & Markusen, E. (1982). Death at a distance: A study of family survivors. *Omega, 13,* 191–225.

Paffenbarger, R. S., Hyde, R. T., Wing, A. L., & Hsieh, C. (1986). Physical activity, all cause mortality and longevity of college alumni. *New England Journal of Medicine, 314,* 605–613.

Palmore, E. (1975). *The honorable elders: A cross-cultural analysis of aging in Japan.* Durham, NC: Duke University Press.

Palmore, E., & Maeda, D. (1985). *The honorable elders revisited.* Durham, NC: Duke University Press.

Panek, P. E., Barrett, G. V., Sterns, H. L., & Alexander, R. A. (1977). A review of age changes in perceptual information processing ability with regard to driving. *Experimental Aging Research, 3,* 387–449.

Panek, P. E., & Reardon, J. R. (1986). *Age and gender effects on accident types for rural drivers.* Paper presented at the meeting of the Gerontological Society of America, Chicago.

Panek, P. E., & Sterns, H. L. (1985). Self-evaluation, actual performance, and preference across the life-span. *Experimental Aging Research, 11,* 221–223.

Papalia, D. E. (1972). The status of several conservation abilities across the life-span. *Human Development, 15,* 229–243.

Papalia, D. E., & Bielby, D. (1974). Cognitive functioning in middle and old age adults: A review of research based on Piaget's theory. *Human Development, 17,* 424–443.

Papalia, D. E., Salverson, S. M., & True, M. (1973). An evaluation of quantity conservation performance during old age. *International Journal of Aging and Human Development, 4,* 103–109.

Papalia-Finley, D. E., Blackburn, J., Davis, E., Dellmann, M., & Roberts, P. (1980). Training cognitive functioning in the elderly—Inability to replicate previous findings. *International Journal of Aging and Human Development, 12,* 111–117.

Parasuraman, R. (1987, November). *Aging and sustained attention.* Paper presented at the National Institute on Aging Conference on Aging and Attention, Washington, DC.

Parasuraman, R., & Giambra, L. (1991). Skill development in vigilance: Effects of event rate and age. *Psychology and Aging, 6,* 155–169.

Parasuraman, R., Nestor, P., & Greenwood, P. (1989). Sustained-attention capacity in young and older adults. *Psychology and Aging, 4,* 339–345.

Pargament, K. I. (1990). God help me: Toward a theoretical framework of coping for the psychology of religion. *Research in the Social Scientific Study of Religion, 2,* 195–224.

Pargament, K. I., Ensing, D. S., Falgout, K., Olsen, H., Reilly, B., Van Haitsma, K., & Warren, R. (1990). God help me (I): Religious coping efforts as predictors of the outcomes to significant negative life events. *American Journal of Community Psychology, 18,* 793–824.

Pargament, K. I., Olsen, H., Reilly, B., Falgout, K., Ensing, D., & Van Haitsma, K. (1992). God help me (II): The relationship of religious orientations to religious coping with negative life events. *Journal of the Scientific Study of Religion, 31,* 504–513.

Park, D. C., Cherry, K. E., Smith, A.D., & Lafronza, V.N. (1990). Effects of distinctive context on memory for objects and their locations in young and elderly adults. *Psychology and Aging, 5,* 250–255.

Park, D. C., Morrell, R. W., Frieske, D. A., Blackburn, A. B., & Birchmore, D. (1991). Cognitive factors and the use of over-the-counter medication organizers by arthritis patients. *Human Factors, 33,* 57–67.

Park, D., Morrell, R. W., Frieske, D., & Kincaid, D. (1992). Medication adherence behaviors in older adults: Effects of external cognitive supports. *Psychology and Aging, 7,* 252–256.

Park, D. C., Puglisi, J. T., & Smith, A. D. (1986). Memory for pictures: Does an age-related decline exist? *Psychology and Aging, 1,* 11–17.

Park, D. C., Puglisi, J. T., & Sovacool, M. (1983). Memory for pictures, words, and spatial location in older adults: Evidence for pictorial superiority. *Journal of Gerontology, 38,* 582–588.

Park, D. C., Puglisi, J. T., & Sovacool, M. (1984). Picture memory in older adults: Effects of contextual detail at encoding and retrieval. *Journal of Gerontology, 39,* 213–215.

Park, D. C., Royal, D., Dudley, W., & Morrell, R. (1988). Forgetting of pictures over a long retention interval in young and older adults. *Psychology and Aging, 3,* 94–95.

Park, D. C., Smith, A. D., Lautenschlager, G., Earles, J., Frieske, D., Zwahr, M., & Gaines, C. (1994, April). *Mediation of long-term memory performance across the life span.* Paper presented at the Cognitive Aging Conference, Atlanta.

Parkes, C. M. (1972). *Bereavement.* New York: International Universities Press.

Parkes, C. M. (1975). Determinants of outcome following bereavement. *Omega: Journal of Death and Dying, 6,* 303–323.

Parmelee, P. A., & Lawton, M. P. (1990). The design of special environments for the aged. In J. E. Birren & K. W. Schaie (Eds.), *Handbook of the psychology of aging* (3rd ed., pp. 464–488). San Diego: Academic Press.

Pascual-Leone, J. (1990). Essay on wisdom: Toward organismic processes that make it possible. In R. J. Sternberg (Ed.), *Wisdom: Its nature, origins, and development* (pp. 244–278). Cambridge, UK: Cambridge University Press.

Pasley, K., & Ihinger-Tallman, M. (1987). *Remarriage and stepparenting.* New York: Guilford.

Passuth, P. M., & Bengtson, V. L. (1988). Sociological theories of aging: Current perspectives and future directions. In J. E. Birren & V. L. Bengtson (Eds.), *Emergent theories of aging* (pp. 333–355). New York: Springer.

Pastalan, L. A. (1982). Research in environment and aging: An alternative to theory. In M. P. Lawton, P. G. Windley, & T. O. Byerts (Eds.), *Aging and the environment: Theoretical approaches* (pp. 122–131). New York: Springer.

Patel, V. L., & Groen, G. J. (1986). Knowledge based solution strategies in medical reasoning. *Cognitive Science, 10,* 91–116.

Patterson, C. J. (1995). Lesbian mothers, gay fathers, and their children. In A. R. D'Augelli & C. J. Patterson (Eds.), *Lesbian, gay, and bisexual identities over the lifespan* (pp. 262–290). New York: Oxford University Press.

Pattison, E. M. (1977a). The dying experience—Retrospective analysis. In E. M. Pattison (Ed.), *The experience of dying* (pp. 303–315). Englewood Cliffs, NJ: Prentice-Hall.

Pattison, E. M. (Ed.). (1977b). *The experience of dying.* Englewood Cliffs, NJ: Prentice-Hall.

Pauls, J. (1985). Review of stair safety research with an emphasis on Canadian studies. *Ergonomics, 28,* 999–1010.

Pearlin, L. I., & Johnson, J. (1977). Marital status, life strains, and depression. *American Sociological Review, 42,* 704–715.

Pearlman, J., Stotsky, B. A., & Dominick, J. R. (1969). Attitudes toward death among nursing home personnel. *Journal of Genetic Psychology, 114,* 63–75.

Peele, S. (1984). The cultural context of psychological approaches to alcoholism: Can we control the effects of alcohol? *American Psychologist, 39,* 1337–1351.

Peplau, L., & Gordon, S. L. (1985). Women and men in love: Sex differences in close heterosexual relationships. In V. O'Leary, R. K. Unger, & B. S. Wallston (Eds.), *Women, gender, and social psychology* (pp. 257–292). Hillsdale, NJ: Erlbaum.

Pepper, S. C. (1942). *World hypotheses.* Berkeley, CA: University of California Press.

Perfect, T. J. (1994). What can Brinley plots tell us about cognitive aging? *Journal of Gerontology: Psychological Sciences, 49,* P60–P64.

Perkins, H. W., & Harris, L. B. (1990). Familial bereavement and health in adult life course perspective. *Journal of Marriage and the Family, 52,* 233–241.

Perlmuter, L. C., & Monty, R. A. (1989). Motivation and aging. In L. W. Poon, D. C. Rubin, & B. Wilson (Eds.), *Everyday cognition in adulthood and late life* (pp. 373–393). Cambridge: Cambridge University Press.

Perlmutter, M. (1978). What is memory aging the aging of? *Developmental Psychology, 14,* 330–345.

Perlmutter, M., Adams, C., Berry, J., Kaplan, M., Person, D., & Verdonik, F. (1987). Aging and memory. In K. W. Schaie (Ed.), *Annual review of gerontology and geriatrics* (Vol. 7, pp. 57–92). New York: Springer.

Perlmutter, M., Metzger, R., Miller, R., & Nezworski, T. (1980). Memory for historical events. *Experimental Aging Research, 6,* 47–60.

Perry, W. I. (1970). *Forms of intellectual and ethical development in the college years.* New York: Holt, Rinehart & Winston.

Pershagen, G., Hrubec, Z., & Svensson, C. (1987). Passive smoking and lung cancer in Swedish women. *American Journal of Epidemiology, 125,* 17–24.

Peterson, B. E., & Klohnen, E. C. (1995). Realization of generativity in two samples of women at midlife. *Psychology and Aging, 10,* 20–29.

Peterson, J. T. (1990). Sibling exchanges and complementarity in the Philippine highlands. *Journal of Marriage and the Family, 52,* 441–451.

Peterson, J. W. (1990). Age of wisdom: Elderly Black women in family and church. In J. Sokolovsky (Ed.), *The cultural context of aging* (pp. 213–227). New York: Bergin & Garvey.

Pezdek, K. (1983). Memory for items and their spatial locations by young and elderly adults. *Developmental Psychology, 19,* 895–900.

Pfost, K. S., & Fiore, M. (1990). Pursuit of nontraditional occupations: Fear of success or fear of not being chosen? *Sex Roles, 23,* 15–24.

Phillis, D. E., & Stein, P. J. (1983). Sink or swing? The lifestyles of single adults. In E. R. Allgeier & N. B. McCormick (Eds.), *Changing boundaries: Gender roles and sexual behavior* (pp. 202–225). Palo Alto, CA: Mayfield.

Piaget, J. (1970). Piaget's theory. In P. H. Mussen (Ed.), *Carmichael's manual of child psychology: Vol. 1* (3rd ed., pp. 703–732). New York: Wiley.

Piaget, J. (1972). Intellectual evolution from adolescence to adulthood. *Human Development, 15,* 1–12.

Pillemer, K. (1993). The abused offspring are dependent. In R. J. Gelles & D. R. Loseke (Eds.), *Current controversies on family violence* (pp. 237–249). Newbury Park, CA: Sage.

Pillemer, K., & Moore, D. W. (1989). Abuse of patients in nursing homes: Findings from a survey of staff. *The Gerontologist, 29,* 314–320.

Pillemer, K., & Suitor, J. J. (1992). Violence and violent feelings: What causes them among family caregivers? *Journal of Gerontology: Social Sciences, 47,* S165–S172.

Pincus, L. (1976). *Death and the family: The importance of mourning.* New York: Pantheon.

Pino, C. J., Rosica, C. M., & Carter, T. J. (1978). The differential effects of relocation on nursing home patients. *The Gerontologist, 18,* 167–172.

Plath, D. W. (1980). *Long engagements: Maturity in modern Japan.* Stanford, CA: Stanford University Press.

Plude, D. J. (1986, August). *Age and visual search for features vs. conjunctions.* Paper presented at the meeting of the American Psychological Association, Washington, DC.

Plude, D. J., & Doussard-Roosevelt, J. A. (1989). Aging, selective attention, and feature integration. *Psychology and Aging, 4,* 98–105.

Plude, D. J., & Doussard-Roosevelt, J. A. (1990). Aging and attention: Selectivity, capacity, and arousal. In E. A. Lovelace (Ed.), *Aging and cognition: Mental processes, self-awareness, and interventions* (pp. 97–133). Amsterdam: North-Holland.

Plude, D. J., & Hoyer, W. J. (1981). Adult age differences in visual search as a function of stimulus mapping and processing level. *Journal of Gerontology, 36,* 598–604.

Plude, D. J., & Hoyer, W. J. (1985). Attention and performance: Identifying and localizing age deficits. In N. Charness (Ed.), *Aging and human performance* (pp. 47–99). Chichester, England: Wiley.

Plude, D. J., Murphy, L. J., & Gabriel-Byrne, J. (1989, August). *Aging, divided attention, and visual search.* Paper presented at the meeting of the American Psychological Association, New Orleans.

Polit, D. (1984). The only child in single-parent families. In T. Falbo (Ed.), *The single-child family* (pp. 178–210). New York: Guilford.

Pollack, R. D., Overton, W. F., Rosenfeld, A., & Rosenfeld, R. (1995). Formal reasoning in late adulthood: The role of semantic content and metacognitive strategy. *Journal of Adult Development, 2,* 1–14.

Ponzio, F., Calderini, G., Lomuscio, G., Vantini, G., Toffano, G., & Algeri, S. (1982). Changes in monoamines and their metabolite levels in some brain regions of aged rats. *Neurobiology of Aging, 3,* 23–29.

Poon, L. W. (1985). Differences in human memory with aging: Nature, causes, and clinical implications. In J. E. Birren & K. W. Schaie (Eds.), *Handbook of the psychology of aging* (2nd ed., pp. 427–462). New York: Academic Press.

Poon, L. W. (Ed.). (1986). *Handbook for the clinical memory assessment of older adults.* Washington, DC: American Psychological Association.

Poon, L. W., & Fozard, J. L. (1980). Age and word frequency effects in continuous recognition memory. *Journal of Gerontology, 35,* 77–86.

Poon, L. W., Gurland, B. J., Eisdorfer, C., Crook, T. H., Thompson, L. W., Kaszniak, A. W., & Davis, K. L. (1986). Integration of experimental and clinical precepts in memory assessments: A tribute to George Talland. In L. W. Poon (Ed.), *Handbook for clinical memory assessment of older adults* (pp. 3–10). Washington, DC: American Psychological Association.

Poon, L. W., & Schaffer, G. (1982). *Prospective memory in young and elderly adults.* Paper presented at the meeting of the American Psychological Association, Washington, DC.

Pope, A. M., & Tarlov, A. R. (Eds.). (1991). *Disability in America: Toward a national agenda for prevention* (pp. 309–327). Washington, DC: National Academy Press.

Popkin, S. J., Gallagher, D., Thompson, L. W., & Moore, M. (1982). Memory complaint and performance in normal and depressed older adults. *Experimental Aging Research, 8,* 141–145.

Posner, J. D., Gorman, K. M., Gitlin, L. N., Sands, L. P., Kleban, M., Windsor, L., & Shaw, C. (1990). Effects of exercise training in the elderly on the occurrence and time to onset of cardiovascular diagnoses. *Journal of the American Geriatrics Association, 38,* 205–210.

Posner, M. I., & Boies, S. J. (1971). Components of attention. *Psychological Review, 78,* 391–408.

Post, F., (1987). Paranoid and schizophrenic disorders among the aging. In L. L. Carstensen & B. A. Edelstein (Eds.), *Handbook of clinical gerontology* (pp. 43–56). New York: Pergamon Press.

Pratt, O. E. (1980). The fetal alcohol syndrome: Transport of nutrients and transfer of alcohol and acetaldehyde from mother to fetus. In M. Sandler (Ed.), *Psychopharmacology of alcohol* (pp. 229–258). New York: Raven.

Pratt, O. E. (1982). Alcohol and the developing fetus. *British Medical Bulletin, 38,* 48–52.

Price, D. L., Whitehouse, P. J., Struble, R. G., Clark, A. W., Coyle, J. T., DeLong, M. R., & Hedreen, J. C. (1982). Basal forebrain cholinergic systems in Alzheimer's disease and related dementias. *Neuroscience Commentaries, 1,* 84–92.

Price, J. G. (1991). Great expectations: Hallmark of the midlife woman learner. *Educational Gerontology, 17,* 167–174.

Prinz, P. N., & Raskind, M. (1978). Aging and sleep disorders. In R. Williams & I. Karacan (Eds.), *Sleep disorders: Diagnosis and treatment* (pp. 303–322). New York: Wiley.

Protinsky, H., & Hughston, G. (1978). Conservation in elderly males: An empirical investigation. *Developmental Psychology, 14,* 114.

Pruchno, R. A., Moss, M. S., Burant, C. J., & Schinfeld, S. (1995). Death of an institutionalized parent: Predictors of bereavement. *Omega, 31,* 99–119.

Pruchno, R. A., & Resch, N. L. (1988). Intrainstitutional relocation: Mortality effects. *The Gerontologist, 28,* 311–317.

Puder, R., Lacks, P., Bertelson, A. D., & Storandt, M. (1983). Short-term stimulus control treatment of insomnia in older adults. *Behavior Therapy, 14,* 424–429.

Puglisi, J. T., & Park, D. C. (1987). Perceptual elaboration and memory in older adults. *Journal of Gerontology, 42,* 160–162.

Quadagno, J. (1982). *Aging in early industrial society: Work, family and social policy in nineteenth century England.* New York: Academic Press.

Quayhagen, M. P., & Quayhagen, M. (1988). Alzheimer's stress: Coping with the caregiving role. *The Gerontologist, 28,* 391–396.

Quigley, M. W. (1979, June 19). Executive corps: Free advice pays off for both sides. *Newsday,* 9.

Quinn, J. F., & Burkhauser, R. V. (1990). Work and retirement. In R. H. Binstock & L. K. George (Eds.), *Handbook of aging and the social sciences* (pp. 303–327). New York: Academic Press.

Quinn, R. P., & Staines, G. L. (1979). *The 1977 quality of employment survey.* Ann Arbor: Institute for Social Research, University of Michigan.

Rabbitt, P. (1977). Changes in problem solving ability in old age. In J. E. Birren & K. W. Schaie (Eds.), *Handbook of the psychology of aging* (pp. 606–625). New York: Van Nostrand Reinhold.

Rabinowitz, J. C., Ackerman, B. P., Craik, F. I. M., & Hinchley, J. L. (1982). Aging and metamemory: The roles of relatedness and imagery. *Journal of Gerontology, 37,* 688–695.

Rabinowitz, J. C., Craik, F. I. M., & Ackerman, B. P. (1982). A processing resource account of age differences in recall. *Canadian Journal of Psychology, 36,* 325–344.

Rabins, P. V. (1992). Schizophrenia and psychotic states. In J. E. Birren, R. B. Sloane, & G. D. Cohen (Eds.), *Handbook of mental health and aging* (2nd ed., pp. 463–475).

Rackoff, N. S., & Mourant, R. R. (1979). Driving performance of the elderly. *Accident Analysis and Prevention, 11,* 247–253.

Raeburn, P. (1995, November 7). Genetic trait may delay Alzheimer's. *News Journal* (Wilmington, DE), p. A3.

Ragland, O. R., & Brand, R. J. (1988). Type A behavior and mortality from coronary heart disease. *New England Journal of Medicine, 318,* 65–69.

Ragozin, A. S., Basham, R. B., Crnic, K. A., Greenberg, M. T., & Robinson, N. M. (1982). Effects of maternal age on parenting role. *Developmental Psychology, 18,* 627–634.

Rahman, O., Strauss, J., Gertler, P., Ashley, D., & Fox, K. (1994). Gender differences in adult health: An international comparison. *The Gerontologist, 34,* 463–469.

Ramig, L. A., & Ringel, R. L. (1983). Effects of physiological aging on selected acoustic characteristics of voice. *Journal of Speech and Hearing Research, 26,* 22–30.

Raphael, B. (1983). *The anatomy of bereavement.* New York: Basic Books.

Rapoport, R., & Rapoport, R. N. (1975). *Leisure and the family life cycle.* London: Routledge and Kegan Paul.

Raskind, M. A., & Peskind, E. R. (1992). Alzheimer's disease and other dementing disorders. In J. E. Birren, R. B. Sloane, & G. D. Cohen (Eds.), *Handbook of mental health and aging* (2nd ed., pp. 477–513). San Diego: Academic Press.

Rawlins, W. K. (1992). *Friendship matters.* Hawthorne, NY: Aldine de Gruyter.

Redmore, C. D., & Loevinger, J. (1979). Ego development in adolescence: Longitudinal studies. *Journal of Youth and Adolescence, 8,* 129–134.

Reed, D., Satariano, W. A., Gildengorin, G., McMahon, K., Fleshman, R., & Schneider, E. (1995). Health and functioning among the elderly of Marin County, California: A glimpse of the future. *Journal of Gerontology: Medical Sciences, 50A,* M61–M69.

Reedy, M. N., Birren, J. E., & Schaie, K. W. (1981). Age and sex differences in satisfying love relationships across the adult life span. *Human Development, 24,* 52–66.

Reese, H. W., & Rodeheaver, D. (1985). Problem solving and complex decision making. In J. E. Birren & K. W. Schaie (Eds.), *Handbook of the psychology of aging* (2nd ed., pp. 474–499). New York: Van Nostrand Reinhold.

Register, J. C. (1981). Aging and race: A Black-White comparative analysis. *The Gerontologist, 21,* 438–443.

Regnier, V. (1983). Urban neighborhood cognition: Relationships between functional and symbolic community elements. In G. D. Rowles & R. J. Ohta (Eds.), *Aging and milieu: Environmental perspectives on growing old* (pp. 63–82). New York: Academic Press.

Reinke, B. J., Holmes, D. S., & Harris, R. L. (1985). The timing of psychosocial change in women's lives: The years 25 to 45. *Journal of Personality and Social Psychology, 48,* 1353–1364.

Reisberg, B., Ferris, S. H., Anand, R., de Leon, M. J., Schneck, M. K., & Crook, T. H. (1985). Clinical assessment of cognitive decline in normal aging and primary degenerative dementia: Concordant ordinal measures. In P. Pinchot, P. Berner, R. Wolf, & K. Thau (Eds.), *Psychiatry* (Vol. 5, pp. 333–338). New York: Plenum.

Reisberg, B., Ferris, S. H., Borenstein, J., Sinaiko, E., de Leon, M. J., & Buttinger, C. (1986). Assessment of presenting symptoms. In L. W. Poon (Ed.), *Handbook for clinical memory assessment of older adults* (pp. 108–128). Washington, DC: American Psychological Association.

Reisberg, B., Ferris, S. H., de Leon, M. J., & Crook, T. H. (1982). The global deterioration scale for assessment of primary degenerative dementia. *American Journal of Psychiatry, 139,* 1136–1139.

Reynolds, C. F., Kupfer, D. J., Taska, L. S., Hoch, C. C., Sewitch, D. E., & Spiker, D. G. (1985). Sleep of healthy seniors: A revisit. *Sleep, 8,* 20–29.

Reynolds, D. K., & Kalish, R. A. (1974). Anticipation of futurity as a function of ethnicity and age. *Journal of Gerontology, 29,* 224–231.

Rhyne, D. (1981). Basis of marital satisfaction among men and women. *Journal of Marriage and the Family, 43,* 941–955.

Rice, D. M., Buchsbaum, M. S., Hardy, D., & Burgwald, L. (1991). Focal left temporal slow EEG activity is related to verbal recent memory deficit in a non-demented elderly population. *Journal of Gerontology: Psychological Sciences, 46,* P144–P151.

Rice, E. H., Sombrotto, L. B., Markowitz, J. C., & Leon, A. C. (1994). Cardiovascular morbidity in high-risk patients during ECT. *American Journal of Psychiatry, 151,* 1637–1641.

Rice, G. E., & Meyer, B. J. F. (1985). Reading behavior and prose recall performance of young and older adults with high and average verbal ability. *Educational Gerontology, 11,* 57–72.

Rice, G. E., & Okun, M. A. (1994). Older readers' processing of medical information that contradicts their beliefs. *Journal of Gerontology: Psychological Sciences, 49,* P119–P128.

Richards, O. W. (1977). Effects of luminance and contrast on visual acuity, ages 16 to 90 years. *American Journal of Optometry and Physiological Optics, 54,* 178–184.

Richardson, V., & Kilty, K. M. (1989). Retirement financial planning among black professionals. *The Gerontologist, 29,* 32–37.

Riedel, B. W., Lichstein, K. L., & Dwyer, W. O. (1995). Sleep compression and sleep education for older insomniacs: Self-help versus therapist guidance. *Psychology and Aging, 10,* 54–63.

Riegel, K. F. (1973). Dialectic operations: The final period of cognitive development. *Human Development, 16,* 371–381.

Riegel, K. F. (1976). The dialectics of human development. *American Psychologist, 31,* 689–700.

Riggs, D. S., & O'Leary, K. D. (1992). *Violence between dating partners: Background and situational correlates of courtship aggression.* Unpublished manuscript, State University of New York, Stony Brook.

Rikli, R., & Busch, S. (1986). Motor performance of women as a function of age and physical activity level. *Journal of Gerontology, 41,* 645–649.

Riley, M. W. (1979). Introduction. In M. W. Riley (Ed.), *Aging from birth to death: Interdisciplinary perspectives* (pp. 3–14). Boulder, CO: Westview.

Riley, M. W., & Foner, A. (1968). *Aging and society: An inventory of research findings.* New York: Russell Sage Foundation.

Riley, V. (1981). Psychoneuroendocrine influences on immunocompetence and neoplasia. *Science, 212,* 1100–1109.

Rindfuss, R. R., & Stephen, E. H. (1990). Marital noncohabitation: Separation does not make the heart grow fonder. *Journal of Marriage and the Family, 52,* 259–270.

Ritzer, G. (1977). *Working: Conflict and change* (2nd ed.). Englewood Cliffs, NJ: Prentice-Hall.

Roach, M. (1985). *Another name for madness.* New York: Houghton Mifflin.

Roberto, K. A., & Scott, J. P. (1986). Equity considerations in the friendships of older adults. *Journal of Gerontology, 41,* 241–247.

Roberts, J. D. (1980). *Roots of a black future: Family and church.* Philadelphia: Westminster.

Roberts, P., & Newton, P. M. (1987). Levinsonian studies of women's adult development. *Psychology and Aging, 2,* 154–163.

Roberts, R. E. (1987). An epidemiological perspective on the mental health of people of Mexican origin. In R. Rodriguez & M. T. Coleman (Eds.), *Mental health issues of the Mexican origin population in Texas* (pp. 55–70). Austin, TX: Hogg Foundation for Mental Health.

Robertson, J. F. (1976). Significance of grandparents: Perceptions of young adult grandchildren. *The Gerontologist, 16,* 137–140.

Robertson, J. F. (1977). Grandmotherhood: A study of role concepts. *Journal of Marriage and the Family, 39,* 165–174.

Robinson, B., & Thurnher, M. (1979). Taking care of aged parents: A family cycle transition. *The Gerontologist, 19,* 586–593.

Robinson, J. K. (1983). Skin problems of aging. *Geriatrics, 38,* 57–65.

Rockstein, M., & Sussman, M. (1979). *Biology of aging.* Belmont, CA: Wadsworth.

Rodeheaver, D., & Datan, N. (1988). The challenge of double jeopardy: Toward a mental health agenda for aging women. *American Psychologist, 43,* 648–654.

Rodeheaver, D., & Thomas, J. L. (1986). Family and community networks in Appalachia. In N. Datan, A. L. Greene, & H. W. Reese (Eds.), *Life-span developmental psychology: Intergenerational relations* (pp. 77–98). Hillsdale, NJ: Erlbaum.

Rodin, J., & Langer, E. J. (1977). Long-term effects of a control–relevant intervention with the institutionalized aged. *Journal of Personality and Social Psychology, 35,* 897–902.

Rodin, J., McAvay, G., & Timko, C. (1988). A longitudinal study of depressed mood and sleep disturbances in elderly adults. *Journal of Gerontology, 43,* P45–P53.

Rogers, A., Watkins, J. F., & Woodward, J. A. (1990). Interregional elderly migration and population redistribution in four industrialized countries: A comparative analysis. *Research on Aging, 12,* 251–293.

Rogers, C. S., & Levitin, P. M. (1987). Osteoarthritis. In C. S. Rogers, J. D. McCue, & P. Gal (Eds.), *Managing chronic disease* (pp. 299–305). Oradell, NJ: Medical Economics Press.

Rogers, J., & Bloom, F. E. (1985). Neurotransmitter metabolism and function in the aging central nervous system. In C. E. Finch & E. L. Schneider (Eds.), *Handbook of the biology of aging* (2nd ed., pp. 645–691). New York: Van Nostrand Reinhold.

Rogers, W. A., Bertus, E. L., & Gilbert, D. K. (1994). Dual-task assessment of age differences in automatic process development. *Psychology and Aging, 9,* 398–413.

Roper Organization. (1980). *The 1980 Virginia Slims American women's opinion poll.* Storrs: Roper Center, University of Connecticut.

Rosenberg, E. B. (1992). *The adoption life cycle.* Lexington, MA: Lexington Books.

Rosenthal, C., & Marshall, V. (1988). Generational transmission of family ritual. *American Behavioral Scientist, 31,* 669–684.

Rosenthal, M. J., & Goodwin, J. S. (1985). Cognitive effects of nutritional deficiency. In H. H. Draper (Ed.), *Advances in nutritional research* (Vol. 7, pp. 71–100). New York: Plenum.

Rosin, H. M., & Korabik, K. (1990). Marital and family correlates of women managers' attrition from organizations. *Journal of Vocational Behavior, 37,* 104–120.

Rosin, H. M., & Korabik, K. (1991). Workplace variables, affective responses, and intention to leave among women managers. *Journal of Occupational Psychology, 64,* 317–330.

Rosow, I. (1967). *Social integration of the aged.* New York: Free Press.

Rosow, I. (1985). Status and role change through the life cycle. In R. H. Binstock & E. Shanas (Eds.), *Handbook of aging and the social sciences* (2nd ed., pp. 62–93). New York: Van Nostrand Reinhold.

Ross, J. K. (1977). *Old people, new lives.* Chicago: University of Chicago Press.

Rossi, A. S. (1980). Aging and parenthood in the middle years. In P. B. Baltes & O. G. Brim, Jr. (Eds.), *Life-span development and behavior* (Vol. 3, pp. 137–205). New York: Academic Press.

Roth, W. F. (1991). *Work and rewards: Redefining our work-life reality.* New York: Praeger.

Rowe, J. W., & Kahn, R. L. (1987). Human aging: Usual and successful. *Science, 237,* 143–149.

Rowles, G. D. (1980). Growing old "inside": Aging and attachment to place in an Appalachian community. In N. Datan & N. Lohman (Eds.), *Transitions of aging* (pp. 153–170). New York: Academic Press.

Rowles, G. D. (1983). Geographical dimensions of social support in rural Appalachia. In G. D. Rowles & R. J. Ohta (Eds.), *Aging and milieu: Environmental perspectives on growing old* (pp. 111–130). New York: Academic Press.

Rowles, G. D., & Ohta, R. J. (1983). Emergent themes and new directions: Reflections on aging and milieu research. In G. D. Rowles & R. J. Ohta (Eds.), *Aging and milieu: Environmental perspectives on growing old* (pp. 231–240). New York: Academic Press.

Royce, A. P. (1982). *Ethnic identity: Strategies of diversity.* Bloomington: Indiana University Press.

Rubenfeld, M. I., & Gilroy, F. D. (1991). Relationship between college women's occupational interests and a single-sex environment. *Career Development Quarterly, 40,* 64–70.

Rubin, D. C., & Kozin, M. (1984). Vivid memories. *Cognition, 16,* 81–95.

Rubinstein, R. L. (1987). Never-married elderly as a social type: Reevaluating some images. *The Gerontologist, 27,* 108–113.

Rudzitis, G. (1984). Geographical research and gerontology: An overview. *The Gerontologist, 24,* 536–542.

Russo, R., & Parkin, A. J. (1993). Age differences in implicit memory: More apparent than real. *Memory and Cognition, 21,* 73–80.

Ryan, C. (1982). Alcoholism and premature aging: A neuropsychological perspective. *Alcoholism: Clinical and Experimental Research, 6,* 22–30.

Ryan, E. B., Giles, H., Bartolucci, G., & Henwood, K. (1986). Psycholinguistic and social psychological components of communication by and with the elderly. *Language and Communication, 6,* 1–24.

Ryan, E. B., Hamilton, J. M., & See, S. K. (1993). Patronizing the old: How do younger and older adults respond to baby talk in the nursing home? *International Journal of Aging and Human Development, 41,* 89–107.

Ryan, E. B., Meredith, S. D., MacLean, M. J., & Orange, J. B. (1995). Changing the way we talk with elders: Promoting health using the Communication Enhancement Model. *International Journal of Aging and Human Development, 41,* 89–107.

Rybash, J. M., Hoyer, W. J., & Roodin, P. A. (1986). *Adult cognition and aging.* New York: Pergamon.

Ryckman, R. M., & Malikioski, M. (1975). Relationship between locus of control and chronological age. *Psychological Reports, 36,* 655–658.

Ryff, C. D. (1989). Happiness is everything, or is it? Explorations on the meaning of psychological well-being. *Journal of Personality and Social Psychology, 57,* 1069–1081.

Ryff, C. D. (1991). Possible selves in adulthood and old age: A tale of shifting horizons. *Psychology and Aging, 6,* 286–295.

Ryff, C. D., & Essex, M. J. (1992). The interpretation of life experience and well-being: The sample case of relocation. *Psychology and Aging, 7,* 507–517.

Ryff, C. D., Lee, Y. H., Essex, M. J., & Schmutte, P. S. (1994). My children and me: Mid-life evaluations of grown children and of self. *Psychology and Aging, 9,* 195–205.

Rykken, D. E. (1987). Sex in the later years. In P. Silverman (Ed.), *The elderly as modern pioneers* (pp. 125–144). Bloomington: Indiana University Press.

Sadavoy, J., & Fogel, B. (1992). Personality disorders in old age. In J. E. Birren, R. B. Sloane, & G. D. Cohen (Eds.), *Handbook of mental health and aging* (2nd ed., pp. 433–462). San Diego: Academic Press.

Safilios-Rothschild, C. (1977). *Love, sex, and sex roles.* Englewood Cliffs, NJ: Prentice-Hall.

Salamon, S. (1982). Sibling solidarity as an operating strategy in Illinois agriculture. *Rural Sociology, 47,* 349–368.

Salthouse, T. A. (1984). Effects of age and skill in typing. *Journal of Experimental Psychology: General, 113,* 345–371.

Salthouse, T. A. (1985). Speed of behavior and its implications for cognition. In J. E. Birren & K. W. Schaie (Eds.), *Handbook of the psychology of aging* (2nd ed., pp. 400–426). New York: Van Nostrand Reinhold.

Salthouse, T. A. (1988). The role of processing resources in cognitive aging. In M. L. Howe & C. J. Brainerd (Eds.), *Cognitive development in adulthood* (pp. 185–239). New York: Springer-Verlag.

Salthouse, T. A., (1991). *Theoretical perspectives on cognitive aging.* Hillsdale, NJ: Erlbaum.

Salthouse, T. A., (1991, August). *Status of working memory as a mediator of adult age differences in cognition.* Invited address presented at the American Psychological Association, San Francisco.

Salthouse, T. A. (1992). *Mechanisms of age-cognition relations in adulthood.* Hillsdale, NJ: Erlbaum.

Salthouse, T. A. (1994). The aging of working memory. *Neuropsychology, 8,* 535–543.

Salthouse, T. A., & Babcock, R. L. (1991). Decomposing adult age differences in working memory. *Developmental Psychology, 27,* 763–776.

Salthouse, T. A., Kausler, D. H., & Saults, J. S. (1988). Utilization of path analytic procedures to investigate the role of processing resources in cognitive aging. *Psychology and Aging, 3,* 158–166.

Salthouse, T. A., & Somberg, B. L. (1982). Isolating the age deficit in speeded performance. *Journal of Gerontology, 37,* 59–63.

Salzman, C. (1975). Electroconvulsive therapy. In R. Shader (Ed.), *Manual of psychiatric therapeutics* (pp. 115–124). Boston: Little, Brown.

Salzman, C. (1984). *Clinical geriatric psychopharmacology.* New York: McGraw-Hill.

Salzman, C., & Shader, R. I. (1979). Clinical evaluation of depression in the elderly. In A. Raskin & L. F. Jarvik (Eds.), *Psychiatric symptoms and cognitive loss in the elderly* (pp. 39–72). Washington, DC: Hemisphere.

Samet, J., Hunt, W., & Key, C. (1986). Choice of cancer therapy varies with age of patient. *Journal of the American Medical Association, 255,* 3385–3390.

Sanders, C. M. (1980–81). Comparison of younger and older spouses in bereavement outcome. *Omega: Journal of Death and Dying, 11,* 217–232.

Sandler, D. P., Everson, R. B., & Wilcox, A. J. (1985). Passive smoking in adulthood and cancer risk. *American Journal of Epidemiology, 121,* 37–48.

Sands, L. P., & Meredith, W. (1992). Blood pressure and intellectual functioning in late midlife. *Journal of Gerontology: Psychological Sciences, 47,* P81–P84.

Sangree, W. (1989). Age and power: Life course trajectories and age structuring of power relations in East and West Africa. In D. Kertzer & K. W. Schaie (Eds.), *Age structuring in comparative perspective* (pp. 23–46). New York: Springer.

Sanjek, R. (1984). *Crowded out: Homelessness and the elderly poor in New York City.* New York: Coalition for the Homeless.

Saunders, C. (1977). Dying they live: St. Christopher's Hospice. In H. Feifel (Ed.), *New meanings of death* (pp. 153–179). New York: McGraw-Hill.

Schacter, D. L. (1987). Implicit memory: History and current status. *Journal of Experimental Psychology: Learning, Memory, and Cognition, 13,* 501–518.

Schacter, D. L, Harbluk, J. L., & McLachlan, D. R. (1987). Retrieval without recollection: An experimental analysis of source amnesia. *Journal of Verbal Learning and Verbal Behavior, 23,* 593–611.

Schachter, S. (1982). Recidivism and self-cure of smoking and obesity. *American Psychologist, 37,* 436–444.

Schaie, K. W. (1965). A general model for the study of developmental change. *Psychological Bulletin, 64,* 92–107.

Schaie, K. W. (1977). Quasi-Experimental designs in the psychology of aging. In J. E. Birren & K. W. Schaie (Eds.), *Handbook of the psychology of aging* (pp. 38–58). New York: Van Nostrand Reinhold.

Schaie, K. W. (1977–78). Toward a stage theory of adult cognitive development. *International Journal of Aging and Human Development, 8,* 129–138.

Schaie, K. W. (1983). The Seattle longitudinal study: A twenty-one year exploration of psychometric intelligence in adulthood. In K. W. Schaie (Ed.), *Longitudinal studies of adult psychological development* (pp. 64–155). New York: Guilford.

Schaie, K. W. (1984). Historical time and cohort effects. In K. A. McCluskey & H. W. Reese (Eds.), *Life-span developmental psychology: Historical and generational effects* (pp. 1–45). New York: Academic Press.

Schaie, K. W. (1990). Intellectual development in adulthood. In J. E. Birren & K. W. Schaie (Eds.), *Handbook of the psychology of aging* (3rd ed., pp. 291–309). San Diego: Academic Press.

Schaie, K. W. (1995). *Intellectual development in adulthood: The Seattle longitudinal study.* New York: Cambridge University Press.

Schaie, K. W. (1996). Intellectual functioning in adulthood. In J. E. Birren & K. W. Schaie (Eds.), *Handbook of the psychology of aging* (4th ed., pp. 266–286). San Diego: Academic Press.

Schaie, K. W., & Hertzog, C. (1983). Fourteen-year cohort-sequential studies of adult intelligence. *Developmental Psychology, 19,* 531–543.

Schaie, K. W., & Hertzog, C. (1985). Measurement in the psychology of adulthood and aging. In J. E. Birren & K. W Schaie (Eds.), *Handbook of the psychology of aging* (2nd ed., pp. 61–92). New York: Van Nostrand Reinhold.

Schaie, K. W., Orchowsky, S., & Parham, I. A. (1982). Measuring age and sociocultural change: The case of race and life satisfaction. In R. C. Manuel (Ed.), *Minority aging, sociological and social psychological issues* (pp. 223–230). Westport, CT: Greenwood.

Schaie, K. W., Plomin, R., Willis, S. L., Gruber-Baldini, A., & Dutta, R. (1992). Natural cohorts: Family similarity in adult cognition. In T. Sonderegger (Ed.), *Psychology and aging: Nebraska symposium on motivation, 1991* (pp. 205–243). Lincoln: University of Nebraska Press.

Schaie, K. W., & Strother, C. R. (1968). A cross-sequential study of age changes in cognitive behavior. *Psychological Bulletin, 70,* 671–680.

Schaie, K. W., & Willis, S. L. (1986). Can decline in adult intellectual functioning be reversed? *Developmental Psychology, 22,* 223–232.

Schaie, K. W., Willis, S. L., & O'Hanlon, A. M. (1994). Perceived intellectual performance change over seven years. *Journal of Gerontology: Psychological Sciences, 49,* P108–P118.

Scheibel, A. B. (1982). Age-related changes in the human forebrain. *Neurosciences Research Progress Bulletin, 20,* 577–583.

Scheidt, R. J., & Schaie, K. W. (1978). A situational taxonomy for the elderly: Generating situational criteria. *Journal of Gerontology, 33,* 848–857.

Schiedt, R. J., & Windley, P. G. (1985). The ecology of aging. In J. E. Birren & K. W. Schaie (Eds.), *Handbook of the psychology of aging* (2nd ed., pp. 245–258).

Schermerhorn, R. A. (1970). *Comparative ethnic relations: A framework for theory and research.* Chicago: University of Chicago Press.

Schiffman, S., & Covey, E. (1984) Changes in taste and smell with age: Nutritional aspects. In J. M. Ordy, D. Harman, & R. B. Alfin-Slater (Eds.), *Aging: Vol. 26. Nutrition in gerontology* (pp. 43–64). New York: Ravin.

Schmitt, F. A., Murphy, M. D., & Sanders, R. E. (1981). Training older adults free recall rehearsal strategies. *Journal of Gerontology, 36,* 329–337.

Schneider, E. L., & Reed, J. D. (1985). Modulations of aging processes. In C. E. Finch & E. L. Schneider (Eds.) *Handbook of the biology of aging* (2nd ed., pp. 45–76). New York: Van Nostrand Reinhold.

Schneider, L. S. (1995). Efficacy of clinical treatment for mental disorders among older persons. In M. Gatz (Ed.), *Emerging issues in mental health and aging* (pp. 19–71). Washington, DC: American Psychological Association.

Schneider, M. S. (1986). The relationship of cohabiting lesbian and heterosexual couples: A comparison. *Psychology of Women Quarterly, 10,* 234–239.

Schooler, K. K. (1982). Response of the elderly to environment: A stress-theoretical perspective. In M. P. Lawton, P. G. Windley, & T. O. Byerts (Eds.), *Aging and the environment: Theoretical approaches* (pp. 80–96). New York: Springer.

Schuknecht, H. (1974). *Pathology of the ear.* Cambridge, MA: Harvard University Press.

Schultz, N. W. (1980). A cognitive-developmental study of the grandchild-grandparent bond. *Child Study Journal, 10,* 7–26.

Schulz, R. (1978). *The psychology of death, dying and bereavement.* Reading, MA: Addison-Wesley.

Schulz, R. (1985). Emotion and affect. In J. E. Birren & K. W. Schaie (Eds.), *Handbook of the psychology of aging* (2nd ed., pp. 531–543). New York: Van Nostrand Reinhold.

Schulz, R., & Hanusa, B. H. (1978). Long-term effects of control and predictability enhancing interventions: Findings and ethical issues. *Journal of Personality and Social Psychology, 35,* 1194–1201.

Schulz, R., & Hanusa, B. H. (1979). Environmental influences on the effectiveness of control- and competence-enhancing interventions. In L. C. Perlmuter & R. A. Monty (Eds.), *Choice and perceived control* (pp. 315–337). Hillsdale, NJ: Erlbaum.

Schulz, R., Tompkins, C. A., & Rau, M. T. (1988). A longitudinal study of the psychosocial impact of stroke on primary support persons. *Psychology and Aging, 3,* 131–141.

Schwab, D. P., & Heneman, H. G., III. (1977). Age and satisfaction with dimensions of work. *Journal of Vocational Behavior, 10,* 212–222.

Scialfa, C. T., Guzy, L. T., Leibowitz, H. W., Garvey, P. M., & Tyrrell, R. A. (1991). Age differences in estimating vehicle velocity. *Psychology and Aging, 6,* 60–66.

Scott, R. B., & Mitchell, M. C. (1988). Aging, alcohol, and the liver. *Journal of the American Geriatrics Society, 36,* 255–265.

Scozarro, P. P., & Subich, L. M. (1990). Gender and occupational sex-type differences in job outcome factor perceptions. *Journal of Vocational Behavior, 36,* 109–119.

Sears, P. S., & Barbee, A. H. (1978). Career and life satisfaction among Terman's gifted women. In J. C. Stanley, W. C. George, & C. H. Solano (Eds.), *The gifted and the creative: Fifty year perspective* (pp. 28–66). Baltimore: Johns Hopkins University Press.

Seltzer, J. A. (1991). Relationships between fathers and children who live apart: The father's role after separation. *Journal of Marriage and the Family, 53,* 79–102.

Seltzer, M. M., & Karnes, J. (1988). An early retirement incentive program: A case study of Dracula and Pinocchio complexes. *Research on Aging, 10,* 342–357.

Sendbeuhler, J. M., & Goldstein, S. (1977). Attempted suicide among the aged. *Journal of the American Geriatrics Society, 25,* 245–248.

Shainess, N. (1984). *Sweet suffering: Woman as victim.* Indianapolis: Bobbs-Merrill.

Shanas, E. (1972). Adjustment to retirement. In F. M. Carp. (Ed.), *Retirement* (pp. 219–244). Berkeley, CA: Behavioral Publications.

Shand, A. E. (1920). *The foundations of character.* London: Macmillan.

Shapiro, D. H. (1985). Meditation and behavioral medicine: Application of a self-regulation strategy to the clinical management of stress. In S. R. Burchfield (Ed.), *Stress: Psychological and physiological interactions* (pp. 307–328). Washington, DC: Hemisphere.

Sheehy, G. (1976). *Passages.* New York: Dutton.

Sheehy, G. (1981). *Pathfinders.* New York: Morrow.

Sheehy, G. (1995). *New passages: Mapping your life across time.* New York: Random House.

Shekelle, R. B., Gale, M., & Norusis, M. (1985). Type A score (Jenkins Activity Survey) and risk of recurrent heart disease in the aspirin myocardial infarction study. *American Journal of Cardiology, 56,* 221–225.

Shelton, B. A., & John, D. (1993). Ethnicity, race, and difference: A comparison of white, black, and Hispanic men's household labor time. In J. C. Hood (Ed.), *Men, work, and family* (pp. 131–150). Newbury Park, CA: Sage.

Shephard, R. J. (1978). *Physical activity and aging.* Chicago: Yearbook Medical.

Shephard, R. J. (1981). Cardiovascular limitations in the aged. In E. L. Smith & R. C. Serfass (Eds.), *Exercise and aging: The scientific basis* (pp. 19–30). Hillsdale, NJ: Erlbaum.

Shephard, R. J. (1982). *Physiology and biochemistry of exercise.* New York: Praeger.

Sheppard, H. L. (1976). Work and retirement. In R. H. Binstock & E. Shanas (Eds.), *Handbook of aging and the social sciences* (2nd ed., pp. 286–309). New York: Van Nostrand Reinhold.

Sherrington, R., Rogaev, E. I., Liang, Y., Rogaeva, E. A., Levesque, G., Ikeda, M., Chi, H., Lin, C., Li, G., Holman, K., Tsuda, T., Mar, L., Foncin, J.-F., Bruni, A. C., Montesi, M. P., Sorbi, S., Rainero, I., Pinessi, L., Nee, L., Chumakov, I., Pollen, D., Brookes, A., Sanseau, P., Polinsky, R. J., Wasco, W., Da Silva, H. A. R., Haines, J. L., Pericak-Vance, M. A., Tanzi, R. E., Roses, A. D., Fraser, P. E., Rommens, J. M., & St. George-Hyslop, P. H. (1995). Cloning of a gene bearing missense mutations in early-onset familial Alzheimer's disease. *Nature, 375,* 754–760.

Sherwood, S., Ruchlin, H. S., & Sherwood, C. C. (1989). CCRCs: An option for aging in place. In D. Tillson & C. J. Fahey (Eds.), *Support of the frail elderly in residential environments.* Glenview, IL: Scott Foresman.

Shield, R. R. (1988). *Uneasy endings: Daily life in an American nursing home.* Ithaca, NY: Cornell University Press.

Shimamura, A. P. (1986). Priming effects in amnesia: Evidence for a dissociable memory function. *Quarterly Journal of Experimental Psychology, 38A,* 619–644.

Shimamura, A. P., Berry, J. M., Mangels, J. A., Rusting, C. L., & Jurica, P. J. (1995). Memory and cognitive abilities in university professors: Evidence for successful aging. *Psychological Science, 6,* 271–277.

Shinar, D., McDowell, E. D., Rackoff, N. J., & Rockwell, T. H. (1978). Field dependence and driver visual search behavior. *Human Factors, 20,* 553–559.

Shirom, A., & Mazeh, T. (1988). Periodicity in seniority-job satisfaction relationship. *Journal of Vocational Behavior, 33,* 38–49.

Shneidman, E. S. (1973). *Deaths of man.* New York: Quadrangle/New York Times.

Shock, N. W. (1977). Biological theories of aging. In J. E. Birren & K. W. Schaie (Eds.), *Handbook of the psychology of aging* (pp. 103–115). New York: Van Nostrand Reinhold.

Siedler, H., & Malamud, N. (1963). Creutzfeld-Jakob disease: Clinicopathologic report of 15 cases and review of the literature. *Journal of Neuropathology and Experimental Neurology, 22,* 381–402.

Siegel, J. M. (1990). Stressful life events and use of physician services among the elderly: The moderating effect of pet ownership. *Journal of Personality and Social Psychology, 58,* 1081–1086.

Siegel, R. K. (1980). The psychology of life after death. *American Psychologist, 35,* 911–931.

Siegler, I. C., & Gatz, M. (1985). Age patterns in locus of control. In E. Palmore, E. Bosse, G. Maddox, J. Nowlin, & I. C. Siegler (Eds.), *Normal aging 3* (pp. 259–267). Durham, NC: Duke University Press.

Siegler, I. C., George, L. K., & Okun, M. A. (1979). A cross-sequential analysis of adult personality. *Developmental Psychology, 15,* 350–351.

Silverman, P. (1987). Community settings. In P. Silverman (Ed.), *The elderly as modern pioneers* (pp. 185–210). Bloomington: Indiana University Press.

Simmons, L. W. (1945). *Role of the aged in primitive society.* New Haven, CT: Yale University Press.

Simons, A. D., McGowan, C. R., Epstein, L. H., Kupfer, D. J., & Robertson, R. J. (1985). Exercise as a treatment for depression: An update. *Clinical Psychology Review, 5,* 553–568.

Simonton, D. K. (1990). Creativity and wisdom in aging. In J. E. Birren & K. W. Schaie (Eds.), *Handbook of the psychology of aging* (3rd ed., pp. 320–329). San Diego: Academic Press.

Singleton, W. T. (1979). Safety and risk. In W. T. Singleton (Ed.), *The study of real skills: Vol. 2. Compliance and excellence* (pp. 137–156). Baltimore: University Park Press.

Sinnott, J. D. (1984a). *Everyday memory and solution of everyday problems.* Paper presented at the meeting of the American Psychological Association, Toronto.

Sinnott, J. D. (1984b). Postformal reasoning: The relativistic stage. In M. L. Commons, F. A. Richards, & C. Armon (Eds.), *Beyond formal operations: Late adolescent and adult cognitive development* (pp. 298–325). New York: Praeger.

Sinnott, J. D. (1986). Sex roles and aging: Theory and research from a systems perspective. *Contributions to human development* (Vol. 15). New York: Karger.

Sinnott, J. D. (1994a). New science models for teaching adults: Teaching as a dialogue with reality. In J. D. Sinnott (Ed.), *Interdisciplinary handbook of adult lifespan learning* (pp. 90–104). Westport, CT: Greenwood Press.

Sinnott, J. D. (1994b). The relationship of postformal thought, adult learning, and lifespan development. In J. D. Sinnott (Ed.), *Interdisciplinary handbook of adult lifespan learning* (pp. 105–119). Westport, CT: Greenwood Press.

Sinnott, J. D. (1994c). The future of adult lifespan learning: Learning institutions face change. In J. D. Sinnott (Ed.), *Interdisciplinary handbook of adult lifespan learning* (pp. 449–465). Westport, CT: Greenwood Press.

Sivak, M., & Olson, P. L. (1982). Nighttime legibility of traffic signs: Conditions eliminating the effects of driver age and disability glare. *Accident Analysis and Prevention, 14,* 87–93.

Sivak, M., Olson, P. L., & Pastalan, L. A. (1981). Effect of driver's age on nighttime legibility of highway signs. *Human Factors, 23,* 59–64.

Sjogren, T., Sjogren, H., & Lindgren, A. G. H. (1952). Morbus Alzheimer and morbus Pick. *Acta Psychiatrica Scandinavica, 82(Suppl.),* 68–108.

Slivinske, L. R., & Fitch, V. L. (1987). The effect of control enhancing intervention on the well-being of elderly individuals living in retirement communities. *The Gerontologist, 27,* 176–181.

Small, B. J., Hultsch, D. F., & Masson, M. E. J. (1995). Adult age differences in perceptually based, but not conceptually based implicit tests of memory. *Journal of Gerontology: Psychological Sciences, 50B,* P162–P170.

Smallegan, M. (1989). Level of depressive symptoms and life stresses for culturally diverse older adults. *The Gerontologist, 29,* 45–50.

Smith, A. D. (1975). Aging and interference with memory. *Journal of Gerontology, 30,* 319–325.

Smith, A. D. (1977). Adult age differences in cued recall. *Developmental Psychology, 13,* 326–331.

Smith, A. D. (1995). Memory. In J. E. Birren & K. W. Schaie (Eds.), *Handbook of the psychology of aging* (4th ed., pp. 236–250). San Diego: Academic Press.

Smith, A. D., & Park, D. C. (1990). Adult age differences in memory for pictures and images. In E. A. Lovelace (Ed.), *Aging and cognition: Mental processes, self-awareness, and interventions* (pp. 69–96). Amsterdam: North-Holland.

Smith, D. B. D. (1990). Human factors and aging: An overview of research needs and application opportunities. *Human Factors, 32,* 509–526.

Smith, E. L., & Serfass, R. C. (Eds.). (1981). *Exercise and aging: The scientific basis.* Hillsdale, NJ: Erlbaum.

Smith, J., & Baltes, P. B. (1990). Wisdom-related knowledge: Age/cohort differences in responses to life-planning problems. *Developmental Psychology, 26,* 494–505.

Smith, M., Colligan, M., Horning, R. W., & Hurrell, J. (1978). *Occupational comparison of stress-related disease incidence.* Cincinnati: National Institute for Occupational Safety and Health.

Smith, S. W., Rebok, G. W., Smith, W. R., Hall, S. E., & Alvin, M. (1983). Adult age differences in the use of story structure in delayed free recall. *Experimental Aging Research, 9,* 191–195.

Snyder, C. J., & Barrett, G. V. (1988). The Age Discrimination in Employment Act: A review of court decisions. *Experimental Aging Research, 14,* 3–47.

Sokolovsky, J. (1990). Bringing culture back home: Aging, ethnicity, and family support. In J. Sokolovsky (Ed.), *The cultural context of aging* (pp. 201–211). New York: Bergin & Garvey.

Sokolovsky, J., & Cohen, C. (1983). The cultural meaning of being a "loner" among the inner-city elderly. In J. Sokolovsky (ed.), *Growing old in different societies* (pp. 189–201). Belmont, CA: Wadsworth.

Soldatos, C. R., Kales, J. D., Scharf, M. B., Bixler, E. O., & Kales, A. (1980). Cigarette smoking associated with sleep difficulty. *Science, 207,* 551–553.

Solnick, R. L., & Corby, N. (1983). Human sexuality and aging. In D. S. Woodruff & J. E. Birren (Eds.), *Aging: Scientific perspectives and social issues* (2nd ed., pp. 202–224). Pacific Grove, CA: Brooks/ Cole.

Somberg, B. L., & Salthouse, T. A. (1982). Divided attention abilities in young and old adults. *Journal of Experimental Psychology: Human Perception and Performance, 8,* 651–663.

Somers, A. R. (1987). Insurance for long-term care: Some definitions, problems, and guidelines for action. *New England Journal of Medicine, 317,* 23–29.

Sontag, S. (1972, September 23). The double standard of aging. *Saturday Review,* pp. 29–38.

Spasoff, R. A., Kraus, A. S., Beattie, E. J., Holden, D. E. W., Lawson, J. S., Rodenburg, M., & Woodcock, G. M. (1978). Longitudinal study of elderly residents of long-stay institutions 1: Early response to institutional care. *The Gerontologist, 18,* 281–292.

Spayd, C. S., & Smyer, M. A. (1988). Interventions with agitated, disoriented, or depressed residents. In M. A. Smyer, M. D. Cohn, & D. Brannon (Eds.), *Mental health consultation in nursing homes* (pp. 123–141). New York: New York University Press.

Speare, A., Jr., Avery, R., & Lawton, L. (1991). Disability, residential mobility, and changes in living arrangements. *Journal of Gerontology: Social Sciences, 46,* S133–S142.

Speare, A., Jr., & Meyer, J. W. (1988). Types of elderly residential mobility and their determinants. *Journal of Gerontology, 43,* S74–S81.

Spilich, G. J. (1985). Discourse comprehension across the life span. In N. Charness (Ed.), *Aging and human performance* (pp. 143–190). Chichester, England: Wiley.

Spirduso, W. W. (1980). Physical fitness, aging, and psychomotor speed: A review. *Journal of Gerontology, 35,* 850–865.

Spirduso, W. W., & MacRae, P. G. (1990). Motor performance and aging. In J. E. Birren & K. W. Schaie (Eds.), *Handbook of the psychology of aging* (3rd ed., pp. 183–200). San Diego: Academic Press.

Spitze, G., Logan, J. R., Joseph, G., & Lee, E. (1994). Middle generation roles and the well-being of men and women. *Journal of Gerontology: Social Sciences, 49,* S107–S116.

Spitzer, M. E. (1988). Taste acuity in institutionalized and noninstitutionalized elderly men. *Journal of Gerontology, 43,* P71–P74.

Spitzer, R. L., Endicott, J., & Robins, E. (1978). Research Diagnostic Criteria: Rationale and reliability. *Archives of General Psychiatry, 35,* 773–782.

Spokane, A. R. (1985). A review of research on person-environment congruence in Holland's theory of careers. *Journal of Vocational Behavior, 26,* 306–343.

Sporakowski, M. J., & Axelson, L. J. (1984). Long-term marriages: A critical review. *Lifestyles: A Journal of Changing Patterns, 7*(2), 76–93.

Stanford, E. P., & DuBois, B. C. (1992). Gender and ethnicity patterns. In J. E. Birren, R. B. Sloane, & G. D. Cohen (Eds.), *Handbook of mental health and aging* (2nd ed., pp. 99–117). San Diego: Academic Press.

Stanford, E. P., Happersett, C. J., Morton, D. J., Molgaard, C. A., & Peddecord, K. M. (1991). Early retirement and functional impairment from a multi-ethnic perspective. *Research on Aging, 13,* 5–38.

Stanford, E. P., & Lockery, S. A. (1984). Aging and social relations in the black community. In W. H. Quinn & G. A. Hughston (Eds.), *Independent aging: Family and social systems perspectives* (pp. 164–181). Rockville, MD: Aspen.

Stanford, J. L., Weiss, N. S., Voigt, L. F., Daling, J. R., Habel, L. A., & Rossing, M. A. (1995). Combined estrogen and progestin hormone replacement therapy in relation to risk of breast cancer in middle-aged women. *Journal of the American Medical Association, 274,* 137–142.

Stark, E. (1992, May). *From dependency to empowerment: Framing and reframing the battered woman.* Paper presented at the Second Annual Conference: Domestic Violence: The Family/Community Connection, State University of New York Division of Nursing, Stony Brook, NY.

Stein, P. (1978). The lifestyles and life changes and the never married. *Marriage and Family Review, 1,* 1–11.

Steinmetz, S. K. (1993). The abused elderly are dependent. In R. J. Gelles & D. R. Loseke (Eds.), *Current controversies on family violence* (pp. 222–236). Newbury Park, CA: Sage.

Stelmach, G. E., Amrhein, P. C., & Goggin, N. L. (1988). Age differences in bimanual coordination. *Journal of Gerontology: Psychological Sciences, 43,* P18–P23.

Stelmach, G. E., Goggin, N. L., & Garcia-Colera, A. (1987). Movement specification time with age. *Experimental Aging Research, 13,* 39–46.

Stenback, A. (1980). Depression and suicidal behavior in old age. In J. E. Birren & R. B. Sloane (Eds.), *Handbook of mental health and aging* (pp. 616–652). Englewood Cliffs, NJ: Prentice-Hall.

Stephens, J. (1976). *Loners, losers, and lovers.* Seattle: University of Washington Press.

Stephens, L. R. (Ed.). (1975). *Reality orientation* (rev. ed.). Washington, DC: American Psychiatric Association.

Stern, C., Prather, P., Swinney, D., & Zurif, E. (1991). The time course of automatic lexical access and aging. *Brain and Language, 40,* 359–372.

Sternberg, R. J. (1985). *Beyond IQ: A triarchic theory of human intelligence.* Cambridge: Cambridge University Press.

Sternberg, R. J. (1986). A triangular theory of love. *Psychological Review, 93,* 119–135.

Sternberg, R. J., Conway, B. E., Ketron, J. L., & Bernstein, M. (1981). People's conceptions of intelligence. *Journal of Personality and Social Psychology, 41,* 37–55.

Sterns, H. L., Barrett, G. V., Alexander, R. A., Valasek, D., Forbringer, L. R., & Avolio, B. J. (1978). *Training and evaluation of older adult skills critical for effective driving performance.* Final report prepared for the Andrus Foundation of the NRTA/AARP. Cited in Sterns et al. (1985).

Sterns, H. L., Barrett, G. V., Alexander, R. A., Valasek, D., & McIlvried, J. (1984). *Research to improve diagnostic testing and training of older drivers.* Interim report prepared for the Andrus Foundation of the NRTA/AARP. Cited in Sterns et al. (1985).

Sterns, H. L., & Sanders, R. E. (1980). Training and education of the elderly. In R. R. Turner & H. W. Reese (Eds.), *Life-span developmental psychology: Intervention* (pp. 307–330). New York: Academic Press.

Stevens, J. C., & Cain, W. S. (1985). Age-related deficiency in the perceived strength of six odorants. *Chemical Senses, 10,* 517–529.

Stevens, J. C., & Cain, W. S. (1986). Smelling via the mouth: Effect of aging. *Perception and Psychophysics, 40,* 142–146.

Stevens, J. C., & Cain, W. S. (1987). Old-age deficits in the sense of smell as gauged by thresholds, magnitude matching, and odor identification. *Psychology of Aging, 2,* 36–42.

Stevens-Long, J. (1988). *Adult life* (3rd ed.). Mountain View, CA: Mayfield.

Steward, R. J., & Krieshok, T. S. (1991). A cross-cultural study of vocational identity: Does a college education mean the same for all persisters? *Journal of College Student Development, 32,* 562–563.

Stigsdotter Neely, A., & Bäckman, L. (1993a). Maintenance of gains following multifactorial and unifactorial memory training in late adulthood. *Educational Gerontology, 19,* 105–117.

Stigsdotter Neely, A., & Bäckman, L. (1993b). Long-term maintenance of gains from memory training in older adults: Two 3½-year follow-up studies. *Journal of Gerontology: Psychological Sciences, 48,* P233–P237.

Stigsdotter Neely, A., & Bäckman, L. (1995). Effects of multifactorial memory training in old age: Generalizability across tasks and individuals. *Journal of Gerontology: Psychological Sciences, 50B,* P134–P140.

Stine, E. L. (1990). The way reading and listening work: A tutorial review of discourse processing and aging. In E. A. Lovelace (Ed.), *Aging and cognition: Mental processes, self-awareness, and interventions* (pp. 301–327). Amsterdam: North-Holland.

Stine, E. L., & Wingfield, A. (1987). Process and strategy in memory for speech among younger and older adults. *Psychology and Aging, 2,* 272–279.

Stine, E. L., Wingfield, A., & Poon, L. W. (1986). How much and how fast: Rapid processing of spoken language in later adulthood. *Psychology and Aging, 1,* 303–311.

Storandt, M., & Wittels, I. (1975). Maintenance of functioning in relocation of community-dwelling older adults. *Journal of Gerontology, 30,* 608–612.

Storandt, M., Wittels, I., & Botwinick, J. (1975). Predictors of a dimension of well-being in relocated healthy aged. *Journal of Gerontology, 30,* 97–102.

Storck, P. A., Looft, R., & Hooper, F. H. (1972). Interrelationships among Piagetian tasks and traditional measures of cognitive abilities in mature and aged adults. *Journal of Gerontology, 27,* 461–465.

Straus, M. A., Gelles, R. J., & Steinmetz, S. K. (1980). *Behind closed doors: Violence in the American family.* Garden City, NY: Anchor/Doubleday.

Strauss, A. L., & Glaser, B. G. (1970). *Anguish.* Mill Valley, CA: Sociology Press.

Strayer, D. L., & Kramer, A. F. (1994). Aging and skill acquisition: Learning-performance distinctions. *Psychology and Aging, 9,* 589–605.

Strayer, D. L., Wickens, C. D., & Braune, R. (1987). Adult age differences in the speed and capacity of information processing: 2. An electrophysiological approach. *Psychology and Aging, 2,* 99–110.

Streib, G. F., & Schneider, C. J. (1971). *Retirement in American society.* Ithaca, NY: Cornell University Press.

Stroebe, M. S., & Stroebe, W. (1983). Who suffers more? Sex differences in health risks of the widowed. *Psychological Bulletin, 93,* 279–301.

Suls, J., & Wills, T. A. (1991). *Social comparison: Contemporary theory and research.* Hillsdale, NJ: Erlbaum.

Surwillo, W. W., & Quilter, R. E. (1964). Vigilance, age, and response time. *American Journal of Psychology, 77,* 614–620.

Swanson, J. L. (1992). Vocational behavior, 1989–1991: Lifespan career development and reciprocal interaction or work and nonwork. *Journal of Vocational Behavior, 41,* 101–161.

Sweer, L., Martin, D. C., Ladd, R. A., Miller, J. K., & Karpf, M. (1988). The medical evaluation of elderly patients with major depression. *Journal of Gerontology, 43,* M53–M58.

Swenson, C. H., Eskew, R. W., & Kohlhepp, K. A. (1981). Stages of the family life cycle, ego development, and the marriage relationship. *Journal of Marriage and the Family, 43,* 841–853.

Swenson, C.H., & Trahaug, G. (1985). Commitment and the long-term marriage relationship. *Journal of Marriage and the Family, 47,* 939–945.

Taietz, P. (1975). Community complexity and knowledge of facilities. *Journal of Gerontology, 30,* 357–362.

Taietz, P., & Milton, S. (1979). Rural-urban differences in the structure of services for the elderly in upstate New York counties. *Journal of Gerontology, 34,* 429–437.

Talley, T., & Kaplan, J. (1956, December). The Negro aged. *Newsletter of the Gerontological Society, 6.*

Tanfer, K. (1987). Patterns of premarital cohabitation among never-married women in the United States. *Journal of Marriage and the Family, 49,* 483–497.

Tannen, D. (1990). *You just don't understand.* New York: Morrow.

Tanner, L. (1993, June 16). AIDS a leading killer of young adults. *The News Journal* (Wilmington, DE), p. A5.

Tate, N. (1983). The black aging experience. In R. McNeely & J. Colen (Eds.), *Aging in minority groups.* Beverly Hills, CA: Sage.

Taylor, R., & Chatters, L. (1986). Church-based informal supports. *The Gerontologist, 26,* 637–642.

Teachman, J. (1986). First and second marital dissolution: A decomposition exercise for whites and blacks. *Sociological Quarterly, 27,* 571–590.

Teaff, J.D., Lawton, M.P., Nahemow, L., & Carlson, D. (1978). Impact of age integration on well-being of elderly tenants in public housing. *Journal of Gerontology, 33,* 126–133.

Templer, D.I. (1972). Death anxiety in religiously very involved persons. *Psychological Reports, 31,* 361–362.

Templer, D., Ruff, C., & Franks, C. (1971). Death anxiety: Age, sex, and parental resemblance in diverse populations. *Developmental Psychology, 4,* 108–114.

Teri, L., Truax, P., Logsdon, R.G., Uomoto, J., & Zarit, S. (1990). *Assessment of behavioral problems in dementia: The Revised Memory and Behavior Problems Checklist.* Unpublished manuscript, University of Washington, Seattle.

Terkel, S. (1974). *Working.* New York: Pantheon.

Terpenning, M.S., & Bradley, S.F. (1991). Why aging leads to increased susceptibility to infection. *Geriatrics, 46*(2), 77–80.

Teski, M. (1981). *Living together: An ethnography of a retirement hotel.* Washington, DC: University Press of America.

Tetrick, L.E., Miles, R.L., Marcil, L., & Van Dosen, C.M. (1994). Child-care difficulties and the impact on concentration, stress, and productivity among single and nonsingle mothers and fathers. In G.P. Keita & J.J. Hurrell, Jr. (Eds.), *Job stress in a changing workforce* (pp. 229–239). Washington, DC: American Psychological Association.

Thal, L.J. (1988). Treatment strategies. In M. K. Aronson (Ed.), *Understanding Alzhei-*

mer's disease (pp. 50–66). New York: Scribner's.

Thomas, D.A. (1990). The impact of race on managers' experiences of developmental relationships (mentoring and sponsorship): An intra-organizational study. *Journal of Organizational Behavior, 11,* 479–492.

Thomas, G.S., & Rutledge, J.H. (1986). Fitness and exercise for the elderly. In K. Dychtwald (Ed.), *Wellness and health promotion for the elderly* (pp. 165–178). Rockville, MD: Aspen.

Thomas, J.L. (1985). Visual memory: Adult age differences in map recall and learning strategies. *Experimental Aging Research, 11,* 93–95.

Thomas, J.L. (1986a). Age and sex differences in perceptions of grandparenthood. *Journal of Gerontology, 41,* 417–423.

Thomas, J.L. (1986b). Gender differences in satisfaction with grandparenting. *Psychology and Aging, 1,* 215–219.

Thomas, J.L. (1988). Predictors of satisfaction with children's help for younger and older elderly parents. *Journal of Gerontology: Social Sciences, 43,* S9–S14.

Thomas, J.L., Bence, S.L., & Meyer, S.M. (1988, August). *Grandparenting satisfaction: The roles of relationship meaning and perceived responsibility.* Paper presented at the meeting of the American Psychological Association, Atlanta.

Thomas, P.D., Hunt, W.C., Garry, P.J., Hood, R.B., Goodwin, J.M., & Goodwin, J.S. (1983). Hearing acuity in a healthy elderly population: Effects on emotional, cognitive, and social status. *Journal of Gerontology, 38,* 321–325.

Thomas, V., & Striegel, P. (1994–95). Stress and grief of a perinatal loss: Integrating qualitative and quantitative methods. *Omega, 30,* 299–311.

Thompson, A.D. (1978). Alcohol and nutrition. *Clinics in Endocrinology and Metabolism, 7,* 405–428.

Thompson, I. (1994). Woldenburg Village: An illustration of supportive design for older adults. *Experimental Aging Research, 20,* 239–244.

Thompson, L., & Walker, A.J. (1989). Gender in families: Women and men in marriage, work, and parenthood. *Journal of Marriage and the Family, 51,* 845–871.

Thompson, L.W., & Gallagher, D. (1986). Treatment of depression in elderly outpatients. In G. Maletta & F.J. Pirozzolo (Eds.), *Advances in neurogerontology: Vol. 4. Assessment and treatment of the elderly patient* (pp. 151–173). New York: Praeger.

Thompson, L.W., Gallagher-Thompson, D., Futterman, A., Gilewski, M.J., & Peterson, J. (1991). The effects of late-life spousal bereavement over a 30-month interval. *Psychology and Aging, 6,* 434–441.

Thomson, E., & Colella, U. (1992). Cohabitation and marital stability: Quality or commitment? *Journal of Marriage and the Family, 54,* 259–267.

Thorne, A. (1989). Conditional patterns, transference, and the coherence of personality over time. In D.M. Buss & N. Cantor (Eds.), *Personality psychology: Recent trends and emerging directions* (pp. 149–159). New York: Springer-Verlag.

Thorne, A., & Klohnen, E. (1993). Interpersonal memories as maps for personality consistency. In D. Funder, R. Parke, C. Tomlinson-Keasey, & K. Widaman (Eds.), *Studying lives through time: Personality and development* (pp. 223–253). Washington, DC: American Psychological Association.

Thorson, J. A. (1995). *Aging in a changing society.* Belmont, CA: Wadsworth.

Thurstone, L.L. (1938). *Primary mental abilities.* Chicago: University of Chicago Press.

Tice, C.J., & Perkins, K. (1996). *Mental health issues and aging.* Pacific Grove, CA: Brooks/Cole.

Tice, R.R. (1987). Summary and discussion of Part V. In H.R. Warner, R.N. Butler, R.L. Sprott, & E.L. Schneider (Eds.), *Modern biological theories of aging* (pp. 211–215). New York: Raven Press.

Timiras, P. (1994). Cardiovascular alterations with age. In P. Timiras (Ed.), *Physiological basis of aging and geriatrics* (2nd ed., pp. 199–214). Boca Raton, FL: CRC Press.

Tobin, J.J. (1987). The American idealization of old age in Japan. *The Gerontologist, 27,* 53–58.

Tobin, S.S., & Lieberman, M.A. (1976). *Last home for the aged.* San Francisco: Jossey-Bass.

Toffler, A. (1970). *Future shock.* New York: Random House.

Tomlinson, B.E., Blessed, G., & Roth, M. (1970). Observations on the brains of demented old people. *Journal of the Neurological Sciences, 11,* 205–242.

Tomlinson-Keasey, C. (1972). Formal operations in females from eleven to fifty-four years of age. *Developmental Psychology, 6,* 364.

Tomporowski, P.D., & Ellis, N.R. (1986). Effects of exercise on cognitive processes: A review. *Psychological Bulletin, 99,* 338–346.

Treat, N.J., Poon, L.W., Fozard. J.L., & Popkin, S.J. (1978). Toward applying cognitive skill training to memory problems. *Experimental Aging Research, 4,* 305–319.

Treisman, A., & Gelade, G. (1980). A feature-integration theory of attention. *Cognitive Psychology, 12,* 97–136.

Troll, L.E. (1971). The family of later life: A decade review. *Journal of Marriage and the Family, 33,* 263–290.

Troll, L.E. (1975). *Early and middle adulthood: The best is yet to be—Maybe.* Pacific Grove, CA: Brooks/Cole.

Troll, L.E., & Bengtson, V. (1982). Intergenerational relations throughout the life span. In B.B. Wolman (Ed.), *Handbook of developmental psychology* (pp. 890–911). Englewood Cliffs, NJ: Prentice-Hall.

Trujillo, K.M., Walsh, D.M., & Brougham, R.R. (1991, June). *Age differences in exercise motivations.* Paper presented at the annual meeting of the American Psychological Society, Washington, DC.

Tucker, J.S., Friedman, H.S., Tsai, C.M., & Martin, L.R. (1995). Playing with pets and longevity among older people. *Psychology and Aging, 10,* 3–7.

Tun, P.A., & Wingfield, A. (1995). Does dividing attention become harder with age? Findings from the Divided Attention Questionnaire. *Aging and Cognition, 2,* 39–66.

Tuokko, H., Gallie, K.A., & Crockett, D.J. (1990). Patterns of deterioration in normal and memory impaired elderly. *Developmental Neuropsychology, 6,* 291–300.

Turner, B.F. (1982). Sex-related differences in aging. In B.B. Wolman (Ed.), *Handbook of developmental psychology* (pp. 912–936). Englewood Cliffs, NJ: Prentice-Hall.

Turner, B.F. (1987). Mental health and the older woman. In G. Lesnoff-Caravaglia (Ed.), *Handbook of applied gerontology* (pp. 201–230). New York: Human Sciences Press.

Turner, R.M., & Ascher, L.M. (1982). Therapist factor in the treatment of insomnia. *Behavior Research and Therapy, 17,* 107–112.

Udry, J.R. (1971). Marital alternatives and marital disruption. *Journal of Marriage and the Family, 43,* 889–897.

Uhlenberg, P. (1987). A demographic perspective on aging. In P. Silverman (Ed.), *The elderly as modern pioneers* (pp. 145–160). Bloomington: Indiana University Press.

Unger, R.K. (1979). *Female and male.* New York: Harper & Row.

United States Bureau of the Census. (1995). *Statistical abstract of the United States.* Washington, DC: Government Printing Office.

United States Bureau of the Census. (1991). *Statistical abstract of the United States.* Washington, DC: U.S. Government Printing Office.

United States Department of Health and Human Services. (1984). *The health consequences of smoking: Chronic obstructive lung disease* (DHHS Publication No. PHS-50205). Washington, DC: U.S. Government Printing Office.

United States Department of Health and Human Services. (1988). *Vital statistics of the United States, 1985: Vol. 2. Mortality* (Part A). Hyattsville, MD: Author.

United States Department of Health and Human Services. (1995). *Vital statistics of the United States, 1992: Vol. 2. Mortality* (Part A). Hyattsville, MD: Author.

United States Department of Labor. (1988). *Bureau of Labor Statistics.* Washington, DC: U.S. Government Printing Office.

United States Department of Labor. (1995). *Bureau of Labor Statistics Report.* Washington, DC: Author.

United States Department of Transportation. (1986). *1983–1984 Nationwide personal transportation study* (Vol. 11). Washington, DC: Author.

United States Office of Technology Assessment. (1984). *Technology and aging in America.* Washington, DC: U.S. Government Printing Office.

United States Public Health Service. (1993). From L. S. Schneider, Efficacy of treatment for geropsychiatric patients with severe mental illness. *Psychopharmacology Bulletin, 29,* 501–524.

United States Senate Special Committee on Aging. (1989). *Developments in aging: 1988.* Washington, DC: U.S. Government Printing Office.

Vaillant, G. E. (1977). *Adaptation to life.* Boston: Little, Brown.

Vaillant, G. E., & Vaillant, C. O. (1990). Natural history of male psychological health: 12. A 45-year study of predictors of successful aging. *American Journal of Psychiatry, 147,* 31–37.

VandenBos, G.R., DeLeon, P.H., & Pallack, M.S. (1982). An alternative to traditional medical care for the terminally ill. *American Psychologist, 37,* 1245–1248.

van Geert, P. (1987). The structure of Erikson's model of eight stages: A generative approach. *Human Development, 30,* 236–254.

Van Hoose, W.H., & Worth, M.R. (1982). *Adulthood in the life cycle.* Dubuque, IA: William C. Brown.

Van Maanen, J., & Schein, E.H. (1977). Career development. In R.J. Hackman & J.L. Suttle (Eds.), *Improving life at work* (pp. 30–95). New York: Goodyear.

Verbrugge, L.M. (1994). Disability in late life. In R.P. Abeles, H.C. Gift, & M.G. Ory (Eds.), *Aging and quality of life* (pp. 79–98). New York: Springer.

Verbrugge, L.M. (1995). New thinking and science on disability in mid- and late life. *European Journal of Public Health, 5,* 20–28.

Verbrugge, L.M., & Jette, A.M. (1994). The disablement process. *Social Science and Medicine, 38,* 1–14.

Verhaeghen, P., & Marcoen, A. (1994). Production deficiency hypothesis revisited: Adult age differences in strategy use as a function of processing resources. *Aging and Cognition, 1,* 323–338.

Verhaeghen, P., Marcoen, A., & Goossens, L. (1993). Facts and fiction about memory aging: A quantitative integration of research findings. *Journal of Gerontology: Psychological Sciences, 48,* P157–P171.

Vernon, S.W., & Roberts, R.E. (1982). Use of the SADS-RDS in a tri-ethnic community survey. *Archives of General Psychiatry, 39,* 47–52.

Verrillo, R.T., & Verrillo, V. (1985). Sensory and perceptual performance. In N. Charness (Ed.), *Aging and human performance* (pp. 1–46). Chichester, England: Wiley.

Verwoerdt, A. (1980). Anxiety, dissociative and personality disorders in the elderly. In E.W. Busse & D.G. Blazer (Eds.), *Handbook of geriatric psychiatry* (pp. 368–380). New York: Van Nostrand Reinhold.

Verwoerdt, A. (1981). *Clinical geropsychiatry* (2nd ed.). Baltimore: Williams & Wilkins.

Vickio, C.J., & Cavanaugh, J.C. (1985). Relationships among death anxiety, attitudes toward aging, and experience with death in nursing home employees. *Journal of Gerontology, 40,* 347–349.

Vickio, C.J., Cavanaugh, J.C., & Attig, T. (1990). Perceptions of grief among university students. *Death Studies, 14,* 231–240.

Vijg, J., & Papaconstantinou, J. (1990). EURAGE workshop report: Aging and longevity genes: Strategies for identifying DNS sequences controlling life span. *Journal of Gerontology, 45,* B179–B182.

Villa, R.F., & Jaime, A. (1993). La fé de la gente. In M. Sontomayor & A. Garcia (Eds.), *Elderly Latinos: Issues and solutions for the 21st century.* Washington, DC: National Hispanic Council on Aging.

Viney, L.L. (1987). A sociophenomenological approach to life-span development complementing Erikson's sociodynamic approach. *Human Development, 30,* 125–136.

Waddell, K.J., & Rogoff, B. (1981). Effect of contextual organization on spatial memory of middle-aged and older women. *Developmental Psychology, 17,* 878–885.

Wagenaar, W.A., & Groeneweg, J. (1990). The memory of concentration camp survivors. *Applied Cognitive Psychology, 4,* 77–87.

Walker, J.I., & Brodie, H.K.H. (1980). Neuropharmacology of aging. In E. W. Busse & D.G. Blazer (Eds.), *Handbook of geriatric psychiatry* (pp. 102–124). New York: Van Nostrand Reinhold.

Walker, L.E.A. (1984). *The battered woman syndrome.* New York: Springer.

Wall, P. D. (1975). Signs of plasticity and reconnection in spinal cord damage. In R. Porter & D. W. Fitzsimons (Eds.), *Outcome of severe damage to the central nervous system* (pp. 35–54). Amsterdam: Elsevier.

Wall, S., & Arden, H. (1990). *Wisdomkeepers: Meetings with Native American spiritual elders.* Hillsboro, OR: Beyond Words Publishing.

Wall, S. D., Brant-Zawadski, M., Jeffrey, R. B., & Barnes, B. (1981). High frequency CT findings within 24 hours after cerebral infarction. *American Journal of Neuroradiology, 2,* 553–557.

Wallace, A. F. C. (1971). Handsome Lake and the decline of the Iroquois matriarchate. In F. L. K. Hsu (Ed.), *Kinship and culture* (pp. 367–376). Chicago: Aldine-Atherton.

Wallace, J. (1985). Behavior modification methods as adjuncts to psychotherapy. In S. Zimberg, J. Wallace, & S. B. Blume (Eds.), *Practical approaches to alcoholism psychotherapy* (2nd ed., pp. 109–130). New York: Plenum.

Wallace, J. I., & Schwartz, R. S. (1994). Involuntary weight loss in the elderly. In R. R. Watson (Ed.), *Handbook of nutrition in the aged* (pp. 99–111). Boca Raton, FL: CRC Press.

Wallerstein, J. S., & Kelly, J. B. (1980). *Surviving the breakup: How children and parents cope with divorce.* New York: Basic Books.

Walsh, D. A., Krauss, I. K., & Regnier, V. A. (1981). Spatial ability, environmental knowledge, and environmental use: The elderly. In L. S Liben, A. H. Patterson, & N. Newcombe (Eds.), *Spatial representation and behavior across the lifespan,* (pp. 321–357). New York: Academic Press.

Walsh, E. K., & Cavanaugh, J. C. (1984, November). *Does hospice meet the needs of dying clients?* Paper presented at the meeting of the Gerontological Society of America, San Antonio.

Wanberg, C. R. (1995). A longitudinal study of the effects of unemployment and quality of reemployment. *Journal of Vocational Behavior, 46,* 40–54.

Wanberg, C. R., & Marchese, M. C. (1994). Heterogeneity in the unemployment experience: A cluster analytic investigation. *Journal of Applied Social Psychology, 24,* 473–488.

Wantz, M. S., & Gay, J. E. (1981). *The aging process: A health perspective.* Cambridge, MA: Winthrop.

Ward, R. A. (1984a). *The aging experience: An introduction to social gerontology* (2nd ed.). New York: Harper & Row.

Ward, R. A. (1984b). The marginality and salience of being old: When is age relevant? *The Gerontologist, 24,* 227–232.

Ward, R. A., & Kilburn, H. (1983). Community access and life satisfaction: Racial differences in later life. *International Journal of Aging and Human Development, 16,* 209–219.

Wattis, J. P. (1983). Alcohol and old people. *British Journal of Psychiatry, 143,* 306–307.

Wattis, J. P., & Seymour, J. (1994). Alcohol abuse in elderly people: Medical and psychiatric consequences. In R. R. Watson (Ed.), *Handbook of nutrition in the aged* (2nd ed., pp. 317–329). Boca Raton, FL: CRC Press.

Watts, F. N. (1995). Depression and anxiety. In A. D Baddeley, B. A. Wilson, & F. N. Watts (Eds.), *Handbook of memory disorders* (pp. 293–317). Chichester, England: Wiley.

Webb, W. B. (1975). *Sleep: The gentle tyrant.* New York: Spectrum.

Webb, W. B. (1982). Sleep in older persons: Sleep structures of 50- to 60-year-old men and women. *Journal of Gerontology, 37,* 581–586.

Webb, W. B., & Campbell, S. S. (1980). Awakenings and the return to sleep in an older population. *Sleep, 3,* 41–46.

Webb, W. B., & Levy, C. M. (1982). Age, sleep deprivation and performance. *Psychophysiology, 19,* 272–276.

Webb, W. B. & Swinburne, H. (1971). An observational study of sleep in the aged. *Perceptual and Motor Skills, 32,* 895–898.

Wechsler, D. (1958). *The measurement and appraisal of adult intelligence* (4th ed.). Baltimore: Williams & Wilkins.

Weg, R. B. (1983). The physiological perspective. In R. B. Weg (Ed.), *Sexuality in the later years* (pp. 39–80). New York: Academic Press.

Weibel-Orlando, J. (1990). Grandparenting styles: Native American perspectives. In J. Sokolovsky (Ed.), *The cultural context of aging* (pp. 109–125). New York: Bergin & Garvey.

Weiner, M. B. Brok, A. J., & Snadowski, A. M. (1987). *Working with the aged* (2nd ed.). Norwalk, CT: Appleton-Century-Crofts.

Weiner, R. D. (1979). The psychiatric use of electrically induced seizures. *American Journal of Psychiatry, 136,* 1507–1517.

Weingartner, H., Cohen, R. M., & Bunney, W. E. (1982). Memory-learning impairments in progressive dementia and depression. *American Journal of Psychiatry, 139,* 135–136.

Weingartner, H., & Silberman, E. (1982). Models of cognitive impairment: Cognitive changes in depression. *Psychopharmacology Bulletin, 18,* 27–42.

Weishaus, S., & Field, D. (1988). A half century of marriage: Continuity or change? *Journal of Marriage and the Family, 50,* 763–774.

Weisman, A. D. (1972). *On dying and denying.* New York: Behavioral Publications.

Weiss, R. S. (1975). *Marital separation.* New York: Basic Books.

Weitzman, L. J. (1985). *The divorce revolution: The unexpected social and economic consequences for women and children in America.* New York: Free Press.

Weksler, M. E. (1990). Protecting the aging immune system to prolong quality of life. *Geriatrics, 45*(7), 72–76.

Welch, D. C., & West, R. L. (1995). Self-efficacy and mastery: Its application to issues of environmental control, cognition, and aging. *Developmental Review, 15,* 150–171.

Welford, A.T. (1977). Motor performance. In J. E. Birren & K. W. Schaie (Eds.), *Handbook of the psychology of aging* (pp. 450–496). New York: Van Nostrand Reinhold.

Welford, A. T. (1988). Reaction time, speed of performance, and age. In J. A. Joseph (Ed.), *Central determinants of age-related declines in motor functioning* (pp. 1–17). New York: New York Academy of Sciences.

Wells, C. E. (1979). Pseudodementia. *American Journal of Psychiatry, 136,* 895–900.

Wells, L., & Macdonald, G. (1981). Interpersonal networks and post-relocation adjustment of the institutionalized elderly. *The Gerontologist, 21,* 177–183.

Wentkowski, G. (1985). Older women's perceptions of great-grandparenthood: A research note. *The Gerontologist, 25,* 593–596.

Wessler, R., Rubin, M., & Sollberger, A. (1976). Circadian rhythm of activity and sleep-wakefulness in elderly institutionalized patients. *Journal of Interdisciplinary Cycle Research, 7,* 333.

West, R. L. (1995). *Compensatory strategies for age-associated memory impairment.* In A. D. Baddeley, B. A. Wilson, & F. Watts (Eds.), *Handbook of memory disorders* (pp. 481–500). London: Wiley.

West, R. L. (1984, August). *An analysis of prospective everyday memory.* Paper presented at the meeting of the American Psychological Association, Toronto.

West, R. L. (1986a). Everyday memory and aging. *Developmental Neuropsychology, 2,* 323–344.

West, R. L. (1986b). *Memory fitness over 40.* Gainesville, FL: Triad.

West, R. L., & Walton, M. (1985, March). *Practical memory functioning in the elderly.* Paper presented at the National Forum on Research in Aging, Lincoln, NE.

Wetzler, M. A., & Feil, N. (1979). *Validation therapy with disoriented elders who use fantasy.* Cleveland: Edward Feil Productions.

Whitbourne, S. K. (1985). *The aging body.* New York: Springer.

Whitbourne, S. K. (1986). *The me I know: A study of adult identity.* New York: Springer-Verlag.

Whitbourne, S. K. (1987). Personality development in adulthood and old age: Relationships among identity style, health, and well-being. In K. W. Schaie (Ed.), *Annual review of gerontology and geriatrics* (Vol. 7, pp. 189–216). New York: Springer.

Whitbourne, S. K. (1996a). *Development of a scale to measure identity processes in adults.* Unpublished manuscript, University of Massachusetts.

Whitbourne, S. K. (1996b). *Identity and adaptation to the aging process.* Unpublished chapter, University of Massachusetts.

Whitbourne, S. K. Culgin, S., & Cassidy, E. (1995). Evaluation of infantilizing intonation and content of speech directed at the aged. *International Journal of Aging and Human Development, 41,* 109–116.

White, A. T., & Spector, P. E. (1987). An investigation of age-related factors in the age-job satisfaction relationship. *Psychology and Aging, 2,* 261–265.

White, L. K., & Booth, A. (1985). The quality and stability of remarriages: The role of stepchildren. *American Sociological Review, 50,* 689–698.

Whitlock, F. A. (1986). Suicide and physical illness. In A. Roy (Ed.), *Suicide* (pp. 151–170). Baltimore: Williams & Wilkins.

Wickens, C. D., Braune, R., & Stokes, A. (1987). Age differences in the speed and capacity of information processing. 1: A dual task approach. *Psychology and Aging, 2,* 70–78.

Wiener, J. M. (1988, Winter). Financing options for long-term care. *Living-at-Home,* pp. 1–3.

Wiener, Y., & Vaitenas, R. (1977). Personality and developmental correlates of voluntary and mid-career change in enterprising occupations. *The Gerontologist, 17,* 132.

Wiens, A. N., & Menustik, C. E. (1983). Treatment outcome and patient characteristics in an aversion therapy program for alcoholism. *American Psychologist, 38,* 1089–1096.

Williams, A. F., & Carsten, O. (1989). Driver age and crash involvement. *American Journal of Public Health, 79,* 326–327.

Williams, J. E., & Best, D. L. (1990). *Measuring sex stereotypes* (2nd ed.).

Williams, J. H. (1977). *Psychology of women.* New York: Norton.

Williams, S. A., Denney, N. W., & Schadler, M. (1983). Elderly adults' perception of their own cognitive development during the adult years. *International Journal of Aging and Human Development, 16,* 147–158.

Williamson, G. M., & Schulz, R. (1990). Relationship orientation, quality of prior relationship, and distress among caregivers of Alzheimer's patients. *Psychology and Aging, 5,* 502–509.

Willis, S. L. (1990). Current issues in cognitive training research. In E. A. Lovelace (Ed.), *Aging and cognition: Mental processes, self-awareness, and interventions* (pp. 263–280). Amsterdam: North-Holland.

Willis S. L., Jay, G. M., Diehl, M., & Marsiske, M. (1992). Longitudinal change and prediction of everyday task competence in the elderly. *Research on Aging, 14,* 68–91.

Willis, S. L., & Nesselroade, C. S. (1990). Long-term effects of fluid ability training in old-old age. *Developmental Psychology, 26,* 905–910.

Willis, S. L., & Schaie, K. W. (1992, November). *Maintaining and sustaining cognitive training effects in old age.* Paper presented at the annual meeting of the Gerontological Society of America, Washington, DC.

Willis, S. L., & Schaie, K. W. (in press). Cognitive functioning in middle age. In S. W. Willis & J. Reid (Eds.), *Middle aging.* San Diego: Academic Press.

Willis, S. L., Schaie, K. W., & Lueers, N. (1983, April). *Fluid-crystallized ability correlates of real life tasks.* Paper presented at the meeting of the Society for Research in Child Development, Detroit.

Wilson, B., & Moffat, N. (Eds.). (1984). *Clinical management of memory problems.* Rockville, MD: Aspen.

Wingfield, A., & Stine, E. L. (1986). Organizational strategies in immediate recall of rapid speeds by young and elderly adults. *Experimental Aging Research, 12,* 79–83.

Wiseman, R. F. (1981). Community environments for the elderly. In F. J Berghorn, D. E. Schafer, and Associates (Eds.), *The dynamics of aging* (pp. 377–390). Boulder, CO: Westview.

Wiswell, R. A. (1980). Relaxation, exercise, and aging. In J. E. Birren & R. B. Sloane (Eds.), *Handbook of mental health and aging* (pp. 943–958). Englewood Cliffs, NJ: Prentice-Hall.

Wittels, I., & Botwinick, J. (1974). Survival in relocation. *Journal of Gerontology, 29,* 440–443.

Wittkowski, J. (1981). *Attitudes toward death and dying in older persons and their dependence on life satisfaction and death-related experiences.* Paper presented at the International Congress of Gerontology, Hamburg.

Wolf, E. (1960). Glare and age. *Archives of Ophthalmology, 60,* 502–514.

Wolf, R. S., Godkin, M. A., & Pillemer, K. A. (1986). Treatment of the elderly: A comparative analysis. *Journal of Long Term Home Health Care, 5*(4), 10–17.

Wolfson, C., Handfield-Jones, R., Glass, K. C., McClaran, J., & Keyserlingk, E. (1993). Adult children's perceptions of their responsibility to provide care for dependent elderly parents. *The Gerontologist, 33,* 315–323.

Woodruff-Pak, D. S. (1988). *Psychology and aging.* Englewood Cliffs, NJ: Prentice-Hall.

World Health Organization. (1980). *International classification of impairments, disabilities, and handicaps.* Geneva: Author.

Wright, L. K. (1991). The impact of Alzheimer's disease on the marital relationship. *The Gerontologist, 31,* 224–237.

Yanik, A. J. (1988). *Vehicle design considerations for older drivers* (SAE 885090). Warrendale, PA: Society of Automotive Engineers.

Yanik, A. J. (1994). Barriers to the design of vehicles for mature adults. *Experimental Aging Research, 20,* 5–10.

Yankelovich, D. (1981). *New rules: Searching for self-fulfillment in a world turned upside down.* New York: Random House.

Yates, F. A. (1966). *The art of memory.* Middlesex, England: Penguin.

Yee, D. (1985). A survey of the traffic safety needs and problems of drivers 55 and over. In J. L. Malfetti (Ed.), *Drivers 55+: Needs and problems of the older drivers: Survey results and recommendations* (pp. 96–128). Falls Church, VA: AAA Foundation for Traffic Safety.

Yesavage, J. A. (1983). Imagery pretraining and memory training in the elderly. *Gerontology, 29,* 271–275.

Yesavage, J. A., Sheikh, J., Tanke, E. D., & Hill, R. (1988). Response to memory training and individual differences in verbal intelligence and state anxiety. *American Journal of Psychiatry, 145,* 636–639.

Yllo, A. (1978). Nonmarital cohabitation. *Alternative Lifestyles, 1,* 37–54.

Yllö, K. A. (1993). Through a feminist lens: Gender, power, and violence. In R. J. Gelles & D. R. Loseke (Eds.), *Current controversies on family violence* (pp. 47–62). Newbury Park, CA: Sage Publications.

Young, L. J., Percy, C. L., & Asire, A. J. (Eds.). (1981). *Incidence and mortality data: 1973–1977* (National Cancer Institute Monograph 57, DHHS No. NIH 81-2330). Washington, DC: U.S. Government Printing Office.

Zabrucky, K., & Moore, D. (1994). Contributions of working memory and evaluation and regulation of understanding to adults' recall of texts. *Journal of Gerontology: Psychological Sciences, 49,* P201–P212.

Zabrucky, K., & Moore, D. (1995). Elaborations in adults' text recall: Relations to working memory and text recall. *Experimental Aging Research, 21,* 143–158.

Zarit, S. H. (1982). Affective correlates of self-reports about memory of older people. *International Journal of Behavioral Geriatrics, 1,* 25–34.

Zarit, S. H., & Anthony, C. (1986). Interventions with dementia patients and their families. In M. Gilhooly, S. Zarit, & J. E. Birren (Eds.), *The dementias: Policy and management* (pp. 104–121). Englewood Cliffs, NJ: Prentice-Hall.

Zarit, S. H., Cole, K. D., & Guider, R. L. (1981). Memory training strategies and subjective complaints of memory in the aged. *The Gerontologist, 21,* 158–164.

Zarit, S. H., Eiler, J., & Hassinger, M. (1985). Clinical assessment. In J. E. Birren & K. W. Schaie (Eds.), *Handbook of the psychology of aging* (2nd ed., pp. 725–754). New York: Van Nostrand Reinhold.

Zarit, S. H., & Zarit, J. M. (1983). Cognitive impairment. In P. M. Lewinsohn & L. Teri (Eds.), *Clinical geropsychology* (pp. 38–80). New York: Pergamon Press.

Zegans, L. S., (1982). Stress and the development of somatic disorders. In L. Goldberger & S. Breznitz (Eds.), *Handbook of stress: Theoretical and clinical aspects* (pp. 134–152). New York: Free Press.

Zelinski, E. M., Gilewski, M. J., & Anthony-Bergstone, C. R. (1990). Memory Functioning Questionnaire: Concurrent validity with memory performance and self-reported memory failures. *Psychology and Aging, 5,* 388–399.

Zelinski, E. M., Gilewski, M. J., & Thompson, L. W. (1980). Do laboratory tests relate to self assessment of memory ability in the young and old? In L. W. Poon, J. L. Fozard, L. S. Cermak, D. Arenberg, & L. W. Thompson (Eds.), *New directions in memory and aging* (pp. 519–544). Hillsdale, NJ: Erlbaum.

Zepelin, H. (1973). A survey of age differences in sleep patterns and dream recall among well-educated men and women. *Sleep Research, 2,* 81.

Zgola, J. M. (1987). *Doing things: A guide to programming activities for persons with Alzheimer's disease and related disorders.* Baltimore: Johns Hopkins University Press.

Zick, C. D., & McCullough, J. L. (1991). Trends in married couples' time use: Evidence from 1977–78 and 1987–88. *Sex Roles, 24,* 459–488.

Zimberg, S. (1985). Principles of alcoholism psychotherapy. In S. Zimberg, J. Wallace, & S. B. Blume (Eds.), *Practical approaches to alcoholism psychotherapy* (pp. 3–22). New York: Plenum.

Zisook, S., & Schucter, S. R. (1994). Diagnostic and treatment considerations in depression associated with late life bereavement. In L. S. Schneider, C. F. Reynolds, B. D. Lebowitz, & A. J. Friedhoff (Eds.), *Diagnosis and treatment of depression in late life: Results of the NIH Consensus Development Conference.* Washington, DC: American Psychiatric Press.

Zsembik, B. A., & Singer, A. (1990). The problem of defining retirement among minorities: The Mexican Americans. *The Gerontologist, 30,* 749–757.

NAME INDEX

GLOSSARY/SUBJECT INDEX

Attention (continued)
feature integration theory of, 158–159
selectivity in, 159–161
sustained, 163–164
switching, 160

Attentional capacity Refers to the amount of information that can be processed at any given time. 158, 162–163

Autoantibodies Antibodies that attack the body itself. 81–82

Autobiographical memory, 196–197

Autoimmunity The process by which autoantibodies are produced, which may be partially responsible for aging. 81–82

Automatic attention response The automatic capturing of attention by a stimulus. 165

Automatic processes Processes that are fast, reliable, and insensitive to increased cognitive demands. 165–167

Autosomal dominant A type of genetic transmission in which only one gene from one parent is necessary for a person to acquire a trait or a disease. 336

Average longevity The length of time it takes for half of all individuals born in a certain year to die. 111–115

Backward masking, 156

Balance, 94–95

Battered woman syndrome The situation in which a woman believes that she cannot leave an abusive situation and may even kill her abuser. 364–367

Behavior therapy A type of psychotherapy that focuses on and attempts to alter current behavior. Underlying causes of the problem may not be addressed. 325

Benzodiazepines A type of medication used to treat anxiety disorders. 327

Bioethics The study of the interface between human values and technological advances in health and life sciences. 493–495

Biological age A definition of age that focuses on the functional age of biological and physiological processes rather than on calendar time. 14

Biological forces One of four basic forces on development that includes all genetic and health-related factors. 5

Biological theories of aging, 71–74

Bipolar disorder A type of psychopathology characterized by both depression and mania. 324

Blood pressure, 83, 86

Bones and joints, 101–102

Brain, 74–80
changes in neuron, 75–78
imaging techniques, 78–80
psychological effects, 80

Brain death A definition of death that relies on eight criteria including the lack of an EEG for 24 hours. 492

Brain imaging, 78–80

Burnout The feeling that results when the pace and the pressure of one's occupation becomes more than one can bear, causing a depletion of a person's energy and motivation. 415

Cancer, 136–139

Cardiac arrhythmias Irregularities in the heartbeat. 84

Cardiovascular disease, 83–86

Cardiovascular system, 82–86

Career plateauing The lack of promotional opportunity from the organization or the person's decision not to seek advancement. 424–425

Caregiving, 341–345, 376–377, 391–392

Case studies An intensive investigation of individual people. 24

Cataracts Opaque spots in the lens of the eye which seriously limit the amount of light transmitted. 88

Causal attributions Explanations people construct to explain their behavior, which can be situational, dispositional, or interactive. 305–306

Cellular theories of aging, 72–73

Cerebral hemorrhage The breaking of a blood vessel in the brain. 85–86

Cerebrovascular accident (CVA) An interruption of the blood flow in the brain. 85–86

Cerebrovascular disease A form of cardiovascular disease that involves the blood vessels in the brain. 85–96

Cholesterol, 135

Chronic disease, 83–87, 101–102, 140–143

Chronic obstructive pulmonary disease (COPD) A family of age-related lung diseases that block the passage of air and cause abnormalities inside the lungs. 87

Chronological age A definition of age that relies on the amount of calendar time that has passed since birth. 14

Climacteric The transition during which a woman's reproductive capacity ends and ovulation stops. 95–97

Clinical death A definition of death based on the lack of a spontaneous pulse and respiration. 492

Clinical memory testing, 220–222

Cognitive-process approach An approach to intelligence emphasizing the ways in which people conceptualize problems and focusing on modes or styles of thinking. 237, 251–263
Kitchener & King's theory, 257–259
Piaget's theory, 252–255
postformal thought, 256–263
Schaie's theory, 262–263

Cognitive therapy A type of psychotherapy aimed at altering the way people think as a cure for some forms of psychopathology, especially depression. 325–326

Cognitive training, 223–228, 249–251

Cohabitation Two individuals living together who are not married but who are in a relationship. 370–371

Cohort effects One of the three basic influences examined in developmental research, along with age and time-of-measurement effects, which reflect differences due to experiences and circumstances unique to the historical time in which one lives. 17–22, 244–246

Communication with older adults, 473–474

Communication enhancement model, 473–474

Communities, 455–457

Comparable worth The notion that people should be paid equally for similar work regardless of gender. 420

Competence In person-environment interactions, the theoretical upper limit of a person's ability to function. 451

Comprehension of language, 179, 181–183

Computed tomography (CT) scan, 78

Configurational learning Process requiring people to combine spatial and temporal information so that they can recognize a location when they view it from a different perspective. 205

Confounding Any situation in which you cannot determine which of two (or more) effects is responsible for the behaviors you observe. 17–22

Congruence model In person-environment interactions, the notion that people need to find the environment in which they fit and that meets their needs the best. 452–453, 468–471

Contextual approach to dying, 503–504

Contextual model A model that views people as dynamic, active, not reducible to parts, and not headed toward a specific end point. 11–12

Continuity-discontinuity controversy The debate over whether the same rules (continuity) or different rules (discontinuity) are used to explain change in human development. 9–10

Coping In the stress and coping paradigm, a complex, evolving process of dealing with stress that is learned. 118–119

Correlation A relation or association between two variables. 23–24

Costa & McCrae's model of personality, 278–283

Cortical death A definition of death based on the lack of brain activity in the cortex. 493

Creutzfeld-Jakob disease, 340

Cross-cultural issues
age-set systems, 58–59
definitions of age, 54–55
demographics, 37–38
egalitarian societies, 56–57

CREDITS

This page constitutes an extension of the copyright page. We have made every effort to trace the ownership of all copyrighted material and to secure permission from copyright holders. In the event of any question arising as to the use of any material, we will be pleased to make the necessary corrections in future printings. Thanks are due to the following authors, publishers, and agents for permission to use the material indicated.

Figure Credits

CHAPTER 1

20: Figure 1.3 "A Cross-Sequential Study of Age Changes in Cognitive Behavior," by K. W. Schaie and C. R. Strother, 1968, *Psychological Bulletin, 70,* 671–680. Copyright © 1968 by the American Psychological Association. Reprinted with permission.

CHAPTER 2

39: Figure 2.3 "Aging and Worldwide Population Change," by G. C. Meyers. In R. H. Binstock and E. Shanas (Eds.), *Handbook of Aging and the Social Sciences,* Second Edition, p. 180, Van Nostrand Reinhold. Copyright © 1985 Duke University Center for Demographic Studies. Reprinted with permission from the author.

CHAPTER 3

90: Figure 3.2 "Dark Adaptation as a Function of Age: 1. A Statistical Analysis," by R. A. McFarland et al., 1960, *Journal of Gerontology, 15,* 149–154. Copyright © 1960 The Gerontological Society of America. Reprinted with permission. **91:** Figure 3.3 Reprinted with permission from "Aging of the Sensory Systems," by E. Meisami. In P. Timiras (Ed.), *Physiological Basis of Aging and Geriatrics,* Second Edition, pp. 115–131. Copyright © 1994 CRC Press, Boca Raton, Florida.

CHAPTER 4

133: Table 4.1 "Sleep Disturbances," by R. R. Bootzin and M. Engle-Friedman, in L. L. Carstensen and B. A. Edelstein (Eds.), *Handbook of Clinical Gerontology,* pp. 238–251. Copyright © 1987 Pergamon Press. Reprinted with permission. **141:** Figure 4.3 Reprinted from *Social Science and Medicine, 38,* L. M. Verbrugge and A. M. Jette, "The Disablement Process," 1–14. Copyright © 1994, with kind permission from Elsevier Science Ltd, The Boulevard, Langford Lane, Kidlington 0X5 1GB, UK. **144:** Figure 4.4 Adapted from "Gender Differences in Adult Health: An International Comparison," by O. Rahman et al., 1994, *The Gerontologist, 34,* 463–469. Copyright © 1994 The Gerontological Society of America. Adapted by permission.

CHAPTER 5

169: Figure 5.1 "Movement Specification Time with Age," by G. E. Stelmach, N. L. Goggin, and A. Garcia-Colera, 1987, *Experimental Aging Research, 13,* p. 42. Copyright © 1987 by Beech Hill Enterprises, Inc. Reprinted with permission. **170:** Figure 5.2 "Brinley Plots and Theories of Aging: The Explicit, Muddled, and Implicit Debates," by A. D. Fisk and D. L. Fisher, 1994, *Journal of Gerontology: Psychological Sciences, 49,* p. 87. Copyright © 1994 The Gerontological Society of America. Reprinted with permission. **172:** Figure 5.3 "Aging and Information Processing Rate," by J. Cerella. In J. E. Birren and K. W. Schaie (Eds.), *Handbook of the Psychology of Aging,* Third Edition, p. 203. Copyright © 1990 Academic Press. Reprinted with permission. **175:** Figure 5.4 "Effects of Age and Skill in Typing," by T. A. Salthouse, 1984, *Journal of Experimental Psychology: General, 113,* 345–371. Copyright © 1984 by the American Psychological Association. Reprinted with permission of the author. **181:** Figure 5.5 "Hearing and Aging: Implications of Recent Research Findings," by M. Bergman, 1971, *Audiology, 10,* 164–171. Copyright © 1971 S. Karger AG. Reprinted with permission.

CHAPTER 6

199: Table 6.1 "Comprehension and Retention of Television Programs by 20- and 60-year-olds," by J. C. Cavanaugh, 1983, *Journal of Gerontology, 38,* 190–196. Copyright © 1983 The Gerontological Society of America. Reprinted with permission. **205:** Figure 6.1 "Aging, Spatial Performance, and Spatial Competence," by K. C. Kirasic and G. L. Allen, 1985, in N. Charness (Ed.), *Aging in Human Performance.* Chichester, England: Wiley. Copyright © 1985 by John Wiley & Sons, Inc. Reprinted with permission of the publisher. **213:** Figure 6.2 "Adult Age Differences in Free Classification and Free Recall," by D. F. Hultsch, 1971, *Developmental Psychology, 4,* 338–342. Copyright © 1971 by the American Psychological Association. Reprinted with permission of the author. **224:** Figure 6.3 "Imagery Pretraining and Memory Training in the Elderly," by J. A. Yesavage, 1983, *Gerontology, 29,* 271–275. Copyright © 1983 by S. Karger. Reprinted with permission.

CHAPTER 7

233: Excerpt "The Old Alchemist" is from *In the Ever After: Fairy Tales and the Second Half of Life,* by Allan B. Chinen. Copyright © 1989 by Chiron Publications. Reprinted with permission. **240:** Figure 7.1 "The Course of Adult Intellectual Development," by K. W. Schaie, 1994, *American Psychologist, 49,* 304–313. Copyright © 1994 by the American Psychological Association. Reprinted with permission. **241:** Figure 7.2 Adapted from "The Hazards of Cognitive Aging," by K. W. Schaie, 1989, *The Gerontologist, 29,* 484–493. Copyright © 1989 The Gerontological Society of America. Adapted with permission. **242:** Table 7.1 "The Aging of Human Abilities," by J. L. Horn. In B. B. Wolman (Ed.), *Handbook of Developmental Psychology,* pp. 847–870. Copyright © 1982 Prentice-Hall. Reprinted with permission. **244:** Figure 7.3 "Organization of Data on Life-Span Development of Human Abilities," by J. L. Horn. In L. R. Goulet and P. B. Baltes (Eds.), *Life-Span Developmental Psychology: Research and Theory,* p. 463. Copyright © 1970 Academic Press. Reprinted with permission. **245:** Figure 7.4 "The Course of Adult Intellectual Development," by K. W. Schaie, 1994, *American Psychologist, 49,* 304–313. Copyright © 1994 by the American Psychological Association. Reprinted with permission. **258:** Table 7.2 Adapted from *Developing Reflective Judgment: Understanding and Promoting Intellectual Growth and Critical Thinking in Adolescents and Adults,* by P. M. King and K. S. Kitchener, pp. 14–16. Copyright © 1994 Jossey-Bass Inc., Publishers. Adapted with permission. **260:** Figure 7.5 "Reasoning on Social Dilemmas Varying in Emotional Saliency: An Adult Developmental Perspective," by F. Blanchard-Fields, 1986, *Psychology and Aging, 1,* p. 329. Copyright © 1986 by the American Psychological Association. Reprinted by permission. **265:** Figure 7.6 Adapted from Nancy Wadsworth Denney, "Aging and Cognitive Changes," in *Handbook of Developmental Psychology,* B. B. Wolman (Ed.), copyright © 1982, p. 820. Adapted by permission of Prentice Hall, Inc., Upper Saddle River, New Jersey.

CHAPTER 8

286: Table 8.1 From *The Life Cycle Completed, A Review,* by Erik H. Erikson. Copyright © 1982 by Raikan Enterprises, Ltd. Reprinted by permission of W. W. Norton & Company, Inc. **298:** Figure 8.1 "S. K. Whitbourne, *The Me I Know: A Study of Adult Identity,* copyright © 1986, Springer-Verlag New York. Reprinted with permission. **302:** Figure 8.2 "Possible Selves in Adulthood and Old Age: A Tale of Shifting Horzons," by C. D. Ryff, 1991, *Psychology and Aging, 6,* 286–295. Copyright © 1991 by the American Psychological Association. Reprinted with permission.

CHAPTER 9

343: Figure 9.1 *Profiles in Caregiving: The Unexpected Career,* by C. S. Aneshensel et al. Copyright © 1995 Academic Press. Reprinted with permission.

CHAPTER 10

363: Figure 10.1 "Age and Sex Differences in Satisfying Love Relationships Across the Adult Life Span," by M. N. Reedy, J. E. Birren, and K. W. Schaie, 1981, *Human Development, 24,* 52-66. Copyright © 1981 S. Karger AG, Basel. Reprinted with permission. **365:** Figure 10.2 "Through a Psychological Lens: Personality Traits, Personality Disorders, and Levels of Violence," by K. D. O'Leary. In R. J. Gelles and D. R. Loseke (Eds.), *Current Controversies on Family Violence,* pp. 7–30. Copyright © 1993 Sage Publications. Reprinted with permission. **378:** Table 10.1 "Perceived Causes of Divorce: An Analysis of Interrelationships," by M. D. Cleek and T. A. Pearson, 1985, *Journal of Marriage and the Family, 47,* 179–191. Copyright © 1985. Reprinted with permission.

CHAPTER 11

408: Table 11.1 John Holland, *Making Vocational Choices: A Theory of Vocational Personalities and Work Environments,* copyright © 1985, pp. 19–22. Adapted with permission of Prentice Hall, Inc., Upper Saddle River, NJ. **410:** Figure 11.1 *Career Motivation in Mid-Life Managers,* by A. Howard and D. W. Bray, 1980, paper presented at the annual meeting of the American Psychological Association, Montreal. Reprinted with permission of the author.

CHAPTER 12

452: Figure 12.1 "Ecology and the Aging Process," by M. P. Lawton and L. Nahemow. In C. Eisdorfer and M. P. Lawton (Eds.), *The Psychology of Adult Development and Aging,* p. 661. Copyright © 1973 by the American Psychological Association. Reprinted with permission. **468:** Table 12.1 "Who Leaves—Who Stays: Residency Policy in Housing for the Elderly," by J. Bernstein, 1982, *The Gerontologist, 22,* 305–313. Copyright © 1982 The Gerontological Society of America. Reprinted with permission. **469:** Table 12.2 "A Congruence Model of Person-Environment Interaction," by E. Kahana. In M. P. Lawton et al. (Eds.), *Aging and the Environment: Theoretical Approaches.* New York: Springer, 1982. Reprinted with permission of Dr. Eva Kahana. **474:** Figure 12.2 "Changing the Way We Talk With Elders: Promoting Health Using the Communication Enhancement Model," by Ryan et al., 1995, *International Journal of Aging and Human Development, 41,* 89–107, Baywood Publishing Company, Inc. **476:** Table 12.3 "Types of Elderly Residential Mobility and Their Determinants," by A. Speare, Jr., and J. W. Meyer, 1988, *Journal of Gerontology, 43,* 574–581. Copyright © 1988 The Gerontological Society of America. Reprinted with permission.

CHAPTER 13

497: Figure 13.1 "Epidemiology of Suicide in the Elderly," by J. L. McIntosh, 1992, *Suicide and Life-Threatening Behavior, 22,* 15–35, Guilford Publications. **513:** Table 13.1 "Perceptions of Grief Among University Students," by C. J. Vickio, J. C. Cavanaugh, and T. Attig, 1990, *Death Studies, 14,* p. 236. Copyright © 1990 Hemisphere Publishing Corporation. Reprinted with permission. **516:** Figure 13.3 "Older Adult Family Stress and Adaptation Before and After Bereavement," by F. N. Norris and S. A. Murrell, 1987, *Journal of Gerontology, 42,* 609, 610. Copyright © 1987 The Gerontological Society of America. Reprinted with permission of the publisher and author.

Photo Credits

CHAPTER 1

1: Edward Hopper, *Cape Cod Evening,* 1939. John Hay Whitney Collection © 1996 Board of Trustees, National Gallery of Art, Washington, 1939, oil on canvas, 30¼ × 40¼; framed; **6:** © David Young-Wolff / PhotoEdit; **15:** © Kathy Sloane / Jeroboam; **17:** © Jean- Claude LeJeune / Stock Boston.

CHAPTER 2

32: Laura Wheeler Waring, *Anna Washington Derry,* 1927. National Museum of American Art, Washington DC/Art Resource, NY; **40:** © Deborah Kahn, 1984 / Stock Boston; **45:** © Joel Gordon; **56:** © P&D Maybury-Lewis / Anthro-Photos; **61:** © Ilka Hartmann/Jeroboam.

CHAPTER 3

68: (left) Rembrandt *Self Portrait as a Young Man.* © Alinari / Art Resource, NY; **68:** (right) Rembrandt *Self Portrait as an Old Man.* Foto Marburg / Art Resource, NY; **79:** © James P. Dwyer / Stock Boston; **92:** © Alan Carey / The Image Works; **99:** © Cleo / PhotoEdit.

CHAPTER 4

108: Fairfield Porter, *The Tennis Game,* 1972. Lauren Rogers Museum of Art, Laurel, Mississippi; **111:** © Anestis Diakopoulos / Stock Boston; **119:** © Michael Newman / PhotoEdit; **129:** © Bohdan Hrynewych / Stock Boston; **132:** © Felicia Martinez / PhotoEdit.

Chapter 5

152: © M. C. Escher / Cordon Art, Baarn, Holland. All rights reserved; **161:** © Bachmann / PhotoEdit; **174:** © David Young-Wolff / PhotoEdit; **178:** © Lara Hartley.

CHAPTER 6

188: Andrew Wyeth, *Children's Doctor,* 1949. Collection of the Brandywine River Museum, Gift of Betsy James Wyeth. © 1996 Andrew Wyeth; **192:** © Ilka Hartmann / Jeroboam; **200:** © Jeff Greenberg / PhotoEdit; **204:** © Karen Preuss / The Image Works; **223:** © Lara Hartley.

CHAPTER 7

232: Jack Beal, *Sydney and Frances Lewis,* 1975. Washington and Lee University, Lexington, Virginia; **235:** © Mark Antman / The Image Works; **253:** © David Carmack 1990 / Stock Boston; **261:** © Robert Kapa / Magnum.

CHAPTER 8

274: Giovanni Costetti, *Pensive Woman,* Alinari / Art Resource, NY; **279:** © Hazel Hankin, 1991 / Stock Boston; **287:** © Michael Malyszko / Stock Boston; **291:** © Rick Reinhard / Black Star; **297:** © Mosby / Payne Hahn / Stock Boston, 1977.

CHAPTER 9

312: Alberto Giacometti, *The Artist's Mother,* 1950. Oil on canvas. 35⅜ × 24″. The Museum of Modern Art, New York. Acquired through the Lillie P. Bliss Bequest. Photograph © 1996 The Museum of Modern Art, New York; **319:** © Tony Freeman / PhotoEdit; **342:** © Martha Tabor; **348:** © Nita Winter.

CHAPTER 10

355: Phillips Collection, Washington DC / Superstock; **359:** © Marianne Gontarz; **379:** © Bob Daemmrich / PhotoEdit; **387:** © Melanie Carr / Zephyr Pictures; **395:** © Joel Gordon.

CHAPTER 11

402: Jacob Lawrence, *Builders,* 1980. Courtesy SAFECO Insurance Companies, Seattle, Washington and courtesy of the artist and Francine Seders Gallery, Seattle, WA; **412:** © Judy Canty / Stock Boston; **420:** © SuperStock, Inc.; **433:** © Mark Richards / PhotoEdit; **441:** © Gale Zucker / Stock Boston.

CHAPTER 12

448: Grandma Moses, *Moving Day on the Farm,* 1951. Copyright © 1987, Grandma Moses Properties Co., New York; **456:** © David S. Strickler / The Image Works; **459:** © Melanie Carr / Zephyr; **463:** © Bob Collins / The Image Works; **464:** © Steve Skjold.

CHAPTER 13

486: Andrew Wyeth, *Beckie King,* 1946. Dallas Museum of Art, Gift of Everett L. DeGolyer; **490:** © Owen Seumptewa; **511:** © Spencer Grant / Stock Boston; **514:** © AFP / Bettman.

CHAPTER 14

526: Marc Chagall, *En avant,* 1917, gouache on paper 38.1× 48.7 cm, Art Gallery of Ontario, Toronto. Gift of Sam and Ayala Zacks; **531:** © J. Berndt / Stock Boston 1986; **535:** © Elizabeth Crews.

Optional:

Your name: ______________________________ Date: ______________________________

May Brooks/Cole quote you, either in promotion for *Adult Development and Aging*, Third Edition, or in future publishing ventures?

Yes: __________ No: _________

Sincerely,

John C. Cavanaugh

FOLD HERE

NO POSTAGE NECESSARY IF MAILED IN THE UNITED STATES

BUSINESS REPLY MAIL

FIRST CLASS PERMIT NO. 358 PACIFIC GROVE, CA

POSTAGE WILL BE PAID BY ADDRESSEE

ATT: *John C. Cavanaugh*

Brooks/Cole Publishing Company
511 Forest Lodge Road
Pacific Grove, California 93950-9968

FOLD HERE

TO THE OWNER OF THIS BOOK:

I hope that you have found *Adult Development and Aging*, Third Edition, useful. So that this book can be improved in a future edition, would you take the time to complete this sheet and return it? Thank you.

School and address: ______________________________

Department: ______________________________

Instructor's name: ______________________________

1. What I like most about this book is: ______________________________

____

____

2. What I like least about this book is: ______________________________

____

____

3. My general reaction to this book is: ______________________________

____

4. The name of the course in which I used this book is: ______________________________

____

5. Were all of the chapters of the book assigned for you to read? ______________________________

If not, which ones weren't? ______________________________

6. In the space below, or on a separate sheet of paper, please write specific suggestions for improving this book and anything else you'd care to share about your experience in using the book.

____

____

____

____

____